UNIVERSITY CASEBOOK SERIES — Continued

CONSTITUTIONAL LAW, Seventh Edition (1965) with 1966 Supplement
Noel T. Dowling, Professor of Law, Columbia University.
Gerald Gunther, Professor of Law, Stanford University.

CONTRACT IN CONTEXT (1952)
Addison Mueller, Professor of Law, University of California at Los Angeles.

CONTRACTS, (1965) (Successor Volume to Patterson, Goble & Jones, Cases on Contracts) with Statutory Supplement
Harry W. Jones, Professor of Law, Columbia University.
E. Allan Farnsworth, Professor of Law, Columbia University.
William F. Young, Professor of Law, Columbia University.

CONTRACTS AND CONTRACT REMEDIES, Fourth Edition (1957)
Harold Shepherd, Professor of Law Emeritus, Stanford University, and
Harry H. Wellington, Professor of Law, Yale University.

CONTRACTS AND CONTRACT REMEDIES (1959)
John P. Dawson, Professor of Law, Harvard University, and
Wm. Burnett Harvey, Dean of the Law School, Indiana University.

CONVEYANCES, Second Edition (1941)
Marion R. Kirkwood, Professor of Law Emeritus, Stanford University.

COPYRIGHT, Unfair Competition, and Other Topics Bearing on the Protection of Literary, Musical, and Artistic Works (1960)
Benjamin Kaplan, Professor of Law, Harvard University, and
Ralph S. Brown, Jr., Professor of Law, Yale University.

CORPORATE REORGANIZATION, with Statutory Supplement (1950)
The late E. Merrick Dodd, Professor of Law, Harvard University, and
DeForest Billyou, Professor of Law, New York University.

CORPORATIONS, Third Edition—Unabridged (1959) with 1965 Supplement
Ralph J. Baker, Professor of Law, Harvard University, and
William L. Cary, Professor of Law, Columbia University.

CORPORATIONS, Third Edition—Abridged (1959) with 1965 Supplement
Ralph J. Baker, Professor of Law, Harvard University, and
William L. Cary, Professor of Law, Columbia University.

CREDITORS' RIGHTS, Fifth Edition (1957)
The late John Hanna, Professor of Law Emeritus, Columbia University, and
James Angell MacLachlan, Professor of Law Emeritus, Harvard University.

CREDITORS' RIGHTS AND CORPORATE REORGANIZATION, Fifth Edition (1957)
The late John Hanna, Professor of Law Emeritus, Columbia University, and
James Angell MacLachlan, Professor of Law Emeritus, Harvard University.

CRIMINAL JUSTICE, THE ADMINISTRATION OF, CASES AND MATERIALS ON, 1966
Francis C. Sullivan, Professor of Law, Loyola University.
Paul Hardin III, Professor of Law, Duke University.
John Huston, Professor of Law, Syracuse University.
Frank R. Lacy, Professor of Law, University of Oregon.
Daniel E. Murray, Professor of Law, University of Miami.
George W. Pugh, Professor of Law, Louisiana State University.

CRIMINAL JUSTICE, Second Edition, 1964
Fred E. Inbau, Professor of Law, Northwestern University, and
Claude R. Sowle, Dean of the Law School, University of Cincinnati.

CRIMINAL LAW AND ITS ADMINISTRATION (1940), with 1956 Supplement
The late Jerome Michael, Professor of Law, Columbia University, and
Herbert Wechsler, Professor of Law, Columbia University.

CRIMINAL LAW AND PROCEDURE, Third Edition (1966)
Rollin M. Perkins, Professor of Law, University of California, Hastings College of the Law.

DAMAGES, Second Edition (1952)
The late Charles T. McCormick, Professor of Law, University of Texas, and
William F. Fritz, Professor of Law, University of Texas.

DECEDENTS' ESTATES AND TRUSTS, Second Edition (1961)
John Ritchie III, Dean and Professor of Law, Northwestern University,
Neill H. Alford, Jr., Professor of Law, University of Virginia, and
Richard W. Effland, Professor of Law, University of Wisconsin.

University Casebook Series

ACCOUNTING AND THE LAW, Third Edition (1964), with Problem Pamphlet
The late James L. Dohr, Director, Institute of Accounting, Columbia University,
Ellis L. Phillips, Jr., Professor of Law, Columbia University.
George C. Thompson, Professor, Columbia University Graduate School of Business, and
William C. Warren, Dean of the Law School, Columbia University.

ACCOUNTING, LAW AND (1949)
Donald Schapiro, Instructor in Law, Yale University, and
Ralph Wienshienk, Visiting Lecturer in Law, Yale University.

ACCOUNTING, MATERIALS ON, Third Edition (1959)
Robert Amory, Jr., Esq.,
W. Covington Hardee, Esq.,
David R. Herwitz, Professor of Law, Harvard University, and
Donald T. Trautman, Professor of Law, Harvard University.

ADMINISTRATIVE LAW, Fourth Edition (1960), with Problems Supplement
Walter Gellhorn, Professor of Law, Columbia University, and
Clark Byse, Professor of Law, Harvard University.

ADMIRALTY (1954)
The late Stanley Morrison, Professor of Law, Stanford University, and
The late George W. Stumberg, Professor of Law, University of Texas.

BANKRUPTCY ACT (Annotated) 1965 Edition
James Angell MacLachlan, Professor of Law Emeritus, Harvard University.

BILLS AND NOTES (1956), with Statutory Supplement
William D. Hawkland, Dean of the Law School, State University of New York at Buffalo.

BUSINESS ORGANIZATION: EMPLOYMENT—AGENCY—PARTNERSHIP—ATTORNEYS, Third Edition (1965)
Alfred F. Conard, Professor of Law, University of Michigan, and
Robert L. Knauss, Associate Professor of Law, University of Michigan.

BUSINESS ORGANIZATION: CORPORATIONS (1948)
A. A. Berle, Jr., Professor of Law, Columbia University, and
William C. Warren, Dean of the Law School, Columbia University.

BUSINESS PLANNING (1966)
David R. Herwitz, Professor of Law, Harvard University.

CIVIL PROCEDURE, see Procedure

COMMERCIAL AND INVESTMENT PAPER, Third Edition (1964) with Statutory Materials
Roscoe T. Steffen, Professor of Law, University of California, Hastings College of the Law.

COMMERCIAL LAW, CASES & MATERIALS ON, (1965) with Statutory Supplement
E. Allan Farnsworth, Professor of Law, Columbia University.
John Honnold, Professor of Law, University of Pennsylvania.

COMMERCIAL TRANSACTIONS—Text, Cases and Problems, Third Edition (1964)
Robert Braucher, Professor of Law, Harvard University, and
Arthur E. Sutherland, Jr., Professor of Law, Harvard University.

COMPARATIVE LAW, Second Edition (1959)
Rudolf B. Schlesinger, Professor of Law, Cornell University.

CONFLICT OF LAWS, Fifth Edition (1964)
Elliott E. Cheatham, Professor of Law, Vanderbilt University,
Erwin N. Griswold, Dean of the Law School, Harvard University,
Willis L. M. Reese, Professor of Law, Columbia University, and
Maurice Rosenberg, Professor of Law, Columbia University.

CONSTITUTIONAL LAW, Second Edition (1963) with 1966 Supplement
Edward L. Barrett, Jr., Dean of the Law School, University of California at Davis,
Paul W. Bruton, Professor of Law, University of Pennsylvania, and
John O. Honnold, Professor of Law, University of Pennsylvania.

UNIVERSITY CASEBOOK SERIES — Continued

DOMESTIC RELATIONS, Fourth Edition (1961), with Statutory Supplement
   Albert C. Jacobs, President, Trinity College, and
   Julius Goebel, Jr., Professor of Law Emeritus, Columbia University.

DOMESTIC RELATIONS—Civil and Canon Law (1963)
   Philip A. Ryan, Professor of Law, Georgetown University, and
   Dom David Granfield, Associate Professor, Catholic University of America.

EQUITY, Fourth Edition (1958)
   The late Zechariah Chafee, Jr., Professor of Law, Harvard University, and
   Edward D. Re, Professor of Law, St. John's University.

ETHICS, see Legal Profession

EVIDENCE, Fifth Edition (1965) with 1966 Supplement
   John M. Maguire, Professor of Law Emeritus, Harvard University.
   Jack B. Weinstein, Professor of Law, Columbia University.
   James H. Chadbourn, Professor of Law, Harvard University.
   John H. Mansfield, Professor of Law, Harvard University.

FEDERAL COURTS, Fourth Edition (1962) with 1966 Supplement
   The late Charles T. McCormick, Professor of Law, University of Texas,
   James H. Chadbourn, Professor of Law, Harvard University, and
   Charles Alan Wright, Professor of Law, University of Texas.

FEDERAL COURTS AND THE FEDERAL SYSTEM (1953)
   Henry M. Hart, Jr., Professor of Law, Harvard University and
   Herbert Wechsler, Professor of Law, Columbia University.

FEDERAL RULES OF CIVIL PROCEDURE, 1966 Edition

FEDERAL TAXATION, see Taxation

FREE ENTERPRISE AND ECONOMIC ORGANIZATION, Third Edition (1966)
   two volumes: I. Concentration & Restrictive Practices, II. Regulation of Prices, Entry & Service
   Louis B. Schwartz, Professor of Law, University of Pennsylvania.

FUTURE INTERESTS AND ESTATE PLANNING (1961) with 1962 Supplement
   W. Barton Leach, Professor of Law, Harvard University, and
   James K. Logan, Dean of the Law School, University of Kansas.

FUTURE INTERESTS (1958)
   Philip Mechem, Professor of Law Emeritus, University of Pennsylvania.

INSURANCE, Fourth Edition (1961)
   The late Edwin W. Patterson, Professor of Law, Columbia University, and
   William F. Young, Professor of Law, Columbia University.

INTERNATIONAL TRANSACTIONS AND RELATIONS (1960)
   Milton Katz, Professor of Law, Harvard University, and
   Kingman Brewster, Jr., President, Yale University.

INTRODUCTION TO LAW, see Legal Method

JUDICIAL CODE: Rules of Procedure in the Federal Courts with Excerpts from the Criminal Code, 1965 Edition
   Henry M. Hart, Jr., Professor of Law, Harvard University, and
   Herbert Wechsler, Professor of Law, Columbia University.

JURISPRUDENCE (Temporary Edition Hard Bound) (1949)
   Lon L. Fuller, Professor of Law, Harvard University.

LABOR LAW, Sixth Edition 1965 with Statutory Supplement
   Archibald Cox, Professor of Law, Harvard University, and
   Derek C. Bok, Professor of Law, Harvard University.

LABOR RELATIONS (1949)
   The late Harry Shulman, Dean of the Law School, Yale University, and
   Neil Chamberlain, Professor of Economics, Columbia University.

LEGAL DRAFTING (1951)
   Robert N. Cook, Professor of Law, University of Cincinnati.

LEGAL METHOD, Second Edition (1952)
   Noel T. Dowling, Professor of Law Emeritus, Columbia University,
   The late Edwin W. Patterson, Professor of Law, Columbia University, and
   Richard R. B. Powell, Professor of Law, University of California, Hastings College of the Law.
   Second Edition by Harry W. Jones, Professor of Law, Columbia University.

LEGAL PROFESSION, Second Edition (1955)
   Elliott E. Cheatham, Professor of Law, Vanderbilt University.

UNIVERSITY CASEBOOK SERIES — Continued

LEGISLATION, Second Edition (1959)
Horace E. Read, Vice President, Dalhousie University,
John W. MacDonald, Professor of Law, Cornell Law School, and
Jefferson B. Fordham, Dean of the Law School, University of Pennsylvania.

LOCAL GOVERNMENT LAW (1949)
Jefferson B. Fordham, Dean of the Law School, University of Pennsylvania.

MODERN REAL ESTATE TRANSACTIONS, Second Edition (1958)
Allison Dunham, Professor of Law, University of Chicago.

MUNICIPAL CORPORATIONS, see Local Government Law

NEGOTIABLE INSTRUMENTS, Second Edition (1965), with Statutory Supplement
E. Allan Farnsworth, Professor of Law, Columbia University.

NEW YORK PRACTICE (1964)
Herbert Peterfreund, Professor of Law, New York University,
Joseph M. McLaughlin, Professor of Law, Fordham University.

OIL AND GAS, Second Edition (1964)
Howard R. Williams, Professor of Law, Stanford University,
Richard C. Maxwell, Dean of the Law School, University of California, Los Angeles, and
Charles J. Meyers, Professor of Law, Stanford University.

ON LAW IN COURTS (1965)
Paul J. Mishkin, Professor of Law, University of Pennsylvania.
Clarence Morris, Professor of Law, University of Pennsylvania.

OWNERSHIP AND DEVELOPMENT OF LAND
Jan Krasnowiecki, Professor of Law, University of Pennsylvania.

PATENT, TRADEMARK AND COPYRIGHT LAW (1959)
E. Ernest Goldstein, Professor of Law, University of Texas.

PLEADING & PROCEDURE: STATE AND FEDERAL, 1962 with Federal Rules Supplement
David W. Louisell, Professor of Law, University of California at Berkeley, and
Geoffrey C. Hazard, Jr., Professor of Law, University of Chicago.

PROCEDURE—CIVIL PROCEDURE (1961), with Federal Rules Supplement and Procedure Portfolio
James H. Chadbourn, Professor of Law, Harvard University, and
A. Leo Levin, Professor of Law, University of Pennsylvania.

PROCEDURE—CIVIL PROCEDURE (1953), with Federal Rules Supplement
Richard H. Field, Professor of Law, Harvard University, and
Benjamin Kaplan, Professor of Law, Harvard University.

PROCEDURE—CIVIL PROCEDURE (1962), with Federal Rules Supplement
Maurice Rosenberg, Professor of Law, Columbia University,
Jack B. Weinstein, Professor of Law, Columbia University.

PROCEDURE PORTFOLIO (1962)
James H. Chadbourn, Professor of Law, Harvard University, and
A. Leo Levin, Professor of Law, University of Pennsylvania.

PROPERTY, Second Edition (1966)
John E. Cribbet, Professor of Law, University of Illinois,
William F. Fritz, Professor of Law, University of Texas, and
Corwin W. Johnson, Professor of Law, University of Texas.

PROPERTY (1954)
Howard R. Williams, Professor of Law, Stanford University.

PROPERTY—PERSONAL (1953)
S. Kenneth Skolfield, Professor of Law Emeritus, Boston University.

PROPERTY—PERSONAL, Third Edition (1954)
Everett Fraser, Dean of the Law School Emeritus, University of Minnesota
—Third Edition by
Charles W. Taintor II, late Professor of Law, University of Pittsburgh.

UNIVERSITY CASEBOOK SERIES — Continued

PROPERTY—REAL—INTRODUCTION, Third Edition (1954)
Everett Fraser, Dean of the Law School Emeritus, University of Minnesota.

PROPERTY—REAL PROPERTY AND CONVEYANCING (1954)
Edward S. Bade, Professor of Law Emeritus, University of Minnesota.

PUBLIC UTILITY LAW, see Free Enterprise

RECEIVERSHIP AND CORPORATE REORGANIZATION, see Creditors' Rights

RESTITUTION, Second Edition (1966)
John W. Wade, Dean of the Law School, Vanderbilt University.

SALES AND SECURITY, Fourth Edition (1962), with Statutory Supplement
George G. Bogert, James Parker Hall Professor of Law Emeritus, University of Chicago.
The late William E. Britton, Professor of Law, University of California, Hastings College of the Law, and
William D. Hawkland, Dean of the Law School, State University of New York at Buffalo.

SALES AND SALES FINANCING, Second Edition (1962) with Statutory Supplement
John O. Honnold, Professor of Law, University of Pennsylvania.

SECURITY, Third Edition (1959)
The late John Hanna, Professor of Law Emeritus, Columbia University.

SECURITIES REGULATION (1963) with 1966 Supplement
Richard W. Jennings, Professor of Law, University of California at Berkeley,
Harold Marsh, Jr., Professor of Law, University of California at Los Angeles.

TAXATION, FEDERAL, Sixth Edition (1966)
Erwin N. Griswold, Dean of the Law School, Harvard University.

TAXATION, FEDERAL ESTATE AND GIFT, 1961 Edition with 1965 Supplement
William C. Warren, Dean of the Law School, Columbia University, and
Stanley S. Surrey, Professor of Law, Harvard University.

TAXATION, FEDERAL INCOME, 1960 Edition integrated with 1961 Supplement and a 1964 Supplement
Stanley S. Surrey, Professor of Law, Harvard University, and
William C. Warren, Dean of the Law School, Columbia University.

TORTS, Second Edition (1952)
The late Harry Shulman, Dean of the Law School, Yale University, and
Fleming James, Jr., Professor of Law, Yale University.

TORTS, Third Edition (1962)
William L. Prosser, Professor of Law, University of California, Hastings College of the Law, and
The late Young B. Smith, Professor of Law, Columbia University.

TRADE REGULATION, Third Edition (1960)
Milton Handler, Professor of Law, Columbia University.

TRADE REGULATION, see Free Enterprise

TRUSTS, Third Edition (1958)
George G. Bogert, James Parker Hall Professor of Law Emeritus, University of Chicago.

TRUSTS AND SUCCESSION (1960)
George E. Palmer, Professor of Law, University of Michigan, and
Richard V. Wellman, Professor of Law, University of Michigan.

UNITED NATIONS LAW, with Documentary Supplement (1956) and Recent Cases Supplement (1963)
Louis B. Sohn, Professor of Law, Harvard University.

WILLS AND ADMINISTRATION, 5th Edition (1961)
Philip Mechem, Professor of Law Emeritus, University of Pennsylvania, and
The late Thomas E. Atkinson, Professor of Law, New York University.

WORLD LAW, see United Nations Law

University Casebook Series

EDITORIAL BOARD

LON L. FULLER
DIRECTING EDITOR
Professor of Law, Harvard University

EDWARD L. BARRETT, Jr.
Dean of the Law School, University of California at Davis

DEREK C. BOK
Professor of Law, Harvard University

JEFFERSON B. FORDHAM
Dean of the Law School, University of Pennsylvania

HARRY W. JONES
Professor of Law, Columbia University

PAGE KEETON
Dean of the Law School, University of Texas

BAYLESS A. MANNING
Dean of the Law School, Stanford University

WILLIAM L. PROSSER
Professor of Law, University of California, Hastings College of the Law

JOHN RITCHIE, III
Dean of the Law School, Northwestern University

EUGENE V. ROSTOW
Professor of Law, Yale University

SAMUEL D. THURMAN
Dean of the Law School, University of Utah

WILLIAM C. WARREN
Dean of the Law School, Columbia University

BUSINESS PLANNING

MATERIALS
ON THE
PLANNING OF CORPORATE TRANSACTIONS

By

DAVID R. HERWITZ

Professor of Law, Harvard University

Brooklyn
THE FOUNDATION PRESS, INC.
1966

DR. NORMAN A. WIGGINS

Copyright © 1966
by
THE FOUNDATION PRESS, INC.
All rights reserved

Herwitz Cs.Bus.Planning UCB

PREFACE

These materials are a product of the development of the Business Planning course here at the Harvard Law School. Three factors were primarily responsible for the creation of that course and the resulting approach taken in these materials. One was the growing demand on student time made by the tax and corporate courses, as a result of the great proliferation of materials in these fields. This was accentuated in the third year, particularly because of the trend in the basic second-year courses toward emphasizing general principles rather than specific detail, thus increasing the burden of coverage thrown on the third-year courses. A second factor was the notion that combining the corporate and tax aspects of business transactions in a single course could serve to provide the students with a more realistic view of the lawyer's work in these areas. Third, and perhaps most important, was our desire to utilize the "problem method", which we had found to be a stimulus to greater interest and effort on the part of the students, especially in the third year. We hoped that by using the problem method in a planning setting we could give the students both the experience of bringing legal materials to bear upon an actual problem and some feel for the process of exercising judgment and reaching a decision.

Accordingly, the Business Planning course was organized around a series of separate, rather detailed problems, drawn principally from actual experience or litigated cases. Each problem calls for selecting and planning the transaction which meets the needs of the parties, in the light of the applicable corporate, tax, and securities considerations. The classroom focus is expected to be almost exclusively on the problems, with the relevant legal doctrine coming into the class discussion only as it relates to the analysis of the particular problem under consideration.

The problems have been selected and arranged with an eye not only to illuminating the most important types of corporate transactions but also to providing some orderly coverage. Thus, Problem No. 1 involves the organization of a private corporation, and Problem No. 2 the organization of a public corporation. Problem No. 3 uses the conflict between the active stockholders of a close corporation and the inactive family of a deceased principal stockholder as a vehicle for analyzing stock dividends, recapitalizations, and stock repurchases. Problem No. 4 involves the impact of repurchase of stock on corporate control in a quasi-public corporation, with particular attention on the tax side to the attribution of stock ownership rules and the accumulated earnings tax; the second part of the problem presents the liquidation of a corporation. Problem No. 5 deals with the whole range of problems relating to corporate combinations; and Problem No. 6 involves the division of a corporation.

Obviously, a problem course of this type could have been conducted with the existing casebooks in the separate basic courses as the sources for the background legal material. Indeed, we did just that here for several years, using the two excellent and comprehensive casebooks, Baker & Cary, Cases and Materials on Corporations (3d ed. 1959), and Surrey & Warren, Federal Income Taxation (1960 ed.). However, our original notion that the students could be left largely on their own to "research" the problems in the casebooks did not work out well, particularly on topics to which the students had not previously been exposed. In order to aid the students in their preparation, and to provide a better focus for the discussion in each class session, we decided to develop the outlines identifying the topics and relevant source material which now accompany each of the problems. These outlines in turn rather highlighted the inconvenience of skipping around, both between and within the two casebooks, to get at the relevant material. Moreover, the second-year casebooks tend to rely more on principal cases than is necessary for a third-year course, where a generous use of all kinds of text seems appropriate. (This is especially true as to topics covered at least to some extent in second-year, for which a brief review note may be ample.)

The presentation of the materials in the book has been largely shaped in response to this background. The functional division of the chapters parallels the coverage of the problems; and the arrangement of the material within each chapter coincides with the order of discussion suggested in the outlines. As to the relative emphasis given to the various topics, that reflects not only the customary appraisal of relative importance and interest by the editor but also some estimate of whether the students are likely to have had much exposure to the subject. Thus the fact that Chapter 1 includes little more than a thumbnail review of such important topics as pooling agreements and voting trusts, while the less common subject of allocating special control over certain areas of operation is developed in some detail, reflects my judgment that the former have probably been dealt with at length in the basic Corporations course whereas the latter has not. In the same vein, rather full treatment has been given to most of the areas of corporate finance, such as dividends and reduction of capital, because at few if any schools do these subjects get more than cursory treatment in the basic course.

One requisite of the problem method is the selection of some particular corporation statute as the governing law applicable to the

PREFACE

problems. Even as early as 1960 the Model Business Corporation Act had become both an obvious and an attractive choice for that purpose; and events since then have confirmed that choice, with about half the states now having corporation statutes more or less patterned after the Model Act. The Model Act has also been the focus of some of the most useful writing in the corporate field of late (some of which is reproduced in these materials). So far as primary authority is concerned, cases decided under the Model Act are beginning to appear in some of the earliest adopting states. In addition, since the Model Act was largely patterned after the Illinois Corporation Act, authority under that statute is likely to be at least highly persuasive under the Model Act, which accounts for the special emphasis on Illinois authorities in the materials.

One question which always arises in connection with the problem method is whether to use the same problem for more than one year, in view of the risk that students will obtain the "solutions" from former students. Experience here suggests that this danger is more apparent than real. After all, there are no "official" solutions to problems of this kind; rather they simply constitute exercises in informed judgment. Moreover, since this is a third-year course, by hypothesis the "former students" are not around the following year. In any event, so far as I am aware, in more than five years of dealing with pretty much the same problems here the use of notes of former students has not proved to be any problem (if indeed it has occurred at all). Accordingly, present plans call for reprinting the same problems in the Supplement each year, but updating them to keep them current.

A couple of hopes for this permanent edition which were expressed in the preface to the temporary edition have not yet been realized. The first relates to the important subject of covenants not to compete, which is introduced in Chapter 6 but is not really presented by the real estate corporation involved in Problem No. 6. An alternative corporate division problem involving a typical operating business would be useful, but since I rarely reach Problem No. 6 anyway I have not found the opportunity to develop such an alternative. Second, the problems still do not present any significant collapsible corporation or personal holding company issues, which accounts for the very sketchy character of the materials on those subjects.

Merely to acknowledge my debt to my colleagues in the original Business Planning undertaking, Professors Ernest J. Brown, Abram J. Chayes, and Louis Loss of the Harvard Law School, and Assistant Secretary of the Treasury, Stanley S. Surrey, does not do justice to their contribution to the development of Business Planning. Suffice it to say that they are entitled to credit for much of whatever is of

PREFACE

value here, but they do not bear any responsibility for any shortcomings there may be in these materials. I would like also to express my appreciation to the authors of the two fine casebooks mentioned earlier for their generous permission to adapt portions of their materials for inclusion here.

September 1, 1966

DAVID R. HERWITZ

SUMMARY OF CONTENTS

	Page
CHAPTER 1. ORGANIZATION OF A CLOSE CORPORATION	1

Section
1. Enterprise Valuation 1
2. Allocation of Managerial Control 29
3. Allocation of Interests in a New Enterprise 44
4. Tax Aspects of Incorporation 76

CHAPTER 2. ORGANIZATION OF A PUBLIC COMPANY 189

Introduction 189
1. Federal Regulation of Public Issues of Securities 190
2. State Regulation of Securities: "Blue Sky" Laws 249
3. Problems of Compensation Income for the Promoters of a Public Company 262
4. Note on Special Problems in Planning Senior Securities .. 287

CHAPTER 3. DIVIDENDS AND OTHER CORPORATE DISTRIBUTIONS 303
Introduction 303
1. Liquidation Preferences and Stated Capital 303
2. The Fund Available for Dividends 313
3. Reduction of Capital 350
4. Tax Aspects of Corporate Dividends 371
5. Tax Aspects of Stock Dividends 379
6. Recapitalization Under Corporate Law 389
7. Tax Aspects of Recapitalization 398
8. Repurchase of Stock 414
9. Tax Incidents of Stock Repurchases 464
10. The Accumulated Earnings Tax 558
11. Note on Personal Holding Companies 594

CHAPTER 4. CORPORATE LIQUIDATIONS 613
1. Liquidation, Dissolution, and Sale of Assets 613
2. Dissolution Upon Deadlock [Set out in Chapter 6] 630
3. Tax Aspects of Corporate Liquidations 630

CHAPTER 5. CORPORATE COMBINATIONS 679
Introduction 679

1. Mechanics of Corporate Combinations 680
2. Fairness in Combination Transactions 747

SUMMARY OF CONTENTS

CHAPTER 5. CORPORATE COMBINATIONS—Continued

Section		Page
3.	Financial Aspects of Corporate Combinations	782
4.	Tax Incidents of Combination Transactions	801
5.	Carryover of Tax Attributes in Combination Transactions	836

CHAPTER 6. CORPORATE DIVISIONS 887

Introduction 887
1. Dissolution Upon Deadlock 888
2. Role of Goodwill and Covenants not to Compete 907
3. Tax Aspects of Corporate Divisions 919

Index 935

TABLE OF CONTENTS

	Page
CHAPTER 1. ORGANIZATION OF A CLOSE CORPORATION	1

Section
1. Enterprise Valuation 1
    A. Introduction 1
    B. Valuation of a Large Enterprise 7
        1. Capitalization of Earnings 13
        2. Asset Valuation 19
    C. Valuation of a Small Enterprise 26
2. Allocation of Managerial Control 29
    A. Allocation of Directorships 29
    B. Assuring Long-Term Employment 38
    C. Allocation of Control Over Designated Areas of Operation 40
3. Allocation of Interests in a New Enterprise 44
    A. Note on the Characteristics of Various Types of Stocks and Bonds 44
    B. The Authorization and Issuance of Stock 49
    C. The Use of Debt Securities 67
        1. Subordination of Shareholder Debt 69
        2. Imposition of Unlimited Liability Upon Shareholders 75
4. Tax Aspects of Incorporation 76
    A. Issuance of Stock—Tax Incidents to the Corporation 76
    B. Issuance of Stock—Tax Incidents to the Recipient .. 76
    C. Tax Incidents of Issuance of Debt 106
    D. Choice Between Stock and Debt 120
        1. Differences at the Corporate Level 120
        2. Differences to the Holder—Annual Return and Gain Upon Disposition 121
        3. Differences to the Holder—Treatment of Investment Loss 121
            a. Losses on Stock 121
            b. Losses on Debt 124
            c. Loss on Shareholder Guaranty of Corporate Debt 132
            d. Attempts to Arrange Character of Loss on Liquidation 132
    E. Limitations on the Amount of Stockholder-Owned Debt 133
        1. Form of the Obligation—Hybrid Securities 134

Herwitz Cs.Bus.Planning UCB   XV

TABLE OF CONTENTS

CHAPTER 1. ORGANIZATION OF A CLOSE CORPORATION—Continued

Section
4. Tax Aspects of Incorporation—Continued
   E. Limitations on the Amount of Stockholder-Owned Debt —Continued

                                                Page

      2. Inadequate Capitalization—Ratio of Debt to Equity 135
      3. Pro Rata Holding of Debt and Stock 136
      4. The Search for New Standards: "Intent" and "Risk" 138
      5. Creation of Debt Upon the Incorporation of a Going Business 145
      6. Substitutes for Stockholder Debt 147
   F. Subchapter S 149
   G. Multiple Corporations 157
      1. Introduction 164
      2. Sections 1561–1563 164
      3. Section 269 168
         a. Scope of the Section 168
         b. Application of § 269 to the Incorporation of a Going Enterprise 170
         c. Principal Purpose Test 170
      4. Section 1551 177
         a. Scope of the Section—Pre-1964 177
         b. Post-1964 Scope of § 1551 178
         c. Purpose 180
      5. Sections 61(a) and 482 181

CHAPTER 2. ORGANIZATION OF A PUBLIC COMPANY 189

Introduction 189

1. Federal Regulation of Public Issues of Securities 190
   A. Distribution Techniques—Underwriting 190
   B. The Securities Act of 1933 192
   C. Exemptions Available for Modest Financings 202
      1. Non-Public Offerings—Section 4(1) 202
      2. The Intra-State Exemption—Section 3(a)(11). 219
      3. Exemption for Small Issues—Section 3(b) 223
         a. In General 223
         b. Offering Circulars 227
      4. Combination of Exemptions—Integration and the "Issue" Concept 245
   D. Securities Act Problems in Issuing Stock for Professional Services 246
2. State Regulation of Securities: "Blue Sky" Laws 249
   A. Techniques of Regulation 249
   B. The Uniform Securities Act 259

TABLE OF CONTENTS

CHAPTER 2. ORGANIZATION OF A PUBLIC COMPANY—Continued

Section
2. State Regulation of Securities: "Blue Sky" Laws—Continued

Page
3. Problems of Compensation Income for the Promoters of a Public Company _____ 262
4. Note on Special Problems in Planning Senior Securities __ 287
   A. Annual Return on Senior Securities _____ 287
      1. Dividends on Preferred Stock _____ 287
      2. Interest on Debt Securities _____ 289
   B. Rights on Liquidation _____ 290
      1. Preferred Stock _____ 290
      2. Debt Securities _____ 291
   C. Voting Rights _____ 291
   D. Convertibility _____ 293
      1. In General _____ 293
      2. Problems of Convertible Securities and Warrants 295
   E. Redemption _____ 297
   F. Sinking Funds _____ 299
   G. Contractual Restrictions _____ 300

CHAPTER 3. DIVIDENDS AND OTHER CORPORATE DISTRIBUTIONS 303

Introduction _____ 303

1. Liquidation Preferences and Stated Capital _____ 303
2. The Fund Available for Dividends _____ 313
   A. In General _____ 313
   B. Unrealized Appreciation as a Source of Dividends __ 320
      1. Randall v. Bailey _____ 320
      2. Analysis of Randall v. Bailey _____ 322
      3. The Role of Accounting _____ 326
      4. The Aftermath of Randall v. Bailey in New York 328
      5. Unrealized Appreciation Outside New York ____ 332
      6. Revaluation Under the Model Act _____ 335
      7. Methods of Valuation _____ 340
   C. Stock Dividends _____ 341
      1. In General _____ 341
      2. Stock Dividends—A Further Analysis _____ 343
      3. Stock Dividends Out of Revaluation Surplus ____ 349
3. Reduction of Capital _____ 350
   A. Historical Background _____ 350
   B. Mechanics of a Reduction _____ 351
   C. Impact of a Reduction of Capital _____ 358
      1. Upon Creditors _____ 358
      2. Impact of a Reduction Upon Preferred Stockholders _____ 362

TABLE OF CONTENTS

CHAPTER 3. DIVIDENDS AND OTHER CORPORATE DISTRIBUTIONS—Continued

Section
3. Reduction of Capital—Continued
   C. Impact of a Reduction of Capital—Continued   Page
      3. Respective Rights of Preferred and Common in Reduction Surplus _____ 365
4. Tax Aspects of Corporate Dividends _____ 371
   A. Corporate Distributions in General _____ 371
   B. Computation of Earnings and Profits _____ 373
   C. Disguised Dividends _____ 374
   D. Dividends in Kind _____ 374
5. Tax Aspects of Stock Dividends _____ 379
   A. Historical Background _____ 379
   B. Current Law—Receipt of Stock Dividends _____ 384
   C. Current Law—Disposition of Dividend Stock _____ 385
      1. The Operation of § 306 _____ 385
      2. Some Current § 306 Issues _____ 388
6. Recapitalization Under Corporate Law _____ 389
7. Tax Aspects of Recapitalization _____ 398
   A. In General _____ 398
   B. Distributions Having the Effect of a Dividend _____ 400
   C. Preferred Stock Recapitalizations _____ 403
      1. Recapitalizations Equivalent to a Stock Dividend 403
      2. Stock Dividends as Recapitalizations _____ 405
      3. Non Pro Rata Recapitalizations _____ 406
   D. Securities Recapitalizations _____ 410
8. Repurchase of Stock _____ 414
   A. Power to Purchase _____ 414
   B. Fiduciary Limitation on Repurchase of Stock _____ 441
9. Tax Incidents of Stock Repurchases _____ 464
   A. Historical Background _____ 464
   B. Impact of a Redemption Upon the Withdrawing Shareholders _____ 471
      1. In General—§ 302 _____ 471
      2. Redemption to Pay Estate Taxes—§ 303 _____ 481
      3. Redemption Through Related Corporations—§ 304 _____ 482
      4. Partial Liquidation—§ 346 _____ 482
   C. Special Tax Aspects of an Installment Repurchase _____ 487
      1. Deferred Payment Transactions in General _____ 490
         a. "Open" Versus "Closed" Transactions _____ 490
         b. The Role of Accounting Method _____ 493
         c. Accounting for Gain on the Repayment of an Obligation _____ 496
      2. The Discount Factor in Deferred Obligations _____ 503
      3. The Installment Method of Accounting _____ 519
      4. Section 483 _____ 526

TABLE OF CONTENTS

Chapter 3. Dividends and Other Corporate Distributions —Continued

Section
9. Tax incidents of Stock Repurchases—Continued

		Page
D.	Impact of a Redemption Upon the Remaining Stockholders	532
E.	Tax Incidents of a Redemption to the Corporation	538
	1. Recognition of Gain or Loss Upon a Redemption Distribution in Kind	538
	2. Deductibility of Redemption Expenses	540
	a. The "Partial Liquidation" Cases	540
	b. The "Straight Redemption" Cases	543
	c. Distinguishing Between Expenses of the Corporation and Expenses of the Individual Stockholders	545
	d. Deductibility of Expenses for Tax Advice— § 212(3)	546
	3. Effect of a Redemption on Earnings and Profits	554

10. The Accumulated Earnings Tax 558
    A. In General 558
    B. Purpose, Burden of Proof, and the Role of the Reasonable Business Needs Issue 565
       1. Apart From the § 535(c) Credit 565
       2. The Impact of the § 535(c)(1) Credit 578
       3. Proof of Reasonable Business Needs 580
    C. Accumulation of Earnings in Connection With a Redemption 582
11. Note on Personal Holding Companies 594

Chapter 4. Corporate Liquidations 613

1. Liquidation, Dissolution, and Sale of Assets 613
   A. Introduction 613
   B. The Requirement of Stockholder Approval for a Sale of Assets 615
      1. In General 615
      2. Sale of Assets Pursuant to a Dissolution 622
   C. Rights of Creditors Upon a Sale of Assets, Liquidation or Dissolution 624
2. Dissolution Upon Deadlock [Set out in Chapter 6] 630
3. Tax Aspects of Corporate Liquidations 630
   A. In General 630
   B. Note on Collapsible Corporations 657

Chapter 5. Corporate Combinations 679

Introduction 679
1. Mechanics of Corporate Combinations 680

TABLE OF CONTENTS

CHAPTER 5. CORPORATE COMBINATIONS—Continued

Section
1. Mechanics of Corporate Combinations—Continued

		Page
A.	In General	680
B.	Securities Regulation Aspects	693
	1. In General	693
	2. Rule 133	695
C.	The De Facto Merger Doctrine	697
D.	Liquidation of the Acquired Corporation	723
	1. In General	723
	2. Special Problems in the Liquidation of a Controlled Subsidiary	724
	a. Straight Dissolution	724
	b. The "Short Merger" Procedure	730
	3. Effect of Liquidation Preferences	735
	4. Alteration of Preferred Stockholders' Liquidation Preference	737

2. Fairness in Combination Transactions ... 747
   A. Fairness Between the Constituent Corporations ... 747
   B. Fairness Among Classes of Stock of the Same Corporation ... 761
      1. In General ... 761
      2. Standards for Testing Inter-Class Fairness in Recapitalizations ... 765
         a. The Absolute Priority Approach ... 765
         b. The Investment Value Approach ... 767
         c. The Appraised Valuation Approach ... 773

3. Financial Aspects of Corporate Combinations ... 782
   A. Introduction ... 782
   B. Standards for Deciding Whether a Transaction is a Purchase or a Pooling ... 787
      1. The Approach of the AICPA ... 787
      2. The View of the SEC ... 793
   C. Parent-Subsidiary Accounting Problems ... 795
   D. Purchase and Pooling Under the Corporation Statutes ... 796

4. Tax Incidents of Combination Transactions ... 801
   A. General Background ... 801
      1. Non-Recognition and Basis for Corporate Transferors and Transferees ... 802
      2. Non-Recognition and Basis for Shareholders and Security Holders ... 803
   B. Judicial Limitations on Qualification as a Reorganization ... 804
      1. In General ... 804
      2. Continuity of Interest ... 805

xx

TABLE OF CONTENTS

CHAPTER 5. CORPORATE COMBINATIONS—Continued
    B. Judicial Limitations on Qualification as a Reorganization—Continued

Section
4. Tax Incidents of Combination Transactions—Continued

		Page
	3. Continuity of Business Enterprise	811
	4. Use of a Subsidiary in Reorganization Acquisitions	813
C.	Special Problems in B Reorganizations	814
	1. In General	814
	2. Liquidation of a Subsidiary Acquired in a AB Reorganization	824
	a. Recognition of Gain or Loss	824
	b. Basis Aspects in the Tax-Free Liquidation of a Subsidiary	825
D.	Special Problems in C Reorganizations	828
	1. Exceptions to the "Solely for Voting Stock" Requirement	828
	2. Acquisition of "Substantially All" of the Acquired Corporation's Property	829
	3. Liquidation of the Acquired Corporation	831
	4. Effect of Ownership by the Acquiring Corporation of Stock in the Acquired Corporation	832
	5. Claims of Dissenting Stockholders	833

5. Carryover of Tax Attributes in Combination Transactions 836
    A. In General 836
    B. Carryover of Earnings and Profits 837
    C. Net Operating Losses 841
        1. Mechanics of the Operating Loss Carryover Provisions 841
        2. Carryover of Operating Losses in Corporate Combinations 847
            a. Survival of Operating Losses Under Prior Law 847
            b. The 1954 Code Treatment 848
        3. Limitations on Loss Carryovers in Combination Transactions 851
            a. Section 382(b) 851
            b. Section 382(a) 857
            c. The Libson Shops Doctrine 858
            d. Section 269 858
            e. Consolidated Returns 861
        4. Limitations on Loss Carryovers in Non-Reorganization Transactions 872

TABLE OF CONTENTS

	Page
CHAPTER 6. CORPORATE DIVISIONS	887

Introduction 887

Section
1. Dissolution Upon Deadlock 888
2. Role of Goodwill and Covenants not to Compete 907
   A. In General 907
   B. Implied Covenants not to Compete 910
   C. Tax Aspects of Covenants not to Compete 913
3. Tax Aspects of Corporate Divisions 919
   A. In General 919
   B. Qualification Under § 355 921
   C. The Liquidation-Reincorporation Problem 934

Index 935

TABLE OF CASES

The principal cases are in italic type. Cases discussed in notes and footnotes are in roman type. References are to pages.

A.B.C.D. Lands, Inc. v. Commissioner, 377
Abelow v. Midstates Oil Corp., 730, 759
Abercrombie v. Davies, 35
Ach v. Commissioner, 185
Advanced Research Associates, Inc., 211
Advance Machinery Exchange, Inc. v. Commissioner, 183
Airlene Gas Co. v. United States, 177
Alcorn Wholesale Co. v. Commissioner, 171
Alcott v. Hyman, 712
Aldon Homes, Inc. v. Commissioner, 181
Allen v. Commissioner, 274
Alprosa Watch Corp. v. Commissioner, 168, 848
American Bantam Car Co. v. Commissioner, 81
American Hosp. & Life Ins. Co. v. Kunkel, 428
American Smelting & Refining Co. v. United States, 507
Annabelle Candy Co. v. Commissioner, 544, 917
Apollo Industries, Inc. v. Commissioner, 581
Applestein v. United Board & Carton Corp., 692, 710, 711.
Archbold v. United States, 478
Architectural Building Products, Inc. v. Cupples Products Corp., 689
Arnold v. Phillips, 74, 144
Atlantic City Electric Co. v. Commissioner, 810
Atzingen-Whitehouse Dairy, Inc. v. Commissioner, 543

Ballentine Motor Co. v. Commissioner, 183
Baltimore v. Commissioner, 274
Bangor & Aroostook Ry. Co. v. Commissioner, 374
Barrett v. Denver Tramway Corp., 763, 766
Barrow Manufacturing Co. v. Commissioner, 577, 581
Bass v. Commissioner, 404, 405
Bateman v. Commissioner, 810

Bausch & Lomb Optical Co. v. Commissioner, 832
Baxter v. Lancer Industries, Inc., 332
Bazley v. Commissioner, 412, 804
Becher v. Commissioner, 812
Bedford v. Commissioner, 412
Benas v. Title Guaranty Trust Co., 359
Benintendi v. Kenton Hotel, 39
Bennett v. Propp, 448
Bentsen v. Phinney, 812
Berckmans v. Commissioner, 262, 275
Berghash v. Commissioner, 654
Berks Broadcasting Co. v. Craumer, 332
Berner v. United States, 277
Berry, Estate of v. Commissioner, 511
Bijou-Pensacola Corp. v. United States, 145
Blumenthal v. Roosevelt Hotel, Inc., 691
Bolmer Bros., Inc. v. Bolmer Const. Co., 330
Bonsall v. Commissioner, 921
Bowman v. Armour & Co., 393, 412, 511
Boyle v. Commissioner, 477
Bradbury v. Commissioner, 473
Brake & Electric Sales Corp. v. United States, 145
Brandon v. United States, 846
Brill v. Blakeley, 365
British Motor Car Distributors, Ltd. v. Commissioner, 168
Broadway Drive-In Theater v. United States, 137
Brook v. Commissioner, 118
Brown v. Commissioner, 117, 404, 405, 495
Brown v. Watson, 52
Burke v. Commissioner, 929
Burnet v. Logan, 491
Burr Oaks Corp. v. Commissioner, 97
Bush Hog Manufacturing Co. v. Commissioner, 178, 187
Cameron Industries, Inc., 245
Campbell v. Carter Foundation Production Co., 118
Campbell v. Commissioner, 129
Campbell v. Wheeler, 78
Campbell County State Bank v. Commissioner, 183

TABLE OF CASES

Camp Wolters Enterprises v. Commissioner, 116
Cardinal Finance Co. v. Commissioner, 656
Carpenter v. United States, 551
Cary v. Commissioner, 479
Casey v. Commissioner, 578
Catalina Homes, Inc. v. Commissioner, 150
Central Bldg. & Loan Ass'n, 640
Chamberlin v. Commissioner, 380
Charles Ilfeld Co. v. Hernandez, 871
Charter Wire, Inc. v. United States, 146
Cheff v. Mathes, 452, 460
Chicago Corp. v. Munds, 24, 691, 778
Childs Company, 296
Christie v. Fifth Madison Corp., 435
Cisler v. Commissioner, 520
City Bank of Washington, 637
City of. See under name of city.
Civic Center Finance Co. v. Kuhl, 809
Clem v. Campbell, 274
Coady, 924, 929
Coastal Oil Storage Co. v. Commissioner, 168, 169, 177, 859
Cole v. National Cash Credit Ass'n, 688, 760.
Colony, Inc., The v. Commissioner, 137
Colton v. Williams, 283
Commerce Photo-Print Corp. v. Commissioner, 543
Commissioner v. Capento Securities Corp., 412
Commissioner v. Carter, 491
Commissioner v. Caulkins, 505
Commissioner v. Court Holding Co., 100, 631
Commissioner v. Day & Zimmerman, 825
Commissioner v. Doering, 546
Commissioner v. Estate of Bedford, 400
Commissioner v. Estate of Ogsbury, 286
Commissioner v. Fender Sales, Inc., 77
Commissioner v. First State Bank of Stratford, 375
Commissioner v. Gilbert, 142
Commissioner v. Godley, 378
Commissioner v. Gross, 186, 330, 378
Commissioner v. Haserot, 482
Commissioner v. Hirshon Trust, 378
Commissioner v. H. W. Porter & Co., 76
Commissioner v. LoBue, 280
Commissioner v. Morgan, 505
Commissioner v. National Bellas Hess, Inc., 90, 96.
Commissioner v. Neustadt's Trust, 410

Commissioner v. Smith, 280
Commissioner v. South Lake Farms, Inc., 642
Commissioner v. Stone's Estate, 282
Commissioner v. Turnbow, 814
Commissioner v. Virginia Metal Products, Inc., 870
Commissioner v. Wilson, 925
Commonwealth Title Ins. & Trust Co. v. Seltzer, 442
Commonwealth & Southern Corp., 306, 364
Cortland Specialty Co. v. Commissioner, 805
Costello v. Fazio, 69, 145
Cottrell v. Pawcatuck Co., 24, 760
Cowden v. Commissioner, 494
Cox v. Commissioner, 97
Crowell-Collier Publishing Co., 213, 215
Culbertson v. Commissioner, 492
Curry v. Commissioner, 119
Curtis v. United States, 933
Cutter Labs, Inc. v. Twining, 432

Darcy v. Brooklyn & N. Y. Ferry Co., 624
Davis v. Penfield, 413
Daytona Marine Supply Co. v. United States, 146
Dean v. Commissioner, 409
Dees v. Commissioner, 268, 275
Deutsch v. Commissioner, 535
D. F. Bernheimer & Co., 211
Diamond Brothers Co. v. Commissioner, 137, 145
Dillier v. Commissioner, 172
Dill Mfg. Co., 587
Dimbula Valley (Ceylon) Tea Co. v. Laurie, 334
Distributors Finance Corp. v. Commissioner, 827
Dorminey v. Commissioner, 130
Drybrough v. Commissioner, 78

Easson v. Commissioner, 79
Eastern Gas and Fuel Associates, Matter of, 771
Eaton v. White, 266
E. I. du Pont de Nemours & Co. v. United States, 89
Eisenberg v. Commissioner, 846
Eisner v. Macomber, 341, 379
Electric Regulator Corp. v. Commissioner, 581

TABLE OF CASES

Ellingwood v. Wolf's Head Oil Refining Co., 292
Ennis v. Commissioner, 493
Esrenco Truck Co. v. Commissioner, 157
Essex Universal Corp. v. Yates, 442
Euclid-Tennessee, Inc. v. Commissioner, 885

Fahs v. Florida Machine & Foundry Co., 93
Fairfield S. S. Corp. v. Commissioner, 649
Family Record Plan, Inc., 641, 643
Farmers Union Corp. v. Commissioner, 538
Farris v. Glen Alden Corp., 699, 703, 704, 705, 706
Fedcal Distributing Co. v. Commissioner, 171
Federal Grain Corp. v. Commissioner, 96
Federal United Corp. v. Havender, 392
Federal Water Service Corp., 769, 770
Felder v. Anderson, Clayton & Co., 24
Fenco, Inc. v. United States, 578, 581
Ferris v. United States, 476
Fidanque v. American Maracaibo Co., 711
First Nat. Bank of St. Elmo, Illinois v. United States, 376
First Savings & Loan Ass'n v. Commissioner, 490
Fischer v. Commissioner, 404
Five Star Manufacturing Co. v. Commissioner, 545
Floyd v. Scofield, 642
Fors Farms, Inc. v. United States, 149
Fotocrafters, Inc. v. Commissioner, 578
1432 Broadway Corp. v. Commissioner, 136
Fox v. Harrison, 537
Franzblau v. Capital Securities Co., Inc., 763

Galler v. Galler, 39
Gamman v. Commissioner, 151
Garlove v. Commissioner, 131
Gazette Publishing Co. v. Self, 587
Gearing, Matter of, 36, 40
Geeseman v. Commissioner, 280
General Alloy Casting Co. v. Commissioner, 149
General Inv. Co. v. American Hide & Leather Co., 459
General Utilities & Operating Co. v. Helvering, 375

George v. Commissioner, 833
George L. Castner Co. v. Commissioner, 495
Gerdes v. Reynolds, 442
Gidwitz v. Lanzit Corrugated Box Co., 904
Gilbert v. Commissioner, 140, 497
Gloninger v. Commissioner, 537
Gloucester Ice & Cold Storage Co. v. Commissioner, 138
Glover Packing Co. of Texas v. United States, 884
Goldman v. Postal Telegraph, Inc., 737
Gooding Amusement Co. v. Commissioner, 139
Goodman v. Global Indus., 431
Goodnow v. American Writing Paper Co., 317, 325
Goss v. Commissioner, 536
Graham v. Louisville Transit Co., 366
Gravois Planing Mill Co. v. Commissioner, 541
Gregory v. Helvering, 804
Groman v. Commissioner, 813
Gulledge v. Commissioner, 131
Guttmann v. Illinois Central R. Co., 288

Hall v. Geiger-Jones Co., 249
Hamburgers York Road v. Commissioner, 184
Hamilton Mfg. Co. v. United States, 361
Hammond Iron Co. v. Commissioner, 538
Hamrick v. Commissioner, 78, 822
Hardstone Brick Co. v. Department of Commerce, 257
Hariton v. Arco Electronics, Inc., 698, 708
Hartman Tobacco Co. v. Commissioner, 92
Hartzell v. Commissioner, 407
Haskell Mfg. Co. v. United States, 362
Hawkinson v. Commissioner, 402
Hay v. Hay, 290
Hays Corp. v. Commissioner, 824
Hedberg-Freidheim Contracting Co. v. Commissioner, 578
Heilbrunn v. Sun Chem. Corp., 701
Heller v. Commissioner, 804, 805
Heller Trust v. Commissioner, 495
Helvering v. Gowran, 380
Helvering v. Griffiths, 380
Helvering v. Minnesota Tea Co., 805, 831
Helvering v. Southwest Consolidated Corp., 399, 822, 833
Helvering v. Sprouse, 380
Helvering v. Tex-Penn Oil Co., 277, 492

TABLE OF CASES

Helvering v. Winston Bros. Co., 833
Herbert's Estate v. Commissioner, 496
Heringer v. Commissioner, 277
H. F. Ramsey Co. v. Commissioner, 861, 885
Hiawatha Home Builders, Inc. v. Commissioner, 177
Hickok v. Commissioner, 413
Himmel v. Commissioner, 476
Hollywood Baseball Ass'n v. Commissioner, 76
Holsey v. Commissioner, 532
Holstein v. Commissioner, 96
Holtz v. Commissioner, 132
Honigman v. Green Giant Co., 764
Hottenstein v. York Ice Machinery Corp., 779, 781
Howard Case, 820
Humphrys v. The Winous Co., 31

Idaho Power Co. v. United States, 402
Idol v. Commissioner, 536, 539
Imler v. Commissioner, 485
I. T. 2674, XII—1, p. 511

Jackson v. Nicolai-Neppach Co., 888
Jacques Coe & Co. v. Minneapolis-Moline Co., 774, 691
J. A. Maurer, Inc. v. Commissioner, 135
James Armour, Inc. v. Commissioner, 652
James Bros. Coal Co. v. Commissioner, 514
James Realty Co. v. United States, 168, 169
Janney v. Philadelphia Transp. Co., 30
Jay Ronald Co. v. Marshall Mortgage Corp., 351
J. E. Hawes Corp. v. Commissioner, 656
Jerome v. Cogswell, 351
Jewell v. United States, 79
Jewell Ridge Coal Corp. v. Commissioner, 138
J. Gordon Turnbull, Inc. v. Commissioner, 545
J. I. Morgan, Inc. v. Commissioner, 117
John A. Nelson Co. v. Helvering, 806, 810
John Kelley Co. v. Commissioner, 134, 135
John P. Scripps Newspapers v. Commissioner, 558
Johnston v. Commissioner, 493
Jolley v. United States, 525
Joseph C. Gallagher, 653
Joy Manufacturing Co. v. Commissioner, 77

Kaczmarek v. Commissioner, 94
Katcher v. Ohsman, 39
Kaufmann v. United States, 546
Keller v. Wilson & Co., 391, 742
Kellogg v. Georgia-Pacific Paper Corp., 725
Kelly Trust v. Commissioner, 405
Kennedy v. Carolina Public Service Co., 364
Kimbell-Diamond Milling Co. v. Commissioner, 825
Kingsford Co. v. Commissioner, 511
Kingston v. Home Life Ins. Co., 324
Kinney, Matter of, 363
Kleinberg v. Schwartz, 440
Kneeland v. Emerton, 256
Kniffin v. Commissioner, 98
Knowles v. Commissioner, 277
Kors v. Carey, 443, 460
Koshland v. Helvering, 379
Kruger v. Gerth, 900
Kuchman v. Commissioner, 285
Kuckenberg, 640, 643

LaBelle Iron Works v. United States, 322, 327, 333, 334
LaVoy Supply Co. v. Young, 431
Leavin v. Commissioner, 517
Lehman v. Commissioner, 285
Le Tulle v. Scofield, 806
LeVant v. Commissioner, 278, 284
Levin v. Midland-Ross Corp., 19, 778
Levin v. Pittsburgh United Corp., 613
Levy v. Commissioner, 657
Libson Shops, Inc. v. Koehler, 848, 858, 883
Lich v. United States Rubber Co., 362
Lockwood, Estate of v. Commissioner, 929
Loftus v. Mason, 330
Louisiana Irrigation and Mill Co. v. Commissioner, 377
Lutkins v. Commissioner, 820

McCarthy v. Conley, 482
MacDonald v. Commissioner, 278
MacFarlane v. North American Cement Corp., 762
McGinty v. Commissioner, 537
McNamara v. Commissioner, 283
McShain v. Commissioner, 537
Made Rite Investment Co. v. Commissioner, 172
Mailloux v. Commissioner, 274, 277
Mairs v. Madden, 442

xxvi

TABLE OF CASES

Maloney v. Spencer, 130
Mamula v. Commissioner, 521
Manacher v. Reynolds, 764
Marks v. Wolfson, 19
Marsack, Estate of v. Commissioner, 492, 493
Marsan Realty Corp. v. Commissioner, 97
Martin v. American Potash Chemical Corp., 352
Marwais Steel Co. v. Commissioner, 872
Marx v. Bragalini, 331
Mathews Const. Co., In re, 431
Maxwell Hardware Co. v. Commissioner, 874
May Broadcasting Co. v. United States, 94
Mayellen Apartments Inc., In re, 622
M. C. Parrish & Co. v. Commissioner, 504
Mendham Corp. v. Commissioner, 836
Merlo Builders, Inc. v. Commissioner, 138
Merritt-Chapman & Scott Corp. v. New York Trust Co., 296
Middle States Terminals, Inc. v. Commissioner, 181
Miller v. United States, 493
Miller's Estate v. Commissioner, 135
Mills v. Commissioner, 811, 822
Mills Estate, Inc. v. Commissioner, 540
Moffatt v. Commissioner, 652
Mohawk Carpet Mills, Inc. v. Delaware Rayon Corp., 290
Mojonnier & Sons, Inc. v. Commissioner, 93
Montana Power Co. v. United States, 507
Moore v. Commissioner, 480
Moro v. Soldo, 428
Morris v. Standard Gas & Electric Co., 325
Motel Co. v. Commissioner, 138
Moughon v. Commissioner, 147
Mountain State Case, 582
Mountain States Mixed Feed Co. v. United States, 657
Mountain States Steel Foundries, Inc. v. Commissioner, 414, 332, 545
Mountain Water Co. of La Crescenta, 635
Muchnic v. Commissioner, 406
Murphy v. Guantanamo Sugar Co., 763
Murphy Logging Co. v. United States, 148, 149

Nassau Lens Co. v. Commissioner, 143, 508
Neff v. United States, 480
New Colonial Ice Co. v. Helvering, 848
New England Foundry Corp. v. Commissioner, 178
Newman v. Arabol Mfg. Co., 736
North American Philips Co. v. Commissioner, 492
Northern Trust Co. v. Essaness Theatres Corp., 441, 442

Obre v. Alban Tractor Co., 72
O'Connor v. Commissioner, 93
O. D. 852, p. 543
O'Neill v. Maytag, 458
Opelka v. Quincy Memorial Bridge Co., 614
Orzeck v. Englehart, 701, 711
Otis & Co. v. SEC, 767
Overland Corp. v. Commissioner, 91
Oxford v. Macon Telegraph Publishing Co., 333

Page v. Whittenton Mfg. Co., 364
Paine v. Commissioner, 497, 509
Palmbaum v. Magulsky, 34
Paloma Frocks, Inc. v. Shamokin Sportswear Corp., 42
Parker v. Commissioner, 479
Parker v. United States, 95
Parshelsky's Estate v. Commissioner, 933
Pelton Steel Casting Co. v. Commissioner, 586
Penfield v. Davis, 116
People ex rel. Wedgewood Realty Co. v. Lynch, 324
Perlman v. Feldmann, 7, 24, 761
Petrishen v. Westmoreland Finance Corp., 51
Philadelphia Park Amusement Co. v. United States, 77
Philadelphia Steel & Iron Corp. v. Commissioner, 23
Phillips v. Frank, 499
Phipps Industrial Land Trust v. Commissioner, 495
Phoenix Coal Co. v. Commissioner, 845
Phoenix Electronics, Inc. v. United States, 845
Pinellas Ice & Cold Storage Co. v. Commissioner, 805
Pittsfield Coal & Oil Co. v. Commissioner, 98

TABLE OF CASES

Porges v. Vadsco Sales Corp., 762
Powell's Pontiac-Cadillac, Inc. v. Gross, 633
Prentis v. United States, 117
Pretzer v. United States, 510
Pridemark, Inc. v. Commissioner, 654
Priester v. Commissioner, 535
Putnam v. Commissioner, 132, 148

Quintal v. Greenstein, 324

Radom & Neidorff, In re, 899, 908
Raleigh Properties, Inc. v. Commissioner, 508
Randall v. Bailey, 320, 359
Rank v. United States, 284
Rath v. Rath Packing Co., 714
Raybestos-Manhattan, Inc. v. United States, 690
Raymond I. Smith, Inc. v. Commissioner, 579
Reed v. Commissioner, 137
Reifsnyder v. Pittsburgh Outdoor Advertising Co., 459
Reilly Oil Co. v. Commissioner, 809
Rev.Proc. 62-32, p. 98
Rev.Proc. 63-20, p. 98
Rev.Proc. 64-22, p. 101
Rev.Proc. 64-31, pp. 98, 119, 389, 481
Rev.Rul. 54-396, p. 833
Rev.Rul. 55-59, pp. 811, 822
Rev.Rul. 55-112, p. 410
Rev.Rul. 56-116, p. 403
Rev.Rul. 56-220, p. 811
Rev.Rul. 56-285, p. 845
Rev.Rul. 56-303, pp. 115, 116
Rev.Rul. 56-330, p. 812
Rev.Rul. 56-512, p. 930
Rev.Rul. 56-513, p. 486
Rev.Rul. 56-541, p. 653
Rev.Rul. 56-654, p. 403
Rev.Rul. 57-132, p. 388
Rev.Rul. 57-278, p. 833
Rev.Rul. 57-328, p. 388
Rev.Rul. 57-334, pp. 486, 931
Rev.Rul. 57-490, p. 378
Rev.Rul. 57-518, p. 829
Rev.Rul. 58-402, p. 492
Rev.Rul. 58-603, p. 858
Rev.Rul. 58-614, p. 532
Rev.Rul. 59-60, p. 26
Rev.Rul. 59-84, p. 410
Rev.Rul. 59-197, pp. 403, 932
Rev.Rul. 59-233, p. 478
Rev.Rul. 59-259, p. 95

Rev.Rul. 59-400, p. 931
Rev.Rul. 60-50, p. 655
Rev.Rul. 60-302, p. 81
Rev.Rul. 60-322, p. 486
Rev.Rul. 61-214, p. 656
Rev.Rul. 62-74, p. 491
Rev.Rul. 62-128, p. 97
Rev.Rul. 63-29, 812
Rev.Rul. 63-40, p. 872
Rev.Rul. 63-226, p. 150
Rev.Rul. 63-234, p. 95
Rev.Rul. 63-245, p. 654
Rev.Rul. 64-56, p. 87
Rev.Rul. 64-73, p. 813
Rev.Rul. 64-102, p. 932
Rev.Rul. 64-147, p. 929
Rev.Rul. 64-309, p. 151
Rev.Rul. 65-96, p. 845
Rev.Rul. 65-192, p. 25
Rev.Rul. 65-257, p. 655
Rev.Rul. 65-289, p. 481
Rev.Rul. 66-67, p. 122
Rev.Rul. 66-112, pp. 78, 822
Rev.Rul. 218, p. 846
Richards v. Ernst Wiener Co., 432
Ringling Bros.-Barnum & Bailey Combined Shows v. Ringling, 35
Rio Grande Oil Co. v. Welsh, 392
Roberts v. Whitson, 35
Roberts Co. v. Commissioner, 94
Robinson v. Wangemann, 429, 540
Roebling v. Commissioner, 807
Romer v. United States, 846
Rooney v. United States, 642
Roosevelt Hotel Co. v. Commissioner, 834
Root v. York Corp., 781
Rosenfeld v. Fairchild Engine and Airplane Corp., 442
Rosenthal v. Commissioner, 119
Rowan v. United States, 132, 135, 147
Rubin v. Commissioner, 130
Rudco Oil & Gas Co. v. United States, 377
Ruppert Plumbing & Heating Co. v. Commissioner, 870

St. Louis Southwestern Ry. Co. v. Loeb, 288
Sanders v. Cuba R. R. Co., 288
Sandy Estate Co. v. Commissioner, 582
San Joaquin Light & Power Corp., In re, 729
Schine Chain Theaters, Inc. v. Commissioner, 137, 145
Schmidt, Estate of, v. Commissioner, 97, 657

xxviii

TABLE OF CASES

Scott Building Supply Corp. v. Mississippi State Tax Commission, 333
Scripps Newspapers Case, 578, 580
S. E. C. v. Ralston Purina Co., 202, 207
Seeley v. New York National Exchange Bank, 350
Sensabaugh v. Polson Plywood Co., 37
Shanik v. White Sewing Machine Corp., 392
Shanken v. Lee Wolfman, Inc., 32
Shannon v. Commissioner, 119
Shannon v. Stevenson, 52
Shaw Construction Co. v. Commissioner, 183
Shea v. Commissioner, 132
Shrage v. Bridgeport Oil Co., 724, 729
Siegel v. Commissioner, 169
Silverman Application of, 691
Simmons v. Commissioner, 278
Simpson v. Commissioner, 79
Slater v. Commissioner, 493
Smith v. Good Music Station, Inc., 761
Smith v. San Francisco & N. P. Ry. Co., 34
Southern Engineering and Metal Products Corp. v. Commissioner, 543
Southland Ice Co. v. Commissioner, 828, 834
Southwest Natural Gas Co. v. Commissioner, 807
Specialty Paper and Board Co. v. Commissioner, 278
Spiegel v. Beacon Participations, Inc., 459
Spreckles v. Commissioner, 136
Springfield Street R. Co. v. United States, 845, 846
Squier, Estate of v. Commissioner, 471, 479
Standard Linen Service, Inc. v. Commissioner, 539
Stanton Brewery, Inc. v. Commissioner, 848
State ex rel. Cullitan v. Campbell, 293
State Farming Co. v. Commissioner, 845
Stater Bros., Inc.—Second Street v. Commissioner, 170
Sterling v. Mayflower Hotel Corp., 747
Sterling Industries, Inc. v. Ball Bearing Pen Corp., 41
Stieglitz v. Electrol, Inc., 298
Stiles v. Aluminum Products Co., 620
Stockton Harbor Industrial Co. v. Commissioner, 835
Strassburger v. Commissioner, 380
Strong v. Fromm Laboratories, 896

Talbot Mills v. Commissioner, 134
Taylor v. Axton-Fisher Tobacco Co., 298
Temple v. Bodega Bay Fisheries, 75
Tennant v. Epstein, 288
Tennessee, Alabama & Georgia Ry. Co. v. Commissioner, 827
Texas Bank & Trust Co. of Dallas v. Commissioner, 827
Texoma Supply Co. v. Commissioner, 138
Theater Concessions, Inc. v. Commissioner, 177
Thompson v. Fairleigh, 298
Thornhill v. Commissioner, 284
Tiffany v. Commissioner, 477
Tobey v. Commissioner, 131
Tobin v. Cody, 911
Tombari v. Commissioner, 487
Towne v. Eisner, 379
Treves v. Menzies, 613
Tri-Continental Corp. v. Battye, 24
Trotz v. Commissioner, 95
Trust Co. of Georgia v. Rose, 266, 271, 276
Trustees of Dartmouth College v. Woodward, 742
Turnbow Case, 820
Turner v. Commissioner, 107
Turzillo v. Commissioner, 280

Ultramares Corp. v. Touche, 199
Underhill v. Commissioner, 502, 518
Ungar v. Commissioner, 275
Union Chemical & Materials Corp. v. United States, 282
United Corporation, 307
United Light and Power Co., 770
United States v. Carey, 477
United States v. Cumberland Pub. Service Co., 631
United States v. Duke Laboratories, Inc., 577
United States v. E. I. duPont de Nemours & Co., 403
United States v. Frazell, 66
United States v. General Geophysical Co., 439, 539
United States v. Horschel, 630
United States v. Lynch, 377
United States v. McNally Pittsburg Mfg. Corp., 581
United States v. Marett, 929
United States v. Marshall, 520
United States v. Mattison, 827
United States v. Midland-Ross Corp., 505
United States v. Whitney Land Co., 842

TABLE OF CASES

Van Keppel v. United States, 478
Victorson v. Commissioner, 284, 286
Virginia Ice & Freezing Co., 636

Wabash Railway Co. v. Barclay, 288
Wall v. Commissioner, 532
Wallace Corp. v. Commissioner, 861
Watson v. Commissioner, 27
W. D. Haden Co. v. Commissioner, 133
Weiner v. Commissioner, 497
Wessell v. Guantanamo Sugar Co., 763
Westburn Sugar Refineries, Ltd. v. Inland Revenue, 334
Western Mass. Theatres, Inc. v. Commissioner, 809
Westover v. Smith, 492
West Seattle Nat. Bank v. Commissioner, 644
West View Hills, Inc. v. Lizau Realty Corp., 42
Whipple v. Commissioner, 124
Wilgard Realty Co. v. Commissioner, 93
Williamson v. United States, 642

Wilshire & Western Sandwiches, Inc. v. Commissioner, 136
Wilson v. Commissioner, 832, 933
Wolff v. Heidritter Lumber Co., 430, 437
Wolfson v. Avery, 30
Wood Harmon Corp. v. United States, 635
Woodward v. Quigley, 19
Wouk v. Merin, 290

Young Motor Co. v. Commissioner, 565

Zabriskie v. Hackensack & N. Y. R. R., 743
Zahn v. Transamerica Corp., 298
Zanesville Investment Co. v. Commissioner, 861
Zaubler v. West View Hills, Inc., 43
Zenz v. Quinlivan, 535
Zimmermann v. Tide Water Associated Oil Co., 729
Zipp v. Commissioner, 532

TABLE OF INTERNAL REVENUE CODE SECTIONS

§ 61(a), pp. 181–183
§ 165(g) (2) (C), p. 124
§ 166, pp. 124–133
§ 172, pp. 841–847
§ 212(3), pp. 546–554
§ 267, pp. 482–483
§ 269, pp. 159–161, 168–176, 858–869
§ 301, pp. 371–373
§ 302, pp. 471–481, 486
§ 303, p. 481
§ 304, p. 482
§ 305, pp. 384–385
§ 306, pp. 385–389, 403
§ 307, p. 385
§ 311, pp. 374–378, 538–540
§ 312, pp. 373–374, 554–557, 933
§ 316, pp. 371–373
§ 318, pp. 476–479
§ 331, p. 630
§ 332, pp. 648–652, 824–825
§ 333, p. 630
§ 334(b) (1), p. 825
§ 334(b) (2), pp. 825–828
§ 336, p. 630
§ 337, pp. 630–657
§ 341, pp. 657–678
§ 346, pp. 482–486
§ 351, pp. 77–98, 106–120, 920
§ 354, pp. 399, 803
§ 355, pp. 919–934
§ 356, pp. 399, 803
§ 356(a) (2), pp. 400–403, 810
§ 357(a), pp. 78, 802
§ 357(b), pp. 78–79

§ 357(c), pp. 79–80
§ 358, pp. 79, 803–804
§ 361, p. 802
§ 362(a), p. 80
§ 362(b), pp. 802–803, 824
§ 368(a) (1) (A), pp. 807–811
§ 368(a) (1) (B), pp. 814–824
§ 368(a) (1) (C), pp. 828–835
§ 368(a) (1) (D), pp. 652–654, 919–920
§ 368(a) (1) (E), pp. 398–400, 405–413
§ 368(c), pp. 77, 95–96
§ 381, pp. 836–837
§ 381(c) (1), pp. 847–851
§ 381(c) (2), pp. 837–841
§ 382(a), pp. 857–858, 872–885
§ 382(b), pp. 851–857
§ 421, pp. 281–282
§ 453, pp. 519–526
§ 482, pp. 162–164, 183–187
§ 483, pp. 526–532
§§ 531–537, pp. 558–594
§ 1001, pp. 491–496
§ 1032, pp. 76, 77, 400
§ 1036, p. 399
§ 1232(a) (1), pp. 121, 496–498, 505, 509–510
§ 1232(a) (2), pp. 506, 511
§ 1239, pp. 81, 95
§ 1244, pp. 122–123
§§ 1371–1378, pp. 149–157
§§ 1501–1504, pp. 869–872
§ 1551, pp. 161–162, 177–181
§§ 1561–1563, pp. 164–167

†

BUSINESS PLANNING

Chapter 1

ORGANIZATION OF A CLOSE CORPORATION

SECTION 1. ENTERPRISE VALUATION

A. INTRODUCTION

Often the organization of a new corporation involves the incorporation of a going business, previously carried on in either the proprietorship or partnership form. In such cases a common first step is to value the existing enterprise, in order to determine the amount of the consideration which the corporation is receiving in exchange for its stock, and to prepare its opening books of account. In addition, if the incorporation transaction involves bringing in new parties valuation of the existing business will be needed to arrive at a proper allocation of the interests in the new corporation among the various participants.

A recent publication of the Small Business Administration provides an excellent introduction to the subject of valuing a business.

GOULD & CODDINGTON, HOW DO YOU KNOW WHAT YOUR BUSINESS IS WORTH?

SBA Management Aid No. 166, 1964.

Corporations whose stocks are actively traded on the major exchanges are valued continuously by the investing public. But how do owner-managers of small closely held companies determine how much their business is worth when they, for instance, seek outside financing?

Or how do you value a business for situations such as those involving estate and gift taxes? And what about the value of a company which you may purchase in order to strengthen your own business?

NO SET FORMULA FOR VALUATION

Various methods can be used for computing a company's worth, but no set formula exists. Keep in mind that the buyer, or investor, wants an answer to one question: What percent of return can I get on my investment? Or said another way: What is the value of the future earning power of this company?

The best way to answer that question is by using the capitalized earnings method for evaluating the worth of a company. But first, look at two other commonly used methods: (1) asset valuation, and (2) market valuation.

Asset Valuation

Companies are often evaluated by their assets as reflected in book value, reproduction value, and liquidation value. However, assets are significant only as they enable a company to manufacture and sell products, or services, that will generate profits.

Book value. Sometimes a company's book value does not hold up in the market place. One company, for example, sold for $300,000 even though its net worth or book value was $600,000. The reason: a large part of the assets was tied up in specialized equipment and slow-moving inventory, sales volume was down, and the company's net income after taxes was only $30,000. The purchasers decided that the company to them was worth only 10 times earnings, or $300,000.

Another disadvantage of valuing a company on its net worth is that book value can be high because of retained earnings over a long period of time. The company can still be a poor investment because its current earnings are down and prospects for increased future earnings are dim.

Reproduction value. Many small businessmen value their companies in terms of reproduction value—the current cost of reproducing the assets of the business. They reason like this: The cost of duplicating my business will be higher than what is shown on my balance sheet because many items have been depreciated. Also inflation has increased the prices of certain pieces of machinery.

A disadvantage of reproduction value is that it tends to set a high asking price on a business. Often a man can start a new one with less capital than it takes to buy a company on its reproduction value.

Liquidation value is the amount that would be available to the common stockholders in the event that a small business is liquidated. In liquidation, time is often a factor; outside pressures demand action; and the business is sold at a sacrifice. However, this method has some use in placing a floor under the value of a company—determining the minimum asking price.

Market Value

Quoted prices on stock exchanges constitute market value of common stock. Usually such prices in a broad and active market can be considered the current value of a company. But even so a company is sometimes merged or sold at quite a different value from the current value of its marketable common stocks.

Market value can be subjected for example, to short-term swings caused by rumors, opinions, and other factors. The fickleness of over-the-counter stock prices tends to be even greater than that of the major stock exchanges. For example, the announcement of potential contracts often raises the over-the-counter value of the stock of an electronics company out of proportion to its real value.

Where thin, limited markets exist, differences between the current value and market price of a company's stock are apt to be great. For example, a company with 300,000 shares outstanding might sell at 5 to 10 times earnings and under book value per share because demand for the stock is slight. The industry is highly competitive, the company's sales are down, and profits have been declining. At the same time, another company with 300,000 shares outstanding—but with strong earnings and growth prospects—might sell at 30 to 50 times earnings and many times book value.

CAPITALIZED EARNINGS VALUE

Whether you buy or sell a small company you need to know about the company's ability to earn profits—especially future profits. The capitalized earning approach considers a business as a living, changing organism which uses its assets to produce the greatest possible return on investment.

Two steps are used in capitalizing earnings. First, you find a company's true earning power, based on both its past experience and future probabilities. Second, you capitalize these earnings at a rate which is realistic for the risks involved.

Finding a Company's Earnings

A company's *past earnings* record gives a buyer, or investor, an indication of what he might reasonably expect in the future. He learns about this record from past income statements. Looking at them for a 5-year period helps him to see trends.

The buyer should make adjustments to the income statement for: (1) nonrecurring items that a buyer should not expect to encounter in the future, (2) unusually large bad debts, (3) inventory write-offs, (4) excessive salaries, (5) low salaries that might have to be raised in order to get qualified assistants, and (6) nonbusiness ventures.

The kind of accounting procedure used can also have a direct effect on reported earnings. For example, one company may charge the cost of tools and dies as expense items in the year in which they were bought. Another may amortize the cost of such equipment over a period of years and thereby increase earnings.

When a potential buyer adjusts for nonrecurring items and for varying accounting practices, he is trying to judge what future earnings might be under his ownership. His return on investment has to come from possible *future earnings*.

Therefore, the buyer needs income statement projections based on what he thinks he can do with the company. Often an independent study of the company's prospects for sales helps to give a sound basis for earnings projections.

Even though selling may be your last thought at this point, it is a good idea to look ahead. Make sure that your accounting system records the information necessary for making realistic earnings projections. Thus you can base your negotiations on facts should you ever decide to sell. Also, don't buy, or sell, without having an independent audit of the company's books.

Finally, from the 5-year period, you have to pick one annual earnings figure as the true *earning power* of the business. If the company has a proven record, current earnings can often be used. In well-established companies, *proven past profits* and *projected income* for the current year usually go together to make the true earnings figure. However, when a company is fairly new but with good potential, future earnings estimates are weighed heavily.

What Capitalization Rate Should Be Used?

The rate at which you capitalize a company's average earning power depends on the risks involved. The higher the risk of generating projected earnings—and thus creating a return on the buyer's investment—the lower the capitalization rate.

Suppose, for example, that the earning power of two companies is the same—$100,000. Suppose further that Company A has a proven record of profits and a very substantial annual earnings growth rate. With highly favorable prospects for the future, Company A might be capitalized at 20 times earnings for a value of $2 million. At the start, the investor would get 5 percent return on investment, and the proven growth of earnings would increase his possibility for a greater return in the future.

However, keep in mind that valuation is also subjective—what the buyer thinks the business is worth to him. Some may be willing to pay a much lower multiple of earnings for a closely held company even though the present owners have built an outstanding record for growth and prospects appear favorable.

On the other hand, Company B is relatively small and in a highly competitive industry. The company is growing but has not established itself. A buyer would need a high percentage return—20 percent or more—on investment. If he needed 20 percent, earnings could be capitalized at 5 times for a value of $500,000.

External Influences

When determining the proper capitalization rate, or price-earnings multiple, external influences have to be weighed. Some of them are:

(1) Economy. What effect will the state of business and the regional and national economic outlook have on the company?

(2) Industry. Do industry factors—such as competitive structure, cyclical, seasonal and Governmental influences, and industry glamour—make the company attractive to investors? Unattractive?

(3) Company position. How does the company compare with its competitors in size, growth, margins, order backlog, suppliers, patents, and freight advantages?

(4) Financial strength. How do the company's balance sheets and income statement ratios compare with competitors and with credit statistics for the industry as a whole? A debt-free company, of course, can borrow capital for expansion and diversification.

(5) Management. Is the company's management strong? Does its past performance indicate that it can maintain and increase profits in the future?

(6) Character of investment. In a closely held company—one person or a small group owning more than half the stock—the price-earnings multiple will be lower because of the nonmarketability of the investment.

Factors Which The Buyer Injects

In addition to these external influences, the price-earnings multiple is often determined by factors which the buyer, or investor, may throw into the situation. Some examples are:

(1) Buyer's price-earnings multiple. If an investing company can buy a company at a price-earnings multiple below its own, its stockholder's position is not diluted. For example, if a buying company's stock is selling at 15 times earnings, it can afford to issue stock with a value up to—but not more than—15 times earnings for an acquisition. However, if the buying company pays more than 15 times earnings, its stockholders will earn less per share on the combined earnings.

(2) Competitive investments. When buying for investment, the return on the purchase price of a company must compare favorably with other things—such as stocks, bonds, real estate, or savings deposits—for which the buyer could spend his money.

(3) Job money. Companies are often sold to buyers who want to take over active management, and such a buyer may be willing to pay a little more.

(4) Buyer's needs. Another company might pay a higher price than an individual buyer in order to fill needs such as management, products, brands, patents, franchises, or licensing agreements.

(5) Method of payment. Tax factors have to be considered. Acquisitions effected through merger, sale of stock, or sale of assets for either cash or stock depend on tax factors involved with the corporation's assets and net worth as well as each stockholder's personal position.

(6) Minority stockholders. The value of a minority ownership position in a closely held company is not as great as a majority stockholder because of the additional risks associated with lack of control.

(7) Cash flow. Cash flow—net profits after taxes plus non-cash charges, such as depreciation, depletion, and amortization, has become an important factor in valuation. The cash generated from operations can be used for capital expenditures, reduction of debt, payment of dividends, and expansion. So a company may be sold at a very high multiple of earnings yet at a reasonable ratio to cash flow. This cash "payout" often determines the ultimate value of a business and is becoming increasingly important.

APPLICATION OF METHODS

When determining how much your company is worth, keep in mind that its marketable value may vary according to what you are planning to do.

If you set a value in order to get *public financing*, bear in mind that a public underwriting of securities should be priced so that the investment will be attractive in comparison with stocks of other companies in your industry. Such pricing should also give the stock room to rise after the issue has been floated.

The situation is somewhat different if you seek *private financing*. When buying non-marketable securities, an investor needs a higher return. Usually private venture capital sources seek investments which will double in value and be marketable within 3 years.

In a *private sale* to one individual, he buys on what he thinks he can earn from the company. If he plans to operate the company himself, he may pay more for the intangible benefits of having managerial responsibilities.

Above all, in buying or selling, keep in mind that value varies with individuals. The worth of a going company is largely a subjective matter—what a person thinks the business is worth to him. But even so, the capitalized earnings approach embodies facts which can be used to arrive at a realistic value.

The capitalized earnings method helps you to: (1) find the true earning power of a business and (2) then find the investment necessary to earn a rate of return that is in line with the risks involved. This method also considers all of the external influences—such as the economy and industry conditions—which bear on a company's prospects.

B. VALUATION OF A LARGE ENTERPRISE

Before attempting to apply these valuation techniques to a small business, it should be helpful to see how they operate in the context of large enterprises, where there has been a good deal more recorded experience. For the most recent, comprehensive discussion of valuation of a large enterprise (in the context of statutory proceedings for the appraisal of the stock of dissenting minority stockholders, see page 777 infra), see Note, Valuation of Dissenters' Stock under Appraisal Statutes, 79 Harv.L.Rev. 1453 (1966).

PERLMAN v. FELDMANN
United States District Court, District of Connecticut, 1957.[*]

154 F.Supp. 436.

Discussion

This case was remanded to this court by the Court of Appeals for a determination of the value of the defendants' stock without the appurtenant control over the corporation's output of steel.

. . . Prior to the commencement of the second trial the court ruled that it would not receive evidence of actual events subsequent to August 31, 1950, on the issue of the value of the shares of Newport on that date. The parties urged that this rule was too stringent and stipulated that evidence of subsequent occurrences be admitted for the limited purpose of testing the weight and validity of assumptions and prognoses made by experts as of August 31, 1950. After a lenghty chambers conference and in compliance with the court's position that some reasonable limit should be placed upon the period for which evidence of subsequent events could be admitted, it was understood by the court and the parties that two years from August 31, 1950, would be recognized as the period so limited.

What Judge Hand said in Guggenheim v. Helvering, 2 Cir., 117 F.2d 469, 473, at the end of head note reference (1) is expressive of

---

[*] Findings of Fact and Conclusions of Law omitted.

what the court had in mind with regard to post August, 1950, occurrences:

> "Only so far as present opinion is composed in part of a forecast of the future can the future be supposed to have anything to do with it; and it really has none even then, because a forecast of the future is an entirely different thing from the actual future which will confirm or falsify it."

This court thus placed considerable emphasis upon the reasonableness of what was foreseeable on August 31, 1950. The purchasers took steps to familiarize themselves with corporate earnings and other pertinent data of interest to them right up to the date of exercising the option. There were factors present which in the light of current trends could reasonably be projected into the future. The two-year limitation was not a limit on the range of the opinion anyone interested might have had on August 31, 1950, but was chosen as the fairest method of putting a quantitative limit on the corroborative force of actual future events. . . .

The problem has been to find the fair market value of the Newport Steel Corporation as a going concern, i. e. its enterprise value, on August 31, 1950. For the purpose of evaluating the control block shorn of the power to control the corporation's output of steel, the court has accepted the mathematical sequel of dividing the enterprise value of the corporation by the number of shares outstanding and multiplying the result by the number of shares in the block. What special value there may have been to an investor in being able to manage the corporation without controlling or having any particular interest in using the product or channeling its distribution to end users in which he was interested, is implicit in the factors going to determine enterprise value. In this case it is found that the difference between the value of the block thus arrived at, and the amount paid the individual defendants by the Wilport Company constituted a bonus or premium paid the individual defendants by the Wilport Company to control the corporation's output of steel.

The conclusion as to enterprise value of the Newport Steel Corporation on August 31, 1950, was arrived at by the experts for the plaintiffs and the experts for the defendants by somewhat different means. Each tended to emphasize factors which were helpful to the side for which he was testifying. The plaintiffs' expert gave great weight to records of earnings for several years prior to August 31, 1950 and little weight to changes in means and equipment for production and sales in the few months preceding August, 1950, the changes in demand for products and the reasonably foreseeable consequences of these changes in the period following August 31, 1950. The defendants' expert, on the other hand, relied heavily on a projection into the future of the higher earnings achieved in the recent past plus increased or normalized earnings by the new steel facilities, insufficiently tempered by the negative consideration of increased taxes.

The court has been greatly assisted by observing the tools used by the experts and their procedures in using them; but it has adopted the final conclusion of neither.

In broad aspect the court has concluded that the defendant has sustained its burden of persuading the court of the justification for using earnings of the steel division after May, 1950 and earnings of Caswell-Runyan for ten months preceding August 31, 1950, as the bases for projected future earnings for those divisions as opposed to the longer prior period of several years urged by the plaintiff; but the court is equally well persuaded that any reasonably prudent investor considering the circumstance of the Korean war and the accompanying boom would have foreseen the imposition of an excess profits tax with a consequential increase in taxes to 65% of earnings or a percentage very close to it. It would, if possible, have been preferable to average the earnings for June, July and August, but July was broken up by vacations and its inclusion would improperly distort the figures; therefore, an average of June and August has been used.

By the end of May 1950 the "new facilities" which had been in the process of being installed over the period of the preceding two years, were completed, the last electric furnace having been put in in May. Between then and the end of August the "new facilities" were demonstrating what might reasonably be expected of them. By the end of that time they appeared to stand on the threshold of achieving full or normal production. The Korean War started June 26th. The circumstances leading up to it, and the impact of the war itself created rising prices and a heightened demand for steel and other goods. The plaintiffs object to any emphasis at all on these changed economic conditions, but the resulting boom and the gray market conditions, pointing up the demand for steel, should not be considered as a factor showing that the defendants received a premium for their block of stock and at the same time be denied or disregarded in considering enterprise value as of August 31, 1950. The defendants object to the use of the August figures because they are not as representative of the full earning capacity of the "old facilities" as are the figures for June, and even June obviously could reflect only the circumstances leading up to the inception of the war and not the full impact of the war itself. Yet the consideration of circumstances which cause the averaged figures for June and August to fall short of absolute full capacity are what make them reasonable and realistic.

It was foreseeable that the high demand for steel would continue for at least two years. It was also reasonable to assume that the new facilities would very soon after August 1950 reach full production. To compute the increase in earnings after August, 1950, attributable to the new facilities the method used by the defendants' expert and adopted by the plaintiffs' expert was followed, but the finding was limited to the increase over and above the forecast based upon the June-August average. The result was subjected to the deduction of general expenses based on the formula of the plaintiffs' expert, and this result was treated to the application of the 65% tax rate for earnings after taxes. Failure to discount the projected increased earnings of the "new facilities" to account for any short delay in achieving full production by them is offset by and the estimate of increased earnings is made somewhat more conservative by making no allowance for the 6,300 tons per month of excess capacity of the strip mill which, as the evidence showed, was available for converting ingots of customers or of other steel mills.

The court also considered the detrimental effect of Newport's contract with General Motors whereby General Motors was given an option to take at a formula price 10,000 tons of steel per month for a period of 42 months but the negative weight given this contract is somewhat tempered by the evidence that General Motors was not holding Newport to the contract price but was paying current Newport prices.

With regard to the tax rate, the defendants take the position that an excess profits tax was not then foreseeable, which is not convincing; and the plaintiffs claim they did not use it because their computations were based entirely upon past earnings. However, the plaintiffs did give some claimed weight to it in making an arbitrary 25% reduction of the defendants' expert's new facilities' earnings forecast which the plaintiffs adopted as a starting point for estimated future earnings. In any event, it would be most unlikely that a prospective purchaser of the enterprise on August 31, 1950, would not have foreseen and made allowance for an excess profits tax, which makes it reasonable to assume a total tax of about 65% with which a purchaser would have to reckon.

Although the plaintiffs' expert in some of his methods of computation gave a weight of 25% to asset value and 75% to earnings, it is the court's opinion that a greater weight should be given to the assets factor and that greater weight should be given to assets in the steel division than in the Caswell-Runyan division. While the ultimate use of capital equipment is to gain earnings, in a wartime economy there is a direct accession to the dollar value of plants, machinery and tools, particularly going concerns, from inflationary forces which have accompanied every war in history, and from the cost and difficulty of procuring materials and equipment for setting up new and additional plants. There was evidence that in the summer of 1950 these forces were already at work, and it was reasonable to assume that they would continue. Therefore, instead of the 25% used by the plaintiffs' expert, the court has found that the assets-earnings proportion in the valuation should be 40% assets—60% earnings for the steel division and 33⅓%–66⅔% for Caswell-Runyan.*

---

* [Ed. note] The Findings of Fact indicate that the asset factor for each of these divisions was based upon net book value, which in both cases was substantially in excess of the figure derived by capitalizing earnings.

In deciding what multiplier to use in determining enterprise value on the basis of an earnings figure, that is, what rate of capitalization to use, both experts computed and gave some weight to price-earning ratios of other steel companies' stocks. The plaintiffs' expert used the earnings of selected companies in the period January 1947 to September 1950; the defendants' expert used current earnings of certain companies as of 1950. The plaintiffs' expert used his market-derived multiplier of 5.2 in computing value on past earnings but upped it to 6 for computing value on estimated future earnings. The defendants' expert, proceeding from a much less narrow base, derived his multiplier not only from price-earnings ratio derived from a study of selected steel companies but also from broad factors of judgment and experience applied to the nature and condition of the business, both the beneficial and adverse factors to be encountered in its operation, and its position in the economy. He to some extent considered the impending excess profits tax in arriving at his multiplier. Although he fixed a lower multiplier for the old facilities and a higher one for the new, he actually used a composite multiplier of 5 for the steel division as a whole.

While the defendants' expert's method of deriving the multiplier seems the better conceived, the court does not agree with his judgment that the valuation should omit direct consideration of excess profits taxes and merely give them indefinite weight in arriving at the multiplier. Nor does the defendants' expert appear to be justified when he says that if the excess profits tax had been first deducted from earnings he would have arbitrarily raised the multiplier to a figure about double the 5 which he used.

The excess profits tax, while not precisely known in August, 1950, was reasonably foreseeable at some percentage within a range of reasonableness and could be given express and separate mathematical application. The court has therefore taken the excess profits tax into account in computing the estimated future net earnings after taxes. The multiplier is then applied to those tax reduced net earnings.

After considering the elements testified to by the experts and applying its own judgment to their conclusions, the court is of the opinion that a proper multiplier for the steel division is 5.5, and this is applied not only to the old and new facilities' estimated future average yearly earnings (obtained by annualizing the average of earnings in June and August 1950) but also to the probable increase in earnings of the new facilities, which, though probable, are thus weighted downward to a small degree from any higher multiplier which might be indicated by their newness because the quality of "probability" is not quite as good as the reasonably foreseeable repetition of something already performed at least once. The court is mindful that the choice of any particular multiplier is of necessity somewhat arbitrary, but it is the only way of using earnings to arrive at the main goal of the valuation proceeding—enterprise value.

As to the Caswell-Runyan woodworking division: the use of $696,000, an average of the ten months' earnings from November, 1949, through August, 1950, annualized, for a prognosis as of August 31, 1950, seems justified under the circumstances. It was not necessary to have the hindsight judgment from knowing that the ensuing twelve months' earnings before taxes would total $832,823. The twelve months preceding August 31, 1950, showed earnings before taxes of $733,941.27. The demand for television and radio cabinets was in August continuing in full swing. While an astute purchaser might have foreseen the overproduction of television sets in the second ensuing year followed by a falling off of earnings to $355,752, it is likely that a purchaser would consider that the war-time economy and the accompanying boom would call for something which this division could supply. It was recognized as a volatile business, but the conservative multiplier of 5 used after an application of a 65% tax rate makes full allowance for this characteristic and the exigencies of the business generally.

The Universal Cooler division was on August 31, 1950, the subject of negotiations for a sale which was consummated on October 31, 1950. It was found to be worth its asset or book value and the experts were confirmed by its sale slightly in excess of book value two months later. As the plaintiffs point out, the earnings of this division were extremely erratic, which would indicate that earnings alone cannot always be relied upon for value in an economic atmosphere such as that which existed in August 1950.

The pipe mill was valued at its cost by the defendants' expert, and this was found to be entirely reasonable and proper; but his claims of foreseeable income, as the court found at the first trial, are entirely too speculative and could not be adopted.

The court adopted the defendants' expert's appraisal of the Detroit real estate based upon capitalization of net rental at 8% to arrive at $1,657,000, which had to be reduced by the limiting factor of an option to the federal government to purchase at $1,073,658, which was found to be the value on August 31, 1950.

The plaintiffs' expert devoted considerable testimony to the market price of small lots of Newport and evidently held the opinion that the various prices were strongly corroborative of his analyses and almost conclusive evidence in themselves. This claim is not persuasive, however, for small lot sales were not an indication of Newport's enterprise value on August 31, 1950. They did not reflect the value of controlling a steel company as an investment in an enterprise under the circumstances attendant upon Newport at that time. The sales of stock to Feldmann by his friends and associates were not arms-length transactions but were flavored by the intention of doing Feldmann a favor as a return for past favors. There were meritorious considerations involved which render the transactions of little or no weight in establishing value.

After considering all of the evidence relative to the various divisions of the Newport Steel Corporation the court has adopted what it has conceived to be the methods best adapted to disclose the fair market value of each of the divisions as part of the going concern. The total of the values of each of these divisions has been found to be $15,825,777.53, which is the enterprise value of Newport Steel Corporation. Each share therefore had a fair market value on August 31, 1950, of $14.67 and the premium or bonus per share was $5.33.

1. CAPITALIZATION OF EARNINGS

DEWING, FINANCIAL POLICY OF CORPORATIONS [1]

5th ed. 1953. Vol. I, pp. 281–282, 287–292, 390–391.

Structure of a Going Business. . . . At the outset we should face the fact that—except in the rare cases when a business has outlived its usefulness and should be dismembered and the parts sold—a business operating from day to day and from one year to another is a unity of men and property dedicated to the specific purpose of performing an economic service at a profit. This unity persists as the human beings who operate it come and go, as the material goods are made and sold, and as its fixed properties and machines decay and are replaced by new. This operating unity, continuing over periods of time, is what is meant by the phrase "a going business." The going business is more than an aggregate of parts; and the value of such an enterprise is more than the sum of the exchange value of its material components. This intangible something, inseparable from a going business, is what we call organization. Inherent in the organization are many elements of an intangible character which make possible the continued existence of the normal business. Such a going, organized enterprise is the subject of our main interest. . . .

A corporation operating a normal business will be found to possess three distinguishable parts, each making its necessary contribution to the integrated whole; they are the parts of the normal going business. They may be called the permanent property of the business, the current capital, and finally the group of intangible values which distinguish the going business from the dead business, and which we call the organization. The separate contributing values of these three parts cannot be determined; the business is the joint product of the three, and the

---

[1]. Reprinted by permission of the publisher, The Ronald Press Company, Portions of the text omitted.

value of the business is the value of the three united in the form of a single operating unity.*

* * *

The Capitalization of Earnings. The phrase, capitalization of net earnings, is frequently used both in present-day discussions of business theory and in the current literature of economics. The idea behind it is simple, but the practical application of this idea to a concrete case is complex and difficult.

Nevertheless, in spite of the practical difficulty of determining a definite and precise value for a specific business, the capitalization of earnings is the *only* means at our disposal for determining the value of a going business. This is because the business, as a going enterprise —as a combination of organization, fixed and current capital—was designed primarily to earn profits. Its value is measured by the extent to which it conforms to this purpose. Justice Holmes very wisely and precisely summarized the whole theory of value applied to business enterprise: ". . . the commercial value of property consists of the expectation of income from it."

The capitalization of earnings of a business enterprise is the result of two factors—the earnings and the rate of capitalization. Consequently, the first problem is the determination of a figure which represents the fundamental earning capacity of the business. . . . But the determination of the fundamental earning power of a business, gleaned from a study of its past accomplishments, is only part of the problem.

---

* [Ed. note] Professor Dewing originally took a different view of what was measured by capitalization of earnings, as is indicated by the following footnote from the 1934 edition:

The basic definition of the value of a business was expressed somewhat differently in the 1926 edition of this book. At that time I stated that the value of a business represented a summation of three distinct elements: fixed assets or producers' goods, current assets, and managerial ability. In determining this value current assets were to be "valued" separately, and the final earning capacity of the other two, as evidenced by capitalizing average net earnings, added to the value of the quick assets. Since that time I have given much thought to this subject of valuation; and its importance, for all phases of corporation finance, has risen in my mind. I have also talked with many business men; I have participated, in one way or another, in numerous business consolidations, and I have had the benefit of illuminating criticism from my colleagues. As a result I am convinced that the [present description] is more accurate. . . . For all businesses, barring perhaps such utilities as water and electric companies, a certain irreducible amount of current assets is required for the operation of the business. This amount of current assets is just as much a part of the business as a going concern as its fixed assets or producers' goods. When however, as is true in many businesses, there is an excess of quick assets in the corporation treasury, this excess must be valued separately and added to the capitalized earnings value. Similarly, if there is a deficiency of quick assets, so that the company's current borrowings are in excess of its current assets, then the capitalized earnings value of the business must be reduced by an amount equivalent to the deficiency of quick assets. (3d ed. 1934, Vol. 1, page 135, note f).

If we assume that a statistical study has disclosed the earnings to be capitalized, the rate at which they shall be capitalized is by no means clear. Under our competitive system of economic values, the business is the instrument which creates the earnings, and the valuation of the business is the valuation of this instrument. It is true, too, under our competitive system, that the price which men will pay for this instrument will depend on the relative certainty with which these earnings can be counted upon to continue. In other words, the rate at which a business shall be capitalized, to obtain its value, will depend on the confidence the buyer may feel in the continuation of the earnings. This is the relative risk of the business itself. The greater the risk, the greater the doubt of continued earnings, the lower is the capitalized value of these earnings; and conversely, the lower the risk, the greater the value. Consequently, to proceed further with a study of the rate of capitalization, we must analyze the risk of the business as an instrument for producing earnings.

The risk of a business rests on one dominant factor and on numerous contributing factors of less moment. The dominant factor is the relative importance of management, one of the group of those intangible values into which we have attempted to divide organization. The factors of less moment are the influence of the alternation of business booms and depressions, the uncertainties of trade customs, of sources of supply of the materials of the business, of changes in tariff laws or patent laws, of changes in political theory bringing about new and restrictive legislation. There are other factors peculiar to individual types of enterprise, but these are included in the idea of management in the sense that they present problems which must be met and solved by the management if the business is to continue to be profitable.

In the long run the interest on the capital invested tends to become equal among different kinds of enterprises. That is, the mere rate of return on capital, without considering the risk incident to carrying it on, inclines to be the same for all businesses. Furthermore, in the long run, the larger return obtained in certain risky enterprises is counterbalanced by the greater frequency of losses, while the smaller return to stable businesses less frequently bears the burden of losses. A building may be used as part of the fixed capital of a risky business or as part of the fixed capital of a stable business. It is the same building in either case. Yet if the building is used as a storage warehouse, far less organization, particularly skill of management, is required than if the building is used for the manufacture of fancy dancing slippers. In the combination of capital and management, management is of much less relative importance in the former case than in the latter. In brief, the contribution of skill of management to success is greater in a risky than in a stable business. This difference is reflected, moreover, not only in the larger earnings which the risky business must produce in order to compensate for the greater losses, but also in the fact that, if the business is offered for sale, there are fewer men willing and qualified to buy it and to manage it successfully.

This difference as regards the relative importance of management affects directly the ratio at which net earnings in different kinds of business should be capitalized. For if management is of relatively greater importance to insure success in certain businesses than in others, a buyer will gauge his valuation in accordance with this phase of the business. He will pay comparatively little for the combination of fixed and current assets and past management, represented by the capitalized past earnings, in those businesses in which the importance of good management is so great a prerequisite to success that the future earnings can with difficulty be predicted from the past earnings. Or, stating the same idea differently, the greater the risk of the business, the smaller the ratio between past earnings and present value; and, conversely, the greater the stability of the business—and the less degree to which management is a prerequisite to success—the closer the connection between past earnings and present value. The relative importance of management gives us a key to the relative value of a business in terms of the record of past earnings.

Ratios for Capitalization of Net Earnings in Various Businesses. In the light of the relative importance of management—corresponding to the inherent risks of the business—it is possible to arrange businesses in the order of the ratios by which one may capitalize the past earnings. Those that are very stable, to which skill of management is least essential for success, are at one end of the series; those that are very risky and require unusually great skill of management are at the other end of the series. A gravity system water works is, in the writer's opinion, the easiest kind of business enterprise to administer. It requires much fixed capital but little skill. Even the aldermen of a city can manage the water works with not too destructive inefficiency. At the other end are businesses, like ladies' fancy millinery or drama production, which are so uncertain and risky that only a few people of rare ability are likely to succeed in them. The quantity of assets at the command of the managers of this latter kind is of relatively little importance in forecasting success, and if men of marked ability with highly specialized knowledge withdraw, this skeleton of assets remaining is of little value to other men. Between these two extremes lie the great majority of enterprises. Toward one end of the series would be grouped the large variety of local utilities protected by franchise from direct competition and from confiscatory rates by the Fourteenth Amendment. Toward the other end would be found the extra hazardous businesses involving keen foresight, personal attention to details, and marked power to coordinate all the parts of the enterprise.

The ratios of percentages at which the extremes of this series should be capitalized in order to translate earnings into value must depend on a variety of conditions. Businesses requiring only a small amount of capital will sell for a higher price, relatively, than those requiring a large amount, because there are a greater number of possible buyers; on the other hand, businesses that require large amounts of capital will appeal more strongly to investment bankers and will, therefore, have a readier access to investment funds. Businesses which are pleasant and give the owner a social standing will sell for more than businesses which are disagreeable to conduct or which carry social discredit. Seasonal and fluctuating types of enterprise have certain apparent disadvantages; so have those which require a highly specialized background of training and demand a fund of information available only to a few.

Perhaps the most difficult, and so far as results are concerned, the most important point in any theory of value based on earning power, is the rate at which earnings shall be capitalized. A comparatively large error in computing net earnings—by an over- or an underestimate of depreciation, for example—is not of as much importance in the final result as a comparatively small difference in the rate at which earnings shall be capitalized. Yet the determination of this rate is at best a matter of guesswork, but guesswork supported by the evidence of prices at which businesses of various kinds are being actually valued at any one time. This evidence from current experience with reference to the value of different enterprises can be culled not only from the prices at which enterprises are actually sold, but also from the valuation put upon them by bankers extending credit to them and by investors who are willing to buy their bonds and stocks. In other words, such guesswork is subject to the best kind of pragmatic test, namely the evidence of actual experience.

Summary Statement of Capitalization of Earnings. From these various methods of approach, it is possible to throw industrial businesses into diverse categories in accordance with which we can form some estimate of the value of a business by capitalizing its earnings. These categories could be described in the following manner:

1. Old established businesses, with large capital assets and excellent goodwill—10%, a value ten times the net earnings. Very few industrial enterprises would come within this category.
2. Businesses, well established, but requiring considerable managerial care. To this category would belong the great number of old, successful industrial businesses, large and small—12½%, a value eight times the net earnings.
3. Businesses, well established, but involving possible loss in consequence of shifts of general economic conditions. They are strong, well established businesses, but they produce a type of commodity which makes them vulnerable to depressions. They require considerable managerial ability, but little special

knowledge on the part of the executives—15%, a value approximately seven times the net earnings.

4. Businesses requiring average executive ability—and at the same time comparatively small capital investment. These businesses are highly competitive, but established good-will is of distinct importance. This class includes the rank and file of medium-sized, highly competitive industrial enterprises —20%, a value approximately five times the net earnings.

5. Small industrial businesses, highly competitive, and requiring a relatively small capital outlay. They are businesses which anyone, even with little capital, may enter—25%, a value approximately four times the net earnings.

6. Industrial businesses, large and small, which depend on the special, often unusual skill of one, or of a small group of managers. They involve only a small amount of capital; they are highly competitive and the mortality is high among those who enter the competitive struggle—50%, a value approximately twice the net earnings.

7. Personal service businesses. They require no capital, or at the most a desk, some envelopes and a few sheets of paper. The manager must have a special skill coupled with an intensive and thorough knowledge of his subjects. The earnings of the enterprise are the objective reflection of this skill; and he is not likely to be able to create "an organization" which can successfully "carry on" after he is gone. He can sell the business, including the reputation and the "plan of business," but he cannot sell himself, the only truly valuable part of the enterprise—100%, a value equal, approximately, to the earnings of a single year.

This summary of categories is not a classification in the sense of clearly defined and marked classes. There are innumerable intermediate stages. These seven categories are of the nature of nodal points in the organization of industry, according to the relation of earnings and value. There may be businesses so highly stabilized, so immune to the shocks of industrial depression and incompetent management, that they are worth more than ten times their annual earnings; there may be businesses so peculiar and individual that they are, in the hands of another, not worth even the earnings of a single year.

NOTE ON CAPITALIZATION RATES

The Dewing capitalization-ratio chart may well have become outdated since its most recent republication in 1953, particularly with regard to its assumption that ten times earnings is the highest permissible multiplier for an industrial. As early as 1951 at least one leading authority on stock valuation, Graham & Dodd, Security Analysis (3d ed. 1951), was already recommending a multiplier of 15 for valuing the stocks of first-rank industrials, and the 1962 edition of the same work suggests a general range of multipliers from seven to twenty. See Graham, Dodd & Cottle, Security Analysis (4th ed. 1962) 513. Moreover, the average price-earnings ratio for blue-chip industrials on the New York Stock Exchange is currently more than twenty, to say nothing of such glamour stocks as Polaroid and I. B. M., which have often sold at more than fifty times earnings.

The possible need to jack up the Dewing multipliers has been recognized in one case in Delaware, where the courts have often expressly relied upon the Dewing chart in selecting a multiplier. Marks v. Wolfson, 41 Del.Ch. 115, 188 A.2d 680, 686 n. 7 (Ch.1963). There the Vice Chancellor, in rejecting a minority stockholder's complaint that a price of more than ten times earnings for a corporation's business was too low, commented: "Even allowing for a higher multiplier for the type of business here involved because of changed business conditions since 1953 the value here set would appear to fall well above the limits discussed by Dewing." On the other hand, very shortly thereafter, in Levin v. Midland-Ross Corporation, 41 Del.Ch. 276, 194 A.2d 50 (Ch.1963), the Vice Chancellor, after concluding that the company involved fitted the description in Dewing's paragraph 3, page 17 supra, applied the multiplier of seven there specified without comment. See also Woodward v. Quigley, —— Iowa ——, 133 N.W.2d 38 (1965), where a multiplier of 13.5 was used for a closely-held newspaper company.

2. ASSET VALUATION

PATON & PATON, ASSET ACCOUNTING [2]
1952. pp. 358–366.

VALUATION OF PLANT
* * *

Bases of Valuation. The basis of valuation depends, to begin with, on whether the going-concern or liquidation approach is adopted. This is particularly important when the object of valuation is a complex property layout owned by a particular concern. Specialized plant assets, in general, are worth much more if they can be continued in use in the existing setting than if it is necessary to dispose of them piecemeal, and move them from their present location. This is particularly true of buildings and heavy machine installations. On the other hand the value of such an asset as an automobile of standard make and model, which can serve as well in one location as another, and is readily moved, is the same under either approach.

The most common starting-point in plant valuation, where the going-concern assumption is adopted, is replacement cost. The appraiser generally takes the position that it is the cost of construction or

---

2. Reprinted with permission of the publisher, The MacMillan Company, copyright, 1952. Portions of the text omitted.

acquisition as indicated by current prices,* less estimated depreciation based on careful inspection and analysis, that is of primary significance to management, investors, and other interested parties. In fact this formula has dominated plant appraisals for many years and has received considerable support from commission rulings and court decisions. This stress on replacement cost, on the whole, is not unwarranted. As pointed out in preceding chapters, the influential costs in the economic process are those that are reflected in the immediate level of prices, and this holds for plant costs—in the long run, at any rate—as well as for the current costs of labor and materials. Again the warning should be sounded, however, that replacement cost less depreciation is not a reliable measure of the value of a plant which because of obsolescence, unsatisfactory location, poor arrangement, or other unfavorable conditions would not be reproduced in kind.

The main alternative to the replacement-cost appraisal, for the going concern, is the capitalization-of-income basis. In the last analysis, of course, the value of plant depends on prospective earnings. No one will invest in plant property unless he feels justified in assuming that there is at least a fair prospect of "getting his money back" plus a rate of return that is attractive in view of all the impinging conditions. On the other hand there are serious difficulties in the way of making practical application of this idea to the concrete process of plant valuation. In the first place the task of estimating earnings for any considerable period is loaded with complications and yields results that are none too dependable under the most favorable conditions. Second, in most cases business income must be viewed as a composite result of operation, not assignable to particular structures or machines. Third, the earnings of plant property are in themselves affected by changes

---

* [Ed. note] The authors recommend the specific revaluation approach, under which replacement cost is derived on the basis of applicable current costs of construction and fabrication, rather than the "converted dollars" approach, under which original cost is restated in terms of the change in the general price-level, as measured by some general index such as the consumer-price index compiled by the U. S. Bureau of Labor Statistics. Of course the costs of plant assets constitute an important element in the general price level, but obviously the two do not always coincide. According to the authors (pages 324–325):

> Replacement cost is probably of greater significance to the managers and owners of depreciable assets than original dollar costs restated in terms of the movement of the over-all price level. These parties . . . are especially interested in the impact of changing conditions upon the specific properties they own and operate. . . . Of particular importance is the fact that in a competitive market it is replacement costs rather than costs previously incurred that are generally influential in the process of price determination. This is true of current factors such as materials and labor services and it is also true of the periodic use of plant. . . . [In addition,] specific indices representing the movement of the costs of buildings and equipment in a particular market area are somewhat more readily computed, and somewhat more reliable, than indices designed to measure the change in the value of the dollar for the whole economy.

in costs, and in the particular situation the immediate market value is more likely to be represented by current cost than by prospective income. For most specific business properties, therefore, the income basis of valuation has little practical application.

For obsolescent plants that will probably be continued in use for only a short time, and will be replaced if at all with another type of asset, the earning-power basis may have some application. It also has merit in the case of apartment houses and other rental properties.

Where valuation is undertaken in connection with a liquidation proceeding, or it is assumed that liquidation is imminent, neither cost of replacement nor prospective earnings have much bearing, except in special cases. Here valuation consists of determining the immediate sale value, to other owners in other circumstances, of each of the component items of plant. For some of the movable equipment, useful under varying conditions, such sale value may be represented by replacement cost less estimated depreciation. For specialized heavy equipment the liquidation value may be confined to net salvage, if any. Buildings and other structures generally can't be moved intact, and the break-up salvage value of such properties is usually small. On the other hand, if a buyer can be found who can use a building in its present location, although perhaps for a very different purpose, the sale value may be a substantial amount. Liquidation value, it may be added, constitutes a minimum or floor estimate in any property appraisal.

. . .

General Appraisal Procedures— . . . Actual appraisal of plant assets has been largely in the hands of professional firms specializing in property inspection and valuation. These firms, in general, have developed an exacting technique in the endeavor to put their appraisals on a sound basis. . . .

Pricing Plant . . . **—Replacement Cost.** Pricing usually means determining replacement cost for each element. . . . In dealing with units of standard equipment the appraiser commonly relies upon quotations furnished by manufacturers or other regular sources of supply, supplemented by estimates of transportation and installation charges. Cost of replacement of special machinery, built to order or by the operating firm itself, and for which no regular quotations are available, is determined either by an analysis of the asset into the component factors of labor, materials, and overhead, made by the appraiser with the cooperation of the owner's engineers, or by securing estimates based on similar analyses by reliable machine builders. In appraising buildings and other structures the standard procedure involves the development of detailed construction specifications—in terms of steel, lumber, brick, and so on, and the various kinds of labor required in the direct process of construction, the development of appropriate unit costs for all of these factors, and the systematic estimating of the more indirect items such as architect's fees, engineering, insurance, depreciation of construction equipment, general supervision, taxes and interest during construction, injuries and damages, etc. An alternative and less expensive method consists of finding the extent or capacity of each asset in terms of cubic feet (in the case of a building), horsepower or some other recognized unit for measuring productive capacity (in the case of equipment), and applying in each case the appropriate current unit cost furnished by experienced builders and manufacturers.

Competent appraisers have little difficulty (aside from the amount of work involved) in approximating the amount of the various kinds of materials and supplies required to construct a particular unit of plant, and in determining the appropriate unit costs for the particular market area and physical location. Estimating the number of units of each type of labor required is somewhat more troublesome, particularly in view of the many variations in construction methods. . . . When it comes to the question of general overhead costs, still greater difficulties confront the appraiser, and often there is room for substantial difference of opinion regarding these elements of total cost.

Appraisers have occasionally been guilty of preparing elaborate estimates of replacement cost for buildings and equipment which on account of obsolescence or other conditions would never be replaced in kind, if at all. . . . It is also unreasonable, in computing replacement cost, to use present-day costs of materials represented in the existing asset that are now considered too expensive for use in the type of property being appraised. Fortunately appraisal practice in recent years has been greatly improved at this point. Competent valuation experts recognize the impropriety of blindly going ahead with the preparation of estimates of replacement cost for obsolete assets and in other situations where such costs have no significance. No asset can have a value, from a going-concern point of view, in excess of the cost of the most efficient and up-to-date means available for reproducing the existing capacity, with appropriate deduction for depreciation in view of the age of the property. Such cost, less depreciation, is a ceiling figure. . . .

Estimating Depreciation at Appraisal Date. Professional appraisers, in part as a result of an engineering point of view, stress physical condition as determined by careful field inspection as a basis for estimating depreciation accrued to date of appraisal. Thus the conception of the appraiser is not identical with that of the accountant, and his estimate is likely not to agree with the accrual computed by the accountant. The accountant defines depreciation as the expiration of the cost or value of the property as the useful life passes; he is primarily concerned with the distribution of such cost or value over service life, in a reasonable way, through systematic computations. The appraiser, on the other hand, is trying to find depreciation for valuation purposes on a specific date, and is not inclined to give much attention to the relation of his estimate to the process of spreading cost or value over estimated service life. The appraiser endeavors to measure by inspection the lack of serviceability or utility—the "observed depreciation"—as compared to a brand-new unit of property. He emphasizes the effect of both routine servicing and replacement of parts as a means of off-setting or retarding the march of depreciation. To the appraiser the ultimate unit of property for purposes of depreciation calculations is not simply the building or machine in its entirety but the individual structural components thereof in relation to the whole—a point of view which the accountant will do well to take more seriously. Thus the appraiser properly takes the position that if important structural elements have been recently replaced the existing accrued depreciation has been affected by such replacements. He sometimes pushes this point too far, however, by insisting that there is little or no depreciation in excess of accrued or deferred maintenance. No matter how well a unit of property may be serviced and cared for throughout its life depreciation continues to accrue with advancing age. And physical operating condition alone is not an adequate test of the extent of the depreciation accrued. Most depreciable assets have to be kept in fairly good condition, in order to be used effectively, down to the very day of retirement. The accounting and appraisal interpretations are brought nearer together, it may be added, under a program of accounting which classifies property according to the replaceable component elements, and deals with the renewal of particular elements as replacements rather than as maintenance.

Because of the difficulty of measuring the results of obsolescence, inadequacy, etc. by inspection the appraiser is also somewhat more reluctant than the accountant to take such factors into his reckoning until their effect has become apparent. This means, as a rule, that the appraiser's estimate of depreciation due to these considerations is relatively low.

NOTE ON ASSET VALUATION

As the foregoing excerpt suggests, asset value may continue to play a significant role in the valuation process. For one thing, if a company has no demonstrable earning power and hence the capitalization of earnings approach cannot be used, obviously some form of asset valuation must be relied upon. And even when capitalization of earnings is used to determine the overall enterprise value, it may still be necessary to value the various individual assets in order to determine the appropriate basis of each for depreciation and the like. For this purpose, the tangible assets are normally valued at reproduction cost, at least so long as the overall enterprise value either equals or exceeds the total reproduction cost of the individual assets. Any excess of the enterprise value over the total reproduction cost of tangible assets would then be allocated to goodwill or other intangibles.[3]

3. For an excellent illustration of the valuation of tangible assets for the purpose of allocating an overall purchase price between tangibles and intangibles, see Philadelphia Steel & Iron Corporation v. Commissioner, 23 T.C.M. 558 (1964).

In addition, as Perlman v. Feldmann, page 7 supra, illustrates, in some cases a so-called "asset value factor" is weighted in with the capitalized earnings figure to obtain the final enterprise value. This approach seems to stem principally from a line of Delaware valuation cases arising under the statute giving stockholders who dissent from a merger the right to have their shares appraised and purchased by the corporation. See, e. g., Tri-Continental Corp. v. Battye, 31 Del.Ch. 523, 74 A.2d 71 (Sup.Ct.1950); Chicago Corporation v. Munds, 20 Del.Ch. 142, 172 A. 452 (Ch.1934). The early appraisal cases involved investment companies whose assets consisted of listed securities which could readily be valued. In part because the investment company shares often sold at a substantial discount from the underlying asset value, the courts concluded that the market price of the shares was not the exclusive test of value, see page 777 infra, and that some account should be taken of other valuation factors, particularly asset value.

Whatever may be said of this approach in the valuation of an investment company, obviously a quite different question is presented when an ordinary industrial is being valued. Nevertheless, when appraisal cases involving industrials came along, an asset value factor was routinely included without any real consideration of its appropriateness in that context. On the other hand, in cases involving valuation of an industrial for other purposes, for example to test the fairness of the price at which the business was sold, asset value has been completely ignored and the valuation has been based exclusively upon capitalization of earnings. E. g., Cottrell v. Pawcatuck Co., 36 Del.Ch. 169, 128 A.2d 225 (Sup.Ct.1956). Curiously, each of these two lines of Delaware valuation cases has totally ignored the existence of the other.

If an asset value factor is to be included, how should it be computed? In Perlman v. Feldmann it seems to have consisted simply of the book value of the net assets. The Delaware appraisal cases, on the other hand, after first paying little attention to this issue, now tend to look to replacement value. E. g., Felder v. Anderson, Clayton & Co., 39 Del.Ch. 76, 159 A.2d 278 (Ch.1960). That seems clearly correct. If asset value has any real relevance in the valuation of a substantial enterprise, it is because a prospective purchaser would consider alternative means of obtaining such facilities, including reproducing them elsewhere, and hence the replacement cost may be a relevant component of value. This is particularly so when, as the court in Perlman v. Feldmann put it, the reason for taking asset value into account is the "direct accession to the dollar value of plants, machinery and tools" in a wartime economy, due in part to "the cost and difficulty of procuring materials and equipment for setting up new and additional plants."

Presumably, no account is taken of goodwill or other intangibles in computing the asset value factor, except perhaps to the extent of the cost of any purchased intangibles. There does not appear to be any way of valuing self-developed goodwill except on the basis of some variation of capitalized earnings;[4] and it would hardly make sense to use capitalization of earnings

---

4. The most common method of valuing goodwill separately is the one derived from A.R.M. 34, 2 Cum.Bull. 31 (1920). Under this method the value of goodwill is measured in terms of the excess of average earnings over a reasonable return on the tangible assets employed in the enterprise. Any such excess is regarded as a kind of "super-profit" stemming from goodwill, and the value of the goodwill is determined by capitalizing such super-profit, usually at a substantially higher rate (lower multiplier) than the one used

in deriving the asset value factor when that factor is to be used as a kind of counter-balance to an overall enterprise value based upon capitalization of earnings.

This means that for any enterprise with a material amount of goodwill the asset value factor should be less than the figure derived by capitalizing earnings. In such a case the effect of weighting in the asset value factor is to reduce the impact of the goodwill apparently disclosed by the capitalization of earnings. However, the authorities have not had to face this problem as yet, since it seems that in every case where an asset value factor was included it exceeded the figure derived by capitalizing earnings and therefore resulted in increasing the final value figure. Thus inclusion of an asset value factor has had the effect, if not the purpose, of countering the possibility that too conservative a multiplier was used in capitalizing earnings.

On the other hand, in some circumstances the asset value factor could play the opposite role and offset an overly optimistic capitalization of earnings. Using asset value for this purpose might be particularly appropriate in connection with the new glamourous "space-age" companies which have come to the fore in recent years and have often been valued at figures far in excess of any reasonable asset value. The danger of ignoring asset value in such cases is graphically described in Graham, Dodd & Cottle, Security Analysis (4th ed. 1962) 556–557:

> In past years the main dividing line between shares deemed eligible and ineligible for first-time distribution to the public was the size of the enterprise. Among the millions of small businesses in operation it was never difficult to find a considerable number which were earning a large return on invested capital and had also increased their profits at a high percentage rate over several years past. As is well known, high percentage figures of this sort are more readily attainable by a successful small business, with an investment perhaps under $100,000, than by our large and well-established enterprises with a formidable amount of capital to figure earnings against. But the flourishing small companies were recognized as subject to special hazards growing out of their limited size; and these weaknesses, in the judgment of responsible investment-banking houses, disqualified them from public distribution. This prudent barrier was overcome not long ago, and a flood of little companies began to inundate the market. For most of them the high returns on capital plus apparently impressive growth rates (generally for only a few recent years) permitted an offering price equal to several times the net equity and a subsequent market price well above that.

as the measure of a reasonable return on tangibles. Reliance on this formula seems to have declined in recent years, and its use in the tax field is certain to be curtailed as a consequence of Revenue Ruling 65–192, 65–2 Cum.Bull. 259, which restricts the use of A.R.M. 34 to cases where "no better basis [is] available." See generally, Neuhauser, The Two-Step Method of Valuation: One Step Backwards? 51 Iowa L.Rev. 321 (1966).

We think that the purchase of such issues at a price, say, five or more times their net worth must carry great risks to the buyers as a whole, and that these risks are related directly to the net-worth situation. In past periods of similar offerings—always in the higher ranges of bull markets—the invariable sequel was for most of these unseasoned issues to fall *below* their asset values. They were then, belatedly, recognized as unsuitable for public ownership because of their inadequate size, and their shares found buyers in the market only on a *bargain basis*. This meant that, instead of valuing them more generously than from a privately owned ("Main Street") viewpoint, Wall Street now considered them to be worth a good deal less to its buyers than their value to a private owner. If a similar sequel should follow the present spate of new common-stock offerings, the losses will be that much heavier because of the huge multipliers now being paid soon after issuance, and the carnage will indeed be terrible.

C. VALUATION OF A SMALL ENTERPRISE

In the valuation of small businesses, asset value has continued to play a dominant role. Graham, Dodd & Cottle, op. cit. page 25 supra, at 553, expressly contrast public and private enterprises in this regard, stating that "net worth is a primary factor of value in most privately owned businesses," and adding the explanation that "the private owner has no clear-cut measure of the value of his business other than that shown on his balance sheet." On the other hand, as the SBA publication quoted above illustrates there has been growing recognition that for small businesses, as well as for large ones, earning power may provide the best guide to value. And on the tax side, the Internal Revenue Service has been on record since 1959 as favoring primary consideration for earnings when valuing the stock of a closely-held corporation, at least if it is primarily engaged in selling products or services to the public. Rev.Rul. 59–60, 1959–1 Cum.Bull. 237.

However, application of the capitalization of earnings approach to a small business does pose some special problems. For one thing, the entrepreneurs of a small enterprise, particularly when it is not incorporated, often do not isolate compensation for their own services from the rest of their entrepreneurial return. In such cases it is necessary to determine and deduct reasonable compensation for such services in arriving at the figure for estimated future earnings to be capitalized, since the value of the enterprise should be based upon its earning power in excess of reasonable compensation for any services rendered.[5]

There is more doubt about the extent to which taxes should be deducted in determining the estimated future earnings of the enterprise. Normally, in valuing a corporation estimated corporate income taxes are deducted, as they were in Perlman v. Feldmann, whereas presumably in valuing a proprietorship or partnership no deduction is made for income taxes incurred by the individuals on the earnings of the business.[6] A harder question is whether when an existing proprietorship or partnership is being valued to measure its contribution to a proposed corporation any account should be taken of the corporate taxes to which the earnings will be subjected in the future. Probably for any growing enterprise it would be wise to deduct estimated corporate income taxes. As we shall see later, corporate income taxes are often a modest price to pay to shield the earnings of the enterprise from the graduated tax rates applicable to individuals. But in any event the value of an enterprise should not depend upon whether it is in fact incorporated and hence subject to corporate taxes. Therefore, in practice it seems likely that a lower multiplier would be used if pre-tax earnings are being capitalized than if post-tax earnings are being capitalized, so that the ultimate enterprise value would come out about the same either way.[7] This makes sense since there is at least a substantial risk of ultimately becoming subject to corporate taxes, and so pre-tax earnings are less secure than post-tax earnings.

Choosing the proper multiplier for a small enterprise also poses some special difficulties. There is much less recorded experience with the valuation of such businesses from which some guidance might be obtained. Of course, whenever there is a publicly-held company engaged in a business similar to the one to be valued, the price-earnings ratio of the publicly-held stock will provide some measure of a proper multiplier; but for many small businesses there will be great difficulty in finding a sufficiently "similar" publicly-held company. Although the above Dewing chart affords some guide, it has to be said that the distinctions among the various paragraphs in the lower ranges of the chart, particularly numbers 4, 5 and 6, are far from clear. There is also the question of whether and to what extent the current financial climate calls for an increase in the Dewing multipliers in these lower ranges. Suffice it to say that whatever may be true in the upper ranges of the chart, there is little evidence of any substantial upswing in the value-earnings ratio of small, private businesses. For an example of capitalization of the earnings of a modest enterprise

---

5. See 2 Bonbright, The Valuation of Property 729 (1937).

6. See A.R.M. 145, I–1 Cum.Bull. 24 (1922). But see Watson v. Commissioner, 7 T.C.M. 74, 76 (1948).

7. The SEC has sometimes valued the same enterprise on the basis of both pre-tax and post-tax earnings, using a higher multiplier in the latter case. See Higbee Co., 8 SEC 777, 792 (1941).

(which, however, contains some obvious errors in application), see the valuation set out in the findings of fact in the Turner case, page 107 infra.

One other special problem presented in applying the capitalization of earnings method to a small business relates to the handling of long-term liabilities. In valuing a large enterprise, long-term debt, particularly when it is represented by bonds held by the public, is often treated as part of the ownership of the enterprise, along with the equity, on the theory that the allocation between long-term debt and equity is largely within the control of the parties and should therefore not unduly affect the valuation of the enterprise. Under this view of course the interest on the long-term debt is not deducted in arriving at the "earnings" to be capitalized, and the resulting enterprise value includes both the debt and equity components. The value of the equity interest alone can then be determined by deducting the amount (or, if it is clearly substantially different, the value) of the long-term debt from the total enterprise value figure.

Alternatively, it is possible to value the equity interest directly, by capitalizing just the post-interest income available for the equity. Under this approach it is common to use a somewhat higher capitalization rate (lower multiplier) than would be applied to pre-interest earnings, since the interest "comes off the top," so to speak, and represents the most secure, least risky portion of the total earnings stream.

To illustrate these two approaches, assume that a corporation has $500,000 of long-term debt, paying 6% interest, and an estimated earning power of $200,000 before interest. Under the first alternative the value of the equity interest would be determined by first applying a multiplier, say 12, to the earnings before interest, producing a figure of $2,400,000, and then deducting the $500,000 debt to arrive at an equity value of $1,900,000. Under the second alternative, if the same multiplier of 12 was applied to the post-interest earnings of $170,000 (ignoring any tax effects) available for equity, the result would be a value for the equity of over $2,000,000. The reason for this difference is that the multiplier of 12 is substantially lower than the multiplier of almost 17 which is inherent in the interest rate of 6% on the bonds. But if the multiplier applied to the earnings after interest is reduced to, say, 11, the value of the equity comes out at about the same $1,900,000 produced by the first alternative.

The role of long-term debt in the valuation of a small enterprise is a little more troublesome. For one thing, except for debt held by stockholders, which is often, as we shall see later, almost literally a form of equity, it is not very realistic to think of the long-term debt of a small business as akin to equity. Rather for the small enterprise long-term debt is more often than not just another way of meeting the shortage of working capital which tends to plague small businesses.

Moreover, for a small enterprise, where the overall multiplier is not likely to be even as high as five, there is an enormous jump to the multiplier of 15 or more which is inherent in any normal interest rate on the debt. Accordingly, the first alternative above, under which the earnings before interest are capitalized and the face amount of the long-term debt is deducted, would tend to understate the value of the equity. It seems more sensible to use the second alternative, under which only the post-interest earnings available for the equity are capitalized, and to take account of the presence of any substantial amount of long-term debt in such cases by using a slightly lower multiplier than would otherwise be in order.

SECTION 2. ALLOCATION OF MANAGERIAL CONTROL

A. ALLOCATION OF DIRECTORSHIPS

Obviously, the matter of allocation of control over the affairs of the proposed business enterprise is of prime concern to the parties. There are of course three primary levels of control in the corporate hierarchy: (1) the stockholders, who elect the board of directors, and also have residual power over fundamental corporate changes such as an amendment of the certificate of incorporation or a merger; (2) the directors, to whom is committed general management of the business and affairs of the corporation; and (3) the officers, who in theory execute the policy determined by the directors, but in practice, particularly in a small business, often have wide latitude in determining the course of the operations of the business. Since the principal source of power to control the operations of the corporation resides in the board of directors, allocation of directorships is often the first order of business for each of the interested parties. Obviously, the influence which any particular number of directors may wield depends upon such other factors as the total number of directors and whether there is a provision requiring a higher than majority vote for action by the directors. But regardless of the impact of these factors, each interested party can be expected to press for at least one seat on the board. The following constitutes a capsule review of the techniques most commonly used to achieve this objective.

Cumulative Voting

Under cumulative voting, each shareholder is entitled to cast as many votes as are equal to the number of his shares multiplied by the number of directors to be elected, and he may cast all of such votes for a single director or distribute them among the candidates as he sees fit. E. g., MBA § 31. The formula for determining the number of the total voting shares of a corporation which are needed to elect one director may be expressed mathematically as $\frac{V}{n+1} + 1$ where V is the total number of voting shares of the corporation and n is the number of directors to be elected. Thus if, for example, there were four directors to be elected, it would take one-fifth (20%) of the stock plus one share to be sure of electing one of the directors.

Where cumulative voting is merely permitted rather than required, a shareholder relying on it to control a position on the board must make sure that he cannot be out-flanked by an amendment of the certificate of incorporation to eliminate cumulative voting. And even when cumulative voting is mandatory the value of the right may be impaired through such maneuvers as removal of a director, reduction in the number of directors, or classification of directors. Probably the best defense against these devices is a provision in the certificate prohibiting any such action if the votes cast against it would have been sufficient to elect a director under cumulative voting prior to the proposed change. Cf. MBA § 36A.

Where cumulative voting is mandatory, the use of any other technique for the allocation of the voting control may be subject to challenge as inconsistent with cumulative voting. Indeed, where, as in many jurisdictions, cumulative voting is embodied in the state constitution, even a device expressly permitted in the corporation statute may be invalidated as inconsistent with the constitutional cumulative voting provision. Thus in Wolfson v. Avery, 6 Ill.2d 78, 126 N.E.2d 701 (1955), a longtime provision of the Illinois corporation statute similar to MBA § 35 authorizing the division of directors into several classes with only one class being elected each year was held invalid on the ground that it impaired the right of cumulative voting guaranteed in the Illinois Constitution. On the other hand, in Janney v. Philadelphia Transportation Co., 387 Pa. 282, 128 A.2d 76 (1956), a similar contention was rejected on the ground that the Pennsylvania Constitutional provision requiring cumulative voting was intended simply to give a minority interest an opportunity to acquire representation on the board of directors, but did not purport to insure the maximum effectiveness of the exercise of that right. The court noted that the cumulative voting strength of a minority might be diluted by many techniques other than staggering the terms of directors, such as having a smaller board of directors, making the directors' terms of office longer than one year, or issuing non-voting stock, so that a decision holding classification of directors unconstitutional would presumably have required invalidating these well-recognized techniques also. It may be of some relevance that the provision in the Illinois Constitution requiring cumulative voting has also been construed to require that all stock be entitled to vote, whereas non-voting stock is permissible in Pennsylvania.

Where mandatory cumulative voting is provided by statute rather than in the constitution, other provisions of the corporation statute are of course of equal rank, and hence a provision inconsistent with cumulative voting need not necessarily yield. Thus in Humphrys v. The Winous Co., 165 Ohio St. 45, 133 N.E.2d 780 (1956), a corporation with three directors divided them into three classes as then permitted by the statute, so that only one director was elected each year. This meant that the plaintiff, who owned more than 40% of the voting stock, could not secure any representation on the board, despite the provision requiring cumulative voting in the Ohio corporation statute. Nevertheless, the Supreme Court of Ohio sustained the classification of the directors, holding that the cumulative voting provision did not nullify the classification provision. The court noted that in 1955 the legislature had amended the classification provision to require that each class consist of not less than three directors.

However, the result might be different if a technique was used for allocating voting control which was not only inconsistent with cumulative voting but also not expressly sanctioned by the corporation statute. This issue must be considered before any of the following other devices for allocation of voting control are used in a jurisdiction where cumulative voting is made mandatory by statute.

Classification of Shares

The devices of non-voting shares or several classes of shares are often used to achieve the allocation of directorships desired by the parties. Most corporation statutes, like MBA § 14, permit the creation of several classes of stock, or one or more series of stock within a class, with such voting power, full, limited, or none, as may be provided in the certificate of incorporation. Under such a statute, it seems permissible to arrange for several different classes of common stock which are identical except for the fact that a specified number of the directors are to be elected by each class of shares. Thus if a corporation had three shareholders with unequal holdings of stock, representation for each of them on a three-man board of directors could be assured simply by dividing the stock into three classes and giving each class, regardless of the number of shares in the class, the right to elect one of the three directors. Dividends and liquidation rights would presumably be left on a share for share basis.

It should be noted that the allocation of voting power resulting from classification of shares could reach beyond the election of directors. Under statutes requiring certain types of transactions to be approved by "each class" of stock, such classification could result in giving a stockholder a veto power to which he would not be entitled under "straight" voting. This is much less of a problem under statutes like MBA § 55 which require a class vote only when the proposed transaction has some special impact on the particular class. In Shanken v. Lee Wolfman, Inc., 370 S.W.2d 197 (Tex.Civ.App.1963), each of a corporation's three stockholders owned a separate class of stock, the three classes being identical in all respects except that class A had the right to elect three directors, and classes B and C one director each. There were 150 shares of stock authorized in each class, of which 100 had been issued to the respective stockholders. In connection with a contemplated acquisition of a related enterprise, the holders of classes A and B proposed that the authorized stock of each class be increased to 250 shares, but the plaintiff, who owned all of the class C stock, was able to block any increase in the authorized stock of his class under the Texas counterpart of MBA § 55(a). The other two stockholders then resolved simply to increase the aggregate number of the shares of classes A and B to 325 each. The plaintiff contended that he was also entitled to a class vote on this proposal, under a provision of the Texas statute (patterned on one originally included in the Model Act but dropped in the 1957 amendments) to the effect that "the holders of the outstanding shares of any class entitled to vote upon a proposed amendment by the provisions of the articles of incorporation shall be entitled to vote as a class thereon if the amendment . . . would change the shares of any class, whether with or without par value, into a different number of shares of the same class." *Held*, the proposed amendment did not *change* the original shares in classes A and B into a greater number of shares, but merely *added* 175 shares to each of such classes. The court also ruled that the proposed amendment did not "change the designations, preferences, limitations, or relative rights" of the plaintiff's class C stock within the meaning of the Texas counterpart of MBA § 55(e) because the "*quality and relative rights of the shares* in each class, as distinguished from the relative position of the classes in the capital structure, have remained identical."

As to the issue of whether classification can be squared with cumulative voting, consider the following:

OPINION OF THE ATTORNEY GENERAL OF MISSOURI

No. 238, 1964.

Your official opinion request of June 19, 1964, raises the following question relating to a corporation organized under the provisions of [the Missouri corporation statute].

> "May the Articles of Incorporation (or amendments) provide that each of two classes of voting stock shall elect one-half of the directors of a six-member board of directors, regardless of the number of voting shares in each class of stock?"

Article XI, Section 6 of the Missouri Constitution provides:

> "In all elections for directors or managers of any corporation, each shareholder shall have the right to cast as many votes in the aggregate as shall equal the number of shares held by him, multiplied by the number of directors or managers to be elected, and may cast the whole number of votes, either in person or by proxy, for one candidate, or distribute such votes among two or more candidates; and such directors or managers shall not be elected in any other manner . . . ."

. . . The shareholders' right to "distribute such votes among two or more candidates" clearly means that each voting shareholder has a right to vote cumulatively for any or all directors to be elected and to have those votes counted.

The placing of limitations on the number of directors a class of stock may elect would completely ignore the number of votes within that class of stock and prevent the distribution of such votes as each shareholder desired. This is contrary to Article XI, Section 6 of the Constitution of Missouri, which clearly provides that shareholders may vote for all directors to be elected. In addition, the shareholders of a particular class might thereby be given voting power disproportionate to the number of votes to which such shareholders are entitled under the Constitution. On the other hand, the shareholders might be precluded from exercising their full voting power under the Constitution by not having their votes counted cumulatively towards the election of all directors. Under the Constitution shareholders entitled to vote do so as shareholders of the corporation and not as members of a particular class of stock. Therefore, we are of the opinion that Articles of Incorporation (or amendments) which would arbitrarily limit the voting rights of a particular class of voting stock to the election of one-half of the directors is inconsistent with the constitutional provision of cumulative voting. . . .

Just as classification may be utilized to allocate voting control while dividend and liquidation rights are left on a share for share basis, so it may be used to allocate dividends and liquidation rights while voting is left on a straight per share basis. Thus the certificate of incorporation might provide for three classes of stock, each entitled to a specified percentage of any dividend or liquidating distribution, for example, 50% for class A, 30% for class B, and 20% for class C, regardless of the number of shares in the class. Assuming that voting rights would be left on a per share basis, voting power would be the only matter affected by the number of shares in the respective classes, and hence the numbers could be fixed to achieve whatever voting allocation was desired.

Non-voting stock can also be used to make voting power disproportionate to total equity interest. For example, if three stockholders making unequal capital contributions wanted to have equal voting power, they could each take the same amount of voting stock, while satisfying any additional equity interest with non-voting stock which was identical as to dividends, liquidation rights and the like. However, it must be kept in mind that the use of non-voting stock also affects the allocation of voting power on matters other than election of directors, unless the statute permits shares which are non-voting only as to the election of directors and entitled to vote on all other matters.

Shareholder Voting Agreements

Another common device to fix the composition of the board of directors is an agreement by two or more shareholders to vote their shares as a unit. While such agreements may cover a wide range of matters upon which shareholders have the power to act, they most commonly relate to the election of directors. Here the agreement may specify that the shares are to be voted for particular named persons as directors; or it may provide simply that the shares are to be voted as a unit. In the latter case, the question arises as to how the shares are to be voted in the event of disagreement among the parties. Presumably, in the absence of some express provision covering disagreement, the shares cannot be voted at all if the parties can not agree.

In dealing with such agreements, often referred to as "pooling agreements", the courts have usually been confronted with two questions: (a) whether such agreements are contrary to public policy; and (b) if they are valid, how and against whom they may be enforced. Most of the cases involving such agreements have upheld their validity, at least where the agreement did not go beyond the legitimate sphere of shareholder activity and attempt to bind the discretion of directors as well. However, if the consideration for entering into a pooling agreement gives a private benefit to the shareholder, the pooling agreement may be invalidated. For example, in Palmbaum v. Magulsky, 217 Mass. 306, 104 N.E. 746 (1914), one of three shareholders agreed to cancel a debt owed to him by another shareholder if the latter would vote with him on the question of whether to sell all of the corporate assets. In a subsequent action on the debt, performance of this agreement was held to be no defense on the ground that the agreement "operated as a fraud" upon the third shareholder.

More difficulty has been encountered in determining the appropriate remedy for violation of such agreements. In Smith v. San Francisco & N. P. Ry. Co., 115 Cal. 584, 47 P. 582 (1897), an agreement between three shareholders that they would vote their shares in such manner as should be decided by a ballot among them was held to give the majority on such ballot an irrevocable proxy to vote the shares of the third member of the pool, regardless of the latter's objection. The three stockholders had purchased their stock in reliance upon an understanding that such an agreement would be made immediately after the purchase. But in Roberts v. Whitson, 188 S.W.2d 875 (Tex. Civ.App.1945), the court refused to enforce a pooling agreement between two shareholders which provided that the shares were to be voted jointly and that the decision of arbitrators would control in the event of a disagreement among the parties. In addition to holding that the provision for arbitration constituted an illegal separation of ownership and the power to vote, the court held that mere mutual promises were not sufficient consideration to make the pooling arrangement irrevocable.

The risk of relying on this kind of agreement is perhaps most strikingly illustrated by the now classic case of Ringling Bros.-Barnum & Bailey Combined Shows v. Ringling, 29 Del.Ch. 610, 53 A.2d 441 (Sup.Ct.Del.1947). There two of the three shareholders of the corporation, who owned slightly less than one-third of the stock each, executed an agreement which provided that they would vote their shares jointly and that in the event of any disagreement, they would submit the matter to a named arbitrator whose decision was to be binding upon the parties. After some years of maintaining control over the corporation's affairs by voting together, the parties fell out, and one of them sought to vote her own shares in violation of the directions of the arbitrator. The Chancellor upheld the agreement and found an implied proxy in the willing party to vote the shares of the unwilling party in accordance with the instructions of the arbitrator. On appeal, the Supreme Court also upheld the agreement but refused to find any implied proxy. Accordingly, the court confined relief to prohibiting the unwilling shareholder from voting her shares against the instructions of the arbitrator. The result of this decision was that the third shareholder, who controlled slightly more than one-third of the shares, assumed control of the corporation, the very circumstance which the voting agreement had been designed to prevent.

Another potential danger in a pooling agreement is illustrated by the contention in the Ringling case that the pooling agreement was invalid because it in effect constituted a voting trust which was invalid for failure to conform to the statutory requirements for such instruments. Although the Ringling court rejected this contention, it cannot be ignored, particularly under new corporation statutes like the Model Act which deal extensively with the requirements for a valid voting trust while making no reference whatever to pooling agreements. Moreover, subsequent to the Ringling case the Supreme Court of Delaware, in Abercrombie v. Davies, 36 Del.Ch. 371, 130 A.2d 338 (1957), held that a purported pooling agreement which was little different in practical effect from the one involved in Ringling, although it was admittedly somewhat more complicated and far-reaching, did constitute a voting trust and was therefore invalid for failure to comply with the statutory formalities.

Other Arrangements

There are, of course, a variety of other possibilities for achieving the desired allocation of control in particular circumstances. A voting trust may be a useful technique in some situations, but the scope of this device is limited by statute in many jurisdictions, particularly as to the permissible duration which is normally confined to ten years. See MBA § 32.

Another useful device is the requirement of a higher than majority vote for shareholder action. E. g., MBA § 30. A shareholder unanimity agreement, under which no action can be taken by shareholders except by unanimous consent, is an extreme variation of this approach. However, in view of the normal presumption of majority rule in the absence of express statutory support, the validity of such a provision may be open to question. And even where such a provision is valid it would seem to be effective only to maintain the status quo, rather than as an independent means for securing a position on the board of directors. In other words, if the parties start with the desired allocation of directorships, a unanimity agreement among the stockholders would be effective to maintain that allocation; but in the event of changed circumstances, as for example the death of one of the directors, such a provision would not enable the interests formerly represented by the deceased director to elect his successor, but would only make it possible for them to block anyone they opposed.

Closely allied with the high vote requirement is the high quorum requirement. See MBA § 30. For example, requiring the presence of all of the shareholders for a quorum can be an indirect method for maintaining the status quo, since any shareholder can remain away from the meetings and thus eliminate any possibility of action prejudicial to his interests. Again, however, there is the question of whether such a quorum provision is valid in the absence of specific statutory support. In addition, there may be a question as to whether a shareholder may remain away from meetings for the sole purpose of preventing a quorum. Cf. Matter of Gearing, discussed at page 40 infra.

General Problems

Common to all of the foregoing devices for allocation of control is the question of the effect of a transfer of some or all of the stock of one of the parties, whether by sale, pledge, gift, or death. Of course this problem can be minimized by imposing restrictions upon the transfer of the stock, as is commonly done in close corporations. When a transfer does occur, the subsequent effect of the control arrangement may depend upon whether it is embodied in a corporate regulation, either a certificate of incorporation provision or a by-law, in which event it would presumably bind any transferee, or in a private shareholders' agreement, where it would probably not be binding upon a transferee unless he had notice of the agreement. So a certificate provision calling for cumulative voting (in a jurisdiction where cumulative voting is merely permissive) or for classification of shares would be no less binding upon a transferee than upon the original holder; but if the arrangement was incorporated in a shareholders' agreement a transferee might not be subject to the burdens, or entitled to the benefits, of the agreement.

There may be other distinctions between corporate regulations and outside agreements. Particularly because corporate regulations are likely to bind subsequent transferees of stock, such regulations may be held to a strict standard of compliance with the statutory "norm", whereas the parties to a voluntary shareholders' agreement may be free to waive or limit some of their statutory rights. Thus a particular allocation of voting power in a by-law or certificate of incorporation provision might be condemned as inconsistent with the statutory norm, although the same provision in a shareholders' agreement would be held valid and binding upon the parties to the agreement. The further consequence of this distinction is that when a by-law or certificate of incorporation provision is invalidated, the question may arise as to whether the invalid corporate regulation can be viewed as a contract among the shareholders who adopted it, and upheld to that extent. These problems are nicely illustrated in Sensabaugh v. Polson Plywood Company, 135 Mont. 562, 342 P.2d 1064 (1959), where, despite a provision in the Montana Constitution requiring cumulative voting, a committee of the corporation's directors (including the plaintiff) had proposed an amendment to the by-laws to eliminate cumulative voting in favor of "straight" voting for the election of directors, and the stockholders unanimously approved the amendment. A few years later the plaintiff and a few other stockholders sought to cumulate their votes, and upon being refused the plaintiff brought an action to invalidate the amended by-law as inconsistent with the constitutional provision. The court held unanimously that the constitutional provision prohibited the corporation from depriving the stockholders of the right of cumulative voting by any regulation or act on its part. And one member of the court took the view that a contract among the stockholders calling for "straight" voting would be equally void as inconsistent with the established public policy of the state. However, a majority of the court thought that the stockholders were free to contract with one another to limit or deny the right of cumulative voting even though the corporation could not do so. Therefore, the question was presented as to whether the invalid by-law could be enforced as a contract requiring "straight" voting among the stockholders who had adopted it. On this issue too the court divided, but a majority held that the by-law could not be enforced as a contract:

> "[There] must at all times be borne in mind the difference between stockholders' contracts between themselves without the realm of the corporate structure and those carried on or attempted within. Here we have the majority of the stock-

holders, including plaintiff herein, in 1956 desiring to bind themselves from cumulative voting. If their purpose at that time was, as appears from the record, for the good of the corporation and themselves as stockholders, they could have easily entered into a valid contract between themselves to that end. . . . The Constitutional provision involved here was not designed as a restriction on the rights of stockholders to make their contracts which violate no rule of the common law, and which affect no rights, except their own. Here the stockholders did not do so without the realm of the corporate structure but carried it within, by amending the by-law. By such a method the majority attempted to bind all stockholders, including those not represented at the meeting when the by-law was amended."

Consider how to draft a contract provision requiring "straight" voting for the election of directors. Would it be possible to provide by contract for a voting allocation equivalent to that provided by classification of shares?

B. ASSURING LONG-TERM EMPLOYMENT

Normally, it is contemplated that most if not all of the participants in a closely-held corporation will hold full-time positions with the company and will draw their basic livelihood from it. Hence, once the allocation of control at the board of directors level has been established, the parties are likely to turn their attention to assuring their respective roles as salaried officers or other employees of the corporation. A capsule review of the problems which may arise in accomplishing this seems in order at this point.

The appointment of corporate officers is normally a matter for the board of directors unless specifically reserved to the shareholders by the corporation statute. And the hiring of employees for the corporation, as well as fixing the compensation of corporate agents at whatever level, seems clearly within the mandate of the board of directors to "manage the business". Typically, at the outset of a venture this "statutory norm" presents no obstacle to fixing the original positions and compensation of the parties in accordance with their agreement. However, under many corporate statutes some officers must be reappointed each year. In addition, the board of directors often has the power to remove any officer or agent regardless of cause. E. g., MBA § 45. Hence, each party needs some assurance that the board will not change the status quo in the future.

Of course the hornbook general rule is that the discretion of the directors cannot be bound in advance. Nevertheless, at least in the close corporation area, some variation from this corporate norm is permitted. Thus today a contract among the shareholders of a closely-held corporation which includes provisions allocating positions and salaries among the participants will probably be effective to put the parties in those positions and keep them there, despite the fact that to this extent the future discretion of the directors has been curtailed. See generally, Galler v. Galler, 32 Ill.2d 16, 203 N.E.2d 577 (1964).

An alternative to such a shareholders agreement, at least for positions which do not call for annual appointment, might be found in long-term employment contracts with the corporation. It is now clear that the board of directors has the power to execute an employment contract extending beyond its own term; and in the close corporation area it is likely that the duration of an employment contract, even one for the life of the employee, would not be a ground for invalidating it. However, such a contract might still be subject to the express or implied power of the corporation, acting through the board of directors, to terminate the employment regardless of cause. While such a removal would presumably give the employee a right to contract damages, cf. MBA § 45, this may not be sufficient protection to one who wants to continue to take an active role in the operations of the enterprise in which he has a substantial financial stake. A possible solution to this problem is suggested by the fact that a party who has control of at least one-half of the board of directors would seem to be entirely safe from this quarter, since he can prevent any affirmative action terminating his employment. Every employee who is also a director can obtain the same veto power over changes in his position or salary under a provision requiring a unanimous vote of the board of directors for any action affecting his employment arrangement.

Provisions requiring a higher than majority vote for action by the board of directors of a closely-held corporation have been receiving increasingly sympathetic treatment from the courts. Compare Katcher v. Ohsman, 26 N.J.Super. 28, 97 A.2d 180 (1953), with Benintendi v. Kenton Hotel, 294 N.Y. 112, 60 N.E.2d 829 (1945). In addition, many modern corporation statutes appear to expressly contemplate either a certificate of incorporation or by-law provision requiring a higher than majority vote by the directors. E. g., MBA § 37. And even in a jurisdiction where a requirement of a higher than majority vote for all action by directors might be invalid, such a requirement might be sustained if it were limited to a few particular matters within the board's competence.

At the board of director level, as at the shareholder level, the practical effect of a veto power may be achieved by setting a high quorum requirement for action by the directors. See MBA § 37. A provision requiring the presence of all the directors for a quorum would in effect give every director a veto power, since each could block any action by the board simply by staying away from the meeting. However, unless such a quorum provision can be combined with a rather strict requirement for notice of the business to be transacted at each director's meeting, any director seeking to block a matter would have to avoid every meeting, which would cut down the chances of getting the directors together to thrash out their differences. In addition, a recent New York decision, Matter of Gearing, 11 N.Y.2d 201, 182 N.E.2d 391 (1962), takes a dim view of such use of the quorum requirement, indicating that a director who stays away from directors' meetings in order to prevent the existence of a quorum may later be estopped from attacking action taken without the presence of a quorum.

C. ALLOCATION OF CONTROL OVER DESIGNATED AREAS OF OPERATION

Often the closely-held corporation constitutes a combination of quite different skills represented by the various participants. To what extent may a party be given complete control in the area of his special competence? In analyzing the following possible approaches to such an objective, be sure to consider also whether such an objective is a desirable one.

In view of the ultimate responsibility of the board of directors for "management of the business," it is generally assumed that any authority reposed in a corporate officer or other employee, whether that authority springs from a by-law, an employment contract, a resolution of the board of directors, or from the inherent powers of the particular corporate office involved, is subject to the supervision and control of the board of directors. To be sure, like any agent the corporate officer or employee may have power to bind the corporation well beyond his actual authority; but as between any officer or employee and the board of directors, the authority of the individual is subservient to the ultimate power of the board. Accordingly, even if a by-law expressly conferred very broad authority upon one of the officers, for example in a particular sphere of operations such as sales or production, the exercise of that authority would presumably still be subject to the ultimate control of the board. And it seems unlikely that anything short of a clear statutory mandate would be sufficient to authorize a departure from this normal corporate hierarchy—which is probably a complete answer to the possible implication the other way in the second paragraph of MBA § 44.

Assuming that a by-law, however broadly phrased, would still leave the corporate officer or employee subservient to the will of the directors, what would be the effect of a deadlock among the directors which made it impossible to say what the board's will was? Surely a stalemate among the directors should not necessarily paralyze the operations of the business, and presumably each officer or employee would be empowered to continue to carry on his normal operations. But suppose, for example, the vice-president in charge of sales, operating under a very broad by-law authorization in that area, proposed to pursue some change in sales policy, and the board of directors was evenly divided on the matter. One view of the situation would be that once the board of directors has considered a matter within its competence, it has assumed "jurisdiction" of the matter, and a deadlock means that the matter failed to carry. On the other hand, it might be contended that if the proposed action is within the general authority delegated to the officer, he is authorized to act unless the board affirmatively denies him permission. Under this view, the deadlock of the directors would mean that permission had not been refused, and the officer would remain free to act.

Under the view that the officer's authority remains unimpaired in the face of a board of directors deadlock, any party can be given virtually complete control in a particular area by giving him very broad express authority, together with power to deadlock the board. And it would seem that the power to deadlock can be achieved for any party who is a director by requiring unanimity among the directors for any action on a matter relating to the particular area, so that in effect the person would have a veto power over any interference with his exercise of authority.

There is only scant authority on the question of the power of an officer to act in the face of a deadlocked board, and practically all of what there is comes from the same jurisdiction, New York, relates to the same corporate office, the presidency, and involves the same type of action, the instigation of litigation on behalf of the corporation. In Sterling Industries, Inc., v. Ball Bearing Pen Corp., 298 N.Y. 483, 84 N.E.2d 790 (1949), the plaintiff corporation was owned and controlled equally by two groups, one of which also owned the defendant company. After the plaintiff and defendant had entered into a contract, the plaintiff's president called a special meeting of its board of directors to consider the advisability of instituting suit against the defendant for an alleged breach of that contract. At the meeting, the directors were evenly divided and the president declared that the motion had failed to carry. Nevertheless, the president later caused the plaintiff to institute suit against the defendant. The court held that the suit should be dismissed as unauthorized, on the ground that any actual or implied authority of the president to commence the action was terminated when a majority of the board failed to sanction it. The court relied upon the "statutory norm" that the business of the corporation should be managed by the board of directors, and remitted the president to a stockholder's derivative action.

However, Paloma Frocks, Inc. v. Shamokin Sportswear Corp., 3 N.Y.2d 572, 147 N.E.2d 779 (1958), seems to suggest an important distinction. Here it was the defendant corporation which was owned and controlled by two groups, one of which also controlled the plaintiff corporation. The two corporations entered into a contract which included a provision for submitting any dispute to arbitration. After some performance under the contract, the president of the defendant served a demand on the plaintiff for arbitration under the contract. The plaintiff sought an injunction against the proposed arbitration on the ground that it had never been authorized by the defendant's directors. The president of the defendant conceded that the directors of the defendant had not acted, but contended that a meeting of the board would have been an idle gesture since the group interested in the plaintiff corporation would never have voted for the arbitration and the board would have been deadlocked. *Held*, reversing the lower court which had relied upon the Sterling Industries case, the president of the defendant was authorized to institute the arbitration proceeding. The Court of Appeals purported to distinguish the Sterling case on two grounds, the first being that in Sterling the president had asked the board's permission to bring the suit and had failed to obtain the consent of a majority, whereas in this case the board had never acted at all on the matter. Second, in the instant case the president of the defendant was merely carrying out an existing agreement that all disputes should be submitted to arbitration; although the board of directors presumably had the power to forbid a particular arbitration, they had not done so here.

The first ground of distinction in the Paloma Frocks case was carried to a perhaps drily logical extreme in West View Hills, Inc. v. Lizau Realty Corp., 6 N.Y.2d 344, 160 N.E.2d 622 (1959). There the plaintiff corporation was owned by three equal stockholders who were also its three directors. The same three men had also formerly been equal stockholders and the three directors of the defendant corporation, but shortly before the commencement of this action, the one who was the president of the plaintiff had sold his stock in the defendant to the other two and severed his connections with the defendant. Subsequently, the president of the plaintiff launched it on this suit against the defendant and the two other individuals on a claim that they had caused the plaintiff to perform valuable construction services for the defendant without any compensation. The defendants contended that the suit should be dismissed on the ground that the board of directors of the plaintiff had never authorized it. The Court of Appeals held that the president's authority to commence an action on behalf of the plaintiff corporation was not eliminated because a majority of the board of directors were in a position to withhold authorization. Once again the court distinguished the Sterling case on the ground that there the president's authority to bring suit was effectively terminated by the board's refusal to sanction it, whereas here the board of directors had never taken any action prohibiting the president's bringing of the suit. Two judges dissented, finding that the decision of the majority conflicted with the basic principle that the corporation was to be managed by the board of directors. The dissent contended that however relevant the absence of direct prohibition against the bringing of suit by the directors might be in a deadlock situation, it could hardly be decisive where the president knew that an actual majority of the board opposed the suit. In the view of the dissenting judges, the majority opinion amended the corporation statute to read that the corporation "shall be managed by its board of directors, except when one member of the board, who happens to be president, disagrees with the majority, in which case it shall be managed by the president." Incidentally, the court seemed to ignore the fact that the corporation in question was a Connecticut corporation, as appears in Zaubler v. West View Hills, Inc., 148 Conn. 540, 172 A.2d 604 (1961), where the president obtained an injunction against a withdrawal of the New York suit after he had been removed as president and a director of the corporation by the other two directors.

A similar control allocation might be achieved by making a broad delegation of the powers of the board in particular areas to executive committees, coupled with a provision for deadlocking the full board. Even assuming that such committees would have to consist of more than one director, the composition of each committee could be fixed to maximize the influence of particular persons in particular areas of operation.

Another technique for allocating control over specific areas of the business to particular persons might be the use of multiple corporations. For example, suppose the parties organizing an ordinary manufacturing enterprise want to allocate special control over sales matters to one of the parties and over production matters to another. If separate corporations for sales and production were organized, it would be possible, by the use of non-voting shares, classification, or other techniques discussed earlier, to give the designated persons control of the board of directors of the respective corporations. Under this approach, it would not be necessary to try to put an officer's authority beyond the control of the board of directors. Presumably, the allocation of financial interests in the two corporations among the parties would be identical, since otherwise there would be a real conflict between the two corporations in their mutual dealings, and the whole nature of the over-all enterprise would be drastically changed.

There are, however, some difficulties with this multiple corporation route. For one thing, giving a person control of the board of directors of one of the corporations goes well beyond the allocation of control over a particular sphere of operations such as sales or production. Such control would also encompass all the other areas within the competence of the board of directors, including the payment of dividends. In addition, any party other than the two persons to whom the control over the respective corporations would be allocated would not share in control at all under this approach, whereas with only one corporation there would be room for such a party to wield some influence. Of course such difficulties might be met by confining the power of the designated persons to the specified areas of operations, presumably by the use of veto powers and the like. Or perhaps the separate operating corporations could be made wholly-owned subsidiaries of a common parent, which would be governed by the parties' more general allocation of control. However, if resort to such devices becomes necessary query whether the multiple corporate set-up is worth undertaking, at least so far as allocation of control is concerned.

SECTION 3. ALLOCATION OF INTERESTS IN A NEW ENTERPRISE

A. NOTE ON THE CHARACTERISTICS OF VARIOUS TYPES OF STOCKS AND BONDS [8]

The various types of business units—sole proprietorships, partnerships, business trusts, corporations—all are distinctive modes of organizing business enterprise. *They are modes of allocating three elements of enterprise: (1) the risk of loss, (2) the power of control, and (3) the participation in the proceeds of the business activity.* In corporate enterprises it is the corporate "capital structure" through which this allocation of risk, control, and profit is effected. Capital structure refers to the aggregate of the "securities" issued by the corporation—the instruments, such as shares of stock and bonds, which represent relatively long term investment in the corporation. The distribution of risk, control, and profit is worked out through the fixing of the terms of the various classes of securities and their relative amounts in the capital structure.

The most important characteristics of corporate securities as forms of investment are their variations with regard to: (1) the right to an early claim on the income of the enterprise before other security holders receive any payments; (2) the right to the "residual" income, however large, after others have been paid promised amounts; and (3) the right to vote on personnel and policy in the corporation, and hence the power to control the corporation.

The arrangement of the capitalization section of the balance sheet illustrates the traditional classification of corporate securities based upon the distinction between debt securities and shares of stock (preferred or

---

8. The following material is adapted, with permission, from unpublished materials prepared by Professor Wilbur G. Katz of the University of Wisconsin Law School.

common). For many purposes, however, a more significant distinction is that between "senior" securities, which have a prior and limited claim upon earnings, and securities with a residual interest in earnings. Securities in this second category are often called "equity" securities, a usage traceable to the term "equity of redemption" in connection with mortgaged property. In classifications based on this distinction, senior securities include both debt securities and the typical preferred stock; equity securities include not only common stock but also the "participating preferred stock" described below.

Before describing securities in detail, one point should be emphasized: that the rights of preferred shareholders and bondholders (and of common shareholders if there are several classes of them) are a matter of contract. For a draftsman, the security is whatever he chooses to make it. There are historically certain characteristics which are common to specific types of securities. Even they may vary with business conditions, for the primary consideration is what is most attractive to the market at the time. In a period of prosperity, for example (such as 1956–57), a conversion feature is often found in debentures as well as preferred stock.

The traditional forms of securities will therefore be first described, then some of the more frequent variations and hybrid categories.

Debt Securities

Typical debt securities (bonds, debentures, notes) are issued in bearer form, although provision is often made for registration in the owners' names. They carry no voting rights in the election of directors and are issued with a stated maturity date on which the principal or "face" amount is payable. Gradual reduction of the amount outstanding is often provided, either by serial maturities or by a *"sinking fund."* The latter is an arrangement under which specified amounts are periodically applied to the retirement of the securities. The sinking fund installments are sometimes fixed and unconditional; in other cases they are made partly or wholly contingent upon earnings.

Debt securities are typically *redeemable* at the option of the corporation, usually at the face amount plus a premium which declines as the maturity date approaches. The redemption privilege is important, for when interest rates decline it may become profitable to "refund," i. e., to replace the issue with another carrying a lower interest rate.

Typical debt securities carry an obligation to pay *fixed interest*, i. e., whether or not income has been earned. The interest obligation is usually represented by semi-annual "coupons" (small notes attached to the bonds) which are detached and surrendered in exchange for the semi-annual interest payments.

Debt securities are often issued pursuant to an *"indenture,"* an elaborate contract between the corporation and a trustee for the benefit of the holders of the securities. Indenture provisions are of great variety and have an important bearing upon the risk assumed by the security holder. The federal Trust Indenture Act of 1939 prescribes requirements for indentures and qualifications for indenture trustees.

Holders of debt securities are, of course, creditors and, as such, in the event of default their remedies include those of initiating proceedings for receivership, bankruptcy, or reorganization, although some of these remedies are often limited by provisions of the indenture. It is easy to overemphasize the formal rights of the various security holders. When a corporation becomes bankrupt and unable to meet its financial obligations, a compromise agreement is usually worked out whereby all classes of security holders make some sacrifice, scaling down their interests in order to keep the corporation in operation because it is worth more as a going concern.

Mortgage Bonds. In this type of debt security, the indenture constitutes a mortgage upon described property of the corporation, the indenture trustee being mortgagee for the benefit of the bondholders. Mortgage security theoretically makes available the usual remedies of mortgage foreclosure; but what is of greater practical importance, the mortgage establishes priorities which are respected in large measure in proceedings for corporate reorganization. Mortgage indentures typically contain elaborate covenants covering maintenance and insurance of mortgaged property, payment of taxes, etc., and defining events of default which may justify acceleration of the maturity of the bonds.

Another type of secured obligation is the collateral trust bond. Here the property standing as security consists of other securities pledged to the indenture trustee for the protection of the bondholders.

Debentures. This is the customary term for relatively long-term debt securities which have no mortgage or pledge of corporate property. These obligations rest upon the general credit of the corporation and upon the force of the various indenture covenants, such as prohibitions against incurring further indebtedness, the mortgaging of corporate property to other creditors, the payment of dividends, etc.

Shares of Stock

Stock certificates (unlike typical debt securities) are issued in the name of the holder and transfer is made on his written order and on surrender of the certificate. The relative rights of holders of various classes of stock are usually prescribed in the corporation's certificate of incorporation. Under some statutes, however, preferred stock may be issued in series the respective terms of which may be fixed by the board of directors.

Cumulative Preferred Stock. Holders of typical preferred shares are entitled to dividends at a specified rate per year in priority to dividend distributions on common shares. Typical preferred shares are non-participating in that their holders are limited to dividends at the rate specified regardless of the amount of earnings or of the dividends paid on common shares. Preferred dividends (unlike bond interest) are not payable unconditionally but only from earnings or other funds legally available under the statute governing dividends. Preferred dividends are typically *cumulative*, i. e., if dividends for any year are not paid currently they accumulate (whether earned or not) and must be paid before any dividends may be paid on common shares. Accumulations of preferred dividends are not technically a debt but merely a priority in future dividend distributions. Only when dividends have been declared are they listed among the liabilities on corporate balance sheets, although arrearages should be disclosed parenthetically or by footnote. No interest or additional dividends accrue on the accumulations however long they remain unpaid. As will be seen in a later chapter, directors have wide discretion as to the time of paying dividends and typical preferred shareholders have no remedies comparable to those of holders of debt securities when interest is in arrears.

Investment in typical preferred stock is a long-term investment; there is no "maturity" date on which the stock must be retired. On dissolution or other liquidation of the corporation, preferred stock often has a specified *liquidation preference,* usually an amount approximating the amount of the investment plus dividend arrearages. (Often the preference is slightly greater in the event of "voluntary dissolution" than "involuntary dissolution.") Typical preferred shares, like debt securities, are made redeemable at the option of the corporation and sometimes the charter provides for a sinking fund for the retirement of preferred stock.

Preferred stock frequently carries no ordinary *voting rights* in the election of directors, except in a state like Illinois where all classes of shares must have one vote per share. It is common, however, to provide for *contingent voting rights* when preferred dividends are in arrears. These provisions typically permit the preferred shareholders then to elect a specified number of directors, sometimes a majority of the board. In addition, corporate statutes usually give the preferred stock a class vote on certain fundamental matters such as merger or dissolution, as well as on other proposed changes which may adversely affect the interests of the preferred. And of course the scope of protection to the preferred by class vote may be expanded by appropriate provision in the certificate of incorporation.

Participating Preferred Stock. Among the special classes of stock, the most common are those which entitle the holder to an initial preferred dividend and also (after the junior stock has received its initial dividend) to participation in further distributions on a parity with the junior stock. These are "participating preferred shares" and are sometimes given other names, such as "Class A Common." Provisions applicable to such shares are not standardized, but the initial preferred dividend is now usually made cumulative. It is usual, also, for such shares to have an initial preference on liquidation with further participation after an initial distribution on junior shares.

Common Stock. Typical common stock is easily described since it represents the residual interest in corporate assets, earnings and control. Occasionally common stock is divided into two classes which are identical except that voting rights are in one class exclusively.

Warrants are essentially contracts, pursuant to which the corporation agrees to sell to the holder a certain number of shares at a specified price. They are frequently sold to the public along with an issue of bonds or stock, and are sometimes issued to investment bankers as a bonus, or in a reorganization to holders whose claims were not otherwise recognized.

Convertibles and Other Hybrid Securities

Both debentures and preferred shares are often made convertible at the option of the holder into common shares at a specified rate. The rate is typically such that at the outset the debenture or preferred share is worth more than the common shares into which it is convertible. The value of the conversion privilege lies in the possibility of appreciation of the common shares. Frequently the conversion rate is on a sliding scale with the holder entitled to fewer common shares as conversion is postponed. After the necessary appreciation of the common shares, the market fluctuations of the convertible security follow closely those of the corresponding common shares.

Convertible securities (like other debt securities and preferred shares) are typically made redeemable, but the conversion privilege continues after notice of redemption is given until the date fixed for actual redemption. Thus while an ordinary debenture or preferred share will not frequently reach a market level above its redemption price, this is not true of a convertible. Convertible securities require carefully drafted provisions against "dilution" of the conversion privilege through transactions such as splits of common shares and stock dividends. Under such provisions the number of common shares into which the security is convertible is increased proportionately in the event of such transactions.

As already noted, rights of preferred shareholders and bondholders are largely a matter of contract. It is therefore possible to create stock which approximates the characteristics of debt securities. The most common of these hybrid types is the "income bond" or debenture, a debt security on which interest is payable only to the extent covered by the corporate earnings. In addition, there are subordinated debentures, which are subordinated to other borrowings. None of these features is mutually exclusive and there is practically no limit to the variety of combinations which the draftsman may adopt.

Preferred share provisions sometimes make it mandatory that dividends be declared if earnings are available. Furthermore, preferred shares are sometimes issued with a maturity date on which they must be retired. Here the character of a debt security is approached, although such matured preferred shares do not rank as a debt if the corporation is insolvent.

Capital Structures

In considering capital structures there are at least two separate questions to consider: (1) What should be the relation between the basic equity interests and senior securities? (2) What type of senior securities should be issued?

The answer to the first question will vary widely in accordance with the circumstances of the company and the industry. The S.E.C., for example, has a working policy of 60–10–30; i. e., sixty percent funded debt, ten percent preferred stock, and thirty percent common stock, for public utilities subject to their jurisdiction. (22d Annual Report of the S.E.C. (1956), p. 159.) Earnings must be relatively steady and predictable (as in this industry) in order to justify such a heavy ratio of debt and preferred. On the other hand, if the concern were closely held, and the senior securities were held by the owners of the common, there would be little risk if the company were in default, and hence greater justification for "thin capitalization." Though by no means assured, this device may afford stockholders equal participation with outside creditors in the event of bankruptcy and the further possibility of tax advantages. These points will be considered later in this chapter.

In any event, whenever senior securities are to be issued to outsiders, consideration must be given to the types and amount of the corporation's other outstanding securities. The risk of the holder of a debt security is of course reduced by the existence of substantial junior investment. The assets and earning power provided by the junior investment constitute a safety factor, or cushion, for the holders of the senior securities. It is equally obvious that the risks and dividend prospects of a common shareholder are affected by the amount and character of outstanding senior securities. . . .

B. THE AUTHORIZATION AND ISSUANCE OF STOCK

Every corporation statute has some counterpart of MBA §§ 14, 15 and 48(d), (e), and (f), which give to the parties very broad powers to decide what amount and types of stock a corporation shall have authority to issue. Whatever the parties decide must be set out in the certificate of incorporation, thereby becoming a matter of public record and subject to change only by an amendment of the certificate, which universally requires the consent of the shareholders. See MBA § 53.

The number of shares actually issued does not appear in the certificate of incorporation, although many jurisdictions do require that a report covering each issuance of stock be filed and made a matter of public record. The actual issuance of shares, including the matter of to whom they are to be issued and for what consideration, is generally committed to the board of directors, except that in some jurisdictions, as under MBA § 17, the right to fix the consideration for no-par shares may be reserved to the shareholders. However, even apart from such a provision the directors do not have unlimited discretion over the issuance of stock. The corporation statute invariably imposes some restrictions as to the type of consideration for which shares may be issued, e. g., MBA § 18, as well as the usual requirement that par value shares be issued for no less than par. In addition, the directors as fiduciaries would undoubtedly be subject to general equitable control if they attempted to issue shares unfairly—for example, to themselves or their nominees at an unduly low price, or for the purpose of affecting the balance of control over the corporation.

NOTE ON THE ISSUANCE OF STOCK FOR SERVICES

Among the most troublesome problems in connection with stock issues are those that relate to the issuance of stock for services. They are analyzed in the following article, along with a number of related corporate and tax issues involved in the organization of a close corporation.

HERWITZ, ALLOCATION OF STOCK BETWEEN SERVICES AND CAPITAL IN THE ORGANIZATION OF A CLOSE CORPORATION [9]

75 Harv.L.Rev. 1098 (1962).

1. First Business Setting—Organization of a Brand New Enterprise with Two Participants

It is a familiar rule under corporate law that stock may not be issued for future services. Various aspects of the federal tax laws may also serve to discourage such transactions. Despite this apparent disfavor, it is submitted that the issuance of stock primarily on account of future services is a desirable and even necessary element in many business situations, particularly those involving the organization of a close corporation. To take a fairly typical illustration, assume that S is a person who has little or no capital but does have special service skills, as for example in the design and production of ladies' belts. C is a person with substantial capital to invest in new enterprises, but his time is fully occupied in his own business affairs. C and S decide that a combination of C's capital and S's services could produce a profitable business operation. Certainly such a proposed enterprise would hold little attraction for S if he were expected to become a mere employee of the new organization. And S has good reason to insist upon some substantial proprietary interest. When viewed from the point of view of sound planning and practical business judgment, the ultimate profits of a small business based upon a combination of capital and services should be shared by those who contribute necessary service skills, rather than be allocated exclusively to the contributors of capital. The same is true of the power to control the operations of the new business. So if the new venture took the form of a partnership, S would expect the partnership agreement to give him a substantial share in the future profits of the business, as well as a considerable voice in the management of its affairs, regardless of the amount of capital which he could personally contribute to the enterprise.

If instead the parties chose to form a corporation, S would be no less eager to obtain a reasonable share of the future profits, as well as a right to participate in control. But under the corporate form, control and the right to profits inhere in the stock of the corporation, particularly the basic equity stock. Thus S could satisfy his desires only by obtaining a substantial portion of that stock. But if S could make no more than a nominal capital investment, most of his stock would be received essentially on account of his future service, and thus run head-on into the corporate and tax obstacles. The object of this paper is to demonstrate how sound planning may nevertheless accommodate the justifiable interests of the parties in such circumstances.

2. Future Services as Consideration for Stock

Typically the corporate bar against issuing stock for services has been based upon some provision of the corporation statute such as "no corporation shall issue shares of stock except for money, labor done or property." Since

---

9. Copyright (c) Harvard Law Review Association, 1962. Portions of the text and most of the footnotes omitted. Section headings have been added.

it was generally accepted that even without any statutory authority stock might be issued for consideration other than cash, such provisions appear to have been designed primarily to restrict the quality of consideration eligible for the issuance of stock. This was doubtless originally motivated primarily by concern for the interests of creditors, since the capital contributed by shareholders was expected to serve as a substitute for the personal liability of the owners of the business. And it was later recognized that stockholders too have interests to be protected against the issuance of stock for ephemeral or valueless consideration.

It is obvious that quite apart from any statute it would not be proper to issue stock for future services *in vacuo*, without either a promise to perform such services or some other consideration sufficient to support an ordinary contract. But as an original matter the question whether stock might properly be issued for a promise to perform future services under such a statute is not entirely free from doubt. Although such a promise cannot qualify as "labor done," it is less clear that a promise to perform future services could not constitute "property" within the meaning of the statute. Some of the early cases suggest that the term "property" should be narrowly construed, to the exclusion of intangible items, but today it is clear that intangible property can qualify as valid consideration for the issuance of stock so long as the required value is present. And the acquisition of the specialized, skilled services of a particular person may constitute an item of considerable value to a business enterprise.

The issuance of stock for promised future services might have been justified by analogy to the treatment of cash prepayments for similar purposes. There seems to be no reason why a corporation may not make a substantial advance payment of compensation to a prospective employee. At least under generally accepted accounting principles, such an advance payment would properly be recorded as an asset, reflecting the fact that the corporation had not yet received the benefit of the promised future services. The asset could then be amortized over the period for which the advance payment constituted additional compensation.

Admittedly, such advance payments of compensation would be rare. But it would seem not uncommon to offer a cash bonus to a prospective employee in order to induce him to leave other activity and undertake the proffered new employment. Here again, the advance payment would constitute an asset, at least for accounting purposes, although there might be more difficulty in ascertaining the period over which it should be written off. In the case of a newly organized corporation the funds for such a bonus could be derived only from the issuance of stock to others for cash or property. Since presumably the corporation could issue stock to a prospective employee for cash and then pay the same amount of cash to him as such a bonus, it would seem arbitrary to prohibit the corporation from taking the shortcut of issuing stock directly to the prospective employee in consideration of his undertaking employment.

Just this basis was adopted recently by the Pennsylvania Supreme Court in Petrishen v. Westmoreland Fin. Corp.,[15] one of the rare decisions taking a favorable view of the issuance of stock for a promise of future services. In that case a new corporation was organized to engage in the small-

---

15. 394 Pa. 552, 147 A.2d 392 (1959).

loan business. Under the articles of incorporation the authorized capital stock consisted of 200 shares of $500-par-value stock, of which six persons each purchased ten shares for cash. On the same date, the corporation employed A, who had had considerable experience in the small-loan business, under an agreement which provided *inter alia* that after the corporation had earned a specified amount, ten shares of stock would be issued to A. After A had acted as manager of the corporation's business for over a year, although before the corporation had earned the specified amount, the board of directors caused ten shares of stock to be issued to A. In a suit to upset a subsequent vote of the shareholders, in which A's shares were necessary to make a majority, it was urged that A's vote should not have been counted because his stock had been illegally issued, in contravention of Pennsylvania's constitutional and statutory provisions similar to the language quoted above. In rejecting this contention the Supreme Court relied upon an 1896 Pennsylvania case which had upheld the validity of an agreement to issue stock as an inducement to get a desired person to assume the presidency of a corporation.[17] The court quoted with approval the observation in the earlier opinion to the effect that an issuance of stock to induce one to leave his present employment and come to work for the corporation was no different from a payment of cash for the same purpose upon the condition that the cash be invested in stock of the corporation, and that the latter would clearly be a valid transaction.

Actually the recipient of the challenged stock in the Petrishen case was neither entitled to nor did receive any stock until after he had performed valuable services for the corporation for a substantial period.[19] But the court appeared to treat the case as one involving the issuance of stock solely for an undertaking to render future services, and in any event it is clear that the court fully approved the favorable treatment extended to such a transaction in the earlier case.

Nevertheless, the majority of cases have held that a promise to render future services does not constitute valid consideration for the issuance of stock. A particularly interesting illustration is provided by the New York case of Brown v. Watson,[21] which involved the organization of a new corporation to act as a consultant in such fields as management, engineering, and finance. The promoter of the new enterprise persuaded the defendants to leave other lucrative and promising jobs to come to work for the new corporation. Each of the defendants received a number of shares of $5 par, class A stock of the new corporation in accordance with a resolution of the directors that "to compensate you for the risk you undergo in undertaking this employment, we are transferring to you . . . shares of the Class A stock . . . which presently has no value." Upon the failure of the corporation, the trustee in bankruptcy brought an action against the defendants to recover the par value of the stock they had received allegedly without

---

17. Shannon v. Stevenson, 173 Pa. 419, 34 A. 218 (1896) . . . .

19. Such a transaction would seem to qualify under the "labor done" language of the statute, since the stock is to be issued only after services have actually been performed. . . . But if an executory contract to issue stock in the future is valid, it becomes even harder to justify any distinction between issuance of the stock in advance and payment of cash in advance in similar circumstances. . . .

21. 124 N.Y.S.2d 504 (Sup.Ct.1953), modified in part and reversed in part, 285 App.Div. 587, 139 N.Y.S.2d 628 (1955).

payment. The defendants prevailed temporarily, in the trial court. The court conceded that under the New York statute neither a simple executory contract to perform services for the corporation nor the undertaking to leave previous employment, though perhaps valid consideration for other purposes, could support the issuance of stock. However, the court purported to find an additional element in the undertaking to enter the employment of the new corporation as distinguished from the agreement to render the services. While recognizing that the distinction was a narrow one, the court viewed the promises of these skilled defendants to render their services, so vital to the success of the new corporation, as in the nature of a goodwill item and hence "property" within the contemplation of the statute. The decision of the trial court was cursorily reversed by the appellate division, which in a per curiam opinion held squarely that stock could not be issued in exchange for a promise to enter the employ of the corporation; while special knowledge, experience, and contacts in a particular field might be of some value, they could not be considered "property" within the meaning of the statute.

The traditional concern about future services as consideration for stock lies chiefly in the fact that such services can prove valuable to a business only as a going concern and are totally devoid of realizable value for creditors or stockholders in the event of a liquidation of the enterprise. While of course other intangible items, notably goodwill, may prove worthless upon the failure of an enterprise, promised future services are subject to the special objection that they have no realizable value from the outset.[26] Moreover, future services do not lend themselves readily to any objective standards for measuring the quantity of value involved. This difficulty is aggravated by the fact that such items are commonly transferred by the very people in control of the corporation, who thereby become judges of the amount of their own contributions. And in any event it has been common experience that corporate promoters are more likely to be extravagant when making payments in stock than when laying out hard cash, a factor which serves to limit the force of the analogy drawn earlier to a cash payment of advance compensation, or a bonus for undertaking employment.[30]

The traditional bar against issuing stock for future services cannot be avoided merely by using no-par stock. Despite the suggestion in some of the early cases that no-par stock could be issued even for nothing, there is no longer any doubt that there must be some consideration, and it must qualify under the statute dealing with the types of consideration for which stock may be issued. These statutes, unlike the ones dealing with the required quantity of consideration, refer simply to "stock" without any distinction between par and no-par and there seems little basis for constructing one. Certainly there is no less injury to other shareholders from an overly gen-

26. See Scully v. Automobile Fin. Co., 11 Del.Ch. 355, 101 A. 908 (Ch.1917), where the court, in holding that a plan of doing business was not "property" for which stock could be issued although the corporation had prospered in the use of the plan, made the following observation, which might equally apply to promised future services: "The business idea was not salable or transferable, and had no commercial value, and was not property in any sense." Id. at 358, 101 A. at 909.

30. . . . Similar problems may arise when stock is issued for alleged secret processes or formulas . . . [and the courts have gone both ways on the question of whether] such items can constitute property sufficient to support the issuance of stock.

erous allocation of no-par stock to corporate insiders for future services than from a similar allotment of par value stock. And there is still substantial danger of overvaluation of the consideration received for no-par stock, despite the reduced pressure in that direction resulting from the absence of any required minimum amount per share: ultimately some dollar figure must be assigned to the capital stock issued and the consideration received therefor, if only because of the practical necessity of recording the corporation's financial position in dollar terms. Accordingly, whether or not a recipient of no-par stock for future services would be liable to creditors in the event of subsequent corporate insolvency, he would at least be subject to the threat of cancellation of his stock for failure to pay lawful consideration.

Whatever may have been the historical justification for the prohibition against issuing stock for future services, there seems to be reason to question the need for any continuing flat bar. Today creditors more often recognize that the true security for the payment of their claims lies in the prospective earnings of the debtor corporation; in any event, for accurate reflections of the real financial position of an enterprise they have become accustomed to rely more upon commercial credit reports and the like than on its ostensible capital. And the ever-increasing pressure toward full disclosure of financial transactions has reduced the danger to stockholders from overly generous allocations of stock for questionable consideration.

In any event, a flat bar against the issuance of stock for future services is particularly unwarranted in the case of the close corporation. Here all of the stockholders are ordinarily privy to the agreement for the distribution of stock, and the likelihood of some stockholders overreaching others with extravagant issues of stock for future services is practically nil. So far as creditors are concerned, while it is perhaps true that the smaller the enterprise the more attenion that is paid to the stated asset values, a requirement of conservative valuation of promised future services, as well as full disclosure of the character of such a contribution in the corporation's financial statements, would seem sufficient to protect this group.

Curiously, however, the very extensive comment which has appeared over the past several years calling special attention to the problems of the close corporation does not appear to contain a single reference to the impact on such enterprises of the traditional limitations upon the consideration for which stock may be issued. Similarly, the recent wave of new or revised corporation statutes, some of which contain special provisions affording the close corporation relief from the statutory norm in other cases, has not produced a single legislative exception to the traditional bar against issuing stock for future services. Indeed, a number of the new statutes have followed the lead of the Model Business Corporation Act in adding a section providing expressly that a promise to render future services shall not constitute valid payment for stock. And neither have the courts, which have often recognized the need for permitting greater flexibility in the arrangements among the participants in a close corporation, shown much inclination to relax the statutory bar in this context. Consequently, in the simple illustration above, where S and C want to combine their services and capital respectively to form a new corporation, S could not receive any stock avowedly on account of his agreement to render future services without subjecting himself to some danger of cancellation of his stock as well as some risk of liability to creditors in the event the enterprise fails.

3. Alternatives to Issuance of Stock Expressly for Future Services

Actually, however, the rule forbidding the issuance of stock for future services amounts to little more than a trap for the unwary, in view of the ease with which it can be circumvented. One who is to receive stock primarily on account of future services or other doubtful consideration can validate his stock under the statute dealing with eligible consideration merely by contributing some modest amount of qualified property. The fact that other parties pay a substantially higher price for their shares is of no concern, for there is normally no requirement in the corporation statutes that stock be issued for the same consideration, even when it is issued at the same time. To be sure, an arbitrary sale of stock at different prices to different shareholders at the same time may be actionable. But where there are practical business reasons for such differences in prices and all the shareholders consent with full knowledge, there would seem to be no valid objection to this procedure.

Thus in our illustration, if S and C were to form a new corporation with authorized capital of 1,000 shares of no-par stock, to be divided evenly between them, a consideration of as little as $500 might be set for the shares to be issued to S, even though the consideration for the 500 shares to be issued to C was $50,000. So long as the assets and the paid-in capital on the corporation's financial statements were each carried at no more than $50,500 as a result of the transaction, there would seem to be no basis for attacking it either at the outset or upon the later behest of creditors.

As a practical matter, however, this approach does not normally provide a very satisfactory resolution of the problem. When stock is issued to S for a nominal consideration compared to that paid by C for his stock, there is in effect an immediate transfer by C to S of an undivided pro rata interest in the capital contributed by C. For example, S would be entitled from the outset to one-half of the income earned on C's capital even if it were deposited in a savings bank and S's services contributed in no way to that income. Moreover, upon a subsequent liquidation of the enterprise S would be entitled to one-half of the total net assets even though they represented primarily the capital contributed by C. Under these circumstances it is understandable that C would not be willing to allow S to obtain very much of the stock of the new corporation for his nominal consideration, with the result that S would receive a smaller interest in the future profits of the enterprise than he would want. In effect, S would have to accept a smaller share of the future profits than he desired because he would be receiving an interest in underlying asset value, which he did not particularly desire or need.

Prima facie, S would also end up with a correspondingly limited share of the control which resides in the holders of the stock. But the control pattern can be rearranged quite easily either by using nonvoting stock or by dividing the stock into two classes, each of which has the right to elect a specified number of directors. Alternatively the parties might resort to one of the many other available control devices, such as unanimity agreements, shareholders' pooling agreements, or cumulative voting, although the validity and effect of these devices are somewhat less clear. It would probably be necessary to adopt some control technique in any event unless the parties arrive at an exactly even division of the voting securities, since otherwise the holder of a majority of the stock would be in absolute control of the corporation's affairs.

It would also be possible to rearrange the allocation of the profits of the enterprise, to give S more than the share to which his stock interest would entitle him, in fixing the amount of compensation to be paid to S for services. Obviously S must draw some regular return from the enterprise in any event, since this would be his primary source of livelihood. While S might forego compensation as such and like C look only to his proportionate share of the profits, as is often done in partnerships, such an arrangement is far less feasible under the corporate form. For one thing, if S's withdrawals are treated as a division of profits rather than as compensation for services the corporation would obtain no tax deduction. Moreover, unless C withdrew an equal amount, either actually, or constructively by a credit to his account on the corporation's books, he would lose his rights to that amount, and it would simply be merged with the balance of the retained earnings of the corporation, in which both S and C would ultimately share pro rata.

Accordingly it seems clear that the bargain between S and C as to the division of profits should be premised upon some senior return to S in the form of compensation for his services. Indeed, in corporate financial terms, the profits of the enterprise represent only the earnings remaining after deduction of fair compensation for services rendered. And from a more practical point of view, unless the enterprise is expected ultimately to produce earnings in excess of fair compensation for S's services, it would obviously not be worth undertaking.

Of course determination of what is fair compensation for the particular services in any case may be very difficult. Some help may be obtained from evidence of the price commanded by similar services in the industry. But in the last analysis, this issue must be hammered out by the parties in the course of working out the terms of their venture.

The important point in the immediate context is that S's share of future profits could be satisfied to a substantial extent through compensation by including therein some type of bonus provision based upon a percentage of the annual profits. Such an arrangement could well result in a larger deduction for tax purposes. On the other hand, it is perhaps just as likely that a percentage compensation agreement would incur the twofold disadvantage of depriving the new corporation of necessary working capital while burdening S with additional taxable income which he may not need. And a deferred compensation agreement, which in theory might solve both of these problems, is somewhat impractical, at least at the beginning of so modest an enterprise.

4. Tax Aspects of the All Common Stock Structure *

In addition to receiving less stock and hence a smaller share of future profits than he would like, S would be faced with the possibility of a substantial tax burden as a result of any stock which he does obtain for a price substantially less than that paid by C. Suppose that S receives twenty per cent of the stock of the corporation in exchange for $500, while C contributes $50,000 for the remaining eighty percent of the stock. It seems

---

* [Ed. note] The tax issues discussed in this section are analyzed in greater detail in Chapter 2.

clear that at this point the value of the enterprise, and hence the value of all of its stock, would be equal to the total amount of the cash paid in. Thus S's twenty percent of the stock would be worth $10,100, although he would be paying only $500 for it. Normally, it is true, a purchase of property for less than its fair value does not constitute a taxable event. But quite the contrary obtains in the case of a bargain purchase by an employee from his employer; here it is generally held that such a transaction constitutes compensation income to the employee to the extent of the bargain. The fact that S had not formally taken up employment at the time of the bargain purchase would not seem sufficient to avoid the application of this rule in the instant situation, since such employment would be an integral part of the business plan. And any argument that S's bargain purchase actually constituted a gift of stock from C would doubtless fail, in view of the total absence of any donative intent in the picture. While the corporation would presumably get an offsetting deduction against income, this tax benefit could be substantially less than the tax burden on S, and in any event would not help to provide S with the funds necessary to pay the tax imposed upon him.

Could this potential tax on S be reduced by subjecting his stock to various restrictions on transferability, including perhaps a requirement that the stock be tendered back to the corporation at a stipulated price if S should voluntarily leave the corporation's employment prior to normal retirement? It seems now to be generally accepted that such restrictions can reduce and indeed even eliminate, at least temporarily, the value of the stock received and hence the compensation income at that time. However, all of the authorities to this effect appear to have involved the stock of publicly held corporations, whose stock but for such restrictions would have been freely marketable. In the close corporation situations, particularly of the sort involved here, there is usually little or no market for the shares anyway, so the imposition of such restrictions on transferability would seem far less significant. Indeed, it has been urged that wise planning for the close corporation requires the imposition of restrictions on transferability. And in tax cases too, such restrictions have been recognized as vital to the continuing welfare of the corporate enterprise. It is hard to see how the same kinds of stock restrictions regarded as essential to the continued success of a close corporation could at the same time operate to deprive the stock subjected to them of any fair market value.

To what extent could the interests of the parties be accommodated by tailoring two classes of stock more specifically to their special needs? For example, in addition to giving each class the power to elect one-half of the directors, thus assuring an even division of control, specific provision could be made for division of the profits in accordance with whatever bargain might be reached by C and S. Assuming agreement that the profits should be allocated sixty percent to C and forty percent to S, the certificate of incorporation could provide that dividends should be apportioned on the basis of sixty percent to the class A stock (to be held by C) and forty percent to the class B stock (to be held by S). Provision could also be made that in the event of liquidation, class A and class B would share any distribution up to a total of $50,500 in the ratio of $50,000 to $500, with any excess to be apportioned between the two in the ratio of sixty percent to forty percent. This would protect C's interest in his original contribution while conforming the interests in any accumulated equity to the pattern for allocation of profits.

Assuming that such classification would be valid under the corporation statute, there would still be some difficulties. For one thing, such a scheme would not entirely eliminate the possibility of bargain-purchase income to S. While on a liquidation basis S's stock would be worth no more than what he paid for it, on a potential-earnings basis the situation would be quite otherwise. S's stock would be entitled to receive forty percent of the income from capital of over $50,000, which even on the basis of a five percent return would be $1,000 per year, or twice as much as the total cost of the stock.

5. The Advantages of Senior Securities

In addition, S would still be receiving a senior return in the form of compensation for services as well as sharing in the entire return on C's capital regardless of the contribution made by S's services. To be sure, these factors can be taken into account in deciding upon the basis of allocation of the ultimate profits between S and C. But it is virtually impossible to find any objective criteria for computing the percentage of the future profits which S should yield in consideration of these immediate interests in C's capital contribution, particularly since estimation of the likely amount of total future profit at this stage can be little more than a guess.

It is submitted that the way to a sounder accommodation of the interests of the parties is opened by recognizing that C's capital, no less than S's services, is entitled to a senior return, representing reasonable compensation for its use in the enterprise, prior to the determination of the profits to be allocated between C and S. To put it another way, just as the profits in which C is to share on the basis of his stock interest should be determined only after a reasonable compensation for S's services, so the profits in which S is to share should be determined only after a reasonable return on C's capital. To be sure, determination of a fair return on C's capital may be even more difficult than arriving at fair compensation for S's services. No fixed return would adequately compensate C for the risk involved in putting up practically the entire capital for a new small business. That is precisely why C would demand and be entitled to a substantial share of the equity interest in the enterprise in addition to any senior return he might receive. But the fact that no fixed return on his capital contribution would alone adequately compensate C does not mean that no provision for a senior return on that capital should be made.

What is needed, then, is both a recognition of C's superior rights in the capital contributed by him, particularly in the event of a liquidation, and a senior return upon such capital before determination of the profits to be divided between S and C. These two requirements are the very essence of a senior security. Thus C might receive debt securities with their automatic asset preference and senior return, or preferred stock with a cumulative dividend and a liquidation preference, or some combination of the two, in the total amount of his capital contribution. The return on the senior securities, like S's compensation, would be left to the bargaining arena, but presumably it would be substantial, in recognition of the high degree of risk involved.

The important corollary of interposing senior securities representing C's capital contribution is that the common stock, while still retaining all of its control features, is nevertheless reduced to a basic equity security representing solely the prospective profits in excess of a reasonable return on the capital invested in the enterprise. In view of its extremely speculative character such stock would quite appropriately be issued for purely nominal consideration. Hence it becomes quite simple to allocate the stock between the parties in accordance with whatever bargain is reached as to the division of profits and control. Since the two parties would pay the same price per share for this stock, the question of disproportionate consideration would not even arise; and there would seem to be no basis for finding any compensation income to S for tax purposes since his stock would be worth no more than the amount he paid for it.

Of course this approach does not in itself resolve the difficult question of the basis upon which the common stock should be allocated between the parties. But it is submitted that this mode of analysis can help to bring more clearly into focus just what is being allocated, and why. Normally, the final decision will depend upon a variety of factors, and will of course vary widely from case to case. Absent any objective standards for appraising the relative contributions of capital and services in the particular business involved, the final allocation will probably be controlled largely by the relative bargaining positions of the parties.

6. Tax Aspects of Senior Securities *

As to the type of senior securities to be used in such situations, at first blush debt would seem to be the obvious choice. The senior return on debt in the form of interest would typically be payable in all events regardless of the corporation's earnings, just as is true of S's compensation for services. C's contribution would be on a parity with the claims of outside creditors in the event of failure of the enterprise. And the potential tax advantages in the use of debt, such as deductibility of the interest for corporate tax purposes or the tax-free repayment of such obligations to the bondholder, are too well known to require cataloging here.

To be sure, § 1244 of the Internal Revenue Code of 1954 has somewhat redressed the balance between debt securities and common stock by permitting an ordinary loss deduction for losses sustained on common stock which qualifies under the section, while losses on debt would normally be treated as capital losses. However, § 1244 seems likely to have its primary appeal in connection with investment in marketable securities which can easily be disposed of at capital gains rates if the enterprise prospers. In such situations, § 1244 puts the taxpayer in the position of "heads I win—capital gain; tails the Government loses—ordinary loss." Where the investment is in a small enterprise, on the other hand, and there is no readily foreseeable market, the investor cannot have his cake and eat it too. Put to the choice between the tax-free withdrawal of a substantial portion of his investment afforded by debt securities and the advantageous loss treatment provided by § 1244 stock, the typical investor seems likely to choose the tax advantage relating to success of the enterprise ahead of a benefit dependent upon failure. And in any event, since only common stock is eligible for § 1244 treatment, qualification under that section would require a return to an all-common-stock capitalization with the multifold difficulties which that entails.

* [Ed. note] The tax issues discussed in this section are analyzed in greater detail later in this Chapter.

However, it seems clear that an attempt to treat the bulk of C's contribution as debt would actually result in the loss of most of the expected advantages. Although a full scale analysis of the so-called "thin incorporation" area is outside the scope of this paper, it is not amiss to note the obvious danger in a debt-equity ratio of almost 50 to 1, particularly when the equity is purely nominal and does not come close to covering the working needs of the new enterprise. And it would constitute no defense to an attack from this quarter that only one of the two shareholders held any debt, since such a non-pro-rata debt holding would be easily explained by the fact that the other shareholder was a contributor of services rather than capital. So C's purported debt would probably be regarded as entirely additional equity, with the result that for tax purposes the interest deduction would be lost, any repayment would be treated as a redemption of stock, and the loss upon worthlessness of the claim would be treated as loss on worthless stock. In addition, the debt would doubtless be subordinated to the claims of other creditors in the event of insolvency.

Even with a more modest amount of debt for C, there would be some problems. Presumably, in order to maximize the chances of having the debt recognized as such, the usual indicia of debt instruments would be included, particularly a fixed maturity date, and perhaps also the absence of any subordination to the claims of general creditors. But as between C and S, it is by no means clear that C is entitled to the return of any substantial portion of his capital contribution at some specified future date, at least unless S is also free to withdraw his services in part or in whole from the new corporation and employ them elsewhere.[85] In addition, to the extent that C's contribution is placed on a parity with the claims of outside creditors, it would not enhance the corporation's chances of obtaining outside credit, which is one of the important functions of invested capital. However, this might be of limited importance in situations where, as here, financial institutions would normally require the personal signatures of the principal stockholders on corporate indebtedness.

In any event, it seems clear that a substantial portion of C's senior securities would have to take the form of preferred stock. The preferred stock would presumably have both a cumulative dividend preference and a liquidation preference. It might also include a mandatory dividend feature, requiring the payment of the dividend in every year in which it was earned, thus eliminating the chances of discord among the parties over whether to pay the preferred dividend in any particular year. Of course the advantages of § 1244 stock may loom a good deal larger when compared with preferred stock rather than with bonds. But preferred stock may still provide greater opportunity than common stock for restoring to C some of his capital contribution without unfavorable tax consequences, particularly in view of the non-pro-rata holding of preferred in the instant situation. Moreover, a distortion of the allocation of profits among the parties in the event the enter-

---

85. Of course even if S binds himself by contract to full-time employment with the corporation for an extended period, such an agreement to render personal services would not be specifically enforceable by the corporation. But injunctive relief to prevent S from working elsewhere might well be obtained. . . . And if more stringent measures seem called for, a provision could be adopted requiring S to sell his stock to the corporation at a fairly low stipulated price, should he voluntarily leave the corporation's employ.

prise prospers may be too high a price to pay to achieve the advantages of § 1244 in the event the venture fails.

Introduction of preferred stock into the capital structure of the corporation will also prevent the parties from avoiding the corporate tax by electing to have the corporate earnings taxed to the stockholders individually under subchapter S of the Code, since such treatment is available only to corporations which do not have more than "one class of stock." But this would seem to be of little concern in the instant situation, since presumably C would not be interested in including in his individual high tax bracket a proportionate share of the undistributed net profits of the corporation. Indeed, more generally subchapter S appears to hold little attraction for the typical small corporation where most of the earnings in excess of compensation to the working shareholders is expected to be plowed back into the business.

Once the parties have, in the light of all the relevant factors, decided on the basis for allocating interests in the new corporation, the stock and securities would be issued in accordance with that agreement. Assume for example that S was to receive a fixed salary of $15,000 per year, and C was to receive a senior return of seven percent on his capital contribution, with the remaining net profits to be divided in the ratio of forty percent to S and sixty percent to C. C would contribute $49,400 of his total $50,000 investment in exchange for senior securities with a preference in assets totaling $49,400, and a seven percent return, perhaps divided evenly between bonds and preferred stock. C would also receive sixty percent of the authorized no-par common stock of the new corporation in exchange for the $600 balance of his investment. S would receive the remaining forty percent of the stock for his contribution of $400. Presumably S would also enter into a long-term employment contract in order to secure to both parties their respective rights based upon S's services.

7. Second Business Setting—Incorporation of a Going Enterprise with the Injection of Additional Services and Capital

How does this approach work out in the common but more complicated situation involving the incorporation of an already existing business? Assume that P is the proprietor of a going business which has been making steady progress since its inception a few years earlier. P has decided that the services of another skilled executive plus substantial additional capital must be obtained if the business is to achieve its maximum potential. He has approached S, who has been working for P for some time, during which S has demonstrated the important executive skills needed to supplement P's own talents. However, S has indicated that he would be interested in remaining with the venture over the long term only if he can obtain a substantial proprietary interest. P has also spoken with C, once again an outsider who has substantial capital to invest but whose time is fully occupied with his own business affairs.

Suppose that the three parties decide that the combination of P's existing business, the respective talents of P and S, and substantial capital from C could produce a highly successful enterprise. Obviously here also at the outset the question arises as to the appropriate allocation, among the three participants, of interests in the proposed new venture. While it might be ideal to divide the ultimate profits and control of the enterprise evenly among the three, in practice such an allocation is unlikely to be achieved. No matter what basis for allocating profits and control between capital and services is selected, it seems clear that P must end up with [a substantially larger interest than either S or C, since P would] be contributing as much in services as S, and at least as much capital, in the current value of his business, as C is likely to contribute in fresh money. Thus the parties would probably be aiming at an even division between P on the one hand, and C and S on the other.

Such an allocation of the interests, moreover, would facilitate a reasonable arrangement for division of control over the operations of the enterprise, in the form of a four-man board of directors, consisting of C, S, P, and P's nominee. Under this arrangement, P would have the power to block any action at the board of directors level, which is no less than his due as a fifty percent owner, whereas C and S would have such power only when acting in concert.

The first step in the bargaining process might well be to determine the current value of P's business, to be approximately matched by C's capital contribution. Though obviously a matter ultimately to be negotiated by the parties, the figure would probably be calculated according to either the current replacement value of P's net assets, or a capitalization of the predictable future earnings of P's business, or some compromise between these methods. Assume that the current replacement cost of P's assets, less the outstanding liabilities, amounts to approximately $60,000, and that a reasonable estimate of future earnings for P's proprietorship based primarily upon its past earnings record, is $15,000 per year. Since a capitalization rate of twenty-five percent, or four times earnings, is well within the range of reasonableness, the parties could properly arrive at a figure of $60,000 as the current value of P's proprietorship, to be approximately matched in cash by C.

The next step in the negotiations would be to determine the appropriate basis for allocation of the ultimate profits of the enterprise among the three participants. In the first instance, this question would seem to be of little concern to P, since he should receive a fifty percent interest in profits regardless of the basis for allocating such profits between capital and services. As between C and S the situation is very much as it was in the simpler two-man situation dealt with earlier. Under the corporate form, in the absence of any senior securities, the issuance of any substantial portion of the single class of stock to S essentially on account of his future services not only would be inequitable to C but also would subject S to a substantial risk of compensation income.

8. Tax Aspects of the Incorporation of a Going Business—§ 351

In this kind of situation a further tax difficulty is presented which would directly involve P if, as is often the case, the current value of P's business exceeds the total tax basis of the constituent assets in his hands because of either increased asset values or a good earnings record. P would probably want to qualify the incorporation under § 351 of the Code in order to avoid the recognition of gain in the transaction. But such tax-free treatment will be lost if in the incorporation transaction more than twenty percent of the stock is issued for services, unless the recipient of such stock also contributes some significant amount of cash or other property for stock. Thus in the instant situation, assuming that S could make no more than a nominal investment of cash or other property, receipt by him of more than twenty per cent of the stock would disqualify the transaction under § 351, and P would be forced to recognize for tax purposes the unrealized appreciation in the value of his business.

It is no idle possibility that S would expect more than twenty per cent of the stock of the proposed new enterprise. For example, any allocation of ultimate profits to the contributors of services in excess of the forty per cent assumed earlier in connection with the two-party situation would entitle S to more than twenty percent of the stock for his contribution of one-half of the vital executive services. In addition, receipt of more than twenty per cent of the stock could practically guarantee S a directorship, as he would like. While stock classification or some type of voting agreement might assure S of a position on the board regardless of the amount of stock he holds, cumulative voting, required in many jurisdictions and permitted in most others, would provide an even surer method. With cumulative voting and a four-man board of directors, any stockholder owning at least one share more than twenty percent of the total voting stock can assure himself a position on the board. On the other hand, as we have seen, the issuance of just one share more than twenty percent of the voting stock of the corporation to one who is contributing essentially only services would prevent qualification of the transaction for tax-free treatment under § 351. . . .

9. The Impact of Senior Securities

. . . The question therefore becomes whether the use of senior securities can relieve the threat of nonqualification under § 351, as well as the danger of compensation income to S from his receipt of a substantial stock interest for nominal consideration. Assuming that C will contribute capital in an amount corresponding to the assumed $60,000 current value of P's business, P and C would receive equal amounts of senior securities with a preference in liquidation equal to their respective contributions and whatever senior return is agreed upon by the parties. As we have seen, it would be unwise to cast all of the senior securities in the form of debt, since this would almost surely result in having all of the debt treated as additional equity. One possibility would be to make a pro rata allocation between debt and preferred stock for both C and P. A much more attractive alternative in this situation may be to give to one of the parties all debt securities and to the other all preferred stock. Of course there would have to be some rational basis for so favoring one of the two contributors of capital over the other; but it is submitted that there are excellent business reasons for extending to C this substantial preference over P. As a practical business matter, one who supplies fresh capital to an enterprise is usually entitled to the more favorable consideration since there are simply more enterprises of the type here involved seeking additional capital than there are potential contributors of capital who are willing to invest in such enterprises.

Other considerations also favor giving all of the debt securities to C. In the incorporation of a going enterprise, there may be considerable difficulty in justifying debt treatment for any portion of the funds already committed to the business and hence at least presumptively part of the capital necessary to operate the business. It is likely to be a good deal easier to justify debt treatment for new funds, particularly when they come from an outsider. Moreover, such an allocation would result in a completely disproportionate holding of debt [by the stockholders]; this would increase the likelihood of obtaining an interest deduction for corporate tax purposes which would of course redound to the ultimate benefit of all the parties.

Another factor arises from our assumption that the tax basis of P's assets is less than the current value of his business, which C is being asked to match. For, assuming a tax-free incorporation, the new corporation will take those assets at their old basis in P's hands regardless of their value at the time of incorporation. Thus P's capital contribution would have less than full value for tax purposes, and subordination to C would be one way of reflecting that absence of full economic utility.

10. The Effect of Senior Securities on Compensation Income

Once senior securities have been issued to take care of the major capital contributions by P and C, the common stock would again be reduced to a security representing simply the prospective profits of the enterprise. Such stock could therefore be issued at a nominal price to each of the three parties, in whatever proportion they have decided to allocate the future profits. Assume that fifty percent of the stock is issued to P for $500, twenty-nine percent to C for $290, and twenty-one percent to S for $210. Have we eliminated all risk of compensation income to S? To be sure, here, as in the earlier two-party situation, on a liquidation basis the common stock would be worth no more than what was paid for it, and on this basis there would appear to be no bargain purchase by S. But unlike the earlier situation this venture is not being started from scratch but rather is succeeding to an already existing profitable business. Accordingly it is not so clear that the stock should be valued solely on a liquidation basis. Perhaps it should also be appraised in the light of its right to share in future profits, the existence of which is no longer a matter of sheer speculation. Certainly there is good reason to expect the new enterprise to earn no less than the $15,000 per year estimated for P's proprietorship without any new capital. Of course, the return on the senior securities must be deducted in order to find the profits remaining for the common stock, but on the basis of a seven percent return on $120,000 of such securities, this would amount to only $8,400. Still left would be $6,600 for the common stock, even on the somewhat unlikely premise that the new corporation would not improve upon the earning performance of the preexisting proprietorship. Thus S's twenty-one percent of the stock would be entitled to earnings of almost $1,400 per year, which would make the stock worth substantially more than the $210 paid for it. To the extent of that excess, there would seem to be a bargain purchase to S after all, which could be subject to taxation as compensation income.

Such an analysis does seem to accord with the economic realities of the situation, for it is clear that the parties were intending to confer some substantial economic benefit on S on account of his future services. Surely the parties would not be willing to sell any additional common stock to outsiders at the same price even if it were non-voting stock with no share in control over the enterprise.

Some difficulty is presented by the fact that both P and C also obtained their stock at the same price per share. If S's stock was worth substantially more than the price paid, and hence constituted a bargain purchase, so did the stock of P and C. Of course P also might be receiving a bargain purchase on account of his promised future services. But there would still remain the question of why P should receive over twice as many shares as S at this bargain price when their service contributions were expected to be approximately equal, as well as why C should participate in the bargain purchase at all, since he is not expected to contribute any services. The answer might be that the substantial capital contributions of P and C entitle them to receive some common stock in addition to the senior securities, because the latter do not constitute full consideration for the capital contributed. For example, $60,000 worth of bonds in an enterprise of this size and type, with a capital cushion of only approximately $61,000 below it, would hardly sell on a seven percent, or even ten percent, basis in the market place. Similarly, preferred stock in the same amount, with a cushion of common capital in the amount of only $1,000, and subject to a prior bond claim of $60,000, would command substantially more than a seven percent return. Hence a fair appraisal of the value of the senior securities actually supports the contention that the market value of the common stock is substantially more than the price paid for it. In effect, both P and C are permitted to obtain common stock at a bargain price because the amount purportedly paid for the senior securities is excessive.

Such an analysis again seems to comport with the economic realities of the situation. For as we saw in connection with the earlier two-party situation, it is precisely because the senior securities received by a contributor of capital do not fully compensate him for the risk involved that he is entitled to receive a substantial share in the ultimate profits of the enterprise represented by the common stock.

Nevertheless, establishment of a value for the common stock in excess of the price paid for it would be no easy task. For one thing, in the valuation of a business as small as the one involved here it is still common to rely a good deal more on asset value than on estimated earnings. And one of the important reasons for this is particularly relevant here: the future earnings of such a business often defy reasonable estimation, even when there is a previous earnings history. So in the instant situation, the expanded operations undoubtedly contemplated by the parties might as soon turn the previous profits into losses as increase them. Moreover, even if the hoped-for earnings are realized, there is little chance of any dividends on the common stock in the foreseeable future in view of the normal dependency of this type of business upon retained earnings for both current working capital and any projected expansion, to say nothing of the possible retirement of senior securities. And account must also be taken of the extremely limited market for the common stock of such an enterprise. So it is entirely possible that the parties could defeat any effort to revalue their stock and securities in order to cast the transaction in a mold different from the one expressly adopted by them.

Even if it could be demonstrated that S, and to some extent P, have received a bargain purchase of the common stock essentially on account of future services, there remains one further argument for avoiding the imposition of tax on such compensation at that time. As noted above, the interposition of senior securities ahead of the common stock reduces the latter to what in economic terms amounts primarily to a right to share in the future profits of the enterprise. The receipt of a mere right to participate in future profits, even by an employee from his employer, would not seem to constitute a taxable event. For example, when a young lawyer becomes a partner in an established law firm and hence entitled to some specified percentage of future partnership profits, surely he is not to be taxed upon the discounted value of those future profits; a rule to the contrary would certainly cast a considerable pallor over the now-joyous Christmas occasions on which such ascendency to partnership is typically celebrated. Perhaps the reason in the partnership situation is that the new partner must continue to work for the partnership in order to become entitled to his share of annual profits, and hence "earns" such amounts only as he performs the required services annually.* If so, the receipt of a common stock in a corporation would be analogous only if the employee were bound to resell the stock at his cost upon leaving the corporation's employ, in which event there might well be no compensation income on receipt of the stock anyway because its value would be limited to the resale price. But it seems also to be true that receipt by a cash basis taxpayer of an unsecured right to future payments, particularly where the amount of such payments is unascertainable, is not a taxable event. It is under this view that the analogy of the common stock in the instant situation to a mere right to future profits would have its maximum force. But the fact is that such stock constitutes a good deal more than mere evidence of a right to future profits, despite the interposition of senior securities. Rather the stock constitutes a traditional proprietary interest embodying rights in property and control, however limited, as well as in profits. Hence, if a bargain-purchase element can be isolated in the instant situation, it seems likely that a tax on compensation income would result.

11. The Effect of Senior Securities on Qualification under § 351

A showing that some of the parties obtained their stock at a substantial bargain price, and hence in large part on account of future services, could have important ramifications on the question of tax-free incorporation under § 351. For example, if it were determined that S's twenty-one percent stock interest was actually worth $5,500, it might well follow that he received only a proportionate amount of that stock for his $210 cash contribution, and the remainder on account of future services. In our assumed case, less than one-twentieth of S's total twenty-one percent of the stock could be attributed to the cash payment of $210. Thus S would have received more than twenty percent of the total stock of the new corporation for services, which could lead to disqualification of the transaction under § 351 if it were found that S's nominal cash contribution was designed primarily to qualify the incorporation for tax-free treatment.

12. The Effect of Senior Securities on Basis

The true value of the common stock would also be a critical element in the determination of the basis of the senior securities received by P and C. Under § 358, when a party to a tax-free incorporation under § 351 receives more than one class of stock or securities, the basis of each of the various classes is to be determined in accordance with their respective fair market values at the time received. Thus in the instant situation, P's total basis in the assets contributed by him to the corporation, including the $500 in cash paid for the common stock, would be allocated between his senior securities

---

* [Ed. note] But one who receives a partnership interest in both capital and profits as compensation for past services must include in income the fair market value of the interest upon its receipt. United States v. Frazell, 335 F.2d 487 (5th Cir. 1964), rehearing denied, 339 F.2d 885 (5th Cir. 1964).

and common stock in accordance with the fair market value of each. Obviously, the Government would be anxious to maximize the value, and hence proportionate share of basis, allocated to the common stock, in order to reduce the basis of the senior securities, which are likely to be disposed of in a taxable transaction at an earlier date than the common stock.

This incentive would be even greater where, as in C's case, the senior securities consist of debt obligations, since the customary fixed maturity date of such obligations would increase the likelihood of taxable disposition of the debt prior to disposition of the common stock. Normally the basis for securities purportedly purchased solely for cash would be fixed by the contract price. But once C is included as one of the transferors of property under § 351, as he must be if the transaction is to have any chance to qualify for tax-free treatment, there seems no escape from the basis provisions of § 358 even though C is contributing only cash to the new corporation.

A finding that the common stock was worth more than the amount purportedly paid for it would create a further complication whenever the senior securities accompanying such stock included debt obligations. For if it is established that the amount actually paid for the debt obligations was less than their face value, the difference would presumably constitute original issue discount. In that event, upon a subsequent sale or retirement of the debt obligations the portion of the amount received attributable to the original issue discount would, unless it is de minimis, be taxed as ordinary income. Presumably the corporation would be entitled to amortize any such original issue discount, but this would hardly compensate the bondholders for the ordinary income tax burden inflicted upon them.

Despite the many potential difficulties observed in the foregoing, it is submitted that here, no less than in the two-party situation, utilization of senior securities can help the parties to reach a fair accommodation of their respective interests. Whatever the problems that remain after the interposition of the senior securities, they appear considerably less troublesome than those which would result from using only a single class of stock. And in practical planning terms, the most important advantage of using such senior securities can certainly be achieved in that the parties can thereby obtain a much clearer picture of just what is involved in the allocation of the interests in a new business and how their various interests can be most fairly accommodated.

C. THE USE OF DEBT SECURITIES

Despite the fact that from the point of view of practical corporate financial management long-term debt securities have become increasingly regarded as merely an alternative type of investment in an enterprise, corporate law still distinguishes sharply between all types of creditors' claims on the one hand, and ownership or equity interests on the other. (Of course it is not always so easy to decide on which side of the line a particular hybrid security containing both debt and equity features may fall.) One illustration of this difference in treatment between the two is the fact that the Model Act, like most corporation statutes, does not have any counterpart of §§ 14 and 15 to expressly authorize the issuance of debt securities. Nevertheless, ample authority for the issuance of various kinds of debt obligations can be implied from the counterpart in practically every corporation statute of MBA § 4(h), which gives every corporation the general power to incur liabilities and to evidence such liabilities by notes, bonds, or the like.

The sharp distinction drawn between debt and equity, primarily in connection with priority in the assets of an insolvent enterprise, has been sorely tested in cases involving debt obligations owned by people who are also stockholders. It is of course clear that there is no fixed rule prohibiting a stockholder from also being a creditor of the corporation. But obviously such a dual role can play havoc with the fundamental doctrine that in the event of financial difficulty, the claims of creditors take precedence over the interests of stockholders. The problem is somewhat aggravated by the fact that in most of the cases the stockholder-creditors are in complete control of the corporation and can pretty much dictate the form in which to cast their investment in the corporation. Of course the presence of stockholder-owned debt may lead third parties to withhold credit from the corporation, or at least to require the stockholders to guarantee the corporation's debts, but prospective creditors often do not investigate sufficiently to learn the facts.

This question of the extent to which stockholders may set up part of their contributions as "loans" to the corporation may well be part of a broader inquiry as to the responsibility of the organizers of a corporation to provide it with a reasonable amount of capital for the business which it is to undertake. The imposition of such responsibility can easily be defended as an appropriate price to be paid for the limited liability which the shareholders enjoy. But the application of such a rule would require a difficult factual determination in each case as to what was a reasonable amount of capital. Moreover, what is the effect of a statutory provision like MBA § 48(g) which in dealing with this general subject requires no more than that every corporation have a minimum paid-in capital of $1000 before commencing business? It is to be noted that this section, which is typical of similar provisions in other jurisdictions, completely ignores the type of business to be undertaken as well as any other particular circumstances which may be present.

The following cases represent recent judicial efforts to grapple with the corporate problems presented in the area of a stockholder debt and inadequate initial capitalization.

1. SUBORDINATION OF SHAREHOLDER DEBT

COSTELLO v. FAZIO

United States Court of Appeals, Ninth Circuit, 1958.
256 F.2d 903.[10]

[Fazio, Ambrose, and Leonard were partners in a plumbing supply business which they decided to incorporate. The capital accounts of the partners prior to incorporation were approximately $43,000 for Fazio, $6,000 for Ambrose, and $2,000 for Leonard. In contemplation of incorporation, Fazio and Ambrose reduced their capital accounts to $2,000 each, by obtaining promissory notes from the partnership in the amounts of approximately $41,000 and $4,000 respectively. At the close of its last fiscal year the partnership's current liabilities had exceeded the current assets, and the business had suffered a loss of $22,000, on sales of approximately $390,000, compared to a profit of $40,000 on sales of approximately $665,000 for the preceding year. The new corporation issued 200 shares of no-par common stock, with a stated capital of $10 per share, to each of the three partners, and assumed all the liabilities of the partnership, including the notes to Fazio and Ambrose. Two years later, after suffering continued losses, the corporation was in bankruptcy. Fazio and Ambrose filed claims on their notes as general creditors. The trustee in bankruptcy sought to subordinate their claims on the ground that they really represented a portion of the capital investment in the business. The referee held that the claims should be allowed, the district court affirmed, and the trustee appealed.]

HAMLEY, CIRCUIT JUDGE. . . . Clifford V. Heimbucher, a certified public accountant and management consultant, called by the trustee, expressed the view that, at the time of incorporation, capitalization was inadequate. He further stated that, in incorporating a business already in existence, where the approximate amount of permanent capital needed has been established by experience, normal procedure called for continuing such capital in the form of common or preferred stock.

Stating that only additional capital needed temporarily is normally set up as loans, Heimbucher testified that " . . . the amount of capital employed in the business was at all times substantially more than the $6,000 employed in the opening of the corporation." He also expressed the opinion that, at the time of incorporation, there was "very little hope [of financial success] in view of the fact that for the year immediately preceding the opening of the corporation, losses were running a little less than $2,000 a month. . . ."

---

[10]. Portions of the opinion and all of the footnotes omitted.

William B. Logan, a business analyst and consultant called by the trustee, expressed the view that $6,000 was inadequate capitalization for this company. John S. Curran, a business analyst, also called by the trustee, expressed the view that the corporation needed at least as much capital as the partnership required prior to the reduction of capital.

Robert H. Laborde, Jr., a certified public accountant, had handled the accounting problems of the partnership and corporation. He was called by the trustee as an adverse witness. . . . Laborde readily conceded that the transaction whereby Fazio and Ambrose obtained promissory notes from the partnership was for the purpose of transferring a capital account into a loan or debt account. He stated that this was done in contemplation of the formation of the corporation, and with knowledge that the partnership was losing money.

The prime reason for incorporating the business, according to Laborde, was to protect the personal interest of Fazio, who had made the greatest capital contribution to the business. In this connection, it was pointed out that the "liabilities on the business as a partnership were pretty heavy." There was apparently also a tax angle. Laborde testified that it was contemplated that the notes would be paid out of the profits of the business. He agreed that, if promissory notes had not been issued, the profits would have been distributed only as dividends, and that as such they would have been taxable.

* * *

In any event, when we speak of inadequacy of capital in regard to whether loans to shareholders shall be subordinated to claims of general creditors, we are not referring to working capital. We are referring to the amount of the investment of the shareholders in the corporation. This capital is usually referred to as legal capital, or stated capital in reference to restrictions on the declaration of dividends to stockholders. . . . The corporate accounts and the undisputed testimony of three accounting experts demonstrate that stated capital was wholly inadequate.

* * *

It does not require the confirmatory opinion of experts to determine from this data that the corporation was grossly undercapitalized. In the year immediately preceding incorporation, net sales aggregated $390,000. In order to handle such a turnover, the partners apparently found that capital in excess of $50,000 was necessary. They actually had $51,620.78 in the business at that time. Even then, the business was only "two jumps ahead of the wolf." A net loss of $22,000 was sustained in that year; there was only $66.66 in the bank; and there was an overdraft of $3,422.78.

Yet, despite this precarious financial condition, Fazio and Ambrose withdrew $45,620.78 of the partnership capital—more than eighty-eight per cent of the total capital. The $6,000 capital left in the business was only one-sixty-fifth of the last annual net sales. All this is revealed by the books of the company. . . .

* * *

We therefore hold that the factual conclusion of the referee, that the corporation was adequately capitalized at the time of its organization, is clearly erroneous.

The factual conclusion of the trial court, that the claimants, in withdrawing capital from the partnership in contemplation of incorporation, did not act for their own personal or private benefit and to the detriment of the corporation or of its stockholders and creditors, is based upon the same accounting data and expert testimony.

Laborde, testifying for the claimants, made it perfectly clear that the depletion of the capital account in favor of a debt account was for the purpose of equalizing the capital investments of the partners and to reduce tax liability when there were profits to distribute. It is therefore certain, contrary to the finding just noted, that, in withdrawing this capital, Fazio and Ambrose did act for their own personal and private benefit.

It is equally certain, from the undisputed facts, that in so doing they acted to the detriment of the corporation and its creditors. The best evidence of this is what happened to the business after incorporation, and what will happen to its creditors if the reduction in capital is allowed to stand. The likelihood that business failure would result from such undercapitalization should have been apparent to anyone who knew the company's financial and business history and who had access to its balance sheet and profit and loss statements. Three expert witnesses confirmed this view, and none expressed a contrary opinion.

Accordingly, we hold that the factual conclusion, that the claimants, in withdrawing capital, did not act for their own personal or private benefit and to the detriment of the corporation and creditors, is clearly erroneous.

Recasting the facts in the light of what is said above, the question which appellant presents is this:

> Where, in connection with the incorporation of a partnership, and for their own personal and private benefit, two partners who are to become officers, directors, and controlling stockholders of the corporation, convert the bulk of their capital contributions into loans, taking promissory notes, thereby leaving the partnership and succeeding corporation grossly undercapitalized, to the detriment of the corporation and its creditors, should their claims against the estate of the subsequently bankrupted corporation be subordinated to the claims of the general unsecured creditors?

The question almost answers itself.

* * *

Appellees argue that more must be shown than mere undercapitalization if the claims are to be subordinated. Much more than mere undercapitalization was shown here. Persons serving in a fiduciary relationship to the corporation actually withdrew capital already committed to the business, in the face of recent adverse financial experience. They stripped the business of eighty-eight per cent of its stated capital at a time when it had a minus working capital and had suffered substantial business losses. This was done for personal gain, under circumstances which charge them with knowledge that the corporation and its creditors would be endangered. Taking advantage of their fiduciary position, they thus sought to gain equality of treatment with general creditors.

In [some prior] cases, there was fraud and mismanagement present in addition to undercapitalization. Appellees argue from this that fraud and mismanagement must always be present if claims are to be subordinated in a situation involving undercapitalization.

This is not the rule. The test to be applied . . . is whether the transaction can be justified "within the bounds of reason and fairness." . . .

The fact that the withdrawal of capital occurred prior to incorporation is immaterial. This transaction occurred in contemplation of incorporation. The participants then occupied a fiduciary relationship to the partnership; and expected to become controlling stockholders, directors, and officers of the corporation. This plan was effectuated, and they were serving in those fiduciary capacities when the corporation assumed the liabilities of the partnership, including the notes here in question.

Nor is the fact that the business, after being stripped of necessary capital, was able to survive long enough to have a turnover of creditors a mitigating circumstance. The inequitable conduct of appellees consisted not in acting to the detriment of creditors then known, but in acting to the detriment of present or future creditors, whoever they may be. . . .

* * *

Reversed and remanded for further proceedings not inconsistent with this opinion.

In Obre v. Alban Tractor Co., 228 Md. 291, 179 A.2d 861 (1962), Obre and Nelson pooled certain equipment and cash for the purpose of forming a corporation to engage in the dirt-moving and road building business. Obre transferred equipment independently appraised at $63,874.86, plus $1,673.24 of cash, in exchange for $20,000 in par value of non-voting preferred stock, $10,000 in par value of voting common stock, and an unsecured five-year note for $35,548.10, with interest at 5%. Nelson's contribution was equipment valued at

$8,495.00 and cash of $1,505.00 for which he received $10,000 in par value voting common stock. The corporation experienced financial difficulty from the outset and was insolvent before the end of the second year. No interest was ever paid on Obre's note. The trial court rejected Obre's claim as a general creditor on the ground that the purported loan actually represented a contribution to risk capital, primarily because the corporation could not have carried on its operations without the equipment contributed by Obre.

The Court of Appeals reversed. The court assumed without deciding that even absent some element of fraud, mismanagement or estoppel, the claim of a principal shareholder might be subordinated if the corporation was undercapitalized, citing, among other cases, Costello v. Fazio. However, the court found no showing that $40,000 was inadequate capitalization for an enterprise of this size, "particularly in view of the careful planning that went into determining its capital structure". The parties had wanted their control of the corporation to be equal from the outset, and their ownership eventually to be equal, and the excess of Obre's contribution over the $30,000 in stock received by him was not treated as a capital investment "since this would have made the desired end of eventual equal ownership that much more difficult". The court also noted that the parties' memorandum agreement for the proposed capital structure expressly stated as to the permanent equity capital of $40,000 that "all parties consider [it] entirely adequate for the foreseeable needs of the corporation". The court continued as follows:

> In our view, appellees have failed to show that $40,000 was an unreasonable amount of capital upon which to predicate success in the corporate venture. No evidence was offered to reflect the financial status of the corporation other than its authorized capital stock and the fact that it encountered financial difficulties early in its operations and eventually foundered. This, in our view, failed to establish that the financial set-up of the corporation was a sham, or worked an injustice. . . . What may appear hazardous by hindsight may not have been unreasonable at the outset. It is not unusual in corporate financing to have approximately one-half of contributions put in as risk capital and the balance as loan capital. There can be no question but that, if a third party had advanced the money represented by Obre's note, he would validly be considered a creditor of the corporation.
>
> Our view in no way compromises the position of the corporate creditor. . . . It is obvious that the creditors in this case could have determined (if they actually did not do so) the financial status of the corporation by simply inspecting the stock issuance certificate filed with the State Tax Commission, or by requesting financial reports, or by ob-

taining credit ratings from the sources available. . . . In the instant case, the note to Obre was listed on the monthly financial reports of the corporation as a debt of the corporation. In addition, though interest was never actually paid, the fact that there was a provision for payment of interest on the note further establishes its character as a loan and not a risk capital investment. The fact that the note was taken at the time of incorporation is not significant in view of the failure to establish inadequate capitalization of the corporation.

In Arnold v. Phillips, 117 F.2d 497 (5th Cir. 1941), cert. den. 313 U.S. 583 (1941), Arnold organized a corporation to engage in the brewing business. The corporation had an authorized capital stock of $50,000, all of which Arnold purchased for cash. He then advanced to the company an additional $75,000 in order to enable it to complete the construction of a plant and to commence its operations. After initial success the business began to lose heavily, and Arnold advanced substantial additional sums. He obtained a mortgage on the plant securing both the original loan of $75,000 and the later advances. Upon bankruptcy liquidation, Arnold's claim upon his original loan of $75,-000 was rejected on the ground of inadequate capitalization, but his claim as a secured creditor for the later advances was sustained. The court said:

> The two series of advances differ materially as respects their nature and purpose. Those made before the enterprise was launched were, as the district court found, really capital. Although the charter provided for no more capital than $50,-000, what it took to build the plant and equip it was a permanent investment, in its nature capital. There was no security asked or given. Arnold saw that he could not proceed with his enterprise unless he enlarged the capital. There can be little doubt that what he contributed to the plant was actually intended to be capital . . . a sort of interest-bearing redeemable stock . . . ..
>
> After two years of prosperity, with the original capital thus enlarged demonstrated to be sufficient, with a book surplus of nearly $100,000 after payment of large salaries and dividends in the form of interest, there arose a situation very different from that in the beginning. Adversity then occurring raised a problem not different from that which commonly faces a corporation having losses. It may borrow to meet its needs. Had this corporation borrowed of a bank upon the security of the plant, the debt would no doubt be valid. What would render it invalid when Arnold furnished the money? As to each of these later advances, it is testified without contradiction that it was made after consultation with Otto, the Secretary and Treasurer, and on the security of the deed of

trust. The money went to relieve the needs of the business exactly as it would have done if a bank had advanced it. No other creditor was prejudiced or misled. There are no circumstances which discredit the testimony. They were truly loans and not new capital. . . .

We do not think a case is presented where the corporate entity ought to be disregarded as being a sham, a mere obstacle to justice, or instrument of fraud. It is not denied that a corporation owned by one man save for qualifying shares, is lawful in Texas. That it was created to shield the owner from liability beyond the capital set up by the charter does not show an unlawful or fraudulent intent, for that is a main purpose of every incorporation. It becomes an evidence of fraud only when the capital is unsubstantial and the risk of loss great, or the contributions to capital are greatly overvalued, and the like. It would be hard to say in this case that $50,000 was not a substantial capital, and impossible so to say after holding that the real capital was $125,500, though some was irregularly paid in.

2. IMPOSITION OF UNLIMITED LIABILITY UPON SHAREHOLDERS

In a few cases, notably in California, the court has imposed the extreme sanction of rejecting the corporation as an independent entity altogether, thereby subjecting the shareholders to unlimited individual liability. Of course, such a remedy would usually not be called for in a case where substantial shareholder debt is present since, as the court recognized in Arnold v. Phillips, supra, subordination should provide a complete answer to inadequate capitalization. Moreover, every case in which this relief has been granted has involved, in addition to insufficient capital, some incorporation defect such as failure to complete the necessary filings with state officials, or, as in the most recent California case, Temple v. Bodega Bay Fisheries, Inc., 4 Cal.Rptr. 300, 180 C.A.2d 279 (Dist.Ct. of App.1960), a failure to issue stock in accordance with the permit obtained from the state authorities. The impact of not providing a sound financial basis for the business to be operated is well summarized in the following excerpt from Ballantine on Corporations (rev. ed. 1946) 302–303, which has been quoted with approval in the California cases:

> If a corporation is organized and carries on business without substantial capital in such a way that the corporation is likely to have no sufficient assets available to meet its debts, it is inequitable that shareholders should set up such a flimsy organization to escape personal liability. The attempt to do corporate business without providing any sufficient basis of

financial responsibility to creditors is an abuse of the separate entity and will be ineffectual to exempt the shareholders from corporate debts. It is coming to be recognized as the policy of the law that shareholders should in good faith put at the risk of the business unincumbered capital reasonably adequate for its prospective liabilities. If the capital is illusory or trifling compared with the business to be done and the risks of loss, this is a ground for denying the separate entity privilege.

SECTION 4. TAX ASPECTS OF INCORPORATION

A. ISSUANCE OF STOCK—TAX INCIDENTS TO THE CORPORATION

Section 1032 provides that no gain or loss is to be recognized by a corporation upon the issuance of its stock in exchange for money or property. No distinction is drawn between an original issue and treasury stock, unlike the prior law under which gain or loss was sometimes recognized when treasury stock was reissued. See e. g., Commissioner v. H. W. Porter & Co., 187 F.2d 939 (3rd Cir. 1951). As to the corporation's basis in property acquired in exchange for its stock, that depends upon the tax treatment accorded the transferor of the property and will therefore be considered under (B) below.

When stock is issued as compensation for services, the corporation is entitled to a deduction in the amount of the fair market value of the stock. Hollywood Baseball Ass'n v. Commissioner, 42 T.C. 234 (1964), affirmed, 352 F.2d 350 (9th Cir. 1965); Rev.Rul. 62–217, 1962–2 Cum.Bull. 59. In effect, the transaction is treated as though the compensation had been paid in cash, in an amount equal to the fair market value of the stock, and then the cash was used by the recipient to purchase the stock.

B. ISSUANCE OF STOCK—TAX INCIDENTS TO THE RECIPIENT

Obviously, a simple purchase of stock for cash does not ordinarily result in any tax to the purchaser, and his basis in the stock would be the price paid, under the normal cost principle of § 1012. Conversely, the receipt of stock for services, whether in full, or in part as by way of a bargain purchase, would normally give rise to ordinary income, to the extent of the fair market value of the stock received, or, in the case of a bargain purchase, the difference between that value and the price paid.[11] But the result may be otherwise if the recipient of the stock for services already owns all of the stock of the corporation. Compare Joy Manufacturing Co. v. Commissioner, 230 F.2d 740 (3d Cir. 1956) (a parent corporation which performed services for its wholly-owned subsidiary in exchange for additional stock did not thereby realize any income), with Commissioner v. Fender Sales, Inc., 338 F.2d 924 (9th Cir. 1964) (the two equal stockholders of a corporation realized ordinary income when they received equal amounts of stock in satisfaction of their previously accrued but unpaid salaries).

When stock is acquired in exchange for property, *prima facie* the transaction constitutes a taxable exchange under § 1002, calling for recognition of gain or loss by the transferor of property, in the amount determined under § 1001. The basis of the stock received would again be its cost. In an exchange transaction, the "cost" of the property acquired is normally measured by the fair market value of the property given up; but the fair market value of the property received can also be used, since in an arm's length transaction the value of what is given up should equal the value of what is received. Indeed, in the rare circumstance when the respective values of properties exchanged in a taxable transaction are not equal, and no gift or other special factor is present, the practicalities of tax administration require that the basis of the property received be measured by its value when received rather than by the value of the property given up. Philadelphia Park Amusement Co. v. United States, 130 Ct.Cl. 166, 126 F.Supp. 184 (Ct.Cl.1954).

The corporation's basis in the property received would be determined under the normal cost rule, Reg. § 1.1032–1(d), and would therefore be measured by the fair market value of the stock issued for it.

There are a number of exceptions to the general rule of § 1002 requiring the recognition of gain or loss upon an exchange. One of the most important of these is § 351, which provides for non-recognition in connection with certain transfers of property to a corporation in exchange for its stock or securities. Speaking generally, § 351 precludes the recognition of gain or loss when the transferor or transferors of property receive only stock or securities of the corporation and thereafter they own enough stock to be "in control" of the corporation, which is defined in § 368(c) to mean ownership of 80% of the total combined voting power of the corporation and 80% of all other classes of stock. For the purposes of § 351, the term "stock" does not

---

11. For a detailed analysis of the tax treatment of stock issued for services, see Chapter 2, Section 3.

include either warrants or options, Reg. § 1.351–1(a),(1); but it does include a non-assignable, contractual right to receive additional stock contingent upon future earnings, so that both the right, and ultimately any stock, may be received tax-free. Hamrick v. Commissioner, 43 T.C. 21 (1964), remanded per stipulation, 66–1 U.S.T.C. ¶ 9322 (4th Cir. 1965), approved (in result only) in Rev.Rul. 66–112, noted at page 822 infra. (As to the meaning of "securities", see pages 116–120, infra.)

If, in a transaction which meets the control test of § 351, a transferor of property receives not only non-recognition property, i. e., stock or securities of the corporation, but also "boot," i. e., money or other property, § 351(a) no longer applies to prevent the recognition of gain. However, § 351(b) comes into play to limit recognition of gain on the transaction to the amount of any money plus the fair market value of any other property received. A loss on the transaction would still go unrecognized.

Often, particularly in connection with the incorporation of a going proprietorship or partnership, property is transferred to a controlled corporation subject to liabilities, with the corporation either expressly assuming the liabilities or taking the property subject to them. Absent some special provision, relieving the transferor of liabilities, whether directly, by assuming them, or indirectly, by taking the property subject to them, would constitute other consideration moving to the transferor and hence boot under § 351(b). But the practical effect of such a result would be to nullify one of the primary objectives of § 351, to enable parties to incorporate a going business enterprise without invidious tax consequences. Accordingly, it is provided in § 357 that the assumption of a transferor's liabilities will generally not be treated as boot (subject to a corollary provision in § 358(d) for a corresponding reduction in the transferor's basis in the stock or securities received from the corporation). However, there are two exceptions in § 357: (1) § 357(b), which provides for boot treatment if the principal purpose for the assumption of a liability (or the acquisition of property subject to a liability) was to avoid income tax, or in any event was not a bona fide business purpose; and (2) § 357(c), which was added to the Code in 1954 and requires boot treatment to the extent that the total of the liabilities exceeds the total basis of the property transferred.

The principal purpose exception of § 357(b) is designed to combat such situations as a taxpayer borrowing on property just before its transfer to a controlled corporation and retaining the proceeds while leaving the corporation to repay the loan. E. g., Drybrough v. Commissioner, 42 T.C. 1029 (1964). In addition, any effort to foist upon a controlled corporation purely personal obligations of the transferor, such as liability for his individual income taxes, would invite the application of § 357(b). E. g., Campbell v. Wheeler, 342 F.2d 837 (5th Cir. 1965). But the Government has failed in its efforts to apply § 357(b) to cases where the controlled corporation assumes the purchase money obligation incurred by the transferor when he acquired the property he subsequently transfers to the corporation. Simpson v. Commissioner, 43 T.C. 900 (1965); Jewell v. United States, 330 F.2d 761 (9th Cir. 1964). In the latter case the court commented rather wryly on the twofold test in § 357(b) of whether the principal purpose was to avoid taxes, or in any event was not a bona fide business purpose: "We think that when, if ever, this combination of motives and action occurs, it will be noteworthy. It would require that the action be immune from both tax avoidance motive and business sense."

Section 357(c) can be best understood in the light of the basis provisions governing § 351 transactions. If a transferor receives only non-recognition property, under § 358 his basis in that property is the same as his basis in the property transferred. If the non-recognition property consists of both stock and securities, or more than one class of stock, the carryover basis is allocated among the various classes of stock and securities received in accordance with the fair market value of each. Reg. § 1.358–2(b)(2). When the transferor is required to recognize some gain because of the receipt of boot, his basis in the non-recognition property received is equal to his basis in the property transferred plus the amount of any gain recognized, less the amount of any money and the fair market value of any other boot received. Section 358(a)(1). His basis in the boot would be its fair market value. Section 358(a)(2). If the corporation assumes any liabilities in the transaction, or takes the property transferred subject to liabilities, then although the transferor does not have to recognize gain on that account, his basis in the non-recognition property is reduced by the amount of such liabilities. Section 358(d). To illustrate, if property with a basis of 100 and a present market value of 130 is transferred, subject to liabilities of 40, to a corporation in exchange for stock worth 80 and cash of 10, the transferor would actually have a gain of 30, but it would only be recognized to the extent of 10. His basis in the stock would be 60, computed as follows: 100 (basis of the property transferred) plus 10 (recognized gain) less 10 (cash received) less 40 (liabilities to which the property was subject).

Suppose that in the preceding illustration the current value of the property transferred to the corporation was 230, and the liabilities to which it was subject totalled 140. In that event, the application of § 358 would produce a minus basis for the non-recognition property received by the transferor (100 plus 10, less 10, less 140, or minus 40). Prior to the 1954 Code it was not clear whether a minus basis was permissible or whether instead transactions of this kind required the recognition of enough gain to bring the basis up to zero. In Easson v. Commissioner, 294 F.2d 653 (9th Cir. 1961), the court found no significant objection to a minus basis under the prior law and held that no additional gain had to be recognized. It is this situation with which

§ 357(c) of the 1954 Code deals, and that section now expressly requires a transferor to recognize gain in the amount by which the accompanying liabilities exceed the total basis of the property transferred. See generally, Cooper, Negative Basis, 75 Harv.L.Rev. 1352 (1962).

The corporation's basis in § 351 transactions is governed by § 362. Under that section the basis of the transferred property in the hands of the corporation is the same as it was in the hands of the transferor, increased by the amount of any gain recognized by the transferor. Thus in the preceding example where property with a basis of 100 and present value of 130 was transferred, subject to liabilities of 40, in exchange for stock worth 80 and cash of 10, the corporation's basis in the property acquired would be 110, the sum of 100 (the transferor's basis) plus 10 (gain recognized to the transferor). Notice that the liabilities play no part in the determination of the corporation's basis, whether or not they are assumed. Notice too that the operation of the basis provisions results in their being two potential gains, one to the corporation on the property and the other to the stockholder on his stock, where only one existed before.

For property transferred to the corporation in a § 351 transaction, § 1223(2) allows the corporation to tack the holding period of the transferor. Section 1223(1) allows the transferor to tack on to the holding period for his stock the holding period of the property transferred, if the property was either a capital asset or an asset eligible for capital gain treatment under § 1231. If, as would typically be true in the incorporation of a going business, the transferred assets include some that are eligible for capital gains treatment and others that are not, presumably the stock would be allocated between the two types of property in accordance with their fair market values, in order to determine how much of the stock would be entitled to a tacked holding period and how much would not.

Most of the problems in connection with § 351 have involved the operation of the control test, under which the persons who transferred property to the corporation must have the requisite stock ownership "immediately after" the transfer. This requirement will normally be satisfied upon the incorporation of an existing proprietorship or partnership, since the proprietor or partners usually end up owning all of the stock of the new enterprise. However, occasionally some of the stock is either originally issued, or promptly assigned, to a nontransferor of property, perhaps as compensation for services, or as a gift, or because of a prior commitment by one or more of the persons who did transfer property to the corporation that they would assign some or all of the stock received to the outsider, and such situations present serious problems under the control test. There may also be difficulties with the control requirement in connection with transfers to an already going corporation.

Sometimes a taxpayer wants to *avoid* the non-recognition provisions of § 351, in which event, since the section is not elective, pains must be taken not to comply with the conditions of § 351. For example, the taxpayer may be seeking to recognize a loss on a transfer of assets which have depreciated in value. Or he may want recognition even if a gain is present, in order to obtain the concomitant "step-up" in the corporation's basis in the acquired property to the fair market value of the property, rather than carrying over the transferor's basis, as would be required if § 351 applied; if the gain to be recognized is subject only to the favorable capital gains rate, the taxpayer may be willing to incur that tax in order to give the corporation a stepped-up basis for depreciable assets which would decrease, through depreciation deductions, the corporation's ordinary income. However, before pursuing this course there are several factors that must be carefully weighed. First, the entire tax on the gain must be paid at the outset, whereas the corresponding depreciation deductions will be spread out over the useful life of the property. Second, the gain recognized by the transferor will not produce any corresponding tax benefit to the corporation to the extent such gain is allocable to non-depreciable assets like land and goodwill. Third, under § 1245 any gain on depreciable personal property will be taxed to the transferor as ordinary income rather than capital gain, to the extent of any depreciation previously taken. (A similar though much more limited threat is posed in the case of gain on depreciable real property by § 1250.) And finally, § 1239 may subject the transferor to ordinary income tax on all of his gain on all depreciable property, if the transferor (together with his spouse and minor children and grandchildren) owns more than 80 percent in value of the outstanding stock of the corporation. (Section 1239 may also apply where a transaction qualifies under § 351 but there is partial recognition of gain (including gain recognized pursuant to § 357(c), supra). Rev.Rul. 60–302, 1960–2, Cum.Bull. 223.) Notice the agonizing differences between the control test applicable under § 351, which stresses voting power and is satisfied at exactly 80 percent, and the § 1239 test of *more than* 80% of the *value* of the outstanding stock.

AMERICAN BANTAM CAR CO. v. COMMISSIONER

United States Tax Court, 1948. 11 T.C. 397.
Affirmed per curiam, 177 F.2d 513 (3d Cir. 1949).

[A group of individuals, called the "associates", purchased the assets of a bankrupt automobile company in 1935 for $5,000. The assets were subject to liabilities of $219,099.83. The associates then organized the taxpayer corporation in 1936 to take over the assets. The associates were to transfer the assets subject to the liabilities, plus $500 in cash, to the taxpayer in return for 300,000 shares of no par common stock; 90,000 shares of convertible preferred stock (each share having 3 votes) were to be sold to the public through underwriters at $10 a share; the underwriters were to receive as compensation, in addition to discounts and commissions, certain amounts of the common stock issued to the associates, such amounts to be based on a schedule determined by progress of the sale of the preferred stock. The transfer of the assets to the taxpayer in return for the common stock was made on June 3, 1936, at which time the taxpayer had no working capital, no labor force and no sales organization. On June 8, 1936, pursuant to the oral agreement on the substance of the plan, the associates and the underwriters agreed on a schedule as follows: the underwriters were to receive 22,500 shares of common stock when the first 20,000 shares of convertible preferred had been sold; 16,500 shares of common when the next 15,000 shares of preferred had been sold; 19,500 shares of common upon the sale of each of the next two batches of 17,500 shares of preferred; and 22,000 shares of common when the last 20,000 shares of preferred had been sold. On August 16, 1936, the associates placed their 300,000 common stock shares in escrow until the public offering of the preferred stock was completed. No preferred shares were sold prior to October, 1936; in the balance of 1936, the underwriters (referred to as Grant) sold 14,757 preferred shares; and in 1937, up to October, the underwriters sold 68,861 preferred shares. In October, 1937, the associates transferred to Grant 87,900 common stock shares; Grant sold 1,008 of these to the public. Consequently, as of October 31, 1937 the associates held 212,100 shares of common stock, Grant held 86,892 and the public 1,008; as to the preferred stock, there were 83,618 shares owned by the public.

The issue was whether the taxpayer's basis in the assets acquired from the associates was the cost of the assets to the taxpayer, i. e., their fair market value at the date of acquisition, or the lower basis of the assets in the hands of the associates.]

Opinion

HILL, JUDGE. This case requires the determination of the proper basis for the Austin assets acquired by petitioner on June 3, 1936, in exchange for stock. We must decide whether under the facts here [§ 362(a) (1)] requires petitioner, in computing deductions for depreciation, to take as the basis of the assets so acquired the basis thereof in the hands of the transferors. This section is applicable if the exchange by which petitioner received the Austin assets was one in which gain or loss is not recognized under the provisions of [§ 351]. We therefore must first consider whether, when the associates turned over the Austin assets to petitioner, subject to liabilities of $219,099.83, plus $500 in cash, and in return petitioner issued to the associates 300,-000 shares of its no par common stock, all the requirements of [§ 351] were satisfied.

* * *

It has been held that money turned over to the transferee corporation by the transferors does not prevent a tax-free exchange, for it is includible within the term "property" in [§ 351]. . . .

* * *

The first question, then, is whether the associates had . . . ["control" within the meaning of § 368(c)] over petitioner immediately after the exchange on June 3, 1936. Prima facie, when the various steps taken to organize the new corporation and transfer assets to it are considered separately, the associates did have "control" of the petitioner immediately after the exchange within the statutory definition of the word. We think that from June 3 to June 8, 1936, they owned 100 per cent of all the issued stock, and from June 8, 1936, until October 1937 they owned stock possessing at least 80 per cent of the total combined voting power of all classes of stock. On June 3, 1936, the associates were issued absolutely and unconditionally 300,000 shares of no par common stock. The resolution of the board of directors of petitioner accepting the associates' offer of the Austin assets attached no strings whatsoever to the issuance of the stock to them. It is true that on June 2, 1936, petitioner had an authorized capital stock of 700,000 shares, 600,000 common shares and 100,000 preferred shares, but in determining control only stock actually issued is considered. . . . On June 8, no other common stock had been issued, and a contract regarding possible future assignment of those 300,000 shares already issued was not entered into before that date. No preferred stock had been issued on June 3 nor was a contract for its sale provided until June 8. Statutory words "immediately after the exchange" require control for no longer period; in fact, momentary control is sufficient. . . . Certainly, therefore, the associates had absolute control over the corporation from June 3–8, 1936, due to their complete ownership of all outstanding stock.

It is true that, by virtue of their agreement with the associates on June 8, 1936, the underwriters did at that time acquire the right to earn shares of the common stock issued to the associates by the sale of certain percentages of preferred stock, but the ownership of the 300,000 shares remained in the associates until such sales were completed. It is significant to note that this agreement stated that the associates were the owners of the 300,000 shares. On August 16, 1936, the associates deposited all their shares in escrow with the Butler County National Bank and Trust Company, but they only surrendered possession by the terms of their agreement with the bank and retained all other attributes of ownership.

During all of 1936 the associates retained ownership over the 300,000 shares of common stock and during that interval the underwriters sold only 14,757 shares of preferred stock, which did not entitle them to any common stock under the agreement of June 8, 1936. The corporation's by-laws provided that each share of preferred stock should have three votes, while each share of common stock should have one vote. Therefore, at the end of 1936, out of 344,271 possible stock votes, the total combined voting power of all outstanding stock, the associates owned 300,000 or over 80 per cent. It was not until October 1937, when the underwriter Grant received 87,900 shares of the associates' common stock in fulfillment of the underwriting agreement, that the associates lost "control" of petitioner within the statutory definition of the word. Retention of "control" for such a duration of time satisfies [§ 351].

Petitioner, however, contends that the series of steps organizing the new corporation, transferring assets to it, and arranging for the sale of its preference stock must be considered as parts of the integrated plan formulated in May 1936 and, therefore, considered as parts of a single transaction. It argues that this unified transaction started on June 2, 1936, when petitioner was incorporated, and ended in October 1937, when the public offering of the preferred stock by the underwriters ceased and Grant was awarded 87,900 shares of common stock; that the transfer of common stock to Grant in 1937 was the final step of an indivisible operation and must be viewed concurrently with the preceding steps. On this theory the associates did not obtain control of petitioner, for on consummation of this final step in the general plan the associates had only 212,100 shares of common stock, while Grant had 86,892 shares and the public had 1,008 and there were 83,-618 shares of outstanding preferred stock owned by the public. The 212,100 stock votes held by the associates in October 1937 fell shy of the required 80 per cent to give the requisite control.

In determining whether a series of steps are to be treated as a single indivisible transaction or should retain their separate entity, the courts use a variety of tests. . . . Among the factors considered are the intent of the parties, the time element, and the pragmatic test of the ultimate result. An important test is that of mutual interdependence. Were the steps so interdependent that the legal relations created by one transaction would have been fruitless without a completion of the series?

Using these tests as a basis for their decisions the courts in Hazeltine Corp. v. Commissioner, 89 F.2d 513, and Bassick v. Commissioner, 85 F.2d 8, treated the series of steps involved in each case as parts of a unified transaction and therefore determined that the transferors of assets to the new corporation did not acquire the requisite control. An analysis of the fact situations involved shows salient distinguishing features from the present facts. In each of the above cases there was a written contract prior both to the organization of the new corporation and the exchange of assets for stock which bound the transferors unconditionally to assign part of the stock acquired to third parties after the exchange. Thus at the moment of the exchange the recipient of the stock did not own it, but held it subject to a binding contractual obligation to transfer a portion. The court in each case thought that the incorporation and exchange would never have been agreed upon without the supplemental agreement turning over stock to a third party. In such situations it is logical for the courts to say that the exchange and the subsequent transfer are part of one and the same transaction, so that the transferor never actually owned the shares he later assigned.

A close examination of the facts surrounding the exchange in the present case makes it clear that the exchange of assets for stock and the subsequent transfer of a portion of that stock to Grant therein involved should not be considered part of the same transaction so as to deprive the associates of "control" immediately after the exchange. The facts are distinguishable from those existing in the Hazeltine and Bassick cases on three grounds. First, there was no written contract prior to the exchange binding the associates to transfer stock to the underwriters. At the most there was an informal oral understanding of a general plan contemplating the organization of a new corporation, the exchange of assets for stock, and marketing of preferred stock of the new corporation to the public. A written contract providing for the transfer of shares from the associates to the underwriters did not come until five days after the exchange. Secondly, when the transfer of shares to the underwriters was embodied specifically in a formal contract, the underwriters received no absolute right to ownership of the common stock, but only when, as, and if, certain percentages of preferred stock were sold. How clearly contingent was the nature of their rights is illustrated by the fact only one underwriter, Grant, met the terms of the agreement and became entitled to any shares. Thirdly, the necessity of placing the 300,000 shares in escrow with a bank is indicative of complete ownership of such stock by the associates following the exchange.

The standard required by the courts to enable them to say that a series of steps are interdependent and thus should be viewed as a single transaction do not exist here. It is true all the steps may have been contemplated under the same general plan of May 1936; yet the contemplated arrangement for the sale of preferred stock to the public was entirely secondary and supplemental to the principal goal of the plan—to organize the new corporation and exchange its stock for the Austin assets. The understanding with the underwriters for disposing of the preferred stock, however important, was not a *sine qua non* in the general plan, without which no other step would have been taken. While the incorporation and exchange of assets would have been purposeless one without the other, yet both would have been carried out even though the contemplated method of marketing the preferred stock might fail. The very fact that in the contracts of June 8, 1936, the associates retained the right to cancel the marketing order and, consequently the underwriters' means to own common stock issued to the associates, refutes the proposition that the legal relations resulting from the steps of organizing the corporation and transferring assets to it would have been fruitless without the sale of the preferred stock in the manner contemplated.

Finally to say that the separate steps should be viewed as one transaction so that ownership of 87,900 shares never passed to the associates has the disadvantage of inferring that the interested parties intended to suspend ownership of 300,000 shares from June 3, 1936, until such time as the underwriters definitely did or did not earn the right to such shares—as it turned out, until October 1937. It is much more logical to say that ownership of all 300,000 shares rested in the associates until the conditions precedent had been fulfilled by the underwriters, and that when the associates turned over the stock to Grant they were exercising their rights of ownership acquired on June 3, 1936. To allow petitioner's contention is to permit a 15-month time lag after the exchange before determining "control immediately after the exchange". Such a proposition defeats the very language of the statute.

* * *

Thus we conclude that in the present case the exchange of assets for stock between the associates and petitioner on June 3, 1936, was a separate completed transaction distinct from the subsequent transfer of common stock to Grant so that the associates were in control of petitioner immediately after the exchange within the provisions of [§ 351].

* * *

What then is the basis for depreciation purposes of property acquired by a corporation by a tax-free exchange under [§ 351]? Section [362(a)(1)] answers this question. The basis is the same as it would be in the hands of the transferor. In the instant case the basis of the Austin assets in the hands of the associates was the cost of those assets to them. They paid $5,000 cash and received the property subject to liabilities of $219,099.83. Thus the basis in their hands was $224,099.83. Therefore, the basis for the Austin assets to the petitioner is also $224,099.83, as contended by the respondent.

NOTE ON § 351

1. Composition of the Control Group—"Property" under § 351

Since the applicability of § 351 turns on how much stock is owned by persons who transferred property to the corporation, it is important to determine what constitutes "property" for this purpose. The two most important items about which there might be some question are cash, which, as the American Bantam opinion indicates, is included, and services, which, as is now expressly provided in the last sentence of § 351(a), are not. The primary purpose in excluding services seems to have been to make sure that § 351 could not enable a recipient of stock for services to escape the recognition of compensation income, a purpose with which there can be little quarrel. However, the approach taken also has the effect of preventing stock issued to someone who has only contributed services from being included in the control group for the purpose of testing control under § 351. Thus if in conjunction with transfers of property to a corporation more than 20 percent of its stock is issued to one who contributes only services, the control test cannot be satisfied. This seems like an unnecessary obstacle to the issuance of stock for services, particularly since the burden of non-qualification under § 351 falls upon some other party who has transferred appreciated property to the corporation and does not affect the contributor of services at all.

From the point of view of a transferor of property, the role of § 351 is presumably to distinguish between a mere change in the form of his investment and a transaction which amounts to a sale or exchange. It is hard to see why a transferor of property to a corporation should be required to recognize gain any more when more than 20 percent of the stock is issued to some other party for services than when more than 20 percent of the stock is issued to someone else for other property, or *a fortiori* for cash. Quite the reverse, it would seem that a transfer of appreciated property to a new corporation in exchange for, say, one-half of its stock comes much closer to a sale when the other half of the stock is issued for cash than when the other half of the stock is issued on account of services, particularly future services to be rendered to the new corporation. Accordingly, it is submitted that stock issued for services to the corporation should be includible in the control group for the purpose of testing control under § 351, although of course this should not preclude the recognition of compensation income upon the receipt of stock for services. As a matter of fact, this is just the treatment accorded to stock issued for services to one who has also transferred property to the corporation: the stock issued for services is counted in the control group, Reg. § 1.351–1(a)(2), but nevertheless constitutes taxable income to the recipient, § 351(d)(4), a result which further emphasizes the doubtfulness of excluding stock issued for services from the control group in other situations.

Where do secret processes or other types of trade secrets fit into the property-services dichotomy?

REVENUE RULING 64–56

1964–1 Cum.Bull. 133.

The Internal Revenue Service has received inquiries whether technical "know-how" constitutes property which can be transferred, without recognition of gain or loss, in exchange for stock or securities under section 351 of the Internal Revenue Code of 1954.

The issue has been drawn to the attention of the Service, particularly in cases in which a manufacturer agrees to assist a newly organized foreign corporation to enter upon a business abroad of making and selling the same kind of product as it makes. The transferor typically grants to the transferee rights to use manufacturing processes in which the transferor has exclusive rights by virtue of process patents or the protection otherwise extended by law to the owner of a process. The transferor also often agrees to furnish technical assistance in the construction and operation of the plant and to provide on a continuing basis technical information as to new developments in the field.

Some of this consideration is commonly called "know-how." In exchange, the transferee typically issues to the transferor all or part of its stock.

* * *

Since the term "know-how" does not appear in section 351 of the Code, its meaning is immaterial in applying this section, and the Service will look behind the term in each case to determine to what extent, if any, the items so called constitute "property . . . transferred to a corporation . . . in exchange for stock."

The term "property" for purposes of section 351 of the Code will be held to include anything qualifying as "secret processes and formulas" within the meaning of sections 861(a)(4) and 862(a)(4) of the Code and any other secret information as to a device, process, etc., in the general nature of a patentable invention without regard to whether a patent has been applied for . . . and without regard to whether it is patentable in the patent law sense. . . . Other information which is secret will be given consideration as "property" on a case-by-case basis.

The fact that information is recorded on paper or some other physical material is not itself an indication that the information is property. See, for example, Harold L. Regenstein, et ux. v. Commissioner, 35 T.C. 183 (1960), where the fact that a program for providing group life insurance to federal Government employees was transmitted in the form of a written plan did not preclude a finding that the payment was a payment for personal services.

It is assumed for the purpose of this Revenue Ruling that the country in which the transferee is to operate affords to the transferor substantial legal protection against the unauthorized disclosure and use of the process, formula, or other secret information involved.

Once it is established that "property" has been transferred, the transfer will be tax-free under section 351 even though services were used to produce the property. Such is generally the case where the transferor developed the property primarily for use in its own manufacturing business. However, where the information transferred has been developed specially for the transferee, the stock received in exchange for it may be treated as payment for services rendered. See Regenstein, supra, where the taxpayer developed a plan for selling insurance which he ultimately sold to certain insurance companies. The court held that the consideration received was payment for services.

Where the transferor agrees to perform services in connection with a transfer of property, tax-free treatment will be accorded if the services are merely ancillary and subsidiary to the property transfer. Whether or not services are merely ancillary and subsidiary to a property transfer is a question of fact. Ancillary and subsidiary services could be performed, for example, in promoting the transaction by demonstrating and explaining the use of the property, or by assisting in the effective "starting-up" of the property transferred, or by performing under a guarantee relating to such effective starting-up. . . . Where both property and services are furnished as consideration, and the services are not merely ancillary and subsidiary to the property transfer, a reasonable allocation is to be made.

Training the transferee's employees in skills of any grade through expertness, for example, in a recognized profession, craft, or trade is to be distinguished as essentially educational and, like any other teaching services, is taxable when compensated in stock or otherwise, without being affected by section 351 of the Code. However, where the transferee's employees concerned already have the particular skills in question, it will ordinarily follow as a matter of fact that other consideration alone and not training in those skills is being furnished for the transferor's stock.

Continuing technical assistance after the starting-up phase will not be regarded as the performance under a guarantee, and the consideration therefore will ordinarily be treated as compensation for professional services, taxable without regard to section 351 of the Code. . . .

Assistance in the construction of a plant building to house machinery transferred, or to house machinery to be used in applying a patented or other process or formula which qualifies as property transferred, will ordinarily be considered to be in the nature of an architect's or construction engineer's services rendered to the transferee and not merely rendered on behalf of the transferor in producing, or promoting the sale or exchange of, the things transferred. Similarly, advice as to the lay-out of plant machinery and equipment may be so unrelated to the particular property transferred as to constitute no more than a rendering of advisory services to the transferee.

The transfer of all substantial rights in property of the kind hereinbefore specified will be treated as a transfer of property for purposes of section 351 of the Code. The transfer will also qualify under section 351 of the Code if the transferred rights extend to all of the territory of one or more countries and consist of all substantial rights therein, the transfer being clearly limited to such territory, notwithstanding that rights are retained as to some other country's territory.

The property right in a formula may consist of the method of making a composition and the composition itself, namely the proportions of its ingredients, or it may consist of only the method of making the composition. Where the property right in the secret formula consists of both the composition and the method of making it, the unqualified transfer in perpetuity of the exclusive right to use the formula, including the right to use and sell the products made from and representing the formula, within all the territory of the country will be treated as the transfer of all substantial rights in the property in that country.

The unqualified transfer in perpetuity of the exclusive right to use a secret process or other similar secret information qualifying as property within all the territory of a country, or the unqualified transfer in perpetuity of the exclusive right to make, use and sell an unpatented but secret product within all the territory of a country, will be treated as the transfer of all substantial rights in the property in that country. . . .

In accord with the view that a secret process can constitute property for tax purposes are such cases as E. I. du Pont de Nemours & Co. v. United States, 288 F.2d 904 (Ct.Cl.1961), indicating that a secret process can be a "capital asset," which is defined in terms of "property" in § 1221 of the Code. Query whether there is any relevance under § 351 in the further holding of the du Pont case that there was no sufficient "sale or exchange" for the purposes of § 1222 where all that the transferee received was the right to use the secret process, with the transferor retaining the right to license others. Suffice it to say that Rev.Rul. 64–56 seems to be a good deal less stringent in this regard.

The question of whether any property interest has been transferred is hardest when the secret process is alleged to have been conveyed by one who is also to become a long-term employee of the corporation. If the transferor's future services are closely related to the operations in which the alleged secret process will be used, obviously the line between a mere promise of future services and an alleged transfer of a secret process could be exceedingly fine. But as long as the benefits to be derived from the secret process do not depend exclusively upon the services of the particular transferor, property treatment would seem to be at least a possibility.

2. Computation of Control—"Immediately After" under § 351

The critical question under the control test is whether the transferors of property own the required 80% of the corporation's stock "immediately after" the transfers. This calls for a computation of the total stock outstanding and the amount owned by the transferors of property, apparently as of a particular point in time. But as the American Bantam case indicates, the words "immediately after" are not to be taken too literally; and in some circumstances it may be appropriate to take account of projected changes in either the amount of stock owned by the transferor group or the total stock outstanding.

a. *The Effect of a Proposed Public Offering.* It is to be noted that the court in the American Bantam case drew no distinction, so far as the impact on the control test was concerned, between the contemplated public offering of additional stock by the corporation and the prospective transfer of some of the stock received by the original transferors of property. A similar case is Commissioner v. National Bellas Hess, Inc., 220 F.2d 415 (8th Cir. 1955), where too the taxpayer had been organized to take over the assets of an insolvent enterprise. Pursuant to the plan of reorganization, the creditors of the insolvent corporation, who had become in effect the owners of the corporation's property, transferred the property to the taxpayer in exchange for 300,000 shares of its stock. The plan also provided that a management group, consisting of executives of the old corporation who were helping to arrange the reorganization and had agreed to work for the taxpayer, should have an option for three years to purchase the 300,000 shares of stock from the creditors at a stipulated price. Shortly after incorporation the taxpayer started trying to sell stock to the public, and within three months some 345,000 shares of common stock had been sold. The management group did not exercise its option, but it was assigned to a third party who arranged to amend the option so that it could be exercised at the rate of 100,000 shares per year. Accordingly, the creditors ceased to be stockholders of the taxpayer three years after its organization. The court held, for the taxpayer, that the transaction satisfied the control test, so that the taxpayer was entitled to carry over the predecessor's basis in the property instead of having to use the *lower* fair market value of the property at the date of acquisition. Relying upon the American Bantam case, the court found that the factors which ultimately divested the creditors of control were not interdependent elements of the incorporation transaction. As to the management group's option to purchase the stock received by the creditors, the fact that the group never did exercise the option established that it was not an integral element in the transaction. And as to the sale of stock to the public, the court thought that even though contemplated from the outset its prospects were so uncertain that the incorporation transaction could not have depended upon it. On petition for rehearing, the Commissioner pressed additional evidence indicating that the taxpayer was required by the terms of the plan to sell at least 250,000 shares of stock to the public within six months; but the court concluded that the control test was still satisfied since the taxpayer was given a substantial period in which to comply, and no interest in the stock to be issued was created in any one during the interim. 225 F.2d 340 (8th Cir. 1955).

Despite the failure of these cases to draw any distinction between a contemplated issuance of more stock by the corporation and a prospective transfer of stock by the original control group, the fact is that they may be quite different in their impact on the control test. For when the corporation issues additional stock for cash or other property, to the public, for example, as in American Bantam, the new shareholders are also transferors of property to the corporation. Therefore, if the stock issued to them is to be taken into account at all in applying the control test, it is arguable that these new stockholders should be included in the transferor group, so that their stock would count in determining whether the transferors have the requisite 80%. One argument the other way is that § 351 was not intended to apply to the formation of a public corporation with marketable stock, which is certainly a far cry from the mere change in form of investment involved in, say, the organization of a close corporation to take over a small proprietorship. Or, in a somewhat related vein, it might be contended that the control group is supposed to embrace those persons who act in concert to organize the corporation and transfer property to it, and therefore can not include members of the public who simply invest in the stock of new enterprise. While there is no authoritative support for either of these propositions, there have been some stirrings in these directions. For example, the Service will not issue rulings on whether § 351 applies to the organization of so-called "swap-funds," that is, investment companies formed by a group of unrelated persons who transfer their previously-owned marketable securities to the new corporation in exchange for its stock. See Rev.Proc. 64–31, § 3.01(10) (b), page 100 infra. Unfortunately, no light was shed on these issues by the American Bantam and National Bellas Hess cases because the possibility of including the stock to be issued to the public as part of the control group was totally ignored. The same was true in the more recent case of Overland Corp. v. Commissioner, 42 T.C. 26 (1964).

As to the standard to be applied in determining whether such a proposed public offering should be taken into account in computing the total stock outstanding, the court's stress on the concept of "interdependence" in the American Bantam case clearly indicated that something less than a binding contractual commitment might suffice. Yet the court did exclude the prospective offering in American Bantam, although it is hard to imagine how a prospective public offering could have been more closely tied to the original incorporation without being the subject of a binding commitment. The court paid curiously little attention to the fact that since the corporation had no working capital and no business organization, it was entirely dependent upon the proposed public offering to get its business started. This would seem to be "interdependence" with a vengeance. Of course the particular proposed public offering might have failed, as the court seemed to suggest, or some alternative method of financing might have been substituted. But this would normally be true in every case where there is no binding commitment and would therefore leave little scope for the "interdependence" notion. The National Bellas Hess decision is even more troublesome in this respect: the holding that the fact that the reorganization plan required a public offering was not conclusive because no interest in the stock to be issued to the public was created in anyone in the interim seems virtually equivalent to requiring a contractual commitment as a condition to taking the prospective offering into account. It is therefore not surprising that in the more recent Overland Corporation case, supra, the court held that in circumstances much like those in National Bellas Hess the public offering called for by the reorganization plan was an integral part of the incorporation transaction, with the result that the control test was not satisfied (since the public was not included as part of the control group).

Notice that if a proposed issuance of additional stock, whether in the form of a public offering or otherwise, is taken into account its impact on the computation of the control fraction will normally be quite different from that of a prospective transfer of stock by members of the control group. For the issuance of additional stock reduces the control fraction by increasing the denominator (the total stock outstanding), whereas a transfer of stock by the control group reduces the fraction by decreasing the numerator (the amount of stock owned by the group).

b. *The Effect of a Prospective Transfer of Stock by One or More of the Control Group.* When it is a prospective conveyance of stock by one or more members of the control group that is at issue, obviously the prospective transferees of the stock can not be included in the control group since they are not transferors of property to the corporation. Therefore, there is only the question of whether the prospective conveyance of stock is either committed at the time of the transfers of property or is so integral a part of the overall transaction that it should be taken into account. Here the "interdependence" concept may be even harder to apply, since normally neither the incorporation of an enterprise nor its subsequent financing depends upon what the original transferors of property to the corporation do with the stock they receive. However, that is not true of a case like Hartman Tobacco Co. v. Commissioner, 45 B.T.A. 311 (1941), where the plan of financing for a new corporation called for the issuance of more than 20% of the stock for cash to underwriters who in turn intended to sell the stock to the public as soon as possible. The court sustained the contention of the Commissioner that the stock acquired by the underwriters counted in applying the control test (except to the extent of any binding resale commitments at the time it was received). This gives the same narrow cast to the interdependence notion in this area as the American Bantam and National Bellas Hess cases reflected in the context of additional offerings of stock by the corporation.

A number of the cases involving a transfer, directly or indirectly, by members of the control group have stemmed from the organization of a corporation to take over an existing proprietorship where the former proprietor ends up with less than 80% of the stock of the new corporation. It is clear that if the proprietor simply gives away more than 20% of the stock, for example to his children, the control test would still be satisfied, and it does not matter that the making of such gifts was the primary purpose of incorporation. Wilgard Realty Co. v. Commissioner, 127 F.2d 514 (2d Cir. 1942). The same is true if the proprietor voluntarily uses some of his stock to discharge some previous debts, and it makes no difference that the stock is issued directly to the outsiders instead of being first issued to the proprietor and then transferred by him. O'Connor v. Commissioner, 16 T.C.M. 213 (1957). In O'Connor the taxpayer organized a corporation to exploit certain of his patents, which were to be transferred to the corporation in exchange for 51,000 shares of its stock. No stock was immediately issued, but shortly thereafter, at the taxpayer's request, 11,000 of the 51,000 shares were issued to certain persons who had previously advanced money to him to help finance work on the patents. Although this left the taxpayer with less than 80% of the corporation's stock, the court held that the control test was satisfied. Since there was no evidence that the taxpayer's creditors had obtained any interest in either the patents or the stock to be issued in exchange for them, the taxpayer had become the sole owner of the 51,000 shares of stock, regardless of whether the stock was actually issued to him. He was then free to deal with the stock as he wished, and the fact that he caused some of his stock to be issued to others designated by him did not affect the control which he had "immediately after" the exchange.

On the other hand, the control test is not satisfied where outsiders receive more than 20% of the stock upon incorporation pursuant to a binding obligation of the proprietor. In Mojonnier & Sons, Inc. v. Commissioner, 12 T.C. 837 (1949), a father had promised his sons and a foreman that if they continued to work in his business they would receive some stock when he incorporated the business a few years later. Upon the later incorporation, stock was issued directly to the sons and the foreman, and the father received less than 80% of the total. *Held,* at the behest of the corporate taxpayer which was seeking a stepped-up basis, the predecessor of § 351 did not apply because of the absence of control. The Commissioner's argument that the father had in effect received all the stock and then made gifts to the others was rejected, the court stating that the transfers of stock were not gifts but were rewards for past services made directly to the others in accordance with the prior agreement.

In a case like Mojonnier, could it be argued that as a result of the father's commitment to transfer stock to the others in reward for past services they had acquired at least an equitable interest in the father's business, and accordingly qualified as transferors of property themselves? In Fahs v. Florida Machine & Foundry Co., 168 F.2d 957 (5th Cir. 1948), a father and son entered into an agreement under which if the son continued to work in his father's business he was eventually to receive a one-half interest in it. Some three years later the father organized the taxpayer corporation and conveyed to it all of the assets of his business, receiving in exchange just over 50% of the stock, with the rest of the stock going to the son. In contending that the transfer of the father's business had been tax-free and hence the corporation was not entitled to a stepped-up basis for the property, the Commissioner urged that the son had actually acquired an equitable one-half interest in the business under the earlier agreement, so that he was a joint transferor with his father at the time of the incorporation transaction. This was curtly dismissed by the court as "not borne out by the evidence." [12] But cf. Roberts Co. Inc. v. Commissioner, 5 T.C. 1 (1945), where it was held that attorneys who had undertaken to establish the interest of their clients in certain land, in consideration of a contingent fee entitling them to a specified percentage of whatever interest they could establish, had obtained a property interest which qualified them as part of the transferor group when the property was conveyed to a corporation.

Under the Fahs view, § 351 becomes virtually an elective provision in such situations since the applicability of the section turns entirely upon whether or not an interest in the property to be transferred to the corporation is assigned to the outsider before incorporation, although there is little or no difference between these two situations so far as ultimate economic impact is concerned. To illustrate further, consider the case of May Broadcasting Co. v. United States, 200 F.2d 852 (8th Cir. 1953), where a corporation which owned a radio station in addition to other enterprises agreed to make a one-fourth interest in the station available to a third party. In pursuance of this agreement, the taxpayer was organized and the owner of the radio station transferred it to the taxpayer in exchange for all of its stock. After a nine month delay due to the necessity of obtaining FCC approval of the transaction, one-fourth of the stock of the taxpayer was sold to the third party in accordance with the previous agreement. The court held, for the taxpayer, that the transaction did not qualify as a tax-free incorporation because the ultimate loss of control was pursuant to a contract existing at the time of incorporation. Yet it seems clear that if the transaction in the May Broadcasting Co. case had taken the form of a sale by the owner of the radio station to the third party of an undivided one-quarter interest in the station, followed by a joint transfer of the station to the new corporation in exchange for three-quarters and one-quarter of its stock respectively, § 351 would have been satisfied. Similarly, if the owner of the radio station had transferred the property to the new corporation for three quarters of its authorized stock, while the third party transferred cash for the remaining one-quarter of the stock, the transaction would doubtless have qualified under § 351. Query whether there are sufficient differences among these alternatives to warrant differences in tax treatment.

Suppose that upon incorporation there is a binding commitment that the corporation issue more than 20% of its stock to a third party when he has completed certain services to be performed for the corporation. In Kaczmarek v. Commissioner, 21 T.C.M. 691 (1962), the taxpayer formed a corporation for the purpose of developing a piece of real estate he owned. The taxpayer received 75% of the new corporation's authorized stock, and agreed with his lawyers that they would receive the remaining 25% when they had completed certain legal work relating to rezoning the property, preparing certain leases and the like. More than a year later the taxpayer and his lawyers had a falling out which the taxpayer settled by paying the lawyers cash in exchange for their rights to acquire stock. *Held*, the control test was satisfied. The court concluded that the proposed issuance of stock to the lawyers was not an interdependent step in the incorporation transaction, par-

---

12. The court also held that the taxpayer corporation was not estopped from using a stepped-up basis because of the failure of the father to report the gain on the transaction in the year of incorporation, even though that year was now barred by the statute of limitations.

ticularly in view of the fact that the lawyers never did complete the services or actually receive the stock. On the other hand, Parker v. United States, 242 F.Supp. 117 (D.La.1965), holds that an employee's subscription for 20% of the stock of a corporation organized to take over a proprietorship prevented the former proprietor from owning "more than 80 percent" of the stock within the meaning of § 1239, even though the employee was only to receive the stock as he paid for it and had only paid $7500 of the total subscription price of over $23,000 at the time of incorporation. Cf. Trotz v. Commissioner, —— F.2d —— (10th Cir.1966) (a 21% stock interest issued to an employee upon the incorporation of the taxpayer's proprietorship was not "owned" by the taxpayer for the purpose of § 1239 even though the stock was pledged to secure a loan from the taxpayer and in effect could be acquired by the taxpayer at book value at any time.)

3. Computation of Control—Several Classes of Stock

Application of the control test becomes more complex for a corporation which has more than one class of stock. When there are several classes of voting stock, § 368(c) lumps them all together for the purpose of determining the "total combined voting power." Non-voting stock, on the other hand, is subject to a separate test based upon the number of shares; but it is not clear whether when there are several classes of non-voting stock they should be lumped together for the purpose of determining whether the control group has the requisite "80 percent of the total number." The position of the Service is that in such circumstances the control test requires 80% of *each* class. Rev.Rul. 59–259, 1959–2 Cum.Bull. 115.

Combining separate classes of voting stock for the purpose of computing total combined voting power presents some difficulties when the various classes have different voting powers. Presumably some kind of weighting formula is called for. Thus where stock has been classified to permit each class to elect a specified number of directors, each class of stock would be weighted in accordance with the percentage of the board of directors which the class is entitled to elect. I.T. 3896, 1948–1 Cum.Bull. 72. In that ruling a parent corporation owned all of its subsidiary's common stock, which was entitled to elect six of the seven directors, and 55.5% of the preferred stock, which was entitled to elect one director; and the question was whether the parent owned "stock possessing at least 95 per centum of the voting power of all classes" within the meaning of § 141(d) of the 1939 Code. According to the ruling, six-sevenths, or 85.71% of the total voting power should be attributed to the common stock, and one-seventh, or 14.29%, to the preferred stock. Since the parent owned 100% of the common stock, it was regarded as owning the entire 85.71% of voting power attributable to that stock; as to the 14.29% of voting power attributable to the preferred, the ruling treated the parent as owning 7.93%, by virtue of its 55.5% ownership of the preferred. Therefore, the total voting power owned by the parent was 85.71% plus 7.93%, a total of 93.64%, which fell short of the necessary 95%. Rev.Rul. 63–234, 1963–2 Cum.Bull. 148, assumes without discussion that the approach of I.T. 3896 would be followed in applying the control test of § 368(c).

There is more question as to whether and how such voting arrangements as pooling agreements and voting trusts would affect the computation of control. In Commissioner v. National Bellas Hess, Inc., 220 F.2d 415 (8th Cir. 1955), the court stated that "control relates to equitable ownership," in holding that the deposit of stock in a voting trust did not affect the computation of control. Accord, Federal Grain Corp. v. Commissioner, 18 B.T.A. 242 (1929). But these cases were decided under an earlier counterpart of § 368(c) which defined control in terms of "ownership of at least 80 per centum of the voting stock" instead of the present "ownership of stock *possessing* at least 80 percent of the total combined voting power." (Emphasis supplied.) Perhaps in determining how much voting power is "possessed" by certain stock, as the statute now seems to require, account must be taken of any existing voting trust or other agreement. Thus a voting agreement designed to give a particular stockholder more power in the election of directors than the number of his shares would otherwise afford might call for the application of a weighting formula analogous to that applied in classification situations by I.T. 3896. Compare the regulation recently promulgated under § 1563, § 1.1563–1(a)(6), which provides that in measuring the voting power of stock for purposes of a control test much like that of § 368(c) the terms of the stock as set out in the certificate of incorporation provide the starting point, but account will be taken of voting agreements which vary the formal voting rights possessed by the stock.

4. Effect on Control of Disproportionate Issuance of Stock

Unlike present § 351, the predecessor section required that the stock and securities received by each transferor be substantially in proportion to his interest in the total property transferred to the corporation. This proportionate interest requirement, like the above-mentioned restriction on counting stock issued for services in the control group, probably arose out of a concern that compensation (or perhaps gift) elements in a disproportionate incorporation would go untaxed. Accordingly, when in 1954 the proportionate interest requirement was dropped as a factor in the non-recognition of gain, it was expressly provided in the cross references in § 351(d) that an examination should be made of any disproportionate allocation of stock and securities to determine whether any compensation or gift was present. In pursuance of this approach, Reg. § 1.351–1(b)(1) states that where there is a disproportionate allocation of stock and securities, the transaction will be taxed "in accordance with its true nature," and "in appropriate cases the transaction may be treated as if the stock and securities had first been received in proportion" to the property transferred, and then distributed to the ultimate recipients by way of gift or compensation. Query whether and to what extent such a constructive reallocation would affect the control computation—this question is avoided in the Regulation examples since all of the parties there are transferors of property to the corporation and therefore it does not make any difference for control test purposes which of them is regarded as having received the stock.

It is clear that control does not have to be allocated among the transferors of property in proportion to their respective interests in the property transferred. E. g., Holstein v. Commissioner, 23 T.C. 923 (1955) (control test satisfied where in effect A transferred property worth $16,710 for 210 shares of common stock and 16,500 shares of non-voting preferred while B transferred $210 in cash for 210 shares of common). Nor is there any re-

Sec. 4   TAX ASPECTS OF INCORPORATION   97

quirement that every transferor of property receive some voting stock. Thus if in a case like Holstein, supra, A had received only non-voting preferred and B had received all the voting common, § 351 would still have been satisfied. Burr Oaks Corp. v. Commissioner, 43 T.C. 635 (1965); see Marsan Realty Corp. v. Commissioner, 22 T.C.M. 1513, 1524, note 6 (1963). But query the result if A received only debt securities, while B received all the stock—such a transaction would seem to fall perilously close to the sale side of the line. Cf. Curry v. Commissioner, 43 T.C. 667 (1965) discussed at page 119 infra.

5. Contributions to Capital

When a shareholder contributes property to a corporation and receives no shares of stock in return, presumably the transaction constitutes a contribution to capital, and there is no occasion for recognizing either gain or loss. But even if a constructive "exchange" could be found because of the increase in value in the existing shares, § 351 would usually be applicable to provide non-recognition treatment. The transferor would add his basis in the contributed property to his basis in his stock, and the corporation under § 362(a)(2) would take the transferor's basis in the property.

When property is transferred as a contribution to capital by persons other than shareholders, as when a community organization makes property available to a corporation to induce it to locate in the area, § 362(c), added to the Code in 1954, makes the basis of the property to the corporation zero.

6. Accounting Aspects of § 351 Transactions

Just as § 351 does not prevent the recognition of compensation income which may be involved in an incorporation transaction, so there may be other ordinary income items which are "realized" by virtue of the incorporation transaction and are not shielded from recognition by the section. Normally, this kind of problem will not arise if the unincorporated enterprise was on the accrual method of accounting since any receivables would already have been recognized for tax purposes; and the subsequent receipt of cash by the corporation should not result in any tax consequences to it. See Cox v. Commissioner, 43 T.C. 448 (1965). However, if there is a reserve for bad debts when the receivables are transferred to the new corporation, the Service takes the position that the reserve must be "restored" to the income of the transferor, on the ground that the transferor can no longer incur the loss for which the reserve was created; and this "restoration" to income is not a "gain on the transfer of property" within the meaning of the non-recognition provision of § 351. Rev.Rul. 62–128, 1962–2 Cum.Bull. 139. But this view was recently rejected in Estate of Heinz Schmidt v. Commissioner, 355 F.2d 111 (9th Cir. 1966) where the Court of Appeals, reversing the Tax Court, assumed that the "price" paid by the transferee corporation for the accounts receivable was equal to their net book value (after deduction of the reserve) and concluded that in such cases there was no "income" to be restored. (See pages 656, 657, infra, for a more extensive discussion of the restoration of the reserve for bad debts to income, in the context of IRC § 337 which provides non-recognition upon the sale of assets pursuant to a corporate liquidation.) The Schmidt case expressly left open the question of whether the transferee corporation had the right "at the commencement of its business, to set up the same reserve as an offset to the receivables entered upon its books."

If the unincorporated venture was on the cash basis, on the other hand, any "earned" but unpaid receivables transferred to the corporation would not have been recognized as yet by the transferor; and until rather recently it seemed to be the view of the Service that the transfer of such items to the corporation constituted a realization of income by the transferor which too was not a "gain on the transfer of property" covered by § 351. However, in Kniffin v. Commissioner, 39 T.C. 553 (1962), it was held that § 351 did prevent recognition of income to the transferor in such circumstances; the court also held that the assumption of transferor's liability for unpaid expenses did not constitute a "payment" of the expenses by the transferor entitling him to a deduction for such amounts. Presumably, as was assumed in Pittsfield Coal & Oil Co. Inc. v. Commissioner, 25 T.C.M. 11 (1966), the corporation must include in its income the amounts collected on the receivables, since they are not capital assets, § 1221(4), and would have the same zero basis in the hands of the corporation that they had in the hands of the transferor. Similarly, it would seem that the corporation should be able to deduct its payments on the assumed liabilities for expenses. Cf. Rooney v. United States, 305 F.2d 681 (9th Cir. 1962) (taxpayers who transferred an agricultural crop to a newly-organized corporation were required to allocate the expenses of raising the crop to the corporation rather than deducting them on their individual returns). Apparently the Service has now abandoned its efforts to force recognition of income items by cash basis transferors, in view of its acquiescence in Kniffen. 1965–45 Int.Rev.Bull. 5. See generally, Dauber, Accounts Receivable in Section 351 Transactions, 52 A.B.A.Journ. 92 (1966).

NOTE ON RULINGS AND OTHER ASPECTS OF PRACTICE BEFORE THE INTERNAL REVENUE SERVICE

Obviously, the multifold problems associated with § 351 make it desirable whenever possible to obtain a ruling from the Service before the transaction is undertaken. But as already alluded to above, there are some § 351 issues on which the Service will not rule; and there are some others on which it is reluctant to issue rulings. Accordingly, this is an appropriate place at which to set out the most recent general promulgation of the Service on whether and when rulings will be issued, together with two other recent pronouncements relating to the administration of tax laws. See generally, Note, The Availability and Reviewability of Rulings of the Internal Revenue Service, 113 U. of Pa.L.Rev. 81 (1964).

REVENUE PROCEDURE 64–31
1964–2 Cum.Bull. 947.

SECTION 1. PURPOSE.

The purpose of this Revenue Procedure is to supersede Revenue Procedure 62–32, C.B.1962–2, 527, Revenue Procedure 63–20, C.B.1963–2, 754,

Sec. 4   TAX ASPECTS OF INCORPORATION   99

and to set forth an up-to-date, section-by-section list of those areas of the Internal Revenue Code of 1954 in which the Internal Revenue Service will not issue advance rulings or determination letters.

SEC. 2. BACKGROUND.

It is the policy of the Service to answer inquiries of individuals and organizations, whenever appropriate in the interest of sound tax administration, as to their status for tax purposes and as to the tax effects of their acts or transactions, prior to their filing of returns or reports as required by the revenue laws.

There are, however, certain areas where, because of the inherently factual nature of the problems involved, or for other reasons, the Service will not issue advance rulings or determination letters. These areas are set forth in two sections of this Revenue Procedure. Section 3 reflects those areas in which advance rulings and determinations will not be issued. Section 4 sets forth those areas in which they will not ordinarily be issued. Each section reflects a number of specific questions and problems as well as the general areas.

With respect to the items listed, Revenue Rulings or Revenue Procedures may be published in the Internal Revenue Bulletin from time to time to provide general guidelines as to the position of the Service.

This list should not be considered as all inclusive. The elimination of items previously described in Revenue Procedure 62–32 should not be construed as meaning that the Service will rule on those items, but merely that the Service will consider such requests and may decline to rule in advance on any question whenever warranted by the facts and circumstances, particularly where it is not clear to the Service that the parties to the transaction are dealing at arms length. Whenever a particular item is added to or deleted from the list, appropriate notice thereof will be published in the Internal Revenue Bulletin. . . .

SEC. 3.   AREAS IN WHICH RULINGS WILL NOT BE ISSUED.

.01 *Specific questions and problems.*

. . .

2. Section 163.—Interest.—Whether advances to thin corporations constitute loans or are equity investments.

. . .

4. Section 269.—Acquisition Made to Evade or Avoid Income Tax.—Whether an acquisition is within the meaning of section 269.

5. Section 302.—Redemption of Stock.—(a) Whether section 302(b) applies where the consideration given in redemption by the corporations consists entirely or partly of its notes payable, and the shareholder's stock is held in escrow or as security for payment of the notes with the possibility that the stock may or will be returned to him in the future, upon the happening of specified defaults by the corporation.

(b) The tax effect of the redemption of stock for notes, or the liquidation of a corporation by a series of distributions, where the distributions in liquidation or the payments on the notes are to be made over a long future period.

6. Sections 311 and 336.—Taxability of Corporation on Distribution; General Rule.—Upon distribution of property in kind by a corporation to its shareholders, in complete liquidation under section 331 (where under the facts a sale of the property by the corporation would not qualify under section 337), in partial liquidation under section 346, or in redemption of stock under section 302(a), followed by a sale of the property, whether the sale can be deemed to have been made by the corporation under the doctrine of Commissioner v. Court Holding Company, 324 U.S. 331, . . .

7. Section 331.—Gain or Loss to Shareholders in Corporate Liquidations.—The tax effect of the liquidation of a corporation, preceded or followed by the reincorporation of all or a part of the business and assets, where the shareholders of the liquidating corporation own more than a nominal amount of the stock of the new transferee corporation; or where a liquidation is followed by the sale of the corporate assets by the shareholders to another corporation in which such shareholders own more than a nominal amount of the stock.

8. Section 337.—Gain or Loss; Certain Liquidations.—The application of this section to gains realized by a corporation upon the sale of property, in connection with its liquidation, to another corporation, where more than a nominal amount of the stock of both the selling corporation and the purchasing corporation are owned by the same persons.

9. Section 346.—Partial Liquidation.—The amount of working capital attributable to the business or portion of the business terminated which may be distributed in partial liquidation.

10. Section 351.—Transfer to Controlled Corporation.—(a) What will constitute stock or securities where part of the consideration received by the transferors consists of bond, debentures or long-term notes of the transferee in an amount, which when compared to the capital stock of the corporation, gives rise to the question of a "thin corporation."

(b) Whether the transfer of appreciated stocks or securities to a newly organized investment company in exchange for shares of the stock of such investment company, as a result of solicitation by promoters, brokers or investment houses, will constitute nontaxable exchanges within the meaning of this section.

(c) Whether the transfer of appreciated real estate, or interests therein, to a newly organized real estate investment trust, within the meaning of section 856(a) of the Code, in exchange for shares or interests in such trust, as a result of solicitation by promoters, brokers, or investment houses, will constitute nontaxable exchanges within the meaning of this section.

* * *

16. Section 1551.—Disallowance of Surtax Exemption and Accumulated Earnings Credit.—Whether a transfer is within section 1551 of the Code.

* * *

.02 *General Areas.*

1. The results of transactions which lack bona fide business purpose and have as their principal purpose the reduction of Federal taxes.

2. A matter upon which a court decision adverse to the Government has been handed down and the question of following the decision or litigating further has not yet been resolved.

* * *

SEC. 4. AREAS IN WHICH RULINGS WILL NOT ORDINARILY BE ISSUED.

.01 *Specific questions and problems.*

. . .

2. Section 306.—Disposition of Certain Stock.—Whether the distribution or disposition or redemption of "section 306 stock" in a closely held corporation is in pursuance of a plan having as one of its principal purposes the avoidance of Federal income taxes within the meaning of section 306 (b) (4).

3. Section 341.—Collapsible Corporations.—Whether a corporation will be considered as a "collapsible corporation," that is, whether it was "formed or availed of" with the view of certain tax consequences.

4. Section 351.—Transfers to Controlled Corporation.—The tax effect of the transfer where part of the consideration received by the transferors consists of bond, debentures or any other evidences of indebtedness of the transferee.

* * *

.02 *General Areas.*

1. Any other matter where the determination requested is primarily one of fact, e. g., market value of property.

2. The tax effect of any transaction to be consummated at some indefinite future time.

SEC. 5. SCOPE OF APPLICATION.

This Revenue Procedure is not to be considered as precluding the submission of requests for technical advice in any of the above areas from the office of a District Director of Internal Revenue to the National Office.

REVENUE PROCEDURE 64-22

1964–1 Cum.Bull. (Part 1) 689.

Statement of Some Principles of Internal Revenue Tax Administration.

The function of the Internal Revenue Service is to administer the Internal Revenue Code. Tax Policy for raising revenue is determined by Congress.

With this in mind, it is the duty of the Service to carry out that policy by correctly applying the laws enacted by Congress; to determine the reasonable meaning of various Code provisions in light of the Congressional purpose in enacting them; and to perform this work in a fair and impartial manner, with neither a government nor a taxpayer point of view.

At the heart of administration is interpretation of the Code. It is the responsibility of each person in the Service, charged with the duty of interpreting the law, to try to find the true meaning of the statutory provision and not to adopt a strained construction in the belief that he is "protecting the revenue". The revenue is properly protected only when we ascertain and apply the true meaning of the statute.

The Service also has the responsibility of applying and administering the law in a reasonable, practical manner. Issues should only be raised by examining officers when they have merit, never arbitrarily or for trading purposes. At the same time, the examining officer should never hesitate to raise a meritorious issue. It is also important that care be exercised not to raise an issue or to ask a court to adopt a position inconsistent with an established Service position.

Administration should be both reasonable and vigorous. It should be conducted with as little delay as possible and with great courtesy and considerateness. It should never try to overreach, and should be reasonable within the bounds of law and sound administration. It should, however, be vigorous in requiring compliance with law and it should be relentless in its attack on unreal tax devices and fraud.

OPINION NO. 314 OF THE ABA COMMITTEE ON PROFESSIONAL ETHICS

April 27, 1965. 51 A.B.A. Journ. 671.

Ethical Relationship Between the Internal Revenue Service and Lawyers Practicing Before It

The Internal Revenue Service is an instrumentality of the executive branch of the Government, and therefore lacks some of the basic attributes of disinterestedness and impartiality which characterize a true court. Canon 26 imposes upon a lawyer practicing before the service the duty not to mislead it deliberately or affirmatively by false or misleading statements. At the same time no canon of ethics imposes upon a lawyer any duty (except to prevent the commission of a crime) to disclose information acquired as a result of the attorney-client relationship which would tend to reveal the weakness of his client's case, to prejudice his client's rights, or to bring on a controversy with the Government.

Canons 1, 15, 16, 22, 26, 29, 32, 37, 41, 44

The Committee has received a number of specific inquiries regarding the ethical relationship between the Internal Revenue Service and lawyers practicing before it. Rather than answer each of these separately, the Committee, believing this to be a matter of general interest, has formulated the following general principles governing this relationship.

Canon 1 says: "It is the duty of the lawyer to maintain towards the Courts a respectful attitude." Canon 15 says that the lawyer owes "warm zeal" to his client and that "The office of attorney does not permit, much less does it demand of him for any client, violation of law or any manner of fraud or chicane." Canon 16 says: "A lawyer should use his best efforts to prevent his clients from doing those things which the lawyer himself ought not to do, particularly with reference to their conduct towards Courts . . ." Canon 22 says: "The conduct of the lawyer before the Court and with other lawyers should be characterized by candor and fairness."

All of these canons are pertinent to the subject here under consideration, for Canon 26 provides: "A lawyer openly, and in his true character, may render professional services . . . in advocacy of claims before departments of government, upon the same principles of ethics which justify his appearance before the Courts . . .".

Certainly a lawyer's advocacy before the Internal Revenue Service must be governed by "the same principles of ethics which justify his appearance before the Courts". But since the service, however fair and impartial it may try to be, is the representative of one of the parties, does the lawyer owe it the same duty of disclosure which is owed to the courts? Or is his duty to it more nearly analogous to that which he owes his brother attorneys in the conduct of cases which should be conducted in an atmosphere of candor and fairness but are admittedly adversary in nature? An analysis of the nature of the Internal Revenue Service will serve to throw some light upon the answer to these questions.

The Internal Revenue Service is neither a true tribunal, nor even a quasi-judicial institution. It has no machinery or procedure for adversary proceedings before impartial judges or arbiters, involving the weighing of conflicting testimony of witnesses examined and cross-examined by opposing counsel and the consideration of arguments of counsel for both sides of a dispute. While its procedures provide for "fresh looks" through departmental reviews and informal and formal conference procedures, few will contend that the service provides any truly dispassionate and unbiased consideration to the taxpayer. Although willing to listen to taxpayers and their representatives and obviously intending to be fair, the service is not designed and does not purport to be unprejudiced and unbiased in the judicial sense.

It by no means follows that a lawyer is relieved of all ethical responsibility when he practices before this agency. There are certain things which he clearly cannot do, and they are set forth explicitly in the canons of ethics.

Canon 15 scorns the false claim that it is the duty of the lawyer to do whatever may enable him to succeed in winning his client's cause no matter how unscrupulous, and after making it clear that the lawyer owes entire devotion to the interest of his client, Canon 15 concludes as follows:

> . . . But it is steadfastly to be borne in mind that the great trust of the lawyer is to be performed within and not without the bounds of the law. The office of attorney *does not permit,* much less does it *demand* of him for any client, violation of law or any manner of fraud or chicane. He must obey his own conscience and not that of his client [emphasis supplied].

Canon 22, relating to candor and fairness, states that

> It is unprofessional and dishonorable to deal other than candidly with the facts . . . in the presentation of causes.

> These and all kindred practices are unprofessional and unworthy of an officer of the law charged, as is the lawyer, with the duty of aiding in the administration of justice.

Canon 29 provides in part that a lawyer

> should strive at all times to uphold the honor and to maintain the dignity of the profession and to improve not only the law but the administration of justice.

Canon 32 states that

> No client . . . is entitled to receive nor should any lawyer render . . . any advice involving disloyalty to the law whose ministers we are. . . . [He] advances the honor of his profession and the best interests of his client when he . . . gives advice tending to impress upon the client and his undertaking exact compliance with the strictest principles of moral law. . . . [A] lawyer will find his highest honor in a deserved reputation for fidelity to private trust and to public duty, as an honest man and as a patriotic and loyal citizen.

In addition, the preamble to the canons concludes as follows:

> No code or set of rules can be framed, which will particularize all the duties of the lawyer . . . in all the relations of professional life. The following canons of ethics are adopted by the American Bar Association as a general guide, yet the enumeration of particular duites should not be construed as a denial of the existence of others equally imperative, though not specifically mentioned.

The problem arises when, in the course of his professional employment, the attorney acquires information bearing upon the strength of his client's claim. Although a number of canons have general bearing on the problem (Canons 15, 16, 22 and 26), Canon 37 regarding client confidences and Canons 29, 41 and 44 regarding perjury, fraud and deception and the withdrawal of an attorney are most relevant.

For example, what is the duty of a lawyer in regard to disclosure of the weaknesses in his client's case in the course of negotiations for the settlement of a tax case?

Negotiation and settlement procedures of the tax system do not carry with them the guarantee that a correct tax result necessarily occurs. The latter happens, if at all, solely by reason of chance in settlement of tax controversies just as it might happen with regard to other civil disputes. In the absence of either judicial determination or of a hypothetical exchange of files by adversaries, counsel will always urge in aid of settlement of a controversy the strong points of his case and minimize the weak; this is in keeping with Canon 15, which does require "warm zeal" on behalf of the client. Nor does the absolute duty not to make false assertions of fact require the disclosure of weaknesses in the client's case and in no event does it require the disclosure of his confidences, unless the facts in the attorney's possession indicate beyond reasonable doubt that a crime will be committed. A wrong, or indeed sometimes an unjust, tax result in the settlement of a controversy is not a crime.

Similarly, a lawyer who is asked to advise his client in the course of the preparation of the client's tax returns may freely urge the statement of positions most favorable to the client just as long as there is reasonable basis for those positions. Thus where the lawyer believes there is a reasonable basis for a position that a particular transaction does not result in taxable income, or that certain expenditures are properly deductible as expenses, the lawyer has no duty to advise that riders be attached to the client's tax return explaining the circumstances surrounding the transaction or the expenditures.

The foregoing principle necessarily relates to the lawyer's ethical obligations—what he is *required* to do. Prudence may recommend procedures not required by ethical considerations. Thus, even where the lawyer believes that there is no obligation to reflect a transaction in or with his client's return, nevertheless he *may*, as a tactical matter, advise his client to disclose the transaction in reasonable detail by way of a rider to the return. This occurs when it is to the client's advantage to be free from either a *claim* of fraud (albeit unfounded) or to have the protection of a shorter statute of limitations (which might be available by the full disclosure of such a transaction in detail by way of a rider to the return).

In all cases, with regard both to the preparation of returns and negotiating administrative settlements, the lawyer is under a duty not to mislead the Internal Revenue Service deliberately and affirmatively, either by misstatements or by silence or by permitting his client to mislead. The difficult problem arises where the client has in fact misled but without the lawyer's knowledge or participation. In that situation, upon discovery of the misrepresentation, the lawyer must advise the client to correct the statement; if the client refuses, the lawyer's obligation depends on all the circumstances.

Fundamentally, subject to the restrictions of the attorney-client privilege imposed by Canon 37, the lawyer may have the duty to withdraw from the matter. If for example, under all the circumstances, the lawyer believes that the service relies on him as corroborating statements of his client which he knows to be false, then he is under a duty to disassociate himself from any such reliance unless it is obvious that the very act of disassociation would have the effect of violating Canon 37. Even then, however, if a direct question is put to the lawyer, he must at least advise the service that he is not in a position to answer.

But as an advocate before a service which itself represents the adversary point of view, where his client's case is fairly arguable, a lawyer is under no duty to disclose its weaknesses, any more than he would be to make such a disclosure to a brother lawyer. The limitations within which he must operate are best expressed in Canon 22:

> It is not candid or fair for the lawyer knowingly to misquote the contents of a paper, the testimony of a witness, the language or the argument of opposing counsel, or the language of a decision or a textbook; or with knowledge of its invalidity, to cite as authority a decision that has been overruled, or a statute that has been repealed; or in argument to assert as a fact that which has not been proved, or in those jurisdictions where a side has the opening and closing arguments to mislead his opponent by concealing or withholding positions in his opening argument upon which his side then intends to rely.
>
> It is unprofessional and dishonorable to deal other than candidly with the facts in taking the statements of witnesses, in drawing affidavits and other documents, and in the presentation of causes.

So long as a lawyer remains within these limitations, and so long as his duty is "performed within and not without the bounds of the law", he "owes 'entire devotion to the interest of the client, warm zeal in the maintenance and defense of his rights and the exertion of his utmost learning and ability', to the end that nothing be taken or be withheld from him, save by the rules of law, legally applied" in his practice before the Internal Revenue Service, as elsewhere (Canon 15).

C. TAX INCIDENTS OF ISSUANCE OF DEBT

The creation of a debt obligation in exchange for money constitutes a simple borrowing transaction which is not taxable to either the borrower or the lender. This is true whether the debt is evidenced by a formal instrument, such as a note or bond, or is merely represented by an open account indebtedness on the corporation's books. The lender's basis in the debt would be the amount he advanced in exchange for it.

When property is acquired in exchange for debt, the transaction amounts to a purchase on credit, which is likewise not a taxable event for the purchaser. However, as to the transferor of the property, the transaction, whether viewed as a sale on credit or an exchange of one type of property for another (i. e. a claim against the transferee), would be taxable in the absence of some statutory exception. The basis of both parties would be determined under the normal cost rule.

When property is transferred to a corporation in exchange for debt obligations, the important statutory exception which may be applicable to prevent the recognition of gain to the transferor is § 351, which it will be recalled provides non-recognition treatment for "securities" as well as stock. The term "securities," which also appears in the reorganization provisions, is nowhere defined in the Code. While some of the earlier cases seemed to require some proprietary or ownership interest to qualify as "securities", there is no longer any doubt that the term embraces pure debt obligations. As a matter of fact, it seems quite clear that the term includes only debt obligations. For one thing, since the word "securities" is used in conjunction with the word "stock", "securities" would be somewhat redundant if it also included stock. In addition, the treatment of "securities" received in reorganization transactions under § 354 of the Code expressly turns upon the "principal amount" of the securities, a phrase which is meaningful only in relation to debt obligations.

However, even for debt obligations which do qualify as securities, tax-free treatment is also dependent upon satisfaction of the control test, in which the securities would normally play no part since the test is based upon ownership of stock and voting power. Thus for non-recognition treatment the recipient of the securities must himself have the requisite control of the corporation, or be a part of a group of transferors who acquire the necessary control in the transaction which includes the issuance of the securities.

If § 351 does apply, then, as in the counterpart situation where stock is received tax-free, under § 362(a) the corporation takes the property received in exchange for the securities at its basis in the hands of the transferor, and under § 358 the transferor carries over his basis in the property to the securities received. (If the transferor receives both stock and securities, his carryover basis is allocated between the two in proportion to their respective fair market values. Reg. § 1.358–2(b)(2).)

If debt obligations which do not qualify as securities are received in a transaction to which § 351 otherwise applies, the obligations would be treated as "other property" under § 351, with the result that gain (but not loss) would be recognized to the extent of the fair market value of the obligations. As a corollary, under § 362(a) the basis of the property received by the corporation in exchange for the obligations would be increased by the amount of the gain recognized by the transferor, and the latter's basis in the debt obligations would be their fair market value.

TURNER v. COMMISSIONER

United States Tax Court, 1961.
20 T.C.M. 468.[13]

Memorandum Findings of Fact and Opinion

TIETJENS, JUDGE: The Commissioner determined a deficiency in petitioners' income tax for 1957 in the amount of $11,670.36. The issues presented are (1) whether there was a recognized gain upon the incorporation of a sole proprietorship; . . . .

Findings of Fact

Some of the facts have been stipulated and are incorporated herein by reference.

Petitioners are husband and wife and reside in Martinsville, Virginia. For the calendar year 1957 they filed a joint income tax return with the director of internal revenue for the district of Virginia.

Rufus F. Turner, hereinafter referred to as petitioner, as a sole proprietor, had engaged in the operation of a fresh produce wholesale grocery business for 36 years in Martinsville under the name of Cash Produce Company. Also associated with the business were petitioner's wife, Marguerite H. Turner, who had been employed for 26 years as a bookkeeper, and James R. Ingram, petitioner's son-in-law, who had been employed for 7 years and was petitioner's principal assistant.

On November 14, 1956, petitioner incorporated the sole proprietorship under the name of Cash Produce Company, Inc., hereinafter referred to as Cash Produce. The corporation transacted no business until January 1, 1957. A stock statement was filed with the Virginia State Corporation Commission on December 6, 1956, advising it of a

---

13. Footnotes by the court omitted.

plan to issue 135 shares of common stock for $6,750 in cash. Also in December 1956, petitioner conferred with his attorney and his certified public accountant with respect to the manner in which to accomplish the proposed transfer of the proprietorship assets to the new corporation. At that time the accountant made the following computation of the proprietorship goodwill:

Net earnings (before income taxes)—

1952	$ 29,887.34
1953	18,468.80
1954	19,536.61
1955	24,830.86
1956	21,535.87
Total	$114,259.48
Less income taxes—25% average	28,564.87

Total net earnings	$ 85,694.61	
5 year average	$ 17,138.92	
Net earnings capitalized at 10%		$171,389.20
Less net invested capital at 12-31-56 excluding goodwill (75,534.48 + 21,535.87)		97,070.35
Goodwill at date of incorporation		$ 74,318.85
Rounding off	$ 74,300.00	

On January 1, 1957, with the exception of real estate and certain other fixed assets, all of the assets of the sole proprietorship together with certain liabilities were transferred to Cash Produce in exchange for 1,365 shares of common stock. These assets had a cost basis of $49,593.46. A summary of the balance sheet of the proprietorship as of December 31, 1956 was as follows:

Current Assets			$ 47,077.44
Fixed Assets		$ 91,455.07	
Less Depreciation		$ 36,490.09	54,964.98
Other Asset			230.10
TOTAL ASSETS			$102,272.52
Current Liabilities			$ 5,202.17
R. F. Turner, Capital:			
Balance 1-1-56		$116,013.78	
Earnings for year 1956		21,535.87	
		$137,549.65	
Drawings for 1956		40,479.30	97,070.35
TOTAL LIABILITIES			$102,272.52

* * *

A financial statement for Cash Produce as of January 1, 1957 was prepared by the accountant on January 19, 1957, and transmitted to the Produce Reporter Company, Wheaton, Illinois which publishes

Sec. 4 TAX INCIDENTS OF DEBT 109

a credit rating reference book of produce firms. The following is the balance sheet from that financial statement:

CURRENT ASSETS			
Cash		$ 9,092.61	
Accounts receivable—customers		12,339.46	
Merchandise inventory—at the lower of cost (determined by the first-in-first-out method) or market		25,645.37	$ 47,077.44
FIXED ASSETS			
Store fixtures, furniture, equipment and vehicles— at cost		$25,002.29	
Less accumulated depreciation		17,514.20	7,488.09
INTANGIBLE ASSETS			
Good Will		$74,300.00	
Incorporation expense		230.10	74,530.10
TOTAL ASSETS			$129,095.63
CURRENT LIABILITIES			
Accounts payable:			
Trade	$2,312.01		
Other	625.02	$ 2,937.03	
Accrued liabilities:			
Salaries and wages	$2,024.58		
Taxes (other than taxes on income)	240.56	2,265.14	$ 5,202.17
NONCURRENT LIABILITY			
Note payable to officer—unsecured and without interest			$ 48,893.46
CAPITAL			
Common stock—authorized, 3,000 shares of $50 par value; issued and outstanding, 135 shares		$ 6,750.00	
Subscriptions to common stock, 1,365 shares		68,250.00	75,000.00
TOTAL LIABILITIES			$129,095.63

Thereafter petitioner received the following reply from the Produce Reporter Company in regard to the financial statement submitted:

> The statement of Cash Produce Company, Inc., does present several problems from a rating standpoint.
>
> The item of "good will" is very correctly listed as an "intangible asset", it is the type asset which is eliminated from credit consideration in arriving at Blue Book financial ratings.
>
> When your good will and incorporation expenses of $74,530.10 are eliminated from your statement, that January 1, 1957 Corporation financial statement then shows a net worth of less than $500.

We believe we have a feel of what your accountant and tax attornies [sic] have attempted to accomplish in handling your incorporation on a basis which provides for a corporation note payable "to officer" of $48,893.46. Such an arrangement does, however, deplete completely the corporation's financial responsibility for credit rating purposes.

Your accountant can, of course, advise you on the advisability of issuing corporate stock for that indebtedness to officers.

Frankly, Mr. Turner, we hesitate very much to recommend a subordination agreement covering the notes payable to officers and do so only as a last resort.

In the event your accountants or attornies [sic] would want to prepare a subordination agreement which would clearly set forth that no payments are to be made on indebtedness to officers as long as there are any trade obligations and indicate clearly that you will notify Produce Reporter Company prior to the time any payment is made on that indebtedness, then such a subordination agreement could be accepted.

It is the type exception, however, which is "loaded" with possibilities of misunderstanding for the future.

* * *

In response to this letter petitioner wrote the following:

As principal stockholder, president and manager of Cash Produce Co., Inc. the undersigned will continue to honor credit extension with the same integrity and ability as in the past, and to personally guarantee payment of the corporations debts in the same manner as prior to incorporation.

Though you suggest in your letter that a subordination agreement as to the corporations debt to me is "loaded" with possibilities of misunderstanding, you may accept this letter over my signature below as such an agreement, to the effect that any trade obligations will most certainly be paid before any liquidation of this debt. Any drawings I made from the corporation above the minimal salary allowance provided for me will be charged against my annual profit-sharing. Furthermore, your letter ignored the fact that the note payable to officer of $48,893.46 was created by the charge for goodwill, and that the goodwill was a capitalization at 10% of the average net profits of the past five years. . . .

Nevertheless, to eliminate goodwill from credit consideration as you state, should also require elimination of the debt which it created, leaving a remaining net worth of

$49,363.36. To the latter should be added, if not more, by the subordination described above, the value of the business real estate which I retained in my own right in the amount of $47,476.89, giving a total net worth for credit purposes (excluding other personal assets) in the amount of $96,840.25, exclusive of goodwill.

* * *

As evidence of the $48,893.46 designated on the balance sheet submitted to the Produce Reporter Company as "NONCURRENT LIABILITY, Note Payable to officer—unsecured and without interest", the accountant prepared the following instrument which was executed sometime between January and November 1957:

Notice of Indebtedness

January 1, 1957

For value received, We, Cash Produce Co., Inc., do hereby promise to pay to Mr Rufus F. Turner, his heirs or assigns, the amount of Forty-eight thousand, eight hundred, ninety-three dollars and forty-six cents, ($48,893.46) without interest, payable at the office of the corporation on or after February 1, 1958; also the corporation is not to furnish security of any type for this indebtedness. It is also agreed that the payee may draw funds from the corporation at any time upon the pledge of this note as security, said drawings to be deducted from the amount of this liability prior to settlement.

Accepted and agreed to the above this date January 1, 1957.

(S) Rufus F. Turner   Cash Produce Co., Inc.
—————————————
        Payee

(S) Rufus F. Turner
—————————————
        Registered
        Agent
        President

This instrument was not adopted or ratified by any formal resolution of the stockholders or the board of directors of Cash Produce.

A meeting of the board of directors of Cash Produce was held on February 25, 1957. Relevant parts of the minutes of that meeting are as follows:

WHEREAS, Rufus F. Turner, sole proprietor and owner, trading and doing business previously as the Cash Produce Company, Martinsville, Virginia, has the below mentioned personal property assets of $129,095.63, and said Rufus F. Turner, owner and sole proprietor, being subject to liabilities of $54,095.63, he having previously purchased for cash 135 shares at $50.00 per share for $6,750.00 cash; therefore, total liabilities outstanding by purchase of said stock being the sum of $60,845.63, and the difference between said assets and liabilities being net assets and net worth of $68,250.00, and he has offered to sell the personal assets of said Cash Product [sic] Company for the below sum, subject to said liabilities, with the remaining value in net assets and worth of $68,250.00 to the Cash Produce Company, Incorporated payable in common stock of the corporation, representing the difference between the assets subject to said liabilities.

WHEREAS the said Rufus F. Turner, owner, has offered to transfer the said current, fixed and intangible personal property assets of said Cash Produce Company with the assumption of said liabilities to the Cash Produce Company, Incorporated, in exchange for $68,250.00 to be paid in 1365 shares of the capital stock of the corporation of the par value of $50.00 each, and it is necessary for this Board of Directors to determine the value of such property in current money of the United States of America, as well as to accept or reject the said offer:

NOW, THEREFORE, BE IT RESOLVED:

First, that this Board, in the exercise of its best skill and judgment, fixes and determines the value of the said property in current money of the United States in accordance with the Financial Statement of Cash Produce Company, . . . a copy of which is hereby attached and incorporated [14] . . . .

Second, that the said offer of the said Rufus F. Turner, owner, trading as the Cash Produce Company, Martinsville, Virginia, be, and the same hereby is, accepted, in the sale of the above valued assets of $129,095.63, subject to the liabilities of $54,095.63, to the Cash Produce Company, Incorporated, and that 1365 shares of the Common stock of the par value of $50.00 each in the total sum of $68,250.00 of said Corporation be issued, (in addition the amount $6,750.00 has previously been issued to him by said Corporation for cash) and the remaining amount of $68,250.00 now be issued to Rufus F. Turner by said Corporation, to cover the actual net worth and net assets as shown in the First Resolution above.

A fiscal year ending July 31 was adopted by Cash Produce. Petitioner's wife, as bookkeeper, incorrectly credited the $48,893.46 to "Accounts Payable" and subsequently certain drawings of petition-

---

14. [Ed. note] Identical to the one set out above.

er were debited to this account with the result that the financial statement of Cash Produce for its fiscal year disclosed notes payable as $42,090.29. This error was corrected in January 1958 when the accountant audited petitioner's drawing account in preparation of the joint income tax return.

On November 15, 1957, the accountant left the firm by which he had been employed and shortly thereafter opened his own office in Martinsville. On January 1, 1958, petitioner and Cash Produce became the accountant's clients. On or about January 8, 1958, the accountant's immediate supervisor of his former firm telephoned him and also advised petitioner by letter that the incorporation of Cash Produce was, in the supervisor's opinion, taxable rather than tax free.

On January 14, 1958, a debenture bond in the amount of $48,893.46 issued by Cash Produce to petitioner was filed with the Virginia State Corporation Commission. Although this debenture bond was dated January 1, 1957, it was prepared by Cash Produce's attorney from a form supplied by the accountant a few days prior to the filing. Pertinent provisions of this debenture bond are as follows:

> Cash Produce Company, Incorporated, a Corporation organized and existing under the laws of the State of Virginia, (hereinafter called the "Corporation"), for value received, hereby promises to pay to Rufus F. Turner, or order, his heirs or assigns, the total sum of $48,893.46, bearing interest at three per cent (3%) per annum, and being payable as follows: $5,000.00 on January 1, 1962, and $5,000.00 on the first day of each year thereafter until the total sum of $48,893.46 herein owed is paid unto the said Rufus F. Turner, or order, his heirs or assigns, together with 3% interest per annum and with the first payment of interest being due and payable on said sum on January 1, 1958 and on the first day of each year thereafter.
>
> The issue of the within corporate debenture is made and executed pursuant to the articles of incorporation of the said Corporation and in pursuance of a resolution of said Corporation passed on the 1st day of January, 1957 and said debenture herein being debenture No. 1.
>
> * * *
>
> This debenture is of an authorized issue debenture due as hereinabove set forth of the Corporation (hereinafter called debenture) of the aggregate principal amount of Forty-Eight Thousand Eight Hundred Ninety-Three Dollars and Forty-Six Cents ($48,893.46), duly authorized by resolution of the Board of Directors of the Corporation adopted January 1, 1957.

The liability reflected in the debenture bond was recorded on the books of Cash Produce by the accountant as a "Long Term Liability" with the explanation "Indenture due Rufus F. Turner from transfer of assets at date of incorporation." Although entered on the books in January 1958 it was dated January 1, 1957.

* * *

The Commissioner explained in the statement accompanying the statutory notice of deficiency:

It is held that you realized a gain of $74,300.00, recognized as a long-term capital gain to the extent of $48,893.46 (taxable at 50%), which represents the fair market value of non-interest bearing note received as part payment in the transfer of your net equity in assets to the Cash Produce Company, Incorporated. Therefore, taxable income has been increased in the amount of $24,446.73.

* * *

Opinion

. . . In contesting the Commissioner's determination the petitioner argues (1) that the incorporation was entirely tax free as the "Notice of Indebtedness" was not a legal instrument, but only a memorandum prepared for petitioner's personal satisfaction until a debenture bond was issued and that the petitioner's receipt of such debenture bond on January 14, 1958 was an integral and concluding step in the plan of incorporation; (2) that the notice of indebtedness does not constitute "other property" within the concept of section 351; (3) that even if the notice of indebtedness is "other property" it had no fair market value; (4) that if it is "other property" and in addition had a fair market value, nevertheless no gain was realized upon the receipt of the stock and "other property" because the value of the property received was not in excess of the net adjusted cost basis of the tangible assets transferred; and (5) that the notice of indebtedness represented an equity interest equivalent to stock.

[The court first held that the "Notice of Indebtedness" constituted an enforceable note rather than a mere memorandum having no legal significance, and that the issuance of the note had been duly authorized by the board of directors of the corporation.]

The next approach taken by petitioner is that the notice of indebtedness does not constitute "other property" within the meaning of section 351(b). This contention is not predicated upon an agreement that the notice of indebtedness was a security under section 351 (a), but rather that the notice of indebtedness was received by petitioner only as evidence of an existing obligation and not in payment of an obligation. We agree with petitioner that the notice of indebtedness is written evidence of an existing enforceable obligation. However, we do not agree that this is not "other property" within the purview of section 351(b). Petitioner cites *Jay A. Williams*, 28 T.C. 1000 (1957), and extracts from context our statement that "A note received only as security, or as an evidence of indebtedness, and not as payment, may not be regarded as income". In *Williams* we dealt with the question of whether a note received in payment of services was income to the recipient. We held the note was not income as it was established to our satisfaction that the note was not received in payment of the outstanding debt due the taxpayer for the performance of services and that "a simple change in the form of indebtedness from an account payable to a note payable is insufficient to cause the realization of income by the creditor".

It is obvious that petitioner by this contention has completely misconceived the import of the note in this case. The question presented here is not whether the receipt of the note resulted in ordinary income under section 61(a) . . . . but whether gain was recognizable on the incorporation as a result of the receipt of the note under section 351. Our afore-going conclusion was that the notice of indebtedness was an enforceable note and the cases have uniformly held that a note of such duration does not comply with the statutory concept of a security. . . . Inasmuch as it does not qualify as a security under section 351(a), it is "other property" under section 351(b). Rev.Rul. 56–303, 1956–2 C.B. 193.

Petitioner continues, that even if the notice of indebtedness is "other property" it had no fair market value. He says that it is apparent from the financial condition of the corporation and the testimony of the parties concerned that there was no immediate intention or ability to pay the obligation. The evidence does not disclose an inability on the part of the corporation to pay the note. Although there was evidence regarding the value of the note it was focused primarily on the aspect of its value as collateral security for a loan. There is a question as to whether it could be discounted; however, it should be kept in mind that, as previously indicated, this note was not an ordinary note whose value would increase as the maturity date approached, but was *sui generis*, as its provision that "the [petitioner] may draw funds from the corporation at any time upon the pledge of [the] note as security, said drawings to be deducted from the amount of [the] liability prior to settlement" made it in effect a drawing account. As we see it, the fair market value of the note was at all times its stated value as petitioner at any time could have withdrawn such amounts, the only barrier to such withdrawals being the voluntary, self-imposed subordination agreement which could have been rescinded at any time by petitioner. We do not think that the evidence introduced establishes that the amount determined by Commissioner to be the fair market value is arbitrary or unreasonable.

Petitioner in another phase of his assault upon Commissioner's determination argues that if we should find that the note has a fair market value nevertheless petitioner realized no gain on the transfer for the reason that the value of the stock and "other property" received was not in excess of the net adjusted cost basis of the tangible assets transferred. Simply stated, petitioner contends that the $74,300 which was ascribed to goodwill at the time of the incorporation was incorrect and that no goodwill existed or was transferred, or, if any was transferred, its value was negligible. The Commissioner says that the sole proprietorship possessed transferable goodwill with a value of $74,300. This presents a paradox as petitioner now attempts to retreat from his original position by relying on [authorities] in which the Commissioner challenged the transfer of goodwill. Conversely, the Commissioner here does not challenge, but acquiesces in the original amount designated by petitioner as goodwill. In addition to the aforementioned case and ruling, petitioner also calls attention to the testimony of a representative of Produce Reporter Company who stated that goodwill had no value in arriving at a rating for a produce business. A query from the Court revealed that this rating was from the standpoint of a creditor rather than a possible purchaser and that all assets were viewed in regard to their basis at liquidation in order to ascertain their worth to creditors in the event of such liquidation. This sheds little light upon the problem.

We are convinced that the corporation acquired something more in value at the incorporation of the sole proprietorship than the tangible assets transferred, which was goodwill, and petitioner has not shown the Commissioner's determination of the amount of this goodwill to be erroneous. . . . It follows that the Commissioner's determination must be sustained. . . .[15]

NOTE ON "SECURITIES"

Just what types of debt obligations qualify as "securities" is not so easy to say. The term does seem to contemplate written, perhaps even relatively formal, instruments, so that mere open account indebtedness would not qualify. In addition, the authorities appear to require a reasonably long duration for the obligation before it can qualify as a security. The theory is that when short-term debt obligations are received, the transaction comes so close to a sale for cash that gain should be recognized. Present thinking seems to be that it would be incautious to expect security classification for obligations with a duration much less than five years. Compare Rev.Rul. 56–303, 1956–2 Cum.Bull. 193 (notes of under four years duration held not securities) with Penfield v. Davis, 105 F.Supp. 292 (N.D.Ala.1952), aff'd 205 F.2d 798 (5th Cir. 1953) (five year debentures redeemable at a premium prior to maturity held securities). But it is clear that the duration of the obligations is not necessarily determinative. As the Tax Court put it in Camp Wolters Enterprises v. Commissioner, 22 T.C. 737 (1954), aff'd 230 F.2d 555 (5th Cir. 1956):

> The test as to whether notes are securities is not a mechanical determination of the time period of the note. Though time is an important factor, the controlling consideration is an over-all evaluation of the nature of the debt, degree of participation and continuing interest in the business, the extent of proprietary interest compared

---

15. The decision of the Tax Court on this issue was affirmed in 303 F.2d 94 (4th Cir. 1962).

with the similarity of the note to a cash payment, the purpose of the advances, etc. It is not necessary for the debt obligation to be the equivalent of the stock since [§ 351] specifically includes both "stock" and "securities."

So in Prentis v. United States, 64–1 USTC para. 9417 (S.D.N.Y.1964), an "overall evaluation of the transaction" led the court to conclude that a six months note there involved constituted a security.

Currently the most troublesome problem of "securities" classification arises in connection with transactions which take the form of a "sale" of property to a controlled corporation, with the purchase price payable in installments over a specified period and evidenced by an installment debt obligation. In principle there seems no reason why such an obligation can not constitute a "security" within the meaning of § 351, assuming that it otherwise meets the tests for such classification. The fact that the transaction is expressly cast in the form of a "sale" should not preclude "security" classification since, as already noted, at least in theory any transfer of property in exchange for debt obligations, however described, amounts to a sale on credit. Nevertheless, in a number of cases involving a purported "sale" of property to a controlled corporation on a deferred payment basis represented by an installment obligation the court seemed to assume that qualification under § 351 depended upon whether the installment obligation really constituted equity rather than debt, e. g., J. I. Morgan, Inc. v. Commissioner, 30 T.C. 881 (1958) reversed on another issue, 272 F.2d 936 (9th Cir. 1959), thus apparently ignoring the possibility that the obligation was valid debt but nevertheless subject to tax-free treatment under § 351 because it qualified as a "security". And at least two cases have expressly rejected security classification for installment obligations received in "sales" transactions on grounds that make it look as though the "sale" form of transaction was determinative. In Brown v. Commissioner, 27 T.C. 27 (1956), a father and son who were partners in a logging and lumber business decided to incorporate. Since the son contemplated an expansion of the business which the father did not favor, the father was reluctant to contribute his entire present interest in the business as an equity investment in the corporation. Therefore, it was agreed that the two would contribute to the corporation for stock only the current assets of the partnership, that is, the cash, accounts receivable and inventory. These assets would have been sufficient to enable the corporation to carry on a lumber sales and marketing business if it had chosen to do so. Thereafter, the partners sold the logging and milling assets to the corporation for approximately $600,000, payable in ten equal installments with interest at the rate of 4%. Payments under the installment obligation were not dependent upon earnings, and title to the property transferred was reserved by the sellers as security for the performance of the obligation. The issue was the basis of the logging facilities in the hands of the corporation, which in turn depended upon whether the transfer of those assets had been tax-free under § 351. The Commissioner contended that the exchange of the current assets for stock and the transfer of the logging facilities for the installment obligation were interdependent parts of a single transaction to which § 351 applied, and that the installment obligation either amounted to preferred stock or at least qualified as a security under § 351. But the court held, for the corporate taxpayer which was seeking the higher basis for the assets, that although the installment obligation represented *bona fide* debt, it did not constitute a security under § 351:

> Securities, as that term is used in [§ 351], have been held to be instruments in the nature of bonds, debentures, or other obligations representing long-term advancements to the issuing corporation. . . . The question whether an evidence of indebtedness constitutes a security does not depend for its resolution upon a simple determination of the length of time the obligation is to run, but depends rather upon an over-all evaluation of the nature of the debt so as to ascertain whether or not the instrument issued evidences a continuing interest in the affairs of the corporation. . . . The installment contract in question was not intended to insure the partners a continued participation in the business of the transferee corporation, but was intended rather to effect a termination of such a continuing interest. We are aware of no decision in which an installment sales contract reserving title in the seller has been held to qualify as a security . . . . Although in certain particulars the contract may resemble a bond, essentially it partakes of the nature of a contract of sale, and in our view does not constitute a security within the meaning of [§ 351].

The Brown decision was expressly followed in Brook v. Commissioner, 23 T.C.M. 1730 (1964), which rejected security treatment for an installment obligation received from a controlled corporation in exchange for the transfer of an exclusive franchise to assemble and sell a newly-developed type of binding for books, although the installment obligation was not secured by the franchise or anything else. On the other hand, Campbell v. Carter Foundation Production Co., 322 F.2d 827 (5th Cir. 1963), allowed security treatment for installment notes received upon a "sale" of property to a controlled corporation; the notes were characterized as "the substantial equivalent of equity securities," although at the same time the court sustained the deductibility of the interest paid on the notes. See generally, Comment, Section 351 Transfers to Controlled Corporations: The Forgotten Term—"Securities", 114 U. of Pa.L.Rev. 314 (1965).

Notice that in these cases where the purported "sale" of property to the corporation occurs sometime after the organization of the corporation there may be, in addition to the "security" issue, a question as to whether the "sale" transaction and the earlier transfer or transfers of property to the corporation in exchange for stock constitute interdependent parts of a single transaction which should be integrated for the purpose of applying § 351. For even if the installment obligation does qualify as a security § 351 will not apply unless the control test is satisfied, which in turn may well depend upon whether the sale transaction is integrated with the earlier transfers for stock. And if the installment obligation does not qualify as a security the amount of gain to be recognized and the manner of reporting it may depend upon whether the two transactions are integrated. In a separate sales transaction, of course, the taxable gain is the difference between the amount received and the basis of the property transferred; and the seller will usually be able to elect the installment method of reporting. See pages 519–521, infra. On the other hand, if the two transactions are integrated, any "seller" who also transferred property for stock would have to recognize his total gain on the combined transactions, to the extent of the fair market value of the installment obligation, which would constitute "other property" under § 351(b). In addition, it is far from clear that the installment method of reporting could be utilized in these circumstances.

Some cases, particularly some quite recent ones, have taken an even more extreme position with regard to these purported sales transactions, holding that a bona fide sale is simply not the kind of transaction covered by § 351. In Shannon v. Commissioner, 29 T.C. 702 (1958), the court stated that once the transaction was found to be a sale, "it follows for the same reasons that it was not an exchange within the meaning of" § 351, and therefore it was not necessary to determine whether the installment obligation received might be deemed a security "if the transaction were other than a sale." No authority was cited for the proposition that a transfer by way of sale was not subject to § 351. The same result was reached in Curry v. Commissioner, 43 T. C. 667 (1965), where a husband and wife who owned 60 percent of the equity in a building and their son and daughter who owned the remaining 40 percent "sold" the building for $50,000 cash and $1,500,000 in installment obligations to a corporation which had been organized by the son and the daughter's husband, each of whom had invested $22,500 for 45% of its stock, the remaining 10% of the stock having been issued to the father for $5,000. The court expressly followed Shannon, but also purported to rely upon such cases as Brown, supra, without any clear recognition that those cases involved the question of whether the debt obligation received in a purported "sale" transaction qualified as a security, rather than whether § 351 applied to such transactions at all. This led the court to conclude that the non-applicability of § 351 to sales transactions was "too well-settled" to be overturned. However, the court also endorsed the rule on the merits:

> If respondent's position were adopted, section 351 would apply even where an unrelated third party was the stockholder of the corporation. Assume, for example, a transaction identical to that involved in the instant case except that A. T. & T. was the sole shareholder of [the corporation]. We cannot believe that Congress intended nonrecognition of gain in such a case. Indeed, respondent would undoubtedly be quick to object if taxpayers tried to prevent recognition by such a device. Yet it is clear that, in a sale effected in this manner, the transfers of cash for stock and property for notes are interdependent steps of a single plan. It is not a ground for distinction that two of the stockholders in the instant case were also transferors of realty, since we have found the parties were capable of independent action and intended a bona fide sale.

The Curry decision was followed in Rosenthal v. Commissioner, 24 T.C.M. 1373 (1965), which also contains the warning that if the price paid in the sale transaction, including the face amount of the obligations, exceeds the fair market value of the property received, the excess may be taxable as a dividend.

Any planning in this area becomes even more hazardous in the light of the announced Service policy that rulings will "ordinarily" not be issued as to "the tax effect of the transfer where part of the consideration received by the transferors consists of bonds, debentures or any other evidences of indebtedness of the transferee", Rev.Proc. 64–31, 1964—2 Cum.Bull. 947, § 4.01.4, page 101 supra; and apparently rulings will never be issued on the question of "what will constitute stock or securities where part of the consideration received by the transferor consists of bonds, debentures or long-term notes of the transferee in an amount which, when compared to the capital stock of the corporation, gives rise to the question of a 'thin corporation'." Id. at § 3.01.10(a) page 100 supra.

D. CHOICE BETWEEN STOCK AND DEBT

As under corporation law, so under the tax laws a sharp distinction is drawn between debt and equity—and again, the comparison substantially favors debt. Without attempting to make a complete catalogue of the differences in tax treatment between debt and stock, the following review of the more important differences should serve to illustrate the range of issues which underlies any choice between the two.

1. DIFFERENCES AT THE CORPORATE LEVEL

Perhaps the best-known tax consideration bearing on the choice between debt and equity is the fact that the annual return on debt in the form of interest is deductible by the corporation, while dividends on stock (with the exception of certain public utility preferred stocks) are not. Also deductible as interest is any original issue discount incurred upon the issuance of the debt. The subject of original issue discount is a complex one, and will be considered in detail in Chapter 3. Suffice it here to observe that in the simple case where an obligation is issued for a price less than the face amount of the obligation, the difference constitutes discount and should be charged off ratably over the life of the obligation, Reg. § 1.61–12(c)(3); and the same may be true when debt obligations are issued in exchange for property rather than cash, to the extent that the face amount of the obligations exceeds the fair market value of the property. In the case of a taxable exchange of property for debt obligations, any discount on the obligations would be deducted from the face amount of the obligations to determine the amount realized, and hence the gain to be recognized, by the transferor; and the cost basis of the property received by the corporation would be measured in the same way.

Upon the repayment of a debt obligation, income from cancellation of indebtedness may arise if the debt is settled at less than face, or a loss may result from retirement at a premium. Apart from such factors, however, neither income nor earnings and profits are affected by the repayment of debt. As to stock, redemption is not normally a taxable event for the corporation, Reg. § 1.311–1(a), but a reduction in earnings and profits may result, §§ 312(a) and 312(e).

One other factor worth noting here is that the accumulation of corporate earnings to repay *bona fide* debt will generally not run afoul of the accumulated earnings tax, but accumulation to redeem stock may incur serious risks under that tax, as we shall see later.

2. DIFFERENCES TO THE HOLDER—ANNUAL RETURN AND GAIN UPON DISPOSITION

The most important difference between stock and debt from the holder's point of view is that the taxability of dividends as ordinary income depends upon whether they are covered by earnings and profits, whereas interest on debt constitutes income to the recipient in any event. Moreover, where the recipient is an individual, dividends are subject to a $100 exclusion, § 116, for which there is no counterpart for interest. If the recipient is a corporation, dividends are subject to an 85% intercorporate dividend deduction (which in some circumstances under the 1964 amendments may be 100%), § 243, while interest is fully taxable.

With regard to gain on a sale or exchange, both debt obligations (in whatever form, except for accounts receivable arising in the ordinary course of business) and stock would normally qualify as capital assets, so that gain would be capital if the holding period was satisfied. However, there is one qualification in the case of debt: if the obligations were originally issued at a discount of any substance, under § 1232(a)(2), the portion of gain equivalent to the original issue discount would be taxable as ordinary income.

One of the most important differences between stock and debt arises in connection with the treatment of payments made in retirement or redemption. As to debt obligations, no matter what their form, the receipt of payment is a return of capital to the extent of the holder's basis in the obligation. Moreover, for corporate debt evidenced by a written instrument, § 1232(a) treats payments in redemption as if they were received upon a sale or exchange of the instrument, so that gain will normally be capital, except to the extent of any original issue discount. Distributions in redemption of stock, however, run a serious risk of being taxed as a dividend under § 302, a subject which will be considered at length in Chapter 3.

3. DIFFERENCES TO THE HOLDER—TREATMENT OF INVESTMENT LOSS

a. Losses on Stock

In general, any loss on stock, whether incurred upon a sale or exchange, a redemption, or worthlessness, will be capital loss, long-term or short-term depending upon the holding period. There is, however, one very important exception—§ 1244, which provides ordinary loss treatment for up to $25,000 of loss ($50,000 on a joint return) on stock which qualifies under that section. To qualify as so-called "§ 1244 stock," the stock must be common stock of a "small business corporation," as defined in the statute, and must be offered pursuant to a plan adopted by the corporation after June 30, 1958. The plan must specify the period during which the stock will be offered, which period must end not later than two years after the adoption of the plan, and according to the regulations, § 1.1244(c)–(1)(c), the plan must be in writing. Rev.Rul. 66–67, 1966–12 I.R.B. 9, states that the minutes of a board of directors meeting can qualify as a § 1244 plan, if they "contain all of the required elements" of such a plan; but a resolution which did not limit the offering period for stock to two years, nor specify the maximum consideration which could be received for the stock, did not qualify.

Section 1244 stock can only be issued for money or other property, which excludes services; by special statutory definition, stock and securities are also excluded, which means among other things that stock issued upon the conversion of a security can not qualify. There is also one condition that can not be tested until the date of the loss on the stock: the corporation must not, for a period up to five years prior to the loss on the stock, have derived as much as 50% of its gross receipts from inactive sources such as dividends, rents and royalties (unless its total deductions exceeded its gross income).

The definition of a "small business corporation" turns entirely upon the amount invested in the corporation — the number of shareholders and classes of stock are irrelevant. To qualify, the corporation must meet both of the following tests at the time of the adoption of the plan: (1) the sum of the aggregate amount which may be offered under the plan and the aggregate amount of money and other property (taken into account at its basis to the corporation upon receipt, less any liabilities assumed or to which the property was subject) received by the corporation after June 30, 1958 for stock, or as a contribution to capital or paid-in surplus, must not exceed $500,000; and (2) the sum of the aggregate amount which may be offered under the plan plus the equity capital of the corporation (defined as the total amount of cash plus the *basis* of the other property of the corporation, less any liabilities, *exclusive of liabilities to shareholders*) must not exceed $1,000,000. In effect, then, the maximum amount of § 1244 stock which any corporation can have is the lesser of $500,000 and the excess of $1,000,000 over the corporation's equity capital to date.

Section 1244 contains some rather strict rules prohibiting overlapping stock offerings. First, at the time of the adoption of the plan to issue § 1244 stock the corporation must not be offering any other stock for any purpose, regardless of whether such other offering qualifies under § 1244. Thus any outstanding stock options, warrants or securities convertible into stock would have to be exercised or terminated before a valid § 1244 plan could be adopted. Second, once the plan has been adopted the corporation must not make any subsequent offering of stock of any kind until the offering under the plan has been completed; any other offering of stock after the adoption of a plan will prevent any stock thereafter issued under the plan from qualifying under § 1244, although stock previously issued under the plan is not affected. According to the regulations, § 1.1244(c)–1(h)(1), if any stock is issued under the plan for ineligible consideration, such as securities or services, that would constitute a subsequent offering which would disqualify any further stock issued under the plan from § 1244 treatment. Although the regulations do not say so, the logical consequence of this position may well be that no § 1244 stock can be issued under a plan which permits the issuance of any stock for ineligible consideration, since it is the offering of stock for ineligible consideration that is critical, not the issuance, and such offering may start at the very outset of the plan.

There may also be problems with the "common stock" requirement. Presumably, any express preference either in dividends or upon liquidation would be a disqualification. But particularly in connection with liquidation rights there may be arrangements which are arguably preferential in substance though not in form. For example, suppose that X acquires half of the common stock of a corporation for $90,000, while Y, who is expected to provide important services to the venture, is to receive the other half of the stock for $10,000. In order to take account of this substantial difference in the amount of capital invested, the parties might arrange for the creation of two classes of stock which would be identical except that upon liquidation the first $100,000 of assets would be allocated between the two classes in the ratio of 9 to 1; any excess over $100,000 would be distributed on a share for share basis. Or the parties might achieve the same effect by giving one class nine times as many shares as the other (accompanied by an appropriate allocation of voting power by classes rather than based on the number of shares), and then providing that upon liquidation the first $100,000 is to be distributed on a share for share basis, with any excess divided equally between the two classes. Would the class with the greater liquidation benefits qualify as "common stock" under § 1244?

Two other exceptions to capital loss treatment relate to investments in or by companies organized pursuant to the Small Business Investment Act of 1958, described briefly at page 189 infra. Section 1242 provides for ordinary loss on stock of a Small Business Investment Company, and § 1243 provides for ordinary loss on investments by such companies in convertible debentures or in stock acquired pursuant to conversion of such debentures.

b. Losses on Debt

In the case of a sale or exchange of a debt obligation (which includes, by virtue of § 1232, the retirement of an obligation evidenced by a written instrument), whether the loss is ordinary or capital will depend upon the character of the obligation in the hands of the taxpayer. Normally, for any taxpayer who is not a dealer a debt obligation, whatever its form, will constitute a capital asset under § 1221, unless it is a receivable acquired in the ordinary course of business, § 1221(4).

The treatment of loss upon worthlessness of a debt is a good deal more complicated. See generally, Redman, Bad Debts: Establishing Worthlessness; Effect of Security; Rules Applicable to Foreclosure and Repossession, 22 N.Y.U.Fed.Tax Inst. 315 (1964); Smith and Tovey, Federal Tax Treatment of Bad Debts and Worthless Securities (1964). If the debt obligation is evidenced by a written instrument which is either registered or in coupon form, it falls within the special definition of "security" in § 165(g)(2)(C), and any loss upon worthlessness is treated as if it arose from a sale or exchange of the obligation on the last day of the taxable year. If the obligation is not covered by § 165(g)(2)(C), the treatment of loss due to worthlessness is governed by § 166, dealing with bad debts. When such debt is held by a corporation, any loss due to worthlessness will be ordinary. But losses of an individual are subject to the distinction drawn in § 166 between business and non-business bad debts, with loss on the latter limited under § 166(d) to short-term capital loss treatment regardless of the holding period involved. Because of the great difficulty experienced by the lower federal courts in applying the distinction between business and non-business bad debts, particularly in cases involving advances by a taxpayer to a corporation in which he was also a stockholder, the Supreme Court finally had to take a hand in the matter:

WHIPPLE v. COMMISSIONER

Supreme Court of the United States, 1963.
373 U.S. 193, 83 S.Ct. 1168.

MR. JUSTICE WHITE delivered the opinion of the Court.[16]

Section [166(a)] of the Internal Revenue Code . . . provides for the deduction in full of worthless debts other than nonbusiness bad debts while § [166(d)] restricts nonbusiness bad debts to the treatment accorded losses on the sale of short-term capital assets. . . .

---

16. Portions of the opinion and all of the footnotes omitted.

The question before us is whether petitioner's activities in connection with several corporations in which he holds controlling interests can themselves be characterized as a trade or business so as to permit a debt owed by one of the corporations to him to be treated . . . as a "business" rather than a "nonbusiness" bad debt.

Prior to 1941 petitioner was a construction superintendent and an estimator for a lumber company but during that year and over the next several ones he was instrumental in forming and was a member of a series of partnerships engaged in the construction or construction supply business. In 1949 and 1950 he was an original incorporator of seven corporations, some of which were successors to the partnerships, and in 1951 he sold his interest in the corporations along with his equity in five others in the rental and construction business, the profit on the sales being reported as long-term capital gains. In 1951 and 1952 he formed eight new corporations, one of which was Mission Orange Bottling Co. of Lubbock, Inc., bought the stock of a corporation known as Mason Root Beer and acquired an interest in a related vending machine business. From 1951 to 1953 he also bought and sold land, acquired and disposed of a restaurant and participated in several oil ventures.

On April 25, 1951, petitioner secured a franchise from Mission Dry Corporation entitling him to produce, bottle, distribute and sell Mission beverages in various counties in Texas. Two days later he purchased the assets of a sole proprietorship in the bottling business and conducted that business pursuant to his franchise as a sole proprietorship. On July 1, 1951, though retaining the franchise in his own name, he sold the bottling equipment to Mission Orange . . . of which he owned approximately 80% of the shares outstanding. In 1952 he purchased land in Lubbock and erected a bottling plant thereon at a cost of $43,601 and then leased the plant to Mission Orange for a 10-year term at a prescribed rental. Depreciation was taken on the new bottling plant on petitioner's individual tax returns for 1952 and 1953.

Petitioner made sizable cash advances to Mission Orange in 1952 and 1953, and on December 1, 1953, the balance due him, including $25,502.50 still owing from his sale of the bottling assets to the corporation in July 1951, totaled $79,489.76. On December 15, 1953, petitioner advanced to Mission Orange an additional $48,000 to pay general creditors and on the same day received a transfer of the assets of the corporation with a book value of $70,414.66. The net amount owing to petitioner ultimately totaled $56,975.10, which debt became worthless in 1953 and is in issue here. During 1951, 1952 and 1953 Mission Orange made no payments of interest, rent or salary to petitioner although he did receive such income from some of his other corporations.

Petitioner deducted the $56,975.10 debt due from Mission Orange as a business bad debt in computing his 1953 taxable income. The

Commissioner, claiming the debt was a nonbusiness bad debt, assessed deficiencies. The Tax Court, after determining that petitioner in 1953 was not in the business of organizing, promoting, managing or financing corporations, of bottling soft drinks or of general financing and money lending, sustained the deficiencies. A divided Court of Appeals affirmed, . . . and upon a claim of conflict among the Courts of Appeals, we granted certiorari.

I.

The concept of engaging in a trade or business as distinguished from other activities pursued for profit is not new to the tax laws. As early as 1916, Congress, by providing for the deduction of losses incurred in a trade or business separately from those sustained in other transactions entered into for profit, § 5, Revenue Act of 1916, c. 463, 39 Stat. 756, distinguished the broad range of income or profit producing activities from those satisfying the narrow category of trade or business. This pattern has been followed elsewhere in the Code. See, e. g., [§§ 162 and 212]. It is not surprising, therefore, that we approach the problem of applying that term here with much writing upon the slate.

In Burnet v. Clark, 287 U.S. 410 (1932), the long-time president and principal stockholder of a corporation in the dredging business endorsed notes for the company which he was forced to pay. These amounts were deductible by him in the current year under the then existing law, but to carry over the loss to later years it was necessary for it to have resulted from the operation of a trade or business regularly carried on by the taxpayer. The Board of Tax Appeals denied the carry-over but the Court of Appeals for the District of Columbia held otherwise on the grounds that the taxpayer devoted all of his time and energies to carrying on the business of dredging and that he was compelled by circumstances to endorse the company's notes in order to supply it with operating funds. This Court in turn reversed and reinstated the judgment of the Board of Tax Appeals, since "[t]he respondent was employed as an officer of the corporation; the business which he conducted for it was not his own. . . . The unfortunate endorsements were no part of his ordinary business, but occasional transactions intended to preserve the value of his investment in capital shares. . . . A corporation and its stockholders are generally to be treated as separate entities." . . .

The question [of whether a taxpayer's activities in investing and managing his own estate constituted a trade or business] was squarely up for decision in Higgins v. Commissioner, 312 U.S. 212 (1941). Here the taxpayer devoted his time and energies to managing a sizable portfolio of securities and sought to deduct his expenses incident thereto as incurred in a trade or business under § [162]. The Board of Tax Appeals, the Court of Appeals for the Second Circuit and this Court held that the evidence was insufficient to establish taxpayer's activities as those of carrying on a trade or business. "The petitioner merely kept records and collected interest and dividends from his securities, through managerial attention for his investments. No matter how large the estate or how continuous or extended the work required may be, such facts are not sufficient as a matter of law to permit the courts to reverse the decision of the Board." 312 U.S., at 218.

Such was the state of the cases in this Court when Congress, in 1942, amended the Internal Revenue Code in respects crucial to this case. In response to the Higgins case and to give relief to Higgins-type taxpayers, . . . [§ 162] was amended not by disturbing the Court's definition of "trade or business" but by following the pattern that had been established since 1916 of "[enlarging] the category of incomes with reference to which expenses were deductible," . . . to include expenses incurred in the production of income.

At the same time, to remedy what it deemed the abuses of permitting any worthless debt to be fully deducted, as was the case prior to this time, . . . Congress restricted the full deduction under § [166] to bad debts incurred in the taxpayer's trade or business and provided that "nonbusiness" bad debts were to be deducted as short-term capital losses. . . . The upshot was that Congress broadened § [162] to reach income producing activities not amounting to a trade or business and conversely narrowed § [166] to exclude bad debts arising from these same sources.

The 1942 amendment of § [166] therefore, . . . was intended to accomplish far more than to deny full deductibility to the worthless debts of family and friends. It was designed to make full deductibility of a bad debt turn upon its proximate connection with activities which the tax laws recognized as a trade or business, a concept which falls far short of reaching every income or profit making activity.

II.

Petitioner, therefore, must demonstrate that he is engaged in a trade or business, and lying at the heart of his claim is the issue upon which the lower courts have divided and which brought the case here: That where a taxpayer furnishes regular services to one or many corporations, an independent trade or business of the taxpayer has been shown. But against the background of the 1942 amendments and the decisions of this Court in the [cases like Burnet and Higgins], petitioner's claim must be rejected.

Devoting one's time and energies to the affairs of a corporation is not of itself, and without more, a trade or business of the person so engaged. Though such activities may produce income, profit or gain in the form of dividends or enhancement in the value of an investment, this return is distinctive to the process of investing and is generated by the successful operation of the corporation's business as distinguished from the trade or business of the taxpayer himself. When the only return is that of an investor, the taxpayer has not satisfied his burden of demonstrating that he is engaged in a trade or business since investing is not a trade or business and the return to the taxpayer, though substantially the product of his services, legally arises not from his own trade or business but from that of the corporation. Even if the taxpayer demonstrates an independent trade or business of his own, care must be taken to distinguish bad debt losses arising from his own business and those actually arising from activities peculiar to an investor concerned with, and participating in, the conduct of the corporate business.

If full-time service to one corporation does not alone amount to a trade or business, which it does not, it is difficult to understand how the same service to many corporations would suffice. To be sure, the presence of more than one corporation might lend support to a finding that the taxpayer was engaged in a regular course of promoting corporations for a fee or commission, . . . or for a profit on their sale, . . . but in such cases there is compensation other than the normal investor's return, income received directly for his own services rather than indirectly through the corporate enterprise, and the principles of [cases like Burnet and Higgins] are therefore not offended. On the other hand, since the Tax Court found, and the petitioner does not dispute, that there was no intention here of developing the corporations as going businesses for sale to customers in the ordinary course, the case before us inexorably rests upon the claim that one who actively engages in serving his own corporations for the purpose of creating future income through those enterprises is in a trade or business. That argument is untenable in light of [the aforementioned cases], and we reject it. Absent substantial additional evidence, furnishing management and other services to corporations for a reward not different from that flowing to an investor in those corporations is not a trade or business under § [166(d)]. We are, therefore, fully in agreement with this aspect of the decision below.

III.

With respect to the other claims by petitioner, we are unwilling to disturb the determinations of the Tax Court, affirmed by the Court of Appeals, that petitioner was not engaged in the business of money lending, of financing corporations, of bottling soft drinks or of any combination of these since we cannot say they are clearly erroneous.

. . . Nor need we consider or deal with those cases which hold that working as a corporate executive for a salary may be a trade or business. . . . Petitioner made no such claim in either the Tax Court or the Court of Appeals and, in any event, the contention would be groundless on this record since it was not shown that he has collected a salary from Mission Orange or that he was owed one. Moreover, there is no proof (which might be difficult to furnish where the taxpayer is the sole or dominant stockholder) that the loan was necessary to keep his job or was otherwise proximately related to maintaining his trade or business as an employee. . . .

We are more concerned, however, with the evidence as to petitioner's position as the owner and lessor of the real estate and bottling plant in which Mission Orange did business. The United States does not dispute the fact that in this regard petitioner was engaged in a trade or business but argues that the loss from the worthless debt was not proximately related to petitioner's real estate business. While the Tax Court and the Court of Appeals dealt separately with assertions relating to other phases of petitioner's case, we do not find that either court disposed of the possibility that the loan to Mission Orange, a tenant of petitioner, was incurred in petitioner's business of being a landlord. We take no position whatsoever on the merits of this matter but remand the case for further proceedings in the Tax Court.

Vacated and remanded.

MR. JUSTICE DOUGLAS dissents.

NOTE ON BUSINESS BAD DEBTS

1. Is the Taxpayer Engaged in Business?

In a footnote to its opinion in Whipple the Court expressly disapproved a number of prior lower court decisions, most of which had rested primarily upon a finding of so-called "promoter" status, that is, sufficient activity in promoting and financing various incorporated ventures to constitute a business separate and distinct from the businesses carried on by the corporations themselves. For example, in Campbell v. Commissioner, 11 T.C. 510 (1948), the taxpayer had prevailed upon a showing that he had organized, financed and operated twelve separate corporations in the retail coat business. It would appear that the Whipple opinion intended to lay the promoter approach permanently to rest, except for taxpayers engaged in promoting ventures for compensation.

As a matter of technical construction of the statute, and perhaps in terms of sound tax administration as well, this result standing alone seems unobjectionable. It becomes less clear, however, with the Court's apparent acceptance of the view that leasing property to a corporation does constitute a separate trade or business. It is not immediately apparent why a taxpayer who rents a single piece of property to a corporation is carrying on a business, while the taxpayer who lends funds, even to several corporations, is not. Although lending money is normally a more passive activity than leasing property, the distinction between the two is at most a matter of degree, and may even disappear entirely in the case of a "net lease" where the lessee assumes all responsibility for the property and the lessor simply collects rent. To be sure, continuous activity in the leasing of property can constitute a business by any standard; and indeed equipment leasing has recently become a substantial industry. But the same is true of money lending, and the question remains why so much more should be required to establish a money-lending business than a leasing business. The practical impact of such a distinction may be that any well-advised taxpayer who decides to incorporate a business will retain some of the operating assets in his own hands and lease them to the corporation—a practice which might have some other significant tax advantages as well. See page 149 infra.

Another footnote to the Whipple opinion cited two cases, Maloney v. Spencer, 172 F.2d 638 (9th Cir. 1949), and Dorminey v. Commissioner, 26 T.C. 940 (1956), as apparent examples of the "substantial additional evidence" needed to establish a separate business for the taxpayer, in order to justify business bad debt treatment. In Maloney the taxpayer had originally operated three vegetable processing plants as an individual, but he thereafter incorporated three corporations and leased the plants to them. Under the terms of the leases, which of course were not at arms' length, the taxpayer was also required to provide "adequate financing for the needs of" the corporations. Pursuant to this requirement the taxpayer made advances to the corporations, and the court permitted business bad-debt treatment for these advances upon the finding that he was engaged in the business of "acquiring, owning, expanding and leasing food processing plants." Notice that the court in Maloney did not particularly stress the "leasing" business as such in reaching its decision; rather, the court seemed to be following the "promoter" approach, and indeed among the cases relied upon was one of the promoter decisions expressly disapproved by the Supreme Court in Whipple.

In Dorminey v. Commissioner, the taxpayer was engaged in business as a wholesale produce dealer, both as a sole proprietor and through several wholly-owned corporations. He customarily made advances to a number of different enterprises which were either customers or suppliers of his produce business. The taxpayer controlled some of the concerns to which he made advances, while in others he had no financial interest at all. The advances in question had been made to a corporation which the taxpayer had organized to engage in the business of importing bananas because of his difficulty in obtaining a steady supply of bananas for his produce business. The new corporation ran into financial difficulties and was forced to borrow from the taxpayer as well as outsiders. By the time of the ultimate failure of the new corporation, the taxpayer had advanced almost $16,000. The Tax Court held that these advances had been made to assure a supply of bananas for the taxpayer's sole proprietorship, and accordingly allowed business bad-debt treatment. But here again it is troublesome to note that in deciding Dorminey the Tax Court seemed to rely primarily upon "promoter" cases, including two which were expressly disapproved in Whipple.

2. Is the Debt Sufficiently Related to an Admitted Business?

One factor which the Maloney and Dorminey cases have in common is that the taxpayer was carrying on an active business as a sole proprietor, in addition to his interests in controlled corporations. In such cases the taxpayer is admittedly carrying on a business personally, and if his advances to other enterprises are sufficiently related to his admitted individual business there is no need to find any other basis to sustain business bad-debt treatment. This view received a substantial boost in the post-Whipple case of Rubin v. Commissioner, 22 T.C.M. 1089 (1963), where the taxpayer was engaged as a sole proprietor in the business of distributing various types of products to supermarkets. He organized a new corporation to manufacture sportswear for sale to supermarkets, and made advances to the new enterprise. The court held that these loans by the taxpayer were designed to help his own sales business and were accordingly entitled to business bad-debt treatment.

The Whipple opinion sheds very little light on the question of when an advance to another enterprise is sufficiently related to an admitted business of the taxpayer, since it contains no guidance as to the standards to be applied in making the determination. While both the Maloney and Dorminey cases did find the necessary relationship, those cases were not cited for this proposition, and in any event neither case contains any useful analysis of this issue.

At bottom the question of whether a debt is sufficiently related to the taxpayer's business would seem to depend upon whether the advances were primarily intended to further the taxpayer's individual business or to support and enhance his interest in the corporation to which the advances were made. Obviously, the line between these two may be a very fine one. In Gulledge v. Commissioner, 249 F.2d 225 (4th Cir. 1957), the taxpayer was engaged in the business of operating a peanut farm. He joined with other peanut growers in organizing a corporation to establish a processing plant in their area, for the purpose of facilitating the sale of their crops. The taxpayer and his associates furnished the new corporation with equity capital and also advanced additional sums. Upon the failure of the new corporation, the taxpayer claimed a business bad debt for the advances, which the court denied:

> . . . It is true that the taxpayer and the other stockholders were induced to contribute to the capital of the corporation in the hope that the establishment of a peanut mill in their neighborhood would enable them to secure a better price for their peanuts, and hence it may be said in a broad sense that the business of the farmers and the business of the corporation was related. It does not follow, however, that the business of the corporation was incidental to the business of the taxpayer and that the loss of the money loaned by him to the corporation was incurred in the operation of his farms. The two businesses were separate and distinct. The taxpayer owned the one directly while in the other he had merely the interest of a stockholder. The corporation was not merely a department of the business of his farm. Not only was the corporation a separate business and taxable entity, but it was set up to purchase and process not only the taxpayer's crop but also the peanuts of all the other growers in the locality; and it was formed in the expectation that it would return a profit to its founders.

In Garlove v. Commissioner, 24 T.C.M. 1049 (1965), the court allowed business bad-debt treatment to a lawyer for an advance to a corporation in which he was a minority stockholder, director, and inactive officer. The court found that the lawyer had made the loan in order to help support a good client, as well as to accommodate the two principal stockholders of the corporation who were also regular clients. The court regarded it as unreasonable to infer that the taxpayer would have advanced $15,000 merely to protect his investment in the corporation, which amounted to only $7,000. Compare Tobey v. Commissioner, 22 T.C.M. 1157 (1963), where business bad-debt treatment was denied for the advances made to a corporation by a lawyer who had been instrumental in developing, promoting and financing this and other enterprises but did not own a majority of the stock of any of them. The court relied upon the Whipple decision, saying

> The plain teaching emerging from the [Whipple case] is, that in order to prevail in the instant case, the petitioner must show that he intended to develop the business enterprises in which he engaged as going businesses for sale to customers in the ordinary course. But, petitioner does not even claim to have had such an intention . . ..

---

c. Loss on Shareholder Guaranty of Corporate Debt

As a result of the decision in Putnam v. Commissioner, 352 U.S. 82 (1956), a shareholder who must pay an obligation of his corporation which he has guaranteed is regarded as then standing, through subrogation, in a creditor position vis-a-vis the corporation. Upon the failure to recover from the corporation, the shareholder's loss is treated as resulting from the worthlessness of the debt due him from the corporation. Thus, the foregoing cases dealing with when a business bad-debt deduction is available for advances to a corporation are equally applicable to losses on a guaranty. See Holtz v. Commissioner, 256 F.2d 865 (9th Cir. 1958), rejecting business bad-debt treatment for payments on a guaranty despite the fact that the taxpayer had either made or guaranteed some 250 loans for four corporations which he owned. On the other hand, amounts paid by a shareholder-guarantor for release from liability under a guaranty at a time when the corporation was not in any danger of insolvency have been held to be deductible as an ordinary loss under § 165(c)(2). Shea v. Commissioner, 36 T.C. 577 (1961), affirmed per curiam, 327 F.2d 1002 (5th Cir. 1964).

---

d. Attempts to Arrange Character of Loss on Liquidation

The differences between stock and debt as to deductibility of losses have led to some attempts at juggling by taxpayers. In Rowan v. United States, 219 F.2d 51 (5th Cir. 1955), the stockholders of a corporation whose liabilities exceeded its assets planned to liquidate it. However, the stockholders had also made open account advances to the corporation which they feared the Commissioner might treat as contributions to capital, thus giving them only a long-term capital loss on the advances. Accordingly, they subscribed to new stock, had the corporation pay its debts to them with the resulting cash, and then liquidated the corporation 20 days later, claiming a short-term capital loss on the new stock. The District Court disregarded the new stock as having no business purpose and held that the advances did constitute capital contributions, thus allowing only a long-term capital loss. The Court of

Appeals, however, made the juggling unnecessary by holding that the advances qualified as debt, though non-business, so that the stockholders were entitled to short-term capital loss anyway.

W. D. Haden Co. v. Commissioner, 165 F.2d 588 (5th Cir. 1948), involved an attempt by a parent corporation to obtain ordinary loss treatment for losses realized upon the liquidation of its subsidiary. The parent owned the preferred stock of the subsidiary and had also made advances of over $80,000. The subsidiary purported to use $60,000 of the assets remaining after the payment of all other creditors to redeem the preferred stock, which did not leave enough to pay the full amount of the indebtedness to the parent. The parent sought to deduct the unpaid balance as a bad-debt ordinary loss, but the deduction was disallowed on the ground that the debt obligation ranked ahead of the preferred stock and therefore the assets of the subsidiary should have been applied to the debt first.

E. LIMITATIONS ON THE AMOUNT OF STOCKHOLDER-OWNED DEBT

As might be expected, the substantial tax advantages enjoyed by debt has placed considerable strain on the line between debt and equity. The problem is particularly acute in the area of stockholder-owned debt since as a practical matter the stockholders may well be in position to dictate the form in which to cast their contributions to the corporation, and often it is clear that some debt has been created primarily on account of the potential tax advantages. In such cases, there is much to be said for treating the stockholder-owned debt as additional equity for tax purposes even where there has been the most meticulous compliance with the formal requirements for the creation of debt. On the other hand, it is certainly possible for stockholders to make loans to their corporation which will be recognized as valid corporate debt for tax purposes. As the following materials indicate, the test for determining when stockholder advances will be accepted as valid debt is far from clear—but it is worthwhile attempting to discern what criteria are presently being employed. For an excellent review of the authorities, see Goldstein, Corporate Indebtedness to Shareholders: "Thin Capitalization" and Related Problems, **16 Tax L.Rev. 1 (1960).**

1. FORM OF THE OBLIGATION—HYBRID SECURITIES

Before reaching the special tax notions relating to stockholder debt, there may well be a threshold question as to whether the particular instrument constitutes debt even under corporate law, when the instrument is a "hybrid," that is, one having some of the formal characteristics of both debt and stock. In John Kelley Co. v. Commissioner, 326 U.S. 521, 66 S.Ct. 299 (1946), the terms of the "income debenture bonds" there involved included interest at 8%, non-cumulative, and payable only if earned; twenty-year maturity; subordination to all creditors, but priority over stockholders; and no right to participate in management. The companion case of Talbot Mills v. Commissioner, involved "registered notes" calling for interest ranging from 2% to 10%, depending upon the amount of earnings; payment of the interest could be deferred, but it was cumulative; the term of the notes was 15 years; and they could be subordinated to other creditors. The test stated by the Tax Court and ultimately approved by the Supreme Court was as follows:

> The determining factors are usually listed as the name given to the certificates, the presence or absence of maturity date, the source of the payments, the right to enforce the payment of principal and interest, participation in management, status equal to or inferior to that of regular corporate creditors, and intent of the parties.

Applying this approach the Tax Court classified the securities in the Kelley case as debt, and those in Talbot Mills as stock, and the Supreme Court, deferring to the expertise of the Tax Court under the Dobson rule, approved both decisions.

The frequent use of hybrid securities in the earlier cases seems to have represented an effort to obtain the tax benefits of debt classification while avoiding such non-tax burdens of debt as a fixed interest rate or a fixed maturity date. To be sure, such instruments sometimes result from the demands of a prospective investor-lender — for example, for a minimum guaranteed annual return plus a further participation based upon earnings. But generally speaking, particularly in the case of stockholder-held debt, there is no difficulty in complying with the formal requisites of debt, especially since the shareholders can always forbear to press their strict legal rights as creditors. Accordingly, taxpayers have by and large abandoned the use of these ambiguous hybrid instruments in favor of formal debt instruments carrying fixed interest payments, a fixed maturity date, no voting rights, and limited, if any, subordination to other creditors. But this merely served to move the debt-equity battleground to new terrain, as it became recognized that even the most meticulous compliance with the formal requisites of debt would not preclude treating purported stockholder advances as really amounting to additional capital contributions.

2. INADEQUATE CAPITALIZATION—RATIO OF DEBT TO EQUITY

As on the corporate side, so for tax purposes both the absolute size of the capital contribution and its relative size in comparison with the amount of any purported stockholder debt are important factors. In the John Kelley Co. case, supra, the Supreme Court had observed that since "material amounts of capital were invested in stock, we need not consider the effect of extreme situations such as nominal stock investments and an obviously excessive debt structure." This statement started many courts on a search for debt-equity ratios in an effort to find some objective basis for determining how much of their total contribution to a corporation stockholders should be permitted to be set up as debt. This gave rise to the term "thin incorporation," meaning a corporation whose relative equity contribution was too small.

Since the ratio of debt to equity in the companion Talbot Mills case was 4:1 and the Supreme Court had apparently not regarded that as an "extreme situation," that ratio was often thought to mark the boundary of a "safe area." However, the court decisions were far from consistent, and the acceptability of a particular ratio often seemed to depend upon the absolute size of the actual equity investment. See generally, Caplin, The Caloric Count of a Thin Incorporation, 17 N.Y.U.Fed.Tax Inst. 771 (1959), 43 Marq.L.Rev. 31 (1959).

In addition, there were a number of problems in the computation of the ratio. For example, while the debt component does not normally include outside debt, the result may be different where the outside debt is guaranteed by stockholders. See J. A. Maurer, Inc. v. Commissioner, 30 T.C. 1273, 1290, n. 2 (1958). On the other hand, in measuring the equity component apparently the actual value of the consideration contributed for stock, including any intangible items such as the goodwill associated with a going business, may and perhaps must be taken into account. E. g., Miller's Estate v. Commissioner, 239 F.2d 729 (9th Cir. 1956).

Today it appears that the debt-equity ratio simply constitutes one factor to be considered along with all the other circumstances of the case. And some courts have apparently rejected the debt-equity ratio entirely. In Rowan v. United States, 219 F.2d 51 (5th Cir. 1955), the court, in sustaining open account advances by shareholders as valid debt, commented as follows:

> It would obviously work an unwarranted interference by the courts in ordinary and perfectly proper business procedures for us to say that there can be established, as a matter of hindsight, a ratio of stockholder owned debt to the capital of the debtor corporation. No stockholder could safely advance money to strengthen the faltering steps of his corporation

(which, of course, may be greatly to the benefit of other creditors) if he is faced with the danger of having the Commissioner, with the backing of the courts, say, "he had no right to launch a corporate business without investing in it all the money it needed, and investing it in the way that is most disadvantageous to himself, both as relates to taxation and as to other creditors."

---

3. PRO RATA HOLDING OF DEBT AND STOCK

Obviously, the most troublesome situations in the debt-equity area involve pro rata holdings of stock and debt, since it is here that the choice between debt and stock has the least independent, non-tax significance and is therefore most likely to have been motivated by hoped-for tax advantages. Accordingly, the courts have been quickest to deny debt classification when the purported debt obligations are held pro rata by the stockholders. In 1432 Broadway Corporation v. Commissioner, 4 T.C. 1158 (1945), aff'd per curiam, 160 F.2d 885 (2d Cir. 1947), where a family group had contributed rental property and cash to a new corporation in exchange for over a million dollars in debentures and a few shares of no-par stock, the Tax Court put it this way:

> The entire contribution was a capital contribution rather than a loan, but by the form adopted the corporation was in a position to feign that its rent income was used as a means of discharging its debenture obligation, giving it a tax deduction, and not as a distribution of dividends, which would not be deductible. . . . The distribution of the rent income, whether called interest or principal on debentures or dividends on shares, would go to the same persons in the same proportions, since each had the same proportionate number of both, and it would matter not to them whether the distribution was called dividends or interest. But to the corporation on the accrual method it mattered materially whether the distribution was called interest, thus being deductible in computing its taxable net income, even though not actually paid, or dividend, which would be without a favorable tax effect. . . . It is idle to argue that the debentures were transferable and must therefore be judged separately from the shares, for they were issued to the same persons as held the shares, and in the same proportions, and they were not in fact transferred. . . .

On the other hand, pro rata holding of debt obligations is not an absolute barrier to recognition of debt status. E. g., Wilshire & Western Sandwiches, Inc. v. Commissioner, 175 F.2d 718 (9th Cir. 1949); Spreckles v. Commissioner, 8 T.C.M. 1113 (1949) (debt held by sole stockholder). Conversely, a disproportionate holding of debt and stock will not prevent the debt from being classified as additional equity if other factors so warrant. In Reed v. Commissioner, 242 F.2d 334 (2d Cir. 1957), the majority shareholder, owning 165 shares, advanced $130,000 over several years while the minority stockholder, owning 135 shares, made no advances. Apparently only some $300 was paid in for the stock. In denying debt classification to the advances by the majority stockholder the court said:

> It is true that the advances made by the taxpayer were not proportionate to his stockholdings,—a condition which, if present, often affords cumulative support for a finding that the advances constituted contributions of risk capital. But here the amounts paid in for capital stock were so small as to be purely nominal and the taxpayer's contribution in cash was balanced by highly skilled services contributed by other stockholders. In such a case, neither reason nor authority requires that for purposes of federal tax law advances by a stockholder shall constitute risk capital only if contributed in proportion to existing stockholdings.

Similarly, in Broadway Drive-In Theater v. United States, 220 F. Supp. 707 (E.D.Mo.1963), the court dismissed the fact that one of the four principal stockholders made no advances to the corporation with the comment that he "was in the position of contributing managerial services as he was president and had previous experience in operating drive-in theaters."

Quite apart from the presence of any such services element, the courts have regularly refused to sustain purported debt simply because it was disproportionate to the stock holdings. Thus in The Colony, Inc. v. Commissioner, 26 T.C. 30 (1956), other issues in 244 F.2d 75 (6th Cir. 1957), 357 U.S. 28 (1958), the court remarked that the disproportionate holdings of stock and debt were entitled to "no greater weight than if petitioner had issued disproportionate amounts of common and preferred stock." Accord, Gale v. Commissioner, 15 T.C.M. 518 (1956). In Schine Chain Theaters Inc. v. Commissioner, 22 T.C.M. 488 (1963), aff'd per curiam, 331 F.2d 849 (2d Cir. 1964), the court refused debt classification to advances of over a million dollars made by the holder of 55% of the stock of the corporation, although the five holders of the remaining 45% made no advances at all. Similarly, in Diamond Brothers Co. v. Commissioner, 322 F.2d 725 (3d Cir. 1963), substantial advances made by the holder of 50% of the corporation's stock were denied debt treatment although the other stockholders had not made any advances. The Court of Appeals approved the Tax Court's findings "that the parties intended that the advances would be repaid only if [the corporation] prospered, that the funds advanced were to be put at the risk of [the corporation's] business, and that petitioner hoped primarily for an increase in the value of its stock holdings in [the corporation] rather than for repayment," and held that accordingly the advances were really an investment rather than a loan.

Can debt classification be denied when advances are made by one who is not a stockholder at all? In Gloucester Ice & Cold Storage Co. v. Commissioner, 298 F.2d 183 (1st Cir. 1962), the court seemed to think that a negative answer was required. Yet in The Motel Co. v. Commissioner, 22 T.C.M. 825 (1963), affirmed, 340 F.2d 445 (2d Cir. 1965), debt classification was denied for an initial advance of $100,000 by a non-stockholder—but the putative creditor was the father of the principal stockholder and took an active role in the affairs of the corporation, and the total equity capital was only $10,000. A later advance by the father of over $200,000 was recognized as bona fide debt, largely because after the earlier $100,000 advance was treated as equity the corporation had a substantial equity investment. In Merlo Builders, Inc. v. Commissioner, 23 T.C.M. 185 (1964), the court denied debt classification for advances of $50,000 to each of three corporations by persons who were unrelated to the stockholders of the corporations. The court noted that the corporations had only a nominal equity capital, and found that the purported creditors were the real entrepreneurs in the enterprise, so that their purported loans should be regarded as investments.

If debt held pro rata by common stockholders is classified as equity, does the status of the debt change if it is transferred to a person outside the common stock group? Texoma Supply Co. v. Commissioner, 17 T.C.M. 147 (1958), seemed to assume that equity classification would continue. How about the converse situation, where the stock and debt of a corporation are originally issued to different persons but subsequently the same party acquires both. In Jewell Ridge Coal Corp. v. Commissioner, 318 F.2d 695 (4th Cir. 1963), the court stated that when the same people acquired both a controlling stock interest in a corporation and also some of its debt obligations, the purchase of the obligations could be treated as an additional capital investment, thus precluding debt classification.

4. THE SEARCH FOR NEW STANDARDS: "INTENT" AND "RISK"

With the recognition that neither ratios nor the relationship of debt to stockholdings were conclusive, other standards for distinguishing between a capital investment and a bona fide loan were sought. Some courts moved toward more subjective factors, such as whether the taxpayer intended to treat his debt claims as an outside creditor would. Thus in Gooding Amusement Co., Inc. v. Commissioner, 23 T.C. 408 (1954), aff'd 236 F.2d 159 (6th Cir. 1956), where all of the debt and stock of a corporation was held pro rata by a husband, wife and infant daughter, but the ratio was only about 1:1, the Tax Court put it this way:

> It is, in our opinion, unreasonable to ascribe to the husband petitioner, F. E. Gooding, an intention at the time of the issuance of the notes ever to enforce payment of his notes, especially if to do so would either impair the credit rating of the corporation, cause it to borrow from other sources the funds necessary to meet the payments, or bring about its dissolution. . . . The fact that the majority of the notes here involved, all of which have long since matured, have not been paid lends corroboration to our finding that at no time material to our consideration did the noteholders intend to enforce payment of their notes or assert the rights of bona fide creditors. If the state of mind of the noteholders was as above indicated, it is apparent that their position with respect to the amount represented by the principal of the notes was akin to that of the ordinary shareholder, who understands that his investment is subject to the risks of the venture and prior claims of creditors. The incidence here of the subordination of the Goodings' notes to the claims of others is too marked to permit us to find that a bona fide debtor-creditor relationship was established between the corporation and its controlling stockholders.

However, it should be noted that a switch to emphasis upon the taxpayer's intention does not necessarily mean a retreat from objective tests to purely subjective criteria. Obviously, as the Gooding excerpt indicates, the best clue to the likely intention of the parties may come from an objective appraisal of the financial position of the enterprise. In making such an appraisal, it is to be recalled that traditionally debt is expected to be more secure than equity — that is of course why the return on debt is correspondingly lower than on equity. Hence there is much to be said for the view that the riskier the investment, the more it takes on the character of a capital contribution rather than a loan.

Moreover, at least for any relatively small business, which is an inherently risky proposition, any outside creditor would normally insist that the debtor be able to repay the loan fairly promptly, which means that some source other than long-term future profits must be available. After all, if a creditor must depend upon the realization of future profits just like an equity investor, there is no reason for him to settle for a smaller return than that accorded to an equity investor. Therefore, any "advance" which could not be expected to be repaid in a relatively short time may fairly be regarded as "at the risk of the business," and hence a capital investment rather than a bona fide loan.

This relationship between the riskiness of a purported advance and the taxpayer's intention with respect to it is nicely illustrated in the series of opinions stemming from Gilbert v. Commissioner, 248 F.2d 399 (2d Cir. 1957), which for variety of judicial expressions on the debt-equity issue has never been equalled. The corporation involved in that litigation was organized by Gilbert and Borden in June, 1946, with an authorized capital stock consisting of 1000 shares of $100 par preferred and 20,000 shares of $1 par common. Borden paid $40,000 cash for 4,000 shares of common, and Gilbert acquired 4,000 shares of common in exchange for his going business which was valued by the directors at $40,000, including approximately $35,000 for goodwill. It was understood between the two stockholders that the financing of the corporation "would be generally on about a 50-50 basis."

Most of the available cash was promptly used to purchase the stock of other enterprises which the corporation took over. Shortly after the corporation was organized a bank loan was obtained "in order to provide funds with which to conduct the operation of the corporation," and both Gilbert and Borden individually guaranteed the note and also pledged some personally-owned securities as collateral. Other personally-owned securities were loaned at various times by Gilbert and Borden to the corporation and its subsidiaries for use as collateral in obtaining loans from outside sources. In addition, throughout the period from the corporation's inception until it was liquidated at the end of the taxable year 1948, Gilbert, his wife, and Borden made substantial advances to the corporation "for necessary operating expenses." These loans were normally evidenced by demand promissory notes, with interest at 3½%, payable semi-annually. While the amount of the advances of the parties varied from time to time, in general an approximate equality was maintained between the Gilberts and Borden.

During its existence the corporation was actively engaged in the prosecution of a number of different ventures, but none of them worked out very well, and the company never made any profit. No interest was ever paid on any of the notes issued to the parties, nor was any interest credited on the books until shortly before the end. The corporation failed in 1948, and in their joint return for that year the Gilberts claimed a bad debt deduction for their outstanding advances of approximately $80,000. The Tax Court held that the advances made by the husband "were, in reality, contributions of risk capital and did not give rise to bona fide debts on the part of the corporation." As to Mrs. Gilbert, the Tax Court found her advances to be bona fide loans (but deductible only as non-business bad debts under the predecessor of § 166(d) of the 1954 Code). Only Mr. Gilbert appealed.

In remanding the case to the Tax Court, the Court of Appeals for the Second Circuit delivered three separate opinions. Judge Medina, in the primary opinion, ruled that a remand was necessary because the Tax Court had failed to state the reasons for its conclusion that Gilbert's advances did not give rise to bona fide debts. In Judge Medina's view, the critical issue under the tax law was whether there was a reasonable expectation of repayment regardless of the success of the venture, or whether instead the advances were actually placed at the risk of the business — in other words, the degree of risk involved. Judge Medina urged that the risk factor was really at bottom in the other factors which had been stressed in previous decisions. Thus inadequate original capitalization makes any subsequent advance extremely risky; an agreement to keep loans proportional to stockholdings suggests a lack of confidence that the loans will be repaid; and the question of whether outsiders would be willing to make such advances plainly turns upon the degree of risk involved. Judge Medina also ruled that neither the taxpayer's intention that the advances should be loans, on the one hand, nor his motive to minimize taxes, on the other, should be regarded as crucial.

Judge Waterman, after expressing agreement with Judge Medina's approach, added some further observations, particularly with reference to the Commissioner's contention that the corporation had been inadequately capitalized from the start. In his view, the "thin corporation" standard was applicable only in "extreme situations such as nominal stock investments and an obviously excessive debt structure"; once it was established that the parties' equity investment was more than nominal, "the means by which the corporation's activities are financed is a matter to be handled in whatever way seems most advantageous to it." For Judge Waterman, this left only two factors supporting the conclusion of the Tax Court: (1) that the advances were made in proportion to the equity investments of the parties, and (2) that the advances had been continuously made without regard to normal creditor safeguards under the circumstances. He concluded that the question of whether these factors were sufficient to preclude characterization of the advances as loans for income tax purposes should be answered by the Tax Court in the first instance.

Judge Learned Hand dissented on the ground that the opinions of the majority still left the proper test undefined, because they did not state the facts that should be determinative. For him, the critical question was whether the taxpayer had entered into a transaction which did not appreciably affect his beneficial interests except to reduce his taxes, in which event the transaction should be disregarded for tax purposes. Accordingly, he proposed the following statement of the applicable test, under which the taxpayer would have the burden of proving that he qualified:

"When the petitioners decided to make their advances in the form of debts, rather than of capital advances, did they suppose that the difference would appreciably affect their beneficial interests in the venture, other than tax-wise?"

Upon remand, the Tax Court, 17 T.C.M. 29 (1958), again held that Mr. Gilbert's advances did not qualify as bona fide debts for tax purposes, and made the following additional "findings of ultimate facts":

1. At the time of the organization of Gilbor, Inc., and thereafter petitioners and Borden anticipated and understood that the funds received by Gilbor, Inc., upon the issuance of its capital stock would not be sufficient to finance the conduct of its business.

2. No outside investor would have made the necessary advances of funds to Gilbor, Inc., without adequate security, which security Gilbor, Inc., was itself unable to provide.

3. It was at that time understood and agreed between petitioners and Borden that they would make the advances to Gilbor, Inc., necessary to the conduct of its business (or furnish collateral to it), and that these advances would be made by Borden and by petitioners in proportions which were substantially equivalent to the proportion of the stock of Gilbor, Inc., owned by Borden and of the stock owned by Benjamin Gilbert. The advances were made in such proportion.

4. The advances made by petitioner Benjamin Gilbert to Gilbor, Inc., were made by him without regard to the normal creditor safeguards.

5. Petitioner Benjamin Gilbert made no efforts to enforce the obligations evidencing the advances made by him to Gilbor, Inc.

6. At the time the advances here in question were made to Gilbor, Inc., by Benjamin Gilbert, it was not reasonable to expect that they would be repaid unless the business ventures of Gilbor, Inc., should prove to be successful.

7. As a matter of substantial economic reality, the advances to Gilbor, Inc., made by Benjamin Gilbert were placed at the risk of the business of Gilbor, Inc., and constituted risk capital.

Upon appeal, the Tax Court's decision was affirmed by a panel which did not include any of the judges who had participated in the previous decision. Commissioner v. Gilbert, 262 F.2d 512 (2d Cir. 1959). After stating that no one element was determinative in deciding whether particular advances should be treated as equity rather than debt, the court then held that in view of (1) Gilbert's obvious knowledge that the purported advances might well be swallowed up by the corporation's capital requirements, (2) the attempt to keep the advances closely proportionate to stockholdings of the parties, and (3) the continuation of "loans" after the company was obviously in serious financial difficulty and unlikely to be able to repay, Gilbert had not sustained his burden of establishing that the Tax Court's decision was erroneous.

The court also rejected Gilbert's complaint that the Tax Court had arrived at three different and inconsistent results in treating Gilbert's advances as capital contributions, his wife's advances as non-business bad debts, and Borden's as business bad debts. The court observed that each person had a sufficiently different relationship to the corporation to justify the different conclusions.

It is interesting to note that in its very next confrontation of the debt-equity issue, Nassau Lens Co., Inc. v. Commissioner, 308 F.2d 39 (2d Cir. 1962), the Court of Appeals for the Second Circuit once again found it necessary to remand to the Tax Court "for further findings". The Tax Court had relied primarily upon the absence of any "business purpose" in denying debt classification to notes received by a sole proprietor upon the incorporation of his business. The Court of Appeals rejected this standard:

> It is all very well to say that it makes little "economic" difference whether the investment here was divided between debt and equity or was entirely allocated to equity. But by the same reasoning it may make little "economic" difference to Pildes whether he has an unincorporated business or a corporation in which he is the sole stockholder. And if one wanted to carry the argument far enough, presumably the Commissioner would be free to make *ad hoc* attacks on a whole variety of transactions involving closely held corporations. But the Code does not so empower the Commissioner, for it recognizes and treats corporations as separate entities and affords significance to the type of investment chosen in them so long as that investment has substantial economic reality in terms of the objective factors which normally surround the type chosen. . . .
>
> Upon remand the first question for determination is whether Pildes did in fact create a debt. If the Tax Court finds that a valid debt was created, then the next question is whether it should be treated as debt for the purpose of taxation. This depends on whether the creation of the debt had a result similar to the one Congress had in mind when it drafted the statute involved, or if the intent is

unclear, whether there is a patent distortion of normal business practice. The standards to be applied have been extensively discussed in other decisions of this Court, and need be mentioned only briefly here. The starting point is, of course, whether there is an intent to repay, for in the absence of that no debt can be said to exist. . . . Other factors to be considered relate to the extent to which the debentures bear a substantial risk of the enterprise and, like risk capital, are tied up indefinitely with the success of the venture. . . . Relevant considerations are whether the debt instruments are subordinate to those held by outsiders or whether they specify a relatively fixed date upon which the creditor may demand a definite sum regardless of the profits earned. . . . The Tax Court should also give consideration to the debt-equity ratio and the question of whether outside investors would have made similar advances. . . .

Tax saving motives are, of course, not irrelevant and may be considered by the Tax Court. They may not, however, be given conclusive effect but should be given weight commensurate with the extent to which "they contribute to an understanding of the external facts of the situation." . . . In short, a departure from normal business patterns combined with a tax avoidance motive usually will be sufficient to justify treating the "loan" as equity. Either factor alone, however, is not enough.

This current emphasis on the risk factor has given rise to one unfortunate by-product: it seems to condemn advances made by stockholders to an obviously failing enterprise in a last-ditch effort to resuscitate it. Certainly, such advances could not pass the screen of the additional findings in the Gilbert case, supra at page 142, since under such circumstances "no outside investor would [make] the necessary advances," the advances would be made "without regard to the normal creditor safeguards," and it would be "not reasonable to expect that they would be repaid unless the business ventures . . . should prove to be successful." Yet there is a strong case to be made for sustaining such advances as bona fide debt. Indeed, Arnold v. Phillips, page 74 supra, in a non-tax setting sustained debt status for later advances to meet corporate needs in the face of operating losses, while holding that initial advances should be treated as additional equity. The injection of fresh funds into a failing enterprise may well represent the only chance of keeping the enterprise going long enough to get back on its feet. But outsiders can hardly be expected to advance funds at such a time; and a rule which treats all advances by stockholders at such times as equity will certainly discourage them from extending such a helping hand. The ultimate losers under such a rule could well be the outside creditors, as the court noted in the Rowan case, page 135 supra, when it warned against a rule which would discourage a stockholder from advancing "money to strengthen the faltering steps of his corporation (which, of course, may be greatly to the benefit of the other creditors)."

Nevertheless, there appears to be only one tax case in which an express distinction in favor of subsequent advances has been drawn. Bijou-Pensacola Corp. v. United States, 172 F.Supp. 309 (N.D.Fla.1959). And two recent cases, Diamond Brothers Co. v. Commissioner, page 137 supra, and Schine Chain Theaters, Inc. v. Commissioner, page 137 supra, actually stressed the continuation of the advances in the face of steadily worsening financial conditions as a factor cutting against debt classification.

5. CREATION OF DEBT UPON THE INCORPORATION OF A GOING BUSINESS

Under the first additional finding of fact in the opinion on remand in the Gilbert case, page 142 supra, one of the factors cutting against debt classification is that the funds in question were needed by the corporation "to finance the conduct of its business." Applying that test to the incorporation of a going enterprise, it is certainly arguable that whatever amount is already at work in the unincorporated enterprise is demonstrably needed to carry on the business and could therefore not be used as consideration for the issuance of debt. Such a view would be consistent with the result reached on the corporate side in Costello v. Fazio, page 69 supra, where the intimation is clear that the essential assets of a going business must be treated as a capital investment in the corporation organized to take over the business.

A contention along these lines has been advanced by the Government in a number of recent tax cases, but except for a couple of district court opinions it has not received a very sympathetic reception. In Brake & Electric Sales Corp. v. United States, 185 F. Supp. 1 (D.Mass.1960), aff'd, 287 F.2d 426 (1st Cir. 1961), a sole proprietor organized a new corporation to take over his business, and invested $20,000 cash in exchange for all of its stock. The proprietor then transferred to the corporation all of the assets of the proprietorship (except for some real estate, which was subsequently leased to the corporation) in exchange for a note for $90,000 and the assumption of liabilities of approximately $27,000. In denying a deduction for the interest paid on the notes, on the ground that the notes actually represented an additional capital investment, the District Court stated:

> . . . The $90,000 transaction represented the transfer to the corporation of substantially all of the assets

shown on the books of the individual proprietorship, except for cash and the real estate. They were assets essential to the conduct of the business and . . . it could not have been carried on without them. A transfer of this character seems rather to be a permanent investment in the risk of the business rather than the temporary loan which the parties represented it to be.

However, in affirming the Court of Appeals took pains to point out that no single factor was determinative of the result. The fact that the property exchanged for the debt obligations consisted of essential operating assets of the predecessor proprietorship drew only the following comment in a footnote:

We think that the nature of the assets, and their continued necessity to the running of the business are relevant considerations in determining the intent of the parties in making the transfer, to be taken together with the other evidence of lack of realistic expectation of payment in cash when due according to the face of the note. . . . The factors of the nature of the assets and their importance to the operation of the business would not be very strong evidence of intent to make a risk-capital investment in every case but they are some evidence to be taken together with the other circumstances of the case.

In Charter Wire, Inc. v. United States, 309 F.2d 878 (7th Cir. 1962), in circumstances much like those in the Brake & Electric case the trial court had stressed the fact that the purported debt was issued in exchange for all of the partnership's operating assets "without which the business could not be carried on," but the Court of Appeals merely referred to this element as "another factor that may be used to weigh the balance." The Court of Appeals seemed to attach at least as much weight to such other factors as the pro rata holding of stock and debt, and the subordination of the debt to bank loans over a substantial period of time. In Daytona Marine Supply Co. v. United States, 61–2 USTC para. 9523 (S.D.Fla.1961), where again the Government had attacked debt created upon the incorporation of a going enterprise, the court said:

The government in this case appears in reality to be contending for a new or novel rule of law to the effect that no bona fide indebtedness for Federal tax purposes can be created where the organizers of a new corporation cause operating assets to be transferred to it as a part of its initial capitalization in return for the issuance of bonds and stock. The Court knows of no such rule of law and no direct authority in support thereof has been cited by Counsel for the Defendant. I do not think it appropriate to enunciate such a rule in this case.

Accord, Vantress v. Commissioner, 23 T.C.M. 711 (1964).

Assuming no absolute bar to the creation of some debt upon the incorporation of a going enterprise, that leaves the validity of such debt to be tested by the same standards as are applicable in other situations. Here the test of whether outside creditors might have made similar advances is particularly instructive. For a modest-size enterprise, this test poses a considerable obstacle to any *long-term* debt, since it would be rare indeed for an outside creditor, other than perhaps the Small Business Administration operating pursuant to a specific statutory mandate, to extend credit to a small business for any extended period. On the other hand, small enterprises often do have considerable *short-term* debt, quite apart from the open account indebtedness to suppliers which is always present. For example, machinery and equipment can often be purchased on the basis of a deferred payment obligation running over a period of several years (and generally secured by a chattel mortgage on the property). Sometimes additional working capital can be obtained on a term basis by factoring accounts receivable. Hence the injection of a reasonable amount of short-term debt, perhaps similarly secured, upon the incorporation of a going business might well pass the "outside creditor" test.

The case for recognition of such debt may be strengthened by actually casting the transfer of particular assets in the form of a "sale" to the corporation on a deferred payment basis evidenced by the debt obligation received, see pages 117–120, supra, instead of just having a package deal under which all the assets of the business are exchanged for stock and debt obligation of the corporation (plus assumption of accompanying liabilities). However, it would be wise to confine the "sale" approach to the type of assets which would be most likely to be sold to the corporation by an outsider in similar circumstances. In some of the cases involving challenged debt created upon incorporation of a going business the court has given considerable weight to the type of property for which the debt obligations were issued. Compare Rowan v. United States, page 135 supra (stressing the fact that the advances were for *"working capital* (not, it will be noted, purchase of capital assets)" in sustaining debt treatment), with Moughon v. Commissioner, 22 T.C.M. 94 (1963) (rejecting debt classification for bonds issued in exchange primarily for goodwill and other intangibles which were "permanent assets of the corporation" and "were placed at the risk of the corporate business.")

6. SUBSTITUTES FOR STOCKHOLDER DEBT

One obvious alternative to advances by stockholders is outside borrowing by the corporation. Presumably the corporation could deduct the interest paid to outsiders, and although the stockholders would not be receiving that interest they should be able to earn a corresponding amount by investing the funds they were not required to advance to the corporation. More important, by not putting those funds into the corporation in the first place the stockholders would not face the problems involved in trying to get the funds out later without a dividend tax. However, the plain fact is that in these close corporation situations the corporation would rarely be able to borrow any significant amount of money from an outsider, at least absent a personal guaranty of the indebtedness by the stockholder. Hence the real question is how stockholder-guaranteed debt is to be treated under the thin capitalization doctrine. While there appear to have been no cases in point to date, it would certainly be rash to assume that a switch from direct advances to guaranteed outside loans would solve all the problems in this area. In the long run stockholder-guaranteed debt seems likely to be just as unsuccessful in assuring deductibility of interest payments (or freedom from dividend treatment for repayment of the debt) as it proved to be with regard to providing ordinary loss treatment for payments under the guaranty upon the worthlessness of the debt, under the Putnam case, page 132 supra. Moore and Sorlien, Adventures in Subchapter S and Section 1244, 14 Tax L.Rev. 453, 493, note 108 (1959), put it this way:

> It is possible that the reason for the paucity of authority on this point is the difficulty of focusing the attack. Nearly always a thin capitalization is placed under fire by denying the corporate deduction for interest paid the shareholder-noteholder. Sometimes the attack is on payment of the capital, which could be treated as a dividend or equity redemption substantially equivalent to a dividend. If a bank is the creditor, an additional step must be taken by the Commissioner, as the corporation will point out that the interest has been paid to a bank and ask how in the world the Commissioner can deny *that* deduction. The answer would have to be that the shareholder, by endorsing the note, has placed himself in a dual position — creditor of the corporation and debtor to the bank. In effect, then, the interest is paid to the shareholder, who in turn pays it to the bank. If the capitalization were thin, the analysis would be that the "interest" paid by the corporation was a dividend to the shareholder, who receives an equivalent deduction for interest paid the bank. Thus, the bank pays tax on the interest, the shareholder is even, and the corporation loses its interest deduction. Lest this reasoning be thought too strained, the Supreme Court dictum in the Putnam case . . . appears to support the conclusion and places in some jeopardy what had been thought by many to be a fairly simple escape-hatch to the thin capitalization doctrine.

Accord, Bittker, Federal Income Taxation of Corporations and Stockholders (1959) 124–125. Compare Murphy Logging Co. v. United

States, 239 F.Supp. 794 (D.Ore.1965) (treating shareholder-guaranteed debt as a loan to the shareholders and in effect a capital contribution by them to the corporation), with Fors Farms, Inc. v. United States 66–1 U.S.T.C. ¶ 9206 (W.D.Wash.1966) (sustaining shareholder-guaranteed debt against attack); see also General Alloy Casting Co. v. Commissioner, 23 T.C.M. 887 (1964), where substantial bank loans guaranteed by stockholders were not even challenged although much smaller direct stockholder loans were treated as equity.

A more attractive alternative to stockholder debt may lie in having the stockholder retain some of the operating assets and lease them to the corporation. The corporation would deduct the rental payments, which would presumably amount to approximately as much as the interest on any debt which might have been created plus the depreciation deduction the corporation would have enjoyed if it had owned the assets. And the stockholders would in effect receive tax-free repayments of principal by virtue of being able to deduct depreciation on the assets from the rental payments. However, here too there is the danger that the Service and the courts will refuse to be bound by the form of the transaction. There is no reason why stockholders should be more free to lease operating assets to a corporation than to "lend" them by way of an exchange for debt obligations, and the same policy which enables a court to treat an alleged debt obligation as additional capital may prove sufficient to justify similar treatment for an alleged lease.

F. SUBCHAPTER S [*]

Subchapter S, §§ 1371–1378 of the Code, is designed to permit closely-held corporations to avoid the corporate tax on income, at the cost of making stockholders subject to tax on the corporation's income whether or not it is distributed to them. Although the provision is sometimes described as permitting a corporation to elect partnership tax treatment, this is not very accurate since the tax mechanics are quite different — a Subchapter S corporation is governed essentially by corporate tax rules, not partnership rules. In 1966 Subchapter S was amended in several respects, including the addition of §§ 1375(f) and 1378 to the Code. P.L. 89–389. See generally, Schwartz, New Subchapter S Law Passed: Relaxed Rules Require Re-examination of Election, 24 Journ. of Tax. 370 (1966). The 1966 amendments will be further detailed below. The following is a summary description of Subchapter S.

---

[*] Adapted, with permission, from Surrey and Warren, Federal Income Taxation—Cases and Materials (1960 ed.) 1455–1469.

Qualification under Subchapter S. Any domestic corporation, including an association or business trust taxed as a corporation, may elect Subchapter S treatment, as long as it has no more than ten shareholders, no shareholder who is not an individual or an estate, and no more than one class of stock. According to the regulations, a corporation with a voting trust as a stockholder is barred from a Subchapter S election, just as is true in the case of an ordinary private trust. Reg. § 1.1371–1(e). But see Catalina Homes, Inc. v. Commissioner, 23 T.C.M. 1361, 1368 (1964). Unlike § 1244, the amount of the corporation's assets is not a factor in qualifying under Subchapter S; but like § 1244, there are tests turning on the nature of the corporation's gross receipts. In effect they preclude Subchapter S treatment for any corporation deriving more than 20% of its gross receipts from royalties, rents, dividends, interest, annuities, and sales of securities (with an exception, added in 1966, for the first two years in which the corporation conducts any trade or business, if such "passive" income in those years was less than $3000).

As to the number of stockholders, a husband and wife holding stock jointly are counted as only one. When stock is held by a nominee, agent, guardian or custodian, the beneficial owner is considered the shareholder.

As to the requirement of one class of stock, Reg. § 1.1371–1(g) indicates that any variation in outstanding stock with respect to rights and interest in the control, profits, or assets of the corporation is regarded as resulting in more than one class of stock. There is one exception: "if two or more groups of shares are identical in every respect except that each group has the right to elect members of the board of directors in a number proportionate to the number of shares in each group, they are considered one class of stock". While this exception is obviously intended to leave some leeway for "classification of shares" without automatically precluding Subchapter S treatment, it seems likely to be of minimal effect since quite often one of the reasons for adopting a classification of shares is to give some stockholders greater power in the election of directors than the proportionate number of their shares would otherwise entitle them. Any doubt that the Service will insist upon proportionate allocation of voting power for qualification under Subchapter S seems to be eliminated by Rev.Rul. 63–226, 1963–2 Cum.Bull. 341. That ruling states that even where all of the outstanding stock of the corporation is of the same class, the existence of any "voting control device or arrangement, such as a pooling or voting agreement or a charter provision granting certain shares a veto power or the like, which has the effect of modifying the voting rights of part of the stock so that particular shares possess disproportionate voting power as compared to the dividend rights or liquidation rights of those shares and as compared to the voting, dividend and liquidation rights of the other shares of stock of the corporation outstanding," will lead to a finding of more than one class of stock. The ruling rejected Subchapter S treatment for a corporation whose shareholders had entered into an agreement providing that any shareholder not actively engaged in the business of the corporation would grant an irrevocable proxy to vote his shares to one or more active shareholders.

Reg. § 1.1371–1(g) also notes that if instruments purporting to be debt obligations are classified as additional equity, they will constitute a second class of stock, thus creating an additional hazard for corporations which may be too "thin". Accord, Catalina Homes, Inc. v. Commissioner, 23 T.C.M. 1361 (1964). However, Gamman v. Commissioner, 46 T.C. No. 1 (1966), in a court-reviewed opinion (with five dissents), expressly rejected the unqualified position taken in the regulations, holding instead that whether debt treated as equity constitutes a second class of stock is a question of fact in each case. The majority then found that since the notes in the instant case were held pro rata by the stockholders and did not as a practical matter give them any additional rights or interest in the corporation the notes did not represent a second class of stock.

On the other hand, Rev.Rul. 64–309, 1964–2 Cum.Bull. 333, preserves some needed flexibility in the "one class of stock" requirement. That ruling holds that where preferred stock was required to be issued for not more than $100 to the FHA by a corporation whose mortgage was insured by the FHA, and such stock was clearly intended merely to give the FHA voting control over the corporation in the event of default by the corporation under its agreement with the FHA, the preferred was not a second class of stock for the purposes of Subchapter S because it did not represent an equity interest in the corporation.

Manner of Election and Termination. The election to come under Subchapter S is made by the corporation, but all shareholders must consent. The election for any taxable year must be made during the first month of that year or the last month of the preceding year. The election remains in effect until terminated.

An election may be *voluntarily* terminated by action of all the shareholders. Such termination, however, will be effective only for future years if made later than the first month of the current year. An election is *involuntarily* terminated if any new shareholder fails to consent to Subchapter S status within 30 days after becoming a shareholder, or if the corporation ceases to meet the qualifications for a Subchapter S corporation. An involuntary termination is effective as of the beginning of the year in which the terminating event occurs.

An obvious question is whether voluntary action to achieve an "involuntary termination" will be effective. For example, can an immediate cessation of Subchapter S status be achieved by giving one share of stock to a person who does not consent within 30 days, or by transferring a share of stock to a trust, or by having the corporation issue a second class of stock? There are some implications in Reg. §§ 1.1374–2(b) (1) and 1.1372–5 that such events will be recognized. Suppose an election is made in one year with an agreement to revoke or terminate it next year — is the election effective? These issues are important, since there may be some tax advantages in a "one-year" election.

On the other side, shareholders desiring a continuation of Subchapter S status face the problem of how to prevent an involuntary termination resulting from a transfer of stock by another shareholder for the purpose of terminating the election. Would the typical restriction on stock transfer provide a sufficient barrier, or simply leave the other shareholders with a rather dubious claim for damages?

Once a Subchapter S election terminates, the corporation or any successor may not reelect prior to the fifth year after effective termination, unless the Commissioner consents to an earlier election. Reg. § 1.1372–5 states that he will ordinarily not consent where the termination was planned or reasonably within the control of the shareholders.

Overall Effect of Election. As respects the *corporation*, a Subchapter S election ends its liability for any federal income tax, although it must continue to file an annual information return.

As respects the *shareholders*:

(1) They continue to be taxed on actual distributions of the corporation, whether as dividends, in partial liquidation, etc., as before, except that:

> (a) no dividend exclusion is allowed for dividend distributions out of current earnings and profits;
>
> (b) a "capital gain pass-through" treatment is accorded in some circumstances where there is capital gain at the corporate level;
>
> (c) distributions out of previously taxed undistributed income are given special treatment.

(2) The shareholders will be taxed on their proportionate interest in any undistributed current income of the corporation. In effect, that income is treated as a year-end dividend, without dividend exclusion.

(3). The shareholders may obtain and utilize any net operating loss of the corporation incurred during the year.

Mechanics of Subchapter S Treatment. As to undistributed corporate income, each person who is a shareholder on the last day of the corporate taxable year is taxed on his pro rata portion of the undistributed corporate taxable income. If the taxable years of a corporation and a shareholder differ, he includes his share for his taxable year within which the corporate taxable year ends. Obviously this focus on shareholdings on the last day of the year raises tax avoidance possibilities through year-end transfers.

The undistributed corporate taxable income is determined by first computing the regular taxable income of the corporation, but disregarding any net operating-loss deduction and dividends-received deduction. There is then subtracted any *money* actually distributed as a dividend during the taxable year to the extent the distribution is out of current earnings and profits. In general effect, the undistributed income is current corporate income less current cash distributions. The constructive dividend at the end of the year is the amount of the undistributed taxable income which if distributed would have been a dividend to the shareholder. Notice that distributions in kind are not subtracted from taxable income to determine undistributed corporate taxable income, though to the extent of the earnings and profits allocable to those distributions they can be taxable to the shareholder.

These rules require an allocation of the current earnings and profits. Reg. §§ 1.1373–1(d) and (e) provide that current earnings and profits are first allocable to actual distributions of money and then ratably to constructive dividends and to actual distributions in kind and then to any distribution in exchange for stock.

The shareholder's basis for his stock is increased by the amount taxable to him as a constructive dividend, if actually included in his income. Thus, in effect there is a constructive distribution and a constructive contribution to capital.

As a consequence of this constructive dividend, the corporation possesses funds which have already been taxed to its shareholders, so that some device is needed to prevent the shareholders from again being taxed if there is a distribution of those funds. The statute in effect sets up for each shareholder a corporate "account" consisting of the amount of undistributed taxable income already taxed to him. This amount of previously taxed income is the total of his constructive dividends for prior years, less his share of corporate operating losses in prior years, and less any prior distributions from this account. Any distribution from this account while Subchapter S status exists is a non-dividend distribution, to be applied against stock basis, with any excess producing capital gain. Obviously, this device requires rules of allocation when a distribution is made. Reg. § 1.1375–4(b) provides that money dividends in excess of current earnings and profits are charged first to this previously taxed income account and then to accumulated earnings and profits. Distributions in kind and distributions in exchange for stock are never charged to this account.

While later money distributions are thus protected where prior undistributed income has been taxed, there are obstacles affecting the overall protection afforded by this device. The account is personal to the shareholder, and his account disappears if he ceases to be a shareholder, whether by sale, gift or death. (If he retains some stock, however, the whole account still remains.) Moreover, if the election terminates, all accounts up to then are wiped out and not reinstated with a new election. Also, any corporate losses passed through to the shareholders reduce the account for years subsequent to the loss. Hence if shareholders are looking forward to a distribution of some funds tax-free because allocable to that account, it is necessary, if a loss year occurs, to make the distribution during that year before the account is reduced by the loss. If the account is wiped out by the distribution, the amount of the loss of the year must be offset against future constructive dividends before the account can again reach a plus figure.

As a result of these obstacles, shareholders may prefer to have the constructive dividend actually distributed and then, if the corporation really needs the funds, lend them to the corporation. In this way, the amounts could, in the future when conditions permit, be paid in redemption of the debt and thus avoid dividend status without the complications of the rules governing the previously taxed income account. But such "debt" may create its own problems, such as whether the purported debt is really a second class of stock, or whether the distribution and contribution should be disregarded as a sham transaction.

Prior to the 1966 amendments a Subchapter S corporation which did not want to accumulate its current earnings had to distribute them before the end of the current year, since any distribution of money is deemed to come first from the earnings and profits of the year in which the distribution is actually made. However, under the new § 1375(f) most distributions of money during the first 2½ months after the close of a taxable year will be treated as distributions of the undistributed taxable income of the previous year.

Capital Gain Pass-Through. Prior to 1966 any capital gains included in the taxable income of a Subchapter S corporation could be passed through as capital gains to the shareholders. This created the possibility of a significant advantage in a "one-shot" election under Subchapter S, for a corporation which could forsee substantial capital gains for a particular year or two. However, new § 1378 has significantly curtailed this possibility by imposing a capital gains tax on the corporation (in addition to the one on the shareholders) on any capital gains in excess of $25,000, if the corporation's ordinary income is less than its net capital gains for the year *and* it has not been a Subchapter S corporation for the three preceding taxable years (or since its inception).

Net Operating Loss Pass-Through. If a Subchapter S corporation has an operating loss, it passes through to the shareholders (but capital losses do not pass through). The corporate loss is made available on a pro rata daily allocation basis to each shareholder holding stock on that day, unlike the constructive dividend which is allocated to year-end shareholders. This daily allocation of the loss is designed to avoid the problem of stock acquisitions made to obtain prior corporate losses. The shareholder can use this loss as part of a net operating loss deduction at his level. However, the amount of the loss which can be utilized at the shareholder level is limited to the total of the shareholder's investment in the corporation, i. e., the total of his stock and debt investment as of the close of the corporate year (or earlier if he ceased to be a shareholder before then). Any excess of loss simply disappears. The shareholder's investment basis is reduced by his share of a loss, with stock basis being reduced first. Any subsequent constructive dividends increase the basis of stock; but debt basis is never increased, even though debt basis may have been reduced by an earlier loss. At the corporate level, the loss of the year cannot be utilized in determining any corporate net loss carryover or carryback from that year.

The possible advantages of a "one-shot" Subchapter S election in connection with a net operating loss were not affected by the 1966 amendments. Hence where substantial losses are in prospect such an election could prove beneficial by enabling the shareholders to take immediate personal advantage of the losses instead of leaving them to be utilized by carry-forward or carryback at the corporate level.

Treatment of Family Groups. The Secretary is given authority to reallocate any actual or constructive dividend received by a Subchapter S shareholder among those other shareholders who are members of his family (spouse, ancestors, and lineal descendants), if he determines that such action is necessary to reflect the value of services rendered by any of those shareholders. Thus, if a father-shareholder works for too low a salary in an effort to shift income via dividends to his shareholder children, the portion of their dividends which represent a fair salary to the father is allocated to the father *as a dividend*. The corporation's taxable income is thus not reduced. Reg. § 1.1375–3. Presumably the father is then subject to gift tax. Curiously, under the statute the father must be a shareholder for this reallocation to occur. Does it follow that no reallocation could be made if the father performing the services was not a stockholder?

The regulations also provide for reallocation of non-pro-rata distributions of actual dividends. As respects constructive distributions, suppose a father gives stock to his son on the last day of the year; does this shift the constructive dividend to the son? Reg.

§ 1.1373–1(a)(2) states that a donee or purchaser is not considered a shareholder unless the stock is acquired in a bona fide transaction and the donee or purchaser is the real owner of the stock, and further that transactions between members of a family will be closely scrutinized.

Advisability of Electing Subchapter S. The question of whether to elect Subchapter S status obviously depends upon the particular circumstances. In the relatively rare case of a close corporation which distributes most of its taxable income to its stockholders in the form of dividends, Subchapter S status should prove distinctly advantageous, since it eliminates the tax at the corporate level. In the more common case where the stockholders in effect draw out all of the profits in the form of salaries, so that in fact no corporate tax is incurred, Subchapter S status may still be desirable since it would eliminate any dispute as to the reasonableness of the salaries. (Similarly, where stockholder-owned debt is in the picture, Subchapter S makes it unnecessary to consider whether the debt was really equity so that the deduction for "interest" should be disallowed.) Moreover, if a working stockholder dies and his family can thereafter share in the corporate profits only by way of dividends, while the other stockholders are still receiving salaries, Subchapter S status may make the adjustment somewhat easier.

However, in the most common case of all, where the corporation must accumulate a substantial portion of its profits to meet its business needs, the desirability of Subchapter S is basically a matter of tax arithmetic, and generally the arithmetic would seem adverse to Subchapter S. The corporate rate is 22% on the first $25,000, and 48% on any excess, which rates are reached by married individuals at about $12,000 and $44,000 of taxable income respectively. Quite commonly, therefore, the corporation's tax bracket will be lower than that of the shareholders, particularly if the shareholders' incomes were to be augmented by constructive dividends under Subchapter S; in that event it is normally better to permit the business to accumulate its necessary funds at the corporate rate. Indeed, shielding the business income from the high individual tax rates is one of the most common reasons for incorporating a small business in the first place.

To be sure, the foregoing arithmetic takes no account of the fact that Subchapter S would lead to a lower capital gains tax upon a later sale of stock, by virtue of the increase in stock basis which accompanies taxability of the constructive dividends. However, it is doubtful that this factor would in the end swing many corporations over to Subchapter S. The long-term future is generally too uncertain for present planning. Among other things, the unrealized appreciation on the stock might go untaxed by virtue of inclusion of the stock in the stockholder's estate.

Even when the arithmetic makes the question quite close, there are some other problems under Subchapter S which may cut against the election. One is the conflict that may develop among the shareholders because of the uneven impact of Subchapter S treatment, depending as it does upon the individual circumstances of each shareholder. In addition, there is the great complexity of Subchapter S, which unquestionably demands greater time and attention, and hence substantially greater expenditures for legal and accounting services, than would be required for regular corporate operation.

The issues may be somewhat different where the question is whether the availability of Subchapter S should lead an existing partnership or proprietorship to incorporate. Subchapter S does enable the parties to obtain whatever non-tax advantages may inhere in operation as a corporation without incurring any additional tax. And on the tax side, operation as a corporation offers the opportunity for more favorable pension plans than are available to partners or sole proprietors, as well as some fringe benefits like group life insurance or the sick pay exclusion which are open only to corporations. But these advantages must be weighed against the cost of incorporating and the likely increased expense and diminished flexibility which may result from operating as a corporation. Obviously, the ultimate balance will vary with the particular circumstances of the case.

G. MULTIPLE CORPORATIONS

THE ESRENCO TRUCK CO v. COMMISSIONER

United States Tax Court, 1963. 22 T.C.M. 287.

[In 1948 Pliescott entered the poultry rendering business as a sole proprietor, operating his own processing plant in Maryland. He also owned a number of trucks which he used to pick up the raw materials and to deliver his finished products. The business prospered, and for the next three fiscal years, ending July 31, 1949, 1950, and 1951, he had sales of approximately $172,000, $225,000, and $359,000, and net income of $59,000, $41,000 and $90,000 respectively. During these years Pliescott's trucks were involved in a number of highway accidents, and by 1952 he had become concerned about the possibility of incurring personal liability in the event of a serious accident. He was also aware that one of the risks of the rendering business was the possibility of producing a contaminated product which could destroy a whole flock of poultry and thereby lead to substantial damage claims. Pliescott consulted his attorney about incorporating his business and was advised to separate the business into three corporations — one to hold title to his real estate, a manufacturing corporation to perform the rendering operations, and a trucking corporation to haul the raw materials and finished products. Pliescott's accountant was consulted as to the tax consequences of forming three corporations, and he advised that they would be favorable.

Accordingly, in 1952 Pliescott organized three separate corporations: Associates, to which the real estate was transferred; Eastern, which received the operating assets used in carrying on the rendering business; and Esrenco, which took over the trucks used to haul the goods. Only a nominal amount of cash was transferred to each of the corporations, but Pliescott also advanced approximately $20,000 to Eastern. Pliescott and his wife became respectively the president and secretary of each of the three corporations, and two of the three directors.

Originally, Esrenco was intended to act solely as a trucking company, but it developed that this would subject Esrenco to ICC regulation. Accordingly, the arrangement was changed to one under which Esrenco purchased raw materials, hauled them to Eastern's plant, and sold them to Eastern for processing. Eastern then sold its finished products to Esrenco which in turn sold them to its customers. Esrenco's profits on sales of raw material to Eastern and sales of finished products to its customers were comparable to what it would have earned as a contract-hauling company, and it derived no profit from transactions in which it merely purchased and resold without actually hauling the goods purchased to the ultimate buyer.

All three corporations maintained their offices in a small building leased by Associates to Eastern, and Eastern charged Esrenco and Associates on a pro rata basis for office space and secretarial and bookkeeping services. Separate books, bank accounts, and social security records were maintained for each corporation. Transactions between Esrenco and Eastern were handled by entries in intra-company accounts, and payments were made by periodically transferring amounts from the bank account of one company to the bank account of the other, usually by checks drawn to even amounts. Advertising expenses of the business were borne by Eastern, and only Eastern maintained a listing in the telephone directory.

For the taxable year 1958 the Commissioner added Esrenco's entire taxable income of almost $30,000 to that of Eastern (of more than $100,000) relying upon § 482. The Commissioner also denied both Esrenco and Associates a surtax exemption, relying upon §§ 269 and 1551.]

Opinion [17]

KERN, JUDGE. Respondent first contends that "the principal purpose" for Pliescott's acquisition of control of Associates and Esrenco was avoidance of Federal income taxes within the meaning of section 269 by securing the benefit of exemptions from surtax which he would not otherwise have enjoyed. Petitioners contend that neither Esrenco nor Associates was formed or availed of for the principal purpose of avoiding Federal income tax, but that each corporation was separately organized and operated solely for valid business reasons, *i. e.*, to separate the risks inherent in the rendering operation from those involved in the trucking operation, and to separate the risks of such operations from the ownership of realty.

Section 269 disallows any deduction, credit, or allowance obtained through acquisition or control of a corporation if the principal purpose of the acquisition was for the purpose of evasion or avoidance of Federal income tax. There is no dispute that Pliescott's ownership of 100 percent of the stock of Esrenco and 50 percent of the stock of Associates [the other 50 percent being owned by his wife] constituted control as defined in the statute. The surtax exemption provided in section 11(c) is among the deductions, credits, or allowances contemplated which may be disallowed pursuant to section 269. . . . Further, the deductions, credits, or allowances may be disallowed to an acquired corporation which is created primarily for the purpose of avoiding tax. . . .

Therefore, the narrow question to be decided is whether petitioners have carried their burden of demonstrating that a tax avoidance purpose did not exceed in importance any other purpose. . . .

Respondent would have us discount the reasons given by Pliescott for the acquisition of Esrenco. Respondent notes the tax advantage gained by Pliescott in acquiring Esrenco and argues, citing Army Times Sales Co., 35 T.C. 688, that such results once accomplished must have been intended. In reaching the conclusion in Army Times Sales Co., supra, that a sole stockholder's purpose in acquiring control of a corporation was to avoid Federal income tax by securing the benefits of deductions which he would not otherwise have enjoyed, we said at page 704:

> The judicial ascertainment of someone's subjective interest or purpose motivating actions on his part is frequently difficult. One method by which such ascertainment may be made is to consider what the immediate, proximate, and reasonably to be anticipated consequences of such actions are and to reason that the person who takes such actions intends

---

17. Portions of the opinion and all of the court's footnotes except number 5 omitted.

to accomplish their consequences. This reasoning is implicit in the . . . homely English adage "actions speak louder than words."

In that case we found oral testimony to the effect that a business purpose motivated the acquisition of a corporation to be implausible in the light of evidence of record that the acquired corporation was insolvent and a failure as a business venture. In the instant case there are no such compelling circumstances to lead us to doubt Pliescott's oral testimony that his actions were motivated by business purposes.

Respondent's argument that Pliescott must have intended to enjoy the benefits of exemption from surtax overlooks the requirement in section 269 that the principal purpose for the acquisition of a corporation must have been to avoid Federal income taxes. . . . From the record before us we conclude that Pliescott's primary concern was to gain the maximum protection against risks inherent in the manufacture of rendered products and in the hauling of those products.

Respondent questions the bona fides of Pliescott's business judgment by arguing that product contamination was a remote possibility, that insurance coverage would limit risks from trucking accidents, and that fire hazards were not reduced by incorporation. While there is some merit in these arguments they do not cast doubt on the fact that it was the exercise of sound business judgment which led to the acquisition of Esrenco. Pliescott's concern for accident and product liability was not illusory. The record establishes that the best caliber of drivers could not be employed in the rendering business. Numerous accidents resulted in the insurer's cancellation of Pliescott's accident insurance in 1953. Further, the production of a contaminated product in the rendering business, although a remote possibility, was not unknown, and was feared most as a risk of the rendering business by one of Pliescott's competitors.

It is also significant that it was Pliescott's attorney who decided that three corporations rather than one should be organized. By such an arrangement it was the expectation of Pliescott and his advisor that the damages for liability arising from the manufacture of a contaminated product would be limited to the assets of the rendering company, that the damages for liability arising from the truck accidents would be limited to the assets of the trucking company, and that the real estate would be isolated from such risks. Pliescott's attorney, after his decision and advice to Pliescott, consulted with Pliescott's accountant as to whether there would be any disadvantageous tax consequences by forming three corporations. Upon the accountant's assurance that the tax consequences were favorable rather than unfavorable the plan was executed.

The evidence of record establishes that Pliescott's purpose in acquiring Esrenco was for bona fide business reasons and that Esrenco would have been created absent any tax advantage. We therefore hold that the stock of Esrenco was not acquired for the principal purpose of tax avoidance by securing additional exemptions from surtax which Pliescott would not otherwise have enjoyed. . . .

If Associates is to sustain its burden of proof that it was not acquired for the principal purpose of tax avoidance, it must establish that it was acquired for a business purpose. Associates was formed in order to hold title to real estate owned by Pliescott and his wife and collect rents therefrom. The alleged business purpose for its formation was to insulate the land from risks inherent in the manufacturing and trucking operations of the rendering business. Associates never had any employees and it did not pay any salary to Pliescott, except for small salary payments in the fiscal years ended in 1953 and 1954. No formal leases were executed for the property leased to Eastern and Esrenco, and in 1957, when Eastern was put out of operation as a result of fire, Eastern paid no rent to Associates. Associates' rental income from other sources was insignificant. From this evidence we find that Associates was a mere corporate shell to hold title to real estate and served no bona fide business purpose. We therefore conclude that it was acquired to secure an exemption from surtax which Pliescott would not have enjoyed. On this issue we hold for respondent.

The next issue is whether Esrenco should be denied the surtax exemption under section 1551. Respondent contends that Esrenco was formed for the purpose of acquiring rendered products from Eastern and leasing garage buildings from Associates; that after the transfer of these properties Pliescott controlled all three corporations, and that petitioners have failed to establish by a clear preponderance of the evidence that the securing of the surtax exemption was not a major purpose of the transfers.

Petitioners' contention is that Esrenco was not formed for the purpose of acquiring rendered products from Eastern, that the sale of goods from Eastern to Esrenco and the leasing of garage space from Associates do not constitute transfers within the contemplation of section 1551, and finally that the securing of a surtax exemption was not a major purpose of such transfers.

Since we are of the opinion that the securing of a surtax exemption was not a major purpose of the transfers of the properties here in question,[5] it is not necessary for us to decide the other contentions of the parties on this issue.

5. [Footnote by the court] We question whether the sales of rendered products by Eastern to Esrenco constituted transfers of property within the intendment of section 1551. It seems to us that the statute means transfers of capital assets held as property by the transferor at or about the time of the incorporation or reactivation of the transferee corporation and not to periodic sales of manufactured products created long after the time of such incorporation or reactivation.

Whether the securing of a surtax exemption is a major purpose of a transfer is a question of fact to be resolved upon a consideration of all the circumstances relevant to the transaction, and the burden of proving by the clear preponderance of the evidence that securing the exemption from surtax was not a major purpose of the transfer is placed upon petitioner by statute.

In Truck Terminals, Inc., [33 T.C. 876] at 885, we concluded:

> . . . that the "major" quality of a "purpose" within the framework of the statutory sections here involved is to be determined in the light of the effect which consideration of securing the exemption and credit had upon producing the decision to create or activate the new corporation.

The record in the instant case established to our satisfaction that the benefit of the surtax exemption did not produce the decision to create Esrenco. In the instant case, as in Hiawatha Home Builders, Inc., 36 T.C. 491, an accountant advised of the tax advantages to be gained by the formation of the new corporation. But we were persuaded in that case, as we are here, that the securing of a tax advantage was not the major purpose of the creation of the petitioner and that the corporation would have been formed if no tax saving resulted. We decide this issue for the petitioners.

We next direct our attention to respondent's alternative argument made under the provisions of section 482. Respondent determined that the taxable income of Esrenco for the fiscal year ended July 31, 1958, constitutes income to Eastern. Respondent contends "that Eastern produced all the income of the rendering business, and the mere fact that Esrenco on its tax return reported part of such income and deducted expenses attributable to such income does not control."

Petitioner contends . . . section 482 does not furnish authority for consolidating the taxable income of two corporations. . . .

* * *

With respect to the scope of the respondent's authority under section 482, and its predecessor, section 45 of the Internal Revenue Code of 1939, we said in Ballentine Motor Co., Inc. [39 T.C. 348 (1962), affirmed 321 F.2d 796 (4th Cir. 1963)]:

> We believe that net income may in certain instances be properly allocated under section 45 and currently section 482. If net profits are shifted (one device at which the statute was specifically directed), it would be a logical short cut to allocate them instead of allocating "gross income, deductions, credits, [etc.]." The other devices of income shifting mentioned by the committee reports similarly suggest allocation of such income. The statute allows allocation of gross income and deductions, and to the extent this is permitted we believe it may be done as "net income."

We do not construe [certain prior cases] to prevent this type of allocation. . . . In [those cases] respondent's principal arguments were that the income was earned by sham corporations, and in each case this argument was rejected on the facts. Here he is contending that income was shifted to a valid and subsisting corporation but that the transfer was to evade taxes and resulted in a distortion of income.

The issue therefore resolves itself into whether respondent properly determined that the taxable income of Esrenco in the amount of $29,618.21 for the taxable year ended July 31, 1958, constitutes income to Eastern within the provisions of section 482.

Section 482 and its predecessor, section 45 of the Internal Revenue Code of 1939, have been interpreted to confer broad discretionary power upon the Commissioner to allocate income or deductions if he determines that such allocation is necessary in order to prevent evasion of taxes or clearly to reflect income. . . . The congressional committee reports show that Congress intended the statute to prevent the evasion of taxes by the shifting of profits, the making of fictitious sales, and other methods frequently adopted for the purpose of "milking." . . .

Respondent argues that Esrenco performed no bona fide separate business function. Respondent also questions the bona fides of the sales between Eastern and Esrenco. [The court then quoted Reg. § 1.482–1(b) (1).] Thus, section 482 is based on the recognition of various corporate entities but allows the Commissioner to prevent distortions in income between controlled corporations. . . .

In Seminole Flavor Co., [4 T.C. 1215 (1945)] the petitioner manufactured flavor extracts. The advertising, sale, and supervision of the bottling of its products were taken over from petitioner by a partnership composed of petitioner's stockholders, whose interests in the partnership were identical with their stock interests in the petitioner. We held that section 45 of the Internal Revenue Code of 1939 had no applicability because the partnership was formed for valid business reasons, and operated as a separate entity. See also Buffalo Meter Co., 10 T.C. 83, 89, wherein it was said that "[t]he important consideration is that the partnership was real for all purposes and that it has at all times functioned as an entirely separate economic entity."

In the instant case Esrenco was formed for valid business reasons, which we discussed above with respect to the determinations made pursuant to sections 269 and 1551. Further, it has been established that Esrenco operated at all times as a separate economic entity. It actually bought and sold the goods it hauled, and its profits were limited to the services it performed. It paid Eastern for its pro rata share of the cost of office space and secretarial and bookkeeping services. Esrenco also owned its own trucks, had its own employees, and kept separate books, bank accounts, and social security records.

On the basis of the record before us we have found that:

> Esrenco's charges to Eastern for raw materials sold to it reflected a profit comparable to that which Esrenco would have earned as a contract-hauling company, and it also earned a similar price differential on finished goods purchased from Eastern and resold. Esrenco derived no profit from transactions in which it merely purchased and resold without actually hauling the goods purchased to the ultimate buyer. Both the rates charged for hauling and the prices paid for finished goods varied, the latter being governed by world-wide market conditions which subjected it to wide fluctuation.

Therefore, this issue is governed by the principles applied in Seminole Flavor Co. and Buffalo Meter Co., both supra. There is no question but that the transactions between Eastern and Esrenco were fair and at arm's length. We therefore conclude that respondent exceeded his authority by allocating Esrenco's taxable income for the fiscal year ended July 31, 1958 to Eastern. . . .

---

1. INTRODUCTION

The Esrenco case highlights the fact that using more than one corporation to carry on a business enterprise can produce significant tax savings because the first $25,000 of each corporation's income is exempt from surtax and is therefore taxed at a lower rate. As a result, taxpayers have often attempted to use more than one corporation in an effort to obtain additional surtax exemptions and thereby get more income taxed at the lower rate. However, as the Esrenco case illustrates, there are a number of provisions in the Code which may be used by the Commissioner to limit, either directly or indirectly, the number of surtax exemptions which may be enjoyed by a group of related corporations; and this anti-exemption arsenal was expanded by the Revenue Act of 1964.

2. SECTIONS 1561–1563

It seems appropriate to start with the limitation on surtax exemptions imposed by §§ 1561–1563, added in 1964, since this limitation is absolute in the circumstances where it applies and does not depend upon purpose or any other subjective factor. To understand the role of §§ 1561–1563 it is important to recall that the Revenue Act of 1964 not only reduced the overall tax rate for corporations but also sharply decreased the rate applicable to the first $25,000 of corporate income. Under the pre-1964 law, the first $25,000 was taxable at 30%, with any excess over $25,000 taxable at 52%. For years after 1964 the first $25,000 is taxable at only 22%, with the excess taxable at 48%. The result of this increase in the gap between the rate applicable to the first $25,000 and the rate on the excess is a proportionate increase in the value of each surtax exemption. An additional surtax exemption may now save as much as $6,500 (26% x $25,000) per year, as compared with the annual saving of $5500 (22% x $25,000) under prior law. However, in 1964 Congress was in a mood to discourage rather than encourage the proliferation of corporations, as is evidenced by the amendments to § 1551, discussed below. Accordingly, §§ 1561–1563 were enacted to limit the benefits of this rate change in the case of certain groups of related corporations. In essence such groups are restricted to a single surtax exemption unless every member of the group agrees to pay an additional 6% tax, that is, a total of 28%, on its first $25,000 of income.

Briefly speaking, the new provisions apply to any *affiliated* group of corporations, consisting of a parent and one or more controlled subsidiaries, or any *controlled* group, consisting of two or more brother-sister corporations owned by a single individual, trust, or estate, or any combination of the two types of groups. Although the primary objective seems to have been to make sure that this substantial tax reduction being granted to small business in 1964 would not be available to "medium and large enterprises which use, or might choose to use, the multiple corporate form of organization," see S. Rep.No. 830, 88th Cong., 2d Sess. 149 (1964), the new provisions apply as well to a group of small corporations as to a large multi-corporate enterprise.

These provisions contribute yet another to the maddening variety of definitions of control in the Code. Apparently rather than choose between the voting power approach of § 368(c) and the value test of § 1239, § 1563 defines control in terms of ownership of at least 80% of *either* the voting power or the value of the outstanding stock. Section 1563 also contains its own set of constructive stock ownership rules to be used in applying the control test. In addition, § 1563 provides for the exclusion of certain stock in applying the control test, notably stock owned by employees of a component corporation if such stock is subject to substantial restrictions or limitations which run in favor of the component corporation, or the parent corporation or common owner, as the case may be. According to Reg. § 1.1563–2 (b)(2)(iii), in the case of an affiliated group this qualification covers "any legally enforceable condition which prohibits the employee from disposing of his stock without the consent" of the component corporation or the parent, and it is not necessary that the corporation have a discriminatory concession with respect to the price of the stock. Reg. § 1.1563–2(b)(4)(ii) contains a similar provision as to controlled groups, but with an exception for cases in which the restriction on the employee's stock is matched by a "reciprocal" restriction on stock owned by the common owner of the group—i. e. typical cross options in a close corporation. The regulations also provide that in measuring the voting power of stock the terms of the stock as set out in the certificate of incorporation provide the starting point, but account will be taken of voting agreements which vary the formal voting rights possessed by the stock. Reg. § 1.1563–1(a)(6).

If a controlled group of corporations exists, three basic alternatives are available to the corporations which make up the group. They are described in the Report of the House Ways and Means Committee, H.Rep.No. 749, 88th Cong., 1st Sess. 118 (1963), as follows:

>   (1) The corporations in the group may forgo the use of multiple surtax exemptions, i. e., they each file separate income tax returns and allocate one $25,000 surtax exemption among the members of the group . . . .
>
>   (2) Corporations in the group may elect to pay a penalty tax and file a multiple surtax exemption return. Under this election each member of the group (subject to the tax avoidance provision) may claim a separate $25,000 surtax exemption, but each must also agree to pay an additional tax of 6 percent on the first $25,000 of its taxable income. With the generally applicable rates of 22 percent on the first $25,000 of taxable income and . . . 48 percent on income over $25,000, this means a total tax for such companies of 28 percent on the first $25,000 of income and . . . 48 percent . . . on income over $25,000.
>
>   (3) A controlled group which also qualifies as an "affiliated group" of corporations may, as under present law, file a consolidated income tax return.
>
>   This third alternative is similar to the first alternative in that only one $25,000 surtax exemption is available to the corporations filing the consolidated return. However, there are additional benefits in filing a consolidated return arising from the ability to declare and receive dividends between members of the group without tax, and to offset losses of one company against another.

The arithmetic of the matter makes it relatively easy to determine when it would be advantageous to elect the multiple exemptions, 6% penalty alternative instead of apportioning a single surtax exemption among the members of the group. Under the single exemption alternative, the first $25,000 of income of the group would be taxed at 22%, but any excess would be taxed at 48%. Under the multiple exemption alternative, the tax rate on the group's first $25,000 would be 6% higher, at a tax cost of $1500; but the rest of the group's normal tax net income (that is, the total of taxable income not exceeding $25,000 for each corporation) would be taxed at a rate of 20% lower, 28% instead of 48%. Since 20% of $7500 is $1500, it follows that whenever the total normal tax net income of the group exceeds

$25,000 by more than $7500, that is, whenever the total of such income is more than $32,500, the multiple exemption alternative will be preferable.

The new provisions seem remarkably generous in the amount of time which they allow taxpayers to make their choices. The parties have up to three years after the due date of the return for the year in question to elect the multiple exemption alternative, or to terminate a previous election. Once this alternative has been elected, it continues in force until it has been terminated, either voluntarily, or involuntarily as by the addition to the group of a new member which does not consent to the election. However, once an election has been terminated the multiple exemption alternative cannot be elected again by the group for five years.

As to the alternative of apportioning a single exemption among the members of the group, the parties have up to one year before the statute of limitations has run on the year in question to adopt a plan of apportionment or to amend one previously adopted. Once a plan has been adopted it remains in effect until amended or terminated. Whenever no apportionment plan is in effect the exemption will be apportioned equally among the members of the group.

An affiliated parent-subsidiary group has two other elections available to it which would also limit the group to a single surtax exemption. One is an election to file consolidated returns under § 1501, an alternative which was made substantially more attractive in 1964 by the elimination of the additional 2% tax which used to be imposed on this privilege. The other is an election, under the 1964 amendments to § 243, to have a 100% intercorporate dividend deduction on dividends received from members of the affiliated group, instead of the normal 85% intercorporate dividend deduction. Under either of these elections the affiliated group is limited to one surtax exemption.

It is important to note that election of the multiple exemption alternative under §§ 1561–1563 does not preclude the application of any of the Commissioner's traditional weapons, such as §§ 269, 1551, or 482, to limit or deny exemptions. See S.Rep. No. 830, 88th Cong., 2d Sess. 150 (1964); Reg. § 1.1561–1(b). But if any member of a group which has elected the multiple exemptions, 6% penalty alternative under §§ 1561–1563 were to be denied its exemption, that corporation would no longer be subject to the 6% penalty. § 1562(b)(1)(B).

See generally, Dunn, Affiliated and Related Corporations: Elections for a Multiple Corporation Group under the Revenue Act of 1964, 23 N.Y.U. Fed.Tax Inst. 255 (1965); Jones, Effect on Multiple Corporation Elections of Acquisition or Creation of New Corporations, and of Disposition or Liquidation of Old Corporations, 23 N.Y. U. Fed.Tax Inst. 279 (1965).

3. SECTION 269

a. Scope of the Section

Section 269 originally got off to a very slow start in this area, principally because the Tax Court adopted the view that § 269(a)(1) could be used to deny "a deduction, credit or allowance" only to the person who acquired control of the corporation, and not one belonging to the corporation itself. E. g., Alprosa Watch Corp. v. Commissioner, 11 T.C. 240 (1948) (holding § 269(a)(1) inapplicable to an acquired corporation's own loss carryover). This construction seemed to be premised upon the view that the phrase "which such person . . . would not otherwise enjoy" modified "deduction, credit or other allowance." Whatever the grammatical force of this view, it ignored the fact that § 269 was designed primarily to prevent "the practice of . . . acquiring corporations with current, past, or prospective losses or deductions, deficits, or current or unused excess profits credits, for the purpose of reducing income and excess profits taxes," see S. Rep.No.627, 78th Cong., 1st Sess. 58 (1943), and this objective could not be accomplished unless the statute reached the attributes of the acquired corporation. Moreover, the grammar of the statute was by no means all one way. If the phrase "which such person . . . would not otherwise enjoy" is viewed as modifying the word "benefit," the statute reaches to the attributes of the acquired corporation, since the benefit of those attributes is certainly "enjoyed" by the persons who acquire the corporation. The Service continued to press for this construction of § 269(a)(1), and it finally prevailed in Coastal Oil Storage Co. v. Commissioner, 242 F.2d 396 (4th Cir. 1957), where the court held that § 269(a)(1) could be utilized to disallow the surtax exemption of a newly-created subsidiary. This view has been uniformly followed by the authorities since then. E. g., James Realty v. United States, 280 F.2d 394 (8th Cir. 1960) (surtax exemption); British Motor Car Distributors, Ltd. v. Commissioner, 278 F.2d 392 (9th Cir. 1960) (loss carryover).

Even if § 269(a)(1) does reach the tax attributes of the acquired corporation, the question may still be asked whether the surtax exemption is one of the "deductions, credits or allowances" covered by the statute. In 1943, when the predecessor of § 269 was first enacted, there was no such thing as a "surtax exemption"—the two-bracket rate structure for corporations did not come in until 1950. Moreover, § 269 does not expressly refer to "exemptions," a problem which the regulations attempt to solve by treating the term "allowance" as broad enough to encompass all types of tax attributes. Reg. § 1.269–1(a).

Quite apart from semantics, there may be reason to doubt that § 269(a)(1) was intended to apply to those tax attributes of the acquired corporation which, like the surtax exemption, result simply from existence as a corporation. Certainly the primary target of the section was the special tax benefits of the particular acquired corporation, such as "current, past or prospective losses or deductions, deficits, or current or unused excess profits credits." See S.Rep.No.627, 78th Cong., 1st Sess. 58 (1943). Confining the section to such items would be more consonant with the "would not *otherwise* enjoy" language, which seems to look to something other than the tax attributes which inhere in any corporation. More important, failure to so confine the section means that it could be applied to deny the surtax exemption in a case where only a single corporation has been created. This possibility can not be dismissed on the ground that there would always be enough non-tax purposes for a single incorporation to preclude the application of § 269. Often the primary purpose for incorporating a growing enterprise is the desire to be able to accumulate funds in the business at corporate rather than individual tax rates, and of course the surtax exemption would be an integral factor in any such planning. Perhaps the answer to this is that the "would not otherwise enjoy" language would not be satisfied where the only "benefit" involved is the tax rate applicable to all corporations. Cf. I.T. 3757, 1945 Cum. Bull. 200, ruling that § 269 does not apply to the formation of a foreign selling subsidiary to take advantage of the lower tax rate provided under §§ 921 and 922 for corporations whose income is derived from Latin America; accord, Siegel v. Commissioner, 45 T.C. No. 55 (1966).

On the other hand, if the surtax exemption was excluded from the operation of § 269(a)(1), the section would no longer apply to a case like Coastal Oil, supra, where an existing corporation transfers a part of its business to a newly-organized subsidiary. There it is easier to say that an *additional benefit* is being sought, by bringing into conjunction with income already subject to the corporate tax an additional surtax exemption which would not "otherwise" be enjoyed. But it should be noted that the transfer of property to a subsidiary in order to obtain an additional surtax exemption is expressly covered by § 1551 (discussed below); and the very enactment of § 1551 (in 1951) to deal with surtax exemptions lends further support to the view that § 269 does not apply to this item.

Nevertheless, it no longer seems open to serious challenge that, as the Esrenco opinion flatly states, § 269(a)(1) may be invoked to deny surtax exemptions. Accord, e. g., James Realty Co. v. Commissioner, supra; Reg. § 1.269-3(b)(2). In addition, in cases involving the transfer of property to a newly-created subsidiary § 269(a)(2) may be applicable. Coastal Oil Storage Co. v. Commissioner, supra, (alternative holding). The Tax Court in Coastal Oil had rejected § 269(a)(2) on the ground that the subsidiary's right to a surtax exemption did not depend upon its receipt of property from the parent corporation, but the Court of Appeals held that the subsidiary "could not have enjoyed the benefit of the surtax exemption . . . but for the acquisition of the property producing the income from or against which the exemption [is] claimed."

b. APPLICATION OF § 269 TO THE INCORPORATION OF A GOING ENTERPRISE

Assuming that § 269(a)(1) does reach surtax exemptions, there are still some problems with its application to the incorporation of a going business. As already noted, although theoretically possible it is most unlikely that the surtax exemption would be denied to a single corporation, at least where the incorporators have no other incorporated enterprise. Should the result be different when the incorporators do own another corporation, but it is engaged in a wholly unrelated activity? Certainly there is nothing express in § 269 which would support a bald policy of "only one [corporation] to a customer." Accordingly, cases like Esrenco, which assume that § 269 can reach the creation of multiple corporations to take over an existing unincorporated enterprise, must rely upon either the interrelationship of the activities being carried on by the several corporations, or the simultaneity of the incorporation transactions, to bring § 269 into play.

As to the significance of the timing factor, what would happen if the taxpayer staggered the organization of a series of related corporations over a period of years? For example, in a case like Esrenco the individual taxpayer might have incorporated the manufacturing activity first, while continuing to carry on the rest of the enterprise as an individual; then, perhaps a year later, the trucking corporation might have been organized; and finally, in the third year, a real estate corporation could have been organized to take over the real property. It seems clear that § 269 would not apply to the organization of the manufacturing corporation in the first year, since at that point the taxpayer would only be enjoying the benefit of one surtax exemption. When the taxpayer later incorporates the other activities, is he bound, from the point of view of § 269, to use the already existing corporation? Absent a finding of "constructive" simultaneous incorporation, based upon the existence of a fixed plan of seriatim incorporations from the outset, application of § 269 would have to depend entirely upon the relationship of the activity then being incorporated to the one already being carried on in corporate form; and the question may well be asked whether the "would not otherwise enjoy" language, or anything else in § 269, provides the necessary standards for making this kind of relationship judgment.

c. PRINCIPAL PURPOSE TEST

As the Esrenco case indicates, once a transaction is brought within the scope of § 269 the taxpayer has the burden of proving that tax avoidance was not "the principal purpose," i. e., "that a tax avoidance purpose did not exceed in importance any other purpose." Taxpayers have had a fair measure of success in satisfying this burden in cases involving multiple surtax exemptions. For example, in Stater Bros., Inc.—Second Street v. Commissioner, 21 T.C.M. 780 (1962), the court sustained separate surtax exemptions for each of 11 corporations created to take over the 11 separate retail food markets owned and operated by two brothers. The court emphasized the fact that each of the markets had a different manager whose compensation arrangement was contingent upon the profits earned in his particular store. In Fedcal Distributing Co. v. Commissioner, 22 T.C.M. 935 (1963), the court allowed a surtax exemption to each of four corporations created to take over a retail liquor proprietorship which operated four separate liquor concessions under separate licenses. The former proprietor satisfied the court that he was primarily interested in separating the ownership of the several licenses, for the purpose *inter alia* of being able to sell one or more of the licenses by selling the stock of the corporation owning it, thereby avoiding the need to obtain the consent of the local licensing board which was required for the direct sale of a license. In Alcorn Wholesale Co. v. Commissioner, 16 T.C. 75 (1951), the proscribed tax avoidance purpose was found absent in the reorganization of a single corporation, King Grocery Company, which operated five wholesale grocery houses in different towns in Mississippi, into five separate brother-sister corporations. The court emphasized the following non-tax purposes for the transaction:

> (1) To increase the combined borrowing capacity. Under Mississippi law, a bank can only loan one person or corporation 15 per cent of that bank's aggregate paid-in capital and surplus. (2) To limit the liability so that a financial disaster to one petitioner arising from a tort judgment or other event would not affect the other petitioners. (3) To permit the handling of competitive lines of merchandise. Where an exclusive franchise had been granted for the sale of a product to some competitor of King Grocery Company in one of the trade areas, King Grocery Company was unable to obtain a franchise for the sale of that product in another of the trade areas. After the reorganization, the petitioner corporations could separately obtain franchises for the sale of competing products. (4) To eliminate the prejudice against absentee ownership. King Grocery Company was known as a Tupelo, Mississippi, concern and so was considered an absentee owner in other trade areas. After the reorganization, the naming of the stores after the counties in which they were located implied to the public that they were locally owned.

In 1954 subsection (c) was added to § 269 in an effort to strengthen the purpose element of the section. The import of this provision is far from clear, but it is obviously aimed mainly at the acquisition of an existing corporation rather than the creation of a new one. Accordingly, analysis of this provision will be postponed until the discussion of corporate acquisitions in Chapter 5.

Despite the relative success enjoyed by taxpayers to date on the purpose issue, there is no warrant for undue confidence, as is strikingly illustrated by the most recent case in point, involving the organization of four corporations to take over the business of a partnership:

DILLIER v. COMMISSIONER [18]

United States Tax Court, 1964. 41 T.C. 762

TURNER, JUDGE. . . . Although in his determinations the respondent disallowed the surtax exemptions of all four of the Made Rite corporations, counsel for the respondent in his opening statement conceded that one surtax exemption should be allowed, either to one of the corporations or apportioned among the four corporations.

It is clear that Dillier, Kaelin, Johnson, Halter, and Curnow organized and by their stockholdings acquired control of the petitioner corporations, and that by forming four corporations, rather than one, three additional surtax exemptions were made available. The respondent has determined that the principal purpose for this arrangement was the avoidance of Federal income tax by securing the benefit of the additional surtax exemptions. The burden of showing facts which will justify a conclusion to the contrary is on the petitioners.

It is the contention of the petitioners that each of the four Made Rite corporations was a viable business entity and actually engaged in a substantive business activity: That Sausage sold meat products; that Manufacturing processed or manufactured meat products; that Investment owned and leased real estate; and that Transportation owned and leased trucks.

The facts show that the stock of each of the four Made Rite corporations was held in equal amounts by each of the five stockholders, and that when the corporations began to transact business, they operated a single, integrated business enterprise. Meat supplies were purchased and processed into sausage products, ham, and bacon, and the finished products were sold to retail outlets by driver-salesmen working in assigned territories. This was the same business that had theretofore been operated by a single entity, the partnership. The same division of duties among the five former partners prevailed as under the partnership.

The meat products manufactured or processed by Manufacturing were sold only through Sausage, and all receipts therefrom were deposited in the Sausage bank accounts. Although Sausage was purportedly an independent company selling meat products, it sold only the products of Manufacturing, with minor exceptions, and

---

[18]. Findings of fact, portions of the opinion and all of the court's footnotes omitted. The decision of the Tax Court was affirmed by the Court of Appeals for the Ninth Circuit, sub nom. Made Rite Investment Co. v. Commissioner, 357 F.2d 647 (9th Cir. 1966).

carried no inventory on its books. The entire inventory of the business was recorded on the books of Manufacturing, and "sales" from Manufacturing to Sausage were determined by calculations made after Sausage had sold the products to customers. All of the rental income of Investment represented intercompany payments from Manufacturing and Transportation, except for small amounts received from rental to unrelated parties of a parking lot and a few residential units. All of the rental income of Transportation represented intercompany payments from Sausage. No vehicles owned by Transportation were rented to outsiders.

The four corporations used a single office, at which the records for all four were kept. The signs upon the main plant and office building were limited to "Camellia Brand" and "Made Rite Sausage." The only listing for the business in the telephone directory was made in the name of Sausage.

It was the testimony of Johnson, who was the petitioners' principal witness, that at the time of incorporating the four Made Rite corporations it was his understanding that the business would get additional surtax exemptions if four corporations were formed rather than one, although it was his further testimony that this was not a decisive factor in making the decision. Johnson recited a number of alleged business purposes which he claimed motivated the organization of multiple corporations. Although some of the reasons advanced were unclear, the principal ones appear to be as follows: (1) That problems potentially arising from the death of a stockholder would be reduced; (2) that labor problems would be minimized; (3) that more accurate accounting figures for each function of the business would be obtained; (4) that limited liability would be obtained for each corporation; (5) that the adoption of profit-sharing or incentive plans would be facilitated; (6) that unequal cash withdrawals by the partners would be eliminated; and (7) that the discounting of secured notes issued to the stockholders could provide funds to pay off certain personal obligations of the stockholders.

An examination of the alleged business purposes reveals their lack of substance. According to Johnson, it had been felt that, in the event of the death of a stockholder, his heirs might be persuaded to retain the stock of the corporations holding the real estate and trucks. The benefit of this arrangement to the business would apparently be that if the heirs so decided, it would be necessary to raise cash only to acquire the decedent's stock in the sales and manufacturing companies. The purported intention to hold the real estate and trucks for this purpose is not supported by the facts, however, which show that the trucks were sold and leased back and that efforts were made by the petitioners to do the same with the real estate. No reason was given as to why the stock of separate corporations holding the real estate and trucks would be more attractive to the heirs than the stock of a single corporation conducting the entire business, except to say that the two corporations would have "fixed income." However, the record shows that no dividends were paid by either Investment or Transportation during the taxable years. The record further shows that the trucks provided no income except through their use in the meat packing business, which the petitioners maintain was speculative, and that the real estate did not provide a significant amount of outside income. If the heirs did not wish to retain their stock in these two corporations, Johnson testified, the real estate or trucks could be sold to raise cash to pay the heirs. No explanation is given as to why the real estate or trucks, if held in a single corporation, could not as readily have been sold to raise the needed cash.

With respect to labor problems, the contention appears to be that if the employees of either the manufacturing corporation or the sales corporation went on strike, the other corporation could continue to operate, since its employees would be members of different unions. Johnson testified, however, that the Made Rite business had "never had a strike of any consequence," and that "in the last thirty years we have had only a couple of days lost because of strikes." It was his further testimony that when there had been a strike by the members of the Teamsters Union, who worked for Sausage, their picket line had been honored by the members of the Butchers Union, who worked for Manufacturing. The facts also show that the employees of the partnership belonging to the Packers Union became employees of Manufacturing, but that neither the Packers Union nor the association which had bargained with that Union on behalf of the partnership were ever advised of the change of employer.

We see little merit in the contention that the use of multiple corporations was necessary to provide accurate accounting figures for each department. Proper allocation of income and expenses could have been attained by a divisional accounting system, and it does not appear that the allocation between the corporations was made with precision. For example, rental payments for the five executive automobiles were all accrued against Sausage, even though some of the five stockholders were purportedly rendering services primarily to other corporations. As a further example, no office expenses were charged to Investment.

Johnson testified that at the time the corporations were organized the Made Rite business faced increasing competition from national meat packing firms. He stated that in the event the manufacturing operations became unprofitable, those operations could be discontinued and the sales company could continue to operate, selling products to be manufactured by others under the Made Rite label. By reason of the multiple corporations, the liability of the manufacturing corporation would be limited to the extent of its own assets. Yet the facts show that when Manufacturing sought sizable lines of credit from a bank in 1957 and 1958 the other three Made Rite corporations guaranteed repayment of the funds to be advanced by the bank and the five stockholders subordinated the notes they personally held against the corporations to the obligations to the bank.

The argument concerning the adoption of incentive or profit-sharing plans is also without foundation in the record. According to Johnson's testimony, the partners anticipated "that with the sales and manufacturing as separate organizations we could set up profit sharing incentive plans so that junior executives, which we would develop, would be in a position to share in the results of their efforts." There is no evidence, however, that the corporations ever adopted any such plan or seriously considered doing so. Nor is there evidence as to the identity of the "junior executives" for whose benefit the plans were to be instituted. The only executives appear to have been the five stockholders, who received approximately equal total compensation from the various Made Rite corporations, regardless of the profits or losses of the particular corporation or corporations purportedly employing them.

Neither of the final two alleged business purposes for the multiple corporations demonstrates any reason why a single corporation would not have been sufficient. Johnson testified that it had been a practice of the partners to make withdrawals of cash from the partnership to pay their individual taxes, and that the unequal withdrawals which resulted had caused friction among the partners. With the corporate setup, he said, "any dividend or any money coming out of the corporations would be in proportion to the shareholder's interest and not in proportion to his tax burden as an individual." The facts show that the stock of each of the four corporations was issued to the five stockholders in equal amounts. Therefore, the five would receive equal dividends in the same manner as though they had owned equal shares in a single corporation. Johnson also testified that the stockholders learned that a bank would discount corporate notes held by them and secured by real estate, and they could use the funds so received to pay off certain outstanding personal obligations. While it has been shown that the notes issued by Investment to the stockholders were secured by a first deed of trust on the plant and surrounding real property, no reason is advanced why it was necessary to place the real estate in a separate corporation in order to use it as security for the notes.

We are convinced, from our study of the record, that the alleged business objectives did not in fact motivate the organization of the multiple corporations. The one purpose of apparent substance was the obtaining of the additional surtax exemptions of which Johnson had cognizance.

As supporting their contention that the obtaining of additional surtax exemptions was not the principal purpose of organizing the multiple corporations, the petitioners also point to the fact that one surtax exemption was voluntarily given up when Sausage elected to report its income for the years 1958 and 1959 as a small business corporation under subchapter S of chapter 1 (secs. 1371–1377) of the Code. Subchapter S, which had not been enacted at the time the corporations were organized, provides in general for taxing the income of an electing corporation directly to its stockholders. Since there is no tax to the corporation, there is correspondingly no surtax exemption. An examination of the facts show that the net income of Sausage was $37,922 in 1958 and $73,162.91 in 1959, and that dividends in the amount of $25,000 in 1958 and $57,078 in 1959 were paid to the stockholders. No dividends were paid by any of the other Made Rite corporations during those years. By making the election, therefore, it was possible to make all dividend payments to the stockholders from Sausage and avoid corporate taxation on the amounts so paid, retaining in the meantime the benefit of the surtax exemptions of the other corporations. Certainly this procedure did not make the three additional surtax exemptions less beneficial. The year 1958 was the first year for which such an election could have been made, as subchapter S became effective for the taxable years beginning after December 31, 1957.

The respondent in his determinations of deficiencies did not exercise the authority granted to him under section 269(b) to allow a surtax exemption to one of the corporations or to allocate a single exemption among the four corporations. Instead, he disallowed the exemptions of all four corporations. Counsel for the respondent has conceded, however, that one surtax exemption should be allowed, and we think that the exemption should be allowed to Sausage. Sausage was the successor in name to the partnership. It did all of the selling and except for comparatively small amounts received as rent on a parking lot and a few residential units, the income of the entire operation was realized on the sales so made. All of the receipts from sales were deposited by Sausage in its bank account, and except for the aforesaid amounts of rent the income of the other three corporations consisted entirely of book allocations and intercompany transfers made directly or indirectly from Sausage. In light of the record, we have concluded that Sausage is entitled to surtax exemptions for the years 1956 and 1957, and we so hold. No corporate tax was payable by Sausage for 1958 and 1959, by virtue of its election to report its income under subchapter S, and therefore no surtax exemptions were available to it for those years.

The determinations of the respondent denying surtax exemptions to Manufacturing, Investment and Transportation for the years 1956 through 1959 are sustained. . . .

4. SECTION 1551

a. Scope of the Section—Pre-1964

The pre-1964 version of § 1551, which was involved in the Esrenco case, applied only to what is now covered in paragraph (a)(1) of the section. Section 1551 differed from § 269 in at least two important respects: (1) § 1551 applied expressly to surtax exemptions (together with accumulated earning tax credits); and (2) § 1551 applied only when there was a transfer of property from an existing corporation to a new (or newly-activated) corporation. Quite clearly, the provision was aimed primarily at cases like Coastal Oil, supra, where a corporation transfers part of its going business to a new subsidiary; and indeed in the Coastal Oil case the court relied on § 1551 to deny the surtax exemption for that part of the taxable period which came after the enactment of the provision in 1951. However, § 1551 was not limited to transfers to a subsidiary—a transfer by a corporation to another corporation controlled by the stockholder of the transferor corporation was also covered.

As to what types of "transfer" of property were contemplated by pre-1964 § 1551, obviously a straightforward exchange of property for stock of a subsidiary was the primary object of the provision. In addition, a transfer of property by lease was held subject to the statute. Theater Concessions, Inc. v. Commissioner, 29 T.C. 754 (1958). There was more difficulty with the question of whether the statute reached *sales* of property. Literally, of course, a sale does constitute a transfer of property. However, the question of whether § 1551 covered sales was complicated by the exception in the statute for transfers of money. The apparent reason for this exception was to make sure that § 1551 would not stifle legitimate expansion carried out through the organization of new subsidiaries. See Joint Committee Staff Summary of Provisions of the Revenue Act of 1951, 1951-2 Cum.Bull. 287, 303. But the existence of this exception cast doubt on whether the statute applied when a parent transferred cash to a subsidiary and then sold property to the subsidiary for that cash—and hence on whether the statute applied to sales at all. In an early district court case, Airlene Gas Co., Inc. v. United States, 58-2 USTC para. 9805 (D.Ky.1958), the court took the view that § 1551 did not extend to purchases of property; but the court was obviously influenced by the fact that the transaction there involved had begun some months before § 1551 was enacted, and had clearly been carried out for bona fide business reasons. More recently, in Hiawatha Home Builders, Inc. v. Commissioner, 36 T.C. 491 (1961), without any reference to the Airlene decision the Tax Court stated flatly that § 1551 did apply to sales of property. The court noted the express exception for transfers of money in § 1551, and concluded that "if Congress had intended to except any further transfers, it would have spelled out the exceptions." See accord, New England Foundry Corp. v. Commissioner, 44 T.C. 150 (1965).

Strangely enough, none of these cases made any reference to the statement in Reg. § 1.1551–1(d) that "the transfer of cash for the purpose of expanding the business of the transferor corporation through the formation of a new corporation is not a transfer within the scope of section 1551 irrespective of whether the new corporation uses the cash to purchase from the transferor corporation stock in trade or similar property." Although at first blush this statement could be taken as an indication that a purchase by a subsidiary, at least with cash received from its parent, is not subject to § 1551, a narrower reading might confine it to cases of purchasing inventory-like property for the purpose of expanding the business.

b. POST–1964 SCOPE OF § 1551

Any doubt about the applicability of § 1551 to sales of property would seem to have been eliminated by the 1964 addition of § 1551(a) (2), which expressly applies to "indirect," as well as direct, transfers. An example given in the Report of the House Ways and Means Committee, H.Rep.No.749, 88th Cong., 1st Sess. A211 (1963), expressly describes as "an indirect transfer of property" a case in which a corporation transfers cash to its newly-organized subsidiary and the subsidiary then uses the cash to purchase stock in trade from the parent corporation. (Notice that in treating a sale as an indirect transfer the Committee Report somewhat undercuts the view that such a transaction was already covered by the pre-1964 version of the statute, although it seems likely that in picking the example of a sale of stock in trade the Report is trying to preserve the position that sales of other types of property were already covered.) There is more doubt as to whether § 1551(a)(2) embraces the type of periodic sales of goods in the ordinary course of business which the court in the Esrenco case seemed to think was outside the scope of § 1551(a) (1). See note 5, page 161 supra. But it must be kept in mind that the creation of a sales corporation may involve a transfer of intangible property, such as goodwill and customers lists, or a dealer's franchise, from the old corporation to the new one, and such a transfer could fall under § 1551(a)(2), although the Tax Court has expressed doubt as to the applicability of the pre-1964 version of § 1551(a) (1) in such circumstances. See Bush Hog Manufacturing Co., Inc. v. Commissioner, 42 T.C. 713, 726–727, note 5 (1964).

Another example of an indirect transfer of property given by the House Report is a case where stockholders acquire property (other than money) from their corporation and as part of the same transaction transfer such property to a new corporation created for the purpose of receiving it. This is evidently in response to the decision in the Airlene Gas Co. case, supra, that the pre-1964 version of the statute did not apply to such a case.

An even more important 1964 change was the addition of § 1551 (a)(3) which extends the statute to transfers by individuals—specifically, transfers of property (other than money) by five or fewer persons in control of a corporation to a new (or newly-activated) corporation controlled by the same persons. Although subsection (a)(3) was enacted with virtually no fanfare, it represents a very substantial expansion in the scope of § 1551 and in the anti-exemption universe as a whole. Among other things it would seem to plug the loophole which, as was noted earlier, may exist under § 269 if a multi-incorporation of a going enterprise is staggered over several years. Note that § 1551 (a)(3) does not require any relationship, business or otherwise, between the property transferred to the new corporation and the operations of the existing one or more corporations—in other words § 1551 (a)(3) does impose a kind of "one corporation to a customer" rule for any group of five or less who already own a corporation, unless only cash is being transferred to the new corporation.

The new provision presents a number of problems of interpretation. Foremost is the question of whether it applies in the case of simultaneous organization of two or more corporations, as when multiple corporations are formed to take over a going enterprise. Literally, § 1551(a)(3) seems to require that at least one controlled corporation be in existence before the exemption of a new (or newly-activated) corporation may be challenged. Of course, as a theoretical matter, the organization of two or more corporations would rarely if ever be precisely simultaneous; and in any event it is at the time of the *transfer of property* to the challenged corporation that the statute requires the existence of another controlled corporation, a condition which would surely be satisfied. On the other hand, it is certainly arguable that if simultaneous incorporation was one of the targets of this provision some language more clearly calculated to reach such situations would have been included. Moreover, the absence of any reference to simultaneous incorporation in the Committee Reports tends to suggest that such situations were not intended to be covered. Resolution of this issue will have to await the issuance of regulations under § 1551 (a)(3).

Another question under § 1551(a)(3) is whether the individuals who control the first corporation must all transfer property other than money to the challenged corporation in order for the section to apply. Literally, that is what the statute seems to require. Under this construction, the statute would not be applicable if some of the control group transfer cash to the challenged corporation (unless of course the cash were used to acquire property from another controlled corporation, in which event the transaction would presumably fall within § 1551(a)(2)). However, some doubt is cast upon this construction of § 1551(a)(3) by the comment in the Committee Reports, S.Rep.No. 830, 88th Cong., 2d Sess. 155 (1964), and H.Rep.No.749, 88th Cong., 1st Sess. 202 (1963), to the effect that "for purposes of determining whether the transferor is considered to be in control of the transferee corporation, the individual who makes the transfer, together with no more than four other individuals, must own" the requisite value or voting power of the stock of the two corporations. This interpretation could greatly expand the scope of § 1551(a)(3) by making it applicable to a case where, for example, one of the five owners of one corporation transfers property to a new corporation, while the others transfer money, or perhaps nothing at all, for their stock. Here again further guidance must be awaited in the regulations.

In order to exclude from § 1551(a)(3) cases where two or more corporations are owned by the same group of people but in such different proportions as to be outside the purpose of the statute, § 1551(b)(2)(B) introduces a new wrinkle into the control test. That provision adds to the general control test of at least 80% of the voting power or the value of the stock of each corporation (subject to the attribution rules of § 1563) the requirement that more than 50% of the voting power or the value of the stock of each corporation be owned in identical percentages in the two corporations by the individuals in the group. In other words, when any individual in the control group owns a different percentage of stock in the two corporations, for this computation only the smaller percentage is taken into account. So if A owns 65% of X Corp. and 35% of Y Corp., while B owns 35% of X and 65% of Y, the identical ownership of each is 35%, for a total identical ownership of 70%, and the test of § 1551(b)(2)(B) would be satisfied.

---

c. Purpose

Unlike § 269, which applies only when tax avoidance is *the principal* purpose, § 1551 comes into play whenever the desire to secure an additional surtax exemption (or accumulated earnings credit) is as much as "a major purpose" of the transaction. This obvious effort to strengthen the Government's hand on the purpose issue is coupled with a provision expressly casting upon the taxpayer the burden of disproving the presence of such a major purpose "by the clear preponderance of the evidence", thus reinforcing the normal presumption of correctness which attaches to any determination by the Commissioner. In theory this "major purpose" test of § 1551 might have been expected to constitute a considerable obstacle to taxpayers seeking to acquire additional surtax exemptions. For it is not enough to escape § 1551 that the taxpayer show a valid business purpose for the transaction, although that was usually sufficient to ward off § 269; since tax saving might still be a major purpose even though business reasons are also present, the taxpayer must go on to establish the negative proposition, i. e., that securing an additional exemption was *not* a major purpose. Nevertheless, in practice taxpayers have had astounding success under § 1551, and in the vast majority of cases to date they have succeeded in convincing the courts that there was no major tax purpose. For example, in the most recent case in point at this writing, Middle States Terminals, Inc. v. Commissioner, 25 T.C.M. 203 (1966), involving the transfer of a partially-constructed Chicago terminal to a newly-formed corporation by an Ohio truck terminal corporation (which also owned a terminal in Cincinnati), the court found that the "only reason" for the transaction was the insistence upon separate entities by the bank which financed both terminals so that "it would be easier to proceed against the separately-held property in the event either of the terminals got into financial difficulties". For other representative cases in the almost unbroken line of taxpayer successes, see Hiawatha Home Builders, Inc. v. Commissioner, 36 T.C. 491 (1961); Cronstroms Manufacturing, Inc. v. Commissioner, 36 T. C. 500 (1961); Midwest Metal Stamping Co., Inc. v. Commissioner, 24 T.C.M. 1533 (1965).

5. SECTIONS 61(a) AND 482

The other two important weapons in the Commissioner's anti-multiple-corporation arsenal are §§ 61(a) and 482. While these provisions do not directly limit or deny surtax exemptions, they may lead to the same result since under these sections the income of one corporation may be attributed to another in certain circumstances, in effect eliminating the benefit of the former's surtax exemption. Such attribution under § 61(a) rests upon the fundamental tax doctrine that income is to be taxed to the one who earns or otherwise creates the right to receive it. Thus, if a corporation serves no real economic function it may be disregarded as a sham and its income taxed to the enterprise that really produced it. Section 61(a) has been most commonly invoked in connection with real estate enterprises where taxpayers have often attempted to use many corporations, particularly in the development of housing projects. Thus in Aldon Homes, Inc. v. Commissioner, 33 T.C. 582 (1959), the shareholders of a real estate corporation had formed 16 additional corporations (referred to as "Alphabet" corporations because their names started with a different letter of the alphabet from A through P), each of which was to acquire house lots from the principal corporation. Construction of the houses on these lots was to be carried out by another affiliated corporation, and sales of the completed houses were to be handled by still another corporation; but the overall planning of all these related activities was done by the principal corporation. The court agreed with the Commissioner that the income of the Alphabet companies resulting from sale of the completed houses was attributable to the principal corporation under the predecessor of § 61(a):

> After careful consideration of all the evidence presented and of the authorities cited, however, we have concluded that the sixteen alphabet corporations, Aldon through Pewang, were not organized for any purpose other than the obtaining

of tax benefits; that they did not carry on the business activities which resulted in the profits from the development of Tract 17169, nor any substantial business activities, and consequently did not earn the income in question; that, though legal entities in form, for purposes of taxation, they were unreal or shams and are to be disregarded.

Petitioners argue that the development of Tract 17169 through 16 corporations rather than through one served a number of business purposes: (1) That it enabled the avoidance of a possible general claim against the entire project in the event the development of any portion of the tract was a business failure; (2) that it limited possible tort liability; (3) that it eased the handling of mechanics' liens; and (4) that it facilitated the attraction of capital by reducing corporate taxes and thereby increasing the return to the parties. We are convinced, however, from our study of all the facts and circumstances that none of the alleged advantages in the use of multiple corporations in the development of Tract 17169 constituted any actual business purpose in the instant case. The alleged business purposes impressed us simply as a lawyer's marshaling of possible business reasons that might conceivably have motivated the adoption of the forms here employed but which in fact played no part whatever in the utilization of the multiple corporate structure. . . .

* * *

Holding corporate meetings, adopting by-laws, electing officers and directors, and issuing stock and other securities, through necessary steps in preparation for the carrying on of business activities, were merely formal acts of organization and were not substantive income-producing activities. Nor did the keeping of separate books for each of the corporations, of itself, constitute such business activity. All 16 of the alphabet corporations were organized and dissolved in unison. Their original incorporators were identical and their articles of incorporation and minutes of meetings were substantially identical. The stock of the corporations was held almost exclusively by Metz, Woodrow, and Oberndorfer, the controlling stockholders of Aldon. The same office staff, occupying the same office space, kept the books for all the corporations.

* * *

The alphabet corporations were but the mechanical instruments which amplified the tune, the melody and lyrics of which had been composed and written by Aldon, and it was Aldon, through its controlling stockholders, which controlled the tempo and the finale—the distribution of the profits. It is not to be overlooked that Metz, Woodrow, and Oberndorfer were not only the controlling stockholders of Aldon but that separately or together they were also the controlling stockholders in each of the alphabet corporations, and so, had absolute control of the instruments which played the tune.

Accord, Shaw Construction Co. v. Commissioner, 323 F.2d 316 (9th Cir. 1963), where the parties attempted to use 88 corporations, together with three trusts and one partnership, in carrying out a real estate development.

As to § 482, until recently that provision had proved rather ineffective so far as limiting the benefits of multiple surtax exemptions is concerned. The discussion of § 482 in the Esrenco case, supra, reflects the traditional view that the provision is primarily designed to prevent shifting of items of income or expense between controlled enterprises as a result of non-arm's-length dealings between the two. The courts had uniformly refused to find any warrant in § 482 for simply ignoring a corporation and attributing all of its income and expenses to some other corporation, except where the parties themselves had ignored the separate existence of the various enterprises by commingling the assets, failing to keep separate accounts, or arbitrarily shifting income among the enterprises without regard to which one actually did the work (in which event of course § 61(a) could normally also be invoked). E. g., Advance Machinery Exchange, Inc. v. Commissioner, 196 F.2d 1006 (2d Cir. 1952). Otherwise, a typical application of § 482 was like that in Campbell County State Bank v. Commissioner, 311 F.2d 374 (8th Cir. 1963), where the stockholders of a bank used its premises and facilities to run an insurance partnership without paying anything to the bank, and § 482 was used to allocate some of the bank's expenses to the partnership, thus increasing the bank's taxable income. (Notice that in such circumstances the parties could conceivably have been subjected to an even more onerous tax burden by viewing the value of the cost-free use of corporate facilities by the shareholders as a dividend to them from the corporation, taxable as ordinary income.)

It was also generally assumed that § 482 did not permit a straightforward allocation of the net income of one corporation to another, since that would really amount to ignoring the separate existence of the first corporation rather than merely reallocating particular items of income or expense between controlled entities which had not dealt at arm's length. However, the Ballentine Motor Co. case, referred to in the Esrenco opinion, supra, rejected any fixed bar against the allocation of net income, holding instead that this procedure could be viewed as merely a short-cut for the allocation of total gross income and deductions. Actually, the decision in the Ballentine Motor Co. case did not constitute much of a departure from the traditional view of § 482. The case involved the transfer at cost of an inventory of automobiles, which was assured of profitable sale at retail, from a profitable corporate dealership to a related corporate dealer having accumulated losses; after enough of the inventory had been sold to absorb the transferee's losses, the remaining inventory was returned to its original owner. Obviously, in an arm's length transaction there was no reason why the profitable corporation should have allowed the loss corporation to obtain the assured profit inherent in the inventory transferred.

However, more recently the Tax Court approved an allocation of net income under circumstances which suggest a substantially expanded role for § 482 that could make the section a formidable weapon in the anti-exemption battle. In Hamburgers York Road v. Commissioner, 41 T.C. 821 (1964), the stockholders of a successful downtown retail men's wear store decided to open a suburban store. A new corporation was organized for this purpose, at least in part because of the desire of one of the three groups of inter-related stockholders of the old corporation to have a larger stock interest in the new store than they had in the existing one. The stockholders of the old corporation acquired the stock of the new corporation in the agreed-upon new proportions for a total of $20,000, and this amount, together with advances of $40,000 from a bank and $25,000 from one of the stockholders, constituted the new corporation's working capital. The new corporation did not acquire any tangible assets from the old corporation. The officers and directors of the two corporations were virtually identical, and, except for the services performed by its own manager and men's clothing buyer, all of the new store's functions, including general buying, alterations, credit and collection services, and accounting, were handled by employees of the old corporation, with the old corporation being reimbursed by the new one.

The court found that the two stores constituted a single integrated enterprise, with the suburban store operated substantially as a branch of the downtown store; that the earnings of the integrated enterprise were primarily attributable to the long-established business reputation and good will of the old store, its business organization and procedures, the brands of merchandise which it handled, and its advertising programs; and that there was no substantial business purpose for the separate incorporation of the new store. Accordingly, the court concluded that the principal purpose for creating a second corporation was to obtain an additional surtax exemption, that the business relationship between the two stores was not at arm's length, and that pursuant to § 482 it was necessary to allocate all of the taxable income of the new corporation to the old corporation in order to prevent evasion of taxes and to reflect clearly the taxable income of the two corporations.

It is the court's emphasis in the Hamburgers York Road case upon the *purpose* for incorporating the new store which marks the apparent departure from previous § 482 authority. For it has generally been thought that the purpose for which a particular entity was created is irrelevant under § 482. Normally, as the court put it in the Esrenco opinion, "section 482 is based on the recognition of various corporate entities", with the question under § 482 being the nature of the dealings among these corporations; and obviously on that question the purpose for which any particular corporation was created would have little bearing.

To be sure, the court in Hamburgers York Road also found that the business relationship between the two corporations was not at arm's length, as evidenced by the fact that the old corporation allowed the new one to enjoy without charge the benefits associated with the former's good will, trade name, experienced buying and selling organizations, customer lists, and advertising formats. Accordingly, there was certainly warrant for allocating to the old corporation under § 482 some amount—a kind of constructive rent—for the use of these valuable intangibles. But it is less easy to agree with the court that the old corporation would not have charged an outsider any less than its total net profits for this privilege. Surely this goes too far, for what outsider would ever agree to pay all of its profits for the privilege of using another's intangibles—or tangibles either, for that matter. Moreover, the court's view ignores the contributions which the new corporation itself made to earning its profits, such as its $20,000 of capital and the desirable premises which it held under lease, to say nothing of the fact that it was the new corporation which was subject to the risk of loss, inherent in the operation of any business, and on that account alone entitled to some share of the profits.

The court sought to minimize the importance of the contributions made by the new corporation, observing that the lease on the new premises could have been obtained by the old corporation and was in fact guaranteed by it, and that the new corporation's capital was not particularly significant and came from the stockholders of the old corporation who might just as easily have contributed it to the old corporation. These responses suggest some confusion between a § 482 proceeding and an attack under § 269 or § 1551. Under the latter sections it is certainly appropriate to consider whether there was any non-tax reason for the creation of the second corporation, or whether the old corporation could have done everything the new corporation did. But under § 482, the question would seem to be what in fact the new corporation did do, rather than what some other entity might have done—and in that context the new corporation seems clearly entitled to "credit" for at least so much of its profits as are attributable to its own contributions, such as its capital and its premises.

A less extreme view of the reach of § 482 was taken by the Tax Court in a case decided shortly after Hamburgers, Ach v. Commissioner, 42 T.C. 114 (1964), affirmed, 358 F.2d 342 (6th Cir. 1966). There an individual who had successfully operated a women's wear proprietorship for many years "sold" her business to a corporation, owned by her son, which had accumulated large operating losses in the conduct of an entirely different type of business and owed a large sum of money to her husband. The sale price was only $30,000, payable in installments, which was clearly inadequate since it was about equal to one year's earnings of the proprietorship. The former proprietress was not a stockholder of the corporate transferee, but she continued to run the women's wear business as a full-time employee and chairman of the board of directors, although she received no compensation. While agreeing with the Commissioner that the circumstances called for an allocation of income from the corporation to the former proprietress as an individual, the court refused to allocate all of the corporation's profits to her. Noting that the Commissioner's power under § 482 was limited to correcting a *distortion* of income, the court held that some of the income from the dress business was properly attributable to the corporation, because it stemmed from assets now owned by the corporation and the services of the corporation's employees (other than the former proprietress). Admittedly these items were substantially less important than the value of the former proprietress's management services, but they were not insignificant, and the court finally concluded that these items accounted for 30% of the profits, leaving 70% of the profits to be allocated to the former proprietress. The Hamburgers York Road case was not mentioned.

While the Ach decision appears to be more in keeping with the traditional view of § 482 than Hamburgers York Road, Ach presents some knotty questions of its own. First, would the value of the former proprietress's services have constituted a sound basis upon which to determine the amount to be allocated to her, were it not for the fortuitous fact that she was not a stockholder of the corporation and did not draw any compensation? If she had been a substantial stockholder, the court would have had to consider whether allocation of some of the corporation's profits to her based on the value of her services was really any different from insisting that a stockholder receive compensation for services, which courts have been somewhat reluctant to do. E. g., Commissioner v. Gross, 236 F.2d 612 (2d Cir. 1956). Moreover, if she had received reasonable compensation, no additional allocation to her would have been called for under the court's approach, since then her services would have belonged to the corporation just like those of the other employees, and would have been part of the corporation's own contribution to its profits. But this would wholly ignore the fact that she sold the business for a price far less than its value (quite apart from the value of her service). Is the answer to this that the inadequate sales price in these circumstances does not independently justify any allocation of profits, but rather should be viewed as resulting in either a contribution to capital, if the transferor is a substantial stockholder, or if not, as a gift to those who are stockholders, to the extent of the bargain purchase?

There is also the more general question of for how long an allocation of the corporation's profits such as the one ordered in the Ach case is to continue, and whether the allocation percentage must be redetermined from year to year. It seems unlikely that the ratio of the value of the services of the former proprietress to the value of the contributions made by the corporation itself would remain static, particularly if the business continues to grow; but the prospect of a recomputation every year is not very inviting.

The last of the 1964 triumvirate of § 482 cases, Bush Hog Manufacturing Co., Inc. v. Commissioner, 42 T.C. 713 (1964), involved an attack upon eight sales companies created by the stockholders of a manufacturing company. The Commissioner also relied upon §§ 269, 1551, and 61(a), but his determination under these provisions failed in the face of the court's finding that the sales corporations had been set up for valid business purposes rather than tax avoidance. So far as § 482 was concerned, the court seemed to hue to the traditional view of that provision in holding that it was not applicable because "there was no evidence of an artificial shifting of income and deductions" among the corporations (although presumably the result would have been the same even if the court had adopted the broader Hamburgers York Road approach to § 482, in view of the court's finding on the purpose issue in connection with §§ 61(a), 269 and 1551). See generally Murdoch, The Scope of the Power of the Internal Revenue Service to Reallocate under Section 482, 6 B.C.Ind. & Com.L.Rev. 717 (1965).

Whatever may be § 482's future on the domestic scene, the section seems clearly destined to play an increasingly important part in the foreign income area, where, pursuant to the 1962 additions to the Code, §§ 951–964, allocation of income and deductions between related foreign and domestic enterprises may well be critical. This has already resulted in the promulgation of some proposed additional regulations under § 482 seeking to refine the standards for arm's-length dealings between related entities, 30 Fed.Reg. 4256–4259 (1965); and more new regulations, relating particularly to allocation in connection with transfers of intangible property, are on the way. T.I.R. No. 725, April 30, 1965. See generally, Waris, What's New in Section 482?, 43 Taxes 614 (1965); Cohen, Section 482: Treasury's Efforts to Teach an Old Dog Some New Tricks, 43 Taxes 835 (1965).

*

Chapter 2

ORGANIZATION OF A PUBLIC COMPANY

Introduction

The special problems of organizing a publicly-held corporation flow primarily from the federal and state securities statutes which govern raising investment capital from the public. Accordingly, before analyzing the problems involved in soliciting funds from the public, it may be useful to review briefly some of the alternative sources of funds which may be available to help meet the capital requirements of either a going concern or a proposed new venture.

1. **Banks and Insurance Companies.** Banks are still the primary source of outside financing for small and medium-sized businesses. However, more often than not the bank will insist upon some security; and unless the enterprise is fairly substantial the principal stockholders may well have to co-sign the obligation. In addition, bank loans are almost always short-term. Insurance companies are also an important source of financing, and they are often willing to extend credit for a longer period; but insurance company financing is rarely available to a small business.

2. **Finance Companies, Factors, etc.** These concerns are primarily sources of short-term financing, secured by either inventory or accounts receivable. However, such arrangements can in effect amount almost to long-term financing, if provision is made for constant repayment and reëxtension of credit as the accounts receivable or inventory turn over. Some financing is also done on the security of equipment, by either conditional sale or chattel mortgage; there is also a growing tendency to finance such items indirectly by simply leasing instead of purchasing them.

3. **Small Business Investment Companies.** The Small Business Investment Act of 1958 authorized the creation of Small Business Investment Companies, organized for the purpose of supplying long-term financing to small business concerns through the medium of long-term loans or investments in equity securities or convertible debentures. These SBIC's are private corporations with paid-in capital of at least $300,000, of which up to half can be obtained on attractive terms from the Small Business Administration. By the middle of 1963 almost 700 such companies had been formed in various parts of the country. However, there is as yet little information concerning either the practices or experiences of such companies. See generally, Comment, The Small Business Investment Company: An Attempt to Fill the Equity Gap, 9 Vill.L.Rev. 109 (1963). Suffice it to say that because of the comparative novelty of these enterprises, as well as the myriad of federal regulations to which they

are subject, a good deal of time and expense may be needed to work out a satisfactory financing deal with an SBIC.

4. **State and Local Financing Assistance.** Many states and municipalities have financial assistance programs of various kinds designed to attract new industry to the particular area. These programs vary widely and may offer such diverse incentives as free land for a plant-site, rent-free use of existing facilities, relief from local taxes, and aid in training workers. Some of these incentive programs are the products of specific legislation; others, particularly at the municipal level, are a good deal more informal, and the extent of the incentives in any particular case may be largely a matter of bargaining between the parties. While of course established businesses are the favorite targets of such programs, incentives may also be extended to a new enterprise, particularly one which holds the promise of creating a substantial number of new jobs.

Normally, state and local government agencies cannot provide actual cash financing. However, in many localities the local banks join forces to form a separate organization capable of helping to encourage new industry to locate in the area by making more speculative, and perhaps longer-term, loans than would be customary for banks. Such organizations, sometimes called Industrial Development Commissions, usually work closely with the appropriate state agencies in the effort to attract new business. However, these Commissions generally stick fairly close to ordinary banking practices; accordingly, they typically require mortgage security, and often a steep interest rate as well, sometimes as high as ten per cent.

SECTION 1. FEDERAL REGULATION OF PUBLIC ISSUES OF SECURITIES

A. DISTRIBUTION TECHNIQUES—UNDERWRITING

The following excerpts from Professor Loss' classic work in the securities field, Securities Regulation,[1] provide a helpful introduction to the two basic methods of distributing securities:

FIRM-COMMITMENT UNDERWRITING

With respect to public financing otherwise than by rights offerings, the most prevalent type of American "underwriting" is the "firm-commitment" variety. It is not

---

[1]. Loss, Securities Regulation (2d ed. 1961) 163–164, 171–173 (hereinafter cited as Loss). Reprinted with the permission of the publisher, Little, Brown & Co. Footnotes omitted.

technically underwriting in the classic insurance sense. But its purpose and effect are much the same in that it assures the issuer of a specified amount of money at a certain time (subject frequently to specified conditions precedent in the underwriting contract) and shifts the risk of the market (at least in part) to the investment bankers. The issuer simply sells the entire issue outright to a group of securities firms. . . . They in turn sell at a price differential to a larger "selling group" of dealers. And they sell at another differential to the public. . . .

BEST-EFFORTS UNDERWRITING

Companies which are not well established are not apt to find an underwriter who will give a firm commitment and assume the risk of distribution. Of necessity, therefore, they customarily distribute their securities through firms which merely undertake to use their best efforts. Paradoxically, this type of distribution is also preferred on occasion by companies which are so well established that they can do without any underwriting commitment, thus saving on cost of distribution. The securities house, instead of *buying* the issue *from* the company and reselling it as principal, *sells* it *for* the company as agent; and its compensation takes the form of an agent's commission rather than a merchant's or dealer's profit. There may still be a selling group to help in the merchandising. But its members likewise do not buy from the issuer; they are sub-agents. This, of course, is not really underwriting; it is simply merchandising.

AMERICAN INVESTMENT BANKING IN GENERAL

There is nothing immutable about these . . . methods of distribution. The investment banking industry, being very much alive, is continually studying and developing new techniques. . . . Then there are the companies which, through choice or necessity, attempt to distribute their securities without using any underwriters at all. The issues so offered are typically at one end or the other of the quality spectrum. A considerable portion of the best stocks and convertible bonds is sold through rights offerings of one kind or another without the use of underwriters. And at the other extreme are those companies, usually promotional ventures, which have no alternative but to peddle their securities through their own officers, directors and employees. . . .

B. THE SECURITIES ACT OF 1933

The Securities Act of 1933 was enacted as a result of the public sentiment aroused by practices used in distributing securities in the period 1920–1930. Federal intervention was necessary because state regulation was neither uniform in its terms nor uniformly enforced. Moreover, it was difficult for a state to protect its citizens from sellers across state lines, since often the offending promoter or salesman was physically outside the state and hence beyond the reach of its process.

The primary objective of the Securities Act was to protect investors by requiring full and fair disclosure of material facts concerning securities publicly offered, and by preventing misrepresentation and fraud in their sale. The Act gives the SEC power to supervise the required disclosure, but the Commission is not called upon to pass on the merits of securities. Thus any security may be offered for sale if it is effectively registered, and the truth is told concerning it. However, by rigorous enforcement of the disclosure requirements in the case of dubious issues, the SEC is in position to force the company to indicate clearly just how doubtful the venture is. (Unfortunately, events during the boom market up to the spring of 1962 indicated that full disclosure is not always enough and that in such periods the public will buy securities almost without regard to their intrinsic merits.)

SECURITIES ACT OF 1933

Definitions

Sec. 2. When used in this title, unless the context otherwise requires—

(1) The term "security" means any note, stock, treasury stock, bond, debenture, evidence of indebtedness, certificate of interest or participation in any profit-sharing agreement, collateral-trust certificate, preorganization certificate or subscription, transferable share, investment contract, voting-trust certificate, certificate of deposit for a security, fractional undivided interest in oil, gas, or other mineral rights, or, in general, any interest or instrument commonly known as a "security," or any certificate of interest or participation in, temporary or interim certificate for, receipt for, guarantee of, or warrant or right to subscribe to or purchase, any of the foregoing.

(2) (Definition of "Person") . . .

(3) The term "sale" or "sell" shall include every contract of sale or disposition of a security or interest in a security, for value. The term "offer to sell", "offer for sale", or "offer" shall include every attempt or offer to dispose of or solicitation of an offer to buy a security or interest in a security, for value. The terms defined in this paragraph and the term "offer to buy" as used in subsection (c) of section 5 shall not include preliminary negotiations or agreements between an issuer (or any person directly or indirectly

controlling or controlled by an issuer, or under direct or indirect common control with an issuer) and any underwriter or among underwriters who are or are to be in privity of contract with an issuer (or any person directly or indirectly controlling or controlled by an issuer, or under direct or indirect common control with an issuer). Any security given or delivered with, or as a bonus on account of, any purchase of securities or any other thing, shall be conclusively presumed to constitute a part of the subject of such purchase and to have been offered and sold for value. The issue or transfer of a right or privilege, when originally issued or transferred with a security, giving the holder of such security the right to convert such security into another security of the same issuer or of another person, or giving a right to subscribe to another security of the same issuer or of another person, which right cannot be exercised until some future date, shall not be deemed to be an offer or sale of such other security; but the issue or transfer of such other security upon the exercise of such right of conversion or subscription shall be deemed a sale of such other security.

(4) The term "issuer" means every person who issues or proposes to issue any security; . . .

. . .

(10) The term "prospectus" means any prospectus, notice, circular, advertisement, letter, or communication, written or by radio or television, which offers any security for sale or confirms the sale of any security . . . .

(11) The term "underwriter" means any person who has purchased from an issuer with a view to, or offers or sells for an issuer in connection with, the distribution of any security, or participates or has a direct or indirect participation in any such undertaking, or participates or has a participation in the direct or indirect underwriting of any such undertaking; but such term shall not include a person whose interest is limited to a commission from an underwriter or dealer not in excess of the usual and customary distributors' or sellers' commission. As used in this paragraph the term "issuer" shall include, in addition to an issuer, any person directly or indirectly controlling or controlled by the issuer, or any person under direct or indirect common control with the issuer.

(12) The term "dealer" means any person who engages either for all or part of his time, directly or indirectly, as agent, broker, or principal, in the business of offering, buying, selling, or otherwise dealing or trading in securities issued by another person.

Exempted Securities

Sec. 3. (a) Except as hereinafter expressly provided the provisions of this title shall not apply to any of the following classes of securities:

. . .

(3) (Commercial Paper)

(4) (Securities of Charitable Organizations)

. . .

(9) Any security exchanged by the issuer with its existing security holders exclusively where no commission or other remuneration is paid or given directly or indirectly for soliciting such exchange;

. . .

(11) Any security which is a part of an issue offered and sold only to persons resident within a single State or Territory, where the issuer of such security is a person resident and doing business within, or, if a corporation, incorporated by and doing business within, such State or Territory.

(b) The Commission may from time to time by its rules and regulations and subject to such terms and conditions as may be prescribed therein, add any class of securities to the securities exempted as provided in this section, if it finds that the enforcement of this title with respect to such securities is not necessary in the public interest and for the protection of investors by reason of the small amount involved or the limited character of the public offering; but no issue of securities shall be exempted under this subsection where the aggregate amount at which such issue is offered to the public exceeds $300,000.

Exempted Transactions

Sec. 4. The provisions of section 5 shall not apply to any of the following transactions:

(1) Transactions by any person other than an issuer, underwriter, or dealer; transactions by an issuer not involving any public offering; . . .

(2) Brokers' transactions, executed upon customers' orders on any exchange or in the open or counter market, but not the solicitation of such orders.

Prohibitions Relating to Interstate Commerce and the Mails

Sec. 5. (a) Unless a registration statement is in effect as to a security, it shall be unlawful for any person, directly or indirectly—

(1) to make use of any means or instruments of transportation or communication in interstate commerce or of the mails to sell such security through the use or medium of any prospectus or otherwise; or

(2) to carry or cause to be carried through the mails or in interstate commerce, by any means or instruments of transportation, any such security for the purposes of sale or for delivery after sale.

(b) It shall be unlawful for any person, directly or indirectly—

(1) to make use of any means or instruments of transportation or communication in interstate commerce or of the mails to carry or transmit any prospectus relating to any security with respect to which a registration statement has been filed under this title, unless such prospectus meets the requirements of section 10, or

(2) to carry or to cause to be carried through the mails or in interstate commerce any such security for the purpose of sale or for delivery after sale, unless accompanied or preceded by a prospectus that meets the requirements of subsection (a) of section 10.

(c) It shall be unlawful for any person, directly or indirectly, to make use of any means or instruments of transportation or communication in interstate commerce or of the mails to offer to sell or offer to buy through the use or medium of any prospectus or otherwise any security unless a registration statement has been filed as to such security, or while the registration statement is the subject of a refusal order or stop order or (prior to the effective date of the registration statement) any public proceeding or examination under section 8.

Registration of Securities and Signing of Registration Statement

Sec. 6. (a) Any security may be registered with the Commission under the terms and conditions hereinafter provided, by filing a registration statement. . . .

. . .

Civil Liabilities on Account of False Registration Statement

Sec. 11. (a) In case any part of the registration statement, when such part became effective, contained an untrue statement of a material fact or omitted to state a material fact required to be stated therein or necessary to make the statements therein not misleading, any person acquiring such security (unless it is proved that at the time of such acquisition he knew of such untruth or omission) may, either at law or in equity, in any court of competent jurisdiction, sue—

(1) every person who signed the registration statement; (2) every person who was a director . . . (3) every person who, with his consent, is named in the registration statement as being or about to become a director . . . (4) every accountant, engineer, or appraiser, or any person whose profession gives authority to a statement made by him . . . (5) every underwriter with respect to such security.

If such person acquired the security after the issuer has made generally available to its security holders an earning statement covering a period of at least twelve months beginning after the effective date of the registration statement, then the right of recovery under this subsection shall be conditioned on proof that such person acquired the securities relying on such untrue statement in the registration statement or relying upon the registration statement and not knowing of such omission, but such reliance may be established without proof of the reading of the registration statement by such person.

(b) [Defenses of Persons Other than Issuer]

. . .

(3) That [as regards any part of the registration statement (A) not purporting to be made on the authority of an expert or (B) purporting to be made upon his authority as an expert] he had, after reasonable investigation, reasonable ground to believe and did believe . . . that the statements therein were true and that there was no omission to state a material fact required to be stated therein or necessary to make the statements therein not misleading; and [as regards any part of the registration statement (C) purporting to be made on the authority of an expert or (D) purporting to be a statement by an official person] he had no reasonable ground to believe and did not believe . . . that the statements therein were untrue or that there was an omission . . . or that such part of the registration statement did not fairly represent the statement. . . .

. . .

Civil Liabilities Arising in Connection With Prospectuses And Communications

Sec. 12. Any person who—

(1) offers or sells a security in violation of section 5, or

(2) offers or sells a security (whether or not exempted by the provisions of section 3, other than paragraph (2) of subsection (a) thereof), by the use of any means or instruments of transportation or communication in interstate commerce or of the mails, by means of a prospectus or oral communication, which includes an untrue statement of a material fact or omits to state a material fact necessary in order to make the statements, in the light of the circumstances under which they were made, not misleading (the purchaser not knowing of such untruth or omission), and who shall not sustain the burden of proof that he did not know, and in the exercise of reasonable care could not have known, of such untruth or omission, shall be liable to the person purchasing such security from him, who may sue either at law or in equity in any court of competent jurisdiction, to recover the consideration paid for such security with interest thereon, less the amount of any income received thereon, upon the tender of such security, or for damages if he no longer owns the security.

. . .

Fraudulent Interstate Transactions

Sec. 17. (a) It shall be unlawful for any person in the offer or sale of any securities by the use of any means or instruments of transportation or communication in interstate commerce or by the use of the mails, directly or indirectly—

(1) to employ any device, scheme or artifice to defraud, or

(2) to obtain money or property by means of any untrue statement of a material fact or any omission to state a material fact necessary in order to make the statements made, in the light of the circumstances under which they were made, not misleading, or

(3) to engage in any transaction, practice, or course of business which operates or would operate as a fraud or deceit upon the purchaser.

. . .

(c) The exemptions provided in Section 3 shall not apply to the provisions of this Section.

State Control of Securities

Sec. 18. Nothing in this title shall affect the jurisdiction of the securities commission (or any agency or office performing like functions) of any State or Territory of the United States, or the District of Columbia, over any security or any person.

Special Powers of Commission

Sec. 19. (a) The Commission shall have authority from time to time to make, amend, and rescind such rules and regulations as may be necessary to carry out the provisions of this title including rules and regulations governing registration statements and prospectuses for various classes of securities and issuers, and defining accounting, technical and trade terms used in this title. . . .

. . .

NOTE ON THE SECURITIES ACT [2]

1. The Structure of the Act

Apart from the definitions (§ 2) and the exemptions (§§ 3, 4), the general structure of the Act hinges upon § 5, which makes it unlawful to sell a security unless a registration statement is in effect and unless accompanied or preceded by a prospectus. §§ 6–10 relate to the procedure, and information required in registration.

The sanctions imposed are both civil (§§ 11, 12), criminal (§§ 17, 24) and administrative—through action by the Securities and Exchange Commission (§ 8), subject to review and enforcement by the courts (§§ 9 and 19–21). Careful analysis in advance by the SEC, coupled with the omnipresent threat of civil liability, has resulted in a very small volume of litigation involving misstatements in registration statements and prospectuses. Most of the registration problems are handled informally by letter, telephone, or conference.

2. Section 17—The General Anti-Fraud Section

Section 17 is somewhat independent of the general structure of the Act. With minor exceptions the exemptions of §§ 3 and 4 do not apply to § 17. Whether or not securities are registered, subsection (a)—which is a general anti-fraud provision—makes unlawful any form of fraud, untruth, or omission of a material fact, with respect to the sale of any securities in interstate commerce or by use of the mails. Subsection (b) is directed against "touting." It was designed particularly to meet the evils of the tipster sheet, as well as stories in newspapers or periodicals that purport to give an unbiased opinion but which in reality are bought and paid for.

There has been considerable doubt whether § 17 may be used as a basis for civil liability, in the way that § 10 of the Securities Exchange Act of 1934 often has been. However, as an anti-fraud statute, it has been relied upon repeatedly in obtaining indictments and injunctions against prospective wrongdoers.

3. The Civil Liabilities Sections

Quite apart from the general fraud prohibition of § 17, there are three specific civil liability sections in the Securities Act: §§ 11, 12(1) and 12(2). They greatly improve the legal position of an investor seeking redress for losses in a suit against persons connected with the sale or issuance of a security. Section 11 provides for civil liability of an issuer, and also numerous others participating in the preparation of the *registration statement*, for losses sustained by a purchaser by reason of misstatements or omissions. Section 12(1) is operative when anyone *offers* or *sells* a security in violation

---

2. The following material is adapted, by permission, from Baker & Cary, Cases and Materials on Corporations (3d ed., unabridged 1959) 1098–1105, 1124–1133.

of the registration and prospectus provisions of § 5; and § 12(2) imposes liability for sale of a security, whether registered or exempt from registration, by means of material misstatements or omissions of fact.

a. *Prior to the Act.* For an investor to recover his losses in a common law deceit action was an arduous task. The buyer had to prove that the defendant *misrepresented* a *material fact*; that the defendant knew or should have known of its falsity (though this element of *scienter* was not required for rescission); that the buyer *relied* upon the *misrepresentation*; that his loss was a *consequence* of it; and that the defendant was in privity with the buyer. This burden of proof was particularly stringent in the securities area, because of the twin difficulties of accurately valuing a security and establishing the cause of a price decline, and because the defendant-seller generally possessed exclusive knowledge of much of the essential information.

b. *Purpose and Effect of the Civil Liability Sections.* The primary objective of the Securities Act is honest and accurate securities marketing. The civil liability sections aid in advancing this objective by broadening the law of deceit, particularly in terms of the group of persons subject to liability. This threat of personal liability of directors and other participants, taken together with the SEC's rigorous supervision over registration statements, and the possibility of a stop order, with its disastrous effect on marketing the security, has tended to promote precision in the material contained in registration statements.

Doubtless this is one of the reasons for the small number of civil cases which have actually been brought under the Act. There are, however, some other reasons, such as the reluctance of the average investor to "throw good money after bad", the high costs of litigation, and the prosperity that the economy has enjoyed since World War II. Also, there are some major deterrents to suit within the terms of the statute itself. For example, § 11(e), requiring an undertaking for costs where the judge feels the suit or defense "to have been without merit," has made potential litigants think twice before marching into court. The plaintiff's burden of proving the untruth, and the various defenses open to the defendants, make success less certain. And there is also the short statute of limitations in § 13 of the Act, applying to both § 11 and § 12.

c. *Section 11—Civil Liabilities on Account of False Registration Statement.* Section 11 particularly was opposed by the securities industry which wrongly feared it would stifle legitimate financing. *Prima facie*, liability is imposed on the issuer and a wide variety of persons participating in the registration statement, if it contained a material untruth or omission — scienter, reliance and privity are no longer part of the plaintiff's case.

However, § 11 does allow the issuer and all others named in § 11(a) certain defenses: (a) that the plaintiff knew of the untruth at the time of acquisition of the securities; (b) where the issuer has made generally available an earnings statement covering a period of at least twelve months beginning after the effective date of the registration statement, that the plaintiff has failed to prove that he relied on untrue items in the registration statement (but the plaintiff may establish such reliance without proving that he read the registration statement); (c) that the damages did not result from the misrepresentation in the registration statement.

Any person other than the issuer is not liable under § 11(a) if he proves that he had reasonable grounds to believe in the truth of the statement or, in the case of statements by experts or officials, that he had no reasonable grounds to believe them untrue. The standard of reasonableness under § 11(c) is the normal common law test: "A prudent man in the management of his own property".

It is in the imposition of liability on the persons named in § 11(a) other than the issuer that the section makes its revolutionary departure from common law, for the privity requirement is fully abandoned. In effect, § 11 responded to the call of Chief Justice Cardozo in Ultramares Corp. v. Touche, 255 N.Y. 170, 174 N.E. 441, 74 A.L.R. 1139 (1931), where, after suggesting that a finding of gross negligence might support an action, he refused to hold the defendant accountants liable to third parties for mere negligence in failing to discover the manipulations in the defendant company's books while drawing financial reports, and added: "A change so revolutionary must be wrought by legislation."

d. *Section 12(1)—Civil Liabilities for Failure to Register or Use a Prospectus.* This subsection imposes on the seller of a security (or one controlling the seller under § 15) a virtually absolute liability, in rescission or for damages, to the *immediate purchaser* if the sale or offer was made in violation of the registration or prospectus requirements of § 5 and instruments of interstate commerce were used. The only defense open to the seller is the statute of limitations, § 13. In other words, the seller is liable if he sells a security which should have been registered under § 5 of the Act but was not, or if he sends a prospectus that is defective under § 10, or fails to send such a prospectus at all in violation of § 10. § 12(1) appears to be the most emphatic and clear-cut civil liability provision in the Act.

e. *Section 12(2)—Liability for Misstatements or Omissions of Material Facts in Sales or Offers of Securities.* Section 12(2) is a general liability provision and applies even when the securities are exempt from registration. Under § 12(2) the seller (or one controlling the seller under § 15) is liable to his immediate purchaser if the seller sells or offers any security by the use of any instrument of interstate commerce and has made a material misrepresentation by omission or commission. Note that under § 12(2) the purchaser must prove his own lack of knowledge, whereas under § 11, supra, the defendant bears the burden of proving the plaintiff's knowledge. The purchaser is entitled to rescission, or money damages if he has already disposed of the security at a loss.

Section 12(2) furnishes the seller a defense that was not available in common law rescission, if he can "sustain the burden of proof that he did not know and in the exercise of reasonable care could not have known" of the misrepresentation. However, it is not clear just what it would take to satisfy this burden. Presumably, the seller could rely on the issuer's registration statement, where there is one, for 9 months after the effective date, and thereafter on the issuer's annual reports, if they are filed with the Commission. See generally, Loss, 1708–1712.

4. The Registration Process [3]

Registration involves filing with the Commission a statement describing such matters as the names of persons who participate in the direction, management, or control of the issuer's business; their security holdings and remuneration, including option, bonus, or profit-sharing privileges; the character and size of the business enterprise; its capital structure and past history and earnings; its financial statements, certified by independent accountants; underwriters' commissions; payments to promoters made within two years or intended to be made; acquisitions of property not in the ordinary course of business, and the interest of directors, officers and principal stockholders therein; pending or threatened legal proceedings; and the purposes to which the proceeds of the offerings are to be applied. The "prospectus" constitutes a part of the registration statement which in effect amounts to a summary of the more important matters.

The staff of the Division of Corporation Finance examines each registration statement for compliance with the standards of disclosure and usually notifies the registrant by an informal letter of any material non-compliance. This permits the registrant to file an amendment before the statement becomes effective, which would normally occur twenty days after the filing of the statement.

This 20-day waiting period is designed to provide investors with an opportunity to become familiar with the proposed offering. While in theory the 20-day period starts anew upon the filing of any amendment to the registration, in practice, by virtue of the Commission's power to shorten the waiting period, it usually amounts to little more than twenty days from the time of original filing.

The question of what types of informational or quasi-promotional activities might be carried on during the waiting period has been one of the most troublesome under the Act. Prior to the 1954 amendment, the Act made unlawful the *offer* or sale of a security until a registration statement had become *effective*. From the legislative history of the Act it seemed clear that Congress intended to permit the dissemination of information during the waiting period so that the public would become informed of the essential facts relating to the proposed issue. Yet in practice the free flow of information was restricted because of the fear that communications to prospective customers might be construed as illegal "offers".

After some administrative efforts to resolve this problem, in 1954 the statute was amended to explicitly permit written *offers* to sell and solicitations of *offers* to buy during the waiting period by means of a preliminary prospectus filed with the Commission prior to its use. However, the prohibition against making an actual sale or contract of sale of a security prior to the effective date of the registration statement was not changed. In addition, a new section 5(c) was enacted to expressly make it unlawful to *offer* a security prior to the original filing of a registration statement. Under this provision, care must be taken to assure that publicity efforts made in advance of the filing of a registration statement do not in fact amount to the beginning of a public offering, in violation of section 5(c).

---

3. Adapted from SEC 22d Annual Report (1956) 49–52.

5. The Special Impact of the Securities Act on Promoters

What is said in MacChesney and O'Brien, Full Disclosure under the Securities Act, 4 Law and Contem.Prob. 133, 136 (1937), is still apt today:

"In a new corporation . . . the share of the promoter is of special interest and significance as the percentage of dilution of the stock for promotional payments is apt to be great. Form . . . [S–1, Item 11] is designed to force disclosure of the promotion process so that the investor may know what he is paying for this type of service. The form when answered properly will bring out the names and addresses of the promoters, the stock interest, whether beneficial or of record, payments to promoters and the nature of the consideration given therefor, a statement of the intention of such persons with respect to subscription to additional stock and the prices at which such subscriptions will be executed, and details of any property purchases already made from promoters and any property purchases to be made by use of the proceeds of the issue registered. The Commission has, in many instances, compelled the identification of certain payments ostensibly going to an individual not named as promoter, or disguised as a payment for tangible assets, as promotional payments. Administration has made these requirements of disclosure not merely formal. A superficial statement of what has been given and what has been received is not enough. The real character of the promotional operation must be clearly presented."

The term "promoter" itself is broadly defined under Rule 405 as any person who directly or indirectly takes the initiative in founding and organizing the business, or who in connection with its founding and organization directly or indirectly receives for services and/or property ten percent or more of any class of securities.

The following excerpt, from SEC 18th Annual Report (1952) 18, illustrates how these disclosure requirements may operate in connection with the promoters of a speculative new enterprise:

Speculative hazards disclosed.—A corporation organized under the laws of Delaware to acquire all of the stock of a foreign corporation, which had been organized to explore for sulphur under a concession from a foreign government, filed a registration statement covering 400,000 shares to be offered the public at $1.00 per share. The staff insisted that full disclosure be made of material facts concerning the participation of inside promoters. As a result, the registrant incorporated in its amended prospectus an "Introductory Paragraph" which described the basis of the insiders' participation in sharp contrast to the basis upon which public investors were to be offered a share in the venture, as indicated in the following quotation therefrom:

"[The registrant] has no operating history, and neither owns nor controls any known sulphur deposits. The offering price of $1.00 per share for the 400,000 shares of Common Stock to be sold was determined arbitrarily and such price does not necessarily have any relation to the value of the shares offered. There is presently no established market for the Common Stock.

"The purchasers of such 400,000 shares of Common Stock who will provide all of the cash required for the purposes of this financing as described later in this prospectus, will acquire only 31.25% of the total Common Stock then outstanding.

"[The foreign corporation] and its controlling stockholders who are identified later in this Prospectus as promoters acquired a total of 800,000 shares of Common Stock and will receive in addition $100,000 in cash from the proceeds of this financing and a royalty of $1.00 per short ton of sulphur produced for the assignment of certain rights in concessions of unproven value on which the cost in cash to these promoters has been $12,882.84. The holdings of Common Stock of such promoters will therefore constitute 62.50% of the outstanding stock on completion of this financing.

"The directors of (the registrant) who are also later identified in this Prospectus as promoters have received 80,000 shares of Common Stock for services rendered and to be rendered, or 6.25% of the outstanding stock on completion of this financing.

"Thus a total of 68.75% of the Common Stock will be held by persons designated as promoters."

C. EXEMPTIONS AVAILABLE FOR MODEST FINANCINGS

1. NON-PUBLIC OFFERINGS—SECTION 4(1)

S.E.C. v. RALSTON PURINA CO.

Supreme Court of the United States, 1953.
346 U.S. 119; 73 S.Ct. 981.

MR. JUSTICE CLARK, delivered the opinion of the Court.[4]

Section 4(1) of the Securities Act of 1933 exempts "transactions by an issuer not involving any public offering" from the registration requirements of § 5. We must decide whether Ralston Purina's offerings of treasury stock to its "key employees" are within this exemption. On a complaint brought by the Commission under § 20(b) of the Act seeking to enjoin respondent's unregistered offerings, the District Court held the exemption applicable and dismissed the suit. The Court of Appeals affirmed. The question has arisen many

---

4. Some of the Court's footnotes omitted.

times since the Act was passed; an apparent need to define the scope of the private offering exemption prompted certiorari. . . .

Ralston Purina manufactures and distributes various feed and cereal products. Its processing and distribution facilities are scattered throughout the United States and Canada, staffed by some 7,000 employees. At least since 1911 the company has had a policy of encouraging stock ownership among its employees; more particularly, since 1942 it has made authorized but unissued common shares available to some of them. Between 1947 and 1951, the period covered by the record in this case, Ralston Purina sold nearly $2,000,000 of stock to employees without registration and in so doing made use of the mails.

In each of these years, a corporate resolution authorized the sale of common stock "to employees . . . who shall, without any solicitation by the Company or its officers or employees, inquire of any of them as to how to purchase common stock of Ralston Purina Company." A memorandum sent to branch and store managers after the resolution was adopted advised that "The only employees to whom this stock will be available will be those who take the initiative and are interested in buying stock at present market prices." Among those responding to these offers were employees with the duties of artist, bakeshop foreman, chow loading foreman, clerical assistant, copywriter, electrician, stock clerk, mill office clerk, order credit trainee, stenographer, and veterinarian. The buyers lived in over fifty widely separated communities scattered from Garland, Texas, to Nashua, New Hampshire and Visalia, California. The lowest salary bracket of those purchasing was $2,700 in 1949, $2,435 in 1950 and $3,107 in 1951. The record shows that in 1947, 243 employees bought stock, 20 in 1948, 414 in 1949, 411 in 1950, and the 1951 offer, interrupted by this litigation, produced 165 applications to purchase. No records were kept of those to whom the offers were made; the estimated number in 1951 was 500.

The company bottoms its exemption claim on the classification of all offerees as "key employees" in its organization. Its position on trial was that "A key employee . . . is not confined to an organization chart. It would include an individual who is eligible for promotion, an individual who especially influences others or who advises others, a person whom the employees look to in some special way, an individual, of course, who carries some special responsibility, who is sympathetic to management and who is ambitious and who the management feels is likely to be promoted to a greater responsibility." That an offering to all of its employees would be public is conceded.

The Securities Act nowhere defines the scope of § 4(1)'s private offering exemption. Nor is the legislative history of much help in staking out its boundaries. The problem was first dealt with in

§ 4(1) of the House Bill, H.R. 5480, 73d Cong., 1st Sess., which exempted "transactions by an issuer not with or through an underwriter; . . . ." The bill, as reported by the House Committee, added "and not involving any public offering." . . . This was thought to be one of those transactions "where there is no practical need for [the bill's] application or where the public benefits are too remote." . . . The exemption as thus delimited became law.[6] It assumed its present shape with the deletion of "not with or through an underwriter" . . . a change regarded as the elimination of superfluous language. . . .

Decisions under comparable exemptions in the English Companies Acts and state "blue sky" laws, the statutory antecedents of federal securities legislation, have made one thing clear—to be public an offer need not be open to the whole world. In Securities and Exchange Comm'n v. Sunbeam Gold Mines Co., (C.A.9th Cir. 1938), 95 F.2d 699 this point was made in dealing with an offering to the stockholders of two corporations about to be merged. Judge Denman observed that:

"In its broadest meaning the term 'public' distinguishes the populace at large from groups of individual members of the public segregated because of some common interest or characteristic. Yet such a distinction is inadequate for practical purposes; manifestly, an offering of securities to all red-headed men, to all residents of Chicago or San Francisco, to all existing stockholders of the General Motors Corporation or the American Telephone & Telegraph Company, is no less 'public', in every realistic sense of the word, than an unrestricted offering to the world at large. Such an offering, though not open to everyone who may choose to apply, is none the less 'public' in character, for the means used to select the particular individuals to whom the offering is to be made bear no sensible relation to the purposes for which the selection is made. . . . To determine the distinction between 'public' and 'private' in any particular context, it is essential to examine the circumstances under which the distinction is sought to be established and to consider the purposes sought to be achieved by such distinction." 95 F.2d, at 701.

The courts below purported to apply this test. The District Court held, in the language of the Sunbeam decision, that "The purpose of the selection bears a 'sensible relation' to the class chosen," finding that "The sole purpose of the 'selection' is to keep part stock ownership of the business within the operating personnel of the business and to spread ownership throughout all departments and activities of the business." The Court of Appeals treated the case as involving

---

6. The only subsequent reference was an oblique one in the statement of the House Managers on the Conference Report: "Sales of stock to stockholders become subject to the act unless the stockholders are so small in number that the sale to them does not constitute a public offering." H.R.Rep. No. 152, 73d Cong., 1st Sess. 25.

"an offering, without solicitation, of common stock to a selected group of key employees of the issuer, most of whom are already stockholders when the offering is made, with the sole purpose of enabling them to secure a proprietary interest in the company or to increase the interest already held by them."

Exemption from the registration requirements of the Securities Act is the question. The design of the statute is to protect investors by promoting full disclosure of information thought necessary to informed investment decisions. The natural way to interpret the private offering exemption is in light of the statutory purpose. Since exempt transactions are those as to which "there is no practical need for [the bill's] application," the applicability of § 4(1) should turn on whether the particular class of persons affected needs the protection of the Act. An offering to those who are shown to be able to fend for themselves is a transaction "not involving any public offering."

The Commission would have us go one step further and hold that "an offering to a substantial number of the public" is not exempt under § 4(1). We are advised that "whatever the special circumstances, the Commission has consistently interpreted the exemption as being inapplicable when a large number of offerees is involved." But the statute would seem to apply to a "public offering" whether to few or many.[11] It may well be that offerings to a substantial number of persons would rarely be exempt. Indeed nothing prevents the commission, in enforcing the statute, from using some kind of numerical test in deciding when to investigate particular exemption claims. But there is no warrant for superimposing a quantity limit on private offerings as a matter of statutory interpretation.

The exemption, as we construe it, does not deprive corporate employees, as a class, of the safeguards of the Act. We agree that some employee offerings may come within § 4(1), e. g., one made to executive personnel who because of their position have access to the same kind of information that the act would make available in the form of a registration statement.[12] Absent such a showing of special circumstances, employees are just as much members of the investing "public" as any of their neighbors in the community. Although we do

11. See Viscount Sumner's frequently quoted dictum in Nash v. Lynde, " 'The public' . . . is of course a general word. No particular numbers are prescribed. Anything from two to infinity may serve: perhaps even one, if he is intended to be the first of a series of subscribers, but makes further proceedings needless by himself subscribing the whole." (1929) A.C. 158, 169.

12. This was one of the factors stressed in an advisory opinion rendered by the Commission's General Counsel in 1935. "I also regard as significant the relationship between the issuer and the offerees. Thus, an offering to the members of a class who should have special knowledge of the issuer is less likely to be a public offering than is an offering to the members of a class of the same size who do not have this advantage. This factor would be particularly important in offerings to employees, where a class of high executive officers would have a special relationship to the issuer which subordinate employees would not enjoy." 11 Fed.Reg. 10952.

not rely on it, the rejection in 1934 of an amendment which would have specifically exempted employee stock offerings supports this conclusion. The House Managers, commenting on the Conference Report, said that "the participants in employees' stock-investment plans may be in as great need of the protection afforded by availability of information concerning the issuer for which they work as are most other members of the public." H.R.Rep.No.1838, 73d Cong., 2d Sess. 41.

Keeping in mind the broadly remedial purposes of federal securities legislation, imposition of the burden of proof on an issuer who would plead the exemption seems to us fair and reasonable. . . . Agreeing, the court below thought the burden met primarily because of the respondent's purpose in singling out its key employees for stock offerings. But once it is seen that the exemption question turns on the knowledge of the offerees, the issuer's motives, laudable though they may be, fade into irrelevance. The focus of inquiry should be on the need of the offerees for the protections afforded by registration. The employees here were not shown to have access to the kind of information which registration would disclose. The obvious opportunities for pressure and imposition make it advisable that they be entitled to compliance with § 5.

Reversed.

THE CHIEF JUSTICE and MR. JUSTICE BURTON dissent.

SECURITIES ACT RELEASE NO. 4552 [5]

November 6, 1962.

NON-PUBLIC OFFERING EXEMPTION

The Commission today announced the issuance of a statement regarding the availability of the exemption from the registration requirements of Section 5 of the Securities Act of 1933 afforded by the second clause of Section 4(1) of the Act for "transactions by an issuer not involving any public offering," the so-called "private offering exemption." Traditionally, the second clause of Section 4(1) has been regarded as providing an exemption from registration for bank loans, private placements of securities with institutions, and the promotion of a business venture by a few closely related persons. However, an increasing tendency to rely upon the exemption for offerings of speculative issues to unrelated and uninformed persons prompts this statement to point out the limitations on its availability.

Whether a transaction is one not involving any public offering is essentially a question of fact and necessitates a consideration of all surrounding circumstances, including such factors as the relationship

---

5. Footnotes omitted.

between the offerees and the issuer, the nature, scope, size, type and manner of the offering.

(Number of Offerees)

The Supreme Court in S.E.C. v. Ralston Purina Co., 346 U.S. 119, 124, 125 (1953), noted that the exemption must be interpreted in the light of the statutory purpose to "protect investors by promoting full disclosure of information thought necessary to informed investment decisions" and held that "the applicability of Section 4(1) should turn on whether the particular class of persons affected need the protection of the Act." The Court stated that the number of offerees is not conclusive as to the availability of the exemption, since the statute seems to apply to an offering, "whether to few or many." However, the Court indicated that "nothing prevents the Commission, in enforcing the statute, from using some kind of numerical test in deciding when to investigate particular exemption claims." It should be emphasized, therefore, that the number of persons to whom the offering is extended is relevant only to the question whether they have the requisite association with and knowledge of the issuer which make the exemption available.

(Identity of Offerees)

Consideration must be given not only to the identity of the actual purchasers but also to the offerees. Negotiations or conversations with or general solicitations of an unrestricted and unrelated group of prospective purchasers for the purpose of ascertaining who would be willing to accept an offer of securities is inconsistent with a claim that the transaction does not involve a public offering even though ultimately there may only be a few knowledgeable purchasers.

(Offering to Employees)

A question frequently arises in the context of an offering to an issuer's employees. Limitation of an offering to certain employees designated as key employees may not be a sufficient showing to qualify for the exemption. As the Supreme Court stated in the Ralston Purina case: "The exemption as we construe it, does not deprive corporate employees, as a class, of the safeguards of the Act. We agree that some employee offerings may come within Section 4(1), e. g., one made to executive personnel who because of their position have access to the same kind of information that the Act would make available in the form of a registration statement. Absent such a showing of special circumstances, employees are just as much members of the investing 'public' as any of their neighbors in the community." The Court's concept is that the exemption is necessarily narrow. The exemption does not become available simply because offerees are voluntarily *furnished* information about the issuer. Such a construction would give each issuer the choice of registering or making its own voluntary disclosures without regard to the standards and sanctions of the Act.

(Sale to Promoters)

The sale of stock to promoters who take the initiative in founding or organizing the business would come within the exemption. On the other hand, the transaction tends to become public when the promoters begin to bring in a diverse group of uninformed friends, neighbors, and associates.

(Size of Offering)

The size of the offering may also raise question as to the probability that the offering will be completed within the strict confines of the exemption. An offering of millions of dollars to non-institutional and non-affiliated investors, or one divided, or convertible into many units would suggest that a public offering may be involved.

(Facilities Used in Public Offering)

When the services of an investment banker, or other facility through which public distributions are normally effected, are used to place the securities, special care must be taken to avoid a public offering. If the investment banker places the securities with discretionary accounts and other customers without regard to the ability of such customers to meet the tests implicit in the Ralston Purina case, the exemption may be lost. Public advertising of the offering would, of course, be incompatible with a claim of a private offering. Similarly, the use of the facilities of a securities exchange to place the securities necessarily involves an offering to the public.

(Acquisitions for Investment)

An important factor to be considered is whether the securities offered have come to rest in the hands of the initial informed group or whether the purchasers are merely conduits for a wider distribution. Persons who act in this capacity, whether or not engaged in the securities business, are deemed to be "underwriters" within the meaning of Section 2(11) of the Act. If the purchasers do in fact acquire the securities with a view to public distribution, the seller assumes the risk of possible violation of the registration requirements of the Act and consequent civil liabilities. This has led to the practice whereby the issuer secures from the initial purchasers representations that they have acquired the securities for investment. Sometimes a legend to this effect is placed on the stock certificates and stop-transfer instructions issued to the transfer agent. However, a statement by the initial purchaser, at the time of his acquisition, that the securities are taken for investment and not for distribution is necessarily self-serving and not conclusive as to his actual intent. Mere acceptance at face value of such assurances will not provide a basis for reliance on the exemption when inquiry would suggest to a reasonable person that these assurances are formal rather than real. The additional precautions of placing a legend on the security and issuing stop-transfer orders have proved in many cases to be an effective means of preventing illegal distributions. Nevertheless, these are only precautions and are not to be regarded as a basis for exemption from registration. The nature of the purchaser's past investment and trading practices or the character and scope of his business may be inconsistent with the purchase of large blocks of securities for investment. In particular, purchases by persons engaged in the business of buying and selling securities require careful scrutiny for the purpose of determining whether such person may be acting as an underwriter for the issuer.

(Period of Retention)

The view is occasionally expressed that, solely by reason of continued holding of a security for the six-month capital-gain period specified in the income-tax laws, or for a year from the date of purchase, the security may be sold without registration. There is no statutory basis for such assumption. Of course, the longer the period of retention, the more persuasive would be the argument that the resale is not at variance with original investment intent, but the length of time between acquisition and resale is merely one evidentiary fact to be considered. The weight to be accorded this evidentiary fact must, of necessity, vary with the circumstances of each case. Further, a limitation upon resale for a stated period of time or under certain circumstances would tend to raise a question as to original intent even though such limitation might otherwise recommend itself as a policing device. There is no legal justification for the assumption that holding a security in an "investment account" rather than a "trading account," holding for a deferred sale, for a market rise, for sale if the market does not rise, or for a statutory escrow period, without more, establishes a valid basis for an exemption from registration under the Securities Act.

(Change of Circumstances)

An unforeseen change of circumstances since the date of purchase may be a basis for an opinion that the proposed resale is not inconsistent with an investment representation. However, such claim must be considered in the light of all of the relevant facts. Thus, an advance or decline in market price or a change in the issuer's operating results are normal investment risks and do not usually provide an acceptable basis for such claim of changed circumstances. Possible inability of the purchaser to pay off loans incurred in connection with the purchase of the stock would ordinarily not be deemed an unforeseeable change of circumstances. Further, in the case of securities pledged for a loan, the pledgee should not assume that he is free to distribute without registration. The Congressional mandate of disclosure to investors is not to be avoided to permit a public distribution of unregistered securities because the pledgee took the securities from a purchaser, subsequently delinquent.

(Institutional Investors)

The view is sometimes expressed that investment companies and other institutional investors are not subject to any restrictions regarding disposition of securities stated to be taken for investment and that any securities so acquired may be sold by them whenever the investment decision to sell is made, no matter how brief the holding period. Institutional investors are, however, subject to the same restrictions on sale of securities acquired from an issuer or a person in a control relationship with an issuer insofar as compliance with the registration requirements of the Securities Act is concerned.

(Integration of Offerings)

A determination whether an offering is public or private would also include a consideration of the question whether it should be regarded as a part of a larger offering made or to be made. The following factors are relevant to such question of integration: whether (1) the different offerings are part of a single plan of financing, (2) the offerings involve issuance of the same class of security, (3) the offerings are made at or about the same time, (4) the same type of consideration is to be received, (5) the offerings are made for the same general purpose.

(Related Series of Offerings)

What may appear to be a separate offering to a properly limited group will not be so considered if it is one of a related series of offerings. A person may not separate parts of a series of related transactions, the sum total of which is really one offering, and claim that a particular part is a non-public transaction. Thus, in the case of offerings of fractional undivided interests in separate oil or gas properties where the promoters must constantly find new participants for each new venture, it would appear to be appropriate to consider the entire series of offerings to determine the scope of this solicitation.

(Strict Construction)

As has been emphasized in other releases discussing exemptions from the registration and prospectus requirements of the Securities Act, the terms of an exemption are to be strictly construed against the claimant who also has the burden of proving its availability. Moreover, persons receiving advice from the staff of the Commission that no action will be recommended if they proceed without registration in reliance upon the exemption should do so only with full realization that the test so applied may not be proof against claims by purchasers of the security that registration should have been effected. Finally, Sections 12(2) and 17 of the Act, which provide civil liabilities and criminal sanctions for fraud in the sale of a security, are applicable to the transactions notwithstanding the availability of an exemption from registration.

NOTE ON NON-PUBLIC OFFERINGS

1. **Number of Offerees.** The reference in the Ralston case to the Commission's use of "some kind of numerical test in deciding when to investigate particular exemption claims" was apparently directed to what has long been thought to be a "rule of thumb" used by the Commission to the effect that an offering to no more than 25 persons does not constitute a public offering. This rule of thumb was alluded to as early as the 1935 opinion of the General Counsel referred to in footnote 12 of the Ralston opinion, which was addressed to a proposed offering of almost $2,000,000 of preferred stock to 25 persons. The General Counsel declined to express an opinion as to whether a public offering was involved, emphasizing the necessity of considering all of the surrounding circumstances. However, he also referred to an earlier opinion expressed by his office that "under ordinary circumstances an offering to not more than approximately 25 persons is not an offering to a substantial number and presumably does not involve a public offering." Such a rule of thumb has also been expressly recognized on several occasions since the Ralston decision. For example, in 1957 a member of the Commission stated: "As a rule of thumb, the Commission has considered that an offering made to not more than 25 or 30 persons, who take the securities for investment and not for distribution, is generally a private transaction not requiring registration."[6]

As to the current status of this rule of thumb, Sec. Act Rel. No. 4552 seems an almost studied effort at ambiguity on the question of whether there has been any change in the Commission's practice in this regard. But two subsequent promulgations do suggest that the notion of a rule of thumb as to a permissible maximum has been discarded. First, in D. F. Bernheimer & Co., Inc., Sec. Exch. Act Rel. No. 7000 (1963), involving an offering by a broker-dealer of convertible debentures to 22 of its customers, of whom most were already stockholders of the issuer and some 18 ultimately purchased, the Commission held that no right to an exemption had been established, without so much as a reference to the small number of offerees involved. A few months later, in Advanced Research Associates, Inc., Sec. Act Rel. No. 4630, Sec. Exch. Act Rel. No. 7117 (1963), where an offering

---

6. Orrick, Some Observations on the Administration of the Securities Laws, 42 Minn.L.Rev. 25, 33 (1957).

of 97,000 shares of common stock was made to 21 friends and relatives of the promoters, 18 of whom actually purchased, the Commission stated expressly that "a private offering exemption is not established by merely showing that the offering was made to a small group." In the latter case, as in the earlier one, the Commission emphasized the "criteria enunciated" in Ralston: "While certain of the purchasers who had a close relationship to [the issuer] presumably had access to full information, respondent has not established, in our opinion, that every offeree and purchaser had 'access to the kind of information which registration would disclose' and did not need 'the protections afforded by registration'."

Hence it may be doubted that Professor Loss would still summarize the situation, as he did before these releases, in the following manner:

> In short, notwithstanding the theoretical possibility under the Ralston approach that an offering even to a handful of persons selected at random might be a "public offering" if they were not able to "fend for themselves", it seems relatively safe to assume that an offering to not more than some twenty-five persons will be considered exempt—at least so far as Commission intervention as distinct from civil liability under Section 12(1) is concerned—and that the other factors become important only when it is desired to approach a greater number of offerees.[7]

It is often possible to obtain an advance indication as to the likelihood of Commission intervention on an exemption issue of this kind by a request for a so-called "no action" letter. This process has been well summarized in Jennings and Marsh, Securities Regulation—Cases and Materials (1963) 316, note 28:

> The Commission often receives letters from Counsel, on behalf of a client, setting forth facts concerning a proposed sale of securities with an opinion of Counsel to the effect that registration under the Securities Act is not required on the basis of a claimed exemption and a request that the Commission advise whether they concur in the opinion. The Commission may or may not give a no-action letter in reply to these requests. If it does so, an authorized member of the Staff will sign the letter which in substance states that, on the basis of the facts set forth in the letter, no action will be recommended to the Commission, if the proposed sales are made, in the manner described, without registration under the act, in reliance on Counsel's opinion that registration is not required.

2. The Investment Requirement. Both Sec. Act Rel. No. 4552 and Sec.Exch.Act Rel.No. 7000 emphasize the need for the issuer to ascertain that the buyers in a purported "private" offering are taking the securities for investment and not for distribution. As Release No. 4552 indicates, the buyer's contemporaneous statement as to his investment intention, though relevant, is not conclusive on this issue. Similarly, the length of time for which the buyer actually holds the securities is not controlling as to his intention at the time of acquisition, but is "merely one evidentiary fact to be considered." As with respect to the allowable number of offerees, however, so with the period of retention there may be a rule of thumb operating, although here the Commission has never made any public pronouncement to

---

7. Loss, op. cit. at page 664.

that effect, and assiduously avoided any intimation of it in Release No. 4552. Professor Loss suggests that "holding for as long as two years or so will normally be well-nigh conclusive" of an original investment intention, and even a one-year holding presumably creates something of an inference in that direction. Loss, at 672. And of course, as the release indicates, even a resale well within one year is not necessarily inconsistent with an original investment intention, if the buyer can show a bona fide and substantial change in his circumstances not initiated by him. Here too is an issue on which it may be possible to secure a no-action letter, if the buyer can establish his case to the satisfaction of the Commission's staff.

An excellent illustration of the resale problem is afforded by the situation involved in Crowell-Collier Publishing Co., Sec.Act Rel.No. 3825 (1957). In 1955, Crowell-Collier was under serious financial pressure and needed additional funds. Having been advised that flotation of additional common stock would not be feasible because of the company's loss record, the company arranged with Elliott & Company, a registered broker-dealer, to sell privately some $3,000,000 of convertible debentures. The conversion rate was fixed at $5.00 per share when the stock was trading over the counter at $5\frac{1}{2}$ to $6\frac{1}{4}$. However, prior to the actual placement of the debentures, the company put out a press release announcing that $3,000,000 of debentures had been sold, that operations for the first 6 months of 1955 had showed a profit, and that the management of the company was being reorganized. Largely as a result of that release, the stock had risen some 3 points by the time the debentures were actually sold.

Relying upon the advice of counsel, the company sought to limit the offering to 25 offerees in order to qualify the transaction for exemption under § 4(1). Commitments were ultimately obtained from 27 persons, including 4 broker-dealer firms. By the time of the actual closing, however, about $\frac{1}{3}$ of the buyers, including the 4 broker-dealer firms, had secured others to join them as participants in their commitments, with the result that there were at least 79 purchasers representing 86 individuals and firms.

Substantial conversion of the debentures began almost immediately after the passage of the six month, capital-gains time period. Not long thereafter, in May, 1956, the Elliott firm arranged for the sale of another $1,000,000 of the company's convertible debentures to some twenty-two purchasers (including three other broker-dealer firms), some of whom had participated in the first offering and had already converted the earlier debentures and sold the common stock. The three broker-dealer participants in the 1956 issue immediately resold some of those debentures to at least fifteen additional persons.

All of the original buyers of both issues, as well as substantially all of those who bought from them, gave investment letters covering the debentures (but not the stock into which the debentures were convertible.)

The Commission held that no exemption under § 4(1) was available for the issuance of the debentures (or for the ultimate resale of the underlying stock either). The Commission emphasized the following factors as indicating a public offering: establishment of the conversion price below the market; the fact that the investment representations as to the debentures imposed no restriction on conversion and sale of the underlying stock; issuance of the debentures in bearer form and small denominations; the speculative character of the securities; the presence of broker-dealer firms among the original buyers; the precarious financial position of the issuer; the Elliott firm's insistence upon immediate listing of the stock on the American Stock Exchange; the substantial number of conversions which occurred between the two issuances of debentures; the sale of the second block of debentures at a premium of $600 per $1000 debenture, reflecting the emphasis on the conversion feature rather than the investment quality of the debentures; and the concurrent issuance of warrants and options to partners of the Elliott firm who transferred them to relatives and others. The Commission also discussed the relationship between the investment intention required for an exemption under § 4(1) and the period for which securities are subsequently retained in fact. After an analysis much like that which now appears in the relevant paragraph of Sec.Act Rel.No. 4552, supra, the Commission summed up the matter as follows:

> Purchasing for the purpose of future sale is nonetheless purchasing for sale and, if the transactions involve any public offering even at some future date, the registration provisions apply unless at the time of the public offering an exemption is available.

3. **The Use of Private Placement.** As the Crowell-Collier case illustrates, the exemption for private offerings under § 4(1) is by no means limited to small financings. Actually, over one-third of the tremendous volume of large corporate financings in the post-war years have been privately placed, mostly with institutional investors such as life insurance companies. However, it should be noted that exemption from registration is not the primary reason for the growth of private financing, although that doubtless played an important part in the early development of private placement in the 1930's. Today, particularly in connection with debt financing, the greatest attraction of private placement seems to lie in the opportunity to sit down and negotiate the terms of the deal with the institutional lender. One important consequence of such face to face negotiations is the ability to secure a final commitment on the interest rate at a relatively early stage, after which the risk of market fluctuation is on the lender. In a public flotation of securities through underwriters, on the other hand, the risk of market fluctuation remains on the issuer throughout the period required for preparation of the registration statement and the twenty-day waiting period after filing, since normally the investment bankers will not make a firm commitment as to price terms until just before the time of the public offering.

Another important ingredient of dealing directly with an institutional investor is the opportunity to work out special "tailor-made" terms for the particular transaction. For a public offering, any departure from the traditional format would be likely to prove costly in terms of market reception. In a private deal such special terms can be bargained out in the give and take of negotiation without any need for undue sacrifice by the borrower. Moreover, to the extent that the borrower may have certain rather special problems or prospects which must be clarified to a prospective lender, a registration statement for a public offering may constitute a rather blunt instrument as compared with a face-to-face discussion with financially sophisticated representatives of potential institutional lenders.

Private placement may also be a good deal less expensive than a public offering. In addition to substantially lower flotation costs, private placement may make it possible to either avoid or greatly reduce the fees of indenture trustees which are a necessary ingredient of any large public issue of debt securities. Moreover, all of the other regular expense items, such as accounting and legal fees, and printing expenses, are characteristically higher for a public offering than a private placement. See generally re private placement, Corey, Corporate Financing by Direct Placement, 28 Harv. Bus.Rev. 67 (Nov.-Dec., 1950); Steffen, The Private Placement Exemption: What to Do About a Fortuitous Combination in Restraint of Trade, 30 U. of Chi.L.Rev. 211 (1963).

4. Convertible Securities

a. *Exemption under § 4(1)*. The Crowell-Collier case also illustrates the special difficulties which convertible securities present under § 4(1), since an apparent private offering of the debentures may result ultimately in a public distribution of the underlying stock. By the time of the Crowell-Collier case, the Commission had rejected the view that a convertible security should be regarded as a single "package" of alternative rights, so that an exemption under § 4(1) for the original issue would cover a subsequent sale of the stock received upon conversion to the same extent as if the stock had expressly been the subject of the exempt private offering. Instead, the Commission had decided to follow what Professor Loss calls the "two-security approach", Loss, at 677, under which registration of the underlying stock is required when a privately placed convertible security is converted by a substantial holder with a view to distribution of the stock. In 1959, in Sec. Act Rel.No. 4162, the Commission promulgated a proposed Rule 155 designed to clarify the treatment of convertible securities, and accompanied the proposal with the following summary of the views of its staff, based on a comprehensive study of the problem:

> I. It has been generally understood that a conversion is an exchange within the meaning of section 3(a)(9), with the result that the actual transaction of conversion is exempt if the other conditions of the section are satisfied. It is clear, however, that there is nothing in the intrinsic nature of securities issued in a transaction falling within section 3(a)(9) which justifies consideration of such securities as permanently exempt from registration without regard to any other factors.

> II. A security which is immediately convertible consists of the convertible security and a right to acquire the underlying security, thus involving a continuous offering by the issuer of the underlying security. A purchaser of the convertible security acquires it and the right and no more. If he offers to sell the convertible security, he offers to sell the right, thus transferring the issuer's offer of the underlying security, originally limited to the persons to whom the convertible security was initially offered, into an offer to all persons to whom the convertible security is now offered. The issuer's offer of the underlying security terminates upon exercise or expiration of the right. At any one time a person can own only one security or the other; he can never own both. Consequently, it cannot be said that a purchase of the convertible security includes a simultaneous purchase of the underlying security. In the case of

a debenture convertible into an equity security, the purchaser remains a creditor until he chooses to become an owner of the equity security; the two interests never merge. The transaction of conversion is an exchange for value and, therefore, a sale under the Securities Act and under accepted commercial practice and understanding.

III. An issuer has a direct, intimate and continuing connection with any offer it is making of a security, whether by virtue of a right, conversion privilege or otherwise, so long as that offer continues. As to the issuer, then, for purposes of section 5 and exemptions therefrom under section 4(1), the entire transaction of offer and sale in the situation under discussion is open and incomplete until the public offering and sale of both securities are completed, or the possibility of a public offering is terminated.

IV. The issuer's right to rely upon the exemptive provisions of section 4(1) must be tested against the economic, financial and legal characteristics of the transaction, with particular reference to the motives and expectations upon the part of both the issuer and the initial purchasers which are a cause and a result of the decision to employ a convertible security in the transaction.

V. An issuer contending that there will be no public offering in the entire transaction assumes a heavy burden of proof. This burden can presumably be carried where the issuer surrounds the transaction with restrictions designed to preclude the possibility that, without registration, the underlying security will be offered to the public, either directly or by virtue of a public offering of the convertible security. It is not sustained simply by obtaining from purchasers assurances that they are acquiring the convertible security with no present intention to distribute that security, or even with no present intention to distribute the underlying security. If the purchaser should state upon acquisition of the convertible security, or if the issuer should understand, that it is the intention of the purchaser to distribute the underlying security directly, or by a public offering of the convertible security, if and when the relation between the market price of that security and the conversion price made it profitable to do so, the issuer could not successfully maintain that no public offering was involved in the entire transaction. In the ordinary case of a private placement of a convertible security, it must be presumed that this will in fact be the intention of the usual purchaser, absent restrictions preventing him from doing so, even though that intention is not expressly stated. Likewise, it must be presumed that the issuer understands that such is the intention of the purchaser. If not, the conversion privilege does not serve its normally intended purpose.

VI. These assumptions lead to the conclusion that the purchaser of a convertible security in a private placement may be a statutory underwriter in a subsequent distribution by him of either security. . . .

VII. These views are consistent with fundamental principles announced in various prior statements of the Commission. One of these principles is that the essential purpose of the first and second clauses of section 4(1) is to draw the line between an isolated transaction or transactions with particular persons on the one hand, and transactions which are in reality part of a distribution of securities. In any attempt to reach a conclusion in this area, the entire transaction and not merely a part of it must be considered. Applying this principle, a transaction having inherent in it the probability that, before its completion, a large block of securities will be distributed to the general public appears to be of such a nature as not to be entitled to exemption under section 4(1).

VIII. This does not mean that registration necessarily, or even properly, should be required at the time when the convertible security is privately placed. There are at least three reasons for not requiring registration at this point: first, there is no present public offering and there may never be one; second, the original sale of the convertible security might be regarded as a preliminary agreement with an underwriter as to the underlying security; or third, the second clause of section 4(1) might be regarded as available until events demonstrate that a public offering is involved. When, however, the public offering materializes, registration might be necessary. What will be required is to establish arrangements initially for keeping the issuer informed of intended distributions and restraining their consummation until registration has been accomplished.

IX. For purposes of the provisions of sections 2(11), 4(1) and 5 of the Securities Act, the transaction involved in the private placement by an issuer of a convertible security is not completed until the disposition of the underlying security is determined. The scope and purpose of these sections extend to a public offering of such security and registration should be effected prior to any public offering of such security or of the convertible security unless the circumstances of the acquisition and retention of the convertible and of the underlying security are such that the provisions of section 5 do not apply.

In 1962 Rule 155 was finally adopted in much the same form in which it had been originally proposed: [8]

Definition of "Transactions by an Issuer Not Involving Any Public Offering" in section 4(1) of the Act for certain transactions with respect to convertible securities.

(a) The phrase "transactions by an issuer not involving any public offering" in section 4(1) of the Act shall not include (1) any public offering of a convertible security (which at the time of such offering is immediately convertible into another security of the same issuer) by or on behalf of any person or persons who purchased the convertible security directly or indirectly from an issuer as part of a non-public offering of such security, or (2) any public offering by or on behalf of any such person or persons of the security acquired on conversion of a convertible security, unless

8. 17 C.F.R. 230.155 (1962).

the security so acquired was acquired under such circumstances that such person or persons are not underwriters within the meaning of section 2(11) of the Act.

(b) The phrase "transactions by any person other than an . . . underwriter" in section 4(1) of the Act shall, in the situations covered in paragraph (a), be deemed to include transactions by the initial, and any intermediate, holder of the convertible security or of the underlying security who (1) has not acquired the convertible or underlying security with a view to the distribution of either of them, and (2) is not effecting, is not causing to be effected, and has not arranged for, a public offering of either security within the meaning of and subject to paragraph (a) of this section.

(c) This section shall apply to transactions of the character described in paragraph (a) of this section only with respect to convertible securities issued after February 7, 1962.

b. *The Trust Indenture Act of 1939.* When, as is normally true, the convertible securities are initially debt, the Trust Indenture Act (15 U.S.C.A. §§ 77aaa–77bbbb), may be called into play. That Act prohibits the public sale of bonds, debentures, notes and similar debt securities unless they are accompanied by a trust indenture which conforms to the standards of the Act, designed to safeguard the rights and interests of the security holders.

The Act was passed after studies by the Commission had revealed the frequency with which trust indentures failed to provide minimum protection for security holders and absolved so-called trustees from minimum obligations in the discharge of their trust. The Act requires that the indenture trustee be free of conflicting interests which might interfere with the faithful exercise of its duties on behalf of the security holders. The Act also requires that the trustee be a corporation meeting a minimum combined capital and surplus test; imposes high standards of conduct and responsibility upon the trustee; requires the issuer to supply evidence to the trustee of compliance with the indenture terms and conditions, such as those relating to the release or substitution of mortgaged property, issuance of new securities or satisfaction of the indenture; and provides for reports and notices by the trustee to security holders. Other provisions of the Act prohibit impairment of the security holders' right to sue individually for principal and interest except under certain circumstances and require the maintenance of a list of security holders which may be used by them to communicate with each other regarding their rights.

The Act does not apply to any issue of securities which is itself exempt under § 3(a) (11) or 4(1) of the Securities Act, nor to any offering of $250,000 or less in principal amount of securities issued otherwise than under an indenture in any twelve month period, nor to an offering of $1,000,000 or less in principal amount of securities issued under an indenture in any thirty-six month period.

2. THE INTRA-STATE EXEMPTION—SECTION 3(a) (11)

SECURITIES ACT RELEASE NO. 4434
December 6, 1961.

SECTION 3(a)(11) EXEMPTION FOR LOCAL OFFERINGS [9]

The meaning and application of the exemption from registration provided by Section 3(a) (11) of the Securities Act of 1933, as amended, have been the subject of court opinions, releases of the Securities and Exchange Commission, and opinions and interpretations expressed by the staff of the Commission in response to specific inquiries. This release is published to provide in convenient and up-to-date form a restatement of the principles underlying Section 3(a) (11) as so expressed over the years and to facilitate an understanding of the meaning and application of the exemption.

* * *

"Issue" Concept

A basic condition of the exemption is that the *entire issue* of securities be offered and sold exclusively to residents of the state in question. Consequently, an offer to a non-resident which is considered a part of the intrastate issue will render the exemption unavailable to the entire offering.

Whether an offering is "a part of an issue", that is, whether it is an integrated part of an offering previously made or proposed to be made, is a question of fact and depends essentially upon whether the offerings are a related part of a plan or program. . . . Thus, the exemption should not be relied upon in combination with another exemption for the different parts of a single issue where a part is offered or sold to non-residents.

The determination of what constitutes an "issue" is not governed by state law. . . . Any one or more of the following factors may be determinative of the question of integration: (1) are the offerings part of a single plan of financing; (2) do the offerings involve issuance of the same class of security; (3) are the offerings made at or about the same time; (4) is the same type of consideration to be received; and (5) are the offerings made for the same general purpose.

Moreover, since the exemption is designed to cover only those security distributions, which as a whole, are essentially local in character, it is clear that the phrase "sold only to persons resident" as used in Section 3(a) (11) cannot refer merely to the initial sales by the issuing corporation to its underwriters, or even the subsequent resales

---

9. Portions of the text and all footnotes omitted.

by the underwriters to distributing dealers. To give effect to the fundamental purpose of the exemption, it is necessary that the entire issue of securities shall be offered and sold to, and come to rest only in the hands of residents within the state. If any part of the issue is offered or sold to a non-resident, the exemption is unavailable not only for the securities so sold, but for all securities forming a part of the issue, including those sold to residents. . . . It is incumbent upon the issuer, underwriter, dealers and other persons connected with the offering to make sure that it does not become an interstate distribution through resales. It is understood to be customary for such persons to obtain assurances that purchases are not made with a view to resale to non-residents.

Doing Business Within the State

In view of the local character of the Section 3(a) (11) exemption, the requirement that the issuer be doing business in the state can only be satisfied by the performance of substantial operational activities in the state of incorporation. The doing business requirement is not met by functions in the particular state such as bookkeeping, stock record and similar activities or by offering securities in the state. . . .

If the proceeds of the offering are to be used primarily for the purpose of a new business conducted outside of the state of incorporation and unrelated to some incidental business locally conducted, the exemption should not be relied upon. . . . So also, a Section 3(a) (11) exemption should not be relied upon for each of a series of corporations organized in different states where there is in fact and purpose a single business enterprise or financial venture whether or not it is planned to merge or consolidate the various corporations at a later date. . . .

Residence Within the State

Section 3(a)(11) requires that the entire issue be confined to a single state in which the issuer, the offerees and the purchasers are residents. Mere presence in the state is not sufficient to constitute residence as in the case of military personnel at a military post. . . . The mere obtaining of formal representations of residence and agreements not to resell to non-residents or agreements that sales are void if the purchaser is a non-resident should not be relied upon without more as establishing the availability of the exemption.

An offering may be so large that its success as a local offering appears doubtful from the outset. Also, reliance should not be placed on the exemption for an issue which includes warrants for the purchase of another security unless there can be assurance that the warrants will be exercised only by residents. With respect to convertible securities, a Section 3(a) (9) exemption may be available for the conversion. . . .

Resales

From these general principles it follows that if during the course of distribution any underwriter, any distributing dealer (whether or not a member of the formal selling or distributing group), or any dealer or other person purchasing securities from a distributing dealer for resale were to offer or sell such securities to a non-resident, the exemption would be defeated. In other words, Section 3(a)(11) contemplates that the exemption is applicable only if the entire issue is distributed pursuant to the statutory conditions. Consequently, any offers or sales to a non-resident in connection with the distribution of the issue would destroy the exemption as to all securities which are a part of that issue, including those sold to residents regardless of whether such sales are made directly to non-residents or indirectly through residents who as part of the distribution thereafter sell to non-residents. It would furthermore be immaterial that sales to non-residents are made without use of the mails or instruments of interstate commerce. Any such sales of part of the issue to non-residents, however few, would not be in compliance with the conditions of Section 3(a)(11), and would render the exemption unavailable for the entire offering including the sales to residents. . . .

This is not to suggest, however, that securities which have actually come to rest in the hands of resident investors, such as persons purchasing without a view to further distribution or resale to non-residents, may not in due course be resold by such persons, whether directly or through dealers or brokers, to non-residents without in any way affecting the exemption. The relevance of any such resales consists only of the evidentiary light which they might cast upon the factual question whether the securities had in fact come to rest in the hands of resident investors. If the securities are resold but a short time after their acquisition to a non-resident this fact, although not conclusive, might support an inference that the original offering had not come to rest in the State, and that the resale therefore constituted a part of the process of primary distribution; a stronger inference would arise if the purchaser involved were a security dealer. It may be noted that the non-residence of the underwriter or dealer is not pertinent so long as the ultimate distribution is solely to residents of the state.

Use of the Mails and Facilities of Interstate Commerce

The intrastate exemption is not dependent upon non-use of the mails or instruments of interstate commerce in the distribution. Securities issued in a transaction properly exempt under this provision may be offered and sold without registration through the mails or by use of any instruments of transportation or communication in interstate commerce, may be made the subject of general newspaper advertisement (provided the advertisement is appropriately limited to indicate that offers to purchase are solicited only from, and sales will be made only to, residents of the particular state involved), and may even be delivered by means of transportation and communication used in interstate commerce, to the purchasers. Similarly, securities issued in a transaction exempt under Section 3(a)(11) may be offered without compliance with the formal prospectus requirements applicable to registered securities. Exemption under Section 3(a)(11), if in fact available, removes the distribution from the operation of the registration and prospectus requirements of Section 5 of the Act. It should be emphasized, however, that the civil liability and anti-fraud provisions of Sections 12(2) and 17 of the Act nevertheless apply and may give rise to civil liabilities and to other sanctions applicable to violations of the statute.

Conclusion

In conclusion, the fact should be stressed that Section 3(a)(11) is designed to apply only to distributions genuinely local in character. From a practical point of view, the provisions of that section can exempt only issues which in reality represent local financing by local industries, carried out through local investment. Any distribution not of this type raises a serious question as to the availability of Section 3(a)(11). Consequently, any dealer proposing to participate in the distribution of an issue claimed to be exempt under Section 3(a)(11) should examine the character of the transaction and the proposed or actual manner of its execution by all persons concerned with it with the greatest care to satisfy himself that the distribution will not, or did not, exceed the limitations of the exemption. Otherwise the dealer, even though his own sales may be carefully confined to resident purchasers, may subject himself to serious risk of civil liability under Section 12(1) of the Act for selling without prior registration a security not in fact entitled to exemption from registration. In Release No. 4386, we noted that the quick commencement of trading and prompt resale of portions of the issue to non-residents raises a serious question whether the entire issue has, in fact, come to rest in the hands of investors resident in the state of the initial offering.

The Securities Act is a remedial statute, and the terms of an exemption must be strictly construed against one seeking to rely on it. . . . The courts have held that he has the burden of proving its availability. . . .

NOTE ON THE INTRA-STATE EXEMPTION

In practice, the Commission's very narrow construction of the intrastate exemption has made it rather dangerous to rely upon that exemption. As Sec.Act Rel.No. 4434 indicates, the Commission takes the position that a single offer, to say nothing of a sale, to a non-resident destroys the exemption for the entire "issue". The harshness of this view is compounded by the Commission's insistence that the residence requirement in § 3(a) 11 means "domicil" in the conflict-of-laws sense, under which the subjective intent to remain in the jurisdiction is controlling, not the more objective criterion of the existence of a relatively permanent dwelling place. The domicil test makes the burden of compliance far more onerous, particularly for the salesmen of securities who as a practical matter must make these decisions in the first instance. Professor Loss observes that in effect such a narrow reading of the exemption virtually makes the issuer an insurer of every offeree's state of mind, and of every salesman's integrity as well. "Unless the standard is one of due care—which includes reasonable supervision of all selling agents and may well require something more than an automatic acceptance of the buyer's representation—the exemption is virtually read out of the statute. Perhaps it should be. But that presumably is why Congress sits. Meanwhile, although it is usually impractical to litigate with the Commission when an issuer is primarily interested in completing its financing, a seller against whom a claim is made for rescission or damages under § 12(1) would be well advised to defend if he thinks he used reasonable care." Loss, at 604–605.

3. EXEMPTION FOR SMALL ISSUES—SECTION 3(b)

a. IN GENERAL

The major exemption for small business financing is found in the Commission's Regulation A promulgated pursuant to § 3(b) which authorizes the Commission to create exemptions for issues of $300,000 or less, subject to such terms and conditions as it may prescribe. Actually, Regulation A provides not so much an exemption as a simplified form of registration for most issues up to $300,000. "Registration" under Regulation A consists of filing (with the appropriate regional office of the SEC rather than in Washington) a rather simple "notification" covering mainly the terms of the present offering, any recent past or proposed future financings, the names of directors and officers, the method of flotation, and the planned use of the proceeds. Although this notification does not become formally "effective" on a particular date, as in the case of a registration statement, the Regulation does provide for a ten day waiting period; and in practice the regional office is likely to process the notification in a manner much like that applied to a registration statement in Washington.

An additional requirement of Regulation A, added by amendment in 1953, is that whenever the total issue exceeds $50,000, neither a written offer, nor a sale, of securities may be made unless there is or has been made available to the offeree an "offering circular", which in effect amounts to a telescoped prospectus.

Because of the flurry in uranium stock and resulting abuses, Regulation A was further revised in 1956. More severe restrictions were imposed on promotional companies (i.e., those which have not had net income in either of the last two years from "operations, of the character in which the issuer intends to engage"). For such companies an offering circular must be used even for issues under $50,000. In addition, the maximum allowable amount under Regulation A may as a practical matter be less than $300,000, because these companies, in applying the $300,000 maximum, are required by Rule 253(c) to add to the amount of a proposed public offering the amount of any securities issued for property or services, no matter to whom, plus the amount of any securities issued to certain specified insiders, regardless of for what consideration, unless some "effective" arrangement is made to keep such securities off the market for at least a year, as by an escrow arrangement.[10]

Excerpts from Regulation A follow:

REGULATION A—GENERAL EXEMPTION

Rule 251. Definitions of Terms Used in This Regulation

* * *

Promoter. The term "Promoter" includes—

(a) Any person who, acting alone or in conjunction with one or more other persons, directly or indirectly takes the initiative in founding and organizing the business or enterprise of an issuer:

(b) Any person who, in connection with the founding or organizing of the business or enterprise of an issuer, directly or indirectly receives in consideration of services or property, or both services and property, 10 percent or more of any class of securities of the issuer or 10 percent or more of the proceeds from the sale of any class of securities. However, a person who receives such securities or proceeds either solely as underwriting commissions or solely in consideration of property shall not be deemed a promoter within the meaning of this paragraph if such person does not otherwise take part in founding and organizing the enterprise.

* * *

---

10. According to Sec. Act Rel. No. 4413 (1961) 3, note 5, the escrowee must be "independent", with the result that a person who was a director and stockholder of the issuer could not qualify.

Among the other proposals made by the SEC in 1955–56 were (1) to require that the financial statements in offering circulars be certified by independent public accountants; and (2) to require some arrangement, such as a temporary escrow of the offering proceeds, to assure that investors would get part or all of their money back if the offering was not successful. In dropping the first of these proposals, the SEC pointed out that only limited financial information was available in promotional situations anyway, so that the hoped-for benefits of this proposal would probably not outweigh the added expense burden imposed on small businesses. As to (2), the SEC apparently accepted the assertions that such a provision would "result in a confusing and complex rule." Rel. U–225 (1956) 2.

Rule 253. Special Requirements for Certain Offerings

(a) The following provisions of this rule shall apply to any offering under this regulation of securities of any issuer which—

(1) was incorporated or organized within 1 year prior to the date of filing the notification required by Rule 255 and has not had a net income from operations; or

(2) was incorporated or organized more than 1 year prior to such date and has not had a net income from operations, of the character in which the issuer intends to engage, for at least 1 of the last 2 fiscal years.

* * *

(c) In computing the amount of securities which may be offered hereunder, there shall be included, in addition to the securities specified in Rule 254—

(1) all securities issued prior to the filing of the notification, or proposed to be issued, for a consideration consisting in whole or in part of assets or services and held by the person to whom issued; and

(2) all securities issued to and held by or proposed to be issued, pursuant to options or otherwise, to any director, officer or promoter of the issuer, or to any underwriter, dealer or security salesman;

Provided, That such securities need not be included to the extent that effective provision is made, by escrow arrangements or otherwise, to assure that none of such securities or any interest therein will be reoffered to the public within 1 year after the commencement of the offering hereunder and that any reoffering of such securities will be made in accordance with the applicable provisions of the Act.

(d) None of the securities to be offered hereunder shall be offered for the account of any person other than the issuer of such securities.

* * *

Rule 254. Amount of Securities Exempted

(a) The aggregate offering price of all of the following securities of (i) the issuer, (ii) its predecessors and (iii) all of its affiliates which were incorporated or organized, or became affiliates of the issuer, within the past 2 years, shall not exceed $300,000:

(1) all securities of such persons presently being offered under this regulation, or under any other regulation adopted pursuant to section 3(b) of the Act, or specified in the notification required by Rule 255 as proposed to be so offered;

(2) all securities of such persons previously sold pursuant to an offering under this regulation, or under any other regulation

adopted pursuant to section 3(b) of the Act, commenced within 1 year prior to the commencement of the proposed offering; and

(3) all securities of such persons sold in violation of section 5(a) of the Act within 1 year prior to the commencement of the proposed offering.

Notwithstanding the foregoing, the aggregate offering price of all securities of such persons so offered or sold on behalf of any one person other than the issuer or issuers of such securities shall not exceed $100,000, except that this limitation shall not apply if the securities are to be offered on behalf of the estate of a deceased person within 2 years after the death of such person.

(b) The aggregate offering price of securities which have a determinable market value shall be computed upon the basis of such market value as determined from transactions or quotations on a specified date within 15 days prior to the date of filing the notification, or the offering price to the public, whichever is higher; provided, that the aggregate gross proceeds actually received from the public for the securities offered hereunder shall not exceed the maximum aggregate offering price permitted in the particular case by paragraph (a) above.

(c) Where securities which have no determinable market value are offered in exchange for outstanding securities, claims, property, or services, the aggregate offering price thereof shall be computed at the public offering price of securities of the same class for cash, or if no cash offering is to be made, then upon the basis of the value of the securities, claims, property or services to be received in exchange, as established by bona fide sales made within a reasonable time, or in the absence of such sales, upon the basis of the fair value of the securities, claims, property or services to be received in exchange, as determined by some accepted standard.

(d) The following securities need not be included in computing the amount of securities which may be offered under this regulation:

(1) Unsold securities the offering of which has been withdrawn with the consent of the Commission by amending the pertinent notification to reduce the amount stated therein as proposed to be offered;

(2) Securities acquired or to be acquired, otherwise than for distribution, by a single holder of the majority of the outstanding voting stock of the issuer in connection with a pro rata offering to stockholders;

* * *

b. Offering Circulars

The following are illustrative excerpts from two Offering Circulars prepared pursuant to Regulation A. The Kilbanon circular is set out practically in full; about all that has been omitted is the accountant's certificate and the footnotes to the financial statements. Substantially more has been omitted from the Chomerics circular, but most of the supplement to that circular, covering the most recent financial data on the company as of the offering date, has been included.

OFFERING CIRCULAR

KILBANON CORPORATION

114 Concord Road

Wayland, Massachusetts

(A Massachusetts Corporation, Incorporated May 13, 1960)

COMMON STOCK
(No Par Value)
20,000 Shares
Offering Price: $5.00 Per Share(1)

This is a new issue of securities, being offered as a speculation.
(See Caption "Directors, Officers and Stockholders")

	Offering Price to Public	Underwriting Discounts or Commissions	Proceeds to Issuer
Per Share	$5.00	None	$5.00
Total Offering 20,000 Shares	$100,000	None(2)	$100,000(3)

(1) The price has been arbitrarily determined and bears no relation to book value. There is no assurance that the stock offered hereby may be resold at or near the offering price.

(2) The issuer intends to offer these shares directly to the public. There is no market for the company's securities at present, and there is no assurance that a market will exist in the future.

(3) The issuer will pay all the expenses of the offering estimated not to exceed $5,000, including the cost of printing the Offering Circular, the preparation of the stock certificates, the stock issue tax, the fees and expenses of the issuer's counsel and accountants, and costs incurred in qualifying the shares offered hereunder for offer and sale under the securities or Blue Sky Laws of certain states.

THESE SECURITIES ARE OFFERED PURSUANT TO AN EXEMPTION FROM REGISTRATION WITH THE UNITED STATES SECURITIES AND EXCHANGE COMMISSION. THE COMMISSION DOES NOT PASS UPON THE MERITS OF ANY SECURITIES NOR DOES IT PASS UPON THE ACCURACY OR COMPLETENESS OF ANY OFFERING CIRCULAR OR OTHER SELLING LITERATURE.

The date of this Offering Circular is September 1, 1961.

THE COMPANY

The Company was incorporated under the laws of the Commonwealth of Massachusetts in May 1960. Its principal assets consist of Inventory and Accounts Receivable. It operates from 114 Concord Road, Wayland, Massachusetts, a private residence, and maintains a modest show-room located at 292 Madison Avenue in New York City. It has, at present, no full-time employees and the business of the Company is managed on a part-time basis by Augustine M. Masiello and Donald V. Pryor, both of whom have been serving without compensation. (See Remuneration).

THE BUSINESS OF THE COMPANY

The Company is engaged in the sales of imported knit-wear and sports-wear to retail specialty stores primarily in New England and New York State and, to a limited extent, in the Mid-Atlantic and Mid-Western areas. It is a sales company and has not engaged in manufacturing. The sales are contracted on the basis of samples made to order by manufacturers in Ireland with which the Company has established working relationships, without being bound under any contractual arrangement. Orders are submitted to those manufacturers in quantities in large measure based upon orders already booked. The Company has concentrated on merchandise in classical styles proven to be of perennial appeal and has avoided highly stylistic merchandise.

During its first fiscal year of approximately six months duration ending December 31, 1960, gross sales totaled $8,522.23. Between January 1 and June 30, 1961, gross sales increased to $15,015.06. As of June 30, there were firm orders on hand for July, August and September, 1961, shipments in the approximate amount of $29,000. The number of accounts has increased from 38 in December, 1960, to 102, as of June 30, 1961. No one account represents more than 20% of the Company's business.

The Company's products and the range in retail prices are as follows:

Item	Fall-Winter Line	Spring-Summer Line
Skirts	$17.95–$29.95	$14.95–$17.95
Sweaters	14.95– 16.95	—
Suits	55.00– 65.00	45.00– 50.00
Coats	55.00– 90.00	—
Blouses	14.95	4.95– 5.95

The Fall-Winter Line is made up of tweeds and woolens. The Spring-Summer Line includes cottons, linens and light tweeds.

COMPETITION

The Ladies' Garment Industry is competitive. The Company believes that its sources of supply abroad produce for it quality clothing at comparatively lower costs and that its practice of placing its bulk orders in large measure after orders places the Company in an advantageous position with respect to competition. The Company has specialized in hand-woven Irish tweeds displaying originality in weaves and colors fashioned in classic styles of proven demand. This phase of the garment industry has not yet been subjected to the intense competition characteristic of other aspects of the industry. There is no assurance that the Company will remain in its present advantageous position or that other larger companies with greater resources will not enter this phase of the industry.

MANAGEMENT

Donald V. Pryor, President, graduate of Tufts University with a Degree in Business Administration in 1948, has been Sales Manager of the Walpole Company of Boston and, since 1953, has been engaged as a Manufacturer's Agent representing manufacturers of ladies' leather goods and ladies' sportswear.

Augustine M. Masiello, Treasurer of the Corporation, is a graduate of Iona College with a Degree in Business Administration. Following two years employment with Rusch and Company, Factors, he became Office Manager in 1954 of Far Eastern Fabrics of New York, importers of silk and other textiles from the Orient. In 1956, he was employed by G. T. Inc. of Boston as a Buyer of fabrics. G. T. Inc. is a leader in the men's and women's sportswear field with a present annual volume in excess of $2,000,000. At the end of 1958, he became a Manufacturer's Agent.

Both Mr. Pryor and Mr. Masiello have, in the aggregate, eleven years experience in the New England and New York State areas and are well-known to buyers of better specialty shops and department stores in these areas.

The other Directors are Emily U. Masiello and Joan C. Pryor.

REMUNERATION

No remuneration has been paid to the Directors and Officers of the Company to the present time and none is owed. Except for re-imbursement of expenses, no salary, commission or other compensation has been paid to Mr. Masiello or Mr. Pryor. It is contemplated that both of them will be able to arrange their personal affairs in order to devote full time to the business of the Company in approximately six months. Until such time as he shall devote his full time to the Company, each has agreed to continue to serve without compensation, receiving re-imbursement for expenses, and commissions of six to eight per cent on sales made by them. No remuneration will be paid with the proceeds of the immediate offering.

DIRECTORS, OFFICERS AND STOCKHOLDERS

The Directors, Officers, and Stockholders of the Company and the number of shares of stock held by each and the consideration paid therefor are as follows:

Name and Address	Position	Shares Owned Beneficially and of Record	Percentage of Ownership Before	Percentage of Ownership After	Amount Paid
Donald V. Pryor 50 Red Barn Road Wayland, Massachusetts	President and Director	12,500	41.7	25	$2,000
Augustine M. Masiello 114 Concord Road Wayland, Massachusetts	Treasurer & Director	12,500	41.7	25	$2,000
Emily U. Masiello 114 Concord Road Wayland, Massachusetts	Clerk and Director	none	none	none	none
Joan C. Pryor 50 Red Barn Road Wayland, Massachusetts	Director	none	none	none	none
Richard J. McDermott 12 Squirrel Hill Road Wayland, Massachusetts	—	5,000	16.6	10	$1,000
		30,000	100%	60%	$5,000

All of the foregoing may be considered as promoters.

There are no outstanding options to purchase stock.

Before the offering contemplated hereby, the book value of the holdings of the officers, directors and promoters was approximately 31¢ per share. The book value of these shares will be increased at no cost to these persons to approximately $2.18 per share if the offering is successful. Accordingly, an investment of $5 per share will be reduced to a book equity of $2.18 per share.

Assuming all of the 20,000 shares offered hereunder shall be issued, the existing directors, officers and promoters, as a group, will hold 60% of the outstanding shares at a cost of $5,000, and the public will hold 40% of the outstanding shares at a cost of $100,000.

CAPITAL STOCK

Originally, the authorized capital stock of the Company consisted of 1,000 shares of common stock, no par value, of which 120 shares were issued and outstanding as of June 23, 1961. Of these 120 shares Donald V. Pryor and Augustine M. Masiello held 50 shares each and Richard J. McDermott held 20 shares which he purchased in June 1961 at a price of $50 per share. On June 23, 1961, the authorized capital stock was increased from 1,000 common shares, no par value, to 100,000 common shares, no par value, and the outstanding stock was split by issuing 249 shares additional for each of the 120 shares then outstanding, thereby causing the outstanding shares to number 30,000. No additional consideration has been paid by the Stockholders for the increase in their present holdings. See Note E of Financial Statements.

The shares of common stock of the Company presently outstanding are, and the shares of its common stock offered hereunder upon the issuance thereof will be, fully paid and non-assessable. The holders thereof have one vote for each share held of record. No shareholder has cumulative voting rights. Upon liquidation of the Company, the holders of the common stock are entitled to share ratably in the net assets available for distribution.

It is intended that the Transfer Agent will be The State Street Bank and Trust Company of Boston, Massachusetts.

APPLICATION OF PROCEEDS

The net proceeds from the sale of the shares offered herein by the Company will be added to the working funds of the Company and used generally for corporate purposes as set forth below. The Officers are presently engaged in negotiations with The Industrial Development Authority in Dublin, Ireland, seeking to obtain grants for the establishment of a factory and other facilities in Ireland for the manufacture of sportswear and other clothing. Under present legislation, the Irish Government is authorized to make special grants and provide other facilities that may, under certain conditions, amount to as much as two-thirds of the cost of the factory site and buildings, and as much as one-third to one-half of the cost of machinery and equipment. Under the applicable laws now in force, there is complete remission of the tax on profits of manufacturing companies derived from new or increased exports for ten years. Because such negotiations are in the preliminary stages, it is difficult to predict their outcome. If such negotiations shall prove successful, it is possible that the Company may further increase its margin of profit on merchandise sold in this Country and improve its competitive position. Although it is not possible, at this time, to estimate accurately what portion of the proceeds of this Offering may be necessary for this purpose, the Officers believe that about $55,000 will be required.

All real estate, if any, and machinery, equipment and production facilities to be acquired in Ireland will be owned or leased and operated by a corporation to be established under the laws of Ireland. All or not less than two-thirds of the capital stock to be issued by said corporation will be held by the Company and the remaining interest, if any, will be issued to one or more persons who reside or intend to reside in Ireland and who, in the opinion of the Officers, may be in a position to assist in acquiring, organizing or operating the contemplated production facilities there. The sum of $55,000 allocated in the schedule below is to be advanced to or invested in the proposed foreign subsidiary which in turn will acquire the production facilities.

The remainder of the proceeds is expected to be utilized for the purposes of establishing a more effective show-room in New York City, creating a sales force, increasing the working capital in anticipation of increased sales, augmenting inventories and establishing a more adequate business office in the Greater Boston area.

The Company proposes to use the net proceeds of its Offering for the following purposes and substantially in the respective amounts hereinafter set forth:

Proposed Production Facilities (Foreign Subsidiary)	$55,000
Sales Staff	3,000
Show-room, New York City	5,000
Administrative Office	3,000
General Corporate Operations	29,000
	$95,000

The Officers and Directors will seek the prior approval of the Stockholders in the event of any significant deviation from the purposes above stated.

DIVIDENDS

To date, the Company has paid no cash dividends on its common stock and does not contemplate the payment of dividends in the immediate future. The payment of dividends and the amount thereof will depend upon future earnings, the financial condition of the Company, general economic conditions, and particularly the needs of the Company for expansion.

THE OFFERING

The offering herein is being made directly by the Company. It comprises 20,000 shares of the authorized 100,000 shares of the capital stock of the Company. The Company has not entered into any Underwriting Contract with any persons or firm.

LITIGATION

The Company is not a defendant in any pending litigation and knows of no threatened litigation against the Company.

TAX CONSIDERATION

The common stock of the Company may qualify under certain circumstances as "Section 1244 Stock" within the meaning of Section 1244 of the Internal Revenue Code of 1954. Under the Small Business

Tax Revision Act of 1958, amending the Internal Revenue Code of 1954, any individual sustaining a loss on the sale, exchange, or worthlessness of "Section 1244 Stock" is entitled to treat such loss, within certain maximum limits, as an ordinary loss instead of a capital loss. This treatment applies only to losses of an individual in shares purchased directly from the issuer and does not apply to losses sustained by Transferees of any such purchaser. While the stock being offered hereunder is intended to qualify as Section 1244 Stock, the opinion of the Company must not be relied upon, in view of the recent origin of said provision and the regulations issued thereunder, and the need for further clarification thereof.

COUNSEL FOR COMPANY

Counsel for the Company in connection with this offering is Haig Der Manueulian, Esq., of Schlesinger & Manuelian, 18 Tremont Street, Boston, Massachusetts.

FINANCIAL STATEMENTS

Financial Statements of the Company have been prepared in accordance with generally accepted accounting principles and practices by Harold J. Gibbons, 64 Reed Avenue, Everett, Massachusetts, who has been retained by the Company since its inception.

EXHIBIT A

KILBANON CORPORATION

FINANCIAL CONDITION
JUNE 30, 1961

ASSETS

CURRENT ASSETS
Cash			$5,051.20
Accounts Receivable	$8,281.70		
Less—Allowance for Bad Debts and Discounts	333.37		7,948.33
Inventories: (Note A)			
Finished Goods	3,776.95		
On Consignment	613.75		
Samples	925.01		
In Transit	4,010.19		9,325.90

TOTAL CURRENT ASSETS $22,325.43

OTHER ASSETS
  Insurance Deposit 50.00

DEFERRED CHARGES
Stock Reorganization Expense (Note B)	1,750.00	
Miscellaneous	74.28	1,824.28

TOTAL ASSETS $24,199.71

LIABILITIES AND NET WORTH

CURRENT LIABILITIES
Accounts Payable	$7,201.38	
Loans Payable (Note C)	2,000.00	
Notes Payable (Note D)	5,000.00	
Accrued Federal Income Tax	636.68	

TOTAL CURRENT LIABILITIES $14,838.06

NET WORTH
Capital Stock—No Par Value (Note E)
  Authorized 100,000 Shares
Issued and Outstanding 30,000 Shares	5,000.00
Paid in Surplus	2,951.07
Earned Surplus—Unappropriated	1,410.58

TOTAL NET WORTH 9,361.65

TOTAL LIABILITIES AND NET WORTH $24,199.71

Commitments and Contingent Liabilities—See Note F

The notes appended are an integral part of this report.

EXHIBIT C

KILBANON CORPORATION

STATEMENT OF INCOME

SIX MONTHS ENDED JUNE 30, 1961 AND YEAR (SEVEN MONTHS) ENDED DECEMBER 31, 1960

	Jan. 1 to June 30 1961	May 13 to Dec. 31 1960
SALES	$15,015.06	$ 8,522.23
COST OF SALES (Note G)	10,260.45	5,642.98
GROSS PROFIT ON SALES	4,754.61	2,879.25
OPERATING EXPENSES (Note H)		
Cash Discounts Allowed	638.56	584.46
Legal and Audit	210.00	456.33
Bad Debts	—	130.00
Sales and Shipping Expenses	248.32	328.48
Commissions	49.35	—
Taxes	55.75	—
Interest	17.89	—
Miscellaneous	78.17	249.28
Travel	—	2,540.01
TOTAL OPERATING EXPENSES	1,298.04	4,288.56
INCOME BEFORE FEDERAL INCOME TAX	3,456.57	(1,409.31)
PROVISION FOR FEDERAL INCOME TAX	636.68	—
NET INCOME FOR PERIOD	$ 2,819.89	$(1,409.31)

The notes appended are an integral part of this report.

OFFERING CIRCULAR

CHOMERICS, INC.
(a Delaware Corporation)
(Incorporated July 24, 1961)

40,000 Shares Common Stock
($.10 par value)

The Common Stock offered hereby is speculative.

Particular reference is made to "Introductory Statement".

THESE SECURITIES ARE OFFERED PURSUANT TO AN EXEMPTION FROM REGISTRATION WITH THE UNITED STATES SECURITIES AND EXCHANGE COMMISSION. THE COMMISSION DOES NOT PASS UPON THE MERITS OF ANY SECURITIES NOR DOES IT PASS UPON THE ACCURACY OR COMPLETENESS OF ANY OFFERING CIRCULAR OR OTHER SELLING LITERATURE.

Since prior to this offering, there has been no public offering of the securities of the issuer, no public market exists for the common stock and the creation of such public market is not guaranteed as a result of the purchase and sale of the shares offered hereby. There are no arrangements for the return of funds to purchasers in the event that less than all of the shares offered hereby are sold.

	Price to Public(1)	Underwriting Discounts and Commissions(2)	Proceeds to Company
Per share	$5.00	None	$5.00
Total	$200,000	None	$200,000(3)

(1) The offering price has been arbitrarily determined and bears no relation to the earnings or assets of the Company nor to the book value. See "Introductory Statement".

(2) The Company has entered into no underwriting agreement covering the shares offered hereby.

(3) Assuming all of the shares offered hereby are sold and before deducting expenses to the Company estimated at $11,500, including the cost of printing the Offering Circular, the preparation of the stock certificates, the stock issue tax, the fees and expenses of the issuer's counsel and accountants, and costs incurred in qualifying the shares offered hereunder for offer and sale under the securities and Blue Sky Laws of certain States.

The date of this Offering Circular is July 2, 1962.

INTRODUCTORY STATEMENT

Chomerics, Inc., (the "Company") was incorporated in Delaware on July 24, 1961 and has its executive offices and plant at 341 Vassar Street, Cambridge, Massachusetts. The Company has been organized to serve as a supplier of special plastics and plastic compositions to industrial consumers, especially the electronics industry, and to be a specialist in the application of plastic systems in electrical environments. The Company will work toward the development of new plastic compositions in response to particular customer problems and in so doing the Company will act as plastic technologists. Some of these products will be new to the electronics and electrical industry and the market for them cannot be predicted with any degree of certainty at this time.

As indicated, the Company is relatively new in the business it intends to pursue, has no history of earnings or operations, and has no established competitive position; consequently, investors therefore assume the usual risks associated with any new enterprise. The Company has developed a conductive plastic system which it feels is equal in performance in most applications to silver filled plastics and the Company presently anticipates that this will be its first major product line.

Although the Company has conducted various market surveys which indicated a broad potential market for its conductive plastic system, no assurance can be given that the Company will be successful in selling its products or in realizing profits.

The offering price of the securities offered hereby has been determined upon the basis of the funds estimated by the Company to be reasonably required to commence commercial operations and is not based on book value, earnings, asset value or any other recognized criterion of value.

The Company has issued 84,000 shares of its Common Stock for cash in the aggregate amount of $81,400. At the time of incorporation the original founders of the Company, Messrs. Lee A. Strimbeck, Robert F. Jasse, Melvin Nimoy and John E. Ehrreich, who are presently officers and directors of the Company, each purchased 12,500 shares of Common Stock at $.10 per share and Richard J. McDermott and Roye Levin, Financial Advisors to the Company, each purchased 5,000 shares at $.10 per share and each of the foregoing because of their activity in the formation of the Company, may be deemed to be "Promoters" as that term is defined in the Securities Act of 1933, as amended. Subsequently, on September 14, 1961, 20,000 shares of the presently issued and outstanding Common Stock were sold as an investment to a limited number of persons at a price of $3.75 per share. (See "Prior Sale of Common Stock")

Prior to the sale of the 40,000 shares of Common Stock offered hereby, the book value as of January 31, 1962, was approximately $.48 per share based upon the 80,500 shares then outstanding. Assuming the sale of all of the shares at the public offering price of $5.00 per share, the book value based upon the new number of shares to be outstanding will be approximately $1.69 per share. Persons who purchase shares at the public offering price will, on the foregoing assumption, sustain an immediate dilution in their equity amounting to an estimated $3.31 per share based on the difference between the purchase price and the estimated book value subsequent to the offering, and conversely, the present shareholders including the officers and directors, will benefit from the above increase in book value in an amount equal to $1.21 per share, such benefit being at the expense of those who purchase at the offering price.

After this offering is completed the Common Stock owned by Promoters, Officers and Directors of the Company will represent approximately 50.6 per cent of the total outstanding Common Stock for which they have paid an aggregate amount of $6,150 while the public purchasers will have paid an aggregate of $200,000 for 40,000 shares or approximately 32.9 per cent of the total outstanding shares. In addition, Messrs. Lee A. Strimbeck, John E. Ehrreich, Melvin Nimoy and Robert F. Jasse have been granted Restricted Stock Options for the purchase of 20,000 shares of the Company stock (see "Restricted Stock Options" herein).

APPLICATION OF PROCEEDS

On the assumption that all of the shares of Common Stock offered hereby will be sold, the net proceeds from the sale of such shares are estimated at a maximum of $188,500 after deducting the expenses of the offering. It is expected that such net proceeds will be used in the following approximate amounts in the priority indicated. The first $15,000 will be used to purchase additional plant equipment required for the Company to enter into full-scale production of its products developed to date; the next $10,000 will be used to purchase additional laboratory equipment; the next $25,000, for future research and development; the next $50,000, to discharge outstanding Promissory Notes, the proceeds of which were used to meet current expenses. The balance of the proceeds of this offering will be added to the working capital of the Company and used for general corporate purposes.

CAPITALIZATION

The capitalization of the Company as of January 31, 1962, and as adjusted to give effect to the sale of all of the shares offered hereby and the application of a portion of the proceeds to the payment of Notes as set forth under "Application of Proceeds" is as follows:

Title of Class	Amount Authorized	Amount Outstanding	Amount to Be Outstanding
Convertible Promissory Notes (8%) due December 31, 1962(1)	$50,000	$50,000	None
Common Stock (par value $.10)	1,000,000(2)	84,000(3)	124,000(4)

(1) See Note 5 to Financial Statements.

(2) 20,000 shares have been reserved by the Board of Directors for issuance pursuant to Restricted Stock Options. Options covering a total of 20,000 shares have been granted to date. (See "Restricted Stock Options.")

(3) Including 3,500 shares held in Treasury. On February 28, 1962, the Board of Directors voted to sell a total of 1,000 shares of Treasury stock at a price of $.10 per share to Dr. Edwin Gilliland and Mr. Andrew Rouse, both of whom are members of the Board of Directors.

(4) Excluding 10,000 shares reserved for conversion of eight (8%) per cent convertible notes.

BUSINESS

General

Chomerics, Inc. was incorporated in Delaware on July 24, 1961. The Company's long-range objective is to develop, manufacture and sell plastic specialties to select industrial markets. The Company is first concentrating its efforts on the supplying of nonfabricated plastic specialties, principally formulated resin mixtures, to the electronics industry.

* * *

DESCRIPTION OF SECURITIES

Common Stock

The only class of capital stock authorized is the Common Stock, par value ten cents ($.10) per share.

Holders of Common Stock are entitled to receive such dividends as may be from time to time declared by the Board of Directors out of any funds of the Company legally available for that purpose, and holders are to share pro rata in the distributable assets of the Company in the event of any liquidation, dissolution or winding up. The holders of the Common Stock do not have preemptive rights.

The Board of Directors does not intend to declare any dividends on the Common Stock for the indefinite future.

The voting rights are vested exclusively in the holders of the Common Stock, each stockholder being entitled to one vote for each share held, and the holders of the Common Stock have no preemptive rights, subscription rights, conversion rights or redemption rights.

The shares of Common Stock to be issued and sold as provided herein will be upon the issue and sale thereof, fully paid and non-assessable.

The transfer agent for the Common Stock is STATE STREET BANK AND TRUST COMPANY.

Eight (8%) per cent Convertible Promissory Notes

On December 15, 1961, the Company sold at par, $50,000 principal amount of its eight (8%) per cent convertible Promissory Notes due December 14, 1963 to six persons. The proceeds were used as working capital.

The Notes are convertible at the rate of $5.00 per share at any time prior to 90 days from the date of this Offering Circular and thereafter the company has the right with respect to any then unpaid principal, to repay the same in cash. It is the Company's present intention to repay any remaining principal from the proceeds of this Offering. (See "Application of Proceeds".)

If and when the Notes are converted, the noteholders would receive 10,000 shares of Capital Stock at a cost equivalent of $5.00 per share. Said notes were issued pursuant to a private offering and neither the notes nor the underlying Common Stock are included in this present offering. Persons holding the notes have represented to the Company that the notes and the underlying Common Stock were purchased for investment purposes only and not for resale or distribution.

Prior Sale of Common Stock

On September 14, 1961, the Company sold 20,000 shares of Common Stock in one transaction for $75,000 at a price of $3.75 per share to twenty-six (26) persons. All of the purchasers were either relatives, friends or acquaintances of the Company and its "Promoters" (see "Introduction"). The Common Stock was sold pursuant to a private offering and is not included in this present offering. Persons purchasing the stock represented to the Company that the stock was purchased for investment purposes only and not for resale or distribution.

CHOMERICS, INC.

SUPPLEMENT TO OFFERING CIRCULAR DATED JULY 2, 1962

The purpose of this supplement is to present the financial statements of Chomerics, Inc. as of a more recent date and to include a Profit and Loss Statement not previously included in view of the fact that actual operations did not commence until September 15, 1961. The Profit and Loss Statement presented herewith reflects the period from the date of incorporation July 24, 1961, to May 31, 1962.

This supplement further reflects a Statement of Cash Receipts and Disbursements from the date of incorporation to May 31, 1962, and a Balance Sheet as of May 31, 1962. All of the foregoing statements have been prepared from the books of the Company without audit. In the opinion of the Company all adjustments necessary to a fair statement of results for such periods have been included.

As of May 31, 1962, the Company had a working capital deficit of $39,256 and a deficiency in capital of $72,477. The book value as of May 31, 1962 is approximately $.11 per share based upon the 81,000 shares then outstanding Assuming the sale of all of the shares offered at the public offering price at $5.00 per share, the book value based upon the new number of shares to be outstanding will be approximately $1.73 per share. Persons who purchase shares of stock at the public offering price will, on the foregoing assumption, sustain an immediate dilution in their equity amounting to an estimated $3.27 per share based on the difference between the purchase price and the estimated book value subsequent to the offering.

Dated July 18, 1962

CHOMERICS, INC.

Balance Sheet
May 31, 1962
(Unaudited)

ASSETS

CURRENT ASSETS:
Cash		$17,428.63
Accounts Receivable-Trade		3,319.50
Inventories at Cost:		
Raw Materials and Finished Goods	$ 7,503.97	
Supplies	272.96	7,776.93
Prepaid Expenses:		
Rent	$ 1,170.00	
Other	1,117.43	2,287.43
Total Current Assets		$30,812.49

PROPERTY AND EQUIPMENT (Note 1):
Production Machinery and Equipment	$ 6,605.60	
Laboratory Equipment	7,529.25	
Office Furniture and Equipment	100.00	
Leasehold Improvements	4,711.75	
Total	$18,946.60	
Less: Accumulated Depreciation	2,853.21	
Net Property and Equipment-Cost		16,093.39

OTHER ASSETS AND UNRECOVERED DEVELOPMENT COSTS:
Unrecovered Development Costs (Note 7)	$28,087.63	
Patent Applications (Note 2)	491.00	
Unamortized Organization Expense (Note 3)	1,361.46	
Due from Officers and Directors (Note 4)	1,635.19	
Utility Deposits	210.00	
Total Other Assets and Unrecovered Development Costs		31,785.28
TOTAL		$78,691.16

The notes to financial statements are an integral part of this statement.

Balance Sheet
May 31, 1962
(Unaudited)

LIABILITIES

CURRENT LIABILITIES:
8% Convertible Promissory Notes (Note 5)	$55,000.00
Accounts Payable-Trade	10,511.18
Accrued Expenses and Payroll and Local Taxes	4,557.24
Total Current Liabilities	$70,068.42

COMMITMENTS (Note 6) .... —

Total Liabilities $70,068.42

STOCKHOLDERS' EQUITY

Common Stock, Par Value $.10
Authorized: 1,000,000 shares

Issued: 84,000 shares	$ 8,400.00
Paid in Surplus	$73,000.00
Retained Earnings (Deficit)	(72,477.26)
Total	$ 8,922.74
Less: Treasury Stock-Cost 3,000 shares	300.00
Total Stockholders' Equity	8,622.74
TOTAL	$78,691.16

The notes to financial statements are an integral part of this statement.

CHOMERICS, INC.

STATEMENT OF PROFIT AND (LOSS) AND RETAINED EARNINGS (DEFICIT) FROM DATE OF INCORPORATION JULY 24, 1961, TO MAY 31, 1962.

(Unaudited)

GROSS SALES	$10,415.53
COST OF SALES	4,056.80
GROSS PROFIT	6,358.73
OVERHEAD EXPENSES	
SELLING EXPENSES	36,044.63
GENERAL AND ADMINISTRATIVE	26,826.50
FACTORY ADMINISTRATION	13,957.07
DEPRECIATION	625.06
AMORTIZATION	1,382.73
TOTAL EXPENSES	78,835.99
NET LOSS FOR PERIOD	$72,477.26
RETAINED EARNINGS	
BEGINNING OF PERIOD	.00
DEFICIT IN RETAINED EARNINGS	
END OF PERIOD	$72,477.26

4. COMBINATION OF EXEMPTIONS—INTEGRATION AND THE "ISSUE" CONCEPT [11]

Both Releases 4552 and 4434 make it clear that in determining whether an exemption is applicable to a particular offering, consideration must be given to whether that offering is separable from other financings of the issuer or is in reality merely a part of a larger offering or "issue". If the latter is true, no exemption is available unless the entire issue qualifies for it. In other words, an issuer may not divide what is actually a single offering into two or more parts in order to qualify one part under one exemption and another part under some other exemption.

Although Releases 4552 and 4434 do not deal with exemption under Regulation A, the integration concept is equally operative there, being imported into the word "issue" in § 3(b) just as it is in § 3(a)(11). (In the private offering exemption of § 4(1), which does not contain the word "issue", the concept presumably comes in by way of either the word "transactions" or the word "involving".)

Both Releases 4552 and 4434 set out the standards for determining when purportedly separate offerings are really so related that they should be "integrated" into a single issue for the purpose of applying the various exemption provisions. One of the most common problems of this kind has arisen in connection with the stock issued to the promoters of a promotional enterprise. According to Professor Loss, at pages 618–619, the Commission's traditional policy under Regulation A has been to consider stock issued to promoters for property or services and taken by them for investment not to be part of the same "issue" as stock concurrently offered to the public for cash. And in order to avoid favoring the issuance of stock to promoters for non-cash consideration, the Commission came to regard stock issued to promoters as a separate "issue" even when they paid cash like anybody else.

So far as § 4(1) is concerned, it appears that the Commission follows the same policy of treating promotional stock issued for property or services as a separate "issue".[12] Presumably, the Commission would apply the same policy to promotional stock under the intrastate exemption of § 3(a)(11), since that section uses the same term "issue" as in § 3(b). Of course as to Regulation A itself this traditional policy has now been revised pursuant to Rule 253(c), supra, with its requirement that *all* stock issued to promoters of a promotional company be included in applying the $300,000 maximum permitted by Regulation

---

11. See generally, Loss, at 594, 618–619, and 687–689.

12. See Loss, at 689, note 140: "But this is not true as to shares sold to a few persons for cash in a 'preunderwriting offering' designed to raise funds to pay the costs in connection with [the] contemplated public offering. Cameron Industries, Inc., Sec. Act Rel. 4159 (1959) 6."

A, unless the condition for keeping such shares off the market is satisfied.

It should be noted that preserving an exemption for the offering to outsiders by preventing the integration of the promotional stock, as by an escrow arrangement under Rule 253(c), is only half the battle. It is also essential to establish an exemption for the promotional stock itself, presumably under § 4(1), or possibly § 3(a) (11); and for this purpose it is important to be sure that such exemption is not lost as a result of integration of the outsider offering with the promotional stock. A valid exemption for the promotional stock is of particular importance when the outsider offering is under Regulation A, because of the provision in Rule 254(a) (3) to the effect that any stock illegally issued during the prior year must be included in computing the amount of the Regulation A offering. Under this provision, if the promotional stock does not qualify for an exemption it would have to be integrated with the Regulation A offering as illegally issued stock, even though there may be an arrangement pursuant to Rule 253(c) to keep the promotional stock off the market for a year. As a matter of fact, Professor Loss suggests (at page 619, note 4) that the escrow provision of Rule 253(c) may have been as much designed to protect the private offering exemption for stock issued to promoters as to control the application of the "issue" concept under Regulation A.

D. SECURITIES ACT PROBLEMS IN ISSUING STOCK FOR PROFESSIONAL SERVICES

1. The Accountant. The Securities Act pretty well precludes the issuance of stock to an accountant for his services in connection with the organization of the corporation if he is to perform any services in connection with the registration of any of the company's stock under the Act. Schedule A of the Act provides that the financial statements required to be included in a registration statement must be "certified by an independent public, or certified public accountant". The Commission has adopted a very strict objective approach to the independence requirement, and has held that the test is not met wherever the circumstances create a reasonable doubt that the accountant "will or can have an impartial and objective judgment on questions confronting him." Acc.Ser.Rel. No. 81 (1958) 3. In accordance with this test, Rule 2–01(b) of Regulation S–X provides that the accountant may not hold "any direct financial interest" in the registering corporation, which would seem to preclude the ownership of even a single share of stock of the corporation. Presumably, a compensation arrangement entitling the accountant to receive stock for his services would be equally inconsistent with the independence requirement.

In addition to the bar against any financial interest, Rule 2–01 (b) forbids any connection with the registering corporation or any affiliate as a "promoter, underwriter, voting trustee, director, officer, or employee". Moreover, according to Professor Loss (pages 343–344) an accountant who has any significant business or family relationship with the corporation, or who takes too great a part in the original accounting determinations or decisions of management, is likely to be regarded as lacking the necessary independence.

For a long time the American Institute of Certified Public Accountants took a somewhat less restrictive view of the independence requirement. Although the AICPA did not dispute either the vital importance of the accountant's independence, or the fact that his duty is to safeguard the public rather than to advance the interests of his client, it did resist the imposition of flat bars, on the ground that the particular facts and circumstances of each case should control. However, after consideration of the matter at a number of successive annual meetings, in 1962 the AICPA adopted a rule prohibiting a member of the organization from certifying any financial statement, even for a closely-held company, if he "had, or was committed to acquire, any direct financial interest in the enterprise" or "was connected with the enterprise as a promoter, underwriter, voting trustee, director, officer or key employee". AICPA Code of Professional Ethics, Rule 13, set out in 113 J. Accountancy (April, 1962) 29–30.

As a practical matter, the bar against any direct financial interest may prove less troublesome than the Commission's prohibition against taking too substantial a part in the original accounting and management decisions. It is certainly not uncommon for an accountant to be brought in at the inception of a new enterprise to help on general financial matters, including setting up the original books for the enterprise. As a practical matter, the accountant so engaged usually either already is, or becomes, closely associated with the promoters, and does play a significant role in reaching decisions in the formative stages. But under the Commission's view such an accountant would apparently be precluded from certifying the financial statements for registration purposes, although that may have been one of the reasons for bringing in the accountant in the first place.

2. **The Lawyer.** As a part of the registration material, the issuer must include an opinion of counsel that the stock being sold will be legally issued, fully paid, and non-assessable, together with the name and address of counsel rendering the opinion. There does not appear to be any bar against having such an opinion as to the legality of the issue rendered by an attorney who has a financial interest in the corporation, although presumably that fact must be disclosed. This difference in attitude toward lawyers and accountants was recently referred to as follows, in Sec.Act Rel. No. 4465 (1962), which holds

that an accountant's partnership with the issuer's legal counsel [13] precludes the accountant from having the necessary independence:

> "Though owing a public responsibility, an attorney in acting as the client's advisor, defender, advocate and confidant enters into a personal relationship in which his principal concern is with the interests and rights of his client. The requirement of the Act of certification by an independent accountant, on the other hand, is intended to secure for the benefit of public investors the detached objectivity of a disinterested person. The certifying accountant must be one who is in no way connected with the business or its management and who does not have any relationship that might affect the independence which at times may require him to voice public criticism of his client's accounting practices." [14]

If ownership of stock of the issuer does not bar a lawyer from rendering an opinion as to the legality of a proposed new issue, it would seem that, *a fortiori*, a right to receive stock for services would not disqualify him. But perhaps the answer is otherwise if the lawyer is to receive stock from the very issue upon whose legality he is passing. And apart from the question of what position the Commission might take, the lawyer himself might well hesitate to render an opinion upon a stock issue in which he personally is to participate.

Of course the question of whether a lawyer should take stock as compensation for his services is part of the broader question of whether it is desirable for a lawyer to hold a financial interest in an enterprise which he represents. A somewhat related question is whether a lawyer should serve on the board of directors of a client corporation. There are no clear guideposts on these issues, and in the absence of special circumstances the lawyer would appear to be free to decide for himself which course to adopt.

3. The Stockbroker.

There is of course no bar against a broker holding an interest in a company whose stock he is helping to sell.

---

13. Such a partnership between an accountant and a lawyer would seem to be a violation of Canon 33. See Opinion No. 297 of the ABA Professional Ethics Committee, 112 J. Accountancy (July, 1961) 73–74.

14. Compare Invest. Co. Act Rel. No. 214 (1941), expressing the General Counsel's opinion that the regular counsel for an investment company on a general retainer was too closely related to the management to be one of the "independent" persons required by the Investment Company Act to constitute at least 40% of the board of directors:

"The usual work of such counsel and the questions which confront him relate to the management of the company. He provides the legal advice which guides the management of the company in its activities. The purpose of [the Act]—to provide an independent check on management—can hardly be accomplished if a person so closely related to the management is permitted to be included in the minority portion of the board which is designed to check independently on management activities."

However, the registration material must fully disclose the nature and amount of all commissions or discounts paid or to be paid, directly or indirectly, to underwriters and selling agents. There seems little doubt that this is broad enough to reach an arrangement under which the selling agent is permitted to buy "cheap stock" along with the promoters prior to the offering to outsiders at a higher price. Such an arrangement also poses the question of whether a dealer in securities can satisfactorily establish the necessary investment intention; if not, the inclusion of his stock in the "issue" to the promoters would presumably defeat the private offering exemption which would normally be relied upon for that issue. See Sec.Act Rel. No. 4552, supra.

SECTION 2. STATE REGULATION OF SECURITIES: "BLUE SKY" LAWS [15]

A. TECHNIQUES OF REGULATION

Prior to the enactment of the federal Securities Act in 1933, virtually every state had adopted legislation designed to protect the public from "speculative schemes which have no more basis than so many feet of 'blue sky'." See Hall v. Geiger-Jones Co., 242 U.S. 539, 550, 37 S.Ct. 217, 220, 61 L.Ed. 480 (1917). Since § 18 of the Securities Act provides that "Nothing in this title shall affect the jurisdiction of the Securities commission . . . of any State . . . over any security or any person," state and federal regulation have continued side by side.

The impact of these laws is by no means limited to cases where the offering is exempt from registration under the federal act, since many of the state laws go beyond the disclosure requirements of the federal statute. Experience has shown that disclosure is often not enough, for naive investors seldom examine the available facts and commonly are not sophisticated enough to make proper use of them if they do. However, the form and content of the additional protection afforded by the local blue sky laws vary greatly from state to state. Three different methods of regulation are employed: the fraud approach, dealer registration, and securities registration. These three methods are used in different combinations in the various states; and within the three methods there are important differences in procedures and standards, to say nothing of variations in such matters as the

---

15. Some of the following material is adapted, by permission, from Baker & Cary, Cases and Materials on Corporations (3d ed., unabridged 1959) 1133–1142.

scope of exemptions and the definitions of operative terms such as "security" and "sale."

1. **The Fraud Approach.** From the point of view of administration this is probably the simplest method. In the ordinary case neither the dealer nor the administrator need take any action because of the statute. This form of blue sky law normally provides in quite broad terms that certain practices, usually described in terms of "fraud", shall be the grounds of criminal prosecution, or suspension of trading by or at the suit of the administrator, or both. While the administrator normally has broad investigatory powers, they are unlikely to be exercised in the absence of complaint or suspicious circumstances. It is probably for this reason that the fraud method is thought not to be sufficient in itself, and there appear to be no states which rely solely upon this approach.

2. **Dealer Registration.** Virtually every state has some form of requirement that dealers, including generally brokers, salesmen and the like (and sometimes issuers), must register as a prerequisite to dealing in securities within its borders. However, the amount, detail and nature of the information that must be submitted vary widely among the states. Moreover, there are basic differences of approach even within this type of blue sky provision.

In a few states registration is little more than a formality. In New York, for example, a dealer need only file statements setting forth his name and address, his connections in the securities business for the preceding five years, the names of the last three issues sold by him or by a dealer with which he was associated, and the details of any revocation of his registration, or any criminal conviction or injunction in connection with the securities business. If the applicant is not an individual, similar information must be given in respect of all partners or corporate officials. There is no provision for denying or revoking registration.

The Pennsylvania statute, by way of contrast, requires the dealer to file not only certain specified information but also any information the Commission may require. The dealer must also submit satisfactory evidence of his financial responsibility and good repute. Registration becomes effective in thirty days if the Commission takes no action, but the Commission has power to deny registration if it "finds that the applicant is not of good repute, or that the proposed plan of business of the applicant is unfair, unjust, or inequitable, or that the applicant is not of sufficient financial responsibility to deal safely with the public."

In the majority of states, registration may be denied or revoked for cause, and the administrator sometimes has considerable discretion in determining whether a dealer shall be permitted to do business within the state. In addition, it is not uncommon to require either a minimum capital or a bond.

3. **Securities Registration ("Qualifying" an Issue).** The large number of statutory schemes encompassed within this heading cannot all be described fully. What they have in common is the prohibition against dealing in securities, unless they are exempt, until the issue has been qualified in accordance with the statutory procedure. The procedures prescribed and the standards adopted vary considerably from state to state. In general, they are aimed particularly at unseasoned speculative securities being offered to the general public.

At one extreme are the few states which require no more than that certain information be filed. New York asks for little more than identification of the issuer. A few other states require not much more, but do give the administrator power to investigate and call for additional data; and he may issue a stop order pending the outcome of his investigation.

In most states, however, the statute calls for affirmative administrative approval of the proposed issue. In many of these jurisdictions, a streamlined type of registration called "notification", which requires little more than a simple notice of intention, is available for quality stock issues, while full registration, often called "qualification", is necessary for other issues. In general, the streamlined notification procedure is limited to seasoned securities. In Kansas, for example, securities may be registered by notification where the issuer has been in business for over five years and meets a specified annual net earnings test. A number of states, following the Uniform Securities Act, discussed infra, also have a special simple procedure, called "co-ordination", for registering a security which has already been registered with the SEC.

NOTE ON THE STATUTORY STANDARDS

1. In General

The statutory standards for full registration, i. e., qualification, under the various statutes are typically set forth in broad terms, and as a result the administrator normally has great discretion in approving issues sought to be registered under such statutes. The great variety of these statutory standards, as well as the exemptions which may be available, are well summarized in the following excerpts from the definitive work in this field:

LOSS AND COWETT, BLUE SKY LAW [16]
1958. Pages 67–83.

STANDARDS APPLIED AND CONDITIONS IMPOSED IN THE REGISTRATION OF SECURITIES

We have already noticed the variety of statutory standards governing the effectiveness of registration statements for securities, and the breadth of some of them. Obviously such phrases as "sound business principles," "grossly unfair terms," and "fair, just, and equitable" leave a good deal to the administrator's imagination. In an attempt to determine how these and other standards are applied in practice, the questionnaire which was sent to all the administrators asked them "to describe briefly the various criteria which you apply in actual practice" when registration is sought for (a) issues of promotional companies, (b) oil, gas, or mining issues, (c) mutual fund shares, (d) any other types of securities treated as special categories in the particular state, and (e) securities not falling in any special category. The best responses were directed to the first category—promotional issues.

Apart from one administrator who replied, "I don't know what you mean by promotional companies," the answers ranged, as might have been expected, from a naked repetition of the statutory standards to an attempt to formulate seemingly objective tests and rules of thumb:

(1) Although the question was followed by the underscored statement that "We are familiar with your statutory standards and would like you to discuss in your answer the manner in which you have applied these standards," about a dozen administrators substantially repeated the language of the statute. Apparently they have made no particular effort to probe into their decisional processes. Or perhaps they have concluded that any delineation of the statutory standards would be either impractical or illusory. . . .

(2) . . . [The criteria] most commonly referred to were the remuneration (direct or indirect) of promoters, the ratio of the promoters' equity to that of the public investors,* and the character and experience of the

---

16. Reprinted by permission of the publisher, Little, Brown & Co. Footnotes omitted.

* [Ed. note] Ohio, which has a reputation for strictness in security regulation, refused to permit the sale in 1950 of 600,000 shares of Class A stock of Holiday Brands, Inc. at $3.00 a share, because 285,000 shares of Class B stock were to be sold to the promoters at 5 cents a share. The provision that both classes of stock would be treated equally if the company liquidated was deemed unfair to the buyers of Class A stock. N. Y. Times, May 8, 1950, p. 28, col. 5.

At the 1955 meeting of the National Association of Securities Administrators, the following resolution relating to so-called "cheap stock" was adopted (38 Proceedings NASA 113–115):

"The sale of securities to the underwriters or promoters, at prices substantially below the public offering price, at a time in close proximity to the public offering date, will hereafter be looked upon with great disfavor and will be considered as a basis for denial of the application except in unusual circumstances such as favorable developments after the date of sale to underwriters or promoters and before the public offering dates, sufficient to justify the differential in price. The burden of justifying such sales shall rest upon the applicant."

promoters and the proposed officers and directors. Almost as many administrators referred to the size of the underwriting and selling commissions, some in terms of a maximum of 15 or 20 percent of the public offering price. Several administrators used such phrases as "the economic potential" of the venture, "the possibility of success," "reasonable investment merits," and "the nature of the promotion." There were also scattered references to the types of securities being offered (presumably from the point of view of reasonable capital structure and effect on control) and the accuracy of the disclosure. And there were isolated references to the reasonableness of the offering price, the adequacy of the proceeds, the nature of the venture, the amount of capital to be raised, arm's-length dealings between the promoters and the company, and the relative voting and dividend rights of the promoters and public investors (as distinct from the more frequent references to the relative *equity interests* of the two groups).

(3) About a dozen administrators (it is always difficult to know where to draw the line) have tried, to a greater or lesser extent, to formulate seemingly objective tests of more or less general applicability to all kinds of securities, including promotional issues. In seven of these states there are published rules. In the other five states, and to some extent in the seven, the administrators expressed these tests in reply to the questionnaire. . .

A few administrators have adopted rule-of-thumb *percentage tests* designed to keep the promoters' equity within bounds. Thus, California, New Mexico and Texas by rule restrict the promoters' participation so that, in general, an "ultimate equality" is achieved between shares sold for cash or its equivalent and promotional shares. A Mississippi rule limits "patents, goodwill, services, and other intangibles" to 30 percent. The Florida administrator follows the policy, without formal rule, of requiring a *tangible* investment from promoters of at least 25 percent of the amount of securities offered to the public. A Texas rule requires, in the case of "speculative" securities, that at least 10 percent of the proposed capital stock be paid for in cash by the organizers and promoters before any stock is offered to the public. And in Utah, where the corporation law requires that 10 percent of the capital stock be paid in but does not specify how, a special rule for uranium issuers requires that 25 percent of the required subscription be paid in cash.

As an additional anchor to windward, the California regulations "ordinarily" limit promotional stock to common shares, with a further provision to the effect that promotional securities of a new enterprise financing through a single class of stock may have no greater voting rights in the aggregate than the securities issued for cash or its equivalent. Under an Idaho rule the promotional security cannot be of greater rank than the security sought to be qualified. And an Alabama rule provides that there must be an "equitable participation" between promotional and other shares; that the organizers or promoters "must in every case contribute, either by way of cash or other valuable consideration, a substantial portion of the proposed capital"; and that no promotional shares "will ordinarily be sanctioned" when "principal financing is undertaken by the sale of non-cumulative or non-participating or redeemable shares."

In New Hampshire, where the statute does not lay down anything more than a "public interest" standard, if that, the administrator nicely solves the problem of promotional issuers by simply insisting, except in unusual circumstances, that all out-of-state stocks offered for sale have a three-year dividend record and that all out-of-state bonds offered have a BAA rating. The problem of the apparently legitimate but new *local* company is handled by conditioning the license so that sales may be made only to people in the locality or restricting the amount which may be offered.

A number of administrators apply tests which, in one way or another, are designed to assure a *sound capital structure*. Thus, a rule in Mississippi—which could mean a good deal or very little depending upon the administrative approach to questions of valuation—provides that "No permit will be issued unless the assets be equal to or greater than the outstanding capital stock and other liabilities." Under a Michigan rule stock with an asset preference will not be registered if its equity is more than double the equity of the junior stock unless (1) it has the right to participate with the junior stock as to dividends and management "in such manner as shall be satisfactory to the Commission" or (2) it is to be sold "in a restricted offering upon terms and conditions satisfactory to the Commission." Published administrative rulings in Ohio construe the statutory standard "grossly unfair terms," somewhat similarly, to cover cases where the common stock equity held by the management is very small in relation to the preferred, the preferred having no vote irrespective of the extent of default in the payment of cumulative dividends, unless the purchasers of preferred are "fully informed persons." And the Florida Securities Commission "does not look with favor upon new corporations issuing interest securities or preferred stock, except in rare cases which are justified by a reasonable excess of assets over liabilities to the extent of meeting principal requirements." In the case of fixed-interest securities the Florida Commission requires in any event "a sinking fund and an earnings history commensurate with the obligations the corporation is creating."

* * *

Another category of fairly specific criteria developed in a few states has to do with the *selling price* of the securities. . . . The Ohio administrator has ruled, in effect, that an offering to the public is "grossly unfair" under the statute when a substantially simultaneous offering is made to employees or promoters at a substantially lower price. In Iowa, Michigan and New Mexico the administrator is authorized, without elaboration, to "limit the price" at which shares, whether par or no-par, may be sold. And there are virtually identical sets of rules in Alabama and California which permit preferred shares to be issued only for cash or for assets whose value "is established to the satisfaction of" the administrator . . . (and) permit no-par shares to be issued only at a price or for a consideration which fairly represents their "true worth". . . . Interestingly enough, the two administrators differ in their attitudes toward stock which has a par value. Under the Alabama rules any *premium* over par must be justified, and under the California rules any *discount* must be brought within the grounds of exception specified in the Corporations Code. . . .

Other fairly specific administrative animadversions were reflected in the replies to the questionnaire: The Michigan administrator objects to unduly burdensome long-term contracts, whether relating to employment, royalties, sales, property leases, or other matters. The Ohio administrator considers, among other things, whether the articles or by-laws contain any prejudicial restrictions permanently affecting the rights of stockholders, or whether there are restrictions on the transferability of shares, such as a requirement that they be offered to the company before they may be sold on the market. And we have already noticed that 1946 statement of policy of the National Association of Securities Administrators which looks with "great disfavor" upon the issuance of stock options to persons other than buyers of securities. According to the 1955 report of the Association's Options and Warrants Committee, this statement of policy is followed in at least twenty-seven states, though usually with some modifications. That year the Association extended the statement of policy to cover so-called "cheap stock" sold to underwriters.

* * *

These several administrative approaches to the *standards*, ranging from the very general to the fairly specific—and they cannot be more than illustrative—are supplemented in some states by a variety of *conditions* which the administrator imposes when granting registration:

(1) The most commonly imposed condition is one which sets a *maximum selling commission or "load."* The registration certificate or permit will prescribe the maximum number of shares and the commissions deductible from the sale price. Although this practice often has express statutory sanction, sometimes it is sought to be justified under one of the more general statutory standards. Moreover, whereas many statutes and rules provide that commissions shall not exceed a maximum percentage of the offering price, the commissions allowed by the administrator are frequently far lower. The figure will vary in accordance with the type of security involved.

* * *

(2) Thirty jurisdictions prescribe *escrow* requirements of one kind or another, most of them giving the administrator discretionary authority; sixteen jurisdictions provide separately for the impounding of cash proceeds under certain conditions; and a few statutes which do not refer specifically to escrow or impounding do authorize the administrator to impose such conditions or restrictions upon registration as he believes consistent with the public protection. At any rate, thirty-four administrators stated in their replies to the questionnaire that they considered themselves empowered to require escrow under certain circumstances, and a somewhat smaller number thought they had the authority to require impounding of the proceeds of the issue until a designated percentage of the issuer's capital needs has been reached. Most administrators impose an escrow condition infrequently. The most common use is in connection with the issuance of securities to promoters or other persons for intangibles. The impounding device is used even less frequently. California is apparently the only state which regularly resorts to that practice, traditionally conditioning permits for local or promotional companies in that manner. The investor is thus meant to be afforded a "fair run" for his money. Sometimes the mere threat of an escrow or impounding condition persuades an applicant to withdraw his application.

* * *

(4) An administrator will sometimes withhold clearance until he has received assurances or commitments regarding such matters as the intended use of the proceeds, limitations of executive salaries, or future company policy in various respects. Although the registration certificate or permit

is silent as to these matters, the registrant is aware that any deviation from his representations without prior clearance may result in the institution of proceedings—or at the very least make life difficult the next time he files an application.

* * *

EXEMPTIONS

The word "exemptions" opens a big subject, because they are manifold and variegated. One or two illustrations will have to suffice in pointing out that here, too, statutory language is sometimes one thing and administrative practice another.

One of the acute areas concerns sales to a limited number of persons. Very few of the statutes incorporate the federal exemption for non-public offerings as such. Some sort of "isolated sale" exemption is almost universal. But most of the statutes explicitly limit this exemption to the sale of an outstanding security by its owner. In any event, even if other courts do not follow the strict view of the Massachusetts court that the exemption does not cover two sales which are reasonably contemporaneous, (Kneeland v. Emerton, 280 Mass. 371, 183 N.E. 155 (1932)) this type of exemption is narrow at best. Moreover, only about half of the statutes contain special exemptions for offers or sales to a limited number of persons, or up to a limited amount of money, at least when the issuer is past the organizational stage. What, then, are the owners of the incorporated corner grocery to do if they want to raise additional capital from a few relatives and friends in order to remodel the store and no exemption is available? In the first place more likely than not it will never occur to the individuals involved, or even their lawyer, that anything like a blue sky law is remotely involved in this kind of financing. In the second place, if the lawyer happens to think of the blue sky law, checks it, finds no apparent exemption, and calls the administrator, he may well be told to go right ahead because "the act is not intended for this kind of case"—all of which may make him wonder whether he has not embarrassed the administrator by bringing the matter to his attention and whether it would not be better next time, or perhaps in another state, to go ahead in a similar situation without calling at all. A variation of this problem occurs when a company makes an offer in a number of states, either to its own stockholders (whether or not pursuant to preemptive rights) or by way of an exchange offering to stockholders of another company, and there are only four or five offerees in a particular state.

An even more prevalent problem is that of unsolicited broker-dealer transactions in securities which have not been registered in the particular state. Such transactions are specifically exempted in only ten or twelve states. Suppose a customer reads about a security in some financial publication or hears about it from a friend. He telephones a broker-dealer or agent and gives him an order. If the broker-dealer or agent is a careful person, he will check to see whether the security has ever been cleared for sale in his state. But suppose he finds it has not been. He is reluctant to reject the order, because the customer may not understand, particularly if the fellow next door is not so careful or so conscientious and does accept the order. It is probably impossible for him to qualify the security within the short time given him by the customer to buy it. Again, the broker-dealer may discover on checking the statute that the question whether an unsolicited transaction is exempted is not altogether clear. So once more the administrator is put in the position of either saying "No" and knowing that other broker-dealers are not bothering to ask him and that there is not much he can do about it, or saying "Yes" when the statute is ambiguous or perhaps quite clear that no such exemption exists.

In both these instances, even though the administrator turns his head the other way, the statute more likely than not declares that all sales in violation of any of its provisions are voidable. Indeed, the courts are apt to say so even if the statute does not. And, regardless of the administrator's policy not to enforce the statute in certain cases, or his inability to do so as a practical matter, the courts in civil actions will have to take the statute as they find it. This is one of the sources of the innocently assumed contingent civil liabilities which are discussed in a later chapter.

2. The Effect of Broad Standards

Obviously, the broader the statutory standards, the greater the power of the administrator. The hesitancy of the courts to interfere with this broad discretion is illustrated by such authorities as Hardstone Brick Co. v. Department of Commerce, 174 Minn. 200, 219 N.W. 81 (1928). There a petition to sell stock in Minnesota had been denied, pursuant to statutory power "to deny an application for registration if the securities are fraudulent or if it appears . . . that the sale thereof would work a fraud on purchasers thereof, . . . or for good cause appearing . . ." In upholding the denial the court said:

> 1. This court can make but a limited review of the determination of the department. If it keeps within its jurisdictions and its action is not arbitrary or oppressive or unreasonable or without evidence to support it, the court cannot interfere. . . .
>
> * * *
>
> 3. The department was justified in finding that the sale of stock would operate as a fraud on the purchasing public. Cochran was to have various commissions for the sale of the machinery which was to be used in the manufacture of the brick. He was to have a royalty on the product. There was evidence that the machinery was to be purchased at an exorbitant price. The commission could well find that there was no particular demand for brick in the vicinity and that a brick-making plant, especially with so large a capitalization, could not be successful. The incorporators, with one exception, were retired farmers in comfortable circumstances. They knew nothing of brick making. They had no valuable experience in business. The other incorporator knew nothing of brick making and his business experience was not such as to suggest that he would be useful in the management of the business. It is not necessary that an actual fraudulent purpose be found. We do not say that the evidence would not sustain a finding of such purpose. It is for the commission to find just what a corporation purposing to float its stock has behind it. And there was nothing promising success [here]. . . .

As might be expected, the broad powers of blue sky administrators have aroused some adverse comment. The following excerpts are taken from the article, "BLUE SKY RED TAPE", which appeared in the July, 1957, issue of Fortune Magazine at page 122:

Dr. Lynn Bollinger, president of Helio Aircraft Corp., estimates that his company has spent four of its nine years of life wading through red tape. Besides having to cope with complex CAA and SEC requirements, which Bollinger feels are difficult to meet but necessary, Helio ran into a monumental snarl in attempting to comply with state blue-sky laws. . . .

In 1948, Bollinger and Otto C. Koppen developed the Courier, a $28,000 executive airplane that can fly at 30 mph, or 160; take off from a football field, land on a tennis court. At the time Bollinger was heading an aviation research project at Harvard Business School. (Koppen is still in charge of aeronautical-design at M.I.T.) The test plane they built lived up to Koppen's predictions, but more development was necessary and the two teachers, having spent $20,000 of their own funds, ran out of money.

. . . In three stock flotations under Regulation "A" . . . Helio raised almost $900,000. But when Bollinger tried to register Helio's stock outside the East he discovered that it was, as a practical matter, almost impossible to comply with the blue-sky laws of most of the southern, midwestern, and western states. The laws, says Bollinger, were "too complex, too contradictory, and often too capricious."

The first ground rule for a small company without an earnings record, Bollinger learned, is never to apply for a security registration in a troublesome state. If the application is refused, the refusal prejudices registration in other states. Instead, an "informal opinion" is requested from each state security commissioner. If the opinion is unfavorable, there is little that the company can do. "I might have exerted pressure in a few states," says Bollinger, "but then the state commissioner would have been waiting. All he would have to do is suspend our stock on suspicion of misrepresentation. The order might be rescinded the next day, but the damage would be done." Bollinger also discovered that:

In one far-western state, the commissioner raised questions about accounting procedures already approved by the SEC. This clearly was not his real objection, so Bollinger hired a local lawyer to talk to the commissioner. "They've got plenty of money back East," the commissioner told the local man. "If that stock is any good why are they trying to sell it out here?"

In two southern states Helio stock would have qualified for sale—but only if Bollinger and the other "promoters" had put all their personal stockholdings in escrow in *each* state.

In one midwestern state the commissioner did qualify Helio for sale, but appended one requirement: every prospective purchaser would have to be approved by the state security commissioner. A local broker, who agreed to sell the issue, promptly withdrew.

In another midwestern state the only way to find out whether Helio stock would be qualified was to answer the ninety-two detailed questions on the state's application blank. Helio's lawyers foresaw several weeks of work, and several thousands of dollars worth of auditing fees. The attorneys told Bollinger it was not worth the effort. . . .

B. THE UNIFORM SECURITIES ACT

A growing recognition of the need for much greater standardization of the blue sky requirements, both procedural and substantive, of the various states led to the development of the Uniform Securities Act, drafted by Professor Loss and Mr. Edward M. Cowett. The Act was approved by the Commissioners on Uniform Laws in August, 1956, and has since been adopted in whole or in part, in many states. Briefly, the Uniform Act adopts all three of the regulatory approaches reflected in the current Blue Sky statutes: the prohibition of fraudulent practices, the registration of dealers and the like, and the registration of securities. In the registration of securities, the Act provides for both the streamlined notification technique for quality issues and full qualification registration for other issues. In addition, it was the Uniform Act which introduced the concept of registration by co-ordination, that is, the simplified procedure for registration of securities which have already been registered under the federal act. The following excerpts from the Uniform Securities Act (and the Draftsmen's Commentary, which appears in Loss and Cowett) illustrate the operation of the Act, with particular reference to its impact on the organization of promotional companies:

§ 301. [*Registration Requirement.*] It is unlawful for any person to offer or sell any security in this state unless (1) it is registered under this act or (2) the security or transaction is exempted under section 402.

§ 305. [*Provisions Applicable to Registration Generally.*]
* * *

(g) The [Administrator] may by rule or order require as a condition of registration by qualification or coordination (1) that any security issued within the past three years or to be issued to a promoter for a consideration substantially different from the public offering price, or to any person for a consideration other than cash, be deposited in escrow; and (2) that the proceeds from the sale of the registered security be impounded until the issuer receives a specified amount. The [Administrator] may by rule or order determine the conditions of any escrow or impounding required hereunder, but [he] may not reject a depository solely because of location in another state.

§ 306. [Denial, Suspension, and Revocation of Registration.]

(a) The [Administrator] may issue a stop order denying effectiveness to, or suspending or revoking the effectiveness of, any registration statement if [he] finds (1) that the order is in the public interest and (2) that

* * *

(F) the offering has been or would be made with unreasonable amounts of underwriters' and sellers' discounts, commissions, or other compensation, or promoters' profits or participation, or unreasonable amounts or kinds of options;

* * *

DRAFTSMEN'S COMMENTARY

. . . The *standards* in § 306(a) are a cross-section of the existing standards somewhere between the two extremes: the simple "fraud" test exemplified by the Georgia statute and the "fair, just and equitable" or "sound business principles" language of states like California and formerly Kansas. This is not a mere practical compromise. Administrative flexibility is important in this area, but it must always be balanced against the proper claim of legitimate business to as great a degree of specificity as the public interest will permit. Clause (F) of § 306(a) refers to "unreasonable" *selling expenses or promoters' participation or options;* this one clause should take care of many of the classic abuses which led to the development of such a thing as blue sky law. Among other grounds for action under § 306(a), Clause (E) contains a *fraud* standard, Clause (A) contains a *full disclosure* standard, and Clause (B) refers to *violations* by the issuer and various other persons. It is difficult to think of a case of abuse which would not be covered by one or another of these standards, particularly when buttressed by the authority given the Administrator elsewhere in the Act . . . [*inter alia*] to condition any registration by qualification or coordination upon the escrowing of certain securities and the impounding of the proceeds (§ 305(g)) . . .

The efficacy of these several devices to take care of those borderline cases which are not quite fraudulent under § 306(a)(2)(E) and do not involve unreasonable selling expenses, promoters' participation or options under § 306(a)(2)(F), but which would be attacked in some states today under some vague standard like "fair, just and equitable," must not be underestimated. For example, the fact that this Act is not fundamentally a disclosure statute like the Securities Act of 1933 does not require that the effectiveness of the disclosure device be overlooked. The SEC has demonstrated what a vigorous administration of a full disclosure standard can achieve without more. When this device is added to the other standards of § 306(a), particularly Clause (F), it does not seem necessary to subject *all* issues of securities to a vague standard like "public policy" or "sound business principles" in order to be able to strike at the occasional issue of dubious character which does not fall squarely within Clause (B), (D), (E), or (F) of § 306(a).

Sec. 2 "BLUE SKY" LAWS

§ 402. [Exemptions.]

(a) The following securities are exempted from sections 301 and 403:

. . .

(8) any security listed or approved for listing upon notice of issuance on the New York Stock Exchange, the American Stock Exchange, or the Midwest Stock Exchange . . . ; any other security of the same issuer which is of senior or substantially equal rank;

. . .

(b) The following transactions are exempted from sections 301 and 403:

(1) any isolated non-issuer transaction, whether effected through a broker-dealer or not;

. . .

(9) any transaction pursuant to an offer directed by the offeror to not more than ten persons . . . in this state during any period of twelve consecutive months, whether or not the offeror or any of the offerees is then present in this state, if (A) the seller reasonably believes that all the buyers in this state are purchasing for investment, and (B) no commission or other remuneration is paid or given directly or indirectly for soliciting any prospective buyer in this state . . . but the [Administrator] may . . . withdraw or further condition this exemption, or increase or decrease the number of offerees permitted, or waive the conditions in Clauses (A) and (B) . . . ;

(10) any offer or sale of a preorganization certificate or subscription if (A) no commission or other remuneration is paid or given directly or indirectly for soliciting any prospective subscriber, (B) the number of subscribers does not exceed ten, and (C) no payment is made by any subscriber;

. . .

§ 403. [*Filing of Sales Literature.*] The [Administrator] may by rule or order require the filing of any prospectus, pamphlet, circular, form letter, advertisement or other sales literature addressed or intended for distribution to prospective investors, unless the security or transaction is exempted by section 402.

SECTION 3. PROBLEMS OF COMPENSATION INCOME FOR THE PROMOTERS OF A PUBLIC COMPANY

BERCKMANS v. COMMISSIONER
United States Tax Court, 1961. 20 T.C.M. 458.

[Petitioner had been a successful executive in the brewery business for many years when in 1950 he became the president and general manager of the Frankenmuth Brewing Company in Michigan. Frankenmuth had outstanding 750,000 shares, of which petitioner owned about 21,000. Despite two very successful years with Frankenmuth, petitioner advised the other directors that the future of a small local brewery was not promising and that a program of expansion would be necessary for the long-run survival of the company. The other directors agreed, and an active campaign was undertaken to find other breweries which might be acquired.

On June 10, 1953, International Breweries, Inc. was incorporated in Michigan under the direction of Frankenmuth which paid the cost of incorporation. The new company had an authorized capital of 5000 shares of $10 par value common stock. It was contemplated that the new corporation could be used as a vehicle for future acquisitions or mergers.

Through the middle of 1954 no attractive acquisition opportunities were found by the representatives of Frankenmuth, and the new corporation remained entirely inactive. At about that time, it was learned that the Iroquois Beverage Corporation of Buffalo, New York might be available for about $6,000,000, but the owners of that company made it clear that they would be interested only in selling the assets of the company for cash. This led the officers of Frankenmuth to consider both long-term loans from private lenders and a public issue of stock as means for financing a possible acquisition of Iroquois. The petitioner undertook discussions with Shields & Co., a New York underwriting firm, about possible arrangements for such financing.

In the late fall of 1954 a majority of the directors of Frankenmuth advised the petitioner that they preferred to sell the Frankenmuth business rather than attempt to acquire Iroquois or any other breweries. The petitioner was authorized to seek a purchaser for the business of Frankenmuth at a price which would yield the shareholders at least $4.00 per share.

With a view to the possibility of having International acquire both the Frankenmuth and Iroquois businesses, petitioner undertook further discussions with Shields. A tentative plan of financing was developed, composed of some long-term private loans and a public offering of 500,000 shares of International at $9.50 per share, to net the company $8.50 per share. It was also contemplated that Shields and petitioner would acquire 60,000 shares of International stock for a total of $60,000.

In March of 1955, Frankenmuth requested a ruling from the Internal Revenue Service that any loss resulting from the proposed sale by Frankenmuth of all its assets to International could be recognized for income tax purposes. A favorable ruling was ultimately received on April 29, 1955. In the middle of April, Iroquois wrote a letter of intent to International indicating its willingness to urge its stockholders to approve a sale of all of its assets for cash in the amount of $6,000,000. Frankenmuth wrote a similar letter indicating its willingness to urge its stockholders to approve a sale of its assets to International for the net sum of $2,800,000.

Immediately thereafter, the petitioner arranged for a change in the capital structure of International to increase its authorized capital stock to 600,000 shares of $1.00 par value. The petitioner then subscribed for 36,667 shares of the capital stock of International for $1.00 per share, and Shields subscribed for 23,333 shares of such stock at the same price. The $60,000 received by International was for the purpose of providing funds for the estimated expenses of carrying out the contemplated transactions, including printing, legal, accounting, and engineering expenses, state and federal securities registration expenses, and the cost of brewery and other licenses. Such expenses eventually amounted to about $130,000. In early May, after appropriate votes of directors and shareholders, both Frankenmuth and Iroquois executed formal agreements for the sale of all their respective assets to International. The Iroquois agreement was expressly contingent upon International's obtaining the necessary funds through private loans and a public offering of its stock, and the consent of Iroquois' labor unions to the assignment to International of the collective bargaining agreement.

At about the same time, Shields completed the organization of its underwriting group, consisting of thirty-nine different underwriting houses, to handle the sale of 500,000 shares of International stock to the public. Shortly thereafter a registration statement was filed with the SEC, which statement ultimately became effective on May 31, 1955. On May 7, the petitioner and International entered into an employment agreement which provided for a salary of $50,000 per year to petitioner through December 31, 1960. On May 27, a large insurance company made available a term loan of $1,400,000, and on the same day International entered into a $500,000 revolving credit agreement with a Detroit bank.

On May 31, 1955, Shields, as representative of the underwriters, entered into an agreement with International for the purchase of the stock which was to be sold to the public. As is customary in the trade, none of the members of the underwriting group, including Shields, were even conditionally committed in any way prior to the date of that contract. Under this contract, Shields' obligation was conditioned upon a number of circumstances obtaining at the date of the closing of the proposed public offering of International stock, including such items as Blue Sky approval in Michigan; consummation of the proposed private loans; possession of all necessary licenses and permits for the maintenance and operation of the proposed brewery business; an opinion of counsel that there were no defects in the title to any real property to be acquired by International; absence of any substantial adverse change in the condition of Frankenmuth or Iroquois, financial or otherwise; and absence of any unfavorable market conditions which in the sole judgment of Shields would render it impractical or inadvisable to consummate the sale of the stock as contemplated. Shields regarded each of these conditions as vital and would not have waived any of them, nor would it have proceeded with the public stock offering if any one of the conditions had not been fulfilled. While presumably some effort would have been made to postpone the closing to allow an unsatisfied condition to be fulfilled, a lengthy postponement would not have been possible with respect to this particular underwriting.

However, all of the conditions were promptly satisfied, and the public offering of International stock occurred immediately after May 31, 1955. The offering was over-subscribed. The acquisition of the Frankenmuth and the Iroquois assets by International was consummated on June 3, 1955, at which time International received all appropriate deeds, bills of sale, assignments, and related documents from the two companies. On the same day International received $4,250,000, the proceeds from the sale of 500,000 shares of International stock to the underwriters at the net price of $8.50 per share. International also received the $1,400,000 proceeds of the insurance company loan, and the $500,000 from the Detroit bank. Out of these proceeds, plus the liquid assets obtained from Iroquois, International paid Iroquois the sum of $6,000,000 for its assets, and Frankenmuth the sum of $2,800,000 for its assets.

The Commissioner determined that the petitioner's acquisition on April 15, 1955, of 36,667 shares of International at $1.00 per share constituted a bargain purchase. Accordingly, the Commissioner asserted a deficiency based upon the difference between $1.00 per share and the fair market value of the stock on April 15. The Commissioner originally contended that the fair market value of the stock on April 15 was $9.50, but in his amended answer in the Tax Court the Commissioner pressed for a value of only $7.00 per share.]

Opinion

HARRON, JUDGE. . . . At the time petitioner purchased and paid for his stock, International was an inactive corporation, which might acquire going businesses or which might simply remain nothing but a shell. It had no business, no earnings, no management record, no experience and no assets, except $60,000 in cash which Berckmans and Shields paid for stock. It was incurring liabilities for expenses, but nothing else. Immediately after the stock purchase, International had assets consisting solely of $60,000 cash, represented by 60,000 shares of stock having a par value of $1.00 a share, and possibly an even lower book value because of its accrual of legal, printing, engineering, and other expenses. International had no other assets, tangible or intangible; it did not have contracts with Frankenmuth, Iroquois, New England Life, Manufacturers Bank, or Shields and any members of the proposed underwriting group.

As of April 15, 1955, neither Shields nor any other underwriter had executed or entered into any contract in connection with the purchase, underwriting and public offering of International stock; Shields had not completed the organization of an underwriting group. The stock had not been registered with the Securities and Exchange Commission or under any state Blue Sky laws, and therefore, it could not have been offered, legally, to the public at that time. . . . Both proposed purchases [of assets from Frankenmuth and Iroquois] were subject, on April 15, 1955, to numerous contingencies, including the ability of International to raise the necessary funds through institutional loans and a stock offering. In the case of Frankenmuth, the proposed sale of its assets also was contingent upon obtaining an income tax ruling, and upon obtaining the approval of at least 80 per cent of the stockholders. . . . Neither of the two lending institutions involved, New England Life and Manufacturers Bank, on April 15, 1955, had bound themselves in any way or given International even any preliminary letters of intent . . . .

The first registration statement was not filed with the Securities and Exchange Commission until almost four weeks after the critical valuation date, April 15, 1955, and Shields and the underwriters did not enter into any contract with International until May 31, 1955, only 3 days before the closing of the purchase of the Frankenmuth and Iroquois assets. Even the underwriter's contract was subject to numerous contingencies and conditions. . . .

The principal differences between the parties in their approaches to valuation, and their subsequent conclusions, are not in what remained to be done, but rather in divergent appraisals of the probabilities (on the critical date) that what remained to be done, would be done. In other words, the substantive disagreement is not one of fact, but one of prediction on April 15 as to the likelihood that the proposed combination of Frankenmuth and Iroquois into International would be accomplished.

The petitioner's expert witnesses, Gilbreth and Parcells, both predicated their opinions upon the existence of the above described contingencies. Gilbreth is in the investment banking and securities underwriting business in Detroit, and Parcells is president of a corporation engaged in the same business.

Parcells testified that it was necessary that the contingencies be resolved favorably to International in order that the stock would have value. He testified that the stock was in no event worth more, on April 15, than its inherent value, and concluded that the fair market value of the stock was "something less than $1 per share."

Gilbreth testified that because of the conditions of uncertainty with respect to the possibility of a public offering, and especially the unpredictability of the securities market at such time as a closing date might be reached, he would not arrive at a value higher than the amount paid for the stock on April 15, or the amount of net asset value on that date. It was Gilbreth's opinion that International's stock was worth no more than $1 per share on the critical date.

. . . the respondent's expert witness, Snyder (the executive vice-president of a corporation engaged in the business of underwriting and selling securities), testified that while he took into consideration some, but not all, of the contingencies considered by the petitioner's witnesses, he saw very little probability that any contingency would fail to be resolved in favor of International. Snyder conceded that his confidence of a successful outcome for the entire series of transactions, as of April 15, 1955, was largely based on Berckman's purchase of the stock and Shield's continued participation in the venture at that point. Snyder reasoned that unless the participants to the proposed public offering felt success assured, the attempt would have been discontinued before the critical date. In our opinion, Snyder's view was to a substantial extent influenced by what he regarded as the apparent hope of and confidence of the petitioner, Shields, and their associates in the outcome. Snyder testified that the stock of International had a value on April 15, 1955, of between $6 and $7 per share.

We find Snyder's opinion of value on the critical date too optimistic and not sufficiently realistic about the existing contingencies. It appears to be influenced by hindsight knowledge about the successful completion of a complex series of transactions.

The respondent's position is neither novel nor without precedent. The facts here are to some extent similar to those in Trust Company of Georgia v. Rose, 25 F.2d 997, affd. 28 F.2d 767, and Eaton v. White, 70 F.2d 449. In both of those cases sales of stock to private purchasers were very shortly followed by sales to the public at higher prices. In each case, the Commissioner determined the value of the stock sold just prior to a public offering to be the amount per share for which the respective shares were sold to the public. In each case, the courts refused to find that the public sale prices represented the values of the shares sold prior to the public offerings. It was said in Trust Company of Georgia, supra at page 999:

> The 13,677 shares in which it is supposed the trust company made a taxable gain, were bindingly contracted for on August 21, 1919, at $5 . . . . While it was *believed* on that day that the other stock could be disposed of at a price that would provide the balance of the cash necessary to buy the old company, and that thereby all of the stock would be made worth more than $5, or even $35, per share, nevertheless on that day the stock had no market value, and its future was wholly uncertain.

We conclude that the facts in this case require a similar finding. The event giving value to the stock of International was the successful public offering of May 31, 1955. The offering itself was dependent, among other factors, on the virtually simultaneous completion of loans to International from a bank and an insurance company, the sales to International of the assets of Iroquois and Frankenmuth, and the purchase by the underwriting group of 500,000 shares of International for $8.50 per share. The completion of each of these transactions was interrelated. All of these transactions were conditioned upon the successful resolution of numerous contingencies, including the survival of certain of the principals, the passage of a bill before the Michigan legislature, the receipt of a favorable revenue ruling, the availability of a corporate name, issuance of a registration statement by the Securities and Exchange Commission, and the existence of favorable market conditions. An adverse development in any one of these situations very likely would have proved fatal to the entire operation. No contractual commitments were in existence on April 15, 1955, whereunder any of the participants, including the lenders, the underwriters, and the stockholders of Iroquois and Frankenmuth, were in any way committed to proceed with their undertakings. The entire series of transactions continued to stand in a precarious and delicate balance until at least May 31, 1955.

Upon careful consideration of all the evidence and the factors discussed above, it is held that on April 15, 1955, and at all times prior to April 30, 1955, the value of the stock of International did not exceed $1 per share. . . .

DEES v. COMMISSIONER

United States Tax Court, 1962. 21 T.C.M. 833.

[In 1952 one Miller contacted the petitioner to discuss the formation of an insurance company in Texas. Miller believed that petitioner had the experience and reputation in the banking business needed for the successful formation of such a company. After some discussions, the parties organized the Western Republic Life Insurance Company (hereinafter sometimes referred to as "Insurance"). They also formed Western Republic Life Underwriters, (hereinafter "Underwriters") which was to raise the necessary capital for Insurance by the public sale of both its own stock and stock of Insurance. By the end of 1953, approximately 50,000 shares of Underwriter's common stock had been sold to insiders for a total of $52,150, and 25,000 shares of its Class A common stock had been sold to the public at prices ranging from $16.00 to $20.00, netting to Underwriters after sales commissions approximately $12.80 per share.

In March of 1953, when the insurance company commenced business, it had issued 2500 shares of $10.00 par value stock for a total of $37,500. On August 15, 1953 Insurance issued another 7500 shares of its $10.00 par value stock for $80,000, so that it then had outstanding 10,000 shares, with paid-in capital of $100,000 and paid-in surplus of $17,500. Underwriters owned 9,995 shares of the outstanding 10,000 shares of the insurance company.

On October 14, 1953, Insurance increased its authorized capital stock from 10,000 shares of $10.00 par value to 300,000 shares of no-par stock. The outstanding 10,000 shares of $10.00 par value stock were exchanged for 100,000 shares of no-par stock. At the same time Underwriters acquired an additional 100,000 shares of the no-par stock of Insurance for $1.50 per share, so that the insurance company had outstanding a total of 200,000 shares of stock represented by paid-in capital of $250,000 and paid-in surplus of $17,500. Underwriters owned 199,950 shares of the insurance company's outstanding 200,000 shares.

In November, 1953, Underwriters undertook to sell 50,000 of the insurance company's remaining 100,000 shares of no-par stock to the public. The promotion by Underwriters of insurance company stock was similar to that used by Underwriters in the sale of its own Class A common stock. At the peak of the promotional period Underwriters had about thirty-five agents carrying on a high-pressure sales campaign for insurance company stock in twenty-two principal cities in Texas. The selling price for insurance company stock varied between $16.00 and $25.00 per share, of which it was agreed that Underwriters would remit to Insurance $12.80 per share.

By the end of 1953 about 1100 shares of insurance company stock had been sold and issued at a price of $16.00 per share. In addition, another 3625 shares had been subscribed for at a price of $20.00 per share, payable in installments of 25% down and the balance over three years. During 1954 approximately 30,000 more shares of stock were sold and issued for $16.00 to $20.00 per share, and approximately 20,000 more shares were sold on three year subscription contracts at $20.00 to $25.00 per share.

Prior to the organization of either Underwriters or Insurance it had been orally agreed among the parties that petitioner would be entitled to purchase a reasonable amount of insurance company stock at the average price paid for the stock by Underwriters. It was also understood that none of such stock would be sold during the promotion period. In pursuance of this understanding, on December 21, 1953, petitioner purchased from Underwriters 5000 shares of insurance company stock for $1.50 per share. On April 21, 1954, petitioner purchased another 5000 shares of insurance company stock, paying $1.00 per share. On the same date petitioner also received without payment an additional 3800 shares as compensation for services rendered.

By December 21, 1953, the date of petitioner's first purchase, Insurance had issued 199,950 shares to Underwriters for an average price of $1.25 per share, and 1024 shares had been sold to the public at $16.00 per share. By the time the petitioner purchased the additional 5000 shares on April 21, 1954, an additional 7000 shares had been sold to the public at approximately $16.00 per share, and more than 9000 shares had been sold to the public on three year subscription contracts at $20.00 to $25.00 per share.

Prices for insurance company stock were not quoted in the over-the-counter market compilations during the years 1953, 1954, and 1955. During that period the market for the stock was created solely by the efforts of the agents who were selling the stock on an individual solicitation basis. The book value per share of Insurance's stock on December 31, 1953, 1954, and 1955 respectively was $3.07, $3.02, $2.50. On its federal income tax returns, Insurance reported a loss for 1953, and a nominal taxable income for the years 1954 and 1955.

The Commissioner determined that the fair market value of insurance company stock purchased by the petitioner on December 21, 1953 and April 21, 1954 was substantially in excess of the prices paid on those dates, and that the petitioner had realized bargain purchase income in the amount of the difference.]

Opinion [17]

Issue 1

SCOTT, JUDGE. The first issue is whether petitioner's acquisition from Underwriters of 5,000 shares of insurance company stock on

---

17. Portions of the opinion and all footnotes omitted.

December 21, 1953, and his further acquisition from Underwriters of 8,800 shares of insurance company stock on April 21, 1954, constitutes income to petitioner in the amounts of the excess, if any, of the fair market value of the stock on the dates of acquisition over the amounts paid therefor.

Petitioner contends that he purchased 5,000 shares of insurance company stock on December 21, 1953, for $1.50 per share and 5,000 shares on April 21, 1954 for $1 per share, which was in each instance the fair market value of the stock on the dates of purchase, but that even if the fair market value of the stock was in excess of $1.50 and $1 per share on the respective dates, he realized no income from the transactions until he sold the stock. Petitioner takes the position that 3,800 of the shares of insurance company stock acquired by him on April 21, 1954, was compensation for services rendered but that the fair market value thereof on that date was not more than $1.50 per share.

Petitioner does not contend that any dates other than those on which he acquired the stock should govern in determining whether he realized income from the transactions. Petitioner acquired the 10,000 shares of stock pursuant to an agreement . . . [permitting him] to buy from Underwriters a reasonable amount of insurance company stock at the average price paid for such stock by Underwriters. Petitioner contends that this was an arm's-length agreement fixing a bona fide price at which he would be entitled to purchase stock, that there was no correlation between the purchase of the stock and the services he rendered to insurance company, that the purchases were not intended to be a form of compensation, and that he was otherwise adequately compensated for the services he rendered.

Respondent argues that the agreement allowing petitioner to buy the stock at the average price paid therefor by Underwriters was entered into in recognition of the services to be rendered by him to insurance company in contributing his name, prestige, and experience to the insurance enterprise, and that petitioner's acquisitions of stock pursuant to the agreement were in payment for the actual services he rendered in assisting in acquiring bank loans for Underwriters and in selling, or at least assisting in the selling, of insurance policies for insurance company. . . .

It was evident when the stock purchase agreement was made, that the price to be paid by petitioner for the stock would be a price well below the price at which the stock would be offered to the public and would in all probability, depending on when petitioner elected to exercise his right, be below the fair market value of the stock. It is clear that the parties considered the agreement to provide for a bargain purchase by petitioner. It is also clear that it was contemplated that petitioner would lend assistance to insurance company to be entitled to exercise the right.

... The price Underwriters was to pay for insurance company's stock was governed by the amount of funds Underwriters would have available, and the price Underwriters paid for insurance company stock in order to give insurance company its initial capital was unrelated to any market value of the purchased stock. Absent other factors, the natural result of sales of insurance company stock to the public and the receipt by insurance company of $12.80 for each share so sold would be an increase in value of the stock. As such public sales were made, the book value of each share outstanding would rise above the $1.25 average paid by Underwriters for the 199,950 share block of insurance company stock it owned. There was apparently no time limit on petitioner's option to purchase insurance company stock at the $1.25 average figure. It may be noted that petitioner did not exercise his option until there had been some sales at the public offering price of $16 with a resulting increase in the net worth of insurance company. Also, at the time of petitioner's first purchase, the indications were that the public offering of insurance company stock would be successful.

The purchases were not arm's-length transactions, and the option rights given petitioner were intended by the parties to result in a bargain purchase for petitioner. The purchase agreement and the purchases made pursuant thereto were either a means of inducing petitioner to embark on the venture or compensating him for services rendered. In either circumstance, the bargain purchases are to be treated as compensation. . . .

Petitioner relies upon Trust Co. of Georgia v. Rose, 25 F.2d 997 (N.D.Ga., 1928), affd. 28 F.2d 767 (C.A. 5, 1928) as supporting his position that income is not received upon a bargain purchase of stock. In that case a new corporation was set up to acquire the stock and assets of an old corporation. The taxpayer therein was a moving force arranging the acquisition of the stock of the old corporation and the creation of the new corporation. The taxpayer in August 1919 with others entered into a syndicate agreement whereby the parties thereto agreed to purchase 83,000 shares of common stock of the new corporation at $5 per share and to underwrite the remaining 417,000 shares for sale to the public at $35 per share. The taxpayer received 13,677 shares of common stock at $5 per share. The difference between the $5 per share the taxpayer paid for the 13,677 shares and the public selling price for the stock was determined by the Commissioner to be income to the taxpayer upon the purchase of the stock. The court held that any gain arising out of the acquisition of the stock would not be taxable until the taxpayer sold the stock.

In the Trust Co. of Georgia case, the court held that the transaction there involved was a purchase in good faith, that on the date the taxpayer contracted to buy the stock it had no market value and its future was wholly uncertain. The Trust Co. of Georgia case did not involve an employer-employee type relationship, the taxpayer was not being induced to perform or compensated for performing services for another but was, as a syndicate member and as a prime mover, acting on its own behalf. The Trust Co. of Georgia case is distinguishable on a factual basis from the instant case.

Issue 2

The second issue concerns the fair market value of insurance company stock on December 21, 1953, and April 21, 1954.

Respondent has determined that insurance company stock was worth $12.80 per share and $16 per share on the respective valuation dates. Petitioner contends that the stock was not worth more than the $1.50 and $1 per share amounts he paid for the stock on the dates of purchase.

In support of his position, respondent points to the sales made to the public under the stock promotional set up, the fact that the purchasers were making a long-term investment and had faith in the eventual success of the company, and the fact that petitioner and Miller considered the stock a good buy at $16. Petitioner, on the other hand, argues that the public sales of the stock were the result of highly aggressive sales tactics, that for the most part the purchasers were woefully uninformed about the affairs of insurance company, and that, in effect, this ignorance and gullibility on the part of the stock purchasers explains why the stock was sold at the higher price. . . .

The sales to the public which respondent heavily relies upon in support of his determination were the result of extensive high pressure sales activities on the part of Underwriters from November 1953 until November 1955. Underwriters had 25 full-time salesmen and about 10 part-time salesmen selling insurance company stock. The salesmen covered the whole State of Texas. . . . The sales were generally in small quantities of 25, 50, or 100 share lots. The sales effort and promotion used was that of personal solicitation. One purchaser was called upon 15 different times by the same salesman. Most of the purchasers bought their stock without becoming acquainted with the available information as to the financial condition of insurance company. There is no evidence of fraudulent practices, but it is apparent that the salesmen were taking advantage of a situation which one witness described as "insurance fever" in the State of Texas. The salesmen were provided with a "pitch kit" which *inter alia* contained a statement of the amount earned on a hypothetical investment in one insurance company set up in Texas which had experienced a tremendous growth. Apparently, no mention was made of numerous other insurance companies that had suffered financial reverses. A number of other insurance companies were being organized in Texas at the same time apparently under the same type of promotional plan.

At the time petitioner acquired his first 5,000 shares of stock over 95 percent of the outstanding insurance company stock was held by Underwriters who had paid an average price of $1.25 per share. At that time insurance company was still in a formative stage. It had no earnings record, the book value of its outstanding stock was approximately $3 per share. The situation was only slightly changed when petitioner acquired his second 5,000 shares.

Petitioner had agreed with Miller not to sell his insurance company stock during the promotion period. Although no binding agreement is shown by the evidence, we think the evidence shows that petitioner had at least a moral obligation not to sell his stock. The reason for the prohibition, as stated by Miller, was that if the founding fathers did sell their own stock this would undermine the public offering and the stock salesmen would leave the organization. . . .

Upon consideration of all the evidence of the circumstances surrounding the public sales of insurance company stock, we do not believe that such sales are indicative of the fair market value of that stock. . . .

On the other hand, we feel the stock was worth more than the average price paid therefor by petitioner. The book value of the stock was approximately $3 per share on December 31, 1953. At the time petitioner acquired his stock the public promotion was underway and the indications were that it would be successful. As each share was sold to the public, the paid-in surplus of insurance company was increased by $12.80, the implication being that with each succeeding public sale petitioner's share in the paid-in surplus of insurance company would increase. The record also shows that persons with some knowledge of the affairs of insurance company, such as agents, other employees of both Underwriters and insurance company and members of the board of directors of insurance company purchased the stock for $12.80. Miller testified that petitioner at the time he received the stock could have sold it for $5 per share.

Based on all the evidence we hold that the 5,000 shares of insurance company stock acquired by petitioner on December 21, 1953, and the 8,800 shares acquired on April 21, 1954, had a fair market value of $5 and $5.50 per share on the respective dates. . . .

NOTE ON THE ISSUANCE OF STOCK OR OPTIONS FOR SERVICES

1. Outright Issuance of Stock

a. *Tax Incidents to the Recipient.* The underlying premise in both the Berckmans and Dees cases is of course that compensation may be paid in kind as well as in cash, and hence a transfer of stock or other property by an employer to an employee must be carefully scrutinized to see whether any compensation element is present. In the polar case where an employee receives stock from his corporate employer without having to pay anything for it, the employee would normally realize compensation income to the extent of the fair market value of the stock received; and the same is true if a non-employee independent contractor, such as an underwriter, receives stock or other property as compensation for services. Reg. § 1.61–2(d)(4). It is not essential that the recipient of stock have already performed services for the corporation, so long as some future services are contemplated—while the issuance of stock on account of future services may present some problems under corporate law, there is no obstacle to taxing the receipt of such stock as compensation. E. g., Mailloux v. Commissioner, 320 F.2d 60 (5th Cir. 1963) (stock received by taxpayers from promoter of new mining corporation upon their agreement to help promote the company and sell its stock was includible in income upon receipt at its then fair market value); cf. Allen v. Commissioner, 107 F.2d 151 (4th Cir. 1939) (lawyer who received stock from a corporation primarily on account of services to be rendered in the future held taxable on the value of the stock upon receipt).

The only escape from compensation income in such circumstances would lie in finding a gift to the recipient of the stock, and only rarely would it be possible to infer the necessary donative intent on the part of either the corporation or the stockholders. For example, in Baltimore v. Commissioner, 17 T.C.M. 388 (1958), the taxpayer, upon agreeing to become general manager of a newly-organized corporation, received one-fifth of the stock while four other persons each contributed $10,000 for the other four-fifths. In holding that the taxpayer had received income of $8,000, the court rejected the taxpayer's contention that the stock represented a gift, finding that it had been received in consideration for the taxpayer's terminating his previous employment and accepting the position of general manager with the new enterprise.

On the other hand, the necessary donative intent was found in somewhat analogous circumstances in Clem v. Campbell, 62–2 USTC para. 9785 (N.D. Tex.1962). There the taxpayer had joined with thirteen others to organize two related corporations which he was to manage. The taxpayer purchased 10% of the stock of the two corporations for a total of $12,500, which he had borrowed from the other stockholders and agreed to repay in accordance with a fixed schedule. After repaying about $2,000 the taxpayer advised the other stockholders that because of some substantial unexpected expenses, he could not continue to make the scheduled repayments. Shortly thereafter, the other stockholders cancelled most of the amounts still owed to them. *Held*, the cancellation of the taxpayer's indebtedness constituted a gift rather than additional compensation. There was no moral or legal obligation on the part of the other stockholders to pay the taxpayer any additional compensation; the cancellation of the indebtedness was promoted by a genuine desire to make a gift to the taxpayer because of his financial need.

Compensation may also be lurking even though the employee or independent contractor purports to purchase the stock or other property instead of receiving it free, if he is permitted to acquire the property for less than its value. In the case of such a bargain purchase, "the difference between the amount paid for the property and the amount of its fair market value at the time of the transfer is compensation and shall be included in the gross income of the employee or independent contractor." Reg. § 1.61–2(d)(2).

Obviously, whether there has been a bargain purchase depends upon the value of the stock or other property at the time it is acquired, as the Berckmans and Dees cases illustrate. And of course in the case of fungible property like stock, if there has been an arm's-length sale at or near the time of the acquisition by the taxpayer the price paid in such a transaction furnishes the best evidence of the value of the stock. Thus, in the Dees case the court was persuaded that there had been a bargain purchase because by the time the taxpayer bought his shares some stock had already been sold to the public at a price substantially higher than he paid. On the other hand, evidence that a higher price was paid for the stock at a time appreciably after the taxpayer's acquisition, or after a change in the circumstances of the enterprise, would be much less relevant since that is equally consistent with an increase in the value of the stock after it was acquired by the taxpayer, and of course such an increase would not be taxable until the taxpayer disposed of his stock. Hence in Berckmans the court refused to take into account the price of a subsequent public offering of stock which had not yet ripened into a binding commitment between the underwriter and the issuer at the time when the taxpayer acquired his stock.

However, on its facts the Berckmans case was by no means an easy one. In effect the question of whether to take the proposed public offering into account in valuing the stock received by the taxpayer is not unlike the question of whether a proposed public offering should be "integrated" with a prior issue of stock to insiders for the purpose of applying the control test under § 351. It is to be noted that in Berckmans not only did the public offering occur very shortly after the taxpayer acquired his stock—it was also clearly contemplated from the outset. Even more important, since the enterprise in Berckmans consisted of combining two going businesses (rather than, say, starting a brand-new venture) and therefore its value was capable of being reasonably estimated, the prospective public offering was scarcely a sheer speculation. To be sure, at the moment when the taxpayer acquired his stock the prospective public offering was still subject to the "contingencies" stressed by the court. But those contingencies were largely technical; and in any event they related to whether the particular transaction would be carried out as proposed, and not to whether stock could in fact be sold to the public at the proposed price, which is the critical issue so far as valuation is concerned. Moreover, as the Government's expert witness testified, it is unlikely that either the taxpayer or the underwriter would have purchased any stock of the new corporation at any price if either had entertained any real doubt that the transaction would be completed as proposed and that the public offering would be successful. Cf. Reg. § 1.421–6(b)(3)(ii) which provides that where "a stock option is granted to an underwriter prior to a public offering and such grant is expressly or impliedly conditional upon the successful completion of the underwriting, the date on which the option shall be considered 'granted' shall be the date of the successful completion of the underwriting."

Nevertheless, the decision in Berckmans may perhaps be justified on the ground that the spread between the price paid by the insiders and the price paid by the public represents a kind of "entrepreneurial increment" rather than compensation income. That is, when an entrepreneur who has launched a business, with all the attendant risks, is able to persuade others to come in with him at a higher price, the premium paid by the outsiders may be regarded as the cost of being permitted to share in the entrepreneur's venture rather than as compensation for the entrepreneur's future services. Cf. Ungar v. Commissioner, 22 T.C.M. 766 (1963), which dismissed rather lightly the effort to find compensation income to an entrepreneur who received cheap stock from his corporation not long before a public offering. After all, it must still be true that the payment of a large amount of compensation in advance should not lightly be inferred. Therein lies the important difference from the case of the "classical" promoter who is permitted to acquire admittedly "cheap" stock for his efforts in lining up the deal. The promoter's services are usually completed by the time he acquires his stock, or shortly thereafter; and particularly if there is no other form of compensation, it may be expected that the stock acquisition entails some immediate financial advantage representing compensation for services. Unlike the entrepreneur, the promoter would not normally be content simply to "get in on the ground floor," especially since the promoter does not have the opportunity to influence the ultimate success of the enterprise which the entrepreneur has by virtue of serving as one of the chief officers of the company.

Even if there is force in this distinction, it presents some difficulty in a case like Berckmans since the taxpayer there, in addition to being an entrepreneur, had obviously performed some "classical" promotional services in arranging for the combination of the two previously unrelated brewery enterprises. Therefore, the spread between the price he paid and the price paid by the public may well have represented not only some "entrepreneurial increment" but also some compensation for those promotional services. Probably, the best course in such circumstances would be to ignore the promotional activity unless that is the predominant element in the situation. On the other hand, a case like Dees presents no "entrepreneurial increment" issue at all since there the taxpayer only rendered promotional services, and no long-term relationship with the issuer was contemplated.

Is there a special problem in finding bargain purchase compensation income to an independent contractor which performs its services not as an agent for the issuer but rather solely for its own account, as in the case of a "firm commitment" underwriter like the one in the Berckmans case who buys securities from the issuer and sells them as a principal? Some distinction between "firm commitment" underwriters and "best efforts" underwriters, who perform their selling services as agents for the issuer, seems implicit in the decision in the Trust Co. of Georgia case, cited in both the Berckmans and Dees opinions. Particularly the lower court in the Trust Co. of Georgia case emphasized the fact that the underwriter there had not performed services for the issuer, but had rather purchased and sold the issuer's stock for its own account. And the Tax Court in Dees seems to have pursued much the same line in distinguishing the Trust Co. of Georgia case (although the Tax Court somewhat overdrew the distinction by implying that Dees involved an employer-employee relationship). On the other hand, there is certainly nothing in the bargain purchase regulations which invites any distinction between types of underwriting arrangements, and doubtless the Service would vigorously resist any such distinction.

b. *Deductibility by the Grantor.* Normally, a corporation which gives an employee either "free" stock or a bargain purchase will be entitled to a deduction for whatever amount is taxed as compensation income to the employee, subject of course to the "reasonable amount" limitation of § 162(a)(1). However, in some cases the "compensatory" stock may come from the stockholders personally rather than the corporation. Although absent some clear evidence of donative intent the employee would still realize compensation income in such circumstances, e. g., Knowles v. Commissioner, 24 T.C.M. 129 (1965), the stockholders would not qualify for an "ordinary and necessary expense" deduction, under either § 162 or § 212; but they would apparently be entitled to a deduction for "losses incurred in any transaction entered into for profit" under § 165(c)(2). E. g., Berner v. United States, 282 F.2d 720 (Ct.Cl.1960). Presumably, such a deduction should be limited to the basis of the stockholders in the stock transferred, § 165(b), although the Berner case seemed to allow a deduction based upon fair market value.

Alternatively, the transaction might be viewed as though the stock had been transferred by the stockholders to the corporation, as a contribution to capital, and then "paid" by the corporation, thus entitling it to the deduction. However, note that if all of the stockholders did not participate in the transfer of stock to the corporate employee, this view could lead to finding a gift by the stockholders who did participate to those who did not. Cf. Heringer v. Commissioner, 235 F.2d 149 (9th Cir. 1956); Hitchon's Estate v. Commissioner, 45 T.C. 96 (1965).

c. *Effect of Restrictions on Transferability.* In valuing the stock involved in the Dees case, the court, it will be recalled, took some account of what was regarded as at least a "moral" obligation of the taxpayer not to sell any of his stock until the close of the promotional period. Presumably, a legally binding restriction on transferability—for example, an absolute bar against transfer for a specified period, or a right of first refusal in the corporation at a fixed price—would have an even more significant effect on value; for stock which would otherwise be marketable, such restrictions would be likely to greatly depress the value. Indeed, in some cases such restrictions may make it impossible to attribute any fair market value to the stock. Cf. Helvering v. Tex-Penn Oil Co., 300 U.S. 481, 57 S.Ct. 569, 81 L.Ed. 755 (1937). However, such transactions are now governed by Reg. § 1.61–2(d)(5), which provides that where property is transferred by an employer to an employee or independent contractor (after September 24, 1959) as compensation for services and the property is "subject to a restriction which has a significant effect on its value", the compensation is subject to tax only when the restrictions lapse or the property is disposed of, in accordance with the rules set out in Reg. § 1.421–6. The latter section deals with the treatment of restricted stock received upon the exercise of an option, and will be analyzed in detail later in this note. It is enough here simply to observe the two examples of restrictions "significantly affecting value" which are set out in the regulations: (1) a requirement that under certain circumstances the employee resell the stock to the corporation at the price he paid for it; and (2) a provision giving the corporation a right of first refusal at book value before the employee may dispose of the stock during his employment. On the other hand, a right of first refusal in the corporation at fair market value is not regarded as a restriction which has a significant effect on value, and hence the recipient of stock subject to such a restriction would realize compensation income at the time of receipt.

The rule prior to the 1959 change in the regulations for the receipt of property subject to a restriction as compensation was that so long as the property had an ascertainable market value upon receipt it was to be valued as of that time for the purpose of determining the amount of compensation to the recipient. In Mailloux v. Commissioner, page 274 supra, an agreement by the taxpayers that they would not sell any of the stock received by them without the consent of the promoter was held by the Tax Court not to have any substantial effect upon the fair market value. The Tax Court found that the restrictive arrangement was merely for the purpose of maintaining the market value of the stock, for the mutual benefit of all the parties; the court also emphasized both the absence of any absolute prohibition against sale and the fact that the taxpayers had actually disposed of substantial portions of their stock within a year after receipt. However, the Court of Appeals reversed, stating that "where the holder of a highly speculative stock . . . can carry it into the market place only at the indulgence of another, the fair market value of the stock is [not] the same as it would be if the dominion of the holder was free and unfettered." Since the transaction in Mailloux arose before the applicable date of Reg. § 1.61–2(d)(5), supra, (calling for a delay in determining the tax incidents, pursuant to Reg. § 1.421–6) the Court of Appeals then had to decide whether the stock had an ascertainable market value upon its receipt by the taxpayer. The court answered that question in the affirmative, but applied a substantial discount on account of the restriction on transfer. Accord, Simmons v. Commissioner, 23 T.C.M. 1423 (1964).

What about such "practical" restrictions on transferability as that resulting from an investment intention letter covering the stock, pursuant to a claimed exemption from registration under the Securities Act? This could amount to a substantial restraint since the corporation might well refuse to transfer such shares on its books for a substantial period after issuance, at least absent a clearance from the S.E.C., see Israels, Problems Incident to Use of Stop-Transfer Procedures, 18 Bus.Law. 85 (1962); and in any event there are practical restraints in such circumstances which might lead to a finding of a "significant effect on value" which would preclude immediate inclusion in income. See LeVant v. Commissioner, 45 T.C. No. 17 (1965), discussed at page 284 infra (listed stock selling at about $39 per share valued at only 34⅜ because subject to an investment letter); cf. Specialty Paper and Board Co., Inc. v. Commissioner, 24 T.C.M. 1085 (1965) (unregistered stock, listed on the American Stock Exchange and trading at approximately $5 per share, valued at only $2.85 per share when received in exchange for property by the taxpayer subject to an investment letter). See also MacDonald v. Commissioner, 230 F.2d 534 (7th Cir. 1956), where, in a case involving receipt of stock upon the exercise of an option, the court seemed to regard § 16(b) of the Securities and Exchange Act, which entitles the corporation to recover any profits made by insiders on purchases and sales within six months, as a practical restriction on transfer which significantly affected value.

On the other hand, as to stock which has no quoted market price anyway, such as that of a closely-held corporation, it seems less likely that even express restrictions on transfer would significantly affect value. Indeed, quite the reverse, the typical close corporation stock restriction is widely regarded as enhancing the value of the stock, by increasing the likelihood of stable and harmonious management and preventing the intrusion of unwanted outsiders. Accordingly, the presence of a restriction in such circumstances, particularly if it applies to all of the corporation's stock, should probably not preclude immediate inclusion of the value of the stock in the income of the recipient.

2. Stock Options

a. *In General.* In the Dees case, as the court expressly recognized at several points in its opinion, what the taxpayer actually received originally was a stock option, that is, a right to buy a specified amount of the new insurance company's stock at a specified "option price" (here, the average price paid by Underwriters). Such an option would seem to constitute an item of property, with a present value at least equal to any excess of the market value of the stock on the date the option is granted over the option price. (Even if there is no such excess, there is certainly some value in the continuing right represented by the option to purchase stock at a fixed price without having to make any investment or take any risk of loss until and unless the option is exercised.) By analogy to the case of outright acquisition of stock dealt with above, the receipt of an option by an employee from his employer without consideration would result in compensation income, in the amount of the value of the option at the time of receipt. As a corollary, the exercise of the option would not be a taxable event, and the stock acquired would have a basis equal to the sum of the amount included in the employee's income upon receipt of the option plus the option price paid to obtain the stock. A subsequent disposition of the stock would qualify for capital gains treatment, long-term or short as the case might be.

On the other hand, the receipt of an option might be regarded as an "open" transaction, to be closed for tax purposes only when the option is exercised, at which time under traditional bargain-purchase doctrine the employee would have compensation income in the amount of the spread between the option price and value of the stock at that time. One advantage of waiting until the date of exercise to measure and tax the compensation income involved in a stock option is that it would not be necessary to undertake the admittedly very difficult task of valuing the option. Another problem inherent in taxing an option upon receipt is that if the stock declines in value and the option is never exercised, the employee will have been taxed on "income" he never enjoyed, and may be left with only a capital loss as an offset. See IRC § 1234. However, the fact is that the spread between the option price and the market value at the date of exercise depends upon the fortuitous circumstance of when the employee exercises the option, and the vagaries of the market up to that date. Hence the spread at that time may well not be a fair measure of the amount of compensation which the option transaction was intended to confer upon the employee.

Most of the history of the tax treatment of stock options has been a contest between these two competing approaches, taxing the value of the option upon receipt, and taxing the spread between the option price and the value of the stock when the option is exercised.

b. *Historical Development.* The Treasury has long pressed for taxing employee stock options at exercise rather than upon receipt, even though waiting until exercise results in deferring the imposition of tax. That is because such deferral is more than counterbalanced by the fact that so long as the stock appreciates in value (and of course this is the assumption which underlies the granting of options), the spread at exercise will exceed the value of the option upon receipt, and hence the amount taxed as ordinary compensation income will be greater. Accordingly, the original Treasury approach was to ignore the grant of an employee stock option and treat the exercise of the option as the consummation of a bargain purchase as of that date.

The earliest attacks on this position went beyond the issue of when to tax stock options, raising the more basic question of whether options granted to employees necessarily resulted in compensation income at all. A number of courts actually did carve out a distinction for options alleged to be primarily intended to give the employee a proprietary interest in the business rather than additional compensation, and held that such options did not result in compensation income. E. g., Geeseman v. Commissioner, 38 B.T.A. 258 (1938). Unless the option price was less than the value of the stock at the time the option was granted, it was usually inferred that there was no intention to compensate the employee.

For a time, the Commissioner acquiesced in this approach. However, in 1945, the Supreme Court, dealing for the first time with employee stock options, sustained a decision of the Tax Court that the exercise of an option gave rise to ordinary income in the amount of the excess of the value of the stock over the option price at that time. Commissioner v. Smith, 324 U.S. 177, 65 S.Ct. 591, 89 L.Ed. 830 (1945). Although the Smith case might have been read as merely affirming the Tax Court's finding of fact that the option there involved was intended to provide compensation, the Service treated the decision as meaning that an employee option always resulted in compensation income, and reaffirmed its position that the date of exercise of the option was the time to measure and tax such compensation. In any event, Commissioner v. LoBue, 351 U.S. 243, 76 S.Ct. 800, 100 L.Ed. 1142 (1956), finally laid the proprietary interest concept permanently to rest, holding that any employee stock option (other than one qualifying for the special treatment under what is now IRC §§ 421–425) produces compensation taxable as ordinary income to the employee.[18]

Although both LoBue and Smith measured the compensation income from stock options as of the date of exercise rather than receipt, neither case conclusively resolved this question of the proper timing of the tax. In the Smith case, the Court observed: "It of course does not follow that in other circumstances not here present the option itself, rather than the proceeds of its exercise, could not be found to be the only intended compensation." In LoBue, the Court substantially expanded on this theme:

> It is of course possible for the recipient of a stock option to realize an immediate taxable gain. . . . The option might have a readily ascertainable market value and the recipient might be free to sell his option. But this is not such a case. These three options were not transferable and LoBue's right to buy stock under them was contingent upon his remaining an employee of the company until they were exercised. Moreover, the uniform Treasury practice since 1923 has been to measure the compensation to employees given stock options subject to contingencies of this sort by the difference be-

---

18. The proprietary interest concept may still have some vitality in special situations. In Turzillo v. Commissioner, 346 F.2d 884 (6th Cir. 1965), an employee-minority stockholder was allowed capital gain when he in effect released for consideration his chance to become a 50% stockholder by virtue of the corporation's option to redeem the controlling stockholder's stock upon his death.

tween the option price and the market value of the shares at the time the option is exercised.

Two justices dissented, on the ground that the taxable event was the granting of the options and not the exercise:

> When the respondent received an unconditional option to buy stock at less than the market price, he received an asset of substantial and immediately realizable value, at least equal to the then-existing spread between the option price and the market price. It was at that time that the corporation conferred a benefit upon him. At the exercise of the option, the corporation "gave" the respondent nothing; it simply satisfied a previously-created legal obligation.

c. *"Qualified Stock Options."* In 1950 the drive for favorable tax treatment for stock options turned to the legislative side, where substantial success was achieved with the enactment of the predecessor of what is now § 421. That statute provided that for stock options which complied with the requirements of the section, which were denominated "restricted stock options," normally there would be no tax until and unless the stock obtained upon exercise of the option was sold, and then only at capital gains rates. As a corollary, the corporate employer *never* gets any deduction on account of such options.

The enactment of this legislation virtually revolutionized the course of management compensation for publicly-held corporations. It appears that as many as half of the larger publicly-held corporations, and perhaps two-thirds of the corporations listed on the New York Stock Exchange, used restricted stock options to some extent. The sharp decline in stock prices in the spring of 1962 undoubtedly slowed this trend; and indeed many a company with an existing plan went scurrying to find ways and means for amending a stock option plan to take account of the decline in market price while still retaining the tax advantages. However, the market resurgence during the first half of 1963 soon restored stock options to their pre-slump popularity.

This special tax treatment for stock options by no means went uncriticized, see e. g., Griswold, Are Stock Options Getting Out of Hand?, 38 Harv. Bus.Rev. 49 (Nov., 1960). In 1963 President Kennedy's Tax Message in effect called for a repeal of the preferential provisions. However, the legislative response in the 1964 Revenue Act was instead merely to tighten up the provisions by limiting the favored tax treatment for stock options issued after 1964 to those which satisfied the requirements of § 422 for so-called "qualified stock options" (or were part of a broadly-based "employee stock purchase plan" under § 423). Briefly, to qualify under § 422 an option must (1) be granted pursuant to a plan approved by the stockholders and within 10 years thereof; (2) not be exercisable more than 5 years after it is granted; (3) carry an option price which is not less than the fair market value of the stock at the date of the grant; and (4) not be transferable by the grantee (except by will or the laws of intestacy). In addition, the option can not be exercised more than three months after the termination of the grantor's employment, and the stock received upon exercise of the option must be held for at least three years. Finally, employees who own, either actually, or constructively under attribution rules set out in § 425, more than 5% to 10% of the corporation's stock (the exact figure depending upon the amount of the corporation's equity capital) are barred from participating. See generally, Rothschild, The New Stock Option, 17 So.Cal.Fed.Tax Inst. 117 (1965); Baker, Employee Stock Option Plans Under the Revenue Act of 1964, 20 Tax L.Rev. 77 (1964).

d. *Current Status of Unrestricted Stock Options.* Neither the predecessor of §§ 421–425 as enacted in 1950 nor the 1964 amendments thereto gave any guidance as to the proper tax treatment of those options which did not qualify under the statute, often referred to as "unrestricted stock options", and there has continued to be uncertainty as to the time when the compensation income is to be measured and taxed. In the main, the focal issue has been whether the options had a "readily ascertainable market value" when received, in which event, as suggested in LoBue, the tax might be imposed upon receipt rather than exercise. The difficulty of resolving this issue is dramatically illustrated by the difference of opinion between the Court of Appeals for the Third Circuit and the Court of Claims as to whether the very same options had a readily ascertainable market value. In Commissioner v. Stone's Estate, 210 F.2d 33 (3d Cir. 1954), the taxpayer in 1947 paid $1,000 for options to buy 10,000 shares of his employer's common stock at $21.00 a share, at a time when the market price of the stock was $19.75 per share. The taxpayer treated the options as having a value of $6,000, and included $5,000 as compensation income in 1947. In the following year, the taxpayer sold 8,900 options for $82,680, and the Commissioner sought to include the value of the options at that date as compensation income. The Court of Appeals, writing before the LoBue decision, affirmed the decision of the Tax Court that the options had an ascertainable value at the time of receipt. Accordingly, the compensation income was properly reported upon receipt of the options, and not upon a later exercise or disposition of them.

The Court of Claims reached the opposite conclusion in a case involving Stone's employer's deduction for compensation. Union Chemical & Materials Corp. v. United States, 155 Ct.Cl. 540, 296 F.2d 221 (1961). The employer had originally taken a deduction of $5,000 in 1947, which coincided with Stone's inclusion in income of the same amount for that year. However, upon Stone's disposition of the options in 1948, his employer claimed a further deduction to reflect the increased spread between the option price and the fair market value of the shares. The court allowed it, concluding that the options received by Stone had not had a "readily ascertainable market value" as that term was used in the LoBue case (which had been decided in the interim since the Stone's Estate decision). The court did not regard the testimony of the two stockbrokers that the options were worth between $30,000 and $35,000 as establishing that the market value was readily ascertainable. In addition, the court particularly emphasized the fact that the option price exceeded the market price of the stock at the date of receipt of the options, which may indicate a view that the value of an option is never "readily ascertainable" unless the option price is less than the market price.

In an effort to bring some order into this area, the Treasury in 1959 promulgated comprehensive regulations dealing specifically with unrestricted stock options, tacking the new regulations on to the regulations under the pre-1964 version of § 421 dealing with restricted stock options. Reg. § 1.421–6. These regulations were made generally applicable to all options granted after February 26, 1945, (the date of the decision in the Smith case) except as to options to acquire property where the property is subject to a restriction having a significant effect on value, which options are covered only after the date of the regulation. As first promulgated, § 1.-421–6 maintained the original Treasury position that the earliest permissible date for recognizing the compensation income resulting from an unrestricted stock option (or allowing the corresponding deduction) was the exercise date (or more precisely, the date when the taxpayer has an unconditional right to receive the stock, if that is later than the date of exercise, see Reg. § 1.421–6(d)(1)). But in 1961 the Treasury yielded to such contrary authority as the dictum in the LoBue case and accepted the view that the compensation incidents of an option might be recognized upon its receipt if at that date it had a "readily ascertainable fair market value". Reg. § 1.421–6(c). However, this concession was made in quite narrow terms. The regulations provide that except where options are "actively traded on an established market", the option does not have a readily ascertainable fair market value when granted unless the taxpayer can show that all the following conditions exist: (1) the option must be freely transferable; (2) it must be exercisable in full immediately; (3) neither the option nor the stock may be subject to any restriction or condition having a significant effect on fair market value; and (4) the value of the "option privilege", i. e., the continuing call on stock at a fixed price, must be "readily ascertainable", taking into account such matters as whether the value of the underlying stock can be ascertained, the probability of increase or decrease in such value, and the length of the option period.

As to options which do meet these standards, the regulations expressly limit the compensation income to the value of the option at the time of receipt. Indeed, finding compensation income upon a later exercise of such options is precluded even if the employee did not actually include the value of the options in income upon receipt and, further, even if a deficiency for the year of receipt has become barred by the statute of limitations.

Bearing in mind that these regulations are not based upon any statute, their requirements do seem quite strict, and they appear to go somewhat beyond the decided cases in this area. E. g., McNamara v. Commissioner, 210 F.2d 505 (7th Cir. 1954) (options valued and taxed upon receipt although not immediately exercisable in full). However, it is to be noted that the regulations do not, at least expressly, make it a condition to finding a readily ascertainable value for an option that the market price of the stock exceed the option price, as may have been suggested in the Union Chemical decision, supra. Of course, whenever the market price does not exceed the option price, it will be particularly difficult to show that the value of the "option privilege" is "readily ascertainable", as the regulations require; but at least the issue is not foreclosed as a matter of law, so that the courts are left with some leeway. Thus in Colton v. Williams, 62–2 USTC para. 9675 (N.D.Ohio 1962), the court found that an option to buy stock at $3.25 per share granted to a majority stockholder-officer two months after stock was sold to the public at $3.00 per share had an ascertainable fair market value, so that compensation income should be taxed upon receipt of the option and not upon a later exercise. With no mention of the regulations on this point, the court referred to "previous" (but unspecified) authority which the court regarded as indicating that an option could not have an ascertainable fair market value if the option price exceeded the market value of the stock at that date. However, the court found it unnecessary to resolve that question in this case because it was satisfied, on the basis of the substantial over-subscription of the public offering and the expert testimony of an experienced stockbroker, that the value of the stock did exceed the option price by at least 50 cents per share. On the ultimate question of whether the value of the option was readily ascertainable, the court did refer to Reg. § 1.421–6, and found that its standards were met by the evidence of the successful public offering shortly before the granting of the options, the expert testimony of the broker, and the absence of "any evidence against the fact of the option having a value." (Query just what that last item means.) See generally, Horwich, A Tale of Two Dicta: The Non-Restricted Stock Option, 18 U. of Miami L.Rev. 596 (1964).

The court also held that the taxpayer's failure to report any compensation income from the options in the year of receipt was not controlling against him, in view of the confused state of the law in 1951. Here too the court failed to refer to the regulations, although on this issue, as noted earlier, the regulations expressly support the court's conclusion.

However, most of the cases involving pre-Reg. § 1.421–6 transactions have approved the exercise date as the proper time for measuring and taxing the compensation income involved in stock options. E. g., Victorson v. Commissioner, 326 F.2d 264 (2d Cir. 1964) (rejecting the taxpayer's contention that where the option price was 1 mill per share for stock being sold to the public for 50¢ per share, it was so clear that the option would be exercised that the transaction should be viewed as a purchase of stock at the outset); Thornhill v. Commissioner, 37 T.C. 988 (1962). And in what appears to be the first case involving a transaction subsequent to the adoption of Reg. § 1.421–6, the Tax Court expressly relied upon the regulations to reach the same result. LeVant v. Commissioner, 45 T.C. No. 17 (1965). The LeVant case actually involved an exchange of an option for stock of a different enterprise, but the court, citing IRC § 1234(c), found no reason to treat the transaction differently from an exercise of an option. Accord, Rank v. United States, 345 F.2d 337 (5th Cir. 1965) (options redeemed in a complete liquidation of the corporate grantor).

e. *Effect of Restrictions on the Stock.* As we have seen, Reg. § 1.421–6 provides for postponing the taxation of the compensation income resulting from a stock option beyond even the date of exercise of the option, if the stock received upon exercise "is subject to a restriction which has a significant effect on its value." In such circumstances, the regulations call for the recognition of compensatory income at the time when the restriction lapses, or when the stock is transferred in an arm's length transaction, whichever occurs first. The amount of compensation income is equal to the difference between (1) the price paid for the stock upon exercise of the option, and (2) the lesser of (a) the fair market value of the stock at the time of its acquisition (determined without regard to any restriction then existing) and (b) its fair market value at the time when the restriction lapses (or the amount of the consideration received in an arm's length transfer if that occurs before the restriction lapses).

Notice that although the existence of a restriction on the stock may postpone imposition of the tax on compensation income beyond the date of exercise, the amount of such income cannot exceed the spread between the option price and the market value of the stock (without the restriction) as of that date. This apparently generous rule for taxpayers, and indeed the whole complex pattern relating to restrictions affecting the value of stock, represents the response of the Treasury to the two principal decided cases in this area. In Lehman v. Commissioner, 17 T.C. 652 (1951), the stock acquired by the taxpayer upon exercising certain options received from his employer was subject to restrictions which substantially affected its value. The taxpayer apparently regarded the stock as having no ascertainable market value upon receipt and did not report any compensation income at that time. Upon the lapse of the restrictions, the Commissioner sought to tax as compensation income the spread between the price paid by the taxpayer and the market value of the stock *when the restrictions lapsed*. The Tax Court disagreed with the Commissioner as to both the timing and the measure of the tax, holding that: (1) the lapse of the restrictions was not a taxable event since nothing passed to the taxpayer from his employer at that time; (2) the spread between option price and market value as of the date of the lapse of the restrictions bore no necessary relationship to the amount of compensation intended by the employer.

In the other important case, Kuchman v. Commissioner, 18 T.C. 154 (1952), decided only a few months after Lehman, the Commissioner had reverted to his more customary view that the time for taxing options was the date of exercise, even if the stock received was subject to restrictions. The Commissioner computed the amount of compensation income at exercise by simply ignoring the restrictions and using the spread between the option price and the figure equal to the market value of unrestricted stock on that date. However, the Tax Court held that the amount of compensation income could not be determined at the time of exercise in such circumstances because the existence of the restrictions deprived the stock of any ascertainable value on that date.

Notice that the combination of Lehman and Kuchman cleared a neat little path for taxpayers through the unrestricted stock option area. Under Kuchman, subjecting the stock to some restrictions on transfer (which need not be very onerous—in Kuchman itself, they consisted of merely the taxpayer's agreement that he would not sell the stock for a year and would offer it back to the corporation at cost if he left the company's employ within the year) is sufficient to prevent the imposition of any tax upon the exercise of the option; and under Lehman, the lapse of the restrictions on the stock is not a taxable event. Hence only upon a subsequent sale of the stock would there be any tax, and then quite possibly only at capital gains rates.

The regulations seek to forestall this result by accepting the Kuchman rationale while rejecting that of Lehman. (This represents a reversal of theory for the Commissioner, since he originally acquiesced in the Lehman case; a nonacquiescence was substituted upon the adoption of Reg. § 1.421-6.) It is obviously for the purpose of minimizing the conflict with the Lehman case that the regulations limit the amount of compensation income to the spread between option price and market value (without regard to restrictions) at the date of exercise of the option. While this certainly does undercut the "amount" objection of Lehman, the regulations do not meet the argument that lapse of restrictions on stock is not a taxable event, and it remains to be seen whether the courts will follow the regulations on this point. There is some judicial support for the regulation position in a dictum in another pre-Reg. § 1.421–6 case, Commissioner v. Estate of Ogsbury, 258 F.2d 294, 296–297 (2d Cir. 1958), which states, without mentioning Lehman, that an employer's removal of restrictions from stock held by an employee would result in taxable income to the employee.

f. *Coverage of the Regulations.* The scope of Reg. § 1.421–6 has followed a somewhat checkered path. As originally adopted in 1959, the "employees" to whom § 1.421–6 applied included "any person who performs services for compensation". But in July, 1960, the coverage of the regulations was drastically curtailed by an amendment confining the term "employee" essentially to persons meeting the conventional common law "servant" test. In December, 1960, the Treasury proposed amendments to the regulations which would have restored their coverage of independent contractors, but those proposals were withdrawn early in 1961 for "further study". In July, 1963, the Service again proposed to amend the regulations, this time to "treat options received as compensation by independent contractors, and options received as interest by lenders, in the same manner as compensatory options received by employees". See Prop.Reg. § 1.61–15(a), 28 Fed. Reg. 7097–7098 (July 11, 1963). The final regulations, adopted in December, 1963, preserve the extension of Reg. § 1.421–6 to "options granted in whole or partial payment for the services of an independent contractor", but the reference to options received by lenders has been dropped. Reg. § 1.61–15(a). There seems little doubt that the new regulations will be sustained; even prior to their adoption the courts were treating options issued to independent contractors in about the same manner as those received by employees. Victorson v. Commissioner, 21 T.C.M. 1238 (1962), affirmed, 326 F.2d 264 (2d Cir. 1964).

Nevertheless, there is some force in the argument for distinguishing independent contractors from employees, at least to the extent of being more ready to use the date of grant as the time for taxing options issued to independent contractors such as underwriters. In the case of a full-time employee whose services may have some impact upon the future value of the corporation's stock, options provide substantial incentive for maximum effort by the employee in the future, and therefore it is possible to think of him as "earning" the options over the course of time right up to the date of exercise. But obviously this argument for treating the spread at exercise as the "intended compensation" loses a good deal of force in the case of, say, an underwriter, for whom options provide little if any long-range incentive because his services have usually ended by the date of the grant and he has little opportunity to influence the future value of the stock. For such independent contractors it is harder to justify treating the later spread at exercise as the intended compensation; there is more reason to assume that the compensation is limited to the value of the options at the time of the grant. See Brach & Dixon, Tax Treatment of Compensatory Stock Options to Non-Employees: The Valuation Problem, 17 J.Taxation 66, 73–74 (1962).

Such a distinction between independent contractors and regular employees is much like the one suggested above in connection with compensatory bargain purchases. However, it is to be noted that here the distinction would favor the independent contractor over the employee, since in the normal case taxing an option upon receipt results in a smaller amount of ordinary income than taxation at exercise; perhaps this supports the elimination of the distinction so far as options are concerned.

SECTION 4. NOTE ON SPECIAL PROBLEMS IN PLANNING SENIOR SECURITIES

The term "senior securities" encompasses all interests in the corporation having either an earnings or assets claim which is prior to that of the basic common stock equity. Obviously such senior claims may take the form of either debt or equity interests—indeed, as noted in Chapter I, the line between the two has become rather blurred, and at least in economic terms seems less significant than the line between basic equity on the one hand and any type of senior security on the other. Nevertheless, even the most modern corporation statutes give little evidence of any departure from the traditional distinction between debt as a representation of a creditor's claim and equity as the embodiment of a proprietary interest.

So far as the preparation of senior securities is concerned, any type of stock would be governed by MBA § 14 and its counterparts which give the parties very broad power to fix the terms of any stock issued by the corporation; and of course the terms of debt securities are almost exclusively a matter of private agreement between the parties. Accordingly, the preparation of senior securities is primarily a planning exercise, calling for a recognition of the likely problems, a judgment as to how they should be resolved (which may ultimately be determined by negotiations between the parties), and careful draftsmanship to assure that the intention of the parties is clearly expressed. The following material is designed to illustrate both a number of the classic senior security problems which the parties must resolve and the possible fate of careless drafting.[19]

A. ANNUAL RETURN ON SENIOR SECURITIES

1. DIVIDENDS ON PREFERRED STOCK

In the absence of special provisions, of course, the payment of dividends on any stock, preferred or common, is within the discretion of the directors. Hence a "preference" in dividends usually amounts in the first instance to no more than a right to be paid *first*, when and if any dividend payments are made.

A dividend preference may take a variety of forms, ranging all the way from a mere specified preferred dividend, "and no more", to a full right of participation with the common in any further distribution, presumably after the common have first received a dividend equal to the preferred's.

---

[19]. Some of the material in this note is adapted, by permission, from Baker & Cary, Cases on Corporations (3d ed., unabridged 1959) 955–1009.

What happens when the terms of the preferred stock do not specify whether the preferred is limited to the specified dividend? The authorities are divided on whether to presume that preferred are entitled, in addition to any express priorities they may have, to all the rights of the common unless the contrary is expressly provided, see St. Louis Southwestern Railway Co. v. Loeb, 318 S.W.2d 246 (Mo.1958); Christ, Rights of Holders of Preferred Stock to Participate in the Distribution of Profits, 27 Mich.L.Rev. 731 (1929), or to assume that any specified priority in dividends for the preferred precludes any further participation unless it is specifically provided for, the view apparently preferred by most of the commentators. E. g., Tennant v. Epstein, 356 Ill. 26, 189 N.E. 864 (1934); see Stevens, Corporations (1949) 481, Ballantine, Corporations (1946) 506. An analogous question to be considered below is whether the mere existence of a liquidation preference gives rise to a presumption that the preferred is limited to that amount upon a liquidation.

Turning now to the specified preferred dividend itself, the primary question is the extent to which it is cumulative, that is, whether and to what extent unpaid back dividends on the preferred must be paid before any dividends are paid on the junior securities. The range of possibilities extends from the traditional non-cumulative provision, under which there are no rights of any kind in dividends not paid, to the classic cumulative clause, which calls for complete cumulation of unpaid dividends, even those not earned.

However, certain recognized variations of these polar positions tend to bring them closer together, and indeed may even make them virtually identical. Thus a cumulative preference might be regarded as calling for cumulation only as to dividends actually earned, a construction which has sometimes been adopted in liquidation preference cases, as will be discussed below. Such a provision would then be little different from the New Jersey version of non-cumulative preferred under its so-called "dividend credit rule", where it is held that in the absence of express provision to the contrary, a non-cumulative preferred dividend nevertheless cumulates for any year in which it is earned. E. g., Sanders v. Cuba Railroad Co., 21 N.J. 78, 120 A.2d 849 (1956). In that case the court analyzed the rule in the following terms:

> It may be acknowledged that New Jersey's dividend credit rule has not generally been accepted by the other states or in the federal courts. See Wabash Railway Co. v. Barclay, 280 U.S. 197 . . . . In the recent case of Guttmann v. Illinois Central R. Co., 189 F.2d 927, 930 (2 Cir., 1951), . . . Judge Frank expressed the view that nothing in the terms of the ordinary non-cumulative preferred stock contract points to "a contingent or inchoate right to arrears of dividends" and that the contrary notion is an invention "stemming from considerations of fairness, from a policy of protecting investors in those securities." There seems to be little doubt that equitable factors did play a significant part in the development of New Jersey's doctrine. In the Wabash Railway case, supra, Justice Holmes stated that there was a common understanding that dividends which were passed (though there were profits from which they could have been declared) were forever gone insofar as non-cumulative preferred stock was concerned; but he referred to no support-

ing materials and there are those who have suggested a diametrically opposite understanding. See Lattin, Non-Cumulative Preferred Stock, 25 Ill.L.Rev. 148, 157 (1930).

This much is quite apparent—if the common stockholders, who generally control the corporation and will benefit most by the passing of the dividends on the preferred stock, may freely achieve that result without any dividend credit consequences, then the preferred stockholders will be substantially at the mercy of others who will be under temptation to act in their own self-interest. . . . While such conclusion may sometimes be compelled by the clear contractual arrangements between the parties there is no just reason why our courts should not avoid it whenever the contract is silent or is so general as to leave adequate room for its construction. In any event, New Jersey's doctrine has received wide approval in legal writings and there does not seem to be any present disposition in this court to reject it or limit its sweep in favor of the Supreme Court's approach in the Wabash Railway case.

As a further illustration of how close these two rules may come, it might be observed that in the Guttmann case, referred to in the foregoing excerpt from the Sanders opinion, the plaintiff was actually contending for only a rather limited version of the New Jersey dividend credit rule, which would have conditioned the application of the rule not only on the existence of earnings but also their availability for distribution, in the sense of not having been invested in fixed assets or the like; on the other hand, in the Sanders case, it was suggested that the New Jersey court should limit the operation of the dividend credit rule on just such a basis, with the court incidentally displaying little enthusiasm for the suggestion.

The New Jersey dividend credit rule is not the only doctrine which has developed to mitigate or avoid the rigors of the traditional non-cumulative view. For one thing, an ambiguous preferred stock instrument seems likely to be presumed to be cumulative. See Buxbaum, Preferred Stock—Law and Draftsmanship, 42 Cal.L.Rev. 243, 244 (1954). Moreover, assuming a clear non-cumulative provision, a court may be more likely to find that the dividend is "mandatory", that is, that the dividend must be paid for any year in which it is earned, than if the stock were cumulative. Id. at 254. Of course this "mandatory" issue is also one that should be clearly resolved in the drafting, whether or not the stock is non-cumulative.

2. INTEREST ON DEBT SECURITIES

Typically of course the annual interest on debt is payable in all events, at least once a year, without regard to the earnings of the enterprise or the discretion of the directors. However, there are so-called "income" bonds on which interest is payable only to the extent earned, which comes rather close to a mandatory preferred stock. In planning an income bond, questions may arise reminiscent of the distinction between cumulative and non-cumulative preferred: for example, is interest which is not earned, and hence not paid, in a prior year required to be paid in any subsequent year in which the net earnings exceed the interest due for that year?

B. RIGHTS ON LIQUIDATION

1. PREFERRED STOCK

Although preferences on liquidation are still in common use, their practical value is somewhat doubtful, at least in the case of involuntary liquidation. Typically such a liquidation is the fate of a failing enterprise, and at such a time there is rarely anything left over for stockholders, so that preferences among them are of little moment. The situation may be different in the case of a voluntary liquidation, of course—and this may be one reason why some preferred stock contracts differentiate between the two types of liquidation with regard to the existence and the amount of any preference. Where that is the case, any collateral reference to liquidation preferences, for example in a contractual limitation on reduction of capital, must clearly indicate which one is meant. This precaution was carefully observed in the Model Act, e. g., §§ 19, 41(d), 60 and 63, although it is not entirely clear just how or why the particular choices reflected there were made.

It should be noted that while stock may often have a liquidation preference but no dividend preference, a cumulative dividend preference should seemingly always be accompanied by a liquidation preference and that preference should include any unpaid dividends. Otherwise, the junior stockholders, who usually control the management, might be tempted to pass preferred dividends in contemplation of a liquidation and thus deprive preferred stockholders of their dividends.

Assuming a liquidation preference which does include unpaid cumulative dividends, in some such language as "par plus accrued dividends", the question has arisen whether this includes the unpaid dividends for years in which they were not earned. In Hay v. Hay, 38 Wash.2d 513, 230 P.2d 791 (1951), where the corporation being liquidated had never had any earnings, the court held (en banc, with four dissents) that the liquidation preference included the dividends for all prior years, against the objection that this resulted in part of the investment of the common stockholders being distributed to the preferred stockholders. The closeness of this question is further illustrated by Wouk v. Merin, 238 App.Div. 522, 128 N.Y.S.2d 727 (1st Dept. 1954), where the contrary result was reached, once again by a divided court.

A question previously alluded to is whether the existence of a specified liquidation preference exhausts the rights of the preferred on liquidation despite the absence of a specific provision to that effect. In Mohawk Carpet Mills, Inc. v. Delaware Rayon Corp., 35 Del.Ch. 51, 110 A.2d 305 (Del.Ch. 1954), the preferred stock had a specified non-cumulative dividend of 10%, an express right to participate equally with the common in any further dividends after the payment of a 10% dividend on the common, and a liquidation preference of "par value . . . before any payment in liquidation is made" to the common. In holding that the express liquidation preference was "clearly exhaustive", the court emphasized the absence of any express right to participate in liquidation beyond the specified liquidation preference, in contrast with the presence of such a participation provision in connection with dividends. The court did not comment on the fact that under its interpretation the common would have a great incentive to resist the payment of any dividends, at least once a liquidation was contemplated, since upon liquidation the common would get all the accumulated earnings while the preferred merely got back its par value.

2. DEBT SECURITIES

Of course all debt securities have an inherent priority over any form of equity interest. Among themselves, however, in the absence of some special provision all creditor's claims, including accrued but unpaid interest on interest-bearing debt (but not interest on defaulted interest), stand on the same footing.

The most common device for giving one class of creditors priority over another is a security interest, such as a mortgage on some specified property. While an analysis of mortgage bonds or other secured instruments is beyond the scope of these materials, it may be observed that security indentures are among the most complicated (and cumbersome) of legal instruments. Just to illustrate the types of problems which must be considered, the planner must decide whether a particular mortgage is to be "closed", meaning that no more securities may be issued under that lien, or "open-end", meaning there may be successive issues secured by the same lien. At the same time a decision must be reached on what is almost the converse question, i. e., whether to include an "after-acquired property" clause, under which property obtained by the borrower subsequent to the mortgage nevertheless becomes subject to the lien of the mortgage. Such clauses are particularly ticklish because courts tend to read them rather strictly, if indeed they uphold them at all as against intervening lienors —and caution may dictate the inclusion of a requirement that the corporation deliver supplemental mortgages on after-acquired property at stated intervals.

Another illustration of a special provision varying the normal priority of claims is a subordination clause, under which a particular class of creditors agrees to defer its claims to those of another class. Here too there are a host of issues on which some resolution must be reached and then clearly expressed, such as the time and amount of the subordination, and the classes it is intended to benefit.

C. VOTING RIGHTS

One of the clearest illustrations of the traditional distinction between debt and equity is in the area of voting rights. Under most corporation statutes, any type of stock, preferred or common, is normally presumed to be fully entitled to vote, although the modern permissive provisions like MBA § 14 do give the parties broad power to limit or deny the voting power of any class. Moreover, under some statutes even a class of stock which is given no right to vote by the certificate of incorporation nevertheless retains the right to vote on certain fundamental matters such as, for example, merger and consolidation. E. g., Del.Corp.Law § 251; contra, MBA §§ 54, 67.

As to debt securities, on the other hand, only a few states, such as California and Delaware, have provisions expressly permitting such securities to have voting rights. In the absence of such express authority, there is considerable doubt as to the validity of a provision giving voting rights to debt securities. To be sure, a class of debt securities can obtain the virtual equivalent of a class vote on any matter by providing, as a term of the securities, that such matter requires the consent of a specified percentage of the holders of the debt securities. But a private contract may well not be effective to convey regular voting rights, i. e., for the election of directors; and a provision in the certificate of incorporation giving voting rights to debt securities seems likely to founder upon the fairly clear implication in sections like MBA § 14 that voting rights are an attribute of stock, notwithstanding the broad permission in such sections as MBA § 48(i) to include "any provision, not inconsistent with law, which the incorporators elect to set forth in the articles of incorporation for the regulation of the internal affairs of the corporation."

Coming back to the voting rights of preferred stock, it should be noted that even a right to vote on a share for share basis with the common may not constitute "equal" voting rights for the preferred, unless the required investment per share for the two classes is approximately the same. In other words, there is a considerable disparity in voting rights if the preferred stock gets one vote per share constituting an investment of $100, and the common stock gets one vote per share representing $5.

Today the most common practice is to give contingent voting rights to the preferred stockholders, usually in the form of a right to vote upon default in the payment of dividends for a specified period. The extent of the preferred's participation in voting under such circumstances may range anywhere from an exclusive right to elect all the directors, to a right merely to elect one. (For example, New York Stock Exchange Rule A–15 requires, as a condition to listing a preferred stock, that it have the right to elect at least two directors upon a default in six or more quarterly dividends.)

Such contingent voting provisions involve many complications and call for considerable care in drafting. One particularly troublesome problem relates to the circumstances under which a default is cured and the voting power of the preferred terminated. In Ellingwood v. Wolf's Head Oil Refining Co., Inc., 27 Del.Ch. 356, 38 A.2d 743 (Sup.Ct.1944), the contingent voting provision was as follows:

> If at any time the corporation shall be in default in respect to the declaration and payment of dividends in the amount of two years' dividends on the preferred stock, then the holders of a majority of the preferred shall have an election to exercise the sole right to vote for the election of directors and for all other purposes, to the exclusion of any such right on the part of the holders of the common stock, until the corporation shall have declared and paid for a period of a full year a 6% dividend on the preferred stock, when the right to vote for the election of directors, and for all other purposes, shall revert to the holders of the common stock

Prior to 1942 the corporation was in substantial default on its preferred stock, which had assumed the voting power. For 1942 the corporation declared and paid a full 6% on the preferred, but it was still more than two years in default, and the question was whether the right to vote had reverted to the common stock. A majority of the court held for the preferred on the ground that the two year default provision was controlling; the minority thought that the provision relating to payment of a full year's dividend governed, and entitled the common to a return of voting power until and unless the corporation subsequently defaulted for another two years.

Of course, once again the real villain here was poor draftsmanship. On the merits, however, it does seem that normally the preferred should retain the vote until the total default has been reduced below a specified minimum, lest the management be tempted to manipulate the dividend policy primarily for the purpose of restoring voting power to the common from time to time.

The importance of distinguishing between voting rights for preferred as a class and individual voting rights per share is well illustrated by State ex rel. Cullitan v. Campbell, 135 Ohio St. 238, 20 N.E.2d 366 (1939). There the question was the meaning of a charter provision which provided that upon default "the holders of preferred stock shall be entitled to the same voting power as the holders of the common stock". The preferred contended that the meaning of this provision was that as a class they should have the same voting power as that of the common as a class, which would in effect have given the preferred approximately 90 votes per share. The court rejected this contention and held that in the absence of language clearly indicating otherwise, the normal rule that each share, preferred or common, was entitled to one vote would be presumed to apply.

D. CONVERTIBILITY

1. IN GENERAL

FLEISCHER AND CARY, THE TAXATION OF CONVERTIBLE BONDS AND STOCK [20]

74 Harv.L.Rev. 473–476 (1961).

. . . Conversion is the act of exchanging one class of securities for another, the conversion right being created by written contract between the holder of the security and the company which issued it. Although there have occasionally been convertibility provisions authorizing an exchange of a security for a more senior issue,* or for stock of another com-

---

20. Copyright ©, Harvard Law Review Association, 1961. Reprinted by permission. Portions of the text and all footnotes omitted.

* [Ed. note] Some modern statutes forbid any "uphill" conversion into more senior stock. E. g., MBA § 14(e). And of course, a right to convert stock into any type of debt instrument in effect amounts to an option to compel repurchase of the stock, which today is generally regarded as invalid, at least as against creditors. See Ballantine, Corporations (1946) 513.

pany, conversion almost always involves a shift from a security with higher priority into common stock of the same concern. Another characteristic of convertible securities is that the holder typically has the right not only to acquire common stock but also to pay for it in full by turning in the security he presently owns.

In general, there seems to be three main reasons why publicly held corporations issue convertible bonds and convertible preferred stock. First and possibly most important is the desire by management to raise common capital indirectly. "[M]anagements many times view the convertible as a device permitting them to raise funds today at tomorrow's higher common stock prices." The conversion feature has been attractive among growth companies where current market prices of the common shares are regarded as substantially lower than long-range investment value. This may explain the frequent relationship between rising stockmarket prices and a relative increase in the use of convertible securities. To the extent that their recent popularity is attributable to the uninterrupted prosperity since the war, it might correspondingly decline in the event of unfavorable business conditions.

A further advantage of raising equity capital through convertibles is that the new funds will be contributing to income by the time the debentures are converted. In the interim, while the company is putting the new money effectively to work, the charge takes the form of interest—deductible for tax purposes—rather than a reduction in income per share. Thus the dilution of earnings which traditionally accompanies an equity issue is deferred until the firm is making more money.

Another reason for issuing convertible securities is the desire to improve market acceptance of a bond or preferred-stock contract. In the capital market, as with apparel, fashion often prescribes what is readily acceptable to the buyer. The "sweetening" effect of the conversion feature is especially apparent when it is included in subordinated debenture bonds or second-priority preferred stock. In this type of financing it may be useful as a means of keeping down the interest or dividend rate, or of relieving the borrower from a heavy sinking fund or some other burdensome provision.

In the case of many companies, especially those which are closely held, a convertibility provision has more than a mere sweetening function in raising initial capital. In the early stages of a firm's history, the investor may be unwilling to accept stock alone for his contribution and may insist upon the protection of a debt claim. At the same time, he is obviously not satisfied with a high interest rate as an adequate return for the risk involved. In this context the convertible serves dual objectives, and affords the investor a flexibility which new businesses are willing to provide in order to attract needed financing.

Finally, to the investor the convertible bond not only offers the self-evident advantage of a debt security, but is also more attractive from the standpoint of borrowing. Federal Reserve Regulation U restricts loans by banks for the purpose of purchasing or carrying stock but not debt. In 1959, therefore, although a buyer of common had to pay down ninety per cent of the purchase price, he might pay as little as ten per cent if he acquired a debenture convertible into the same number of shares. Investor acceptance has thus played a significant part in the resort of corporations today to convertible securities.

Historically, convertible securities are not a recent development in corporate finance. . . . Until recent times, however, convertibility was not one of the hallmarks of a high-grade corporate issue. Now the tide seems to have shifted. American Telephone and Telegraph Company has been a leader in the field, with an almost continuous policy of offering rights to convertible bonds to its shareholders. Since the war especially, many of the well-established growth companies have resorted to convertible financing—with distinct success.

. . . Currently, the SEC's statistical studies indicate that nearly ten per cent of all bonds and notes offered during the years 1956 to 1960 were convertible, and a recent survey concluded that roughly half the preferred stock offered to the public during 1959 and the first half of 1960 contained a conversion privilege. . . .

2. PROBLEMS OF CONVERTIBLE SECURITIES AND WARRANTS

Despite the above it is clear that convertible securities do not represent a panacea for all corporate financing problems. First of all, the two-fold nature of a convertible is inherently complicated and confusing, particularly for an unsophisticated investor. More important, the prospective dilution of the common stock by conversion often goes unnoticed until it actually occurs, to the possible detriment of those who have acquired common stock in the meantime. And finally, there is the danger that neither component of a convertible security will receive as much care in planning as it needs: for the prospect of conversion may make the senior aspects of the security loom less important, while the inherent deferral of the junior component tends to push that aspect into the background. In other words, the presence of the convertible feature may lead a prospective investor to let down his guard in examining the senior security elements of the instrument, while at the same time he is not paying close enough attention to the junior security features just because they are clothed at the outset in senior security form. Under these circumstances, of course, convertible securities could combine the worst of both the senior and junior financing worlds, rather than the best as is often claimed.

Some of the foregoing disadvantages of convertible securities might be lessened by switching to straight senior securities, to be accompanied by stock warrants, that is, options to buy stock at a specified price. Such a package can give the investor much the same combination of safety and speculative opportunity that a convertible offers, while making it easier to focus separately upon the two components of the package. Normally, the warrants are made transferable so that it is not necessary to actually make the investment called for by the warrant in order to realize upon any market rise. On the other hand, unless the warrants are perpetual, ultimately someone must make that investment, and therein lies one of the chief disadvantages of warrants—that is, the receipt of additional capital by the corporation upon the exercise of warrants is not in any way geared to or based upon the corporation's need for additional funds. As a matter of fact the relationship is quite likely to be inverse. Warrants are most often exercised when the corporation is prospering, at which time the corporation's capital needs can usually be met by other means without difficulty. On the other hand, when the corporation is faring badly and may well be in need of funds, the warrants are not likely to be exercised; worse yet, their existence will substantially impair the corporation's ability to finance with other junior capital.

Another objection to warrants is that they tend to end up in the hands of professionals, which means that the warrants have not really performed any sound investment function. For reasons like these, the SEC has generally taken a dim view of warrants and has opposed their use in reorganization situations falling within its jurisdiction. See Childs Company, 24 S.E.C. 85, 120–122 (1946).

Turning to the problems of planning convertible securities or warrants, one obvious requisite is that the company be in position to honor any conversions (or exercises of warrants) by maintaining sufficient authorized but unissued (or perhaps treasury) shares. Other important substantive issues include the amount of the conversion or exercise price, and the duration of the conversion or warrant privilege. Obviously, these factors are somewhat interrelated—for example, it is not uncommon to provide in the case of a long-term convertible or warrant that the conversion or exercise price shall increase with the passage of time. In any event, ultimately such factors of general financial import as price and term must be fixed in the light of all the relevant market factors, as well as the comparative bargaining power of the parties.

One of the most intricate of all problems relating to senior securities is the matter of protecting convertible securities or warrants against dilution. For example, when stock is split two for one, the holder of a security convertible into that stock presumably should be entitled to receive twice as many shares when he converts. Similar problems arise in the event of a stock dividend, recapitalization, or issuance of stock pursuant to employee stock options, or indeed whenever additional common stock is issued for a consideration less than the conversion or warrant price. Because protection against dilution under general legal principles is far from clear in these circumstances, today it is common to include express contractual provisions dealing with the matter. In view of the many situations which must be covered, and the intricacies of the relationships involved, these "anti-dilutions" provisions are among the most complicated in corporate finance. An excellent illustration of this is provided by the case of Merritt-Chapman & Scott Corp. v. New York Trust Co., 184 F.2d 954 (2d Cir. 1950), where even a very lengthy and detailed anti-dilution provision failed to make clear whether the effect of a stock dividend on outstanding warrants was to increase the number of shares which the warrant holder was entitled to receive for the specified price, or to leave the number of shares unchanged but reduce the exercise price proportionately.

It is also common to include a contractual provision protecting conversion and warrant rights against destruction or impairment by merger, consolidation, or the like. The format often used to protect convertibles in the event of merger is to provide that the convertible security is to become convertible into whatever interest would have been received in the merger if the convertibles had been converted prior thereto.

E. REDEMPTION

Many modern bond and preferred stock issues contain provisions permitting the corporation at its option to redeem, that is, to pay off and eliminate from the corporation's capital structure, all or part of the issue. Obviously, it is of great advantage to the issuing corporation to be able to get rid of an outstanding issue when it can be attractively replaced. For example, if the cost of money has declined since the original issue, the corporation can reduce its charges (or dividend requirements, in the case of preferred stock) by calling the outstanding issue and floating a new one at a lower yield. Or an outstanding issue, particularly of debt securities, may contain some onerous provisions such as restrictions on later financing, which could be eliminated by floating a new issue.

Of course, in view of the costs inherent in a refinancing, the advantages of the new issue must be reasonably significant in order to make a change worthwhile. Nevertheless, the ability to adjust the corporation's capital structure to varying economic conditions is considered an extremely important adjunct of fund raising. Accordingly, a corporation is normally willing to pay a premium for the right to exercise a redemption privilege. This is usually accomplished by setting the redemption, or "call", price at a figure somewhat in excess of the original issue price of the securities. Sometimes, particularly when the prospective lender has substantial bargaining power, as in the case of a large insurance company, the borrower may be required to forego the redemption privilege for some specified period after issue, if not entirely.

Since the redemption of outstanding debt securities constitutes the discharge of a liability, there are no limitations as to permissible sources for the funds. Redemption of preferred stock, on the other hand, does constitute a repurchase of its own stock by a corporation, which is normally permitted only out of surplus. But there is an important distinguishing feature of redeemable stock, in that the prospect of such repurchase is recognized and publicized from the very outset, which serves to forewarn third parties that this investment may not be a permanent one. Accordingly, under most corporation statutes redemption of redeemable stock constitutes an exception to the normal restrictions on repurchase and instead may be charged against the stated capital attributable to the shares being redeemed. E. g., MBA §§ 5, 60. However, if the redemption price includes a call premium, or accrued but unpaid dividends, these components may stand on a different footing and may have to be covered by surplus. E. g., Del.Corp.Law § 243; contra, MBA §§ 60, 61.

In the absence of provision to the contrary, the question whether and when to exercise the power to redeem would normally be a matter for the board of directors. Here is another point where difficulty can be caused by laying too great stress on the equity character of preferred stock, and not enough on its practical similarity to debt. In the case of straightforward debt securities, it would scarcely be suggested that in deciding whether to redeem the directors should take account of the interests of the holders of the debt securities. But when it comes to redeeming preferred stock, there is a danger that a need to consider the best interests of the preferred stock may be inferred from various abstract legal principles, such as that directors must act for the benefit of all the stockholders, and directors may not favor one class of stockholders over another. However, the fact is that the very purpose of including a redemption provision is to permit the junior stockholders to eject the redeemable seniors from the enterprise when it suits the convenience of the juniors. Viewed in this light, surely it should be no objection to a redemption that the directors own, or are controlled by the owners of, a majority of the junior shares, despite the contrary intimation in the classic case of Zahn v. Transamerica Corporation, 162 F.2d 36 (3d Cir. 1947).[21] On another branch of the same litigation, the Kentucky court, in Taylor v. Axton-Fisher Tobacco Company, 295 Ky. 226, 173 S.W.2d 377 (1943), seemed to show greater awareness that the redemption provision was primarily for the benefit of the junior stockholders, when it decided that a redemption call once made could not be altered or revoked by the directors against the will of the junior stockholders. Even there, however, the court seemed to concede that directors could originally exercise the redemption privilege by making it optional with the holders of the redeemable stock, which certainly seems like a doubtful construction of a provision designed for the benefit of the junior stockholders.

On the other hand, substantial holdings of the redeemable stock on the part of the directors would seem to create a significant conflict of interest with regard to exercise of the redemption privilege. Obviously, a redemption which is beneficial to the redeemable stock is likely to be a disservice to the junior securities, and vice versa. Thus it would appear that the court in Stieglitz v. Electrol, Inc., 60 N.Y.S.2d 490 (Sup.Ct.,Sp.T. 1945), gave too short shrift to the argument by a junior shareholder that a redemption authorized by a three to two vote of the directors should be enjoined because two of the three directors who voted in favor were holders of the redeemable stock. In denying relief the court seemed to rely simply on the general proposition that in the absence of fraud or the like, directors were not precluded from voting on questions involving stock just because they were stockholders; the court did not appear to even notice the special inter-class conflict involved.

A number of redemption problems call for special care in planning and drafting. One is the manner of selecting the stock to be redeemed when less than the entire class is called. In order to prevent possible discrimination within the class, it is common today to provide for redemption "pro rata", or "by lot", so as to insure equal treatment of members of the same class.

Another area of concern relates to the period during which the redemption privilege may be exercised, if it is not available immediately after the issuance of the stock and/or it does not run forever. An object lesson in careless drafting is provided by Thompson v. Fairleigh, 300 Ky. 144, 187 S.W.2d 812 (1945), where the charter provided that the preferred stock could be retired at a stipulated price "at the end of five years from

---

21. The actual result in that case seems clearly sound, however, i. e., that since the redeemable stock was also convertible, the directors should have given the stockholders sufficient information to enable them to make a sound decision on whether to convert instead of surrendering their stock for redemption.

July 1, 1925". Twelve years later, when the preferred stock was worth much more than the redemption price, the corporation's effort to redeem the preferred failed. Relying upon the rule that "where one party is given the right of election he is bound to exercise it promptly and may not delay in order to speculate on future contingencies", the court decided that the right must be exercised within a reasonable time, and that twelve years was not reasonable.

In addition, some decision should be made and clearly spelled out as to the status of the holders of redeemable stock at various stages in the redemption process, with particular regard to such matters as the right to vote or receive dividends during the period between the call and the date fixed for surrender of the securities. Similarly, if the redeemable stock is also convertible, the precise relationship between the exercise of the redemption privilege and the option to convert should be clearly indicated.

F. SINKING FUNDS

An increasingly common alternative to a right of redemption is a provision for systematic retirement of outstanding bonds (and not infrequently preferred stock as well). This is often accomplished by creating a sinking fund, that is by setting aside a sum each year to be used to purchase, or "sink", the issue in question. (Serial bonds, i. e., debt with serial maturities, is a common alternative for periodically reducing an issue of debt securities, but of course this method is not available for preferred stock.) Sinking funds for bonds are typically paid over to a trustee, who may be the trustee under the bond indenture; for preferred stock, the funds are usually handled directly by the company. The funds are generally used to buy in the securities involved, usually in the open market, although the securities are normally made redeemable lest exclusive reliance on open market purchases drive the market price too high.[22] Sinking funds may thus achieve two purposes: first, to reduce the amount of the stock or bonds outstanding and thereby improve the position of the remainder of the issue; and second, to support the market for the issue.

The need for a sinking fund may vary with the industry involved. Where technological change occupies a significant role, affecting not only plant and equipment but also the line of products manufactured, the use of a sinking fund to periodically reduce the claim (or interest) of the senior security holders seems wise from both the point of view of the company and that of the investors. Similarly, if the company is engaged in mining or other exploitation of wasting assets, a sinking fund may afford essential protection by reducing the outstanding issue as the value of the property shrinks.

22. Open market purchases of stock on which there are accrued but unpaid cumulative dividends may pose some special problems of fairness, since there could be a temptation to pass dividends in order to depress the market price of the stock, as well as to conserve the cash with which to make the acquisition. See generally, Buxbaum, Preferred Stock—Law and Draftsmanship, 42 Cal.L.Rev. 243, 267–268 (1954).

Among the questions posed in the preparation of a sinking fund provision is that of the appropriate accounting "source" of the funds, that is, the account to which they are to be charged. As a strictly legal matter, it would seem that any source eligible for reacquisition of the securities should be available for the sinking fund. Obviously, there would be no problem with regard to debt securities; for preferred stock, on the other hand, there would be the question of whether sinking funds would be limited to surplus, or could be "backed" by stated capital, as in the case of straight redemption. However, in practice sinking-fund contributions are often tied to annual net earnings, which of course introduces quite different, although equally troublesome, problems.

As to remedies for failure to perform a sinking fund agreement, in the case of debt securities it should surely constitute a default under the accompanying indenture, although the trustee might be slow to invoke foreclosure or other default remedies on this account alone. On the preferred stock side, a mandatory injunction would seem to be about the only suitable remedy, and presumably even an individual stockholder would have standing to maintain such an action.

G. CONTRACTUAL RESTRICTIONS

Senior security contracts often include special provisions restricting the conduct of the corporation in various areas. While theoretically the permissible scope of such contractual restrictions is virtually unlimited, in practice they tend to be designed principally to maintain adequate working capital and a cushion for senior securities. In other words, the emphasis is primarily on minimizing the flow of cash out of the corporation in the form of dividends, other distributions to junior stockholders, excessive salaries or the like.

BUXBAUM, PREFERRED STOCK—LAW AND DRAFTSMANSHIP [23]
42 Cal.L.Rev. 255–257 (1954).

The basic protection of shareholders against destruction of their proprietary interest is today provided by the financial restrictions found in nearly all articles. The statutory and decisional law concerning these provisions is nonexistent; for they are hyper-legal, offering protection beyond the law's minima. Only construction questions can arise here and generally careful draftsmanship has avoided even these.

Restrictions against dividends to junior stock fall into a few major categories. Some contracts require the existence of a certain amount of total assets, whether in the aggregate or per share. Others require the retention of a certain amount of working capital after the dividend is paid.

23. Reprinted by permission of the California Law Review. Footnotes omitted.

A third group require a certain surplus position for payment of dividends, which will protect against stock dividends. They are all expressed negatively. A covenant to maintain set margins is a practical absurdity and would give shareholders the right to litigate over their company's financial status at a level far below the usual "breaking point" of equitable insolvency. The most common provision forbids a dividend declaration unless after the putative payment the aggregate dividend payments on all stock from, say, January 1, 1950 are still less than the sum of $X plus the consolidated net income earned since January 1, 1950 plus proceeds from the sale of junior stock since that date (or net proceeds, after cost of junior stock acquired in any way). The same equation is often expressed so that the consolidated net income (with or without the $X) is to exceed all payments on all stock plus the cost of all junior shares acquired (or usually, net cost after proceeds from the sale of junior shares).

Careless drafting may indirectly destroy the effect of the safeguard. If instead of "all payments to all stock" the phrase read merely "dividend distributions," sinking fund payments or nondividend distributions could be made without entering into the equation, thus destroying the provision's value. Or if the provision were that all payments should not exceed the sum of dated consolidated net income *plus proceeds from the sale of junior stock*, common stock could be refunded by an acquisition and reissue, bloating the amount legally available for junior dividends (by raising the limit which these dividends may not exceed) though the clause intends to count only net proceeds after cost of acquiring any junior stock. Though open to abuse, this latter aberration is still common.

Certain legitimate exceptions may of course be made in these clauses. Thus when the dividend restriction reads "all payments to all junior stock shall not exceed . . ." etc., it normally exempts refunding—the acquisition of junior shares out of proceeds from the sale of new junior shares. Otherwise these payments to acquire the old shares are "payments on junior stock" which reduce the permissible dividend payments. Further, dividends payable in junior stock are usually exempt from the restriction "all payments. . . ." However, if dated consolidated surplus, not net income, is used in the equation, payments may in effect be limited anyway—if the applicable state law requires capitalization of earned surplus upon the declaration of stock dividends.

A more direct provision implementing the Delaware type of statute requires that after the putative payment consolidated net current assets equal 150% of this and all prior stock's liquidation preferences. Several variations of this type of protection are used: after the dividend, consolidated net current assets are to remain above $X, or (rarely, since it is little used) above consolidated funded debt; or that consolidated net tangible assets remain 200% of consolidated fixed liabilities plus preferred stock (at par). Except for the size of the protection these are all of the same sort. Often the clause provides that assets are to equal a multiple of several items, which usually intends a multiple of the aggregate of these items. A sentence creating the latter in the disjunctive, as "assets to be two times fixed liabilities, plus preferred stock" is therefore, whether intended or not, an evasion of the supposed protection. A simple yet proper protection which does not run this risk is often found, expressed absolutely or relatively: after the putative payment capital and surplus shall remain above $X; or that the year's total dividend and other distributions be no more than one-third of that year's net income. Unless the latter were construed as a general expression of dividend policy, requiring that so much be paid out, these are effective means of protecting the preferred's share in the corporate assets.

As to all these clauses, it is vital that all payments, distributions, acquisitions, etc., include those of subsidiaries; otherwise the provisions can be totally avoided. Also many of these clauses are based on the dollar ratio between certain items—net current assets, tangible assets, etc.—which are vague until defined. The definition is a contractual matter detailed in most articles. Thus defective definitions of these concepts might weaken the supposed protection. If the articles are silent as to meaning, the more or less standard accounting interpretations would govern in litigation. It is because the courts honor any contractual definition, no matter how unusual accounting-wise, that exact definition becomes important.

Chapter 3
DIVIDENDS AND OTHER CORPORATE DISTRIBUTIONS

Introduction

From the very beginning, state corporation statutes have imposed limitations on dividends and other distributions to stockholders. These limitations were generally framed, directly or indirectly, in terms of the par value of the stock issued to stockholders, which was assumed to be a measure of the minimum original investment by the stockholders in the enterprise. The theory was that this amount, often referred to as "legal capital", ought not to be voluntarily returned to the stockholders because creditors of the corporation, who could look only to the corporate assets and not to the individual liability of the stockholders, should be able to rely upon such legal capital as a safety margin for the payment of their claims.

As the material in the next few sections of this chapter illustrates, much of the historic development in the area of corporate finance has been directed to the interpretation and application of this "legal capital" concept. For example, the primary issue in the classic "watered stock" cases was whether the issuance of stock of a specified par value did in fact constitute a representation that an amount equal thereto had been invested by the stockholders. In the dividend cases, the central issue has usually involved some aspect of the "measuring rod" function of legal capital, in connection with a limitation of dividends to the excess of net assets over legal capital. And of course the reduction-of-capital cases raise the question of how and when this "legal capital" measuring rod can be reduced.

SECTION 1. LIQUIDATION PREFERENCES AND STATED CAPITAL

Today, most modern corporation statutes provide specifically as to how legal capital, now commonly called "stated capital", is to be determined under various circumstances. E. g., MBA § 19. The effect of such statutes is to give the parties very broad power to fix the stated capital figure, either by setting the par value, in the case of par stock, or, as to no-par stock, by allocating a portion of the consideration received to capital surplus. However, the statutes often impose some limitations with regard to the stated capital attributable to stock having a liquidation preference. Thus MBA § 19 limits the amount which may be allocated to capital surplus in the case of no-par preferred stock with a liquidation preference to the excess, if any, of the consideration received for such stock over the liquidation preference. In the same vein, § 63 imposes restrictions upon the reduction of the stated capital attributable to no-par stock whenever the corporation has any stock with a liquidation preference outstanding.

These provisions in the Model Act dealing expressly with certain aspects of the relationship between the liquidation preference of no-par stock and the stated capital attributable to such stock suggest some other questions about that relationship which the Act does not expressly resolve. Thus it might be asked whether the Act impliedly forbids the issuance of no-par stock with a liquidation preference for a consideration less than the amount of the preference. A less extreme possibility is that the Act by implication requires that the stated capital attributable to such stock be fixed at not less than the amount of the liquidation preference, regardless of the amount of consideration for which the stock was issued. If either of these limitations are to be found, obviously it must be by inference from the express provisions in the Act, such as §§ 19, 41(d) and 63; and before drawing such inferences it would be important to compare the objectives and beneficiaries of such proposed implied limitations with the objectives and beneficiaries of the express provisions. There is also the question of where low-par stock with a substantial gap between par value and liquidation preference stands in the light of a provision like MBA § 19 which deals expressly only with no-par stock so far as allocation to capital surplus is concerned. The following materials may shed some light on these various issues:

KATZ, ACCOUNTING PROBLEMS IN CORPORATE DISTRIBUTIONS [1]

89 U. of Pa.L.Rev. 776–778 (1941).

One problem in accounting for preferred shares furnishes another illustration of the influence of accounting requirements in the reform of corporate practices. This is the problem of preferred shares with a par or stated value less than the amount of the preference on involuntary liquidation. This type of preferred shares has been referred to by Commissioner Healy as "that excrescence, that abomination which charter-mongering states — corporation 'Reno's' . . ., have put upon us . . . in their 'liberalization' of corporation

---

1. Reprinted by permission of the University of Pennsylvania Law Review. Most of the footnotes omitted.

laws." Commissioner Healy gave as an example shares sold for $50, having a par value of $40, and entitled to an annual dividend of $3 and to a $50 preference on liquidation. In such a case, the shares are almost invariably carried on the balance sheet at the par value of $40 with the $10 additional consideration shown as capital surplus.

A more extreme case was presented by the financing of Dodge Brothers, Inc., in 1925. Here preference shares without par value were set up on the balance sheet at $1 per share despite a liquidation preference of $105 per share and a $7 annual dividend rate. It was with respect to this balance sheet that Professor Ripley used the terms "prestidigitation", "acrobatics", and "accounting monstrosity".

The SEC now requires that a spot-light be focused upon such acrobatics. The following information with respect to preferred shares must be set forth in balance sheets or in explanatory notes:

> "Preferences on involuntary liquidation, if other than the par or stated value, shall be shown. When the excess involved is significant there shall be shown (i) the difference between the aggregate preference on involuntary liquidation and the aggregate par or stated value; (ii) a statement that this difference, plus any arrears in dividends, exceeds the sum of the par or stated value of the junior capital shares and the surplus, if such is the case; and (iii) a statement as to the existence, or absence, of any restrictions upon surplus growing out of the fact that upon involuntary liquidation the preference of the preferred shares exceeds its par or stated value." [52]

In recent security issues, the statement made in most prospectuses, pursuant to the requirement of clause (iii), is that "there are no restrictions upon surplus growing out of the fact that upon involuntary liquidation the preference of the preferred shares exceeds its par or stated value." The chief accountant of the Commission has suggested that the requirement of a statement of such restrictions on surplus arose "out of the feeling that, if surplus had been contributed by the preferred shareholders,[53] a court of equity might enjoin dividends, at least to common shareholders, which reduced such surplus below an amount necessary to satisfy the liquidating value of the preferred shares . . . ." It is possible, however, that restrictions on surplus might exist in other situations; it is possible that a dividend on common shares might be enjoined in any case where the difference between the aggregate liquidation preferences and the aggregate stated value of the preferred shares exceeds the total stated value of the common shares. . . .

---

52. SEC Regulation S–X [Rule 3.19(d)(3)] . . . .

53. In some states part of the consideration received for preferred shares may be set up as paid-in surplus only if the amount allocated to stated capital is equal to the aggregate liquidation preference. . . .

COMMONWEALTH & SOUTHERN CORPORATION, 13 S.E.C. 84 (1943), involved a Delaware corporation subject to the jurisdiction of the Commission as a registered public utility holding company. Since the corporation had shown a profit for the current year, the management wanted to pay a dividend on the preferred stock, but they were concerned about the possible impact of the substantial diminution in the value of the company's investments in its various subsidiaries. The management was prepared to rely upon the "nimble dividend" provision of Del.Corp.Law § 170, which permits dividends out of current net profits even if the corporation has an overall deficit unless "the capital of the corporation . . . shall have been diminished by depreciation in the value of its property, or by losses, or otherwise, to an amount less than the aggregate amount of the capital represented by the issued and outstanding stock of all classes having a preference upon the distribution of assets." However, the management was concerned that some dissident stockholder might contend that the diminution in the value of the assets of the corporation had reached so far that this proviso was in operation. Accordingly, the company sought the permission of the Commission to reduce the capital of its 1,500,000 shares of preferred stock from $100 a share to $10 a share, basing its request upon advice of counsel that any question as to the legality of the dividends under Delaware law would be avoided by such a reduction. No change was proposed in the cumulative dividend rate of $6 per share, the redemption price of $110, or the liquidation preference of $110 per share plus accrued dividends (which at that time amounted to about $25 per share). The company was prepared to restrict the resulting capital surplus of $135,000,000 so that it could not be used for the payment of dividends on, or repurchase of, common stock. It was also agreed that no use would be made of the capital surplus which would reduce it to an amount less than $90 per share of preferred stock, and that there would be no change in these restrictions without the approval of 60% of the preferred stock.

In denying the company's application for approval of the proposed reduction, the Commission expressed doubt that the reduction would validate the proposed dividend. After pointing out that the phrase "capital represented by" the preferred stock in the Delaware statute had not been construed by the Delaware courts, the Commission continued as follows:

> Counsel employed by the company testified before us that in his opinion the phrase means the stated or par value of the preferred. The legislative history of the Section affords support to this view.[2] The argument for the other view

---

2. [Ed. note] The legislative history of Del. § 170 is rather more forceful than might be inferred from this mild comment. Prior to its amendment in 1929 the quoted proviso was in terms of "the aggregate amount to which the holders of . . . stock of all classes having a preference upon the

runs as follows. The stock has a liquidating preference of $100, a redemption value of $110, and a dividend rate of $6 per share. The indications are that it actually contributed capital to the corporation at the rate of $100 per share. It is unrealistic to say that the question whether the capital represented by this stock is impaired should be judged on the basis of $10 per share. Is the capital represented by these shares $100 or $10? The least significant of all the figures mentioned is the $10. It has no relation to the liquidation value, the redemption value, the dividend rate, or the capital contributed—it represents nothing but a lawyer's inventiveness. If the real purpose of the Delaware statute is to protect the preferred capital, actually contributed, from being dissipated in the form of dividends, the construction given the statute by the counsel called by the management will accomplish the directly opposite result.

The Commission disapproved its earlier opinion in United Corporation, 11 S.E.C. 67 (1942), where a Delaware holding company was permitted to reduce the stated value of its no-par preference stock from $50 to $5 per share, while the assets preference of the redemption price remained at $50.

CALIFORNIA CORPORATIONS CODE

§ 1900. **Requirement of stated capital; computation; agreed consideration defined.** Every stock corporation shall have a stated capital which shall be an amount made up of the sum of the following amounts, less the amounts of any reductions of stated capital made as authorized by this division:

(a) The aggregate par value of par value shares which have been issued from time to time . . . .

(b) The aggregate amount specified in dollars of the agreed consideration received or to be received by the corporation for all shares without par value which have been issued from time to time, except any portion of the consideration for such shares without liquidation preference which has been expressly designated by the board of directors upon or prior to issue as paid-in surplus. In the absence of such designation by the board of directors, the entire amount of the consideration for shares without par value shall be credited to stated capital. The entire amount of the agreed consideration for shares

distribution of assets would be entitled upon such distribution". Comparison of that language with the present wording makes it clear that the draftsman recognized the possibility of a difference between the stated capital attributable to preferred stock and its liquidation preference, and wanted to be sure that the former rather than the latter controlled.

without par value having a liquidation preference shall be credited to stated capital.[3]

(c) Such amounts as are transferred from surplus to stated capital upon declaration of a share dividend or by resolution of the board of directors.

* * *

§ 1506. **Transfer from surplus to stated capital; amount transferred; notice to shareholders.** If a dividend declared in shares having a par value is paid, the aggregate par value of the shares shall be deducted from the surplus from which the dividend is declared and added to stated capital.

If a dividend declared in shares without par value is paid, there shall be deducted from the surplus from which the dividend is declared and added to stated capital the aggregate involuntary liquidation preferences of any preferred shares included in the dividend, and an amount per common share (or share having no liquidation preference) included in the dividend equal to the per-share stated capital attributable immediately preceding the payment of the dividend to the outstanding shares of the class to which the shares included in the dividend belong, or if no such shares are outstanding, then there shall be deducted from the surplus from which the dividend is declared and added to stated capital the estimated fair value of the shares issued as a dividend, as determined and stated by resolution of the board of directors.

Upon the payment of a share dividend from earned surplus, an amount equal to the excess, if any, of the estimated fair value of the shares issued as a dividend, as determined and stated by resolution of the board of directors, over the amount required to be transferred to stated capital in accordance with this section may be deducted from earned surplus and added to paid-in surplus.

---

3. Ballantine and Sterling, California Corporation Laws (4th ed. 1962) 329–330 contains the following observation with regard to this last sentence of § 1900(b):

> The directors cannot now designate or credit as paid-in surplus any portion of the consideration for shares without par value having a liquidation preference, although under the former law the excess of any consideration received over the lowest aggregate liquidation price of such shares could have been so credited. In view of the fact that it is only rarely that a corporation can sell its preferred shares without par value for a consideration in excess of the liquidation preference of such shares, it seemed better to provide in the statute that no part of the consideration received for preferred shares without par value shall be credited to paid-in surplus.

OPINION NO. 473 OF THE ATTORNEY GENERAL OF ILLINOIS

1933 A.G.O. 618.

Hon. Edward J. Hughes, Secretary of State:

Dear Sir:

I have your letter of August 29, 1933, enclosing letter from De-Frees, Buckingham, Jones & Hoffman of Chicago, Illinois, in which you desire my opinion as to the construction of Sections 17, 19 and 60 of the Business Corporation Act, particularly as to whether the above sections considered as a whole establish the fact that it was the intent of the Legislature to establish as a principle the public policy in this state that the retirement and redemption price of stock having a preferential right cannot exceed the stated capital, or if the Legislature intended that this principle should apply only to decreases made in stated capital after the corporation had commenced functioning under its charter, and not to provisions made at the time of the organization of the corporation in the first instance; the particular question involved in the instant case being whether or not shares of no par value preferred stock may be issued in an amount less than the involuntary liquidating price of such shares.

These questions require a consideration of Sections 17, 19 and 60 of the Business Corporation Act, the pertinent provisions of said Sections being as follows:

"Sec. 17. Shares without par value may be issued for such consideration as may be fixed from time to time by the board of directors unless the articles of incorporation reserve to the shareholders the right to fix the consideration."

"Sec. 19. **Determination of amount of stated capital.** A corporation may determine that only a part of the consideration for which its shares may be issued, from time to time, shall be stated capital *provided* that in the event of any such determination:

* * *

"(b) If the shares issued shall consist wholly of shares without par value, all of which shares have a preferential right in the assets of the corporation in the event of its involuntary liquidation, then the stated capital represented by such shares shall be not less than the aggregate preferential amount payable upon such shares in the event of involuntary liquidation.

"(c) If the shares issued consist wholly of shares without par value, and none of such shares has a preferential right in the assets of the corporation in the event of its involuntary liquidation, then the stated capital represented by such shares shall be the total consideration received therefor less such part thereof as may be allocated to paid-in surplus. . . . "

* * *

"Sec. 60. **Regulations governing reductions of stated capital and distribution of assets.** No reduction of stated capital shall be made which would reduce the stated capital represented by shares without par value having a preferential right in the assets of the corporation in the event of involuntary liquidation to an amount less than the aggregate preferential amount provided from time to time to be payable upon such shares in the event of such involuntary liquidation.

"Paid-in surplus, whether created by reduction of stated capital or otherwise, may be distributed in cash or in kind to the shareholders entitled thereto, subject to the following additional restrictions and in the following manner:

"(a) No such distribution shall be made to any class of shareholders unless all cumulative dividends accrued on preferred or special classes of shares entitled to preferential dividends shall have been fully paid.

"(b) No such distribution shall be made to any class of shareholders which will reduce the remaining net assets below the aggregate preferential amount payable in event of voluntary liquidation to the holders of shares having preferential rights to the assets of the corporation in the event of liquidation."

I understand that a specific case has arisen in which it is desirable that a new corporation be formed to take over certain bonded indebtedness of an existing corporation and that the general creditors are willing to accept preferred stock in lieu of their claims, provided that in case of any voluntary or involuntary liquidation of the new corporation, such creditors shall receive the face amount of their present claims; that it is impossible to issue preferred no-par stock for the full amount of the claims of the general creditors, as the stated capital of the corporation would then exceed the value of the property of the corporation.

It was the evident intention of the Legislature, as indicated by the express language of Section 60, to provide that the rights of shares having preferential rights in the assets of the corporation be protected in the event of liquidation, before any amount be paid to the stockholders not enjoying such preferential rights. This protection was expressly extended such preferential stock in paragraph (b) of said Section, which prohibits the payment of dividends out of paid-in surplus to the detriment of such preferred stock.

Section 19 provides that the corporation *may* determine that only a part of the consideration for which its shares may be issued shall be stated capital, *provided that in the event of any such determination,* if the shares consist wholly of shares without par value having preferential right in the assets of the corporation, in the event of involuntary liquidation, then the stated capital represented by such shares shall be not less than the aggregate preferential amount payable upon such shares in such event.

It was the apparent intention of the Legislature that the use of the word "may" does not make it mandatory upon the corporation to make any allocation to paid-in surplus; and this construction is further borne out by the proviso "provided that in the event of any such determination" that such shares (in such event) shall be in an amount not less than the aggregate preferential amount payable on the same in the event of such involuntary liquidation.

It is my opinion that the corporation is not required to make such allocation (to paid-in surplus) and that in default of such affirmative action in making such allocation to paid-in surplus, the entire consideration received in whatever amount it may be, remains and is stated capital and the requirement of paragraph b of Section 19 applies only in the event that the corporation determines that only a part of the consideration for which its shares are issued be stated capital;

. . . .

The provisions of all the sections considered indicate that it was the intention of the Legislature to protect the holders of stock enjoying preferential rights in the assets of the corporation in the event of involuntary liquidation, from any diminution of value of their stock by reducing the stated capital represented by their shares to an amount less than the involuntary liquidating value.

It also was the evident intention of the Legislature to limit the redemption of stated capital after the corporation had commenced functioning under its charter to an amount which would not jeopardize the rights of stock having the preferential right. This provision is intended to protect such class of stock in cases where the corporation already in existence and having greater assets than the involuntary liquidating value of its no par value preferred stock might otherwise attempt to reduce the aggregate stated capital represented by such shares below the involuntary liquidating value of the same and thus reduce the assets relied upon for the protection of such shares in the event of such liquidation. This procedure is prevented on account of the fact that stock in the hands of the public, entitled to preferred rights, may be adversely affected by diminishing its value by action of the board of directors. In the instant case, the rights of the preferred stockholders are expressly protected, both by contract and by provisions in the certificates issued, by providing therein that in the event of involuntary liquidation, such stock be accorded the preference, in order and amount to which it is entitled relative to the common stock not entitled to such preferential rights and, accordingly, I can see no objection to the plan suggested.[4]

---

4. In Opinion No. 727, 1934 A.G.O. 397, the question presented to the Attorney General of Illinois was whether, for the purpose of computing franchise taxes based on "stated capital", § 19 (b) of the Illinois Act constituted a definition of stated capital attributable to no-par shares with a liquidation preference which controlled the general definition in § 2(k) [the counterpart of MBA § 2(j)]. The Attorney General ruled that § 2(k) governed, stating that § 19(b) "was not intended as a definition of the term 'Stated

HILLS, MODEL CORPORATION ACT [5]
48 Harv.L.Rev. 1355–1356, 1363–1364 (1935).

26. Shares having a distribution preference . . . including shares with and without par value, [should be] . . . treated alike and covered by the same provision. Existing statutes treat shares with par value separately from shares without par value, but there is no real basis for a difference, since shares without par value may or may not have a preference to assets comparable with a par value. . . .

. . . Shares without par value which have a distribution preference should not be issued for a consideration less than the highest amount of distribution preference thereof. The majority of existing statutes allow the board of directors to issue shares without par value for an unlimited amount of consideration, greater or less than their preference to assets in the event of liquidation or dissolution. That privilege has been abused to the detriment of equity shares and shares having junior preferences by the issuance of shares for less than their distribution preference. Some recent corporation laws place a minimum limit on the amount of consideration which must be credited to stated capital, but none assure the attainment of a consideration equal to the minimum of stated capital to be derived therefrom. . . . A provision requiring receipt of consideration of a value not less than the highest amount of distribution preference cannot be fairly criticized. . . .

* * *

27. Shares subject to redemption may be redeemed from stated capital. It follows that the amount of consideration received on the issuance of redeemable shares, and the amount thereof credited to stated capital, must be not less than the highest redemption price. It is not uncommon to have different redemption prices for the same shares graduated according to successive periods of time. The highest price at any time payable should be the minimum amount of consideration, unless the policy of paying a fair premium for exercising the privilege of redemption is to be recognized as a reasonable business objective, ...

* * *

46. Precedent decrees the capitalization of surplus upon the payment of a share dividend from shares previously unissued. The

---

Capital', but was meant as a protection to the holders of shares without par value who purchased the same upon the assumption that it had a definite involuntary liquidation price, which they were entitled to believe would be held for their protection without depletion."

5. Copyright (c), Harvard Law Review Association, 1935. Reprinted by permission. Hills' Model Act is not related in any way to the MBA.

writer has not followed that precedent with respect to shares without a distribution preference. Under existing corporation laws, the payment of shares having a par value increases stated capital by the aggregate par value of the shares issued, but the payment of shares without par value increases stated capital by an undetermined amount to be fixed by a variety of methods. The writer has again classified all shares as shares with or without a distribution preference. Shares with a distribution preference should be capitalized in an amount not less than their preference, but shares without a distribution preference need not be capitalized unless the board of directors so determines.

* * *

Shares having a distribution preference and shares subject to redemption (with or without par value) should be capitalized at the highest amount to which they may become entitled as they forthwith acquire a preference or an opportunity to be redeemed out of stated capital. On the other hand, there is no sound reason for requiring the capitalization of surplus on the payment of a dividend of shares not entitled to a distribution preference and not subject to redemption. Such shares, whether paid to shareholders of the same or a different class, represent a further subdivision of net assets in excess of all preferences. If paid to shareholders of the same class, as in the great majority of cases, a dividend of such shares is no more than a subdivision of issued shares and the equity represented thereby. The board of directors has authority at any time to transfer all or a part of surplus to stated capital and can do so in conjunction with a share dividend if it so elects.

SECTION 2. THE FUND AVAILABLE FOR DIVIDENDS

A. IN GENERAL

HACKNEY, THE FINANCIAL PROVISIONS OF THE MODEL BUSINESS CORPORATION ACT *

70 Harv.L.Rev. 1358, 1363–1375, 1389–1392 (1957).

I. DIVIDENDS AND EARNED SURPLUS

The heart of the Model Act is its limitation of ordinary dividends and purchases of treasury shares to unreserved and unrestricted earned surplus.[3] . . .

---

* Copyright (c), Harvard Law Review Association, 1957. Reprinted by permission. Portions of the text and most of the footnotes omitted.

3. . . . The term "unreserved" is designed to exclude the reserves of earned surplus which under § 64 the board may create for any proper pur-

Concepts of Capital and Income.—Historically there have been, other than an insolvency test, two methods of defining the funds available for dividends: one which "prohibits distributions except from a surplus as normally computed on a corporate *balance sheet*," and one which "prohibits payments except from current or past *net profits* most frequently determined by a corporate profit and loss statement."

The question immediately arises: What is the difference in principle between a profits (or income) test and a balance-sheet test for dividends? The answer, one essentially of interpretation and not of computation,[50] lies in the difference between the term "capital," which to the economist and accountant is a concept roughly dichotomous to income, and the term "legal capital," which to the lawyer is a concept specifically defined by statute and having no necessary relationship to income. The economist's concept lies behind the development of the profits or income test, while the concept of "legal capital" is reflected in the balance-sheet test. Conceptually, capital can be thought of as the capital assets themselves, or their value at a specified time. Income then consists of all other assets—those generated by, and existing in addition to, the capital assets. On the other hand, capital loses its dichotomous relationship with income when stated capital is defined by statute as the dollar value of assets required to be provided and retained for the protection of creditors—as though all assets (capital or otherwise) are to be thrown into a grain bin and dividends therefrom to be prohibited when the top surface of the assets falls below a certain level. The classic dividend questions illustrate the problems arising from these different approaches.

If assets equal to balance-sheet capital were not actually provided —if the stock was watered or issued at a discount—can the fruits of the enterprise, its earnings, nevertheless be deemed available for dividends as income? If assets were contributed to the corporation in excess of the required capital, must they be deemed not available for dividends as not being income? If the assets constituting the economic or contributed capital of the corporation appreciate in value, has there been income or just change in the value of the corporation's capital— whether or not realized—with no effect on income? If the corporation's economic or contributed capital has been impaired, or dimin-

poses and may abolish under appropriate circumstances. . . . The term "unrestricted" is designed to exclude the restrictions on surplus by § 5 when a corporation acquires its own shares. . . .

50. By the nature of double-entry bookkeeping, accounting for income earned during past years will have a direct effect upon balance-sheet surplus, and, conversely, accounting practices followed in preparing the balance sheet will be reflected in the income statement. . . . Thus the real question in contrasting the computation of income and of balance-sheet surplus as dividend sources lies in the problem whether asset values in a balance-sheet test are to be determined solely according to the conventions of accounting which are today aimed principally at accurately reflecting income and may distort the balance-sheet-asset values as a consequence. . . .

ished through losses, or has lessened in value, or has been sold at a loss, but the earning capacity of the capital remains unaltered, are all the fruits thereof still income, or can there be no income until the capital impairment has been repaired by the retention of earnings?

In the nineteenth century, when statutory or legal capital was not specifically defined by statute, the same questions arose under both the capital-impairment and the profits forms of statute. The introduction of no-par-stock statutes in the 1910's created further complications which brought to the fore the possibility of dividends clearly not from earnings yet still not from legal capital.

The policy question whether huge quantities of paid-in surplus should be available for dividends led to the more basic question whether mere impairment of legal capital was a satisfactory test on which to base the legality of dividends. A capital-impairment test may have seemed satisfactory when the principal if not the sole objective of dividend regulation was to maintain a cushion against insolvency for the benefit of creditors. However, following the late 1920's the objectives of dividend regulation were broadened to include the protection of the shareholders against a diminution of their actual investment, the protection of different classes of shareholders against each other, the prevention of inferences misleading to existing shareholders or to potential investors or creditors which might result from unjustifiable dividends, and even the maintenance of the financial soundness of large business corporations in the interest of their employees and customers. The correct computation of income and the limitation of dividends to income, it was said, helped to achieve these aims; and with growing pressure from many quarters—the stock exchanges, the accounting societies, the federal government through statutes and administrative regulations—the feeling grew that dividends should ordinarily reflect and be based solely upon earnings.

In attempting to formulate statutory language limiting dividends to income, two distinct approaches were found possible.

One is, like the capital-impairment restriction, a balance-sheet test. The surplus of net assets in excess of capital is obtained and then analyzed and any which is not paid-in or other capital surplus is deemed accumulated income. This test involves the elimination of the economic and accounting concept of capital and the substitution of the statutory concept of stated or legal capital. The second approach attempts to avoid all confusion over the definition of capital by restricting dividends solely to income. The method of computation is to take the balance of all the corporate income statements to date and deduct dividends and other transfers therefrom, with the remainder being earned surplus.

The Model Act definition, it seems, utilizes the aggregate-income-statement method of arriving at earned surplus. It does not use the balance sheet as a source of reference but directs one to take the balance of net profits, income, gains, and losses over a period of time. The Model Act's adoption of the American Institute of Accountants' definition of earned surplus argues strongly that just as accounting today is mainly concerned with the fairest possible presentation of periodic net income, regarding the balance sheet merely as a connecting link between successive income statements, so earned surplus as used in the act is intended to signify a composite income statement from the year of inception and not simply a balance-sheet increase in net assets.

* * *

In 1935, it was reported that thirty-seven states and the District of Columbia had balance-sheet tests for the payment of dividends (with current-earnings alternatives in several). . . . most revisions and codifications of corporation laws since then have followed the same course and imposed balance-sheet tests.[54] In 1941, only one state, Texas, had a pure profits test for dividends. It thus seems that the Model Act dividend source embodies a marked shift from the consistent balance-sheet pattern of American dividend statutes which has been developing for the last fifty years.

The new Model Act provision will not make the computation of funds available for dividends any easier. In jurisdictions which now allow dividends out of any surplus, corporations with long and complex financial histories may find it extremely difficult after the Model Act becomes effective to segregate surplus according to its source. . . .

* * *

Nor is it clear what is meant by the Model Act definition's repetitive terms, "net profits," "income," and "gains and losses." . . . while these terms have had varying meanings in the past there is an increasing tendency to regard the terms "income" and "profit and loss" as coextensive. There is no indication of how the term "gains" might differ in meaning from "profits" or from "income," nor why the word "earnings" is left out of the definition, nor why the word "net" must precede "profits" but not "income," "gains," or "losses." . . .

If to the average accountant the word "income" describes a general concept, not a specific and precise thing, then it is even less clear what it would be construed to mean by the courts. There are many concepts of net income, only one of which is an accounting concept.

---

54. . . . At least three of the four states which had adopted an earned-surplus test prior to the Model Act probably intended to impose a balance-sheet test and not an income test. The draftsmen of the California revision, Cal.Stat.1931, c. 862, § 346, have indicated that they intended the earned-surplus restriction there to be based on a balance-sheet test, more restrictive than plain surplus. See Ballantine & Sterling, California Corporation Laws § 132 at 177 (1949) (earned surplus is the "balance or excess of assets over liabilities including stated capital, such excess being derived from profits or earnings"); . . .

The Model Act has not explicitly referred to accounting practice as the criterion to be followed in the determination of income,[68] and properly so, for it would seem that dividend regulation is no longer the chief or even one of the principal aims of current accounting principles involving the reporting of income. . . .

The Meaning and Computation of Earned Surplus.—The definition of earned surplus employed by the Model Act undoubtedly has value; it certainly describes the figure which appears on a corporate balance sheet beneath capital and capital surplus. However, as a statutory dividend test, it must do more than describe the end product; it must prescribe the method of computation to be used to ascertain that figure. Tested against some of the standard dividend problems which have appeared to date, the Model Act definition answers some clearly and well, while others it either overlooks or seems to answer badly.

The issuance of stock for water or for overvalued assets raises the classic dividend question: What is capital and what is income? The Goodnow v. American Writing Paper Co.[74] answer is that capital is the value of the actual assets received upon issuance of the stock, whether or not watered, and that there can be net profits despite the existence of a capital deficit. There are few other cases in point. If there can be net profits without freezing earnings equal to the original water, then it follows that there might well be earned surplus. It is certainly open to argument that the water gives rise to no loss within the definition, so that all earnings after incorporation constitute available earned surplus.

The converse of the question presented in the Goodnow case is whether capital, defined by Goodnow as the assets received, means all economic or contributed capital so as to include a premium in excess of legal capital. Under the Model Act, such a premium clearly is not earned surplus, but is subject to the restrictions imposed upon capital surplus. An analogous question has been whether dividends could be

---

68. It would have been simple to include a provision to the effect that income was to be computed in accordance with generally accepted (or sound) accounting principles applied on a consistent basis; but this was not done. The source of the Model Act definition of "earned surplus" being the accountants' own definition, . . . the question is raised how far accounting principles will control . . . . The third full paragraph of § 43 of the Model Act provides that directors may safely rely upon the book value of corporate assets and upon financial statements represented to be correct by the proper corporate officer or outside accountants . . . . The meaning of this provision could be that financial statements prepared in accordance with generally accepted accounting principles are to be the ultimate test, but that directors are not to be personally liable if in good faith they rely upon another's incorrect preparation of those financial statements. In the absence of an explicit statutory reference to generally accepted accounting principles, however, it is not believed that a court would limit itself to finding as a fact whether the corporation had followed those principles. The determination of what is meant by "earned surplus," like all problems of statutory construction, would involve essentially a question of law. . . .

74. 73 N.J.Eq. 692, 69 A. 1014 (Ct.Err. & App.1908).

paid from earnings of the current accounting period despite an existing deficit from operating or other losses, the argument being that such dividends would not be out of capital but out of the profits created by such capital as it existed at the beginning of the accounting period in question. In America, under both a capital-impairment restriction and a net-profits limitation, this argument has been rejected, at least in the absence of a showing of alternative statutory sources. The Model Act makes it clear that the fund currently available must be a balance or net figure after taking into consideration past operating losses. However, the status under the Model Act of other types of losses which may by-pass the income statement is not so certain.

* * *

In English law, certain gains and losses accruing from transactions in capital or fixed assets are not deemed to affect profits but are accorded special treatment as accretions to or diminutions of capital and therefore do not affect the funds available for dividends. There seems to be only one case in American law which has adopted this approach, and there is little doubt that it will not be followed. The Model Act definition of earned surplus, by including all gains and losses, makes it clear that gains and losses on disposition of capital assets are an element of earned surplus.

* * *

Capital Surplus.—As defined in the Model Act, surplus has two components—earned and capital. Earned surplus is defined specifically, and capital surplus is all other surplus. Capital surplus, of course, turns out to be principally that portion of contributed capital which is in excess of what is defined as stated capital in section 2(j).[148]

The Model Act follows modern accounting thought in emphasizing two different types of surplus classified according to source. In this view it is apparent that capital surplus resembles capital more than it does surplus, and the act so treats it. As capital (but not stated capital) this capital surplus is surrounded by most of the restrictions which apply to stated capital, while as surplus (but not earned surplus) it is given but few of the qualities of earned surplus. . . .

Capital surplus is not treated in all respects as identical with capital. . . . [I]n a quasi-reorganization, a deficit may be charged off to capital surplus after earned surplus, if any, has been exhausted; with authority from charter provision or shareholder vote and for some purposes with no such authority, purchases and acquisitions of treasury shares may be made from capital surplus; and capital surplus may be capitalized in connection with the distribution of a stock divi-

---

148. Specific provision is made for creation of capital surplus on the issuance of shares, Model Act § 19, including conversions and exchanges, id. § 17; by transfer from earned surplus by action of the board, id. § 64 . . ; and by reduction of stated capital, id. § 64. Any other proper source of capital surplus is automatically provided for because any increase in net assets which is not earned surplus becomes capital surplus.

dend. Capital surplus may also be capitalized in order to help support a conversion or exchange of shares for shares. The Model Act also contains the usual provision allowing the transfer of any surplus to stated capital at any time by resolution of the board.

There would seem to be a serious question under the Model Act whether other uses of or charges to capital surplus are proper in view of the express provisions for the charges just reviewed. Particularly is this true in the light of the second paragraph of section 64 which grants to the board power at any time to transfer earned surplus to capital surplus—apparently it was thought that the board might not otherwise have the power to do so. The problems are usually stated in terms of whether certain charges may be made to capital surplus in spite of the presence of an earned surplus, but the Model Act would raise the additional question whether some of the charges are losses so that they may be applied against capital surplus under section 64 even in the absence of earned surplus. For example, writing off good will, which has undisputed continuing value, to capital surplus has been justified by accountants. Organization and financing expenses and even early interest payments and other costs are sometimes charged to paid-in surplus arising from the sale of stock at a premium. Discounts on some share may be charged to paid-in surplus arising from the issue of other stock. Expenditures incident to reorganization or recapitalization are usually charged against the capital surplus resulting from the reorganization. Premium and call expense on redemption of preferred stock is frequently charged against the paid-in surplus on new stock issued in order to refund the old. Where a write-down of assets is a reversal of an original write-up or a correction of an indefensible original overvaluation of the same assets, good accounting practice seems to allow the charge to be made, notwithstanding an existing earned surplus, against a capital surplus created at the time of the original acquisition of the assets for stock. The paid-in surplus may have been initially created in the light of uncertainties about recorded figures for newly acquired assets and designed as the means of making later adjustment in the figures. Some writers urge that a write-down of fixed assets due to a generally declining price level should be permitted against capital surplus despite the existence of an earned surplus. Furthermore, federal and state administrative agencies sometimes allow or require write-downs of assets to be charged against capital surplus despite the existence of an earned surplus, and it would be unfortunate if state law did not permit such a charge. More important than any specific question is the possibility that the act might be construed to contain a general prohibition against the use of capital surplus for any but the purposes enumerated in the act. Accounting or legal theory as to the propriety of charges to capital surplus is constantly changing, and statutory rigidity might unnecessarily hamper proper developments in the field.

B. UNREALIZED APPRECIATION AS A SOURCE OF DIVIDENDS

1. RANDALL v. BAILEY

The starting point for any consideration of the propriety of dividends from revaluation surplus is the classic case of Randall v. Bailey, 288 N.Y. 280, 43 N.E.2d 43 (1942). In that case, the corporation had written up its shipping terminal facilities to the amount at which the land and buildings were assessed for local property taxes, and dividends had been paid on the basis of the resulting appreciation of more than seven million dollars. In an action by the trustee in bankruptcy to hold directors liable for such dividends, the question presented was succinctly stated by the Court of Appeals as follows: "May unrealized appreciation in value of fixed assets held for use in carrying on a corporate enterprise be taken into consideration by directors in determining whether a corporate surplus exists from which cash dividends may be paid to stockholders?" The applicable statute, which governed the payment of dividends in New York from 1923 to September 1, 1963, (the effective date of the new Business Corporation Law) was § 58 of the Stock Corporation Law:

> No stock corporation shall declare or pay any dividend which shall impair its capital or capital stock, nor while its capital or capital stock is impaired, nor shall any such corporation declare or pay any dividend or make any distribution of assets to any of its stockholders, whether upon a reduction of the number of its shares or of its capital or capital stock, unless the value of its assets remaining after the payment of such dividend, or after such distribution of assets, as the case may be, shall be at least equal to the aggregate amount of its debts and liabilities including capital or capital stock as the case may be.

In holding for the defendants, the trial court first observed that if "the part of the statute containing the words 'unless the value of its assets' etc. is to be read as relating back to the beginning of the section, the lack of merit in plaintiff's contention is apparent." However, the court concluded that "the structure of the statute is such as to make that reading grammatically impossible", which meant that the regular recurring dividends here involved were governed solely by the "capital impairment" test imposed by the first portion of the statute.

The plaintiff pitched his argument primarily on the theme that only realized gains could be taken into account for dividend purposes (notwithstanding the fact that he was contending at the same time that unrealized diminution in the value of assets, here investments in subsidiaries, *did* have to be taken into account). In rejecting this construction of the statute, the trial court concluded that although such an argument might have had force under the "surplus profits" language used in earlier New York statutes, the complete abandonment of that language in favor of the "capital impairment" limitation in § 58 indicated an effort to abolish any limitation based on realization. The test now, said the court, is "whether or not the value of the assets exceeds the debts and the liability to stockholders," for which purpose "all assets must be taken at their actual value." The court then continued as follows:

> I see no cause for alarm over the fact that this view requires directors to make a determination of the value of the assets at each dividend declaration. On the contrary, I think that is exactly what the law always had contemplated that directors should do. That does not mean that the books themselves necessarily must be altered by write-ups or write-downs at each dividend period, or that formal appraisals must be obtained from professional appraisers or even made by the directors themselves. That is obviously impossible in the case of corporations of any considerable size. But it is not impossible nor unfeasible for directors to consider whether the cost of assets continues over a long period of years to reflect their fair value, and the law does require that directors should really direct in the very important matter of really determining at each dividend declaration whether or not the value of the assets is such as to justify a dividend, rather than do what one director here testified that he did, viz. "accept the company's figures." The directors are the ones who should determine the figures by carefully considering values, and it was for the very purpose of compelling them to perform that duty that the statute imposes upon them a personal responsibility for declaring and paying dividends when the value of the assets is not sufficient to justify them. What directors must do is to exercise an informed judgment of their own, and the amount of information which they should obtain, and the sources from which they should obtain it, will of course depend upon the circumstances of each particular case. [23 N.Y.S.2d at 184.]

The decision of the trial court was affirmed by the Court of Appeals, which, however, differed in its construction of the statute and concluded that both portions of the statute applied to all dividends. On the basis of this construction, (as well as the legislative abandonment of the "surplus profits" language, and a state dividend tax decision to be noted below) the court approved the view that § 58 looked to the current value of assets. However, curiously enough the court then ended its opinion by importing the concept of "surplus" into the picture, although that term is nowhere used in § 58:

> The Legislature having declared that dividends may be paid when there is no impairment of capital or capital stock caused thereby and when the value of the corporate assets remaining after the payment of such dividends is at least equal to the aggregate amount of its debts and liabilities including capital or capital stock as the case may be, Stock Corporation Law, § 58, in other words from its surplus, our inquiry turns to the question whether surplus may consist of increases resulting from a revaluation of fixed assets. Surplus has been well defined as follows in Edwards v. Douglas, 269 U.S. 204, 46 S.Ct. 85, 70 L.Ed. 235, Brandeis, J.: "The word 'surplus' is a term commonly employed in corporate finance and accounting to designate an account on corporate books. . . . The surplus account represents the net assets of a corporation in excess of all liabilities including its capital stock. This surplus may be 'paid-in-surplus,' as where the stock is issued at a price above par; it may be 'earned surplus,' as where it was derived wholly from undistributed profits; or it may, among other things, represent the increase in valuation of land or other assets made upon a revaluation of the company's fixed property. See LaBelle Iron Works v. United States, 256 U.S. 377, 385, 41 S.Ct. 528, 65 L.Ed. 998."

2. ANALYSIS OF RANDALL v. BAILEY

Since the basic themes involved have implications which go well beyond the particulars of New York § 58, it is worth analyzing the views taken of that statute by the two New York courts. At the outset, it must be observed that the trial court's construction of § 58 seems rather inconsistent with the court's conclusion that the two parts of the statute were directed to different types of dividends. If the legislature took the trouble to separate out the two types of dividends, and then to phrase the respective tests in quite different language, (i. e., "impair capital" as against "value of assets"), it hardly makes sense to conclude that the two tests meant the same thing.

Moreover, there was reason to expect that the legislature would want to single out for special treatment dividends resulting from a reduction of capital, which would seem to be the subject of the second portion of the statute. A reduction of capital calls for special attention to the interests of creditors because the "safety-margin" for their claims, which is what stated capital represents, is being reduced. In such quasi-liquidation situations, the legislature might well require that the *value* of assets be up to snuff before any distribution to stockholders is made, while being content to rely on an accounting cost basis for ordinary dividends. See Reduction of Capital, Section 3 infra.

Turning to the Court of Appeals, it did not have to deal with the foregoing issue once it decided that both portions of the statute were applicable to the dividends involved. However, the court failed to provide any real answer to the trial court's view that this reading was "grammatically impossible". Certainly the court's reliance on the fact that both portions of the statute expressly applied to "any dividend" is not very persuasive, particularly since that phrase is followed by the modifying "whether upon" clause in the second portion of the statute, and the real question at issue was the significance of that clause.

A more important question is whether a finding that both portions of § 58 applied to all dividends was as adverse to the plaintiff's case as the court and the parties seemed to think. Apparently it was accepted that because of the plaintiff's emphasis on the realization test, it was imperative for him to avoid the "value of its assets" language in the statute. But this overlooked the fact that the "value" language does not purport to create an affirmative source of dividends. Rather, both portions of the statute are phrased in negative terms, and each constitutes a *prohibition*, not a permission. In other words, the effect of finding both portions of the statute applicable to a dividend is simply that there are then two hurdles which must be overcome before a dividend is in the clear; but such a finding can scarcely expand the power to pay dividends.

Furthermore, if there are two hurdles to clear, presumably they must be different. Since the second part of the statute is clearly addressed to a minimum required value of assets, the only meaning left for the first portion of the statute is a required minimum of assets computed on the basis of cost less depreciation in accordance with generally accepted accounting principles. The result of this construction would be that the corporation could not pay a dividend unless *both* the value and the adjusted cost basis of its net assets exceeded stated capital. In short, unrealized appreciation would not provide any affirmative source of dividends; but any diminution in value of assets would have to be taken into account. And this of course was the very interpretation which the plaintiff was urging in this case.

Recognition of the possible force of this line of argument may well be what led the Court of Appeals to translate the statutory test under § 58 into "surplus" terms at the end of its opinion. Indeed, the first sentence of the concluding paragraph in the opinion actually states the two portions of § 58 in negative terms, and in the conjunctive. So the court was perhaps seeking to replace those two negatives with a single affirmative fund, to lay a basis for reading-in permission to use revaluation surplus.

Turning to a different issue, it should be observed that the courts which decided Randall v. Bailey may have been influenced by the fact that as of the date of the challenged dividends liability under the New York statute was not limited to negligence, willfulness or bad faith. That is, directors were virtually insurers of the propriety of a dividend, and a finding that the statute had been violated would presumably have resulted in liability on the directors no matter how ambiguous the statute or how careful the directors. See Quintal v. Greenstein, 142 Misc. 854, 256 N.Y.S. 462 (Sup.Ct.1932), aff'd without opin., 236 App.Div. 719, 257 N.Y.S. 1034 (1st Dept. 1932) (in an action charging directors with improper dividends, *held*, "defenses of good faith and due care, however worded, are insufficient in law.") In other jurisdictions, courts have sometimes read into ambiguous or silent statutes a requirement that at least negligence on the part of the directors be shown before holding them liable. See Baker & Cary, Cases and Materials on Corporations (3d ed.1959) 1355–1359. In 1939, in conformity to a general statutory trend toward limiting the liability of directors to cases of willful or negligent conduct, New York § 58 was amended to give the directors an affirmative defense if they could show that they had "reasonable grounds to believe and did believe, that such dividends or distribution would not impair the capital of such corporation."

Notwithstanding the citation by both courts in Randall v. Bailey of New York authority which allegedly required, or at least supported, the decision, it is fair to say that there was no compelling authority one way or the other, either within or without New York. Actually, the only cited New York cases where unrealized appreciation on corporate assets was even present were cases like People ex rel. Wedgewood Realty Co. v. Lynch, 262 N.Y. 202, 186 N.E. 673, 262 N.Y. 644, 188 N.E. 102 (1933), a state dividend tax case which the Court of Appeals referred to as "decisive"; and of course cases involving the tax treatment of distributions to stockholders do not necessarily turn on the validity of the distributions under corporate law.

Probably the best known prior authority outside New York was a dictum in Kingston v. Home Life Insurance Company, 11 Del.Ch. 258, 272, 101 A. 898, 904 (Ch. 1917), affirmed without note of this point, 11 Del.Ch. 428, 104 A. 25 (Sup.Ct.1918), to the effect that an estimated increase in the value of a company's office building did not provide a source for the payment of dividends. However, in stating that such unrealized appreciation, "however accurately the increase be estimated, is not a net profit arising from the business of the company", the Chancellor did not do full justice to the Delaware statute, which as of that date permitted a corporation to pay dividends "out of surplus or net profits arising from its business." Unless "surplus" and "net profits arising from its business" were synonymous, they represented two separate funds;[6] and since they were phrased in affirmative terms, unlike New York § 58, either one was sufficient to support a dividend. Hence it was incumbent upon the court to inquire whether unrealized appreciation might constitute "surplus" within the meaning of the statute, even if it did not qualify as "net profits arising." Since the Kingston decision the Delaware statute has been substantially rewritten, and now permits a corporation to pay dividends "out of its net assets in excess of its capital", or if the corporation has a deficit, to pay so-called "nimble dividends," that is, out of net profits for the current or preceding fiscal year. Del.Corp.Law § 170(a). The question of dividends out of revaluation surplus has not arisen in Delaware since the revision of the statute. Morris v. Standard Gas & Electric Co., 31 Del.Ch. 20, 63 A. 2d 577 (Ch.1949), which is often cited as permitting dividends out of unrealized appreciation, see e. g., Note, Cash Dividends Payable from Unrealized Appreciation on Fixed Assets—A Reconsideration of Randall v. Bailey, 20 U. of Pitt.L.Rev. 632, 638 (1959), actually does no more than determine that the proviso to § 170, prohibiting nimble dividends if the net assets of the corporation "have been diminished by depreciation in the value of its property" to an amount less than the stated capital attributable to stock with a liquidation preference, had not been touched off by the *decline* in asset values which had taken place. Notice the analogy between a proviso which makes the special privilege of nimble dividends turn on value of assets, and the suggested construction of New York § 58 making the special privilege of paying dividends pursuant to a reduction of capital turn on value of assets.

6. See Goodnow v. American Writing Paper Co., 73 N.J.Eq. 692, 694, 69 A. 1014, 1015 (Ct.Er. and App.1908), discussed at page 317 supra, where the court expressed the view that under the New Jersey statute of 1896, permitting a corporation to pay dividends "from the surplus or net profits arising from its business . . .", there was "room to contend that the words 'net profits' were intended to be synonymous with the word 'surplus';" but under the 1904 amendment, which added a comma after "surplus" and made the language read "from its surplus, or from the net profits arising from the business . . .", the court thought that "this contention is no longer possible; . . . [t]he evident intention of the change is to point out two funds from which dividends may be made." Query, however, how much doubt there really was as to the two-fund nature of the 1896 statute. It had succeeded an earlier version phrased in terms of "from the surplus profits arising from the business", and the insertion of the words "or net" certainly seems designed to create two funds. See Kehl, Corporate Dividends (1941) 59–60. Moreover, the Goodnow court virtually ignored the phrase "arising from its business", which presumably only modified "net profits", and not "surplus". Interestingly enough, the "arising" phrase was dropped from the Delaware statute a month before the Kingston decision, a fact not noted by the Chancellor despite the fact that the dividend issue was essentially a prayer for an injunction against future improprieties.

3. THE ROLE OF ACCOUNTING

The trial court in Randall v. Bailey paid no attention to accounting practice with regard to unrealized appreciation in deciding whether such appreciation constituted a source of dividends under the New York statute. Rather the court's view was that "the question is not one of sound economics, or of what is sound business judgment, or financial policy or proper accounting practice, or even what the law ought to be. . . . The problem is one of statutory construction." Of course this view overlooks the fact that the words of a dividend statute are typically terms of accounting art, not legal art, and their meaning comes primarily from the accounting background from which they spring. Even the phrase "impair capital" used in New York's § 58, while perhaps less familiar in accounting than "net assets", "net profits", or "surplus", is nonetheless an obvious reference to a balance sheet computation, which takes us immediately into the accounting domain. Since it can hardly be assumed that the legislature was wholly unaware of the accounting significance of the accounting terms which it used, the traditional first step in statutory construction—the quest for legislative intention—must at least start with the accounting background. In other words, the initial inquiry under § 58 might well have been the extent to which unrealized appreciation on fixed assets is normally recognized on the corporate books for accounting purposes.

This is not to say that the proper construction of the dividend statute as to unrealized appreciation, or any other issue for that matter, should be entirely controlled by accounting views or practice. There is as much danger in giving too great weight to accounting implications as in giving too little. Unless the accounting significance of a term is so clear that no other meaning could rationally be attributed to the legislature—and such complete freedom from ambiguity is as rare in accounting as in the law—the accounting implications simply represent one factor to be taken into account. Like any other inferences which may be drawn from the language used in the statute, they may have to yield to contrary implications flowing from the statutory purpose. Thus the difference between the policy underlying dividend regulation, to accommodate fairly the interest of creditors as well as the interests of shareholders *inter se,* and the primary purpose of financial accounting, to disclose meaningfully the financial condition of an enterprise, might well lead to different views on unrealized appreciation. But certainly as a first step in interpreting the statute it is essential to know whether accounting encourages, simply permits, or actually condemns the recognition of unrealized appreciation in financial statements.

The Court of Appeals in Randall v. Bailey seemed to move in this direction of looking to accounting for guidance: after importing the term "surplus" into the test under § 58, the court cited the accounting definition of surplus, as set forth in an opinion by Mr. Justice Brandeis, to show that it included unrealized appreciation on the company's property. See page 322 supra. Unfortunately, this venture into "accounting" background was led somewhat astray by the court's adoption of Justice Brandeis' citation of the LaBelle case as an authority apparently recognizing revaluation surplus. Actually, the Supreme Court in LaBelle seemed to take a rather dim view of recognizing unrealized appreciation on fixed assets. In holding that an excess profits tax could constitutionally fail to give the taxpayer any credit for unrealized appreciation in the value of its assets, the Court said:

> The principal line of demarcation—that based upon actual costs, excluding estimated appreciation—finds reasonable support upon grounds of both theory and practice, in addition to the important consideration of convenience in administration, already adverted to. There is a logical incongruity in entering upon the books of a corporation as the capital value of property acquired for permanent employment in its business and still retained for that purpose, a sum corresponding not to its cost but to what probably might be realized by sale in the market. It is not merely that the market value has not been realized or tested by sale made, but that sale cannot be made without abandoning the very purpose for which the property is held, involving a withdrawal from business so far as that particular property is concerned. Whether in a given case property should be carried in the capital account at market value rather than at cost may be a matter of judgment, depending upon special circumstances and the local law. But certainly Congress, in seeking a general rule, reasonably might adopt the cost basis, resting upon experience rather than anticipation.

In any event, if the accounting view of unrealized appreciation is to be taken into account, it should be obtained from accounting, rather than legal, authorities. Generally speaking, in accounting there are no binding primary authorities like decided cases, although accounting opinions of the SEC, called Accounting Series Releases (ASR's), as well as those of other administrative agencies, control the preparation of financial statements subject to the jurisdiction of the respective agencies. For the accounting profession at large, the nearest thing to an official authority has been the Accounting Research Bulletins (ARB's), and more lately, Opinions of the Accounting Principles Board, of the American Institute of Certified Public Accountants (AICPA).[7] And despite some increased support of late

---

[7] The fifty-two Accounting Research Bulletins (ARB's) published between 1939 and 1961 represent the opinions of the Committee on Accounting Procedure and the Committee on Terminology of the AICPA on matters as to which there were divergences in accounting procedures and terminology.

for recognizing and recording unrealized appreciation, see Accounting Research Study Nos. 3 and 6, referred to in note 7, supra, the fact remains that the most recent official promulgation, Opinion No. 6 of the Accounting Principles Board (1965), reaffirms the traditional accounting view that "property, plant and equipment should not be written up by an entity to reflect appraisal, market or current values which are above cost to the entity." The SEC too has continued in its long-standing policy of insisting that accounting for fixed assets be based upon cost. See Rappaport, SEC Accounting Practice and Procedure (2d ed.1963) 3.9–3.16.

4. THE AFTERMATH OF RANDALL v. BAILEY IN NEW YORK

The decision in Randall v. Bailey proved to have some very important practical ramifications, particularly in the real estate field. Under that decision a corporation may ignore depreciation for dividend purposes so long as the actual value of the property does not decline, since it is the value of property and not its book value which controls. This factor has been combined with accelerated depreciation for tax purposes to produce a so-called "tax-shelter" real estate corporation. To illustrate, a corporation which acquires an apartment property can normally obtain a high enough depreciation rate so that with accelerated depreciation the enterprise will show a loss for tax purposes for at least the first few years, even though it is economically successful. During that period, the value of the prop-

The bulletins were designed to establish a professional standard on accounting questions, but they were merely advisory recommendations to the profession rather than binding regulations.

In 1953 ARB No. 43 was published as a collation of the thirty-four ARB's issued by the Committee on Accounting Procedure, which were revised and restated as separate chapters of ARB No. 43. At the same time, the eight ARB's which had been issued by the Committee on Terminology were amplified and restated in Accounting Terminology Bulletin No. 1. Since 1953 ARB Nos. 44–51 and ATB Nos. 2–4 have been issued separately.

Starting in 1958, there was a complete overhaul of the AICPA's machinery for research and pronouncements on accounting principles. Pursuant to a report by a Special Committee on Research Program, an Accounting Principles Board was created for the purpose of supervising an expanded research program by the accounting research staff, and issuing "opinions" on accounting principles. The report also proposed that the research should lead to the publication of Accounting Research Studies in particular problem areas which would provide a vehicle for discussion and analysis prior to the issuance of pronouncements by the Accounting Principles Board. It was expressly recommended that two of the first projects by the accounting research staff should be "a study of the basic postulates underlying accounting principles generally, and a study of the broad principles of accounting." In response to this recommendation, Accounting Research Study No. 1, "The Basic Postulates of Accounting", by Professor Moonitz, then the Director of Accounting Research of the AICPA, was published in 1963, followed one year later by Research Study No. 3, "A Tentative Set of Broad Accounting Principles for Business Enterprises", by Professors Moonitz and Sprouse. To date, five other Accounting Research Studies have been published, including No. 6, "Reporting the Financial Effects of Price-Level Changes".

erty may remain the same, or even increase, as a result of successful operations and/or a rise in the price level. In such a case, depreciation could be ignored for dividend purposes, and so far as the dividend statute is concerned the corporation could distribute an amount equal to its net income *before* depreciation. To be sure, as a practical matter (and maybe as a matter of contract obligation under the terms of a mortgage, particularly one insured by the FHA) the corporation would probably be limited to distributing its "surplus cash" for the year—that is, an amount equal to net income before depreciation less any repayment of principal on long-term indebtedness (which of course would not be a current expense in accounting terms but does reduce the cash on hand available for distribution). But surplus cash is still greater than corporate net income, at least whenever depreciation for the year exceeds the amortization of principal, as is almost invariably the case.

The important point is that whatever the distributions amount to, they are "sheltered" from dividend tax on the stockholders because of the absence of any corporate earnings and profits, which are a *sine qua non* of taxable dividends. See Section 4, infra. Eventually of course under accelerated depreciation the corporation's annual charge will decline to the point where the corporation will show a profit for tax purposes, and both the corporation and the stockholders will be subject to tax. However, at that point the corporation can sell its property, incurring merely a capital gains tax on the excess of the sales price over the basis of the property (except for a limited "recapture" of depreciation under IRC § 1250). Or the corporation might acquire additional property and use the high depreciation on the new property to offset the income on the old, thus producing a spiral effect which is regarded in some quarters as one of the primary reasons for the present high cost of real estate. It may also be possible to liquidate the corporation and pay no corporate tax at all (provided that the collapsible corporation provisions of IRC § 341 do not apply.)

A somewhat similar use of revaluation was involved in the so-called "windfall profits" cases, where distributions were also made to stockholders despite the absence of corporate earnings. Those cases usually started with a substantial over-estimation of the expected cost of a new construction project, for the purpose of getting an FHA-insured construction mortgage for an amount in excess of the actual cost. Once the project was completed, it was revalued to a figure at least equal to the amount actually borrowed (which was quite often by then a fair appraisal of the value of the property, on the basis of occupancy and other factors); and the excess mortgage proceeds were then distributed to the stockholders, free of any dividend tax since the corporation typically had little or no earnings and profits at the time of the distribution. The Government tried strenuously to plug this loophole by establishing that any distribution to stockholders was taxable as a dividend so long as it did not "impair capital" under corporate law, but the courts refused to depart from the traditional view that cash distributions to stockholders are taxable only to the extent of earnings and profits, which are not augmented by unrealized appreciation. Commissioner v. Gross, 236 F.2d 612 (2d Cir. 1956).

The 1954 Code closed this loophole, at least as to the proceeds of loans insured by government agencies like the FHA, by providing that any corporation which makes a distribution to its stockholders, at a time when it has such a loan in an amount in excess of the basis of the property securing the loan, shall have its earnings and profits increased by the amount of such excess. While this provision does not apply to traditional financing, it does virtually eliminate the straight windfall profits cases, since it would rarely be possible to induce a completely private lender to advance funds amounting to more than the construction costs actually incurred.

The use of revaluation to validate the distribution of the "windfall profits" under corporate law did not pass without adverse comment. In Loftus v. Mason, 240 F.2d 428 (4th Cir.1957), the circumstances were much like those in Gross except that the certificate of incorporation limited dividends to "net earnings of the corporation", and the FHA claimed that the distribution of the excess mortgage proceeds was a violation of that provision. The court held that the distribution clearly violated the certificate limitation, so that it was unnecessary to discuss the general question of the effect of a "reappraisement of corporate property" upon the payment of dividends. However, the court apparently could not resist adding the observation that "in application of sound accounting principles dividends may ordinarily be declared only out of actual earnings or profits and not upon a theoretical estimate of an unrealized appreciation in value of assets", citing the Kingston and LaBelle cases, with a "cf." for Randall v. Bailey.

What of the case where a corporation indirectly "realizes" on an increase in the value of its property by obtaining a new, larger mortgage on the property, after which the additional proceeds received are distributed to the stockholders? On the corporate side, this would be an *a fortiori* case under Randall v. Bailey;[8] and even where that case is not followed, this kind of independent verification of the existence, and indirectly the amount, of unrealized appreciation might induce a court to permit recognition of it for dividend purposes. There is also the question of whether such a transaction would increase

---

8. See Bolmer Bros., Inc. v. Bolmer Const. Co., 114 N.Y.S.2d 530 (Sup.Ct.Sp.T.1952), where the court held that in computing the "surplus" to which New York Penal Law § 664(5) confined repurchases of stock, the actual value rather than the book value was controlling. In determining the value of the corporation's principal asset, an apartment house, the court relied primarily upon expert testimony, making no special point of the fact that the outstanding first mortgage was increased shortly before the repurchase transaction. Curiously, Randall v. Bailey was not even cited.

earning and profits for tax purposes, a matter which will be considered in more detail in Section 4, infra. Marx v. Bragalini, 6 N.Y.2d 322, 160 N.E.2d 611 (1959), decided under the New York State income tax which is patterned after the federal, held that earnings and profits were not increased, in an opinion containing some observations on unrealized appreciation which seem to undercut the decision in Randall v. Bailey, though that case was not mentioned.

> The exclusion of unrealized appreciation from "earnings and profits" as a source of taxable dividends is soundly and wisely based, for to make the determination of the corporation's "earnings and profits" at the time of each corporate distribution depend upon a revaluation of all the corporate assets would create serious administrative difficulties. There is probably no problem in the administration of the tax laws which is fraught with more uncertainty, is more time-consuming and expensive, or leads to less satisfactory results than the problem of the valuation of property. Nothing short of a clear legislative mandate would persuade us to decide that it is necessary to have a current valuation of all corporate assets, wherever located, for the purpose of determining the taxability of corporate distributions.

This attitude toward valuation is in particularly marked contrast to the view of the trial judge in Randall v. Bailey, who saw "no cause for alarm over the fact that this view requires directors to make a determination of the value of the assets at each dividend declaration."

The most recent chapter in the revaluation story in New York has been written by the legislature, with the enactment of the new Business Corporation Law as of September 1, 1963. That act completely recasts the dividend and other financial provisions in terms much like those used in the Model Act, with the definitions of "surplus", "net assets", and "capital surplus" modelled closely upon the Model Act provisions. The same is true of "earned surplus", except that the New York version expressly excludes "unrealized appreciation of assets" from the definition. However, the basic permission to pay dividends under N.Y.B.C.L. § 510(b) differs from that of the Model Act, since it merely limits dividends to "surplus only, so that the net assets of the corporation remaining . . . shall at least equal the amount of its stated capital. . . ." Hence the distinction between earned surplus and other types of surplus becomes relevant only for the purpose of the statutory requirement that notice be sent to the stockholders of the source of any dividends which do not come from earned surplus. N.Y.B.C.L. § 510(c).

While the statute does not expressly provide that unrealized appreciation may be included in capital surplus (where it would be available for regular dividends, subject to the notice requirement), that seems a fair inference from the express exclusion of unrealized appreciation from earned surplus. And confirmation of this view is provided by the following statement in the Explanatory Memorandum on Business Corporation Law of the Joint Legislative Committee: "There is no basic change in the present law that permits dividends to be paid out of any surplus, including unrealized appreciation of assets." New York Legislative Document No. 12, Appendix C, 62 (1961). On the other hand, it is to be noted that nowhere does the new statute refer to the "value of assets", a phrase which loomed large in the decision by the Court of Appeals in Randall v. Bailey. Moreover, this was intentional, as evidenced by the following comment appearing in the Revisers' Notes and Comments relating to the definition of "net assets": "The expression 'value of assets' has been avoided . . . to eliminate any construction that would require appraisal of assets rather than reliance on ordinary accounting figures for computations of surplus." In view of the possibility of conflicting inferences from these various sources, it may be too early to consign Randall v. Bailey and its New York progeny to the history books.

5. UNREALIZED APPRECIATION OUTSIDE NEW YORK

Since the decision in Randall v. Bailey, there does not appear to have been a case squarely presenting the issue of dividends out of revaluation surplus under a silent statute. Berks Broadcasting Co. v. Craumer, 356 Pa. 620, 52 A.2d 571 (1947), did specifically condemn such dividends, but the Pennsylvania statute as of that time expressly excluded unrealized appreciation on fixed assets from the eligible sources for dividends, and there was no occasion for even referring to Randall v. Bailey. However, there have been two cases approving unrealized appreciation as a source for the repurchase of stock, under tests quite similar to those applicable to the payment of dividends. In Mountain States Steel Foundries, Inc. v. Commissioner, 284 F.2d 737 (4th Cir. 1960), set out at page 414 infra, one issue was the deductibility for tax purposes of interest paid by a corporation on obligations incurred in the repurchase of its own stock, and this was thought to turn on the validity of the repurchase transaction for corporate purposes. The court held that the governing statute, which provided that no corporation should "use its funds or property for the purchase of its own shares . . . when such use would cause any impairment of . . . capital", did not require "a blind acceptance of book values as real", but rather looked to the realistic current value of assets. Randall v. Bailey was cited with apparent approval. Similarly, in Baxter v. Lancer Industries, Inc., 213 F.Supp. 92 (E.D. N.Y.1963), on the issue of the existence of adequate surplus for the repurchase of stock, the court said: "What little authority there is suggests that actual values, albeit conservatively applied, rather than book values, are determinative".

In the very different context of state franchise taxes, which are often predicated on some such measure as Mississippi's "capital stock, surplus and undivided profits", several courts have required inclusion in the tax base of unrealized appreciation on fixed assets, at least where it is recorded on the corporation's books. Thus in Scott Building Supply Corporation v. Mississippi State Tax Commission, 235 Miss. 22, 108 So.2d 557 (1959), as a condition to a loan the RFC required the corporation to have an appraisal made of its tangible property, and thereafter to base its periodic reports to the RFC on those appraised values. The corporation entered the excess of the appraised values over the book values on its books, with a corresponding credit to revaluation surplus. The court held that this amount was included within the term "surplus", relying principally upon the same excerpt from the opinion of Justice Brandeis in Edwards v. Douglas as that quoted by the Court of Appeals at the end of its opinion in Randall v. Bailey. The court was also evidently influenced by the independent legal significance of the appraisal made in the instant case, on which it commented as follows:

> The revaluation of the corporate assets in this case was not a revaluation based merely on the subjective feeling of management that the recorded book values of the buildings and the equipment were so grossly unrealistic that they should be revised. The revaluation was based upon an appraisal of the assets made by an independent appraiser pursuant to the requirement of the Reconstruction Finance Corporation, and the revaluation increase was entered on the appellant's books of account and the balance sheet submitted to the Reconstruction Finance Corporation. It is not claimed that the corporate assets were overvalued as a result of the appraisal, or that the "revaluation surplus" shown on the books did not reflect properly the amount of the increase in value of the capital assets shown by the appraisal.

In Oxford v. Macon Telegraph Publishing Co., 104 Ga.App. 788, 123 S.E.2d 277 (1961), the corporation had made an appraisal of the value of both its tangible and intangible assets, and had recorded the unrealized appreciation on its books, with a credit to capital surplus and capital stock. In connection with a state license tax based upon the "true net worth" of the corporation, the Georgia court ruled, first, that "surplus" included an increase in value arising from a revaluation of fixed assets (again relying upon that same quotation from Justice Brandeis in Edwards v. Douglas); second, that such increase in valuation was generally recognized as "revaluation surplus"; and third, that where such "revaluation surplus" was included in the regular balance sheets of the corporation, it formed a part of "true net worth". It may be of interest to note that in this case it seems to have finally been recognized that the La Belle case did not provide much support for revaluation, despite its citation by Justice Brandeis in this oft-quoted excerpt; in fact, La Belle was here advanced by the taxpayer as authority against recognition of revaluation. However, the Georgia Court emphasized the observation in La Belle that recognition of revaluation "may be a matter of judgment, depending upon special circumstances and the local law", and concluded that "the Georgia legislature might and did adopt a different basis for calculating a corporation's net worth" than that used in the statute involved in La Belle.

Two recent English cases have divided on the propriety of dividends out of unrealized appreciation on fixed assets which had been recorded on the books as expressly provided by the governing statute. In Westburn Sugar Refineries Ltd. v. Inland Revenue, 1960 S.L.T. 297 (Scot. Ct. of Sess.), which ruled against such dividends, the principal opinion for the majority put it this way:

> . . . [P]articularly in the case of an appreciation which is neither realized nor immediately realizable it would be illegal to distribute the surplus. This certainty accords with the uncontradicted evidence in this case of the practice among chartered accountants. It appears to me that were the Courts to hold otherwise it would involve opening the door to dangerously premature distributions of the funds of a company which a change in economic or trading conditions might prove to be disastrous after the lapse of a few years. For nowadays particularly the values of fixed assets may fluctuate heavily.

A dissenting opinion accepted this general rule but argued that to the extent of depreciation taken to date on the assets, the excess of appraised value over current book value should be available for dividends.

On the other hand, in Dimbula Valley (Ceylon) Tea Co. Ltd. v. Laurie, [1961] 2 W.L.R. 253 (Ch.), the court expressly declined to follow the Westburn Sugar case, stating:

> For myself, I can see no reason why, if the valuation is not open to criticism, . . . a surplus so ascertained should not be distributed. . . . After all, every profit and loss account of a trading concern which opens and closes with a stock figure necessarily embodies an element of estimate. The difference between ascertaining trading profits by, amongst other things, estimating the value of the stock in hand at the beginning and end of the accounting period, and ascertaining capital profits by comparing an estimated value of the assets with their book value, appears to me to be a difference of degree but not of principle. Moreover, if a company has fluid assets available for payment of a dividend, I can see nothing wrong in its using those assets for payment of a dividend, and at the same time, as a matter of account,

treating that dividend as paid out of a capital surplus resulting from an appreciation in value of unrealised fixed assets. The proper balance of the company's balance-sheet would not be disturbed by such a course of action. The company would be left with assets of sufficient value to meet the commitments shown on the liability side of its balance-sheet, including paid-up share capital. A company is not required by law to keep any part of its assets in any particular form. I do not say that in many cases such a course of action would be a wise commercial practice, but for myself I see no ground for saying that it is illegal.

6. REVALUATION UNDER THE MODEL ACT

SEWARD, EARNED SURPLUS—ITS MEANING AND USE IN THE MODEL BUSINESS CORPORATION ACT [9]

[9]. Reprinted by permission of the Virginia Law Review Association. Portions of the text and most of the footnotes omitted. Mr. Seward was a member, and later chairman, of the ABA committee which prepared the Model Act.

[12]. See § 43 . . . .

38 Va.L.Rev. 440–443 (1952).

The accounting definitions in the Model Act do not fix a particular time as of which they shall be applied and they do not state what standards of value are to be utilized. . . . "Net assets," the key term of the definition, is defined to mean "the amount by which the total assets of a corporation, excluding treasury shares, exceed the total debts of the corporation." The test is a current one, and while a standard of values is not prescribed, the book values clearly are not determinative. Consequently a decrease in values will reduce surplus, and an increase in values will augment it. Realization of the gain or loss by sale or other disposition is not prerequisite to its effect upon surplus. . . .

The fact that the test of value is a current one does not require frequent revaluations of assets on the corporate books. The book values may be relied upon unless there is good reason to believe them to be incorrect.[12]

The next question, of course, is whether changes in the value of assets affect earned surplus or capital surplus.

It is accepted accounting procedure that losses when realized or determined, whether by sale or by appraisal, be written off against earned surplus before any inroads are made on capital surplus. To test this practice under the Model Act reference must be made to the definition of earned surplus. . . . The diminution in value is a "loss" even though not realized by a sale.* Hence it it a charge against earned surplus. Only when earned surplus has been exhausted may any portion of a loss be charged to capital surplus.

If a diminution in value of assets is a loss which reduces earned surplus, does it follow that an increase in the value of assets augments earned surplus? There has been much written about the inadvisability of declaring dividends out of unrealized appreciation in asset values, and concededly such dividends, as a general rule, are not good practice. The legality, however, and not the advisability of such procedure is the issue in the present discussion. Under the Model Act such a dividend would be legal only if unrealized asset appreciation, when properly recognized and determined, increases the balance of the earned surplus account.

When an asset is sold at a price above the book value there is a profit, and whether it was a fixed asset or inventory, the profit would increase earned surplus. In the absence of a sale or other disposition of the asset, there can be no "profit" and no "income"; but there may nevertheless be a "gain." The general connotation of that word (as distinguished from its use in taxation where a gain in a capital asset must be realized by some disposition to be considered taxable) includes appreciation in value.

The thinking of much of the accounting profession, however, is that unrealized appreciation ought to be reflected in capital or capital surplus and not in earned surplus. This presents some logical inconsistencies when compared with the general view of the profession that unrealized losses should be charged first against earned surplus. If assets are revalued for good reason and it is found that some have increased in value while others have decreased, should the losses only be charged against earned surplus while the gains are charged to capital surplus? May the gains and losses be offset? Should the losses be recognized and the gains ignored?

One of the sage principles of accounting is that assets be carried at cost, or at any lower value which conditions require. A statement as to appreciation in value prior to disposition is regarded in the nature of prophecy. Appreciation, moreover, is often a function of the changing value of the dollar. Not only do values change but the standard of measurement is not stable. Hence accountants hesitate to depart from the cost basis for assets. Inevitably, however, situations will arise when values of assets will be so far out of keeping with the facts that corrections are necessary.

It has become accepted practice in financial statements to overstate bad aspects of a business and to understate good aspects. That is a conservative and advisable approach. Accounting is not an exact science, and new theories of liability, particularly under the Securities

---

* [Ed. note] No authority is cited by the author for this proposition.

Act, have made both accountants and lawyers very cautious. Conservative though it may be to discourage the practice of recognizing a gain resulting from appreciation of an asset prior to actual disposition, it is difficult to escape the logic as a legal matter of routing both gains and losses in such transactions through the earned surplus account.[18]

Furthermore, under the Model Act if unrealized gains are added to capital surplus rather than to earned surplus an inaccurate and accounting result would arise upon the sale of the revalued asset. The difference between book value and sale price is a proper addition to earned surplus. If the portion of the increase in value recognized in the revaluation is credited to earned surplus, then at the time of the sale, only the balance of the profit would be carried to earned surplus. That would give the earned surplus account its proper balance. But if part of the increase had already been carried to capital surplus, how would the earned surplus account be given its proper balance? The Model Act does not permit transfers from capital surplus to earned surplus unless the earned surplus account has a deficit position.

This indicates the correctness of the above analysis that unrealized gains, if recognized, should be carried to earned surplus. Hence, even though conservative accounting and business policy, in the absence of extremely unusual circumstances, recommend against such procedure, a board of directors acting under the Model Act would have the power to augment earned surplus by recognizing appreciation in the value of assets.

Section 40 of the Model Act was based upon § 157.41 of the Illinois Business Corporation Act, but paragraph (c) of that section was not adopted:

> (c) No dividend, except a dividend payable in its own shares, shall be declared or paid out of surplus arising from unrealized appreciation in value, or revaluation, of assets.

The omission lends support to the argument that unrealized appreciation in asset values is available as earned surplus, and is not subject to the restrictions applying to capital surplus.

---

18. It would be appropriate, as a matter of accuracy and disclosure, to have a separate division of the earned surplus account to reflect such transaction.

HACKNEY, THE FINANCIAL PROVISIONS OF THE MODEL BUSINESS CORPORATION ACT [10]

70 Harv.L.Rev. 1377–1383 (1957).

Unrealized appreciation might arguably add to the funds available for dividends under either a balance-sheet-surplus test or an income test. In the former case, the assets might simply be written up, or in the absence of a technical write-up, be taken at their fair value for dividend purposes, and thereby the amount of net assets in excess of capital would be increased. Under an income test, the funds available for dividends might be increased on a write-up either directly by a credit to earned surplus or to the profit-and-loss account, or indirectly when the written-up assets constitute inventory, because the higher the value of goods remaining on hand at the end of the year, the lower the cost of goods sold, and the higher the income. In all these situations, if permissible under the law, funds would become available for dividends because of book entries. . . . The Model Act contains no express prohibition against using unrealized appreciation or revaluation surplus in computing surplus, as contained in so many of the statutes in the last thirty years. It is thus arguable that under the Model Act unrealized appreciation may be written up on the books and surplus can be created therefrom. The Model Act definition of earned surplus does not use the word "value," but the third paragraph in section 43 would seem to accomplish the same thing since it provides in effect that the board in good faith may, in determining the amount available for dividends, consider the assets to be of their book value.

Clearly, accounting principles would not permit approval of a balance sheet which includes as earned any surplus arising from revaluation of assets or unrealized profit; accordingly, when outside accountants audit a corporation's books, it would seem that under section 43 directors would be precluded from paying dividends from unrealized appreciation. George C. Seward . . . argues that unrealized appreciation in asset values is available under the Model Act as earned surplus . . . Nevertheless, in view of the virtual unanimity on the subject among accountants, the bar, and the reported cases, . . . it seems unlikely that any court would allow a write-up of fixed assets to create an earned surplus available for dividends, unless it felt compelled to do so by a specific statutory provision. . . . Some courts might well hesitate on a policy basis even to allow the creation of capital surplus by revaluation, because of the permissible uses of capital surplus under the Model Act. . . . Nevertheless, as previously shown, the Model Act would seem to allow

---

10. Copyright (c), Harvard Law Review Association, 1957. Reprinted by permission. Portions of the text and all footnotes omitted.

a write-up of assets, the resulting surplus being construed as part of capital surplus under section 2(m).*

The most recent comment on this subject is Gibson, Surplus, So What?—The Model Act Modernized, 17 Bus.Law. 476 (1962). Mr. Gibson, Mr. Seward's successor as chairman of the ABA Committee on Corporate Laws, and the man chiefly responsible for the thoughtful 1962 amendments to the Model Act, seems to agree with Mr. Seward:

> [Since "surplus" has a] vital role in corporate policy, the average prudent director may well inquire what surplus is. The Model Act reassuringly informs him that it is the "excess" of net assets over stated capital.
>
> But how do net assets exceed stated capital? In length, breadth, or thickness? None of these standards would satisfy the creditor, who is the person primarily to be protected, or even the stockholder, who is the person secondarily to be protected. Value is obviously the governing standard, though the Act refrains with studied care from any reference to that standard except in saying that a director shall not be personally liable for dividend distributions if believing in good faith that the assets have a "value" at least equal

---

* [Ed. note] When unrealized appreciation has been entered on a corporation's books, the question then arises whether the revaluation or capital surplus may ultimately be transferred to earned surplus, either gradually, as depreciation is taken on the appreciated figure for the asset, or in a lump sum when the asset is retired. The argument for doing so is that the appreciation has in effect been "realized" through the depreciation process, much as if the asset had been sold for its appreciated value. Moreover, this approach would only put earned surplus at the same level it would have been at if there had been no revaluation with its increased depreciation deduction from income. Accounting Research Bulletin No. 5 dealt extensively with this issue, concluding that even if the revaluation surplus did ultimately become "a part of earned surplus, it would seem that it should not form the basis of ordinary dividends, but should be regarded as appropriated surplus . . . ." ARB No. 5, ¶ 14 (1940). The successor to ARB No. 5, Ch. 7B of ARB No. 43, is silent on the matter, except for a qualified assenting opinion stating that where unrealized appreciation is recognized "the credit item should be treated as permanent capital and would therefore not be available for subsequent transfer to earned surplus as *realized* through depreciation or sale." (Notice the gulf between this view and Mr. Seward's concern, supra page 337, that if unrealized appreciation is once credited to capital surplus, it will not be possible to get it over to earned surplus even if the property is sold.) See generally, Fitts, The Relation of Depreciation to the Determination of Surplus and Earnings Available for Dividends, 33 Va.L.Rev. 581, 597–599 (1947) (approving "a periodic transfer to earned surplus" as depreciation is taken on the unrealized appreciation); Dodd & Baker, Cases and Materials on Corporations (2d ed. 1951) 1035 n. 33 (noting doubts about the practice, "at least where senior securities have been issued, or even traded in, in reliance upon financial statements reflecting the write-up, and the securities continue to be outstanding"); Vatter, Corporate Stock Equities—Part II, which appears in Backer, Handbook of Modern Accounting Theory (1955) 385, 420–423.

to the amount stated on the books. But one reference is enough. Value of fixed assets is thus the eventual and governing test of surplus and hence of permissible dividends under the Model Act.

However, Mr. Gibson then goes on to decry this view on the ground that a value approach presupposes a liquidity of assets which simply does not exist in the modern industrial corporation. He recommends that instead the test for dividends should be based upon earnings, either accumulated or current, for which he assumes a change in the Model Act would be required. Of course a change would be necessary to authorize "nimble dividends", that is, dividends out of current earnings despite the existence of an overall deficit. But so far as limiting dividends to accumulated earnings is concerned, it may well be argued that this is the very test embodied in the term "earned surplus" under the Model Act; and the strong case against using values as a basis for dividends might as well be addressed to construing the Model Act, as to amending it.

7. METHODS OF VALUATION

Where value of assets is significant for dividend purposes, how is it to be measured? Among the possible approaches are appraised value (for each asset or class of assets); secondhand replacement cost, where such a market exists; reproduction cost new less depreciation (presumably based on engineering "observation" rather than straight-line or other accounting depreciation); or overall enterprise valuation, based upon capitalization of projected earning power. The authorities offer little guidance on the issue. In Randall v. Bailey, valuation of the corporation's land and building seemed to be based primarily upon assessed valuations used for local property tax purposes; however, it appears that evidence as to both reproduction cost, and enterprise value based on capitalization of earnings, was also taken into account. The other cases afford little clarification as to what is the significant measure of value for these purposes. And among the commentators, only Hackney appears to recognize the difficulties involved in measuring value.

Actually the method of valuation proposed could well be a critical factor on the question of whether to permit dividends on the basis of revaluation. For example, if liquidation value, i. e., immediate realizable value, were the criterion, there might be little objection to regarding any excess of that conservative measure of value over book value as available for dividends. Conversely, however, reproduction cost, though doubtless highly significant in measuring the amount of invested capital for the purposes of computing the ratio of earnings to invested capital, affords little basis for paying dividends, particularly if the earnings potential of the assets is such that no one would actually reproduce them.

C. STOCK DIVIDENDS

1. IN GENERAL

A distribution by a corporation of its own stock to its stockholders without consideration has always been a troublesome item in corporate finance. Although often termed a stock "dividend", such a distribution is in fact almost the antithesis of a dividend in cash: not only does the corporation not part with any of its assets, but also the distribution of stock is normally accompanied by a "capitalization" of surplus, i. e., a transfer of surplus to stated capital, which actually reduces the corporation's legal power to pay cash dividends. At least from the point of view of the recipient, then, a typical dividend of common on common (which is the case assumed throughout unless otherwise noted) amounts simply to a division of the same "pie" into a larger number of small slices. Accordingly, it has generally been agreed that a stock dividend does not constitute income to the recipient. ARB No. 43, Ch. 7B; May, Stock Dividends and Concepts of Income, 96 J. Accountancy 427 (1953); cf. Eisner v. Macomber, 252 U.S. 189, 40 S.Ct. 189, 64 L.Ed. 521 (1920) (stock dividend not income for tax purposes). But see Wilcox, Accounting for Stock Dividends: A Dissent from Current Recommended Practice, 96 J. Accountancy 176 (1953).

There has been much less uniformity as to the proper manner of reflecting a distribution of stock on the corporation's books. See generally, Manne, Accounting For Share Issues Under Modern Corporation Laws, 54 Nw.U.L.Rev. 285, 317–327 (1959). Of course there is no dispute that to the extent of an increase in the stated capital of the corporation, which always accompanies a distribution of par stock, an amount equal thereto must be transferred from some surplus account to stated capital in order to "back" the new stock and preclude its being watered. This requirement is embodied in practically every state statute. E. g., MBA § 40(d) (1). As to the question of how much surplus, if any, to transfer to stated capital in the case of no-par shares, that is normally left to the discretion of the directors. E. g., MBA § 40(d) (2). But agreement ends on the question of whether this requirement is enough. The AICPA has attempted to set up standards for determining the circumstances under which something more may be required, at least for accounting purposes:

STOCK DIVIDENDS AND STOCK SPLIT–UPS
Accounting Research Bulletin No. 43, Ch. 7B (1953).

1. The term *stock dividend* as used in this chapter refers to an issuance by a corporation of its own common shares to its common

shareholders without consideration and under conditions indicating that such action is prompted mainly by a desire to give the recipient shareholders some ostensibly separate evidence of a part of their respective interests in accumulated corporate earnings without distribution of cash or other property which the board of directors deems necessary or desirable to retain in the business.

2. The term *stock split-up* as used in this chapter refers to an issuance by a corporation of its own common shares to its common shareholders without consideration and under conditions indicating that such action is prompted mainly by a desire to increase the number of outstanding shares for the purpose of effecting a reduction in their unit market price and, thereby, of obtaining wider distribution and improved marketability of the shares.

3. This chapter is not concerned with the accounting for a distribution or issuance to shareholders of (a) shares of another corporation theretofore held as an investment, or (b) shares of a different class, or (c) rights to subscribe for additional shares or (d) shares of the same class in cases where each shareholder is given an election to receive cash or shares.

* * *

Stock Dividends

10. . . . [A] stock dividend does not, in fact, give rise to any change whatsoever in either the corporation's assets or its respective shareholders' proportionate interests therein. However, it cannot fail to be recognized that, merely as a consequence of the expressed purpose of the transaction and its characterization as a *dividend* in related notices to shareholders and the public at large, many recipients of stock dividends look upon them as distributions of corporate earnings and usually in an amount equivalent to the fair value of the additional shares received. Furthermore, it is to be presumed that such views of recipients are materially strengthened in those instances, which are by far the most numerous, where the issuances are so small in comparison with the shares previously outstanding that they do not have any apparent effect upon the share market price and, consequently, the market value of the shares previously held remains substantially unchanged. The committee therefore believes that where these circumstances exist the corporation should in the public interest account for the transaction by transferring from earned surplus to the category of permanent capitalization (represented by the capital stock and capital surplus accounts) an amount equal to the fair value of the additional shares issued. Unless this is done, the amount of earnings which the shareholder may believe to have been distributed to him will be left, except to the extent otherwise dictated by legal requirements, in earned surplus subject to possible further similar stock issuances or cash distributions.

11. Where the number of additional shares issued as a stock dividend is so great that it has, or may reasonably be expected to have, the effect of materially reducing the share market value, the committee believes that the implications and possible constructions discussed in the preceding paragraph are not likely to exist and that the transaction clearly partakes of the nature of a stock split-up as defined in paragraph 2. Consequently, the committee considers that under such circumstances there is no need to capitalize earned surplus, other than to the extent occasioned by legal requirements. It recommends, however, that in such instances every effort be made to avoid the use of the word *dividend* in related corporate resolutions, notices, and announcements and that, in those cases where because of legal requirements this cannot be done, the transaction be described, for example, as a *split-up effected in the form of a dividend.*

* * *

13. Obviously, the point at which the relative size of the additional shares issued becomes large enough to materially influence the unit market price of the stock will vary with individual companies and under differing market conditions and, hence, no single percentage can be laid down as a standard for determining when capitalization of earned surplus in excess of legal requirements is called for and when it is not. However, on the basis of a review of market action in the case of shares of a number of companies having relatively recent stock distributions, it would appear that there would be few instances involving the issuance of additional shares of less than, say, 20% or 25% of the number previously outstanding where the effect would not be such as to call for the procedure referred to in paragraph 10.

2. STOCK DIVIDENDS—A FURTHER ANALYSIS

Much of the difficulty in this area has stemmed from the failure to recognize that although a distribution of stock and a transfer from surplus to stated capital are often combined in a stock dividend, the two are not necessarily related. Quite the contrary, each can occur wholly independent of the other; and presumably they achieve different objectives. Thus it is not necessary to issue additional shares in order to capitalize surplus — the directors may at any time transfer any type of surplus to capital. MBA §§ 2(j), 19, 64. On the other hand, it is not so easy to say what is accomplished by such capitalization. While it does pro tanto reduce the power of the directors to pay dividends, capitalization is hardly necessary for this purpose since the directors could simply decline to pay dividends anyway. And while capitalization may serve as notice to shareholders that the directors have decided to reduce the amount of dividends which the corporation could pay, this seems of importance only on the doubtful assumption that shareholders regard a corporation's entire surplus as being actually available for dividends. Perhaps the best that can be said for such capitalization of surplus is that it reflects a judgment by management that the amount involved must be permanently committed to the enterprise.

It is also perfectly possible to issue additional shares pro rata to existing shareholders without any capitalization of surplus. For example, existing par shares may be replaced with twice as many shares having one-half the par value, constituting a "split-up" in the true sense of the word. And in the case of no-par shares, there would seem to be no obstacle to issuing additional shares without capitalizing any surplus, in the absence of an express statutory requirement.[11]

However, at least in theory there would seem to be little point to such a stock distribution. The result should simply be a decline in the per share market value proportionate to the increase in the number of shares, with the total value of all the stock outstanding remaining the same. After all, the value of the enterprise has not changed — nor have the respective interests of the shareholders, although such interests are now represented by a greater number of shares. And it should make no difference whether the distribution of stock is accompanied by a transfer from surplus to stated capital. Such an intra-proprietorship-account transfer, whether or not in conjunction with a distribution of stock, does not affect either net assets or earning power and so should have no impact on value.

Nevertheless, the fact is that in practice the stock market, which really determines the economic impact of a stock dividend (of a publicly-held company), has its own way of operating. Even in the case of

---

11. Query whether MBA § 40(d)(2) is intended to require capitalization of at least some surplus in conjunction with a no-par stock dividend. See Hackney, The Financial Provisions of the Model Business Corporation Act, 70 Harv.L.Rev. 1357, 1386, note 136 (1957):

. . . A corporation may have a stated capital of a round figure which it dislikes to disturb; it would prefer to pay a stock dividend and merely shift some earned surplus (equal to the market value of the shares) to capital surplus. A stock split of no-par shares may be accomplished by charter amendment, Model Act § 53(i), without the capitalization of any surplus. Interpreting § 40(d) so as not to require the capitalization of any surplus on the issuance of no-par shares allows the board of directors to accomplish the same thing without amendment. The Model Act does not seem to contemplate a per-share stated capital or stated value for no-par shares, similar to per-share par value, which can only be changed by the shareholders; the articles of incorporation must state merely the total authorized number of shares and the par value of each or that they are without par value. See Model Act § 48(d).

Hackney's observations are certainly sound, but they do not seem to take any account of the contrary implication in the language of § 40(d)(2). However, the question may well be academic as a practical matter, for it would appear that whatever number of new no-par shares is desired can be issued by the board of directors without any capitalization of surplus simply by treating the transaction as a "split-up" under the last paragraph of § 40.

a large stock distribution, where, as Chapter 7B of ARB No. 43 points out, the market will necessarily be affected, the decrease in market price may not be proportionate to the increase in the number of shares. There are some important "market" factors which come into play here. First, since many stockholders are more attracted to lower-priced stocks, and would simply rather buy 100 shares at $50 than 50 shares at $100, lowering the market price of stock may in and of itself increase the demand for it. Thus a 2 for 1 stock distribution on a stock selling at say, 90, might well result in an ultimate market price significantly above 30.

Secondly, a stock distribution often heralds an increase in total cash dividends. For example, a company about to increase its cash dividend by 20% might accomplish the same thing by declaring a 20% stock dividend and then maintaining the same per share dividend rate. (Some managements favor this method of increasing dividends because it may attract less attention from interested observers such as labor unions and the like.) Of course the larger the size of the stock distribution, the smaller the likelihood of a pro rata increase in dividends; but even 2 for 1 and 3 for 1 distributions have frequently been accompanied by at least some overall dividend increase.

Finally, there is that most peculiarly "market" phenomenon of all — that is, that in a long-term bull market of the type we have been experiencing for quite some time, announcement of a proposed stock distribution is likely to boost the market price of a stock *ipso facto*, without regard to such underlying economic factors as the likelihood of a more attractive price range or an increase in dividends.[12] Indeed, particularly among the so-called "glamour" issues, a kind of reverse psychology has developed in connection with the relationship of stock dividends to cash dividends; stock distributions may be hailed as an indication that cash dividends will not be paid because the earnings are being plowed back in the business, which in turn is regarded as a badge of that much-sought-after category, the "growth" company.

However, it is to be noted that Chapter 7B does not suggest that any account be taken of the overall increase in the value of stockholders' holdings which so often accompanies a large-size distribution of stock. Yet the accounting for a small-size stock distribution seems to be based entirely, although not expressly, upon this increase-in-value phenomenon. For when Chapter 7B speaks of a distribution small enough not to "have any apparent effect upon the share market price", it is not to be taken literally. Any distribution of additional shares reduces the market value per share. What happens is that, just as in the

---

12. The most recent studies seem to indicate that in the case of a substantial stock distribution, the market run-up is likely to disappear unless some increase in cash dividends is forthcoming. And of course an increase in cash dividends would independently support a price rise, without the need of any distribution of stock. See Barker, Effective Stock Splits, 34 Harv.Bus.Rev. (Jan.–Feb., 1956) 101; Barker, Stock Splits in A Bull Market, 35 Harv.Bus.Rev. (May–June, 1957) 72.

case of a large-size distribution, the prospect of the distribution causes a run-up in the market, and that increase is enough to offset the decline in price resulting from the distribution itself, because the relatively small distribution produces only a small decline.

Why should the increase in value accompanying a relatively small stock distribution be treated so differently from the increase which occurs in the case of large-scale distribution? The price rise associated with stock dividends does not appear to be any more permanent — as in the case of larger distributions, the increase in market price is likely to last only where the distribution of stock is accompanied by an increase in cash dividends.[13] Of course, there is something special about an increase in value which is exactly equal to the old market price per share times the number of dividend shares received, so that the market price of the stock is not changed by the distribution of stock. For it is under these circumstances that a stockholder can sell his dividend shares without reducing the total market value of his investment in the company (although of course such a sale would reduce his percentage interest in the enterprise). And it is this phenomenon that leads some shareholders to view a stock dividend as equivalent to a distribution of earnings in the amount of the fair market value of the dividend stock, which in turn is largely responsible for the recommendation that an equivalent amount of earned surplus be capitalized.

However, quite apart from its inconsistency with the treatment of split-ups, this approach creates some problems. Since a stock dividend does not in fact constitute income to the recipient, as the first portion of Chapter 7B, omitted from the above excerpts, specifically concludes, why, as a dissent to Chapter 7B asks, should the corporation's accounting be "based upon the assumption that the stockholder may think otherwise"? To put it a little differently, regardless of whether shareholders regard a stock dividend as a distribution of earnings, the fact is that most corporation statutes require no more than the minimal stated capital "backing".[14] Of course it is not uncommon for an accounting rule to go beyond the corresponding legal rule; the disclosure function of accounting is not limited merely to portraying a corporation's legal position. However, here the accounting rule goes well beyond mere disclosure. In fact its avowed aim is to change the corporation's legal position by reducing its earned surplus and accordingly its capacity to pay dividends, which seems like a rather doubtful role for accounting to attempt to play.

Curiously, Chapter 7B does not appear to mention what is perhaps the strongest argument for capitalizing earned surplus to the extent of

---

13. See Barker, Evaluation of Stock Dividends, 36 Harv.Bus.Rev. (July-Aug., 1958) 99.

14. However, some statutes, like the Model Act, do expressly contemplate the possibility of capitalizing more than the bare legal minimum. For example, notice the phrase "at least", added to MBA § 40(d)(1) in 1957. See generally, Sprouse, Accounting Principles and Corporation Statutes, 35 Acc.Rev. 246 (1960).

Sec. 2   FUND AVAILABLE FOR DIVIDENDS   347

the fair market value of the dividend shares, i. e., that the transaction should be viewed as if it were a cash dividend followed by an issuance of new stock for cash. Such a transaction would of course ultimately result in a transfer of earned surplus equal to the fair market value of the dividend stock to stated capital and/or capital surplus. However, both a cash dividend and a new issue of stock would have independent legal consequences, such as federal income taxes on the former, which make it awkward to adopt such a constructive view of a stock dividend.

The case against requiring capitalization of earned surplus to the extent of an amount equal to fair market value of a stock dividend is put this way by Paton and Paton, in their excellent analysis of the relationship between stock distributions and capitalization of earnings:[15]

> The market-price formula has no logical basis. The possibility of capitalizing earnings rests on the conception of a stockholders' equity consisting of two main sections: (1) capital and (2) retained earnings. The act of capitalization consists of a formal transfer from the second compartment to the first. The market value per share at any time represents the current appraisal in the financial market of the *entire* equity per share, including both capital and retained earnings. Accordingly there is no rhyme or reason in a proposal to use the market value of *both* sections as a unit of measure in effecting a transfer from *one* section to the other. Without much doubt the sponsoring of this type of formula results in part from a misconception as to the nature of the capitalization process, when accomplished through the issue of additional shares. Continued use of the term stock "dividend" has created a persistent impression, not unnaturally, that something of "value" is transferred to the shareholder by the act of multiplying the number of units he holds.
>
> The preferable accounting procedure, accordingly, is to determine the number of shares needed to capitalize a given amount of retained earnings by using as a divisor the *capital* book value per share (either par or stated value or, more logically, average amount received per share from stockholders). . . .[16]

In the light of the foregoing analysis, what is the impact of a distribution of stock "out of capital surplus", as is authorized by many

---

15. Paton and Paton, Corporation Accounts and Statements (1955) 125. Reprinted by permission of the publisher, The MacMillan Company.

16. It is not clear why the authors reach the view that the amount to be capitalized on a stock dividend is the average amount received on shares of that class from the stockholders. The logic of their analysis seems to call for no capitalization at all, except as compelled by legal requirements. Such a proposal, i. e., that no capitalization of surplus be required except when the dividend stock either is redeemable or has a liquidation preference, was made in Hills, Model Corporation Act, 48 Harv.L.Rev. 1334, 1363–4, note 46, set out at pages 312–313, supra.

statutes either directly, or, as in the Model Act, indirectly, by not confining stock dividends to earned surplus? To an accountant, such a transaction may well be regarded as a "weird performance, and one having no relation whatever to the capitalization of earnings." [17] Since accountants regard capital surplus as much more akin to capital than to surplus, capitalization of capital surplus, that is, a transfer of capital surplus to stated capital, is looked at somewhat askance. However, the fact remains that under corporation statutes capital surplus, although often not as available for distribution as earned surplus, is invariably less restricted than stated capital, which means that a transfer from capital surplus to stated capital is not without significance.

Nevertheless, authorization to declare stock dividends out of capital surplus can create problems. The theory often advanced is that since no distribution of assets is involved, whatever reasons there may be for confining property dividends to earned surplus do not apply to stock dividends. But such reasoning assumes that a distribution of stock is to be judged, at least in the first instance, by the standards applicable to dividends of property, whereas we have seen that a stock dividend is really just a combination of a stock split-up and a capitalization of surplus. This difference in view is more than just theoretical. For example, under a statute like MBA § 40(d), the question may arise as to whether the necessary backing for a stock dividend may be "charged" against capital surplus even though some earned surplus exists. If a stock dividend is viewed as a type of "distribution" out of surplus, the question would presumably be decided in the light of the express requirement in both § 64 and the last paragraph of § 41 that earned surplus must first be exhausted in the circumstances involved in those sections (although it is far from clear which way those express provisions cut in cases not covered by those sections). On the other hand, if it is recognized that a stock dividend simply combines a stock split with a capitalization of surplus, there is no reason for any particular priority since capital surplus is fully as eligible for capitalization as earned surplus.

There are, however, some cases where the limitations on property dividends might be thought more clearly applicable to stock dividends. For example, if a dividend in redeemable preferred was charged to capital surplus, and thereafter was redeemed out of capital, as is permitted under most statutes, the ultimate impact of the transaction would be little different from a cash dividend out of capital surplus. And of course if the amount transferred to stated capital upon the stock dividend was less than the redemption price, to that extent the transaction is no different from a dividend out of stated capital. (However, it must be observed that the prospect of indirectly paying a dividend out of stated capital is much less earth-shaking than it might once have been, because of the present ease with which stated

---

17. See Paton and Paton, Corporation Accounts and Statements (1955) 124.

capital can be transformed into capital surplus by a reduction of capital. See Reduction of Capital, Section 3, infra.)

A similar problem may be presented when a dividend is declared in stock having a liquidation preference. As was suggested in Section 1, supra, when such stock is issued for consideration, the question arises whether the stated capital attributable to such stock should have to be set at not less than the liquidation preference. If an affirmative answer is given there, then when stock having a liquidation preference is distributed as a dividend, the amount of surplus transferred to stated capital should similarly be at least equal to the liquidation preference of the stock.

As a matter of fact, since dividends in preferred stock are normally declared on common, these problems are really part of the larger question of how to treat a dividend in one class of stock distributed to the holders of another class. Such distributions really constitute recapitalizations which affect the relative rights of the shareholders, at least if there was already more than one class of stock outstanding. Here there would seem to be considerable force in analogizing the transaction to a cash dividend followed by a purchase of the new stock at fair market value, which argues for a capitalization of earned surplus to the extent of the fair market value of the dividend stock. See Manne, op. cit. supra page 341, at 326–327. In any event, this is a far cry from a mere split-up, and indeed may well be too fundamental a matter to be left entirely to the directors. MBA § 40(e) provides some protection here by prohibiting a dividend in shares of another class without the approval of a majority of the outstanding shares of that class. However, this provision does not appear to cover a case where two classes of stock are outstanding and a stock dividend is declared in a third class which was not previously outstanding but does affect the relative interests of the other two classes.

3. STOCK DIVIDENDS OUT OF REVALUATION SURPLUS

Not infrequently, corporation statutes expressly permit stock dividends out of unrealized appreciation while prohibiting dividends in cash or property out of that source. One such statute is Illinois § 41(c) which, as Mr. Seward pointed out, the draftsmen of the Model Act failed to follow. See page 337 supra. On the other hand, the California statute expressly forbids stock dividends as well as cash dividends out of unrealized appreciation. Cal.Corp.Code § 1505.

Under a statute like the Model Act, which does not expressly refer to unrealized appreciation, but does allow stock dividends out of any type of surplus, the question is whether unrealized appreciation can be a source of any type of surplus. This in turn means that the real issue is whether the Act contemplates recognition of unrealized appreciation at all, since if it does, the appreciation quite clearly must feed some type of surplus.

Of course, the wisdom of permitting stock dividends out of revaluation surplus is a quite different issue, but it may be a relevant one, at least where the statute is ambiguous. As we have seen, there may be doubt about the wisdom of authorizing stock dividends "out of" any type of capital surplus; but presumably, exactly the same result can often be accomplished by combining a transfer of capital surplus to stated capital with a stock split-up. And as to whether unrealized appreciation should be included in capital surplus, the fact that capital surplus can be used to back stock dividends would seem to be a less important objection than some of the other uses to which capital surplus can be put, such as a partial liquidation under § 41, or a repurchase of stock under § 5.

SECTION 3. REDUCTION OF CAPITAL

A. HISTORICAL BACKGROUND

As we have seen, the traditional role of stated capital has been that of a measuring rod, to be applied to net assets in order to determine how large a dividend could be paid "out of surplus," or "without impairing capital." Accordingly, it may come as a surprise to see how easily this stated capital measuring rod can be reduced. Actually, authorization to reduce capital has been included in corporation statutes from the very beginning, although under somewhat different circumstances. The original purpose of capital reduction under the general incorporation statutes [18] may perhaps best be inferred from the early rule that upon a reduction of stated capital, the corporation was required to distribute assets to the shareholders in the amount of the reduction. E.g., Seeley v. New York National Exchange Bank, 8 Daley 400 (N.Y.C.P. 1878), aff'd, 78 N.Y. 608 (1879). The implication of this rule is that reduction of stated capital was designed to enable a corporation which had more assets than it could usefully or

---

18. Probably the earliest occasions for reduction of stated capital stemmed from the requirement that a corporation organized pursuant to a special act could not commence business or enforce individual subscriptions until the entire authorized capital had been subscribed. The theory seems to have been that the authorized capital was the amount regarded as necessary to launch the enterprise successfully, and therefore no shareholder should be held to his subscription if that amount of capital had not been raised. But the rule proved to be a substantial impediment to incorporation, and it became common to provide for reduction of the authorized capital, presumably down to the amount which had in fact been raised. By the time of the general incorporation statutes, the requirement that a corporation's entire authorized capital be subscribed had disappeared.

profitably employ in its business — perhaps because the enterprise had never assumed its full proportions, or because of a desire to retrench — to return those excess assets to the shareholders despite the absence of a sufficient surplus. Obviously, if the reason for reducing capital was the existence of excess assets which the corporation could no longer usefully employ, it followed that those assets should be returned to the stockholders.

However, it was soon recognized that if a corporation's capital was already impaired at the time of the reduction, whether by losses, diminution in the value of property, or otherwise, the amount of assets to be distributed to the stockholders should be reduced by the amount of the impairment, so that the corporation would be left with assets equal to the capital as reduced, and the impairment would be eliminated. E. g., Jerome v. Cogswell, 204 U.S. 1, 27 S.Ct. 241 (1907). This link between capital impairment and reduction of stated capital paved the way for the development of what is today the most common use of reduction of stated capital — to eliminate an existing impairment of capital. See para. C(1) infra. And there appears to be no longer even a vestige of the requirement that a reduction of stated capital result in a distribution to stockholders. E.g., Jay Ronald Co., Inc. v. Marshall Mortgage Corp., 291 N.Y. 227, 52 N.E.2d 108 (1943).

B. MECHANICS OF A REDUCTION

As for the mechanics of carrying out a reduction of capital, the original view, developed when there was only par stock, and stated capital was thought to be tied directly to par times the number of shares outstanding, was that capital reduction should be tied to a reduction of either the par value per share or the number of shares outstanding. Since the par value of authorized stock was fixed in the certificate of incorporation, while the number of shares outstanding was not, reduction of par required an amendment to the certificate, whereas a change in the number of shares outstanding did not. All that the latter required was an acquisition of some of its shares by the corporation, which might be accomplished by a pro rata surrender of stock by all of the shareholders, and a cancellation of the shares reacquired. Unfortunately, this led some people to think that a reduction of capital was effected by any acquisition of stock, including a repurchase.[19]

[19]. This confusion greatly hampered the development of the law relating to repurchase of stock, until it was finally recognized, often under the impetus of a change in a corporation statute, that a repurchase of stock really constituted a combination of an acquisition of stock plus a distribution of as-

Such a view overlooked the fact that reduction of the stated capital measuring rod could be effected only in accordance with specific statutory authorization. That is, neither reduction of par value nor reduction in the number of par shares outstanding could in and of itself effect a valid reduction of capital; conversely, a reduction of capital pursuant to statutory formalities might be accomplished without either one of those two steps. Thus in the case of no-par stock, which does not call for any required minimum amount of stated capital, neither a change in the stated capital per share nor a change in the number of shares outstanding is required to produce a reduction of capital. And today the same may be true even where only par stock is present, if stated capital is greater than par times the number of shares outstanding because of a previous transfer from some type of surplus to stated capital.

In the light of the foregoing, consider the approaches to reduction of capital reflected in the following authorities, as well as the Model Act pattern embodied in §§ 53–55 and 62–64.

STATE EX REL. RADIO CORP. OF AMERICA v. BENSON

Superior Court of Delaware, 1924.
32 Del. (2 W.W.Harr.) 576, 128 A. 107.

PENNEWILL, C. J., delivering the opinion of the court:

The plaintiff filed in this court a petition praying for the issuance of a peremptory writ of mandamus to the defendant directed, commanding him to forthwith file in the office of the Secretary of State a certain certificate evidencing and embodying a proposed amendment to its Certificate of Incorporation.

The defendant refused to accept and file said certificate because the proposed amendment was adopted in compliance with Section 26 of the general incorporation law of the State (Rev. Code 1915, Sec. 1940) when, in his opinion, to legally accomplish the purpose sought, it should have been adopted in compliance with Section 28 of said law (Section 1942) and because the filing of such a certificate would be contrary to the established practice in the office of the Secretary of State.

---

sets, and that such a transaction could not be safely governed by the reduction of capital provisions alone. See Section 8 infra. Unfortunately some statutes perpetuate this confusion by specifically including as a method of reducing capital "the purchase of shares for retirement", in addition to actual retirement itself. Del.Corp. Law § 244(b). See Martin v. American Potash Chemical Corp., 33 Del.Ch. 234, 92 A.2d 295 (Sup.Ct.1952). In effect what this amounts to is a combination of a reduction of capital together with a repurchase of stock out of the capital surplus thereby created, which is apparently permitted under the Delaware statute anyway. Del. Corp.Law § 160.

The total authorized capital stock of the plaintiff corporation, at the time of the adoption of the proposed amendment, was five million shares of preferred stock of the par value of five dollars a share, amounting in the aggregate to twenty-five million dollars, and seven million five hundred thousand shares of common stock without nominal or par value.

Of the authorized stock there had been issued three million, eight hundred and ninety thousand, two hundred and seventy-six shares of preferred stock, and five million, seven hundred and eleven thousand, three hundred and two shares of common stock having no par value. By the amendment it is proposed that the total authorized capital stock of the corporation shall be five hundred thousand shares of "A" preferred stock of the par value of fifty dollars per share, amounting in the aggregate to twenty-five million dollars; and one million, five hundred thousand shares of "A" common stock, without nominal or par value.

It is further provided in the amendment that the entire voting power of the corporation shall be lodged in the holders of the preferred stock and the holders of the common stock without nominal or par value, and that the holders of the "A" preferred stock are to have ten votes for each full share thereof, or one vote for each one-tenth share thereof, represented by fractional certificates of said "A" preferred stock; holders of "A" common stock are to have five votes for each full share thereof, and one vote for each one-fifth share thereof, represented by fractional certificates of "A" common stock.

The parts of Sections 26 and 28 of the general incorporation laws material to the issue here involved are as follows:

> Section 26. [Now § 242.] "Any corporation of this State, . . . may, from time to time, when and as desired, amend its charter of incorporation . . . by increasing or decreasing its authorized capital stock; or by changing the number and par value of the shares of its capital stock;" etc.
>
> Section 28. [Now § 244.] "Any corporation organized under this chapter may reduce its capital stock at any time by a vote of, or by the written consent of stockholders representing two-thirds of its capital stock," etc. ". . . No such reduction, however, shall be made in the stock of any corporation until all its debts which are not otherwise fully secured shall have been paid and discharged. . . . The decrease of capital stock issued may be effected by retiring or reducing any class of the stock, or by drawing the necessary number of shares by lot for retirement, or by the surrender of every shareholder of his shares, and the issue to him in lieu thereof of a decreased number of shares, or by

the purchase at not above par of certain shares for retirement, or by retiring shares owned by the corporation or by reducing the par value of shares."

To amend a certificate of incorporation under section 26, a majority vote of the stockholders is required.

The Secretary of State has the right, and it is his duty, to refuse to file an amendment to a certificate of incorporation that is sought to be made under a section of the law that does not authorize the proposed amendment, but if the thing sought to be done might be legally done under the amendment offered, the Secretary has no right to refuse to file it because he thinks the corporation may do something thereunder which could only be legally done under a different section of the law.

If the purpose of the corporation, in securing the desired amendment, was to decrease the number of the shares of its capital stock, without reducing the capital represented by the stock, a procedure under section 26 would seem to be appropriate and permissible, because the section provides that a corporation may amend its charter by decreasing its authorized capital stock or by changing the number and par value of the shares of its capital stock.

The State admits that the amendment is good so far as it relates to the reduction in the number of shares, and the increase in the par value of preferred stock, because, after the provisions of the amendment are carried into effect, the capital, as distinguished from shares, would be the same, and the financial interests of creditors and stockholders would not be affected. But it is insisted that the amendment is not good as to the no par stock.

The question is whether section 26, under which the amendment was adopted, authorized a decrease in the number of the shares of no par stock issued, as well as authorized and unissued? We think it does because shares of no par stock represent aliquot or proportionate parts of the capital, and when decreased in the same proportion, they represent the same aliquot or proportionate parts of the capital.

It being possible for the corporation, under section 26, to issue the shares of no par stock as proposed in the amendment, we will assume that it will be done in the manner in which it can be legally done, so that only the shares will be reduced and the capital remain unchanged.

If the decrease in the number of shares is to be made in a way that would diminish the capital it represents, as by the disbursement of a portion of capital assets among stockholders, the procedure to amend must be as provided in section 28.

When the two sections are read together and carefully considered, it seems clear that section 26 was designed primarily for the convenience of the corporation, and section 28 for the protection of the creditors and stockholders of the corporation.

It is a well-known fact that corporations sometimes desire to greatly reduce the number of the shares of their capital stock for business reasons only, and no creditor can be injured thereby if the capital of the corporation is not decreased. But it is otherwise if not only the shares, but the capital they represent is reduced. And manifestly that is the reason for the requirement in section 28, that no reduction shall be made in the capital stock of a corporation until all its debts are paid. It means that the capital of the corporation, which is the creditors' security, shall not be impaired. It will be observed that the procedure provided in section 28 for reducing capital stock is very different, and much more strict and exacting, than that provided in section 26 for decreasing capital stock and changing the number and par value of its shares; and the only reasonable explanation is, that if the corporation wants to reduce its capital stock in some way that will diminish its capital and thereby impair the creditors' security, the strict requirements of section 28 must be met. But if the purpose is simply to change the number of shares for the convenience of the corporation, without diminishing the capital, then the easier procedure of section 26 may be followed.

Whether section 26 or section 28 applies in a particular case depends, not upon the character of the stock to be decreased, whether with or without par value, but upon the manner and effect of the proposed reduction.

The test by which the application of section 26 or section 28 may be determined, is whether the security of creditors or stockholders will be in any wise impaired by the proposed amendment. If the capital which the stock in question represents would not be reduced, the amendment may be under section 26, otherwise it must be under section 28.

Such construction of the law, we think, makes the two sections harmonious, and should remove any confusion or uncertainty that may exist respecting the proper application of the law to any proposed amendment for reducing the capital stock, or changing the number and par value of the shares of the capital stock of a corporation.

The conclusion of the Court is, that it being possible for the plaintiff corporation to issue the new no par stock under section 26, the amendment proffered to the Secretary of State should have been accepted and filed. If the corporation should attempt, under the amendment, to reduce its capital stock in such a way as to diminish its capital, which could be legally done only under section 28, the act would be not only unauthorized, but unlawful.

For the reason stated, the motion of the defendant to discharge the rule and dismiss the petition is refused.

OPINION NO. 766 OF THE ATTORNEY GENERAL OF ILLINOIS

1935 A.G.O. 85.

Hon. Edward J. Hughes, Secretary of State:

Dear Sir:

I have your letter of April 18, 1935 enclosing therewith Articles of Amendment to the Articles of Incorporation of The Aridor Company, in which you ask whether or not a resolution passed by the stockholders amending the Articles of Incorporation as provided in Section 52 of the Business Corporation Act so as to change the number of authorized shares to be issued or the par value thereof, has the effect of decreasing the stated capital, unless there is passed at the same meeting of stockholders, a resolution specifically decreasing the stated capital.

You advise that it has been insisted that the reduction in par value or the number of shares to be issued, does not carry with it as a corollary thereto, the determination of the amount of stated capital in its reduced amount; in other words, the question is, should the resulting effect upon stated capital be spelled out in the amendment resolution, when the reduction is made in connection with an amendment reducing the par value of shares?

The pertinent portions of Section 52 [counterpart of MBA § 53] are as follows:

"Sec. 52. **Right to Amend Articles of Incorporation.** A corporation may amend its articles of incorporation, from time to time, in any and as many respects as may be desired, *provided* that its articles of incorporation as amended contain only such provisions as might be lawfully contained in original articles of incorporation if made at the time of making such amendment, and, if a change in shares or an exchange or reclassification of shares is to be made, such provisions as may be necessary to effect such change, exchange, or reclassification as may be desired and as is permitted by this Act.

"In particular, and without limitation upon such general power of amendment, a corporation may amend its articles of incorporation, from time to time, so as: . . .

"(e) To increase or decrease the par value of the authorized shares of any class having a par value, whether issued or unissued.

"(f) To exchange, classify, reclassify, or cancel all or any part of its shares, whether issued or unissued."

Section 55 sets out the method of reporting the action of the stockholders' meeting to the Secretary of State, as follows:

"Sec. 55. **Articles of Amendment.** The articles of amendment shall . . . set forth:

"(a) The name of the corporation.

"(b) The amendment so adopted.

* * *

"(e) If such amendment provides for an exchange, reclassification, or cancellation of issued shares, or a reduction of the number of authorized shares of any class below the number of issued shares of that class, then a statement of the manner in which the same shall be effected.

"(f) If such amendment effects a change in the amount of stated capital or the amount of paid-in surplus, or both, then a statement of the manner in which the same is effected and a statement, expressed in dollars, of the amount of stated capital and the amount of paid-in surplus as changed by such amendment.

"If issued shares without par value are changed into the same or a different number of shares having par value, the aggregate par value of the shares into which the shares without par value are changed shall not exceed the sum of (1) the amount of stated capital represented by such shares without par value, and (2) the amount of surplus, if any, transferred to stated capital on account of such change, and (3) any additional consideration paid for such shares with par value and allocated to stated capital."

It will be noted that subsection (f), above, provides for the setting out of the amendment adopted, *in haec verba*, which, if it involves a reduction in par value of the value of the shares, will conclusively show the change in the capital structure.

Subsection (f) provides for the setting out of the rearranged capital structure, involving a statement, expressed in dollars, of the amount of stated capital and paid-in surplus, as changed.

Sections 52 and 55 must be read together. Section 55(f) is designed to report the consequences of the amendment. If the change in capital structure, reflected in dollars, were to be inserted in subsection (b), there would be no purpose in (f).

Section 2(k) defines "stated capital" applicable to par value shares at any particular time as, "the sum of the par value of all shares then issued having a par value." Therefore, the amount of the stated capital applicable to par value shares must be determined at all times by multiplying the number of the outstanding shares having a par value, by the par value of such shares.

Sections 19 and 60 provide for the restatement of stated capital and paid-in surplus, to be made by the board of directors. The amendment requires such restatement or reallocation, but the result of such restatement is not a proper part of the amendment.

If the amendment affected shares without par value, the resulting changes in stated capital and paid-in surplus should properly be made a part of the amendment resolution, in order that it be complete and not misleading. However, this is not necessary in the case of changes in par value shares, as the result involves a mere matter of computation in such case. In fact, the resolution of amendment adopted by the stockholders fixing the amount of the stated capital at any sum not in accordance with the par value and number of shares would be ineffective, and a resolution fixing the amount of stated capital at the identical sum determined as provided by the Act, would be surplusage and unnecessary.

It is my opinion that the change made by the amendment in the amount of the stated capital and paid-in surplus of the corporation is correctly set forth in Article Sixth of the Articles of Amendment, as required by Section 55(f) of the Act and that the resolution adopted by the stockholders need not set forth the change in the amount of the stated capital and paid-in surplus effected by such amendment.

C. IMPACT OF A REDUCTION OF CAPITAL

1. UPON CREDITORS

The earlier capital reduction statutes clearly recognized that the rights of creditors might be imperiled by a reduction of the safety margin represented by stated capital; accordingly, authority to reduce capital was normally conditioned upon some requirement like the payment of all debts not otherwise fully secured, as in the Delaware statute involved in the Benson case. The modern tendency, however, has been to afford less and less protection to creditors in connection with capital reduction. Thus today in Delaware it is quite possible that creditors will not even hear of a proposed capital reduction, since now the only requirement is the rather ineffectual one of publishing notice in the local county newspaper. Del. Corp. Law § 244(e). And the Model Act does not even contain that modest safeguard.

Actually, however, it is not the reduction of stated capital itself which can adversely affect creditors; the danger lies in the possible distribution or other use of the reduction surplus thereby created. Thus the real question is the uses to which reduction surplus can be put. Generally speaking, reduction surplus is just another type of capital surplus, as MBA § 64 expressly provides. That means that under some statutes, such as Delaware's "out of its net assets in excess of its capital", reduction surplus is as eligible for dividend distributions as earned surplus. And even when the use of capital surplus is more restricted, as under the Model Act, the effect of any distribution that is made is in essence to return to the shareholders a portion of the safety margin upon which creditors were supposed to have been entitled to rely.

Is there any basis for inferring special limitations on the distribution of reduction surplus? For example, the view might be adopted that because of the special risk to creditors entailed in a reduction of capital, the amount of reduction surplus available for distribution to stockholders should be determined only after taking account of any decline in the value of assets, whether or not recognition of such decline in value would have been required under normal circumstances.[20] Some judicial support for this approach may be derived from Benas v. Title Guaranty Trust Co., 216 Mo.App. 53, 267 S.W. 28 (St.L.Ct.App.1924), involving a corporation which reduced its capital by $1,500,000 and declared a dividend in property worth $1,150,000. The corporation's books showed net assets in excess of capital as reduced of substantially more than the amount of the dividend; but on the basis of the actual value of its assets the corporation had had a deficit of almost $700,000 prior to the reduction of capital and accordingly had a surplus of only $800,000 after it. The court held, against the objection of minority stockholders, that the board of directors had not only the power but the duty to rescind the $1,150,000 dividend because it would have violated the prohibition against impairment of capital. However, it is not clear that in requiring recognition of the current value of the corporation's property the court intended to announce a special rule for cases involving reduction of capital. Since the court scarcely mentioned the reduction of capital, Benas may well simply represent a decision in accord with Randall v. Bailey that in all circumstances it is the actual value rather than book value of property which determines the amount of surplus available for dividends.

When the purpose for which reduction surplus is created is the elimination of a deficit rather than a distribution to shareholders, the threat to creditors is less immediate; but it is just as real, since future earnings will be freed for distribution instead of having to be retained to make up the deficit. As to whether and when reduction surplus can be used for this purpose, here again the first question might be whether capital surplus generally can be used to eliminate a deficit and thereby provide a "fresh start" for the corporation. Of course in jurisdictions like Delaware where capital surplus seems to be just as free for distribution as earned surplus, this question is largely academic because in any event the net balance of the sur-

---

20. Note that this is the very result produced by the trial court's construction of New York § 58 in Randall v. Bailey, under which the second portion of the statute, expressly calling for valuation of assets, was confined to capital reduction situations. See page 322 supra.

plus accounts is available for dividends. But where the primary source of dividends is earned surplus (or any other fund based upon accumulated profits), it becomes important to decide to what extent a deficit in that account can be written off against capital surplus.

As is so often true in corporate finance, considerable guidance may be obtained by looking to the accounting approach on this problem. There, the first question is whether this problem can be sidestepped entirely by charging a particular loss directly against capital surplus in the first instance, thereby avoiding the creation of a deficit in earned surplus. Obviously, this can not be done in the case of normal operating losses which are automatically closed to earned surplus. But in the past it was sometimes done as to special nonrecurring losses, or diminutions in the value of property. To forestall this practice, the following Rule No. 2 was adopted by the AICPA in 1934:

> Capital surplus, however created, should not be used to relieve the income account of the current or future years of charges which would otherwise fall to be made thereagainst. This rule might be subject to the exception that where, upon reorganization, a reorganized company would be relieved of charges which would be required to be made against income if the existing corporation were continued, it might be regarded as permissible to accomplish the same result without reorganization provided the facts were as fully revealed to and the action as formally approved by the shareholders as in reorganization.[21]

Chapter 7(A) of ARB No. 43 states that adjustments of the kind described in the exception in the Rule constitute a "quasi-reorganization", and goes on to prescribe the requirements for such a transaction in the following terms:

> 3. If a corporation elects to restate its assets, capital stock, and surplus through a readjustment and thus avail itself of permission to relieve its future income account or earned surplus account of charges which would otherwise be made thereagainst, it should make a clear report to its shareholders of the restatements proposed to be made, and obtain their formal consent. It should present a fair balance sheet as at the date of the readjustment, in which the adjustment of carrying amounts is reasonably complete, in order that there may be no continuation of the circumstances which justify charges to capital surplus.

---

21. While Rule No. 2 refers expressly only to relieving the *income account* of proper charges, by common consent the Rule is regarded as equally forbidding the use of capital surplus to relieve *earned surplus* of proper charges against it (such as items which by-pass the income statement). See Baker and Cary, Cases on Corporations (3d ed., unabridged 1959) 1303.

4. A write-down of assets below amounts which are likely to be realized thereafter, though it may result in conservatism in the balance sheet at the readjustment date, may also result in overstatement of earnings or of earned surplus when the assets are subsequently realized. Therefore, in general, assets should be carried forward as of the date of readjustment at fair and not unduly conservative amounts, determined with due regard for the accounting to be employed by the company thereafter. . . .

6. When the amounts to be written off in a readjustment have been determined, they should be charged first against earned surplus to the full extent of such surplus; any balance may then be charged against capital surplus.

* * *

10. After such a readjustment earned surplus previously accumulated cannot properly be carried forward under that title. A new earned surplus account should be established, dated to show that it runs from the effective date of the readjustment, and this dating should be disclosed in financial statements until such time as the effective date is no longer deemed to possess any special significance.[22]

It may be noted that the accounting view of a quasi-reorganization provides some additional support for the idea that a reduction of capital is a good time to recognize any diminution in the value of the corporation's property. The accounting approach clearly calls for a complete shakedown of asset values to current levels, at least whenever reduction surplus is to be used to eliminate a deficit in earned surplus.

Conversely, however, as paragraph 4 of Chapter 7A indicates it is also important to guard against writing assets down to figures below current values in the course of a quasi-reorganization. There might be some temptation to do that in a case where there is ample stated capital to absorb such a reduction and the company is not looking to end up with a net balance in reduction surplus available for distribution. The objective would be to lower the depreciation charges in future years, thus increasing net income and hence the balance in earned surplus from and after the quasi-reorganization. This would of course be a clear violation of Rule No. 2. See generally, Comment, Writing Down Fixed Assets and Stated Capital, 44 Yale L.J. 1025 (1935).

There have only been a few cases in this area. In the most recent one, Hamilton Mfg. Co. v. United States, 214 F.2d 644 (7th Cir. 1954), the court seemed somewhat hostile to the idea of using capital surplus to wipe out an operating deficit and thereby obtain a fresh

---

[22]. The SEC takes much the same view of a quasi-reorganization. See Rapport, SEC Accounting Practice and Procedure (2d ed. 1963) 3.28–3.30.

start on "net profits", the statutory source of dividends. However, the impact of the case is sharply limited by the fact that actually the corporation involved had not sought to effect a quasi-reorganization; at most the issue was somewhat obliquely presented (in connection with a special tax laid on undistributed earnings) as to whether such a transaction could have served to free current earnings for dividends under state law. Two earlier cases, Haskell Mfg. Co. v. United States, 91 F.Supp. 26 (D.R.I.1950), and Lich v. United States Rubber Co., 39 F.Supp. 675 (D.N.J.1941), aff'd without opin., 123 F.2d 145 (3d Cir.1941), neither of which was cited in the Hamilton case, seemed to take a more favorable view of quasi-reorganization.

In many jurisdictions the statute specifically authorizes the use of capital surplus to write off a deficit in earned surplus. E.g., MBA § 64. Query the extent to which these statutes incorporate the standards imposed on quasi-reorganization by the accounting authorities. Perhaps the most important question in this connection is whether earned surplus must always be exhausted before capital surplus is resorted to, as the accounting authorities require. Under MBA § 64 this question is specifically answered in the affirmative. On the other hand, under Illinois § 60A, which provides that a "corporation may, by resolution of its board of directors, reduce its paid-in surplus by charging against its paid-in surplus (1) all or any part of any deficit arising from operating or other losses or from diminution in value of its assets . . .", the Attorney General of Illinois ruled that paid-in surplus could be used to write off a loss due to diminution in the value of assets, despite the existence of earned surplus which might have been used. Opinion No. 682, 1934 A.G.O. 273. Doubt about the soundness of this ruling has been expressed in 1 Ill.Bus.Corp.Act Ann. (2d ed.1947) 268:

> This opinion involves a construction of the words "any deficit arising from operating or other losses or from diminution in value of its assets" as including a net loss of any period regardless of the amount of accumulated profits of prior periods. The soundness of this opinion may be questioned, since the words quoted above might be interpreted to involve the recognition of the existence of a "deficit" only when losses or shrinkage in value of assets have eliminated any earned surplus.

2. IMPACT OF A REDUCTION UPON PREFERRED STOCKHOLDERS

The impact of a reduction of common capital upon the holders of preferred stock with a liquidation preference is quite analogous to the effect of any capital reduction on creditors, since the stated capital attributable to the common serves as a cushion for the liquidation preference in much the same way that all capital serves as a safety margin for the claims of creditors. As with creditors, preferred stockholders are normally assumed to have contracted in the light of the express permission to reduce capital contained in the statute; and accordingly, something more than the mere existence of a liquidation preference is needed before a contractual restriction on reducing capital will be inferred. However, reduction of capital could touch off the provision in practically every state corporation statute which gives a class vote, or sometimes even a right to require the corporation to purchase the stock at its appraised value, in the event of an amendment to the certificate of incorporation which is prejudicial to the interests of the class. To illustrate, in Matter of Kinney, 279 N.Y. 423, 18 N.E.2d 645 (1939), the court held that a certificate amendment reducing the stated capital attributable to common stock by 90%, as a result of changing the common from no-par stock with a stated value of $10 per share to par stock with a par value of $1, fell within a New York statute which entitled preferred stockholders to receive the appraised value of their shares in the event of an amendment altering a "preferential right". Said the court:

> We are thus brought to a consideration of the provision of the amended certificate which reduced the stated capital of the corporation . . . the resulting reduction in the stated capital, totaling $1,440,000, being thereby transferred to surplus. Prior to such transfer, the eight-dollar cumulative preferred stock was in a position to benefit from the earning power of such capital, and in the event of liquidation or dissolution such capital would be available for distribution to such stockholders, subject only to diminution by losses in business operations. It could not have been used for dividends or for the purchase of any shares of stock. When this sum of $1,440,000, amounting to about one-third of the capital of the corporation, was transferred from capital to surplus, the eight-dollar cumulative preferred stock lost its right to rely upon this portion of capital. The capital structure was so altered that it was placed within the power of the corporation to deprive forever the preferred stockholders of their preferential rights in regard to this portion of the capital structure. In brief this $1,440,000 was in itself a security of approximately twenty-eight dollars for each share of the old preferred stock and has now by this amendment of the certificate of incorporation become a surplus that may no longer support such stock.

Although most state statutes provide only a class vote instead of an appraisal remedy to stockholders whose preferential rights are adversely affected, the Kinney decision would appear to be equally pertinent on that issue. Thus under the Model Act a certificate amendment reducing common capital by reducing the par value of outstanding shares might well be thought to "change the . . . preferences" of preferred stock with a liquidation preference within the meaning of § 55(e), which provides for a class vote in such circumstances. However, there is a difficulty here which seems to have been entirely overlooked in the Kinney case. Under most corporation statutes, including both the New York statute and the Model Act, a class vote or other special class right is conditioned upon a *certificate amendment* which adversely affects the class. That puts reduction of capital into a somewhat anomalous position, because in many cases reduction of capital can be accomplished without any amendment of the certificate. E.g., MBA § 63. In such cases it is clear that any remedy conditioned upon amendment of the certificate is not available, despite the fact that the impact on the preferred is exactly the same as if the reduction of capital had involved an amendment of the certificate. And since the rights of preferred stock in connection with reduction of capital should presumably be the same whether there is an amendment of the certificate or not, perhaps this suggests that, despite the Kinney decision, capital reduction pursuant to a certificate amendment should be held not to touch off a provision like MBA § 55.[23]

Suppose the proposal is to reduce the stated capital attributable to the preferred. Of course no change in the contractual terms of the preferred stock without fair compensation could be imposed upon an unwilling preferred stockholder; for example, a compulsory pro rata reduction in the number of the preferred shares, which of course would effectively reduce the total annual dividend of the preferred, and the total liquidation preference, would not be sustained. See Kennedy v. Carolina Public Service Co., 262 F. 803 (N.D.Ga.1920). But it is possible to reduce the stated capital attributable to preferred stock without purporting to affect any of the other terms of preferred. See Commonwealth & Southern Corp., page 306, supra. In that event, there would be a good deal less reason for concern on the part of the preferred, since their interest depends upon their contractual terms, and not the amount of capital attributable to the preferred. Accordingly, there may be doubt about the wisdom of the requirement in Page v. Whittenton Mfg. Co., 211 Mass. 424, 428, 97 N.E. 1006, 1007 (1912), to the effect that in the absence of statute common capital must "be first resorted to to the point of extinction before the preferred stock can be compelled to contribute" to a reduc-

---

23. In Delaware this problem is even more acute. Presumably in order to confirm the decision in the Benson case, supra, that any reduction of capital must be carried out under § 244 of the Delaware law, and not § 242 relating to certificate amendments, § 242 was changed to expressly require that any amendment of a certificate effecting a change in issued shares "shall set forth that the capital of the corporation will not be reduced under or by reason of the amendment". In the face of that language, it seems clear that even if capital is reduced in conjunction with a certificate amendment, the reduction of capital can not be the basis for a class vote under the provision in § 242 authorizing such a vote in the case of a *certificate amendment* which "would alter or change the preferences" of the class.

tion of capital. In any event, such a rule is self-defeating, since normally no reduction of the capital attributable to any class can be effected without the support of the common's voting power, and the common are certainly not going to vote their own "suicide."

It follows, then, that it is the total stated capital remaining after a reduction of capital which is of primary significance, and not the particular amounts allocated to the various classes. Further confirmation of this view under the Model Act may be found in the fact that the provision in § 63 prohibiting reduction of capital below the liquidation preferences of preferred stock relates to total stated capital rather than preferred capital alone. There are, however, some difficulties with this latter provision which might be noted here. First, there is no counterpart limitation applicable to a reduction of capital pursuant to certificate amendment under § 53, which introduces another unfortunate distinction between par and no-par stock in the area of the relationship between stated capital and liquidation preferences. In addition, the measure of the limitation on reduction of capital in § 63 seems inconsistent with the provisions of § 19 relating to stated capital upon original issue. On the one hand, the § 63 limitation is more strict, since there is no prohibition against starting out with stated capital upon original issue less than liquidation preferences; on the other hand, the § 63 limitation is more lenient than the provision for allocation of consideration in § 19, which looks solely to preferred stated capital rather than total stated capital as in § 63.

Finally, query how desirable an absolute restriction against reducing stated capital below the total liquidation preferences is. As a practical matter, it may simply mean that if the preferred should be willing to permit a deeper cut, they would have to accept a cut in their liquidation preference as well.

Despite what has been said, however, it does make some difference whether it is the preferred capital rather than the common which is reduced. First, the preferred are more likely to get a class vote upon a reduction of preferred capital, e. g. Brill v. Blakeley, 308 N.Y. 951, 127 N.E.2d 96 (1955), particularly if, as has typically been true, the preferred is par stock and hence subject to statutes like MBA § 55(b) which provide such a vote to any class whose par is changed. In such a case, incidentally, the preferred ought to be very wary of approving a reduction in preferred capital while any substantial amount of common capital remains, for the very reason that the latter may be subject to further reduction without any approval by the preferred.

---

3. RESPECTIVE RIGHTS OF PREFERRED AND COMMON IN REDUCTION SURPLUS

The other possible area of difference between reduction of preferred capital and reduction of common relates to the distribution of any net reduction surplus which may result. Once more this is part of the broader question of the extent to which there are limitations on the distribution generally of various types of capital surplus.[24] In the absence of statute, there seems little doubt that paid-in surplus on junior shares is not restricted to distribution to preferred; and the same would appear to be true as to capital surplus created by reduction of surplus. Although in the reduction case there is some force in the argument for a freeze on dividends to the junior stockholders until the impairment of the senior "cushion" resulting from the reduction of common capital has been restored, it seems unlikely that such a freeze could be implied merely from the inter-class contract between the preferred and the common.

It is much easier to imply equitable limitations on the use of capital surplus stemming from the preferred, whether upon original issue or pursuant to a reduction of capital.[25] Presumably, any prohibition would apply to not only direct distribution of such capital surplus to the junior stock, but also such indirect benefits to the juniors as charging preferred dividends to that capital surplus despite the existence of earned surplus (or some other capital surplus), thus preserving the latter for dividends to the junior. Cf. MBA § 41 (last paragraph).

Nevertheless, there are some difficulties with this analysis, particularly under a modern statute like the Model Act which appears to have taken some account of these inter-class conflicts but is completely silent on this item. Note, for example, that § 41(d), which specifically limits distributions of capital surplus in terms of preferred liquidation preferences, neither expresses nor invites any further distinction based upon the original source of the capital surplus.[26] Hence the result may be that even as to capital surplus contributed by the preferred, they obtain no special rights except such as are expressly provided in the preferred share contract embodied in the certificate of incorporation.

GRAHAM v. LOUISVILLE TRANSIT CO.

Court of Appeals of Kentucky, 1951. 243 S.W.2d 1019.

CULLEN, Commissioner. In an action against a representative group of its preferred shareholders, and a representative group of its common shareholders, Louisville Transit Co. and its board of directors sought a declaration as to the right of the company to pay dividends

---

24. See generally the excellent analysis of these problems in Baker and Cary, op. cit. note 21 supra, at 1254–1256, 1295–1303, 1320.

25. Id. at 1255, note 9, and 1297.

26. For a thorough analysis of distribution and other problems under provisions for "partial liquidation" like MBA § 41, see Note, Dividends from Contributed Capital and Protection of Preferred Shareholders, 65 Harv.L. Rev. 1203, 1211–1217 (1952).

out of a surplus that was created upon the organization of the company. . . .

* * *

Louisville Transit Co. is a new Kentucky corporation that grew out of a consolidation of The Louisville Railway Company and the Capital Transit Company, both of which were Kentucky corporations. The new corporation came into existence on May 7, 1951. . . .

Immediately prior to the consolidation, The Louisville Railway Company had outstanding, 32,954 shares of preferred stock, with a par value of $100 per share. The stock had a five percent per annum dividend preference, payable "out of the net earnings of the company," and the dividends were cumulative. There was no right of preference on dissolution. No dividends had been paid since 1930, and the arrearage of cumulative dividends amounted to $100 per share. There were 80,942 shares of common stock, with a par value of $100 per share, on which no dividends had been paid since 1930.

In 1941, the railway company had created a capital deficit of almost $9 million by reducing the book value of its operating properties, because of obsolescence, and by writing off abandoned property. Earnings and profits subsequent to 1941, in the amount of almost $4 million, had reduced the deficit so that at the time of consolidation the deficit was $4,890,969.

Immediately prior to the consolidation, Capital Transit Company had outstanding, 50 shares of common stock with a par value of $100 per share, of which 40 shares were owned by The Louisville Railway Company. Capital Transit Company had a surplus of $8,936.

In the consolidation, each share of preferred stock of The Louisville Railway Company (having a par value of $100 and a dividend arrearage of $100) was exchanged for $2.50 in cash and one share of preferred stock of Louisville Transit Co., with a par value of $80. Each share of common stock of the railway company (having a par value of $100), was exchanged for one share of common stock of Louisville Transit Co., with a par value of $10. Each publicly-owned share of common stock of Capital Transit Company (having a par value of $100) was exchanged for ten shares of common stock of Louisville Transit Co.

As a result of the reduction of capital stock accomplished in the consolidation, Louisville Transit Co. came into existence with a surplus of $2,950,442.55. That is the surplus which is involved in this action.

The preferred stock in Louisville Transit Co. is entitled to a five percent annual dividend, payable quarterly, "out of funds legally available for the payment of dividends," and cumulative after April 1, 1950, in preference to dividends on the common stock. The preferred stock also is entitled to a preference on dissolution, in an amount equal to all accrued, unpaid dividends, and an amount equal to twice the amount per share paid to the common shareholders, not to exceed a maximum of $80 per share. The preferred stock is redeemable at par plus accrued, unpaid dividends.

Between the time of organization of Louisville Transit Co. and the time of bringing the action, the company realized earnings and profits in the amount of $128,997. The accrued dividends on the preferred stock amounted to $197,724. Thus, the basis for an actual controversy existed as to the right to pay, out of the surplus, the amount by which the earnings were insufficient to meet the accrued dividends.

It is alleged in the petition, and not denied in the answer, that at the present time, the portion of the surplus proposed to be distributed in dividends is not needed in the conduct of the company's business.

Reaching now the issues raised on the appeal, it appears at the outset that all parties agree that the surplus is available for distribution among the stockholders; the only controversy being as to respective rights of the preferred and the common shareholders in such distribution. The company and its board of directors contend that the surplus is available for the payment of dividends the same as if it had been accrued by earnings of the company since its organization. The preferred stockholders maintain that the surplus is a "paid-in" surplus and that by reason of their rights to preference on dissolution, they are entitled to have set aside and preserved, before the payment of any dividends on the common stock, an amount equal to the total par value of all the preferred stock. The common stockholders take the position that the surplus is distributable, not in the form of dividends, but in the way of a distribution of *capital*, and that the distribution must be on an equitable basis, either in proportion to the respective "contributions" made by the two classes of stockholders in the exchange of the old stock for the new, or in proportion to the respective holdings of common and preferred stock. However, it appears that the common stockholders are primarily interested in overcoming the contention of the preferred stockholders, and they do not strongly urge any right other than their right to receive a dividend too, if the preferred stockholders are given a dividend.

We have been cited to no authority, and have been unable to find any, on the specific question of the status, and availability for payment of dividends, of a surplus created upon the organization of a consolidated corporation, through a reduction in the capital of the consolidating corporations. However, a closely analogous situation was presented in Haggard v. Lexington Utilities Co., 260 Ky. 261, 84 S.W. 2d 84, in which a corporation translated a deficit into a surplus by means of a reduction of its capital stock. In that case the capital of the corporation became impaired by reason of losses on investments. The amount of the impairment was $1,700,000. Subsequently, the corporation reduced its capital stock, as a result of which a surplus was created. Between the time the capital became impaired and the time of the reduction of the stock, the corporation had net earnings of $200,000, which were included in the surplus. This Court held that the $200,000 constituted "earned surplus" and was available for the payment of dividends, subject to no restrictions except as set forth in the articles of incorporation.

We discern no distinction in principle between the situation in the Haggard case and that in the instant case. The fact that the instant case involves a new corporation, whereas in the Haggard case the old corporation continued in existence, does not suggest a basis for distinction, where in both cases the sources of the surplus was earnings. It is admitted in this case that The Louisville Railway Company between the time its capital became impaired in 1941, and the time of the consolidation in 1951, had net earnings of almost $4 million, which is substantially in excess of the surplus that was created on organization of the new corporation.

If the surplus of the Louisville Transit Co., under authority of the Haggard case, is "earned surplus," then the contentions of the preferred and common stockholders, as to their respective preferences in the surplus, must fail. The argument of the preferred shareholders is predicated on the theory that the surplus is a "paid-in" surplus resulting from a reduction of capital stock. The argument of the common stockholders is that the surplus is the equivalent of contributed capital. Actually, the common shareholders take inconsistent positions in their argument, because they contend that the surplus is not "capital" within the meaning of KRS 271.265, prohibiting the payment of dividends out of capital, yet they argue that the surplus should be distributed on the same basis as if it were capital.

It is clear that the only rights possessed by the shareholders in Louisville Transit Co. are those given them under the articles of incorporation. . . .

The only reason for looking behind the organization of the new corporation is to determine the character of the surplus created upon the organization. Upon so looking behind, we find that the surplus, under authority of the Haggard case, may be characterized as earned surplus. Therefore, regardless of who might have been entitled to the earnings had the old corporation continued to exist, the surplus of the new corporation, attributable to such earnings, is distributable on the same basis as if the surplus had been derived entirely from earnings of the new corporation, and the respective rights of the shareholders of the new corporation, in the distribution, are as provided in the articles of incorporation.

If we do not look behind the organization of the new corporation, but consider only what happened at the time of organization, the surplus would fall in the class of a paid-in surplus resulting from the receipt of assets, upon issuance of the stock of the corporation, in excess of the par value of the stock. There is ample authority for the proposition that premiums realized from the sale of stock may be regarded as profits out of which dividends may be paid. . . .

The preferred shareholders, in support of their contention that portions of the surplus equal to the par value of their stock must be set aside as a reserve, cite a note in 31 Columbia Law Review, at page 851, to the effect that a paid-in surplus resulting from a reduction of capital stock should be held as security for the payment of the principal and dividends of the preferred stock, where the preferred stock is non-voting and has a preference on dissolution. The answer to this is found in the fact that if the organization of the Louisville Transit Co. is looked behind, the surplus takes the character of an earned surplus, under the Haggard case; and if the organization of the new corporation is not looked behind, the surplus is not one created by a reduction of capital stock, but rather is one created by the sale of stock above par. Also, the preferred stock of The Louisville Railway Company had voting rights, and did not have a preference on dissolution, so the factual situation on which the law review note is predicated does not exist here.

Under the articles of incorporation of the Louisville Transit Co., dividends on the preferred stock are payable out of "any funds legally available for the payment of dividends." The articles place no restriction on the payment of dividends on the common stock, other than that the dividends on the preferred must first be provided for. So there is no contractual inhibition to the treatment of the surplus as a simple earned surplus for the purpose of dividend payments.

The governing statute, KRS 271.265, does not limit dividend sources to current earnings. The only restrictions imposed by the statute are that dividends may not be declared or paid if the corporation is insolvent or if the payment would render the corporation insolvent or would diminish the amount of the "capital" of the corporation. We think it is clear that "capital," as used in this statute, means capitalized assets, and has the same meaning as "capital stock." The surplus of the Louisville Transit Co. is not "capital" within the meaning of the statute.

It perhaps should be noted that no creditors of the corporation are involved in this action. According to the pleadings, the surplus is a bona fide surplus, in that the real value of the assets of the corporation is equal to the book value. The judgment of the circuit court authorizes the use of the surplus for the payment of dividends when the amount paid "is not needed in the conduct of Louisville Transit Co.'s business." We construe this to include the meaning that the surplus must be a bona fide surplus based on real values.

The judgment is affirmed.

For more on capital reduction, see Note, The Current Law Regarding Reduction of Capital: Its Methodology, Purposes and Dangers, 110 U.Pa.L.Rev. 723 (1962); Note, Reduction of Capital Stock and Distribution of Capital Assets upon Reduction, 35 A.L.R.2d 1149 (1954).

SECTION 4. TAX ASPECTS OF CORPORATE DIVIDENDS

A. CORPORATE DISTRIBUTIONS IN GENERAL

The starting point for the income tax treatment of corporate distributions to shareholders is § 301, which covers, generally speaking, all distributions by a corporation to its shareholders in their capacity as shareholders except (1) distributions of stock of the corporation, or rights to such stock, and (2) distributions in redemption of stock under certain circumstances, including partial and complete liquidation. As to those distributions which are covered, § 301 distinguishes between corporate distributions which are *dividends in the tax sense*, within the meaning of § 316, and those which are not. Taxable dividends must be included in gross income under §§ 301(c)(1) and 61(a)(7), while distributions which are not dividends in the tax sense are applied against the basis of the stock under § 301(c)(2), with any excess treated as a gain from the sale or exchange of property under § 301(c)(3)(A).

The definition of a dividend in the tax sense in § 316(a) is based primarily upon the concept of corporate "earnings and profits": any distribution to a shareholder is a dividend if it is (1) out of earnings and profits accumulated after February 28, 1913,[27] or (2) out of the earnings and profits of the current year (*computed as of the close of the year*, regardless of when the distribution was made) whether or not there are any accumulated earnings and profits. Section 316(a) eliminates most tracing requirements by specifying that whenever there are any earnings and profits, a distribution is deemed to be out of the earnings and profits rather than from any other source—and from the most recent earnings and profits. Moreover, in many situations it is clear that the distribution is covered by one of the two sources of earnings and profits, in which event it is not necessary to

---

27. This limitation based upon the date of the enactment of the 1913 Income Tax Act represents a legislative policy decision rather than a constitutional requirement, Lynch v. Hornby, 247 U. S. 339, 38 S.Ct. 543, 62 L.Ed. 1149 (1918), and is no longer of much practical significance anyway.

determine the exact amount of either one. However, in some cases the precise dollar amount of at least one of the two sources does become crucial, in which event the question of how to compute earnings and profits must be resolved. See topic B, infra.

Taxable dividends received by individuals (including trusts and estates) are subject to an exclusion of the first $100 of dividends received. A husband and wife are each entitled to a $100 exclusion, but such exclusion may only be applied against dividends received by the particular spouse or on jointly owned stock. As to corporations receiving taxable dividends, § 243 provides a deduction in the amount of 85% of any dividends received—in other words, only 15% of intercorporate dividends are included in taxable income. In addition, members of an "affiliated group" of corporations which file separate returns may elect to obtain a 100% dividends received deduction (subject to certain terms and conditions, including the limitation of the affiliated group to one surtax exemption and one minimum accumulated earnings credit).

As already indicated, there are some types of distributions which are not subject to § 301, but are governed by some other specific Code provision. See § 301(f). For example, the effect of § 302 is to except distributions in redemption of stock from § 301. But this exception only applies if the redemption distribution is not essentially equivalent to a dividend, which makes the whole matter somewhat circular. A redemption distribution which is not equivalent to a dividend is treated as *in exchange* for the stock, which brings the capital gain or loss provisions into play. Similarly § 331 excepts distributions in a complete or partial liquidation of a corporation, where again the distribution is treated as in exchange for the stock. The definitions of complete and partial liquidations, while having non-tax antecedents, are tax words of art, and are both extremely important and quite complex. In addition, the definition of partial liquidation in § 346 is also in terms of a distribution not essentially equivalent to a dividend, thus being as circular as the redemption definition.

Distributions of a corporation's own stock, or rights to such stock, are governed by §§ 305, 306 and 307, which expressly make such distributions nontaxable. However, as will be seen later, under certain circumstances the stockholder may have ordinary income rather than capital gain when he disposes of the dividend stock.

These non-dividend corporate distributions are among the most troublesome transactions in the tax law, since they are right on the borderline between capital gain and ordinary income. If corporate earnings are distributed to stockholders, ordinary taxable dividends will result. If instead the corporation retains its earnings there are no tax incidents to the stockholders, even though the value of their stock is likely to rise; and upon a subsequent sale of the stock, the gain due to the accumulated earnings will simply be a part of the total gain on the transaction, which will normally be taxed at capital gains rather than ordinary income rates. What the stockholders would most like is to obtain some of the corporate earnings at capital gains rates without having to give up their stock interest, as they have to do in the case of a sale; and it is here that such borderline transactions as stock redemptions, partial liquidations and stock dividends occur.

In addition to this basic pattern there are two polar factors which are operative in this area. On the one hand, § 1014(a) provides that upon the death of a stockholder his stock gets a new basis equal to its value at that time, which means that if stock is held until death and then sold the earnings accumulated up to the date of death will not even have produced a capital gain tax. On the other hand, § 531, to be discussed in detail later, imposes a special additional tax on any corporation which accumulates its earnings for the purpose of avoiding income tax to stockholders, and the threat of this tax may constitute powerful pressure toward the distribution of taxable dividends.

B. COMPUTATION OF EARNINGS AND PROFITS

Despite the fact that the whole dividend structure is bottomed on the "earnings and profits" concept, that term is nowhere defined in the Code. While § 312 does describe the effect of certain transactions, such as redemptions and corporate divisions, on earnings and profits, it does not give any comprehensive picture of how earnings and profits are to be determined.

It is clear that earnings and profits for the year are not the same as taxable income—the increase in corporate earned surplus would be a more accurate, though still far from exact, measure of earnings and profits. Thus Reg. § 1.312–6, which helps to fill some of the void here, expressly provides for the inclusion in earnings and profits of exempt income, which would include such items as tax-exempt interest and life insurance proceeds. Similarly, certain special deductions allowed in the determination of net income, such as for dividends received, are not deductible in determining earnings and profits. And depletion must be based on cost, rather than the percentage method permitted in computing taxable income. On the other hand, many items not permitted as deductions in computing taxable income, such as federal income taxes, excess charitable contributions, and unreasonable compensation, are deductible in determining earnings and profits.

On matters of timing, earnings and profits follow taxable income much more closely. Thus Reg. § 1.312–6 provides that the same method of accounting used in determining taxable income should be used in determining earnings and profits. Similarly, gains and losses are recognized for earnings and profits purposes at the same time they are recognized as taxable income, thus importing the whole tax-free exchange pattern into the earnings and profits area. This same notion has been applied, without any express support in the regulations, to postpone reflecting in earnings and profits a gain from cancellation of indebtedness which had not yet been recognized in the determination of taxable income. Bangor & Aroostook Ry. Co. v. Commissioner, 193 F.2d 827 (1st Cir. 1951).

See generally, Rudick, "Dividends" and "Earnings or Profits" Under the Income Tax Law: Corporate Non-Liquidating Distributions, 89 U.Pa.L.Rev. 865 (1941); Albrecht, "Dividends" and "Earnings or Profits," 7 Tax L.Rev. 157 (1952); Bittker, Federal Income Taxation of Corporations and Shareholders (1959) 141–149.

C. DISGUISED DIVIDENDS

It is clear that a distribution may be a dividend for tax purposes although it is not a formal dividend under state law, and even though it is not pro rata among the stockholders. Some cases involve a payment to a stockholder which purports to be something other than a dividend, i. e., interest, rent, or compensation. In these circumstances characterization of the payment as a dividend will normally not affect the shareholder (except perhaps for the dividend exclusion) because the payment represents ordinary income to him anyway, and the real issue is the deductibility of the payment by the corporation. In other situations, the disguised dividend may take the form of a benefit obtained by the shareholder as a result of corporate action— for example, a "bargain" sale or lease by the corporation to a stockholder. Lying somewhere between these two situations is one of the most troublesome types of case, the loan to a controlling stockholder, which as a practical matter gives the stockholder the benefit of corporate funds to the same extent as a dividend.

D. DIVIDENDS IN KIND

1. **Effect upon the Corporation.** When a corporation distributes property rather than cash as a dividend to its stockholders, there are a number of problems which test the tax relationship between a cor-

poration and its stockholders. One of the most important early questions was whether a corporation which distributed property that had appreciated in value as a dividend was required to include the unrealized appreciation in its income. Although the case of General Utilities & Operating Co. v. Helvering, 296 U.S. 200, 56 S.Ct. 185, 80 L.Ed. 154 (1935), is widely regarded as having answered this question in the negative, actually the Court did not pass on that question, because it had not been raised in the lower courts. Rather the Court simply affirmed the finding of the trial court that the corporation had not declared a dividend in a specified dollar amount and then satisfied the dividend obligation by distributing property (a case in which concededly the spread between the dollar amount of the dividend and the basis of the property distributed would have been taxable to the corporation). In any event, the 1954 Code confirmed the view usually attributed to General Utilities by providing in § 311 that apart from the three exceptions there noted, "no gain or loss shall be recognized to a corporation on the distribution, with respect to its stock, of . . . property."

However, § 311 does not eliminate all the problems in this area. For example, where, as in the General Utilities case itself, the property distributed to the stockholders is promptly sold to a third party, in accordance with arrangements previously made by the corporation, it is at least open to argument that the corporation rather than the stockholders really made the sale. (It was on this basis that the Court of Appeals had decided for the Government in General Utilities; but this argument too had not been raised in the trial court, and accordingly the Supreme Court refused to consider it.) Moreover, the Senate Finance Committee Report, S.Rep.No.1622, 83rd Cong., 2d Sess. (1954) 247, expressly seeks to preserve some flexibility in this area:

> Your committee does not intend, however, . . . to alter existing law in the case of distributions of property, which has appreciated or depreciated in value, where such distributions are made to persons other than shareholders or are made to shareholders in a capacity other than that of a shareholder. . . . [In addition] your committee does not intend to change existing law with respect to attribution of income of shareholders to their corporation as exemplified for example in the case of Commissioner v. First State Bank of Stratford (168 F.2d 1004 [5th Cir. 1948]).

In the Bank of Stratford case referred to in the Committee Report a bank had charged off certain notes as worthless prior to 1942, thereby obtaining a tax benefit. When it appeared in 1942 that substantial payments would be made on the notes, the bank declared the notes as a dividend in kind and transferred them to the stockholders. The Commissioner successfully included in the bank's income for 1942 the amounts collected by the stockholders during that year on the notes. In holding that the dividend in kind in effect represented an anticipatory assignment of income, since the notes when collected would have been income to the bank, the court said:

> Like Banquo's ghost, the question that will not down is this: May a bank detach interest coupons from negotiable bonds owned by it, assign the coupons to its shareholders as a dividend in kind, and avoid the payment of income tax on the interest subsequently collected by the assignee of the coupons? In other words, by means of a dividend in kind, may a corporation avoid income taxes by doing exactly what was done (without success) by an individual by means of a gift in Helvering v. Horst, 311 U.S. 112, 61 S.Ct. 144? If so, a corporation need not ever again pay an income tax on interest derived from coupons detached from negotiable bonds.
>
> . . .
>
> The avoidance of taxes may be perfectly legitimate, but it cannot be done by the anticipatory assignment of notes representing income, as a dividend in kind, and the subsequent collection of said notes by the assignees. The respondent is a banking corporation, organized and operated for profit. The acquisition of profits for its shareholders was the purpose of its creation. The collection of interest on loans was a principal source of its income. The payment of dividends to its shareholders was the enjoyment of its income. A body corporate can be said to enjoy its income in no other way. Like the "life-rendering pelican" it feeds its shareholders upon dividends. Whether they are in the form of notes or money is immaterial if the dividend is out of earnings, or consists of property purchased from earnings or which is regarded as earnings for accounting purposes. The respondent exercised its power to procure payment of its income to another, which was "the enjoyment, and hence the realization," of its income.
>
> The distinction between General Utilities v. Helvering, supra, and this case lies in the difference in the character of the respective properties distributed as dividends in kind; one represented a capital asset, the other represents income. In the former, the fruit was on the trees; in the latter, the tree itself represents fruit of prior years that was not taxed. The distinction is the same as would have existed in the Horst case if the father had given his son the bond with the unearned-interest coupons attached.

A somewhat similar case is First National Bank of St. Elmo, Illinois v. United States, 194 F.2d 389 (7th Cir. 1952), where a bank, after litigation over oil royalties on land held by it, reached a settlement under which it would receive previously impounded royalties in return for the surrender of certain claims, and thereupon trans-

Sec. 4   TAX ASPECTS OF DIVIDENDS   377

ferred its rights to its stockholders as a dividend in kind. The impounded royalties later paid to the stockholders were held taxable income to the bank.

A classic illustration of the tax avoidance possibilities in this area appears in Rudco Oil & Gas Co. v. United States, 113 Ct.Cl. 206, 82 F.Supp. 746 (1949), in which a family corporation, having determined that its cash position justified a dividend of approximately $60,000, conveyed its interests in oil and gas leases to its shareholders to be held by them until the lessees had paid that sum. By the end of the year over $59,000 had been paid, and the shareholders reconveyed the interests to the corporation. The court held that the amount received by the stockholders was taxable to the corporation (as well as a dividend to the shareholders), since the conveyance was merely "the assignment of future income . . ., a transaction without purpose or intended consequences except in relation to income tax liability."

Does the rationale of the foregoing cases reach the situation where a corporation distributes its inventory as a dividend in kind to its stockholders who thereafter sell it to a third party? In United States v. Lynch, 192 F.2d 718 (9th Cir. 1951), a corporation in the business of growing and marketing apples declared a dividend in kind to its three stockholders of 22,000 boxes of apples. The stockholders then agreed with the corporation that it should sell the apples for their account. Although the corporation was liquidated two months later, the court found that the dividend was not intended to be a liquidation distribution. In taxing the net profit from the sale of the apples to the corporation, the court said:

> The dividend in question was not the kind of a distribution contemplated by [the predecessor of § 316(a)], and must be ignored for tax purposes. Distribution of corporate inventory with the expectation of immediate sale by the shareholders pointedly suggests a transaction outside the range of normal commercially-motivated and justifiable corporate activity, yet we have here a stronger case, because the sale was to be made by utilizing the corporation's facilities in the ordinary course of its business; the shareholders did not engage in a separate and independent business in which the apples were to be used. The shareholders, under the circumstances of this case, cannot avoid payment of the price Congress has decreed must be paid for use of the corporate entity.

Accord, A.B.C.D. Lands, Inc. v. Commissioner, 41 T.C. 840 (1964). In Louisiana Irrigation and Mill Co. v. Commissioner, 14 T.C.M. 1252 (1955), the Tax Court refused to find income to the corporation upon a distribution of appreciated inventory to its stockholders. However, it should be noted that in this case the Commissioner had predicated the realization of income by the corporation exclusively upon the fact that appreciated inventory was distributed to the stockholders — he did not rely at all upon later sale of that inventory by the stockholders, despite the fact that the corporation had made arrangements to facilitate such sale by the stockholders. Hence the court found the Lynch and Stratford cases inapplicable because they involved attribution to the corporation of income received by the stockholders. And as to the corporate realization of income simply as a result of distributing property to stockholders, the court cited General Utilities and held that no different result was called for merely because it was inventory that was distributed. Accord, Rev.Rul. 57–490, 1957–2 Cum.Bull. 231. See generally, Comment, The Imputed Sale and Anticipatory Assignment of Income Doctrines: Their Effect on IRC §§ 311 & 336, 15 Buffalo L.Rev. 154 (1965).

2. **Tax Incidents to the Shareholders.** *Prima facie*, a dividend in kind should be treated just as though it were a dividend in cash in an amount equal to the fair market value of the property distributed. However, the earnings and profits limitation on taxable dividends produces some complications where the dividend in kind involves appreciated property. If the corporation's earnings and profits exceed the basis of the property distributed, but are less than its fair market value, is the full market value nevertheless taxable as a dividend? Commissioner v. Hirshon Trust, 213 F.2d 523 (2d Cir. 1954), and Commissioner v. Godley, 213 F.2d 529 (3d Cir. 1954), both answered that question in the affirmative under the pre-1954 law. It seems to have been conceded that under the General Utilities rule the unrealized appreciation on the distributed property did not increase earnings and profits, just as it did not increase taxable income. However, both courts concluded that since in the case of a dividend in kind the statute called for a reduction in earnings and profits only in the amount of the corporation's basis in the property, and not its fair market value, the entire distribution was "out of earnings and profits", and therefore constituted a dividend in the tax sense. Once the whole distribution constituted a taxable dividend, it was subject to the ordinary rule that a dividend in kind is taxable to the stockholders at its fair market value.[28]

As an original matter, the status of the Hirshon-Godley rule under the 1954 Code was not entirely clear. The express retention in § 312 (a) of the rule limiting the charge against earnings and profits in the case of a dividend in kind to the basis of the property certainly left room for importing the Hirshon-Godley rule. However, there were some implications the other way, not only in the committee reports, see S.Rep.No.1622, 83rd Cong., 2d Sess. (1954) 248, but also in the

---

28. Subsequently, the Commissioner sought to interpret Hirshon and Godley as holding that any corporate distribution constitutes a dividend in the tax sense so long as it does not impair capital, in order to tax a cash distribution which exceeded earnings and profits but was not "out of capital" in corporate terms; but the court refused to so far abandon the earnings and profits concept. Commissioner v. Gross, 236 F.2d 612 (2d Cir. 1956).

statute itself, such as §§ 312(b) and (g) which expressly provide for increasing earnings and profits in connection with a limited number of specified appreciated property situations. In any event, Reg. § 1.316–1(a)(2) expressly rejects Hirshon-Godley by restricting the amount of any dividend for tax purposes to the amount of the corporation's earnings and profits. And this result is further confirmed by the fact that the Hirshon-Godley rule was retroactively overruled as respects pre-1954 years, except for situations which after 1954 would fall under §§ 312(b) or (g). Public Law 629, 84th Cong., 2d Sess. (1956).

When a corporate shareholder receives appreciated property, § 301 (b)(1)(B) restricts the amount of the dividend to the basis of the property distributed, and § 301(d)(2) in turn carries over that basis to the recipient corporation. These provisions are designed to prevent the transferee-corporation from obtaining a stepped-up basis equal to market value while incurring a tax cost of only the relatively modest intercorporate dividend tax.

SECTION 5. TAX ASPECTS OF STOCK DIVIDENDS

A. HISTORICAL BACKGROUND

A brief view of the tortuous history of stock dividends under the tax law may help to set the 1954 Code provisions in perspective. An appropriate starting point is Towne v. Eisner, 245 U.S. 418, 38 S.Ct. 158, 62 L.Ed. 372 (1918), holding that under the 1913 Act, which was silent about stock dividends, a dividend of common on common was not intended to be taxed. The 1916 act expressly made stock dividends taxable, but Eisner v. Macomber, 252 U.S. 189, 40 S.Ct. 189, 64 L.Ed. 521 (1920), held that a dividend of common on common was not taxable as income under the Sixteenth Amendment.

From 1921–1935 successive revenue acts expressly exempted stock dividends from tax; but this only served to shift the constitutional issue to the basis arena. Thus in Koshland v. Helvering, 298 U.S. 441, 56 S.Ct. 767, 80 L.Ed. 1268, 105 A.L.R. 756 (1936), a taxpayer who owned non-voting, cumulative preferred received a dividend in voting common, after which her preferred was redeemed. The Commissioner applied the regulation calling for an allocation of basis to stock received tax-free as a stock dividend, thus increasing the amount of the gain realized upon the redemption of the preferred. However, the Court agreed with the taxpayer that a dividend of common on preferred was constitutionally taxable as "income", despite Eisner v.

Macomber, because it changed the proportionate interests of the stockholders, so that the allocation-of-basis regulation did not apply. Similarly, in Helvering v. Gowran, 302 U.S. 238, 58 S.Ct. 154, 82 L.Ed. 224 (1937), the Court held that a dividend of preferred on common, where some preferred was already outstanding, was outside the Macomber rule because it changed the proportionate interests of the stockholders, which meant that no part of the taxpayer's basis in the common stock was allocable to the dividend preferred.

From 1936 to 1953, the statutory rule provided that a stock dividend "shall not be treated as a dividend to the extent that it does not constitute income to the shareholders within the meaning of the Sixteenth Amendment." Under this statute the Treasury sought to overthrow Eisner v. Macomber, but failed when the Supreme Court held, in a series of three cases decided in 1943, that the statute codified the rule of that case. The Court reaffirmed the proportionate interest test and held that dividends of common on common, Helvering v. Griffiths, 318 U.S. 371, 63 S.Ct. 636, 87 L.Ed. 843 (1943), preferred on common where only common was outstanding, Strassburger v. Commissioner, 318 U.S. 604, 63 S.Ct. 791, 87 L.Ed. 1029, 144 A.L.R. 1335 (1943), and non-voting common on voting and non-voting common, Helvering v. Sprouse, 318 U.S. 604, 63 S.Ct. 791, 87 L.Ed. 1029, 144 A.L.R. 1335 (1943), were all non-taxable under the statute because they did not change the proportionate interests of the stockholders.

In the foregoing cases, no special point was made of the purpose for the stock dividend, or any prospective later use for sale, gift or otherwise. The net effect, therefore, seemed to be that it was possible to "bail out" substantial amounts of accumulated corporate profits by issuing a non-taxable stock dividend, say of preferred on common, and then selling the preferred to a third party, at merely a capital gains tax cost. The common stockholders would still have the basic equity interest (presumably including voting power) represented by the common; and in any event a redeemable feature would make it possible to get rid of the preferred stock if and when that should prove to be desirable. In 1947 the Treasury Department, recognizing the seriousness of this preferred stock bail-out problem, sought to meet the situation by refusing to issue rulings favorable to such an arrangement. Because of the very high stakes involved — a dividend tax on the proceeds of a bail-out would leave very little for the stockholders — most lawyers would not risk a bail-out transaction, and the Treasury succeeded in keeping these transactions to a minimum. See generally, Darrell, Recent Developments in Nontaxable Reorganizations and Stock Dividends, 61 Harv.L.Rev. 958 (1948).

However, in 1953, almost on the eve of the 1954 revision, this stalemate ended when the Court of Appeals for the Sixth Circuit reversed the Tax Court and granted capital gains treatment to a classic bail-out transaction effected in 1946. Chamberlin v. Commissioner, 207 F.2d 462 (6th Cir. 1953). The case involved a preferred stock dividend by a prosperous close corporation which had previously arranged with an insurance company to purchase the preferred from the stockholders and had in fact tailored the terms of the preferred to meet the specifications of the insurance company. The Commissioner contended that the preferred stock dividend was taxable; but the court concluded that under the Supreme Court cases the dividend of preferred on common was non-taxable and neither the purpose to sell the dividend stock nor the actual sale changed that result.

Obviously, the result in Chamberlin made the bail-out area a matter of high priority in the 1954 revision. The following is an excellent analysis of the problem and some of the possible methods of dealing with it, directed toward the American Law Institute Federal Tax Statute proposal, which in material terms was much like the treatment ultimately adopted in the 1954 Code.

COHEN, SURREY, TARLEAU AND WARREN, A TECHNICAL REVISION OF THE FEDERAL INCOME TAX TREATMENT OF CORPORATE DISTRIBUTIONS TO STOCKHOLDERS [29]

52 Col.L.Rev. 9–14 (1952).

2. Common Stock Dividend on Common Stock. One possible course of revision, frequently urged, is that all stock dividends be made taxable as ordinary income. The shareholder is receiving an item which, it may be assumed, represents accumulated corporate profits, and it is therefore urged that the time of receipt is an appropriate point at which to impose the tax. The shareholder's basic investment is represented in his original shares and any reckoning of gain or loss on the investment, as distinguished from interim receipts of corporate profits as dividend income, can await the disposition of the original shares. This all-out approach meets its first obstacle, however, in the case of a common stock dividend issued on identical common stock. It can here be contended that mere receipt of additional pieces of identical paper hardly warrants a policy decision to impose a tax on their value. Furthermore, corporate reasons for this kind of stock dividend, such as the easier marketability of lower-value stock, a wider distribution of stock, or a lower dividend rate, are usually not such as to lead to shareholder taxation.[36] More important, for policy purposes can issuance of a stock dividend be sufficiently distinguished from a split-up of stock? The corporate reasons which lead to the choice between dividend and split-up do not seem relevant to the decision to tax

---

29. Reprinted by permission of the Columbia Law Review. Most of the footnotes omitted.

36. Where the stock dividend is an annual affair, replacing *pro tanto* a regular cash dividend, the argument for taxability is stronger. The text deals principally with those stock dividends which represent a significant change in the capital structure. Since establishment of a dividing line between the two is impractical, the treatment of the annual stock dividend must follow that accorded to the stock dividends discussed in the text.

in the one case and not in the other. If the capitalization of earnings is relied on as a basis of distinction between stock dividends and split-ups, would it not become necessary under such a policy to impose a tax on the shareholder when there is a capitalization of earnings without any distribution of stock? Moreover, a decision to tax the stock dividend probably would lead to all split-ups and no stock dividends.

Finally, the ordinary income-capital gain issue is not really present. True, if not taxed on receipt the stockholder can later sell his stock dividend and obtain capital gain treatment for the increase in value of his investment resulting from the capitalized corporate earnings. But under accepted principles he can achieve the same result by selling a part of his original stock if no stock dividend has been distributed. Since in both cases he is altering his basic position with respect to voting power and participation in earnings and assets, the stock-dividend-and-sale transaction is more akin to a sale of stock than to receipt of a cash dividend. In short, any statutory revision should leave untaxed a dividend of common stock identical with the common stock on which it is distributed. Such an "identical pieces of paper" standard would not be difficult to apply.

3. Preferred Stock Dividends. The next area involves the receipt of a dividend in stock that is different from the stock on which it is distributed. Consider the distribution of a preferred stock dividend on common stock, with no other stock outstanding. Here the arguments leading to non-taxation of a dividend in identical stock are not applicable. There is no problem of distinguishing between alternative corporate courses of conduct, as in the split-up case. Further, a definite ordinary income-capital gain issue is present. Suppose the shareholder sells the preferred stock dividend. How should the cash so obtained be taxed? He still has his voting control and his residual interest in earnings and assets. The cash represents capitalized corporate earnings and is in reality a cash return on the investment which he retains. If he is accorded capital gain treatment he can in effect convert ordinary income into capital gain. While in the sale case cash has not left the corporation, earnings have been capitalized in the preferred stock issue and the shareholder does have cash in his hands. Is the situation appreciably different from a distribution of cash to the shareholder, taxable as ordinary income, followed by an issue of preferred stock in exchange for cash? Once the preferred is redeemed, is the result materially different from a distribution of a cash dividend without any preferred stock in the picture? Or, suppose the shareholder later sells the preferred stock, not to an outside buyer, but to the corporation itself. Here also is the net result significantly different from a simple cash distribution?

It has been urged that these considerations point to treating as a taxable dividend a distribution of preferred stock on common stock when only common stock was previously outstanding. If we followed this course, we would end with a revision under which all stock dividends would be taxable upon receipt except for the "identical pieces of paper" common stock dividend on common stock already discussed. The rule would be fairly simple, and would eliminate improper capital gain advantage in the stock dividend area.

It would probably eliminate preferred stock dividends too. The high individual income tax rates would make such distributions far too expensive in most cases. Whether this result is desirable depends in part on whether there are business or family uses of the preferred stock dividend mechanism which are entitled to recognition in the determination of tax policy. But before we consider this question, we should note that the main argument for taxability is premised on the consequences of a sale by the shareholder, whether to other persons or to the corporation itself by way of redemption. Suppose, however, that the shareholder does not sell his dividend stock, but instead retains it or disposes of it in another fashion. If the danger is that the profit from a sale may be treated as capital gain, then a tax imposed at the time of receipt of the dividend stock may be quite wide of the mark if there exist future desirable courses of conduct other than sale. Stated differently, it can be argued that mere receipt of the preferred stock dividend is not an appropriate occasion for imposing the tax. The shareholder has two pieces of paper in place of one, but he possesses no greater interest than he had before, other than the power now to move on to a tax advantage through a sale. Until he so moves, is the potentiality enough to warrant treating the receipt of the dividend as the occasion for taxing the shareholder on the profits of the corporation? It must not be overlooked that the dividend is not in cash and, while a non-cash receipt may obviously be income, in such a situation it is necessary to consider whether it is proper policy to impose on a non-cash receipt a tax that must be paid in cash. We thus should consider whether there are sound business or family needs served by the preferred stock dividend.

It is urged that these needs exist in several family and business arrangements which occur rather frequently. Suppose a father owns all the common stock of a family corporation. He desires on retirement or death to leave the ownership to his children, but in so doing would like to have his sons run the business while his daughters obtain a more secure interest without participating in management. A preferred stock dividend would solve his problem, since he could then leave the common stock to the sons and the preferred stock to the daughters. Such a rearrangement of family ownership does not appear to give the family an unfair tax advantage. Yet a tax on the father's receipt of the dividend, urged because he might gain an advantage through sale of the dividend, would prevent issuance of the preferred stock and consummation of the arrangement, although it did not involve a sale of the preferred stock. To take another example, the sole shareholder may desire to transfer the active management and an equity interest to junior executives. In order both to reduce the price of the common stock so as to enable them to purchase it and to obtain an investment interest for himself, he has the corporation distribute a preferred stock dividend. He then retains the preferred stock and sells the common stock to the junior executives.

These two situations indicate that a preferred stock dividend has uses which are not dependent on a sale of the preferred stock. There may be other such desirable arrangements, or at least other arrangements which the tax laws need not discourage. Most of these would involve a closely-held or family corporation, though on occasion a widely-held company does declare a preferred stock dividend. While the latter type of corporation probably would not experience any serious disadvantage if the tax law in effect prevented preferred stock dividends, planning for the closely-held family corporation would be handicapped in some situations, perhaps seriously. If possible, therefore, a revision should seek not to impede distribution of preferred stock dividends, while at the same time preventing the occurrence of undesirable tax consequences on a sale of the preferred stock. These two objectives can be satisfied by not taxing the preferred stock dividend at the time of receipt, but taxing as ordinary income the amount obtained on a sale if the common stock shareholder does in fact sell the preferred stock. Action by the shareholder involving neither a sale nor a redemption by the corporation would thus permit him to stay clear of ordinary income consequences.[40] . . .

B. CURRENT LAW—RECEIPT OF STOCK DIVIDENDS

Section 305 provides a blanket exclusion of stock dividends from taxable income, except for the limited case in § 305(b) where the stockholder can choose between stock and cash. Obviously, taxpayers can be expected to do some maneuvering in this area, seeking maximum advantage of the absence of tax; and this in turn may lead to quite a strain on § 305(b) as the one express control. In this connection, suppose a corporation has two classes of common stock which are identical except that only stock dividends are paid on one class and only cash dividends on the other. Are the stock dividends taxable under § 305(b)? What about the more common situation of a corporation which declares "regular" stock dividends and offers to arrange for the sale of the dividend stock for any stockholder who wishes? Often this is merely an offshoot of the general practice of making arrangements for stockholders who would stand to receive fractional shares to either

---

40. The existence of preferred stock in the hands of others does not alter these conclusions. The reasons developed in the text for not taxing the preferred stock dividend on its receipt are unaffected by the fact that preferred stock is already outstanding.

sell their fractional interests or purchase enough to make whole shares. Are there § 305(b) "elections" lurking here?

Section 307 carries forward the principle that a taxpayer's basis in his old stock should be allocated between the old stock and the new, in proportion to their respective fair market values. Here, by the way, treatment of the distribution of stock rights departs slightly from that applicable to distributions of stock, since there are two situations involving rights where there is no allocation of basis: (1) if the value of the rights amounts to less than 15% of the value of the stock, and no election under § 307(b) is made; and (2) if the rights are allowed to lapse (in which event there will be no deductible loss).

C. CURRENT LAW—DISPOSITION OF DIVIDEND STOCK

1. THE OPERATION OF § 306

Section 306 represents the 1954 legislative response to the preferred stock dividend bail-out problem. The purpose and effect of this complex statutory pattern is described in the following excerpts from the Senate Finance Committee Report:

SENATE FINANCE COMMITTEE REPORT

S.Rep. No. 1622, 83d Cong., 2d Sess. 46, 242–245 (1945).

Your committee has also acted to close a possible loophole of existing law known as the "preferred stock bail-out". . . . Your committee's approach to this problem imposes a tax on the recipient of the dividend stock at the time of its sale. This dividend stock would be called "section 306 stock" and any stock received as a dividend would be section 306 stock to the extent of its allocable share of corporate earnings at the time of issuance, except common stock issued with respect to common stock.

The tax imposed at the time of the sale of the stock is at ordinary income rates to the extent of its allocable share of earnings and profits of the corporation at the time the stock dividend was declared. Any amount received for the section 306 stock which exceeds the earnings and profits attributable to it will be taxed as capital gain. If, instead of selling the section 306 stock, the shareholder redeems it, the proceeds received will be taxed as a dividend to the extent of corporate earnings at the time of redemption. . . . [C]ertain exceptions to this basic rule of ordinary income treatment with respect to dispositions of section 306 are provided. . . .

If the section 306 stock is sold the amount realized is treated as gain from the sale of property which is not a capital asset to the extent of the stock's ratable share of earnings and profits of the issuing corporation at the time of its distribution. Thus, assume that a shareholder owns 1,000 shares of the common stock of a corporation and that they are the only shares of its stock outstanding. Assume also that the shareholder acquires 1,000 shares of preferred stock with a fair market value for each share of $100 issued to him as a dividend on his common stock at a time when the corporation has $100,000 in accumulated earnings. There is no tax to the shareholder at the time of receipt of the stock but it is characterized as section 306 stock. If it is sold for $100,000 the shareholder will be taxed on the entire sale proceeds at the rates applicable to ordinary income.

The determination of the section 306 stock's ratable share of earnings at the time of its distribution is to be made in accordance with its fair market value at such time. It should also be noted that it would be immaterial that $100,000 were distributed to the stockholder as a dividend on his common stock subsequent to the distribution of the stock dividend. The stock dividend is nevertheless section 306 stock because of the corporate earnings in existence at the time of its distribution. A shareholder may, in such a case, only dispose of his section 306 stock through redemption by the issuing corporation and thereby avoid its inherent ordinary income characteristics. See discussion of paragraph (2) of subsection (a), below.

Subparagraph (B) of paragraph (1) provides that if the amount received from the sale of section 306 stock exceeds the amount treated as ordinary income, such excess shall, to the extent of gain, be accorded capital-gain treatment. Thus, if in the preceding example the stock had been sold for $110,000 (instead of $100,000) the $10,000 would be taxed at the rates applicable to capital gain.* Subparagraph (C) of paragraph (1) provides that in no event is any loss to be allowed with respect to the sale of section 306 stock.

Paragraph (2) of subsection (a) provides that if the section 306 stock is redeemed, the amount realized is to be treated as a distribution of property to which section 301 applies. Thus, if the section 306 stock was distributed at a time when there was an amount of corporate earnings attributable to it equal to its full fair market value at that time, but if there are no corporate earnings, accumulated or current, at the time of redemption, the amount received on redemption of section 306 stock would be treated under section 301 as a return of capital. No loss would be allowed in such a case under section 301.

It should be noted that where section 306 stock is redeemed the rules of section 302(a) and (b), relating to cases where amounts re-

---

* [Ed. note] This example seems to be in error since an appropriate portion of the shareholder's basis in the common stock should be allocated to the preferred stock and then offset against the $10,000.

ceived in redemption of stock will be taxed at capital gain rates, are not applicable. Section 306 operates independently of section 302 and contains its own rules concerning instances where your committee does not consider it appropriate to tax proceeds received with respect to section 306 stock at the rates applicable to ordinary income.

* * *

Paragraph (4) of subsection (b) excepts from the general rule of subsection (a) those transactions not in avoidance of this section where it is established to the satisfaction of the Secretary that the transaction was not in pursuance of a plan having as one of its principal purposes the avoidance of Federal income tax. Subparagraph (A) of this paragraph applies to cases where the distribution itself, coupled with the disposition or redemption was not in pursuance of such a plan. This subparagraph is intended to apply to the case of dividends and isolated dispositions of section 306 stock by minority shareholders who do not in the aggregate have control of the distributing corporation. In such a case it would seem to your committee to be inappropriate to impute to such shareholders an intention to remove corporate earnings at the tax rates applicable only to capital gains.

Subparagraph (B) of subsection (b) (4) applies to a case where the shareholder has made a prior or simultaneous disposition (or redemption) of the underlying stock with respect to which the section 306 stock was issued. Thus if a shareholder received a distribution of 100 shares of section 306 stock on his holdings of 100 shares of voting common stock in a corporation and sells his voting common stock before he disposes of his section 306 stock, the subsequent disposition of his section 306 stock would not ordinarily be considered a tax avoidance disposition since he has previously parted with the stock which allows him to participate in the ownership of the business. However, variations of the above example may give rise to tax avoidance possibilities which are not within the exception of subparagraph (B). Thus if a corporation has only one class of common stock outstanding and it issues stock under circumstances that characterize it as section 306 stock, a subsequent issue of a different class of common having greater voting rights than the original common will not permit a simultaneous disposition of the section 306 stock together with the original common to escape the rules of subsection (a) of section 306.

Section 306(c) sets forth the definition of section 306 stock. . . . [Section 306(c) (1) (C)] would remove from the category of section 306 stock, stock owned by a decedent at death since such stock takes a new basis under section 1014.

Paragraph (2) of subsection (c) excepts from the definition of section 306 stock any stock no part of the distribution of which would have been a dividend at the time of distribution if money had been distributed in lieu of the stock. Thus, preferred stock received at the time of original incorporation would not be section 306 stock. Also, stock issued at the time an existing corporation had no earnings and profits would not be section 306 stock.

Subsection (d) provides that stock rights shall be treated as stock for purposes of this section and if stock is acquired through the exercise of stock rights, such stock shall be treated as section 306 stock to the extent the rights themselves had the character of section 306 stock at the time of distribution.

2. SOME CURRENT § 306 ISSUES

There has been virtually no litigation under § 306 thus far, but certain trouble spots have already emerged. First, it should be noted that although a *sale* of § 306 stock may result in ordinary income, such income is not "dividend" income. Accordingly, such provisions as the $100 dividend exclusion for individuals and the dividends-received deduction for corporations do not apply; and the earnings and profits of the corporation at the time of the sale are neither relevant to, nor reduced by, the taxation of ordinary income to the stockholders. On the other hand, *redemption* of § 306 stock is subject to the dividend rules. Query whether there is anything in the policy of § 306 which calls for this difference in treatment.

Second, there is a question whether the amount taxable as ordinary income in the case of a sale of § 306 stock is measured by the amount of earnings and profits on the date of the distribution of the § 306 stock, or the amount of earnings and profits at the end of the year in which the distribution occurred. Most of the commentators seem to assume the former—and there are some implications that way in the regulations. Cf. Reg. § 1.306–3(a). On the other hand, the constructive cash dividend test in § 306(a)(1)(A)(ii) would seem to import the general rule of § 316 under which earnings and profits for the current year are measured at year-end. This view finds support in Example 1 in Reg. § 1.306–1(b)(2) which refers to the earnings and profits of a calendar year corporation on December 31 although the distribution of § 306 stock occurred on December 15.

The "taint" on § 306 preferred stock can be sidestepped by a contribution of the stock to a charitable organization. The shareholder avoids any tax with respect to the § 306 stock, there being no sale, but may still treat its market value as a charitable contribution. Rev. Rul. 57–328, 1957–2 Cum.Bull. 229.

Section 306(c)(1)(A) turns on the interpretation of the term "common stock," but there is no general definition supplied by the Code or regulations. Doubtless non-voting common stock is still "common stock". But common stock which is convertible into other than common stock is not "common stock," Reg. § 1.306–3(f); and neither is stock redeemable at the option of the corporation at a price in excess of its book value. Rev.Rul. 57–132, 1957–1 Cum.Bull. 115. In addition, any preference possessed by a class of stock would presumably make it "other than common stock." [30]

Section 306(b)(4), excepting from the operation of § 306 any transaction free of a principal purpose of avoiding tax, seems unlikely to be of any real help in the planning context. Little light is shed on this provision by the regulations, which content themselves with merely repeating some of the examples given in the Senate Finance Committee Report. More important, the question of whether § 306(b)(4) applies to a particular transaction is one of the "areas in which rulings will not ordinarily be issued" by the Service, according to para. 4.01(2) of Rev.Proc. 64–31, 1964–2 Cum.Bull. 947, set out at page 101 supra.

SECTION 6. RECAPITALIZATION UNDER CORPORATE LAW

While the term "recapitalization" may include practically any change in the capital structure of a going concern, it most often refers to a transaction involving a change in the rights of existing stockholders, either by alteration of the terms of outstanding stock or by the issuance of new securities in exchange for the old. Incidentally, the distinction between a *change* in existing stock and an *exchange* of new shares for the old ones is often far from clear. For example, what is the difference between a reduction in the par value of outstanding shares under MBA § 53(e) and the issuance of new shares with a lower par value in exchange for the old shares pursuant to § 53(f)—or between a "change" of par shares into no-par shares under § 53(h) and an "exchange" of new no-par shares for the old par shares under § 53(f)—bearing in mind that as a practical matter a "change" transaction is quite likely to be accompanied by the issuance of new shares reflecting the changes effected. In the same vein, there would seem to be virtually no difference between a stock dividend of, say, one new share for each old share outstanding, and a recapitalization exchange of two new shares for each old share outstanding.

While there are a variety of purposes which may be served by recapitalization, by far the most common objective of the transactions which have come before the courts is the elimination of unpaid dividend arrearages on cumulative preferred stock. (Although of course such arrearages do not constitute a debt and hence do not represent any threat to the existence of the corporation, they do prevent the pay-

---

30. For a consideration of this same issue in the context of the "common stock" requirement of § 1244, see page 123 supra.

ment of dividends on common stock and therefore impede new common stock financing.) The following enlightening description of recapitalizations and the manner in which they are effected comes from the late Professor Dodd's classic article on the standards of fairness applicable to such recapitalizations:

DODD, FAIR AND EQUITABLE RECAPITALIZATIONS [31]

55 Harv.L.Rev. 780–789 (1942).

There are two situations in which the management of a business corporation is likely to attempt to revamp the capital structure so as substantially to modify present and future rights of existing security holders: (1) reorganizations of insolvent corporations, involving modification of the rights of creditors, including bondholders, and (2) recapitalization of solvent corporations, involving modification of the relative rights of classes of shareholders. . . .

* * *

Recapitalization differs radically from reorganization in that it involves only the rights of persons who, as shareholders, have in general no right to receive payment at any time prior to the liquidation of the enterprise. Liquidation cannot normally be accomplished without the assent of those who have voting control over the enterprise, which in most instances means the common shareholders. . . .

[With one minor exception] recapitalization, unlike reorganization, is never necessary for the purpose of relieving the corporation from legal demands which it is unable to meet. Although there are intimations to the contrary in some judicial opinions, it is unlikely that any corporation has been ruined as a result of its inability to modify claims to accrued dividends or to make any other readjustments in its capital structure.

* * *

The need for permitting corporations to modify their charters so as to adapt themselves to circumstances which were unforeseen when the enterprise was created is so obvious that modern corporation statutes invariably authorize the majority or some larger percentage of the shareholders to amend the charter in various ways, usually including the adoption of amendments which create new classes of shares and amendments which change the preference of an existing class of shares. In enacting such statutes, legislatures have sometimes attempted to safeguard the interests of a particular class by requiring the affirmative vote of a majority of the members of that class for the adoption of the amendment, and they have sometimes

---

31. Copyright (c), Harvard Law Review Association, 1942. Reprinted by permission. Portions of the text and all footnotes omitted. The special problem of recapitalization to eliminate preferred stock dividend arrearages will be dealt with in more detail in Chapter 5.

attempted to safeguard the interest of dissenters by giving them the right to receive the fair value of their shares in cash if they do not desire to continue with the enterprise in its amended form. But the prescribed method of amendment has been, almost universally, that of a shareholders' vote rather than that of judicial proceedings, which has always been characteristic of reorganizations. Corporation statutes which confer some particular power on a group within the corporation, whether shareholders or directors, do not ordinarily admonish the group in question that they are to exercise their powers only so as to produce results which are fair and equitable, and statutes which permit recapitalizations are no exception to the rule.

Attempts have been made to use these statutes to adopt two different types of amendments which reclassify shares in such a manner as to eliminate or modify accrued dividend rights. The first type of amendment affects such rights directly by providing for their elimination or modification, or for the substitution therefor of some other right, such as the right to receive additional preferred or common shares in lieu of accruals. The courts have on the whole been unwilling to construe the statutes as authorizing amendments of this type unless the statutory language is very explicit.

The other type of amendment is more complicated. A plan is proposed which includes the creation of prior preferred shares and the offer of such shares, sometimes with a bonus of common, to the holders of the existing preferred shares in return for the surrender of their claim to accruals. Those who decline retain their accruals but become subordinated to the holders of the new prior preferred shares and are subjected in some instances to certain other disadvantages. The courts, with some notable exceptions, have tended to uphold this type of amendment, often relying largely on language in the original charter which impliedly authorized the creation of prior preferred shares.

As the foregoing excerpt indicates, any recapitalization transaction may present a preliminary question as to whether the statute authorizes the use of the particular mechanics to achieve the particular objective. For example, it has been held that elimination of dividend arrearages on cumulative preferred stock can not be accomplished by amendment of the certificate under a statute permitting certificate amendment by "increasing or decreasing its authorized capital stock or reclassifying the same, by changing the number, par value, designations, preferences, or relative, participating, optional, or other special rights of the shares, or the qualifications, limitations, or restrictions of such rights, . . .". Keller v. Wilson & Co., Inc., 21 Del.Ch. 391, 190 A. 115 (Sup.Ct.1936); Consolidated Film Industries, Inc. v. Johnson, 22 Del.Ch. 407, 197 A. 489 (Sup.Ct.1937). On the other hand, the Delaware court did find authority to eliminate such arrearages under the merger statute, even in the course of a merger with a wholly-owned subsidiary. Federal United Corporation v. Havender, 24 Del.Ch. 318, 11 A.2d 331 (Sup. Ct.1940). Notice that the Model Act specifically authorizes a corporation to "cancel or otherwise affect" dividend arrearages by certificate amendment. MBA § 53(k).

Where the recapitalization calls for an exchange of shares, there is a threshold question relating to the mechanics for carrying out the exchange. For example, Model Act § 53(f) authorizes an amendment of the articles of incorporation "to exchange . . . all or any part of its shares, whether issued or unissued"; and § 55(d) provides a class vote in the event that an amendment would "effect an exchange, or create a right of exchange, of all or any part of the shares of another class into the shares of such class". But it is far from clear just how an amendment to the articles can in and of itself "exchange" shares.[32] Nor is it easy to see why an amendment to the articles would be used to "create a right of exchange", unless that right constituted one of the continuing terms of that class of stock within the meaning of § 14.

This problem seems to have been recognized in Model Act § 53, which provides, in cases where an exchange of shares is to be made, for inclusion of "such provisions as may be necessary to effect such . . . exchange". Even without such statutory assistance, in practice the parties have generally by-passed whatever theoretical difficulties there might be by utilizing the concept of a "plan of recapitalization", in which such classic amendment matters as the creation of new shares are joined with such non-amendment items as an exchange of shares. Thus in Shanik v. White Sewing Machine Corp., 25 Del.Ch. 371, 19 A.2d 831 (Sup.Ct.1941), where the court upheld a plan to get rid of preferred arrearages by offering a package consisting of one share of new prior preferred and 3 shares of new common stock for each old share of preferred, only the creation of the new prior preference stock (and the change of the old common stock into 2/5 of a share of new common stock) were included in the amendment of the certificate, although the overall "plan" adopted by the shareholders included the provision permitting each preferred stockholder to exchange his old preferred for the package of new preference stock and common. But see the involved arrangements in the Hartzell case, page 407 infra, apparently undertaken in order to avoid feared impediments to the proposed exchange transaction under the corporation statute.

32. But see the amendment provision in Rio Grande Oil Co. v. Welsh, 101 F.2d 454 (9th Cir. 1939), which provided expressly, in connection with an exchange of five new no-par common shares for each old $25 par common share outstanding, that the holders of the old shares "shall surrender the same to the corporation for cancellation and shall receive and accept in place thereof certificates for shares of the new capital stock".

The following case illustrates a "recapitalization" transaction found not to be authorized by the governing statute:

BOWMAN v. ARMOUR & CO.
Supreme Court of Illinois, 1959.
17 Ill.2d 43, 160 N.E.2d 753.

HERSHEY, JUSTICE. This is an equity proceeding for a declaratory judgment seeking to determine the validity of a 1954 amendment to the articles of incorporation of the defendant, Armour and Company, an Illinois corporation. The plaintiffs-appellants here seek to have the amendment declared invalid and further seek a declaration that action taken pursuant to that amendment be declared ineffective.

The original plaintiffs, as well as the intervenors, are owners of cumulative convertible prior preferred stock of Armour and Company, hereinafter referred to as "Armour." The stock will, in this opinion, be referred to as the "prior stock." The plaintiffs assert that the 1954 plan of recapitalization contained in the amendment operates to deprive them of rights and privileges as holders of the prior stock contrary to constitutional inhibitions.

The case was heard below on an agreed statement of facts, documents, and testimony. The trial court, in a written opinion, found the issues for the defendants and held the recapitalization plan as embodied in the amendment to the articles of incorporation to be valid and further held that the applicable sections of the Business Corporation Act that were construed as the statutory basis for the authorization of the amendment were constitutional.

Constitutional questions having been presented below and decided, this court has jurisdiction on direct appeal.

In 1954, prior to the plan of recapitalization here under attack, the capital structure, debt and surplus of Armour and Company, in thousands of dollars, were:

Long-term debt	$124,699
Prior stock	50,000
Common stock	20,329
Capital and paid-in surplus	33,619
Earned surplus	134,079
	$362,726

The prior stock had, by the terms of the stock certificates and the articles of incorporation, these material features: It had a stated value of $100 per share. Cumulative dividends of $6 per year were to be paid when and if declared and each share was convertible for six shares of common stock and could, at the option of the company, be redeemed at a price of $115 per share plus accumulated dividends.

Each share of the prior stock had one vote in corporate matters and enjoyed certain preferences in the event of liquidation, whether voluntary or involuntary.

The plan of recapitalization proposed to amend the articles of incorporation by a vote of two thirds of the holders of each class of stock providing that the board of directors would be authorized to redeem the prior stock "at a price of $120.00 per share, payable in (i) debentures of like principal amount of the company, maturing November 1, 1984, bearing interest at the rate of 5% per annum cumulative from November 1, 1954, and to be subordinated to other *indebtedness* of the Company, and having such sinking fund provisions and other terms and conditions as the board of directors of the company may determine, (ii) one transferable warrant for the purchase of one share of common stock of the Company, at such price or prices and having such other terms and conditions as the board of directors of the company may determine, (iii) and no more."

The debentures were to mature in 30 years and the stated interest rate of 5 per cent was payable out of earnings. The redemption as authorized by the amendment would, upon the exercise of the power to redeem as contained in the amendment, be compulsory. The amendment was voted upon by the shareholders and adopted by a vote of more than two thirds of each class of outstanding stock, the shareholders voting by class.

Questions relating to the necessity of the recapitalization, the tax advantages to the corporation, the fairness of the plan, the financial consequences of its adoption on the prior stockholders and the infringement of "contractual" or "vested" rights, as well as constitutional rights, have been ably presented on the appeal of this case. However, in view of the fact that our interpretation of the applicable provisions of the Business Corporation Act is determinative of this appeal, it is unnecessary to consider the question of fairness or, in fact, to consider any question other than statutory interpretation and *laches*.

The charter or articles of incorporation of an Illinois corporation is a contract of a three-fold nature. It is operative as between the corporation and the State and it creates rights and duties as between the corporation and its shareholders, as well as between the shareholders themselves. . . . The express nature of the contract is not limited to the specific language found in the articles of incorporation but the contract in its entirety includes the statutory provisions in force when the charter is granted as though those statutory provisions were literally recited in the contract. . . . The holders of the prior stock thus held rights and privileges as expressed in the articles prior to the amendment subject at all times to variation, modification or change to the extent that the articles could be amended from time to time as authorized by the Business Corporation Act.

Section 52 of the Business Corporation Act . . . provides in part as follows:

"Right to amend articles of incorporation. A corporation may amend its articles of incorporation, from time to time, in any and as many respects as may be desired, provided that its articles of incorporation as amended contain only such provisions as might be lawfully contained in original articles of incorporation if made at the time of making such amendment, and, if a change in shares or an exchange or reclassification of shares is to be made, such provisions as may be necessary to effect such change, exchange, or reclassification as may be desired and as is permitted by this Act.

"In particular, and without limitation upon such general power of amendment, a corporation may amend its articles of incorporation, from time to time, so as:

. . .

"(g) To change the designation of all or any part of its shares, whether issued or unissued, and to change the preferences, qualifications, limitations, restrictions, and the special or relative rights in respect of all or any part of its shares, whether issued or unissued."

The authority for the amendment here in question must be found in the quoted portion of section 52 subject to the general limitation that the amendment, in order to be valid, must be by the affirmative vote of two thirds of the outstanding shares of each class of stock issued. (See sec. 53(c) and sec. 54, Business Corporation Act.) In this connection, it is established and uncontroverted that more than two thirds of each class voted for the amendment.

It is, of course, a fundamental rule of statutory construction that the grant of power contained in the Business Corporation Act, like any other grant of power, is to be strictly construed and the enumeration of the series of powers therein contained exclude other powers not fairly incidental to the powers expressly granted. . . .

The grant of power to amend found in section 52 of the act and, specifically material to this case, the power found in subparagraph (g) is very broad. Amendments, however, must be limited to matters that would be permitted in the original articles, and section 14 of the Business Corporation Act relating to preferences in original articles clearly contemplates the issuance of shares redeemable at the option of the company at a price not exceeding the price fixed by the articles of incorporation. . . .

* * *

The language of subparagraph (g) of section 52, authorizing amendment of articles of incorporation makes rights and privileges of preferred stock defeasible to the extent that amendments are authorized. The question here is not one of the existence of the power to amend nor is the question here one of the authority to divest certain rights and privileges. Rather, the question is whether this quoted language gives to Armour the right to amend to the extent that holders of the prior shares are required to surrender their ownership in said stock and accept in lieu thereof the earnings bonds as specified.

The amendment, whether it is viewed as effecting a purchase of the prior stock with bonds or as a compulsory redemption thereof, obviously contemplates that the fundamental relationship of stockholder as between the holders of the prior stock and Armour will be changed and the prior stockholders will become mere creditors of the company.

A share of stock in a corporation is a unit of interest in the corporation and it entitles the shareholder to an aliquot part of the property or its proceeds to the extent indicated. The interest of a shareholder entitles him to participate in the net profits in proportion to the number of his shares, to have a voice in the selection of the corporate officers and, upon dissolution or liquidation, to receive his portion of the property of the corporation that may remain after payment of its debts. A change in preferences, qualifications or relative rights may increase or decrease the right to participate in profits, the right to participate in distribution of the assets of the corporation on dissolution or liquidation, or other indicia of ownership manifest by the ownership of corporate stock. But the change here contemplated is more than that; it is a compulsory redemption or a purchase of the stock rather than a divestiture of certain rights and privileges.

The plan of recapitalization here is not a divestiture of rights or privileges or an increase or decrease in relative rights of shares but it is, as we have said, a compulsory redemption or purchase that results in a change of the status of the shareholder from that of a shareholder to that of a creditor. The ownership of some equity in the corporation is not modified or changed leaving some resulting ownership, but it is liquidated and a corporate owner prior to the amendment finds that subsequent to the amendment he is a creditor.

A corporation has no inherent right to redeem its preferred stock and can do so only if authorized by law. . . . Section 14 of our Business Corporation Act provides for the issuance of preferred shares and further provides that the same may be redeemed "at not exceeding the price fixed by the articles of incorporation. . . ." The articles of Armour expressly provided that the prior stock could be redeemed at a price of $115 per share plus accrued dividends.

This provision, in effect, was the grant of an option by the owners of the prior stock to Armour authorizing redemption on the stated terms. Notwithstanding this provision, it is the contention of the defendants in this case that the holders of the prior stock can be forced to permit the redemption on the basis of the issuance of earnings bonds.

It is the position of the plaintiffs that the only way the stock can be redeemed is by compliance with the provisions of the article and the payment in dollars of the sum therein provided. The plaintiffs assert that the word "price," as used in the statute, is definable only to mean money and not bonds or other evidences of debt.

It is a well established rule that in the absence of contrary statutory definition, words used in a statute are used in their popularly understood meaning. . . . The word "price" has a narrower meaning and is more restricted in scope than the word "consideration," and "price" has been defined as the amount of money given or received in exchange for anything. . . .

The word "price" is used in the redemption language of section 14 and is also found in section 15 of the Business Corporation Act with reference to the issuance of preferred or special shares in a series. It is there provided that there may be variations between series of stock as to price. Further, in section 18 of the Business Corporation Act, the word "price" is not found, and in that section it is obvious that when the legislature wished to broaden the meaning of the term it did not use the word "price" but used the word "consideration" and defined it to include many things—money, property, labor or services actually performed.

A consideration of these sections can lead us only to the conclusion that when the legislature makes reference to the payment of money it uses the word "price." When it is concerned with a broader definition it found adequate words to express its intention.

We have carefully considered the cases cited from other jurisdictions with reference to redemption or retirement of stock out of bonds and a fair statement of the reasoning there found may be found in section 5315 of Volume 11, Fletcher Cyclopedia of Corporations, stating the general rule to be that preferred shares convertible by the holder into bonds or credit obligations, call, in effect, for a purchase by the corporation of its own shares, and like provisions for compulsory redemption should be expressly prohibited. The case there discussed of Berger v. United States Steel Corp., 63 N.J.Eq. 809, 53 A. 68, relates to the redemption of preferred stock by the issuance of bonds therefor and was based upon a specific and peculiar statutory provision, and even in that case it is to be noted that rather strict limitations were imposed as a condition precedent to such redemption and it was required that the holder of the stock sought to be redeemed consent thereto.

It seems to us to be evident that the effect of the amendment here sought to be sustained was, in fact, a purchase with bonds by the Armour company of its own outstanding preferred stock without the consent of the owners of said stock. While the Business Corporation Act does, under certain circumstances, permit a corporation to purchase its own stock, it can do so only when the shareholder is willing to sell, and no amendment passed with the approval of a two-thirds vote of the shareholders can force him to sell.

Further, that section 52(g) should be construed as we have indicated is made more clear by referring to the express safeguards found in the Business Corporation Act applicable to merger. Section 61 expressly provides that on merger the shares of each merging corporation may be converted into shares or other securities or obligations of the corporation. Section 70 provides safeguards for shareholders who may dissent from the merger by permitting them to obtain the fair market value of their shares. To construe section 52 as to authorize the recapitalization plan here under consideration would mean that a minority shareholder would not have the protection on recapitalization that the legislature has provided on merger, even though the recapitalization plan could more drastically affect his interest than would a merger. It is obvious to us that the legislature did not intend to authorize a recapitalization program by amendment of the nature and to the extent of the one here involved but, rather, by the language of section 52(g) contemplated only changes in relative rights, privileges, restrictions or limitations. . . .

SECTION 7. TAX ASPECTS OF RECAPITALIZATION

A. IN GENERAL

As indicated in the corporate discussion, although a recapitalization generally involves some type of exchange of stock or securities between a corporation and its stockholders, rather than a "distribution" in the ordinary sense, many exchange transactions which constitute recapitalizations are virtually the same in ultimate effect as ordinary distribution transactions. For example, a recapitalization consisting of an exchange by common stockholders of all of their old common for proportionate amounts of new preferred and common would be practically the same as a stock dividend of new preferred on the old common. The same would be true if each holder of old common exchanged a pro rata portion of his common for new preferred; a change in the number of common shares owned by each stockholder is of no moment, so long as the proportionate interest of each in the basic equity remains the same.

Again, a pro rata distribution of debt securities to common stockholders would presumably constitute a dividend in kind and as such be includible in ordinary income. Should the transaction be treated differently if instead the shareholders exchange all of their old common for proportionate amounts of new debt securities and common, or if the shareholders exchange a pro rata portion of old common for debt securities?

The origins of special tax treatment for recapitalizations are rooted in the early recognition that certain types of corporate readjustments which left the interests of corporate investors in "corporate solution" did not constitute a sufficient change in the nature of the taxpayer's investment to warrant imposition of tax. Such transactions, described as "reorganizations", range all the way from the absorption of one existing corporation by another engaged in a completely different business to a mere change in the state of incorporation of a going concern; and from the outset, the definition of "reorganization" has included "recapitalization", as it does in § 368(a) (1) (E) today.

On the other hand, there has never been any definition of "recapitalization" in the statute, or in the regulations either. Perhaps the term when first used was regarded as having some fairly well-defined corporate significance, but in fact, as we saw earlier, that has really never been so; even today recapitalization is more of an informal concept than a well-defined term of corporate art. The present regulations, in lieu of any effort at comprehensive definition, simply provide five examples of exchange transactions which are classified as recapitalizations. And the nearest thing to a judicial definition is the description of a recapitalization in Helvering v. Southwest Consolidated Corp., 315 U.S. 194, 202, 62 S.Ct. 546, 551, 86 L.Ed. 789 (1942), as a "reshuffling of a capital structure within the framework of an existing corporation."

In any event, if a transaction does fall within the term "recapitalization" it thereby qualifies as a "reorganization" for tax purposes, which means that it becomes subject to the special "tax-free" reorganization pattern. The pivotal provision in this pattern is § 354 which excepts from the normal recognition of gain or loss under § 1002 certain transactions in which stock or securities are exchanged with a corporation solely for new stock or securities pursuant to a reorganization.[33] Section 354 is supplemented by § 356 which provides for partial non-recognition when such an exchange involves the receipt of some "boot", that is, property not permitted to be received tax-free. Section 356 also deals with the circumstances under which boot may be treated as a dividend, rather than as a payment in exchange for property which would be eligible for capital gain treat-

---

33. It is to be noted that § 354 may overlap § 1036 as to exchanges involving merely new preferred for old preferred, or new common for old common. But where such an exchange occurs outside of a reorganization, as would presumably be true of any exchange among individual shareholders, tax-free treatment can only come from § 1036.

ment. (If only boot, i. e., no non-recognition property, is received, then even if the transaction does constitute a reorganization, the tax treatment of what is received must be determined under the other distribution sections, 301, 302, 331, and 346.) Section 358 prescribes the basis rules for exchanges governed by §§ 354 and 356.

Such recapitalization exchanges are also tax-free to the corporation, but no special provision to that effect is needed because from the corporation's point of view, these transactions simply represent a new issuance of stock or securities. Section 1032 precludes the imposition of any tax upon an issuance of stock by a corporation, including when the new stock is issued in exchange for old stock, Reg. § 1.1032–1(b); and under § 311 the same is true when it is new securities that are issued in exchange for the old stock. (The effect on the corporation of an exchange of new debt securities for old debt is less clear; if the principal amount of the new debt securities is smaller than the principal amount of the old debt securities, cancellation of indebtedness income under § 108 might be present.)

On the other hand, any transfers of property between two or more corporations, as occurs in the more complicated types of reorganization such as mergers or corporate divisions, do require some special provision to avoid being taxed. Section 361 performs this operation (supplemented by § 357); and the corollary basis rules applicable to such tax-free inter-corporate transfers of property are provided in § 362(b), in conjunction with § 358. However, since recapitalization involves only a single corporation, these sections do not come into play; accordingly, further analysis of them can await discussion of corporate combinations and separations later in these materials.

B. DISTRIBUTIONS HAVING THE EFFECT OF A DIVIDEND

As previously noted, when boot is distributed to stockholders in the course of a reorganization exchange, at a minimum there should be recognition of gain to the extent of the boot, and § 356(a)(1) so provides. But something more than partial recognition of gain is called for when such a transaction really amounts to the distribution of a dividend. Here § 356(a)(2) comes into play, subjecting to dividend tax any distribution of boot which "has the effect . . . of a dividend."

The classic case construing the "effect of a dividend" test is Commissioner v. Estate of Bedford, 325 U.S. 283, 65 S.Ct. 1157, 89 L.Ed. 1611 (1944), which involved a recapitalization of Abercrombie & Fitch. At the start of 1937 the company had a surplus deficit as the result of stock dividends charged against surplus in the late 1920's and losses incurred in the 1930's. In order to get into position to pay its current earnings as dividends, the company adopted a plan of recapitalization designed to eliminate its $100 par value cumulative preferred stock by exchanging for each three shares of such stock 3½ shares of new $75 par value preferred, 1½ shares of $1 par value common, and $452.40 in cash. For its 3,000 shares of old preferred stock, the taxpayer received 3500 shares of new preferred, 1500 shares of common, and $45,240 in cash, which had a total value exceeding the taxpayer's basis in the old preferred by almost $140,000. Admittedly, this gain was taxable to the extent of the cash received; but the Commissioner contended that the cash was taxable as a dividend under the predecessor of § 356(a)(2), and the Supreme Court agreed:

> Although Abercrombie & Fitch showed a book deficit in the surplus account because the earlier stock dividends had been charged against it, the parties agree that for corporate tax purposes at least earnings and profits exceeding the distributed cash had been earned at the time of the recapitalization. That cash therefore came out of earnings and profits and such a distribution would normally be considered a taxable dividend. . . . It has been ruled in a series of cases that where the stock of one corporation was exchanged for the stock of another and cash and then distributed, such distributions out of earnings and profits had the effect of a distribution of a taxable dividend under [the predecessor of § 356(a)(2)] . . . . The Tax Court has reached the same result, that is, has treated the distribution as a taxable dividend, in the case of the recapitalization of a single corporation. . . . We can not distinguish the two situations and find no implication in the statute restricting [it] to taxation as a dividend only in the case of an exchange of stock and assets of two corporations.

Taken literally, the Bedford case might mean that any distribution of boot to a shareholder pursuant to a reorganization should be taxed as a dividend to the extent of the shareholder's ratable share of earnings and profits. After all, the language of the opinion is rather sweeping; and the Court ominously ignored the fact that the taxpayer owned no common stock so that this was far from a "classic" dividend equivalence case. Moreover, such a broad construction would have the advantage of substituting an objective standard for the uncertainty which would otherwise be inherent in a provision like § 356(a)(2).

Nevertheless, the fact remains that Congress would presumably have expressly provided for such "automatic" dividend treatment if that had been the desired result. In addition, this construction seems doubtful because it would result in reorganization distributions being at a material disadvantage in comparison to redemptions and partial liquidations where the statutory guard against disguised dividends, expressed in terms of "essentially equivalent to a dividend," has never received anything like this "automatic" construction. See generally pages 479–480, infra.

Moreover, the Bedford result can be reconciled with a less extreme view of dividend equivalence despite the fact that the taxpayer owned only preferred stock. Indeed, since the dividends on the preferred stock in Bedford were in arrears, and the arrearages exceeded the amount of the cash received, Bedford comes close to being a "classic" dividend equivalence case after all. As a matter of fact, as is pointed out in Darrell, The Scope of Commissioner v. Bedford Estate, 24 Taxes 266 (1946), in the absence of dividend arrearages preferred stockholders would not normally have any "ratable share of the undistributed earnings and profits of the corporation" which is the touchstone of § 356(a)(2). Darrell indicates that informal rulings to that effect have been issued by the Commissioner since the Bedford decision.

The only two judicial expressions since Bedford have taken a dim view of the automatic dividend rule. In Idaho Power Co. v. United States, 142 Ct.Cl. 534, 161 F.Supp. 807 (1958), where it was the taxpayer who sought dividend treatment for a distribution of boot in a recapitalization (in order to obtain the deduction under § 247 for dividends paid on preferred stock by a public utility company), the court held that the existence of earnings and profits did not automatically result in dividend treatment. The court then found no dividend when 7% preferred which apparently had no significant arrearages and was redeemable at $110 per share, was surrendered in exchange for new 4% preferred and $8 in cash, and 88% of the preferred stockholders owned no common. In Hawkinson v. Commissioner, 235 F.2d 747 (2d Cir. 1956), the court expressly rejected an automatic dividend interpretation of Bedford, stressing instead the factor of pro rata distribution as the basis for dividend treatment. On the other hand, the regulations seem to adopt the automatic dividend rule, at least judging by the first example in Reg. § 1.356–1(c), which assumes dividend treatment for cash received in a reorganization exchange without any analysis of the surrounding circumstances.

These are some important differences between dividend treatment under § 356(a)(2) and that imposed by the general provision of § 301. One already mentioned is the restriction of the dividend under § 356(a)(2) to the taxpayer's "ratable share" of earnings and profits, which has no counterpart under § 301. Of even more importance is the limitation of the dividend treatment under § 356(a)(2) to the amount of the gain on the exchange transaction. This limitation seems hard to justify. The amount of the taxpayer's potential gain on his investment is not relevant in other dividend situations, and no reason appears why it should be here. The presence of such differences between §§ 356(a)(2) and 301 can only cause difficulty. At the moment, there are signs that the Service will try to by-pass the gain limitation of § 356(a)(2) by moving directly under § 301. See Rev.Rul. 61–156, 1961–2 Cum.Bull. 62; cf. Reg. § 1.301–1 (*l*).

The Service apparently does not consider § 356(a)(2) "dividends" eligible for the dividend exclusion or the dividends-received deduction. See United States v. E. I. duPont de Nemours & Co., 177 F.Supp. 1, 9 (N.D.Ill.1959); Reg. § 1.243–1(a).

C. PREFERRED STOCK RECAPITALIZATIONS

1. RECAPITALIZATIONS EQUIVALENT TO A STOCK DIVIDEND

As previously noted, a recapitalization may amount in effect to a preferred stock dividend—for example, if common stockholders exchange all of their old common for new preferred and common, or exchange some of their old common for new preferred. It seems clear that such transactions should be treated the same for tax purposes as an express stock dividend; and this is accomplished by § 306(c)(1)(B) which applies the "section 306 stock" taint to preferred stock received in a reorganization where "the effect of the transaction was substantially the same as the receipt of a stock dividend." This test is quite analogous to the above-mentioned test of whether boot received in a reorganization will be treated as a dividend under § 356(a)(2); and the regulations, § 1.306–3(d), in a seeming overstatement of this analogy, restate the test for § 306 stock in terms of whether cash received in lieu of the stock in question would have been treated as a dividend under § 356(a)(2). Cf. Note, Exclusion from Section 306 Treatment in Unifying Reorganizations, 76 Harv.L.Rev. 1627 (1963).

The revenue rulings thus far appear to treat as § 306 stock any preferred received by a shareholder whose proportionate common stock interest remains substantially as large as before. E. g., Rev. Rul. 56–116, 1956–1 Cum.Bull. 164; Rev.Rul. 59–197, 1959–1 Cum. Bull. 77. Notice also that a recapitalization producing § 306 stock can occur even though there is no direct exchange of stock. Thus, in Rev. Rul. 56–654, 1956–2 Cum.Bull. 216, a corporation with outstanding common and preferred stock amended its charter to increase the liquidation preference of the preferred. According to the ruling, such a transaction constitutes an exchange of all the preferred and some of the common for new preferred, which means that the increase in value of the preferred stock is subject to the "section 306" taint.

There are a few pre-1954 cases dealing with whether a purported recapitalization really constituted a stock dividend. This issue arose at that time because some stock dividends, unlike recapitalizations, were not tax-free; in addition, stock dividends involved some special basis considerations not present in recapitalizations. Query how much influence these cases will have in the construction of § 306(c)(1)(B).

In Bass v. Commissioner, 129 F.2d 300 (1st Cir. 1942), the corporation involved had outstanding 600,000 shares of no-par common stock with a stated capital of $10 per share, making a total stated capital of $6,000,000. A plan was adopted under which the shareholders turned in their 600,000 shares of common in exchange for 30,000 shares of new preferred stock, with a stated capital of $100 per share, and 300,000 shares of no-par common with a stated value of $10 per share. Immediately thereafter the common stock was split two for one so that the stockholders ended up again owning 600,000 shares of common. However, the common now had a stated capital of only $5 per share, the total stated capital of the corporation having remained at $6,000,000. The Commissioner determined that the transaction amounted to an outright dividend of preferred on common and was sustained by the Tax Court. However, the Court of Appeals reversed, primarily on the ground that a true stock dividend always involves some transfer from surplus to stated capital, whereas here the total stated capital had not been changed.

In Fischer v. Commissioner, 46 B. T. A. 999 (1942), the corporation had 7000 shares of $100 par value common stock outstanding. The corporation reorganized its capital structure into 35,000 shares of $10 par value common, and 14,000 shares of $25 par value preferred, which left the total authorized capital stock at $700,000 as before. The purpose of the plan was to make it possible to sell some of the stock held by the present stockholders to the public, and it was thought that a public issue could be made more attractive if the stock could be sold in units of four shares of preferred and one share of common. The stockholders exchanged all of their old common stock on the basis of five shares of new common and two shares of new preferred for each old common share. The Tax Court rejected the Commissioner's contention that this transaction constituted a taxable stock dividend rather than a recapitalization. The court stressed the fact that there had actually been an exchange of stock, and found a valid "business purpose" in the effort of the stockholders to create a public market for their stock without giving up control of the enterprise.

In Brown v. Commissioner, 26 B.T.A. 901 (1932), a transaction described in the resolution of the board of directors as a "stock dividend" consisted of increasing the authorized capital stock of the corporation from 1000 shares of $100 par common stock to 5000 shares of $100 par preferred and 10,000 shares of $100 par common, followed by the issuance of the new stock on the basis of 5 shares of new preferred and 10 shares of new common for every share of old common surrendered. The increase in stated capital of $1,400,000 was supported by a transfer from a newly created revaluation surplus. The Tax Court held that the transaction constituted a stock dividend, emphasizing the increase in stated capital, and the fact that each shareholder ended up with a pro rata amount of new preferred while his proportionate interest in the corporation remained absolutely and relatively the same.

---

2. STOCK DIVIDENDS AS RECAPITALIZATIONS

What about the converse question, i.e., whether a stock dividend can constitute a recapitalization. Certainly a stock dividend meets the general test of a "reshuffling of a capital structure within the framework of an existing corporation", since new stock is issued and is accompanied by an appropriate transfer to stated capital from some surplus account. To be sure, it is no longer necessary to find that a stock dividend constitutes a recapitalization in order to make receipt of the dividend stock tax-free, since § 305 now assures that result. However, if a stock dividend could be regarded as a recapitalization, then perhaps a subsequent exchange of stock among the shareholders, at least where that is contemplated as an integral companion of the stock dividend from the outset, could be treated as a tax-free exchange "in pursuance of the plan of" recapitalization within the meaning of § 354(a).

Again, what sparse authority there is on the question of treating a stock dividend as a recapitalization stems from the pre-1954 law. In Frank J. Kelly Trust v. Commissioner, 38 B. T. A. 1014 (1938), remanded by stipulation, 106 F.2d 1002 (8th Cir. 1939), the court rejected a contention that an outright stock dividend constituted a distribution pursuant to a recapitalization, holding there was no evidence that the distribution of the dividend stock was made "in pursuance of a plan" of recapitalization within the meaning of the predecessor of § 354. In Brown v. Commissioner, supra, the court declined to rule on the petitioner's contention that the transaction there constituted a recapitalization. However, the court noted that the statutory provisions relating to stock dividends and recapitalizations "literally overlap", and implied that the stock dividend characterization should probably control where applicable. And in Bass v. Commissioner, supra, the court observed that a stock dividend might be a recapitalization because it did involve a change in the capital structure (although the court noted that this would not bring the predecessor of § 354(a) into play to make the distribution of stock tax-free because of the absence of any "exchange").

3. NON PRO RATA RECAPITALIZATIONS

Is it necessary to finding a recapitalization that all members of the same class of stockholders participate pro rata in the exchange transaction? This question arose in one of the earliest preferred stock recapitalization cases, Muchnic v. Commissioner, 29 B.T.A. 163 (1933). There the corporation involved had 20,000 shares of no-par common stock outstanding when its charter was amended in 1925 to authorize the issuance of 5,500 shares of 7% cumulative, redeemable preferred stock. The new preferred was offered to the common stockholders in exchange for common at the rate of six-tenths of a share of preferred for each share of common. Seven of the sixteen stockholders of the company accepted the offer, exchanging 9,166 shares of common for 5,499.6 shares of preferred. The taxpayer, who was a member of the controlling family group, and with his wife owned about 40% of the common, did not participate in this exchange. By 1929, all of the preferred had been redeemed, and all of the common stock acquired by the company in the exchange had been reissued by sale or stock dividend. In 1929, the company again gave the opportunity to its stockholders to exchange their common for the preferred upon the same basis as before. This time only the taxpayer and his wife accepted the offer, each of them turning in 2500 shares of common for 1500 shares of preferred.

The Commissioner sought to tax the gain on the 1929 exchanges but the Board held that the transaction constituted a recapitalization upon which no gain or loss should be recognized under the predecessor of § 354. The Board first rejected the Commissioner's contention that if any reorganization occurred, it was when the corporation amended its charter to authorize the issuance of preferred stock, rather than when such preferred stock was issued in exchange for common. The Board cited language in both corporate and tax authorities indicating that an exchange of preferred stock for common which effected a change in the capital structure of the corporation constituted a recapitalization (and hence a reorganization). The Board then concluded as follows:

> Respondent contends, however, that the instant exchanges fall short of effecting a recapitalization for the reason that not all of the stockholders participated. The answer to that is one of fact; two stockholders made the exchange offered by the company to all, and as a result the capitalization of the company was changed. Before the exchanges, it had outstanding 20,000 shares of common stock having a stated value of $500,000. After the exchanges, it had outstanding 15,000 shares of common stock having a stated value of $375,000 and 3,000 shares of preferred stock of a par value of $300,000; thus disclosing an increase

in its liability upon stock of $75,000. Moreover, there was a "readjustment of existing interests." New priorities as to the company's assets and earnings were assumed upon the issue of the preferred stock, which, together with the reduction in the common stock outstanding, effected a revision of the existing interests of the common stockholders. It cannot be denied that such readjustments affecting the capital of the company constitute a recapitalization.

Although the Commissioner's complaint about the non pro rata nature of the transaction in Muchnic received short shrift, the fact remains that such a non pro rata recapitalization is really essentially equivalent to a transaction consisting of a pro rata stock dividend followed by exchanges among the individual stockholders to reach whatever proportionate holdings of new and old stock are desired. The similarity between these two approaches is dramatically illustrated by the case of Hartzell v. Commissioner, 40 B. T. A. 492 (1939). There the petitioner was one of thirteen stockholders who owned all of the authorized capital stock of a corporation, consisting of 10,000 shares of $100 par value common stock. Six of the stockholders were over 60 years old, and they owned a total of 7,550 shares; the younger seven stockholders, including the petitioner, owned the remaining 2,450 shares. Of the older stockholders, one was president and one was treasurer; the younger stockholders included the general manager, the secretary, and the heads of each of the five departments of the business. All of the older stockholders had children, none of whom were identified with the affairs of the company. The younger stockholders were apprehensive that upon the death of the older stockholders their stockholdings might go to their children, with the result that voting control of the company would pass into the hands of people totally unfamiliar with its affairs. They were also concerned that under such circumstances, they might be displaced from their positions with the company and be left with nothing but their minority stock interests.

The two groups of stockholders discussed this situation from time to time, and ultimately agreed upon a plan under which the older stockholders would own preferred stock while the younger stockholders would obtain all of the common stock of the company. The stockholders instructed an attorney to work out the details of such a plan. The attorney drafted an agreement calling for a pro rata distribution of both new preferred stock and new common to each stockholder, after which the younger stockholders were to transfer their preferred stock to the older stockholders in exchange for the latter's common stock. The stockholders objected to this approach, stating that they had assumed that "before they got through with the reorganization" the older stockholders would own all the preferred stock and the younger stockholders would own all the common stock. However, the attorney explained that the provision in the agreement calling for an initial pro rata distribution of the new preferred and common to each stockholder was merely a "detour" to comply with Ohio laws in filing the certificate of reorganization, and that the ultimate result sought by the stockholders would be accomplished by the subsequent exchange of preferred and common stock between the older and younger groups of stockholders. The attorney also pointed out that it would not be necessary to have an actual exchange of the stock among the stockholders, since the same result could be accomplished by having the company issue directly to each stockholder the amount of preferred or common stock which he was supposed ultimately to own.

After this explanation, all of the stockholders signed the agreement, on February 10, 1931. The agreement provided that the corporation should be reorganized so that its authorized capital stock would consist of 12,000 shares of 7% cumulative $100 par preferred, and 5000 shares of no-par common stock which was to have a stated value of $50 per share; that 11,700 shares of the new preferred stock and 4,900 shares of the new common stock should be issued in exchange for the outstanding 10,000 shares of old common stock on the basis of 1 and 17/100 shares of preferred and 49/100 shares of common for each share of old common; and that the stated capital of the reorganized corporation at the time of filing the necessary certificate of reorganization with the Secretary of State of Ohio should be $1,415,000, consisting of the total par value of the 11,700 of preferred stock to be issued under the plan plus the $50 per share to be allotted to stated capital for each of the 4,900 shares of common stock. The agreement further provided that it was the desire of all the stockholders that the older stockholders would own all the preferred stock and that the younger stockholders should own all of the common stock, and that accordingly the older stockholders would exchange the common stock to which they would be entitled under a pro rata distribution for the preferred stock to which the younger stockholders would be entitled. The agreement also provided that instead of actually issuing to each stockholder his pro rata portion of both preferred and common stock, the company was authorized and directed to distribute directly to each stockholder the amount of preferred or common respectively which each was supposed ultimately to own, "thereby accomplishing the results agreed to by all the stockholders without the necessity of an actual exchange".

The agreement also contained a number of protective features for the preferred stock, such as a provision for redemption of 2% of the preferred stock each year, to the extent of available surplus profits, at $110 per share plus unpaid dividends; a provision that upon any default in the payment of preferred dividends, the entire voting power should be vested in the preferred; and a limitation upon common stock dividends to $5.00 per share per year as long as any preferred stock remained outstanding.

On February 18, 1931, a special meeting of the board of directors was held at which the board unanimously adopted a plan of reorganization identical to the one in the agreement of the stockholders, except that there was no reference to the matter of the ultimate exchange of preferred and common between the two groups or to the accomplishment of this objective by means of direct issuance by the company of all the preferred to the older stockholders and all the common to younger stockholders. Thereafter, at a special stockholders' meeting, the plan of reorganization adopted by the board of directors was unanimously approved and adopted, and the president and secretary were instructed to file with the Secretary of State of Ohio a certificate of reorganization containing a copy of the plan. At the same meeting, a second and separate resolution was unanimously adopted to the effect that the corporation should issue all of the preferred stock directly to the older stockholders and all of the common directly to the younger stockholders.

Pursuant to the plan, the petitioner ended up with 900 shares of new common stock in lieu of his 450 shares of old common. He reported no gain on the transaction, treating it as an exchange made in pursuance of a plan of recapitalization under the predecessor of § 368(a)(1)(E) and hence tax-free under the predecessor of § 354. However, the Commissioner viewed the transaction as consisting of two separate and independent steps: a pro rata exchange of new preferred and common for old common, which he conceded did constitute a recapitalization; and a subsequent exchange among the shareholders in their individual capacities, which he contended was not part of the recapitalization, and did not become so merely because the parties caused the corporation to effect the exchanges for them, by issuing all of the preferred stock directly to the older stockholders and all of the common stock directly to the younger stockholders. Accordingly, the Commissioner determined that the exchanges among the shareholders were taxable under the predecessor of § 1002.

The Tax Court found for the taxpayer, holding that the ultimate effect of the overall transaction was an exchange by some of the stockholders of all of their common stock for new preferred, which constituted a recapitalization under the Muchnic case, supra. The court viewed the intermediate step of pro rata exchange of new preferred and common for old common as a mere "detour", which was used only because of feared impediments in the Ohio statute and did not preclude finding that the entire transaction amounted to a recapitalization.

Since the Hartzell case, the authorities have been uniform in treating such non pro rata exchanges by some of the common stockholders of a corporation of all of their common stock for new preferred stock as tax-free recapitalizations. Thus in Dean v. Commissioner, 10 T.C. 19 (1948), all of the stock of a corporation was owned by a family group, consisting of the active manager of the corporation, and his wife, sister and nieces. The manager was anxious to induce the inactive women stockholders to surrender their voting stock, partly to make the remaining stock more saleable, and thus more attractive for use in inducing new executive talent to accept employment with the corporation, and partly to avoid the possibility that voting control would fall into the hands of the inexperienced women if the manager should die. Accordingly, a plan was adopted under which all of the shareholders were given the privilege of exchanging one share of old common for one and ¼ shares of new preferred, having a $5 cumulative dividend and a preference on liquidation. All of the women stockholders accepted the privilege of exchanging their old common stock for the new preferred while the manager did not exchange any of his stock. The directors of the company then limited the $5 preferred stock to the shares already issued, and authorized a new $4 preferred stock to be issued for sale to investors and additional common stock to be made available to employees. The Tax Court held that the exchange by the women stockholders of all of their old common for new preferred constituted a tax-free exchange pursuant to a recapitalization.

In addition, the Commissioner has affirmatively ruled on several occasions that a non pro rata exchange of new preferred for old common constitutes a recapitalization, so that the exchanges between the common stockholders and the corporation are tax-free under § 354. E. g., Rev.Rul. 55–112, 1955–1 Cum.Bull. 344; Rev.Rul. 59–84, 1959–1 Cum.Bull. 71.

D. SECURITIES RECAPITALIZATIONS

The term "recapitalization" also embraces transactions involving exchanges of debt securities. Perhaps the most comprehensive examination of this issue appears in Commissioner v. Neustadt's Trust, 131 F.2d 528, 529 (2d Cir.1942), involving an exchange of outstanding 20-year, 6% debentures for a like amount of 10-year, 3¼% convertible debentures of the corporation:

> It is not disputed that the corporation's offer to its old debenture holders constituted a plan of reorganization if there was a "recapitalization." This term, which has been in the tax law since 1921, has never been defined in the Revenue Acts. Nor have the Treasury Regulations attempted any definition except by way of illustration. . . .
> In Helvering v. Southwest Consolidated Corp., 315 U.S. 194, 202, 62 S.Ct. 546, 552, 86 L.Ed. 789, Mr. Justice Douglas

remarked that "recapitalization" contemplates a "reshuffling of a capital structure within the framework of an existing corporation." But this advances solution of the problem only by substituting the necessity of defining the phrase "a capital structure" instead of the word "recapitalization." The commissioner contends that only a change in authorized or outstanding capital stock of a corporation can properly be denominated a recapitalization or a reshuffling of the capital structure. He describes an exchange of old debentures for new debentures in the same corporation as a mere refinancing operation. In support of this view reference is made to definitions suggested by certain commentators. . . . But in common financial parlance the long term funded debt of a corporation is usually regarded as forming part of its capital structure. Instances of such usage may be found in Graham & Dodd, Security Analysis, 1934, p. 461; Kraft & Starkweather, Analysis of Industrial Securities, 1930, pp. 153, 154; Paul & Mertens, Law of Fed. Inc. Taxation, 1934, Vol. 2, p. 208; Fletcher, Cyclopedia on Corporations, 1938 Ed. Vol. 15, § 7215. The Security and Exchange Commission has required the funded debt of a corporation to be listed under the caption of "capital securities." The Interstate Commerce Commission treats funded debt as part of the corporate capital structure. . . . A court is justified in believing that when Congress employs in a tax law words having a well defined meaning in the business world, it used them with that meaning in the absence of clear evidence to the contrary. . . . There is no evidence to the contrary. On the other hand the purpose of the statutory nonrecognition of gain or loss from reorganization transactions, favors ascribing to the word "recapitalization" a broad rather than a restricted meaning. Such purpose, as indicated by the Congressional reports printed in the margin, was apparently twofold: To encourage legitimate reorganizations required to strengthen the financial condition of a corporation, and to prevent losses being established by bondholders, as well as stockholders, who have received the new securities without substantially changing their original investment. The transaction in the case at bar meets both of these tests. By changing the interest rate and date of maturity of its old bonds and adding a conversion option to the holders of the new, the corporation could strengthen its financial condition, while the bondholders would not substantially change their original investments by making the exchange. "Recapitalization" seems a most appropriate word to describe that type of reorganization and it is the very kind of transaction where Congress meant the recognition of gain or loss to be held in suspense until a more substantial change in the taxpayer's original investment should occur. We hold that the exchange of securities was made pursuant to a plan of "recapitalization."

Similarly, an exchange of new stock, preferred or common, for outstanding bonds constitutes a recapitalization. E.g., Commissioner v. Capento Securities Corporation, 140 F.2d 382 (1st Cir. 1944); Reg. § 1.368–2(e) (1).

More difficulty is presented by transactions involving the exchange of new debt securities for outstanding stock. For one thing, such a transaction really amounts to a repurchase of stock on credit, see Bowman v. Armour & Co., page 393 supra; and repurchase transactions have always been approached rather gingerly for tax as well as corporate purposes. More important, such transactions present a classic bail-out possibility—indeed, even more so than preferred stock dividends because debt securities are more liquid than preferred stock and easier to sell (or redeem). Under the pre-1954 law this problem was particularly serious because there was then no counterpart of §§ 354(a)(2) and 356(d), and the literal language of the predecessor of § 354(a)(1) made the receipt of debt instruments in a reorganization tax-free so long as they qualified as "securities." However, the Supreme Court went far toward closing this loophole with its decision in Bazley v. Commissioner, 331 U.S. 737, 67 S.Ct. 1489, 91 L.Ed. 1782, 173 A.L.R. 905 (1947), involving an exchange of new no-par common and ten-year, callable debentures for old $100 par common. The Court held that a transaction which produced "for all practical purposes, the same result as a distribution of cash earnings of equivalent value, cannot obtain tax immunity because cast in the form of a recapitalization-reorganization. . . . A 'reorganization' which is merely a vehicle, however elaborate or elegant, for conveying earnings from accumulations to the stockholders is not a reorganization under [§ 368(a) (1)]."

The Bazley decision created some concern because of the difficulty of pinning down just what had been decided. It did not seem to be a "business purpose" decision since, although each of the lower courts had divided over whether it was necessary to show a corporate business purpose for the transaction, as distinguished from a stockholder business purpose such as the one here of making a portion of the investment more marketable, the Supreme Court had made no reference to that issue. Perhaps the most troublesome element was the Court's cryptic statement that "even if this transaction were deemed a reorganization, the facts would equally sustain the imposition of the tax on the debentures [under the predecessor of § 356 (a).]," citing the Bedford case, page 400 supra. Did this mean that the debt instruments in Bazley did not constitute "securities" within the meaning of the predecessor of § 354(a)? Such a holding would have important implications in other areas where the "securities" issue is present. However, it seems more likely that the Court simply felt the need to block this gaping bailout loophole, particularly where the recipients of the debentures were also the controlling stockholders and hence were in position to cause the corporation to exercise its right of redemption at any time.

On the other hand, non pro rata exchanges of new securities for outstanding stock have uniformly been held to qualify as recapitalizations eligible for tax-free treatment under the pre-1954 law. E.g., Hickok v. Commissioner, 32 T.C. 80 (1959) (rejecting the contention, *inter alia*, that an "upstream" exchange, i.e. of new debt for outstanding stock, did not constitute a recapitalization because it weakened rather than strengthened the corporation); Davis v. Penfield, 205 F.2d 798 (5th Cir.1953).

The solution of the 1954 Code is to treat as boot any excess in principal amount of securities received over securities surrendered, which of course means all securities received when none are surrendered. Generally speaking, under § 356 either gain will be recognized to the extent of the value of such excess securities or that amount will be taxed as a dividend. (If no non-recognition property is received, § 356 does not apply, and the transaction is left to be taxed under one of the other distribution provisions, §§ 301, 302, 331 or 346.)

Notice that the 1954 Code pattern substantially increases the possible area of operation for the so-called "automatic" dividend construction of § 356(a) (2). Thus a surrender by a stockholder of all of his common stock in exchange for new preferred and securities could, under a strict "automatic" view, lead to divided treatment of the securities under § 356(a) (2). But such a case actually helps to demonstrate the unsoundness of any automatic rule—for it is hard to see any dividend when an investor changes from a basic equity position to ownership of only senior, fixed income, interests. In such a case it seems clear that the presence of securities as part of the package of senior interests does not have the "effect" of a dividend; and similarly, no part of the preferred stock would have the effect of a stock dividend within the meaning of § 306(c) (1) (B).

SECTION 8. REPURCHASE OF STOCK

A. POWER TO PURCHASE

MOUNTAIN STATE STEEL FOUNDRIES, INC. v. COMMISSIONER [34]

United States Court of Appeals, Fourth Circuit, 1960. 284 F.2d 737.

HAYNSWORTH, CIRCUIT JUDGE. Deficiencies of income tax for the fiscal years 1951–1954 were asserted against this corporate taxpayer upon (1) the disallowance of deductions for interest paid upon notes given in part payment of the purchase price of the stock of dissident stockholders upon the ground that the stock purchase agreement impaired the capital of the corporation and was invalid under state law, and (2) the assessment of the [accumulated earnings tax under the predecessor of §§ 531–537] upon the ground that by the redemption of the stock the corporation had been availed of for the purpose of avoiding surtaxes upon its remaining shareholders by accumulation of earnings. In an unreviewed decision, the single judge of the Tax Court sustained the commissioner upon both questions.

Since we are of the opinion there was no income tax deficiency, we do not consider the Tax Court's computation of the [accumulated taxable income under the predecessor of § 535], a computation with which both parties find fault.

The transaction which gave birth to these problems was consummated in an effort to resolve difficulties arising out of the death of a partner in an antecedent partnership. The story should start with the beginning.

Ben Miller and Harold F. Stratton, of Parkersburg, West Virginia, were the principal partners in a partnership engaged in manufacturing steel castings. Miller died in 1945, and his widow and two daughters then became owners of his fifty per cent interest in the partnership, the other fifty per cent interest being owned by Stratton, his sister and two nephews.

On July 1, 1947, the business was incorporated. Mountain State Steel Foundries, Inc., the taxpayer acquired all of the partnership assets in exchange for which it issued one thousand shares of its common stock, having a par value of $100 each, to the Millers and a like number of shares to the Strattons. It assumed all of the partnership obligations.

---

34. Some of the court's footnotes omitted.

The Millers were not happy with the situation. Except that Mrs. Miller was a member of the Board of Directors, they took no active part in the conduct of the business, but felt the need of larger and more certain income than prospective dividends would provide. The business is said to have been subject to wide fluctuations in earnings. Additionally, the Strattons, who were active in the business and derived income from it through salaries, were interested in expanding and improving the business and its fixed assets and in utilizing a portion of current earnings in good years for that purpose.

This conflict in the interests of the stockholders led Mrs. Miller to demand that the business be sold. Stratton sought to find a purchaser for all of the stock or the corporate assets on a basis which would enable the stockholders to realize $1,700,000. Later, he reduced his asking price to $1,500,000. Some people were interested in the plant, but not at those prices.

In 1950, an accountant, who did work for the taxpayer and its stockholders, suggested to Mrs. Miller that the corporation might buy the Miller stock if she and her daughters would accept payment over a substantial number of years. Mrs. Miller thought well of the idea, and approached the Strattons about it. An agreement was then worked out for the corporation to purchase all of the Miller stock at a price of $450,000, payable $50,000 in cash and the balance, with interest at four per cent per annum, payable in level payments of $11,000 each six months until April 1, 1977 and of $5,000 each six months thereafter until April 1, 1994.[2]

The corporation has met its maturing obligations under these notes. The interest increment of its payments during its fiscal years 1951–1954, respectively, was $11,969.99, $15,757.00, $15,504.77 and $15,242.37. On its income tax returns for those years it deducted those amounts as interest paid.

The Commissioner disallowed these deductions on the theory that the purchase of the stock impaired the capital of the corporation in violation of § 3051(31–1–39) of the West Virginia Code of 1955 and that, because of that statute, the obligations with respect to which the interest was paid were unenforceable and invalid. He further imposed the [accumulated earnings] tax on the theory that, since the Strattons might have bought the stock, had the Millers been willing to accept their personal obligations, and declared additional dividends to provide them with funds to meet their individual obligations, the corporate redemption of the Miller stock established, during each of the tax years, a use by the Strattons of the corporation for the avoidance of personal surtaxes by corporate accumulation of income.

---

2. Mrs. Miller received $30,000 of the cash payment and a note for $195,000, the principal and interest being payable at the rate of $6,000 each six months, or until April 1, 1977. Each daughter received $10,000 in cash and a note for $102,500, the principal and interest being payable at the rate of $2,500 each six months or until April 1, 1994. The taxpayer reserved the right to anticipate these payments after April 1, 1961.

After the Tax Court approved the Commissioner's theories on both aspects of the case, the taxpayer brought an action in the state court against the Millers seeking a declaratory judgment as to its obligations. This proceeding resulted in a decree of the Circuit Court of Wood County, West Virginia, in which it was held that the redemption of the stock did not impair the capital of the corporation within the meaning of § 3051 of the West Virginia Code and that the corporate notes were valid and enforceable. On the basis of this decree, the taxpayer sought leave to file a motion for further trial in the Tax Court. This was denied for lack of merit, apparently on the ground that the state court action was collusive or not really adversary. It does appear that the taxpayer's position in the state court action was that its officials believed the notes to be valid, binding obligations, but that no further payments would be made on them until the court determined and declared the rights and duties of the parties. Honestly, it hardly could have taken any other position.

[Part I *]

The Interest Deduction

By statute,[3] West Virginia has authorized a corporation organized under her laws, other than a banking institution, to purchase, hold and sell shares of its own capital stock. There is a proviso, however, that funds and property of the corporation may not be used to purchase its own shares if the use would impair the capital of the corporation.

The Tax Court was apparently of the opinion that the net worth of the corporation should have been reduced by the full amount of the purchase price as soon as the repurchase agreement was entered into and that the question of impairment should be determined by reference to book figures without regard to the real value of the assets. The Circuit Court for Wood County, West Virginia, on the other hand, held that the real value of the assets, which it found to be substantially more than the book figures, was crucial under the statute. The Commissioner finds the entries in the books so authoritarian that he conceded on argument that if the taxpayer had written up the value of its fixed assets on the basis of an appraisal in line with the testimony in this case and in the state court proceeding, there would have been no capital impairment. He does not question the disparity between real and book values; to him, it is the failure to

---

* [Ed. note] Division of the opinion into "Parts" is by the editor.

3. § 3051 of West Virginia Code of 1955. ". . . Every corporation organized under this chapter, or existing under the laws of this State, shall have the power to purchase, hold, sell and transfer shares of its own capital stock: Provided, that no such corporation shall use its funds or property for the purchase of its own shares of capital stock when such use would cause any impairment of the capital of the corporation; . . ."

have recorded the real value on the books which occasioned the asserted impairment of the capital.

We think a determination of the substantive rights of creditors, stockholders and the corporation, in the application of this statute, should not be so circumscribed by managerial decision to make or withhold particular entries on the books or by the accounting procedures followed by management, procedures which may, or may not, have been realistic or enlightened. Write ups by appraisal are frequently suspect. As a practice they are now usually frowned upon. The suggestion is startling that such a ministerial act, which alters the real situation not in the least, could enlarge corporate power to purchase its stock.

When the legislature spoke of impairment of capital, we think it had a more objective standard than a computation which is the product of years of financial history of an enterprise. If write ups by appraisal be subject to criticism in the world of corporate finance, a blind acceptance of book values as real is much more vulnerable. An overstatement of assets because of a failure to charge off obsolescent equipment should not enlarge the power of the corporation to buy its stock, nor should an understatement because of appreciation in values and the decline in the worth of money restrict it.

Corporate power to purchase its own stock has been frequently abused. Done by corporations conducting faltering businesses, it has been employed to create preferences to the detriment of creditors and of the other stockholders. It was to protect and preserve the margin of safety supplied by the real value of contributed capital that such statutes were enacted. That purpose is not served if the statute is applied in terms of unrealistic values, whether higher or lower than real values. At least until the highest court of West Virginia should otherwise decide, we think for our collateral purpose the statute should be construed as prohibiting the purchase of its own stock if the use of its funds for the purpose would deplete the realizable value of its assets to a point below the total of its liabilities and capital.

What little can be found in decided cases applying similar statutes suggests that actual values, rather than book figures, are critical to the inquiry. Though impressive argument may be made that unrealized gain should not be available justification for dividends, similar language in statutes restricting dividend distributions has been similarly construed.[6]

If we are to look to actual values in applying the statute, the spirit of the statute requires that they be conservatively determined. Opinion evidence of appreciation should be received with skepticism if insolvency ensues. Here, however, no one questions the fact that

6. Randall v. Bailey, . . . ; Morris v. Standard Gas & Electric Co., 31 Del.Ch. 20, 63 A.2d 577.

the real worth of the plant substantially exceeds its depreciated cost.[7] In subsequent years this small manufacturing enterprise has continued to prosper. Its subsequent earnings have been sufficient to maintain a good current position, meet the obligations to the Millers, pay for substantial plant additions and improvements and pay moderate dividends. Its subsequent history is one of prosperity, not of decline. No creditor has suffered loss or delay.

[*Part II*]

We think the Tax Court also misapplied the statute in declaring unenforceable an executory agreement without regard to the "use" of funds which the statute proscribes. Literally read, the statute prohibits use by a corporation of its funds to purchase its own stock if such use will impair the capital. It says nothing of executory agreements which create no rights enforceable in competition with the rights of creditors. Nor do we find anything in the purpose of the statute to protect creditors' rights which requires an extension of the literal language to executory agreements which have not, and in performance cannot, impair the preferred rights.

It is now well-established that the claims of former stockholders under such executory agreements are subordinate to the claims of other creditors existing at the time of performance.[8] When a corporation purchases a portion of its outstanding stock with an agreement to pay for it at a subsequent time, it may not perform its promise if the use of its funds in performance will impair its capital. This is true though earlier performance at the time of consummation of the executory agreement would have occasioned no impairment of the capital.

The promise, therefore, is conditional.[9] The corporation's promise is to pay provided at the time of payment it has sufficient surplus that disbursement of the funds will occasion no impairment of capital. In effect, the statute is read into the agreement. The mere existence of an executory promise to pay so conditioned that it may not be per-

---

7. For tax purposes, the corporation was required to use as its basis for its fixed assets the depreciated cost of its antecedent partnership. Starting with those figures, it showed on its balance sheet at the end of its fiscal year, 1950, a gross plant account of $543,235.46, a depreciation reserve of $345,355.59 and net book value of fixed assets of $197,879.87. It had approximately $150,000 of current assets to pay $20,000 of current liabilities. It had, according to the books, earned surplus of $132,527.53, which, added to the capital account of $200,000, gave it a net worth of $332,527.53. If, as the testimony indicates, its fixed assets had a realizable sales value of at least $1,000,000, its real net worth was more than $1,100,000.

8. See, among others, . . . In re Fecheimer Fishel Co., 2 Cir., 212 F. 357; . . . Richards v. Ernst Wiener Co., 207 N.Y. 59, 100 N.E. 592; . . .

9. This was the express holding in Topken, Loring & Schwartz, Inc. v. Schwartz, [noted at page 437, note 52, infra].

Sec. 8   REPURCHASE OF STOCK   419

formed if performance will impair the capital, hardly may be said, itself, to have impaired the capital.[11]

In most of the cases which have dealt with the problem, the corporation, when it made the promise, had an apparent surplus sufficient to support it. In Christie v. Fifth Madison Corp.,[12] however, the corporation had no surplus when the promise was made. Since the promise was held to be conditioned by the statute, it was held to be a lawful obligation.

Whether the corporate surplus is more or less than the obligation conditionally undertaken, the application of the statute should be the same. In either case, existing creditors suffer no injury when the conditional promise is given. If creditors are prejudiced, it is performance in the use of corporate funds in violation of the statute which works the harm. Those creditors existing at the time of performance are the ones who need the protection of the statute, not those earlier creditors whose claims were unaffected by the executory promise.

What happened here is illustrative. When the agreement was executed in 1950, no creditor was injured. The corporation has prospered since then. With subsequent earnings, it has met its maturing obligations under this agreement, paid for plant additions and improvements and maintained a good cash position. The 1950 creditors' claims long ago were paid in full. If the corporation should suffer financial reverses, creditors of a future day may be exposed to prejudice by further performance of this agreement. For the benefit of those future creditors who may need the protection of the statute, the impact of the statute should be felt at the time of performance, to which its language is directed. In the meanwhile, when corporate use of corporate funds adversely affects no creditor, the statutory language need not be expanded to thwart the reasonable purposes of the corporation and of its present and former stockholders.

As we stated in connection with the other branch of this problem, we deal with the statute only collaterally. If the literal language of the statute is to be expanded to have the effect for which the Commissioner contends, it should be done by West Virginia's legislature or her courts. We find no justification for our interpreting the statute, for our purpose, to have so expanded and so technical an application.

The Commissioner seeks to support the holding of the Tax Court upon the additional ground that the transaction brought no new money

11. Perhaps the condition is more accurately expressed as being that performance should not occasion a violation of the statute. In liquidation, the claim of the promisee, deferred to the claims of all general creditors, would be preferred over the interests of the remaining stockholders. Until the claims of all other creditors are fully satisfied, however, the practical effect of the condition may be stated in the language of the statute.

12. 123 N.Y.S.2d 795 [noted at page 435 infra].

into the corporation. He relies upon cases dealing with hybrid securities where the courts have disregarded the labels attached by the parties to securities and to distributions to the security holders. In such cases the fact that no fresh money came into the corporate treasury when the securities were issued may be of importance. Here, however, the Commissioner does not contend that the Millers are not creditors, or that the notes should be treated as preferred stock. His basic contention is that they are creditors, holding notes, the issuance of which impaired the capital. Under the circumstances, the fact that issuance of the notes brought no new money into the till is irrelevant.

[Part III]

The Avoidance of Surtax upon Stockholders Through Accumulation of Earnings

The Tax Court upheld the imposition of the [accumulated earnings tax] because of the fact that an accountant suggested the purchase of the Miller stock by the corporation. It reasoned that he must have known that if the corporation had paid additional dividends to the Strattons in an amount equal to the disbursements to the Millers, the Strattons would have had larger surtax obligations. It was of the opinion the purchase of the Miller stock served no corporate purpose, and that the Strattons must have learned of the tax considerations from their accountant and must have acted as they did for the purpose of avoiding additional surtax on their personal income.

There was no finding that the Millers, who suggested the corporate purchase to the Strattons, would have been willing to accept the personal obligations of the Strattons or that the Strattons would have been willing to obligate themselves and their estates to make payments extending over a period of 44 years. There was no finding that in any year accumulated earnings were unreasonable or in excess of the needs of the business.[14] There was only the opinion that these disbursements served no legitimate corporate purpose and were arranged by the Strattons with a purpose of avoidance of surtaxes.

We disagree with the premise of the Tax Court that these disbursements served no corporate purpose.

The problem which confronted the widow and daughters of Ben Miller and the Strattons is one that frequently arises upon the death of one co-venturer in a relatively small business enterprise. Many of those enterprises are worth substantially more to those who are able and anxious to manage them, deriving livelihoods from salaries, than to passive investors who must look only to prospective dividends for a return upon their investment. The Miller stock clearly was worth much less as a continuing investment to Mrs. Miller than it would have been worth to Ben Miller had he survived and remained

---

14. See Young Motor Company Inc. v. Commissioner, 1 Cir., 281 F.2d 488.

active in the management of the business. It was natural that she should demand that the business be sold or liquidated, and it would have been essentially unfair to have left her and her daughters indefinitely in a position in which they could expect relatively small and uncertain income from what everyone regarded, with reason, as a valuable property.

This sort of situation leads to demands for dividends out of consideration of the stockholders' personal financial need, perhaps without appropriate regard for the need of the corporation to make capital expenditures in order to maintain a competitive position. On the other hand, those stockholders active in the management of the business deriving salaries from it may be able to afford indulgence of an ambition to enlarge future earnings through still larger current capital expenditures, an indulgence which other stockholders may ill afford.

When the stockholders have such conflicting interests, the corporation and its future are necessarily affected. When the situation results in demands that the business be sold or liquidated, as it did here, the impact of the conflict upon the corporation is direct and immediate. That it is of concern to employees is illustrated by the brief *amicus curiae* of United Steelworkers, the bargaining agent of the taxpayer's employees, filed in support of the taxpayer's position. The resolution of such a conflict, so that the need of the corporation may govern managerial decision, is plainly a corporate purpose.

Many business men now anticipate such problems and provide solutions through agreements, and implementing devices, to take out the estate of a co-venturer, who dies, on a basis designed to be fair to the estate, to the enterprise and to the surviving co-venturers. It has been held that corporate disbursements to pay insurance premiums to provide a fund with which to purchase stock from the estate of the person whose life is insured do serve a corporate, business purpose.[15] If disbursements to create a fund with which to purchase stock serve a corporate purpose, surely the disbursement of the created fund in purchasing the stock serves the same purpose.

For a long time there was controversy over the tax consequence to shareholders when a corporation made disproportionate distributions in partial redemption of its stock. Congress finally acted in this field.[16] Among other things, it specifically provided that a partial redemption of the shares held by an estate would be treated as a sale, not as a distribution of earnings, if the amount of the distribution did not exceed the estate's liabilities for estate and inheritance taxes, interest and funeral and administration expenses.[17] When Congress specifically provided favorable tax treatment for such transactions and sought to encourage them to facilitate the administration

---

15. Emeloid Co. v. Commissioner, 3 Cir., 189 F.2d 230; . . .

16. 26 U.S.C.A. §§ 302 et seq.

17. 26 U.S.C.A. § 303.

of estates, it hardly could have intended to penalize the corporation for doing the favored act.

We need not say that under no circumstances may a stock purchase be relevant to a question arising under [the accumulated earnings tax]. When it is done out of cash accumulations which reasonably may be thought excessive, such a purchase, along with other factors, may be considered appropriately in arriving at ultimate findings.[18] The fact of redemption, of itself, however, furnishes no basis for imposition of the [accumulated earnings] tax. In the circumstances in which they were made, the disbursements in payment for the stock, themselves, do not support a finding that they were withdrawn from excess funds accumulated from earnings beyond reasonable corporate need. Nor is the situation altered by the fact that the Strattons may have been aware that travel along another route would have cost something more in taxes. If they had a choice of routes, they were not required to choose the one which would be most costly to them in taxes.

Reversed.

NOTE ON ACCOUNTING FOR TREASURY SHARES

1. In General

HACKNEY, THE FINANCIAL PROVISIONS OF THE MODEL BUSINESS CORPORATION ACT [35]

70 Harv.L.Rev. 1392–1396 (1957).

Acquisition: Effect on Funds Available.—Section 5 of the Model Act nicely provides that purchases of its own shares can only be made by a corporation to the extent of its earned surplus (and under certain conditions to the extent of its capital surplus), and that such purchases result in a restriction on such surplus so long as the shares are held. Sections 5 and 40 allow dividends and further purchases only out of or to the extent of unrestricted surplus. This result is today certainly considered the best one; the mechanics of achieving the result, however, are unique in that most other statutes provide for a reduction of surplus or a purchase out of surplus and not a mere restriction. It is believed that the restriction technique is superior.[166] Unfortunately, however, the 1950 version

---

18. See Pelton Steel Casting Co. v. Commissioner, 7 Cir., 251 F.2d 278.

35. Copyright (c), Harvard Law Review Association, 1957. Reprinted by permission. Most of the footnotes omitted.

166. Dividends and other distributions upon shares under §§ 40 and 41 are made "out of" particular surplus which results in a reduction thereof. By contrast, purchases under § 5 are made "to the extent of" particular surplus, which does not require an actual reduction but imposes a restriction on surplus to the same extent. Most other statutes accomplish the same restriction by defining net assets so as to exclude treasury shares, thereby reducing surplus by the cost of the shares. See, e. g. Ill.Rev.Stat. c. 32 § 157.2(m) (1955). Some of the objections to this technique are: (a) It is not explicitly stated which surplus —capital or earned—is reduced by

of the Model Act purported to freeze surplus used for the purchase of treasury shares by excluding treasury shares from the definition of net assets, resulting in a decrease in surplus; the restriction approach was not used. Then in 1953 section 5 was amended so as to add the restriction approach now found there, but there was no change in the definition of net assets. It thus appears that after aggregate surplus has been decreased on a purchase, the remaining surplus is charged with a restriction upon its use for dividends or further purchases—apparently inadvertently doubling the adverse effect caused by the purchase.[167]

It would seem that the exclusion of treasury shares from the definition of net assets is only of value where some form of balance-sheet surplus by itself is the dividend source. Such an exclusion accomplishes absolutely nothing and only confuses the issue when dealing with an earnings test.[168] It is believed that in view of the excellent approach of section 5 of the act, it is definitely erroneous to exclude treasury shares from the definition of net assets in section 2.[169]

their purchase. (b) Some or all of the adverse effect upon surplus is usually deemed erased upon disposition of the treasury shares; however, if earned surplus is actually reduced and not simply frozen by the purchase, accountants would instinctively rebel at what appears to be a creation of earned surplus on resale, see note 172 infra, whereas no problem is presented by the mere lifting of a restriction. (c) The reduction-of-surplus technique might well mean that the corporation's method of accounting for treasury shares is dictated by the statute. A recent survey, American Institute of Accountants, Accounting Trends and Techniques in Published Corporation Annual Reports (1956), shows that of 277 surveyed companies carrying treasury shares, only a handful presented them as outright deductions from surplus; almost all showed them either as a deduction from the total of capital stock and surplus or as a deduction from issued stock. Would a balance sheet be incorrect under a "purchase out of surplus" statute if it failed to show an outright reduction but did footnote the unavailability of surplus for dividends arising from the purchase? What would be the liability for incorrectly showing the reduction of surplus? As long as the surplus out of which the shares are acquired is made unavailable for dividends and further purchases, it is believed that the method of accounting should be left to the accountants if the freeze upon surplus is reflected and stated capital is not misstated.

167. The only way in which the reduction of surplus arising from the definition of net assets in § 2(i) and the restriction on surplus imposed by § 5 (b) can be reconciled is to require a reduction in every case and to say that the reduction effectuates the restriction and so a further restriction is unnecessary. The restriction language in § 5(b) then would become completely superfluous, and the status of the surplus which would arise upon disposition of the shares is again put in doubt. This was obviously not the intention of the 1953 amendments to the Model Act. [Ed. note: The South Carolina version of MBA § 5, So.Car. Bus.Corp. Act § 5.17 (1962), provides for a direct reduction of earned surplus, but permits earned surplus to be restored upon a subsequent resale. See Folk, The Model Act and The South Carolina Corporation Law, 15 S.C.L.Q. 275, 342–3 (1963).]

168. Wisconsin, which adopted the Model Act, recognized this. After defining net assets so as to exclude treasury shares, it then restored the cost of treasury shares as an asset in computing capital surplus in order to avoid a restriction plus a reduction in surplus. Wis.Stat. § 180.02 (1955) (first passed in 1951).

169. This is not to say that treasury stock—"a bloodless turnip to the corporate creditors"—is an asset. . . . Clearly it cannot in most cases properly be carried as an asset. The Model Act would seem to prohibit the ac-

Disposition: Effect on Funds Available.—Section 5, after imposing a restriction on surplus so long as treasury shares are held, then provides in clause (b) that "upon the disposition or cancellation of any such shares the restriction shall be removed pro tanto." Although the general principle stated in this provision is in accordance with good accounting and sound corporate practice, questions arise as to the details of its application in practice. For example, the vital phrase, "removed pro tanto", could mean either that if 100 shares were bought and 50 are disposed of, ½ of the restriction is lifted regardless of price, or if 100 shares were bought for $100 and 50 are resold for $80, 4/10 of the restriction is lifted. The first interpretation seems to be the one intended. The language imposing the restrictions explicitly imposes it only "so long as such shares are held as treasury shares," so it appears that the second half of clause (b) simply states the converse of the first half — lifting the restriction upon disposition — making it clear that the entire restriction is not lifted if only some of the shares are resold. Even if the second interpretation is the intended one, it is believed that the mere phrase "pro tanto" is insufficient to spell out the proper treatment of surplus in all cases of disposition of treasury shares. Three groups of related questions arise upon the three possible types of disposition of treasury shares.

Resale.—It is not explicitly provided what happens when the treasury shares are resold for an amount less than the price at which they were acquired by the corporation. Correct practice, it seems, would require that the restriction be removed only to the extent of the consideration received by the corporation, and also that the restriction, to the extent not so lifted, be converted into an actual permanent reduction of the surplus out of which acquired. In other words, directors are legally free to sell treasury shares at any price, but in order to prevent withdrawal of capital at the expense of creditors, surplus must be permanently withdrawn on resale in an amount equal to any excess of per-share purchase price over disposal price. Under the Model Act, the restriction imposed by section 5 seems to be lifted in its entirety as already shown. Surplus, however, has been properly reduced by the amount of the loss. The question as to which surplus is so reduced is not explicitly answered.

Similarly, the Model Act fails to provide which surplus is augmented upon a resale for a price in excess of cost. Most accountants have long maintained that no income can be realized from the purchase and resale of treasury stock, and that the excess of receipts over disbursements would go to capital surplus.[172] A few accountants and many lawyers would say

172. . . . The SEC and AIA pronouncements deal only with increase in surplus arising from resale at more than cost, requiring the difference between sales price and cost to go into capital surplus. However, both Accounting Research Bulletin No. 43 and Accounting Series Release No. 6 state that accounting for purchase and resale of treasury shares should be similar to acquisition and retirement followed by issue of new shares. If purchases of treasury shares can be made only out of earned surplus, then this treatment might result in the conver- counting treatment sometimes adopted of showing treasury shares as a deduction from over-all net worth, which clearly seems proper, or as a deduction from issued shares on the balance sheet which does not seem improper where the issued-shares figure (which usually constitutes stated capital) still appears and the earned-surplus restriction is noted. . . .

there has been a clear gain. . . . Under the net-income approach of the Model Act disagreement is bound to arise as to whether the resale should be considered economically, philosophically, or otherwise to give rise to a profit, and it would be virtually impossible to advise on the question without a court decision.

Cancellation.—If the canceled treasury shares had been acquired at an amount equal to or less than the stated capital attributable thereto, the preferred accounting treatment seems clear: the entire restriction is lifted because of the reduction in stated capital caused by the cancellation.[175] However, if $100-par shares were acquired for $102 and then canceled, the question above posed again arises: Should the $102 restriction upon surplus be removed only to the extent that an amount of stated capital is applied to the cancellation, so that the remaining $2 restriction upon surplus would be converted into a permanent reduction of surplus? The Model Act comment to section 5 states that a cancellation "will make the restricted surplus available." This seems contrary to the comment to section 5 of the 1950 version which stated the correct rule:

> A cancellation of treasury shares . . . will make the restricted earned surplus available to the extent that the amount thereof does not exceed the amount of the reduction of stated capital thus effected. If the shares cancelled were purchased for an amount in excess of the stated capital applicable thereto, the surplus will permanently be reduced by the amounts of such excess.

Finally, if $100-par stock has been acquired for $98 and then canceled, net assets in excess of stated capital have been increased by $2. Surplus has been increased, but again there is no provision in the Model Act specifying whether there has been gain and hence earned surplus or whether the $2 credit should be to capital surplus.

2. Cancellation of Treasury Shares

As indicated in note 175 and the accompanying text in the foregoing excerpt, Hackney assumes that upon the cancellation of treasury stock it is the previously restricted earned surplus which survives the transaction, and not the capital surplus which under § 64 arises from the reduction of capital resulting from the cancellation of stock. Rudolph, Accounting for Treasury Shares Under the Model Business Corporation Act, 73 Harv.L.Rev. 323, 328 (1959), makes the same assumption; and in keeping with Hackney, he laments the fact that "it would be possible for the directors, without any special authorization, to use a limited amount of earned surplus over and over for this purpose until, theoretically, the assets, at book value, had been reduced to bare equivalence to liabilities."

sion of earned surplus into capital surplus in the amount of cost in excess of stated capital as well as creation of additional capital surplus in the amount of sales price in excess of cost. . . .

175. It is important, however, that the board of directors not be given the sole power to cancel treasury shares and thus remove the earned-surplus restriction, for then with an earned surplus to buy the first share it could buy and cancel continuously, with no statutory restriction of any kind. . . .

While it is true that the last sentence of the Comment to § 5 supports this construction, the language of § 5 itself does not require this result; and the result seems inconsistent with the spirit of the general rule of § 64 that the surplus resulting from a reduction of capital shall be capital surplus. In effect, there is a gap in the statutory pattern here. Under § 5, the cancellation of treasury shares removes the restriction on the earned surplus, while under § 64 the cancellation produces capital surplus. But one of these two surpluses must be *reduced*, to correspond to the elimination of the "treasury stock" account, and the statute does not say which.

Curiously enough, Hackney recognizes this issue in the analogous case of a resale of treasury stock for less than the acquisition cost. See page 424 supra. Actually, cancellation could be regarded as a type of resale-for-less-than-cost case, by viewing cancellation as a disposition of the shares for a consideration of zero. Under the view that the excess of the cost of treasury shares over the proceeds of disposition reduces earned surplus, earned surplus would here be reduced by the entire cost of the shares (thus offsetting the removal of the restriction on earned surplus in the same amount). The result would be that the capital surplus resulting from the reduction of capital upon the cancellation of the treasury stock would survive the transaction, rather than earned surplus; and further repurchases of treasury stock from that source would be subject to the limitations on the use of capital surplus under § 5. See Sprouse, Accounting for Treasury Stock Transactions: Prevailing Practices and New Statutory Provisions, 59 Col.L.Rev. 882, 892–893, (1959), where this construction of the Model Act is assumed without discussion.

NOTE ON INSTALLMENT REPURCHASE TRANSACTIONS

HERWITZ, INSTALLMENT REPURCHASE OF STOCK: SURPLUS LIMITATIONS *

79 Harv.L.Rev. 303–326 (1965).

In effect, the Mountain State holding means that an installment repurchase transaction is to be treated as if the successive installments constituted a series of independent repurchase transactions, each of which is to be tested separately under the statute. Of course, the precise question presented for decision in the Mountain State case was whether the total face amount of the installment obligations has to meet the surplus test at the outset, and not whether each installment has to pass the test. But these two issues are obviously interdependent in that the statutory test must be applied at one of the two points, and therefore a decision that the statute need not be satisfied at the outset necessarily means that each installment must be tested independently.[7] The purpose of this Comment is to explore these two alternatives in an effort to determine whether the installment-by-installment approach adopted in Mountain State is sound.

---

*Most of the footnotes omitted.

7. A third alternative might be that an installment repurchase obligation must satisfy the surplus test both at the outset and at the time of each installment. But the structure of the repurchase statutes affords little basis for applying the statutory limitation to the same transaction at two different points in time.

I. Historical Background—The Insolvency Cutoff

Perhaps the best starting point for this analysis is a brief historical survey of the treatment of repurchase transactions. While from the very beginning state corporation statutes have generally restricted dividends to surplus in order to preserve the capital invested in the enterprise as a safety margin for creditors, the same limitations were not originally applied to the repurchase of stock. Of course, it is now clearly recognized that there is no less an invasion of the safety margin for creditors when capital is returned to shareholders through a repurchase of their stock than when the return takes the form of a dividend. But most American courts, absent an express statute, refused to limit repurchases to surplus, contenting themselves instead with imposing such vague conditions as that there be "no prejudice to the rights of creditors." To be sure, there was early recognition that the repurchase of stock could not be treated as a reduction of legal capital unless there had also been compliance with the statutory formalities for a capital reduction transaction, so that a repurchase of stock did not affect the stated capital measuring rod used in determining how much surplus there was. But this rule was offset by treating the repurchased shares as an asset replacing the cash or other property exchanged for them, leaving net assets also unaffected by the transaction.

Today, of course, it is almost universally recognized that stock should not be viewed as an asset in the hands of the issuer. Once reacquired, such "treasury" stock is no different from authorized but unissued stock, which has never been accorded asset status. And insofar as creditors are concerned, they usually become worried about the makeup of the assets of a corporation as a source for payment of their claims only when they are not being paid in ordinary course, and at such times treasury stock is almost certain to be worthless.

In any event, it was generally assumed that under the majority "no prejudice" rule, once a corporation became insolvent repurchase of stock was no longer permissible. Probably repurchase by an insolvent corporation would be voidable as a fraudulent conveyance anyway, since payment would be in exchange for an "asset" demonstrably worthless. On the other hand, a repurchase completed while the corporation was still solvent was not invalidated by subsequent insolvency. It does not appear to have mattered that insolvency followed closely upon the repurchase transaction, as must have often happened when the selling stockholders were knowledgeable insiders trying to rescue some portion of their investment from a corporation known to be on the brink of failure. Perhaps the result would have been different had there been a showing that the repurchase transaction had helped to cause the subsequent insolvency, but there is no evidence of any disposition to import causation concepts into this area.

Obviously, under the prevailing approach it was necessary to determine whether repurchase had preceded insolvency or vice versa — a question that in turn required a determination of not only the date of insolvency [13] but also the date when the repurchase "occurred" for this purpose.

---

13. In addition to the inherent difficulty of a precise factual determination of this kind, there was also uncertainty as to just what the govern-

This posed a special problem in cases in which payment of the redemption price was deferred: was the critical time when the repurchase agreement was executed, or the date on which the price was due? The nearest analogy seemed to be presented by the cases involving resale options, that is, options granted to stockholders (usually at the time they purchased their stock) to require a corporation to repurchase the stock at a specified price. Most of these cases involved attempts by stockholders to exercise their options after the corporation became insolvent, and in this situation the courts showed little hesitancy in holding that the exercise came too late. Exercise of a resale option does not differ from the execution of a new repurchase agreement, particularly from the point of view of creditors, who will rarely have had any notice of the option prior to its exercise.

Thus the resale option cases were of little help in cases in which a solvent corporation executed a binding repurchase agreement, whether in pursuance of an option or otherwise, but became insolvent before completing payment of the redemption price. Solvency at the date of payment was apparently not required under fraudulent conveyance doctrine, since as long as the original repurchase agreement was valid when made, the existing indebtedness constituted sufficient basis for the payment. Indeed, the transaction might well have been viewed, as equivalent to an outright repurchase for cash on the date of the repurchase agreement, coupled with a simultaneous loan of the repurchase price to the corporation by the former stockholder, in which case the obligation to repay would presumably not have been subordinated to the claims of other creditors in the event of subsequent insolvency. Moreover, requiring solvency at the date of payment immediately poses the question of what to do when a corporation wrongfully fails to pay on the agreed date, at a time when it is still solvent, but has become insolvent by the time the promisee brings an action.[16]

Nevertheless, most of the courts insisted on solvency at the date of payment. Once a corporation became insolvent, any payment on a repurchase obligation was regarded as "prejudicial" to the interests of other creditors, and the unpaid balance on the obligation was subordinated

ing standard for insolvency was. State courts usually adopted the so-called "equity insolvency" test of inability to meet debts as they mature, . . . and that definition is expressly adopted in Model Act § 2(n). But a few state courts and most federal courts adopted the "bankruptcy insolvency" test, patterned after the definition in § 1(19) of the Bankruptcy Act, . . . under which a person is insolvent "whenever the aggregate of his property . . . shall not at a fair valuation be sufficient in amount to pay his debts." Today, the matter may be governed in many states by the definition of insolvency in Uniform Fraudulent Conveyance Act § 2(1), which seems to lie somewhere between the liquidity measure of the equity test and the overall balance sheet valuation apparently called for under the bankruptcy approach: "A person is insolvent when the present fair salable value of his assets is less than the amount that will be required to pay his probable liability on his existing debts as they become absolute and matured."

16. See American Hosp. & Life Ins. Co. v. Kunkel, 71 N.M. 164, 173, 376 P.2d 956, 962 (1962); cf. Moro v. Soldo, 143 N.Y.S.2d 863 (Sup.Ct.1955) (under installment-by-installment approach the critical question is whether there is sufficient surplus on the date a particular installment is due; the corporation's lack of surplus or insolvency at the time of trial is not material).

to their claims. An excellent illustration is the oft-cited case of Robinson v. Wangemann,[18] in which the court reversed the allowance of a claim against a bankrupt corporation based on a note given by the corporation for the purchase of some of its stock:

> Arthur Wangemann loaned no money to the corporation. The note he accepted for his stock did not change the character of the transaction nor did the renewals have that effect. A transaction by which a corporation acquires its own stock from a stockholder for a sum of money is not really a sale. The corporation does not acquire anything of value equivalent to the depletion of its assets, if the stock is held in the treasury, as in this case. It is simply a method of distributing a proportion of the assets to the stockholder. The assets of a corporation are the common pledge of its creditors, and stockholders are not entitled to receive any part of them unless creditors are paid in full. When such a transaction is had, regardless of the good faith of the parties, it is essential to its validity that there be sufficient [excess of assets over liabilities] . . . to retire the stock, without prejudice to creditors, at the time payment is made out of assets. In principle, the contract between Wangemann and the corporation was executory until the stock should be paid for in cash. It is immaterial that the corporation was solvent and had sufficient [excess of assets over liabilities] . . . to make payment when the agreement was entered into. It is necessary to a recovery that the corporation should be solvent and have sufficient [excess of assets over liabilities] . . . to prevent injury to creditors when the payment is actually made. This was an implied condition in the original note and the renewals accepted by Arthur Wangemann.

Decisions such as Robinson v. Wangemann were doubtless due at least in part to an increasing concern on the part of the courts that the "no prejudice" rule might be too liberal; and naturally there was particular resistance to letting former shareholders share in any guise with regular creditors in the assets of an insolvent enterprise. Moreover, at least when the selling stockholders were insiders, a delay between the execution of the repurchase agreement and the payment date might really amount to a hedge against financial disaster for the selling stockholders, since the insiders were in a position to rescind the repurchase if the fortunes of the corporation took a turn for the better. In addition, the analogy to a repurchase for cash followed by a loan of the redemption proceeds to the corporation was not very convincing, since more often than not the corporation was already in a precarious financial condition at the time of the repurchase transaction. Thus the corporation typically had neither the necessary cash nor the power to borrow it elsewhere, particularly for the purpose of repurchasing stock; and the idea that stockholders who had just sold out for cash would lend the money back to such a corporation was equally unrealistic.

There is also a special reason for applying the insolvency test to each installment when, as was usually the case, the equity insolvency test is involved. Under that test, with its emphasis on current liabilities, pre-

---

18. 75 F.2d 756 (5th Cir.1935).

sumably only so much of the repurchase obligation as is due currently (or within the relatively near future) is to be taken into account. As previously noted, if the total face amount of the obligation is not tested at the outset, then obviously each installment should be.

To be sure, application of the insolvency test on an installment-by-installment basis presents some special difficulties of its own, particularly once some installments have been paid. For example, where do the parties stand if an insolvency cutoff is applied in midstream — can the former stockholder get back any or all of his stock? This problem is likely to be of little practical importance, however, for once a corporation has become insolvent there is rarely much reason to worry about who owns its stock.

There were occasional chinks in the fairly solid wall of judicial opinion refusing to allow enforcement of a repurchase obligation on a parity with claims of general creditors after a corporation has become insolvent. Perhaps the most forceful statement of the contrary view appears in Wolff v. Heidritter Lumber Co.,[21] in which the court, after distinguishing the cases refusing to allow exercise of a resale option after insolvency, argued as follows:

> [If a purchase of stock] . . . would be valid if the money were then and there paid out of the corporate treasury, it is not perceived why the purchase would be invalidated if the company instead of giving its check in payment gave its note or its other obligation for deferred payment. The contract would be complete; the corporate assets necessary to pay debts would be no differently affected; the corporation's creditors would have no greater right to complain. The stockholder would become a creditor, an unpaid creditor instead of a paid vendor; but the debt due him, being valid then, would not become invalid by reason of the company subsequently becoming insolvent before the date of the debt's maturity. . . .
>
> . . . [O]n reason and authority the conclusion seems inescapable that a corporation may purchase shares of its own stock, for "legitimate corporate purposes," and may, instead of paying cash therefor, issue its obligation payable at a future date, and that the vendor holding such obligation becomes forthwith a creditor, instead of a stockholder, of the company and entitled to rank equally with other creditors in the event of subsequent insolvency of the company, provided that at the time of the purchase the company has sufficient assets to pay its creditors in full and provided the purchase is not made in disregard of the equitable rights of other stockholders.

Plainly there is much to be said for this reasoning, at least when, as was true in the Wolff case, the corporation is prosperous enough at the time of the transaction to make the analogy to a cash repurchase and a loan of the proceeds not too farfetched. And the Wolff case is particularly significant, since the installment repurchase transaction involved in

---

21. 112 N.J.Eq. 34, 163 A. 140 (Ch. 1932).

that case not only gave the selling stockholder the right to retain the shares until completion of the payments but also entitled him to rescind the transaction at any time prior to completion by simply repaying the amounts received to date. In effect, the selling stockholder was in much the same position as the holder of a resale option prior to its exercise, the very type of case that the court in Wolff had expressly distinguished. Nevertheless, the Wolff approach garnered very few adherents over the years, and at this point the insolvency cutoff rule may well be regarded as a settled matter of public policy which is unlikely to be overturned absent an express statutory mandate.[23]

II. APPLICATION OF THE SURPLUS LIMITATION

It is against this background that the question arose as to whether a statutory surplus test should be applied to the total of an installment repurchase obligation when executed or to each installment as paid. Obviously, there is at least a surface analogy between the surplus test and the insolvency test, which invites the easy assumption that the rule should be the same in the two cases, with the surplus test also applied on an installment-by-installment basis. Thus in Mountain State the court proceeded directly from the proposition that "the claims of former stockholders under such executory agreements are subordinate to the claims of other creditors existing at the time of performance" (for which it cited a number of authorities most of which involved the insolvency cutoff), to the proposition that "when a corporation purchases a portion of its outstanding stock with an agreement to pay for it at a subsequent time, it may not perform its promise if the use of its funds in performance will impair its capital," without any discussion of possible distinctions between the two situations.

Similarly, in California, where repurchase is both generally confined to earned surplus and expressly conditioned upon solvency, the courts seem to have moved from an insolvency cutoff to a surplus cutoff without any real consideration of possible differences between the two situations. In the case of In re Mathews Constr. Co.,[26] the court rejected a claim on a repurchase obligation, stating: "An agreement by a corporation to repurchase stock, though valid at the time entered into, becomes invalid if, at the time of payment, there is no surplus. . . . Bankruptcy having intervened, obviously there can be no surplus from which payment for repurchased stock may be made." The court relied on Goodman v. Global Indus.,[28] in which the defendant, in a suit on a resale option, contended that as of the time of the trial the claimed repurchase would render the corporation insolvent. In answer to the plaintiff's argument that the corporation's financial position when the action was brought rather than when trial began should control, the Goodman court observed that the question was immaterial because the plaintiff had "neither alleged nor

23. *But see* LaVoy Supply Co. v. Young, 84 Idaho 120, 369 P.2d 45 (1962), which seems to permit a deferred repurchase obligation to share on a parity with the claims of other creditors in the assets of an insolvent corporation, without any recognition of the problem involved.

26. 120 F.Supp. 818 (S.D.Cal.1954).

28. 80 Cal.App.2d 583, 182 P.2d 300 (1947).

proved the existence of an earned surplus *at any time.*" However, the court went on to quote from Ballantine and Sterling, California Corporation Laws, as follows: [30]

> If the earned surplus from which purchase is allowed to be made . . . shrinks to a deficit at the time of performance, the agreement becomes unenforceable against the corporation. A corporation may make a contract to purchase its own shares at a time when it has an earned surplus justifying it, but if, before the time the seller gets around to the performance of the contract, the surplus has vanished by losses or shrinkage in value of assets, the purchase cannot be completed.

It is far from clear that this excerpt supports the view of the California court in the Goodman case that the corporation's financial condition at the time of trial rather than at the time the action was brought is controlling, at least if the corporation was at fault in not paying at the time of the plaintiff's demand. But the more important point is that the excerpt itself relies primarily upon cases involving insolvency, including particularly Robinson v. Wangemann, without any recognition of the possible distinctions between the surplus and insolvency situations.[33]

The development of a surplus cutoff rule may well have been influenced by the fact that, as was true with the insolvency test, a number of the early cases involved resale options. In this area, the analogy to the insolvency test is perfectly sound; the surplus test too must be applied no earlier than at the time the exercise of the option is sought. Presumably, that is all the court meant in the leading case of Richards v. Ernst Wiener Co.,[34] when it quoted with apparent approval the following statement by the lower court with reference to a resale option: "If when the time came defendant had a sufficient surplus the contract would be enforced. If it had not the contract could not be enforced." Nevertheless, the Richards case has often been cited, as it was in [footnote 8] to the Mountain State opinion, for the proposition that when a repurchase agreement has been executed but payment of the purchase price is deferred, the surplus test must be satisfied at the time of payment.

In fact, there are some important differences between the insolvency and capital impairment situations which must be considered before concluding that the two should be treated alike. It is true that, as under the insolvency test, if the surplus test is not applied at the outset then each installment must be tested or else the statutory limitation would have no impact at all. But, unlike the insolvency test, the surplus test does not look only to current liabilities and thus there is no obstacle to applying the

---

30. Ballantine & Sterling, California Corporation Laws 174 (1938 ed.).

33. In the most recent California case dealing with the limitation on repurchases, Cutter Labs., Inc. v. Twining, 221 Cal.App.2d 302, 313–14, 34 Cal. Rptr. 317, 323–23 (Dist.Ct.App.1963), the court, citing the Goodman and Mathews cases, repeated the view that a valid repurchase agreement "may become unenforceable if at the time for performance no surplus exists."

The recent cases in other jurisdictions have uniformly followed the installment-by-installment view, each time without any real consideration of the issue. E.g., Kleinberg v. Schwartz [see note 65, infra]; In the Matter of Trimble Co., 339 F.2d 838 (3d Cir. 1964); Burk v. Cooperative Fin. Corp., 62 Wash.2d 740, 384 P.2d 618 (1963).

34. 207 N.Y. 59, 100 N.E. 592 (1912).

surplus test to the total face amount of an installment obligation at the outset. Moreover, the Mountain State opinion makes quite clear that its decision not to apply the surplus test at the outset is a consequence of its conclusion that each installment must pass the test, rather than the other way round. Therefore, it makes sense to examine the installment-by-installment rule on its own merits.

An appropriate starting point is the analogy, rejected in connection with the insolvency test, between an installment repurchase transaction and a repurchase for cash accompanied by a loan of the redemption proceeds back to the corporation. When the corporation has sufficient surplus to cover the total repurchase obligation at the outset, such a view of the transaction is no longer so unrealistic. And under this view it would follow that as long as the surplus test is satisfied at the outset, it makes no difference how much surplus there is at the date of each installment. Does fairness to creditors require a contrary view? While it was concern for the interest of creditors that led to installment-by-installment testing for insolvency, it is much harder to justify a flat bar against payments simply because surplus has declined since the execution of the agreement to an amount less than the next installment due. Payment of an installment that impairs capital is surely a far cry from putting former stockholders on a parity with creditors in the liquidation of an insolvent enterprise.

No doubt any distribution that impairs capital is a matter of some concern to creditors, and particularly so when it follows a period of losses, as may well have occurred if a surplus large enough to cover the total obligation at the outset is no longer sufficient to cover a particular installment. But in weighing this concern, it is important to keep in mind that nowadays the general ban on distributions that impair capital is often more apparent than real. Under modern statutes, stockholders commonly have the power to make what is in effect a distribution out of capital simply by reducing stated capital and then distributing the resulting capital surplus, measured by the amount of net assets in excess of the capital as reduced. It seems harsh to bar a corporation from continuing to honor a bona fide repurchase obligation in circumstances in which, absent such an obligation, the corporation could put itself in a position to make a voluntary distribution to stockholders. Indeed, in such circumstances perhaps the corporation should be obliged to take the necessary steps to reduce its capital in order that it can continue to make the agreed payments. Of course, thoughtful counsel could foresee this problem and plan for it in the repurchase agreement.[39] But the important point is that such a problem would not even arise if the surplus test were applied only to the total obligation at the outset.

Another problem created by a surplus cutoff rule relates to the position of the selling stockholder if and when the bar is applied in midstream. Unlike the analogous problem under an insolvency cutoff, here the matter is of considerable practical importance, since a corporation may carry on indefinitely despite an impairment of capital. Accordingly, it is neces-

---

39. Close corporation stock repurchase agreements commonly require the parties to vote to take whatever steps are necessary to reduce the capital of the corporation when that is necessary or desirable for carrying out the repurchase agreement. . . .

sary to make sure that the selling stockholder does not end up in a kind of limbo, without the status of either creditor or stockholder. The situation in the Mountain State case itself illustrates the point. If, after some of the promised payments had been made, capital impairment barred any further installments, would the Miller family have been limited to waiting hopefully for a return to the black that would permit the resumption of payments? Is there any way in which the family could have resumed its former status as a 50% stockholder? If the cessation of payments constituted a default under the agreement, and the stock had been pledged to secure performance, presumably the Millers would have the ordinary remedies of a pledgee, but these would not usually include the right automatically to repossess the pledged property. Moreover, when the stock owned by the former stockholders represents a significant stake in control, and a fortiori when the stockholders owned 50% as in Mountain State, a return of the stock makes sense only if they recover all of it. Otherwise, they will be in the same position as if they had sold just a portion of their stock, even though they presumably would not have agreed to do that. On the other hand, it would hardly be fair to the corporation (or perhaps more accurately, to the remaining stockholders) to provide that the selling stockholders may regain all of their stock at any time when there is a default prior to final payment, since such a rule could result in a windfall to the selling stockholders unless they were compelled to return all prior payments. These questions are a good deal easier to state than to answer. Doubtless here also astute counsel could plan for them in advance, although a solution fair to both sides is not immediately apparent.[40] But again the important point is that this whole chain of complications stems directly from a surplus cutoff rule, and could therefore be avoided by adopting the contrary view.

Another problem that must be faced when the surplus test is applied on an installment-by-installment basis is the relative position of the holder of a repurchase obligation vis-à-vis subsequent creditors with knowledge of the repurchase commitment. While the authorities have uniformly assumed that a creditor is not excluded from the protection of the statutory repurchase limitation merely because his claim arose after the repurchase transaction, some cases have indicated that if such creditors had specific knowledge of the repurchase commitment the opposite result might be reached. Distinctions based upon knowledge are always difficult to draw, particularly since they involve that even more slippery concept, notice; and nowhere is the difficulty better illustrated than in the context of ascertaining what information certain financial statements have disclosed, and deciding whether they were or should have been examined. Moreover, this issue has an unfortunately circular character since, at least until there is an authoritative decision to the contrary, it is entirely possible that a

---

40. One possibility might be to provide some mechanics whereby, during any extended default on a repurchase obligation, the former shareholders would regain voting control—or at least voting power equal to what they formerly had—though not the equity in the shares. This result might be achieved by such devices as contingent voting rights for the repurchase obligations (if state law permits), or a pledge of the repurchased shares to secure the obligations, with contingent voting rights for the pledgees, or a voting trust arrangement.

subsequent creditor with knowledge of the repurchase obligation will simply assume that his claim will have priority.

Application of the surplus test on an installment-by-installment basis also poses some knotty problems in accounting for a repurchase transaction. Although a repurchase of stock does not necessarily require a reduction of surplus, it does at least necessitate a restriction on surplus in the amount of the purchase price, in order to prevent the use of the same surplus for the payment of dividends or for other repurchases. Obviously, in the case of an installment repurchase transaction, there are the same questions as to when and how this surplus restriction should be applied as there are in applying the surplus test itself. Since the surplus restriction requirement is really a corollary of the surplus test, presumably the same schedule should be adopted for both purposes, so that if the surplus test is applied on an installment-by-installment basis, surplus need only be restricted to the extent of each installment as paid. But the result of this approach would be that even if the corporation had ample surplus to cover the total repurchase obligation at the outset, it would not be required to restrict that much surplus, and instead would be free to use it for dividends or other repurchases. Indeed, absent some contractual restriction, either express or implied, a former stockholder holding an installment repurchase obligation might be powerless to prevent the corporation from so dissipating its surplus as to render itself unable to make future installment payments when due.

A related problem arises in connection with accounting for the cancellation of treasury stock. Ordinarily, upon cancellation an amount equal to the stated capital attributable to the shares canceled is charged to the stated capital account, thereby reducing stated capital to that extent; any excess of the purchase price over the stated capital attributable to the shares is charged to surplus, thus reducing that account to the extent of the excess. In the case of an installment repurchase transaction, the question would arise whether all of the stock obtained by the corporation could be canceled, with a proportionate reduction in stated capital, even though the repurchase was subject to the condition subsequent that each installment satisfy the surplus test. In an orderly repurchase universe, the corporation would not be permitted to cancel more stock than had actually been paid for on a prorata basis; but it is not clear that this result would be reached under the statutes, particularly when the cancellation provisions simply apply to "reacquired shares" and do not reflect any recognition of the possibility that the shares have not been fully paid for.[46]

* * *

There is also a serious problem as to how to deal with the interest payments that may be called for in connection with an installment repurchase obligation. In the only case that expressly involved the matter, Christie v. Fifth Madison Corp.,[48] it was assumed without discussion that under installment-by-installment testing the periodic interest payments as well as the principal payments were required to pass the surplus test. As a

---

46. E.g., Model Act § 62: . . . As a practical matter the answer may be that the repurchased shares would normally be pledged to secure the repurchase obligation, so that none of the shares could be canceled until payment in full was completed.

48. 123 N.Y.S.2d 795 (Sup.Ct.1953).

logical matter, the installment-by-installment approach, which sees the payment of cash as all-important, may make a reluctance to distinguish between interest payments and principal payments quite understandable, particularly since the interest rate and schedule of payments are so much within the control of the parties. Nevertheless, application of the surplus test to the interest payments is unsupportable if the interest has been deducted in computing the corporation's net income (as would typically be true), since it would mean that interest was really being taken into account twice in applying the surplus test. Perhaps the Christie decision implies that the interest on a repurchase obligation is not to be treated as a deduction in determining net income, on the ground that it is only a contingent liability. Such a view would certainly lend support to the Commissioner's attempt, as in the Mountain State case, to deny deduction of such "interest" for tax purposes.

This problem too would be largely avoided if the surplus test were applied to the total repurchase obligation at the outset rather than on an installment-by-installment basis. Once the total principal amount of the repurchase obligation had been validated under the surplus test at the outset, the repurchase obligation would be a binding, unconditional debt of the corporation, and the interest component of the subsequent individual installments would be treated no differently from interest on any other debt. To be sure, this approach might leave some room for maneuver by the parties by virtue of their control over the allocation between interest and principal. Thus a corporation contemplating a repurchase of stock for an amount in excess of its then available surplus, payable in installments at a specified interest rate, might rewrite the transaction to reduce the principal amount to a figure covered by existing surplus while increasing the interest rate enough to make the annual installments approximately the same as before. But any blatant attempt to escape the spirit of the surplus test would scarcely go unnoticed, and while some difficult borderline cases can be imagined, in general the courts would have little difficulty in policing such transactions.

Another question not considered by the cases which, like Mountain State, adopt the installment-by-installment view of the surplus test, is the relative position of the holders of repurchase obligations vis-á-vis the remaining shareholders. Although it may be that no solicitude for the interests of other stockholders is called for in a situation like that of Mountain State, in which the other stockholders expressly consent to the repurchase transaction, this situation will often not exist. And while creditors are obviously the primary beneficiaries of surplus limitations on repurchases of stock, there is no reason to think that the statute was not also intended to protect stockholders against repurchases that impair capital. Hence it is difficult to accept the flat assertion of the Mountain State opinion that "in liquidation, the claim of the promisee, deferred to the claims of all general creditors, would be preferred over the interests of the remaining stockholders." Since the total obligation would have never theretofore been subjected to the surplus test, it would seem more appropriate to treat the liquidation as an acceleration of the individual installments and hence limit the priority of the repurchase obligation over the claims of remaining stockholders to the total amount of surplus then available.

The foregoing analysis leads to the conclusion that application of the surplus test to the total repurchase obligation at the outset is not only feasible but also avoids a number of difficult problems inherent in the installment-by-installment approach. Are there any critical disadvantages in applying the test at the outset? None has been suggested in any of the cases adopting the installment-by-installment approach, apart from the basic concern reflected in cases such as Mountain State that application of the surplus test at the outset would make it impossible to effect desirable repurchase transactions (particularly in close corporation situations) for lack of sufficient surplus at the time of the original agreement. But it is perfectly possible to uphold such transactions without insisting upon an installment-by-installment construction of the statute in those cases in which there is sufficient surplus at the start. There is nothing to prevent a corporation that does not have enough surplus at the time of the agreement to validate the total repurchase obligation from executing a concededly conditional repurchase agreement under which each installment would in fact constitute a separate repurchase transaction. In effect this arrangement would be equivalent to the installment-by-installment approach. In such cases, counsel would have to be on their guard to consider and plan against the various difficulties which that approach entails. But in those cases in which the surplus at the outset was sufficient, counsel would no longer have to be concerned about the amount of the corporation's surplus thereafter.[52]

There remains, however, the question of what would happen to the insolvency cutoff rule if the surplus test were applied at the outset. This question presents no problem under the installment-by-installment approach to the surplus test, since insolvency would almost certainly be accompanied by insufficient surplus to permit further payments. But if the surplus test is applied at the outset and is satisfied at that point, it might well be held that the repurchase obligation enjoys for all purposes the same status as any other claim against the corporation and is not subject to any condition subsequent. In other words, when a corporation is not merely solvent but actually has at the outset a surplus at least equal to the total repurchase obligation, the logic of the reasoning in Wolff v. Heidritter [supra] that the obligation is thereafter beyond attack becomes quite compelling. Moreover, the very existence of an express surplus restriction in the statute could be regarded as "occupying the field" and thereby precluding any judicial limitation similar to the insolvency cutoff.

---

52. Even under the "outset" view, there may be a question as to when the repurchase transaction "occurred" for purposes of the surplus test, particularly in connection with close corporation agreements calling for the repurchase of stock upon the death or retirement of a stockholder. As in the analogous case of an option, it seems clear that the test should be applied when the corporation's obligation to purchase matures, and not at the earlier date when the buy-sell agreement is executed. For a time a pall was cast upon these close corporation agreements by the case of Topken, Loring & Schwartz, Inc. v. Schwartz, 249 N.Y. 206, 163 N.E. 735 (1928), which indicated that such buy-sell arrangements were unenforceable because the possibility that the corporation would not be able to perform, for lack of surplus, made the whole arrangement "lacking in consideration." But the decision was narrowly construed by later New York cases, e.g., Greater New York Carpet House, Inc. v. Herschmann, 258 App.Div. 649, 17 N.Y.S.2d 483 (1940); has not been followed by other jurisdictions, see, e.g., Cutter Labs., Inc. v. Twining, 221 Cal. App.2d 302, 314, 34 Cal.Rptr. 317, 324 (Dist.Ct.App.1963); and has since been overruled by statute in New York. N. Y.Bus.Corp.Law § 514.

This conclusion would be virtually inescapable if the insolvency cutoff rule were viewed as primarily designed to offset the undue liberality of the majority "no prejudice" rule, since the cutoff would no longer be needed with the advent of the stricter surplus test. On the other hand, it seems at least as likely that the real impetus for the insolvency cutoff came from the reluctance of the courts to permit former stockholders to share in any guise on a parity with creditors in the assets of an insolvent corporation. If this is true, the cutoff might well be preserved no matter when or how the surplus test is applied. There is still no clear indication from the courts themselves on this matter, since no case as yet has applied the surplus test at the outset. But it is certainly instructive that in cases arising under surplus statutes, when insolvency was present the insolvency cutoff has been applied in much the same terms as in the prestatutory days and without the slightest recognition of possible differences between the old and new contexts. Hence it seems quite likely that, even after the passage of the surplus statutes, the insolvency cutoff is too well settled to overturn without an express statutory mandate.

Of course, no matter what may appear to be the most desirable approach to the surplus test, there is still the question in any particular case whether the words of the governing statute will bear that result. Thus, in rejecting the "outset" test, the Mountain State court laid considerable stress on the words "use its funds" in the West Virginia statute. The court thought these words indicated that the statute came into play only when the corporation made an actual payment in cash or property for the repurchase of stock. To be sure, these words do tend to focus on payment as distinguished from a mere obligation to pay in the future. On the other hand, to do full justice to the statute it is important to note that the complete phrase is "use its funds or property"; and it could well be argued that the execution of a repurchase obligation, which certainly constitutes property in the recipient's hands, amounts to a use by the corporation of its property within the meaning of the statute.

The Model Act provision, [§ 5], phrased in terms of a limitation on a corporation's "purchases of its own shares," seems at first glance even more ambivalent on this issue than the Delaware-type provision. However, there is an important guide to what the term "purchase" means, or perhaps more accurately to what it does not mean, in the insolvency proviso at the end of the section in which the word "payment" is used in apparent contradistinction to the word "purchase." That this was no mere happenstance seems established by the fact that the words "or payment for" did not appear in the original version of the proviso, but were added in the 1957 revision of the act. Here is an excellent illustration of the value of "a page of history," for in the light of the foregoing analysis the purport of what might otherwise have been a most puzzling change becomes unmistakably clear. The draftsman wanted to codify the insolvency cutoff, and he evidently assumed, or at least feared, that the term "purchase" would only cover the execution of the original agreement, and not the actual payments that might come later. But no change was made in the basic surplus restriction, so that only "purchases," and not "payments," are covered, and accordingly the inference is well-nigh irresistible that the surplus test is to be applied to the total repurchase obligation at the outset, and not to any subsequent payments as they are made. In any event, the Model Act provision clearly invites, if it does not require, a full reconsideration of the surplus cutoff rule, which so far no court has undertaken.

III. Some Observations on Planning

Naturally, counsel for shareholders reselling their stock to a corporation have sought to plan around the insolvency and surplus cutoff rules. Once again a tax case provides an excellent example. In United States v. General Geophysical Co.,[59] the taxpayer corporation and the family of its deceased founder agreed that the seventy-seven percent stock interest held by the latter would be redeemed for cash and notes. The corporation's earned surplus was sufficient to cover the total purchase price. However, counsel for the retiring stockholders advised against the proposal on the ground that, under Robinson v. Wangemann [supra], the repurchase notes would be subordinated to the claims of other creditors in the event the corporation became bankrupt. In an effort to avoid this risk the parties decided to have the corporation redeem the stock in exchange for cash and corporate properties having a market value equal to the principal amount of the previously proposed notes. A few hours after the transfer, the corporation repurchased the properties for notes in the same amount as had originally been agreed on for the repurchase of the stock, securing the notes by a mortgage covering those and other properties of the corporation. While there had been no prior formal agreement by the former stockholders to resell the properties to the corporation, this prospect had been discussed, and prior to the redemption transaction, documents for a resale had been prepared in case that course was followed.

The tax issue was whether the corporation could use as its basis for depreciating the reacquired properties the price paid to the retiring stockholders, which was substantially in excess of the corporation's former basis in those properties. Since the corporation was not required to recognize any gain upon the transfer of the properties in redemption of its stock,* use of the higher basis would have represented a considerable tax windfall. The taxpayer pointed to the important nontax reason that had led to the transaction and persuaded the district court that the reacquisition of the properties should be recognized as a purchase giving rise to a new basis for tax purposes. However, the court of appeals reversed. It conceded that there had been a valid business purpose for the transaction, but observed that this only sufficed to preclude a summary finding that the arrangement constituted a mere subterfuge. The real question, said the court, was whether there had been a sufficient interruption in the ownership of the properties to produce a new basis. And it was concluded that there had not been a sufficient interruption, in view of the facts (1) that the corporation had made no physical delivery of any of the properties; (2) that it had parted with only bare legal title to the property and only for a few short hours; and (3) that while the retiring stockholders may have been legally free not to resell the properties to the corporation, it was a foregone conclusion that they would sell them to someone—the very reason for the original sale of their stock was that they no longer wished to own or manage these properties—and the taxpayer corporation was the logical purchaser since the properties constituted almost fifty per cent of its assets and were fully integrated into its operations.

---

59. 296 F.2d 86 (5th Cir.1961) [discussed at page 539 infra].

*[Ed. note] See IRC § 311 and Reg. § 1.311–1(a), discussed at pages 538–540, infra.

The more important question in the present context is whether this transaction would have achieved its alleged primary purpose of avoiding the insolvency cutoff. It is hard to believe that it would have. For the same factors relied upon by the court of appeals in concluding that there was an insufficient interruption of ownership to justify a change in tax basis would seem to call equally for a decision that the nature of the transaction had not really changed from a repurchase of stock to a repurchase of property. Certainly from the point of view of creditors there is no basis for treating the transaction in General Geophysical differently from a straightforward installment repurchase of stock. And the courts, at least of late, have been no less quick in corporate cases than in tax cases to look through the form of a transaction to find its real substance.

The mortgage given to the retiring stockholders in General Geophysical suggests another possible planning device in this area, since a mortgage could also be given in connection with a normal installment repurchase. But it seems clear that the existence of a mortgage would not enhance the status of a repurchase obligation in the event of insolvency. In general, a mortgage securing an obligation stands no better than the obligation itself. And it must be remembered that the very purpose of the insolvency cutoff rule is to assure the creditors of an insolvent enterprise a priority over former stockholders in the distribution of assets. Accordingly, such shareholders could scarcely be allowed to tie up the assets with a security device so that the creditors could not obtain them.

A quite different type of planning effort was involved in the most recent case to date in the repurchase area, Kleinberg v. Schwartz,[65] in which the parties made a thinly-disguised attempt to conceal the fact that the corporation was actually the purchaser of the shares. A lack of family harmony among the three owners of a close corporation had resulted in a decision by two of them to sell out. However, counsel for the retiring stockholders expressed concern about the possible consequences of a corporation buying its own stock, while the remaining stockholder objected to being named as the purchaser because of the tax disadvantages that would result. Accordingly, the parties designated as the purchaser an inactive corporation that they had formed years before, with the remaining stockholder guaranteeing the buying corporation's performance. But the buyer was a mere paper corporation without assets, and all payments for the stock actually came from the funds of the original corporation, which simply deposited the necessary sums in the buyer's account. Accordingly, the court had little difficulty in concluding that the original corporation was the real purchaser of the shares, and the defendant retiring stockholder was held liable to the receiver of the now insolvent corporation under a statute requiring stockholders to refund amounts paid to them for their stock to the extent that such payments impair capital.

It is a relevant concluding note for this Comment to observe that the Kleinberg opinion strongly endorsed application of the surplus test on an installment-by-installment basis. While there was some doubt that the corporation had sufficient surplus to cover the total obligation at the outset anyway, the court did not rest its decision on that. Rather the court commented that "the authorities seem to be unanimous in holding that the fact that

---

65. 87 N.J.Super. 216, 208 A.2d 803 (App.Div.), [affirmed per curiam 46 N.J. 2, 214 A.2d 313 (1965)].

the corporation had a surplus when the agreement to purchase was made is not sufficient to defeat the rights of creditors of the corporation, if it does not have a surplus at the time the payments are actually made." Regrettably, like its predecessors in this field, the Kleinberg court did not perceive any distinction between the insolvency cutoff rule and a surplus cutoff rule, indiscriminately citing cases of both types. This is all the more disappointing since Kleinberg presented a unique opportunity to deal with the problems analyzed in this Comment, in that the New Jersey court was faced with the leading authority denying the existence of even an insolvency cutoff, Wolff v. Heidritter [supra]. But the court instead purported to distinguish Wolff on the ground that it involved the question whether the holder of a repurchase obligation could share on a parity with creditors, whereas Kleinberg dealt with the liability of a stockholder for amounts paid to him out of capital for his shares.

Since the basic question is exactly the same in both situations, that is, when the limitation upon repurchases is to be applied to an installment repurchase transaction, this reconciliation of the two cases is scarcely satisfactory. Indeed, it should be easier to subordinate the balance still due on a repurchase obligation than to require a former shareholder to disgorge amounts already received, particularly when, as appeared to be true in Kleinberg, the former shareholder is unaware that the payments violated the statutory limitation on repurchase. And the result in Kleinberg points up one more disadvantage of installment-by-installment testing since it means that stockholders who receive installment repurchase payments may have to assume the risk of the financial condition of the corporation at the date of each installment rather than just at the outset of the repurchase transaction.

B. FIDUCIARY LIMITATION ON REPURCHASE OF STOCK

As indicated in the foregoing material, in the past a repurchase of stock by a corporation was often a device for favoring insiders by giving them more for their stock than other stockholders could obtain. But of course today the application of normal fiduciary standards would mean that if insiders are on both sides of a transaction, as where the directors cause the corporation to repurchase their own stock, the transaction would be open to attack for unfairness.

Repurchase of stock can also be used to favor insiders if stock is acquired from outsiders at unfairly low prices. The benefit to the insiders from this process is somewhat diluted compared to purchase by the insiders personally, but this is offset by the fact that corporate repurchase eliminates the need to commit any individual funds. However, despite some doubt expressed in earlier cases, it seems clear today that insiders have the same obligation to act fairly, including making appropriate disclosure, when they cause the corporation to repurchase stock as when they purchase it themselves. E. g., Northern Trust Co. v. Essaness Theatres Corp., 348 Ill.App. 134, 108 N.E. 2d 493 (1952). This is certainly the view taken under SEC Rule 10b–5, which is generally operative today in this area. See Loss, Securities Regulation (2d ed. 1961) 1453–1454.

A third situation in which corporate repurchase of stock may be used to benefit insiders is in connection with retention of control. Suppose, for example, that a management, enjoying generous but defensible salaries, learns that a third party is bidding to take over control of the corporation. One alternative of course would be to forego any contest and sell out to the third party. But even this apparently simple course presents a host of problems: there is the need to investigate the background of the buyer or run the risk of his bad faith, e. g., Gerdes v. Reynolds, 28 N.Y.S.2d 622 (Sp.T.1941); the possibility of having to arrange the same terms for all other stockholders who want to sell or face liability to them, cf. Commonwealth Title Ins. & Trust Co. v. Seltzer, 227 Pa. 410, 76 A. 77 (1910); Perlman v. Feldman, 219 F.2d 173 (2d Cir. 1955); and the question of whether and how control can be promptly transferred, as for example by seriatim resignations and replacement by nominees of the buyer, e. g., Essex Universal Corp. v. Yates, 305 F.2d 572 (2d Cir. 1962). See generally, Andrews, The Stockholder's Right to Equal Opportunity in the Sale of Shares, 78 Harv.L.Rev. 505 (1965).

If instead the present management decides to fight it out with the prospective intruder, a different series of problems arises. Presumably, the management does not have to act as a go-between for the other stockholders and transmit offers from the buyer to them; and indeed, it seems open to the management to use private funds to purchase enough stock to block the third party. E. g., Mairs v. Madden, 307 Mass. 378, 30 N.E.2d 242 (1940). In addition, the incumbent management can certainly respond in kind to a proxy contest, and charge the expense to the corporation in most instances. E. g., Rosenfeld v. Fairchild Engine and Airplane Corp., 309 N.Y. 168, 128 N.E. 2d 291 (1955).

What about using the corporation's funds either to purchase the stock already owned by the third party, thereby eliminating him from the scene and avoiding a possible contest, or to finance a general program of repurchase of stock in order to block the third party's efforts to acquire sufficient stock (or proxies) to assume control? On these issues there has been a substantial run of litigation in Delaware during the past few years.

KORS v. CAREY

Court of Chancery of Delaware, 1960.
39 Del.Ch. 47, 158 A.2d 136.

[Lehn & Fink Products Corporation is a manufacturer of cosmetics and household drugs whose stock is listed on the New York Stock Exchange. In March of 1956, United Whelan, a national drug store chain which was a customer of Lehn & Fink, started buying the latter's stock and by March 1, 1957, its holdings totaled over 45,000 shares. The Lehn & Fink management became concerned about United Whelan's purchases and had a meeting with United's president and largest stockholder, Charles Green. Green indicated that United's retail business policy was to try to make special deals with various manufacturers, a policy which Lehn & Fink has consistently resisted. While no demands of any kind were made by United at that meeting, it continued to acquire Lehn & Fink stock, and by the end of 1957 United held 60,200 shares, representing approximately 16% of the total outstanding.

The Lehn & Fink management was aware that Green had waged a number of proxy fights against the managements of a number of different business enterprises, including his successful one for control of United in 1951. (At the trial in the instant action Green conceded that the purpose of Lehn & Fink stock purchases had been to gain control of the company.) The Lehn & Fink management decided that United Whelan should be eliminated as a stockholder, and late in 1957 Lehn & Fink authorized a broker to consummate a purchase of the stock held by United. United never inquired of either the broker or Lehn & Fink as to the identity of the purchaser and never knew that it was Lehn & Fink. United's stock was purchased in February, 1958, for $28 per share, at which time the stock was selling in small lots at about $25½ per share. The brokerage commissions amounted to 50 cents per share.

The plaintiff, a minority stockholder of Lehn & Fink, brought this action against the directors of the company on the ground that Lehn & Fink's purchase of its own shares was not made for a proper corporate purpose and involved both an excessive price and excessive brokerage fees, legal fees, and other costs. The plaintiff sought an accounting for the loss allegedly caused to the corporation (and also an order for sale of the repurchased stock although she did not press for that immediately). United Whelan, having been originally named as a nominal defendant, filed a cross claim against Lehn & Fink seeking rescission of the stock sale on various grounds, including the failure of Lehn & Fink to disclose its identity as the purchaser. The market price of Lehn & Fink stock at the time of the trial ranged from $45 to $48 per share.]

MARVEL, Vice Chancellor [after setting out the facts].[36] The individual defendants have advanced a number of reasons for their decision to acquire United Whelan's stock, including the unlikely one of a desire to have stock available for the acquisition of desirable business assets notwithstanding the existence of 600,000 authorized but unissued shares which could be utilized for such a purpose. I conclude . . . that the real basis for the decision to eliminate United as a stockholder (a decision which crystalized slowly but which was apparently inevitable as early as mid-1956 when United Whelan's steady accumulation of Lehn & Fink stock became obvious) is found in a fundamental divergence in these two corporations' business policies. The record clearly demonstrates that no middle ground for accommodating the views of United Whelan with those of the incumbent management of Lehn & Fink could possibly be found. It was accordingly apparent very early in the game that one or the other of these two opposing forces must necessarily give way either voluntarily or as a result of a battle for control, and what appear to me to be the compelling reasons for the decision to buy out United find their roots in a firm resolve to preserve management policy and independence and an established relationship with customers as such had been developed over the years by past and present directors of Lehn & Fink. For instance, it is contended by the individual defendants, and there is evidence to sustain the contention in principle, that for a substantial customer of Lehn & Fink to have continued to hold a large number of shares of stock of that corporation would have tended to alienate Lehn & Fink's other chain store customers, who, it is claimed, must in order to survive, avoid dependency on the whims of a competitor for adequate supplies of name cosmetics for the promotion of which substantial sums of money have been committed. A variation of this same fear of customer dissatisfaction is found in the views of the directors of Lehn & Fink's that United Whelan did not measure up to Lehn & Fink either in its finished product or in business principles, and that to have United's voice dominant in the affairs of Lehn & Fink would inevitably not only be injurious to the latter's sales but would, because of Green's aggressive principles, which emphasize flexibility and experimental change in corporate purpose, perhaps threaten Lehn & Fink's very existence as an expanding manufacturer of high quality cosmetics. Lehn & Fink's directors were also concerned not only about the chance of being led into a course of conduct involving possible violations of the Robinson-Patman Act by reason of United's insistence on special promotional schemes but also about the need of being required in self-protection to prepare for the possibility of an anti-trust action against United Whelan under § 7 of the Clayton Act on the theory that as a customer it could not lawfully be in a position of being able through stock ownership to influence Lehn & Fink's policy. In brief, a comparison of the over-all business record

---

36. Footnotes by the court omitted.

of United Whelan, including its earnings and how they were achieved (as well as those of other corporations in which Charles Green is a dominant force), with that of Lehn & Fink's demonstrated that the continuance of United Whelan as a dominant force in Lehn & Fink posed a serious threat to the welfare of the latter corporation and its stockholders.

Plaintiff, in answer to these contentions, derides the motives of the individual defendants, pointing out that Lehn & Fink's aging president and dominant management stockholder, Edward Plaut, is concededly desirous of having his son succeed him in office and that in greater or lesser degree all of the Lehn & Fink directors have an interest in retaining management in office. Plaintiff argues that Lehn & Fink's directors, on learning of United's continuing purchases of stock, became the victims of unreasoning panic, imagining that the possible loss of a proxy fight would somehow spell the end for Lehn & Fink, when actually the only matters thereby placed in jeopardy were defendants' selfish interests, plaintiff insisting that the purchase complained of was made secretly and surreptitiously for the improper purpose of retaining jobs and control of corporate power. Plaintiff insists that under the circumstances disclosed at trial any buying out of United Whelan's stock should have been made by means of a spending of personal rather than corporate funds by the individual defendants.

There is no doubt, however, about the right of a Delaware corporation in a proper case to purchase, hold, sell and transfer shares of its own capital stock provided the spending of its own funds in any such transaction does not cause an impairment of its capital, . . . and no contention is made that the purchase here attacked to any extent did so. Plaintiff, while conceding that statutory authority exists, strenuously contends that such power has been abused. She cites a number of leading cases which are concerned with situations in which the spending of corporate funds by corporate officers for the purpose of securing or retaining corporate control have been condemned . . . . Plaintiff's proof, however, in my opinion fails to establish a case of fraud, misconduct or abuse of discretion such as would compel a court of equity to find the individual defendants guilty of a breach of their fiduciary duty and cause the purchase in question to be declared to have been made for no proper corporate purpose. . . . . In other words, directors, while bound to deal with stockholders as a class with scrupulous honesty, may in the exercise of their honest business judgment adopt a valid method of eliminating what appears to them a clear threat to the future of their business by any lawful means . . . . Thus, it is established in Delaware that directors may validly spend corporate funds for the defense of corporate policy in a proxy fight . . . . Furthermore, a reduction of capital through the purchase of shares at private sale is not illegal as a matter of law simply because the purpose or motive of the purchase is to eliminate a substantial number of shares held by a stockholder at odds with management policy, ". . . provided of course that the transaction is clear of any fraud or unfairness. . . .", Martin v. American Potash & Chemical Corp., 33 Del.Ch. 234, 92 A.2d 295, 302, 35 A.L.R.2d 1140.

Faced with these principles in a suit which in essence seeks to impugn a corporate decision to preserve an established management's business policy, plaintiff has labored diligently in pre-trial, at trial, and in her briefs to establish that the individual defendants in authorizing the purchase complained of were not only guilty of misconduct but also abused their discretion . . . . However, I am satisfied that not only has no fraud been established but that plaintiff has failed to carry the burden of proving any misconduct or abuse of discretion on the part of the Lehn & Fink directors. While the actual decision to buy out United Whelan was arrived at quickly late in January, 1958, the factors which went into the decision had been carefully weighed and evaluated over the preceding months during which various methods of coping with United's potential bid for control were under more or less constant discussion by board members not only inter sese but with professional experts such as members of the faculty of the Harvard Business School and officials of Georgenson & Co., proxy solicitors. Without regard to the many bits of questionable evidentiary information which appear in the record, there is no doubt in my mind but that the business methods of Charles Green, which stress liquidity, the spending of substantial sums for aggressive promotional schemes, and a readiness to sacrifice an established mode of doing business for quick profits, presented a threat of a possible future business course which was entirely at odds with Lehn & Fink's traditions. In short, my opinion is that the action of the board in authorizing the purchase complained of in a transaction in which the identity of Lehn & Fink as the buyer was not fraudulently concealed is legally unassailable by a minority stockholder on grounds of fraud, misconduct or abuse of discretion. Furthermore, under the circumstances presented, neither the price paid per share nor the commission allowed the broker in a private transaction, were in my opinion unreasonable, and the other expenses involved in preparing for the final show-down with Mr. Green cannot be said to be excessive. They are in fact modest compared to the moneys which would have been required to defend management policy in an all-out proxy fight.

As to plaintiff's contentions that the Lehn & Fink directors were selfishly voting for the retention of their offices and the emoluments thereof, I conclude, having heard the testimony of the principals involved and considered their personal evaluation of the dilemma posed by the existence of a substantial block of their stock in the hands of United Whelan, that plaintiff has not succeeded in overcoming the presumption that directors form their judgment in good faith . . . . While it appears that the five active members of Lehn & Fink's management currently receive salaries ranging from sums in excess of $35,000 per annum to Mr. Edward Plaut's of slightly more than $100,000 per year, that consultant directors receive compensation ranging from $3,200 to $12,100 and that substantial legal fees have been paid to lawyer-directors, I find no evidence that a selfish desire to retain jobs on the part of the non-managerial Lehn & Fink directors was a factor in their decision. Furthermore, assuming that Edward Plaut, who had most at stake in preserving the status quo at Lehn & Fink, was strongly influenced by family considerations in reaching his decision, nonetheless I am not persuaded that he so dominated the board that its non-managerial members were unable to make their own decisions about the purchase under attack.

Finally, even assuming that the purpose of all the individual defendants was primarily a selfish desire to retain control and jobs through the device of negativing United Whelan's potentiality by a buying out, how has plaintiff been injured? United Whelan, having by its sale patently waived its opportunity to seek control, plaintiff, who never exercised voting control alone or with any group or faction cannot . . ., successfully claim any injury to the shareholders generally as a result of the transaction complained of. On the contrary, the record discloses a substantial increase in value on the part of Lehn & Fink's traded shares since February 1958, an appreciation which is reflected, of course, in the market value of the treasury shares involved in this litigation, and there is no evidence of mismanagement or the like on the part of the incumbent board since these shares were acquired and the possibility of a Green-controlled board eliminated. While plaintiff vigorously contends that the buying out deprived the general body of stockholders of their right to make a choice between the type of management which they might have expected to receive from a board under the influence of Mr. Green as opposed to the incumbent board, the franchise to vote in corporate elections is basically an individual right to vote directly or cumulatively . . . and no more. There being no voting trusts or pooling agreements here involved, it necessarily follows that United Whelan having voluntarily sold stock which might have been the basis for a proxy battle, plaintiff has no possible basis for complaining about a so-called lost opportunity to vote for a Green sponsored management. To be sure the opportunity was lost, however, in losing the opportunity plaintiff and those in her class were deprived of no rights. Judgment for the individual defendants will be entered on the issue of director liability raised in the complaint and answer.

[The Court also denied any relief to United Whelan on the ground that the identity of the purchaser had never been misrepresented to United, and there was no affirmative duty of disclosure on the part of Lehn & Fink.]

BENNETT v. PROPP

Supreme Court of Delaware, 1962. 187 A.2d 405.

[Noma Lites, Inc. is a Delaware corporation engaged in the business of selling decorative lighting equipment. Its stock is listed on the American Stock Exchange. Sadacca owned about 11% of Noma's approximately 950,000 outstanding shares and was chairman of the board of directors. In late 1958 the Noma management learned that Textron was seeking to acquire the assets of American Screw Company, 20% of whose stock was owned by a Canadian subsidiary of Noma. To block Textron's efforts, the Canadian subsidiary bought enough additional American Screw stock to bring its holdings up to 51%. Shortly thereafter, on Saturday, November 22, Sadacca received word from Royal Little, the chairman of the board of Textron, that Textron was about to try to acquire more than 50% of Noma's stock. On the following Monday Sadacca started buying Noma stock in the market. After an unsatisfactory conference with Little on Tuesday, Sadacca resumed his purchases on Wednesday and his total purchases for the two days approximated 200,000 shares. The only other director of Noma who was even aware of Sadacca's activities was Ward, the president. During that period the price of Noma stock rose from 9 to 13, and the average price paid by Sadacca was $11.67. These purchases were made in Sadacca's own name, apparently because he was fearful of the possible effect upon the market of purchases in Noma's name. On Saturday, November 29, at a special meeting of the Noma board, Sadacca reviewed the prior events and indicated that he had purchased the stock for Noma's account. Without discussion of any other alternatives, such as Sadacca's personal assumption of the stock purchases, the board adopted a resolution approving and ratifying Sadacca's actions in purchasing stock "in behalf of the corporation". The board then considered the means for raising the more than $2,300,000 needed to finance this acquisition, and ultimately consummated a short-term loan from a factor, the terms of which included interest at one-thirtieth of one per cent per day, a pledge of the purchased stock and other collateral, and an assignment of accounts receivable.

The plaintiff, a minority stockholder, brought this action alleging that Sadacca, Ward and the other directors had caused Noma to waste its corporate assets in a purchase of unneeded Noma stock solely for the purpose of perpetuating Sadacca's control of Noma. The Vice Chancellor held that all the defendants (except one director who did not vote on the November 29 resolution) were liable to account to Noma for its damages, and the defendants appealed.]

SOUTHERLAND, Chief Justice [after reviewing the facts and the decision below].

First, [the defendants] urge that Sadacca's purchases, and the directors' ratification, were justified because Little's actions posed a serious threat to Noma's welfare. They rely on the Vice Chancellor's prior decision in Kors v. Carey, Del.Ch., 158 A.2d 136.

Second, they urge that the imminence of the deadline [for payment for the stock] confronted the directors with an emergency of a serious nature. If Noma failed to pay for the shares bought by Sadacca, the brokers would sell the shares to protect themselves and would seek to hold Noma responsible for any loss. Noma's credit would be adversely affected. The directors' decision to ratify was thus one made in the exercise of business judgment, and they may not be held liable. . . .

1. The Vice Chancellor rejected the directors' first contention, and we think that he was right. Sadacca's purchases were made to preserve the control of the corporation in himself and his fellow directors. His statement to his board in the November 29 meeting practically admitted as much; at all events we have no doubt about it. The use of corporate funds for such a purpose is improper.

* * *

An exception to the rule was recognized in Delaware in Kors v. Carey, ...

This decision does not help the directors here. Little's attempt to buy American Screw had already been defeated. His letter of November 21 to Sadacca posed no immediate threat. In our opinion, contrary to plaintiff's, it was a thinly-veiled attempt to induce Sadacca and his fellow stockholder-directors to sell out to Little. There was no immediate indication that Little would start to buy large amounts of stock in the market. The argument that Little was dangerous because of his record as a "liquidator" was answered by the Vice Chancellor. He found from the evidence that the attacks at the trial on Little were largely afterthoughts.

In any event, the directors made no finding of immediate threat. They were not even consulted.

The case of Martin v. American Potash & Chemical Corp., . . . also relied on, involved a reduction of capital. The statute applicable to that case permits the purchase of shares for retirement at private sale. The fact that the purchase was prompted by existing dissension in the board was held not to render it illegal.

The decision is obviously distinguishable on two grounds. First, a reduction of capital surrounded by the statutory safeguard of a notice and a stockholders meeting is quite different from the purchases of common stock made here under the general power conferred by § 160 of the corporation law, 8 Del.C. § 160. Second, the elimination of a dissentient faction for genuine business reasons, as in the Kors case, is quite a different thing from the purchase of stock for control purposes before any real threat to corporate policy has occurred. The Potash case is also of no help to defendants.

It is our opinion that Sadacca's sudden decision to buy 200,000 shares of stock in two or three days was not only an unauthorized act on behalf of Noma, but was unjustified on the facts.

We must bear in mind the inherent danger in the purchase of shares with corporate funds to remove a threat to corporate policy when a threat to control is involved. The directors are of necessity confronted with a conflict of interest, and an objective decision is difficult. See the comments on the instant case in 62 Col.L.Rev. 1096, 1100. Hence, in our opinion, the burden should be on the directors to justify such a purchase as one primarily in the corporate interest. See 70 Yale L.J. 308, 317. They sustained that burden in the Kors case; they have not done so here.

It is our opinion that so far as the directors' defense depends on the rule of the Kors case it must fail.

2. The alternative defense is that of a business decision made in a sudden emergency to protect the corporation from serious injury. The defendant's contention may be thus summarized:

At the meeting of November 29 most of the directors learned for the first time what Sadacca had done. They were suddenly and unexpectedly confronted with a situation which threatened financial embarrassment and possible disaster to Noma. The commitment must be met. The day was Saturday, the larger part must be met by Monday. Under the circumstances they did the best they could; they raised the money, ratified the transaction, and preserved Noma's credit. In their business judgment it was the only thing to do. In the exercise of that judgment the law protects them from liability. So runs the argument.

* * *

This defense impresses us as having merit. It will not do, as plaintiff argues, to say that the brokers had no case. It is reasonable to believe that they would certainly have sought to hold Noma; and who can say what the consequences might have been? Sadacca had confronted his directors with a *fait accompli*, as the Vice Chancellor put it. But the Vice Chancellor in effect held that the directors' emergency did not relieve them from the duty of exploring other methods of coping with the situation. In our view, the pressure of time excused them from such efforts. They may not have made the best decision; we cannot say. Perhaps a telephone call to the brokers might have given time for negotiation; on the other hand it might well have precipitated serious litigation Monday morning. Upon the whole, we think that the directors cannot be blamed for deciding to take up the stock in the interest of protecting the corporation from dangerous litigation.

* * *

But this conclusion does not, as defendants' counsel appear to assume, dispose of the case as to Sadacca or as to Ward. Their positions are different. They will be separately considered.

First, as to Sadacca. We are of opinion that the resolution ratifying Sadacca's acts was not effective to legalize the purchases. The directors were without power to ratify them, for they were illegal when made. . . . It follows that the resolution has legal validity only to the extent of authorizing the officers to take up the stock to save the corporation from financial difficulty. Under § 160 they had legal power to do it, and because of the special circumstances we think that the power was not abused. But Sadacca remains liable for his acts.

Second, as to Ward. We have already exonerated the directors who learned about the matter for the first time at the meeting, on the ground that they were confronted with the necessity for a sudden decision in an emergency. We have thus made an exception to the general rule that directors who use corporate funds to preserve control commit a wrong. This exception depends upon the two circumstances proved in this case: prior ignorance and immediate emergency. If either of these circumstances had been absent the directors approving and ratifying Sadacca's purchases would clearly have been jointly liable with him to the corporation.

Ward's prior knowledge of these purchases is sufficient to deprive him of the benefit of the exception. He was the president of the corporation. He had enough time before the following Monday to consult with his fellow officers and directors, to consult counsel, and to take steps to make some arrangements with the brokers beneficial to Noma. As president, he could surely have called a directors' meeting. He did nothing. Apparently he did not even inquire of Sadacca how many shares Sadacca had bought, how much had been paid for them, or how Sadacca expected to finance the purchases. One gets the impression from the record that he was entirely subservient to Sadacca.

We think that his knowledge of the purchases, his silence and failure to act, coupled with his vote on the resolution, constituted a course of conduct amounting to approval of and participation in Sadacca's wrongful acts. This is not to hold Ward guilty of negligence as counsel seem to think the Vice Chancellor did. It is to hold that his actions made him jointly and severally liable with Sadacca for the tort of using corporate funds to maintain control.

We are of opinion that, with the exception of Ward, the directors who voted for the resolution must be exonerated of wrong doing; and that Sadacca and Ward must be held liable for any damages proximately suffered by Noma as a result of Sadacca's unlawful acts.
. . .

CHEFF v. MATHES

Supreme Court of Delaware, 1964. 199 A.2d 548.

[The Holland Furnace Company is a Delaware corporation engaged in the manufacture and sale of furnaces, air conditioners, and other home heating equipment. In 1957 Holland had outstanding approximately 883,500 shares of stock which were listed on the New York Stock Exchange. The company had seven directors: Cheff, who owned about 6,000 shares and was also the chief executive officer, at an annual compensation of $77,400; Mrs. Cheff, who was a daughter of a founder of the company and who owned, in addition to approximately 5,800 shares of Holland outright, almost 50% of Hazelbank United Interest, Inc., an investment vehicle for members of the Cheff-Landwehr family group which owned almost 165,000 shares of Holland stock; Landwehr, Mrs. Cheff's nephew, who owned about 24,000 shares of Holland personally, and approximately 9% of Hazelbank; Trenkamp, general counsel of the company who was not on an annual retainer but did receive substantial sums for legal services; and three "outside" directors who had joined the board at the request of Mr. Cheff: Ames, a partner in a Chicago investment firm; Boalt, an officer of a cosmetics concern; and Spatta, the president of a large manufacturer of earth-moving equipment. None of the directors except Cheff and Trenkamp received any compensation from Holland other than a director's fee of $200 per meeting.

Holland's method of operation from its inception was to sell its products directly to consumers through its own retail salesmen, without any intermediate dealers. This practice, which was unique in the furnace business, was regarded by the management as a vital factor in the company's success. Holland employed approximately 8,500 persons and maintained 400 branch sales offices located in 43 states. However, the business had not been prospering since the postwar period, with sales declining from over $41 million in 1948 to less than $32 million in 1956. In addition, the company's marketing methods had been made the subject of serious charges by the Federal Trade Commission. But in 1956 there was apparently some reorganization of the sales department, including the closing of certain unprofitable branch offices, which the management believed would arrest the decline in sales.

Beginning late in June, 1957, the trading activity in Holland stock increased substantially, rising from a previous monthly average between 10,000 and 25,000 shares to a figure of almost 40,000 shares for the last week in June. The price per share rose to $12, a high for the year. During that same week Mr. Cheff met with one Maremont, the president of Maremont Automotive Products, Inc., and chief executive officer of a number of other concerns, who inquired about the feasibility of a merger between Motor Products and Holland. However, Cheff indicated that because of difference in sales practices between the two companies a merger did not seem feasible, whereupon Maremont indicated that he had no further interest in Holland.

The high level of activity in Holland stock continued into July, and although at first they did not connect it with Mr. Maremont, the Holland officers learned later in July that Maremont had acquired some 55,000 shares of Holland stock. Accordingly, the Holland board decided to investigate Mr. Maremont and learned that he had "been a participant, or had attempted to be, in the liquidation of a number of companies." On August 23, 1957, at his request Maremont met with Mr. Cheff. Maremont indicated that he thought Holland's method of distribution was obsolete, and that "furnaces could be sold as he sold mufflers, through half a dozen salesmen in a wholesale way." Immediately after this meeting Cheff caused Holland to engage in active buying of its own stock and some 1900 shares had been purchased by August 29. On August 30, the Holland board adopted a resolution calling for a stock option plan and authorizing the president to purchase for the corporation up to 71,000 shares for such a plan at a price not to exceed $16.50 per share. Recent purchases by officers of 4900 shares of stock for the corporation were ratified, and a fund of some $500,000 for further purchases by the corporation was set up. In addition, Mrs. Cheff indicated that she was willing to invest an equal amount of her own funds to prevent a Maremont takeover, and authorized her brokers to purchase Holland stock for her individual account.

According to evidence subsequently introduced by the Holland officers, the appearance of Maremont on the scene created a good deal of unrest among the employees of Holland, with a number of employees in the field considering leaving because of their fear of the consequences of a Maremont acquisition. Several branch managers approached corporate officers for reassurances that Maremont would not be allowed to gain control. At the same time the company received a Dun and Bradstreet report which indicated that Maremont's practice was to achieve quick profits by sale or liquidation of companies acquired by him.

A New York broker was engaged to act as agent for Holland and for Mrs. Cheff personally in the purchase of Holland stock in equal proportions, and the broker was advised that as much as $1,500,000 of stock might be acquired, to be divided in equal thirds among Mrs. Cheff, Holland, and Hazelbank. In the meantime, Mr. Maremont had written to each Holland director on September 13, noting the decline in Holland's fortunes over the recent years and recommending that a broad engineering survey be made "for the benefit of all the stockholders." During September Holland and Mrs. Cheff each acquired approximately 23,000 shares, while Motor Products added 31,000 shares to its holdings, with the stock rising to more than $16 per share, its highest price in over two years. On September 25, by which time Holland had acquired some $380,000 worth of its stock, both Mrs. Cheff and Holland discontinued the purchases.

In early September Maremont had offered to sell his Holland holdings to the corporation for $14.00 per share but shortly thereafter he withdrew his offer. At the end of September he wrote to Mrs. Cheff's sister, a stockholder of Hazelbank, offering either to sell his Holland stock to Hazelbank and the Cheff family group, or to buy their stock. However, some of the Hazelbank stockholders were reluctant to acquire any more Holland stock, and Maremont's proposal was referred to the Hazelbank finance committee for further study. On October 14 Trenkamp met with Maremont and reached a tentative agreement that his 155,000 shares of Holland stock would be acquired for $14.40 per share, the closing price of the stock the previous day having been $11. At that point it was not clear who would purchase the stock and in what proportions, since Trenkamp was authorized to act for Holland, Hazelbank and Mrs. Cheff individually. On October 23, the Holland board met to consider the Maremont purchase, and the threat posed by Maremont was reviewed. The board was advised by Mrs. Cheff that either she or Hazelbank would take up any of the Maremont stock which Holland did not buy; the board was also informed that to finance the purchase of the entire Maremont block of stock Holland would have to borrow substantial sums.

The Holland directors, after reaching a consensus that purchase of the Maremont stock was the only alternative to a costly proxy fight, authorized the purchase by Holland of all of the Maremont stock. The directors concluded that the repurchase would sufficiently reduce the total dividend requirement to offset the interest on the borrowed funds, and that it would not be necessary to curtail the company's operations in any way.

In February, 1958, this minority shareholder's suit was commenced against the Holland directors, charging that the 1957 repurchase of stock by Holland had been for the purpose of perpetuating the control of the incumbent directors, and seeking, *inter alia,* to hold the directors liable for damages. The price of Holland stock had fallen back to about $10 per share after the purchase from Maremont; thereafter it reached a high of over $15 per share in early 1959 and then steadily decreased until it had fallen below $2 per share when the stock was delisted in 1964.

The Vice Chancellor found that the repurchase of stock had been made for the purpose of retaining corporate control and held Mr. Cheff, Mrs. Cheff, Landwehr and Trenkamp liable. He rejected the proffered reasons for the repurchase that the corporation wanted to have stock available for a proposed option plan or that the corporation was seeking to utilize its excess funds, since he found that the corporation already had ample treasury stock, and also had a new subsidiary in the finance business which could profitably utilize additional capital. However, the Vice Chancellor absolved the other directors of liability because they did not have an important stake in the affairs of Holland; in addition, he found that they did not understand, prior to the meeting on October 23 at which Holland's repurchase of Maremont's stock was authorized, that an alternative existed in the form of a purchase of some or all of that stock by Mrs. Cheff or Hazelbank. The defendants appealed.]

CAREY, JUSTICE [after setting out the facts].

Under the provisions of 8 Del.C. § 160, a corporation is granted statutory power to purchase and sell shares of its own stock. . . . The charge here is not one of violation of statute, but the allegation is that the true motives behind such purchases were improperly centered upon perpetuation of control. In an analogous field, courts have sustained the use of proxy funds to inform stockholders of management's views upon the policy questions inherent in an election to a board of directors, but have not sanctioned the use of corporate funds to advance the selfish desires of directors to perpetuate themselves in office. . . . Similarly, if the actions of the board were motivated by a sincere belief that the buying out of the dissident stockholder was necessary to maintain what the board believed to be proper business practices, the board will not be held liable for such decision, even though hindsight indicates the decision was not the wisest course. See Kors v. Carey, Del.Ch., 158 A.2d 136. On the other hand, if the board has acted solely or primarily because of the desire to perpetuate themselves in office, the use of corporate funds for such purposes is improper. See Bennett v. Propp, Del., 187 A.2d 405. . . .

Our first problem is the allocation of the burden of proof to show the presence or lack of good faith on the part of the board in authorizing the purchase of shares. Initially, the decision of the board of directors in authorizing a purchase was presumed to be in good faith and could be overturned only by a conclusive showing by plaintiffs of fraud or other misconduct. See Bankers Securities Corp. v. Kresge Department Stores, Inc., D.C., 54 F.Supp. 378. In Kors, cited supra, the court merely indicated that the directors are presumed to act in good faith and the burden of proof to show to the contrary falls upon the plaintiff. However, in Bennett v. Propp, supra, we stated:

> "We must bear in mind the inherent danger in the purchase of shares with corporate funds to remove a threat to corporate policy when a threat to control is involved. The directors are of necessity confronted with a conflict of interest, and an objective decision is difficult. . . . Hence, in our opinion, the burden should be on the directors to justify such a purchase as one primarily in the corporate interest." (187 A.2d 409, at page 409).

* * *

To say that the burden of proof is upon the defendants is not to indicate, however, that the directors have the same "self-dealing interest" as is present, for example, when a director sells property to the corporation. The only clear pecuniary interest shown on the record was held by Mr. Cheff, as an executive of the corporation, and Trenkamp, as its attorney. The mere fact that some of the other directors were substantial shareholders does not create a personal pecuniary interest in the decisions made by the board of directors, since all shareholders would presumably share the benefit flowing to the substantial shareholder. . . . Accordingly, these directors other than Trenkamp and Cheff, while called upon to justify their actions, will not be held to the same standard of proof required of those directors having personal and pecuniary interest in the transaction.

As noted above, the Vice Chancellor found that the stock option plan, mentioned in the minutes as a justification for the purchases, was not a motivating reason for the purchases. This finding we accept, since there is evidence to support it; in fact, Trenkamp admitted that the stock option plan was not the motivating reason. The minutes of October 23, 1957 dealing with the purchase from Maremont do not, in fact, mention the option plan as a reason for the purchase. While the minutes of the October 1, 1957 meeting only indicated the stock option plan as the motivating reason, the defendants are not bound by such statements and may supplement the minutes by oral testimony to show that the motivating reason was genuine fear of an acquisition by Maremont. See Bennett v. Propp, cited supra.

Plaintiffs urge that the sale price was unfair in view of the fact that the price was in excess of that prevailing on the open market. However, as conceded by all parties, a substantial block of stock will normally sell at a higher price than that prevailing on the open market, the increment being attributable to a "control premium". Plaintiffs argue that it is inappropriate to require the defendant corporation to pay a control premium, since control is meaningless to an acquisition by a corporation of its own shares. However, it is elementary that a holder of a substantial number of shares would expect to receive the control premium as part of his selling price, and if the corporation desired to obtain the stock, it is unreasonable to expect that the corporation could avoid paying what any other purchaser would be required to pay for the stock. In any event, the financial expert produced by defendant at trial indicated that the price paid was fair and there was no rebuttal. Ames, the financial man on the board, was strongly of the opinion that the purchase was a good deal for the corporation. The Vice Chancellor made no finding as to the fairness of the price other than to indicate the obvious fact that the market price was increasing as a result of open market purchases by Maremont, Mrs. Cheff and Holland.

The question then presented is whether or not defendants satisfied the burden of proof of showing reasonable grounds to believe a danger to corporate policy and effectiveness existed by the presence of the Maremont stock ownership. It is important to remember that the directors satisfy their burden by showing good faith and reasonable investigation; the directors will not be penalized for an honest mistake of judgment, if the judgment appeared reasonable at the time the decision was made. . . .

In holding that employee unrest could as well be attributed to a condition of Holland's business affairs as to the possibility of Maremont's intrusion, the Vice Chancellor must have had in mind one or both of two matters: (1) the pending proceedings before the Federal Trade Commission concerning certain sales practices of Holland; (2) the decrease in sales and profits during the preceding several years. Any other possible reason would be pure speculation. In the first place, the adverse decision of the F.T.C. was not announced until *after* the complained-of transaction. Secondly, the evidence clearly shows that the downward trend of sales and profits had reversed itself, presumably because of the reorganization which had then been completed. Thirdly, everyone who testified on the point said that the unrest was due to the possible threat presented by Maremont's purchases of stock. There was, in fact, no *testimony* whatever of any connection between the unrest and either the F.T.C. proceedings or the business picture.

The Vice Chancellor found that there was no substantial evidence of a liquidation posed by Maremont. This holding overlooks an important contention. The fear of the defendants, according to their testimony, was not limited to the possibility of liquidation; it included the alternate possibility of a material change in Holland's sales policies, which the board considered vital to its future success. The *unrebutted* testimony before the court indicated: (1) Maremont had deceived Cheff as to his original intentions, since his open market purchases were contemporaneous with his disclaimer of interest in Holland; (2) Maremont had given Cheff some reason to believe that he intended to eliminate the retail sales force of Holland; (3) Maremont demanded a place on the board; (4) Maremont substantially increased his purchases after having been refused a place on the board; (5) the directors had good reason to believe that unrest among key employees had been engendered by the Maremont threat; (6) the board had received advice from Dun and Bradstreet indicating the past liquidation or quick sale activities of Motor Products; (7) the board had received professional advice from the firm of Merrill Lynch, Fenner & Beane, who recommended that the purchase from Motor Products be carried out; (8) the board had received competent advice that the corporation was over-capitalized; (9) Staal and Cheff had made informal personal investigations from contacts in the business and financial community and had reported to the board of the alleged poor reputation of Maremont. The board was within its rights in relying upon that investigation, since 8 Del.C. § 141(f) allows the directors to reasonably rely upon a report provided by corporate officers. . . .

Accordingly, we are of the opinion that the evidence presented in the court below leads inevitably to the conclusion that the board of directors, based upon direct investigation, receipt of professional advice, and personal observations of the contradictory action of Maremont and his explanation of corporate purpose, believed, with justification, that there was a reasonable threat to the continued existence of Holland, or at least existence in its present form, by the plan of Maremont to continue building up his stock holdings. We find no evidence in the record sufficient to justify a contrary conclusion. The opinion of the Vice Chancellor that employee unrest may have been engendered by other factors or that the board had no grounds to suspect Maremont is not supported in any manner by the evidence.

As noted above, the Vice Chancellor found that the purpose of the acquisition was the improper desire to maintain control, but, at the same time, he exonerated those individual directors whom he believed to be unaware of the possibility of using non-corporate funds to accomplish this purpose. Such a decision is inconsistent with his finding that the motive was improper, within the rule enunciated in Bennett. If the actions were in fact improper because of a desire to maintain control, then the presence or absence of a non-corporate alternative is irrelevant, as corporate funds may not be used to advance an improper purpose even if there is no non-corporate alternative available. Conversely, if the actions were proper because of a decision by the board made in good faith that the corporate interest was served thereby, they are not rendered improper by the fact that some individual directors were willing to advance personal funds if the corporation did not. It is conceivable that the Vice Chancellor considered this feature of the case to be of significance because of his apparent belief that any excess corporate funds should have been used to finance a subsidiary corporation. That action would not have solved the problem of Holland's overcapitalization. In any event, this question was a matter of business judgment, which furnishes no justification for holding the directors personally responsible in this case.

NOTE ON REPURCHASE OF STOCK TO MAINTAIN CONTROL

1. **Rule 10b–5.** Whatever the propriety of such a repurchase transaction, a shareholder can not normally challenge it under SEC Rule 10b–5. O'Neill v. Maytag, 339 F.2d 764 (2d Cir. 1964). As the court put it, "Where the duty allegedly breached is only the general duty existing among corporate officers, directors and shareholders, no cause of action is stated under Rule 10b–5 unless there is an allegation of facts amounting to deception." See generally, Comment, Rule 10b–5 and Purchase by a Corporation of Its Own Shares, 61 Nw.U.L.Rev. 307 (1966).

2. **Pro Rata Offer to All Shareholders.** Would a pro rata offer to repurchase from all other shareholders at the same price cure an otherwise vulnerable repurchase from a potential insurgent? Of course as a practical matter such an offer might be beyond the financial capacity of the corporation to fulfill, if any substantial percentage of the stockholders accepted. But

Sec. 8 REPURCHASE OF STOCK 459

in any event it is to be noted that in none of the foregoing cases did the plaintiff complain of the absence of a pro rata offer, or press for that as a remedy. And as a general proposition the fact that stock is being repurchased from some stockholders does not entitle other stockholders to demand pro rata treatment. See e. g., Spiegel v. Beacon Participations, Inc., 297 Mass. 398, 431, 8 N.E.2d 895, 914 (1937) ("No provision of law required the directors, in making these purchases of stock . . . to buy them ratably from the stockholders"). Some early New Jersey cases which intimated the existence of such a requirement, e. g., General Inv. Co. v. American Hide & Leather Co., 98 N.J.Eq. 326, 129 A. 244 (Ct. E. & A. 1925), may be explained by the fact that they involved repurchase of stock as a method of reducing capital, as authorized by some corporate statutes, and of course a requirement for pro rata distribution in connection with a reduction of capital stands on a very different footing and establishes no precedent for an ordinary repurchase transaction.

However, there is at least one dissenting opinion taking the contrary view and insisting that a pro rata offer is required. In Reifsnyder v. Pittsburgh Outdoor Advertising Co., 396 Pa. 320, 152 A.2d 894 (1959), the plaintiff was a minority stockholder of the defendant corporation ("Pittsburgh"), owning 130 of the outstanding 15,000 shares. Approximately 61% of Pittsburgh's stock was owned by General Outdoor Advertising Company ("General"), which elected all of the directors of Pittsburgh and operated it as a subsidiary. In 1955 a consent decree entered in an anti-trust proceeding required General to dispose of its Pittsburgh stock at "not less than a fair market value". Thereafter, negotiations began between Pittsburgh and General looking to purchase by Pittsburgh of the stock held by General. The Pittsburgh board of directors made a survey of its real estate and determined that the reappraised book value of its stock was approximately $233 per share. The General officers originally asked for $2,400,000 for General's stock, but finally agreed to accept $2,150,000 ($232.38 per share) and a deal was closed at that price. Shortly thereafter the Pittsburgh directors called a special meeting of the stockholders to authorize the company to purchase General's stock for $2,150,000 and to borrow $2,000,000 in order to finance the transaction. Actually, Pittsburgh was able to obtain only enough funds to purchase 13,600 of the shares held by General, but Pittsburgh's president offered to purchase the other 1400 shares personally at the same price. At the stockholders' meeting the purchase and borrowing by Pittsburgh, as well as the purchase by Pittsburgh's president, were approved, with the plaintiff casting the only negative votes.

At the stockholders' meeting the plaintiff protested the purchase by Pittsburgh, claiming that the price of $232.38 per share was excessive. He also complained of the purchase by Pittsburgh's president, for the rather anomalous reason that the price was too low. Pittsburgh's president offered the 1400 shares to the plaintiff at the same price, but the offer was declined.

Immediately after the meeting the plaintiff instituted this minority shareholder's suit charging that the directors had violated their fiduciary duty to the corporation by causing it to pay an excessive price for the stock of its former majority stockholder. The Chancellor found that the price per share "was fair, reasonable and not excessive", and that "Pittsburgh's officers and directors acted in good faith and with ordinary prudence and skill".

On appeal, the court held that the action should be dismissed because an indispensible party, General, had not been joined. However, before deciding the case on that point a majority of the court joined in an elaborate dictum upholding the transaction on the merits. The opinion appeared to approve the decision of the Pittsburgh directors to purchase the General stock "in order to continue the present management and to prevent an outsider or competitor from getting control of the company". The court noted that two independent appraisers had testified that the purchase price was fair and reasonable; and the court added "that the wisdom of this purchase has been made apparent by the fact that since that time the corporation has been very successful."

Two Justices took sharp issue with the majority with regard to the transaction on the merits:

> . . . I feel that whenever a corporation offers to purchase all of the shares of the majority or all the shares of a controlling interest in a corporation, the corporation is obligated to offer to acquire, at the same price, all the shares of any dissenting shareholder or group of shareholders.
>
> Fair dealing, fiduciary responsibility, and the direct obligation of loyalty owed to all the shareholders, would dictate that a shareholder who did not want to go along with this "bale-out" of the majority should be given the option of disposing of his shares on the same terms and on the same conditions as the retiring majority. Otherwise, the majority shareholders would have at their command a ready purchaser (the corporation) for their holdings—a market that is denied to the minority. And what is even more important, when the corporate market is created by the majority shareholder as it was in the instant case, it becomes more difficult for the minority to dispose of its holdings since the corporation's liquid assets have been depleted to provide the purchase price for the majority stock. In addition to eliminating the element of unfairness that may or may not exist when the majority "bales" itself out, the extension of the same offer of purchase to the minority would eliminate the difficult proof problem of breach of fiduciary duty or of anticipated future harm to the corporation, and also would prevent disputes over what a proper sales price for the stock would be. It might be argued that this offer may force the dissolution of the corporation in some cases. That is all the more reason why the majority should not be permitted to liquidate its holdings through the utilization of the corporate assets without also extending the same opportunity of sale to the minority shareholder. Here the majority stockholder has abandoned its fiduciary responsibility to the minority and this Court should not, even by way of dicta, countenance such action.

3. **Corporate Need for the Stock.** In both the Kors and Cheff cases the defendants attempted to justify the challenged repurchases on the basis of alleged corporate need for the stock—in Kors for acquisition purposes, and in Cheff for a contemplated stock option plan. In each case the court gave short shrift to the contention at least partly because the corporation already had ample stock available, in the form of either unissued stock or treasury stock.

Are there any circumstances which might justify repurchase of stock for use in connection with options (or acquisitions) despite the existence of ample stock in the corporation's hands? At the outset, it should be observed that any new issue of stock by a corporation to persons other than existing stockholders changes the proportionate interests of existing stockholders. But in the normal case, when the stock is issued for a fair price existing stockholders are not adversely affected, since their smaller percentage interest in the corporation is offset by the fact that the total value of the corporation has proportionately increased. Even when the new stock is issued pursuant to a stock option, in which event the price of the stock would normally be less than its then current market value, at least theoretically the corporation has received other consideration for the rights being exercised, so that again there is no adverse "dilution." Therefore, absent some special circumstances, an alleged concern that the exercise of outstanding options or warrants would "dilute" the interests of existing stockholders does not constitute a very forceful justification for repurchase of stock.

However, if a corporation with outstanding stock options did not have the capacity profitably to employ the additional capital it would receive upon the exercise of the options, then the existing stockholders might well suffer a real dilution of their interests. Thus, if the corporation were earning a certain percentage on its invested capital, but could not earn the same return on additional capital, the issuance of additional stock would necessarily lead to a decrease in the earnings per share, and quite likely to a decline in the market price for the stock. Under such circumstances the corporation might appropriately purchase its stock in the market (at least if the stock was then attractively priced) in order to avoid the overcapitalization expected to result from the exercise of the outstanding options. This would appear to be a perfectly legitimate corporate use of the funds, since presumably the corporation would be buying at current market prices from willing sellers, without taking advantage of any inside information or otherwise doing any injustice to the selling stockholders. And such repurchases might be equally justifiable even where a corporation has no plans to issue more stock, if the corporation is already "overcapitalized", that is, it has on hand more funds than it can profitably utilize.

It appears that an argument much along these lines was made in the Cheff case, with the defendants arguing that the corporation was "overcapitalized". However, this argument was treated rather summarily by the court on the ground that the corporation had plenty of use for its funds in its recently created subsidiary finance company. This brusque treatment makes it clear that the overcapitalization argument is at best a rather slender reed. Moreover, the overcapitalization argument could hardly serve as a justification for buying in an artificially high market; purchasing at such a time was independently condemned in the Cheff case.

4. **Special Position of Non-Inside Directors.** An attempt to impose personal liability upon directors for allegedly improper corporate repurchases raises the distinction between a director's duty of *loyalty* to his corporation and his duty of *care*. Under the duty of loyalty, the director is required to give primary, if not exclusive, consideration to the best interests of the corporation, and in any case where the director favors his own interests over those of the corporation he becomes a virtual insurer of any resulting loss. On the other hand, under the duty of care, while the standard may be various-

ly stated, the net effect is that the director is given wide latitude in the exercise of his judgment on behalf of the corporation and will generally be protected even for quite unwise conduct, so long as he was trying to advance the best interests of the corporation.

This dichotomy between the duty of loyalty and the duty of care is rather sharply illustrated in the decided repurchase cases themselves. Thus in both the Kors and Cheff cases the defendant directors claimed a variety of alleged corporate needs for stock as justifications for the challenged repurchase transactions. If any of these claimed reasons had been established as the real purpose for the repurchase transactions in those cases, presumably the directors would have escaped liability even if they had been wrong about the alleged corporate needs; for the posture of the matter would then have been that the directors had been either foolish or stupid, but presumably they would have been within the cloak of protection afforded by the business judgment rule.

However, in both Kors and Cheff the court rejected the various justifications claimed by the defendants because it seemed clear that a different purpose had in fact motivated the challenged transactions, namely the desire to get rid of a potentially troublesome minority stockholder. Of course this too can constitute a legitimate corporate reason for the repurchase transactions, so that the directors become entitled to the protection of the business judgment rule even if their decision turns out to be unwise. However, the special difficulty with this motive for repurchase, and the reason why directors are often reluctant to rely upon it alone, is that elimination of a troublesome minority stockholder may derive as much from the personal desire of the controlling directors to retain their control as from a concern for the corporation's welfare. Ultimately, in the Kors case the court concluded that the objective of the repurchase transactions did stem primarily from a concern for the corporation's welfare; and, of course, there was no need to consider whether the repurchase was prudent, in view of the special circumstance in Kors that the price of the stock had gone up and the corporation had suffered no damage. Conversely, however, in the Bennett case the court concluded that the primary motive for the repurchase transactions was the desire of the principal defendant to maintain his own controlling position. In the light of that finding, it became equally unnecessary to decide whether the decision to repurchase had been a sound one from the corporation's point of view, but for a very different reason from that in Kors—in Bennett, since the decision was not in fact made "from the corporation's point of view," the defendant was charged with virtually absolute responsibility for the loss caused to the corporation.

Obviously, however, directors cannot be held to have acted in their own self-interest instead of for the best interests of the corporation unless it is established that in fact the directors had some personal stake in the transaction (or, at any rate, some reason to act in concert with those who did). This is simple enough so far as directors who are part of the management are concerned, in cases involving elimination of a troublesome minority stockholder group, since such directors are obviously anxious to maintain their executive positions, salaries and the like. But the situation is very different for those directors who do not receive any benefits from the corporation by way of substantial compensation or otherwise. Such directors can scarcely be accused of acting in their own self-interest, for they have no special interest to preserve or advance in the transaction. They may, of course, have been very careless, or stupid, or too servile to the wishes of the controlling group; and any one of these findings may be a basis for imposing liability. But the important point here is that such liability would be predicated upon a breach of the duty of care more than on a breach of the duty of loyalty; and, in that setting, the directors would be entitled to the protection afforded by the business judgment rule or the like.

This seems to have been the line taken by the Vice-Chancellor in the Cheff case when he dismissed the action as to those directors who had no personal stake in the transaction, while imposing liability on the inside group which had officerships, large stockholdings, or other personal interests at stake. Indeed, the Vice-Chancellor may have gone a little too far, since he did not appear to even consider the possible liability of the "disinterested" directors for breach of their duty of care. (Of course the disloyalty—negligence dichotomy became moot in the Cheff case when the Supreme Court reversed and absolved all the directors; and it is hard to know what to make of the Supreme Court's criticism of the Vice-Chancellor's distinction between interested and disinterested directors, because of the puzzling role of the fact that some of the shareholders had expressed a willingness to buy Maremont's stock on their own.) More attention was paid to this element in the Bennett decision where the court released the directors who had not participated in the original repurchase transaction only after finding that they had not violated their duty of care in "ratifying" the challenged stock repurchases.

Does this analysis square with the Supreme Court's insistence in the Bennett case that the president of the corporation, Ward, was held liable not for negligence but "for the tort of using corporate funds to maintain control"? That this "tort" is not absolute is clear from the court's release of the other directors from liability—so it would seem that either negligence or disloyalty is an essential ingredient. Yet it does not appear that the court was finding Ward guilty of disloyalty in the normal sense—for the court stressed "his silence and failure to act" in connection with Sadacca's purchases rather than any affirmative desire to preserve his own position. Perhaps the answer is that Ward was so subservient to Sadacca that his conduct transcended imprudence and even inattentiveness, and amounted to "disloyalty" in the sense of putting Sadacca's interests ahead of those of the corporation.

SECTION 9. TAX INCIDENTS OF STOCK REPURCHASES

A. HISTORICAL BACKGROUND

HERWITZ, STOCK REDEMPTIONS AND THE ACCUMULATED EARNINGS TAX [37]
74 Harv.L.Rev. 886–898 (1961).

The roots of the present scheme for taxation of stock redemptions lie in the Revenue Act of 1924. That statute defined "amounts distributed in partial liquidation" to include distributions "in complete cancellation or redemption of . . . stock," * and provided that such distributions should be treated as in full payment in exchange for the stock, thus extending the benefits of capital gains treatment to such transactions.[56] There is no clear indication of what kinds of cor-

---

[37]. Copyright (c), Harvard Law Review Association, 1961. Most of the footnotes omitted.

*[Ed. note] For convenience, this provision and its successors will sometimes be referred to as the "definitional section."

[56]. The concept of "partial liquidation" was new in the Revenue Act of 1924. Until that time, distributions in cancellation of redemption of a portion of stock had apparently been treated in the same way as distributions in complete liquidation of a corporation. However, distributions in complete liquidation had themselves had a checkered career up to 1924. Before 1918, no special treatment was accorded to liquidating distributions; they were governed by the general provision which treated every distribution out of the earnings and profits of a corporation as a dividend. E. g., Revenue Act of 1916, § 31(a), ... Accordingly, gain on liquidation was taxed as a dividend to the extent of accumulated earnings and profits. Actually, this was advantageous to the shareholders, since dividends were subject only to the surtax, not to the normal tax, whereas gains from the sale or exchange of property were subject to both the surtax and normal tax . . . .

This advantage was eliminated in the Revenue Act of 1918, ch. 18, § 201(c), . . . which provided that amounts distributed in the liquidation of the corporation should be treated as payments in exchange for the stock. The act made no reference to either partial liquidations or redemptions. The Revenue Act of 1921, ch. 136, 42 Stat. 227, dropped the provision dealing with liquidating distributions, thus restoring the pre-1918 pattern. Frank D. Darrow, 8 B.T.A. 276 (1927). Presumably, the reason for this change was to prevent liquidation distributions from qualifying for the newly instituted alternative tax on capital gains. . . . But such transactions did become eligible for this favored treatment in 1924, when the exchange treatment for distributions in complete liquidation was reinstated and extended to distributions in partial liquidation. . . .

That proved to be a temporary highwater mark for partial liquidations. In 1926, because of concern about the use of partial liquidations to distribute accumulated earnings and profits without dividend tax, § 201(c) of the Revenue Act of 1924, [set out in the text just prior to note 80, infra] which had dealt only with cancellation or redemption of stock issued as a stock dividend, was amended to provide for dividend treatment whenever "a corporation cancels or redeems its stock . . . at such time and in such manner as to make the distribution and cancellation or redemption in whole or in part essentially equiva-

porate transactions were intended to be favored by this provision. Certainly the basic term "partial liquidation" provides no assistance in this regard. It was not a phrase drawn from the common corporate parlance of the day; there appears to be no use of the term "partial liquidation" in the corporate statutes, decisions or treatises of that period.[57] Indeed, even the term "liquidation" seems to have been an uncommon one in the corporate materials, which were more accustomed to use "dissolution" to refer to the complete winding up of a corporation's affairs. The corporate materials are also barren of any reference to "partial dissolution," which might well have been considered as much a self-contradictory concept as "partial incorporation."

The term "partial liquidation," standing alone, might have referred to any pro rata distribution out of the capital of the corporation—that is, any distribution which reduced the amount of the corporation's net assets below the amount of capital originally invested by the shareholders in the enterprise. Such a return to the shareholders of a portion of the original investment would constitute a *pro tanto* dissolution of the enterprise. . . . [By] 1924 almost every corporation statute contained authorization to reduce stated capital, . . . thus making it possible for the corporation to distribute to shareholders a portion of the original capital contribution. Such a

---

lent to the distribution of a taxable dividend." Revenue Act of 1926, ch. 27, § 201(g). . . . [For convenience this provision and its successors will sometimes be referred to as the "essentially-equivalent section."]

This pattern remained unchanged until the Revenue Act of 1934, which stripped distributions in both complete liquidation and partial liquidation of their eligibility for capital gains treatment. . . . In 1936, favorable capital gains treatment was reinstituted for distributions in complete liquidation, but not for distributions in partial liquidation. . . . Not until 1942 were partial liquidations restored to the same footing as complete liquidations. . . . See H.R.Rep. No. 2333, 77th Cong. 2d Sess. 93 (1942):

> Inequity results . . . under the existing law in the case of unquestionable bona fide redemptions of stock not equivalent in any way to the distribution of a taxable dividend. It is believed that the proper application of section 115(g) [the "essentially-equivalent section"] will prove adequate to prevent taxable dividends disguised as liquidations from receiving capital gain treatment.

57. A partial return of capital to the shareholders was usually treated under the heading of "reduction of capital." See, e. g., I Cook, Corporations § 279 (8th Ed. 1923). . . .

The term "partial liquidation" had, however, appeared in several published rulings of the Treasury promulgated prior to the enactment of the Revenue Act of 1924. In I.T. 2034, III-1 Cum.Bull. 47 (1924), the term was applied to a series of distributions in complete liquidation of a corporation; this meaning was expressly included in the statutory definition of the term in the Revenue Act of 1924, ch. 234, § 201(g), 43 Stat. 255. In Sol.Op. 115, 5 Cum.Bull. 47 (1921), the term "partial liquidation" was applied to a transaction consisting of a consolidation of two banks, in the course of which both banks contributed less than all of their assets to the new enterprise and distributed the remaining assets pro rata to their respective shareholders in exchange for a portion of their stock. In I.T. 1543, II-1 Cum.Bull. 17 (1923), a transaction involving an assignment of accounts receivable by a corporation to its shareholders pro rata in exchange for a portion of their stock was described as "partial liquidation."

distribution could appropriately be described as a "partial liquidation." And as a matter of fact the portion of the definition of "partial liquidation" under the Revenue Act of 1924 relating to distributions in "cancellation" of stock almost surely referred to capital-reduction transactions, since cancellation of stock is normally conditioned upon full compliance with the statutory formalities for reduction of capital.

Still, it is hard to believe that capital-reduction transactions played any important role in the extension of favorable exchange treatment to "partial liquidations" under the 1924 statute. Presumably, only a corporation which did not have sufficient surplus otherwise to justify a distribution to shareholders would resort to a capital reduction in order to clear the way for a distribution.* Actually capital reduction seems to have been designed primarily to enable a corporation which had more assets than it could usefully or profitably employ in its business—perhaps because the enterprise had never assumed the full proportions expected, or because of a contraction in the scope of its operations—to return those excess assets to the shareholders despite the absence of sufficient surplus. But such a return of the original capital investment to the shareholders required no special legislation to escape the dividend tax. And if the corporation had a substantial surplus, so that there would be a possibility of a heavy dividend tax in the absence of some saving legislation, there would be no occasion for capital reduction since the excess assets could be returned to the shareholders by way of an ordinary dividend.

The question then arises as to what type of corporate transaction was contemplated by the language in the definition of "partial liquidation" referring to "redemption . . . of . . . stock." One obvious possibility is a corporate repurchase of stock other than for cancellation or retirement and hence outside any capital-reduction proceeding. Preliminarily, this presents some difficulties of construction. By the 1920's there was increasing recognition that repurchase of stock (apart from an authorized capital-reduction proceeding) should be limited to the amount of surplus available for dividends in order to prevent impairment of capital. Nevertheless, it was still common at that time to disregard this stricture by treating the reacquired stock as an asset, "treasury stock," to be carried with the rest of the corporation's assets on the balance sheet.[71] The alleged justification for this procedure was that the treasury stock had been reacquired not for retirement but rather to be held by the corporation, presumably pending a later resale.

Of course, a repurchase of stock to be held in the treasury did not constitute a "cancellation" of stock under the tax statute, since by

---

*[Ed. note] See note 89, infra.

71. Since treasury stock is not really an asset in any sense in the corporation's hands, this procedure masked the fact that net assets had been diminished by the amount of the distribution in reacquisition of the stock. . . .

hypothesis there would be no cancellation or retirement of the reacquired stock. But there is room for doubt as to whether the term "redemption" covers this kind of transaction. For one thing, the failure to use the more common corporate term "repurchase" is puzzling, since the attention then being paid to this subject must have made that term a familiar one. The word "redemption" could be limited to the very narrow sense of retirement of stock by the exercise of a power to call it expressly granted by the original contract.[73] Or, perhaps under the doctrine of *ejusdem generis,* "redemption" could be confined, somewhat less narrowly, to reacquisition of stock for retirement. Such an argument might be buttressed by the observation that the statutory language, "cancellation or redemption," is itself a definition of the term "partial liquidation": A traditional repurchase of stock other than for retirement does not partake at all of the nature of a liquidation, since the reacquired stock is expected to be sold later to replenish the corporation's coffers.

On the other hand, the words "cancellation" and "redemption" are used in the alternative in the statute, and it may be proper to assume that some difference of meaning was intended. Certainly there is nothing in the word "redemption" itself which requires a physical cancellation or retirement of the stock involved. Moreover, the economic significance of the transaction to the selling shareholders upon whom the tax is imposed is not in any way affected by whether the corporation retires the stock which is reacquired or holds it in the treasury.

Furthermore, the legislative background of the statute provides strong evidence that the term "redemption" was intended to be broad enough to cover ordinary repurchase transactions. The language used to define "partial liquidation" under the 1924 Act seems to have been based upon section 201(d) of the Revenue Act of 1921, which provided:

> A stock dividend shall not be subject to tax but if after the distribution of any such dividend the corporation proceeds to cancel or redeem its stock at such time and in such manner as to make the distribution and cancellation or redemption essentially equivalent to the distribution of a taxable dividend, the amount received in redemption or cancellation of the stock shall be treated as a taxable dividend to the extent of the earnings or profits accumulated by such corporation after February 28, 1913.*

This section, incidentally, appears to have been the first example of the use of the term "redemption" in the tax statutes. Although

---

73. See Commissioner v. Snite, 177 F. 2d 819, 823 (7th Cir.1949): "A true redemption of stock, preferred or common, occurs when it is called and retired."

*[Ed. note] This is the earliest predecessor of the "essentially-equivalent" section.

here too it is curious that the term "repurchase" was not employed, it would be even more curious if the term "redemption" had been used in so limited a sense that the intended bite of the section could be avoided simply by holding repurchase stock in the treasury instead of retiring it. Rather the term "redemption" must have been designed to include repurchase transactions under the 1921 statute; and there is no basis for inferring a narrower meaning in the 1924 Act.[80]

A more difficult question under this statute is whether pro rata distributions in reacquisition of stock were eligible for this favored tax treatment. Actually, so far as cancellation of stock pursuant to a capital reduction is concerned, such a transaction normally must be made available to all the shareholders pro rata, in the absence of a specific statutory provision to the contrary; but as we already have seen, capital-reduction transactions were obviously not a primary object of the 1924 legislation anyway. But it could be argued that even ordinary repurchase transactions had to be pro rata to qualify as redemptions under the statute. Unless the repurchase was pro rata from all the shareholders, the transaction would seem to lack an essential ingredient of a liquidation proceeding, and hence would not fit under the governing general term, "partial liquidation." Of course it is hard to believe that the legislature meant to single out for favored treatment any type of stock-reacquisition transaction which involved pro rata distribution to all of the shareholders by a corpora-

---

80. The courts have been far from uniform in their construction of these provisions. . . . Most of the early cases . . . held that a reacquisition of stock came within the language "cancellation or redemption," regardless of whether the reacquired stock was cancelled or held in the treasury. . . . However, several courts, particularly the Court of Appeals for the Second Circuit, took the view that there was no "cancellation or redemption" . . . when the repurchased stock was to be held in the treasury instead of being cancelled. . . . The effect of these decisions was that such a transaction was not a "partial liquidation" and hence did not qualify for whatever treatment was accorded partial liquidations under the particular revenue act. Most of these cases involved taxable years between 1934 and 1942, during which time partial liquidations were not eligible for the favorable capital-gains treatment extended to such transactions between 1921 and 1934, and after 1942. See note 56, supra. Thus in these cases the Commissioner was the party arguing that the transaction constituted a "partial liquidation" within the meaning of the governing revenue act, while the taxpayer was contending that the transaction constituted an ordinary sale of a capital asset by the shareholder to the corporation. This juxtaposition of the parties is somewhat reminiscent of the even more striking departure from the norm, judged by modern standards, which occurred prior to 1924, when taxpayers actually argued for ordinary dividend treatment for partial—liquidation distributions in order to escape the normal tax. See note 56 supra.

Although this alleged distinction between a "sale" and a "partial liquidation" ceased to be important in the cases under [the definitional section] after favorable capital-gains treatment for partial liquidations was reinstituted in 1942, its impact began to be felt in the cases under [the essentially-equivalent section] . . . However, more recently most of the courts, including the Court of Appeals for the Second Circuit, have abandoned this distinction in favor of the view that a repurchase of stock to be held in the treasury nevertheless constitutes a "redemption." This is also the result under the 1954 Code. Int.Rev.Code of 1954, § 317. . . .

tion with accumulated earnings. Even in 1924 it must have been clear that such a transaction had no corporate significance which distinguished it from an ordinary dividend. And of course this is even more obvious when the transaction consists of an ordinary repurchase of stock which is limited under state law to the amount of available surplus. It is equally clear that a pro rata redemption of stock does not materially affect the interest of any of the shareholders. Hence, there is no analogy between the sale of stock by a shareholder (or even a pro rata sale by all of the shareholders) to a third party and a pro rata repurchase by the corporation.

Nevertheless, the broad language used in defining "partial liquidation" in section 201(c) of the 1924 statute left little doubt that pro rata reacquisition transactions could qualify, whether or not they were the exclusive beneficiaries of this favored treatment. This was certainly the view of Congress in 1926, when [the original version of the "essentially-equivalent" section was expanded to cover redemptions of stock not issued as a stock dividend]. The purpose of this amendment was clearly to subject pro rata stock redemptions to dividend treatment.

As a matter of fact, the phenomenon of pro rata repurchase of stock by a corporation with accumulated earnings probably developed almost exclusively as a result of the apparent tax inducement to this kind of transaction provided by the 1924 Revenue Act. An even more absurd companion piece was the practice, which likewise seems to have been unknown prior to the 1924 statute, of a corporation with substantial accumulated earnings undergoing a capital reduction effected by a pro rata repurchase of stock from all the shareholders. As we have seen, such a capital reduction is an entirely unnecessary proceeding from a corporate point of view;[89] and the independent legal significance of such a proceeding would be extremely limited, consisting of only a slight impairment of the corporation's ability to obtain credit in the future by virtue of its reduced stated capital and modest statutory burdens with regard to existing creditors. The explanation for undertaking such a useless formality must be that imaginative counsel thought their chances for qualifying a transaction as a "partial liquidation" under the 1924 statute would be strengthened by clothing it in corporate paraphernalia containing some liquidation elements.

89. An exception might be noted for the case in which the corporation has capitalized accumulated earnings by a stock dividend, and subsequently its stated capital as thus increased has become impaired. Although for tax purposes the corporation's accumulated earnings and profits would not have been affected by the stock dividend, for corporate purposes a reduction of capital would be necessary to enable the corporation to make any distribution to shareholders. . . . Even in this type of case, however, reduction of capital to eliminate the existing impairment of capital does not require any accompanying distribution. . . .

[If pro rata stock reacquisitions are eliminated], what kinds of transactions were left to be covered by the statutory phrase "partial liquidation"? There are certain types of non pro rata repurchases which could be regarded as akin to a liquidation and hence within the contemplation of that term. Take the case of the closely held corporation, where one of the small number of stockholders wishes to sell his interest. Here the alleged corporate advantage of ready transferability of interest in the enterprise may prove to be more myth than reality. In fact, the market for such shares may be limited to the other shareholders and the corporation itself. If the other shareholders are unwilling to purchase such shares either directly, or indirectly through a corporate repurchase, the shareholder who desires to sell may find himself frozen into the enterprise even more completely than a partner in similar circumstances. Unlike a partner, a shareholder has no power to terminate the enterprise unless he happens to have the necessary statutory majority. Even if the remaining shareholders are willing to purchase the shares, it is frequently true that only the corporation is in a position to finance the transaction.

From the point of view of the selling shareholder, a sale to the corporation is no different from a complete liquidation of the corporation. Presumably, the purchase price would approximate what the selling shareholders would receive upon a sale of the business pursuant to an orderly liquidation. A corporate repurchase thus permits the liquidation of a particular shareholder's interest without involving the corporation in the expense and complications inherent in a complete liquidation, and without incurring a tax on the other shareholders.

Here is a transaction to which it certainly would have been rational to extend the favorable tax treatment applicable to complete liquidations. Moreover, it seems to fit the statutory language: Such a transaction could well be regarded as a "partial liquidation"—a vertical rather than horizontal partial liquidation. And including distributions both in cancellation and in redemption of stock would be consistent with a legislative purpose aimed primarily at this type of transaction, since the tax incidents of the transaction should not depend on whether or not the corporation retires the stock—a factor beyond the control of the selling shareholder.

If favorable tax treatment for stock redemptions had been expressly limited at the outset to transactions involving all of the stock of one or more shareholders, most of the difficulties which have beset this area over the years would have been avoided. But perhaps that would have been too harsh a standard. It is at least arguable that non-pro rata redemptions which substantially affect the ownership interests among the shareholders should also be eligible for such treatment, even though there is no complete termination of the interest of any shareholder. There are even some pro rata redemptions which could appropriately be included, as for example where the proceeds of a termination of one or more of a corporation's separate businesses are distributed in redemption of stock. Although favorable treatment for this kind of transaction may well stem originally from a misconception of the scope and function of a capital reduction under corporate law, such treatment is defensible. It simply amounts to treating the liquidation of a portion of a business which could have been carried on as a separate enterprise as though it had been so carried on. Of course it is true that the corporation has enjoyed whatever benefits flow from carrying on the separate enterprises in a single corporation, such as offsetting the gains and losses of the various parts of the business. But since the tax advantages of multiple corporations are usually regarded as outweighing the potential disadvantages, it would not be untoward to extend to the single corporation a privilege automatically enjoyed by the multicorporation operation.

B. IMPACT OF A REDEMPTION UPON THE WITHDRAWING SHAREHOLDERS

1. IN GENERAL—§ 302

ESTATE OF ARTHUR H. SQUIER v. COMMISSIONER

United States Tax Court, 1961. 35 T.C. 950.

[At the time of the decedent's death early in 1954, he owned just over 50% of the stock of a corporation engaged in the industrial supply business. Decedent's wife owned approximately 9%, a trust for his grandchild owned 4%, and the remaining 37% of the stock was owned by one Schilling. In 1952 the decedent, Schilling, and the corporation had entered into a stock purchase agreement under which, upon the death of either of the individuals, their representatives had the option to sell to the corporation up to 30% of their stock at a price based upon book value.

Shortly after the decedent's death, an officer of the decedent's corporate executor was elected a director of the corporation to replace the decedent. The decedent's wife demanded that her son-in-law be named the new president of the corporation, but the executor refused, partly because of doubts as to whether the son-in-law had the necessary maturity and experience to manage the corporation, and partly because it was feared that the long-time general manager of the corporation might leave if the son-in-law became president. Instead, the general manager was made president, with the support of Schilling, which created considerable friction among the parties.

Early in 1955, in order to raise some needed additional cash the executor exercised the option to sell 30% of the estate's stock to the corporation. This redemption reduced the estate's interest in the corporation to approximately 41%, while increasing decedent's wife's interest to about 11%, the trust's interest to about 5%, and Schilling's interest to about 43%.

Shortly after the redemption, Schilling became ill and had to limit his activities. Because of concern about the relations among the stockholders, the executor sought to persuade the shareholders to sell out to some outside purchaser, which the parties finally did late in 1955.

For the last five years the corporation's net income had averaged more than $100,000 per year, and it had paid dividends of approximately $10,000 per year. The Commissioner determined that the redemption of stock from the estate in 1955 was essentially equivalent to a dividend.]

RAUM, JUDGE: The contentions of the parties have revolved largely around the applicability of our recent decision in Thomas G. Lewis, 35 T.C. [71].

We are satisfied that had this case arisen under Section 115(g) of the 1939 Code, rather than under Section 302 of the 1954 Code, the redemptions herein would not be treated as essentially equivalent to the distribution of a taxable dividend. Does the 1954 Code require a different result here? In the Lewis case we found that the 1954 Code did call for a holding that the redemption there considered was essentially equivalent to a taxable dividend. Our conclusion was based to a significant extent upon the fact that when the attribution rules of Section 318 were applied the estate in that case would have to be treated as the sole owner of 100 per cent of the corporate stock, and that an appraisal of the record facts upon that assumption called for a finding that the redemption was essentially equivalent to a taxable dividend.

We do not reach the same conclusion on this record, even after applying the attribution rules of section 318. In this case, a substantial minority interest, not covered by the attribution rules, was held by Otto Schilling, and it rose from 36.70 per cent before the redemption in controversy to 43.18 per cent thereafter. Moreover, the record herein reveals a sharp cleavage between the executor and members of the Squier family, and in spite of the attribution rules as to stock "ownership", the redemptions herein in fact resulted in a crucial reduction of the estate's *control* over the corporation. Accordingly, notwithstanding the attribution rules, the redemptions in this case did result in a substantial dislocation of relative stockholdings in the corporation and also in fact brought about a significant change in control. We think these circumstances serve to distinguish the Lewis case. In addition, there are certain other considerations which to some degree further differentiate this case from Lewis. Thus, unlike the Lewis case where there was a history of failure to pay dividends over a long period, the corporation in the present case had annually declared a dividend (albeit a conservative one) for a number of years prior to the redemptions. Moreover, the redemptions herein did not result in a pro rata distribution since Otto Schilling's large minority interest received nothing—a circumstance that was absent in the Lewis case upon application of the attribution rules. Taking the entire record into account we are satisfied that even after applying the attribution rules here the redemptions in controversy were not essentially equivalent to the distribution of a taxable dividend.

In Bradbury v. Commissioner, 298 F.2d 111 (1st Cir. 1962), the petitioner had organized a new corporation to carry on a lumber manufacturing business formerly conducted by her deceased husband. The petitioner originally obtained all of the stock of the new corporation, but after gifts to her daughter and son-in-law she ended up owning 177 shares, while her daughter owned 86 shares, and her son-in-law 25. From its inception, the corporation maintained an open account for petitioner on its books, which represented advances made to her from time to time at her request. Although petitioner's salary and her share of any dividends were credited to this account, petitioner was continuously indebted to the corporation. After 1953 the corporation paid no dividends, and by July of 1956, the petitioner owed the corporation some $21,000. Shortly before that date, it became necessary for the corporation to replace some obsolete facilities, and the corporation sought to borrow the necessary funds from a bank which had extended short-term financing from time to time. The officers of the bank indicated that they "did not like" the large indebtedness due to the corporation from the petitioner, and recommended that petitioner's account be "cleaned up some way". Thereafter, on July 2, 1956, petitioner transferred 44 shares of her stock to the corporation, which credited her account with approximately $22,500, giving her a slight credit balance. On the basis of the financial statements reflecting this transaction, the bank made a loan to the corporation of $12,000 for a five year term.

The Commissioner determined that this redemption was essentially equivalent to a dividend, and was sustained by the Tax Court. In affirming the decision of the Tax Court, the Court of Appeals applied the attribution of ownership rules of § 318 to attribute the stock of petitioner's daughter to her, with the result that petitioner's percentage ownership of stock before the redemption was 91.3% and after amounted to 89.7%. The court said:

> These figures abundantly demonstrate that despite a transaction which resulted in an economic benefit to petitioner of some $22,489.28, the total effect of the redemption was to effectuate no basic change in the ownership or control of the corporation.

In terms of economic realities the relationship between the shareholders *inter se* and *vis a vis* the corporation remained basically unaltered. Moreover, while the economic increment flowed solely to petitioner and, thus, was not strictly speaking a *pro-rata* distribution, in view of the dominant position of petitioner—owning 91.3 percent of the stock—it was virtually so. . . .

The determination that a distribution in redemption has worked an essentially *pro rata* distribution and produced no material or significant shift in the corporate-shareholder relationship does not, of course, terminate inquiry into whether the transaction which produced these results was or was not essentially equivalent to a dividend. We simply say that in the hierarchy of criteria which may be adduced as evidentiary of this ultimate conclusion these factors must be accorded a preeminent position. And, where they are present, the record must contain conspicuously countervailing considerations to dispel the aura of dividend equivalence which their presence irresistibly impels. We do not find these countervailing considerations present here.

As noted previously, petitioner's principal rebuttal to the determination of dividend equivalence is the assertion that the instant redemption was actuated by a legitimate business purpose. In essence she argues that the generating force behind the transaction was a desire to benefit or assist the corporation as opposed to the purpose of benefiting her as an individual shareholder. She argues that the finding of the Tax Court that the redemption was not prompted by a business purpose was erroneous and that a proper finding in this regard would remove the transaction from the essential equivalence proscription.

We believe that the record justifies petitioner's contention that the transaction was undoubtedly impelled by a legitimate business purpose of the Bradbury Corporation. We believe that the Tax Court placed undue emphasis on the fact that in the past the bank was in the practice of making short term loans to the corporation on specific consignments of lumber despite the presence of the substantial debit balance in the personal account of petitioner. Surely, different considerations might be involved where the bank was asked to grant the corporation a long term construction loan. Consequently, we are entirely willing to believe the petitioner when she says that the fundamental reason behind her transfer of stock was to accord with the stated wishes of the bank that the account be "cleaned up." To be sure the record indicates that petitioner was herself responsible for selecting the specific mode of cleansing which was ultimately settled upon and so in that sense the proximate cause of the transaction stemmed from the shareholder level rather than the corporate level.

However, on this record to concede that the cancellation of the petitioner's indebtedness might be regarded as a corporate business purpose and that it was the efficient cause of the transaction is not to foreclose a finding of "essential equivalence." We believe that United States v. Fewell, 255 F.2d 496 (5 Cir. 1958), where it was held that showing of a business purpose for the redemption, viz., to improve the credit standing of the corporation, does not conclusively prevent a determination of dividend equivalence, establishes the true rule. As the court stated in Fewell: ". . . we are convinced that the mere existence of a single bona fide corporate purpose will not, standing alone, conclusively determine that the transaction does not result in an essential equivalent of the distribution of a taxable dividend." Id. at 500. . . .

In a proper case, the presence of a legitimate corporate business purpose may well be relevant as an offsetting factor to a determination of dividend equivalence. However, we believe that for business purpose to be of really meaningful import the dichotomy between shareholder and corporation must be more sharply drawn than is the case here. In a case such as the instant one, while, on the verbal level, there may be a conceptually distinct corporate and shareholder purpose, as a matter of economic import, it is unrealistic to attempt to segregate them. The separateness of the shareholders in a widely held corporation or the minority position of a particular shareholder in a closely held corporation make considerations of legitimate corporate business purpose a more eminently vital consideration than here where the shareholder is but the shadow of the corporation. Here in terms of business purpose, the shareholder cannot realistically be divorced from the board of directors. It would, consequently, be unwarranted to turn the presence or absence of dividend equivalence on a distinction where there is really no difference. The record indicates that petitioner as the dominant stockholder of the Bradbury Corporation incurred the $22,000 debit balance with the corporation as a result of withdrawing money to meet her personal expenses. Had she initially redeemed her stock to obtain this money the transaction would undoubtedly be treated as a dividend. The only real distinction between such a case and the instant transaction is that it is now asserted that the bank's request that the indebtedness be eliminated furnishes a corporate business purpose. However, in substance there is no material distinction between the two situations; in each the redemption can be ultimately traced to the fact that the stockholder obtained an economic benefit from the corporation in satisfaction of her personal needs.

NOTE ON § 302

a. **Introduction.** The 1954 Code provided redemption transactions with two "safe harbors" from dividend treatment: the "substantially disproportionate" test of subsection (b)(2), which requires a specified decrease in the taxpayer's percentage ownership of voting stock (and all common stock as well, if non-voting common is present); and the complete termination test of subsection (b)(3), which requires all of the taxpayer's stock to have been redeemed. However, even if these tests are not met the taxpayer may still avoid dividend treatment under the general standard of § 302(b)(1), which requires that the distribution be "not essentially equivalent to a dividend."

b. **Substantially Disproportionate Redemption.** Under prior law it had generally been held that when a redemption substantially altered the taxpayer's voting strength, dividend treatment was not justified. E.g., Ferris v. United States, 133 Ct.Cl. 257, 135 F.Supp. 286 (1955) (ownership of voting stock reduced from 63% to 48.5%). Section 302(b)(2) attempts to provide greater certainty in this area with its mathematical test of "substantially disproportionate", which will assure non-dividend treatment if satisfied. The two components of this test are, first, that the taxpayer's percentage ownership of voting stock be reduced to less than 80% of his former percentage (with the same requirement as to the taxpayer's percentage ownership of all common stock if some of the common stock is non-voting); and second, after the redemption the taxpayer must own less than 50% of the total combined voting power of the corporation's stock. Notice that although a qualifying redemption of voting stock can also carry with it a simultaneous redemption of non-voting stock, Reg. § 1.302–3(a), a redemption of some of a taxpayer's non-voting stock, whether preferred or common, cannot by itself qualify under subsection (b)(2) and is left instead to § 302(b)(1). Of course the question of how disproportionate the redemption was is also relevant under the general non-equivalent standard, but it becomes much harder to judge when non-voting stock is involved. See Himmel v. Commissioner, 338 F.2d 815 (2d Cir. 1964), holding, after a thoughtful analysis of the issue, that a redemption of a portion of a taxpayer's preferred stock was sufficiently disproportionate to satisfy the non-equivalence test of § 302(b)(1).

Pursuant to § 302(c)(1), the substantially disproportionate test must be judged in the light of the attribution of ownership rules of § 318, which provide an extensive network of constructive ownership of stock. Thus stock may be attributed between members of a family, or between a trust or estate and its beneficiaries, or a partnership and its partners, or a corporation and its controlling stockholders. There may also be reattribution of stock—that is, stock which is "owned" constructively by virtue of the attribution rules may itself be attributed to someone else under the rules. However, there are some limits on reattribution. From the outset the statute precluded reattribution under the family attribution rules. And reattribution was further narrowed by the 1964 amendments to § 318 which eliminated so-called "sidewise" reattribution, that is, attribution from a beneficiary to an estate or trust for the purpose of reattributing the stock to another beneficiary, or from a partner through the partnership to another partner, or the like. See § 318(a)(5)(B) and (C).

The rule of § 302(b)(2)(D) that the proportionality of a distribution must be tested by the overall consequences of all the related steps in a plan was also recognized under prior law. Thus in the related cases of Boyle v. Commissioner, 187 F.2d 557 (3d Cir. 1951), and Tiffany v. Commissioner, 16 T.C. 1443 (1951), a corporation with three equal stockholders redeemed all but 300 shares from two of them, A and B, and all of the stock of C. B then transferred his remaining shares to D and E, who were already associated with the corporation; D and E also bought some stock from the corporation, so that A, D and E ended up owning the stock in equal thirds just as A, B and C had originally. While it was held in Tiffany that the redemption transaction was not a dividend to B, because he no longer retained any interest in the corporation, in Boyle the redemption was held to constitute a taxable dividend to A. But query the result in the Boyle case, since the parties only ended up where they would have if the corporation had redeemed all of the stock of B and C and then A had sold one-third of his stock to each of D and E, in which event there would have been no basis for finding a dividend to A. On the other hand, United States v. Carey, 289 F.2d 531 (8th Cir. 1961), which in somewhat similar circumstances reached the result contrary to Boyle, seems clearly to have gone too far the other way in insisting that a transaction involving the redemption of an equal number of shares from equal shareholders must have the same tax consequences to the stockholders, so that since the redemption was not taxable as a dividend to one of them (because he had immediately sold the rest of his stock to a third party in a related transaction), it could not be taxable as a dividend to the other, even though he retained the rest of his stock.

c. **Complete Termination of Interest.** Since the complete termination of a shareholder's interest is the polar example of a disproportionate distribution, such a distribution was generally not subject to dividend treatment under prior law. This view is now expressly codified in § 302(b)(3), subject, however, to the § 318 attribution rules. But § 302(c)(2) provides for a waiver of the *family* attribution rules of § 318(a)(1) in certain circumstances, subject to a series of intricate qualifications. First, the distributee must end up with no interest in or position with the corporation other than as a creditor (which raises a number of issues with regard to whether purported "debt" is really debt, see Reg. § 1.302–4(d)). Second, the distributee must not acquire any such interest in or position with the corporation within ten years after the date of the redemption distribution (exclusive of an acquisition of stock by bequest or inheritance). As a corollary of this second qualification the distributee is required to file with his return an agreement that he will notify the Government of any such acquisition; and there is an accompanying extension of the statute of limitations for the assessment of any deficiency resulting from such an acquisition to at least one year beyond the date on which the distributee does give such notice. Third, the waiver of the family attribution rules is not available if the stock redeemed was acquired by the distributee within a prior 10-year period from a person whose stock would be attributable to the distributee (as where a wife-distributee had received the redeemed stock from her husband) or where a person whose stock would be attributable to the distributee acquired stock from the distributee during the 10-year period (as where it is the stock of the husband which is redeemed in the example just given). This third qualification is in turn subject to the limitation that it only applies if the transfer in question was tax-avoidance motivated.

In addition to these express qualifications a further limitation on the waiver of family attribution rules under § 302(c)(2) has been introduced by Rev.Rul. 59–233, 1959–2 Cum.Bull. 106, which holds that the waiver applies only to a family attribution which is the last link in the chain of attribution to the distributee, and not to an attribution under the family rules at some earlier point in the attribution chain. The ruling involved a redemption of the stock owned by a trust created under the will of a deceased mother for the benefit of her children. The father was the only other stockholder of the corporation, and by attribution of his stock to the children and then to the trust the latter constructively owned 100% of the stock. According to the ruling, since the family attribution (from the father to the children) was not the last link in the attribution chain, it was not waived under § 302(c). Notice that if the redemption of stock had been from the father instead of the trust, Rev.Rul. 59–233 would not present any obstacle since now the attribution chain would be from trust to children to father, and the family attribution would be the last link in the chain.

It is far from clear just how the Service arrived at its conclusion in Rev.Rul. 59–233. The ruling purports to rely on the Senate Report (No. 1622, 83d Cong., 2d Sess. 235–236), but there does not appear to be the slightest support for it there, unless it be the fact that the example used to illustrate § 302(c)(2) involves a family attribution which does happen to be the "last link" to the distributee. And so far as the statute itself is concerned, the generality of the § 302(c)(2) language, that "section 318(a) shall not apply", would seem to cut against any limitation of the sort imposed by the ruling.

A difficulty has arisen in connection with the requirement that the distributee file an agreement to notify the Government of any acquisition of a prohibited interest in, or position with, the corporation within the specified ten-year period after the redemption. In Archbold v. United States, 201 F. Supp. 329 (D.N.J.1962), affirmed per curiam, 311 F.2d 228 (3d Cir. 1963), the distributee had never filed the required agreement, but she offered to do so after a deficiency had been proposed in connection with the redemption. The court held that the Government was not bound to accept such a late filing. Under the court's view of the statute, unless an agreement was filed there was no extension of the period for assessment of deficiencies. Therefore, the court reasoned, if the distributee was free to file late, he could safely not file at the outset and run for luck that his return would not be audited within the regular three-year statute of limitations, in which event he could then acquire an interest or position with impunity.

However, in Van Keppel v. United States, 206 F.Supp. 42 (D.Kan.1962), affirmed 321 F.2d 717 (10th Cir. 1963), the trial court rejected the Archbold construction of the provision relating to the statute of limitations:

> Section 302(c)(2) provides for the assessment of tax deficiencies within one year after notice of reacquisition is given. The statute does not say that the one-year statute of limitation is ap-

plicable only if an agreement has been filed. It says the one-year statute of limitation applies if the taxpayer reacquires an interest within ten years. . . . If the statute of limitation extends to one year after notice, regardless of filed agreement, both the taxpayer and the Government are fully protected. Obviously, a filed agreement would make it easier for the Director to detect reacquisitions; but detection is not the essence of section 302(c)(2), since the taxpayer must notify the Director in order to set the one-year statute of limitations in motion.

In affirming, the Court of Appeals for the Tenth Circuit chose to distinguish Archbold, rather than to expressly disagree with its construction of the statute. The court noted that in the Van Keppel case the taxpayer contended that the failure to file the agreement was inadvertent; and the fact was that the moment the absence of an agreement was discovered during an audit, the taxpayer had promptly submitted an agreement to the Director which he did not reject. In the Archbold case, on the other hand, no agreement ever had been filed.

This issue came before the Tax Court for the first time in Cary v. Commissioner, 41 T.C. 214 (1963), in a situation where, as in Van Keppel, the failure to file an agreement was alleged to be inadvertent, and as soon as the absence of an agreement was discovered in the course of an audit an agreement was submitted which was not rejected by the Director. In an opinion reviewed by the full Court it was held that the requirement of filing an agreement was "directory rather than mandatory", and only substantial rather than strict compliance was required. The court expressly rejected the Archbold construction of the statute of limitations provision, and adopted the view taken by the District Court in the Van Keppel case. In addition, the Tax Court noted that the factual distinction relied upon by the Court of Appeals in the Van Keppel case were also present in Cary.

d. **Not Essentially Equivalent to a Dividend.** Since non-equivalence to a dividend was the test under the 1939 Code—indeed, the sole test—the prior case law dealing with non-equivalence continues to be relevant. But this provides scant comfort, since the prior authorities, like those under the present law, do not really afford much guidance about this general test. What does seem to emerge from the cases is that the single most important criterion of non-equivalence (apart from contraction of the enterprise, which under present law is relevant to partial liquidation under § 346, discussed below) is how disproportionate the redemption transaction was. As the Squier case illustrates, even though a redemption is not sufficiently disproportionate to qualify under the safe harbor of § 302(b)(2), it may still be disproportionate enough to satisfy the non-equivalence test. This is particularly so where, as in Squier, it is only by virtue of the attribution of ownership rules that the transaction fails to come within the "substantially disproportionate" safe harbor, and in fact the parties between whom stock is being attributed clearly do not have the community of interests which the attribution rules presume. Accord, Parker v. Commissioner, 20 T.C.M. 893 (1961). Conversely, where, as in the Bradbury case, the redemption transaction leaves the interests of the parties substantially unaffected, the chances of escaping a finding of essential equivalence are very slim indeed.

This primary dependence upon how disproportionate the redemption was seems entirely sound, since after all the starting point here is that a precisely pro rata redemption is exactly the same as a dividend. Therefore, essential equivalence properly turns upon how close to pro rata the transaction was. In any event, efforts to import notions of corporate business purpose into the essential equivalence area have not, as the Bradbury case illustrates, proved very helpful. Actually, the plain fact is that there is rarely any corporate purpose served by a redemption transaction. Take the Bradbury case itself, where it was urged that the impetus for the redemption transaction came from a bank which wanted the taxpayer's indebtedness "cleaned up" before the bank would advance funds. A somewhat similar contention was made in the Fewell case, cited in Bradbury, where it was argued that eliminating the indebtedness of stockholders to the corporation would "improve the credit standing" of the corporation. But how could a corporation be better off as a result of, in effect, surrendering a claim against a stockholder in exchange for something which has no value in the corporation's hands (i. e., its own stock)? See Moore v. Commissioner, 23 T.C.M. 103, 106 (1964) ("Furthermore, it is hard to understand how the cancellation of a debt owed to the corporation improves the corporation's financial picture.") This is particularly striking in the Bradbury case, since the corporation purported to give up a claim against the taxpayer for *$22,000 outright* in order to be able *to borrow approximately $12,000.*

One alleged corporate business purpose which has proved effective in some cases is that of enabling the corporation to acquire some stock which can subsequently be made available to key employees. See e. g., Commissioner v. Snite, 177 F.2d 819 (7th Cir. 1949). But obviously the corporation does not have to redeem stock to have some available for such purposes; it can use authorized but unissued stock, and if there is none, there is generally no difficulty in amending the certificate of incorporation to authorize additional shares. This was recently recognized in a strong opinion in Neff v. United States, 157 Ct.Cl. 322, 305 F.2d 455 (1962), vacating an earlier opinion to the contrary in the same case, 157 Ct.Cl. 304, 301 F.2d 330 (1962), which may well sound the death knell with regard to using the purpose of obtaining stock for resale as a justification for a proportionate redemption. See generally Moore, Dividend Equivalency—Taxation of Distributions in Redemption of Stock, 19 Tax.L.Rev. 249 (1964).

e. **Effect of Redemption on Basis.** Suppose a distribution in redemption of stock is made under circumstances which would make it essentially equivalent to a dividend, but there are no current or accumulated earnings and profits. Despite the verbal difficulty of calling such a distribution "essentially equivalent to a dividend", it is governed by §§ 302(d) and 301(c) rather than § 302(a). Reg. § 1.302–2(a). The distribution would thus be applied against the basis of all of the distributee's stock, including the redeemed stock, with taxable gain resulting only if the entire basis is exceeded, rather than being applied only against the basis of the stock redeemed.

When the entire amount of a redemption distribution is treated as a dividend, no allowance is made for the basis of the redeemed stock; but under Reg. § 1.302–2(c) such basis may be added to the basis of other stock held by the taxpayer. But what happens to that basis if the distributee does not own any other stock, as, for example, where a father owns common stock and a redemption of preferred stock from his son is considered a taxable dividend by virtue of the attribution rules? If the son's stock had come, directly or indirectly, from the father, presumably the father would be permitted to add the basis of the preferred to the basis of his other stock. Reg. § 1.302–2(c), Ex. 2. And if the father was not the source of the preferred, directly or indirectly, perhaps the transaction would not be regarded as essentially equivalent to a dividend, despite the attribution rules.

f. Rulings on Redemption Transactions. Particularly because of the high stakes so often involved, redemptions present an obvious case for seeking advance rulings from the Service as to the tax incidents of a proposed transaction. However, planning in the redemption area cannot quite be relegated to merely preparing requests for rulings. For one thing, the Service's general presumption against ruling on essentially factual questions will normally preclude obtaining an advance ruling on whether a redemption transaction is "essentially equivalent to a dividend." And there are also some narrower redemption issues on which rulings will not be available. See Rev. Proc. 64–31, § 3.01(5), page 99 supra.

---

2. REDEMPTION TO PAY ESTATE TAXES—§ 303

Section 303, first adopted in 1951, precludes dividend treatment for certain redemption distributions for the purpose of paying estate taxes, subject to the conditions of the section. By making the treasury of a closely-held corporation available as a source of funds at the death of a principal shareholder, the problem of meeting estate taxes may be materially eased.

The provision was justified as follows in Sen. Rep. No. 2375, 81st Cong., 2d Sess. (1950) 54:

> "It has been brought to the attention of your committee that the problem of financing the estate tax is acute in the case of estates consisting largely of shares in a family corporation. The market for such shares is usually very limited, and it is frequently difficult, if not impossible, to dispose of a minority interest. If, therefore, the estate tax cannot be financed through the sale of the other assets in the estate, the executors will be forced to dispose of the family business. In many cases the result will be the absorption of a family enterprise by larger competitors, thus tending to accentuate the degree of concentration of industry in this country."

Rev.Rul. 65–289, 1965–2 Cum.Bull. 86, holds that where stock was redeemed in exchange for an installment note having a fair market value equal to the face amount, there was a "distribution of property" within the meaning of § 303, "even though the note is not property of the corporation prior to delivery".

3. REDEMPTION THROUGH RELATED CORPORATIONS—§ 304

Section 304 is designed to prevent escape from the redemption-dividend rules by using related corporations to purchase stock. For example, suppose that the sole stockholder of Corporation A sells some of his A stock to Corporation B, a subsidiary of A. Under § 304, such a transaction is treated as a distribution from Corporation A. Or suppose that a stockholder owns all the stock of both A and B, and he sells some of his A stock to B. Here § 304 treats the transaction as a redemption of B stock and a contribution to its capital of A stock. (Under the attribution rules, this situation would also constructively involve a parent-subsidiary relationship, and hence might be treated the same as the first case.) See generally, Lanahan, Redemptions Through Use of Related Corporations, 18 N.Y.U.Fed. Tax Inst. 741 (1960). As to the treatment of a transaction which literally falls under both §§ 304 and 351, see Commissioner v. Haserot, 355 F.2d 200 (6th Cir. 1965).

4. PARTIAL LIQUIDATION—§ 346

McCARTHY v. CONLEY [38]

United States Court of Appeals, Second Circuit, 1965. 341 F.2d 948.

BLUMENFELD, DISTRICT JUDGE. This is an appeal from a summary judgment adverse to the appellant in a suit for refund of income taxes paid to satisfy deficiency assessments for the years 1954, 1955 and 1956. The taxpayer, Mrs. Lora McCarthy, owned 1000 shares of the stock of The Andrew Radel Oyster Company, a family corporation, which she had acquired through inheritance. In December 1954, she sold her shares to the corporation which paid for them with liquid assets it had accumulated out of earnings and profits over a long period. It was the taxpayer's use of a claimed loss on this transaction to offset income for the years in question that the District Director disallowed.

The court below found that there was no genuine issue of fact which would rebut the District Director's determination that the payment made by the corporation for the purchase of her stock was not a distribution in partial liquidation and ruled that the loss deduction was properly disallowed under § 267 of the 1954 Code [which disallows losses on sales or exchanges between related persons except "in cases of distributions in corporate liquidations"]. We agree.

The issues before us have been narrowed somewhat. The government has conceded that the payment received by the taxpayer from the corporation escapes dividend tax treatment as a distribution un-

---

38. Portions of the text and most of the court's footnotes omitted.

der § 302(b)(3) of the 1954 Code. The taxpayer has conceded that since her two sisters and her two brothers owned the remaining 4000 outstanding shares of stock, the transaction out of which the claimed loss arose was between related taxpayers as defined in § 267(b) and that the recognition of any loss is governed by § 267 of the Internal Revenue Code of 1954.

[The court first ruled that although the exception in § 267 for "distributions in corporate liquidations" may have included all redemption transactions under the pre-1954 law (as well as complete liquidations), because under that law all redemptions were characterized as "partial liquidations" (see page 000–000, supra), the result of the 1954 Code's separation of "redemptions" in § 302 from "partial liquidations" in § 346 was to confine the § 267 exception to those redemption transactions which came within § 346.]

Appellant's second argument is that even if the § 267 exception is limited to partial liquidations as defined in § 346, that definition includes all distributions in redemption which are not essentially equivalent to a dividend. This argument differs from her previous one only in that she makes it with reference to the definition of partial liquidation now found in § 346 of the 1954 Code . . . . We were unable to expand the exception in § 267 to make room for distributions not essentially equivalent to a dividend without regard to the definition of "partial liquidation" in § 346. We are equally unable to hold that a distribution not essentially equivalent to a dividend standing alone is a "partial liquidation" within that definition.

It is true that §§ 302 and 346 both contain the phrase "not equivalent to a dividend." But a reading of all the legislative history reveals congressional purpose to effect a *separation* of the two main tests which had formerly been applied to distributions in redemption of stock. Thus, the fact that the distribution received by her was not essentially equivalent to a dividend under § 302 because it resulted in a complete termination of her interest has no relevance here. Section 346 is plainly designed to go further in its demands. This is made all too clear by the specification in § 346(c):

> "The fact that, with respect to a shareholder, a distribution qualifies under section 302(a) . . . by reason of section 302(b) shall not be taken into account in determining whether the distribution, with respect to such shareholder, is also a distribution in partial liquidation of the corporation."

Taxpayer then takes another stand to argue that in any event contraction is not an absolutely essential element for a distribution to qualify under § 346. She relies upon the following portion of the Senate report as support for this contention:

> "Subsection (a) [of § 346] is intended to provide a definition of partial liquidation which replaces that contained in section 115(i) of the 1939 Code. *Primarily,* this definition involves

the concept of 'corporate contraction' as developed under existing law." (S.R.No.1622, 83d Cong. 2d Sess. 262, 3 U.S. Code Cong. & Adm.News 1954, p. 4899.) (Emphasis added)

Had Congress used the word "includes" in the § 346 definition of partial liquidation, we would be faced with 26 U.S.C. § 7701(b) of the 1954 Code: "The terms 'includes' and 'including' when used in a definition contained in this title shall not be deemed to exclude other things otherwise within the meaning of the term defined." But reading the Senate report in context, the word "primarily" is not misleading. It was not used to create a larger category of "partial liquidations," but to accent a predominant characteristic common to all which come within the statutory definition. It means that other requirements also have to be met, not a non-exclusivity allowing the use of all of the old pre-1954 tests. The requirements in § 346(a) (2) are not in the disjunctive. Thus, for a distribution to receive tax treatment as a partial liquidation, three requisites must be met: (1) It must not be essentially equivalent to a dividend; (2) It must be in redemption of part of the stock pursuant to a plan; and (3) It must occur within the taxable year.

However, it is urged that the term "partial liquidation" may include redemptions resulting from activities at the corporate level, or prompted by corporate needs, even though not involving a contraction. See Brodsky, Partial Liquidation: Definition of Partial Liquidation and Rules for Determining Termination of a Business, 15 Institute on Federal Taxation 539, 552 (1957). Examples suggested of such corporate needs are a corporation's desire to improve its credit rating or to make stock available to its employees. We find it unnecessary to pass upon this contention, for the only non-contraction purpose put forth by the taxpayer was a statement by her two brothers that they permitted the redemption to enable them alone to dissolve the corporation, *if they later so desired.* Under no theory could this be considered a corporate purpose. This was nothing other than a shareholder purpose, for it merely satisfied the wish of her brothers to gain control of the corporation to carry out their own ends.

The only question remaining is whether there was a "corporate contraction" pursuant to a "plan" under § 346. Both parties moved for summary judgment. The case was ripe for such disposition. It was not contended that there was a termination of a separate trade or business which would specifically qualify as a partial liquidation under § 346(b). Nor do we find any call for making a value judgment as to how much "corporate contraction" is necessary to constitute a partial liquidation under § 346(a). In determining that there was no genuine issue of fact as to whether there had been a partial liquidation, the court below properly took into account the concept of "corporate contraction" as developed under existing law by focusing attention on what took place at the corporate level. Nothing substantial was offered to challenge the District Director's determination that there was no immediately intended contraction of the corporation's business of producing, harvesting and selling oysters; a sale of certain oyster lands and facilities four years later, on the death of one of the two managing brothers, was properly deemed unrelated by the district judge. The purchase price of $128.50 per share was based on the then value of the *quick assets* of the firm other than inventory, less liabilities.[17] Nor were any balance sheets or operating statements presented in opposition to the appellee's motion for summary judgment.

The transaction in question was clearly not a vertical liquidation which chopped off a part of the productive resources of the enterprise. That portion of corporate capital remained intact. It was a horizontal slice off the top of a nest egg of securities accumulated from past earnings and profits which did not in any degree impair the business activities of the enterprise as they had been carried on before.[18]

Nor, as held by the court below, did anything exist to indicate a "plan."

The judgment is affirmed.

NOTE ON § 346

a. **Corporate Contraction.** The question left open in the McCarthy case as to how much "contraction" is required to qualify under § 346 is a troublesome one. This much is clear: it is not necessary to meet the mechanical test of § 346(b), since both the statute itself and the legislative history confirm that § 346(b) is a kind of "safe harbor", akin to those under § 302, so that capital gain treatment is assured if that subsection is satisfied but may also be obtained even if it is not. Some further guidance is afforded by the Report of the Senate Finance Committee, Sen. Rep. No. 1622, 83d Cong., 2d Sess. (1954) 262, which expressly approved Imler v. Commissioner, 11 T.C. 836 (1948) as a case of "genuine contraction of the business." That case involved a closely-held corporation which owned a seven story building and several smaller buildings, and was engaged in retinning and soldering metals as well as renting its excess space. A fire destroyed the upper two floors of the seven story building in 1941. Because of the shortage of building materials, the corporation did not rebuild those two floors. Since its facilities were no longer adequate to store materials for the retinning and

---

17. Although in excess of the $100 par, this was substantially less than the fair market value of the shares at the time of the deaths of her father and her mother which was the basis she used to compute the loss. Cf. Twining v. Commissioner, 83 F.2d 954 (2d Cir.) . . . .

18. Furthermore, the taxpayer did not deny that profits from the accumulated securities amounted to more than half a million dollars during the decade between 1950 and 1960. It was the proceeds of the sale of some of these securities that were used to effect the redemption, and while it is urged that they had been held as a contingency fund, the following passage from the Senate report on the Tax Code directly rejects that argument: "It is intended that a genuine contraction of the business as under present law will result in a partial liquidation. . . . However, a distribution of a reserve for expansion is not a partial liquidation." . . .

soldering activities, and the scarcity of materials had made those operations unprofitable anyway, the corporation discontinued them. It then distributed $15,000, which included the excess of the fire insurance proceeds over the repair costs, in a pro rata redemption of stock from its stockholders. *Held*, the redemption was not a dividend. The court stressed the bona fide contraction of business operations, the consequent reduction in needed capital, and the fact that except for the fire no distribution would have been made.

However, the question remains whether there must be a discontinuance of some specific line of activity, as in the Imler case, or whether simply reducing the scope of a single business can qualify. Rev. Rul. 60–322, 1960–2 Cum.Bull. 118, seems to require the former, at least where the source of the distribution is the profits earned by the enterprise in the past.

b. **Subsection 346(b).** Under the mechanical test of § 346(b), qualification as a partial liquidation is assured where two or more separate, active businesses have been conducted for at least five years, and one of them is discontinued, with its assets (or the proceeds of their sale) being distributed to the shareholders. A very similar five year, separate business test is employed in connection with corporate divisions under § 355, and will be considered in more detail in connection with that section in Chapter 6. Suffice it to note here that the regulations under § 355 provide some detailed examples of what constitutes "separate" businesses; there is also an illustration in Rev. Rul. 57–334, 1957–2 Cum. Bull. 240, which treats the operation of rental properties located in different states as separate, active businesses under § 346.

c. **Relation between § 302 and § 346.** A transaction may qualify under § 346 and not § 302, and vice versa; normally it would make little difference to the stockholders which section applied. However, there is one difference relating to basis: under § 346, the basis of the stock redeemed is determined by assuming that the number of shares surrendered bears the same ratio to the total number of shares as the amount of the distribution bears to the total value of the corporate assets prior to the distribution, Rev. Rul. 56–513, 1956–2 Cum. Bull. 191; under § 302, presumably the actual shares surrendered govern the determination of basis. In addition, qualification under § 346 precludes § 306 treatment, whereas qualification under § 302, other than as a complete termination of interest under subsection (b) (3), does not.

At the corporate level, a difference between the two sections arises in connection with distributions in kind. Some § 302 distributions in kind will subject the corporation to tax on any unrealized appreciation on the property, see § 311, and as a corollary, earnings and profits will be increased, see § 312(c); but a distribution in kind which qualifies under § 346 will not produce any effect at the corporate level, except where installment obligations are involved. See § 336.

C. SPECIAL TAX ASPECTS OF AN INSTALLMENT REPURCHASE

TOMBARI v. COMMISSIONER *

United States Court of Appeals, Ninth Circuit, 1962. 299 F.2d 889.

ORR, CIRCUIT JUDGE. William A. Tombari and wife on January 23, 1951, sold to Henry C. Lewis and wife the East Mission Pharmacy (hereinafter the Pharmacy) situate in Spokane, Washington, pursuant to the following agreement of purchase. Total purchase price $300,000.00, payable as follows:

(a) $5,000 cash at execution of the agreement.

(b) $75,987.64 ($75,777.15 principal and $210.49 accrued interest) by the assignment of a real estate contract (hereinafter the Arlington contract) of which the Lewises were obligees.[1]

(c) $19,012.36 in cash before delivery of possession of the property.

(d) $67,157.83 by the Lewises assuming a certain mortgage outstanding against the Pharmacy.

(e) $132,842.17 balance to be paid in monthly installments of $1,000 or more.

Stipulated payments (a) through (d) of said agreement were performed in full during 1951 and the purchasers also made installment payments during that year amounting to $12,770.77. Petitioners (Tombari and wife) reported the sale of the Pharmacy on the installment basis [under the predecessor of § 453]. Commissioner challenged this. Petitioners then reported as ordinary income the amounts they collected in excess of their basis (the fair market value) in the Arlington contract, but now claim this to have been in error. The Commissioner held that it was not. Tombari and wife then petitioned the Tax Court for a redetermination. The Tax Court sustained the Commissioner and we are asked to review the decision of that court.

The first issue for our consideration is whether the sale of the Pharmacy could properly be reported on the installment basis. The statute requires that in order for the taxpayers to invoke the installment reporting provisions, the "initial payments" in the transaction

---

*Most of the court's footnotes omitted.

1. It is stipulated, however, that the fair market value of the Arlington contract at the time of the sale was $50,000.00.

must not exceed 30% of the "selling price." The parties agree as to the make-up of the "initial payments:"

Cash received	$24,012.36
Arlington contract	
(fair market value)	50,000.00
Installment payments	12,770.77
Total initial payments	$86,783.13

In dispute at this juncture is the proper manner of computing the "selling price." Petitioners used the fair market value of the Arlington contract in computing the "initial payments," but now make an about face and use face value in making up the "selling price:"

Cash	$ 24,012.36
Arlington contract	
(face value)	75,987.64
Mortgage assumed	67,157.83
Contract balance	132,842.17
Total selling price	$300,000.00

The Commissioner held that the Arlington contract's fair market value should also be used in determining "selling price:"

Cash	$ 24,012.36
Arlington contract	
(fair market value)	50,000.00
Mortgage assumed	67,157.83
Contract balance	132,842.17
Total selling price	$274,012.36

It is apparent that from taxpayers' figures, the "initial payments" are less than 30% of the "selling price," whereas under the Commissioner's computation, the "initial payments" exceed the 30% limit fixed by the statute and hence the transaction does not qualify for installment reporting.

In arriving at the conclusion that the Commissioner's computation is correct, we resort to statutory construction. We must determine the meaning of the term "selling price" as it refers to the valuation of property received, in light of the objectives of this provision of the statute. We are convinced that the fair market value of the Arlington contract, as opposed to the face value accepted by the contracting parties for their own purposes, must govern the computation of "selling price" in this case.

The provision under consideration is a relief measure. It is designed to reduce hardship which otherwise occurs in an installment sale where the whole gain realized on the disposition is taxable in the year of the sale, but more than 70% of the proceeds of that sale is not available to the taxpayer until later years. Thus, under the statute, if 30% or less is paid at the outset, the taxpayer can "spread" his taxable gain over the whole period of the installment arrangement. But to permit the use of a basically speculative figure (as the face value of the Arlington contract here is) in the "selling price" and the more reliable fair market value in the "initial payments," would be to permit installment treatment where the best forecast at the time of the sale indicated no hardship to the taxpayer sufficient for him to invoke the special relief.

Thus, in the instant case if the estimated fair market value of the Arlington contract were to prove accurate upon the contract's final discharge, the taxpayers would have waited to collect less than 70% of the total consideration, a situation not within the contemplation of the special treatment reserved for what the Congress thought to be the more clearcut hardship cases.

What is required in computing the "selling price" is the best possible evaluation of the consideration at the time of the sale. In the case of the Arlington contract, said evaluation was its fair market value, as contrasted to the more speculative face value accepted by the parties to the sale. Tax Court cases, on varying fact situations, look uniformly to the "actual bargain" of the parties, rather than to the possibly conflicting contract recitals, in assessing the applicability of the installment reporting provision. . . . We find this approach to be the proper one here as well.

We next consider the treatment to be accorded to that portion of each payment received by the taxpayers on the Arlington contract, which portion represented the ratable difference between the fair market value (taxpayers' basis) and the more speculative, or face value of that contract. The difference is of course taxable gain, and the question is whether it is to receive capital gain treatment or is to be taxed at ordinary income rates.

We again are required to resort to statutory construction. The Congress has determined that the favored capital gain treatment should apply only in the case of "the sale or exchange of a capital asset." The policy underlying this provision is evidently that of encouraging, within limits, the free flow, conversion, exchange, investment and re-investment of capital funds, uninhibited by the progressive feature of ordinary income tax rates. . . . It is a device which permits the adjustment of capital markets so that they reflect the economic potentialities of various investments rather than the more artificial considerations resting upon the consequences of graduated taxation. It is evident, then, that the treatment to be given in the instant case of the retention and collection of a contract obligation was not intended to be the same as that accorded in the case of a typical sale or exchange. There is thus no foundation for expanding the meaning of "sale or exchange" to include retention and collection.

The cases, while only infrequently stating the policy, uniformly reach a result which recognizes it. The distinction between the sale or exchange of a contract obligation on the one hand, and its payment and discharge on the other, was set forth at an early date by the United States Supreme Court in Fairbanks v. United States, 306 U.S. 436, 59 S.Ct. 607, 83 L.Ed. 855 (1939). It has been followed without deviation since. . . .

Taxpayers urge that the result thus reached is inconsistent with Westover v. Smith, 173 F.2d 90 (C.A.9, 1949). That case, and others of like import,[4] are not controlling here. In Westover, the obligation which was received and was collected subsequent to the original sale transaction had no ascertainable fair market value. As a consequence, the initial transaction was held open and the recognition and taxation of a part of the gain on that transaction was postponed until collection of the obligation. This was done because at the time of the transaction there was no reliable way of determining what the total gain would ultimately be. The collection of the obligation was thus viewed as a part of the original "sale or exchange of a capital asset." Here, on the other hand, a fair market value was stipulated for the obligation and the original transaction was able to be closed promptly. The subsequent collection of the obligation was, as it is ordinarily, a separate and distinct transaction which "is required to stand on its own feet." See Osenbach v. Commissioner of Internal Revenue, 198 F.2d 235 (C.A.4, 1952). That separation of transactions which helps the taxpayer in the deduction of losses, Bingham, supra, must apply also to taxation of gains.

Affirmed.

---

1. DEFERRED PAYMENT TRANSACTIONS IN GENERAL

a. "OPEN" VERSUS "CLOSED" TRANSACTIONS

The tax treatment of a sale of property on a deferred payment basis is one of the most troublesome questions under the Code. The approach may vary according to the character of the property transferred, the accounting method used by the transferor, and the terms and conditions of the deferred payment obligation received.

Looking first at income derived from the sale of inventory property, or any other revenue received in the ordinary course of business, the proper treatment would seem to depend primarily upon the method of accounting employed. For a seller on the accrual basis, any obligation of a solvent buyer, and *a fortiori* a note, must be included in the seller's income at full face value, e. g., First Savings & Loan Ass'n v. Commissioner, 40 T.C. 474 (1963), subject presumably to a reasonable deduction for prospective bad debts. On the other hand, the cash basis taxpayer normally need not recognize income until cash is actually re-

---

4. See, e. g., Burnet v. Logan, 283 U.S. 404, 51 S.Ct. 550, 75 L.Ed. 1143 (1931); Commissioner v. Carter, 170 F.2d 911 (C.A. 2, 1948). . . .

ceived; but it is to be recalled that any taxpayer for whom inventory constitutes a material income-producing factor is normally required to use the accrual method. IRC § 471; Reg. § 1.446–1(c)(2)(i). And even for a cash basis taxpayer it would seem that a receivable which really amounts to the "equivalent of cash" must be included in income when received. Cf. Rev.Rul. 62–74, 1962–1 Cum.Bull. 68 (cash basis taxpayer who won a prize payable in installments without interest out of a fund deposited in escrow required to include the commuted value of the installments in income that year). Checks and negotiable notes would seem to be the equivalent of cash; but such receivables as non-negotiable instruments, contract rights and open-account claims fall on the other side of the line and do not produce income under the cash basis until they are paid.

But it is with isolated sales of non-inventory property that most of the difficulty has arisen. These transactions are governed by §§ 1001 and 1002 which provide that upon the sale or other disposition of property, gain or loss must be recognized in the amount of the difference between the "amount realized" and the basis of the property disposed of. And under § 1001(b), the amount realized expressly includes not only money but also the "fair market value of the property (other than money) received." Under this language it would appear that any obligation received should be valued for the purpose of immediate recognition of gain; and there is no suggestion that any distinction should be drawn between cash and accrual basis taxpayers in this regard.

However, the fact is that as a practical matter it is sometimes very difficult if not impossible to ascertain the fair market value of a particular obligation. Thus in Commissioner v. Carter, 170 F.2d 911 (2d Cir. 1948), upon the liquidation of a corporation the sole stockholder received rights in certain oil brokerage contracts which provided for the payment of commissions on future deliveries by named sellers to named buyers. Since amounts distributed in liquidation generally are treated as payments in exchange for the stock, see § 331, valuation of the brokerage contracts was called for to determine the "amount realized" under § 1001. But in fact there was no rational basis for determining the fair market value of these rights. Under the rule established by the Supreme Court in the classic case of Burnet v. Logan, 283 U.S. 404, 51 S.Ct. 550, 75 L.Ed. 1143 (1931), a case involving the receipt in a liquidation of a right to a specified royalty per ton of iron ore mined, but with no limitation on the number of tons to be mined, in such circumstances the taxpayer may forego attempting to value the obligation and instead simply report the payments as received, first as return of basis until that has been fully recovered, and then as taxable gain. The taxpayer in Carter had followed this procedure, and the question now presented was what type of gain resulted from these payments; and it was held that the payments should be treated as if they had been received in the liquidation, which meant they gave rise to capital gain rather than ordinary income. This is the so-called "open-transaction" doctrine: that is, where the fair market value of an obligation received upon a sale or exchange can not be ascertained, the original sale or exchange transaction remains open, and payments ultimately received under the obligation are treated exactly as they would have been if received at the time of the sale or exchange. E. g., Westover v. Smith, 173 F.2d 90 (9th Cir. 1949). And it is this doctrine which the court in the Tombari case, supra, found inapposite once the obligation had been valued and included in "amount realized" upon receipt.

Obviously, the open transaction approach is highly desirable from the taxpayer's point of view since it allows him to avoid immediate recognition of gain without any offsetting disadvantage. Understandably, therefore, the Service has sought to limit the operation of the open transaction doctrine by maintaining that practically every obligation can and should be valued upon receipt, so that the original sale or exchange transaction can be "closed" at that point. Indeed, the Service even insists on valuing "contracts and claims to receive indefinite amounts of income, such as those acquired with respect to stock in liquidation of a corporation, except in rare and extraordinary cases." Rev.Rul. 58–402, 1958–2 Cum.Bull. 15. This ruling strives to confine Burnet v. Logan narrowly to its facts, by viewing it not as laying down any general rule that contracts for indefinite payments have no ascertainable value, but rather as simply holding that due to the particular uncertainties in that situation the taxpayer was entitled to recover his entire basis before having to recognize any gain.

The general thrust of this ruling is echoed in the regulations under § 1001 which state that "only in rare and extraordinary cases will property be considered to have no fair market value," Reg. § 1.1001–1(a) [39]; and a similar statement appears in Reg. § 1.453–6(a) (2), relating generally to deferred payment sales of real estate. Indeed, these statements seem to impose an even more stringent limitation upon use of the open transaction doctrine, since read literally they would seem to require the taxpayer to establish that the obligation received had no value at all, rather than merely that its value cannot be ascertained. Several courts have followed this view, e. g., Culbertson v. Commissioner, 14 T.C. 1421 (1950); and a number of cases have specifically rejected any effort to recast the test in terms of the market value being "readily ascertainable." E. g., Estate of Marsack

---

39. It is not only debt obligations which pose the question of ascertainable market value upon receipt. For example, unlisted, highly speculative stock may be found to have no ascertainable value when received, so that determination of gain or loss may have to await the disposition of such stock. E. g., Helvering v. Tex-Penn Co., 300 U.S. 481, 57 S.Ct. 569, 81 L.Ed. 755 (1937). However, here there is even greater reluctance to conclude that the fair market value is unascertainable. See North American Philips Co., Inc. v. Commissioner, 21 T.C.M. 1497 (1962).

v. Commissioner, 288 F.2d 533 (7th Cir. 1961). But the fact is that virtually every obligation has *some* value, despite cases like Miller v. United States, 235 F.2d 553 (6th Cir. 1956), which held that the second mortgage notes there involved had no market value. Thus it seems more sensible to construe the regulations by emphasizing the word "fair" in the phrase "no fair market value", so that an obligation need not be valued where there is simply no rational basis for determining what its fair value is. Cf. Slater v. Commissioner, 356 F.2d 668 (10th Cir. 1966), where the court stated the test in terms of whether the obligations "were susceptible of determination of fair market value", but then held the taxpayer to a valuation equal to the minimum guaranty of $500 which taxpayer had originally used in his return, although annual receipts for the next three years averaged *more than $5000*.

    b. THE ROLE OF ACCOUNTING METHOD

Nevertheless, to date development in this area has not been directed primarily toward the issue of ascertainability of fair market value. Instead, the principal influence has been the distinction between cash and accrual methods of accounting, which has been imported into this area of isolated sales of non-inventory property despite the absence of any apparent warrant in either the language or the purpose of § 1001. However, it does so happen that application of the cash basis to a deferred payment sale of the kind under consideration produces the same result as application of the open transaction doctrine, in that the taxpayer is not required to recognize gain until payments are actually received (and then only after he has recovered his basis in the property transferred). So in Johnston v. Commissioner, 14 T.C. 560 (1950), a cash-basis taxpayer sold stock in 1942 under a contract which called for one-half of the estimated purchase price to be paid in 1942 and the balance in 1943. The exact purchase price could not be determined until 1943, but was based upon a method of computation prescribed in the contract. The total amount ultimately received by the taxpayer resulted in a gain, which the Commissioner determined was taxable in 1943. The purchaser was financially capable of paying the full purchase price in 1942, and the taxpayer contended that the obligation to complete the purchase price should have been valued and included in computing the amount realized in 1942. However, the court indicated that determination of the "amount realized" under § 1001 depended upon the taxpayer's method of accounting, and held that a mere "agreement to pay the balance of the purchase price in the future has no tax significance . . . to [the] seller if he is using a cash system."

The Johnston case was followed in Ennis v. Commissioner, 17 T.C. 465 (1951), where it was held that an obligation did not constitute an "amount realized" unless it was the "equivalent of cash." In the court's view that "cash equivalent" test was not met where "the promise to pay was merely contractual [and] was not embodied in a note or other evidence of indebtedness possessing the element of negotiability and freely transferable." A dissent would have distinguished the Johnston case on the ground that there the total purchase price could not be determined at the time of the sale, whereas in Ennis the exact dollar price was fixed from the outset.

The effect of these cases is to move the "closed transaction" test for cash-basis taxpayers from one of whether the value of the obligation is ascertainable to one of whether the obligation is substantially "equivalent to cash." But not surprisingly there have also been some problems in applying the "cash equivalent" test. Under the Johnston and Ennis cases it seems clear that a simple contract promise, not embodied in any separate debt instrument, does not constitute a cash equivalent. This is consistent with the view that the real question is whether the obligation actually represents a separate item of "property" or is simply "evidence" of a promise to pay cash in the future. See generally, Checks and Notes as Income When Received by a Cash-Basis Taxpayer, 73 Harv.L.Rev. 1199 (1960). While this statement of the question does not solve the problem, it does import notions of ordinary commercial custom which could prove helpful. Thus at the opposite pole from a simple contract obligation is a negotiable promissory note of the kind that passes freely in commerce; such an instrument would normally be regarded as the equivalent of cash. For a time it appeared that negotiability was the key to cash equivalence; but Cowden v. Commissioner, 289 F.2d 20 (5th Cir. 1961), seems to reject that view. In Cowden the taxpayer exchanged a lease of oil and gas rights for a contract calling for deferred payments (having first rejected the offer of a lump sum payment). The Tax Court decided that the taxpayer should be taxed in full at the outset because of the lessee's offer to pay the entire sum at once; but the Court of Appeals reversed, holding instead that the test was whether the contract could be regarded as the "equivalent of cash". In remanding the case for a new trial on that issue, the court offered the following guidance:

> The taxpayers urge that there can be no "equivalent of cash" obligation unless it is a negotiable instrument. Such a test, to be determined by the form of the obligation, is as unrealistic as it is formalistic. The income tax law deals in economic realities, not in legal abstractions, and the reach of the income tax law is not to be delimited by technical refinements or mere formalism.
>
> A promissory note, negotiable in form, is not necessarily the equivalent of cash. Such an instrument may have been issued by a maker of doubtful solvency or for other reasons such paper might be denied a ready acceptance in the marketplace. We think the converse of this principle ought to be applicable. We are convinced that if a promise to pay of a solvent obligor is unconditional and assignable, not subject

to set-offs, and is of a kind that is frequently transferred to lenders or investors at a discount not substantially greater than the generally prevailing premium for the use of money, such promise is the equivalent of cash and taxable in like manner as cash would have been taxable had it been received by the taxpayer rather than the obligation.

Although the Cowden case seemed to make cash equivalence turn upon whether the value of the obligation was substantially equal to the face amount (apart from any interest factor for delay in receipt of the money), as well as free transferability in the marketplace, the subsequent cases have appeared to emphasize the latter factor virtually to the exclusion of the former. Thus in a number of cases involving so-called "land contracts" not unlike the one involved in the Ennis case, supra, cash-basis taxpayers have been required to include in income the value of a simple contract obligation upon a showing that a market existed for such land contracts, even though the value of the obligation was substantially less than the face amount. E.g., Phipps Industrial Land Trust v. Commissioner, 22 T.C.M. 1724 (1963) (value of the obligation 20% less than face amount, although it carried a 6% interest rate); Heller Trust v. Commissioner, 24 T.C.M. 1663 (1965) (value of obligations only 50% of face amount).

What about isolated sales of property by accrual-basis taxpayers? Obviously, for such taxpayers the special cash-basis limitations would have no application, and therefore the test in the regulations of whether the obligations had an ascertainable market value could be applied. However, some cases have held that an accrual-basis taxpayer is subject to the general accrual principle that calls for inclusion in income of the full face amount of any obligations received, subject perhaps to some provision for possible bad debts. E.g., Brown v. Commissioner, 9 T.C.M. 1054 (1950) (accrual-basis taxpayer required to include full face amount of note received upon sale of his business, although the note was non-negotiable, apparently conditioned upon future earnings, and obviously worth less than face). George L. Castner Co., Inc. v. Commissioner, 30 T.C. 1061 (1958), similarly insisted upon a strict accrual approach in connection with obligations received by an accrual basis taxpayer upon the sale of personal property. However, the Castner case contains a strong implication to the effect that upon a sale of real property an accrual basis taxpayer need only include the fair market value of the obligations received, relying upon Reg. § 1.453–6 which provides expressly that upon a deferred-payment sale of real estate which does not qualify for the installment method of accounting, the fair market value of the obligations received should be included in the amount realized for the purpose of determining the gain or loss of the seller.

In view of the dictum by the court in the Castner case with regard to Reg. § 1.453–6, it may be worth noting that there are some difficulties with that regulation. For one thing, it is to be noted that § 453 of the Code deals only with the installment method of accounting, and there may be some question as to the validity of a regulation under that section purporting to deal with the tax treatment of a transaction which does not qualify under that section. Moreover, it is hard to see why any such regulation is necessary, since it does little more than repeat what is already provided in this connection in the regulations under § 1001, a seemingly far more appropriate place. It is equally unclear why, once it was decided to deal in the regulations under § 453 with sales which did not qualify under that section, sales of real estate were covered but sales of personal property were not. And finally, since Reg. § 1.453–6 makes no reference to the method of accounting used by the taxpayer, just as is true of the regulations under § 1001, it is not apparent why the regulations under § 453 should be regarded as overriding traditional accrual principles if the regulations under § 1001 do not. On the other hand, as a practical matter there may be some validity in a distinction between obligations received upon the sale of personal property and those received for real property, since by and large the latter are likely to involve larger amounts and to run for longer periods, so that a rule requiring immediate inclusion of the full face amount could be a great deal more onerous. See generally, Taxation of Vendors of Real Property: The Concept of Fair Market Value, 15 Stan.L.Rev. 85 (1962).

c. ACCOUNTING FOR GAIN ON THE REPAYMENT OF AN OBLIGATION

As the Tombari case indicates, when the "closed transaction" approach is applied and the obligation is valued at the time of receipt for inclusion in the "amount realized", the subsequent collection of the obligation is "a separate and distinct transaction". As such, there must be a reckoning of gain or loss to the extent that the total of the payments received on the obligation exceeds its basis (which of course is fixed at the figure at which the obligation was valued upon receipt). E. g., Herbert's Estate v. Commissioner, 139 F.2d 756 (3d Cir.1943) (relinquishment of an obligation upon payment by the debtor constitutes a "disposition" within the meaning of § 1001; in addition, § 61(a) is broad enough to reach any difference between a taxpayer's basis in a debt obligation and the amount obtained upon its payment).

As to the type of gain or loss incurred upon the repayment of an obligation, the Tombari case holds that it is not capital, because of the absence of any "sale or exchange" as required by § 1222. Prior to the enactment of the predecessor of § 1232(a)(1) in 1934, this was the rule for all obligations. Obviously, this placed receipt of payment of an obligation at a considerable tax disadvantage, and some taxpayers resorted to the practice of "selling" the obligation to an accommodating buyer shortly before the due date in an effort to achieve the necessary sale or exchange for capital gain treatment, with varying results. Compare Weiner v. Commissioner, 21 T.C.M. 252 (1962), affirmed *per curiam*, 316 F.2d 473 (3d Cir. 1963) (sale of a demand note of taxpayer's controlled corporation to a factor three months before it was paid ignored for tax purposes, with the transaction treated as though payment had been received from the maker), with Paine v. Commissioner, 236 F.2d 398 (8th Cir. 1956) (sale of note to a bank ten days prior to maturity recognized as a sale for tax purposes).

Whenever gain on the repayment of an obligation would be taxable as ordinary income, it became all the more desirable to obtain open transaction treatment for obligations received upon the sale or exchange of a capital asset, since under the closed transaction approach the taxpayer was caught in a dilemma. If he sought to minimize his immediate capital gain tax by setting a low value on an obligation at the time of its receipt, he would at the same time be fixing a very low basis for the obligation which the payments were almost sure to exceed, with resulting ordinary income treatment. If instead a high value was placed on the obligation, the taxpayer would increase his immediate capital gains tax burden (without of course having received any additional cash with which to pay the tax); and if he overshot the mark by fixing a value in excess of the total of the payments ultimately received, the taxpayer, at least today, would presumably end up with only a capital loss of uncertain tax benefit. See §§ 165(g), 166(d).

This picture was drastically altered when the predecessor of § 1232(a)(1) made capital gain treatment available upon the repayment of certain types of corporate and governmental obligations, by treating such repayments as received "in exchange" for the obligation. (§ 1232(a)(1) does not apply to any obligations of individuals, which explains why the obligation involved in Tombari was still subject to ordinary income treatment.) As to obligations covered by that statute, a taxpayer could safely try to fix a low value upon receipt, since any excess of the payments ultimately received over that value would still qualify for capital gain treatment.

Another question posed under the closed transaction approach is whether all payments should first go to the recovery of basis (of the obligation) with no taxable gain until the total receipts exceed the basis, just as under the open transaction approach all payments are applied first against the basis of the asset sold. As the Tombari case indicates, many cases follow the contrary view that each payment should be allocated proportionately between return of basis and taxable gain, e.g., Gilbert v. Commissioner, 6 T.C. 10 (1946); as a matter of fact, Tombari assumed without discussion that this was the proper course. To illustrate this approach in simple terms, suppose that upon a sale of property an obligation was received calling for the payment of $50 per year for three years, and the obligation was valued and included in "amount realized" under § 1001 at $120. Instead of treating the first two payments as entirely return of basis, with the third payment representing additional return of basis of $20 and gain to the extent of the remaining $30, each payment would be treated as consisting of return of basis to the extent of 120/150 ($40), and taxable gain as to the remaining 30/150 ($10).

In essence, this "pro rata" method of reporting gain puts the taxpayer onto a kind of informal installment basis of accounting for the repayment of the obligation. Whether it favors the taxpayer or the Commissioner varies from case to case, and the position of the parties has often been reversed where the issue is involved. On the one hand, the method does require the taxpayer to start recognizing gain immediately, instead of being able to defer all tax until the entire basis has been recovered, and of course taxpayers are always interested in deferral of tax. On the other hand, the pro rata method approach does permit the gain to be spread over the entire period covered by the obligation instead of being all bunched in the later years; and this could be of great advantage to a taxpayer, particularly if the gain is ordinary income rather than capital gain as was true in the Tombari case.

It is to be noted that this same kind of informal installment method of accounting is at least theoretically possible in connection with the open transaction approach, so long as the total amount of the obligation is fixed and definite (i.e., the reason for applying the open transaction approach is not an inability to determine the total amount to be received, as was involved, for example, in Burnet v. Logan). However, no case appears to have taken this course, perhaps because it is just this type of situation that the formal installment method of § 453 is supposed to cover, and imposition of an informal technique reaching a virtually identical result would be rather questionable. But there is another difference between these two situations which may be important in this connection. Under the open transaction doctrine, whatever gain is ultimately realized includes the increase in the value of the original asset sold over its basis, and there is something to be said for waiting until the basis of that asset has been recovered before assuming the presence of gain. As to an obligation received and valued under the closed transaction doctrine, on the other hand, any gain realized upon the repayment of the obligation stems from the fact that the obligation was valued at less than its full face amount. Such a spread between the value and the face amount of an obligation, often referred to as "discount", generally constitutes nothing more than an adjustment of the interest rate on the obligation (or the recognition of an interest factor where none is expressed); and there may well be more warrant for treating each payment as including a proportionate part of this "interest" income.

A similar question arises where a taxpayer purchases for cash an installment obligation originally received by someone else upon the sale of property, and the price paid by the taxpayer is less than the face amount of the obligation.

PHILLIPS v. FRANK [40]

United States Court of Appeals, Ninth Circuit, 1961. 295 F.2d 629.

JERTBERG, CIRCUIT JUDGE. . . . During the years in question the taxpayer's accounting records were kept on the cash receipts and disbursements' method, and during these years the taxpayer received payments on real estate contracts owned by him. All of said contracts were purchased by taxpayer in the years in question or prior thereto. Taxpayer did not perform any services in the making of the contracts, but only purchased contracts negotiated by others, the unpaid principal balances of which were payable in periodic installments. In each instance, the price paid was an agreed percentage less than the principal amount due on the contract, which percentage was not the same on all contracts. In other words, they were purchased at a discount. Contracts of the type involved were bought and sold by investors, and all of the contracts owned by taxpayer during the years in question were held as investments. Taxpayer considered each contract to have a value equal to the amount paid by him therefor at the time of the purchase. No security for payment of any of the contracts was held by taxpayer other than a right to repossess in case of default by the vendee, and no promissory note was held by the taxpayer for the unpaid balance of the purchase price.

While one of the admitted facts stated in the pretrial order is that the contracts involved in the instant case are of a type bought and sold by investors, the uncontradicted testimony before the district court is that there is no open market for the sale of the contracts in question; and that they were difficult to sell and that it took considerable time—two or three years—to dispose of them. It is further uncontradicted in the record that a large portion of the contracts purchased by the taxpayer were "highly speculative", consisting of second, and in some instances third liens, on the real properties which were the subject of the contracts, which prior liens taxpayer was required to keep "in order" so as to be able to convey title upon payment in full of the contract price. In some instances, taxpayer suffered losses due to defaults by vendees which resulted in repossessions and sales of the properties. Each contract was purchased by taxpayer on an individually negotiated basis in light of such factors as the value of the real property involved, the existence of prior liens, the burdens and responsibilities of the taxpayer, and the financial ability and credit standing of the vendee.

40. Portions of the text and all footnotes omitted.

In posing the question for decision, the district court stated:

"A percentage of each contract payment, in the proportion of the total discount to the total unpaid contract balance, was treated by the Commissioner as discount income taxable as ordinary income. The sole issue presented is whether the Commissioner erred in such determination."

. . .

In disposing of the issue adversely to the taxpayer the district court stated:

"It is universally recognized that interest is earned and becomes taxable income as paid from period to period, regardless of whether thereafter principal be repaid. There is no logical basis or legal authority justifying different treatment of discount income." . . .

It is not completely clear in what sense the district court used the term "discount income" but the clear implication is that the court used the term to mean a charge for the use of money and, therefore, equivalent of interest. Interest in the business world commonly presupposes a debtor-creditor relationship under which a lender advances capital to a borrower who promises to pay the amount borrowed plus an additional amount as compensation for the use of money. Income earned by lending a sum of money less than the face value of the obligation received as consideration for the loan may be equivalent to interest. Such income has been frequently denominated "discount income" and we recognize that such income should have and generally has had the same tax treatment as interest.

In the instant case, taxpayer purchased for cash (no loans being involved) from vendors thereof executory contracts entered into between such vendors and other persons covering the sale and purchase of real properties. None of such vendors agreed to pay or return to taxpayer any sum, either principal or interest. The contracts were acquired by taxpayer unconditionally, not by way of security for loans. All taxpayer received from the vendors as consideration for the purchase money paid to them were assignments of executory contracts. The district court found as a fact that such contracts were purchased by taxpayer. Clearly, the transactions between the taxpayer and the several vendors were sales and purchases. Under the facts of this case it would be a great distortion to hold that any part of the contract payments received by taxpayer for the periods under review from the several vendees constitutes "discount income" and therefore equivalent of interest.

It is clear, however, that the district court regarded the amount of discount from the unpaid principal balance at which each contract was purchased as income to taxpayer and that a portion of such income was received by taxpayer as income taxable to him, as a prorated part of each principal payment on the unpaid principal balance of each contract.

* * *

Seeking to sustain the judgment of the district court the appellee calls to our attention a line of cases in which a vendor sells real property and receives a note or mortgage in payment, or part payment, of the sales price. Under such facts, there is a line of cases which hold that the sale is considered completed even though full payment has not been received. The note or mortgage, regarded as equivalent to cash, is given a fair market value at the time of the sale, and the gain or loss on the sale is determined with reference to said fair market value. Often, the fair market value of the note or mortgage is less than its face value. In such case, the amount of the difference between the face value of the note or mortgage and the fair market value thereof as determined at the time of sale is regarded as ordinary income and periodic payments on the unpaid principal of the note or mortgage received by a cash basis taxpayer must be apportioned between return of principal and income. . . . This rule has been extended to some other situations where payment is deferred. . . . Tombari v. Commissioner of Internal Revenue, 1960, 35 T.C. 250 (receipt by vendor of real property of a contract obligation of a third party).

On the other hand, there is a line of cases which hold that where a vendor of real property sells the same under contract unaccompanied by a promissory note or other evidence of indebtedness or mortgage, the contract obligation of the vendee cannot be said to be cash or its equivalent (the contract obligation having no fair market value) and that no gain is realized by the vendor until the contract payments by the vendee equal the vendor's basis in the property. . . .

The distinction between a vendor who sells real property and receives a note, mortgage, or contract, from the vendee and the investor who purchases at discount such note, mortgage, or contract was recognized in Vancoh Realty Co., [33 B.T.A. 918 (1936)]. Such distinction is also recognized by appellee. On page 16 of appellee's brief, it is stated:

> "The taxpayer seeks to rely upon Ennis v. Commissioner, 17 T.C. 465, but that case is easily distinguishable. The taxpayer in that case was a vendor of real property, and this immediately sets that case apart from the case at bar. . . ."

* * *

We deem it unnecessary to consider the validity of the distinction drawn in "vendor" cases between the so-called "note and mortgage" cases and the so-called "contract" cases in the two lines of cases above mentioned relating to vendors, although we must confess the distinction in some cases, appears to be illusory.

In the instant case, the taxpayer made a purchase not a sale. Hence, no problem is presented as to any gain realized at the time of such purchase. The taxpayer recognizes that when periodic payments on each contract equal the purchase price of such contract, payments received by taxpayer in each year subsequent thereto must be treated as ordinary income in the year of receipt. Such is the law. . . . The simple question presented on this appeal is: Did the cash basis taxpayer receive during the years under review any payments of which a portion should be allocated to and considered for tax purposes as payment of a portion of the profit which the taxpayer hopes to realize? Taxpayer received for his capital invested the right to receive the unpaid balances due on such contract. What were such rights worth when purchased?

There is no evidence in the record that such rights had any market value, fair or unfair, or any other value in excess of taxpayer's costs. There is no evidence in the record that taxpayer at any time could have sold such contracts at a profit. The only source from which he might reasonably expect to realize any part of his profit is from periodic payments subsequent to the return to him of his invested capital. The fact that the likelihood of realizing a profit might increase as the amount of his investment decreases from receipt of periodic payments does not convert any part of such payments into payments on the hoped for or expected profit. Clearly, the payments received by taxpayer during the period under review aggregating less than his costs constitute a return of capital. A return of capital is not income.

The judgment of the district court is reversed.

It is not entirely clear whether the court in the Phillips case decided that as a *matter of law* the informal installment method was not applicable to purchased obligations, or that as a *matter of fact* the obligations there involved were so speculative that the taxpayer should be permitted to recover his entire investment before being required to recognize any gain. However, subsequent cases have made clear that it is a question of fact. In the most recent case in point, Underhill v. Commissioner, 45 T.C. No. 46 (1966), after a careful review of the authorities the court held that "the ultimate test is whether, at the time of acquisition, the person acquiring the obligation (whether by purchase or otherwise) cannot be reasonably certain that he will recover his cost *and* a major portion of the discount." The court listed the following elements to be taken into account in determining whether a particular obligation is speculative: (1) the existence of personal liability of the debtor and/or a guarantee or endorser and his credit standing, resources, and other special factors bearing on his financial responsibility; (2) the marketability of the obligation, which involves the subsidiary consideration of its negotiability; (3) whether or not, at the time of acquisition, the obligor is in substantial default on payments due; (4) the terms of payment and the extent and nature of the security for the obligation, if any, at the time of acquisition—i.e., whether a first, second, or other prior lien—and the character, condition, and the then-market value of the underlying property; and (5) the size of the discount.

What is perhaps of most importance in our immediate context is the Underhill court's parenthetical indication that the same approach is applicable whether the installment obligation is purchased for cash or "otherwise" acquired, which presumably includes receipt of an installment obligation upon a sale of property, at least where a closed transaction is involved. And this certainly seems sound, since notwithstanding the insistence of the court in the Phillips case upon distinguishing between the two, the fact is that receipt of an installment obligation in exchange for property is in essence a type of "purchase" of the obligation, though for property instead of cash.

2. THE DISCOUNT FACTOR IN DEFERRED OBLIGATIONS

The foregoing material indicates the need for a more detailed analysis of the nature of "discount." Let us start with the simple case of a loan of $1000 for one year with interest at 4%.

Obviously, when the creditor receives $1040 one year later, $1000 represents a repayment of principal, and the additional $40 represents interest which the creditor must include in ordinary income. But suppose instead that the creditor lends $1000 upon an obligation calling simply for the payment of $1040 one year later without interest. Here too, the creditor would receive $40 more than he had originally advanced, and the economic effect of the transaction is exactly the same as if there had been an express provision for interest at 4%. In both cases, the excess $40 received by the creditor surely represents compensation for the use of the money by the debtor and therefore constitutes interest.

Looking at such transactions from a different vantage point, no prospective creditor would advance as much as $1040 in exchange for a right to receive $1040 one year later without interest, since the creditor would insist upon some compensation for the use of whatever money he did advance. Speaking more generally, no deferred maturity obligation without interest can command a price as large as the face amount of the obligation. Instead, a prospective creditor would determine the amount which together with interest thereon at an appropriate rate for the period of the loan would equal the face amount of the obligation. In other words, the creditor would attempt to determine the present value of such a deferred payment obligation without interest, by making allowance for interest for the use of whatever money was actually advanced. This is known as "discounting" the obligation to present value. The discounted present value of a deferred maturity obligation without interest may properly be regarded as the "real" principal sum involved in the obligation; and it is this difference between that present value and the face amount of the obligation (which really represents an interest component) that is usually referred to as "discount". (Of course, discount may also be present even where the obligation expressly provides for interest, if the specified interest rate is lower than the appropriate interest rate for the particular obligation.)

Where the appropriate interest rate can be ascertained, the discounted present value of a deferred maturity obligation without interest can be determined from a so-called "discount" table, which gives the present discounted value of $1 payable after a specified number of years at a specified interest rate. In other words, the table has worked out the amount which together with interest at a particular rate for a specified number of years will amount to $1. To determine the value of a right to receive $1040 after one year, assuming that 4% would be the appropriate interest rate for the transaction, one would start with the figure shown on the table as the present value of $1 payable at the end of one year with interest at 4%, which is .9615, and then multiply by $1040. The resulting figure is, as should be expected, $1000.

Of course it is often difficult to ascertain the appropriate interest rate for a particular transaction with any degree of precision, since it depends upon such diverse factors as the financial strength of the particular debtor and the current state of the money market. But it is normally possible to make at least a reasonable estimate of the appropriate interest rate; and that seems preferable to entirely ignoring an interest factor that is obviously present. Moreover, the present value of an obligation may often be obtained from some independent evidence, such as the consideration given for the obligation in an arm's length transaction, or an actual market for such obligations. In effect, in such a case the "market" performs the operation of discounting the obligation to present value. Again, the fair market value of the obligation constitutes the real principal sum involved, and the excess of the face amount of the obligation over the fair market value represents the discount or interest component in the transaction.

This concept of discount is no stranger to the tax law. For example, the regulations have long provided that where "bonds are issued . . . at a discount", the amount of the discount may be amortized over the life of the bonds. Reg. § 1.61–12(c)(3). On the other hand, in the case of deferred maturity obligations issued in exchange for property rather than cash, there has been considerable resistance to finding any interest factor beyond the amount, if any, specified in the agreement. An example is M. C. Parrish & Co. v. Commissioner, 3 T.C. 119 (1944), affirmed, 147 F.2d 284 (5th Cir. 1945), which involved so-called "warrants" issued by the State of Texas representing the obligation of the state to pay for goods and services supplied to it, when funds became available out of general revenues. The taxpayer's business consisted of purchasing such warrants at less than face from those who had rendered the services to the state, and holding them for redemption. Although the warrants did not carry any interest, the taxpayer argued that interest was necessarily present in such deferred payment obligations, and therefore some portion of the redemption price paid by the state came within the exemption for interest on state obligations. In rejecting this contention, the Tax Court drew an analogy to the simple case of a contractor who sold goods to the state and received a warrant which he retained until it was paid. The court regarded it as clear that in such a case the contractor could not be treated as having interest income, since he would have simply received the agreed purchase price for his goods. The court then concluded with the following rather startling observation: "[The contractor] may have added something to the price of his goods to take care of the delay which would transpire before he got his money, but that certainly would not be interest or discount." With all respect, an "addition" to cover a delay in receiving money is just what interest is.

In the meantime, a special obstacle to finding a discount, even on an obligation issued for cash, had developed as a result of the language of § 1232(a)(1). Of course, prior to the enactment of that section there was much less reason to seek out a "discount", since any excess of the payments received over the basis of the obligation was taxable as ordinary income anyway, whether it was characterized as discount or not. Then § 1232(a)(1) seemed to go to the opposite pole with its provision that amounts received in retirement of a debt obligation should be treated as having been received "in exchange therefore", since read literally that makes the entire amount received in payment of the obligation eligible for capital gain treatment, and precludes finding any discount. Just this construction of § 1232(a)(1) was adopted by the Tax Court in Commissioner v. Caulkins, 144 F.2d 482 (6th Cir. 1944), involving ten-year non-interest bearing certificates which had been issued to the taxpayer at a price fixed to make the discount from face amount identical with 5½% compound interest; and the Court of Appeals reluctantly affirmed.

However, the Service refused to accede to this approach with regard to such investment certificates, insisting that § 1232(a)(1) was not intended to transmute what was essentially income from a capital asset into gain upon its disposition. And ultimately the Service prevailed, first in a series of Court of Appeals decisions starting with Commissioner v. Morgan, 272 F.2d 936 (9th Cir. 1959), and once and for all with the decision of the Supreme Court in United States v. Midland-Ross Corp., 381 U.S. 54, 85 S.Ct. 1308, 14 L.Ed.2d 214 (1965).

This construction of § 1232(a)(1) had long since been "codified" in the 1954 Code by § 1232(a)(2), which ferrets out for special treatment any "original issue discount", defined in § 1232(b)(1) as "the difference between the issue price and the stated redemption price at maturity." As a matter of fact, § 1232(a)(2) goes well beyond the cases since it provides ordinary income treatment for the original issue discount in the case of a sale or exchange of the obligation, as well as upon retirement. On the other hand, it is not clear how § 1232(a)(2) relates to installment obligations, which are our particular concern here. Presumably, § 1232(a)(2) is as broad in its coverage as § 1232(a)(1), which is assumed to include installment obligations within its compass; but most of the language of § 1232(a)(2) does seem directed to more traditional, single-maturity obligations, and in fact the *de minimis* provision of § 1232(b)(1) does not seem capable of being applied to an installment obligation.

Returning now to the special problem of deferred maturity obligations issued in exchange for property, it should first be noted that such transactions are now subject to IRC § 483, added to the Code in 1964. Section 483 will be analyzed in detail in paragraph 4 below; suffice it to note here that under § 483 if an obligation is received in exchange for property and does not carry an interest rate of at least 4%, interest will be imputed at a 5% rate. However, it is not clear whether § 483 limits the discount to that amount in such circumstances, and in any event an analysis of the pre-§ 483 law is important in understanding the role of that section.

In theory, there is no less reason to find a discount when obligations are issued for property than in the case of obligations issued for cash. If the fair market value of the property received in exchange for the obligations is less than the face amount thereof, there would seem to be a discount to the same extent as if the obligations had been issued for cash in the amount of the fair market value of the property.[41] Moreover, for tax purposes it is often of much greater importance to be able to recognize a discount element, and tax it as ordinary income to the creditor, where obligations have been issued for property than where they have been issued for cash. For in the cash case, any amount of additional interest income to the creditor which may result from focusing a discount element is likely to be evenly balanced by the equivalent interest deduction received by the debtor. Accordingly, there is normally little reason for the Service to care about how the parties allocate the tax incidents of interest between themselves. It is important only to make sure that the par-

---

41. It has been suggested that the spread between the face amount of a deferred installment obligation and the "cash" value of the property sold may not all constitute compensation for the use of money — it may also reflect the factor of greater hazard and expense in an installment transaction. See Note, Taxing Deferred Returns upon Transfer of a Capital Asset, 63 Harv.L.Rev. 853, 856 (1950). For the purposes of our analysis, it is sufficient to simply note this issue, without attempting to resolve it.

ties themselves behave consistently, in order to prevent any repetition of what happened in the Caulkins case, where the debtor enjoyed the benefit of amortizing an original issue discount while the creditor was able to escape recognizing any interest income.

However, where debt obligations are issued for property the parties may be able in effect to "have their cake and eat it too" as in Caulkins, by resorting to a larger face amount of debt instead of express interest. Absent a finding of discount, the increase in face amount would become part of the cost of the property acquired; and so long as the property was as either depreciable or constituted stock in trade, this additional cost would be deductible by the buyer as either additional depreciation or additional cost of goods sold. Apart from differences in timing, such a deduction would be roughly comparable to a deduction for interest. Meanwhile, however, the seller would be treating the additional face amount of the obligation as part of the sales proceeds (at least under the open transaction approach), and hence as eligible for capital gain treatment. In other words unless a discount can be established and taxed to the seller as ordinary income, the parties would achieve the tax windfall of Caulkins, which they could then allocate between themselves (by adjustment of the purchase price) as they saw fit.

Nevertheless, the courts have been far from uniform in finding a discount where debt obligations are issued for property. One line of cases has involved efforts by debtors to deduct an alleged discount, generally in situations where an increase in the cost of the property acquired would not have produced any tax benefit either because the property was not depreciable or because it was acquired in a tax-free transaction and therefore was limited to a carryover basis in any event. All but one of these cases involved single maturity instruments rather than installment obligations. In American Smelting & Refining Co. v. United States, 130 F.2d 883 (3d Cir. 1942), where the taxpayer issued its own negotiable bonds to acquire stock in its subsidiary held by outsiders, the court ruled that the difference between the fair market value of the stock acquired and the face amount of the bonds constituted discount which the taxpayer was entitled to amortize. But in Montana Power Co. v. United States, 232 F.2d 541, 545–550 (3d Cir. 1956), involving bonds issued in a tax-free exchange for property, two of the seven judges joined in a dictum disapproving the American Smelting decision and suggesting that an exchange of debt obligations for property could not give rise to an original issue discount. This view was subsequently adopted by the Court of Claims in Montana Power Co. v. United States, 141 Ct.Cl. 620, 159 F.Supp. 593 (1958), which involved the same taxpayer's effort to deduct the entire alleged discount upon the retirement of the bonds. See generally, Molloy, Federal Income Tax Aspects of New Trends in Railroad Corporation Finance, 12 Tax L.Rev. 113, 122–138 (1957).

The latest word on this issue seems to be Nassau Lens Co., Inc. v. Commissioner, 308 F.2d 39 (2d Cir. 1962), involving the incorporation of a sole proprietorship. In exchange for the assets of the proprietorship, the newly-organized taxpayer assumed the liabilities and issued its stock, plus 100 notes, "each with an issuance value of $1000" and providing for payment to the holder at maturity ten years later of $1500 without interest. The taxpayer had the option to redeem such notes in any year prior to maturity at a price fixed in accordance with an accompanying schedule which in effect provided for an annual increment roughly corresponding to interest at 4%. The taxpayer sought to amortize the alleged discount of $500 per bond in accordance with the redemption schedule; but the Commissioner disallowed it, primarily on the ground that the purported obligations actually constituted additional equity, but also on the ground that no amortizable discount arises where obligations are issued for property. While remanding the case on the former point, the court rejected the latter contention, and the dictum in the Montana Power Co. case, supra, upon which it was based. Instead, the court approved the earlier decision in American Smelting, supra:

> It may well be true that to a "borrowing buyer" interest or discount payments seem part of the cost of the property. In reality, however, they are the cost of using the money which is needed to purchase the property, a cost not incurred by the buyer with ready cash.

In the one debtor case involving an installment obligation case the parties had so plainly taken interest into account in arranging the terms of the transaction that it would have been difficult not to recognize the discount-interest component. Raleigh Properties, Inc. v. Commissioner, 21 T.C.M. 812 (1962). There the taxpayer purchased a hotel for $3,240,000, consisting of $560,000 in cash, the assumption of a mortgage of approximately $1,140,000, and the remainder payable in installments over a period of nine years. The taxpayer had originally offered to pay $2,800,000, including the same cash payment of $560,000 and assumption of the mortgage, plus interest of 4½% on the remaining deferred portion of the purchase price. However, the sellers insisted that the full amount of the interest on the deferred payments, which was determined to be $440,000, should be included in the face amount of the purchase money note to be held by the sellers. The taxpayer accepted this condition, after it was agreed that a schedule would be prepared which would allow the taxpayer to prepay the remaining deferred portion of the obligation on specified dates at a discount representing what would have been the remaining interest due under the original terms. Such a schedule was prepared on the basis of a 4½% interest rate, and the taxpayer satisfied himself that prepayment of the note at any time in accordance with that discount schedule would mean that his cost was approximately the originally contemplated $2,800,000 plus 4½% interest on the deferred payment portion to the date of repayment. The court permitted the taxpayer to amortize the discount-interest component of $440,000 over the period of the installment obligation. After observing that the question of whether interest was present depended upon the intention of the parties, and that an intention contrary to the express terms of the obligation would not normally be inferred, the court held that here the existence of the discount schedule made it clear that the parties had in fact intended to take interest into account in the transaction.

Turning now to the question of establishing the existence of a discount as against a creditor, for the purpose of requiring him to include it as ordinary income for tax purposes, the problem becomes somewhat more complicated. First of all, it may be appropriate to note a possible distinction between open and closed transactions in this connection. Where the closed transaction approach has been applied to the original receipt of an obligation in exchange for property, so that the obligation has been valued and included in "amount realized" under § 1001, the prior property transaction pretty much drops out of the picture, and there is much to be said for treating the obligation as if it had been purchased for a cash price equal to its value. Indeed, as already noted, the very process of valuing the obligations at the date of receipt (which is required under the closed transaction approach) in effect establishes whether and to what extent a discount is present; and once established, the discount might as well be recognized. Nevertheless, in the leading case of this type, Paine v. Commissioner, 236 F.2d 398 (8th Cir. 1956), the court refused to recognize any discount component. There a corporation had sold ore-bearing lands for a total sales price computed on the basis of the estimated total tons of ore at 25 cents per ton. Most of the purchase price took the form of promissory notes issued by the buyer, in a total face amount equal to the purchase price computed as above, but without interest and in equal series maturing every six months for a period of more than 30 years. The notes were immediately distributed to the stockholders of the seller, at which time they were valued on the basis of a five per cent simple discount rate for the purpose of determining the basis of the notes in the hands of the stockholders. The taxpayer's notes, which were acquired by gift, were sold to a bank ten days before maturity, for a little less than the face value. The taxpayer treated the difference between the sales price and the basis of the notes as capital gain. The Commissioner determined that this increment constituted original issue discount, taxable at ordinary income rates, and was sustained by the Tax Court. That court first ruled that the "actual" purchase price of the land originally sold was equal to the value of the notes as of the date of sale, which was the figure at which they were valued for basis purposes. The court concluded that the "difference between the face value of the notes and the basis is not explainable as, and could not constitute a portion of, the purchase price". In a rather ironical twist, the court then distinguished the Caulkins case, which it was then still following, on the ground that Caulkins was a construction of § 1232(a)(1) dealing with redemption of obligations, whereas here the taxpayer's notes had been sold. However, the Court of Appeals reversed, holding that the entire face amount of the notes represented the purchase price of the land originally sold, and no part of that face amount constituted interest. The court stressed the fact that the face amount of the notes was exactly equal to the purchase price arrived at by the formula based on 25 cents per ton, and suggested that something would have been added to the face amount if a discount-interest component were included. The court also noted that prior to the sale, the seller of the land would have received serial payments under a lease, in effect corresponding to the pace at which the ore could be removed; and the court regarded the serial notes as simply an arrangement to maintain approximately the same schedule. (The court stopped short of the full force of this analogy, failing to note that under a lease arrangement all of the receipts would constitute ordinary income, subject of course to some recovery of basis by depletion or otherwise.)

Turning now to situations in which the open transaction approach is applied, there is in theory no less reason to separate out a discount where one is present. The measure of the discount would of course be exactly the same as under the closed transaction theory, that is, the difference between the value of the property exchanged and the face amount of the obligations received. However, there would be some administrative difficulties. For one thing, it would now become necessary to value the obligations (or what amounts to the same thing, the property exchanged for them) under the open transaction approach where, unlike under the closed transaction approach, such valuation would not otherwise be required. In addition, there would be the question of whether to account for any discount found on the informal installment approach or on the cost recovery basis. The former would be more common under the closed transaction approach; but it might be awkward if, as seems likely, the principal portion of the payments is being accounted for under the cost recovery method. And wherever the reason for applying the open transaction is uncertainty as to the total amount to be received under the obligation, as in Burnet v. Logan, discount could not be established in the normal fashion anyway, since it would not be possible to determine the total face amount of the obligation.[42]

The only case which seems to have directly presented the issue of taxing discount on an obligation received by a seller in an open transaction is Pretzer v. United States, 61–1 USTC § 9477 (D.C.Ariz.1961). There the taxpayer owned property subject to a mortgage and agreed to sell it to a buyer for $275,000, payable in installments roughly corresponding to the payments due on the mortgage. The buyer express-

---

42. It is, however, possible to focus a discount in this type of situation, by in effect treating each payment as though it were a separate obligation. See page 516 infra.

ly refused to pay any interest, and the agreement between the parties did not provide for any. The court rejected the Commissioner's contention that 6% of the sales price actually constituted interest. In holding that the decision of the parties not to include any interest in the transaction was conclusive, the court relied primarily upon an early ruling, I.T. 2674, XII–1 Cum.Bull. 96 (1933), which stated flatly, in a situation much like that in the Parrish case, supra, that where property is sold on a deferred payment basis and the contract does not provide for any interest, no part of the payments may be treated as interest. See also Kingsford Company v. Commissioner, 41 T.C. 646 (1964), where the court refused to find any discount interest on an installment obligation which the taxpayer had elected to report on the installment method under § 453. In Estate of Berry v. Commissioner, 43 T.C. 723 (1965), where it is not clear how the seller was reporting the obligation, discount is taxed to the seller as interest; but the case involved the same transaction as in the Raleigh Properties case, supra, and may be explained on the same basis.

What is the impact of § 1232(a)(2) on the question of finding a discount income on obligations received in exchange for property? First of all, it seems doubtful that this provision applies at all to open transactions, since payments received in those situations are regarded as being simply delayed portions of the purchase price for the property surrendered rather than payments in exchange for (or in retirement of) the debt obligations. But even where § 1232(a)(2) is operative, it provides very little guidance on the matter of discount in property transactions. What little evidence there is seems to cut against applying § 1232(a)(2) in property cases. First, the definition of original issue discount in § 1232(b) in terms of the word "price" suggests a limitation to cash transactions. Cf. Bowman v. Armour & Co., page 393 supra. Second, in 1956 a regulation proposed under § 1232(a)(1) would have expressly recognized as discount the difference between the face amount of debt obligations and the fair market value of property received in exchange therefor, but this proposal was omitted from the final regulations.

NOTE ON ACCOUNTING FOR INTEREST AND DISCOUNT ON INSTALLMENT OBLIGATIONS

To lay a basis for analyzing a complicated installment obligation like that received by Mrs. Moss in Unit 3 of Problem III, it would be useful to examine the relative components of principal and interest in a simpler type of obligation. For example, suppose that a prospective creditor considering making loan of $1000 for one year at 4% interest decides that he does not want to wait until the final maturity date before receiving some of the principal or interest to which he is entitled. For example, the creditor might want to receive one-half of the principal obligation, together with interest accrued to date, in six months, with the remaining one-half of the principal plus additional interest due at the end of the year. In that event, the transaction might take the form of a two-installment obligation, the first installment composed of $500 of principal plus $20.00 of interest, representing interest at 4% on $1000 for a half a year, and the second installment composed of the remaining $500 of principal plus $10.00 of interest, representing interest at 4% on $500 for half a year. (Keep in mind that the amount of interest on a given principal sum at a specified interest rate for half a year is the same as the amount of interest on the same principal sum at one-half the specified interest rate for a full year.)

Here too there is no difficulty in isolating the interest component of the transaction, in the amount of $30.00. Notice that is $10.00 less than in the case where none of the principal is repaid until the end of the year, because the debtor has had the use of only $500.00 for the last six months, instead of the full $1000.

Exactly the same approach can be used for more complicated types of installment transactions, of which the obligations in Unit 3 of Problem No. III are an extreme illustration. Thus Mrs. Moss, instead of arranging to receive 53 semi-annual payments of $6000,[43] might have agreed to take 1/53 of $195,000, together with interest accrued to date, every six months for 26½ years. In that event, Mrs. Moss' first installment, after the first six months, would amount to $7579.24 composed of $3679.24 of principal (1/53 × $195,000), and $3900.00 of interest (interest on $195,000 at 4% for half a year). The second installment, another six months later, would amount to $7505.66, composed of the same amount of principal repayment of $3679.24, plus interest on the balance of the outstanding principal during that period of $3826.42 (interest on $191,320.76 ($195,000 less $3697.24) at 4% for half a year).

However, the parties often prefer to discharge, or as it is commonly called "amortize", a long-term obligation together with the interest thereon by a series of equal installments, payable either annually, or as in the instant problem, semi-annually. Given a specified principal sum and interest rate, there are two dependent variables, the amount of each installment and the number of years over which such installments will continue. That means the parties can either decide upon the amount to be paid each year, which will fix the number of years for which such installments must be paid to amortize the obligation; or they can decide upon the number of years for which installments are to be paid, in which event the amount of each installment over such period will be fixed.

To illustrate the operation involved, assume that the parties have decided to amortize the simple obligation of $1000 at 4% interest by two equal semi-annual installments, instead of the uneven payments of $520 and $510. It should be obvious that the amount of the two equal payments could not be $515, i. e. one-half of the total principal and interest as computed above. Such a schedule would postpone the payment of $5.00 from first installment to the second without providing any compensation for the delay. But the value of a right to receive $5.00 immediately is greater than the value of a right to receive $5.00 at the end of six months, the amount of the difference being the value of interest on $5.00 for six months. So an obligation calling for the payment of $520 at the end of six months,

---

43. For simplicity it is assumed throughout this analysis that the obligation received by Mrs. Moss consisted of exactly 53 semi-annual payments of $6000 each, although in fact it appears that a fractional fifty-fourth payment was called for.

and $510 at the end of a year is worth more than an obligation calling for the payment of $515 at the end of six months and $515 at the end of a year.

Actually, determination of the precise amount of the two equal semi-annual installments which will amortize the principal and interest on an obligation of $1000 at 4% requires resort to a rather complicated mathematical formula. Happily, however, this formula has been reduced to a table from which the answer can readily be obtained. The table gives the amount per annual installment which will amortize the principal and interest on an obligation of $1 at a specified rate of interest in a specified number of annual installments. Since the table normally assumes annual installments, an adjustment is necessary to apply it to our situation which calls for semi-annual installments. Recall that the amount of interest on a given principal sum at a specified rate of interest for half a year is exactly the same as the amount of interest on the same principal sum at one-half the specified interest rate for a full year. Therefore our transaction can be viewed as an obligation of $1000 being amortized in two *annual* installments at 2% interest. Thus in order to find the amount of the two equal semi-annual installments which will amortize $1000 at 4% interest, we can simply take from the table the figure which will amortize $1 at 2% in two annual installments and multiply it by $1000. The resulting figure is $515.05.

Notice that the total of the two payments is $1030.10, which is 10 cents more than when the transaction took the form of paying $520 at the end of the first six months and $510 at the end of the second six months. That is as it should be, since under the equal installments approach the debtor has the use of an extra $4.95 for the second six months, on which the interest at an annual rate of 4% is 10 cents.

When such a schedule of equal installment payments is adopted, the question arises as to the amount of the interest component in each installment. It can not be assumed that the amount of interest included in the first installment is $15.05, one-half of the total interest in the transaction. That would be inconsistent with the general premise noted earlier that each installment includes all interest accrued to date. Rather the interest component in the first payment should still be equal to the total interest to date of $20.00, i. e., the interest on $1000 at 4% for half a year. The important point is that under this form of the transaction, only $495.05 of the principal ($515.05 less $20.00) has been repaid at the end of the first six months, and the debtor still has the use of $504.95 of principal for the next six months. Hence the interest component of the installment paid at the end of the second six months should equal the interest on $504.95 at 4% for half a year, or 2% of $504.95, or $10.10. And these figures prove out, since the total of the two interest components equals $30.10, and the total of the two principal components equals $1000.

Exactly the same mode of analysis is applicable to Mrs. Moss' more complicated installment obligation, consisting of fifty-three semi-annual installments of $6000 each. The determination of the interest component of each installment can be made on exactly the same basis as outlined above. Thus, the installment of $6000 payable at the end of the first six months must include interest at 2% of $195,000, a total of $3900. The rest of that first $6000 installment, $2100, would constitute repayment of principal, so that the remaining balance of the principal outstanding for the next six months would be $192,900 ($195,000 less $2100). Then the interest component in the second $6000 installment, payable at the end of the first year, would be $3858, (2% of $192,900), and the principal component would be $2142. This running calculation can of course be carried out for each of the remaining 51 payments.

It will be noted that under this approach to installment obligations the interest component declines in each successive installment. This of course follows from the fact that each installment also includes some repayment of principal, and hence the amount of principal outstanding for each successive period decreases. This approach is often referred to as accounting for the interest component on the "declining balance" basis, a term which is perhaps more familiar in connection with depreciation accounting.

It might also be observed that for an installment transaction where the total amount of interest for the entire transaction is known, there is an alternative technique for determining the amount of the interest component in each installment, which is just like the sum of the years digits method used in depreciation accounting. To illustrate, take the instant situation where the total amount of interest for the entire transaction can be determined by deducting the principal sum of the obligation, $195,000, from the total of the fifty-three $6000 payments, $318,000, leaving, $125,000 of interest. The next step is to add together all the numbers representing the number of installments, i. e. 1, 2, 3 and so forth through 53, the total being 1431. The interest component in any given installment is then determined by multiplying the figure for the total interest in the transaction by a fraction of which the denominator is 1431 and the numerator is the number of the particular payment from the end. Thus the interest component of the first payment under this sum of the year's digits method would be $53/1431 \times 123,000$, or $4555.55. While this figure is far from precisely accurate, the true figure determined earlier being $3900, at least this technique does serve to account for the entire interest in the transaction on a declining-balance basis.

It is also possible to account for the interest on an installment obligation on the "straight-line" method, that is, by allocating the total amount of the interest equally among the installments. For example, in the instant situation where the total interest is $123,000, each of the fifty-three $6000 payments could be regarded as including interest in the amount of $1/53 \times \$123,000$, or $2320.75. Indeed, according to a recent Tax Court decision the Commissioner is entitled to insist that interest be accounted for on this basis instead of on a sum-of-the-years digits basis. James Bros. Coal Co. v. Commissioner, 41 T.C. 917 (1964). However, that case may turn on its rather special facts (although no point was made of them in the opinion). The taxpayer had agreed to pay 5½% interest on the principal sum borrowed for a full three years (which amount was then included in the face value of the obligation), even though repayment was to be made ratably each month over the thirty-six month period, which means that the actual interest rate was substantially greater than 5½%.

Thus far we have been considering obligations which expressly provide for interest. As we have seen, however, an obligation may include an interest factor even though none is expressed. If the present value of the obligation is less than the face amount, the difference, or discount, represents at least in part the interest component in the obligation.

An installment obligation may similarly involve a discount. For example, assume that a creditor receives an obligation which entitles him to $515.05 six months from date plus $515.05 one year from date, without interest. Certainly such an obligation is worth less than $1030.10; and the difference, or discount, represents the charge for the use of the money during the period. In the absence of any independent measure of the fair market value of the obligation, the discounted present value of the obligation can be determined by estimating the appropriate rate of interest for the obligation and then using tables to find the amount which would be amortized by two semi-annual installments of $515.05 at that interest rate. Notice that this computation is just the converse of the one involved in transforming an obligation to pay a fixed principal sum into a series of installments which will amortize the given principal sum at the specified interest rate. Assuming that 4% would be the appropriate interest rate for this transaction, the discounted present value of the obligation would of course be $1000. Therefore, such an obligation should be treated exactly as if it were expressly a $1000 obligation at 4% being amortized in two semi-annual installments of $515.05, with the amount of the interest component in each installment being determined as before.

Notice that under this approach the discount is accounted for on a declining balance basis, just as is true of an express interest component. Alternatively, as in the case of express interest, discount could be accounted for on the straight-line basis, with the total amount allocated equally among the installments. This method is particularly inviting where the discount can be determined by independent evidence of the fair market value of the obligation. Thus suppose that the foregoing obligation consisting of two semi-annual payments of $515.05 was determined to have a value, on the basis of extrinsic evidence, of $1000. Obviously, it would be possible to resort to the interest tables to find the interest rate at which a fixed principal sum of $1000 would be amortized by two semi-annual payments of $515.05 each (which would, of course, be 4%); and that rate could then be used to determine the interest component in each installment, as before. However, once the discount has been determined without reference to the interest tables, it would be tempting to avoid those tables entirely, and one way of doing so would be to account for the discount on the straight-line basis, allocating the total ratably among the installments. Another alternative would be to use the sum-of-the-years digits method noted above, which would make it possible to account for the discount on a declining-balance basis without having to resort to the interest tables.

The same alternatives are available in the case of a more complex obligation like that received by Mrs. Moss. Assume, for example, that the parties did not start with a fixed principal sum at a specified interest rate which was subsequently transformed into an installment obligation, but rather simply agreed upon an installment obligation consisting of fifty-three consecutive semi-annual payments of $6000 each, without any interest. Obviously, such an obligation would be worth less than the total face amount of $318,000 (53 × $6000), so a discount would be present. In the absence of any independent measure of the fair market value of the obligation, its discounted present value could be determined by estimating the appropriate interest rate and then determining from the tables what amount, at that interest rate, would be fully amortized by fifty-three semi-annual payments of $6000. Here too the obligation would then be treated as if it were actually an obligation in the face amount of that discounted present value, with interest expressly provided at the assumed rate, which obligation was being amortized in fifty-three semi-annual installments of $6000 each; and again the amount of the interest component in each installment would be determined as before. Or, particularly if the amount of the discount was determined by valuing the obligation, the sum-of-the-years digits method might be utilized, or the discount could be allocated ratably among the installments.

There is one other possible view which may be taken of an installment obligation that does not expressly provide for interest. Returning for a moment to the simple obligation involving two semi-annual installments of $515.05, each installment might be regarded as a separate obligation, rather than as a related portion of a single overall obligation. That is, each installment could be treated as a separate deferred maturity obligation issued at a discount. Such a view of the transaction would result in a substantial change in the computation of the interest component in each installment. If the first $515.05 installment payable at the end of six months was regarded as a separate obligation, it would be analyzed in exactly the same terms as the single payment discount obligation of $1040 due at the end of one year dealt with above. In other words, that first $515.05 installment would be discounted to present value by determining from the tables the amount which, together with interest thereon for six months at the rate determined to be appropriate, would total $515.05. Still assuming that a 4% interest rate would be appropriate, the table would disclose that the discounted present value of such an obligation equals $504.95, and the remaining $10.10 would constitute the discount, or interest component in the transaction.

Analyzing the second installment of $515.05 payable at the end of one year as a separate deferred maturity obligation issued at a discount, the question would be what amount plus interest thereon at 4% for one year would total $515.05. (Since we are comparing this approach with a series of semi-annual installments, it is assumed that the interest is compounded semi-annually, that is, that interest attributable to the first six months would itself be entitled to earn interest during the second six months. In other words, to be precisely accurate, the question is what amount plus interest thereon at 4% for six months, plus interest on the sum of those two items for another six months at 4%, would total $515.05.) Here that discounted present value would equal $495.05, and the remaining $20.00 would constitute the discount, or interest component in the transaction.

Notice that when each installment is treated as a separate discount obligation, instead of as a portion of a single overall obligation, the interest component increases with each installment instead of declining. While to be sure the total amount of the interest over the full period covered by the installments would be exactly the same, the difference in the amount of interest found in any particular installment could be very substantial. For example, applying the separate obligation approach to the first two installments of Mrs. Moss' obligation would result in finding interest components of $117.60 and $133.04 respectively, whereas on the declining balance method the interest components amounted to $3900 and $3858.

It seems unlikely that this view of an installment obligation as a series of individual discount obligations would be accepted where, as in the case of Mrs. Moss, the parties did in fact start with a single obligation for a given principal sum, which was thereafter transformed into an installment obligation. But in a case where the parties simply arrange for a series of consecutive equal periodic installments, without starting with a single overall principal sum, such an approach could be adopted. And of course it is only through the use of this type of method that a discount can be determined in cases where, as in Burnet v. Logan, the obligation does not have any fixed principal amount.

As was suggested earlier, an obligation may be issued at a discount even though it does provide for interest, if the specified interest rate is lower than the fair market interest rate for such an obligation. See e. g., Leavin v. Commissioner, 37 T.C. 766 (1962) (original issue discount found where debentures with a 2% interest rate were issued for cash prices substantially less than face.) For example, an obligation for $1000 payable one year from date with interest at 4% would have a present value of less than $1000 if the appropriate rate for such an obligation were 6%. In the absence of other evidence of the fair market value of the obligation, the discounted present value, and hence the real principal sum involved, could be determined from the tables as the amount which together with interest thereon at 6% for one year would total $1040 (the purported principal sum of $1000 plus the express interest of $40). That figure would be $981.14; and the difference between that amount and $1000 would represent the discount involved, and hence an additional element of interest.

So also an installment obligation which includes an express interest component may nevertheless be issued at a discount. For example, take the obligation consisting of two semi-annual payments of $515.05 which resulted from the decision to amortize a given principal sum of $1000 at an express interest rate of 4% in two installments. Assume that the appropriate rate for this transaction is actually 6%. On this basis, the discounted present value of the obligation, and hence the real principal sum involved, would be determined by finding in the tables the amount which at 6% would be amortized by two semi-annual payments of $515.05 each. The figure would be $985.53. The transaction should then be treated exactly as if it expressly consisted of a fixed principal sum of $985.53 at 6% interest being amortized by two semi-annual payments of $515.05, with the interest component of each installment payment being determined in exactly the manner outlined earlier.

Notice that under this approach the discount is treated just like the express interest — indeed, the discount is combined with the express interest — with both accounted for on a declining balance basis. This situation is to be distinguished from those involving a single payment obligation, with interest payable each period up to maturity, where the discount is normally allocated pro rata among the periods covered by the obligation. For example, take an ordinary $1000 bond due five years from date, with interest at 4% payable annually in the interim. If the appropriate interest rate for such a bond was 6%, the bond would presumably command a price of only approximately $944.00, and the difference between that amount and $1000 would constitute the discount on the obligation. For this type of obligation it is perfectly appropriate to allocate the total discount evenly over the five years covered by the bond, just as the express interest is paid in equal installments during these periods. For here there are no repayments of principal prior to the ultimate maturity of the bond, and hence the primary basis for accounting for any component of interest on a declining balance schedule is absent.

On the other hand, as we have seen, it is perfectly possible to account for the discount on an installment obligation on the straight-line basis, and where the discount has been determined by valuing the obligation this method is particularly inviting. This is no less true where the express interest is being accounted for on the declining balance basis; it is not necessary that express interest and discount be accounted for on the same basis. Certainly the cases like Underhill v. Commissioner, page 502 supra, which require a pro rata recognition of discount in each installment, do not suggest that the same schedule must, or even may, be used in accounting for express interest. It may be worth noting, by the way, that under the schedule for reporting discount assumed in those cases the discount may actually be recognized on an ascending-balance basis. Assume, for example, that the obligation dealt with above, consisting of a $1000 obligation at 4% interest being amortized by two semi-annual payments of $515.05 each, is actually worth only $990, so that a discount of $10 is present. Under the pro rata schedule called for by the cases like Underhill, each installment will be treated as including discount in an amount proportionate to the total discount present, so that in the assumed case $10/1000$ of each principal payment would be allocated to discount, and only the remaining $990/1000$ would be recognized as repayment of principal. But remember that although the total amount of each installment is the same, the principal portion of each installment is different, increasing with each successive installment (corresponding to the fact that the express interest portion declines with each successive installment), and accordingly, the application of a fixed ratio of discount to principal will result in the discount being recognized on an ascending-balance basis.

Again, the same analysis would be applicable to a more complicated obligation like Mrs. Moss', if a discount is present. Assume, for example, that the appropriate interest rate for such an obligation would be 6%. To find the discounted present value of the obligation on a 6% basis, and hence the real principal sum involved, we would determine from the tables the amount which at 6% would be fully amortized by fifty-three semi-annual payments of $6000 each. That figure is $158,139.37; and the difference between that figure and $195,000 would constitute the discount on the obligation. To find the interest component in each installment, we could treat the obligation just as if it had started as a fixed principal obligation of $158,139.37, with interest at 6%, which had been transformed into an installment obligation consisting of fifty-three consecutive semi-annual payments of $6000. Thus the interest component in the first installment of $6000, payable after the first six months, would consist of interest at 6% on the principal obligation of $158,139.37 for half a year, or 3% of $158,139.37, which equals $4744.18. The rest of that first $6000 installment, $1255.82, would constitute repayment of principal, with the result that the remaining balance of the principal outstanding for the next six months would be $156,883.55. Hence the interest component of the second $6000 installment, payable at the end of the first year, would be $4706.51 (3% of $156,883.55), and the principal component would be $1293.49. As we have seen before, under this approach the discount element of the interest, together with the express interest component, is accounted for on a declining-balance basis.

If instead we had some independent evidence of the value of Mrs. Moss' obligation, say, $170,000, indicating a discount of $25,000, that amount might be allocated equally among the fifty-three installments. Alternatively, the $25,000 could be allocated among the installments in proportion to the principal amount of each, by treating the apparent principal portion of each installment as constituting discount to the extent of $25/195$, which would result in accounting for the discount on an ascending balance basis.

Again it might also be possible to regard this installment obligation as a series of separate deferred-maturity notes issued at a discount, this time at 6% instead of 4%. And again the result of such an approach would be to account for the total interest involved in the transaction on an ascending balance basis instead of a declining balance basis. For example, on the separate-discount-notes view of the transaction, the interest component of the first installment would amount to $174.76 and the interest component of the second installment would be $344.42. Notice that the total interest for the first year on this basis would amount to only $519.18, as compared with the total of $9450.69 determined under the declining balance basis. But as noted earlier, there seems less warrant for adopting the separate-discount-notes view of an installment obligation when the parties have started with an agreed-upon total principal sum, as in the instant situation, and the presence of an original issue discount would probably not affect this.

3. THE INSTALLMENT METHOD OF ACCOUNTING

Under IRC § 453 a taxpayer may elect to use the installment method of accounting to report gains from casual sales of property on a deferred payment basis. Under this statutory installment method the taxpayer treats a portion of each payment as gain, in an amount which is proportionate to the total expected gain on the transaction. For example, if the taxpayer sells property with a basis of $100 for a total price of $200, payable $50 down, and $50 a year for the following three years, the total expected gain amounts to 50% of the total price; therefore, the taxpayer would treat 50% of each payment (including the downpayment) as taxable gain. In a sense, the installment method constitutes a compromise between the cost recovery under the open transaction approach, and the immediate recognition of the total gain to date which occurs under the closed transaction view.

The Tombari case, supra, illustrates the most important limitation on qualification for the installment method, i. e., the total payments received in the year of sale must not exceed 30% of the total "selling price." The selling price consists of the sum of the entire consideration payable in cash, no matter when it is payable (including any liabilities assumed by the buyer or to which the property is subject), plus the fair market value of any property received (which of course does not include the deferred obligation since that is part of the consideration payable in cash). In computing the payments in the year of sale, any cash received is included, as well as the fair market value of any property received. Naturally, the deferred obligation of the buyer does not count as part of the payments received in the year of sale, and the same is true of any amounts received upon an assignment of the obligation in the year of sale. Reg. § 1.453–4(c). However, as the Tombari case indicates, if the seller receives an obligation of a third party, including an installment obligation, it constitutes "property" under § 453 and hence must be included at its fair market value in determining the amount of the payments received by the seller in the year of sale (as well as in computing the total selling price).

A question has arisen as to how to treat the buyer's assumption of liabilities of the seller in computing the amount of the payments received in the year of sale. Reg. § 1.453–4(c) states expressly that the assumption of a mortgage is not included (except to the extent that the mortgage liability assumed exceeds the basis of the property transferred), but the regulations are silent as to the effect of the assumption of liabilities in connection with sales of personal property. Cisler v. Commissioner, 39 T.C. 458 (1962), seemed to hold that in such circumstances the entire assumption counts as part of the year-of-sale payments; but the property transferred in that case had a zero basis, so the result is equally consistent with the so-called "mortgage rule" of Reg. § 1.453–4(c) under which only the excess of liabilities over basis is included in computing the year-of-sale payments. Since Cisler, the Tax Court has indicated that as to an assumption of liabilities without more the mortgage rule would be followed. See Irwin v. Commissioner, 45 T.C. No. 53 (1966). However, suppose the buyer makes payments during the year of sale on the liabilities assumed—must such payment be counted as part of the payments received by the seller in the year of sale? The two cases which have faced this question thus far have split—the Irwin case, supra, holding that such payments must be included, in an opinion reviewed by the entire Tax Court, and United States v. Marshall, 357 F.2d 294 (9th Cir. 1966), going the other way—so further litigation on the matter seems assured.

Any disposition of an installment obligation, except in cases of death or certain tax-free transactions, results in the immediate recognition of gain, measured by the difference between the basis of the obligation and the amount realized (or the fair market value of the obligation if it was disposed of without consideration). The basis of an installment obligation is the excess of the face amount of the obligation over the amount of income which would be recognized if the obligation were satisfied in full. Any gain or loss on the disposition of an installment obligation is considered as resulting from the sale or exchange of the property in respect of which the obligation was originally received.

While the installment method of § 453 would normally prove much more favorable than the closed transaction approach, it would often not be as desirable as open transaction treatment. But in many cases the taxpayer can not be sure whether his transaction qualifies for the open transaction method or not. Accordingly, a very important planning question in this area is whether a taxpayer can fall back on the installment method if he tries for the open transaction treatment but is found not to qualify. Until rather recently it seemed unlikely that this could be done, but the following case and ruling provide new basis for optimism.

MAMULA v. COMMISSIONER

United States Court of Appeals, Ninth Circuit, 1965. 346 F.2d 1016.

BARNES, CIRCUIT JUDGE: . . . The facts are not in dispute. In April 1959, taxpayer sold two parcels of real property which he had acquired on or about May 2, 1958. One parcel, which had a basis of $51,051.63, was sold for $150,000, taxpayer receiving from the purchaser a down payment of $5,000 in cash, plus a promissory note in the amount of $145,000, secured by a deed of trust. The other parcel, which had a basis of $27,601.70, was sold for $39,000; taxpayer received a down payment of $5,000 in cash, plus four promissory notes in the respective amounts of $18,000, $10,000, $4,000 and $2,000.

Petitioner's tax return for 1959 was prepared by an experienced certified public accountant who, for five years, had regularly prepared petitioner's federal income tax returns. The accountant advised petitioner that the profits from the sale of the real properties could be reported in any one of three ways: (1) a "closed transaction basis," whereby the entire profit could be reported and the tax paid thereon in the year the sales were consummated; (2) a "deferred basis," whereby no tax would become payable until payments equal to the cost of the property sold had been recovered from the purchasers; or (3) an "installment basis," whereby a portion of each dollar received would be reportable as a tax free recovery of cost and the balance as profit, spread over the life of the payments. Pursuant to petitioner's direction to minimize the 1959 tax liability, the accountant prepared the return with an accompanying schedule adopting the "deferred basis" method. This schedule accurately reflected the transactions in question; and, under the "deferred basis" approach, none of the profit was reflected in 1959 taxable income.

A subsequent audit of petitioner's returns for 1959 and 1960 resulted in a determination by respondent that the "deferred basis" method was improper under Treasury Regulations § 1.453–6 because the promissory notes received from the purchasers had an ascertainable fair market value. . . .

Upon notification that the use of the "deferred basis" method was to be disallowed, petitioner conceded that the method was inappropriate to the transaction in question because of the ascertainable value of the notes. Petitioner then requested that he be permitted to report the income under the installment method described in Section 453 of the Code. Respondent refused to grant such permission, but instead assessed deficiencies against petitioner by including the entire profit as taxable in the year of sale.

The Tax Court upheld respondent's refusal to permit petitioner to use the installment method in the recalculation of his tax liability. The Tax Court held that petitioner's attempt to report on the deferred-payment method resulted in a binding election which precluded him from subsequently reaping the benefits of the installment method. The Court supported this position by the precedent established in Pacific Nat. Co. v. Welch, 304 U.S. 191, 58 S.Ct. 857, 82 L.Ed. 1282 (1938); Jacobs v. Commissioner, 224 F.2d 412 (9th Cir. 1955); and a series of Tax Court opinions.

As an alternative basis for denying petitioner the use of the installment method, the Tax Court noted petitioner's non-compliance with the regulations promulgated under § 453, which required that the election of the installment method be made in the year of the sale and that the computation of the gross profit of the sale be submitted with that year's return. Treasury Regulations § 1.453–8(b).

This petition requests that we review the legality of the alternative holdings of the Tax Court.

The authorities relied upon by respondent and adopted in the Tax Court opinion differ in one elementary manner from the facts in the present case, and we deem it of some importance. Prior instances prohibiting a conversion to the installment method have always involved situations in which the taxpayer had initially elected a valid alternative method of reporting income. Thus, in the Pacific National case, supra, the taxpayer elected the deferred payment method in an appropriate situation, where it clearly and properly reflected his income. He later was denied the right to recalculate his tax liability with the installment method. Either method could have been used; petitioner made his choice, and he and the Commissioner were bound by it. The taxpayer had chosen a method which did not minimize his tax liability, but this alone did not suffice to permit him to make a subsequent recalculation where the method originally chosen did clearly reflect income. The Supreme Court stated:

> "Change from one method to the other, as petitioner seeks, would require recomputation and readjustment of tax liability for subsequent years and impose burdensome uncertainties upon the administration of the revenue laws. It would operate to enlarge the statutory period for filing returns . . ..
> There is nothing to suggest that Congress intended to permit

a taxpayer, after expiration of the time within which return is to be made, to have his tax liability computed and settled according to the other method. By reporting income from the sales in question according to the deferred payment method, petitioner made an election that is binding upon it and the commissioner." 304 U.S. at 194–195, 58 S.Ct. at 858.

We agree with the reasoning of the Supreme Court without reservation, on the facts of the Pacific National case. Once a taxpayer makes an election of one of two or more alternative methods of reporting income, he should not be permitted to convert, of his own volition, when it later becomes evident that he has not chosen the most advantageous method. But we do not think that the Pacific National case, or its reasoning, or any other case cited by respondent, warrants the result reached by the Tax Court in the present case. The controlling facts in the present case are distinguishable from Pacific National and other similar cases to which our attention has been called, and the reasoning of those earlier cases is not appropriate to the case before us.

The present case does not involve an election by a taxpayer to which he is conclusively bound. Indeed, the taxpayer could not be bound by his election for it was a nonallowable choice—it was not allowable and not allowed. No one was bound. We are not here concerned with a taxpayer who uses hindsight to learn that the method he had chosen, though proper, was not the most advantageous to him. We are rather concerned with an instance where the method chosen by the taxpayer is advanced in good faith, and later conceded to have been improper. At the insistence of the government, not the taxpayer, the prior calculations which adopted the improper method must now be set aside, and new calculations, *of necessity*, must be undertaken. The taxpayer has not been accused of any fraudulent activities nor any criminal violations; he rather has been found to have adopted, in good faith, an incorrect method of income recognition. *No forfeiture or penalty is assessed by law for such a mistake.* The only methods subsequently available to him were the installment method, which he now seeks to utilize, and the closed transaction basis, which would have recognized all the profit in 1959, the year of the sales. Taxpayer wishes to recalculate by using the former method, but the respondent and Tax Court have insisted that he recalculate using the latter method.

Requiring the closed transaction basis does not avoid the undue administrative burden which the Supreme Court emphasized and sought to prevent in Pacific National. A recalculation is necessary no matter which method is adopted. Moreover, requiring the closed transaction basis does not shut off a tax avoidance device of conversion. The initial election was invalid and the conversion has occurred at the urging of the Commissioner. The Commissioner and the Tax Court have penalized petitioner for the mistake he previously made, but such a penalty is not authorized by the statute, John P. Reaver, 42

T.C. 72 (1964), and is certainly not suggested by Pacific National or its related cases. See Note 9, Utah L.Rev. 403 (1964).

Although no case cited by either party is on all fours with the present facts, we think the Tax Court reasoning in John F. Bayley, 35 T.C. 288 (1960), and John P. Reaver, supra, parallels our view. In Bayley, the taxpayer did not choose an improper method of calculation, but rather argued that his gain came within the nonrecognition provisions of the Code. The Tax Court, in the portion of its opinion appropriate to the present controversy, stated at page 298:

> "It is our opinion that, in the circumstances here present, petitioners did make a timely election to use the installment method. . . . [T]he first time when petitioners were faced with the necessity of making such an election or choice was when the respondent determined that the gain was includible in income. They then did elect in their amended petition to have the gain computed under the installment method, if it should be determined that the respondent was correct. As above stated, it is our opinion that such election was timely."

* * *

We find the Tax Court in error in its imposition of a penalty on taxpayer by insisting that he use the less favorable method of income recognition in the course of the compulsory recalculation of tax liability for 1959 and 1960.

We also find that the alternative basis relied upon by the Tax Court to deny petitioner access to the installment method is unwarranted. Taxpayer fully disclosed the sales transactions in question in his tax return for the year of sale, 1959. He at that time chose an invalid method of income recognition; he did not use the installment method, so he of course did not attach a schedule showing the installment method calculations. The Regulations in question cannot be construed to apply in an instance where the taxpayer has not chosen the installment method in the year of sale, but has subsequently been permitted to elect it when the method originally elected has been determined to be invalid. The Regulations can only be reasonably construed as applicable where the taxpayer does elect the installment method in the year of sale; if he so elects, the Regulations set out the nature of the schedules that must be attached to that year's income tax return. In light of the unique retroactive election of the installment method sought to be used in this case where there has been good faith and a full disclosure of the transactions in the year of sale, it seems inequitable and unfair that the Regulations should be applied literally, contrary to the purpose and in conflict with the intent originally expressed by the Congress in passing the remedial statute.

The judgment of the Tax Court is reversed, and the case is remanded with instructions to permit the taxpayer to recalculate his tax liability for 1959 and 1960 with the use of the installment method of income recognition for the 1959 real property sales transactions.*

REVENUE RULING 65–297

1965–2 Cum.Bull. 152.

Pending the issuance of revised regulations the Revenue Service will dispose of cases involving the time for electing to report income on the installment method for sales of real property and casual sales of personal property, under section 1.453–8(b) of the Income Tax Regulations pursuant to the following cases: [citing a number of cases including Reaver and Bayley, referred to in the Mamula opinion, but *not* the Mamula case itself though it had been decided two months earlier].

Revenue Ruling 93, C.B. 1953–1, 82, which requires that the election to report a sale of property on the installment method must be made in a timely filed Federal income tax return for the taxable year of the sale, is hereby revoked. Revenue Ruling 56–396, C.B. 1956–2, 298, is modified to eliminate the conclusion that such an election is not valid when made in an untimely filed return.

In the disposition of cases, if, in good faith, the taxpayer failed to exercise the installment method election to report income from sales of real property and casual sales of personal property on a timely filed original return for the year of sale, the Service will recognize as valid, elections made under the following circumstances:

1. Those cases where the sale took place in a taxable year ended before December 18, 1958, if the election was made in the return for the year the first payment from the sale was received. December 18, 1958, is the date the present regulations were effective.

2. Those cases where election of the installment method was made on an amended return for the year of sale not barred by the statute of limitations or the operation of any other law or rule of law, if the facts indicate no election inconsistent with the installment election had been made with respect to the sale.

3. Those cases where the election had been made on a delinquent return for the year of sale.

---

*[Ed. note] Accord, Jolley v. United States, 65–2 USTC ¶ 9559 (D.Nev. 1965), involving a redemption of the taxpayers' stock in 1957 for $270,000, payable $30,000 in cash and $24,000 per year for ten years without interest. The taxpayers apparently decided to report the redemption on the open transaction basis and made no reference to it in their 1957 return. The Commissioner asserted a deficiency for 1957 on the ground that the redemption should have been reported on the closed transaction basis in 1957, with the deferred payment obligation of $240,000 valued at approximately $174,000. After paying the deficiency, the taxpayers sued for a refund on the ground that they were entitled to report the transaction on the installment basis, and the District Court sustained them.

However, an installment election made after the due date (including extensions thereof) for filing the return for the taxable year of the sale will not be recognized as a valid election if the assessment or collection of any portion of the tax for any taxable year resulting from the application of the installment method to such sale is prevented by the operation of the statute of limitations or of any other law or rule of law. . . .

Consideration is being given to the revision of the regulations under section 453 of the Internal Revenue Code of 1954 relating to the election of the installment method for sales of real property and casual sales of personal property. . . .

4. SECTION 483

SENATE FINANCE COMMITTEE REPORT

S.Rep. No. 830, 88th Cong., 2d Sess. 101–103 (1964).

(a) *Present Law.*— Under present law, an individual may sell a capital asset on the installment basis without making any specific provisions for interest payments on installments. In such cases the full difference between the cost or other basis for the property and the sales price usually is treated as capital gain to the seller. The buyer takes as a basis for the property the total sale price paid. For example, an individual taxpayer might sell a capital asset worth $1,000 for $1,300 payable over 10 years. In this case, if no mention is made that part of this payment is to be treated as interest, and the seller elects to report any gain on the installment basis, then each payment might be treated partly as a return of capital and partly as a capital gain. Over the 10-year period, the taxpayer would report $300 of capital gain (assuming he had the full fair market value of $1,000 as his basis for the property). However, had $300 of this $1,300 payment been specified as an interest payment, this amount would have been ordinary income to the seller rather than capital gain. From the buyer's standpoint, the $300 if treated as part of the price of the property would be added to the basis of the property and, in the case of depreciable property be recoverable over the life of the property. He might also, if the property qualified, be eligible for an investment credit with respect to this $300. On the other hand, if this $300 were treated as interest, he could receive an interest deduction for this amount.

(b) *General Reasons for Provision.*— Your committee agrees with the House that there is no reason for not reporting amounts as interest income merely because the seller and purchaser did not specifically provide for interest payments. This treats taxpayers differently in what are essentially the same circumstances merely on the grounds of the names assigned to the payments. In the case of depreciable property this may convert what is in reality ordinary interest income into capital gain to the seller. At the same time the purchaser can still recoup the amount as a deduction against ordinary income through depreciation deductions. Even where the property involved is a nondepreciable capital asset, the difference in tax bracket of the seller and buyer may make a distortion of the treatment of the payments advantageous from a tax standpoint. The House and your committee believe that manipulation of the tax laws in such a manner is undesirable and that corrective action is needed.

(c) *General Explanation of Provision.*— The bill solves the problem referred to above by providing that where property is sold on an installment basis and part or all of the payments are due more than 1 year after the date of the sale or exchange, if no interest payments are specified or if "too low" interest payments are specified then part of each payment due after 6 months is to be treated as interest rather than as part of the sales price.

The interest rate to be used for purposes of this provision is to be a rate provided by regulations prescribed by the Secretary of the Treasury or his delegate. It is anticipated that any rate specified by the Secretary of the Treasury or his delegate will reflect the going rate of interest and will not be higher than the rate at which a person, in reasonably sound financial circumstances and with adequate security could be expected to borrow money from a bank. A rate of 5 percent, for example, would appear appropriate under existing circumstances.

With this interest rate specified by the Secretary, the proportion of each payment which would be considered an interest payment would be determined in the following manner: First, the present value of each installment payment would be determined, based upon the specified interest rate. Second, the deduction of the total of these present values from the total actual payments provided for under the contract then would give the total "unstated" interest payments under the contract.[1] Third, the total unstated interest then is assumed to be spread pro rata over the total payments involved. Thus, if a specific payment represents one-tenth of the total payments, it would be assumed to include one-tenth of the total unstated interest.

For ease of administration and compliance, the regulations are to provide for the discounting of payments on a 6 month basis and are to ignore for this purpose any interest payments due within the first 6 months.

Where an installment contract provides for the payment of some interest, no unstated interest is to be computed unless the interest pay-

---

1. [Footnote by the Committee.] Where an interest rate was provided on the installments but at "too low" a rate, the present value of these interest payments would be determined along with the present value of the remainder of the payments as well. The unstated interest then would represent the present values, including the present values of such interest payments, deducted from total payments to be received under the contract excluding the interest payments.

ments specified are at a rate more than 1 percent below the rate of interest payments which would be computed under this provision in the absence of those payments. Thus, if a 5 percent rate is specified by the Secretary, no unstated interest will be computed where the interest actually provided for under the contract is 4 percent or more. This represents a de minimis rule to prevent the application of this provision in those cases where interest variations are relatively minor.

For purposes of this provision, a payment for property in the form of a note, or other evidence of indebtedness of the purchasers, is not to be treated as a payment. To treat such amounts as payments would permit avoidance of this provision merely by exchanging non-interest-bearing forms of indebtedness for property. However, payments made on such indebtedness for purposes of this provision will be treated as if they were payments made on the contract itself.

Where, at the time of the sale or exchange, some or all of the payments are indefinite as to their size; for example where the payments are in part at least dependent upon future income derived from the property, the "unstated" interest for purposes of this provision will be determined separately with respect to each indefinite payment as it is received, taking into account the time interval between the sale or exchange and the receipt of the payment. Also, where there is a change in the amount due under a contract, the "unstated" interest is to be recomputed at the time of each such change.

The bill specifies five situations in which this provision is not to apply: First, a de minimis rule as to price is provided. Thus, the provision will not apply unless the sale price of the property is in excess of $3,000. . . . Third, in the case of the seller, this provision is to apply only if some part of the gain from the sale or exchange of the property would be considered as gain from a capital asset or as gain from depreciable property. If the property is sold at a loss, this provision will nevertheless apply if, had there been a gain, some part of it would have been considered as gain from a capital asset or from depreciable property. . . .

REPORT OF THE HOUSE WAYS AND MEANS COMMITTEE

H.Rep. No. 749, 88th Cong., 2d Sess. A84–A85 (1963).

Technical Explanation of the Bill

(a) *Amount constituting interest.*—Section 483(a) provides the general rule that part of each payment (under a contract for the sale or exchange of property) to which section 483 applies is to be treated as interest for all purposes of the code. The tax treatment of both the purchaser and the seller may be affected by the rules of section

Sec. 9   TAX INCIDENTS OF REPURCHASES   529

483. Thus, the basis of property in the hands of a purchaser does not include that part of his payments under the contract which is treated as interest under section 483 and he is entitled to interest deductions for such part in accordance with his method of accounting.

The amount to be treated as interest under section 483 is determined by multiplying each payment to which such section applies by a fraction, (1) the numerator of which is the "total unstated interest" under the contract and (2) the denominator of which is the total of all the payments to which section 483 applies which are due under such contract.

(b) Total unstated interest.—Section 483(b) defines "total unstated interest," with respect to a contract for the sale or exchange of property, as an amount equal to the excess of (1) the sum of the payments to which section 483 applies which are due under the contract, over (2) the sum of the present values of such payments and the present values of any interest payments due under the contract. The present value of a payment is determined by discounting such payment from the date the payment is due under the contract back to the date of the sale or exchange. Thus, the present value of a payment is the amount which, if left at interest from the date of the sale or exchange to the date the payment is due, would have increased to an amount equal to such payment. The Secretary of the Treasury or his delegate is to prescribe regulations which provide the manner in which such present value is to be computed as well as the rate of interest to be used. Such regulations are to provide that payments are to be discounted on the basis of 6-month brackets; and that the present value of any interest payment which is due not more than 6 months after the date of the sale or exchange is to be equal to 100 percent of such payment. Thus, a payment is to be discounted from the nearest date which marks a 6-month interval from the date of the sale or exchange. This will make it unnecessary to compute interest on a daily basis.

The computation and allocation of total unstated interest with respect to a contract for the sale or exchange of property is illustrated by the following example:

Example.—S sells Blackacre to P under a contract which provides that P is to make payments in three equal installments of $2,000 each, such installments being due 1, 2, and 3 years, respectively, from the date of the sale. No interest is provided for in the contract. Assume that the Secretary of the Treasury or his delegate has prescribed by regulations that 5 percent per annum compounded semiannually is the rate of interest to be used. Section 483 applies to all three payments the sum of which is $6,000. The present value of the installment due 1 year after the sale is $1,903.63 ($2,000 discounted for 1 year at 5 percent per annum compounded semiannually). The present values of the other two installments are $1,811.90 ($2,000 similarly discounted for 2 years) and $1,724.59 ($2,000 similarly discounted for 3 years). The sum of the present values of the three installments (the payments to which sec. 483 applies) is $5,440.12 and therefore the total unstated interest under the contract is $559.88 ($6,000 minus $5,440.12). The part of each installment treated as interest is $186.63, which is arrived at by multiplying the amount of such installment ($2,000) by a fraction, the numerator of which is $559.88 (total unstated interest) and the denominator of which is $6,000 (total of payments to which sec. 483 applies).

(c) Payments to which section applies.—Section 483(c) defines the payments to which section 483 applies.

In general

Paragraph (1) of section 483(c) provides that, except as provided in section 483(f), section 483 applies to a payment under a contract for the sale or exchange of property if all the following conditions are met:

> Condition (1). Such payment constitutes part or all of the sales price.
>
> Condition (2). Such payment is due more than 6 months after the date of the sale or exchange.
>
> Condition (3). The contract is one that provides that some or all of the payments are due more than 1 year after the date of the sale or exchange.
>
> Condition (4). There is "total unstated interest" under the contract (computed by using a rate provided in regulations prescribed for this purpose by the Secretary of the Treasury or his delegate).

Thus, if a contract provides for one or more payments due more than 1 year after the date of the sale or exchange and the other conditions are met, section 483 applies even to those payments which are due less than 1 year, but more than 6 months, from the date of the sale or exchange.

NOTE ON § 483

Obviously, § 483 is an effort to resolve a number of the problems raised in the foregoing materials, at least so far as installment obligations without interest received in exchange for property are concerned. In effect, the statute calls for determining the principal sum which would be amortized by the specified installments if the obligation provided for interest, compounded semi-annually, at the rate specified by the Secretary, which has now been fixed in the final regulations at the 5% suggested by the Committee Reports. Reg. § 1.483–1(c) (2). The discount, or as § 483 terms it, "unstated interest," thereby disclosed is then to be reported by allocating it ratably among the installments in the proportion that each installment bears to the total of all installments. (This means that in the typical case of equal installments the interest will be accounted for on the straight-line method.) Where the total unstated interest cannot be determined at the outset, as for example where the number or the amount of the installments is indefinite, § 483 adopts the method referred to above as the "separate discount notes" approach, under which the unstated interest is reported on an ascending-balance basis.

While § 483 may serve to bring some order into the interest-discount area for the cases to which it does apply, it also creates some troublesome problems with regard to situations beyond its reach. Perhaps foremost among these is the question of whether § 483 provides the exclusive measure of discount on installment obligations received on the sale of property, so that once that statute has been satisfied (either by applying it or because the minimum 4% rate is met), no additional discount may be established. To illustrate, take the installment obligation received by Mrs. Moss, which provides for express interest at 4% and therefore satisfies § 483. If as assumed above an independent valuation of the obligation showed a value of $170,000, indicating a discount of $25,000, does § 483 now preclude recognizing it as such? This problem is particularly acute in the case of a deferred payment sale which is accounted for on the closed transaction basis. In that situation the obligation must be valued at the time of receipt, and it would seem that under the test of the Underhill case, page 502 supra, the spread between the face amount of the obligation and the figure at which it is valued would constitute discount. But if § 483 provides the exclusive measure of discount in such circumstances, presumably this spread would simply be treated as gain upon the repayment of an obligation, to be taxed at ordinary or capital rates depending on the applicability of § 1232(a)(1).

Notice that in any event § 483 is equally applicable to deferred payment sales which are accounted for on the open transaction basis. If the total amount of the unstated interest subject to § 483 can be determined, the statute would be applied in the same manner as if the closed transaction basis were applicable; if the total amount of the unstated interest cannot be determined at the outset, the separate notes method would be used.

Section 483 is also applicable even though the formal installment method of § 453 has been elected, so that the unstated interest subject to § 483 will be taxed pursuant to that section, leaving only the balance of the installments to be reported in accordance with the schedule of § 453. See Reg. § 1.483–2(a)(2). Notice that this can play havoc with the application of the 30% limitation on the payments received by the seller in the year of sale. For example, prior to § 483 it was assumed that a sale for $10,000, payable $3,000 in the year of sale and $1,000 per year for the following seven years, without interest, would qualify under § 453. With the application of § 483, however, the total purchase price is no longer regarded as $10,000, but rather as $3,000 plus the discounted value of the seven annual payments of $1,000 (i. e., $3,000, plus $7,000 less the unstated interest under § 483), which of course totals less than $10,000; and accordingly the $3,000 downpayment would exceed the permissible 30%. On the other hand, unstated interest is not excluded in computing the "sales price" for the purpose of applying the $3000 minimum of § 483(f)(1). Reg. § 1.483–2(b).

Needless to say, § 483 presents a host of other problems, particularly with relation to its impact upon such diverse areas as tax-free exchanges and stock options. See generally, Frome, *Caveat Vendor:* Interest is Imputed by the Revenue Act of 1964, 31 Brooklyn L.Rev. 297 (1965); Gurko, Unstated Interest under the Revenue Act of 1964, 33 Geo.Wash.L.Rev. 660 (1965).

D. IMPACT OF A REDEMPTION UPON THE REMAINING STOCKHOLDERS

REVENUE RULING 58–614

1958–2 Cum.Bull. 920.

The Internal Revenue Service will follow the decision [in Holsey v. Commissioner, 258 F.2d 865 (3d Cir.1958)], in cases involving similar facts and circumstances.

The decision holds that a remaining shareholder of a corporation does not receive a constructive dividend by way of enhancement in the value of his stock as a result of a purchase by the corporation of another shareholder's stock. In the future, the Service will not treat the purchase by a corporation of one shareholder's stock as a dividend to the remaining shareholders merely because their percentage interests in the corporation are increased. On the other hand, if the stock is in reality purchased by a remaining shareholder and paid for by the corporation, then, regardless of the form of the transaction, the payment will be considered a dividend to the shareholder who made the purchase. This position is in accord with the decisions of H. F. Wall v. Commissioner, 164 F.2d 462, Louis H. Zipp v. Commissioner [259 F.2d 119 (6th Cir.1958)], and similar court holdings.

In these transactions, if a shareholder surrenders stock to a corporation for less than its fair market value, such surrender may be a gift or compensation to the shareholders who remain interested in the corporation. Conversely, if a corporation pays more than fair market value for its stock, the payment may be compensation to the shareholder surrendering stock or may be a gift to him from the shareholders who remain interested in the corporation.

NOTE ON REV.RUL. 58–614

According to Rev.Rul. 58–614, the decision in the Holsey case left intact the Wall-Zipp line of cases to the effect that if the corporation pays for the stock of the withdrawing stockholder on behalf of the remaining stockholders, the latter will be treated as having received a dividend. To appreciate the significance of this assumption, it is necessary to analyze some of the varying factual patterns in this area. Let us start with the simple case of A and B each owning 50% of the stock of the corporation, with A wanting to withdraw from the enterprise by selling his stock for its fair market value of $100,000. Unless B is willing to have an outsider come into the enterprise, either he or the corporation must purchase A's stock. Obviously, if B simply uses his own private resources to purchase

A's stock, there will be no tax incidents to B; but he will have increased his investment in the corporation by $100,000. If B then wanted to draw upon the corporation's funds to replenish his private resources, he could cause the corporation to pay a dividend of $100,000 (assuming that the corporation's surplus position would make such a dividend lawful, and that its cash position would make the dividend feasible). But such a dividend would be fully taxable to B as such, assuming the presence of the necessary earnings and profits. It is into this mold — that is, purchase by the remaining stockholder followed by an ordinary dividend from the corporation to him — that the Commissioner would like to force transactions in this area whenever possible.

At the opposite end of the tax spectrum is the straight redemption by the corporation of A's stock. To be sure, some of the earlier cases suggested that even that transaction might constitute a constructive dividend to B because the redemption benefited him by increasing his percentage stock interest in the corporation (here to 100%). But of course, the short answer to such a contention is that while B does end up owning 100% of the corporation, the corporation is only half as large, having distributed half of its value to A in the redemption transaction. On the other hand, there is the disquieting thought that this is equally true when B purchases A's stock personally for $100,000 and then causes the corporation to distribute a dividend in that amount — there too B ends up as the sole owner of a corporation only half as large.

Actually, it would be rather harsh to treat the entire redemption distribution as a dividend to the remaining stockholder, just as it would be to regard the whole distribution as a dividend to the withdrawing stockholder (which today would be precluded in the case of a non pro rata redemption by § 302). Perhaps the Government would have achieved greater success in its effort to impose some dividend tax on non pro rata redemptions if it had sought to allocate the dividend treatment between the withdrawing and remaining stockholders. One way of accomplishing this would have been to view the redemption transaction as though it had consisted of a pro rata dividend to all stockholders to the extent of accumulated earnings and profits, followed by a purchase of the withdrawing stockholder's stock (now less valuable as a result of the distribution) by the remaining stockholders, using the proceeds of the dividend "received" by them. In other words, in the above situation the redemption distribution of $100,-000 would be taxed as dividend of $50,000 each to the two stockholders, and A would be treated as having sold his stock to B for $50,000. However, this approach seems never to have been advanced in any case, much less adopted; and it would now seem to be foreclosed in non pro rata redemption cases by § 302.

In any event, the Holsey case (plus the Commissioner's acquiescence) now preclude taxing the distribution in a straight-forward corporate redemption as a dividend to the remaining stockholders. Actually, the Holsey case is a particularly strong authority in this area, because the court decided for the taxpayer despite the fact that the option on the withdrawing stockholder's stock which the corporation acquired and exercised had originally been granted to the remaining stockholder. In other words, in Holsey the transaction had taken at least one modest step down the path of a purchase by the remaining stockholder, before emerging as a corporate redemption, which makes it at least a little easier to bring the case under the Wall-Zipp line treating the corporation's payments as made on behalf of the remaining stockholders. To appreciate the significance of this factor, let us consider some of the varying fact patterns in this area. Suppose first that in the above illustration B agreed to personally purchase the stock of A for $100,000 payable in installments; but thereafter B decided that the corporation should make the purchase and assigned the contract to the corporation. This is what happened in the Wall case, and the court held that subsequent payments by the corporation on the installment purchase contract assumed by it constituted dividends to the remaining stockholder. The court stressed the fact that the remaining stockholder was personally liable on the repurchase obligation, and remained so even after he had assigned it to the corporation. This led the court to say that when the corporation made the payments on the obligation, it "paid his indebtedness for Wall out of its surplus. It cannot be questioned that the payment of a taxpayer's indebtedness by a third party pursuant to an agreement between them is income to the taxpayer". Of course the soundness of this general principle is beyond dispute. However, it only applies where the taxpayer has given no consideration for the discharge of his indebtedness by the third party, whereas in Wall, as the taxpayer pointed out, he had assigned to the corporation the benefits of the stock purchase agreement (i. e., the right to receive the stock) which would seem to constitute ample consideration for the corporation's assumption of the corresponding indebtedness. But the court regarded the taxpayer's assignment to the corporation of his right to acquire the stock as little different from a sale by a sole stockholder of a portion of his stock to the corporation, which of course constitutes a classic dividend case.

This hardly did justice to the taxpayer's position. After all, the fact remains that the taxpayer's assignment to the corporation of his right to receive the stock was a complete answer to the discharge of indebtedness theory. Then as to the analogy to a redemption of stock from a sole stockholder, the important point is that the transaction in Wall was also virtually identical in ultimate effect to a direct corporate redemption from the withdrawing stockholder in the first place. Therefore, the real question was which of those two rather close analogies (with very different tax incidents) was to be followed. And this issue can not be resolved against the corporate redemption analogy merely by observing that where there is more than one alternative for achieving a desired result, "the method pursued is determinative for tax purposes without regard to the fact that different tax results would have attached if the alternative procedure had been followed." For it is equally true that the taxpayer in Wall did not actually acquire the stock personally and then have it redeemed by the corporation.

Perhaps what the court was trying to say in the Wall case is that once the transaction has started down the line of a purchase of the withdrawing stockholder's stock by the remaining stockholder, it is then too late to switch over to a corporate redemption and come within that safe harbor (as subsequently established by the Holsey case). If so, the soundness of this view is open to question, since it really amounts to a trap for the unwary, forever depriving a stockholder of the favorable tax treatment available for corporate redemption if he once starts down the stockholder-purchase route. Hence it should not be surprising that the force of the Wall case seems to be on the wane. Even in the recent cases which have purported to follow Wall, there has generally been some additional factor which led the court to impose a dividend tax on the remaining stockholder. Thus in the Zipp case, cited in Rev.Rul. 58–614 and decided just prior to Holsey, it appeared that the two taxpayers had acquired all of the stock of a corporation from their father without making any payment themselves, while he received almost $100,000 from the corporation. Here the analogy to a corporate redemption somewhat breaks down since the two taxpayers had to personally purchase at least some of their father's stock in order to become stockholders at all. To be sure, they could perhaps have purchased only a few shares each from their father, and then had the corporation redeem the rest of his stock, e. g., Zenz v. Quinlivan, 213 F.2d 914 (6th Cir. 1954); but here it might be fair to hold the taxpayers to what they actually did (or perhaps more accurately, what they failed to do).

In Deutsch v. Commissioner, 38 T.C. 118 (1962), the taxpayer had entered into an agreement to purchase all of the stock of a corporation from the widow of the deceased sole stockholder. The agreement called for the taxpayer to make a downpayment of $10,000 in exchange for 35 of the outstanding 350 shares, and to purchase, or cause the corporation to redeem, the remaining shares at the rate of 14 shares every three months for $4200. Except for the original downpayment, the corporation made all the payments, and the Tax Court held that they constituted dividends to the taxpayer. Here too it was a case of an outsider acquiring all of the outstanding stock of a corporation, rather than an existing stockholder becoming the sole stockholder by virtue of the withdrawal of the other stockholder; but unlike in Zipp the taxpayer clearly did purchase the first 35 shares personally. However, the court appears to have been influenced by the fact that the corporation was never a party to the agreement, and never adopted it. In addition, there was an unexplained provision in the agreement calling for the issuance of an additional 300 shares, apparently as a stock dividend, which does suggest that the taxpayer wanted to end up with a substantial number of shares no matter what procedure was followed, and hence does cut in favor of a stockholder-purchase view of the transaction.

In any event, the Tax Court has seemed to be much more willing of late to mitigate the rigors of the Wall decision, at least in cases like the above illustration where in effect one stockholder is withdrawing and the other is becoming the sole stockholder. Thus in Priester v. Commissioner, 38 T.C. 316 (1962), B bound himself to buy A's stock over a two year period but shortly thereafter realized he would have difficulty financing the purchase. Accordingly, B arranged with a third party to take over the contract, with the understanding that he could sell the stock to the corporation at a profit a short time thereafter. The Tax Court found no dividend to B upon the subsequent redemption, holding that the assignment of the contract to the third party was a bona fide transaction which could not be ignored, and that under Holsey the subsequent redemption of the stock from the third party produced no dividend to the remaining stockholder.

Although the court in Priester did not expressly indicate any quarrel with Wall, some change in view would seem to be reflected by the court's willingness to accept the purported sale to the third party. In other situations the Tax Court has been quick to ignore a transitory sale of stock in contemplation of its prompt redemption by the corporation. E. g., Idol v. Commissioner, 38 T.C. 444 (1962), aff'd, 319 F.2d 647 (8th Cir. 1963). In that case, decided by the Tax Court only a few weeks after Priester, the taxpayer had acquired all of the stock of a corporation but still owed a substantial balance on the purchase price. When a third party indicated an interest in acquiring some of the corporation's assets, the taxpayer arranged for a sale of some of his stock to the third party, upon the understanding that the stock would promptly be redeemed in exchange for the corporate assets which the third party wanted. The court virtually ignored the purported sale of stock to the third party and held that the true nature of the transaction consisted of (1) a sale of corporate assets to the third party (on which the corporation was required to recognize gain), together with (2) a distribution of the sale proceeds by the corporation to its sole stockholder in redemption of stock, which constituted a dividend to him. Query whether the result would have been different if the taxpayer had only purchased part of the stock from the prior owner, with the rest of the stock being sold to the third party and then redeemed for the desired assets.

The Tax Court again extended rather sympathetic treatment to a taxpayer caught between Wall and Holsey in Goss v. Commissioner, 22 T.C.M 1219 (1963). There the taxpayer inherited a portion of the stock of a corporation from his father and purchased the rest of the stock from the other beneficiaries under his father's will, borrowing the amount necessary from a third party and pledging the stock acquired as security for the loan. Being unable to meet the payments on the loan, the taxpayer transferred some of the stock to the third party in cancellation of the loan. Immediately thereafter the corporation adopted certain stock restrictions pursuant to which the corporation purchased the third party's stock. The court refused to apply the Wall case to find a dividend to the taxpayer. Instead, the court held that the Priester case was controlling, even though the evidence was not quite as clear as it had been in Priester that the third party had made a substantial profit in the transaction and hence was no mere "straw man".

Assuming that these cases presage some relaxation of the Wall view, they also present some line-drawing problems of their own. For example, harking back to our earlier illustration, suppose that B has actually completed a cash purchase of A's stock when he realizes that a corporate redemption would have been better. Rather than risk an outright redemption at this point, B sells the stock acquired from A to a third party, from whom it is promptly redeemed as contemplated by the parties. Of course if B had been the sole stockholder for some time, such a device would hardly enable him to avoid dividend treatment upon a redemption of his stock. But where it involves stock just acquired from A, is it really any different from what was allowed in Priester?

But if this kind of transaction is to be sustained, what about a direct redemption from the remaining stockholder of stock just acquired from the withdrawing stockholder? Actually, such a redemption has occasionally escaped dividend treatment where it was found that the remaining stockholder really acquired the stock as the agent of the corporation. The leading case to this effect is Fox v. Harrison, 145 F.2d 521 (7th Cir. 1944), where it did appear that the parties had always intended that the corporation purchase all of the stock of the withdrawing stockholder, but since the corporation did not have sufficient surplus to purchase all of the stock, the remaining stockholder acquired a portion of it as a temporary measure, pending the corporation's ability to purchase it. However, the rule of Fox v. Harrison has proved a slender reed upon which to rely, and despite an effort to invoke it in practically every case following the Wall approach, e. g., Deutsch v. Commissioner, supra, the courts have only rarely been satisfied that the purchase by the remaining stockholder was on behalf of the corporation.

On the other hand, an even broader rule than that of Fox v. Harrison is suggested by the decision in McShain v. Commissioner, 22 T.C.M. 1611 (1963). There a contemplated corporate redemption of stock from the withdrawing stockholders was discarded in favor of a purchase by the remaining stockholder because the corporation did not have the necessary liquid funds to finance the acquisition. Subsequently the corporation redeemed most of that stock from the remaining stockholder at the same price. In holding that there was no dividend to the remaining stockholder, the court did not rest on the notion that he had bought as "agent" for the corporation; indeed, Fox v. Harrison was not even mentioned. Rather the court stressed the necessity of considering all the circumstances and added the following significant comment:

> There was no practical difference to [the remaining stockholder] between a corporate redemption of the shares of the retiring shareholders or a purchase by him of the stock of the retiring stockholders followed by a redemption from him of some of the shares purchased at the price he paid for them.

Accord, Peterson v. Commissioner, 23 T.C.M. 63 (1964).

However, two other recent cases attest to the continuing vitality of the distinction between corporate redemption from the withdrawing stockholder and purchase by the remaining stockholder followed by redemption from him. In McGinty v. Commissioner, 325 F.2d 820 (2d Cir. 1963), the corporation borrowed money from a bank and loaned it to the remaining stockholder to use in the purchase of the withdrawing stockholder's stock. Subsequently, the corporation redeemed that stock from the remaining stockholder in cancellation of the loan. The court sustained dividend treatment, finding that although there was some evidence indicating that the redemption was intended to be simultaneous with the purchase from the withdrawing stockholder, the Tax Court was not compelled to find that the two transactions were part of a single plan. The court rejected any suggestion that because the corporation might have redeemed the stock directly the transaction should be viewed as if it had done so.

In Gloninger v. Commissioner, 22 T.C.M. 1635 (1963), affirmed per curiam, 339 F.2d 211 (3d Cir. 1964), the taxpayer was the majority stockholder of a corporation which early in 1954 redeemed about 8% of its stock and later that year was faced with a request by two stockholders owning over 20% of the stock that they be bought out. The taxpayer personally purchased their stock, using the proceeds of a loan from a bank which called for repayment on an installment basis. During the next few years the corporation redeemed some 278 of the 360 shares purchased by the taxpayer from the withdrawing stockholders. The Tax Court sustained dividend treatment, finding that there was no business purpose for the redemption because the objective of eliminating the stockholders who wanted to be bought out was accomplished by the taxpayer's personal purchase, and hence the redemption was not required. Holsey, Wall, and the related cases were not even mentioned.

See generally, Lange, Bootstrap Financing: The Redemption Technique, 18 Tax L.Rev. 323 (1963).

E. TAX INCIDENTS OF A REDEMPTION TO THE CORPORATION

1. RECOGNITION OF GAIN OR LOSS UPON A REDEMPTION DISTRIBUTION IN KIND

IRC § 311 provides that no gain or loss shall be recognized by a corporation upon a distribution of property "with respect to its stock," except where an installment obligation, lifo inventory, or property subject to liabilities in excess of basis, is distributed. While this provision is aimed mainly at dividend distributions, Reg. § 1.311–1(a) states that it also applies to redemption distributions (other than distributions in partial or complete liquidation which are governed by § 336 providing for essentially the same result). However, according to Reg. § 1.311–1(e), § 311 only applies to distributions made by reason of the corporation-shareholder relationship; hence "if the corporation receives its own stock as consideration upon the sale of property by it, or in satisfaction of indebtedness to it, the gain or loss resulting is to be computed in the same manner as though the payment had been made in any other property". Obviously, some such limitation as this is necessary since otherwise a corporation could "sell" its inventory for stock without recognition of gain, and then reissue the stock for cash tax-free under § 1032. But absent a clear tax avoidance scheme of that kind, it is not easy to tell when this proviso would apply, since any redemption distribution in kind is in effect *both* a sale of property by the corporation *and* a repurchase of stock. Such cases as there have been provide little guidance on the matter. Compare Farmers Union Corp. v. Commissioner, 300 F. 2d 197 (9th Cir.1962) (distribution by a corporation of one of its divisions, which it had been trying to sell, to a group of its stockholders in exchange for some of their stock held not a sale on which the corporation could recognize loss), with Hammond Iron Co. v. Commissioner, 122 F.2d 4 (5th Cir.1941) (redemption distribution in kind pursuant to a corporate resolution authorizing the repurchase of stock for cash or property held a sale on which the corporation was entitled to recognize loss).

Sometimes a redemption in kind may cloak what is in fact a sale of corporate assets to a third party, combined with a cash redemption, in which event the corporation will be taxed on any unrealized gain on the assets distributed. Thus where a third party who was interested in purchasing certain assets from a corporation was persuaded to buy stock from the sole stockholder for the same price he would have paid for the corporate assets, upon the understanding that such stock would be promptly redeemed in exchange for the desired assets, the court found a taxable sale of the assets by the corporation (and a dividend to the sole stockholder in the amount of the cash received). See Idol v. Commissioner, discussed at page 536 supra. But Standard Linen Service, Inc. v. Commissioner, 33 T.C. 1 (1959), reached the opposite conclusion in quite similar circumstances except that the corporation had a number of shareholders and they did not all participate in the sale of stock to the third party. The court concluded that "each step of the . . . transaction should be recognized and given its full tax effect, and that its real character was a sale of stock followed by a partial liquidation. The steps taken by the parties had substance and as we see it, were taken in reality and good faith."

The general rule precluding recognition of gain upon a distribution in kind can provide an opportunity for some other significant tax maneuvering. Suppose that a corporation contemplating a cash distribution to its stockholders instead distributed appreciated property, with a current value equal to the amount of the proposed distribution, and then repurchased the property at its current value. Ostensibly, the repurchase would give the corporation a new, higher cost basis for the property, although the corporation would never have paid any tax on the appreciation in value, and both the corporation and the shareholders would end up exactly where they would have been if the corporation had simply distributed cash in the first place. Of course if there was a commitment from the outset to resell the property to the corporation, the purported distribution and sale might be disregarded as a sham, and the corporation would not be entitled to a new basis; but the matter is more difficult where a resale to the corporation, although perhaps quite likely, is not fixed in advance.

Does the notion of business purpose help in this type of case? Suppose that the form of the transaction had been dictated by the desire of the stockholder, whose stock was to be redeemed on an installment basis, to reduce the risk of a surplus or insolvency cut-off, by having a redemption distribution in kind, followed by a resale of the property to the corporation on the same installment terms and conditions originally envisioned for the repurchase of stock. Would this objective constitute a sufficient business purpose to require recognition of the transaction for tax purposes, and hence entitle the corporation to use the higher basis?

These issues came before the court in United States v. General Geophysical Co., 296 F.2d 86 (5th Cir.1961), where it was conceded that a primary purpose of the redemption distribution in kind followed by a resale of property to the corporation on a deferred installment basis was to protect the withdrawing stockholders against the possibility of an insolvency cut-off under Robinson v. Wangemann, page 429 supra. However, the court stressed the fact that although the withdrawing stockholders were technically free not to resell the property to the corporation, it was virtually certain that they would because that property constituted nearly 50% of the assets of the corporation and was totally integrated in its operations. Since there was in fact no physical delivery of any of the assets to the stockholders, and the corporation's control and use of the property were never interrupted, with even the bare legal title surrendered for only a few hours, the court concluded that there was not a sufficient interruption in ownership to produce a new basis. On rehearing, 62–1 USTC para. 9115 (5th Cir.1961), the court emphasized that its decision had not been based on any lack of good faith on the part of the parties, or any doubt as to the business purpose of the transaction, or any quarrel with the idea that it might help to protect the selling stockholders against the insolvency cut-off of Robinson v. Wangemann. Instead the court's view, which it reaffirmed, was that *"for tax purposes* there was not a sufficient severance of the corporation's ownership over the assets for the transaction to create . . . a stepped-up basis."

2. DEDUCTIBILITY OF REDEMPTION EXPENSES

a. THE "PARTIAL LIQUIDATION" CASES

The starting point for the analysis here is the rule that expenses of the reorganization or recapitalization of a corporation must be capitalized, to be deducted (as a capital loss) only if and when the corporation is dissolved, just as was true of the expenses of organizing a corporation until the enactment in 1954 of § 248 permitting organization expenses to be amortized over a period of five years or more. See generally, Note, The Deductibility of Attorneys' Fees, 74 Harv.L. Rev. 1409–1413 (1961). At the opposite end of the spectrum is the rule that the expenses of liquidating a corporation may be deducted against ordinary income when incurred, which is usually justified on the ground that such expenses do not relate to the creation or continuance of a capital asset, or that they represent the cost of accounting to the corporate owner of the enterprise. The opposing rules for liquidation and recapitalization collided in cases of partial liquidation (which under the 1939 Code, it will be recalled, included all stock redemptions), since such transactions contain both liquidation elements, in that some of the stockholders retire from the enterprise and/or some of the corporation's activities are terminated, and recapitalization elements, in that the enterprise continues in altered form. Thus in Mills Estate, Inc. v. Commissioner, 17 T.C. 910 (1951), reversed, 206 F.2d 244 (2d Cir.1953), involving a pro rata redemption distribution of the proceeds of sale of one of a corporation's businesses, the Tax Court commented as follows:

> The expenditures involved herein have characteristics that partake of both lines of decisions. Petitioner's legal expenses were undoubtedly incurred in substantial part in order to amend its charter and reduce authorized capitalization, thereby providing for the acquisition and retirement of its stock followed by the issuance of new stock in reduced amount. This aspect of the transaction certainly brings this case within the [recapitalization] line of authority. However, the actual distribution of assets in partial liquidation was also a significant factor with respect to which the legal fees were paid, and it is difficult to perceive why the cost of a partial liquidation should be any the less an ordinary and necessary business expense than the cost of a complete liquidation.

Accordingly, the Tax Court allocated half of the legal fees and expenses to the recapitalization aspect of the transaction and half to the partial liquidation, and held the latter half deductible. The Court of Appeals reversed, holding that all of the corporate steps taken should be viewed "as a single transaction" which "was essentially a reorganization", and therefore none of the expenses were deductible. The Court of Appeals also intimated some doubt about the rule permitting deduction of liquidation expenses but in view of its decision it did not have to pass on that question.

However, in the most recent case in point, Gravois Planing Mill Co. v. Commissioner, 299 F.2d 199 (8th Cir.1962), the court allowed a deduction for the expenses of a partial liquidation consisting of the redemption of all the stock of one of the stockholders without any contraction of the business of the corporation. In that case Beckemeier, the founder of the business and owner of 200 of the outstanding 400 shares, decided to retire and offered to sell his stock to the corporation in accordance with the existing stock restriction agreement among the stockholders. After some discussion with the other three stockholders, two of whom owned 75 shares and the third 50, it was agreed that Beckemeier should sell 25 shares to the third stockholder, to equalize the holdings of the other three, with the corporation to redeem the balance. Since the corporation was not able to pay the whole amount due from it in cash, Beckemeier agreed to accept as part of the payment a policy of insurance on his life owned by the corporation plus certain real estate owned and occupied by the corporation, on which the corporation was to execute a ten year lease. Thereupon the corporation retained the law firm which Beckemeier had consulted earlier about the problems posed by his retirement. The steps taken thereafter appear from the following chronological statement of services detailed by the law firm in its bill for

$2500: conferences with various of the stockholders; legal research; work on the stock redemption plan; drafting and revising minutes; drafting waivers of notice; conferences with the corporation's accountant; tax advice and preparation of tax opinion; preparation of an amendment to the certificate of incorporation to reduce the corporation's capital; drafting lease and deed; examination of zoning law and building code; execution of papers; and correspondence. This bill was paid by the corporation; the law firm made no separate change to Beckemeier. The court said:

> [H]ere, as distinguished from the Second Circuit's conclusion in Mills Estate (with which we express no agreement or disagreement), the dominant aspect of the Gravois transaction was the liquidation of the Beckemeier shares and not the recapitalization. Beckemeier had reached retirement age and had advised . . . the other shareholders of his desire to retire. The stock was closely held. The same protective consideration which led to the buy-and-sell agreement were present in the face of Beckemeier's incipient withdrawal, were buttressed by his natural feelings of loyalty to his younger associates of long standing, and were exemplified by the equalizing sale to Landgraf. Although there was, of course, a desire on the part of all to keep the organization going, the basic problem with which they struggled was that of the disposition of the outstanding Beckemeier stock and was not one directed to the change or any desired improvement in the form of the corporate structure. Stock retirement, that is, partial liquidation, was the problem and it was the essence of what transpired. If the form, content and wording of corporate minutes are of any significance, those of the shareholders' regular meeting of January 11, 1954, and those of the directors' special meeting of March 2, 1954, lend hearty support to this conclusion. The same is true as to the nature of the legal services described in detail in the bill to Gravois. Of course, the transaction involved a reduction in the corporation's stated capital and a continuance of the corporate activity. And of course the amendment of the articles was filed with the Secretary of State as required by the Missouri statutes. These additional facts, however, are necessary concomitants of this type of partial liquidation. We regard them as constituting only a secondary and not the dominant aspect of the entire transaction.
>
> This, then, brings us to the subsidiary matter of proof. There is no question that the legal services were rendered and the expenses were incurred and both were paid by Gravois, and no challenge has been raised as to their propriety or reasonableness. We find nothing in this record

to justify a conclusion that any part of these was for the benefit of Beckemeier personally. Any possible inference in that direction is overcome by the fact the corporation's obligation to Beckemeier was for a net price per share and, so far as the title certificate expenditure is concerned, by the fact that the purchase of title insurance was protection for Gravois under its deed warranty.

b. The "Straight Redemption" Cases

Curiously enough, there is another, wholly separate line of authorities which deny the corporation any deduction for expenses incurred in a stock redemption without so much as a reference to either "partial liquidation" or "recapitalization." This line of what might be termed "straight redemption" cases simply applies the normal rule that expenses incurred in the acquisition of a capital asset must be added to the cost of the property rather than deducted currently. And the remarkable fact is that no case in either line of authority has ever even acknowledged the existence of the other line.

The "straight redemption" line seems to stem from O.D. 852, 4 Cum.Bull. 286 (1921), where the Service ruled specifically that expenses incurred by a corporation in purchasing its own stock were not deductible, but were "to be considered part of the purchase price of the stock." In Commerce Photo-Print Corp. v. Commissioner, 6 T.C.M. 386 (1947), the court flatly denied a deduction by the corporate taxpayer of the legal expenses incurred in redeeming almost 50% of its outstanding stock. The court stated that so much of the fee as related to the acquisition of the stock should be treated as part of the cost of the stock, and that the portion of the fee relating to the accompanying amendment of the corporation's certificate of incorporation was also not a business expense. The court regarded it as immaterial on this issue that a primary objective of the transaction was to eliminate the friction between the two almost equal stockholders by buying out one of them. Similarly, in Southern Engineering and Metal Products Corp. v. Commissioner, 9 T.C.M. 93 (1950), the court stated categorically that the legal fees expended by the corporation in redeeming all of the stock of one of the two equal stockholders were "not deductible as a business expense of petitioner corporation, but should have been treated as a capital expenditure, i.e., as part of the cost of the stock."

In 1961, less than a year before the decision of the Court of Appeals in the Gravois case, came two more "straight redemption" cases in which the court cursorily rejected the corporation's attempt to deduct legal expenses incurred in connection with the buy-out of some of its stockholders, without so much as a word about partial liquidation or recapitalization. In Atzingen-Whitehouse Dairy, Inc. v. Commissioner, 36 T.C. 173 (1961), a corporate rift was resolved by having the corporate-taxpayer repurchase the stock of two of its three stockholders. In denying the corporation the right to deduct the $6,000 legal fee incurred in that transaction, Judge Raum (who had written the opinion of the Tax Court in the Mills Estate case some years earlier) commented as follows:

> That payment is a capital expenditure which should have been treated as part of cost of the stock purchase. It is not deductible as an ordinary and necessary business expense. The fact that the purchase of the stock was motivated by a desire to eliminate friction between the [stockholders] is immaterial. Certainly, the cost of the stock itself was a capital expenditure rather than a deductible expense, and the accompanying legal fee must be similarly classified.

In somewhat similar circumstances, in Annabelle Candy Co., Inc. v. Commissioner, 20 T.C.M. 873 (1961), reversed on another issue, 314 F.2d 1 (9th Cir.1962), Judge Raum cited his own prior decision in Atzingen-Whitehouse for the proposition that the legal expenses incurred in a redemption should be treated as part of the total capital expenditure. However, it was argued in the Annabelle case that part of the legal services had been directed toward avoiding dissolution of the corporation, with various plans having been considered prior to the adoption of the redemption plan, and that legal fees for this purpose were deductible. The court agreed that such fees might well be deductible, and that an allocation between deductible and non-deductible portions of the legal expense was possible. However, the court added a caveat that since the attorneys for the corporation were also the attorneys for the remaining stockholders, pains had to be taken to make sure that any portion of the fee which was not allocable to the redemption transaction had not in fact been incurred for the benefit of the remaining stockholders personally rather than for the corporation. And in any event in the instant case the court found no substantial evidence that the legal expenses related to any matters other than the redemption, particularly since all of the services described in the attorneys' bill related to the redemption.

It is hard to fathom just how and why these two lines of authority developed separately as they did. As we have seen, unlike the 1954 Code the 1939 Code, under which most of the cases in both lines arose, did not draw any distinction between redemption and partial liquidation—every redemption was a partial liquidation and hence subject to the analogy to complete liquidation. It is true that the earlier partial liquidation cases involved pro rata redemption transactions, while all of the redemption cases have involved only non pro rata redemptions, usually the complete termination of the interest of one or more stockholders. However, this hardly explains the different lines of authority, particularly since the Gravois case itself involved the non pro rata redemption of all of the stock of one stockholder.

More important, it seems clear that, if anything, expenses incurred in connection with a complete termination of the interest of one of the stockholders should be more eligible for deduction than the expenses of a pro rata distribution. Where a stockholder has been bought out, it is at least open to the corporation to argue that the important corporate objective of maintaining harmony was served by the redemption transaction. And if a redemption in such circumstances can constitute a reasonable business need for purposes of the accumulated earnings tax, as held in Mountain State Steel Foundries, Inc. v. Commissioner, page 414 supra, it might well follow that the associated expenses constitute deductible business expenses.[44] In the pro rata distribution case, on the other hand, the only argument available is the rather questionable analogy to the rather questionable rule allowing deduction for the expenses of a complete liquidation.

How does the 1954 Code affect these two lines of authority? As already noted, the 1954 Code does distinguish between "partial liquidations" in § 346 and "redemptions" under § 302, and this might provide some warrant for differentiating between the two with regard to deductibility of redemption expenses. But if so, it would seem that the partial liquidation approach, based on the analogy to complete liquidation, would now be available only for transactions which qualify under § 346, thus excluding, for example, the Gravois case itself.

Section 1032 may also cast some doubt on the "straight redemption" view that the expenses of a redemption should be added to the cost of the stock acquired. Since § 1032 precludes the recognition of gain or loss by a corporation upon any issuance of stock, including treasury stock, the corporation's basis in any stock acquired in a redemption would seem to have little if any significance; query, therefore, how fair it is to add the expenses of the redemption to this same basis "limbo".

c. DISTINGUISHING BETWEEN EXPENSES OF THE CORPORATION AND EXPENSES OF THE INDIVIDUAL STOCKHOLDERS

The warning in the Annabelle case, supra, about the importance of distinguishing between redemption expenses for the benefit of the corporation and those for the benefit of the stockholders is echoed in a closely related context in J. Gordon Turnbull, Inc. v. Commissioner, 41 T.C. 358 (1963). There the corporation sought to deduct fees paid for tax advice on a plan calling for purchase of stock by cer-

---

44. In Five Star Manufacturing Co. v. Commissioner, 40 T.C. 379 (1963), the taxpayer carried this proposition to a "drily logical extreme" with its (unsuccessful) contention that because the redemption there involved was essential to the financial survival of the enterprise, the redemption price itself was deductible.

tain key employees and a redemption of stock from the estate of the deceased majority stockholder. This advice had been originally requested by the key employees on their own behalf, but after the transaction fell through they sent the bill on to the corporation, which paid it in the interests of maintaining good relations with those employees. However, the court found that the expenses had been incurred for the benefit of the employees rather than the corporation and held that the mere fact that the employees might have resigned if the corporation had not paid the obligation did not make it an ordinary and necessary expense of the corporation.

In the Turnbull case it was relatively easy to find that the expenses were "for the benefit of" the employees since they had originally sought the services on their own behalf. But absent some such factor as this, are there any standards for determining who is the "real" or primary beneficiary of services in connection with a redemption? For example, in the classic case of a redemption of 50% of the stock, as in Mountain State, is it not clear that the redemption transaction benefits both groups of stockholders, as well as the corporation? This could become another trap for the unwary, if too much weight is put on such factors as who made the original arrangements for the services in question.[45]

d. DEDUCTIBILITY OF EXPENSES FOR TAX ADVICE — § 212(3)

KAUFMANN v. UNITED STATES

United States District Court, Western District, Missouri, 1963.
227 F.Supp. 807.

DUNCAN, DISTRICT JUDGE. [The Plaintiff and the two Feltenstein brothers owned all the stock of Commerce Loan Company, a highly successful small loan business with forty-one offices located in eleven states. The stockholders decided to sell out and initiated negotiations with the American Investment Company, a nation-wide loan company listed on the New York Stock Exchange. An agreement was reached under which the stockholders of Commerce would exchange all of their stock for approximately $6,000,000 worth of the stock of American.]

Naturally, there was the ever present question of taxation, and consummation of the plan depended to a considerable degree on

---

45. As to any legal expenses which the withdrawing stockholders do in fact incur personally in connection with the redemption of their stock, they would normally be subject to the general rule that expenses incurred in connection with the sale of a capital asset must be applied as an offset against the selling price rather than treated as an ordinary deduction. However, expenses incurred in collecting the price, as distinguished from making the sale, may be deductible under § 212(1). See Commissioner v. Doering, 335 F.2d 738 (2d Cir. 1964) (involving collaterally the open-closed transaction dichotomy); see generally, Note, The Deductibility of Attorneys' Fees, 74 Harv.L.Rev. 1409, 1419–1421 (1961).

Sec. 9   TAX INCIDENTS OF REPURCHASES   547

whether or not the transfer could be made without imposing a prohibitive tax burden upon the owners of the Commerce stock.

Following the signing of the Agreement, Kaufmann and Feltenstein retained the accounting firm of Peat, Marwick, Mitchell & Co., to explore the tax consequences, and to prepare the necessary data and information for submission of the plan to the Reorganization and Dividend Branch of the Tax Ruling Division of the office of the Commissioner of Internal Revenue for a ruling as to whether or not the transfer of stock would be tax free, or subject to taxation as to Kaufmann and the Feltensteins.

The question was duly presented and the ruling of the Bureau was to the effect that the exchange would be tax free. The request for ruling contained 26 pages and 4 schedules. It was presented in explicit detail and conferences were held with representatives of the Internal Revenue Service in Washington. The reply of the commissioner contained 10 pages. Thereafter, the Agreement which had theretofore been executed was carried out and the transfer of stock was made.

Peat, Marwick, Mitchell & Co., submitted a bill for $8,602.81, $7,602.81 of which was for the services in connection with the determination of the tax liability under the agreement for the exchange of the stock, $602.81 of this amount was for out-of-pocket expenses, telephone, travel, blue prints, etc.

The remaining $1,000.00 was for services rendered subsequent to the presentation and ruling to determine the basis of the American stock in the hands of Kaufmann and Feltenstein for future tax income purposes. The accountants took no part in the drafting of the exchange agreement or in the negotiation of its terms.

This amount was paid by Kaufmann and Gerald Feltenstein, and for the taxable year 1957, the plaintiffs [Mr. and Mrs. Kaufmann] took as a deduction . . . [under § 212(3) their] one-half of that amount—$4,301.41. The amount was disallowed by the Bureau, and in due course, the tax was paid and this action was brought.

* * *

It is the Government's contention that:

> "The only activities which are recognized as being 'in connection with the determination, collection, or refund of any tax' are those involved in the preparation of tax returns and in the determination and contesting of the extent of the taxpayer's liability," and that the accountants' functions "were not and could not be a determination of *the extent of* the tax liability of the taxpayer."

It is the plaintiff's contention, on the contrary, that the words [in Reg. § 1.212–1(b)], "or in connection with any proceedings involved in determining the extent of his tax liability," are applicable in a situation such as we have here, and that the amount was expended for the sole purpose of determining whether or not there would be tax liability incident to the transfer of the stock.

The defendant cites a part of [H.Rep. 1337, 83d Cong., 2d Sess. 29, A59 (1954), relating to § 212]:

> "Existing law allows an individual to deduct expenses connected with earning income or managing and maintaining income-producing property. Under regulations costs incurred in connection with *contests* over certain tax liabilities, such as income and estate taxes, have been allowed, but these costs have been disallowed where the *contest* involved gift-tax liability. A new provision added by your committee allows a deduction for expenses connected with determination, collection, or refund of any tax liability.
>
> * * *
>
> "Paragraph (3) is new and is designed to permit the deduction by an individual of legal and other expenses paid or incurred in connection with a *contested* tax liability, whether the contest be Federal, State, or municipal taxes, or whether the tax be income, estate, gift, property, and so forth. Any expenses incurred in *contesting* any liability collected as a tax or as part of the tax will be deductible." (Emphasis supplied)

It is the Government's contention that this legislative history clearly indicates the Congressional intent to limit the provisions of the new paragraph 3 added to Section 212 to actual contested tax liability, and precludes any expenses incident to a determination of tax liability prior to the period when it becomes contested.

Legislative history, of course, may be considered by the courts in determining Congressional intent. However, where the legislative history or the Committee Report are not in accord with the clear meaning of the words used in the Act itself, then the court is bound by the clear and commonly understood meaning of the Act and may not consider the Committee Report.

Paragraph 3 seems to be rather clear in its intent when it says, "in connection with the determination, collection or refund of any tax." The determination is one phase of a tax controversy, the collection is another, and the refund is still another.

The Regulation issued pursuant to this statute follows the language of the statute in using the words, "in connection with the determination of a tax". Further, under the terms of the Regulation, the taxpayer is entitled to deduct expenses paid or incurred in connection with the preparation of his tax return, *"or in connection with any proceedings involved in determining the extent of his tax liability."*

The very purpose of seeking the Bureau's ruling was to determine the question of the parties' tax liability under the proposed agreement. It is a matter of common knowledge in the business world that before the consummation of any substantial business transaction, that the resulting tax consequences are uppermost in the minds of those concerned.

I think it could not be disputed that the very purpose of setting up the Reorganization and Dividend Branch of the Tax Ruling Division of the Office of the Commissioner of Internal Revenue was to advise interested parties of the tax liability arising from a reorganization, such as we are dealing with here. It would also seem to be as much of a business expense to determine that question as to determine the actual tax liability after the reorganization.

The parties cite but one case, and I have found no others where this question has been before the courts. It is Davis v. United States, 287 F.2d 168 (Ct.Cl.1961), on cert. United States v. Davis, 370 U.S. 65, 82 S.Ct. 1190, 8 L.Ed.2d 335, where the decision of the Court of Claims was affirmed in part and reversed in part.

In that case the taxpayer had taken as a deduction the amount of attorneys' fees which he had paid for tax consultation and advice concerning a property settlement incident to a divorce. There was no ruling by the Bureau, as is the case here. Half of the amount deducted had been paid to his counsel and half to counsel for his wife. The Court of Claims allowed the portion paid to the taxpayer's attorney, but disallowed that paid to counsel for his wife. In ruling on the taxpayer's contention of error on that issue, the Supreme Court said:

> "The taxpayer claimed that under § 212(3) of the 1954 Code, which allows a deduction for the 'ordinary and necessary expenses paid . . . in connection with the determination, collection, or refund of any tax,' he was entitled to deduct the entire $5,000. The Court of Claims allowed the $2,500 paid taxpayer's own attorney but denied the like amount paid the wife's attorney. The sole question here is the deductibility of the latter fee; the Government did not seek review of the amount taxpayer paid his own attorney, and we intimate no decision on that point. As to the deduction of the wife's fees, we read the statute, if applicable to this type of tax expense, to include only the expenses of the taxpayer himself and not those of his wife. Here the fees paid her attorney do not appear to be 'in connection with the determination, collection, or refund of any tax of the taxpayer'."

Thus the court affirmed the holding of the Court of Claims that the fees paid for tax advice to the wife were not deductible. The Government had the opportunity to raise the issue as to the deductibility of fees for tax advice to the taxpayer but elected not to do so. It contends here, however, that the decision of the Court of Claims was in error on that point.

In view of the quoted language, there is no indication as to what the court would have done had the question been raised by the Government. Thus, we are without controlling authority and must pioneer in the interpretation of the meaning of the Act.

There is no question here of the reasonableness of the procedure followed by the taxpayers. The problem was an intricate one and created just the sort of situation which the Tax Ruling Division was created to handle. There was a formal presentation, consideration and decision. The ruling handed down by the commissioner is not binding upon him but it is interesting to note the words of the next to last paragraph:

> "It is important that a copy of this ruling be attached to the income tax return for each taxpayer involved for the taxable year in which the transaction is consummated."

Had the expenses deducted here been incurred after a disallowance by the commissioner of the exchange as tax free, they would have been clearly deductible.

I do not think that it can be disputed that the commissioner relied upon the ruling. The sole purpose of the expenditure was the computation of the tax liability, if any, which would arise from the exchange.

It is therefore my conclusion that the deduction taken by plaintiffs of the amount paid relative to the determination of their tax liability arising from the exchange, $3,801.41, is within the terms of the statute.

I do not believe that the same legal or factual situation prevails with respect to the $1,000.00 paid for the determination of the tax basis of the stock received. It will be recalled that the services were divided into two parts, one, a determination of the tax liability incident to the exchange of stock, and two, a determination of the basis of the new stock in the hands of the owners.

There was no controversy at that time as to the tax base of the new stock, and the mere fact that the new owners desired that such a determination be made while the accountants were investigating the situation generally, would not justify the deduction of the amount paid for that service. The base was computed for the information of the taxpayers or for some possible future use, and not for the purpose of determining any tax.

It is therefore my conclusion that the deduction of the amount paid for the determination of the basis $500.00, is not within the terms of the statute.

Plaintiffs are therefore entitled to recover so much of the tax and interest paid as relate to the deduction of the cost of the determination of the tax on the exchange and interest thereon from the date paid.

In CARPENTER v. UNITED STATES, 338 F.2d 366 (Ct.Cl.1964), the Court of Claims reconfirmed its earlier decision in the Davis case (noted in Kaufmann, supra) to the effect that legal expenses incurred by a husband for advice and planning relating to the tax consequences of proposed alimony payments were deductible under § 212(3). The court said:

> In interpreting this subsection of the statute, Treasury Regulations § 1.212–1(*l*) does not restrict the deductibility of expenses for the employment of tax counsel to contest of a tax liability or preparation of tax returns for a single year. It provides, by way of illustration, four separate examples:
>> "expenses paid or incurred for the tax counsel *or* expenses paid or incurred in connection with the preparation of his tax return
>>
>> *or* in connection with proceedings involved in *determining* the extent of his tax liability
>>
>> *or* in contesting his tax liability." [Emphasis supplied.]
>
> There is nothing in the Regulation to suggest that these four illustrative examples of legal expenses deductible under Section 212(3) are exclusive as to its application. Subsection 1(g) of the same section of the Regulation provides for the deduction of fees paid for services of, among other things, "investment counsel." Obviously, a taxpayer does not employ investment counsel *after* he has made his investments, and he should not be restricted to deduction of expenses for tax counsel solely to discover the tax consequences of what has already transpired or a tax liability already accrued. One of the purposes of a taxpayer in obtaining tax counsel is to avoid tax contests, not to create them, and this also serves the interest of the Government in collecting taxes.
>
> The collection of Federal income taxes is accomplished in the first instance by a method of self assessment . . . . This requires the taxpayer, in the preparation of his income tax return, not merely to submit tax information but to compute his own tax, and under Section 6151 to pay *"such tax."*
>
> No exercise in semantics is required in order to conclude that by this process of self assessment, the Government in the first instance accepts the taxpayer's computation and payment of his own tax as a "determination" thereof. It

may later challenge or contest the tax liability, but Section 212(3) refers to the "determination * * * of any tax," without restriction to a contested liability.

For advice in arriving at this determination, the taxpayer may consult the Internal Revenue Service, or he may under Treasury Regulations § 1.212–1(*l*) employ "tax counsel." One of the legitimate purposes of plaintiff in employing tax counsel was to minimize insofar as was legally possible the tax consequences to plaintiff of the property settlement in the divorce. These were tax consequences first, as to the tax year of 1957 when the divorce settlement was concluded and, second, as to plaintiff's future annual payments of $150,000 to his divorced wife as alimony. These tax consequences were the result of the same transaction, which had to be considered *in toto* in 1957 when plaintiff employed tax counsel. If plaintiff is entitled to deduct expenses for legal assistance in preparing his 1957 tax return, this legal assistance or counsel had to consider and evaluate the entire tax problem, in which 1957 was an inseparable part.

To restrict the deductibility of expense for tax counsel to the computation or contest of a tax liability for completed tax years under the particular facts in this case, would defeat the clear purpose of Section 212(3) and the Regulations § 1.212–1.

Accordingly, plaintiff was entitled to deduct as legal expense under Section 212(3) the portion of his attorney's fees allocable to tax counsel. The allocation by plaintiff's counsel that at least seventy percent of his services related solely to plaintiff's tax problems was conservative and reasonably accurate, and there is no evidence that in making the allocation, plaintiff's counsel acted in bad faith. Accordingly, we accept this allocation as correct. . . .

Judge Davis, dissenting, would have confined the deduction under § 212(3) to tax advice relating to past or settled events, thus excluding expenses for advance planning. After noting the emphasis upon "contested" taxes in the legislative history (quoted in the Kaufmann case, supra) the dissenting opinion continued as follows:

The one suggestion, in the legislative history, that the new subsection should go beyond an actual contest of tax liabilities was the statement made to the Senate Committee by the American Bar Association's Section on Taxation. The Association thought that the language of the House Committee report "appears to confine expenses in connection with tax matters to contested tax liabilities," possibly even for the income tax (which previously had been governed by the existing provisions of the Code). To avoid this result the

Senate Committee was asked to add "computation" before "determination" in Section 212(3), or to "clarify the point that deductions with respect to taxes are not hereafter to be confined to contested taxes." See 1 Hearings before the Senate Committee on Finance on the Internal Revenue Code of 1954, p. 487. Congress did not adopt either branch of this suggestion.

With this background, the words Congress put into the 1954 Code—"expenses paid or incurred during the taxable year . . . in connection with the determination, collection, or refund of any tax"—could have been read as limited strictly to contested tax liabilities. But the Treasury Department, perhaps in response to the position of the Bar Association's Section on Taxation, has issued a regulation going somewhat back of a tax contest (but not, I think, as far as the majority believes). Treas.Reg. on Income Tax (1954 Code), Sec. 1.212–1(l). Certainly the regulation goes back to the time of preparation or consideration of a tax return—a stage which takes place after the occurrence or congealing of the transactions or events to be reflected in the return. It is not entirely clear whether the regulation extends further back to the period when the transactions are still in the process of being planned or the taxable events are still uncertain and *in futuro*. The reference in the regulation to "tax counsel" is ambiguous if read alone. With the significant help of the statutory language and the legislative history, I interpret it, however, not as authorizing the deduction of expenses paid for *any* tax counsel, but only for tax counsel employed in connection with the preparation or consideration of tax returns or with tax proceedings, *i. e.*, tax advice given after the critical events have taken place or been settled. Tax counsel designed to help plan future transactions or arrangements is not covered. I would construe the second sentence of section 1.212–1(l) as if it read:

> Thus, expenses paid or incurred by a taxpayer for tax counsel or *other* expenses paid or incurred in connection with the preparation of his tax returns or in connection with any proceedings involved in determining the extent of his tax liability or in contesting his tax liability are deductible [italicized word added].

This reading of the regulation seems to me strongly indicated, if not required, by the words of section 212(3), by the legislative history, and by the untoward consequence of adopting the broader view. The words of the Code ("determination, collection or refund of any tax") connote an appraisal of tax liability on the basis of past or settled events, not a molding of future events to minimize taxes. Each of the three words deals with a function related to taxes already due or about to become due, not with planning ahead. The legislative history treats exclusively with a still more restricted problem, a tax contest; and even the Bar Association's proposal to add "computation" would not, on a normal reading, carry back further than to activities in preparation for a return. The ultimate consequence of the wider view of the regulation, adopted by this court, is that individual taxpayers will be able automatically to deduct counsel fees paid for the general planning of their holdings and estates so as to minimize income, estate, or gift taxes in the years ahead, or for arranging marital or family affairs with the same end of tax-minimization in the future, or for planning charitable or foundation gifts (and allocation of assets) for such a purpose. Hitherto, the large share of these costs which fall outside section 212(1) and (2) have been personal expenses, barred from deduction by Section 262 . . . . I find nothing to intimate that Congress, in adding section 212(3), intended to overturn this accepted position by placing the expenses of trying to reduce one's future taxes in a different category from all the other personal expenses of living.

3. EFFECT OF A REDEMPTION ON EARNINGS AND PROFITS

In view of the important role of earnings and profits in the general tax scheme, it is appropriate to inquire whether a redemption has any impact on a corporation's earnings and profits. The matter is dealt with in § 312(e), with the provision that the portion of a redemption distribution "which is properly chargeable to capital account shall not be treated as a distribution of earnings and profits." But the statute affords no guidance for determining what portion of a distribution is "chargeable to capital account", and the regulations under § 312 are equally unenlightening. Some help is available from Reg. § 1.562–1(b)(2) dealing with the computation of the dividends paid credit, which in the case of a redemption may turn upon the amount of the distribution properly chargeable to earnings and profits. These regulations indicate that "capital account" for this purpose includes not only the stated capital attributable to the stock but also the stock's proper share of paid-in surplus or the like. But our principal resort must be to the authorities, both primary and secondary:

ALBRECHT, "DIVIDENDS" AND "EARNINGS OR PROFITS" [46]
7 Tax L.Rev. 202–207 (1952).

In Helvering v. Jarvis [189] the fourth Circuit Court of Appeals held that post-1913 earnings could not be considered "capital" within section [312(e)] and that the amount of the redemption distribution would have to be allocated to capital only to the extent that "the ratio between the charge to capital and capital prior to retirement would be the same as the ratio between the number of shares retired and the number of shares outstanding prior to retirement." Thus, where one-tenth of the capital stock of $1,000,000 was redeemed for $1,160,-000, only $100,000 of the redemption payment was allocated to capital, about $90,000 was allocated to the capital account of paid-in surplus, and the remainder of almost $970,000 was allocated to earnings. Having been reduced by the excess over the charge to capital, the remaining earnings plus those accrued in the following year were insufficient to cover a subsequent dividend, which was consequently distributed partially tax-free.

A different approach to the allocation problem was taken in Woodward Investment Company [192]. . . . The corporation made a liquidating distribution to its sole stockholder pursuant to a plan of liquidation which was to be completed in two years. Post-1913 earned surplus was $218,000, and total capital and surplus was $446,-000. The Commissioner argued that since the liquidating distribution was below the cost basis of the stock to the taxpayer's sole shareholder and thus not taxable, the corporation should not be given any credit for a dividend distribution because of the liquidation. He contended in effect that no part of the distribution was allocable to earnings.

The Board disagreed and sustained the taxpayer's view that the distribution was from earnings, and thus a dividend for purposes of the dividends paid credit, to the extent of that portion of $113,000, the taxpayer's basis, which the amount of earned surplus bore to the total capital and surplus of the corporation.[195] This formula was based on the assumption that each of the distributions in the plan of liquidation carried with it a portion of the capital and a portion of the earnings attributable to each share. Although the relevant regulations . . . provided for an allocation to capital of the amount represented by the liquidated stock, the Court could not follow the procedure in the Jarvis case of making such an allocation based on the stated capital value of the retired stock, because no specific shares were retired. The liquidation was a pro rata distribution on all the stock. In a memorandum of the General Counsel, the Bureau ruled

---

46. Reprinted by permission of the Tax Law Review. Portions of the text and most of the footnotes omitted.

189. 123 F.2d 742 (4th Cir.1941).

192. 46 B.T.A. 648 (1942).

195. 218,000/446,000 or, roughly, 49% of $113,000, which amounted to about $55,000.

that the Woodward and Jarvis cases were not inconsistent but "merely reflect the necessary differences in the application of a general principle to different types of situations." [198]

* * *

Since the Jarvis formula bases the allocation to capital upon the amount of capital represented by the retired shares, it cannot be applied when there is a pro rata distribution on all the shares. Nevertheless, it is clear that the principle of the Woodward case, namely, that every liquidation carries with it a portion of the capital and a portion of the earnings of the corporation, can and should be applied in both types of liquidation.

The Jarvis formula allocates to earnings the entire amount of the redemption payment over and above the allocation to capital of a sum equal to the portion of the capital account represented by the retired shares. Thus, where the redemption price of the stock far exceeds its capital value plus its proportional share of other capital items like paid-in surplus, the Jarvis formula allows a relatively small allocation to capital and a relatively large allocation to earnings. In so far as the corporation's earnings account is reduced, remaining stockholders will enjoy greater freedom from taxation on subsequent distributions. At the same time, the stockholders whose interests are liquidated lose nothing by having their distributions heavily allocated to earnings, since they will escape the ordinary income tax on the dividends anyway. Furthermore, the remaining stockholders will also enjoy the indirect benefit of a dividends paid credit to the corporation under section [562], which is measured by the amount of earnings deemed to have been distributed.

This situation is best exemplified by the Jarvis case itself. It will be remembered that stock representing capital of $100,000 was redeemed in that case for $1,160,000. The allocation to capital was only $100,000, plus $90,000 allocated to paid-in surplus. The remaining $970,000 was charged to corporate earnings, which were reduced so low as a result that a subsequent distribution to remaining shareholders was partly taxfree.

On the other hand, where the liquidation payment is less than the capital represented by the retired shares, under the Jarvis formula the whole payment is charged to capital and there is no allocation to earnings. This leaves the remaining stockholders with an unduly large portion of "earnings or profits," making more of their subsequent distributions taxable as "dividends", and allowing the corporation no dividends paid credit under section [562].

The Woodward theory can be applied to avoid both these extremes by allocating the distribution between capital and earnings according to the capital and earnings position of the corporation at

---

198. G.C.M. 23460, 1942-2 Cum.Bull. 190. . . .

the time the distribution is made. To illustrate, suppose corporation X, with total assets of $2,000,000, a stated capital of $1,000,000, and $500,000 in post-1913 earnings, decides to make a partial liquidation of 50% of its stock. There are ten stockholders, each of whom holds one-tenth of the 10,000 shares, which have a par value of $100 per share and are worth $200 per share at fair market value. Each share represents a stated capital investment of $100, earnings of $50, and appreciation of $50. On liquidation at $1,000,000, $750,000 should be allocated to capital ($500,000 to original capital and $250,000 to appreciation) and $250,000 to earnings. The remaining stockholders with half the capital investment would be left with their due half of the earnings.

If the redemption price is less than the original capital investment, the Woodward principle will again produce a more equitable result than the Jarvis rule. Assume that the fair market value of the stock in the above hypothetical case had fallen to $75, and 50% (or 5,000 shares) of the stock was redeemed at $375,000. Each share of stock would then represent a stated capital of $100, $50 of "earnings or profits," and an actual loss of $25. The adjustment for the liquidation payment should then be made by charging $500,000 against original capital and $250,000 against earnings. Remaining stockholders would then be left with stock having a par value of $500,000, a real value of $375,000 and "earnings or profits" of $250,000.

The chief objection to this approach might be that it is an apparent anomaly to make allocations for a distribution which are not mathematical equivalents to the distribution itself, such as allocating $500,000 to capital and $250,000 to earnings for a liquidating distribution of $375,000. But it really is not at all anomalous to do so, as the essential purpose of the allocation is to adjust capital and earnings to reflect the changed position of the corporation after the liquidation. This can be done accurately by reducing all corporate accounts proportionately when any interest in the corporation as a whole has been retired. The anomaly lies in the attempt of the Jarvis rule to base the allocation on a mathematical equivalency between such entirely disparate quantities as the amount of the liquidating distribution and "stated capital" and "earnings or profits."

For more recent comment on this problem, see Edelstein and Korbel, The Impact of Redemption and Liquidation Distributions on Earnings and Profits: Tax Accounting Aberrations under Section 312(e), 20 Tax.L.Rev. 479 (1965).

SECTION 10. THE ACCUMULATED EARNINGS TAX

A. IN GENERAL

JOHN P. SCRIPPS NEWSPAPERS v. COMMISSIONER [47]

United States Tax Court, 1965. 44 T.C. 453.

Opinion

Respondent determined deficiencies in petitioner's income tax for the taxable years 1957, 1958, and 1959 under section 531 in that petitioner was availed of for the purpose of avoiding the income tax with respect to its shareholders by permitting its earnings and profits to be accumulated instead of being distributed as a dividend. Under the present statutory provisions dealing with the accumulated earnings tax, unless petitioner can prove to the contrary by a preponderance of the evidence, the very fact that its earnings and profits were permitted to accumulate beyond the reasonable needs of its business is determinative of the proscribed purpose. However, to the extent petitioner can establish that it retained all or any part of its earnings and profits to meet the reasonable needs of its business, such amount will be allowed as a credit against its accumulated taxable income, subject to the accumulated earnings tax. It thus becomes necessary to consider whether petitioner's earnings and profits were, during the years in issue, accumulated beyond the reasonable needs of its business. Included within this question is the necessity of determining to what extent the earnings and profits were accumulated for the reasonable needs of the business so as to give proper consideration to the credit. . . . Pursuant to section 537, the term "reasonable needs of the business" includes the reasonably anticipated needs of the business.

In connection with his determination, respondent sent to petitioner a notice of his intention to issue a notice of deficiency imposing the accumulated earnings tax. In response to such notification, petitioner sent to respondent a statement setting forth the grounds upon which it relies to show that the accumulations of its earnings and profits were for the reasonable needs of its business.

Respondent takes the position that the statement submitted by petitioner was too vague and too broad to place the burden of proof as to the reasonable needs of the business on respondent. Petitioner, on the other hand, argues that the facts contained in the statement are sufficient to support the grounds stated. We partially agree with petitioner.

We have carefully read the statement submitted by petitioner and after giving full consideration to the argument of respondent we

---

47. Findings of Fact and footnotes omitted.

are of the opinion that the statement (except as to the second ground) "does suffice to meet the general purpose and intent of the statute, and thereby to shift the burden of proof to the respondent with respect to the grounds alleged therein." . . .

Whether a corporation has permitted its earnings and profits to accumulate beyond its reasonable needs and whether it was availed of for the purpose of avoiding the income tax with respect to its shareholders are both questions of fact. . . . In determining whether petitioner's accumulations of earnings and profits during the years in issue were for the reasonable needs of its business, it becomes necessary to determine whether prior accumulations were, in fact, sufficient to meet petitioner's needs during the current years. Sec. 1:535–3(b) (ii), Income Tax Regs. However, in making the comparison of prior accumulations and current retained earnings and profits with the reasonable needs of the business, it becomes necessary to determine the nature of the surplus. The mere size of the previously accumulated earnings and profits is not in and of itself indicative that they were sufficient to cover the future needs of the business. As was stated by the Court of Appeals for the Fourth Circuit in Smoot Sand & Gravel Corporation v. Commissioner, 274 F.2d 495, 500–501 (1960) . . . :

> the size of the accumulated earnings and profits or surplus is not the crucial factor; rather, it is the reasonableness and nature of the surplus. Part of the surplus may be justifiably earmarked in the form of reserves, for specific, necessary business needs. Again to the extent the surplus has been translated into plant expansion, increased receivables, enlarged inventories, or other assets related to its business, the corporation may accumulate surplus with impunity. . . .

It therefore follows that the utilization of working capital by a business for the purchase of fixed assets, although not an occasion for a charge against earned surplus in an accounting sense, does in fact decrease the amount of funds available for operating purposes. On the other hand, if the accumulation of surplus is reflected in liquid assets which are sufficient to meet the business needs for plant expansion, working capital, and other reasonable contingencies, this is a strong indication that the accumulations of surplus were beyond the reasonable needs of the business. . . .

We therefore approach the examination of petitioner's prior accumulated surplus (December 31, 1956) as well as its current retained earnings and profits with the foregoing principles in mind. In determining the reasonableness of petitioner's retained earnings during the years in issue, we must keep in mind also that the burden of proof with regard to the various grounds set forth in petitioner's statement (except as to the second ground) is on respondent. Petitioner's statement can be broken into two parts. The first part contains four grounds to show that the accumulations of earnings and profits were for the reasonable needs of the business. The second part contains three grounds showing why the accumulations were not beyond the reasonable needs of its business.

We have stated before that what the reasonable needs of a business are is, at first instance, a question for the officers and directors of the corporation. . . . A corporation can finance its growth by various means. One such method is the retention of its earnings and profits until such time as it is ready to expand. . . . Courts should be hesitant to substitute their judgment and attribute a tax avoidance motive unless the facts and circumstances clearly warrant the conclusion that the accumulation of earnings and profits was unreasonable and for the proscribed purpose. . . .

Petitioner maintains, and we agree, that its officers and directors, after considering the needs of the business for expansion, meeting competition and reserves for contingent liabilities, and working capital decided to distribute a portion of its current earnings while retaining the rest. This decision by the directors of petitioner, in our opinion, reflects appropriate exercise of the managerial function when measured by the standards of a prudent businessman. . . .

We have set forth the facts in this case with great detail. An examination of those facts reveals that petitioner has not remained static, but, on the contrary, has grown from a newspaper with a circulation of 5,042 in 1940 to a circulation of 23,804 in 1960. Its total revenues have grown from $140,994 in 1940 to $1,369,725.72 in 1959, while its net income has increased from $28,234.30 in 1945 to $304,759.30 in 1959. Petitioner has not allowed its earnings to lie idle but, instead, has plowed back its earnings for the expansion of its business as well as for the acquiring of larger facilities. From 1950 through and including 1959, petitioner has invested $570,674.89 in additions to its property account, of which $232,432.62 was invested during the years in issue. The fact that this petitioner has financed its growth from retained earnings rather than from the sale of additional stock or commercial borrowing should not place it in a position of being subjected to a penalty tax under section 531. This record is replete with evidence indicating that petitioner's policy of continued growth and expansion has been followed without giving any thought whatsoever to the tax consideration of its shareholders. . . . In 1962, a year subsequent to the years in issue, petitioner, continuing its policy of expansion, spent approximately $170,000 for the purchase of building addition, typesetting machines, and additions to its printing presses. Included within this amount is the sum of $40,000 representing the purchase of the premises petitioner had rented since 1940. Evidence of what petitioner did in later years does affect the weight to be given to the evidence of petitioner's intentions during the years in issue. . . .

We realize that petitioner's directors act in a rather informal manner and that their plans for expansion might not be as specific as desired nor are all their plans reduced to writing and contained in formal minutes. However, the history of petitioner has been to act in an informal manner. The executive committee, which is the core of petitioner's management, meets daily and when necessary can act with deliberate speed. A closely held corporation cannot be held to the same strict formalities of large public corporations. . . . We have found as a fact that petitioner did not have any formal plans for expansion after 1958. However, by this finding we do not mean that petitioner would not be justified in retaining part of its earnings for future expansion. Nor do we mean by this finding that petitioner did not have any plans for expansion subsequent to 1958. As stated earlier, petitioner's entire history reflects a policy of constant growth. It is not always possible for a company in advance to set aside a specific sum to achieve a specific goal. We are of the opinion that petitioner was justified upon the facts of this case and in keeping with its policy of constant and continuous expansion in retaining some of its earnings during the years in issue for future expansion. . . .

Although petitioner published the only daily newspaper in Ventura City, it was not the only daily paper published within the county. It is important to petitioner to keep its circulation up throughout the county as its advertisers want to reach as large a public as possible. Petitioner did have competition from at least two other papers publishing within Ventura County. During 1959, the last year here in issue, petitioner began discussing plans for the acquiring of a newspaper in Thousand Oaks, another city in Ventura County. Formal plans were not adopted until 1960; however, the evidence of record is clear that petitioner during 1959 was aware of the situation and decided to retain some of its earnings to meet this competition. In 1961 petitioner did, in fact, pursuant to its plan, purchase a paper in Thousand Oaks at an initial cost of $35,000. However, this was only a small portion of what was yet to come. Petitioner had anticipated that its cost in establishing the Thousand Oaks paper would run in the neighborhood of $500,000. A new plant addition for this newly acquired paper cost $455,000. Respondent recognizes that setting aside a portion of earnings to meet competition is a reasonable need of a business, but nevertheless argues that petitioner's plans during the years in issue were vague and indefinite. We disagree. Two of petitioner's directors testified that the question of how to properly meet the threat of competition was always a concern of petitioner and that throughout the years in issue petitioner was aware of the need of funds to properly protect itself in other parts of the county. What we said in L. R. Teeple Co., 47 B.T.A. 270, 279 (1942), is equally pertinent here:

> While it is true that petitioner has continuously and profitably operated . . . and there is no indication that it intends voluntarily to make any change in its business, it is also true that the contingencies in question are real, they are and

have been continuously present, and the exercise of sound business judgment would not permit their being ignored.

. . .

We are satisfied that sound business judgment required the consideration of ways to meet competition, that petitioner did have competition, and that the retention of part of petitioner's earnings for this purpose was not unreasonable. . . . Although the facts contained in petitioner's statement regarding this ground were not sufficient to place the burden of proof on respondent, the affirmative evidence of record does convince us that petitioner has met its burden as to this ground.

Continuing with petitioner's statement, it is asserted that earnings were retained to meet the increasing contingent liability petitioner had under its profit-sharing and retirement plans. The details of said plans are set forth in our findings of fact. Suffice to say here that respondent's contention that because the liability was too remote and not capable of being calculated it could not justify the accumulation of surplus, is rejected. The retirement portion of the plan provided for the covered employees to receive, upon their retirement, a certain percentage of the increased value of petitioner's assets (fixed assets and goodwill) from their value as of 1950 to the date of retirement. We have set forth in our findings of fact the financial growth of petitioner. Not only has its annual earnings grown but its total assets have greatly increased. It is true, as respondent states, that if the future of petitioner turns sour, its liability under the retirement plans may be diminished. However, in light of the history of petitioner we are in complete agreement with the directors' action of setting up a reserve to meet this contingent liability. Sound business judgment requires such action. The original reserve was $200,000 set up in 1956. However, in 1959, after examining the financial prospects of petitioner, it was decided by the directors that a reserve of $350,000 was more reasonable.

We agree that "a contingency is a reasonable need for which a business may provide, if the likelihood, not merely the remote possibility, of its occurrence reasonably appears to a prudent business firm." . . . The liability under the facts in this case was contingent only as to the amount not as to the actual liability. No management group would ignore the existence of such a liability, and the setting aside of a reserve out of accumulated surplus for such purpose was entirely proper. The growth of petitioner over the years clearly indicates the presence of goodwill, one of the measuring rods in determining the value of petitioner for purposes of the retirement plan. The goodwill, plus the increased investment in fixed assets, in our opinion, clearly justifies the reserve in the amount set aside. . . .

Petitioner's last ground for the accumulation of its surplus was to provide funds for working capital. The retention of earnings to provide for working capital requirements has been held to be for the reasonable needs of a business. Section 1:537–2(b) (4), Income Tax

Regs.; . . . As an aid in determining whether a corporation's working capital requirements are sufficient to meet its needs, resort has been had to certain general "rules of thumb." It has been held that a ratio of current assets to current liabilities which is in the neighborhood of 2½ to 1 is an indication of a reasonable accumulation of surplus. . . . The other rule of thumb sometimes resorted to states that an accumulation of earnings to meet operating expenses for at least one year is reasonable. . . . However, it has been said that working capital requirements of one business are not necessarily the same as another business and that therefore the rule of thumb should not be given any greater weight than a rule of administrative convenience. . . . With the above general principles in mind, we will analyze petitioner's working capital requirements for the years in issue.

. . . Respondent argues that petitioner's investments in preferred stock of E. W. Scripps Company should be considered a current asset. While we agree that the preferred stock was readily convertible into cash, we do not agree that it should be considered a current asset in this case. Petitioner purchased the stock in order to provide a return equal to the return it was required to pay the employees covered by its profit-sharing plan. At the same time, petitioner intended to partially "fund" its fixed liability under the profit-sharing plan. An asset used to fund a fixed liability can no longer be considered as a current asset. For this reason we have not classified the investment in the preferred stock as a current asset. An analysis of petitioner's balance sheets reveals that the ratio of current assets to current liabilities for the years in issue, as set forth in our findings, averaged 2.63 to 1. This is some indication that the accumulation of petitioner's surplus was not unreasonable. . . .

Petitioner's operating expenses [excluding depreciation] during the years in issue ranged from $882,316.60 in 1957 to $1,049,341.77 in 1959. If we were to apply the rule of thumb in this case, clearly petitioner's accumulated surplus would not be unreasonable. Respondent contends, however, that resort to the rule of thumb in this case is unwarranted because petitioner's accounts receivable turned over approximately ten times a year. Nevertheless, we believe that the rule of thumb does carry some weight in this case where the surplus is less than two-thirds of the annual operating costs. . . .

The second part of petitioner's statement lists three grounds which are claimed to give additional support to the position that the accumulations of earnings and profits during the years in issue were not unreasonable. They are, stated briefly, (1) a history of substantial dividend payments, (2) no loans to stockholders, and (3) no investments in unrelated businesses.

While these factors are strong indications that the accumulations were not for the proscribed purpose, section 1.533–1(a) (2), Income Tax Regs., they are also of some aid in determining whether or not the accumulations were for the reasonable needs of the business. There is no doubt that a good history of dividends, the absence of loans to the controlling stockholders, the absence of investments in unrelated businesses, and the paying of large salaries to the controlling stockholders indicate that the accumulations of earnings and profits were for legitimate business needs. . . .

A close examination and comparison of petitioner's contentions with regard to these grounds with the evidence of record reveal that they are readily present here. Petitioner has a history of dividends being paid starting in 1943 and continuing up to and including the years in issue. The record reveals that the amount of petitioner's dividends, expressed in terms of a percentage of net earnings after Federal taxes, was as high as 107 percent but never below 25 percent. Respondent points to the fact that although petitioner's earnings have increased over the years, its dividends since 1950 have remained constant at $38,400 per year. While this may be true, petitioner itself has not remained constant but has used its increased earnings to expand its operations. It was through the retention of these very earnings that petitioner was able to expand and thereby consistently increase its annual earnings. Petitioner, in our opinion, acted like a prudent businessman in that it distributed a substantial part of its earnings as a dividend and elected to retain the remainder.

Petitioner did not make any loans to Scripps. On the contrary, Scripps on different occasions loaned the petitioner money. This is in petitioner's favor. . . . Furthermore, petitioner did not have any investments in unrelated businesses. The purchase of E. W. Scripps Company stock, which was readily convertible into cash, was not an investment in an unrelated business but the investing of money retained under its profit-sharing plan which was intended as a partial "funding" of its liability thereunder. In addition, the purchasing and carrying of United States Government bonds by petitioner which are readily convertible into cash do not represent an investment in an unrelated business. . . .

Respondent argues that the loan by petitioner to Telegram Tribune Co. and Tulare Newspapers, Inc., two corporations controlled by Scripps, indicates that petitioner had excess cash which could have been distributed instead, as a dividend. While the business of these two corporations can not be said to be the business of petitioner, they are all in the same field (newspapers). The loans made by petitioner are for relatively short terms only and are never used for long-term financing. The loans carry 6 percent interest. Under the facts and circumstances of this case, we are not convinced that these loans require a holding that the accumulations during the years in issue were beyond the reasonable needs of the business.

We have already held that petitioner's statement was sufficient to place the burden of proof as to the reasonableness of the accumulations during the years in issue on respondent with respect to the grounds stated therein (except as to the second ground). Based upon the evidence as a whole, we are not convinced that petitioner's accumulations during the years at issue were unreasonable. Although respondent has been able to show that as to at least one of petitioner's grounds, plant expansion, there were no definite plans in existence subsequent to 1958, we are not persuaded that the total accumulations are unreasonable. We are satisfied that petitioner's directors, acting for the best interest of petitioner, decided after full discussion that the retention of a certain part of each year's earnings was necessary to meet competition, meet contingent liabilities, and for working capital. The remainder of the earnings was available and was actually paid out as dividends. Accordingly, we hold that all of the retained earnings during the years in issue were for the reasonable needs of petitioner's business.

In view of the credit provided for in section 535(c) (1), it is unnecessary for us to consider whether or not petitioner was availed of for the proscribed purpose. We realize that the burden of proof as to this issue remains with petitioner. . . . However, even if petitioner were availed of for the proscribed purpose, it would still be entitled to a credit equal to the amount of earnings and profits for the taxable years which have been retained for the reasonable needs of the business. In this case the credit would be equal to the full amount of the retained earnings. Therefore, under section 535(a) the accumulated taxable income, on which the section 531 tax is imposed, would be zero.

Reviewed by the Court.

Decision will be entered for the petitioner.

B. PURPOSE, BURDEN OF PROOF, AND THE ROLE OF THE REASONABLE BUSINESS NEEDS ISSUE

1. APART FROM THE § 535(c) CREDIT

The modern classic on this subject is Young Motor Company v. Commissioner, 32 T.C. 1336 (1959) (holding for the Government), reversed, 281 F.2d 488 (1st Cir. 1960), decision on remand 21 T. C. M. 711 (1962) (holding for the taxpayer), reversed, 316 F.2d 267 (1st Cir. 1963), on remand, 23 T. C. M. 113 (1964) (holding for the Government), affirmed, 339 F.2d 481 (1st Cir. 1964). As this lengthy citation indicates, the case produced six opinions; since they have served to illuminate the operation of the statute, they are worth reviewing in some detail here.

During the taxable years involved, 1950, 1951, and 1952, the taxpayer was engaged in conducting an Oldsmobile automobile agency.

Young and his wife owned virtually all of the stock of the taxpayer, and Young was the principal operating officer. Since 1945 the taxpayer had been relatively successful, and its net income after taxes for the taxable years in question was $55,262, $37,402 and $16,374, respectively. The taxpayer had never paid any dividends, and Young drew no salary after 1941. The taxpayer occupied real estate which Young owned personally, and was charged rent approximating only actual maintenance costs. From 1945 on, the taxpayer made substantial loans to Young and to enterprises in which he was interested, all but one without security, and all without interest until 1952. In addition, the taxpayer invested other funds in marketable securities which had no direct relationship to its business.

However, General Motors had reserved the right to require the taxpayer to substantially enlarge or improve its facilities or face cancellation of its franchise, which was terminable at will. In 1945 General Motors began to suggest the need for some enlargement of the taxpayer's quarters, and by 1948 General Motors was threatening to cancel the franchise if its demands were not acceded to. In that year the taxpayer contemplated the construction of a new showroom and service station at a cost of $150,000, but General Motors indicated that a larger building would be necessary. Thereafter, the Korean War made it necessary to postpone any new construction. But in 1953 General Motors demanded that the taxpayer invest $500,000 in a new building, and upon the taxpayer's refusal its franchise was in fact cancelled. Not until 1956 did the taxpayer obtain a franchise from a different manufacturer. Under its terms the taxpayer was required to maintain working capital of $400,000, and accordingly it recalled all of its loans to Young and his other enterprises.

The Commissioner asserted a deficiency for each of the three years, 1950–1952, under § 102 of the 1939 Code, the predecessor of present §§ 531–537. The taxpayer filed a statement designed to shift the burden of proof on the reasonable business needs issue to the Commissioner in accordance with the procedure of present § 534 (which had been made applicable to cases arising under § 102 if tried after 1955*). In upholding the imposition of the deficiency, Judge Opper, speaking for the Tax Court, said:

> The burden of proving absence of the ultimate corporate activity prohibited by section 102 is concededly imposed upon petitioner. . . . Assuming in its favor that the evidentiary element of business need has not been rebutted by respondent because of the statement furnished by petitioner, see section 534, I.R.C. 1954, . . . that factor then merely becomes neutral.

---

*Pub.L. No. 367, 84th Cong., 1st Sess. §§ 4, 5 (1955).

An understandable confusion . . . exists between proof of "unreasonable accumulation" which, if present, is prima facie evidence of the prohibited purpose under section 102, I.R.C. 1939; and proof of absence of the condemned purpose, which does not follow automatically from affirmative proof of business need. There is nothing in section 102, either before or after the [new § 534 procedure], which makes the entire case turn on the unreasonableness of the accumulation as related to business needs. These are two separate questions. . . . Had there never been a reference in the Code to reasonable needs of the business, respondent's determination that a corporation's earnings were accumulated for the purposes described in section 102 would still be presumptively correct. If there is no proof by respondent of the unreasonableness of the accumulation as regards business needs and there is no other evidence, petitioner must still fail because the burden of proof of facts sufficient to show the error of respondent's determination is basically upon it as in all comparable proceedings. . . .

There can be no question that petitioner was availed of here to prevent imposition of the surtax upon its shareholders which would have occurred had the earnings been distributed. Our findings make it clear that many thousands of dollars would have been due from them as income taxes if the current earnings had been distributed. This, however, is no more than a preliminary requisite. The statute also calls for the existence of the inhibited purpose.

If this purpose exists it may be accompanied by other legitimate business objectives and still the statute will apply. . . . While it is always difficult to determine the state of a person's mind, and perhaps more especially that of a corporation, we think, on the present record, any corporate intent must be attributable purely to its guiding hand, Young, and that petitioner has failed to carry its burden of showing that one of the purposes of maintaining its relatively large corporate surplus was not to prevent the imposition of surtax upon Young and his wife by means of accumulating its earnings.

There is in fact no testimony anywhere in the record that this was not one of petitioner's purposes. Nor is there . . . any formal action of the board of directors stating a purpose of any kind for the accumulations. It is not unreasonable to assume that petitioner's controlling stockholder would expect and intend the corporate action to have its inevitable result of freeing the stockholder's income from tax by reason of the failure to distribute.

But in addition to the failure to rebut the presumption of correctness, there is affirmative evidence to support the determination. . . . No dividends have ever been paid by petitioner over its 20-odd-year history. Most of the accumulated surplus was loaned to the principal stockholder or his controlled but unrelated businesses. Nearly all the loans were without security, and all, as petitioner states in its brief, "were non interest bearing in the period in question." The stockholder not only permitted the dividends to accumulate but even failed to draw large amounts of salary. And although petitioner occupied property owned by the stockholder, there is evidence that the rent collected was unduly low in the years before us.

In the first reversal by the Court of Appeals (281 F.2d 488), Judge Aldrich started by reviewing the facts other than those relating to the taxpayer's difficulties with General Motors, and then continued as follows:

We agree that under these circumstances an accumulation of a surplus in excess of $300,000 without payment of even a salary to the principal officer and, in effect, sole stockholder, *prima facie* calls for an explanation. However, taxpayer had one. . . . [The Court here reviewed the taxpayer's relationship with General Motors culminating in the cancellation of franchise.]

In spite of this strong showing, the Tax Court held that the burden of proof was on the taxpayer on all issues except the reasonable needs of the business, that this latter was simply a subsidiary matter which need not be considered, and that on the ultimate question taxpayer had not overcome the presumption of correctness of the commissioner's determination that the accumulation was to avoid taxation upon the shareholders.

Taxpayer's position is succinctly stated in its brief. It "recognizes that the failure to pay dividends from the time the corporation had been formed, the investment of assets of the corporation in unrelated securities, the making of personal loans and the failure to charge interest on said loans, the failure of the president to draw a salary or the charging of a rental which could be described as 'unduly low' constituted factors which can be considered when determining the question of whether or not the prohibited purpose existed. The petitioner, however, submits that these factors must be considered in connection with the question of whether or not the accumulation was beyond the reasonable needs of the business, and that it is not proper to eliminate said issue and then, by riveting attention upon these factors, to infer that, because they in fact existed, there was a violation of the statute."

Taxpayer's point is well taken. It is entirely illogical to say that since reasonable business needs of the taxpayer is only a subsidiary, and not the determinative issue in the case, it is proper to disregard it and look simply at the rest of the record. While the ultimate question here is not the reasonable needs of the business, the answer to that question may well be the single most important consideration in concluding whether taxpayer acted with a proper purpose in mind, or the proscribed one. . . . Just as absence of a reasonable business need for the accumulation is "determinative of the purpose to avoid surtax upon shareholders unless the corporation by the clear preponderance of the evidence shall prove to the contrary," so the existence of an actual business need may be the strongest supporting evidence that taxpayer was motivated by a proper purpose. To by-pass that subsidiary question and then in deciding the case to say that taxpayer has failed on the ultimate issue is like saying that we will overlook any question of self defense and then conclude that on the rest of the record a finding of deliberate homicide is justified. No proper appraisal of a taxpayer's purpose can be made without considering all relevant factors. The more particularly is this so when the court proceeds upon the theory that the commissioner's finding against taxpayer is to be presumed correct, and that the burden is upon taxpayer to overcome it.

The Tax Court may have been led into this error by a misconception of the precise issue. In its opinion it referred to preventing the imposition of the surtax upon stockholders as "one" of taxpayer's purposes, and stated, "If this purpose exists it may be accompanied by other legitimate business objectives and still the statute will apply." The court discussed at some length that taxpayer, being controlled by Young, must be taken to have known that declaring dividends would increase Young's surtaxes—a proposition scarcely requiring argument. If knowledge of such a result is to be the test of purpose, then the only corporations that could safely accumulate income would be those having stockholders with substantial net losses. The statute does not say "a" purpose, but "the" purpose. The issue is not what are the necessary, and to that extent contemplated consequences of the accumulation, but what was the primary or dominant purpose which led to the decision. . . . The Tax Court's test was altogether too favorable to the government.

The taxpayer asks us to reverse outright because the stipulated facts show as matter of law that it was within reason to have made this accumulation. Even if we were to agree that the record so indicates, such a finding would not establish that such circumstance was in fact the actuating motive. There may have been others. The ultimate question is not whether the accumulation could be justified as a reasonable business decision, but whether taxpayer's actual dominant purpose was that defined in section 102(a). This is for the trier of facts. . . .

Upon remand, the Tax Court held for the taxpayer (21 T. C. M. 711), on the basis of supplementary findings and conclusions which are described in the subsequent opinion of the Court of Appeals. Once again the Court of Appeals reversed (316 F.2d 267). Said Judge Aldrich:

> On remand the Tax Court took further evidence and made a few supplementary findings, only one of which is of importance. The finding was that taxpayer's accumulations during the years in question were not in excess of the reasonable needs of its business, an issue the court had failed to resolve before, and the relevancy of which we shall shortly consider.[2] The court explained that it made this finding not as an affirmative matter, but because the evidence was "in virtual equipoise," and under the statute the burden of proof as to the issue of reasonable needs was upon the government. It went on to say that, on the other hand, it "cannot conscientiously" find "that the earnings were accumulated 'for' the reasonable needs of the business. . . ."
>
> The court stated that it "affirmatively refrained" from accepting Young's testimony that he did not cause earnings to be distributed because he feared that if he did he might have spent the money.[3] It also rejected taxpayer's counsel's suggestion that if, instead of making loans with its accumulated earnings, taxpayer had distributed them to its stockholders and thereafter had needed to call for the money, there would have been less available because the funds would have been diminished by the tax resulting from the distribution. This argument, to have any force, presupposes

---

2. [Footnotes are by the court.] The court also found that taxpayer's directors never passed upon, or even discussed, any declaration of dividends, and that Young, the managing officer and, with his wife, principal stockholder, did not know about section 102 during the years in question, an ignorance which, understandably, the court considered irrelevant.

3. This was kindly put, especially in view of the evidence that what Young did with the accumulations, in large measure, was to cause taxpayer to lend them, sometimes without interest, to himself, and to other enterprises in which he, but not taxpayer, was interested.

that there had been an active determination of a reasonable need, and in effect assumes the point.

The court then turned to the question of whether taxpayer was improperly motivated despite the fact that the accumulation was not unreasonable. It concluded that the government had not met the burden it felt our opinion had placed upon it of proving that the inhibited purpose was the "dominant" one.[4]

With respect to the first issue raised by the government, we believe that as a theoretical matter the court was wrong in saying broadly that the statutory burden was upon the government to prove that the accumulations were in excess of the reasonable needs of the business. . . .

In the case at bar the taxpayer had submitted the [§ 534 (c)] statement. This called into play the burden of proof provisions of subsection (a)(2), to wit, that the burden of proof was on the government "with respect to the grounds set forth in such statement." This burden is less extensive than the one set by subsection (a)(1). The court failed to note the distinction. As we read the statute the government has the burden of overcoming the taxpayer's assertion that the grounds set up in its statement constituted reasonable needs, but if it meets that burden and overcomes those alleged grounds, then the burden of proving additional grounds, or needs, is on the taxpayer, and taxpayer will fail on this issue if it does not do so.

Our disagreement with the Tax Court on this matter, however, does not change the result. Taxpayer introduced no new grounds of any substance at the trial. The burden as to the grounds on which this issue was tried was properly where the court placed it. . . . We could not say the court was plainly wrong in finding that the government had failed to meet this burden. This finding may stand.

The second issue raised is whether the Tax Court correctly placed on the government the burden of proof as to the ultimate question under section 102 of the 1939 Code, namely, the taxpayer's dominant purpose in making the accumulation. The court stated that it had so placed the burden because it was required to do so by our prior opinion. With all deference to the court, we made no such ruling. . . . There is no statutory provision with regard to

---

[4] The court expressed apparent dissatisfaction with our use of the word dominant, reminding us of our decision in Chicago Stock Yards Co. v. Commissioner, . . . where we said, at p. 948, that it was enough if the evidence indicated that "the forbidden motive of surtax avoidance played a substantial part." To the extent that there may be a difference, we stand on our later wording. . . .

this burden. The normal burden on a petition to the Tax Court for review of a deficiency determined by the Commissioner is on the taxpayer. . . . Probably the best reason for this is that as a practical matter taxes would be very difficult to collect if there was not a presumption in favor of the Commissioner. It is incumbent upon the taxpayer here to find something which removes its case from this principle.

Taxpayer's response is that the Commissioner's determination was simply that the accumulations were within the purview of the statute because they exceeded the reasonable needs of the business and that for the government now to prove that they were within the statute for another reason is all well and good, but as to this there was no previous determination and the burden is upon the government. . . . We do not reach this question because in our view the deficiency notice * . . . is not to be so strictly construed. We read it as asserting primarily that the earnings had been permitted to accumulate for the purpose of preventing the imposition of surtax, the ultimate issue, *and* that the accumulations were beyond the reasonable needs of the business, a supplementary issue because of its effect on the burden of proof under section 102(c), and not as saying that taxpayer had the forbidden purpose, because, and only because, the accumulations were beyond reasonable needs. Although its language might have been better chosen, we believe the reason for including both clauses in the notice was not to restrict it, but because of what the Commissioner stood to lose under section 534(a) if he failed to assert lack of reasonable business needs. If there was an ambiguity, it does not appear that taxpayer was misled. Throughout its petition it treated the issue of unreasonable accumulation and the improper purpose as separate matters. So far as appears, this point was first raised on the present appeal.

We do not read the 1939 Code as placing the burden as to purpose upon the government when the Commissioner had determined that taxpayer was improperly motivated. For many years, prior to 1938 there had been a provision to the effect that the fact that earnings or profits have been permitted to accumulate beyond the reasonable needs of the business "shall be prima facie evidence of a purpose to avoid

---

*[Ed. note] The notice of deficiency, quoted in the court's footnote 1, stated that "your earnings and profits have been permitted to accumulate (instead of being divided and distributed as dividends among your shareholders) beyond the reasonable needs of your business for the purpose of preventing the imposition of surtax on your shareholders."

Sec. 10 ACCUMULATED EARNINGS TAX 573

surtax upon shareholders." . . . While it is possible to infer that this statutory assistance would not have been given to the government unless Congress assumed the government initially had a burden to meet, this is not a necessary inference. "Prima facie evidence" is not usually burden-placing language, . . . and there is no more reason to reach this result by a reverse inference. Consequently we have held that the effect of this provision was merely to increase, to a perhaps immeasurable extent, the burden customarily on a taxpayer to overcome the Commissioner's determination of liability. . . . We made a similar suggestion with respect to the new language of section 102(c) of the 1939 Code (first introduced in 1938, 52 Stat. 483), providing that if an accumulation was unreasonable taxpayer would be found to have the inhibited purpose unless it proved the contrary by a "clear preponderance of the evidence." . . . We see no reason to change this view. The Tax Court erred in ruling that because the government failed to show an accumulation beyond the reasonable needs of the business the burden was on it with respect to purpose. The only legal effect of the government's failure was to deny it the statutory benefit of having the taxpayer's burden as to purpose increased from the preponderance of the evidence to the clear preponderance.

Before sending the case back for a redetermination of the taxpayer's purpose with the proper burden of proof we must comment upon another error. In discussing the evidence on this issue the court said in its second opinion that we had ruled that no consideration could be given to the taxpayer's knowledge of the tax effect of a distribution upon its shareholders. We did not say this. With all deference, we do not see how the court could think we even implied it. What we said was that finding such knowledge, in the absence of an examination of other factors, was not "the test", and that the dominant motive should not be determined without consideration of "all relevant factors." 281 F.2d at 491. It would be particularly unreasonable, when the principal shareholder is the one who makes the corporate decisions, not to consider his personal interests as one of those factors.

The question of whether the burden of proof has been satisfied may call for delicate measurements. The same judge of the Tax Court has sat on two trials of this case. We suggest it would be appropriate under the circumstances to have a new viewer of the evidence. . . .

On remand, Judge Withey for the Tax Court said that although the accumulation of profits was not beyond the reasonable needs of the business the "primary purpose" for the accumulation was to prevent the imposition of the surtax on the stockholders. 23 T. C. M. 113. And the Court of Appeals wrote a belated finis to this weary tale with an affirmance written by Judge Hartigan. 339 F.2d 481.

As the various opinions in the Young Motor Co. case make clear, the ultimate test under the accumulated earnings tax is whether earnings and profits were accumulated for the proscribed purpose of avoiding the tax on shareholders. The accumulation component of the test presents little difficulty, even though, as noted earlier, the Code nowhere defines "earnings and profits," since it is not necessary to compute the precise amount of earnings and profits which have been accumulated, either in the current year or since the corporation's inception. It is enough for the imposition of the tax that some amount of earnings and profits have been accumulated for the proscribed purpose; the tax is then applied to a quite different fund, "accumulated taxable income," as defined in § 535.

On the other hand, the proscribed purpose component of the test has been a continuous source of difficulty. Proof of state of mind is always troublesome, since direct evidence is usually unavailable, and reliance must be placed on inferences from the surrounding circumstances. Thus it became desirable to attempt to relate the subjective issue of the state of mind of those in control of the corporation to some more objective standard for judging conduct. It is here that the reasonable business needs issue comes into the picture: § 533(a) makes accumulation beyond the reasonable needs of the business "determinative of the purpose to avoid the income tax with respect to shareholders, unless the corporation by the preponderance of the evidence shall prove to the contrary."

However, the precise role of the reasonable business needs issue has always been somewhat puzzling. As noted in the second opinion of the Court of Appeals in the Young case, the earliest versions of § 533(a) merely made unreasonable accumulation *"prima facie* evidence" of the proscribed purpose, which would seem to add little if anything to the presumption of correctness which normally attaches to any determination by the Commissioner. In 1938, in an obvious effort to strengthen the Government's hand in dealing with the elusive state of mind issue, the provision was cast in substantially its present form, except that the corporation could disprove the proscribed purpose only by a "clear" preponderance of the evidence. In this form, the statutory presumption was more forceful than the normal presumption of correctness resulting from a determination by the Commissioner, since the statutory presumption could be overcome only by meeting a more onerous burden of proof. However, in the 1954 Code the word "clear" was dropped without explanation, which seems to leave the matter about where it stood prior to 1938.

In addition, as the various opinions in the Young Motor Co. case observed, the presumption of § 535(a) is only a one way street—that is, no presumption against the existence of the proscribed purpose arises from the fact that earnings were not accumulated beyond the reasonable needs of the business.

Despite the rather chimerical role of the reasonable business needs issue in theory, in practice it has almost always been the chief battleground of accumulated earnings tax cases, and most of the cases have been won or lost on this issue. Thus the taxpayer has rarely succeeded in disproving the existence of the proscribed purpose in the face of a showing of accumulation beyond the reasonable needs of the business; and conversely, a showing of reasonable business needs for a challenged accumulation has generally precluded a finding that the proscribed purpose was present. Accordingly, when Congress in 1954 decided to ease the *in terrorem* impact of the accumulated earnings tax, one of the principal changes was the new § 534 procedure permitting the taxpayer to shift the burden of proof on the reasonable business needs issue to the Commissioner. The Senate Finance Committee Report, S.Rep. No. 1622, 83d Cong. 2d Sess. 70–71 (1954), contains the following explanation of the new procedure:

> At the present time if the Commissioner of Internal Revenue proposes a deficiency on the ground that the taxpayer has accumulated earnings and profits in excess of the reasonable needs of the business, the taxpayer has the burden of proof as to the reasonableness of the accumulation. Moreover, if earnings and profits are accumulated in excess of the reasonable needs of the business, the accumulation is deemed to be for the purposes of tax avoidance unless the taxpayer proves otherwise by the clear preponderance of the evidence.
>
> Your committee agrees with the House that this imposition of the burden of proof on the taxpayer has had several undesirable consequences. The poor record of the Government in the litigated cases in this area indicates that deficiencies have been asserted in many cases which were not adequately screened or analyzed. At the same time taxpayers were put to substantial expense and effort in proving that the accumulation was for the reasonable needs of the business. Moreover, the complaints of taxpayers that the tax is used as a threat by revenue agents to induce settlement on other issues appear to have a connection with the burden of proof which the taxpayer is required to assume. It also appears probable that many small taxpayers may have yielded to a proposed deficiency because of the expense and difficulty of litigating their case under the present rules.
>
> Under the House and your committee's bill, the taxpayer may, upon receipt of notice of a proposed deficiency with re-

spect to the accumulated earnings tax, file a statement of the grounds (together with sufficient facts to indicate the basis for the statement) on which the taxpayer relies to establish the reasonableness of the accumulation. If the taxpayer submits such a statement within the proper time, the burden of proof will be upon the Government as to whether the accumulation is in excess of the reasonable needs of the business. If the taxpayer does not file such a statement it must bear the burden of proof as under existing law. In addition, if the taxpayer presents grounds in its statement which are not supported by the facts in the statement, the burden of proof with respect to these grounds must be borne by the taxpayer. If the Secretary or his delegate fails to give the taxpayer notification prior to the issuance of a notice of deficiency, then the Government must bear the burden of proof even though the taxpayer has filed no statement.

Since § 534 did not purport to change the burden of proof on the ultimate issue of purpose, it became tempting for the Government to by-pass the reasonable business needs issue, together with the complications of the new procedure, in favor of going directly to the ultimate purpose issue, on which presumably the normal presumption of correctness of the Commissioner's determination would apply.[48] And here fate took a hand—by a curious coincidence the first case involving the new § 534 procedure was the Pelton case, page 586 infra, involving accumulation of earnings to finance a stock redemption. Since the Commissioner and both courts seemed to regard that objective as *ipso facto* establishing the proscribed purpose, it was particularly inviting to proceed directly to the ultimate issue of purpose. Then, when the Young Motor Co. case came along, the Tax Court regarded it as merely involving a logical extension of the principle that if the existence of the proscribed purpose can be established directly there is no reason to deal at all with the reasonable business needs issue.

It is this total by-passing of the reasonable business needs issue that was condemned by the Court of Appeals in its first opinion in the Young Motor Co. case. Particularly because of its decision that the tax should be applied only when the proscribed purpose was the "dominant" motive for accumulations, the court understandably was anxious to be sure that the trier of fact would weigh all possible purposes for the challenged accumulations. This would necessarily include an alleged business need for the accumulation since that, as the court observed, might be "the strongest supporting evidence" that a proper purpose was the dominant one. On the other hand, the Court of Appeals reemphasized in its second opinion that a finding of rea-

---

48. So the Court of Appeals expressly concluded in its second opinion in the Young Motor Co. case, page 570 supra. Notice, however, the curious ambiguity of the current regulations on this point, § 1.533–1(b) (2nd sentence).

sonable business needs did not preclude a conclusion that in fact the proscribed purpose had been the dominant motive for the accumulations, and that the burden of proof on that issue remained on the taxpayer.

Assuming that the reasonable business needs issue must be considered in every accumulated earnings tax case, there remains the question whether the Government can avoid the § 534 shift in the burden of proof by basing its notice of deficiency entirely upon a determination that the proscribed purpose was present, thus leaving the taxpayer to bring in the reasonable business needs issue as an affirmative defense, upon which it would bear the burden of proof. This seems possible under the literal language of § 534(a), which makes the provision applicable to cases where the deficiency notice is "based in whole or in part on the allegation that all or any part of the earnings and profits have been permitted to accumulate beyond the reasonable needs of the business." But there are at least two indications the other way. First, the Senate Finance Committee Report, page 575 supra, states the condition for using the § 534 burden-shifting procedure in terms simply of a "proposed deficiency with respect to the accumulated earnings tax," without any suggestion that an allegation of accumulation beyond the reasonable needs of the business is required. Second, § 534 itself describes the "preliminary notification" of subsection (b) in terms of "informing the taxpayer that the proposed notice of deficiency includes an amount with respect to the accumulated earnings tax", again without any reference to an allegation that the accumulation exceeded reasonable business needs.

Incidentally, there has been some resistance to the view expressed in the Young Motor Co. case that the accumulated earnings tax applies only when the proscribed purpose is the "primary or dominant" motive for the accumulation of earnings. Thus Barrow Manufacturing Co., Inc. v. Commissioner, 294 F.2d 79 (5th Cir. 1961), sustained a finding by the Tax Court that the taxpayer had been availed of "for the purpose of preventing the imposition of the surtax upon its shareholders", and held that there was "no error in failing to go further and find that that was the primary or dominant purpose of the accumulation". The court went on to say that the "utility of the badly needed presumption arising from the accumulation of earnings or profits beyond the reasonable needs of the business is well nigh destroyed if that presumption in turn is saddled with the requirement of proof of 'the primary or dominant purpose' of the accumulation." It is true that in United States v. Duke Laboratories, Inc., 337 F.2d 280 (2d Cir. 1964), the court rejected the Government's contention that the question presented to the jury with regard to the challenged accumulations should have been phrased in terms of "a purpose" of avoiding the income tax rather than "the purpose"; but the case is still far from an endorsement of the Young Motor Co. position since the jury had also been instructed that the taxpayer had the burden to show "the absence of any intent to avoid the income tax . . . regardless of what other purposes for accumulation the plaintiff may have established", and that the purpose to avoid tax "need not be the sole or dominant intent". In Fenco, Inc. v. United States, 234 F.Supp. 317 (D.Md.1964), affirmed per curiam 348 F.2d 456 (4th Cir. 1965), the District Court noted the existence of a conflict among the authorities as to whether the proscribed purpose had to be the dominant or primary one, or only one of the "determinating" purposes. However, the court was not required to choose between these competing tests since it concluded both that the taxpayer had failed to show that the proscribed purpose was not a "determinating" motive and also that the proscribed purpose was in fact the primary and dominant purpose.

Since the purposes of a corporation are those of the persons in control of it, special difficulty in determining purpose has been encountered where the shareholders are evenly divided on the matter of accumulation versus dividends. In Hedberg-Freidheim Contracting Co. v. Commissioner, 251 F.2d 839 (8th Cir. 1958), the corporation was owned equally by two shareholders, one of whom wanted to distribute dividends while the other did not. The dividends were not distributed, and the tax was imposed. In Casey v. Commissioner, 267 F.2d 26 (2d Cir. 1959), again there were two equal stockholders, this time deadlocked over whether more than $50,000 would be needed for a contemplated activity. Because of the deadlock, more than $50,000 was accumulated, and no dividend was paid. Nevertheless, the tax was not imposed, the court stating that the belief of one shareholder that no more than $50,000 was needed did not mean that any accumulation in excess of that amount was unreasonable.

2. THE IMPACT OF THE § 535(c)(1) CREDIT

According to the opinion in the Scripps Newspapers opinion, supra, the effect of the credit provided in § 535(c)(1) for "such part of the earnings and profits for the taxable year as are retained for the reasonable needs of the business" is to make the existence of reasonable business needs an absolute bar to the imposition of the accumulated earnings tax. Accord, Freedom Newspapers Inc. v. Commissioner, 24 T.C.M. 1327 (1965). Although not cited in either of the two foregoing cases, Fotocrafters, Inc. v. Commissioner, 19 T.C.M. 1401 (1960), also supports this view; the court in that case assumed that so far as post-1954 years were concerned, once reasonable business needs for accumulating earnings had been shown the § 535(c) credit would automatically operate to wipe out accumulated taxable income and hence eliminate any tax. The court expressly distinguished pre-1954 years in the Fotocrafters case, noting that for those years even when reasonable business needs had been established the taxpayer was still required to carry the ultimate burden of proving the absence of the proscribed purpose. See also Raymond I. Smith, Inc. v. Commissioner, 292 F.2d 470 (9th Cir. 1961), where the court commented that "with regard to the 1954 credit, the ultimate determination of proscribed purpose is not involved, but only the determination of whether accumulations were retained 'for the reasonable needs of the business'."

Despite the apparently uniform view of the authorities to date, it is submitted that this construction of the § 535(c) credit is erroneous. Certainly this interpretation of the credit is not required in order to give it a meaningful role, since its avowed purpose was to eliminate the all-or-nothing character of the pre-1954 accumulated earnings tax, under which once any improper accumulation had been shown the tax was levied on the total amount of earnings and profits accumulated for the year. See S.Rep.No.1622, 83d Cong., 2d Sess. 72 (1954). The credit does effectively confine the tax to the amount of the improper accumulation; and there is nothing in either the legislative history or the statute which suggests that the introduction of the credit was intended to accomplish any other purpose.

As a matter of logic, there seems no reason why a taxpayer should receive a credit on account of the existence of reasonable needs for its business if in fact those needs played no part in its accumulation and the actual purpose was to avoid the tax on stockholders. Moreover, the silence of the legislative history is particularly noteworthy. That is, if there had been an express change in the statute even as comparatively modest as providing a presumption in the taxpayer's favor on the purpose issue if it prevailed on the reasonable business needs issues, some comment in the committee reports would presumably have been called for; yet the foregoing cases have construed the credit provision to go far beyond that and in effect to create an irrebuttable presumption on the purpose issue when reasonable business needs are shown to exist, despite the absence of a word of support in the legislative history. Finally, so far as the specific words of the statute are concerned, query whether the current construction gives sufficient weight to the word "for" in the phrase "as are retained for the reasonable needs of the business". The word "for" is often used as shorthand for the phrase "for the purpose of", and by so interpreting it here the credit would be limited to cases where the reasonable needs were not only present but were also in fact the reason for the accumulation.[49]

49. Compare the following excerpt from the second opinion of the Tax Court in the Young Motor Company case:
We have found . . . that the accumulations were not "beyond the reasonable needs of the business". This is the statutory language. We have not found that the earnings were accumulated "for" the reasonable needs of the business, as petitioner requests us to do. That expression of causation, relevant as it might be to indicate an existing and possibly dominant purpose

However, at a minimum it does seem that the credit in effect codifies the holding of the Young Motor Company case that the accumulated earnings tax applies only when the proscribed purpose is the primary or dominant motive for the accumulation. That is, once a business motive for the accumulation of earnings is established, it seems unlikely that the credit could be withheld just because there was also a minor or subsidiary purpose to avoid the tax on shareholders.

Also of importance is the question of burden of proof under § 535(c). Quite evidently, the § 535(c) credit is an affirmative defense on which the taxpayer would bear the burden in the first instance. However, if the § 534 burden-shifting procedure is successfully invoked, presumably the Commissioner would bear the burden of proof on reasonable business needs for all purposes, including the § 535(c) credit. The report of the Conference Committee, H.Rep.No. 2543, 83d Cong., 2d Sess. 49 (1954), contains the following comment upon a Senate amendment inserting the words "all or any part of" before the words "the earnings and profits" in both §§ 534(a) and 534(c):

> The Senate amendment provides that the shift of the burden of proof under section 534 from the taxpayer to the Government applies not only in determining whether the earnings and profits of the corporation have been permitted to accumulate beyond the reasonable needs of the business, but also in determining the extent to which the earnings and profits of a corporation have accumulated during the taxable year beyond the reasonable needs of the business.

It is less clear what effect § 535(c) may have, if any, on the operation of the burden-shifting mechanism. One possibility is that § 535(c) makes it impossible for the Government to by-pass the reasonable business needs issue in its deficiency notice, because a failure to allow any § 535(c) credit would be tantamount to a "determination" that there were no reasonable business needs. However as an illustration of how interrelated these various issues are, the foregoing point would appear to be sound only if § 535(c) is construed to be independent of any "purpose" issue.

---

3. PROOF OF REASONABLE BUSINESS NEEDS

The Scripps Newspapers case illustrates the modern judicial recognition that in testing the reasonableness of accumulations primary attention should be given to the comparison between the amount of the current assets and the foreseeable needs of the enterprise. As that opinion indicates, such rules of thumb as the accumulation of funds to meet operating expenses for one full year must be adjusted in each case for the circumstances of the particular taxpayer. Thus

inconsistent with that proscribed by section 102, is one which, on this record, we can not conscientiously make.

Sec. 10   ACCUMULATED EARNINGS TAX   581

in Barrow Manufacturing Co., Inc. v. Commissioner, page 577 supra, the court gave virtually no weight to this rule of thumb on the ground that "a rapid turnover of inventory and quick and almost certain collection of accounts provided most of the operating funds." See also United States v. McNally Pittsburg Mfg. Corp., 342 F.2d 198 (10th Cir. 1965). In Bardahl Manufacturing Corp. v. Commissioner, 24 T.C.M. 1030 (1965), the court concluded that accumulation to cover a year's operating costs was not justified in the light of the rate of inventory turnover and accounts receivable collections; but the court held that the taxpayer was entitled to accumulate cash to cover its operating costs for a single operating cycle, which amounted to approximately 4.2 months, or the equivalent of 35% of the total operating expenses for a year. For the most detailed analysis of working capital needs undertaken in any case to date, see Apollo Industries, Inc. v. Commissioner, 358 F.2d 867 (1st Cir. 1966).

In determining the reasonable needs of its business, the taxpayer is not limited to the business which it has carried on to date, but may include the needs of any business which it has undertaken or is about to undertake, Reg. § 1.537–3; and the business may be one carried on through a subsidiary, as well as a directly-owned division of the taxpayer, provided the relationship with the subsidiary is such that its business in effect is operated by the taxpayer. While of course vague and unsubstantiated plans to undertake a new business will not suffice to ward off the accumulated earnings tax, just as is true of similar plans to expand an existing business, Reg. § 1.537–1(b), the taxpayer is entitled to some margin for flexibility. As the court put it in Electric Regulator Corp. v. Commissioner, 336 F.2d 339 (2d Cir. 1964):

> If the Treasury decides that the manufacture of "Regohm" is the "business", then it would forever consign petitioner to the manufacture of that product and view its needs accordingly. Courts, however, must not blind themselves to the realities in this age of rapid technological change. The product of today is frequently outmoded tomorrow. The results of research in the electronics, pharmaceutical and chemical fields alone justify this statement. Nor is it always possible for a company in advance to set aside a specific sum to achieve a specific goal. Comments made in the past to the effect that a definite plan actually followed through must be on the company's books and records before moneys assigned thereto become anticipated needs may have been appropriately qualified in particular cases.

As to plans which are sufficiently definite, is the taxpayer entitled to accumulate earnings equal to the total cost in advance? An affirmative answer seems generally to have been assumed, although there is an intimation the other way in Fenco, Inc. v. United States,

348 F.2d 456 (4th Cir. 1965), where the court suggested that the taxpayer's power to borrow for future expansion eliminated the need to accumulate earnings for that purpose.

Sometimes investment of liquid funds in apparently unrelated assets may actually amount to the operation of a second business. Thus in Sandy Estate Company v. Commissioner, 43 T.C. 361 (1964), a corporation whose principal business had been the operation of apartment properties persuaded the court that its very substantial investments in mortgage loans "were not simply isolated investments, unrelated to petitioner's business," but actually constituted the carrying on of a mortgage loan business for which accumulation of its funds was justified.

C. ACCUMULATION OF EARNINGS IN CONNECTION WITH A REDEMPTION

MOUNTAIN STATE STEEL FOUNDRIES, INC. v. COMMISSIONER

[Part III, page 420 supra].

HERWITZ, STOCK REDEMPTIONS AND THE ACCUMULATED EARNINGS TAX [50]

74 Harv.L.Rev. 900–931 (1961).

A. Accumulation of Earnings Subsequent to a Redemption

. . . [In the Mountain State case] the accumulation occurred after the redemption, which was executed early in the first fiscal year for which the accumulated earnings tax was assessed. Thus, although accumulation of earnings was the method of financing the redemption transaction in Mountain State, the specific purpose for the accumulation was the payment of the corporate obligation previously incurred in the redemption.

Retirement of bona fide indebtedness seems clearly to constitute a reasonable need of the business. The regulations [§ 1.537–2(b)(3)] confirm this, but add the qualification that the indebtedness must be "created in connection with the trade or business." Of course, if the stock redemption is regarded as fulfilling a business need within the meaning of the statute, as the court of appeals seemed to imply

---

50. Portions of the text and most of the footnotes omitted.

in the Mountain State case, this qualification would create no problem. But even if the stock redemption were not so regarded, the effect of this qualification might be in doubt. By way of analogy, suppose that a corporation borrows money for a purpose unrelated to its business operations, such as speculation in the stock market. Doubtless it is true that so long as repayment of this obligation could be financed by liquidating the unrelated assets, accumulation of earnings for such repayment could not be justified, since there would be no business need for the accumulation. The matter would stand no differently than an attempt to accumulate earnings for the very purpose of speculating in the market. But suppose that disaster befell the corporation's investments and they became worthless. Now the outstanding obligation is a direct claim against the corporation's business assets, and it is no longer so clear that accumulation of earnings to repay it should be regarded as beyond the reasonable needs of the business. A redemption transaction like that in Mountain State presents a similar situation. Since the redemption obligation constitutes a bona fide binding claim against the corporation, it can be argued that payment of that obligation is a reasonable need of the business for which accumulation of earnings would be justified.

Even if discharge of the redemption obligation were not considered a reasonable need of the business, the existence of that purpose might serve to rebut any presumption that the accumulation of earnings was designed to avoid the tax on shareholders. Discharge of that redemption obligation in accordance with its terms would be essential to the continued existence of the corporation. Quite commonly the redemption obligation would include provisions prohibiting or restricting the payment of dividends during the term of the obligation, as was apparently true in Mountain State; but even without such express restrictions, the financial drain of the redemption obligation is likely to have the practical effect of drastically curtailing, if not entirely precluding, the payment of dividends. Thus, it is hard to find that the dominant motive for the failure to pay dividends was the proscribed purpose of avoiding the tax on shareholders, as required under the test announced in the Young Motor Co. case. Even under a less stringent test, the good faith objective of those in control of the corporation to discharge the binding redemption obligation might be sufficient to sustain the taxpayer's burden of disproving the existence of the proscribed purpose.

In any event, it should be recalled that a redemption in which the interest of one or more shareholders is entirely eliminated—the type involved in . . . Mountain State—may be regarded as akin to a liquidation transaction. That is, the redemption may be viewed as a substitute for a distribution in kind to the selling shareholders of their pro rata share of the corporation's net assets. For example, suppose that stockholders A and B each own fifty per cent of the stock of A-B Corporation which, it will be assumed for the purpose of making the illustration more graphic, carries on its business at two locations of the same size and capacity. If A wishes to sell out the business, and B prefers to continue operating it, an impasse would result since A would normally be unable to compel either a complete liquidation or a sale of all the assets. One obvious solution would be a "partial liquidation," under which A would surrender all of his stock in exchange for one of the plants and one-half of all the other assets in kind, assuming one-half of the liabilities; B would be left to operate the A-B Corporation on a drastically reduced scale. If thereafter A-B Corporation accumulated its earnings in order to expand to the more desirable scale of operations enjoyed prior to the redemption, there would seem to be no occasion for the imposition of the accumulated earnings tax. The regulations have long provided specifically that accumulation of earnings to provide for bona fide expansion will normally satisfy the reasonable-needs-of-the-business test. There seems to be no reason why the A-B Corporation should be denied the right to accumulate earnings for expansion because of the previous redemption transaction. Indeed, it could be argued that such a situation presents a particularly strong justification for accumulation of earnings, since the expansion would be aimed simply at restoring a previous level of operations, the feasibility and desirability of which had been demonstrated by actual experience.

The same result should obtain if shortly after the partial liquidation A-B Corporation borrowed funds to acquire a plant like the one distributed to A and thereafter accumulated its earnings to pay off the obligation incurred. Whether the purpose of the accumulation was characterized as retirement of bona fide indebtedness or expansion of the business, such an accumulation would seem to be justified under the regulations. Should the result be any different if A-B Corporation purchased from A the very assets distributed to him in the partial liquidation, reassuming the liabilities taken up by A, or if the corporation borrowed from A to finance the transaction by making the repurchase from him on credit? Again the repayment of the obligation incurred in expanding the business back to its original size should constitute a perfectly valid business reason for accumulating earnings. But the latter transaction is no different from a redemption of A's stock on credit for a price equal to the value of the net assets which A would have received through a partial-liquidation distribution in kind. The parties would be in exactly the same position as if they had adopted the more cumbersome and expensive procedure of a redemption in kind followed by a repurchase of the assets on credit. Viewing such a redemption transaction in this manner, an accumulation of earnings to discharge the obligation incurred in the redemption again seems justified as a business need. And this analysis would appear to be equally apt whether the redemption involved a minority of the outstanding stock, a majority, or exactly fifty per cent as in the Mountain State case. Hence, whatever may be the soundness of distinctions drawn among these situations in other types of cases, to be discussed later, such distinctions have no place in cases like Mountain State where the challenged accumulation occurs after the redemption transaction has been consummated.

* * *

On the basis of the foregoing, then, it is submitted that the accumulated earnings tax should not be imposed when earnings are accumulated for the purpose of discharging the obligation incurred in a previous good faith redemption of all of the stock of one or more shareholders. More difficulty is encountered when the redemption does not involve a complete termination of the interest of any of the shareholders, since the analogy based upon complete liquidation as to the selling shareholders fails. But a complete termination of interest is not required for favorable tax treatment of the redemption distribution. In addition, any obligation incurred in such a redemption is no less binding on the corporation. Therefore, when the redemption is not pro rata and effects a substantial change in ownership among the shareholders, of the kind contemplated by section 302(b)(2) of the 1954 Code, it might well be appropriate to permit the corporation to accumulate earnings to discharge a bona fide obligation so incurred.

B. Use of Previously Accumulated Earnings for Redemption

A harder question is presented when earnings are accumulated in advance of a redemption. If the accumulation is for the specific purpose of financing the redemption, there may well be no escape from the issue of whether and when a redemption itself may constitute a "reasonable need" within the meaning of the accumulated earnings tax statute. But the situation may be different when the corporation has accumulated its earnings for other business needs and then utilizes the accumulated earnings to redeem some of its stock. Here the Commissioner would be attacking the accumulation of earnings for the years prior to the redemption transaction still open under the statute of limitations, in the light of the actual use made of those earnings.

Of course where, despite the existence of other potential business needs, the real reason for the accumulation of earnings was to finance an expected redemption, the case should be treated as a conceded accumulation of earnings for the purpose of redeeming stock. But if in fact no redemption was even contemplated in the prior years, and the accumulation of earnings was for other purposes which did constitute reasonable needs of the business within the meaning of the statute, the subsequent decision to use the accumulated earnings to finance a redemption should not affect the justification for the accumulation in the prior years. The accumulated earnings tax, like the income tax generally, is applied on an annual basis. Each taxable year stands on its own footing, and the question whether earnings were accumulated beyond the reasonable needs of the business for any given year must be determined in the light of the factors and circumstances relevant to that year. This is further emphasized by section 535(c) (1) of the 1954 Code, which specifically provides for a credit for each taxable year in the amount of the earnings retained for the reasonable needs of the business during that year.

The regulations [§ 1.537–1(b) (2)] confirm this view with the provision that "subsequent events shall not be used for the purpose of showing that the retention of earnings or profits was unreasonable at the close of the taxable year if all the elements of reasonable anticipation are present at the close of such taxable year." This provision makes it clear that an accumulation of earnings in good faith for a reasonable business need during a particular year does not become subject to the special tax if later the purpose for which the earnings were accumulated has to be abandoned. Since there would obviously be no problem requiring special comment in the regulations if the original business objective was abandoned in the face of some other pressing business need, the thrust of the regulation quoted must be that it makes no difference why the original purpose was abandoned, nor indeed whether the previously accumulated earnings are presently needed for any business reason, although of course the issue of whether the corporation ever actually intended to consummate the original objective would remain. Hence, the abandonment of the original corporate purpose in favor of a redemption of all the stock of one or more stockholders should not affect the validity of the accumulation for the original purpose in the prior years, regardless of whether the redemption transaction is itself thought to constitute a reasonable need of the business. Indeed, this might well be a stronger case than one in which the original purpose is abandoned and no substitute is adopted, since the financial drain of a redemption would normally prevent the consummation of the original objective, and thus eliminate the need to explain why the original objective was abandoned.

* * *

C. Accumulation of Earnings in Contemplation of a Redemption

We come finally to the most troublesome case in the area, one like Pelton * in which earnings are accumulated expressly in contemplation of a planned stock redemption. Even here, as we have seen, it is not essential to decide the issue of whether the stock redemption constitutes a business need. It may be feasible to dispose of the case directly on the ultimate issue of the existence of the proscribed purpose, as the Tax Court did in Pelton. However, in view of the decision in the Young Motor Co. case and the added importance of the reasonable-

---

* [Ed. note] Pelton Steel Casting Co. v. Commissioner, 28 T.C. 153 (1957) (imposing the tax), affirmed 251 F.2d 278 (7th Cir.1958).

business-needs issue under section 535 of the 1954 Code, it seems clear that the question whether and when a redemption may constitute a reasonable business need cannot be bypassed indefinitely.

The treatment of this issue in the authorities, at least prior to the decision of the court of appeals in Mountain State, was not particularly enlightening. There is no specific reference to the question in the regulations, although the general reminder that the needs for which earnings are retained must be "directly connected with the needs of the corporation itself" is doubtless relevant. The two earliest cases involving the effect of a redemption transaction under the accumulated earnings tax, Gazette [121] and Dill,[122] indicated that redemption of a minority shareholder's stock to prevent it from falling into potentially unfriendly hands could constitute a reasonable business need. This view, while apparently not disapproved in Pelton, was nevertheless held inapplicable there on the ground that a majority of the outstanding stock, rather than a minority, was redeemed.

The basis of this distinction never clearly emerges from the Pelton opinion, perhaps because that court was not resting on the reasonable-business-needs issue anyway. As will be noted later, the premise that a minority redemption can constitute a reasonable business need may well be doubtful itself. But if the alleged distinction was meant to suggest that the redemption of a majority of the stock outstanding could not constitute as compelling a need "of the corporation itself" within the meaning of the regulations, it may be open to serious question. The alleged corporate business need which was thought in the earlier cases to underlie a redemption of a minority shareholder's stock was that of preventing the stock from falling into the hands of outsiders who might seek to change established lines of policy or otherwise create disharmony in the intracorporate family, with a consequent deleterious effect on operations. But the worst that can befall the corporation if the minority shareholder's stock is not redeemed is that he or his successor will prove a constant nuisance in the conduct of the corporation's affairs. Absent some special feature like a unanimity agreement among the shareholders or directors which gives the minority shareholder power disproportionate to his shareholdings, he cannot disturb the ultimate control of the majority.

Compare the potential for changes in corporate policy and rupture of the existing harmony among the stockholders if a majority of the stock changes hands. The new majority has the power to overhaul completely the corporation's business affairs. Moreover, upon the institution of new plans and programs, the psychological effect upon the holdover minority shareholders, particularly those who have been officers under the previous administration, offers far greater promise of discord than could arise from a mere transfer from one minority

121. Gazette Publishing Co. v. Self, 103 F.Supp. 779 (E.D.Ark.1952).

122. Dill Mfg. Co., 39 B.T.A. 1023 (1939).

shareholder to a new one. Thus, strictly from the point of view of the corporation as a separate entity, redemption of a majority of the stock to keep it from being transferred may be more vital than redemption of a minority interest.

* * *

Nevertheless, there is a basis for distinguishing between majority and minority redemptions. The question of the business needs of a corporation, though clearly more objective than the issue of the purpose for an accumulation of earnings, itself depends in large measure upon the decisions, or more generally the state of mind, of those in control of the corporation—normally the majority shareholders. But in the case of a contemplated redemption of the shares of the majority, the latter are no longer concerned with the needs of the corporation. Rather they are pursuing their personal desire to get out of the company. Hence, if the state of mind of those in control of the corporation is determinative, an accumulation of earnings to facilitate such a redemption may be regarded as actually motivated by the personal needs or desires of the shareholders rather than needs of the business.

On the other hand, it is true that so long as it is a redemption rather than a complete liquidation which is planned, some of the minority shareholders must be willing to carry on the corporation's business. It seems doubtful as a matter of corporate law today that the majority shareholders could compel a corporation to redeem their own shares, to the exclusion of the minority shareholders, unless the latter were willing. And it could be argued that since the effect of the very redemption transaction contemplated is to shift control of the corporation from the majority shareholders to the minority, the purpose to be attributed to the corporation in accumulating earnings for that objective should be that of the minority stockholders, who are anxious to carry on the enterprise. But the fact remains that, in the absence of special circumstances, minority shareholders do not have any legally protectible interest in maintaining particular corporate policies by preventing a transfer of the controlling shares or otherwise. Hence, though the question may be close, it would certainly be defensible to hold that a redemption of the controlling block of a corporation's stock does not amount to a business need of the corporation within the meaning of the statute.

* * *

However, the basic premise thus far—that a redemption of a noncontrolling block of stock does, or at least may, constitute a reasonable business need under the statute—is itself open to challenge. It has already been observed that a minority shareholder cannot normally present any legal obstacle to the carrying-out of the corporation's objectives as determined by the majority. And the practical danger which such a shareholder most often poses, particularly if he is neither an officer nor a director, is the threat to the untrammeled freedom of the majority shareholders in such matters as their own compensation, or dividend policy, which are primarily matters of individual rather than corporate concern. But even if the interest in preventing such conflict could rise to the level of a business need, developing a standard for handling this issue would be no mean task.

To illustrate, take the Gazette case, where the minority stockholder whose stock was redeemed was threatening to sell to particular outsiders whom the controlling shareholders had special reason for keeping out of the corporation. In the actual case the earnings had been accumulated for other reasons, so that the question of accumulation of earnings in contemplation of a redemption was not presented. But suppose that some years earlier the corporate managers had recognized the possibility that the minority shareholder might become dissatisfied and might consider the sale of his stock to an undesirable outsider. Adoption of a program to put the corporation in a position to redeem the stock of the minority shareholder, in case it might become necessary to prevent such a transfer, would seem to be reasonable enough. And the corporation would certainly be in a better position to prevent an undesirable transfer if it could offer to redeem the stock for cash, rather than on some long-term-credit basis. Accumulation of earnings in advance would offer a good deal more security than relying on the chance of being able to finance a cash redemption when necessary by borrowing.

But the question is whether this would be sufficient to establish a business need for accumulation of earnings. If not, would the added fact that the minority shareholder was already contemplating a sale of his stock change the result? Or would it be incumbent upon the corporation to show that there were some outsiders interested in getting into the company who would pose more than the usual threat of disharmony, and perhaps even that the minority shareholder was in negotiation with those particular outsiders?

Compare this kind of case with a situation where there are no particularly threatening outsiders but the existing minority shareholder has himself become obviously dissatisfied and threatens a rupture of the peace in the corporate family. In such a case, a sale by the minority shareholder to an outsider might distinctly improve the situation; but this is by no means certain, and in any event perhaps the minority shareholder has indicated no desire to sell. Would the desire to put the corporation in a position to make an attractive redemption offer to the minority shareholder if relations worsen amount to a business need justifying the accumulation of earnings?

It is true that under section 537 of the 1954 Code the reasonable-business-needs test has been extended to include "reasonably anticipated needs of the business." But this may well still constitute too blunt an instrument to be used successfully in distinguishing among the many various redemption situations, particularly since any redemption is at best a rather problematical business need. Consider the case of the minority shareholder who in perfect amicability indicates that he would like to withdraw from the corporation in the relatively near future, perhaps simultaneously with his contemplated retirement from an executive position. Suppose that the remaining shareholders are quite willing to have the corporation buy him out, if sufficient funds can be made available. Must the minority shareholder actually break the corporate peace or find an unattractive potential buyer for his shares before the corporation would be justified in accumulating its earnings to finance the proposed redemption?

* * *

In any event, the foregoing cases serve to illustrate the difficulty of attempting to apply a test based upon business needs to the redemption transactions of close corporations. Actually, any attempt to differentiate between corporate objectives and shareholder objectives in the area of close corporations is likely to prove futile. Such "incorporated partnerships," toward which the accumulated earnings tax is primarily directed, do not have any purposes or objectives completely independent of those of their stockholders. Moreover, a close corporation often represents far more than a mere incorporated venture to its proprietors. It may well constitute their life's work, and the foundation of their planning for the present and future security of their families. It is in this latter connection that redemption transactions particularly pursuant to stock-restriction agreements, so often play a key role. Such transactions are obviously inspired by the desires of the individual shareholder. And this is no less true of minority redemptions than of majority redemptions. In a minority redemption, the majority group, acting in its own self-interest, causes the corporation to redeem the stock of the minority shareholder who, likewise acting in his own self-interest, has decided to sell out.

It is true that the opinion of the court of appeals in the Mountain State case appears to have placed its stamp of approval upon the business-purpose analysis of redemption transactions under the accumulated earnings tax. As we have seen, the court was not confronted with the question of accumulation of earnings in advance of a contemplated stock redemption; but the court made clear its intention to include that kind of transaction under the business-purpose umbrella by referring with apparent approval to the decision in Emeloid Co. v. Commissioner. . . .

It would probably be unwise, however, to rely too far on the broad implications of the opinion in Mountain State. First of all, that court had no reason to, and therefore did not, consider the potential wholesale accumulation of earnings in advance of a contemplated redemption which those implications might justify. Moreover, in stressing the importance of resolving the conflict between the two equal groups of stockholders in Mountain State, the court emphasized the importance to the corporation of avoiding the alternatives of sale or complete liquidation of the enterprise which might otherwise have been necessary. But the court failed to consider whether the shareholders whose stock was redeemed could in fact have compelled either of those alternatives. If they could not, as may have been true under the West Virginia statute applicable in the Mountain State situation and would certainly be true in many other jurisdictions, then, as suggested above, the necessity for redemption of that stock from the corporation's point of view is a good deal less clear. And in any event, certainly the selling shareholders, who owned a full one-half interest in the corporation, were not concerned with the needs or purposes of the corporation in their demands to be bought out.

* * *

However, the necessary corollary of this approach is that in redemption cases the court must deal directly with the highly subjective issue of the proscribed purpose. . . .

In [that] event, the important question in these cases is whether the redemption transaction itself provides a basis for inferring the proscribed purpose. To this question the court of appeals in Mountain State gave a clear negative answer, remarking that the "fact of redemption, of itself, . . . furnishes no basis for imposition of the § 102 tax." However, this dictum only opens up the issue; it does not conclude it, particularly since that case did not involve the question of accumulation of earnings in advance of and in contemplation of a redemption.

Here the view expressed earlier, that a redemption of all the stock of the shareholder is akin to a complete liquidation as to that shareholder, may be relevant. In the normal case, when earnings are accumulated to finance a redemption, the selling shareholders will receive their share of the earnings so accumulated as a part of the redemption price. That is because the value of the stock interest to be redeemed will generally increase as the earnings are accumulated; only rarely would a price be set for a future redemption which did not provide for adjustments to take account of profits or losses in the interim. But in effect this means that, from the point of view of the selling shareholders, the situation is just about the same as accumulation of earnings in contemplation of liquidation. Certainly accumulation of earnings in order to distribute them in complete liquidation at capital-gains rates could serve no business need; rather it would go very far to demonstrate the existence of the proscribed purpose to avoid the tax on shareholders. Thus it could well be found that the principal purpose of the selling shareholders in the accumulation of earnings for the redemption of their stock is to avoid surtaxes. . .

* * *

[However,] any earnings accumulated after a final agreement on price is reached would redound entirely to the benefit of the holdover shareholder. As a practical matter, if the transaction is actually consummated within the same fiscal year, presumably no question of a dividend would even arise. It should make no difference that the delay happens to carry beyond the end of the current fiscal year, when under normal circumstances a dividend might be in order. A dividend would not ordinarily be paid prior to the redemption out of earnings accrued subsequent to the agreement on redemption price, since the selling shareholders would not be entitled to share in those earnings. If such a dividend were paid, the holdover shareholder would of course expect the selling shareholders to apply their proceeds against the redemption price. But it seems just as clear that the selling shareholders would not agree to any such procedure. Since the redemption price was determined without including any increment on account of current earnings, there is no reason why they should accept as partial payment of that price a dividend out of those earnings, taxable at surtax rate. Thus in this kind of situation it cannot fairly be said that a dividend out of current earnings would lead to a proportionate reduction in the redemption price. Moreover, there is no analogy there to the case of accumulation of earnings to be distributed in liquidation at capital gains rates, since the selling shareholders do not share in the current earnings being accumulated. Hence there is no basis for imputing to either group of shareholders the proscribed purpose to avoid the dividend tax and, accordingly, no basis for attributing that purpose to the corporation.

As a matter of fact, this kind of situation is very much like an accumulation of earnings subsequent to a redemption for the purpose of discharging the obligation incurred, where of course it is clear that the earnings are accumulated solely for the benefit of the holdover shareholder. Treating these two cases differently would put an undue premium on the time of execution of the redemption transaction, a factor which bears no relation to the critical question of the purpose for the accumulation of earnings. It is submitted that the consistent and proper result is reached by regarding the recommendation made earlier in connection with earnings accumulated subsequent to a redemption as merely an illustration of a broader principle: There is no basis for inferring the existence of the proscribed purpose to avoid the tax on shareholders when the challenged accumulation of earnings is for the benefit of the shareholders whose stock is not to be redeemed and who therefore do not stand to obtain those earnings in a redemption transaction at capital gains rates.

* * *

It is arguable that in every case, even one involving the redemption of a small minority interest, the purpose of the selling shareholders to obtain their share of accumulated earnings at capital gains rates should be imputed to the corporation, thus at least paving the way for imposition of the tax on the portion of the accumulated earnings distributed to the selling shareholders. But any advantages of such a rule seem almost certain to be more than offset by the complicated problems of allocating and tracing earnings that would be involved. Moreover, it would be more consistent with general corporate principles to retain the rule that the purpose to be attributed to the corporation is that of the shareholders in control of it. Under that rule, it would follow that whenever earnings are accumulated to finance a redemption of the stock of the shareholders in control of the corporation, and the redemption price reflects the selling shareholders' proportionate share of the earnings so accumulated, it would be proper to infer the existence of the proscribed purpose and hence to impose the tax.

If there is any doubt whether the accumulated earnings augmented the purchase price, . . . the taxpayer would bear the burden of proof on that issue in accordance with its normal burden of disproving a determination by the Commissioner that the proscribed purpose was present. In cases where only a minority interest is redeemed, and the majority shareholders intend to carry on the business of the corporation, it would not be permissible to infer the proscribed purpose merely from the fact of redemption. So far as a redemption of exactly fifty per cent of the stock is concerned, . . . the business motive of the holdover shareholders would be regarded as predominant, and the proscribed purpose would not be inferred.

However, it should be added that, following the recommendation made earlier, a minority redemption would be simply neutral on the reasonable-business-needs issue; in the absence of special circumstances, such a redemption would give rise to neither a section 535(c) credit in favor of the taxpayer nor a section 533 presumption in favor of the Government. And of course it would still be possible in such a case to infer from other circumstances, in accordance with the general principles operative in the accumulated earnings tax area, that the dominant motive for the accumulation of earnings was in fact the proscribed purpose to avoid the tax on shareholders. This might be of particular importance in cases involving a long-term accumulation of earnings in contemplation of a stock redemption, perhaps pursuant to a stock-restriction agreement.

* * *

One other aspect of the majority-minority distinction drawn here deserves mention, particularly because of its important implications for the practicing lawyer in the planning of redemption transactions. Since the accumulated earnings tax is imposed upon the corporation, and would not normally be assessed until some time after the redemption transaction, the ultimate burden of the tax will fall, at least indirectly, upon the holdover shareholders. This is not a very desirable result. After all, the reason for imposing the tax is the fact that the selling majority shareholders are seeking to get their share of current earnings at capital gains rates; and the holdover shareholders do not get the benefit of those accumulated earnings since they are in fact distributed to the selling shareholders in the redemption. But of course the tax cannot be imposed directly upon the selling shareholders under the present statute. It is therefore incumbent upon counsel for the holdover shareholders to ensure that this potential corporate tax liability for prior years is taken into account in the redemption settlement, either as a direct reduction of the redemption price or by way of an indemnification arrangement with selling shareholders.*

SECTION 11. NOTE ON PERSONAL HOLDING COMPANIES

A detailed analysis of the personal holding company problems is beyond the present scope of these materials. However, the following article, by the Tax Legislative Counsel of the Treasury at the time of the drafting and enactment of the Revenue Act of 1964, provides an excellent introduction to the personal holding company provisions and the impact of the 1964 amendments:

LUBICK, PERSONAL HOLDING COMPANIES—YESTERDAY, TODAY AND TOMORROW **

42 Taxes 855 (1964).

It has been recognized from the earliest income tax acts under the Sixteenth Amendment that the existence of corporate income tax rates lower than individual income tax rates requires special provisions to prevent avoidance of taxes on individual incomes. Otherwise individuals would be able through incorporation of their investments, or in some cases, their personal talents, to divert income from themselves (where it would be taxed at high marginal rates) to a separate corporate entity subject to lower tax. A special tax or rate of tax on all undistributed corporate profits might, of course, alter the balance sufficiently to obviate the need for the penalty taxes on unreasonable accumulations and personal holding companies. Indeed it has been said that such a tax in the 1936 Act was more effective in preventing corporate accumulations to avoid personal tax than measures tailored for that purpose. The merits and implications of such a measure, however, involve a broad reconsideration of the whole system of taxation of corporations and shareholders beyond the scope of this paper.

---

*[Ed. note] See 74 Harv.L.Rev. 932–937 for discussion of the special questions presented in the year in which a redemption transaction takes place, particularly (1) whether the payment of a tax by the withdrawing stockholders on their gain in the redemption transaction has any effect on the question of whether the corporation had the purpose of avoiding "the income tax with respect to its stockholders" under § 532(a); and (2) whether the reduction of earnings and profits as a result of the redemption has any effect on the question of whether the corporation permitted its "earnings and profits to accumulate" within the meaning of § 532(a).

** Reprinted by permission of the publisher, Commerce Clearing House, Inc. Most of the footnotes omitted.

This paper will examine the personal holding company provisions of the Code within the scope, then, of the present relationship of corporate and personal income taxes. First one must keep in mind the mathematics of the advantages of incorporation in the absence of provisions to prevent avoidance of tax by shareholders, in order to evaluate the necessity for various of the personal holding company provisions. Assuming 1965 corporate rates of 22 per cent of the first $25,000 of corporate income and 48 per cent of the excess and a marginal individual rate of 70 per cent on income over $100,000 ($200,000 for a joint return), the advantages of incorporation of investment are striking if the personal holding company tax is avoided.

Illustration 1: A portfolio of $3,000,000 of common stocks yielding 4 per cent is placed in corporation X by its sole shareholder, A, whose income is subject to the 70 per cent top marginal rate. Absent personal holding company, provisions and Section 531 penalty tax on accumulated earnings, the tax improvement to A by incorporation is as follows:

Taxation without incorporation

Dividend income	$120,000
X Individual rate	.70
Tax	$ 84,000

Taxation with corporation

Dividend income	$120,000
Less intercorporate dividend deduction—85 per cent	102,000
Taxable income	$ 18,000
Tax at 22 per cent	$ 3,960

If A liquidates corporation X before his death, there is an additional capital gains tax of $29,010, but this is avoidable by holding until death.

The net after taxes without the capital gains tax is over $116,000, which is what A would retain after taxes from a portfolio in excess of $9,500,000. The net after taxes including the capital gains tax is about $87,000. To retain the equivalent without a corporation would require a portfolio of $7,250,000.

If the dividend income is taxable to the corporation at a marginal rate of 48 per cent because it has $25,000 of other income, the corporate tax would be $8,640, and the capital gains tax on liquidation before death would be $27,840. The equivalent retention from stocks held in individual name would require a portfolio of close to $7,000,000.

The situation with interest income, absent the 85 per cent intercorporate deduction, is not so dramatic, but nevertheless advantageous:

Illustration 2: A portfolio of bonds of $625,000 yielding 4% is placed in corporation X by its sole shareholder, A, whose income is subject to the top marginal rate. Absent personal holding company provisions and Section 531, the tax improvement by incorporation is as follows:

Taxation without incorporation

Interest income	$25,000
X Individual rate	.70
Tax	$17,500

Taxation with corporation

Interest income	$25,000
X Normal tax	.22
	$ 5,500

The net after taxes $19,500 would require a portfolio of $1,625,000 held in *A's* name as an individual. If *A* liquidates corporation *X* before his death, there is an additional capital gains tax of $4,875, reducing the saving to $7,125 plus net additional income earned through deferral of capital gains tax. The net after taxes of $14,625 would require a portfolio of over $1,000,000 held individually.

If the interest income is taxable to the corporation at a marginal rate of 48 per cent, the corporate tax would be $12,000, still a current saving of $5,500. $3,250 would be eliminated by a capital gains tax on liquidation (offset by the advantage of deferral). Even paying corporate tax of 48 percent and capital gains tax on the balance, the net to *A* through use of a corporation would be the equivalent of the yield individually to him from an $812,500 portfolio rather than $625,000.

* * *

The need is therefore clearly demonstrated that additional statutory provisions are required to prevent avoidance of individual rates through incorporation. Our present corporate income tax recognizes the corporation as a separate taxpaying business entity, without taxation of shareholders prior to distribution, but to the extent that use of the corporation is without business justification, it should not insulate shareholders from taxation. The separateness of the corporation is recognized in the closely held corporate business situation, as much as the widely held situation, even though the mechanical problems of currently taxing corporate income to the shareholders are nowhere near so formidable as in a widely held corporation. The line has thus been drawn between income retained for the conduct of active business through a corporation, recognized as not improper merely because of the number of shareholders, and hence subject to no tax but the corporate normal and surtax, and that accumulated merely for investment where business considerations do not call for the use of corporate form or retention by the corporation. The objective is to draw a statute that will strike at the latter tax avoidance situations without interfering with legitimate business operations.

Is an Unreasonable Accumulations Provision Sufficient?

The initial approach to tax avoidance through incorporation was along the lines of present Section 531, imposing a penalty on account of corporate accumulations of surplus for the purpose of avoiding surtax on shareholders. The earlier statutes taxed the unreasonable accumulations to the shareholders, but since 1921 the penalty tax has been at the corporate level.

During consideration of the 1964 Act it was suggested that more reliance on Section 531 might be an adequate substitute for strengthening the personal holding company provisions. Both the Treasury and Congressional experts who considered this idea rejected it.

There are a number of reasons why Section 531 is not adequate to do the job required of the personal holding company provisions.

First there is the arithmetic of Section 531 rates. The accumulated earnings tax is $27\frac{1}{2}$ per cent of the accumulated taxable income up to $100,000 plus $38\frac{1}{2}$ per cent of the excess.

Using the $27\frac{1}{2}$ per cent rate, applicable to accumulations based on several million dollars of investment, and assuming the rate is not revised upward which, as indicated below, is probably not justifiable, a top bracket shareholder could be ahead by keeping his investment in corporate solution even with the payment of an accumulated earnings tax. For example, $100 subject to corporate tax of 48 per cent leaves $52 subject to $27\frac{1}{2}$ per cent accumulated earnings tax, or $14.30. The total tax is $62.30 which is almost $8 below the top marginal rate. If the balance of $37.70 were subjected to a capital gains tax, the total taxes would rise to $71.725, but the probability of escape of capital gains tax at death or at least the advantage of deferral until liquidation would make the individual better off.

The foregoing example is based on a 48 per cent corporate rate and a $27\frac{1}{2}$ per cent accumulated earnings tax. If the income were subject to only a 22 per cent or 28 per cent corporate tax (because corporate income does not exceed $25,000), or a 7.2 per cent corporate tax on dividend income (or even 3.3 per cent if less than $25,000), obviously the accumulated earnings tax at any feasible rate becomes an insufficient deterrent to corporate shelter. Add to that the factor that the $27\frac{1}{2}$ per cent accumulated earnings tax will not apply to the first $100,000 of accumulations (and that multiple $100,000 accumulation credits may be available) or that it may not apply at all if some business purpose can be established for nondistribution and it is clear why Section 531 is an ineffectual deterrent regardless of rate.

* * *

The Congress found that to deal with the extreme cases of avoidance an automatic mechanical penalty tax was needed. The accumulated earnings tax was continued for those cases where avoidance could not be automatically inferred from the high percentage of income of the kind not normally required to be received in corporate form (dividends and interest) or where the income accumulated was from the conduct of an active business, but its retention not needed by the business.

Thus Congress decided that to raise the accumulated earnings tax rate would not be an appropriate solution since that tax was needed for many situations other than incorporated pocketbooks and the like. For instance in the operating corporation which accumulates its earnings and profits from its operating business, Section 531 was still needed to apply to the income from active operations properly derived in corporate form without any tax avoidance motive, but thereafter retained in corporate solution to avoid individual taxes. In the personal holding company situation the very use of the corporate form in deriving the income is the avoidance device. Thus a raise in rate would be unduly severe in many cases where the income itself is legitimately derived in corporate form, though it ought to be distributed, especially since this requires subjective judgment.

The problem becomes one of determining clear cases where the need to derive income in corporate form is so slight that the statute is justified in making receipt of such income in corporate form, or at least receipt and retention, prohibitively costly without permitting inquiry into motive. This paper will briefly review the development of the present structure of the personal holding company tax to show how the present provisions originated, evaluate how well they work and indicate some areas to consider for improvement.

Rate of Tax

The personal holding company tax under the 1964 Act is 70 per cent of the undistributed personal holding company income of a personal holding company. Personal holding companies are those companies which, with certain exceptions, meet two objective tests, one with respect to closely held stock ownership and the other with respect to a high percentage of income derived from passive investments or certain other activities where derivation of income in corporate form is indicative of tax avoidance.

* * *

Although income subjected to the 70 per cent personal holding company tax rate, if the corporation also has taxable income subject to corporate tax, will be taxed by at least a few percentage points in excess of the top marginal individual rate, there is no point to achieving exact correlation. Statistics of Income for 1958–9 (the latest computation with respect to personal holding companies) showed 6,285 returns with schedule PH attached and total personal holding company tax receipts of $559,000 from 305 corporations. This confirms the point that the personal holding company tax does not and, is not designed to, raise revenue directly; rather it is intended to force distributions which will be taxable to shareholders at their individual rates. Even a corporation which becomes subject to personal holding company tax can avoid it subsequently through the deficiency dividend procedure. Therefore, the 70 per cent rate is adequate for its purpose to be sufficiently high to compel distributions, and so long as the personal holding company tax remains a tax on the corporation (as distinguished from taxing personal holding company income directly to shareholders as in the case of foreign personal holding companies), there is no reason, nor is it feasible, to complicate it to extract only the exact tax payable as if distributions had been made.

Stock Ownership

In order to be a personal holding company, Section 542(a) (2) provides that:

"At any time during the last half of the taxable year more than 50 per cent in value of its outstanding stock is owned, directly or indirectly by or for not more than 5 individuals."

This has been the provision since the 1934 Act, except that since 1954 certain exempt organizations and charitable trusts have been treated as individuals to prevent avoidance of the stock ownership rules through a donor controlled foundation. Thus if there are nine or fewer individual stockholders, more than 50 per cent of the stock will be owned by five or fewer individuals. If there are ten or more individuals owning stock or a stockholder is a corporation, trust, estate or partnership, the attribution rules of Section 544 must be applied. In addition, under that section certain convertible securities are treated as stock. These rules have remained unchanged in substance since 1937.

The stock ownership test seems to have worked satisfactorily in the personal holding company area. Aside from some general criticism of the complexity of the attribution rules of the Code, there has been no particular movement by either the Treasury or taxpayers to change the rules.

It is unlikely that a corporation with more than nine equal stockholders after application of attribution rules would be able to operate an investment company to accumulate income in avoidance of shareholder taxes. The requirement of diverse ownership among so many families would make it difficult to manage a corporation with the unity of accumulation purpose required. Nor does it seem appropriate to ease the stock ownership requirement, certainly so long as a corporation must be so essentially passive in order to meet the gross income test.

Gross Income

Even if a corporation meets the stock ownership test, as most corporations do, it will not be a personal holding company unless at least 60 per cent of its adjusted ordinary gross income is personal holding company income. Personal holding company income is defined in detail and embraces various kinds of normally passive investment income and some special items of personal service income.

Originally under the 1934 Act a corporation was not a personal holding company unless at least 80 per cent of its gross income was derived from royalties, dividends, interest, annuities or except for a regular dealer, gains from the sale of stock or securities. The 1937 Act continued the 80 per cent requirement, adding a number of categories of personal holding company income, and provided that once caught as a personal holding company for any year under the 80 per cent test, the gross income test was reduced to 70 per cent for subsequent years until the stock ownership requirement was not met for the last half of a taxable year or three consecutive years followed with less than 70 per cent personal holding company income. The additional 70 per cent test for a corporation once tainted was eliminated by the 1954 Act and the 1964 Act retains a single percentage regardless of prior personal holding company status.

The 1964 change in the percentage test is significant in two respects: the reduction of the percentage of personal holding company income from 80 per cent to 60 per cent and the use of "adjusted ordinary gross income" as the base rather than "gross income." Personal holding company income still includes dividends, interest, royalties and annuities; the principal changes are to eliminate capital gains altogether and to make adjustments in gross rents and gross mineral, oil and gas royalties to eliminate deductions for depreciation, depletion, property taxes, interest and rent paid.

The 60 Per Cent Test

The old percentage test was liberal and easy to avoid. A corporation had to have nonpersonal holding company income only slightly more than 20 per cent of its gross income to shelter the balance of its portfolio income. Thus numerous cases were discovered of dividends being sheltered by fairly inactive businesses which produced little or no profit but enough gross income to shelter up to four times as much personal holding company income. One of the more startling cases was the telephone answering service which predictably produced gross income of about $100,000 a year but had equally predictable expenses somewhat in excess of that. It was acquired for a nominal investment because it was not capable of producing any real profit; yet it was able to shelter gross income of up to $400,000 from dividends taxable at intercorporate dividend rates and from a portfolio at a 4 per cent yield of $10,000,000.

Even at the new 60 per cent test a nominal investment in a telephone answering service with $100,000 of gross income can shelter up to $150,000 of dividend income from $3,750,000 of portfolio.

Quite obviously in situations like the telephone answering service, even the 60 per cent test is unduly liberal. What about the 60 per cent test in other situations? Suppose a genuine manufacturing operation which has a bad year. Its gross receipts are not its gross income;[10] if its cost of goods sold approaches its gross receipts, and if it has other income from interest and dividends, it may be caught as a personal holding company. This, of course, was possible under the 80 per cent test; under the 60 per cent test the area of danger is increased. If the other income is rents or royalties, the proportion of adjusted ordinary gross income might change to qualify the rents or royalties as nonpersonal holding company income (more than 50 per cent of adjusted ordinary gross income) and this would automatically satisfy the requirement of more than 40 per cent nonpersonal holding company income. Where the other income is all interest or dividends, or interest or dividends mixed with rentals, or rentals and royalties mixed, the decline in nonpersonal holding company income could conceivably change the normal percentage ratios so that the corporation becomes a personal holding company.

How serious is the problem? Is it so likely to arise as to call the 60 per cent test into question? If the overall operation of the corporation is at a loss (disregarding the dividends received deduction), there would be no undistributed personal holding company income and hence no problem. If there is over-all income but a loss from operations, the corporation can avoid tax by making a distribution of its personal holding company income equal to its over-all profit (disregarding the intercorporate dividend deduction). If there is a small profit from operations, but not enough *gross* income to equal 40 per cent of adjusted ordinary gross, a larger distribution would be needed. It is unlikely that any such distributions would strain corporate resources. Since portfolio investments usually are capitalized at 20 to 25 times earnings and investments in businesses which are uncertain enough to have fluctuations producing this problem are hardly ever capitalized at more than six times average earnings, any corporation facing the problem would have an unusually large investment portfolio in relation to its capital investment in operating assets. Not only could it likely make the distribution required without strain, but one would suspect the large portfolio investment is good evidence that the corporation was at least partially used to avoid tax at the shareholder level.

If the income extrinsic to the primary business operation is rental or royalty, it could be separately incorporated as a subsidiary so as

10. Treas. Reg. Sec. 1.542–2 points out that gross income is not necessarily synonomous with gross receipts. It refers to Section 61 and the regulations thereunder for a definition of gross income. The most serious difficulties in defining gross income arise in cases involving reimbursement for expenses and computation of cost of goods sold. See Maloney, "What is a Personal Holding Company?" (1951) Proceedings New York University 9th Annual Institute on Federal Taxation, 745, 747 et seq.; Levine, "Gross Income in the Personal Holding Company," (1954) 9 Tax Law Review 453.

always to avoid personal holding company income classification under the 50 per cent test.

The conclusion is, therefore, that the 60 per cent test sets a minimum fair percentage allowing most of the gross income to be portfolio income and an overwhelming proportion of the capital investment to be portfolio type and will not interfere with normal conduct of business operations.

Use of Adjusted Ordinary Gross Income

The 60 per cent is applied to adjusted ordinary gross income; the old 80 per cent test applied to gross income. The first difference is that capital gains are eliminated entirely from both sides of the equation.

The 1934 Act included in the tainted income for the 80 per cent test gains from the sale of stock or securities (except in the case of regular dealers). The 1937 Act added gains from future transactions in commodities unless part of bona fide hedging operations by producers or handlers of the commodity which were necessary to the conduct of the business. Presumably these inclusions were based on the notion that this is the sort of income likely to be derived by incorporated pocketbooks and they were originally included at a time when corporate capital gains did not receive different treatment from corporate ordinary income. Although these capital gains continued until the 1964 Act to be considered as personal holding company income in classifying a corporation as a personal holding company, the alternative tax introduced in 1942 for corporations applied in lieu of personal holding company tax as well as corporate normal tax and surtax. Since 1954 undistributed personal holding company income has been reduced by the excess of net long-term capital gain over net short-term capital loss so that capital gains are never subjected to the penalty tax even if not distributed.

Since capital gains other than from security and commodity future transactions were not personal holding company income, a capital gain could be realized on some other asset, such as Section 1231 real estate, which would raise the percentage of nonpersonal holding company income to permit shelter of portfolio investment. By spreading such a capital gain over many years under the installment method, a long-term shelter without business risk was possible.

By excluding capital gains altogether from the gross income test under the 1964 Act, capital gains from the sale of Section 1231 property on the installment method can no longer be used as part of the active income side of the ledger to shelter personal holding company income for many years following a sale; neither will a casual sale of stock or securities at a large capital gain be treated as personal holding company income to throw a corporation into personal holding company status. Because long-term capital gains are taxed at the same maximum rate to corporations and individuals, they do not raise a problem of corporate shelter. It is fair that neither benefit nor burden results from this special type of income.

The second difference which the use of adjusted ordinary gross income introduces is the requirement of adjustments to both the overall income to which the 60 per cent test applies and the items which are included as personal holding company income.

The adjustments apply to reduce gross income from rents, mineral income and, in limited situations, interest income. Gross rents are reduced by depreciation (with an exception designed to cover rentals from short-term leases of cars and other equipment),[12] property taxes, interest paid allocable to the property leased and rent paid. Similarly mineral, oil and gas royalty gross income is reduced by deductions for depreciation and depletion, property and severance taxes, interest and rent. The same reductions apply to income from working interests in an oil or gas well even though such income is not personal holding company income in any case. There is eliminated from adjusted ordinary gross income and hence personal holding company income, interest received on a condemnation award, judgment or tax refund and certain interest received by dealers who make a primary market in United States Government Bonds.

The adjustments were intended to make the measurement of the percentage of personal holding company income as applied to total income a more accurate measure of the activity of the corporation—to determine whether in fact it was simply a shelter for investment type income or truly engaged in an active business enterprise.

For example, evidence was adduced that working interests in oil and gas wells were being used to shelter dividend and interest income. The working interests had been purchased with a knowledge of the oil and gas in place so the income was predictable with little risk. Of course, the extraction activity was carried on by an agent. Since the income from a working interest is not royalty income, but nonpersonal holding company income, only slightly over 20 per cent of gross was needed to shelter large dividend investment income. It was thought that an analogy to manufacturing or mercantile corporations would require reductions from gross income to be equivalent to the reduction from gross receipts by the cost of goods sold. In essence, depletion and property and severance taxes represent the cost of producing the oil and gas for sale. Certainly these costs are at least as, and usually much more, predictable than those of the manufacturing company and hence there is no reason why a corporation whose income is derived from working interests needs to maintain relatively greater

---

12. Sec. 543(b) (2) (A) (i). In this situation depreciation is apt to be an unusually high percentage of gross income and the degree of risk and activity so high, that it is unlikely to serve as a shelter, at least not with the same ease as real estate.

passive reserves in the form of investment portfolio than a manufacturing company.

The adjustments to rents and royalties have a similar justification. Depreciation in the case of a real estate corporation is the cost of the property sold to produce its gross receipts. The adjustments also prevent a corporation from avoiding personal holding company status through inflating its gross income to a point where gross rentals are more than 50 per cent of total gross income. Wash items, such as rent paid under a sublease arrangement whereby the holding company simply acts as an intervening lessee to inflate its gross rentals, are eliminated. Thus, a much greater proportion of rental activity to total income is required to meet the 50 per cent test if rentals or royalties are to be treated as nonpersonal holding company income.

It should be noted, however, that for a corporation which has less than 50 per cent of its income from rentals or royalties, the "adjusted ordinary gross income" concept makes it easier to meet the over-all 60 per cent test. A corporation which has some incidental rental income will be charged only with adjusted rentals as personal holding company income, and while the denominator of the fraction:

$$\frac{\text{personal holding company income}}{\text{adjusted ordinary gross income}}$$

is smaller, the equivalent decrease in the numerator more than offsets this. For example, using the old measuring rod of gross income, a corporation with $35,000 of gross operating income, $25,000 of dividends and $40,000 of gross rentals would have $65,000 personal holding company income out of $100,000 gross income. Under the 1964 Act, if the adjusted rentals are $20,000 the personal holding company income is $45,000 and the adjusted ordinary gross income is $80,000, so that the personal holding company income falls below 60 per cent.

The adjustments to interest can also constitute a liberalization. By and large they eliminate interest items not usually in the control of the recipient and hence have been eliminated from both parts of the fraction in measuring personal holding company status.

The Criteria Used to Classify Items as Personal Holding Company Income

In defining what is personal holding company income Congress has generally sought to classify those sorts of income which are not derived from the active conduct of a business and which do not involve risks requiring incorporation. There is in the usual case no non-tax reason why they ought not to be received directly by the shareholder rather than his corporation. Hence dividends, interest, royalties (other than mineral, oil or gas royalties and copyright royalties), and annuities are clearly personal holding company income and have been since the 1934 Act.

Income from personal services of a taxpayer should not be insulated from personal taxation by purely formal corporate intervention. The same is true in cases where income is shunted to a corporation from its shareholder for use of corporate property, where there is evidence that the arrangement is purely a shelter for portfolio investment.

Rentals from real property involve an area where there are legitimate reasons for incorporation to limit liability, yet this sort of income can in many cases be derived from investment requiring no operational talent and with no need to maintain a large portfolio for working capital. Hence, there are rules which permit accumulation in the corporate shelter if the bulk of the income is from that activity and if the rentals are not used to shelter other passive income. Mineral, oil and gas royalties have been analogized to rentals with more dubious justification.

Finally some sorts of income are personal holding company income unless in addition to constituting the bulk of the corporate income, and not being used to shelter other passive income, there are sufficient expenses incurred to indicate activity, for example, copyright royalties.

Since the personal holding company provisions are designed to force distributions in the clearest cases of avoidance, leaving to the subjective tests of Section 531 the cases which require a more flexible treatment, mechanical rules are required. A test such as that in Section 954(c)(3) excluding rents derived in the active conduct of a trade or business would not work in the personal holding company area because of its uncertainty. Taxpayers need to know as much as possible within the taxable year where they stand because the penalty tax is so severe and it is neither in their interest nor that of the government to encourage litigation to define what is "active."

In a number of situations what is passive income to most taxpayers is clearly properly attributable to an active business which ought not to be deprived of its ability to operate in corporate form merely because it is closely held. Hence, instead of excepting interest and dividends derived from the active conduct of a trade or business, the statute preserves certainty by excepting certain corporations— banks, insurance companies, finance companies, etc.—which derive income from interest and dividends. In such cases the interest and dividends are clearly related to the principal business activity and not simply sheltered income for the shareholders. To qualify for exemption as a finance company, a subjective test of "active business" must be met, but it is reinforced by requiring that the finance company have certain minimum business expenses as evidence of activity and by permitting the finance company to receive only limited passive income of other sorts so that the operating income from interest cannot shelter other personal holding company income.

Kinds of Personal Holding Income

Section 543(a) now lists the items of adjusted ordinary gross income which constitute personal holding company income. Those other than rentals may be briefly summarized.

Paragraph 1 specifies dividends, interest, royalties (other than mineral, oil or gas royalties or copyright royalties) as personal holding company income. Those corporations receiving interest as part of an active business such as banks and finance companies are excepted from classification as personal holding companies as noted above. Certain special kinds of interest are excluded in determining adjusted ordinary gross income as well as personal holding company income, also as noted above.

Paragraph 2 deals with rents and deserves more extended treatment below.

Paragraph 3 includes mineral, oil and gas royalties. . . .

* * *

Subparagraph 4 contains an exception to permit copyright royalties received by music publishers to be classified as nonpersonal holding company income. As added in 1959 copyright royalties do not constitute personal holding company income if they are 50 per cent or more of gross income, the Section 162 deductions (other than compensation and royalties paid to shareholders) constitute at least 50 per cent of gross income and the sheltered income is not more than 10 per cent of gross income. This paragraph was slightly modified in the 1964 Act to perfect the tests originally designed.

The 1964 Act added a new category of personal holding company income—produced film rents where less than 50 per cent of ordinary gross income. Prior to 1964 all film rentals were classified along with ordinary rentals—not personal holding company income if total rentals were at least 50 per cent of gross income. The 1964 Act added a provision that purchased film rentals—amounts received from the distribution and exhibition of a film negative acquired after substantial completion—are to be treated as copyright royalties. Purchased film rentals are thus subjected to the more stringent tests limiting other sheltered personal holding company income to 10 per cent of ordinary gross and requiring substantial related business expense deductions. On the other hand, produced film rentals—where the interest in the film was acquired before substantial completion—were separated from ordinary rentals and left as nonpersonal holding company income if at least 50 per cent of ordinary gross income.

The small likelihood of a purchased film rental being used as a shelter would not seem to justify the distinction from produced film rentals. It would have been better to put all film rentals under paragraph 2 which applies to rentals generally, or failing that, to preserve the pre-1964 treatment of paragraph 5 for all film rentals.

Paragraph 6 originated in the 1937 Act. It treats as personal holding company income amounts received for the use of property of a corporation from a 25 per cent or greater stockholder. The abuse was the incorporated yacht. A shareholder would incorporate his portfolio and along with it, his yacht or country residence and pay rental for the use of the yacht or residence to the corporation. The rental would thus shelter dividends and interest from the portfolio.

The statute applies whether the shareholder obtains the right to use the property directly or by sublease or other arrangement. This language has been construed to apply to all sorts of indirect use of the property. Thus if a corporation leases property to another corporation and both are owned by the same shareholder, the shareholder has been held to be using the property through his lessee corporation and the rental would be personal holding company income to the lessor. The saving feature in the situation of the bona fide business lease between related corporations is provided by a 1954 amendment which prevents application of the paragraph unless the corporation has other nonrental personal holding company income in excess of 10 per cent of gross income (now "ordinary gross income"). Thus if there is no sheltered income, Section 543(a)(6) will not be a problem. However, if there is dividend or interest income over 10 per cent of ordinary gross income, a distribution of the passive income alone will not help.

In addition, in determining undistributed personal holding company income, the base to which the personal holding company tax applies, business expenses and depreciation allocable to the operation of corporate property may not exceed the rental from the property unless the taxpayer establishes that the rent received was the highest available, that the property was held in the course of business carried on bona fide for profit and that either there was reasonable expectation that operation of the property would result in a profit or that the property was necessary to the conduct of the business. Thus excessive deductions cannot shelter dividend income from tax, even where the classification of the rental from property used by the shareholder as personal holding company income is not a serious hurdle to the corporation because the rentals do not produce net income.

Paragraph 7 was also added by the 1937 Act to deal with the incorporated talent device. If the corporation is to furnish personal services under a contract and if the services are required to be performed by a 25 per cent or more stockholder (directly or indirectly) either by the terms of the contract or by designation of someone other than the corporation furnishing the services, the payments are personal holding company income. The provision was originally aimed at actors, cartoonists and the like who incorporated their services to avoid high individual rates and to obtain capital gains rates on liquidation. It can also apply, however, to corporations performing services of all kinds, such as engineering and technical services, where the party performing the services is designated by the purchaser. Should professional service corporations succeed in establishing taxability as corporations, many of them might find this section troublesome where the client or patient seeks the services of a particular corporate employee lawyer or physician.

Paragraph 8 includes as personal holding company income amounts to be taken up as a corporate beneficiary of an estate or trust. It has been carried from the Revenue Act of 1937, where it was added to preclude the argument that gross income from a trust or estate was not personal holding company income. Sections 652(b) and 661(b) of the 1954 Code would now preserve the character of income distributed to the beneficiary, although the trust instrument can allocate the classes of trust income among the beneficiaries. The instrument creating a trust with both individual and corporate beneficiaries and which has some operating income could still allocate the operating income to a corporate beneficiary, which in essence is the same as a passive investor receiving dividends. Hence the provision is still necessary, and in fact ought to be expanded to include the similar situation of a corporation which is a limited partner.

The 1964 Act eliminated two kinds of personal holding company income which before 1964 had been so regarded in applying the 80 per cent test: gains from the sale of stock or securities and commodities futures. The rationale has been stated above. The elimination of all capital gains in applying the 60 per cent income test of personal holding company status is fair since capital gains income gains no advantage by receipt in the corporate entity. Since it is usually sporadic and hence less predictable, the tighter tests applicable to rents and the permissible percentage of personal holding company income should be relied upon to accomplish their aim of classifying the appropriate corporations as personal holding companies, rather than the haphazard receipt of capital gains not in themselves used to avoid individual taxes.

Rents

The original personal holding company provisions of the 1934 Act did not include rents as personal holding company income. Thus by generating gross rents which constituted over 20 per cent of gross income, it was easy to avoid personal holding company status.

A rent roll is comparatively easy to acquire to avoid personal holding company status. Most taxpayers would hesitate to invest in an unfamiliar mercantile business simply to avoid personal holding company status. This is not true of real estate, since most business persons have some experience with it. In view of the availability of mortgage financing, a large investment is not needed. Also the owner can readily and safely employ agents to manage the property for him. This is not easy in the case of a mercantile operation. Thus the most serious avoidance of personal holding company status has been through rentals.

The 1937 Act recognized this by classifying rentals as personal holding company income unless they constituted 50 per cent or more of gross income. The purpose of the 50 per cent rule was to permit a bona fide real estate operation to be conducted in corporate form. The 50 per cent rule, however, did not prevent the widespread use of gross rents to shelter portfolio income. The evidence submitted by the Treasury Department showed that this practice was widespread even among taxpayers with comparatively low incomes.

During the consideration of H.R. 8363 it was suggested that the statute should differentiate between active rentals and passive rentals, the former being treated in all respects as nonpersonal holding company income and the latter in all respects as personal holding company income.

This was rejected for several reasons. First, it is impossible to define active rentals in a meaningful way to preserve the required degree of certainty in this area. Gearing it to a ratio of Section 162 deductions to gross income is not satisfactory. A net lease of $1,000,000 per year can easily be revised to provide for rental of $1,100,000 with a provision that the lessor will provide services up to $100,000 per year. There are so many kinds of rental property that any percentage measure of activity is too crude a yardstick.

Second, by and large, the risks inherent in rental property do not require the same portfolio reserves as other business. The ease of acquiring rent rolls with a small investment and of acquiring management makes even an active rental business a different animal from the ordinary operating business. There is no need to allow rentals to shelter an equivalent amount of dividend and interest income. The 1964 Act prevents the use of rentals to shelter dividends and interest in excess of 10 per cent of gross income. A return of 15 per cent in gross rentals on original investment (a conservative figure) and a return of 4 per cent on portfolio means that if the 50 per cent test is met, close to 30 per cent of capital can be invested in assets producing personal holding company income without classification as a personal holding company under the 10 per cent test. This would seem a sufficient reserve in any case.

The 1964 Act changed the 50 per cent test to require that the adjusted rents be at least 50 per cent of the adjusted ordinary gross income. As indicated above, this is helpful to the non-real estate corporation, but it requires a real estate corporation to use a more realistic measure to show a preponderance of real estate activity. Second, the 1964 Act added a new test, that the other personal holding company income (including for this purpose all copyright royalties and the adjusted income from mineral, oil and gas royalties, but not compensation from a shareholder for use of corporate property) in excess of 10 per cent of gross income be distributed. If both tests are met, the rentals are not personal holding company income and the corporation is not a personal holding company. If either is failed the rents become personal holding company income and if the cause of failure is the 10 per cent test, the combination of at least 50 per cent rentals and 10 per cent other personal holding company income will make the corporation a personal holding company. Thus a real estate corporation cannot use rentals to shelter more than a modest amount of portfolio income; however, if rentals drop unexpectedly so that the portfolio income exceeds the 10 per cent, the corporation can purge itself by a distribution within two and one-half months after the close of its taxable year not of all its income, but only the amount necessary to meet the test. Thus the required distribution, as long as the 50 per cent test has been met, will never be more than a portion of the nonrental personal holding company income.

The new rental provisions should work successfully in curbing the principal abuse in the personal holding company area, the real estate corporation sheltering portfolio income. At the same time the introduction of the pay-out concept to eliminate personal holding company status where a distribution of excessive portfolio income is made should avoid hardship to bona fide operating corporations.

The 50 per cent side of the rental test can lead to anomalous results in some situations, however. It is possible that a corporation by increasing its active business can become a personal holding company. Suppose a corporation with adjusted rentals of $50,000, dividends of $20,000 and mercantile income of $30,000. Assuming distributions which keep dividend income to no more than 10 per cent of gross income, the rentals are not personal holding company income and the corporation clearly is not a personal holding company. If the mercantile income increases to $40,000, however, the rentals cease to equal 50 per cent of adjusted ordinary gross income and, when added to the dividends, make the personal holding company income exceed 60 per cent of adjusted ordinary gross income. Thus by increasing its active income, the corporation has become a personal holding company. This result could be prevented and at the same time the rules as to rentals could be simplified by substituting a single test for the present dual test applied to rentals. Under such a test rentals would not be personal holding company income unless the corporation had other undistributed personal holding company income in excess of 20 or 25 per cent of adjusted ordinary gross income. This would allow rentals from a highly passive net lease to be non-personal holding company income, but that is true under the 50 per cent test. The chief object of including rentals in personal holding company income is to prevent their use as a shelter for other passive income. The suggested single test would accomplish that result more simply than present law and perhaps more effectively since the allowable percentage of undistributed income would be based upon adjusted ordinary gross, rather than ordinary gross income without adjustment.

Over-all Evaluation

The personal holding company rules as refined over 30 years of experience have evolved from a simple, but ineffective set of provisions to prevent tax avoidance, to a complex melange as each taxpayer parry has been met with legislative riposte. Undoubtedly the 1964 changes will not eliminate all unwarranted tax avoidance, but they seem to have dampened considerably the chief avenues of escape. As indicated above more basic reforms such as eliminating the stepped-up basis at death and multiple surtax exemptions would take a major share of the profit out of the use of the holding company as a pure tax minimization device.

Some refinement here and there as has been indicated in this paper at various places might help simplify in places and plug small leaks in others. Nevertheless, the provisions should work well without undue deterrence to properly motivated business activities. Extremely liberal transition provisions, to facilitate liquidation of pre-existing corporations affected by the new rules, and permitting continuance to amortize pre-existing debts, will more than prevent hardship to those who have had the advantage of conducting affairs right up to the line for many years.

It may be worth exploration of the idea of extending the new pay-out concept for excess passive income in the rental area to the basic 60 per cent test itself—that is, if passive income in excess of 10 per cent of adjusted ordinary gross income has been distributed (in the current year, or perhaps on the average over three years) the corporation which fails the gross income test in a particular year would not be affected adversely. With such a rule the 60 per cent test itself could be lowered. On the other hand introduction of new complexities should await a period of experience with the 1964 provisions.

Another idea which might be explored is the one suggested 25 years ago by Harry Rudick that the undistributed income of a personal holding company be taxed directly to its shareholders currently. This would permit a consolidation of the personal holding company and foreign personal holding company provisions, eliminate the deficiency dividend provisions and adjust the penalty to the appropriate one for each stockholder. The historic constitutional fear of disregarding the corporate entity would seem to be no longer a serious problem in the light of the 1962 Act. On the other hand, such a solution would introduce new problems of basis and treatment of distributions. At the same time subchapter S privileges could be extended to corporations receiving personal holding company income. This could be done if no deductions were permitted for pensions and other employee fringe benefits to owner-managers of such corporations and if certain technical provisions to prevent one shot abuses through pass through of losses and capital gains were adopted.

One can expect a settling period as far as personal holding companies are concerned. Here and there Congress will move to correct an unintended hardship and the Treasury may at the same time, induce the elimination of an unintended loophole. By and large, however, the first major changes since 1937 will require a considerable period of experience before radical overhaul is in order.

Chapter 4

CORPORATE LIQUIDATIONS

SECTION 1. LIQUIDATION, DISSOLUTION, AND SALE OF ASSETS

A. INTRODUCTION

Although the term "liquidation" is widely used, it is rarely defined in the corporate statutes, unlike the term "dissolution" which clearly refers to the final termination of corporate existence. E.g., MBA §§ 75–89. An excellent statement of the relationship between liquidation and dissolution appears in Lattin, Corporations (1959) 550:

> "Dissolution" . . . means the termination of the legal existence of the corporation so that the unit may no longer carry on under its former franchises, for it has none with which to function. Liquidation or winding up involves the process of collecting the assets, paying the creditors, and distributing whatever is left, after liquidation expenses, to the shareholders in accordance with their contracts and, if there are no special contracts, then pro rata according to their shareholding interest.

Typically, liquidation and dissolution will be preceded by a sale of substantially all of the corporation's assets, in order to facilitate distribution to the shareholders (unless of course a distribution in kind is desired). However, a sale of all or substantially all of a corporation's assets is not always a prelude to a liquidation—that is, it is perfectly possible to have a sale of all the assets of a corporation without going on to distribute the proceeds to the stockholders in liquidation. Thus a sale of all of the assets of a corporation does not *ipso facto* constitute a "liquidation" within the meaning of, say, a charter provision governing the liquidation preference of preferred stock. E.g., Levin v. Pittsburgh United Corp., 330 Pa. 457, 199 A. 332 (1938) ("The inevitable legal result of a sale of corporate assets is not necessarily dissolution to be followed by complete liquidation. . . . The remaining stockholders in a corporation may . . . embark again upon the same business or, by amending its charter, proceed into new enterprises."); Treves v. Menzies, 37 Del.Ch. 330, 142 A.2d 520 (Ch. 1958) (sale of substantially all of the assets of a corporation for cash did not constitute a "liquidation, dissolution, or winding-up" of the corporation entitling the preferred stockholders to receive their liquidation preference).

Similarly, a vote to sell all of a corporation's assets does not itself provide any authority to liquidate the corporation and distribute the proceeds. In Opelka v. Quincy Memorial Bridge Co., 335 Ill.App. 402, 82 N.E.2d 184 (1948), the corporation, which owned a toll bridge, had outstanding 4000 shares of $100 par cumulative preferred stock with a liquidation preference of par plus accrued dividends, and 10,000 shares of no par common. In 1945, when the unpaid arrearages on the preferred stock amounted to $104.99 per share, the shareholders approved a plan calling for the sale of all of the corporation's assets and the distribution of the proceeds at the rate of $150.00 per share to preferred stockholders and $5 per share to common stockholders. The transaction was attacked by certain preferred stockholders on the ground, *inter alia*, that it violated the preferred stock liquidation preference. The defendants argued that the transaction was justified by the specific authority to sell all the assets of a corporation provided in § 72 of the Illinois Corporation Act (virtually identical to MBA § 72). The court held that the transaction was invalid:

> It is noted that this section provides for the sale of corporate assets other than in the regular course of business, but does not prescribe the method of distributing the consideration received. In fact, . . . [the counterpart of MBA § 72(c) indicates] that the corporation is to receive the sale price: . . . It logically follows that the consideration received by the corporation should be held for or distributed to the stockholders in accordance with their preferential rights as fixed by the charter and stock certificates. It seems to be the rule that approval of the sale of corporate assets does not extend to approval of a scheme of distribution of the sale price in conflict with the terms of the shareholders' contract as embodied in the charter, stock certificates, and the Corporation Act. In the case of Geiger v. American Seeding Machine Company, 124 Ohio St. 222, 177 N.E. 594, 79 A.L.R. 614, . . . [the Syllabus states that] "the sale of the entire assets of a corporation and the distribution of the proceeds of such sale among stockholders are separate matters between separate parties and based upon separate considerations; stockholders of different classes cannot be compelled to give their consent to one as a condition to their concurrence in the other."
>
> . . . Although this question apparently has not been passed upon by the courts of this state, the same distinction is recognized by the draftsmen of the Act in their authoritative commentary appearing in the Illinois Business

Corporation Act Annotated, wherein, with reference to Section 72, the following appears:

> "No provision, however, is contained in the Act permitting submission of a plan for the distribution among the various groups of shareholders of the shares received as consideration for the sale. *In the absence of unanimous consent, it would seem that the distribution of the consideration received can normally be effected only by following the procedure for voluntary distribution.*"

Defendants . . . [argue] that the reality of the situation confronting the Bridge Company called for some inducement to be offered common stockholders to secure their favorable vote for the plan. Inferentially, this suggests a new principle in law, i.e., that which would otherwise be illegal in corporate affairs may be validated by the exigency of a given situation. This revolutionary innovation cannot be adopted, as to do so would jeopardize the rights of the holders of preferred stock of all Illinois corporations, and, for all practical purposes, destroy the market for preferred stock in the future. If this policy is to be adopted, it becomes a matter for the legislature and not the courts. . . .

B. THE REQUIREMENT OF STOCKHOLDER APPROVAL FOR A SALE OF ASSETS

1. IN GENERAL

While liquidation and dissolution invariably require the affirmative vote of the stockholders, there is often a good deal more question as to whether the approval of stockholders is necessary for a sale of assets by the corporation.

SIEGEL, WHEN CORPORATIONS DIVIDE: A STATUTORY AND FINANCIAL ANALYSIS [1]

79 Harv.L.Rev. 534, 537–544 (1966).

A. Sale of Assets

It was generally held at common law that sale of all the assets of a corporation could be undertaken, except in rare circumstances, only upon unanimous vote of the shareholders, although a small body

---

1. Copyright (c) Harvard Law Review Association, 1966. Reprinted by permission. Most of the footnotes omitted.

of law and informed commentary argued that only a majority vote was necessary. Today, every state, with the sole exception of Arizona, has included in its corporation law a provision governing the sale of assets. A majority of these provisions specifically recognize stock of the purchasing corporation as acceptable consideration for the sale; and most others allow the terms of sale to be set by the board of directors, thus presumably permitting stock to be received as consideration. In some states, however, a minority stockholder may not be forced to accept the stock of the purchasing corporation as consideration for the sale.

Sections 71 and 72 of the Model Business Corporation Act are typical sale-of-assets provisions:

* * *

Whether the sale-of-assets component of a corporate division falls within section 72 turns on two issues: (1) Is there a sale of "all or substantially all" of the assets? (2) Is the sale in "the usual and regular course" of the business of the corporation?

1. "All or substantially all."—Few cases have raised squarely the issue of what size or character of sale is covered by sale-of-assets statutes. The meaning of "all or substantially all" as used in the Model Act and a majority of state statutes remains unclear. Some guidance may be drawn from decisions under other statutes, which speak of sales of "all of its property and assets," "its property . . . or any part thereof,"[22] "any of its property . . . essential to the conduct of its corporate business and purposes," and several other formulations. . . . It seems clear that the size of a sale alone will not be determinative of whether the sale falls within the statute requiring shareholder approval. In all cases, the courts have engaged in a close examination of the facts surrounding the sale. The sale in In the Matter of Timmis * of the calendar department of a printing company, together with the goodwill thereof, was held to be effectively "going out of business *pro tanto*," even though the assets of the division sold represented only one-thirteenth of the total assets of the corporation. In requiring stockholder approval, the court emphasized that the corporation was by virtue of the sale indefinitely barred from reentering the calendar business and that this amounted to a permanent contraction of the nature of the business. Such reasoning applied with equal force to the sale by a corporation of its newspaper plant, although the plant did not constitute its entire business. By contrast, the sale by a drugstore chain of one of its stores was held not substantially to contract either the size or the character of the corporate business.

---

22. E. g., the New York statute discussed in In the Matter of Timmis, 200 N.Y. 177, 93 N.E. 522 (1910).

*[Ed. note] See note 22, supra.

. . .

In Klopot v. Northrup,[30] a corset manufacturer sold its surgical corset department, and dissenting stockholders failed in their attempt to bring the sale within the statute. The court noted that the surgical department was new and experimental, and that it did not constitute such an integral part of the assets as to be essential to the corporate operations. Although factual distinctions clarify some of the decisions, differences in the statutory terms have often been determinative. In the Klopot case, some further explanation was necessary to demonstrate why a transaction strikingly similar to that in Timmis led to an opposite result. The Klopot court rested the distinction on the statutes involved:

> Our statute is not like that of New York, which authorizes a corporation, with the consent of two-thirds of its stock, to sell its property, rights, privileges and franchises "or any interest therein or any part thereof" . . . nor like the similar provision of the Maine statute . . . which applied to the sale of the franchises, entire property or any of the property of a corporation "essential to the conduct of its corporate businesses or purposes;" . . . nor even like the Ohio statute . . . which applied to the sale of "all or substantially all" the assets.

The Connecticut statute in Klopot was indeed different; at the time of that decision it applied to sales by a corporation of "all its property and assets, including its good will and franchises." While it may be argued that the "all assets" language of the statute was intended to exclude any sales of less than all assets, the Klopot court itself recognized the possibility that sales of essential assets, or of assets without which business could not be conducted, might fall within the statute. An Illinois court, faced with a similar statute, has held that "all" means "all or substantially all." But even with this modification, it is clear that the statute in Klopot was less inclusive than the enactment in Timmis and that this distinction was decisive.

These decisions suggest that while sales of all assets or essential assets will fall within the ambit of virtually all statutes, whatever their wording, determining whether sale of a corporate division [by a corporation owning two divisions] . . . would be held within the statute will depend on the particular facts and the statute involved. At one extreme, when language is presumptively directed at all sales, as was the New York statute, the Timmis result seems proper. At the other, when a statute appears limited to sales of "all" or "essential" assets, the reasoning of Klopot may be expected to prevail. Although the meaning of the "all or substantially all" test of the Model Business Corporation Act has not been authoritatively resolved, it seems closer in import to the "all assets" criterion. Had the drafters desired the Timmis result, they could have made

---

30. 131 Conn. 14, 37 A.2d 700 (1944).

the test "all or a substantial part." It seems likely that the words "substantially all" were inserted not to expand the class of sales covered, but rather to prevent avoidance of the statute by retention of some minimal residue of the original assets.* . . .

*[Ed. note] Compare the following views as to the meaning of "substantially all of the assets" of a corporation, in the context of the requirement in I.R.C. § 354(b) that to qualify as a D reorganization one corporation must acquire "substantially all of the assets" of the other. In Moffatt v. Commissioner, 42 T.C. 558 (1964), the court said:

> We note preliminarily that "[the] term 'substantially all' is a relative term, dependent on the facts of any given situation". . . . "Whether the properties transferred constitute 'substantially all' is a matter to be determined from the facts and circumstances in each case rather than by the application of any particular percentage". . . . Moreover, in considering the "facts and circumstances" in any given case, it is a matter of importance to take into account the liabilities of the enterprise, so that the retention of what might be a large amount of assets in other situations would be of very little consequence if such assets were held back by the transferor in order to pay off its liabilities. . . .
>
> * * *
>
> Petitioners' position revolves largely around percentages of balance sheet assets of the old company . . . . Their contention is fatally defective because (a) they fail to take into account the important asset of the business that did not appear on the balance sheet at all . . . . .
>
> (a) . . . It is of the utmost importance to remember that the consulting engineering business is basically a service business. . . . As we have found, the most valuable asset of such business is its staff of trained personnel and the past performance and qualifications of its employees. . . . This was an asset of enormous importance . . . ; yet, it nowhere appears on the balance sheet, and was not taken into account in any way by petitioners in evaluating what was transferred . . . . .

In James Armour, Inc. v. Commissioner, 43 T.C. 295 (1964), the court said:

> In the instant case Armour, Inc. immediately prior to the transactions in question had assets of a fair market value of about $1,230,000. Among these assets the principal item in the conduct of the business was the construction equipment which had a value of $620,774.98 which was transferred to Excavating [a new corporation]. Also among the assets transferred were furniture and fixtures and automobiles of a value of $7,802.84. Thus, total assets of a value of $628,577.82 were transferred directly by Armour, Inc. to Excavating. [The court then noted that although real property with a value of approximately $180,000 was transferred to the stockholders of Armour, Inc., it was promptly leased to Excavating.] The remaining assets, consisting of cash and accounts receivable of approximately $425,000, were not acquired by Excavating. Thus, it will be seen that as a result of the transactions, Excavating either acquired title to, or the use of, all the assets essential to the conduct of the business enterprise. It seems clear that the assets which it did not acquire, namely, cash and accounts receivable, were not necessary to the conduct of the enterprise. If such unneeded assets had been distributed to the petitioners prior to the transfer of the essential assets to Excavating there clearly would be no question that substantially all of Armour, Inc.'s assets were acquired by Excavating. . . . The date of distribution is not decisive in such a situation as is here presented.

2. *"Usual and regular course of business."*—The Model Act and the statutes based on it require shareholder approval only for sales outside of the usual and regular course of business. Many statutes limit only the size of the sale and do not have this additional test. The statutes in both Klopot and Timmis were so drafted, but in Timmis the New York court judicially adopted the additional criterion: "Notwithstanding the broad language of [the sale of assets statute] . . . it is obvious that it was not addressed to ordinary sales by a corporation, nor even to those extraordinary in size but still in the regular line of its business . . .." Since the New York statute in Timmis covered the sale of corporate property "or any interest therein or any part thereof," the result of the decision was that any sale, however small, fell within the statute if it was outside the usual and regular course of business of the corporation. Under the Timmis rule, however, the sale of significant assets—as, for example, an entire store—would fall outside the statute if by virtue of its usual nature it were found to be within the ordinary course of business. The Model Act requires stockholder approval in fewer cases than does the Timmis rule, since the sales covered must be both outside the usual and regular course of business and dispositions of all or substantially all the assets of the corporation. However, since the Model Act's "all or substantially all" test remains open to varying interpretation, it is not unlikely that the nature of the sale—whether it is in the ordinary course of business—will be the major factor in determining whether the sale requires stockholder approval.

The courts have experienced some difficulty in defining a corporation's usual course of business: [as the court said in the Timmis case,] "The sale before us was not made in the ordinary course of the business of the corporation, for it was not organized to sell calendar departments, or any department that would involve going out of business *pro tanto.*" Obviously the usual corporation is not organized to dispose of part of its business. Yet sales of major assets such as buildings or machinery in connection with replenishment programs are ordinarily within the powers specified or implied in the certificate of incorporation, although they may not be everyday occurrences. Corporate management would be hamstrung if every such transaction had to be submitted to a vote of shareholders. . . . Where is the line drawn? Sales of substantial assets by real estate corporations or by corporations organized to liquidate a business have been held within their usual course of business. Generally, a charter provision allowing sales of all assets without shareholder approval will also be held to render such sales usual. Absent such a charter provision, however, is there any ordinary business objective of the cor-

Accordingly, we conclude that substantially all of the assets of Armour, Inc., were acquired by Excavating . . ..

poration that might justify a disposition such as the sale of a . . . corporate division?

Several New York decisions have upheld dispositions of assets without stockholder approval when undertaken as part of a relocation plan, as when sale of one plant is followed by purchase of another. These cases have two significant facts in common: in none was goodwill sold, and in none was a new corporation organized. It has already been noted that disposition of goodwill might in itself bring a sale within the statute. Support for this conclusion is found in the Model Act: section 71 does not include dispositions of good will as part of the sales in the usual course of business, while section 72 does include such dispositions in sales outside of the usual course of business. Exclusion of goodwill from the sale will not assure that the sale may be consummated without shareholder approval, since section 72 covers disposition "with or without the good will." Nevertheless, failure to sell the goodwill will be relevant to a decision that the sale is not out of the ordinary course of business.

The fact that a new corporation was not organized also influenced the decisions in the relocation cases. Yet one commentator has suggested that even when the relocation involves a change in the corporate entity (as by formation of a corporation in another state followed by transfer of assets in return for stock thereof), "such a transaction is within the literal language of those statutes . . . [governing] sale of assets, but hardly within their spirit." . . .

STILES v. ALUMINUM PRODUCTS CO.

Appellate Court of Illinois, First District, 1949.
338 Ill.App. 48, 86 N.E.2d 887.

FEINBERG, PRESIDING JUSTICE. Plaintiffs brought their action under Section 73 of the Business Corporation Act, [the counterpart of MBA §§ 73 and 74] to recover the reasonable value of 1240 shares of stock of the defendant company, owned by plaintiffs. . . .

There is practically no dispute as to the facts. It appears from the evidence that defendant was an Illinois corporation incorporated in 1911 and engaged in the manufacture and sale of aluminum and stainless steel cooking utensils, and also in the fabrication of aluminum and other metals. The charter was amended in 1935, giving it power to deal in real estate and securities. After the charter was amended, a subsidiary company known as General Homes Corporation, was organized, which erected some 30 apartments on real estate adjacent to the plants of the corporation, and appears to have been a housing project for the convenience of defendant's employees. The acquisition of the shares of the General Homes Corporation and a few shares of bank stock was the only exercise of the additional powers of the corporation prior to the sale of its assets in question. During the year 1945, negotiations were entered into for the sale of defendant's manufacturing plants, tangible property inventory, business and good will, to the Reynolds Metals Company, a Delaware Corporation. A contract of sale dated December 7, 1945, between defendant and the Reynolds Company was entered into, by which all of its manufacturing plants (four in number), its tools, dies, machinery, equipment, office furniture, trucks, inventory, good will and patents were sold to the Reynolds Company for $1,406,570. It did not sell its stock in General Homes Corporation, nor some stock in the LaGrange Trust and Savings Bank, money in bank, accounts receivable and some marketable securities and a 1942 Oldsmobile sedan. It was stipulated that the value of the assets not sold was $760,622.69. After the contract of sale was entered into, the directors sent out a notice, under Section 72 of the Business Corporation Act, for a stockholders' meeting to authorize the sale. Plaintiffs were substantial stockholders in the defendant company, and at the meeting did not vote in favor of the sale and followed the [appraisal] procedure prescribed by Section 73. . . .

No question is here raised that defendant did not conform to the statute in the matter of the notice and the holding of the meeting of the stockholders or the procedure necessary to effect a sale, nor is there any question raised here that plaintiffs did not comply with the procedure prescribed by said Section 73.

The only question, as we view it, presented upon this appeal is whether the sale in question was one of "substantially all of the assets" of the defendant company, not made in the usual and regular course of its business, within the meaning of Section 72 of said act. Plaintiffs' theory is that the mere exclusion from the sale of a secondhand automobile, some shares of stock in a subsidiary building company, accounts receivable, money in bank, and some marketable securities, does not take it out of the operation of the statute governing the sale of the "substantially all of the assets" of the company.

The primary object of the company was the manufacture of aluminum and stainless steel cooking utensils and the fabrication of aluminum and other metals. It owned four tracts of real estate, each improved with buildings, having an aggregate of 128,000 square feet, in which it carried on its manufacturing business. It had a vast stock of raw material and finished products, valuable patents, licenses, copyrights and good will, all resulting from the years of successful operation of its business, and all included in the sale in question. To hold out from the sale the choses in action described and an old automobile, and thus seek to prevent the sale from being "substantially all of the assets" of the company, within the meaning of the statute, is in our judgment an effort to circumvent the statute and defeat the rights of a dissenting stockholder under Section 73 of the act. . . .

[T]he present statute, while intending to liberalize the power of directors and stockholders to sell all or "substantially all of the assets" other than in the regular course of business, as provided in said act, . . . also intended to protect the minority stockholder who does not vote in favor of such a sale. It affords to him the remedy of recovering the reasonable value of his stock, whatever that may be as of the time of the sale. It will not permit resort to subterfuge, in a sale of assets, to defeat the rights of a dissenting stockholder.

We think upon the showing made that the sale in question was one of "substantially all of the assets" of the corporation within the meaning of the statute, and that plaintiffs are entitled to bring their action. . . .

2. SALE OF ASSETS PURSUANT TO A DISSOLUTION

Does a sale of substantially all of a corporation's assets pursuant to a dissolution of the corporation still require a vote of the stockholders under a sale-of-assets statute like MBA § 72? Often it will not make much difference as a practical matter, since the dissolution will have to be approved by the stockholders, and normally there would be little difficulty in getting their approval for the sale of assets at the same time. However, as we have seen, dissolution is not the same as a sale of assets, and in some circumstances there might be stockholders who would vote for dissolution but not for a sale of assets—for example, if they preferred to receive a distribution in kind. In In re Mayellen Apartments, Inc., 134 Cal.App.2d 298, 285 P.2d 943 (2d Dist. 1955), the court held that once dissolution had been voted, it was no longer necessary to get the stockholders' approval for sale of all the assets because the statutory provisions dealing with dissolution expressly gave the directors power "to sell . . . or otherwise dispose of all or any part of the assets of the corporation, upon such terms and conditions and for such considerations as such board deems reasonable or expedient".

The Model Act provisions relating to this issue are rather puzzling, and if nothing else they further illustrate how complex the interrelationship between sale of assets and dissolution can be. Section 80(b) somewhat parallels the statute referred to in the Mayellen case, but there are some differences that could be important. First, the "wind-up" powers are conferred upon the corporation, rather than directly upon the board of directors, which may be designed to leave open the question of who acts for the corporation. Second, § 80(b) does not expressly authorize any "sale" of assets, much less the sale of substantially all of them. There is also the question of what inference should be drawn from the fact that § 73(b), which provides appraisal remedies for stockholders who dissent from a sale of assets in certain circumstances, was amended in 1962 to expressly include "a sale in dissolution". That the amendment was thought necessary at all, and that no corresponding amendment was made in § 72 itself, certainly suggest that dissolution sales are not covered by § 72, although they have now become subject to the appraisal remedy of § 73.[2] On the other hand, if a sale in dissolution is not subject to § 72, it is hard to see how a right to dissent from it can be very meaningful. In other words, if a sale of all the assets pursuant to a dissolution under § 77 does not require action by the stockholders under § 72, there will not be any occasion for the stockholders to dissent to the sale; on the other hand, a dissent at the time of the vote on dissolution may be premature, since there may not yet have been any decision on whether the assets are to be sold. Perhaps the practical answer is that the stockholders should refuse to approve a dissolution unless it is accompanied by a "plan" which indicates whether the assets will be sold or distributed in kind.

There is another puzzling aspect of § 73(b) which relates to the interaction between a sale of assets and liquidation or dissolution. In view of the fact that a sale of assets does not in and of itself involve or authorize the distribution of the proceeds to stockholders, what is the import of the exception to appraisal rights in § 73(b) for cases where the sale of substantially all of the assets is "for cash on terms requiring that all or substantially all of the net proceeds of sale be distributed to the shareholders in accordance with their respective interests within one year after the date of sale"? Even if the term "net proceeds of sale" in this exception is read literally (rather than as though it said "net assets", which would seem more in keeping with the apparent purpose of the provision to isolate those cases where the stockholders will receive cash in full fairly promptly), it is hard to see how the required assurance of distribution to the stockholders could normally be given unless dissolution of the corporation had already been approved. If so, the proviso would in effect be limited to cases where the vote to sell the assets was conditioned upon a vote to dissolve the corporation, which of course would be wholly meaningless if a vote to dissolve made it unnecessary to have a separate vote to sell the assets. Compare New York Business Corporation Law § 910, where the proviso limiting shareholders' appraisal rights in connection with the sale of substantially all of the assets is expressly predicated on the shareholders' approval being "conditioned upon the dissolution of the corporation and the distribution of substantially all its net assets to the shareholders in accordance with their respective interests within one year after the date of such transaction".

2. Compare New York Business Corporation Law § 1005(a)(3)(A), which expressly precludes the application of the sale-of-assets statute to sales in dissolution, but does require the approval of a majority of the voting stock (as compared with the ⅔ requirement under the regular sale of assets provision) for a sale in dissolution of substantially all of the corporation's remaining assets where the consideration is in whole or in part the stock or securities of the buyer.

C. RIGHTS OF CREDITORS UPON A SALE OF ASSETS, LIQUIDATION OR DISSOLUTION

DARCY v. BROOKLYN & N. Y. FERRY CO.

Court of Appeals of New York, 1909.
196 N.Y. 99, 89 N.E. 461.

WILLARD BARTLETT, J. On November 15, 1900, the plaintiff duly recovered a judgment against the Brooklyn & New York Ferry Company upon a cause of action which had accrued on the 2d day of July, 1897. The execution upon this judgment was returned unsatisfied. The plaintiff found himself unable to enforce it because the defendant corporation on the 22d of August, 1898, had through its board of directors assumed to sell, assign, and transfer the entire corporate property to another corporation known as the Brooklyn Ferry Company of New York for $6,000,000. The present suit was instituted on the theory that the directors had violated their duties in making the transfer in the manner in which they made it and hence could be compelled to satisfy the plaintiff's claim. The consideration for the transfer did not pass from the purchasing corporation to the Brooklyn & New York Ferry Company or its directors, but was turned over directly to the stockholders of the selling corporation and distributed among them. The Brooklyn & New York Ferry Company thereupon immediately ceased doing business, having thus parted with all its franchises, although no proceedings were ever taken to effect a dissolution of the corporation according to law. No notice of the transfer was given to creditors nor was any property retained by the directors with which to meet the plaintiff's claim or any other indebtedness which might legally be established against the corporation. At the time of the transfer, however, the purchasing corporation did agree to assume all the then existing debts and liabilities of the selling corporation. This agreement was the sole provision made by the directors for the payment of the creditors of the corporation which they represented.

The narrative of the transaction leaves no doubt that what the directors of the Brooklyn & New York Ferry Company sought to bring about was a voluntary dissolution of the corporation and the distribution of its assets without taking the steps to that end which are prescribed by law. Notwithstanding their failure to proceed under the statute, they contend that a creditor of a corporation has no standing to compel them to pay a claim of which they were ignorant at the time of the transfer of the corporate property, in the absence of proof of actual fraud on their part. It is true that there is no allegation or finding of fraud; but there is evidence that the officers of the company had knowledge of the injury to the plaintiff which was the basis of his claim. The liability of the directors is predicated, not on the ground that their action in making the transfer was fraudulent, but upon the proposition that it is a violation of duty on the part of the directors of a corporation to divest it of all its property without affording a reasonable opportunity to its creditors to present and enforce their claims before the transfer shall become effective. This is the proposition involved in the judgment in this case which we are asked to reverse. We think it is sound in law, and should be upheld.

There is express statutory authority for the maintenance of an action by a creditor of a corporation against its directors to compel them to pay the value of any property which they have transferred to others by a violation of their duties. . . . The assets of a corporation constitute a trust fund for the payment of its debts. . . . A creditor cannot be deprived of his equitable lien thereon by an agreement between the corporation and a transferee of the property that the latter shall assume and pay all the corporate debts. The consent of the creditor to accept the substituted debtor is essential to make such an agreement valid as against him. Hence the fact that the Brooklyn Ferry Company of New York agreed with the Brooklyn & New York Ferry Company to assume all the debts of the latter did not justify the directors of the selling corporation in disposing of its assets without making some other provision for the payment of its creditors. The plaintiff was left in the position of the creditor so aptly described . . . [thusly]: "When he demands payment of his claim, he is referred to the empty shell which is all that is left of the live corporation whose tangible assets constituted a trust fund for the payment of his claim at the time of its creation." It is not necessary to determine precisely what the directors of a corporation must do in order to protect themselves against liability when they undertake to divest it of all its property and practically dissolve it without taking the proceedings for a voluntary dissolution which are prescribed by law. For the purposes of the present case, it is enough to say that they were bound to give some notice to creditors of the proposed transfer, and they gave none whatever. We think that their failure to do so was "a violation of their duties" under subdivision 2 of section 1781 of the Code of Civil Procedure, and rendered them liable to the plaintiff for the amount of the claim which he established against the corporation as having accrued before the transfer. The motives which induced the omission are immaterial. The entire assets could not lawfully be set over by the selling corporation to the purchasing corporation until some sort of opportunity had been given to the creditors of the latter to present and enforce their claims. The neglect to afford this opportunity is what constituted a violation of the directors' duties, and it matters not that they may have supposed they were not required to do any more than they did for the protection of creditors. . . . Their omission to make adequate provision for the protection of the creditors was proof of their dereliction and good faith constitutes no defense. Indeed, business men have little cause for complaint when, as in this case, they find themselves in trouble because they have attempted to accomplish privately what the law contemplates shall only be accomplished publicly, namely, the voluntary dissolution of a corporation. The judgment enforces a sound lesson in business morals and should be affirmed, with costs.

NOTE ON THE RIGHTS OF CREDITORS

1. Liability of the Transferee of Substantially All of a Corporation's Assets. Obviously, a transferee of a corporation's assets who, as in the Darcy case, assumes the transferor's liabilities is liable for the debts assumed. However, in some circumstances a transferee may find itself saddled with debts of the transferor which it never agreed to assume. The following is a brief analysis of this subject which should also provide some useful background for considering the liability of the transferor's directors in such circumstances, as illustrated by the Darcy case.

NOTE, RIGHTS OF CREDITORS AGAINST A SUCCESSOR CORPORATION [3]

44 Harv.L.Rev. 260 (1930).

It is common for a corporation to transfer all or nearly all of its assets to another corporation. This device may represent an honest revision of fiscal policy, or it may be adopted with a desire to escape embarrassing debts. But regardless of the motive behind these transfers, they are of vital interest to creditors, for it is out of the *quid pro quo* received in return that the debtor must meet its obligations. This consideration may consist of cash, stock in the new corporation, a promise of cash, or an assumption of the obligations of the old corporation. From a creditor's standpoint, any of these, if in fact an adequate return, probably constitutes value. Any one of them, however, may be objectionable if it hinders the creditor in procuring satisfaction of a judgment. Cash and stock are easily concealed and readily taken out of the jurisdiction; and the transferee's promise to pay money may be enforced only by an additional equitable or statutory proceeding. This is equally true of an assumption of liability, except where third party beneficiaries are allowed to sue. But even in such jurisdictions the creditor may be technically justified in regarding the conveyance as a hindrance, for he can not be compelled to accept a substitute debtor, and satisfaction of a judgment against the old debtor entails additional proceedings.

Even though the consideration paid, however, is found to be free from these objections, unsatisfied creditors may justly complain if it does not reach the old corporation. Since the transfer involves the bulk of the corporate assets,[12] the purchaser must be taken to know that the creditors,

---

3. Copyright (c), Harvard Law Review Association, 1930. Reprinted by permission. All footnotes omitted except note 12, which has been supplemented by the editor.

12. Bulk transfers of assets are always viewed with circumspection by the courts. . . . The same considerations have caused the enactment of [so-called "Bulk Sales Acts", requir-

whose existence he should assume, have an interest in the consideration as the source of future satisfaction of their claims. No stockholder is entitled to the corporate assets or their product when any creditor can not be paid. Consequently the creditors may attack the transaction to the extent that the consideration is paid to the stockholders.

Where the transaction is improper, the obvious remedy of the creditors of the old corporation is to treat the transfer as a fraudulent conveyance, and after procuring judgment against the debtor, either to levy execution on, or to bring a bill in equity against, the property or its product. But many courts have not confined the creditors to this traditional remedy and have permitted the original suit to be brought directly against the transferee, subjecting it to a personal liability limited to the value of the assets transferred; and some courts, going still further, impose on the transferee all the obligations of the transferor.

Theories have not been wanting to explain these results. Some courts find an implied promise by the new corporation to pay the debts of the old to the extent of the value of the assets transferred. . . .

[Some cases rest] liability on the ground that there is a *de facto* merger or consolidation. This is fair enough when the old stockholders receive the consideration for the transfer. But if the old corporation itself receives the remuneration and is thereby kept alive, there seems to be nothing in the nature of merger or consolidation.

Finally, the transferee may be held liable because it is merely the old corporation under the mask of the new entity. This seems justifiable if the stockholders of both corporations are the same. But there are objections to this theory. . . . [I]t would seem desirable, if the new corporation has paid value, to free it of its predecessor's obligations despite the identity of the stockholders. Thus there is no liability where the stockholders of the new corporation have acquired their stock for a consideration entirely distinct from their interest in the old corporation. But when the new stock represents in whole or in part an exchange for the old shares, liability is imposed. To this extent the stockholders have received part of the consideration to which the creditors are entitled. In other words, the test of liability is that of a fraudulent conveyance, although the personal judgment is a remedy which goes beyond the law of fraudulent conveyances.

2. **Liability of the Directors of the Transferor.** The basis upon which the directors were held liable in the Darcy case is not entirely clear. The court purported to rest primarily upon the fact that all of the corporation's assets were transferred to a third party without any notice to the creditors, in violation of what was apparently an early version of a Bulk Sales Act. See note 12, page 626 supra. But at least today the directors of the transferor normally are not personally liable for failure to comply with a Bulk Sales Act — the only sanction is that the transferee of the assets takes them subject to the claims of the transferor's creditors.

ing notice to creditors of any bulk transfer of inventory, regardless of the disposition made of the proceeds. E. g., U.C.C. Article 6; see generally Coogan, Hogan and Vagts, Secured Transactions Under the U.C.C. (1964) Ch. 22.]

However, the court in the Darcy case was obviously influenced by the fact that the transfer of the assets was accompanied by an informal liquidation of the corporation, with the consideration received for the assets passing directly to the stockholders. Had the corporation received and retained it, that consideration would have been available to the corporation's creditors for the satisfaction of their claims. Obviously, directors may not distribute all of a corporation's assets to its stockholders without first providing for the claims of creditors. Indeed, absent some special authorization such a liquidating distribution would constitute the clearest kind of illegal dividend, for which directors would of course be liable. But even where such a liquidating distribution is authorized, as in the case of a formal dissolution of the corporation, the directors are no less charged with the responsibility of taking care of the claims of creditors. E. g., MBA §§ 80(b), 43(c). And as further protection to the creditors upon a dissolution, the statutes often require notice to them. E. g., MBA § 80(a).

However, this does not necessarily mean that all liabilities must be paid off in cash before the corporation is liquidated. MBA § 80(b) is typical of the corporation statutes in requiring only that "adequate provision" for the creditors be made. Like most of the statutes the Model Act does not afford any guidance as to what constitutes such "adequate provision". Since the most common, practical substitute for payment of the liabilities in cash is to have them assumed by a responsible third party, it is particularly important to know whether this kind of arrangement constitutes "adequate provision" for creditors. The directors in the Darcy apparently thought that it did, but the court rather vehemently disagreed. However, it is not clear that there was any express statutory "adequate provision" test operative in the Darcy case; and in addition the court's reasoning on this issue is rather unsatisfactory since the "adequate provision" test seems to have been confused with the requirements for a full-fledged novation based upon the consent of the creditors.[4]

---

4. Assuming that the transferee's assumption of liabilities did not constitute "adequate provision", could it have been regarded as producing an asset in the hands of the transferor corporation, i. e., a claim (against the transferee) by the transferor as promisee of a contract for the benefit of a third party (the creditors)? If so, such an asset would obviously not have been distributed to the transferor's stockholders but rather would still be on hand for the benefit of creditors, and perhaps this would be sufficient to forestall liability upon the directors. The Tax Court has rejected this asset notion in a case imposing transferee tax liability upon the stockholders of a corporation which transferred all of its assets in exchange for stock of the buyer and an assumption of liabilities, and then dissolved, distributing all of the stock received to its stockholders. Kimmes v. Commissioner, 22 T.C.M. 232 (1963). The court commented that "such an assumption is not an asset which can be levied upon and hence does not relieve stockholders of a transferor corporation of transferee liability arising out of the receipt of assets of the transferor corporation". See also Coca-Cola Bottling Co. of Tucson, Inc. v. Commissioner, 334 F.2d 875 (9th Cir.1964), where transferee tax liability was imposed upon the transferee-corporation which had purchased the stock of the transferor corporation and then dissolved it to obtain its assets. In addition to holding that the agreement by one of the stockholders of the transferor to indemnify both the transferor and the transferee against any liabilities of the transferor did not amount to an assumption of the liabilities of the transferor or otherwise constitute adequate provision for its creditors, the

In any event, today, more than fifty years after the Darcy decision, the cases as well as the statutes provide little guidance as to just what type of "provision" for the creditors will be regarded as legally "adequate", and in particular whether the assumption of liabilities by a responsible third party will suffice. One of the few efforts to crystallize the meaning of "adequate provision" in this context appears in the California statute, and since courts in other jurisdictions may well look to the pattern adopted there for aid in construing their own silent statutes, the California statute is worth examining here. Section 5000 of the Corporations Code requires the directors to determine "that all the known debts and liabilities of a corporation in the process of winding up have been paid or adequately provided for". Section 5001, entitled "Provision for payment of debts and liabilities," provides as follows:

> The payment of a debt or liability, whether the whereabouts of the creditor is known or unknown, has been adequately provided for if the payment has been provided for by either of the following means:
>
> (a) Payment thereof has been assumed or guaranteed in good faith by one or more financially responsible corporations or other persons, or by the United States government or any agency thereof, and the provision was determined in good faith and with reasonable care by the board of directors to be adequate at the time of any distribution of the assets by the directors . . ..
>
> (b) The amount of the debt or liability has been deposited [with an appropriate depositary].
>
> This section does not prescribe exclusive means of making adequate provision for debts and liabilities.

This problem of appropriate provision for creditors when a corporation is dissolved seems to have come to the attention of the draftsmen of the 1963 amendments to the Pennsylvania Corporation Laws, but no guidance on what would suffice resulted. In 1963 § 2852–1104(C) of the Pennsylvania Statutes, dealing with the winding up of a corporation in voluntary dissolution proceedings, was amended to add the words in brackets:

> C. The board of directors shall, as speedily as possible, proceed to collect all sums due or owing to the corporation, to sell and convert into cash any and all corporate assets the conversion of which into cash is required to pay its debts and liabilities . . . and, . . . out of the assets of the corporation, to pay, satisfy, and discharge [or make adequate provision for the payment, satisfaction, and discharge of] all debts and liabilities of the corporation, according to their respective priorities.

court held that if the indemnity agreement constituted an asset in the hands of the transferor it was transferred to the transferee upon the liquidation of the transferor.

SECTION 2. DISSOLUTION UPON DEADLOCK

[SET OUT IN CHAPTER 6]

SECTION 3. TAX ASPECTS OF CORPORATE LIQUIDATIONS

A. IN GENERAL

NOTE, TAX-FREE SALES IN LIQUIDATION UNDER SECTION 337 [5]

76 Harv.L.Rev. 780 (1963).

Prior to the enactment of the Internal Revenue Code of 1954, the taxation of corporations and shareholders during the process of liquidation was governed by three well-established principles embodied in the existing tax law: first, the distribution of a liquidating corporation's assets was not a taxable event for the corporation;* second, such a distribution of assets was a taxable event for the shareholders as if they had exchanged their stock;** finally, any conversion of as-

---

5. Copyright (c) Harvard Law Review Association, 1963. Reprinted by permission. Most of the footnotes omitted.

*[Ed. note] This rule is now embodied in IRC § 336. There is of course the possibility that in some circumstances income realized by the stockholders upon property received by them in liquidation will be attributed to the corporation, on the theory, inter alia, that the income was really earned by the corporation, see generally Kilbourn, Post-Liquidation Problems, Corporate and Individual, 23 N.Y.U. Fed.Tax Inst. 701 (1965), just as sometimes occurs when property, particularly inventory, is distributed as an ordinary dividend to stockholders and then sold by them. See pages 375–378, supra. However, there seems to be substantially more resistance to the application of this doctrine when there has been a complete liquidation than when the distribution takes the form of an ordinary dividend. See e. g., United States v. Horschel, 205 F.2d 646 (9th Cir.1953), stressing the difference in this connection between a distribution in complete liquidation and a dividend by a company continuing in business.

**[Ed. note] This rule is now embodied in § 331. An exception to full recognition of gain under § 331 is available under the "one month liquidation" procedure of § 333, which provides for non-recognition of gain, and a corresponding carryover of the stockholders' basis in their stock to the corporate assets received, subject to two important provisos: (1) gain will be recognized (and taxed as ordinary income) to the extent of each shareholder's pro rata share of the corporation's accumulated earnings and profits; and (2) generally speaking, any additional gain will be recognized to the extent of any cash or securities received by the stockholder. Normally, an election under § 333 will be beneficial only for a closely held corporation with substantially appreciated assets but little accumulated earnings, as often occurs in the real estate field. See generally McGaffey, The Deferral of Gain in One-Month Liquidations, 19 Tax L.Rev. 327 (1964).

sets into cash resulted in recognition of gain or loss. To avoid double incidence of taxation upon liquidation, the corporation had to distribute its assets in kind, since a sale followed by distribution of the proceeds might result in a tax to the corporation upon the sale and a tax to the shareholders upon distribution. But in cases where shareholders were numerous, distribution in kind could cause difficulty in the disposition of a business. Problems accompanied both the parceling of assets among the shareholders and the distribution of indivisible assets to them as tenants-in-common.

The difficulties of avoiding corporate taxation by distributions in kind were increased by Commissioner v. Court Holding Co., where a closely held corporation had entered into an oral contract for the sale of its assets and had received part payment. On the day fixed for reducing the contract to writing the shareholders realized that the contemplated sale involved a substantial corporate tax and instead had the corporation declare a liquidating dividend of its property, following which they sold the property on substantially the same terms as in the prior contract. On these facts the Tax Court upheld the imposition of corporate income tax concluding that the sale had been made by the corporation notwithstanding the belated transfer to its shareholders; the Supreme Court affirmed. Considering the same issue in United States v. Cumberland Pub. Serv. Co. the Court explained that the question whether the corporation or the shareholders sold the assets was one of fact, to be determined by the trial court "upon consideration of the entire transaction." The two cases placed shareholders in an unfortunate dilemma. The Court's failure to lay down a more definite standard made it dangerous to plan a sale before liquidation, since shareholders could never be sure of the exact circumstances which would cause a sale to be attributed to the corporation. The danger was particularly acute in closely held corporations because of the ambiguity as to whether the negotiator was acting as a corporate officer or as a representative of the shareholders. On the other hand, if the property was distributed in kind without prior negotiation, the shareholders ran a double risk: if unable to find a buyer, the shareholders might be unable to raise the cash necessary to pay the capital gains tax incurred on the distribution; and, in the absence of prior sale, the Treasury might place an excessive valuation on the property for determining the capital gains tax due. The further danger that uninformed taxpayers would allow the corporation to negotiate the sale before obtaining competent legal advice added weight to Congress' conclusion that the two decisions "represent merely a trap for the unwary."

The legislative response to these uncertainties could have taken several forms. Congress might have provided criteria for determining conclusively which sales were attributable to the corporation and which to the shareholders; it might have attributed to the corporation all sales by shareholders within a certain period of time after a liquidating distribution; or it might have required the corporation to recognize gain on all distributions to its shareholders. Instead Congress provided that under certain conditions a corporation was free to sell its assets and distribute the proceeds without incurring a corporate tax. Although the committee reports indicate that the primary purpose of the section was to correct the formalistic problems presented by the Court Holding and Cumberland cases, the provisions in fact go much further: transactions clearly taxable to the corporation under prior law became tax-free under section 337. The draftsmen intended this solution "to provide a definitive rule" which would "eliminate . . . uncertainties." But the volume of recent cases and the inconsistencies in judicial interpretation indicate that, while the statute has resolved some difficulties, it has created others. This Note will explore the intended function of section 337 and the difficulties of determining the precise scope of its application. In part I certain technical prerequisites to the section's operation are discussed; part II delimits the area within the section's protection; and part III analyzes the interplay between section 337 and other relevant sections of the Code.

I. Prerequisites to Protection

A. *Date of Adoption of a Plan*

Under section 337 it is necessary to determine the date when a plan of liquidation is adopted, since the section operates only if the liquidation is completed within a fixed period afterward and protects only sales made following such adoption. The Code nowhere defines a "plan of complete liquidation" nor indicates how one is adopted although the term appears in several sections. As a matter of corporate law, however, voluntary liquidation can occur only with the approval of the shareholders.[18] Hence, passage of a shareholder resolution ordinarily would seem to be the event which marks the adoption of a plan of liquidation. The applicable regulation states that while the date of adoption of a plan of liquidation is "ordinarily" the date of the shareholder resolution, this date is conclusive only if the corporation has previously sold substantially all its property or if the corporation sells no substantial part of its assets prior thereto. In all other cases, i. e., where substantial sales are made both before and after the resolution date, the date of adoption is to be determined from all the facts and circumstances.[19] The Treasury's purpose in establishing these two quite different tests was to provide corporations a sure way to achieve either nonrecognition of a net gain on the disposition of all assets, or recognition of net loss, while thwarting attempts to obtain a double benefit through nonrecognition of gain on appreciated property

---

[18] See [MBA] § 77 (1960), which is typical of the provisions of many state statutes.

[19] Treas.Reg. § 1.337–2(b) (1955).

Sec. 3　　　　　　　　　TAX ASPECTS　　　　　　　　　633

coupled with recognition of loss on property of diminished value. If a shareholder resolution were treated as conclusive of the date of adoption, the latter result could be achieved by straddling the resolution date — selling all loss property before and all gain property after its adoption.

If the resolution date is as a general rule determinative of the date on which a plan of liquidation was adopted, three significant questions arise. First, should the many small corporations whose major decisions are made without corporate formalities be denied the benefit of section 337? Second, should section 337's protection not be available in cases where involuntary disposition of the assets, through condemnation or destruction, make it impossible for the shareholders to adopt a plan before the conversion occurs? Third, is the Treasury warranted in its attempt to prevent doubling of the benefit of section 337 through sales which straddle the resolution? The courts have not as yet succeeded in formulating clear answers to these questions.

Compelling circumstances for a finding that a plan of liquidation was adopted prior to the passage of a shareholder resolution exist where shareholders who control a block of stock sufficiently large to enable them to authorize liquidation can be shown to have agreed earlier to liquidate. Such a question is likely to arise where a closely held, informally operated corporation begins to sell its properties without making a formal resolution. Powell's Pontiac-Cadillac, Inc. v. Gross [21] involved the liquidation of an automobile dealership the sole shareholders of which were its president, his wife and son. Although the corporation had sold all its assets and distributed the proceeds many months before the passage of a formal resolution, the court found that a plan of liquidation was adopted immediately prior to the signing of the contract of sale. The business was sold because its president wished to retire on account of his wife's ill health; hence there was little likelihood that the corporation would continue to operate thereafter. In such a case it is easy to conclude that an actual, though informal, plan of liquidation existed already at the time of the sale. The danger of such speculation is, of course, that the intention may not yet have been formed; continued operation may then have been contemplated. Thus, the chief issue for resolution is whether the undesirability of importing a subjective test based on the elusive factor of intent into a taxing statute must require a corporation which wishes to obtain its benefits to follow a highly formal method of making that intention clear. Congress' refusal to define a plan of liquidation in formal terms may indicate that it did not wish to prevent the courts from making a judgment on that question on the facts of each particular case, as they had done in other contexts.[22] Probably it is

---

21.　60–1 U.S.Tax Cas. ¶ 9317 (D.N.J. 1960).

22.　. . . It is of some significance that the House version of the 1954 Code defined the plan of liquidation in terms of either a shareholder or board of directors resolution to distribute all the company's property and

desirable to permit such corporations to assume the burden of proving the prior informal adoption of a plan for liquidation and to succeed if they sustain their burden of proof. Such factors as the evidence of intent disclosed in the corporate records, the degree of informality habitually practiced in reaching major decisions, the opportunity which existed for formal action, the length of the period in which substantial sales were made, the quantity and character of the property sold, and the size of the corporation, are obviously relevant on this issue. From the history of taxpayers' attempts thus far, it is likely that the courts will not permit abuse of the opportunity.[23]

Where the power to liquidate is not in the hands of the board of directors because they do not control the necessary proportion of stock, it is difficult to see how liquidation can be assured until the shareholders approve. Consequently, the corporation cannot, strictly speaking, adopt a plan of liquidation before obtaining that approval—ordinarily in the form of a resolution. Except in special circumstances,[24] therefore, a voluntary sale made by a corporation whose directors do not possess voting control should not qualify for nonrecognition unless it is made after the resolution. This result should not be considered harsh; the requirements for qualification under the statute are easily complied with in the great majority of cases and should be respected. However, where the property is transferred involuntarily, notably in a condemnation proceeding, the corporation may be unable to control the time of the transfer, and may not act quickly enough to complete the formal process of authorizing liquidation before the "sale" takes place. Although the corporate law problems in finding a plan of liquidation before the shareholders have agreed on this course are as great in cases of involuntary condemnations as they are in cases of normal sales, there would seem to be greater justification for such an interpretation where the formal requirements are not as easily met. The purpose of the plan requirement is prob-

retire all its stock. See H.R. 8300, 83d Cong., 2d Sess., § 336(c) (1954). No comparable provision appears in the Code as enacted.

23. The Powell's case is the only example of a successful taxpayer contention that a plan had been informally adopted, where the sale was voluntarily negotiated. In Whitson v. Rockwood, 190 F.Supp. 478 (D.N.D.1960), the court agreed that the facts and circumstances of a sale should be examined, but found that the evidence did not show an actual plan of liquidation at the time of the sale. [Ed. note. In Rev.Rul. 65–235, 1965–2 Cum. Bull. 88, the service announced that it will no longer insist upon a formal shareholder's resolution and vote for the adoption of a plan of liquidation where more than the statutory percentage of stockholders had agreed at an informal meeting that the corporation sell all of its assets and distribute the proceeds.]

24. If it can be shown that, in addition to the directors, certain nondirector shareholders knew of and approved the board's plan at the time of sale, and their total votes were sufficient to authorize liquidation, the plan might be considered adopted at that time. Similarly, it would be reasonable to include the shares held by the wives of directors in figuring the proportion, although this would create problems when other close relatives or associates are sought to be included in the directors' total.

ably to prevent a corporation from escaping taxation on gain realized from sales made prior to a bona fide decision to liquidate. Without such a requirement all sales of property during the last twelve months of the corporation's life might be tax exempt, a benefit going far beyond what might have been accomplished through liquidating distributions to the shareholders. The danger of such abuse is not great where substantially all the property is taken involuntarily, since the shareholders have no choice but to liquidate or use the funds to acquire replacement property. Consequently, the purpose of the requirement would not be impaired if the gain so realized on condemnations qualified for section 337 protection. The requirement of a plan might be satisfied, in such a case, by a board of directors' resolution prior to condemnation recommending liquidation to the shareholders, provided they approve within a reasonable time afterward.

The Tax Court appears to have accepted this argument in Mountain Water Co. of La Crescenta,[26] in which substantially all the corporation's property was condemned in January, 1955 at an award above its adjusted basis. The board of directors of the company, a cooperative water supplier whose shareholders were its customers, considered appealing the award, but ultimately transferred the property to the condemning authority on April 25. It then sent ballots to the shareholders for a vote on liquidation, tabulating the affirmative result on June 7. The corporation's claim that the gain on the condemnation award should go unrecognized was sustained. The Tax Court explained, drawing analogies from decisions under other sections of the Code, that there could be no single test for determining adoption of a plan. Any other result, it said, would impair the relief Congress intended to afford to taxpayers. Since liquidation was almost inevitable after the condemnation in view of the company's function, the sale should be viewed as the adoption of a plan. The court also quoted the regulation's provision for examination of the facts and circumstances, but failed to observe that this provision purports to apply only to the "straddle" situation, which was not present in the case.

The approach of the Mountain Water Co. decision, however, was not followed by the district court in Wood Harmon Corp. v. United States.[28] Because of the pendency of condemnation proceedings affecting a large part of a corporation's appreciated property, its board of directors recommended that the shareholders approve liquidation. Three days before the shareholders resolved to liquidate, a state court judge signed an ex parte order vesting title in the city. Under local law, this order constituted transfer of the property, although the terms of compensation remained to be set-

26. 35 T.C. 418 (1960), acq., 1961–1 Cum. Bull. 4.

28. 206 F.Supp. 773 (S.D.N.Y.1962), [affirmed 311 F.2d 918 (2d Cir. 1963).]

tled. On the authority of a previous Treasury ruling, the court sustained the Treasury's contention that the date of sale was the date of transfer of title under local law. Its opinion did not consider the possibility that the plan of liquidation had been adopted on or before the date of transfer, in satisfaction of the conditions of section 337.

Where liquidation is occasioned by destruction of the corporation's property by fire or other casualty, a similar problem is presented in more acute form. The likelihood that a liquidation is contemplated at the time of the casualty is extremely small. Nevertheless, if the casualty is major, there is a strong likelihood that liquidation will follow shortly thereafter, with little opportunity for manipulation to obtain the most favorable tax result. In the case providing the principal support for the view that a casualty loss constitutes a sale or exchange within the meaning of section 337, however, the court specifically indicated that the statute's protection will be available only if the destruction occurs after the corporation has adopted an actual plan of liquidation. The present wording of the statute makes this result almost unavoidable, but it would seem desirable for Congress to amend the statute to permit nonrecognition of such gains if the corporation adopts a plan for liquidation within a reasonable time.

In view of the Tax Court's willingness to find a plan of liquidation in the circumstances preceding the shareholder resolution in Mountain Water Co., one might expect decisions sympathetic to the Treasury's attempt to thwart straddle sales by finding an earlier adoption of a plan in the facts and circumstances. If permitted, such straddles would enable a corporation seriously to distort its tax position, not only for the year of liquidation but for preceding years as well through use of the loss carryback provisions of the Code. Furthermore, since many of the assets sold in the final period of operation normally will be section 1231 assets, these losses will offset ordinary income. Even though it was the general purpose of Congress to favor liquidating corporations, it is doubtful that so great a tax benefit was intended at so small a cost. The Commissioner's attempt to disallow recognition of straddle losses therefore would seem to deserve judicial support.

Nevertheless, the taxpayers have prevailed in both cases to date involving an apparent straddle maneuver. In Virginia Ice & Freezing Co.,[39] the first case under section 337, the corporation's board of directors approved the sale at a loss of two of its several plants on the same day that it resolved to hold a meeting ten days later to consider liquidation. At the second meeting, the board passed a resolution recommending liquidation to the twenty-six shareholders, a course which the shareholders unanimously approved at a special meeting

---

39. 30 T.C. 1251 (1958).

shortly thereafter. Within twelve months the other properties were sold at a gain. The Treasury refused to allow recognition of the loss on the two plants, contending that the circumstances showed that a plan had been adopted before the sale was made. This determination was reversed by the Tax Court, which reasoned that there could be no assurance of liquidation until the shareholders approved, regardless of the facts that their vote proved unanimous and that all actions of the board had been unanimously approved for several years. Virginia Ice might be explained on the ground that the directors did not control a majority of the stock, and hence could not assure adoption of the corporate plan. But the recent case of City Bank of Washington,[40] where the court relied on Virginia Ice, is not susceptible of this interpretation. Here a purchaser agreed to buy both the assets and the outstanding shares of the taxpayer, City Bank, under a contract which expressly provided for the taxpayer's liquidation. Three days before the shareholder meeting, at a time when the purchaser had already acquired nearly eighty per cent of the outstanding stock, City Bank sold some treasury notes at a loss for which it claimed a deduction. Despite a specific finding that liquidation was intended long before this date, the Tax Court allowed the loss, reasoning that a "general intention to liquidate" is not the same thing as a plan of liquidation. It emphasized that a contrary result would produce uncertainty inconsistent with the statute's purpose to establish a clear and unambiguous rule.

If it is concluded that the Tax Court's reliance on the resolution date in City Bank unduly favors the taxpayer, and that in other circumstances taxpayers should be permitted to establish early adoption of plans, the question arises whether it is proper to interpret the statute's simple requirement of "adoption of a plan" as determined in some instances by the adoption of a shareholder resolution and in other circumstances by a different test. Logically the question whether and when a plan was adopted should be answered by the same criteria whether it is the Commissioner or the taxpayer who seeks to make the point, and whether or not the taxpayer's sales straddle the resolution date. However, it is doubtful whether it would serve any statutory purpose to allow the Treasury to attack the taxpayer's contention that the shareholder resolution marked the date of adoption of a plan in the cases where the taxpayer sold all its property either before or after the date of resolution without attempting to straddle. In such cases the taxpayer is merely attempting to comply with the formalities of a largely elective section in order to obtain either nonrecognition of net gain or recognition of net loss; either result is clearly contemplated under the statute. In view of the statute's purpose of providing substantial certainty as an aid in planning liquidation, the regulations seem justified to the extent that they bind the Treasury to accept the resolution date for such cases.

40. 38 T.C. [713 (1962)].

B. *Distributions to Creditors*

* * *

The Treasury has ruled . . . that an insolvent corporation which uses all proceeds of sales to pay its creditors cannot enjoy the benefits of section 337 [48]. It reasoned that the section was intended to provide relief only from double taxation, not to eliminate all taxation of corporate liquidations; since the shareholders of an insolvent corporation will receive no distributions and hence can pay no tax, the benefit of section 337 should be withheld from corporate sales. This explanation is not wholly satisfactory: even in solvent corporations some or all shareholders may have no tax to pay on distributions to them, since a shareholder's basis in his stock bears no relation to his pro rata share of the value of the corporation's assets and can well be higher. It has never been suggested that such circumstances would make section 337 inapplicable. Finally, the ruling leads to the conclusion that an insolvent corporation must pay a tax on all gain realized by the sale of its assets, while a corporation which can retain even a nominal amount for distribution to its shareholders will escape all taxation on sales of property made in compliance with the statutory requirements. It is difficult to find a reasonable basis for this result.

* * *

II. SCOPE OF PROTECTION

A. *Statutory Language*

Assuming that a plan of liquidation has been properly adopted and that sales and distributions have been made as required by section 337(a), there arises the question what types of transactions are protected. The section states that "no gain or loss shall be recognized . . . from the sale or exchange . . . of property . . . ," but subsection 337(b) adds that " 'property' does not include" inventory or goods held for sale in the ordinary course of business (except when sold in bulk), or certain installment obligations. The regulation dealing with section 337 interprets the term "property" as including all assets owned by the corporation except those specifically excluded by the subsection, and in a recent series of cases the Tax Court seems to have taken a somewhat similar approach. However, the legislative history suggests that the statute's protection should be more narrowly restricted. Significantly, the Treasury, in apparent disregard of its own regulation, has persuaded the courts that the section's protection does not extend to gain from the sale of certain assets falling outside the express exceptions when that gain is, in effect, of an ordinary-income type. It is questionable whether the

---

48. Rev.Rul. 56–387, 1956–2 Cum.Bull. 189.

term "property" as used in the statute should be construed as broadly as the regulations seem to suggest.

As passed by the House of Representatives the section denied its protection to "any sale . . . in the ordinary course of business", and although the final bill replaced this broad exception with the present enumeration, the report of the Senate Finance Committee summarized the scope of the section by stating: "It is intended that, during the 12 month period, sales in the ordinary course of business shall result in ordinary gain to the corporation as if the corporation were not in the process of liquidating." Thus recorded indications of congressional intent suggest a purpose of preventing corporations from using section 337 to avoid paying a tax on sales or exchanges which represent income from the normal operation of the business. Furthermore, since the enumerated exceptions do not exclude receivables or rights to income, construing property as broadly as the regulations seem to suggest would allow nonrecognition on the sale of receivables arising from the prior sale of excluded types of property, such as inventory, and thus allow a cash basis corporation easily to bring all gain within the statute's protection.

The purpose of the enactment also reinforces the argument against a broad interpretation. The section was enacted to permit a corporation to escape tax on sales followed by distribution to shareholders to the same extent that it would have avoided tax had it distributed the assets in kind. Courts generally have refused to allow corporations to escape taxation by the transfer in kind of receivables arising from sales in the ordinary course of business. Thus to interpret property to cover such receivables would allow corporations to avoid recognition of gain on assets sold that would have been recognized had they been transferred in kind under section 336. It is unlikely that Congress would have intended section 337 to protect sales of a broader class of assets than those the transfer of which would be protected under 336, since such a result would recreate much of the Court Holding-Cumberland formalism in reverse. The following portions of this part discuss the judicial interpretation of the scope of the term property and suggest a rationale by which property should be defined so as to bring the tax consequences of section 337 liquidations into harmony with those under section 336.

B. *Assignment of Income*

Can a liquidating corporation use section 337 to escape taxation during its final year of operation through the sale of assets representing ordinary income which has not yet been reported? The Treasury initially stated its position in a ruling concerning a cash basis corporation in liquidation which had sold receivables along with the interest earned on them, but not yet collected.[61] The question was whether that portion of the sales price representing interest receivable was protected. The ruling first stated that section 337 applies to "all assets except those specifically excluded" by subsection (b), but then concluded that the section is intended to protect only "unrealized appreciation of business property." This conclusion can be defended, but it cannot follow from the stated premise, for many types of assets which represent ordinary income rather than appreciation are not included within the specific terms of the exceptions.[62] The ruling goes on to reason that the sale of the interest is not protected by section 337 because it does not represent appreciation in value, but is actually an assignment of a claim for ordinary income.

Since that ruling the Tax Court has four times faced a similar issue. Although usually limiting the scope of section 337's protection, it appears to have assumed in each case that property includes all assets save those enumerated and has relied on other questionable grounds to reach its conclusions. This has resulted in a failure to develop any consistent rationale for determining the type of gain protected by the section. In Central Bldg. & Loan Ass'n[63] the Tax Court faced a situation identical to that which prompted the Treasury ruling noted above. The court held the interest reportable on the rationale that section 337 gave no protection because there had been no sale or exchange since the interest was actually collected, not sold. This reasoning seems inappropriate, for a sale did take place, a sale of a right to receive future payment of income. Arguing that section 337 is inapplicable because no sale has taken place deflects the focus of attention from the real issue: whether section 337's protection should embrace sales of property representing income already earned by the taxpayer.

Then in Henry A. Kuckenberg[64] a cash basis construction corporation in liquidation claimed section 337's protection for the proceeds of a sale of three construction contracts upon which work had been completed; the Tax Court agreed in a cryptic opinion that the contracts were property within the meaning of section 337, in effect allowing the taxpayer to convert ordinary income earned on work done before liquidation into nontaxable gain through the simple device of selling the right to receive payment. The court appears not to have considered whether such a result was consonant with the purposes of section 337.

61. Rev.Rul. 59–120, 1959–1 Cum.Bull. 74.

62. Such as interest receivable, dividends receivable, or accounts receivable arising from the sale of inventory.

63. 34 T.C. 447 (1960).

64. 35 T.C. 473 (1960), rev'd, 309 F.2d 202 (9th Cir. 1962).

In Family Record Plan, Inc.[65] the Tax Court held that liquidating sales of accounts receivable, representing sales of inventory and services by a cash basis taxpayer, were taxable despite the language of section 337. The court recognized the problem of interpreting the section to protect assignment of income rights earned in the ordinary course of business since such a holding would allow the cash basis taxpayer to escape all ordinary income arising from his business by selling on credit and then selling the resulting obligations after adoption of a plan of liquidation. Nonetheless, the court was reluctant to rest its decision solely on this reasoning; it felt compelled to fit the receivables within the precise exemptions of subsection (b). Since the receivables called for periodic payment, they were held to be installment obligations as excluded by subsection 337(b)(1)(B).[66] But the exceptions of subsection (b) are narrowly and precisely drawn. It would seem more meaningful to construe the exception for "installment obligations" as a reference to obligations reported under the installment method provided in section 453, and not to obligations payable in installments but reported on the cash basis. Because this taxpayer had not elected the section 453 installment method of accounting, the court's reliance on the installment exception seems questionable.[68]

In its treatment of these cases it would have been preferable for the Tax Court not to seek to bring each disputed item within the specific exceptions of subsection (b), but rather to rely on its more general reasoning that section 337 was not intended to protect assignment of income rights already earned in the ordinary course of business. Because interest receivable, accounts receivable, and rights to future income of all types are usually neither goods held for sale in the ordinary course of business nor installment obligations, taxation of this type of gain to a liquidating corporation requires a rationale broader than the terms of the exceptions themselves. Such a rationale is supplied in the words of the statute and is supported by the history of its enactment.

Section 337's definition of "property" in its most significant part is not new in the tax code but was taken almost verbatim from section 117 of the 1939 Code where it served the function of defining capital assets. Section 117, predecessor to the present section 1221, stated that a capital asset is "property . . . but does not include," *inter alia*, "stock in trade . . . inventory . . . or property held . . . primarily for sale to customers . . . .."

---

65. 36 T.C. 305 (1961) (reviewed by the court), aff'd on other grounds, 309 F.2d 208 (9th Cir. 1962).

66. The language of the opinion is sufficiently general to support an inference that the court would have classified all receivables from sales of inventory as installment obligations whether or not they called for periodic payment. . . .

68. In affirming this case on other grounds the Ninth Circuit expressly refused to decide the installment obligation issue, 309 F.2d at 210.

Like section 337, it was designed to give preferential tax treatment to sales of certain types of assets not held for sale in the ordinary course of business. The linguistic similarity and functional analogy of the two sections suggest an intention that the latter be interpreted in conformity with the former, the words of which it adopted. It is also noteworthy that the regulations dealing with the definition of property under section 117 spoke in broad terms similar to the language of the analogous regulation under section 337.

In spite of what at first appears to be a broadly inclusive definition of capital asset in section 117, by 1954 courts had developed various doctrines which considerably restricted the scope of property entitled to favored capital gain treatment. To the extent that it is possible to generalize from these disparate cases, a policy had emerged of limiting the operation of section 117 to investment as opposed to business assets. While "investment property" is difficult to define with precision, it seems clear that sales of claims for salaries or for payments earned through services which would result in ordinary income, if collected instead of sold, could not qualify for capital gain treatment; analogous examples of unqualified exchanges are payments in cancellation of claims for future rent on a lease or for future salary under an employment contract. When the draftsmen of section 337 appropriated the formula of section 117, they must have anticipated its interpretation in the light of the considerable judicial precedent which had clarified and limited its predecessor so as to exclude from the scope of its protection receivables arising from ordinary business transactions.

The Ninth Circuit, in reversing Kuckenberg and affirming the result of Family Record Plan, concluded similarly, but for somewhat different reasons, that contract rights for services performed or for sales of inventory fall outside section 337's protection. Explaining that the purpose of section 337 was to allow a corporation to accomplish by sale and transfer of proceeds what it could have accomplished by transfer in kind under section 336, it pointed out that under existing case law at the time of Cumberland a cash basis corporation was required to recognize as income gain realized on liquidating transfers of receivables arising from sales in the ordinary course of business.[78] Since the two sections are complementary,

---

78. E. g., Floyd v. Scofield, 193 F.2d 594 (5th Cir. 1952); accord, Williamson v. United States, 155 Ct.Cl. 279, 292 F.2d 524 (1961) & cases cited id. at 529–30. [Ed. note: On the other hand, a liquidating distribution of an unharvested crop does not result in income to the transferor; and the transferor is nevertheless entitled to deduct the expenses incurred in preparing the crop, even though this results in a large operating loss which can be carried back and used to offset the profits of earlier years. Commissioner v. South Lake Farms, Inc., 324 F.2d 837 (9th Cir. 1963). But cf. Rooney v. United States, 305 F.2d 681 (9th Cir. 1962) (where sole proprietor transferred unharvested crop to controlled corporation in tax-free transaction under § 351, Commissioner could allocate the expenses of raising the crop that year to the corporation under § 482, thus precluding any net operating loss for the sole proprietor). See generally, Rudolph, The Realization Requirement and Tax Avoidance, 62 Mich.L.Rev. 961, 972–980 (1964).]

courts can properly be guided by the case law applicable to transfers in kind to the conclusion that sales of receivables resulting from the ordinary operation of the business should not come within section 337's protection. This line of reasoning, although more complex, is closely related to the theory that property under section 337 is limited by the restrictions on property qualifying for capital gain treatment. For the Ninth Circuit's reasoning apparently is based on the notion that a corporation in liquidation which distributes its property in kind should not escape tax on gain deriving from the ordinary operation of the business. The benefit of section 337 therefore would be restricted to assets which, if held for six months, would qualify for capital gain treatment under sections 1221 and 1231.

In Kuckenberg and Family Record Plan the Ninth Circuit also relied on what would seem a more questionable explanation for the exclusion of the receivables. Pointing to the power conferred upon the Commissioner by section 446 to require a taxpayer to use a method of accounting which properly reflects income, it asserted that the cash basis taxpayer in liquidation can be required to report as if on the accrual basis in order to prevent tax avoidance through the device of selling on credit and then transferring the receivables in kind to the shareholders under the protection of section 336, or selling them within section 337's protection. Section 446, however, appears intended to affect only going concerns. To require a change in method of accounting seems inappropriate at a time when termination of the corporation's existence is imminent.

A further ground for the necessity of limiting section 337's protection to assets of a type entitled to capital gain treatment derives from the assignment-of-income doctrine, one of the primary weapons developed by the courts under section 117 to prevent transmutation of ordinary income into capital gains. Under this doctrine if a cash basis taxpayer has earned ordinary income which has not yet been paid, sale of the right to receive that payment results in ordinary income to the taxpayer just as if he had collected the sum in cash from his debtor. The character of the income from the sale of the obligation is determined by the nature of the transaction out of which the obligation arose. The doctrine recognizes that the sale of a right to payment is but an alternative means of realizing the proceeds of a transaction and should not alter the character of the gain. Section 337 is susceptible of similar analysis. By its terms protection is denied to gain not derived from the sale of property, gain from property sold in the ordinary course of business, and gain from sales of property prior to the adoption of a plan. If these exceptions are to be effective, then receivables or obligations arising from such transactions must also be excluded. Just as it looks to see whether on disposition of an obligation the taxpayer realized ordinary or capital gain, the court should determine whether the underlying sale would have qualified under section 337. The result would be to protect only gain from the sale of capital assets or 1231 assets made after adoption of a plan, and gain from disposition of receivables arising from such sales.

C. *Bad Debts and Depreciation*

As a general rule the recovery of a bad debt which had previously been deducted from income with a resulting tax benefit constitutes ordinary taxable gain in the year of its recovery. Similarly, during the course of liquidation an allowance for bad debts, representing deductions taken for estimated future bad debt losses, must be returned to income upon the distribution or sale at face value of the receivables. However, where a corporation is liquidating under section 337 the question arises whether such income should come within the scope of its protection. The courts have uniformly denied protection on the ground that the return of an unwarranted deduction to income does not constitute "gain from a sale or exchange." In West Seattle Nat'l Bank [83] the taxpayer challenged such a holding by arguing that the bad debt allowance was an account similar to accumulated depreciation, establishing a new lower basis for the receivables; since the adjusted basis for the receivables would be face value minus the allowance, their sale at face value results in gain from a "sale or exchange" and the allowance goes unrecognized. The Ninth Circuit disagreed, distinguishing bad debt allowances from depreciation on the ground that

> . . . [an allowance for bad debts] is still based upon an *expectation* that loss of value will occur and not upon the fact that such loss has already occurred. It is a prediction of value and not a statement of present fact. . . . A depreciation or depletion reserve is founded not upon the expectation of loss but upon facts. . . . The adjustment reflects the extent to which the asset has actually been exhausted by depletion, wear and tear or obsolescence.

The court's refusal to protect the allowance for bad debts can be supported, but it is extremely difficult to distinguish that account from depreciation on the basis of the argument urged by the court. Depreciation frequently has no relationship to the fact of loss or wear and tear; accelerated depreciation schedules expressly allowed by the 1954 Code and regulations could result in the bulk of an asset's cost being charged against income while its utility to the enterprise is still at a high level.

A more defensible distinction can be drawn from the general theory underlying the treatment of these accounts in the normal business operation. Depreciation represents the allocation of an asset's

---

83. West Seattle Nat'l Bank v. Commissioner, 288 F.2d 47 (9th Cir. 1961).

cost against the income it is expected to help produce during its life. While each deduction from a particular asset's cost reduces that asset's basis, the 1954 Code implicitly recognizes that these deductions need not parallel the actual diminution in the asset's utility. This gradual adjustment of basis results in the recognition of gain any time a depreciable asset is sold for an amount in excess of adjusted basis. On the other hand, the allowance for bad debts represents an attempt to reduce the income from credit sales to that amount which will actually be collected. It is recognized that some part of the receivables created in any year will never be collected; to account properly for this loss, the taxpayer may estimate and deduct it in the year of sale instead of reporting the face value of the receivables when created and later deducting the loss when an account proves uncollectible. Unlike depreciation deductions, the annual adjustment to the bad debts allowance bears no relationship to the basis of individual accounts receivable; no gain is recognized upon the collection of any individual account at face value. Therefore, upon liquidation there would be no reason to allow corporations to treat this anticipation of loss as if it were an adjustment to basis.

In addition to the bar imposed by the requirement of a "sale or exchange," another appropriate ground for requiring recognition of the unused bad debt allowance as gain would be to prevent the taxpayer from making ordinary income tax-free by an annual charge against income of estimated losses which never materialize. In some cases the excessive amount of the charge as compared with the history of actual loss is apparent at the time it is made. This factor constitutes the one significant point of similarity between the allowance for bad debts and accumulated depreciation. To the extent that depreciation deductions exceed the diminution in value of the asset, a sale in excess of adjusted basis in a section 337 liquidation operates to convert ordinary income into tax-free gain. Although depreciation need not be related to actual use of the asset, its charge against income is justified on the assumption that the usefulness of the asset will be consumed in the production of income. Under such an assumption accelerated depreciation during the early part of an asset's estimated life is balanced by a reduced charge during the remaining period of utility. But where the asset subject to accelerated depreciation is held for only a portion of its useful life, tax-free gain from its sale will in part represent the recovery of depreciation charges taken against ordinary income.

Until recently the Code unequivocally permitted such use of depreciation accounts and thus gave taxpayers some limited support for the contention that unused bad debt allowances should receive similar protection. But the Revenue Act of 1962, which adds section 1245 to the Code, goes far toward correcting this tax benefit inherent in the depreciation provisions of the statute and thereby seriously weakens any possible argument for according section 337's protection to allowances for bad debts. Although aimed primarily at eliminating the conversion of ordinary income into capital gain by making gain on the sale of property taxable as ordinary income to the extent of depreciation deductions previously taken, the committee reports on the new section make it very clear that it also applies to sections 336 and 337. Thus a corporation selling certain depreciable assets in liquidation must report as ordinary income any gain on the sale to the extent that the basis of the asset at acquisition exceeds its adjusted basis at the time of disposition. Section 1245 is not a conclusive answer to the problem of conversion of ordinary income into tax-free gain as it has a number of exceptions, of which buildings are perhaps the most important; * and it applies only to depreciation taken after 1962, so that its full force will not be felt for some years to come.

III. Relation to Other Provisions

A. *Collapsible Corporations*

The function of section 337(c), which excludes collapsible corporations as defined in section 341(b) from the rule of section 337(a), can be understood only in the context of the function and operation of the collapsible provision itself. It is well established that section 341 was intended primarily to prevent transformation of ordinary income into capital gain by the use of temporary corporations. Before enactment of its predecessor, section 117(m) of the 1939 Code, it was possible to form a corporation to construct or produce a single venture, such as a motion picture or a housing development, have it complete the venture and liquidate in kind before the property began to produce income. The corporation would recognize no gain on appreciation in the value of the assets distributed, and the shareholders would obtain a high basis for depreciation or amortization at the cost of only a single capital gains tax. Section 341(a) seeks to eliminate this tax avoidance device by requiring the shareholders of a collapsible corporation to pay tax at ordinary-income rates on the gain which they realize from the distribution. A collapsible corporation is defined as one "formed or availed of principally for the manufacture, construction, or production of property," or for the purchase of inventory-type property, "with a view to . . . a distribution to its shareholders, before the realization by the corporation . . . of a substantial part of the taxable income to be derived from such property. . . ."

Until the enactment of section 337, this plan of avoidance could be fully successful only if the assets were distributed in kind rather than sold, since the corporation would have had to recognize any gain

---

* [Ed. note] Of course § 1250 of the Code, added in 1964, now provides for limited "recapture" of depreciation on real estate. For an analysis of the effect of liquidation on the recapture of depreciation, see Gardner, The Impact of Sections 1245 and 1250 on Corporate Liquidations, 17 U.Fla.L.Rev. 58 (1964).

on the sale of its property. Section 337(a) if applicable would make it possible for the corporation to achieve the same result by selling its assets after adopting a plan of liquidation. In order to foreclose this possibility, Congress enacted section 337(c) denying 337's protection to collapsible corporations. As commentators have pointed out, however, its language is unsatisfactory to accomplish the legislative purpose because under the terms of section 341(b), a corporation formed with an intent to sell its property cannot be collapsible; collapsible status depends on a view to distribution of the assets before the corporation realizes income. A corporation formed to take advantage of section 337 intends to realize the income through sale although not to recognize gain. A literal interpretation of section 341(b) thus would make section 337(c) meaningless. The regulations seek to avoid this impasse by stating that where a corporation would have been considered collapsible had it distributed the assets, section 337 (a) will not protect their sale. Even this does not solve the semantic difficulty, for under section 341(b) it is the view to distribution rather than actual distribution which is crucial. Adequate evidence that the shareholders never entertained such a view at any time during the life of the corporation therefore should be enough to escape collapsible status. The dilemma would be most satisfactorily resolved by a regulation interpreting the phrase "prior to realization" as "prior to recognition," or by a change in the statutory language to that effect. However the purpose of the subsection is sufficiently clear, so that this semantic difficulty should not impair a court's ability to interpret the provision meaningfully. Thus the Tax Court in the recent case of Sproul Realty Co.[101] held that a corporation which is used to take advantage of section 337 before reporting any income may not escape taxation on the gain so realized.

Once a corporation has been determined to be collapsible in the sense explained above and hence must recognize the gain on its sales, there seems no reason to tax the shareholders on their liquidating distributions at ordinary-income rates. A revenue ruling agrees that they are entitled to capital gain treatment.[102] The result of the prevailing statutory interpretation and the revenue ruling is thus to establish a different tax result depending on whether liquidation was effected through an in-kind distribution or a sale;. if the former, only a single, ordinary-income tax will be imposed, but at the progressive individual rates; if the latter, two taxes will be imposed, one on the corporation and one on the shareholder at capital gains rates. Plainly, one tax result may be more advantageous than the other, depending on the brackets of the individual shareholders; corporations in danger of being considered collapsible doubtless will take this into account when planning their liquidation. The difference suggests that the present rule denying section 337 treatment to sale by collapsible

---

101. 38 T.C. [844 (1962)].

102. Rev.Rul. 58–241, 1958–1 Cum.Bull. 179.

corporations may be erroneous; to be consistent with the treatment of liquidations effected through distributions in kind, the corporation should be able to enjoy section 337, but the shareholders' gain should be taxed as ordinary income. This suggestion has been made by the congressional advisory committee on subchapter C, in connection with a recommended general revision of the treatment of the collapsible problem.

Section 341(e) (4), added by the Technical Amendments Act of 1958, lends further complexity to the interrelation of sections 337 and 341. The effect of this amendment is to permit corporations satisfying certain objective tests to take advantage of section 337 even though they might otherwise be considered collapsible. In somewhat simplified outline, the tests are: (1) on and after the date of adoption of the plan of liquidation, the net unrealized appreciation in subsection (e) assets—generally those where disposition produces ordinary income (further defined in section 341(e) (5))—may not exceed fifteen per cent of the corporation's net worth; (2) substantially all its assets then held must be sold rather than distributed in kind; (3) no distribution to shareholders may be made of property subject to an allowance for depreciation, amortization or depletion. If a corporation satisfies the criteria of subsection (e) (4), its sales of property will escape tax under section 337. But the distribution of the proceeds to holders of more than five per cent of the outstanding shares will still be taxed at ordinary rates, as provided in section 341(a) (2), unless the sum of the net unrealized appreciation in subsection (e) assets and certain other types of assets described in subsection (e) (1) does not exceed fifteen per cent of the corporation's net worth at any time following its adoption of a plan. The complexities of subsection (e) are so great that no regulations have yet been issued under it despite the passage of five years since its adoption. It should be noted, however, that strong support exists for the adoption of the objective principle of subsection (e), modified to reduce the complexity, as the sole test for collapsible status.

B. *Section 332—Liquidation of Subsidiaries*

The general provision of subsection 337(c) (2) states that section 337 will not apply to protect sales or exchanges pursuant to a plan of liquidation to which section 332 applies.[108] Subject to certain limitations section 332 provides that no gain or loss shall be recognized by a parent corporation upon the complete liquidation of a subsidiary in which the parent owns at least an eighty per cent interest; however, any assets transferred to the parent ordinarily carry over the subsidi-

---

108. Where a corporation acquires eighty per cent of the stock of a subsidiary within twelve months and then liquidates it within two years after acquiring such control, partial protection may be given under § 337(c)(2)(B). See § 334(b)(2).

ary's adjusted basis for computation of depreciation and gain or loss upon future disposition of the assets by the parent.[109] The rationale of section 332 seems to be that since parent and subsidiary both are parts of a single enterprise they should be allowed to combine without an immediate tax consequence as long as the enterprise retains its original basis in the assets. However, if a liquidating subsidiary could sell its appreciated assets for cash, recognizing no gain on the sale by reason of section 337, and then transfer the cash to the parent which in turn is shielded from recognition of gain by section 332, the enterprise could convert assets into cash in the hands of the parent without ever paying tax on the appreciation. For this reason Congress made section 337 inapplicable. The subsidiary therefore recognizes gain if it sells the assets and then distributes cash to the parent; if the subsidiary distributes the assets in kind, the parent takes the subsidiary's basis and recognizes the appreciation as gain when subsequently it converts the assets.

A special problem arises when a parent corporation and its subsidiary are liquidating simultaneously. At issue is whether all the assets of the total enterprise can be sold and the proceeds transferred to the shareholders without tax liability to the corporation. If section 332 applies to the subsidiary's liquidation, assets in kind can be transferred to the parent without tax consequence, and subsequently the parent can avoid taxation by selling the assets in accordance with section 337, so that all gain is eliminated at the corporate level. The subsidiary would be unable to sell its own assets without recognizing gain because of the mutual exclusivity of sections 332 and 337. It is possible, however, that section 332 does not apply to simultaneous parent-subsidiary liquidations. In Fairfield S.S. Corp. v. Commissioner[111] the opinion of Judge Learned Hand suggested that the predecessor to section 332 did not apply when both parent and subsidiary were liquidating, because the purpose underlying the section was to facilitate the formal unification of a continuing enterprise; the section presupposed the continuation of the venture and not its termination.

If the Fairfield suggestion remains viable, and section 332 is inapplicable to simultaneous liquidations of subsidiary and parent, it is nonetheless possible to escape all corporate tax on such a transaction; for if 332 is inapplicable, then the limitations of section 337 (c)(2), which denies the protection of 337 to liquidations subject to the provisions of 332, is inapplicable as well. As to gain attributable to the subsidiary, if it sells its appreciated assets to a third party, thereafter distributing the proceeds to the parent in the course

109. § 334(b)(1). In the unusual situation described in note 108 supra, the parent's basis in the assets distributed to it is determined by reference to its basis in its subsidiary's stock in respect to which the distribution was made. § 334(b)(2).

111. 157 F.2d 321 (2d Cir. 1946). . . .

of liquidation, 337 will bar recognition of gain; if it distributes the appreciated assets in kind to the parent, 336 provides for nonrecognition of gain. As to gain attributable to the parent resulting from the subsidiary's liquidation, section 337 should prevent recognition. The Treasury has ruled [112] that a liquidating distribution of cash made by a sixty-per-cent-owned subsidiary to a liquidating parent was to be deemed a sale or exchange by the parent of its stock in the subsidiary in the course of the parent's liquidation and thus within the protection of section 337.[113] Underlying support for this ruling is found in section 331(a), which establishes the general rule that liquidation of a corporation is to be treated as a sale or exchange of the shareholder's stock for determining tax liability of the shareholder. The parent could then proceed in the course of its own liquidation to sell within 337's protection appreciated assets which it holds, including those distributed to it without recognition of gain upon its subsidiary's liquidation. In short, if for any reason 332 is inapplicable to a simultaneous liquidation of parent and subsidiary, either because of failure to come within the limitations of section 332, such as the eighty per cent ownership requirement, or because of the implication of Fairfield, then sections 336 or 337 will protect sales by the subsidiary to a third party, and liquidating distributions by the subsidiary to the parent, as well as sales by the parent to a third party. The only tax imposed would fall on the parent's shareholders when they receive the liquidating distributions of the parent. If it is agreed that the parent and its eighty-per-cent-owned subsidiary are really a single business entity, it follows that they should be able to dissolve without incurring a series of taxes. Furthermore, since section 332 by its terms is inapplicable to the liquidation of less-than-eighty-per-cent-owned subsidiaries, section 337 would in such cases provide full protection for tax-free liquidation of parent and subsidiary. It would then be inappropriate if the same tax advantage were denied a wholly owned subsidiary by the operation of a section designed to facilitate, not to hinder, the absorption by parents of nearly-totally-owned subsidiaries.

Anomalous though it seems, it is in fact easier under existing law to avoid tax in the simultaneous liquidation of parent and an under-eighty-per-cent subsidiary than where the parent owns substantially all the subsidiary's stock. For if ownership is below eighty per cent, the transaction is clearly outside section 332; the subsidiary can either sell appreciated assets to a third party or distribute them in kind to the parent with the likelihood in either case that section 337 will protect the transaction from tax. When the sub-

---

112. Rev.Rul. 57–243, 1957–1 Cum.Bull. 116.

113. Section 332 was inapplicable in this ruling because the parent's ownership of the subsidiary's stock was below the eighty per cent requirement, but the reasoning of the ruling would seem applicable to any situation in which § 332 for some reason did not apply.

sidiary is wholly owned, however, uncertainty as to whether Fairfield's suggestion remains valid renders the course more hazardous. The subsidiary's assets can still safely be distributed in kind to the parent. One or the other of sections 332 and 337 must apply to eliminate any liability of the parent. But if the subsidiary has inadvertently sold, or prefers to sell, to a third party before distribution and if section 332 is then ruled applicable to the liquidation (overriding Judge Hand's suggestion in Fairfield), section 337(c)(2) would render 337 inapplicable and the subsidiary would be obliged to recognize gain on the sale. What could be accomplished tax-free if the parent were to sell following the subsidiary's distribution in kind results in a tax if instead the assets are sold by the subsidiary. In short, section 337 recreates the Court Holding-Cumberland problem in the context of simultaneous parent-subsidiary liquidations. If section 337's principal purpose is to do away with the uncertainties caused by the decisions in Court Holding and Cumberland, it should not be interpreted in such a way as to recreate the identical problem in a slightly different context.

Courts could solve this problem in two ways. First, if the Fairfield intimation is followed, section 332 will remain inapplicable to liquidations of subsidiaries by liquidating parents and the benefts of section 337 will become available. But it may be difficult to follow Fairfield, for the reasoning which influenced Judge Hand has been undercut by the passage of section 337. The purpose of section 332 was to confer on the liquidation of more-than-eighty-per-cent-owned subsidiaries a special tax benefit which at that time was not available in cases where the parent's ownership was below this proportion. The rationale of Fairfield was that this special benefit should be available to aid only in the consolidation and not in the liquidation of the total enterprise. Since 337 appears to allow a liquidating parent to receive liquidating distributions from a less-than-eighty-per-cent subsidiary without tax, there would be no reason today to deny the benefits of section 332 as to a parent's receipt of distributions from a more fully controlled subsidiary—especially since section 332 was designed to give preferential treatment to a parent whose ownership of a liquidating subsidiary was very substantial. Fairfield therefore seems unlikely to be followed.

A preferable judicial solution would be to rule that section 337(c)(2) does not cover simultaneous liquidations of parent and subsidiary. The purpose of the limitation of section 337(c)(2) was to prevent operating parents from converting their subsidiaries' appreciated assets into cash without ever recognizing gain. That objective has no application where the parent is also liquidating. In fact, section 337 makes such a tax-free liquidation possible so long as the subsidiary distributes to the parent in kind rather than to third persons. If the inapplicability of 337(c)(2) to this situation were recognized this embarrassment of formalism would be eliminated. Alternatively, the section could be amended to provide that subsection 337(c)(2) shall not apply to simultaneous liquidations of parents and subsidiaries, as was recommended by the Subchapter C Advisory Committee.

C. *Reincorporation Transactions*

If the shareholders wish to withdraw substantial accumulated corporate earnings without paying a tax on dividends, they may form a new corporation, have the old corporation transfer to it part of the operating assets in exchange for part of its stock, and distribute in liquidation the assets retained along with the shares of the new corporation. If the plan is successful, the only tax imposed will be on the shareholders at capital gain rates.[115] However, the Treasury may argue that such a transaction is not a liquidation, but in effect a reorganization, the taxation of which should be governed by the reorganization provisions of the Code. This contention was often successful under the 1939 Code, since the transaction seemed to fit the definition of a (D) reorganization [116] as long as the old corporation acquired at least eighty per cent of the new one's stock. The property distributed to the shareholders, other than the stock in the successor, would then be treated as a dividend to the extent of each shareholder's realized gain, provided that its value did not exceed the corporation's earnings and profits. Under the 1954 Code, however, the definition of a (D) reorganization has been narrowed to include only transactions in which substantially all the old corporation's property is transferred to the successor or in which the old corporation does not liquidate but continues in active business. This change has made it easier for shareholders to prevail in seeking liquidation treatment, since the transaction no longer qualifies under any of the four precisely described categories of statutory reorganization.* The enactment of section 337 in the 1954 Code made liquidation treatment even more attractive, for if the transfer of assets is treated as a sale, the successor corpo-

---

115. § 331. If §§ 337 or 351 do not apply to the sale, the corporation may also incur a tax liability.

116. Int.Rev.Code of 1939, § 112(g)(1)(D). If the predecessor corporation had transferred substantially all its assets to the new corporation in exchange solely for voting stock, the transaction would have been a (C) reorganization. Int.Rev.Code of 1939, § 112(g)(1)(C).

*[Ed. note] However, the courts have refused to give a literal construction to the requirement for a (D) reorganization that "substantially all" of the old corporation's assets be transferred to the new corporation and have held that requirement to be satisfied so long as there was a transfer of "all the assets essential to the conduct of the business enterprise". E. g., James Armour, Inc. v. Commissioner, 43 T.C. 295 (1964), and Moffatt v. Commissioner, 42 T.C. 558 (1964), both described in some detail in the footnote on page 618 supra.

ration will acquire these assets at a basis equal to their fair market value, although no tax will be imposed on the transferor.[122]

Under the language of both the 1939 Code and the present statute, it appears that the transaction described will not be characterized as a (D) reorganization if the transferor takes less than eighty per cent of any class of the new corporation's stock. The Treasury seemed to concede this point in Revenue Ruling 56–541, which involved a transaction in which a corporation transferred its property to another newly organized corporation in exchange for forty-five per cent of the common stock, plus cash and notes, and distributed the proceeds to its shareholders in complete liquidation. The ruling held that the corporation's gain was not recognized pursuant to section 337, and that the shareholders realized a capital gain on the distribution to them. On further consideration of the matter, however, this ruling appeared to present too ready a means of tax avoidance; it was revoked prospectively late in 1961.[124] These transactions the Treasury now holds to be reorganizations under clauses (E) ("a recapitalization") or (F) ("mere change in identity, form, or place of organization. . . .") of section 368(a)(1). Furthermore, to the extent that the transferor corporation had earnings and profits at the time of distribution, all property distributed other than stock in the transferee is considered a dividend to all shareholders, even though the value of such "boot" exceeds a shareholder's gain on the exchange. Both aspects of this ruling lack support in the statute and in prior judicial interpretations. A "recapitalization" under clause (E) has been thought to occur only when the change affects merely the extent of existing shareholders' interests in a continuing corporation; clause (F)'s provision for change in identity, form and place has been thought applicable only where there is no substantial change in the proportionate interests of the shareholders. Surely the relinquishment of more than one-half control is a far more drastic alteration than is contemplated by either clause. Moreover, if the reorganization provisions were made applicable by a greatly expanded view of the function of clauses (E) and (F), the statute authorizes taxation of boot as a dividend to any shareholder only to the extent that he realizes gain on the exchange.

The Tax Court appears to have rejected the present Treasury position in its decision in Joseph C. Gallagher,[127] decided in October 1962. Five shareholders of corporation A, who owned sixty-two

---

122. It is possible that the transfer will fall under the provisions of § 351 if the transferor acquires eighty per cent of all classes of stock issued by the corporation. In such a case, the assets will not acquire a new basis in the hands of the transferee. Even if more than twenty-one per cent is issued to other persons, the entire group may be considered transferors of property so as to make § 351 applicable. It would appear possible to avoid § 351 by issuing more than twenty per cent of any class of stock to persons whose sole contribution is services.

124. Rev.Rul. 61–156 [1961–2 Cum.Bull. 62].

127. 39 T.C. 144 (1962).

per cent of its stock, took seventy-two per cent of the stock of newly formed corporation B for cash, with the remaining twenty-eight per cent going to persons having no interest in A. Pursuant to a plan of complete liquidation adopted by its shareholders, A then sold its operating assets to B for cash and distributed the proceeds with its other assets in a series of distributions which ended within twelve months of the resolution date. The Treasury contended that the distribution received by the five shareholders was a redemption equivalent to a dividend under section 302, and alternatively that the transaction constituted an (E) or (F) reorganization. The court held that these provisions could not apply where the transferee's shareholders were substantially different from those of the transferor. It further held that, while the distributions were in redemption of A's stock, the fact that the redemption was incidental to A's liquidation could not be disregarded. Each distribution was a distribution in partial liquidation under section 346(a)(1), and thus could not be equivalent to a dividend.[128] Three judges dissented, on the ground that the liquidation provisions should not be read so as to permit the distribution of earnings at capital gain rates to shareholders who retained a substantial equity interest in the transferred assets.

Since the possible tax liability of A on the sale of its assets was not at issue in Gallagher, the opinion does not indicate whether it realized gain or whether, if it did, it sought nonrecognition under section 337. It seems clear, however, that a plan calling for a "series of distributions in redemption of all of the stock of the corporation" is in fact a "plan of complete liquidation" satisfying that section. Hence, if the final distribution occurs within twelve months, as in Gallagher, the corporation's gain should be shielded from tax.

NOTE ON § 337

1. **Requirement of a Complete Liquidation.** A series of revenue rulings have provided some practical guidance with respect to the requirement of § 337 that all of the corporation's assets (apart from those retained to meet claims) must be distributed in complete liquidation within one year. In Rev.Rul. 63-245, 1963-2 Cum.Bull. 144, a corporation adopted

---

128. The court was attempting by this reference to rule out the possible application of Treas.Reg. § 1.331-1(c), which says that "a liquidation which is followed by a transfer to another corporation of all or part of the assets of the liquidating corporation or which is preceded by such a transfer may, however, have the effect of the distribution of a dividend. . . ." A similar statement appears in Treas. Reg. § 1.301-1(d). These represent the Treasury's attempt to deal with the tax avoidance possibilities of reincorporation transactions. As Gallagher shows, however, their legal effect is doubtful. [Ed note: The Gallagher decision has since been approved by two Courts of Appeals which have affirmed Tax Court decisions following it. Pridemark, Inc. v. Commissioner, 345 F.2d 35 (4th Cir. 1965); Berghash v. Commissioner, —— F.2d —— (2d Cir. 1966).]

a plan of complete liquidation and within twelve months thereafter wound up its affairs, sold its assets, and distributed the proceeds among its stockholders. However, the corporation had a claim for refund of taxes which could not readily be either sold or divided among its stockholders, and accordingly, pursuant to the plan of liquidation, the claim was transferred to an independent trustee for the benefit of the stockholders. Under applicable local law such a trustee was authorized to receive a liquidating distribution for the benefit of stockholders, and to pay it over to the stockholders when it was reduced to cash. The ruling holds that although § 337 is not satisfied if the corporation retains any assets for distribution to stockholders, in the case of an asset which is not reasonably susceptible to sale or distribution it is sufficient for § 337 purposes if the corporation divests itself of the asset within the specified twelve-month period in a manner equivalent to a distribution of the asset to stockholders. The ruling adds that the person chosen to receive the refund claim for the benefit of the stockholders should be someone selected by the stockholders (or by a court), but indicates that this requirement is satisfied if the person is named in the plan of complete liquidation which is approved by the stockholders.

Rev.Rul. 65–257, 1965–46 I.R.B. 28, approves a similar method of dealing with the claims of stockholders who dissent from a sale of all the corporation's assets in connection with a complete liquidation. In the situation posed by the ruling, it appeared that the requisite judicial review of the appraiser's valuation of the dissenting stockholders' stock could not be obtained within the 12-month period specified in § 337. Accordingly, the corporation transferred to an independent escrowee the amount at which the stock had been valued by the appraiser (together with the statutory interest due thereon), prior to the termination of the 12-month period. The escrow agreement provided that the escrowee would pay to the dissenting stockholders the amounts finally determined to be due them, with any remaining proceeds to be distributed pro rata to the nondissenting stockholders. In the event of a deficiency in the escrow funds, the principal nondissenting stockholders were to pay whatever additional amounts might be needed. The ruling states that since the plan approved by the stockholders authorized the officers to take all appropriate steps necessary to effect a complete liquidation, and the transfer to an escrowee was such a step, it would be treated as though it were a transfer to an escrowee selected by the shareholders. Accordingly, the transfer to the escrowee constituted a distribution to the stockholders which completed the distribution of all the corporation's assets within the 12-month period specified by § 337.

In Rev.Rul. 60–50, 1960–1 Cum.Bull. 150, a corporation had adopted a plan of liquidation, sold its only operating asset, and distributed all its net assets to its sole stockholder in exchange for all of his stock. However, the corporate charter was retained, and immediately after the final distribution in liquidation the former stockholder reactivated the corporation to carry on a new business operation, transferring new assets to it in exchange for a new issue of stock. The ruling holds that while the retention of its charter does not in and of itself mean that there has not been a complete liquidation of the corporation, "the immediate reactivation of the old corporation in another business by the transfer of assets to it by its former shareholder has the same effect as though the old corporation was only partially liquidated," so that § 337 did not apply.

2. Restoration of the Reserve for Bad Debts to Income. As indicated in the foregoing Law Review Note, page 644 supra, when accounts receivable are sold for a price equal to their full face value, then just as in the case where accounts are collected in full the reserve for bad debts is no longer "needed" and must be restored to income; and this restoration to income does not constitute "gain from the sale or exchange of property" within the meaning of § 337 and therefore is not shielded from recognition by that provision. This same approach has been taken with regard to the recovery of other amounts previously charged off for tax purposes. Thus Rev.Rul. 61–214, 1961–2 Cum.Bull. 60, holds that where a building corporation sold all of its assets, including a stockpile of coal, plumbing supplies and small tools which had been charged to current expense in prior taxable years, the proceeds attributable to these items were "to be treated as ordinary income to the corporation under section 61 of the Code and not as nonrecognized gain under the provisions of section 337(a) of the Code".

However, typically the price paid by a third party for the accounts receivable of another enterprise is less than the gross face amount of the receivables—it is usually much closer to the net book value of the accounts (i. e., after deduction of the reserve). In such cases it is certainly arguable that since the prediction of loss on the accounts receivable taken as a whole, which is what the reserve for bad debts really represents, has been confirmed, there is really nothing to "restore" to income. Actually, of course, except when there is a nonrecognition provision in the picture, it would not particularly matter if the reserve was required to be restored to income even when the price received for the accounts receivable was only equal to net book value — for there would be an offsetting loss on the accounts receivable equal to the difference between the face amount (their tax basis) and the price received; and since accounts receivable do not constitute capital assets, § 1221(4), the loss would be ordinary and would counterbalance the restoration of the reserve to ordinary income. However, when the sale of the accounts receivable is subject to a nonrecognition provision, such as § 337, the loss on the accounts is prevented from being recognized; but the reserve is restored to income just the same. Despite the seeming unfairness of finding taxable income when there has been no economic gain, the Tax Court has insisted upon the restoration of the reserve in these circumstances. J. E. Hawes Corporation v. Commissioner, 44 T.C. 705 (1965); Cardinal Finance Company, Inc. v. Commissioner, 22 T.C.M. 90 (1963).

In reaching this conclusion the court has repeatedly stressed the view that although an account which has become worthless may be charged against a reserve for bad debts, a loss incurred upon the sale of one or more accounts is a loss arising from the sale or exchange of property and can not be charged against the reserve. However, the cases relied upon by the court for this proposition involve the sale of an isolated claim, with no reserve for bad debts in the picture; to hold that a loss incurred in such circumstances should be treated as a loss from the sale or exchange of property rather than as a bad-debt loss under § 166 certainly seems unexceptional. See, e. g., Levy v. Commissioner, 46 B.T.A. 423 (1942), aff'd 131 F.2d 544 (2d Cir. 1942). This is a far cry from the proposition that a taxpayer which accounts for its receivables arising in the ordinary course of business on the reserve method can not charge against the reserve a loss incurred upon a close-out of all its accounts receivable by sale. In any event, the Tax Court's view has recently been vigorously rejected by the Court of Appeals for the Ninth Circuit, (which had decided the West Seattle National Bank case, page 644 supra, sustaining a restoration of the reserve for bad debts where the price paid for the accounts receivable was equal to the gross face amount thereof). Estate of Heinz Schmidt v. Commissioner, 355 F.2d 111 (9th Cir. 1966). The Schmidt case actually involved the transfer of a proprietorship to a new corporation under § 351 rather than a sale of assets under § 337; but the same issue was involved since the Service contended that the proprietor's reserve for bad debts should be restored to his income, while any offsetting loss on the transfer of the accounts receivable would go unrecognized under § 351. The Tax Court adopted this view, but the Court of Appeals reversed, holding that "whether the sale be for cash or stock, no income is received unless the consideration received exceeds the net amount of the receivables". The court added that when only the net amount of the receivables is received, "the price received merely demonstrates that the estimate of loss was correct. And there is no gain merely because the reserve is no longer 'needed'; rather, the correctness of the reserve as an estimate of loss is confirmed". A district court appears to have reached the Schmidt result in a § 337 case, but without any extensive consideration of the issues or the authorities. Mountain States Mixed Feed Co. v. United States, 65–2 U.S.T.C. para. 9551 (D.Colo.1965).

B. NOTE ON COLLAPSIBLE CORPORATIONS

A full treatment of collapsible corporations is beyond the present scope of these materials. The following article (rather aptly named for inclusion in these materials) is offered for any who may wish some introduction to the subject:

LARKIN, THE BUSINESS PLANNER AND THE COLLAPSIBLE CORPORATION *

6 San.Cl.Law. 26 (1965).

The creature which today is called a "collapsible corporation" was created as a device to secure capital gains treatment for funds which otherwise would have been taxed as ordinary income. In an attempt to change this result, Congress passed what is now Section 341 of the Internal Revenue Code. As it presently exists, Section 341 presents a crazy-quilt plan of fortifications designed to plug the once existing tax loophole. This bewildering

---

* Reprinted by permission of the Santa Clara Lawyer. Most of the footnotes omitted.

set of rules has been much maligned by the commentators. It is not the purpose of this paper to add to the caustic comments which have already been rendered concerning Section 341; nor is it the purpose of this paper to defend that much abused section. Rather, an attempt will be made to view the statutory scheme as it exists today, to review the cases which have interpreted that section and to point out what, if anything, remains of the concept of the "collapsible corporation." This treatment is intended to benefit not only the business planning attorney faced with a potentially dangerous collapsible situation, but also the attorney called upon to defend a client whose capital gains have been disallowed because of a claim of collapsibility.

Background

The motion picture industry was the first to make use of the collapsible corporation scheme. The classic situation is represented by Pat O'Brien,[3] where four people organized a corporation to produce the movie, *Secret Command*. Two actors invested a total of $12,500 into the corporation in return for all the stock. The corporation then borrowed $349,000 to finance the cost of production. Fourteen months later, after the movie was completed and released for distribution but before the corporation had received any income, the stockholders voted to dissolve. The corporation redeemed their stock and assigned to the two actors the corporate assets (all right, title and interest in the picture) as well as all corporate debts. At liquidation, the stockholders valued the assigned movie rights at $150,000 after the salaries and loans had been paid, and treated the difference between this figure and their original investment ($137,500) as capital gain. The Commissioner challenged the transactions on several grounds, but the Tax Court discounted each of these and held that the gains to the shareholders were long-term capital gains not subject to taxation at ordinary rates. The court refused to apply Section 341 inasmuch as all gains were realized before it became effective.

The collapsible scheme was also used to advantage in other situations. For example, a corporation could be formed to develop an undeveloped asset (*e. g.*, a tract of land or a new patent). Instead of liquidating the corporation after development, as was done in O'Brien, the stock would be held at least six months and then sold. The income could then be taxed at capital gains rates while the purchaser could operate and eventually liquidate the corporation, usually at no gain or loss in income because the property was taken at a stepped-up basis.

Another method utilized was to have the corporation borrow more money than was needed for the construction of the income-producing property. Once again, before any income had been realized, the corporation would be liquidated, or the stock sold, at a fair market value. The excess of the money borrowed over the cost of production was distributed to the shareholders as a capital asset. The difference between the amount of the original investment and the amount distributed was then taxed to the shareholders as long-term capital gain.

3. 25 T.C. 376 (1955), acquiesced in part, 1957–1 Cum.Bull. 4.

Not infrequently, the income producing asset was a tract of land upon which a housing project was to be built. Often, when the shareholders were contractors, architects, or real estate dealers, the above-mentioned devices were supplemented as in the following example. An FHA mortgage guaranty would be obtained using the highest cost estimates possible. In actual construction the shareholders would cut these costs by taking considerably less compensation for their services than provided for in the estimates. Consequently, the actual cost of construction often would be less than the ninety per cent FHA guaranty. Following construction, a disinterested appraiser would consider all the factors affecting the new development (the completed status of the buildings, the further development of surrounding land as shopping centers, increased transportation facilities, and the natural inflation during the period of construction) and generally could revalue the buildings at an amount considerably higher than that originally projected during the planning stages. Thus, an apartment house project might be estimated to cost $2,000,000 which would enable an FHA guaranty of $1,800,000 to be obtained. If costs were cut to $1,650,000, the unused funds of $150,000 would be available in cash for distribution to the shareholders at the completion of construction. After being revalued, the property might honestly be worth as much as $2,250,000. If sold at this price, the shareholders would have realized another $450,000 excess.

The Statutory Scheme of Section 341

Congress was aiming at such activities in 1950 when it passed the "collapsible corporation" provisions, Section 117(m) of the 1939 Internal Revenue Code. Section 117(m) was later amended to include inventory-type properties which would increase in value with time (*e. g.*, whiskey, cheese). The effect of the amendment was to broaden the scope of the section to include property purchased as well as property which is manufactured, constructed or produced. Upon being incorporated into the 1954 Code, the section was again expanded; as Section 341, it included inventory assets and "unrealized receivables and fees" as the type of assets which would cause a corporation to be considered collapsible.

Section 341(b) (1) defines a collapsible corporation as one which is formed, or, if already in existence, is availed of:

1. To manufacture, construct, produce or purchase property;
2. With a view to,
a. Distributing gains realized by it to its stockholders before it has realized a substantial part of the taxable income which could be expected to be derived from the property, and
b. Having the shareholders realize such gain.

The late Chief Judge Parker in Burge v. Commissioner [9] gave this explanation of the concept:

> That the term was used to describe a corporation which is made use of to give the appearance of a long-term investment to what is in reality a mere venture or project in manufacture, production or con-

---
9. 253 F.2d 765, 767, 74 A.L.R.2d 664 (4th Cir. 1958). . . .

struction of property, with the view of making the gains from the project taxable, not as ordinary income, as they should be taxed, but as long-term capital gains. Because the basic type of transaction which gave rise to the legislation involved the use of temporary corporations which were dissolved and their proceeds distributed after tax avoidance had been accomplished, the term "collapsible corporation" was employed to describe the corporations used for this form of tax avoidance. . . .

Section 341(a) clearly applies only to gains which would normally be long-term, *i. e.*, held longer than six months. Every method of receiving a long-term capital gain from a stock distribution is covered by Section 341, except a redemption under Section 302(a) which is not considered to be a partial liquidation under Section 346. It is questionable whether this exception has any practical value to the shareholder. However the inapplicability of Section 341 to short-term gains does provide definite assistance, inasmuch as it permits the shareholder with capital losses to use these against short-term capital gains realized on the liquidation.

The gain which the shareholders received from the assets of a collapsible corporation will be treated as ordinary income where the gain is from:

1. The sale or exchange of the corporation's stock;
2. A partial or complete liquidation of a collapsible corporation which will cause the distribution from the liquidation to be treated as received in payment for the stock; or
3. A corporate distribution which falls within the thrust of Section 301(c) (3) (A) because of lack of earnings or profits.

Section 341(b) (2) imputes the consequences of having manufactured, constructed, produced or purchased the property to the corporation if it engages in such activity to any extent, or if its holds property the basis of which is determined by reference to the cost to the person who originally so treated the property. A transfer under Section 351 of an asset constructed entirely by a person for all of the corporate stock would be such a "holding" by a corporation. In such a Section 351 exchange, the basis of the property in the hands of the corporation would be determined, according to Section 362, by the individual's basis. Under the provisions of Section 1031, a similar rule would be applicable to an exchange of assets between two corporations.

Not all property *owned* by the corporation will render it collapsible. While the code clearly includes any property which has been *constructed* by the corporation and which is carried on its books as a capital asset, there are special rules for *purchased* assets. Section 341(b) (3) sets forth these special provisions for "Section 341 assets" and includes:

1. Stock in trade or inventory; or
2. Property held for sale to customers in the ordinary course of business; or
3. Unrealized fees or receivables; or
4. Section 1231(b) property, as long as that property has not been used in connection with the manufacture, construction or production of stock in trade, inventory, or property primarily for sale in the ordinary course of business.

These assets will be considered Section 341 assets only if they have been held for less than three years. The three-year limitation applies to determinations of collapsibility notwithstanding the shorter "six month" rule generally applied to Section 1231 (property used in trade or business) assets.

To determine whether the requisite three-year period has run, the tacking provisions of Section 1223 will be applied, ". . . but no such period shall be deemed to begin before the completion of the manufacture, construction, production, or purchase." Thus, an asset purchased by an individual on January 1, 1962, and transferred to a corporation on July 1, 1964 in return for 100 per cent of the corporation's stock, in turn held by the corporation until after the individual sells his stock on January 2, 1965, will not be considered a Section 341 asset. Care must be taken that the entire process of manufacture, construction, production or purchase has been completed before the three-year period commences inasmuch as the term "construction" has been broadly construed both by the Internal Revenue Service and the courts. [As will be developed in more detail below].

Section 341(b) (3) (C) which deals with unrealized fees and receivables has been interpreted to mean any rights (contractual or otherwise) to receive payment for property otherwise considered to be a Section 341 asset,

> . . . which has been delivered or is to be delivered and rights to payments for services rendered or to be rendered, to the extent such rights have not been included in the income of the corporation under the method of accounting used by it.

While Section 341 assets purport to relate only to purchased assets, there should be no confusion on the point that the "unrealized receivables and fees" provisions of Section 341(b) (3) will also be applied to receivables due the corporation from the sale of goods or performance or sevices.

A rebuttable presumption of collapsibility will arise under Section 341 (c), if, at the time of the sale, exchange or liquidation, the fair market value of the corporation's Section 341 assets is more than half (50%) of the total corporate assets *and also* more than 120 per cent of the adjusted basis of those same assets. Both conditions must be met. The presumption is clearly rebuttable since the Regulations deem the result to follow unless shown to the contrary. Conversely, however, if the corporation's Section 341 assets do not reach the 50 per cent and 120 per cent levels, no presumptions, conclusive or rebuttable, will arise in *favor* of the corporation, *i. e.*, that it is not collapsible. A crucial element in the application of the percentages to the total corporate assets is the required exclusion of cash, stock in other corporations, obligations which are corporate capital assets, and obligations of any state or of the United States as defined in Section 1221(5). Because the Section 341 (c) presumption works only in favor of the government, the need for it has been questioned. As Bittker notes, "Even without the presumption of Section 341(c), the taxpayer has the burden of overcoming the presumption of correctness that accompanies the Commissioner's action in assessing a deficiency." Perhaps the only practical use of the Section 341(c) presumption is that it may provide an objective standard, ". . . likely to appeal to a Revenue Agent in conducting the audit of a taxpayer's return."

Section 341(d) renders the provisions of Section 341 inapplicable to the shareholder, notwithstanding qualifications under the aforementioned conditions which would render a corporation collapsible, if:

1. The shareholder did not own, outright or constructively, more than 5 per cent of the outstanding stock of the corporation at any time after construction had begun, or after a Section 341 asset had been purchased. Outstanding stock will not be considered to include treasury stock. A person will be deemed to be the owner of stock if he is: A shareholder of a corporation which also owns stock, a partner of a shareholder of a collapsible corporation, a beneficiary of a trust or estate which also owns stock, has an option to acquire stock, or if the stock is owned by any member of his family including his spouse, his ancestors, his brothers or sisters (both whole and half-blood) and their spouses, and his lineal descendants and their spouses.

2. The gain recognized on stock of a collapsible corporation from property includible under Section 341 does not exceed 70 per cent of the total gain for any taxable year. This provision is an "all or nothing" provision. If more than 70 per cent of the gain is attributable to the Section 341 property, that gain is taxable; if not, none of the gain is taxable.

3. The gain is realized more than three years after the completion of the production or purchase of the property. This provision is one of the most important limitations on Section 341. In effect, this carryover from the 1939 Code extends the time limitations for long-term capital gains, as applicable to collapsible corporations, from the normal six-month period to three years. The holding period of prior owners of the property may be included in the three-year period. This means that any corporation can be formed with the intention of collapsing it, and, as long as the shareholder does not transfer his stock or receive his gain until three years after the construction has been completed or the purchase made, the other provisions of Section 341 will not apply. A shareholder who can afford to wait three years after the completion of construction to realize his gain, will receive long-term capital gain treatment for his income.

Other provisions limiting the scope of Section 341 are found in subsection (e). A brief summary of this subsection and its "fearfully intricate provisions" is offered, although a complete description of this subsection is beyond the scope of this article. A principal reason for the enactment of this subsection was to avoid adverse results created by the then existing sections. The following language from the Senate Report to subsection (e) is illustrative:

> The collapsible-corporation provision of present law . . . both by their terms and as interpreted, are so broad that in a number of situations *they have exactly the opposite effect from that intended* —instead of preventing the conversion of ordinary income into capital gain, they may instead convert what would otherwise be capital gain into ordinary income.

Prior to the enactment of subsection (e), a taxpayer avoiding use of a corporate form might be taxed only at capital gain rates, while a similar taxpayer making the same transaction through a corporate entity might be taxed at ordinary income rates because of the operation of Section 341(a) through (d). Congress sought to eliminate this anomalous result by the provisions of subsection (e). It provides, in substance, that a corporation will not be deemed to be collapsible if, "the net unrealized appreciation in subsection (e) assets . . . does not exceed an amount equal to 15 per cent of the net worth of the corporation."

Subsection (e) applies to three distinct types of transaction: A sale or exchange of stock (§ 341(e) (1)), a distribution under a total liquidation (§ 341(e) (2)) or a partial liquidation under Section 333 (§ 341(e) (3)). Section 341(e) (4) gives certain collapsible corporations the right to elect the benefits of Section 337 provided that following the adoption of the plan of complete liquidation: (a) the net unrealized appreciation of subsection (e) assets does not exceed fifteen per cent of the corporation's net worth; (b) substantially all the corporate assets are sold within twelve months; and (c) no distribution of property is made for which exhaustion, wear and tear, obsolescence, amortization or depletion deductions are allowable. Exemptions under the first two types of transactions are granted to individual shareholders (limited under the first type to those owning twenty per cent or less of the stock), while those under Section 341(e) (3) and (4) are granted to corporations. It is, of course, necessary to classify and evaluate both the subsection (e) assets and all assets making up the "net worth" of the corporation in order to take advantage of the subsection.

Subsection (e) carefully defines "subsection (e) assets" (§ 341(e) (5)), "net unrealized appreciation" (§ 341(e) (6)), "net worth" (§ 341(e) (7)), "related person" (§ 341(e) (8)), and "property used in the trade or business" (§ 341(e) (9)). Unrealized appreciation of subsection (e) assets may prevent a corporation from taking advantage of the subsection's provisions and, absent other available defenses, can cause a transaction to result in ordinary income to the stockholder. These assets are defined as follows:

1. Corporate property which, if sold by the corporation or by a holder of twenty per cent of the corporation's outstanding stock, would produce ordinary income to the seller. If a twenty per cent holder would not receive capital gains treatment for the gain on the sale (*e. g.*, as a dealer in such property), then his existence will prevent the corporation and its other stockholders from taking advantage of the subsection (e) provisions.

2. Property used in the trade or business (*i. e.*, a Section 1231(b) asset), provided that the aggregate of unrealized depreciation exceeds the unrealized appreciation on all such property.

3. Property used in the trade or business (*i. e.*, a Section 1231(b) asset), provided that such property, if owned by a twenty per cent holder, would produce ordinary income as the result of a sale or exchange.

4. Property consisting of a copyright, literary, musical, artistic or similar asset if it was created, wholly or partially, by the personal efforts of a holder of more than five per cent of the corporation's outstanding stock.

In each of the above-mentioned instances, the constructive ownership rules of Section 544 apply. A corporation or a twenty per cent shareholder cannot take advantage of subsection (e) if the sale is to a "related person." Other corporate assets, although not held for sale, may come within the thrust of Section 341(e) (5) (A) (i) and may be classified subsection (e) assets, *e. g.*, stock of a corporation which is "Section 306 stock," or stock of a corporation which in turn holds stock in a collapsible corporation to which none of the Section 341(d) limitations apply. Finally, Section 341(e) (11) specifically provides that failure of a corporation to meet the requirements of subsection (e) is not to be considered in determining its collapsible status under Section 341(a) through (d). Subsection (e) is difficult to interpret, not only because its wording is complex but also because it has not yet been construed by either a court decision or revenue ruling.

In August 1964, subsection (f) of Section 341 was enacted. The Report of the Senate Finance Committee states:

> . . . [S]ection 341(a) shall not apply to a sale of stock of a corporation if . . . such corporation consents to recognize gain on any future disposition by it of its "subsection (f) assets" . . . and if the sale of the stock is made within the six-month period after the consent is filed.[36]

The new subsection is applicable only to "subsection (f) assets" which are defined as non-capital assets of the corporation; these include land, any interest in real property (exclusive of security interests) and unrealized fees and receivables.

The general rule of collapsibility in Section 341(a) (1) will not apply to a sale of the stock of a corporation holding subsection (f) assets if that corporation consents—in accord with one of the procedures to be established in soon-to-be-released regulations—to the application of subsection (f) (2). The individual shareholder may sell some of his corporate stock without the collapsibility dangers, if the corporation consents to having its future distributions of "341(f) assets" treated as gain from the sale or exchange of such assets. If a transfer is made by means of sale, exchange or involuntary conversion, the gain will be the excess of the amount realized less the adjusted basis of the subsection (f) asset; gain from any other type of disposition will be the amount by which the fair market value of the asset exceeds its adjusted basis.[39]

Although the full import of subsection (f) remains to be seen, some questions have been answered by the terms of the subsection itself and the accompanying Senate Report. A consent will be effective for a six-month period commencing on the date of filing, and will apply to *every* sale of that corporation's stock made by *any* shareholder during the consent period. Once a consent has been filed and a sale of the stock made thereunder, the consent cannot be revoked until the six-month period has expired.[41] A subsequent determination that the corporation was not a collapsible corporation will not vitiate the consent; the corporation will continue to be subject to the special tax treatment of Section 341(f) (2) in regard to any future disposition of its "subsection (f) assets." [42] While the consent is automatically revoked at the end of the six-month period unless the corporation files another consent, no limit has been fixed upon the number of consents which may be filed.

---

36. Section 341(f) has been designated P. L. 88–484. See S.Rep. No. 1241, in U.S. Code Cong. & Ad.News, 88th Cong., 2d Sess. 3081, 3085 (1964). Other treatments of subsection (f) can be found in Hall, The Consenting Collapsible Corporation, 12 U.C.L.A.L.Rev. 1365 (1965); New Collapsible Relief Measure Is More Useful Than Most Men Believe, 22 J.Taxation 148 (1965).

39. Int.Rev.Code of 1954, § 341(f) (2) (A), (B). "Other types of dispositions" include distribution of subsection (f) assets as a dividend (S.Rep. No. 1241, supra note 36, Example 2), or a distribution in a complete or partial liquidation of the corporation (id. at Example 1).

41. S.Rep.No.1241, supra note 36, at 3086.

42. Ibid.

This new section presents no additional considerations for the determination of collapsibility. The Senate Report clearly states that a consenting corporation does not automatically become noncollapsible nor does it become collapsible per se. The subsection applies only to the stockholders who qualify under its provisions.

A special exception to subsection (f) is made for tax-free treatment under Sections 332, 351, 361 and 371(a) of the Code. Also, Section 341(f) (6) provides that the subsection will not apply if the consenting corporation, on the date of the sale, owns more than five per cent of the outstanding stock of another corporation, which has not also filed a consent.

The nonrevocation provisions of a Section 341 consent present problems to the taxpayer who would "wheel and deal" with his corporations. Section 341(f) (5) contains another limiting provision which allows a taxpayer to take advantage of subsection (f) with only one consenting corporation during any five-year period. Thus, a taxpayer who has sold stock in a consenting corporation during a consent period may not, within five years from the date of that sale, take advantage of the provision of Section 341(f) (1) as regards the sale of the shares of stock of any other consenting corporation. He may, however, within the five-year period, take advantage of the original consent or of any subsequent consent when he makes further sales of the stock of the original consenting corporation.

CASE LAW

As is indicated by the statutory scheme of Section 341, the facts of a particular case will largely determine whether the corporation in question will be collapsible. The cases which have thus far arisen have set forth some important principles of law. Of more importance, however, is the fact that they have applied the statutory rules and the regulations to particular fact situations, thus establishing specific guidelines which can be utilized to interpret a potential fact pattern in the future.

It is apparent from a review of the cases that two opposing philosophies have emerged in the area of collapsible corporations. One group of cases invariably looks to the Congressional purpose of preventing the use of the collapsible device to receive capital gains. Many statements of this purpose can be found throughout the various House and Senate Committee reports. This group of cases appears to concentrate on the issue of the "view"; if the taxpayer had the prohibited view, the necessary intent, the case will very nearly be decided at that point. When there are additional issues in the case, these cases will often fall back on the fact that Congress intended to penalize anyone having just such a view, quote from the relevant Congressional report, and decide the additional issue against the taxpayer concluding that Congress could not have meant to allow *any* taxpayer to achieve tax avoidance and thus reach the haven of capital gains treatment. . . .

* * *

Another entirely different approach to the collapsible corporation problem has been expressed. The philosophy of these cases is that the purpose expressed in the Congressional records is not all-controlling, but is to be used as an aid to interpretation of the statute. These cases take into consideration what Congress actually did, *i. e.*, what the final wording of the statutory scheme has finally achieved, as well as what the drafters hoped to do, *i. e.*, the Congressional report statements. The fact that Congress intended to catch these persons in its collapsible corporation net would not necessarily mean that they were, in fact, entrapped by its provisions. Just as, conversely, the provisions succeeded in catching some taxpayers which Congress had no intention of taxing at all. . . .

View

One of the principal factual considerations when dealing with collapsibility is whether the taxpayer-stockholder has taken certain actions "with a view to" acquiring capital gains rates on the income from the transaction. Of course, only the individual taxpayer really knows the answer to this question. His testimony is one indication of whether the view, the requisite intent to receive capital gains, existed, but other factors weigh heavily. One early argument advanced on the issue of view was that the word "principally" in the definition modified the words "with a view to" rather than the words "manufacture, construction, or production." The effect of such an interpretation would have eased the taxpayer's burden considerably since the term "principally" forces a quantitative distinction upon whatever it refers to. If a corporation were required to be formed or availed of "principally" with a view to its collapsing, then a determination would have to have been made in every case as to what portion of its activities were conducted with this view as compared to its other activities. Moreover, the courts would have had to determine what constitutes "principally," *i. e.*, 51 per cent of the corporation's activities, 75 per cent, or even 10 per cent, if the other 90 per cent of the corporate activity was spread out over a multitude of activities, none of which included more than 2 or 3 per cent of the total corporate activity. Unfortunately for subsequent taxpayers, one of the early cases decided the issue noting that the argued for interpretation, ". . . is without support of any rule of law or of grammar with which we are familiar." [62]

Perhaps the greatest conflict with respect to *view* arises over the question of when the view must have been entertained. Under the statute a corporation will be regarded as collapsible if the view existed either at the time of formation or when the corporation is later "availed of." The requisite view need not exist when the corporation is formed; it is sufficient if it exists when the corporation is availed of at some later time. Of the two possibilities set forth in the statute, *i. e.*, "formed" or "availed of," the "availed of" alternative is of much greater importance. Even if the corporation is "formed" for the purpose of collapsing, but is never actually used for this purpose, no gain would be attributable to the shareholders, and thus the purpose of formation would be of little importance. On the other hand, if any corporation, whether or not formed for the explicit purpose, is so "availed of," then, and only then, would gains be attributable to such corporation, thus bringing it within the thrust of Section 341.

The regulation states that the view must exist ". . . at any time *during* the manufacture, production, construction, or purchase . . . ." of the collapsible property. Both the Second and Fourth Circuits think that the regulations are too favorable to the taxpayer and do not hesitate to say so. The Second Circuit has held that the view need only exist when the corpora-

---

62. Burge v. Commissioner, [note 66 infra, at 768, n. 2].

tion is availed of, despite the fact that the regulations prescribe a narrower test which requires that the view be availed of during construction. With respect to the test in the regulations the court has stated: "We are disposed to disagree with so narrow an interpretation. . . ."[65] The Fourth Circuit takes a similar position.[66] It is worthwhile noting, however, that these findings in Burge and Glickman were not necessary to the final outcome of the cases since there was an additional finding that the view existed during the process of construction. Furthermore, in a later decision by the Second Circuit, when again faced with the problem of when the necessary view had to exist, the statement was made that, "Whether when the view to distribute arises after completion of construction the gain on distribution would be treated as ordinary income need not be decided . . . ."[67] Again, the view existed during construction, and although it again appears to be merely dictum, this may be a slight withdrawal from the earlier strict interpretation in Glickman.

The Third and Fifth Circuits interpret the problem much more reasonably in favor of the taxpayer. The Third Circuit in Jacobson v. Commissioner[68] met the problem head on and stated: "The 'view' with which a corporation is used for a particular purpose must necessarily be a view entertained at the time of such use."

The Court continued:
To us this seems so clear on the face of the statute that we would content ourselves with the foregoing brief analysis of the statutory text were it not for the fact that other highly respected courts have been persuaded to a contrary interpretation. [Citing Glickman and Burge] . . . However, there is an additional consideration which to us seems decisive in support of our reading of the statute and against the cited cases. The interpretation which to us seems most natural and reasonable has been adopted administratively and published in a formal Treasury regulation. [Treas.Reg. 1.341-2(a)(3).] . . . Thus, the regulation, adopting what is certainly not an arbitrary interpretation of the statute, treats a corporation as collapsible only if "the view to sale" shall have existed at the time of the construction in which the corporate entity was used, or if circumstances which subsequently induce sale were themselves within contemplation during the period of construction. We are guided by and shall apply the statute as thus reasonably interpreted in the regulations.

The Tax Court opinions have oscillated between the two divergent positions. Numerically, more cases have followed the regulations than have declined to follow them. More significant is the fact that all the Tax Court cases since Jacobson was decided in 1960, have followed that decision on this point. The trend appears to be definitely toward the position that the requisite view must exist during construction. Should a subsequent case reach the opposite conclusion, it would seem to be a ripe question for determination by the Supreme Court.

65. Glickman v. Commissioner, 256 F.2d 108, 111 (2d Cir. 1958).
66. Burge v. Commissioner, 253 F.2d 765 (4th Cir. 1958).
67. Mintz v. Commissioner, 284 F.2d 554, 558 (2d Cir. 1960).
68. 281 F.2d 703, 705 (3d Cir. 1960).

Another question with respect to view that has produced considerable conflict is who must have the requisite view. The regulations state that ". . . those persons in a position to determine the policies of the corporation, whether by reason of their owning a majority of the voting stock of the corporation or otherwise," are required to have the view. It appears that a dissenting minority shareholder, who did not have the requisite view, or even a person who became a shareholder after the view had been entertained by others, could be brought within the ambit of the statutory rules through the intentions of other shareholders who did have the view. In only one instance is the individual minority shareholder relieved of the effect of the statute. This is the exception, previously noted, and found in Section 341(d) (1), which exempts the owner of five per cent or less of the stock from the effects of the section. Note, however, the further limitation of Section 341(d) whereby an owner of stock is deemed to own the stock of other persons closely related to him in business or personally, which narrows the rule considerably. This is important in the collapsible corporation situation which usually involves closely held corporations. In a recent Court of Claims case,[74] and in two recent Tax Court opinions,[75] the courts considered the question of who must have the requisite view. In each case, minority shareholders holding more than five per cent of the stock became disenchanted with the policies of the majority or controlling stockholder, and sold out to the latter. Each time, the majority stockholders continued to hold their stock, and the sale of the stock by the minority shareholders was held not to be a collapsible transaction. In so holding the Court of Claims made the following statement:

> The essence of the Tax Court's rulings [in Solow and Lowery] is that the collapsible corporation provisions are not applicable in a case in which a minority stockholder has his stock redeemed and the majority stockholder continues to own the corporation.[76]

The following criticism of this holding has been advanced: "But this surely must be regarded as an overstatement. Obviously, it cannot be assumed automatically that a less than 50 per cent shareholder is not in control of the policies of the corporation." However, this much seems clear; a transaction will not be considered to be within Section 341 when a minority shareholder, or even a 50 per cent shareholder, who does not control the policies of the corporation (as was the case in Solow), sells his stock to the majority or controlling shareholder, or has his stock redeemed by the corporation while the other shareholder keeps his stock, if the transaction is free from obvious self-dealing between the two parties. This result would appear to be true whether or not the transaction took place before, during, or after the collapsible activity has been completed.

One specific area of conflict that developed involved the question of whether Section 341 applies even if the sale of the corporate assets would have produced capital gain had no corporation existed. The Fifth Circuit in United States v. Ivey [78] held that a shareholder's gain from sale of his stock

---

74. Goodwin v. United States, 320 F.2d 356 (Ct.Cl. 1963).

75. Ralph J. Solow, supra note 70; Sylvester J. Lowery, 39 T.C. 959, aff'd, 335 F.2d 680 (3d Cir. 1964).

76. Goodwin v. United States, supra note 74, at 359.

78. 294 F.2d 799 (5th Cir. 1961), opinion on rehearing, 303 F.2d 109 (1962), where the court stated: "As we see it, the statute cuts both ways. To use the statute as a means of converting into ordinary income gain that would have been capital gain to the individual would be at odds with the statutory

in a collapsible corporation was not taxable as ordinary income if such gain would have been entitled to capital gains treatment had the taxpayer not incorporated. The case was remanded to determine whether in fact the gain would have qualified for capital gains treatment. In Braunstein v. Commissioner [79] the taxpayer argued for the position that had been accepted by the court in the Ivey case. The Second Circuit rejected the view taken by the Fifth Circuit despite their recognition that "this occasionally produces unwarranted taxation of capital gains as ordinary income." Because of the conflict between the circuits the Supreme Court granted certiorari on the limited question of whether Section 341 is inapplicable " . . . where the stockholders would have been entitled to capital gains treatment had they conducted the enterprise in their individual capacities without utilizing a corporation."[81] The Supreme Court first determined that since neither the taxpayer nor the corporation was engaged in the trade or business of selling apartment houses, " . . . the corporations were not used to convert ordinary income into capital gain and the provisions of . . . [Section 341] are inapplicable."[82] The Court gave a brief history of the section and concluded:

> There is nothing in the language or structure of the section to demand or even justify reading into these provisions the *additional* requirement that the taxpayer must in fact have been using the corporate form as a device to convert ordinary income into capital gain. . . .
>
> For example, if we were to inquire whether or not the profit would have been ordinary income had an enterprise been individually owned, would we treat each taxpaying shareholder differently and look only to *his* trade or business or would we consider the matter in terms of the trade or business of *any* or at least a substantial number of the shareholders? There is simply no basis in the statute for a judicial resolution of this question, and indeed when Congress addressed itself to the problem in 1958, it approved an intricate formulation falling between these two extremes. [Citing subsection (e).]

The Supreme Court thus answered the problem posed by the differences between Ivey and the Second Circuit in Braunstein. The impact of the Braunstein decision is of course, diminished as a result of the enactment of subsection (e).

The existence of the requisite "view" is a factual question to be determined by examination of all the relevant facts and circumstances. The regulations point out with compelling clarity that if the sale, exchange or distribution takes place solely because of the occurrence after construction or purchase of an event which could not be contemplated beforehand, the corporation will not be deemed to have been unlawfully availed of with the requisite view.

purpose and incompatible with the principles underlying the distinction between ordinary income and capital gain."

79. 305 F.2d 949 (2d Cir. 1962).

81. 371 U.S. 933 (1962).

82. Braunstein v. Commissioner, 374 U. S. 65, 69, 83 S.Ct. 1663, 10 L.Ed.2d 757 (1963).

This section of the regulations complements the previous statement in the regulations that: "The requirement [that the corporation is availed of with the requisite view] is satisfied whether such action was contemplated unconditionally, conditionally, or as a recognized possibility." When read together, the two sections require the taxpayer to produce evidence of an uncontemplated occurrence which precipitated the disposition of his stock at the exact time it was disposed of in order to negate the conclusion that the view existed. The "recognized possibility" provision in the regulations has been particularly troublesome in the normal FHA case. Often a loan is acquired in an amount which is excessive, or after completion of the building, a reappraisal shows that it should be revalued. The excessive funds which result from either of these two potentialities are treated especially where the taxpayer is a man experienced in the building industry, as either within the contemplation of the taxpayer or as a recognized possibility during the period of construction.

What have the courts been willing to accept as an "uncontemplated occurrence" so as not to taint the transaction with the undesirable view? Jacobson v. Commissioner [87] presents virtually the only instance where an appellate court has accepted the taxpayer's argument that the view was formed after the uncontemplated occurrence. There, construction of the apartment was completed in July of 1950. During the same month, a real estate broker tried to induce the shareholders to sell their apartment houses, but they rejected the offer. Later, the majority shareholder discovered some cracks in the walls of the building and advised the minority stockholders to sell their shares (presumably to him). The minority group countered with an offer to purchase his shares. Finally, both sides agreed to sell their stock. The Commissioner determined that the corporation was collapsible and the Tax Court agreed. The Third Circuit reversed the Tax Court stating:

> The refusal of the stockholders to permit a broker to list or offer the property for sale in July, the fact that the parties had made other long term investments in rental property and the manifest unwillingness of the majority to sell even after Winograd [the majority shareholder] discovered the cracks and recommended sale, are all facts found by the Tax Court. In aggregate they make a very strong and persuasive case in support of the appellant's claim that they had no thought of selling until after the cracks were discovered.

Revenue Ruling 51–575 provides another instance of an uncontemplated occurrence.[89] A corporation completed construction of a housing project under the Wherry Act. Later, the Housing Act of 1956 was passed which required the project to be sold to the proper military authority. The sale of the property, solely because of the enactment of the latter Act, was an uncontemplated occurrence and thus not a collapsible transaction.

In Braunstein v. Commissioner,[92] petitioner claimed that sale of the property was due to unanticipated circumstances which caused a decrease in rents and an increase in operating expenses. The Second Circuit found that: (a) real estate taxes on the property had increased; (b) discontinuance of free rubbish removal by the city cost taxpayers $8,500; (c) to meet

---

87. 281 F.2d 703 (3d Cir. 1960).   92. 305 F.2d 949 (2d Cir. 1962).
89. 1957–2 Cum.Bull. 236.

competition, the corporations were required to furnish free gas and electricity; and (d) there was an increase in vacancy rates. Although some of these expenses were admittedly unexpected, the Second Circuit found, on balance, that the annual surplus of one apartment project was only $1,010 dollars less than projected, the other only $5,100 less. The court stated that, "It is difficult to believe that this small decrease, which is all the taxpayers had cause to expect, would have caused experienced real estate operators like the three taxpayers to sell their stock unless they had a previous view to its sale."

Despite the court's conclusion, a strong argument can still be made that, under proper circumstances, such factors as increased real estate tax, added expenses for rubbish removal, gas, or electricity, price competition, higher vacancy rates than had been expected and other similar expenses, are facts which may negate the conclusion that the view existed before the completion of construction.

The health of one of the parties to the sale has often been a controlling factor. In Elliott v. United States,[94] one of the minority shareholders suffered two strokes and was advised to retire from active participation in the project. He convinced another minority shareholder to sell also, and finally, they both convinced the majority shareholder to give in. Nine months after construction was completed, the sale was consummated. The court held that the requisite view did not exist.

Other examples of uncontemplated occurrences have been upheld. In Wheeler Kelly & Hagny Invest. Co. v. United States,[96] the gain was attributable to a general appreciation in market value. Similarly, in Morris Cohen [97] a factual situation was presented where:

> There is evidence here that the early sale at a profit of the DOM stock was made possible by the selection of nearby land for the location of two large manufacturing plants, a fortunate circumstance not anticipated by the petitioners.

Southwest Properties, Inc.,[99] involved the increase in value of land in question because of the decision of a bank to open near the cite owned by the taxpayers. In Jack Saltzman,[100] the petitioner used the cash which he received from the sale of his property to further invest in his electrical business which he had purchased over a year after the purchase of his office building. In each of the above-mentioned cases, the events were found not to have been anticipated by the taxpayers, thus not tainting their actions with the view necessary to make Section 341 applicable.

It will be recalled that the statute requires that the property be constructed, ". . . with a view to—

    (A) the sale or exchange of stock . . . and,

    (B) the realization by such shareholders of gain attributable to such property.

Both views are necessary in order that the statutory requirement be met. Payne v. Commissioner [102] is the only reported instance where the taxpayer attempted to separate the two views which are required under Section 341.

---

94. 205 F.Supp. 384 (D.Ore.1962).
96. 64–1 USTC ¶ 9260 (1964).
97. 39 T.C. 886 (1963).
99. 38 T.C. 97 (1962).
100. 22 TCM 336 (1963).
102. 268 F.2d 617 (5th Cir. 1959).

The taxpayer in Payne was not successful in his attempt to separate the two views. The failure emphasizes once again that if a view to the sale or exchange of the stock is found, and if in fact a gain does accrue to the stockholder, then aside from very unusual extenuating circumstances, the view to the realization of the gain attributable to the property will be imputed. There seems to be little hope that the separate view distinction may be argued with success in the future.

Construction

The collapsible corporation is one which is "availed of principally for the manufacture, construction, or production of property . . . ." Most of the cases arising under Section 341 are concerned with real estate corporations which have been engaged, directly or indirectly, in the construction of buildings. The question of whether construction is in process at certain stages of the transaction is important in three contexts:

1. If construction has not begun, Section 341 does not apply.[105]

2. If construction has not been completed at the time of the sale, distribution or exchange, the corporation may be regarded as collapsible. The regulations, and several of the cases applying them, concede that if the requisite view arises after construction is completed, the collapsible provisions of Section 341 will not attach.

3. If Section 341(d) is to apply, three years must have passed after construction is completed.

It is thus necessary to know when construction has begun as well as when it has been completed. In all three situations the term "construction" has been broadly construed both by the Internal Revenue Service and the courts.

Activities prior to sale or exchange which have been held to constitute construction include:

1. Successfully petitioning to a zoning board to have land owned by a corporation re-zoned from a residential to a commercial class.[107]

2. Engaging an architect to revise boundary lines on a plat, paying for a building permit, making a deposit for the purchase of water materials, advancing money to the utility company to make connections, and making payments to acquire FHA loans.[108] The Second Circuit felt that it did not have to rely wholly on the filing of applications for permits, loans and the payment of filing fees in order to hold that "construction to any extent" had started since the corporation had also paid for water materials and utility connections. In *dictum* the court declared that it was not saying that the filing alone would not have been enough since real estate development is so heavily dependent upon government licenses and loans. The court then concluded that the word "construction" had to be interpreted broadly since the legislative history showed an equation of "construction" with "adding value to the property."

---

105. Morris Cohen, 39 T.C. 886 (1963).

107. Rev.Rul. 56–137, 1956–1 Cum.Bull. 178.

108. Farber v. Commissioner, 312 F.2d 729 (2d Cir. 1963).

3. Subdividing the corporate property, making provisions for sewers, streets and utilities and arranging for FHA financing of the project. The taxpayers, who had acted on behalf of the corporation, argued in Abbott v. Commissioner,[110] that the statute required the construction to be done by the corporation, whereas in this case much of the construction enhancing the value of the land had been done after the liquidation of the corporation. In finding that construction had begun, the court stated that the entire operation was arranged for and covered by binding agreements that only the corporation was in a position to carry forward at the time these agreements were entered into. The court then stated: ". . . [I]f individuals could thus project the acts which would take place after distribution and dissolution as though the corporation was in no sense a participant, all of the provisions in question would be meaningless."

4. Subdividing land, having the land annexed to a city, and obtaining an FHA commitment, all of which was done by individuals, was held, in Payne [112] to be as much an integral part of construction as is the erection of a building.

5. Contracting to buy land, seeking an FHA mortgage commitment through a mortgage broker, and employing an architect who had completed about 40 per cent of the total plans. These activities of a corporation formed to erect and own apartment houses were sufficient to sustain a finding that it had engaged in construction.[113]

6. Applying for and receiving a zoning change, hiring an architect to draw preliminary plans, negotiating with a city for building permits and acquiring two tenants were held to be construction in Sproul Realty Co.[114]

On the other hand, several recent opinions have held that a certain amount of preliminary activity on the part of a corporation would not constitute "construction." In Morris Cohen [115] the corporation had attempted to have water service supplied to the land, employed a surveyor to make a contour map showing how the property could be developed as commercial land, and filed a petition to have the property rezoned as residential instead of agricultural. During this period two large manufacturing plants were built near the corporation's land, and an unsolicited offer was made to buy either the corporation's stock or its land. The offer was accepted. In finding that there was no construction under Section 341(b), Judge Murdock, speaking for the Tax Court, held:

> The very limited activities of representatives of Sarkisian or of DOM while the petitioners owned its stock did not put either in the real estate business, did not result in any physical danger or improvement to the property of either and, in the case of DOM, did not constitute "construction" even within the broad meaning of that term as used in Section 341(b).

110. 258 F.2d 537 (3d Cir. 1958).

112. 30 T.C. 1044, aff'd, 268 F.2d 617 (5th Cir. 1959).

113. Sterner, 32 T.C. 1144 (1959). See also the Tax Court decision in Abbott, 28 T.C. 795, 805, aff'd, 258 F.2d 537 (3d Cir. 1958), where the statement was made: "Indeed, it may be said that construction of a road is no less 'construction' than building an apartment house."

114. 38 T.C. 844 (1962).

115. 39 T.C. 886 (1963).

Cohen and Vernon M. McPherson,[117] the most recent cases to deal with the problem of preliminary activities and construction, can be reconciled with the earlier cases solely on the basis that they, unlike the earlier cases, did not involve FHA loans.

An even more liberal interpretation of "construction" has been applied to determine the point of completion. If anything remains to be done the courts will find that "construction" has not been completed. The extreme, thus far, is Glickman v. Commissioner,[119] where the buildings in question were entirely finished when the sale was made, but some minor landscaping and a final FHA inspection remained. The FHA had, however, made preliminary inspections and had permitted occupancy as the individual buildings were completed. In addition, the municipal authorities had issued their final certificate of occupancy. The cash distribution was made on January 13 and four days later the final FHA inspection was made. The Second Circuit, in holding that "construction" had not been completed, stretched the term almost to the breaking point by saying, ". . . [T]hat under the correct interpretation of the statute 'construction' should be defined technically to mean all construction required to perform the contract completely."

In Edward Weil,[121] a retaining wall and a parking lot remained to be constructed. In setting the outer limit of the word "construction," the court said, "the final completion could not be fixed earlier than the time when the project was ready to begin earning a 'substantial part' of the 'net income'. . . . " The Weil test is easier for the taxpayer to meet than the Glickman test since, in Glickman, the corporation could have begun, and as a matter of fact had begun, to earn a substantial part of its net income, but technically, had not completely performed the contract. A good example of how the Weil test can work to the taxpayer's advantage is Maxwell Temkin,[123] where repairs to walks, driveways, steps and a considerable amount of landscaping remained to be completed to fulfill the contract. These facts did not prevent the Tax Court from finding the construction had been completed, since the building had been occupied and producing rents for some time. Temkin and Weil, unlike Glickman, did not involve corporations using FHA financing and are, therefore, analogous to Cohen and McPherson, which were concerned with the beginning of construction. A recent revenue ruling [124] dealt with facts similar to those in Glickman. Following completion of construction as set forth in the plans and specifications, minor alterations and corrections (including a change of decor, removal of an obstruction and installation of rest rooms) were made. The alterations did not increase rental area, change the character of the structure or increase the fair market value or realizable net income of the building. This was not considered to be "construction." There is no indication whether an FHA commitment was involved. The ruling may be an indication that the Internal Revenue Service is retreating from its absolute position.

117. 21 TCM 583 (1962), involving employment of a land planning consultant and engineering firm.

119. 256 F.2d 108 (2d Cir. 1958). Cf. Epstein v. United States, 221 F.Supp. 479 (N.D.Ohio 1963), where the point was assumed for discussion but the decision was grounded on another issue.

121. 28 T.C. 809 (1957).

123. 35 T.C. 886 (1963).

124. Rev.Rul. 63–114, 1963–1 Cum.Bull. 74.

The final chapter on the judicial definition of "construction" has not yet been written. As to commencement and conclusion, there remains a sharp split of authority. Perhaps this dichotomy will be rationalized on the basis of the presence or absence of FHA guarantees. This rationale is, of course, a pure fiction. No good reason can be advanced to support the proposition that different rules should apply to two corporations with identical work remaining merely because one has obtained an FHA loan and the other has used conventional bank financing. Such a result is, obviously, a throwback to the philosophy of strict interpretation and congressional intent and an undue reliance on the fact of "view." The better rule of Weil and Temkin should be followed whether or not there was an FHA commitment.

Substantial Part

The Circuits are clearly split as to the interpretation of the words "a substantial part of the taxable income to be derived from such property." Section 341(b)(1), from which these words are drawn, declares that the collapsible provisions will apply when the sale or exchange is made before a substantial part of the corporation's net income has been earned. A major problem has arisen because of the courts' inability to agree on the time when these words should apply. The Fifth Circuit [126] has declared that "substantial part" refers to the income which the corporation has realized up to the time of the sale or exchange. Under this theory, if at the time of the sale or exchange the corporation *has realized* a "substantial part" of the net income to be realized, the corporation will not be collapsible within the meaning of Section 341. The Third Circuit,[127] on the other hand, has stated that "substantial part" means that the corporation cannot have a "substantial part" of its income *yet to be realized* at the time of the sale or exchange. A related problem is: What constitutes a "substantial part" since this term is not defined by the Code or Regulations?

A starting point is provided by the relatively early case of Levenson v. United States [128] wherein the court noted that Congress had given no indication of what per cent of income would be "substantial," and expressed its belief that the phrase would cause interpretive difficulty. The court said that, absent any amendment to the statute, determination would be made on an *ad hoc* basis "by the courts and local tax officials."

Whether pre-sale or post-sale income was to be used to determine if the substantial-part test has been met, was first considered in Abbott. The Third Circuit affirmed the Tax Court, believing that the lower court had followed the post-sale rule, and stated:

> The real question posed by the statute, however, is not whether a substantial part of the total profit was realized prior to dissolution but rather whether that part of the total profit realized *after* dissolution was substantial. This was the test correctly applied by the Tax Court in making its finding that the dissolution took place before a substantial part (nearly 90%) of the total profit was realized.

126. Commissioner v. Kelley, 293 F.2d 904 (5th Cir. 1961).

127. Abbott v. Commissioner, 258 F.2d 537 (3d Cir. 1958).

128. 157 F.Supp. 244 (N.D.Ala.1957).

However, James B. Kelley [132] (the next Tax Court case) indicated that the Third Circuit had misinterpreted the Tax Court's application of the substantial part test. In a sharply divided opinion (five judges dissented, including the judge who wrote Abbott), the Tax Court stated that it had not meant to follow the post-sale test, and did not believe that it had done so. On appeal, the Fifth Circuit affirmed [133] in a very comprehensive opinion. The court noted that the opinion of the Third Circuit in Abbott was a surprise to the Tax Court; it cited the lower court's opinion in Kelley, and took note of the position of the Commissioner and the taxpayer. The court stated, "The grit in the oil is that *a* substantial part has already been realized, but *a* substantial part remains to be realized, leaving plenty of life in the collapsible corporation device." Then, deciding in favor of the taxpayer, the opinion continued, "Section 117(m) requires only that '*a* substantial part' be realized. The indefinite article '*a*' says in plain language that there may be two or more substantial parts."

Kelley provides the better reasoned rule, since it interprets the statutory language clearly and precisely. Nevertheless, the split between the Circuits remains and is emphasized by the fact that the Internal Revenue Service has served notice that it will not follow Kelley [136] as well as by the fact that even the Kelley decisions were not unanimous. However, the present judicial trend clearly follows the Kelley doctrine.[137]

On the issue of what actually *is* a substantial part of the taxable income to be derived from the property, there has been a wide divergence of opinion among the courts. Some have held 50 per cent, 40 per cent, 33 per cent, and 34 per cent constituted a substantial part. On the other hand, 17 per cent, 10 per cent, and 9½ per cent have been held not to be a substantial part. It should be kept in mind that the "substantial part" in issue is a substantial part of the *taxable* rather than *net* income. And it also should be emphasized that the particular facts of the case are important. Thus, the Fifth Circuit has found one-third to be a substantial part and seventeen per cent to be insubstantial. In holding that thirty-four per cent was substantial, the Tax Court found no cases indicating that more than twenty per cent was insubstantial. Below twenty per cent will probably be held insubstantial; above thirty per cent will probably be held substantial. A case involving something between these two figures will be decided on the facts presented. Since no hard and fast rule can be established without legislative direction, in the exceptional case even the 20–30 per cent rule may not stand up. Prior to Kelley, the Internal Revenue Service followed a rule of thumb that over fifty per cent would be considered substantial. In view of the fact that the Service declines to follow Kelley, it can be expected to require at least fifty per cent in the future.

---

132. 32 T.C. 135 (1960).

133. Commissioner v. Kelley, 293 F.2d 904 (5th Cir. 1961).

136. Rev.Rul. 62–12, 1962–1 Cum.Bull. 321. In this regard, cf. Treas.Reg. § 1.341–5(c) (2) (1955).

137. Commissioner v. Zongker, 334 F.2d 44, 45–46 (10th Cir. 1964), refers to the Kelley decision as, "an exhaustive and penetrating treatment . . ." of the statutory meaning which is, "more plausible and certainly less penal." The court in Winn v. United States, 243 F.Supp. 282, 290 (W.D.Mo.1965) stated, "The opinion of Judge Wisdom appears to be unassailable unless one ignores the plain language of the statute . . .."

Present Availability of Section 341

Although several courts and the Internal Revenue Service have taken an overly stringent view of Section 341, there is, as Judge Wisdom has sagely noted "plenty of life in the collapsible corporation device." Regarding the present availability of Section 341, the following factors must be carefully considered:

1. *Negation of the Requisite View.* This can best be achieved by showing that prior to the time the corporation was "availed of," there was an absence of factors which would indicate that the taxpayer intended to utilize this corporation for tax avoidance purposes. For example, one might show; (1) other investments for long-term capital gains in this type of property, (2) absence of two classes of stock "so that one class could be redeemed as soon as the building was completed," (3) no FHA mortgage guaranty during construction. On the other hand, an uncontemplated occurrence after construction has been completed (decrease of rental income, increase of expenses, health reasons, increased valuation of the land because of activities of other landholders nearby) can also show a lack of the necessary view.

2. *Construction.* If the sale or exchange is early in the series of transactions, an argument should be made that construction has not begun, especially if the corporation has not relied upon an FHA guaranty. It also can be argued, on the basis of Maxwell Temkin, that Section 341 does not apply because the "view" did not exist until after the completion of construction.

3. *Substantial Part.* The better-reasoned rule of Commissioner v. Kelley should be followed in regard to when the corporation must earn a substantial part of its taxable income. If the Kelley rule is followed by the courts, a minimum of thirty per cent of the income will have to be earned by the corporation before the sale or exchange. Whereas, if the Abbott rule is followed, fifty per cent would seem to be necessary.

4. *Section 341(d) Limitations.* These exceptions become important only if the corporation is found to be collapsible.

   a. Seventy per cent rule. If less than seventy per cent of the gain is attributable to the collapsible property of the corporation, Section 341 is inapplicable. If a corporation which owns a building is later availed of to construct a second building, and the gain can be equally divided between the two buildings, the seventy per cent exception will absolve the taxpayer from any liability. This may be one of the most important means of escaping the burden of Section 341.

   b. Three year rule. If the corporation holds the property for three years following construction, before the shareholder sells or exchanges his stock, Section 341 does not apply. Care must be taken to see that construction is completed.

   c. Five per cent rule. A taxpayer who owns less than five per cent of the outstanding shares in a corporation is relieved from liability although the corporation is collapsible.

5. *Section 341(e).* In general, subsection (e) provides for an exemption from the collapsible provisions of Section 341 if the net unrealized appreciation of the corporation's subsection (e) assets does not exceed fifteen per cent of the corporation's net worth at the time of: (a) a sale or exchange of stock under Section 341(a) (1), (b) a complete liquidation under Section

341(a) (2), (c) a Section 333 partial liquidation, (d) a Section 337 dissolution. If it is suspected that the provisions of subsection (e) may be applicable to a particular fact situation, care should be taken to investigate this extremely complex subsection. The authorities listed above will undoubtedly prove extremely useful.

6. *Section 333.* If a corporation is found to be collapsible, but is able to take advantage of one of the exceptions in Section 341(d) or 341(e), then it is not a corporation to which Section 341(a) applies, and may qualify under Section 333. This section specifically states that it applies to complete liquidations other than a collapsible corporation to which Section 341(a) applies.

7. *Six-Month Rule.* If the sale or exchange is within six months from the time it was acquired, none of the collapsible corporation provisions will attach, inasmuch as Section 341 applies only to gains which would otherwise be long term capital gains.

8. *Election.* A timely election of Subchapter S is a possible solution to the collapsible problem, if the collapsible property of the corporation is not inventory.

9. *Section 337.* Under certain conditions, a taxpayer might be able to take advantage of Section 337.

10. *Section 341(f) Exception.* These provisions remove from the operation of Section 341, sales of stock during a six-month period after the corporation has consented to a recognition by it of future gain on its subsection (f) assets. The subsection (f) provisions are expected to provide assistance in cases of stock sales in a corporation which is "rapidly growing and expects to continue in business but which holds constructed or produced properties which are worth substantially more than their cost and upon which there has not been substantial realization of the profits to be derived from the properties."[163]

CONCLUSION

The foregoing shows that the collapsible corporation, while considerably limited in scope by statute, judicial decision, and the Internal Revenue Service, from what it once was, has by no means become a useless concept. In an attempt to plug the collapsible corporation loophole, Congress has succeeded only in constructing a confusing statutory framework which fails to do the job. This has resulted in a series of confusing and conflicting decisions by the courts. . . . The device of the collapsible corporation, when employed wisely and with the necessary safeguards, can be an effective tool in the hands of the skilled business-planning attorney.

As to the relationship between the collapsible corporation provisions and qualifying a liquidating sale of corporate assets under § 337, see pages 646–648, supra.

[163]. H.R.Rep. No. 1308 in U.S.Code Cong. & Ad.News, 88th Cong., 2d Sess. 3081, 3082 (1964).

Chapter 5

CORPORATE COMBINATIONS

Introduction

The combination of two or more corporations into a single unified enterprise constitutes one of the most complicated of all corporate transactions. Part of the difficulty in this area stems from the fact that a variety of techniques are available for achieving a combination; accordingly, some analysis of these different methods at the outset is essential. While the term "merger" has often been used to describe all types of combination transactions, strictly speaking "merger" refers to the statutory proceeding under which an existing corporation absorbs one or more other corporations, thereby succeeding to all of their assets, franchises and powers, and becoming liable for all of their debts, and the stockholders of the merged (i. e. disappearing) corporation or corporations receive stock or securities of the surviving corporation in exchange for their previous holdings. Obviously, so far-reaching a procedure as this rests entirely upon express statutory authorization, such as MBA §§ 65–70; and so does that close counterpart of merger, "consolidation," which is in essence nothing more than the merger of all of the existing corporations into a brand-new corporation, specially organized for the purpose. E. g., MBA § 66.

However, these express statutory techniques do not represent the only ways in which to achieve a combination. One obvious alternative for combining two corporations is for one of them to sell all of its assets to the other in exchange for the latter's stock. If the company which acquires the assets also assumes the selling company's liabilities, and the selling company distributes the stock it received to its stockholder in exchange for its own stock in a complete liquidation, the parties would end up in the same position as under a statutory merger.

Another method for amalgamating two corporations is for the acquiring corporation to acquire all (or substantially all) of the stock of the other corporation from the latter's stockholders, in exchange for stock of the acquiring corporation, thus turning all (or substantially all) of the stockholders of the acquired corporation into stockholders of the acquiring corporation. To be sure, this exchange of stock technique does not combine the two businesses under a single corporate roof as in a merger or asset acquisition. But there is little practical difference from the acquiring corporation's point of view between operating the acquired corporation's business directly as an outright-owned division and operating it through a controlled (if not wholly-owned) subsidiary; and in any event, the acquiring corporation would normally have the power to liquidate the subsidiary and thus reach the same end-point as under the other techniques.

SECTION 1. MECHANICS OF CORPORATE COMBINATIONS

A. IN GENERAL

Obviously, these different combination techniques vary quite widely in the corporate mechanics involved. (There may also be some important tax differences, as we will see later, although each of these combination techniques is included in the definition of "reorganization" for tax purposes.) The following represents one of the most thoughtful analyses of the non-tax aspects of these combination techniques, using the definitions applicable to tax-free-reorganizations under the Code as the point of departure:

DARRELL, THE USE OF REORGANIZATION TECHNIQUES IN CORPORATE ACQUISITIONS [1]

70 Harv.L.Rev. 1183–1206 (1957).

The subject to which the ensuing discussion is primarily addressed relates to the practical uses of the so-called tax-free-reorganization provisions of the Internal Revenue Code of 1954 in effecting corporate acquisitions of the stock or assets of existing corporations not already controlled by the acquiring corporation. While this topic is limited in scope, it encompasses an area of considerable practical importance. This is notably true in times which have witnessed the increasing popularity of business combinations.

It has been said on the basis of factual studies that the decision to effect a corporate acquisition is usually influenced more by business than by tax considerations, but that tax considerations usually do play an important role in the selection of the method by which an acquisition is carried out. Proposed corporate acquisitions considered desirable from a purely business standpoint have been known to succeed or to fail primarily because of tax and similar considerations. It is the purpose here to give primary attention to some of the principal factors, both tax and nontax, which bear upon the choice between taxable or

---

1. Copyright ©, Harvard Law Review Association, 1957. Reprinted by permission. Portions of the text and most of the footnotes omitted.

tax-free acquisitions and, if the latter is chosen, upon the selection of the statutory tool most suitable for use in a given situation.

[To qualify for tax-free treatment, a combination transaction must fall within one of the definitions of "reorganization" contained in clauses (A), (B), and (C) of § 368(a) (1), which, speaking generally provide as follows:]

Type (A)—"statutory merger or consolidation." This definition refers to a merger or consolidation effected under the statutory provisions of the applicable local corporation laws.

Type (B)—"the acquisition by one corporation, in exchange solely for all or a part of its voting stock, of stock of another corporation if, immediately after the acquisition, the acquiring corporation has control of such other corporation (whether or not such acquiring corporation had control immediately before the acquisition)." "Control" for this purpose "means the ownership of stock possessing at least 80 percent of the total combined voting power of all classes of stock entitled to vote and at least 80 percent of the total number of shares of all other classes of stock of the corporation."

Type (C)—"the acquisition by one corporation, in exchange solely for all or a part of its voting stock (or in exchange solely for all or a part of the voting stock of a corporation which is in control of the acquiring corporation), for substantially all of the properties of another corporation, but in determining whether the exchange is solely for stock the assumption by the acquiring corporation of a liability of the other, or the fact that property acquired is subject to a liability, shall be disregarded." The basic requirements of this definition are therefore that the acquisition must be solely for voting stock of the acquiring corporation and that substantially all of the properties of the other corporation must be acquired.

* * *

In considering a proposed corporate acquisition, one must be familiar with the glosses the courts have put not only upon the tax statute but also upon state corporation statutes. Indeed, the lawyer should do more; he should try to anticipate what, if any, further glosses may be added in the future. In other words, as with any other legal problem, a proposed corporate acquisition must be considered in lawyer-like fashion in all its facets, with full awareness of the risks that might be encountered under laws which are not static, if the proposed transaction appears to contain elements running counter to any general legal or equitable principle.

In working out an agreement for a contemplated corporate acquisition, the parties concerned must iron out their conflicting interests through negotiation, and this frequently entails considerable give and take. When reference is made in the following discussion to the desire of any particular party, the purpose is simply to provide a convenient introduction to a particular problem and by no means to suggest that such party has sufficient leverage to accomplish the desired end.

It will be necessary on occasion to paint with a broad brush. There are qualifications and refinements to almost any proposition, and this is especially true in the field of corporate reorganizations. In the interest of a better understanding of a difficult and complicated subject, technical refinements have in some respects been sacrificed, and what is said should be considered with this in mind. Without further preliminary discussion, we may now turn to a consideration of some of the principal factors, both nontax and tax, which bear upon the desirability of accomplishing a contemplated corporate acquisition through use of the tax-free-reorganization provisions and upon the choice of reorganization techniques. The factors to be discussed are by no means all-inclusive; other will doubtlessly come to mind. Those mentioned are thought to be the ones that are most commonly present.

I. Factors Other Than Federal Income Taxes

Antitrust Laws.— One of the foremost problems in connection with corporate acquisitions, once the business decision is made that an acquisition is desirable, is the problem of legality under the antitrust laws. Attention to these problems has recently been accentuated by the current activities in this field of the Department of Justice, the Federal Trade Commission, and congressional committees. As shown by the report of the Attorney General's Committee, the application of the antitrust laws is in a developing state and is by no means clear. The most painstaking and exhaustive factual and economic studies are usually required to determine the propriety of contemplated acquisitions; and, in the end, rarely is the answer wholly certain.

However, we are here concerned with the solution only of related problems. In the first place, there is no longer any general distinction for antitrust purposes between asset acquisition and stock acquisition in the elimination of competition or the creation of a monopoly. But in view of the Department of Justice's recent practice of seeking to enjoin proposed business combinations before they become effective, the time that would be required to complete the prospective reorganization may be an important factor in the choice of reorganization procedure when some antitrust risk is involved but the proposed combination is not a *cause celebre* and management upon the advice of counsel is prepared to go ahead without clearing with the Department. The greater the time required to complete the reorganization, the longer the opportunity to enjoin remains open.

Another antitrust problem to be considered in selecting the type of reorganization is the question whether the acquired business is to be kept segregated from the acquiring corporation's business either as a precaution or pursuant to the terms of a court order. . . .

* * *

Stockholders' Approval and Appraisal Rights.— Upon a statutory merger or consolidation, state statutes customarily require formal approval of the agreement of merger or consolidation by the stockholders of all constituent corporations. This usually means the holding of formal stockholders' meetings for this purpose and securing the prescribed favorable vote of the stockholders entitled to vote. Proxy-solicitation expenses, the preparing and filing of proxy statements, and other acts in compliance with applicable rules of the SEC and of any stock exchange on which the stock is listed may thus become necessary. Moreover, state merger-and-consolidation statutes usually give to dissenting stockholders of any of the constituent corporations the right to demand and receive in cash the appraised value of their shares. Though the merger or consolidation may be conditioned on there being no greater than a limited percentage of such dissenters, the dual problem of stockholders' approval and appraisal rights has sometimes proven troublesome.

Upon an acquisition involving the transfer of substantially all corporate assets, whether in a taxable transaction or a type (C) reorganization, approval by a substantial majority of the transferor corporations' stockholders is normally required. Formal approval by the acquiring corporation's stockholders is generally not required unless insufficient authorized stock is available to be issued for the assets, in which event authorization of the additional stock by the acquiring corporation's stockholders may be necessary.[44] State statutes often give appraisal rights to the transferor's dissenting stockholders but usually not to stockholders of the transferee.

Upon a stock acquisition, . . . no formal stockholders' approval is usually necessary, unless the stock to be acquired is owned by a corporation and approval of its stockholders is necessary to authorize the transfer, or unless approval by the acquiring corporation's stockholders is necessary to authorize the additional stock to be issued in the exchange. And there is normally no problem of stockholders' appraisal rights. In the case of a corporation having securities listed on the New York Stock Exchange, however, stockholders' approval will be required if directors, officers, or substantial stockholders have an interest in the acquired corporation or the stock to be issued represents an increase in outstanding shares of twenty percent or more.

Accordingly, upon consideration of these problems only, though a cash purchase might have some advantages from the standpoint of appraisal rights, as between the three types of reorganization the type

---

44. If the stock of the acquiring corporation is or is to be listed on any stock exchange, the rules of the particular exchange with respect to such matters as proxies and stockholders' meetings must of course be observed. For example, the New York Stock Exchange requires that approval of the acquiring corporation's stockholders be obtained when the new shares represent an increase in outstanding shares of 20% or more. N. Y. Stock Exchange, Company Manual at B–17 (1956).

(B) reorganization would normally rank first, the type (C) second, and the type (A) third.

Stockholders' Pre-emptive Rights.— Stockholders' pre-emptive rights are not involved in an acquisition when treasury stock is issued or, normally, in connection with the issuance of new stock in a statutory merger or consolidation. At common law, stock could be issued for an adequate consideration consisting of property other than money without violating stockholders' pre-emptive rights. But some corporate charters and possibly some state laws may modify the common-law rules so that such rights would be involved in connection with the creation and issuance of stock in an asset or stock acquisition whether or not in a tax-free reorganization. This factor, however, is usually not of great significance in corporate acquisitions.

Dilution of Stockholders' Equity.— The problem of equity dilution appears in practice to be very real and to bear very distinctly not only upon the type of reorganization to be used but indeed upon whether a tax-free-reorganization plan should be adopted at all.

The management of an acquiring corporation will normally be reluctant to recommend the creation and issuance of additional common stock to acquire the stock or assets of another corporation if the effect would be to reduce the prospective earnings per share of its own common stock, and may feel the same if the effect would be to reduce the book value or equity of such stock. In such cases the acquiring corporation's management may favor a taxable acquisition or, if the tax-free-reorganization approach is desired for other reasons, may cast about for some method within that area of alleviating this problem. Under the 1954 Code any kind of stock may be issued in a type (A) reorganization; but only voting stock — though it may be of any class or classes — may be issued in an asset or stock acquisition qualifying as a type (C) or type (B) reorganization. In the past, a limited preferred stock, voting or nonvoting according to the requirements, has frequently been used in such cases. Indeed, a special type of acquisition stock is sometimes devised, such as a voting preferred stock convertible into common stock at a value in excess of the current market price for the common. When this latter device is used, the objective of the acquiring corporation is usually the ultimate disposal of the common issued upon conversion of the preferred at more than market value at the time the preferred is issued for the assets. However, under the 1954 Code the issuance in a tax-free reorganization of any stock other than common stock in exchange for common stock, particularly of a closely held corporation, has distinctly less appeal than formerly, because the new stock so issued would normally be section 306 stock. The problem of stock dilution is accordingly now more difficult to solve within the framework of a tax-free reorganization.

* * *

Continuing Minority Interests in the Acquired Corporation.— Opinions may differ as to the advisability of having a corporate subsidiary with minority common stockholders. But ordinarily the existence of such minority interests is strongly disfavored by corporate management because it contains the seeds of potential dispute. Accordingly, the management of an acquiring corporation usually desires to avoid the possibility of any such continuing minority.

This, of course, would be automatically accomplished by a statutory merger or consolidation or an asset acquisition, whether taxable or tax free, for the vote of the required percentage of stockholders in favor of merger or consolidation or in favor of transfer of assets commits all stockholders of the corporation to be acquired, leaving to dissenters their cash appraisal rights. The acquiring corporation would then have nothing further to do with the stockholders of the acquired corporation. This result cannot, however, be ensured by a stock acquisition, whether or not pursuant to a tax-free reorganization, unless all the stockholders of the acquired corporation voluntarily agree to exchange or sell their stock.[57]

Creation of a Substantial Minority Voting Block in the Acquiring Corporation.— The problem of creation of too powerful a minority voting block in the acquiring corporation is often serious in the eyes of the acquiring corporation's stockholders or its management. This problem arises, for example, when the stock of the corporation to be acquired is in the hands of a family or closely related group and the corporation to be acquired is of such size that, if its stockholders receive ordinary common stock of the acquiring corporation, their stock, voted as a block, might be sufficiently powerful to give them effective voting control or at least a veto power. When it is desired to issue stock in an acquisition which qualifies as a tax-free reorganization, the following are among the possibilities that might be considered in this situation.

A nonvoting preferred stock or a nonvoting common stock of the acquiring corporation could be used if permitted by the governing state law, provided the acquisition is effected by statutory merger or consolidation. But if such preferred stock would be section 306 stock, it may not be acceptable. Moreover, there might be stock-exchange objections to the issuance of a nonvoting common stock if the stock is to be listed on a national stock exchange. . . .

Ordinary voting common stock might be issued, but the stock placed in a voting trust having acceptable voting trustees, with voting-trust certificates being given to the stockholders of the acquired corporation. This apparently can be done in any of the three types of tax-

---

57. But even in such a case it may sometimes be possible to eliminate the minority by a subsequent merger or other reorganization [particularly under the so-called "short-form" merger statutes which provide a simplified procedure for merger of an at least 90% owned subsidiary. See pages 730–735, infra.]

free reorganization under discussion inasmuch as, under the existing administrative view, pure voting trusts are in effect looked through for tax purposes and the voting-stock requirements of the reorganization sections are deemed satisfied if the underlying stock is voting stock regardless of who actually exercises the vote. However, one disadvantage of a voting-trust arrangement is that under state law such a trust is ordinarily not valid for more than ten years, and the voting-block problem would therefore be only deferred and not solved. . . .

It might be possible under state law to reduce the potential minority voting block by having the acquiring corporation create two classes of voting stock, each with one vote per share but with the shares of one class having a par value and relative worth many times greater per share than the shares of the other class. Use of the former as the acquisition stock would give the shareholders of the acquired corporation only a fraction of the voting power they would have if there were only one class of voting stock, except when a class vote is required. Perhaps the same result might be accomplished in some states by giving each class the same par or stated value per share, with one class receiving a greater vote per share than the other. This would seem acceptable from a tax-free-reorganization standpoint, since both classes would appear to be voting stock. But if either class had preferential rights as to dividends or assets it probably would be treated as "other than common stock" for purposes of section 306, regardless of what it might be called under state corporation law. Obstacles to having two classes of common stock are more likely to be encountered in connection with state corporate law, corporate-policy considerations, and rules of regulatory bodies or security exchanges.

Nonassignable or Burdensome Contracts and Franchises, Labor Unions, Deferred-Compensation Plans, Etc.—Sometimes the corporation that is to be acquired possesses valuable franchises, leases, or contracts which are not assignable without consent. In such cases a statutory merger or consolidation or, if consent to assignment would even then be required, a stock acquisition has an advantage over an asset acquisition in that the need to obtain consent to assignment is eliminated. Moreover, if assets are to be acquired, the task of attending to all the details involved in the transfer, such as the preparation and execution of deeds, would be simplified if the acquisition were by a statutory merger or consolidation. Again, state bulk-sales laws either would be of no concern or would not apply to an acquisition by statutory merger or consolidation, since the surviving or successor corporation automatically becomes responsible for all liabilities and a statutory merger or consolidation is not generally regarded as involving a sale. But a transfer in exchange for stock, in a type (C) reorganization or otherwise, probably does fall within the "sale" language of the bulk-sales statutes.

On the other hand, existing loan indentures or other agreements may contain restrictions upon a merger or consolidation or transfer of assets. If one or more mortgages are involved, after-acquired-property clauses therein might cause difficulty if a statutory merger or consolidation or asset acquisition were attempted. Undesirable leases or contracts including burdensome patent-license agreements may constitute an obstacle to a statutory merger or consolidation or a stock acquisition. Labor-union problems—the consequences, for example, of bringing a union or a different union into the picture — may present an obstacle to a statutory merger or consolidation or an asset acquisition but not to a stock acquisition. Problems of reconciling and meshing deferred-compensation plans of the corporations (including pension, profit-sharing, and stock-option plans as well as individual employment contracts and bonus policies) may present similar obstacles. Finally, the corporate charter of the corporation to be acquired may itself be important to preserve, as in the case of a banking corporation; or the preservation of the organization and its customers or even of an existing stock-exchange listing may make it desirable that the corporation to be acquired be technically the acquiring or surviving corporation or that its stock be acquired.

State and Local Taxation.— Not infrequently an asset acquisition, unlike a stock acquisition, will give rise not only to state or local excise taxes in connection with the transaction but will also involve some duplication of state or local franchise, business, and property taxes, including sales, use, transfer, or license taxes, and fees applicable to real estate, personal property, motor vehicles, and the like. Sometimes some of these extra taxes can be avoided entirely when the transfer is effected by operation of law through statutory merger or consolidation, and some of the duplication may be eliminated by timing the transfer so that it will occur at the end of the state fiscal or corporate tax year. The provisions of federal and state unemployment-insurance-tax laws relating to the period of employment required for employee coverage may, in combination with the federal credit provisions, involve extra taxes unless the acquisition is carefully timed so as to occur either at the end of the year or, if during the year, after the number of months of employment required for employee coverage has elapsed.

Known, Unknown, and Contingent Liabilities.— Freedom from responsibility for liabilities of the transferor or acquired corporation is frequently an important consideration in the eyes of the management of an acquiring corporation. When this is so, a simple clean-cut purchase of the desired property, leaving the transferor corporation with all responsibility for its own liabilities, has strong appeal. If, on the other hand, the acquisition is solely or largely for stock in a tax-free reorganization, problems may arise, depending upon the particular facts, as to the extent to which the acquiring corporation can escape from responsibility for the transferor or acquired corporation's actual and potential liabilities.

Upon a statutory merger or consolidation, the surviving corporation becomes liable for all obligations of the constituent corporations, whether or not known and disclosed and even though purely contingent at the time of merger or consolidation.* Some protection against contingent and unknown liabilities of a constituent corporation may nevertheless be obtained by providing in the agreement of merger or consolidation for withholding for a specified period of time part of the stock to be issued to the constituent corporation's stockholders, the stock so withheld to be sold at market or to be cancelled at a prescribed value to offset any such liabilities that arise within the specified period. If desired, certificates of contingent interest may be issued to represent the interests of the constituent corporation's stockholders in the stock so withheld. This procedure, however, should be approached with caution and with an awareness of the uncertainties of the tax consequences. . . .

A stock acquisition, whether or not in a type (B) reorganization, also involves the problem of unknown, undisclosed, and contingent liabilities, though the acquiring corporation in that case does not itself become responsible for them. Here, again, the acquiring corporation may be able to protect itself against over-payment for the stock acquired by insisting upon a suitable guarantee or escrow arrangement pending determination of such liabilities.

An asset acquisition, whether in a taxable purchase or in a type (C) reorganization, though usually accompanied by an express assumption of at least some of the transferor corporation's liabilities, has the distinct advantage over the other two procedures of enabling the acquiring corporation to obtain substantially all the assets of the other corporation without becoming responsible for any liabilities not specifically assumed by it under the agreement. But there would nevertheless remain in the case of a type (C) reorganization the problem of possible transferee liability.

Transferee Liability.— When management of the acquiring corporation is fearful of unknown contingent liabilities and cannot get or is not prepared to rely solely on the warranties of the principal stockholders of the corporation to be acquired, the question of potential transferee liability may become important. Though this sub-

---

* [Ed. note] E. g., MBA § 69(e). These statutes usually go on to provide, as § 69(e) does, that "neither the rights of creditors nor any liens . . . shall be impaired" by the merger. It seems generally to be assumed that these statutes require a showing of something akin to an "impairment of contract". Thus a creditor cannot block a proposed combination merely because "the quick asset condition of the consolidated company will, in relation to its liabilities, render it less desirable as a debtor from the viewpoint of current financial soundness than the constituent debtor". Cole v. National Cash Credit Ass'n, 18 Del.Ch. 47, 156 A. 183 (Ch.1931).

ject may be thought to relate primarily to federal income-tax problems, it is included here because of its potentially broader application.

In a type (A) reorganization by statutory merger or consolidation, the surviving corporation automatically, as a matter of corporate law, becomes responsible for all of the acquired corporation's liabilities, including its tax liabilities, whether it expressly assumes these liabilities or not. In a type (B) stock-for-stock reorganization there is no problem of transferee liability since the exchange of stock does not involve a transfer of the acquired corporation's assets.* If the acquired corporation is subsequently liquidated and the assets are distributed to the acquiring corporation as a stockholder, the acquiring corporation will be liable as a transferee under the same circumstances as any other stockholder.

In a type (C) reorganization the problem of transferee liability arises when there is no express assumption of liabilities by the acquiring corporation.[65] When an acquiring corporation purchases substantially all the assets of another corporation for cash in an arm's length transaction without assuming the latter's tax liabilities, it does not ordinarily become subject to transferee liability for such taxes. When, instead of paying cash, the acquiring corporation takes over such assets in exchange solely for stock, its freedom from liability as a transferee is uncertain. If the transaction is regarded as a *de facto* merger, if the acquiring corporation is merely a continuance of the debtor corporation, or if an intention to defraud can be found, there will probably be transferee liability on the part of the acquiring corporation. On the other hand, under the corporation law of some states the acquiring corporation does not become liable for the debts of the transferor corporation merely because the consideration to the transferor corporation is the stock of the receiving corporation. Should the acquiring corporation issue its stock directly to the transferor's stockholders, thus by-passing the transferor corporation as permitted in a type (C) reorganization, the risk of transferee liability on the part of the acquiring corporation becomes greater since, by deliberately by-passing the transferor, the transferee helped make it impossible for the transferor to pay.

On the question of transferee liability of the stockholders of the transferor corporation, the decisions indicate that, whether the transferor corporation actually receives the acquiring corporation's stock for its assets and then distributes it among its stockholders or whether upon acquisition of the assets the acquiring corporation's stock is issued by it directly to the transferor corporation's stockholders, the stockholders of the transferor corporation are liable

---

* [Ed. note] See Architectural Building Products, Inc. v. Cupples Products Corp., 221 F.Supp. 154 (E.D.Wis.1963).

65. Even when there is an express assumption of liabilities, problems of interpretation may arise. . . .

as between themselves and the Government as transferees for any unpaid income taxes of the transferor corporation even though the transferee corporation expressly assumed such liabilities. It has recently been held, however, that the transferor corporation's former stockholders are not so liable when the acquiring corporation acquired the stock of the transferor corporation in exchange for stock of the acquiring corporation and thereafter completely liquidated the transferor corporation. This decision seems sound if the distinction intended to be drawn is between a stock acquisition in a type (B) reorganization followed by complete liquidation of the acquired corporation and an asset acquisition in a type (C) reorganization followed by complete liquidation of the transferor corporation.

Documentary Stamp Taxes.— Federal stamp taxes are generally imposed on the issuance and transfer of stock and bonds. Stock-transfer taxes and other similar taxes are also imposed under the laws of some of the states, but only the federal taxes will be touched upon here.

In a statutory consolidation, an issue tax is due upon the issuance of stock in the resulting corporation to the stockholders of the constituent corporations. In a merger the issue tax normally applies to the stock of the surviving corporation issued to the stockholders of the merging corporation. If, however, the merger is accompanied by a recapitalization and the issuance of new or additional stock to the stockholders of the constituent that becomes the surviving corporation, an issue tax will be due on this stock to the extent that additional capital is dedicated. No transfer tax is imposed on the surrender for cancellation of stock of the constituent corporations for stock of the surviving corporation. However, transfer taxes are imposed upon the transfer of any stocks or bonds included among the assets of the constituent corporations other than any stocks or bonds of the constituent that becomes the surviving corporation. A transfer tax is also imposed on the delivery of the surviving corporation's stock to the stockholders of the other constituent corporations, based on the constructive receipt and distribution of this stock by such constituent corporation.[78] . . .

In the case of a type (C) reorganization, the rules are the same. . . . In a type (B) reorganization, there would of course

---

78. Raybestos-Manhattan, Inc. v. United States, 296 U.S. 60 (1935) . . . . [Ed. note: Actually, the transaction involved in the Raybestos case was not a statutory merger or consolidation, but was an asset acquisition, so that of course there was an actual, and not just a constructive, transfer of the acquiring corporation's stock by the acquired corporation to its stockholders. But the Court referred to the transaction as a "consolidation", and subsequent cases did not detect the misnomer. It is interesting to note that an accompanying transaction in Raybestos did constitute a statutory merger, and the Commissioner did not even assert the transfer tax as to that one. In any event the regulations now clearly call for the transfer tax in statutory mergers and consolidations. Reg. § 47.4321-2(a)(9). See Generally Branda, Going Public: Stamp Taxes, 21 N.Y.U.Inst. Fed.Tax. 1473 (1963).]

be an issue tax on the issuance of new shares of the acquiring corporation and a transfer tax on the transfer of the stock of the acquired corporation in exchange for such new shares.

* * *

A federal stamp tax is also imposed upon conveyances of realty sold. This tax applies to transfers for a consideration in a taxable or tax-free acquisition, but not to transfers pursuant to a statutory merger or consolidation. Along with various state taxes the stamp tax should be taken into account in determining the cost of a reorganization involving such transfers and in formulating the terms and time schedule for the reoganization.

NOTE ON THE APPRAISAL REMEDY FOR DISSENTING STOCKHOLDERS

There are a number of important questions in connection with the appraisal remedy upon which many of the statutes afford little guidance. Perhaps the most critical of these issues is whether appraisal is a dissenting stockholder's *exclusive* remedy whenever it is available. Outside of the handful of jurisdictions whose statutes expressly make the appraisal remedy exclusive, only a few courts have indicated that any substantial limitation on equitable relief would be inferred from the presence of an appraisal remedy, e. g., Blumenthal v. Roosevelt Hotel, Inc., 202 Misc. 988, 155 N.Y.S.2d 52 (Sup.Ct.1952); and even in those jurisdictions an attack for alleged "fraud" might well be entertained. This is the pattern expressly adopted in the new New York statute, N.Y.B.C.L. § 623. It does seem sound to require a stronger showing by a minority stockholder seeking to upset a transaction approved by a majority if an appraisal alternative was available to him. For an excellent analysis of this question, see Vorenberg, Exclusiveness of the Dissenting Stockholder's Appraisal Right, 77 Harv.L.Rev. 1189 (1964).

Another troublesome appraisal problem is valuation of the stock. Perhaps the most important issue here is how much weight to give to "market price" when there is a full and free market. The New York courts tend to regard market price as controlling, e. g., Application of Silverman, 282 App.Div. 252, 122 N.Y.S.2d 312 (1st Dept.1953); but Delaware, which has by far the greatest volume of litigation in this area, treats the market figure as just one of the relevant considerations. Chicago Corp. v. Munds, 20 Del.Ch. 142, 172 A. 452 (Ch.1934). In particular, as we have seen, the Delaware cases have generally insisted that a so-called "asset value" figure be included, to be weighted in the final result along with market value and/or a capitalization of earnings figure. See page 24 supra; Jacques Coe & Co. v. Minneapolis-Moline Co., page 774, infra.

Interest and costs also have a bearing on a dissenting stockholder's appraisal recovery. As to interest, some statutes, like MBA § 74, expressly provide for interest; and the courts have generally reached the same result where the statute is silent. As to costs, practically every statute has some such pattern as that of MBA § 74 which makes the corporation *prima facie* liable for costs, but allows the court to assess some or all of them against the shareholder under some circumstances.

Typically, the statutes elaborate the procedural requirements in great detail, but they differ widely on many particulars and of course fail to resolve a number of others. One recurring question is whether stockholders must be notified of their right to an appraisal. Like most other statutes, the Model Act contains no express requirement of such notification; and this omission cannot be lightly dismissed, in view of the fact that special attention was obviously given to the form and content of the notice applicable to important transactions like merger. E. g., MBA § 67. On the other hand, the court in Applestein v. United Board & Carton Corporation, discussed at pages 710–711 and 720–721, infra, assumed without hesitation that the equally silent New Jersey statute "inferentially required" notice to shareholders of their right to an appraisal. Construction of the state statute may be academic for corporations subject to the SEC proxy regulations, in view of the rule that any proxy solicitation on a matter carrying appraisal rights must include notice of the existence of the right and an outline of the statutory procedure for perfecting it. SEC Reg. X–14, Schedule 14 A, Item 2.

The timing of the procedure which a dissenting stockholder must follow may be a little tricky. For example, MBA § 74 requires the stockholder to file a written objection to the proposed corporate action *prior to or at* the pertinent meeting of the shareholders; in addition the shareholder must make a written demand within ten days after the stockholders' vote. However, the significance of the "objection", as distinguished from the "demand", is not clear in view of the fact that when the statute goes on to provide that a shareholder who fails to seek the appraisal shall be "bound by the terms of the proposed corporate action", it refers only to a failure to make the "demand within the ten day period", and does not mention the earlier requirement of the written objection. The provision eliminating all shareholder rights once appraisal is sought is similarly conditioned only upon the "demand."

There may also be questions as to the kind of stock interest which is eligible for appraisal. Thus unlike the Model Act the new New York corporation statute, following the line of its predecessor, confines the appraisal remedy to voting stock. N.Y.B.C.L. § 910. And under all statutes there are questions of what kinds of beneficial holders may qualify — i. e., voting trust certificate holders, transferees of stock after the record date, etc.

See generally, Manning, The Shareholder's Appraisal Remedy: An Essay for Frank Coker, 72 Yale L.J. 223 (1962).

B. SECURITIES REGULATION ASPECTS

1. IN GENERAL

DARRELL, THE USE OF REORGANIZATION TECHNIQUES IN CORPORATE ACQUISITIONS [2]

70 Harv.L.Rev. 1188–1192 (1957).

Registration Under the Securities Act of 1933 and Compliance With the Securities Exchange Act of 1934 and State Blue-Sky Laws.— The burden and expense of compliance with these laws and the effect upon corporate policies of the disclosure requirements are often quite substantial.

(a) A public offering of additional stock of a corporation to provide funds with which to purchase the stock or assets of another corporation normally entails the preparation and filing of the detailed registration statement required for registration of additional stock under the Securities Act of 1933 and compliance with all applicable rules of the Securities and Exchange Commission with respect to the public offering and sale of the stock.[21] . . .

Under rule 133 of the SEC, the issuance of stock by a corporation to acquire the assets of another corporation in a transaction qualifying under the Internal Revenue Code as a type (A) reorganization or as a typical type (C) reorganization (one followed by immediate liquidation of the transferor corporation) is normally exempt from the registration requirements when, pursuant to state statute or charter provisions, the merger, consolidation, or transfer of assets is submitted to a vote of stockholders binding on all stockholders except for appraisal rights.[23] But the Commission has recently proposed complete reversal of this rule.* The alleged grounds for this proposed change in policy are that, "with the development of the economy and changes in the tax statutes, there has been a tremendous increase in . . . mergers, consolidations and acquisitions of assets which affect materially the rights of security holders" and that, "unless the company's

---

2. Copyright ©, Harvard Law Review Association, 1957. Reprinted by permission. Portions of the text and most of the footnotes omitted.

21. No formal registration is required in connection with the offer of one corporation to purchase for cash the stock of another corporation, but rule X-10B-5 . . . has to be borne in mind. . . .

23. This rule follows a long-standing interpretation of the statute based on the theory that no "sale" is involved in such mergers or acquisitions and, for the purposes of the registration requirements, excludes such transactions from the definitions of the terms "sale," "offer," "offer to sell," and "offer for sale." . . .

* [Ed. note] That proposed new rule was never adopted. However, in 1959 there were some important amendments to Rule 133, which are analyzed immediately following these excerpts from Darrell.

securities are listed on a national securities exchange, in which event a proxy statement under the Commission's proxy rules must be furnished if proxies are solicited, these transactions may occur without the disclosure of adequate information to security holders."

Registration is required for the issuance of stock to acquire stock of another corporation in a type (B) reorganization whenever a public offering is involved. Normally, an exemption from registration would be available in such a transaction only if it could be brought within the limited exemption under the Commission's regulation A, . . . [or if] the stockholders to whom the stock of the acquiring corporation is to be offered in a type (B) reorganization are sufficiently limited in number and informed, and have the requisite bona fide investment intent [to qualify the transaction as a private offering].

(b) The Securities Exchange Act of 1934 and the SEC's rules and regulations thereunder contain registration and reporting requirements applicable to all corporations whose securities are listed upon a national securities exchange. The registration procedures to be followed in connection with reorganizations of these types vary with the circumstances. As an example of the reporting requirements, a form 8–K must be filed within ten days after the close of the month in which a corporation subject to the act makes an acquisition if the acquisition involves a "significant amount" of assets or results in an increase in the amount of stock outstanding and the increase (including all increases not previously reported) exceeds five per cent of the outstanding shares.[29] An acquisition of stock is considered an indirect acquisition of assets of the acquired company if control is acquired.

. . .

Mention might be made in passing of the provisions of section 16(b) of the Securities Exchange Act of 1934. . . . A transfer of stock in exchange for stock in any one of the three types of reorganization under consideration is a sale and the acquisition of the acquiring corporation's stock in such a reorganization is a purchase within the meaning of this provision, except to the extent exempted by SEC rule. The Commission has exempted in rule X–16B–7 certain acquisitions and dispositions of securities pursuant to mergers and consolidations (including mergers accomplished through acquisition by one company of substantially all the assets of another in exchange for stock of the former which is distributed by the latter to its stockholders), whether taxable or nontaxable. But this exemption applies only — and then with qualifications — when the surviving or acquiring corporation (not including the resulting company in a case of consolidation) either owned eighty-five percent or more of the equity securities or held over

---

29. . . . There is an acquisition of a "significant amount" of assets if the net book value thereof exceeds 15% of the total assets of the acquiring corporation, or the gross revenues of the acquired company for its last fiscal year exceed 15% of the aggregate gross revenues of the acquiring corporation for its last fiscal year. . . .

eighty-five percent of the combined assets taken at book value of all the companies involved in the merger or consolidation. . . .

(c) Almost all states have blue-sky laws of one sort or another. . . . The burden of compliance with the differing laws of many states can be a very substantial one, and the choice of acquisition method affects the need for compliance.

Compliance with these laws is generally required in connection with any offering of stock to residents of the respective states. In the case of a stock-for-stock exchange in a type (B) reorganization, qualification of the stock and sometimes registration of the issuing corporation as a dealer are required whenever some specific exemption is not available. While views as to this may vary, the other two types of reorganization with which we are here concerned are generally not regarded as falling within the purview of state blue-sky laws, except in California and possibly in several other states in which regulation is more comprehensive.[40]

2. RULE 133

LOSS, SECURITIES REGULATION [3]

2d ed. 1961, 534–539.

The present Rule 133: . . . the Commission in July 1959 redesignated the existing Rule 133 as 133(a), [and] added paragraphs (b)–(f). . . .

Paragraph (f) merely defines two terms used in the rule: A "constituent corporation" is "any corporation, other than the issuer, which is a party to any transaction specified in paragraph (a)": for example, Company A when it merges into Company B. And an "affiliate" is "a person controlling, controlled by or under common control with a specified person." The rest of the new language, in effect, imposes the status of an "underwriter" on two categories of persons in "no sale" transactions, corresponding with the selling-for and buying-from portions of the definition of "underwriter" in § 2(11) of the act.

(1) Paragraph (b) imposes the status of an "underwriter" on any person who *sells for* the issuer in connection with a distribution. It makes no difference whether he is buying the issuer's securities from security holders of a constituent corporation with a view to their distribution or offering or selling them for such persons, as long as he is acting "pursuant to any contract or arrangement, made in connection with any transaction specified in paragraph (a), with the issuer or

---

40. Section 401(j) (6) (C) of the Uniform Securities Act . . . would not normally require blue-sky qualification or registration in type (A) and type (C) reorganizations.

3. Reprinted by permission of the publisher, Little, Brown & Co. Portions of the text and all footnotes except number 256 have been omitted.

with any affiliate of the issuer." In other words, when A merges into B, a dealer who agrees with B (or an affiliate of B) to distribute the B securities received by A's stockholders is an "underwriter." Here there are no exceptions other than arrangements limited to the matching and combination of fractions among security holders of the constituent corporation and then selling for them whatever fractional or whole interests may need to be sold in order to adjust for fractions which survive the matching process. In effect, paragraph (b) codifies the views expressed in the [two previously decided delisting cases] which . . . represented nothing basically new.

(2) Paragraph (c) imposes the status of an "underwriter" on any constituent corporation (or any affiliate of a *constituent corporation* as of the date of submission of the "no sale" transaction to stockholders) buying from the issuer for distribution; and it expressly provides that the constituent's transfer of the issuer's securities to its own security holders by way of complete or partial liquidation is not a "distribution." The actual language is in terms of any constituent corporation or affiliate which "acquires securities of the issuer in connection with such ("no sale") transaction with a view to the distribution thereof." The word "acquires" was presumably intended to soften the anomaly of a "purchase" by the constituent corporation from the issuer under paragraph (c) when there is no "sale" by the issuer to the constituent corporation under paragraph (a)—although it is difficult to see how the Commission can stretch its power under § 19(a) to define "technical terms" so as to make an "underwriter" out of a person who does not sell for the issuer unless, in the language of § 2(11), he has "purchased from" the issuer. At any rate, paragraph (c), in effect, codifies the views expressed in the Commission's anonymous release of late 1957,* and hence is the only part of the amended Rule 133 which really breaks new ground.[256]

* [Ed. note] That release is described by Professor Loss (532) as follows:
A merger had been authorized by the boards of both companies over the objection of one director of the company to be merged who represented a trust which was the largest single stockholder. It was understood that this trust might effect a distribution of the surviving company's shares which it would receive in the merger. SEC counsel advised that no question would be raised with respect to the merger itself, but that the trust would be a statutory underwriter if it acquired the shares with a view to distribution. Thereupon the issuer registered the shares issuable in the merger. and the prospectus consisted essentially of the information contained in the proxy statement of the surviving company.

256. . . . Actually, if the trust [in the 1957 release] which was the largest single stockholder of the constituent corporation in that case was nevertheless not in a control relationship with that corporation and hence not an "affiliate" as defined in Rule 133(f), it was not an "underwriter" as that term is now defined in Rule 133(c). On the other hand, there is nothing new in Rule 133(c) in so far as it makes an "underwriter" out of a *constituent company* which *sells its assets* for securities of another company which it takes with a view to a distribution rather than a liquidating dividend; for . . . the sale-of-assets case, properly considered, always did involve

Sec. 1 *DE FACTO MERGER DOCTRINE* 697

On that account, paragraph (c), unlike paragraph (b), is subject to an exception which is designed to define a "distribution." This is the function of paragraphs (d) and (e) of the amended rule: There is no "distribution," and hence the constituent corporation or affiliate is not an "underwriter," if it sells during any six-month period, in normal brokers' transactions, not more than one percent of the shares or other units outstanding or, when the security is traded on an exchange, the lesser of that amount or the largest reported volume of trading in any of the four calendar weeks preceding the receipt of the brokerage order. Since these quantitative rules of thumb are modeled on the rule (to be examined later) which interprets the exemption in § 4(2) for unsolicited brokers' transactions, much of the administrative gloss which has been developed there may be expected to carry over to the new Rule 133. Having in mind the brokerage rule, the Commission later referred to paragraphs (d) and (e) as representing

> an effort to recognize that, in a situation where a trading market may be availed of by other persons receiving securities in a Rule 133 transaction, it would be less than realistic to permit a controlling person of a constituent company less latitude in trading transaction than he had before consummation of the Rule 133 transaction and, indeed, less than a controlling person of the issuer itself.

* * *

. . . the new rule, like any legislative reform, will undoubtedly create interpretative problems of its own. What about the Commission's 1957 dictum, for example, to the effect that the "no sale rule" does not apply when the persons negotiating the merger or the like "have sufficient control of the voting stock to make a vote of stockholders a mere formality"? Suppose a majority or two-thirds of the merging corporation's stock is owned by one person and the rest by a hundred small stockholders. Presumably the new portions of Rule 133 will determine the necessity of registration in the event of a resale. And, although the Commission has not withdrawn its dictum, it would be surprising, after all the turmoil, to find it insisting that the submission of the proposed merger to a vote of the stockholders in the hypothetical case is itself an "offer" (and a public one) which must be preceded by registration.

C. THE DE FACTO MERGER DOCTRINE

As Mr. Darrell indicates in his article, the differences in corporate mechanics among the various combination techniques may provide

a private sale from the asset-buying company to the asset-selling company ("constituent") followed by a "no sale" liquidating dividend. . . .

the basis for selection of one method over another. Consider the right of appraisal for dissenting shareholders: while practically every corporation statute affords this remedy to the stockholders of both corporations in connection with a statutory merger, a number of statutes do not provide appraisal in connection with an assets acquisition, and apparently no statute requires it where the exchange of stock technique is employed. Obviously, a management anxious to avoid appraisal proceedings will veer away from the merger technique. However, the fact that the ultimate objective of the other two combination methods is the same as in a merger has led to contentions that although a particular transaction took the form of an asset or stock acquisition, it was really in substance a merger and hence subject to the rules governing such transactions. This is known as the "de facto merger" doctrine.

FOLK, DE FACTO MERGERS IN DELAWARE: HARITON v. ARCO ELECTRONICS, INC.[4]

49 Va.L.Rev. 1261–1289 (1963).

I. Background

The Delaware Supreme Court's recent decision in Hariton v. Arco Electronics, Inc., represents a decisive moment in the development of the *de facto* merger doctrine. This concept has been invoked in connection with two typical techniques of corporate combination other than mergers themselves—sales of corporate assets and stock acquisitions. The archetypal argument, which is often embellished with variations thought suitable to the factual context, is that the transaction, despite attempts to give it another form, is indeed a merger, and therefore certain incidents characteristic of statutory mergers must be attached to it. The usual object of such arguments, unworthy motives aside, is to enjoin the transaction for want of adequate consideration or to enforce shareholder voting or appraisal rights. In Delaware, a merger requires a two-thirds vote of the shareholders of all participating corporations, with appraisal rights for dissenters. A sale of assets, on the other hand, requires only the consent of a majority of the selling corporation's shareholders, with no appraisal rights, and nothing more is needed for a stock acquisition than the approval of the board of directors. Thus, the *de facto* merger concept is primarily a function of the differing features of mergers, assets sales, and stock acquisitions. By treating the last two as covert mergers, the doctrine makes certain consequences of amalgamation identical whatever formal technique is used. . . .

4. Reprinted by permission of the Virginia Law Review Association. Portions of the text and most of the footnotes omitted.

A. *The Hariton Case*

In Hariton v. Arco Electronics, Inc., the purchasing corporation (Loral) acquired the assets of a much smaller enterprise (Arco). The two companies were in complementary phases of the electronics business: Loral was at the research-development-production end and Arco was a distributor. The negotiations were at arms length; there was no stock or director interlock; and concededly the transaction was not "unfair." The "Reorganization Agreement and Plan" called for a transfer of all Arco assets to Loral, the assumption of all Arco liabilities by Loral, and the issue of Loral stock to Arco. In turn, Arco was to dissolve, and it was to distribute the Loral stock to the Arco shareholders.[9] A shareholder of Arco sued to enjoin the transaction on the ground that it was a *de facto* merger, invalid for non-compliance with the merger provisions of Delaware law. In sustaining Arco's motion for summary judgment, the vice-chancellor held that the transaction was a true sale of assets and not a *de facto* merger. . . .

* * *

C. *De facto Mergers: The Pennsylvania Approach*

The pivotal case of recent years, Farris v. Glen Alden Corp.,[19] articulates an approach which the Delaware decisions, culminating in Hariton, reject for the most part without full discussion. At the time that case was decided, Pennsylvania recognized appraisal rights for shareholders of most corporations participating in a merger and for shareholders of a corporation selling all or substantially all of its assets other than in the regular course of business. In Farris, Glen Alden agreed to purchase the assets of List, a holding company for subsidiaries doing a variety of businesses, none of which resembled Glen Alden's activities. The assets of the companies were nearly equal, but List's long-term debt was about seven times that of Glen Alden. Glen Alden agreed to issue a large block of its shares to List, and List in turn agreed to dissolve and distribute the stock to its shareholders. A Glen Alden shareholder sued to enjoin the transaction, asserting that it was a *de facto* merger which failed to comply with Pennsylvania merger requirements. The Pennsylvania Supreme Court, in granting the injunction, held alternatively that (1) the transaction was in substance a merger, and (2) even if it were not, the nominal purchaser (Glen Alden) was the real seller, whose shareholders consequently had an appraisal right under the sale-of-assets statute.

The *de facto* merger holding was based on a variety of factors which the court found in the transaction, including a complete change in the nature of the corporation's business, the doubling of the size of

---

9. Arco had issued an outstanding 486,500 Class A shares and 362,500 Class B shares, a total of 849,000 shares. A single family owned 293,700 of the Class A and all of the Class B, a total of 656,200 shares. At the meeting, 652,050 shares—over 76%—were voted for the plan, and none against it.

. . .

19. 393 Pa. 427, 143 A.2d 25 (1958).

the successor corporation, a shift in control of the board of directors to the selling corporation, the purchaser's assumption of the seller's liabilities, a reduction of the proportionate interest of the purchasing corporation's shareholders in the successor corporation plus a sharp drop in the book value of their shares, and the fact that the selling corporation dissolved and distributed the shares it received to its shareholders. Evidently, in the court's view, no one of these factors alone can transform an assets sale into a merger, but the court did not disclose the precise combination of factors which would. Indeed, some of the factors are to be found in many assets sales of impeccable legitimacy.

The specific features of the transaction in Farris are noted at the outset because they highlight its unusual character. Moreover, the "tests" stated by the court are so inclusive that it becomes difficult to make a satisfactory delineation between a *de facto* merger and a legitimate sale of assets. After stressing the consequences of the transaction and the purposes of the merger statute, the court suggested that the test for a *de facto* merger was whether the transaction (1) destroys the "essential nature" of the purchasing corporation by "fundamentally chang[ing its] corporate character" and (2) "alter[s] the original fundamental relationships of the shareholders among themselves and to the corporation. . . ." If this is true, the shareholder is compelled "against his will [to] accept shares in another" corporation. Charter amendments may also have drastic results, but, although shareholders must approve them, rarely do dissenters have appraisal rights. And directors may embark the corporation on a new and risky enterprise without shareholder approval, let alone appraisal rights.

The court in Farris scrupulously skirted the question whether the appraisal right is constitutional or merely statutory, but in holding a sale of assets to be a *de facto* merger it easily avoided that issue, perhaps intentionally. The effect of the decision is to compel the legislature to be ultra-specific if it wishes to withdraw appraisal rights from any transaction having the form of an assets sale but the substance of a merger. . . .

Alternatively, Farris held the transaction to be "upside-down," finding that Glen Alden was the "real" seller and only nominally the purchaser. As a result, the court said that Glen Alden shareholders had appraisal rights under the sale-of-assets statute. Presumably, the features which evoked the *de facto* merger holding dictated this conclusion, but the most relevant factors seem to be the favored position of the real purchaser (the nominal seller) in directorships in the successor corporation and the disproportionate share of the equity and book value the List shareholders obtained in the successor corporation.

D. *De Facto Mergers: Development of the Delaware View*

Perhaps the foremost case articulating the Delaware position is Heilbrunn v. Sun Chem. Corp.[28] There a large corporation (Sun) acquired a much smaller enterprise through the exchange of its common stock and the assumption of all of the seller's liabilities. The seller agreed to dissolve and distribute the Sun stock to its shareholders, who thus became shareholders of Sun. A shareholder of Sun, the *purchaser* (rather than the seller as in Hariton), sought to enjoin the transaction as a *de facto* merger which did not comply with the merger statute, but the suit was unsuccessful. The court stated its holding in terms of denying a shareholder of the purchaser standing to object to the transaction, reserving any question as to the rights of a shareholder of the seller to invoke the *de facto* merger doctrine. The court easily distinguished the fact situation from that in Farris. The Sun shareholders did not become shareholders of a different sort of enterprise, for both corporations were engaged in the business of manufacturing organic pigments; hence "the business of Sun will go on as before, with additional assets." The transaction was not "upside-down," since the seller was far smaller than the purchaser, although strictly speaking this is irrelevant in Delaware, except so far as it might indicate a *de facto* merger.[31]

More recently, in Orzeck v. Englehart,[32] the Delaware court applied the Hariton and Heilbrunn principles to a corporate fusion accomplished through a stock acquisition and also dealt with the problem of the "upside-down" transaction. Here the purchasing corporation (Olsen) acquired the shares of seven California corporations under Delaware statutory authority. The purchasing corporation "was engaged for many years in the production of airplanes and related enterprises. More recently it has become . . . an 'empty shell.'" The corporations whose shares were purchased "were engaged in the egg business" in California. In rejecting the contention that the transaction was a *de facto* merger, the court extended the propositions advanced in Hariton and relied on the fact that, although the results of a stock acquisition and a merger are virtually identical, the two procedures have an "independent legal significance." Also, the court ruled that the alternative holding of Farris v. Glen Alden Corp.—that the court may realign the parties to an assets sale to determine the true seller—is inapplicable to a stock purchase, since the "incidents and results" of stock purchases and assets sales are "substantially different." According to the court, this is chiefly because an assets sale creates "an identity

---

28. 38 Del.Ch. 321, 150 A.2d 755 (Sup. Ct.1959), affirming 37 Del.Ch. 552, 146 A.2d 757 (Ch. 1958).

31. Since no one has appraisal rights in an assets sale in Delaware, realigning the parties serves no apparent purpose, as it does in a state whose statute grants appraisal rights to the seller's shareholders.

32. 192 A.2d 36 (Del.Ch.1963).

of corporate interests," whereas in a stock purchase "the interests remain separate and distinct."

The Delaware decisions and the Farris case are quite distinct. Apart from the alleged upside-down features of the Olsen stock purchase in Orzeck, the Delaware court has not faced a problem having common features with the Glen Alden transaction. And in turn, the Pennsylvania court has not had to consider the application of the *de facto* merger concept to a stock purchase since its formulation in the Farris case. Consequently, issue has not clearly been joined between the courts yet.

II. SALE OF CORPORATE ASSETS

A. *"Compliance With the Statute"*

The Delaware cases have clearly indicated that a necessary, if not wholly sufficient, condition for sustaining a sale of assets against a *de facto* merger attack is a finding, either explicit or implied, that the transaction complies with the terms of the sale-of-assets statute. . . .

1. *Statutory Formalities.* Both in Hariton and in Heilbrunn, the court impliedly recognizes that substantial non-compliance with the sale-of-assets statute will void the transaction. In each case, the form prescribed by the Delaware statute for a sale of assets was scrupulously observed. Where there is some significant deficiency in this regard, the purported sale of assets may fail, although the transaction will not necessarily be treated as a *de facto* merger. Thus, in [prior cases] transactions cast in the form of a sale of assets were set aside because the consideration for the assets passed, not to the selling corporation, but directly to its shareholders. . . .

* * *

3. *Achieving More Than a Mere Sale of Assets.* Assuming formal compliance with the statute and no breach of duty or other disqualifying conduct, a sale of assets might still be set aside if it accomplishes more than the literal language of the statute permits, *i. e.*, merely selling off the assets. . . .

The question is whether a formally perfect and fair sale-of-assets plan should be vitiated because some other formally perfect and fair procedure, such as liquidation, is coupled with it. At the very least, Hariton means that conditioning a sale of assets upon a mandatory dissolution of the selling corporation does not expose the transaction to attack as a *de facto* merger, despite results which are identical to those of a merger. This result rests on the rejection of a step-transaction doctrine in Hariton. It is also significant, however, that the Delaware cases which have rejected the *de facto* merger doctrine have all involved transactions of a fairly "normal" character, instead of a lopsided transaction such as that in the Farris case. The question is whether form and form alone is controlling, despite the results which follow, and from Hariton it certainly seems to control if the only feature is a result identical to a merger.

B. *Farris v. Glen Alden Corp. and Hariton: A Comparison*

Farris v. Glen Alden Corp. is valuable for discussing a number of factors which induced at least one highly responsible court to treat an assets sale as a *de facto* merger. It is instructive to consider the relevance of each of these factors to the Delaware case development.

(1) The fact that a purchaser's post-transaction business is completely changed evidently weighed heavily in the Pennsylvania court's finding that the combination brought about a substantial change in the nature of the shareholder's investment. However, this may be a completely inappropriate consideration. The very reason for a sale of assets may be not only to enable the purchaser to expand the business it is presently engaged in, but also to allow it to diversify, perhaps moving from a declining into a growth industry. The fact that the change of business takes place by combination, rather than by a charter amendment or internal expansion, seems immaterial, and those who would use the *de facto* merger doctrine to ensure the same results whatever the form might well consider that a change of business by means other than corporate combination would grant none of the rights the *de facto* merger doctrine does. Nor is change of business an identifying mark of a covert merger, for many mergers leave the type of business unchanged. Under the Delaware court's view in Hariton, the change or absence of change in the business of the parties to the assets sale is immaterial if the sale-of-assets statute is strictly complied with.

(2) An increase in the size of the purchaser was also stressed in Farris. But size is not necessarily material, because some size increase is an inevitable result of any assets sale. Certainly, if the purchaser becomes enlarged four- or fivefold after the transaction the situation is unusual, but Farris actually did not present that question, since the corporations there were approximately of equal size. And it will be recalled that Hariton and Heilbrunn each involved a large corporation acquiring a small one. Moreover, the possibility of such an unusual situation occurring in Delaware involves more academic than practical considerations. For if there are no appraisal rights on an assets sale, there is no incentive to adopt the peculiar amalgamation technique condemned in Farris, and if a state allows appraisal rights to the selling corporation's shareholders, there is no reason to cast the transaction in the queer form of a large corporation selling to a small purchaser, e. g., General Motors selling out to Studebaker-Packard, for this merely means more dissenters seeking appraisal rights. But certainly, to take the Farris situation, it is odd to suggest that because the purchaser and seller are of equal size, there can be no genuine sale of assets, only a merger. Whatever its relevance in Pennsylvania, a size

increase seemingly has no bearing on the question of compliance with the statute under the Hariton doctrine.

(3) Another factor relied upon by the Pennsylvania court in Farris was that the purchaser assumed the seller's liabilities. To give weight to this factor is subtly to commit the logical fallacy of saying that because every merger entails the assumption of liabilities, every assumption of liabilities implies a merger. From the standpoint of creditors and, more generally, of the public, it is desirable for the purchaser to assume the seller's liabilities, particularly in light of the confusion about the rights of the seller's creditors after an assets sale. Indeed, the problem is one of encouraging purchasers to shoulder liabilities, not of discouraging it. Additionally, since the assumption of selected liabilities scarcely negatives a "true" assets sale, to assert that the assumption of all liabilities does so is not persuasive.

(4) In Farris, despite the nearly equal size of the two corporations, the purchaser's shareholders had a much smaller proportionate interest after the transaction. However, this point is inconclusive. Whenever the purchasing corporation issues shares for assets, absent pre-emptive rights, the proportionate interest of the old shareholders is necessarily diluted, and it is natural for existing shareholders, particularly in a close corporation, to wish to guard against this. But this reasoning, extended logically, would mean that whenever a purchaser uses its own shares to buy another corporation's assets (as all sale-of-assets statutes permit), there is a *de facto* merger. However, if the assets transferred are approximately equal in value to the original assets of the purchasing corporation and yet the seller acquires an excessive proportion of the purchaser's shares, the facts may point to an excessive consideration calling for judicial inquiry. Nevertheless, were this the case in an avowed merger, the same sort of inquiry would be in order. Hence, this factor is logically irrelevant to the *de facto* merger issue.

(5) The fact that the book value per share of the purchaser's old shareholders was markedly diminished by the asset acquisition may be disposed of in a similar fashion. The implication again is that the purchaser gave an excessive consideration which may be traceable to fraud, breach of duty, pressing needs of the purchaser which induce it to part with a large consideration, or a legally permissible misjudgment on the part of the purchaser's directors.

(6) The Farris court also considered the mandatory dissolution of the seller to be an important factor in its decision, but if Hariton proves only one thing, it is that this feature is not indicative of a *de facto* merger in Delaware.

(7) A final point stressed in Farris—that the nominal seller's directors succeed to a large majority of the purchaser's board posts—also goes to the issue of an excessive consideration.

In sum, these individual factors seem only marginally relevant, at best, to the question when a sale of assets becomes a *de facto* merger. It is doubtful whether any of them would be regarded as persuasive in Delaware, since they do not bear on the question of compliance with the sale-of-assets statute. . . .

A further question is whether some combination of these factors points to a concealed merger, and indeed the court in Farris apparently relies chiefly on the presence of factors (3), (4), (6), and (7). First, if each factor standing alone is only marginally persuasive, grouping together a number of them is not certain to carry conviction. The dilution of the interest of the purchaser's shareholders and the enhanced power of the seller's directors in the new enterprise are defects not logically related to the form of the transaction. On the other hand, the mandatory dissolution of the seller and the assumption of the seller's liabilities by the purchaser are characteristic of a merger. As between these two groups, it is uncertain which is the more significant. If the "oddball" features of the Farris transaction are controlling, then (1) Farris is less significant than it was thought to be, (2) a "normal" sale of assets may well survive a *de facto* merger objection despite important merger-like characteristics, and (3) Farris and Hariton do not inevitably conflict, since the latter is a "normal" type of transaction not sharing some of Farris' unusual features. On the other hand, if the merger-like features are decisive, then (1) most corporate fusions other than a bare assets sale are probably *de facto* mergers, and (2) Hariton is squarely contrary to the holding in Farris. Indeed, the pre-Farris federal court decisions did infer a *de facto* merger simply from the merger-like features of transactions which apparently did not share some of the more unusual characteristics of the List-Glen Alden combination.

Second, a *de facto* merger test based on some combination of factors is unsettling to the security of transactions when it is impossible or difficult to state the disqualifying factors, for no objective standard is available for measuring a proposed transaction in advance. Moreover, every sale of assets is potentially subject to a lengthy hearing probing every possible "*factor*" pointing to a *de facto* merger. Even if the disqualifying factors can be precisely designated, litigation is no less likely to result. Of course, the more disqualifying factors the courts find, the less flexible will be the sale-of-assets procedure. For example, a rule which forbids coupling a sale of assets with a mandatory dissolution of the seller is clear and easy to apply, but its effect is to force every corporate fusion into the mold of a merger. However, even such an apparently straightforward rule creates uncertainty. Is a sale of assets invalid if it is followed by a dissolution of the seller at some later date? The two steps, if such they are, are not formally part of a corporate fusion plan, but a court operating under such a rule must consider whether there is "really" an arrangement which must be interpreted as a *de facto* merger.

Finally, the greater the uncertainty, the greater is the chance of unscrupulous shareholders using their enhanced bargaining position to force concessions.

Third, assuming that some of these factors are indicative of a "real" merger, it is questionable whether a court on its own should declare standards supplementary to whatever standards the statute provides. The Farris excursion left so much uncertainty that the Pennsylvania legislature promptly came to the rescue with a special rule which was, at least, clear cut.[70] The spirit of the Delaware cases, especially Hariton, is to eschew such a judicial attempt. The Hariton decision reflects the belief that the value of maintaining objective standards in this area—the simple statutory formalities and traditional equitable requirements—outweighs any possible benefits of turning up a merger lurking under some assets sale. This is the real significance of the court's invocation of the "equal dignity" and "independence" of each of the statutory techniques for achieving a corporate combination. Apparently, the Delaware court is loath to compel the amalgamators to travel only one of the roads opened by the legislature.

A partial assessment of the Hariton principle is now in order. Its holding, and the doctrine it radiates, is sound. By requiring only adherence to form and minimum standards of fairness, it affords an objective test facilitating corporate planning and at the same time avoids the inherent complexities of a judicial test which seeks a "real" merger beyond the form of the transaction. In addition, it does suitable obeisance to a modern idol of the market-place, "flexibility," for it leaves open some route other than a strict merger for the consolidation of corporations. Dissenting shareholders seeking a buy-out may suffer if Hariton means that most fusions will use the sale-of-assets technique, but there is nothing to show that these interests are so compelling that a court, *absent statute*, should voluntarily give them precedence over the equally weighty competing interests so well served by Hariton. But even beyond this, the Hariton case points to a judgment, not previously articulated by the Delaware courts, on some profoundly basic questions, to which we now turn.

C. *Hariton's Hidden Premises*

1. *The Shareholder's Appraisal Remedy.* Whenever a court holds that a sale of assets is a *de facto* merger, it necessarily recognizes appraisal rights for shareholders of all corporations involved, since they are a characteristic incident of any merger. In holding "plainly correct" the contention that the sale in Hariton "has achieved the same result as a merger," the Delaware court displays, consciously or unconsciously, a profound distrust of appraisal rights, although not a word of this appears in the opinions. In large measure, then, the soundness

---

70. See Pa.Stat.Ann. tit. 15, § 2852–311 (F) (Supp.1962), [described at page 721 infra].

of Hariton turns on the validity of the appraisal remedy and, more particularly, of judicially extending it to a class of transactions for which such a remedy is not expressly granted.

Although it is unnecessary to explore fully the pros and cons of appraisal rights, several points may be mentioned in the context of *de facto* mergers. First, appraisal rights may severely impair the ready cash of the corporation, especially when it is seeking to step up business performance through an amalgamation. Indeed, if the dissenters own a large number of shares, they may block the transaction altogether,[74] although historically the remedy was designed to allow corporate combinations to be carried out. Second, the recognition of appraisal rights results in somewhat arbitrarily carving out a group of transactions—usually mergers—for special treatment, since appraisal rights do not apply in other situations where the shareholder is realistically "hurt" or his investment changed just as much. Apart from the infinite variety of directors' business decisions which can affect a shareholder's interest adversely, there are a number of "fundamental corporate changes" which generate no appraisal right, such as corporate purchases of assets for stock, sales of stock for cash which in turn is used to purchase assets, amendments of the articles of incorporation, dissolution with distributions in kind, and sales of controlling blocks of shares. If the theory of the appraisal remedy is to aid the injured shareholder, appraisal rights should be available in many instances other than mergers, particularly if a shareholder injury is defined as a change in the nature of his investment or in his relationship to the corporation and the other shareholders. If appraisal rights, by eliminating the dissenters, preserve the fiction of unanimous shareholder approval of fundamental corporate changes, the remedy should be more readily available for consistency's sake, and presumably it should under the theory that it is a constitutionally required payment for dissenters also.

If such conceptualistic grounds are insufficient for an express legislative enactment, they should be equally unpersuasive for a court asked to recognize a class of transactions with an extra-statutory appraisal right attached. Indeed, policy considerations play a large role in a court's decision to embrace or reject the *de facto* merger concept, and in making its choice the court impliedly passes judgment on the validity of appraisal rights. A court adopting the *de facto* merger concept should carefully consider whether this is the best way to protect shareholder interests. A court rejecting it, on the other hand, should be assured that it has other tools to protect the affected interests. Assuming that Hariton is a broad declaration for the future, it

---

74. In Farris v. Glen Alden Corp., 393 Pa. 427, 431 n. 5, 143 A.2d 25, 28 n. 5 (1958), it was conceded that if appraisal rights had to be met, "the resultant drain of cash would prevent Glen Alden from carrying out the agreement." . . .

is at least clear that in Delaware appraisal rights will not be the focal point for this protection. . . .

2. *The Nature of the Shareholder's Investment.* Another premise underlying Hariton runs even deeper than its distrust of the appraisal remedy. Stated negatively, it is a rejection of the idea that a shareholder's investment is exclusively defined in terms of his relationship to a unique business enterprise so that (1) he cannot be forced against his will into a relationship with a different enterprise or (2) at least is entitled to sever his original relationship at the corporation's expense. Appraisal rights on mergers and assets sales are consistent with this idea. On analysis, it is a strict application of the corporate entity concept. Aside from occasional appraisal rights for certain charter amendments or on liquidation, or a very rare extension of such rights on a purchase of assets, this idea has not been recognized in "internal" changes in the corporation in which the shareholder originally invested, no matter how great the impact on his investment. Hence, a total change in the business, if not through a "fundamental corporate change" but through internal evolution or a revolutionary decision to alter course, yields no appraisal rights, for the corporate entity remains the same for "legal purposes." On the other hand, such rights cannot be denied where one corporation merges with another doing an identical business, even though the shareholder's investment is unchanged or improved. Consequently, a doctrinaire insistence on the corporate entity concept, here as elsewhere, should be avoided.

The basic premise implicitly adopted in Hariton may perhaps be stated more affirmatively. One does not invest in a unique corporate entity or even a particular business operation, but rather in a continuous course of business which changes over a long period of time. Certainly the best investments are growth investments—investments in enterprises which change with time, technology, business opportunities, and altered demand; and the worst investments are those which diminish in value because the type of business has lost importance and the corporation has been unable to adapt to the changed conditions. Although a shareholder's enthusiasm dwindles when an enterprise changes internally for the worst, no one suggests that he should have an option to compel the return of his investment. Viewed this way, the fact that the change—for better or for worse—comes through marriage, whether by merger or assets sale, seems purely incidental. The fact that the corporate entity in which one invested disappears as a result of a merger or of a sale of assets coupled with dissolution is also beside the point. One's investment may gain immortality when it takes a new form, i. e., a share in a successor enterprise. The fact is that, closely held corporations aside, an investment in a corporation is really an investment in the judgment, business acumen, integrity, and vigor of management, whose personnel and policy change over time. Management ability may have its finest hour in negotiating and implementing arrangements which conceptually change the shareholder's investment and his original relationship to the corporation and its shareholders, but which actually improve his investment.

This is not meant to be a paean in praise of management. It does not mean that management (with or without a majority or more of the shareholders) should be omnipotent or that every distinctive Delaware doctrine, e. g., the narrow scope of fraud, the light treatment of preferred stock rights, is sound. It does seem, however, that an unrealistic importance has been attached to the investor's interest in changes in corporate form. Certainly, "fundamental corporate change" is too undiscriminating a basis on which to adopt a *de facto* merger concept, and in so far as Hariton rejects such a basis, the decision seems entirely sound.

III. Exchange of Shares

A. *Background*

The exchange of shares—one of the commonest techniques for corporate fusions—has been treated differently, both at common law and under statute, from either merger or sale of assets. At common law the dominant policy was the free transferability of shares. This idea was even carried to the point of recognizing, until recently, virtually no limitations short of fraud upon selling even a controlling block of shares, notwithstanding the practical effect of such a sale on the corporation and the other shareholders. Apparently, no court developed a doctrine . . . to protect shareholders from a change in the essential nature of the enterprise in which they invested.[83] Strictly speaking, the law recognized no corporate action in an exchange of shares situation like that in a merger or sale of assets, for the negotiations and sale were carried on by the selling shareholder. This distinction was accurate in theory, but it ignored the fact that the directors and major shareholders of the corporation subject to a "take-over bid" often cooperate with the purchaser and promote or recommend the sale of the shares. No matter how distasteful an objecting shareholder found the shift of control, his investment suffered no "legal" damage entitling him to insist upon unanimous shareholder assent or an appraisal right. Later the courts imposed a type of fiduciary duty upon insiders, including controlling shareholders, which served as a check upon the exchange-of-shares transaction.

Against this background, it is inherently less likely that the *de facto* merger doctrine will threaten a transaction with merger-like features if it is effected through an exchange of shares. No statutes award appraisal rights on share exchanges, and, in general, "the

---

83. In Orzeck v. Englehart, 192 A.2d 36 (Del.Ch.1963), the vice-chancellor specifically rejected a contention that the corporation's purchase of stock in an exchange of shares "has resulted in a change in the essential nature of the enterprise of the corporation," noting that the corporation "became merely a holding company" and did not engage in the business of the corporations whose stock was acquired. . . .

mechanisms for effecting such combinations differ so greatly from those for merger, consolidation and sale of assets" that it is easy to conclude that "the policy of the appraisal statutes should not be deemed to extend into this field." Nevertheless, a share exchange coupled with other statutory procedures may produce a result identical to a merger, and at least one important decision has squarely held the *de facto* merger rule applicable. Applestein v. United Board & Carton Corp.[86] is, in the oddities of its fact situation and the character of its reasoning, very like Farris, on which it heavily relies. In Applestein the sole shareholder of Interstate Container Corporation agreed to exchange all his shares for forty per cent of the stock of the purchasing corporation plus control of its board of directors. The agreement also included an elaborate plan for the complete absorption of Interstate by the purchasing corporation. According to the court, the transaction was either a *de facto* merger or "in practical effect" an acquisition of the nominal purchaser by the controlling shareholder of the selling corporation. Under either theory an objecting shareholder of the purchaser was entitled to appraisal rights and the other incidents of the merger procedure.[89] Applestein's approach is at opposite poles from Hariton, and thus many comments made previously with respect to the Farris case apply to it with equal force.

B. *Exchange of Shares Without More*

It is practically certain that the purchase by corporation *A* of corporation *B* shares from the latter's shareholders, *without more,* will not be a *de facto merger,* at least in Delaware. This transaction has little resemblance to a merger, for corporation *B* continues to own its assets, its business is not changed, it does not dissolve, and its creditors retain the same priority. The only real difference is the substitution of a new shareholder. Unlike a sale of assets, which creates an "identity of corporate interests," in an exchange of shares "the interests remain separate and distinct," whatever that may mean. The new subsidiary may remain alive to perform within the parent's system the kind of business it has always been doing, to retain franchises or other non-saleable rights, or to maximize good will from a trade name and personnel. Similarly the stock acquisition may be simply an investment of surplus funds, or it may be designed to strengthen the competitive hand of the acquirer.

An exchange of shares does not necessarily become a *de facto merger* because the acquiring corporation runs the business in its own interest or integrates it into its system, elects its own nominees to

---

86. 60 N.J.Super. 333, 159 A.2d 146 (Ch.), aff'd per curiam 33 N.J. 72, 161 A.2d 474 (1960).

89. The indicia of a merger found in this transaction included the purchaser's acquisition of all the seller's assets, its assumption of the seller's liabilities, a "pooling of interest" of both, "absorption" of the seller and its dissolution, the purchaser's retention of the seller's directors, officers, and key personnel, and the fact that the seller's sole shareholder succeeded to a large block of the purchaser's stock. . . .

director and officer posts, or assumes its liabilities. Indeed, there may be a "new look" as the new equity interests change the character and conduct of the business. Events of this sort which occur within a corporation do not ordinarily entitle shareholders to dissent, since they are not "fundamental" changes. The fact that they occur after a stock purchase will not retroactively make the transaction a *de facto* merger.

Two Delaware cases are consistent with this analysis. In Fidanque v. American Maracaibo Co.,[100] the court rejected a *de facto* merger contention urged by a shareholder of the acquiring corporation, which had exchanged 36.564 per cent of its outstanding stock for all the outstanding shares of the Case Pomeroy companies. These corporations remained as subsidiaries to carry on certain petroleum activities of the parent for tax reasons, and it was thought that they might become even more active than before the exchange. And in Orzeck v. Englehart, the court again sustained a transaction in which a corporation, at the time an "empty shell" with a large accumulated tax loss carryover, exchanged its stock for the shares of seven California corporations then engaged in the egg business. The court discussed the "independent legal significance" of the forms of corporate fusion authorized by statutes, and held, on this ground, that the transaction was not a *de facto* merger. Although the court noted that the subsidiaries continued in existence and the acquisition plan did not call for their dissolution or merger, the court doubted that this was "of any importance," as, indeed, one would infer from Hariton.

In Delaware, then, the fact that the acquiring corporation gives up a large part of its stock to acquire the shares is immaterial. In Fidanque, it was slightly more than one-third; in Orzeck, it was substantial although not stated. Since a one-third plus block of shares is at least working control of a corporation whose remaining shares are scattered, the Delaware courts have implicitly determined that a shift of control is immaterial to the *de facto* merger question. . . . Yet in Applestein v. United Board & Carton Corp., the New Jersey court found a *de facto* merger when the purchasing corporation used 160,000 of its authorized 400,000 shares to acquire the stock of another corporation, thereby giving the seller forty per cent control with the remaining sixty per cent scattered among more than 1000 shareholders. The individual significance of this fact, however, is unclear, since the court found about a dozen other merger-like features while under the influence of, not to say intoxicated by, Farris.

C. *Exchange of Shares Plus*

If Orzeck v. Englehart is any indicator of Hariton's wider significance, it is likely that many Delaware fusions in the future will be cast in the form of an exchange of shares coupled with some further transaction such as a merger, a sale of assets, or a dissolu-

---

100. 33 Del.Ch. 262, 92 A.2d 311 (Ch. 1952).

tion. Under the Hariton concept, the emphasis upon form, the minimization of merger-like results, the absence of any step-transaction doctrine, and the "overlapping scope" of the merger statute with the sale-of-assets statute all support the conclusion that such transactions would be valid. Nevertheless, the results may differ somewhat depending upon the precise technique combined with the exchange of shares.

1. *Exchange of Shares Plus Merger.* After acquiring stock of corporation B, corporation A effects a merger with B. If this is an ordinary merger, the dissenting shareholders of both corporations will have appraisal rights. On the other hand, if corporation A owns ninety per cent or more of the B stock, it can effect a "short-form" merger, and appraisal rights will only be recognized for the dissenting shareholders of B.[106] Since no more than ten per cent of the shareholders of B could claim appraisal rights, there is some advantage to such a procedure as against an ordinary merger. Assuming all the statutory formalities are complied with, Hariton would no doubt validate a combination effected in this manner, even if it had been planned all along as an integral part of a single transaction.[107] Since the Delaware court disclosed a distrust of appraisal rights in Hariton, it would be odd indeed if this transaction were held to be an ordinary merger entitling the shareholders of A to appraisal rights also.

2. *Exchange of Shares Plus Sale of Assets.* After corporation A acquires corporation B stock, B sells its assets to A for a lawful consideration. Alcott v. Hyman [108] overruled *de facto* merger objections to a similar two-step transaction where the consideration given by A for the B assets was the B stock A had acquired plus cash to cover the value of the securities not tendered. The legality of this procedure was sustained over objections that "non-assenting stockholders [were] frozen out of what had been a profitable business so that on its consummation they merely held an equity in the shell of a once going business, the assets of which had been entirely converted to cash . . . ." Thus, as in Hariton, the transaction was unobjectionable since it met the technical requirements of the sale-of-assets statute in all respects.

The situation becomes more difficult if corporation B sells its assets solely for shares of corporation A. The dissenting B shareholders are then left with a "shell" whose only assets are the shares

---

106. . . . The term "short-form" merger signifies the statutory simplification of the merger procedure where a parent and subsidiary amalgamate. [Such mergers are discussed at pages 730–735 infra.] of the Olson companies into the corporation, and if such merger has, in fact, taken place, that circumstance is no aid to the plaintiff." Orzeck v. Englehart, 192 A.2d 36, 38 (Del.Ch. 1963).

107. "If it be of any importance, the agreement did not call for the merger

108. 40 Del.Ch. 449, 184 A.2d 90 (Del.Ch. 1962).

of A. As a consequence, they are forced to accept A shares. Their only status as against the B shareholders who assented to the original exchange with A is that they hold the A shares indirectly, while the assenting shareholders hold them directly. Hence, this is a device to force dissenting B shareholders to acquiesce in the originally intended exchange of shares. This result becomes even clearer if corporation A, as controlling shareholder, brings about the dissolution of corporation B. Given statutory compliance at each stage and Delaware's rejection of the step-transaction doctrine, plus the holding in the Alcott case, however, this procedure appears valid.

3. *Exchange of Shares Plus Dissolution.* Corporation A acquires the stock of B and then causes B to dissolve, taking B assets for a consideration sufficient to compensate the shareholders of B who did not agree to the original exchange. If the sale of assets occurs before dissolution, the situation is identical to the one just discussed. If it occurs during or as a part of the dissolution, the "outside" B shareholders have no appraisal rights, since they are not available on dissolution in Delaware. Once again, a technique is available for a complete amalgamation of the two corporations without appraisal rights.

These results would follow from Hariton whether or not the additional steps were part of a preconceived plan. In Hariton itself, the sale of assets was coupled with a fully disclosed plan to dissolve the selling corporation and distribute the consideration (stock of the purchaser) to the shareholders. There is no reason why the same principle would not hold when there is an avowed plan to purchase shares coupled with an intention to take further action, even though the upshot of the transaction is equivalent to a merger.

D. *"Upside-Down" Share Exchanges*

As noted earlier, Delaware has apparently not dealt with the Farris-type upside-down sale of assets, but in Orzeck v. Englehart the Delaware court was presented with a similar problem in the context of an exchange of shares. There the vice-chancellor assumed *arguendo* that a *de facto* merger might exist when the nominal seller in a sale-of-assets transaction in fact acquires the buyer, but he staunchly declared that the exchange-of-shares transaction was so different from a sale of assets that the Farris case was inapplicable.[114] Insistence upon the distinctive nature of an exchange of shares, however, is inconsistent with the court's own reliance upon Hariton and Heilbrunn, both sale-of-assets cases. Moreover, an exchange

114. . . . Of course, Applestein v. United Board & Carton Corp. . . . did apply the *de facto* merger doctrine to a share exchange, but as previously mentioned, several factors not present in Orzeck clearly influenced the court's decision.

of shares as well as a sale of assets may be an inverted transaction.[115] The differences between these two kinds of transactions do not affect the scope of the principle implicit in Hariton that several statutory transactions may validly be coupled although the result is virtually identical to a statutory merger. If this interpretation is correct, the fact that the transaction in Hariton was actually built upon a sale of assets is incidental, and that case can apply as well to merger-like results rooted in an exchange of shares. In all events, the premises which underlie the Hariton result can be as meaningfully applied to the one as to the other form of amalgamation.

. . .

RATH v. RATH PACKING CO.[5]

Supreme Court of Iowa, 1965.
—— Iowa ——, 136 N.W.2d 410.

GARFIELD, CHIEF JUSTICE. The question presented is whether an Iowa corporation may carry out an agreement with another corporation, designated "Plan and Agreement of Reorganization," which amounts to a merger in fact of the two without approval of holders of two thirds of its outstanding shares, as provided by [the Iowa statute]. The question is one of first impression in Iowa. We must disagree with the trial court's holding this may be done.

Plaintiffs, minority shareholders of Rath, brought this action in equity to enjoin carrying out the agreement on the ground, so far as necessary to consider, it provides for a merger in fact with Needham Packing Co., which requires approval of two thirds of the holders of outstanding Rath shares and that was not obtained. The trial court adjudicated law points under rule 105, Rules of Civil Procedure, in favor of defendants Rath and its officers, and entered judgment of dismissal on the pleadings. It held approval of the plan by holders of a majority of Rath shares was sufficient. Plaintiffs appeal.

Plaintiffs own more than 6000 shares of Rath Packing Co., an Iowa corporation with its principal plant in Waterloo, Iowa, existing under Code 1962, chapter 496A, I.C.A. (Iowa Business Corporation Act). Rath has 993,185 shares outstanding held by about 4000 owners. It is engaged in meat packing and processing, mostly pork and allied products. Its yearly sales for the last five years were from

---

115. Essentially, an "upside-down" transaction appears to involve either (1) a small purchaser in relation to a large seller, or (2) an excessive consideration. Either of these could occur in an exchange of shares, for a small corporation could either increase its authorized shares tenfold to acquire the shares of a much larger corporation or turn over a disproportionately large number of its own shares for those it was acquiring. These fact situations should be analyzed for what they are; in neither context do they necessarily suggest a *de facto* merger.

5. Portions of the opinion omitted.

about $267,000,000 to $296,000,000. Its balance sheet as of January 2, 1965, showed assets of about $56,500,000, current liabilities of about $20,600,000, and long-term debt of about $7,000,000.

Needham Packing Co. is a corporation organized in 1960 under Delaware law with its principal plant in Sioux City, Iowa. Its total shares outstanding, including debentures and warrants convertible into stock, are 787,907, held by about 1000 owners. Both Rath and Needham stock is traded on the American Stock Exchange. Needham is also engaged in meat packing, mostly beef. Its annual sales were from about $80,000,000 to $103,000,000. Its balance sheet as of December 26, 1964, showed assets of $10,300,000, current liabilities of $2,262,000, and long-term debt of $3,100,000.

Pursuant to authority of Rath's board prior to April 2, 1965, it entered into the questioned agreement with Needham, designated "Plan and Agreement of Reorganization," under which Rath agreed to: (1) amend its articles to double the number of shares of its common stock, create a new class of preferred shares and change its name to Rath-Needham Corporation; (2) issue to Needham 5.5 shares of Rath common and two shares of its 80-cent preferred stock for each five shares of Needham stock in exchange for all Needham's assets, properties, business, name and good will, except a fund not exceeding $175,000 to pay expenses in carrying out the agreement and effecting Needham's dissolution and distribution of the new Rath-Needham stock to its shareholders, any balance remaining after 120 days to be paid over to Rath; (3) assume all Needham's debts and liabilities; and (4) elect two Needham officers and directors to its board.

Under the plan Needham agreed to: (1) transfer all its assets to Rath; (2) cease using its name; (3) distribute the new Rath-Needham shares to its stockholders, liquidate and dissolve; and (4) turn over to Rath its corporate and business records.

If the plan were carried out, assuming the new preferred shares were converted into common, the thousand Needham shareholders would have about 54 per cent of the outstanding common shares of Rath-Needham and the four thousand Rath shareholders would have about 46 per cent.

Under the plan the book value of each share of Rath common stock, as of January 2, 1965, would be reduced from $27.99 to $15.93, a reduction of about 44 per cent. Each share of Needham common would be increased in book value, as of December 26, 1964, from $6.61 to $23.90, assuming conversion of the new Rath-Needham preferred.

In the event of liquidation of Rath-Needham, Needham shareholders would be preferred to Rath's under the plan, by having a prior claim to the assets of Rath-Needham to an amount slightly in excess of the book value of all Needham shares. Needham shareholders are also preferred over Rath's under the plan in distribution of income by the right of the former to receive preferred dividends of 80 cents a share—about five per cent of Needham's book value. Shortly prior to the time terms of the plan were made public Rath and Needham shares sold on the American Exchange for about the same price. Almost immediately thereafter the price of Needham shares increased and Rath's decreased so the former sold for 50 per cent more than the latter.

At a meeting of Rath shareholders on April 26, 1965, 60.1 per cent of its outstanding shares, 77 per cent of those voted, were voted in favor of these two proposals: (1) to amend the articles to authorize a class of 80 c preferred stock and increase the authorized common from 1,500,000 shares ($10 par) to 3,000,000 shares (no par); and (2) upon acquisition by Rath of the assets, properties, business and good will of Needham to change Rath's name to Rath-Needham Corporation and elect as its directors Lloyd and James Needham. Holders of 177,000 shares voted against these proposals and 218,000 shares were not voted. The plan was not approved by the shareholders except as above stated.

Rath officers vigorously solicited proxies for the meeting by personal travel, telephone and through a professional proxy soliciting agency. This action was commenced five days prior to the meeting and four days thereafter a supplement and amendment to the petition were filed.

I. [The court first summarized the merger provisions of the Iowa corporation law (chapter 496A of the Iowa Code) which are patterned after MBA §§ 65–70, 73 and 74.]

The above sections are those on which plaintiffs rely. They contend these statutes specifically provide for effecting a merger and the same result cannot legally be attained at least without approval of the holders of two thirds of the shares and according to dissenters "appraisal rights"—i. e., the right to receive the fair value of their stock by compliance with the specified procedure.

Defendants contend and the trial court held compliance with the above sections was not required and defendants could legally proceed under other sections of chapter 496A which merely authorize amendments to articles of incorporation and issuance of stock. [The court then summarized the Iowa provisions dealing with amendment of the certificate, patterned after MBA §§ 53 and 54 (except that only a majority vote of the stock entitled to vote is required), and the provisions dealing with the issuance of stock, patterned after MBA §§ 17 and 18.]

II. The principal point of law defendants asked to have adjudicated . . . is that the provisions of chapter 496A last referred to are legally independent of, and of equal dignity with, those relating to mergers and the validity of the action taken by defendants is not dependent upon compliance with the merger sections under which the same result might be attained. The trial court accepted this view.

It is clear the view just expressed emanates from the opinion in Hariton v. Arco Electronics, Inc., Del., 188 A.2d 123, the only precedent called to our attention which sustains the decision appealed from. Virtually the only basis for the conclusion Hariton reaches is the statement of the law point these defendants raised. The opinion contains little discussion and cites no authority that supports the decision.

We can agree all provisions of our chapter 496A are of equal dignity. But we cannot agree any provisions of the act are legally independent of others if this means that in arriving at the correct interpretation thereof and the legislative intent expressed therein we are not to consider the entire act and, so far as possible, construe its various provisions in the light of their relation to the whole act. . .

We may also observe that the trial court "concluded the 'safeguards' written into the codes of most states, including Iowa and Delaware, with respect to rights of dissenting shareholders in connection with mergers are based on outmoded concepts of economic realities, particularly in the case of an enterprise such as Rath which is regularly traded on the American Exchange and has a diversified stock ownership with over 4000 shareholders. The court cites especially in this regard articles of Professor Manning, 72 Yale Law Journal 223, and Professor Folk, 49 Virginia Law Review 1261."

If the soundness of this view were admitted, the statutory safeguards should of course be removed by legislative, not judicial action. Our 1959 legislature evidently had a purpose in enacting what we may call the merger sections of chapter 496A as well as those relating to amending articles and issuing stock. We have frequently pointed out it is not the province of courts to pass upon the policy, wisdom or advisability of a statute. . . .

III. The "Plan and Agreement of Reorganization" clearly provides for what amounts to a merger of Rath and Needham under any definition of merger we know.

[The court then quoted a number of definitions of merger in the authorities, including the following.] ". . . a merger signifies the absorption of one corporation by another, which retains its name and corporate identity with the added capital, franchises and powers of a merged corporation." 15 Fletcher Cyc. Corporations, 1961 Revised Volume, section 7041, page 6. . . .

If, as we hold, this agreement provides for what amounts to a merger of Rath and Needham, calling it a Plan and Agreement of Reorganization does not change its essential character. . . .

IV. The power of a corporation to merge must be derived from the law of the state which created it. There must be some plain enactment authorizing the merger, for legislative authority is just as essential to a merger as to creation of the corporation in the first instance. . . . Legislative authority for a merger will not be implied but must be clearly, distinctly and expressly conferred. . . .

* * *

The merger sections of chapter 496A clearly and expressly confer the necessary power to merge. . . . Nothing in the sections dealing with amending articles and issuing stock purports to authorize a merger. They make no reference to merger. The most that may fairly be claimed is that they impliedly confer the required power to merge. But this is insufficient.

V. In seeking the scope and effect of the two sets of sections relied upon at least one fundamental rule of statutory construction is applicable. As stated, the merger sections specifically provide for a particular thing—mergers. The sections authorizing amendment of articles and issuance of stock apply to all amendments and stock issues, whether or not amending the articles or issuing stock is part of a merger, as they may or may not be. As applied to mergers, the sections on which plaintiffs rely are specific provisions, those on which defendants rely are not. . . .

"It is an old and familiar principle . . . that where there is in the same statute a specific provision, and also a general one which in its most comprehensive sense would include matters embraced in the former, the particular provision must control, and the general provision must be taken to effect only such cases within its general language as are not within the provisions of the particular provision. . . ."

* * *

A closely related rule, many times applied by us, is that where a general statute, if standing alone, would include the same matter as a special statute and thus conflict with it, the latter will prevail and the former must give way. The special provision will be considered an exception to or qualification of the general one. . . .

It is apparent that if the sections pertaining to amending articles and issuing stock are construed to authorize a merger by a majority vote of shareholders they conflict with the sections specifically dealing with the one matter of mergers which require a two-thirds vote of shareholders. The two sets of sections may be harmonized by holding, as we do, that the merger sections govern the matter of merger and must be regarded as an exception to the sections dealing with amending articles and issuing stock, which may or may not be involved in a merger.

The construction we give these sections is in accord with the cardinal rule that, if reasonably possible, effect will be given to every part of a statute. . . .

The merger sections make it clear the legislature intended to require a two-thirds vote of shareholders and accord so-called appraisal rights to dissenters in case of a merger. It is unreasonable to ascribe to the same legislature an intent to provide in the same act a method of evading the required two-thirds vote and the grant of such appraisal rights. The practical effect of the decision appealed from is to render the requirements of a two-thirds vote and appraisal rights meaningless in virtually all mergers. It is scarcely an exaggeration to say the decision amounts to judicial repeal of the merger sections in most instances of merger.

It is obvious, as defendants' counsel frankly stated in oral argument, that corporate management would naturally choose a method which requires only majority approval of shareholders and does not grant dissenters the right to be paid the fair value of their stock. The legislature could hardly have intended to vest in corporate management the option to comply with the requirements just referred to or to proceed without such compliance, a choice that would invariably be exercised in favor of the easier method. . . .

VI. 15 Fletcher, Cyc. Corporations, 1961 Revised Volume section 7165.5, page 307, contains this: "However, where a particular corporate combination is in legal effect a merger or a consolidation, even though the transaction may be otherwise labeled by the parties, the courts treat the transaction as a de facto merger or consolidation so as to confer upon dissenting stockholders the right to receive cash payment for their shares." Decisions from several jurisdictions are cited in support. Only Heilbrunn v. Sun Chemical Corp., 37 Del.Ch. 552, 146 A.2d 757, Affd. 38 Del.Ch. 321, 150 A.2d 755, 758, is cited as contra.

Basis of the Heilbrunn decision is the court's declared failure to see how any injury was inflicted on shareholders of a corporation that purchased the assets of another. No opinion was expressed as to whether shareholders of the selling corporation could obtain equitable relief. The Delaware court first decided that question in Hariton v. Arco Electronics, supra, Del., 188 A.2d 123.

We think the precedents which support the statement quoted from Fletcher are sound. Aside from Applestein v. United Board and Carton Corp., supra, 60 N.J.Super. 333, 159 A.2d 146, Affd. 33 N.J. 72, 161 A.2d 474, the case most frequently cited in support of such view is Farris v. Glen Alden Corp., 393 Pa. 427, 143 A.2d 25, 28.
. . .

VII. The trial court thought that while no Iowa case is directly in point, the policy of Iowa law is in accord with its decision, citing [several Iowa cases]. We find no conflict between the conclusion we reach and these precedents. Each of them may be distinguished on the ground the transaction there involved did not amount to a merger nor obligate any corporation to dissolve. This is also true of the three cases from other jurisdictions and Orzeck v. Englehart, Del., 195 A.2d 375, cited by defendants.

* * *

IX. We hold entry of judgment of dismissal on the pleadings was error, that defendants should be enjoined from carrying out the "Plan and Agreement of Reorganization" until such time, if ever, as it is approved by the holders of at least two thirds of the outstanding shares of Rath and in the event of such approval plaintiffs, if they dissent to such plan and follow the [appropriate procedure], shall be entitled to be paid the fair value of their shares in Rath. For decree in harmony with this opinion the cause is—Reversed and remanded.

NOTE ON THE DE FACTO MERGER DOCTRINE

At the outset it is worth noting that the Rath case did not involve what Professor Folk referred to as an "upside-down" transaction, that is, one where the nominal acquiring corporation should really be regarded as the corporation being acquired. For one thing, the purported acquiring corporation in Rath had substantially more book net assets than the acquired corporation. Moreover, so far as control was concerned, although the former stockholders of the acquired corporation could, by converting the preferred stock they received, end up with 54% of the acquiring corporation's common stock, they were obtaining only two seats on the board of directors, in sharp contrast to the Farris and Applestein cases where those associated with the purported acquired corporation took virtually complete control of the acquiring corporation from the very start.

In the Farris case the court expressly adopted as an alternative holding a "turn-around" approach, under which the purported acquiring corporation would be treated as the one whose assets were being acquired. This would have been enough, without any de facto merger doctrine, to give the plaintiff the appraisal rights (and notice thereof) that he was seeking, since under the Pennsylvania statutes the stockholders of a company which sells all of its assets have the same appraisal rights (and voting rights, for that matter) as the stockholders of a party to an express merger.

In the Applestein case, too, the court expressed a willingness to realign the parties if necessary. However, where, as in Applestein, the transaction takes the form of a stock acquisition, it is far from clear what such a realignment would accomplish. For in a stock acquisition there is no express appraisal remedy available to the stockholders of the acquired corporation (at least unless the acquired corporation is subsequently eliminated pursuant to a "short merger" statute like MBA § 68A, see pages 730–735, infra); nor does any statute give the stockholders of the acquired corporation a right to vote. To be sure, the stockholders of the acquired corporation are each free to decide on their own volition whether to accept the exchange offer, which might be viewed as a kind of informal voting right; and upon a subsequent dissolution of the acquired corporation those stockholders who refused the exchange offer and kept their stock can probably get some judicial review of the liquidation distribution to them, see pages 724–730, infra, in effect a kind of informal appraisal right. However, it is hard to see how such rights could be constructively made available to the stockholders of the purported acquiring corporation, either by applying a turn-around approach or otherwise.[6] The court in the Applestein case did not have to deal with these issues since the de facto merger doctrine was in fact adopted there; and in any event it appears that the reference to realigning the parties was simply in response to the argument of the defendants that the de facto merger doctrine only applied to the stockholders of the acquired corporation, an argument which the court quite properly rejected on the merits.

It is to be noted that even in an asset acquisition, a "turn-around" approach would not be effective in a state like Delaware, where no appraisal rights are provided in connection with a sale of assets (and only majority stockholder approval is required, instead of the two-thirds vote needed for a merger). In such circumstances, therefore, and in all stock acquisitions, normally it is only by resort to the de facto merger doctrine that appraisal and/or voting rights can be secured for stockholders who would not otherwise be entitled to them. But the de facto merger doctrine is a somewhat blunt instrument for accomplishing this purpose, at least when, as often appears to be true, the essential objective is to afford protection to the stockholders of a corporation which is relatively small and is being totally submerged in the combination transaction, since the application of the de facto merger doctrine would seem to give the stockholders of *all* the corporations involved the rights and remedies provided by the merger statute.

What is really needed for these situations is an amendment of the corporate statutes to impose some limitations on the power of a corporation to acquire assets or stock of another corporation through the issuance of substantial amounts of its own stock. The first move in this direction seems to have come in Pennsylvania where, in 1959, in what was obviously a response to the Farris decision, the statute was amended to adopt such an approach and eliminate the de facto merger doctrine. Section 2852–908(C), Pa.Stat.Ann. Tit. 15, was amended to provide that "when a corporation acquires assets by purchase, lease or exchange, by the issuance of shares, evidence of indebtedness, or otherwise, with or without assuming liabilities, other than by the [prescribed] procedure for merger or consolidation, . . . the rights, if any, of the dissenting shareholders shall be governed" by § 2852–311 (which deals with the sale of corporate assets) and not by the merger provisions. At the same time, subsection F of § 2852–311 was amended by adding the following:

> "The shareholders of a business corporation which acquires by purchase, lease or exchange all or substantially all of the property of another corporation by the issuance of shares, evidences of indebtedness or otherwise, with or without assuming the liabilities of such other corporation, shall be entitled to the rights and remedies of dissenting shareholders . . . if, but only if, such acquisition shall have been accomplished by the issuance of more than a majority of the voting shares of such corporation to be outstanding immediately after the acquisition."

---

6. Conceivably, a stock acquisition followed by a liquidation of the acquired corporation might be regarded as in effect an acquisition of the assets of the acquired corporation and therefore subject to a "turn-around" approach to the same extent as an actual asset acquisition.

In 1963 a further amendment to subsection F of § 2852–311 changed the condition for giving appraisal rights to "the issuance of voting shares of such corporation to be outstanding immediately after the acquisition sufficient to elect a majority of the directors of the corporation".

While it seems to be a step in the right direction, the new Pennsylvania statute still does not represent a satisfactory resolution of the problem. For one thing, since it provides only an appraisal remedy, and not voting rights, to the stockholders of the purchasing corporation, the new statute has not eliminated the incentive to try to invoke the de facto merger doctrine, or at least a realignment of the parties, which could result in voting rights as well as appraisal. Indeed, it is far from clear just how the Farris case itself would fare under the new statute. It might still be possible for a court to rule that the new statute only applies to a transaction which constitutes a mere "purchase without more", and not to a purported purchase transaction which really amounts to a merger of the two corporations, just as the court in the Farris case in fact ruled, in avoiding the predecessor of § 2852–908(C) which at that time expressly precluded appraisal rights for the stockholders of a corporation which "purchases" the assets of another corporation. And since the new statute is completely silent as to the "upside-down" problem, there is at least room for the alternative holding in Farris that on the basis of the comparative size of the two corporations and the other factors in the transaction, the purported purchaser was really the seller.

The Pennsylvania statute is particularly unsatisfactory with regard to the status of the appraisal remedy for stockholders of an acquiring corporation in a stock acquisition transaction. Literally, the 1959 version of § 2852–908(C), being applicable to any acquisition of "assets", covers stock acquisitions, and hence precludes the application of the merger appraisal provisions in such cases. But subsection F of § 2852–311 applies only to the acquisition of "the property of another corporation", and therefore does not provide any appraisal rights in the case of a stock acquisition. It is not clear why a stock acquisition should be treated differently from an asset acquisition, particularly when the test for appraisal rights is based on a shift in voting control of the acquiring corporation, which can as readily occur in a stock acquisition as in an asset acquisition.

A more promising development is afforded by the 1963 amendments to the Ohio statute, which are designed to provide the same treatment for the stockholders of the acquiring corporation in a combination regardless of whether the transaction takes the form of a stock acquisition, an asset acquisition, or a statutory merger. Under § 1701.84, Ohio Rev.Code (1963), the stockholders of the acquiring corporation in either a stock or an asset acquisition are entitled to both voting rights and appraisal whenever the transaction involves the issuance of a sufficient number of shares of the acquiring corporation's stock to enable the holders thereof to exercise one-sixth or more of that corporation's voting power in the election of directors immediately after the transaction. Pursuant to a corresponding 1963 amendment, the merger sections provide that the stockholders of the surviving corporation are *not* entitled either to vote or to demand appraisal if the amount of stock issued by the surviving corporation does not represent at least one-sixth of the voting power in the election of directors (and if no change is made in the surviving corporation's certificate of incorporation). §§ 1701.79(A), 1701.81(B), Ohio Rev.Code (1963). See generally, Sealy, The 1963 Ohio Acquisition and Merger Amendments, 5 Corp.Prac.Com. 366 (1964).

Even the Ohio statute does not solve all the problems here. For example, assume that a corporation issues a substantial amount of authorized but unissued voting stock for cash in a public offering, and subsequently uses the proceeds to acquire the assets of another corporation. The new statute would not come into play, even though the net effect of these two transactions upon the stockholders of the acquiring corporation would be exactly the same as if the assets had been acquired directly in exchange for the stock, a transaction which of course would be covered by the new statute. However, deciding how to deal with this kind of situation requires consideration of some pretty testing questions in this area. In particular, consider whether stockholders should have any right to vote or appraisal rights when a corporation merely issues a substantial amount of stock for cash, without any subsequent purchase of assets, or when the corporation acquires a new business for cash, without any contemporaneous issuance of stock.

D. LIQUIDATION OF THE ACQUIRED CORPORATION

1. IN GENERAL

Unlike a merger, where the acquired corporation disappears by operation of law, when a combination transaction takes the form of either a stock acquisition or an asset acquisition the acquired corporation remains in existence, unless and until some further step is taken. Thus, in the case of a stock acquisition the acquired corporation becomes a controlled subsidiary of the acquiring corporation; and this parent-subsidiary format can be continued indefinitely if the parties so desire. If instead they prefer to end up with all the assets under a single corporate roof, as in a merger, it is necessary to take the additional step of liquidating the acquired corporation.

In an asset acquisition, of course, all of the assets have already been combined in the acquiring corporation; but the acquired corporation retains its separate existence and identity, as the owner of whatever stock and securities of the acquiring corporation it received in exchange for its assets. Once again, if the parties want to end up as in a merger, with only one corporation and with the former stockholders of the acquired corporation now owning stock of the acquiring corporation, the acquired corporation must be dissolved and its assets (i. e., the stock of the acquiring corporation) distributed to its stockholders in complete liquidation.

In either case, the elimination of the acquired corporation may be accomplished under the normal procedure for voluntary dissolution of a corporation. See generally, pages 613–615, supra. There must, of course, be due regard for the rights of creditors—and since typically there would be an assumption of the acquired corporation's liabilities by the acquiring corporation, either as an integral part of the acquisition transaction, in an asset acquisition, or in connection with the dissolution of the subsidiary pursuant to a stock acquisition, what that really means is facing up to the question of whether such assumption constitutes "adequate provision" within the meaning of the dissolution statutes. See pages 624–629, supra. Once the creditors are taken care of, the remaining assets of the corporation are to be distributed among the stockholders "according to their respective rights and interests". E. g., MBA § 80(b). The assets may be converted into cash to facilitate such a distribution; or, at least when there are no liquidation preferences (which not infrequently expressly require payment in cash), and no contrary stipulation in a "plan of liquidation" approved by the stockholders, the directors would seem to be free to distribute the property of the corporation in kind among the stockholders, except perhaps if a distribution in kind would subject stockholders to unreasonable difficulty and expense in administering property. See Shrage v. Bridgeport Oil Co., 31 Del.Ch. 305, 71 A.2d 882 (Ch.1950) (plan to distribute 1/267,200 interest in each of over 100 oil wells per share held unfairly burdensome to minority stockholders).

2. SPECIAL PROBLEMS IN THE LIQUIDATION OF A CONTROLLED SUBSIDIARY

a. STRAIGHT DISSOLUTION

If in a stock acquisition the acquiring corporation does not obtain all of the stock of the acquired corporation, a simple dissolution of the subsidiary (acquired corporation) accompanied by a liquidating distribution in kind may prove not to be a very effective way to get the subsidiary's business to the parent (acquiring corporation). For under that procedure the minority stockholders of the subsidiary would presumably end up as tenants in common with the parent in the subsidiary's assets, a situation likely to prove inconvenient for all concerned, to say the least. Can this problem be avoided by arranging a "plan of liquidation" of the subsidiary under which the parent would receive all of the operating assets of the subsidiary while the minority stockholders of the subsidiary would receive their pro rata share of the liquidation distribution in cash? This issue recently came before the Federal District Court in Arkansas:

KELLOGG v. GEORGIA-PACIFIC PAPER CORP.[7]
United States District Court, W.D. Arkansas, 1964. 227 F.Supp. 719.

[Crossett Company was an Arkansas corporation engaged in the lumber business, with net assets of more than $100,000,000. A substantial majority of its stock was owned by three families, with the remainder held by the public, including the plaintiffs. During the spring of 1962 Georgia-Pacific began to acquire Crossett stock at $55 per share, starting with the majority stockholders, and by July had acquired 99.6% of the stock. The plaintiffs had an opportunity to sell their stock at $55 per share but refused. Thereafter, on July 30, 1962, at a meeting of the Crossett stockholders not attended by the plaintiffs, a plan of dissolution of Crossett was approved under which Georgia-Pacific was to take as its distributive share all of the assets and the business of Crossett, except for $54.85 per share in cash to be paid to the minority stockholders. The rate of $54.85 per share was apparently based upon the book value of the Crossett stock. The plaintiffs refused to accept the cash payment contemplated by the plan, and brought an action to have the plan declared invalid as a matter of law.]

HENLEY, DISTRICT JUDGE. . . . It is the theory of the plaintiffs that Georgia-Pacific, as the majority stockholder of Crossett, owed plaintiffs, as minority stockholders, a fiduciary duty to manage the affairs and wind up the business of Crossett, including the liquidation of its assets, for the benefit and best interests of all of the stockholders, including the minority; that Georgia-Pacific and the Trustees had no right to adopt a plan of liquidation which would favor Georgia-Pacific at the expense of the plaintiffs; that plaintiffs and Georgia-Pacific were the beneficial owners of all of the assets of Crossett as tenants in common; that having dissolved the corporation Georgia-Pacific and the Trustees, after making provision for the payment of corporate debts (which appears to have been done), were required either to distribute the assets in kind among all of the stockholders in proportion to their stock ownership, or to sell all of the assets on the open market and divide the proceeds on a pro-rata basis. As indicated, plaintiffs contend that Georgia-Pacific had no right to take over the assets and affairs of Crossett as a going concern and require plaintiffs to accept a predetermined cash payment as compensation for their stock ownership.

In resisting the claim of plaintiffs the defendants contend that plaintiffs' interest in Crossett was too small to give them standing to contest the plan of liquidation; that they were dilatory in asserting their objections; that Georgia-Pacific and the Trustees have acted in the utmost good faith and with the utmost regard for the

---

7. Statement of facts and footnotes by the court omitted.

interests of plaintiffs; that the Trustees in working out a method of liquidation were faced with a number of alternatives, and selected the one which was most feasible and which was actually in the best interests of all concerned.

From its consideration of the facts of record in the light of what appear to be governing provisions and principles of law the Court is persuaded that while some of the contentions of the defendants may have some relevancy on the question of what relief is to be granted plaintiffs, none of them can be sustained as far as the legality of the plan of liquidation is concerned, and that plaintiffs are entitled at this time to a binding adjudication that the plan adopted was illegal.

The Arkansas statutes prescribe the method by which the affairs and assets of dissolved domestic corporations are to be liquidated. . . . Without stopping to abstract those statutory provisions in detail, they contemplate that the trustees in liquidation shall collect the corporate assets, pay or provide for the payment of corporate debts and liabilities, and distribute remaining assets in cash or in kind to the former stockholders in proportion to their stock ownership. Those statutes do not contemplate that the trustees in the absence of an agreement among the stockholders shall turn the corporate business and physical assets over to one stockholder or group of stockholders while requiring some other stockholder or stockholders to accept cash as his or their distributive share in liquidation.

As to the legality of the plan of liquidation, the case of Mason v. Pewabic Mining Company, 133 U.S. 50, 10 S.Ct. 224, 33 L.Ed. 524, decided in 1890, appears to be in point here. In that case the Pewabic Mining Company was in distressed financial condition; the majority stockholders of Pewabic were apparently not willing to put any more money into that corporation. Instead, they organized a new corporation which they controlled. It was decided that Pewabic would be dissolved; that Pewabic's assets would be turned over to the new corporation in satisfaction of the stock interest of the majority stockholders, and that the owners of the minority stock would be paid in cash for their stock on the basis of a valuation fixed by the majority. It was held that this method of winding up the affairs of Pewabic was illegal and was subject to injunction. The Court said (pp. 58–59 of 133 U.S., p. 228 of 10 S.Ct., 33 L.Ed. 524):

> "With regard to the main question, the power of the directors and of the majority of the corporation to sell all of the assets and property of the Pewabic Mining Company to the new corporation under the existing circumstances of this case, we concur with the circuit court. It is earnestly argued that the majority of the stockholders—such a relatively large majority in interest—have a right to control

in this matter, especially as the corporation exists for no other purpose but that of winding up its affairs, and that, therefore, the majority should control in determining what is for the interest of the whole, and as to the best manner of effecting this object. It is further said that in the present case the dissenting stockholders are not compelled to enter into a new corporation with a new set of corporators, but have their option, if they do not choose to do this, to receive the value of their stock in money.

"It seems to us that there are two insurmountable objections to this view of the subject. The first of these is that the estimate of the value of the property which is to be transferred to the new corporation and the new set of stockholders is an arbitrary estimate made by this majority, and without any power on the part of the dissenting stockholders to take part, or to exercise any influence, in making this estimate. They are therefore reduced to the proposition that they must go into this new company, however much they may be convinced that it is not likely to be successful, or whatever other objections they may have to becoming members of that corporation, or they must receive for the property which they have in the old company a sum which is fixed by those who are buying them out. The injustice of this needs no comment. If this be established as a principle to govern the winding up of dissolving corporations, it places any unhappy minority, as regards the interest which they have in such corporation, under the absolute control of a majority, who may themselves, as in this case, constitute the new company, and become purchasers of all the assets of the old company at their own valuation.

"The other objection is that there is no superior right in two or three men in the old company, who may hold a preponderance of the stock, to acquire an absolute control of the whole of it, in the way which may be to their interest, or which they may think to be for the interest of the whole. So far as any legal right is concerned, the minority of the stockholders has as much authority to say to the majority as the majority has to say to them: 'We have formed a new company to conduct the business of this old corporation and we have fixed the value of the shares of the old corporation. We propose to take the whole of it, and pay you for your shares at that valuation, unless you come into the new corporation, taking shares in it in payment of your shares in the old one.' When the proposition is thus presented, in the light of an offer made by a very small minority to a very large majority who object to it, the injustice of the proposition is readily seen; yet we know of no reason or authority why those holding a majority of the stock can place a value upon it at which a dissenting minority must sell or do something else which they think is against their interest, more than a minority can do. . . ."

* * *

The correctness of the Pewabic decision is manifest. To say that majority stockholders may dissolve a corporation and proceed to take over the business and principal assets for themselves while at the same time forcing the minority to take mere cash for their interests, the payments to be based on a valuation made by the majority, would be to confer upon the majority the power to confiscate the minority interest, thus depriving the minority shareholders of their interest in an existing business with its attendant possibilities of growth and appreciation in value, an interest which may be worth much more than the present cash value of the minority shares. Such should not be permitted.

In coming to the conclusion that the plan for the liquidation of Crossett which was adopted was illegal the Court does not mean to suggest that Georgia-Pacific or the Trustees have been guilty of any fraud or conscious oppression or conscious violation of any fiduciary duty. On the contrary, the Court assumes, and for summary judgment purposes must assume, that the defendants acted with subjective conscientiousness and fairness, and that the price offered for the minority stock was a fair price. But, those are not the questions before the Court at the moment.

While the interests of plaintiffs in Crossett were very small proportionately, those interests constituted property rights which plaintiffs are entitled to have declared and protected. When Georgia-Pacific decided to bring about the dissolution of Crossett rather than to continue its corporate existence and operations, it assumed the obligation to liquidate Crossett in accordance with law. It had a right to distribute the assets in kind or to put them on the block for sale and divide the proceeds, in either case treating all stockholders alike. It had no right to take over The Crossett Company as a going business and eliminate plaintiffs' interests in that company by cash payments.

To the argument that the method of liquidation selected was the only feasible one and was the alternative most beneficial to plaintiffs there is a conclusive answer. Georgia-Pacific was not required to dissolve and liquidate Crossett. Having chosen to dissolve and liquidate, it was required to do so lawfully. That a lawful liquidation might have produced less money or value to plaintiffs than the method selected is beside the point. Plaintiffs had the right to insist on a lawful liquidation, and they have done so.

The Court is going no further at this time than to declare and adjudicate that Georgia-Pacific's method of liquidating Crossett was not in accordance with law, and that plaintiffs are entitled to some relief. What specific relief should be awarded plaintiffs presents a serious problem which the Court is not now in a position to solve. Although plaintiffs are entitled to a protection of their rights, they have come into a court of equity, and the framing of an appropriate remedy rests to some extent in the discretion of the Court to be exercised within the framework of general principles of equity. The determination of the relief to be awarded plaintiffs may involve a balancing of the comparatively small interests of the plaintiffs, on the one hand, against the very large and significant interests involved on the other hand. Rights of innocent third parties may have intervened, which rights may have to be protected.

Without at all prejudging the matter, it may not be feasible to undo what has been done already. Or it may be that to divest Georgia-Pacific of its ownership of the Crossett properties might inflict undue hardship on Georgia-Pacific without any corresponding benefit to plaintiffs. It is possible that the plaintiffs may have to take money, and they may come out with less than Georgia-Pacific has offered. But, at the very least, they are entitled to the fair value of their stock, determined impartially, and are not required to accept a value fixed by the majority stockholders.

. . . The Court understands from counsel on both sides that in the past some settlement negotiations have been conducted. Those negotiations should be renewed in light of the Court's views herein set forth. If the negotiations are not fruitful, within about thirty days the Court will on short notice call a conference of counsel at which counsel should be prepared to discuss with the Court questions of further proceedings looking toward termination of the litigation by settlement or otherwise.

Accord, In Re San Joaquin Light & Power Corp., 52 Cal.App.2d 814, 127 P.2d 29 (1942) ("while [the statute] permits the distribution of assets other than money where this can be done fairly and ratably and in conformity with the articles, nothing herein in any way indicates an intention to permit a distribution in kind to some of the common stockholders while compelling others to turn in their stock for its present cash value"); Zimmermann v. Tide Water Associated Oil Co., 61 Cal.App.2d 585, 143 P.2d 409 (1943). On the other hand, as previously noted there may be circumstances where a liquidating corporation must offer a cash alternative to minority stockholders, if a straight distribution in kind would work a hardship upon them. See Shrage v. Bridgeport Oil Co., page 724 supra.

Can the problem posed by these cases be met by having the subsidiary sell its assets, at a fair price of course, to the parent corporation? As a practical matter, this would leave the minority stockholders of the subsidiary in the same position as under the approach rejected by the court in the Kellogg case—that is, with cash equivalent to their pro rata share of the value of the subsidiary's assets, as determined by the parent. But it would seem unreasonable to insist that the subsidiary's assets be put up for sale at public auction, thereby forcing the parent to risk losing the assets to a third party. And of course under the sale approach the minority stockholders would have the added protection of being entitled to close judicial scrutiny of the fairness of the price paid, since the parent would be subject to the normal rules applicable to a fiduciary purchasing property from itself. Compare Abelow v. Midstates Oil Corp., 189 A.2d 675 (Del.Sup.Ct.1963), discussed at page 759 infra, where such a sale procedure was sustained.

b. The "Short Merger" Procedure

The difficulties inherent in a straight-forward dissolution of a subsidiary may be avoided under so-called "short merger" statutes, such as MBA § 68A, which authorize a parent corporation owning a specified percentage of the stock of a subsidiary to merge the subsidiary into the parent without any vote or appraisal for the stockholders of the parent, and with only a cash payment to the minority stockholders of the subsidiary. Notice that merger can be a much more convenient way to get rid of a subsidiary than liquidation because a merger avoids any question as to the legal sufficiency of an assumption of liabilities and also eliminates all the paper work, such as deeds and the like, which would otherwise be required to transfer the subsidiary's property to the parent. In connection with the following analysis of short merger statutes, consider whether such provisions might better be viewed as a substitute for liquidation than as a type of merger, and whether that makes any difference.

COMMENT: THE SHORT MERGER STATUTE [8]

32 U.Chi.L.Rev. 596 (1965).

The demand for corporate "flexibility" has generated merger forms less stringent than the old common-law requirement of unanimous shareholder consent. The most recent is the "short merger" statute. Such a statute typically provides that a corporation may merge a ninety or ninety-five per cent owned subsidiary into itself without the consent of the shareholders of either corporation. The formal requirements for merger are simply a resolution passed by

---

8. Reprinted by permission of the University of Chicago Law Review. Portions of the text and most of the footnotes omitted.

the board of directors of the parent corporation, the filing of necessary papers with a state official and notification of the shareholders. The interests of the minority shareholders of the subsidiary may be terminated by an offer of "shares or other securities or obligations of the surviving corporation or . . . cash or other consideration," [3] in lieu of which the minority may force appraisal. Discomfited shareholders of the parent corporation are given no opportunity to dissent because the short merger "should not materially affect their rights." [4] This comment concludes that short merger statutes in their present form are undesirable, and that any advantages which they do offer may be obtained by a simple amendment of the traditional merger statute.

At common law, an equity interest could not be altered, and thus no merger effected, without the unanimous consent of all affected shareholders. However, the growth of corporations, both in magnitude and numbers, dictated that something less than unanimity suffice. In all jurisdictions statutes have been adopted that permit merger with the approval of at least a majority and usually two-thirds of each class of shareholders of both corporations. To allow expression of dissent, the merger plan is required to be presented to meetings of shareholders of both corporations.

Even after majority ratification, however, the dissenting shareholder cannot be forced to go along with the merged enterprise. He has the chance to accept whatever plan of merger the majority approves, but if he chooses not to participate, he can force the corporation to purchase his shares at a value fixed by appraisal. The rationale underlying this option is that in case of a change in his interests, the dissenting shareholder should not have the ability to block action which two-thirds think desirable, but he should have an equally fair chance either to continue participation or sell his shares. The majority is not permitted to force the minority to resort to appraisal by posing an unfair offer.[*] Not only is such an unfair plan of merger unlikely because two-thirds of the shareholders have found it appealing, but the minority shareholder may sometimes have the court of equity enjoin the transaction if it is grossly unfair.

Protection of the minority interests begins to break down, however, even under traditional statutes, whenever one of the corporations to be merged holds an interest in the other sufficiently great to approve the merger. No longer is there an independent majority to help guarantee the fairness of the plan. A meeting of the subsidiary's

---

[3.] ABA-ALI Model Bus. Corp. Act § 68A (1960).

[4.] ABA-ALI Model Bus. Corp. Act § 68A, comment at 348 (1960). The combination of a parent with its ninety-five per cent owned subsidiary certainly would not significantly alter the business in which the parent shareholder had invested. . . .

[*] [Ed. note] As to whether appraisal is the exclusive remedy for stockholders opposed to a merger, see page 691 supra.

shareholders offers no protection because the individual shareholders have too few votes to affect the terms of the merger. If the parent's interest in the subsidiary is very large, for example ninety or ninety-five per cent, there is even little need for a meeting of the shareholders of the parent corporation because a merger will hardly alter their interests.

However, the traditional merger statutes do preserve the "right" of the minority of the subsidiary to receive a fair offer to continue in the enterprise. And although there is no independent majority to help guarantee fairness, the expense of appraisal helps render unprofitable any attempt by the company to abuse its dominant position. Furthermore, the minority shareholder still has equitable remedies available to enjoin a merger until he is given a reasonable chance to continue in the enterprise.

The short merger statute not only retains the objectionable features of any merger involving a controlled corporation, but adds new ones. Not only does it dispense with the requirement of votes by shareholders of either corporation, but it also provides for termination of the interest of the minority shareholders without the requirement that the parent first present an offer of continuing participation.[13]

Such a provision is not different in kind from that in traditional merger statutes allowing an offer of "shares or other securities or obligations. . . ."[14] Under that language the corporation could offer terminable debentures, callable bonds or redeemable preferred shares,[15] and while the minority in this way would receive an offer of "continued participation," the effect would be little different from a cash offer to be paid with interest at a future time.

---

13. It has been suggested that to allow the termination of the shareholder's interest for cash is unconstitutional. . . . Illinois courts have forbidden the conversion of equity into debt securities upon constitutional grounds, despite clear authorization under relevant statutes. Bowman v. Armour & Co., 17 Ill.2d 43, 160 N.E.2d 753 (1959). Such a position would a fortiori bar the conversion of equity into cash; however, the language of the court seems to reflect a vestigial remnant of the old vested interest theory of shareholder's rights and will certainly fall in the face of the overwhelming rejection of that theory in favor of the contract or "social duty" theories of shareholder's rights. . . . Although the social duty theory has not yet been applied in the context of the short merger, the contract theory has been applied to uphold the constitutionality of the short merger upon at least two occasions. Coyne v. Park & Tilford Distillers Corp., 38 Del. Ch. 514, 154 A.2d 893 (1959); Beloff v. Consolidated Edison Co., 300 N.Y. 11, 87 N.E.2d 651 (1949); . . .

14. ABA-ALI Model Bus. Corp. Act § 65 (c) (1960).

15. . . . The legislative history of applicable statutes clearly allows such a conversion. In Delaware, for example, the statute authorizing exchange of shares only for "shares" of the continuing enterprise was amended to permit the exchange of "shares or other securities." . . . Typically, however, states have gone even further and amended statutes permitting exchange of "shares" to read "shares or other securities or obligations." . . .

Similarly, it does not at first appear economically significant that the minority must take cash for their shares rather than receive equity securities of the same value in the continuing enterprise. The minority obviously could use the cash to purchase the shares of the continuing enterprise on the market, or if unavailable, they could buy shares of similar corporations. It might well be asked whether the ownership of shares in a distinct corporation is significantly different from the ownership of an altered interest in the merged entity.

But the major economic impact will be that the minority receiving cash must immediately incur a capital gains tax. The minority shareholder who desires to participate in the enterprise could thus always be forced to settle for securities worth less than the fair value of his interest. He could be threatened that any truly fair offer would be paid only in cash—an offer unimpeachable under the statute but potentially worth even less to him because of the burden of immediate taxation.[17]

Further, where the short merger statute has been adopted, courts have limited minority protection even beyond what the statute permits. On the theory that the short merger statute legislatively sanctions quick elimination of the minority from an enterprise, courts have been hesitant to allow equity to restrain a fraudulent short merger even where it is admitted that the dissenters under a traditional merger statute may avail themselves of full equitable remedies.[18] Although a given dissenter might not resort to equitable relief where the cost of going to court would be disproportionate to the small interest for which he seeks protection, this diminution of equitable remedies portends a toleration of inequitable treatment which would not otherwise be permitted.

* * *

In assessing the desirability of the short merger statutes, their advantages must, of course, be considered. The original impetus for the adoption of short merger statutes apparently was the collapse

17. Of course the amount received in appraisal would be subject to such a tax under either the short merger or the traditional merger. This is not unjust in the latter case because the shareholder who resorts to appraisal in lieu of equitable remedies presumably does so because he wishes to sell his shares, and sale would entail a tax in any case. It is because equitable remedies under the short merger can require no more than payment of cash that such pressure is possible.

18. In Stauffer v. Standard Brands, Inc., 187 A.2d 78 (Del.), affirming 178 A.2d 311 (Del.Ch.1962), the court affirmed the dismissal of a complaint seeking to enjoin a short merger stating that the availability of equitable remedies "refers generally to all mergers, and is nothing but a reaffirmation of the ever-present power of equity to deal with illegality or fraud. But it has no bearing here. . . . [T]he very purpose of the statute is to provide the parent corporation with a means of eliminating the minority shareholder's interest in the enterprise. Thereafter the former stockholder has only a monetary claim." However, the court found it "unnecessary to hold that under no conceivable circumstances could a minority stockholder obtain relief for fraud." . . .

of over-leveraged utility empires during the depression. To facilitate a simplification of holding and operating company relationships, the legislature of New York enacted the short merger to circumvent blocking or delaying tactics employed by small but belligerent minority interests. As similar procedures were made available to all corporations, the check upon arbitrary application furnished by the necessity of obtaining the permission of a state regulatory body, such as a public utilities commission, was eliminated, and the decision whether or not to merge was left in the discretion of the majority.

The original need for such statutes appears to have diminished substantially. The utility empires are now subject to stringent regulation by federal administrative bodies to prevent questionable pyramiding; the activities of holding companies are closely restricted. The delaying tactics of the minority interests, such as spurious derivative litigation, are now less available due to the increased costs of litigation and the more onerous burdens placed by the courts upon those seeking to thwart statutorily authorized corporate action.

The short merger has endured, and shows signs of flourishing, because it offers the opportunity of merger without the needless expense of holding meetings whose outcomes would be pre-determined. Such savings will be significant, however, only where the corporation is of substantial size and where the question would have to be presented at a special meeting. It has been suggested that the short merger may also facilitate an advantageous business deal, or, in the case of a subsidiary with which the parent does a significant amount of business, may promote operating economies. Like possible savings from the elimination of a meeting, however, the benefit gained by shortcutting traditional procedures must be quite limited.

Superfluous costs could be saved, however, by a simple amendment of the traditional merger statute to permit eliminating both parent and subsidiary shareholder meetings and appraisal for parent shareholders when the parent corporation holds a ninety or ninety-five per cent interest in the subsidiary. Such an amendment would make no other change in merger procedure, and it would bring about all the real advantages of the short merger statute without retaining its evils.

Where short merger statutes have already been enacted, their deleterious effects can be minimized by requiring that the parent corporation offer an equity interest unless demonstrably impractical. Further, in the absence of a specific legislative prohibition, equitable remedies should not be abridged and appraisal should not be deemed an exclusive remedy.[31] Construction of the statute to require an offer

---

31. Some jurisdictions which were once willing to hold the appraisal remedy exclusive where the short merger was applied have moved to a position where equitable remedies have been partially restored but in a much-weakened condition. New York, which once clearly held appraisal to be exclusive, Blumenthal v. Roosevelt Hotel, Inc., [202 Misc. 988, 115 N.Y.S.2d 52 (Sup.

of equity securities need not do violence to its language; the provisions permitting offer of "shares or other securities or obligations . . . or cash or other consideration . . ." could be read as options stated in declining order of preference.

The offer of an equity interest will often be easily made out of available unissued or treasury shares. If the corporation is precluded from issuing securities by costly SEC requirements or prior indenture commitments, it will be a simple and inexpensive process to so inform the court. If the corporation is unable or unwilling to demonstrate why it cannot offer equity shares, the court should require further proof of good faith. The merger should be permitted regardless of the demonstrated feasibility of offering an equity interest only on the showing of a substantial reason, such as a previous history of minority obstruction of business operations through spurious derivative suits.[34]

In summary, the short merger may offer a possible saving in costs, but it threatens the minority with both a diminution of equitable remedies and, by permitting the initial offer to be in cash subject to an immediate capital gains tax, the pressure to take an unfair offer. It is suggested that these disadvantages outweigh the remote possibility of savings and that the short merger statutes as presently proposed should thus not be adopted.

3. EFFECT OF LIQUIDATION PREFERENCES

Liquidation of the acquired corporation may be further complicated when it has stock with a liquidation preference outstanding, since if the liquidation preference exceeds the present market value of the stock the holders of the stock may be expected to insist that their preference be honored. This is particularly serious in the case of an asset acquisition, since as a practical matter the only alternative to liquidation is for the acquired corporation to carry on as a kind of holding company (of rather undiversified character), and there is no counterpart of the short merger statute to facilitate the elimination of the acquired corporation. Of course, it might be argued that since the overall transaction amounts in effect to the same thing as a merger,

---

Ct.1952)], retreated from that position in Ribakove v. Rich, 13 Misc.2d 98, 173 N.Y.S.2d 306 (Sup.Ct.1958), but stated in Rank Organization Ltd. v. Pathe Labs., Inc., 33 Misc.2d 748, 227 N.Y.S.2d 562 (Sup.Ct.1962), that the requirement of "good faith" extended only to providing a fair opportunity for appraisal. Delaware has most recently taken the position that the courts will inquire into a short merger but only where the substantive transaction "might be so tainted with illegality as to require invalidation of the merger." Braasch v. Goldschmidt, 199 A.2d 760, 764 (Del.Ch.1964). . . .

34. Of course this process will be costly to the corporation. In view of the much greater expense of dissolution, the alternative method of removing a troublesome minority, this cost seems justified however.

the participation of the preferred stock should be measured in the same way as it is in a merger, that is, by the present value of the stock, rather than by its liquidation preference. But in a merger the statute expressly authorizes the plan of merger to fix the conversion ratio and to provide for the issuance of stock of the acquiring corporation directly to the stockholders of the acquired corporation. On the other hand, as we have seen, a sale of assets does not carry with it any power to distribute the consideration received, much less to determine the basis upon which such consideration should be allocated among the various classes of stock of the acquired corporation. See pages 614–615, supra. Distribution of the assets of a corporation in liquidation can only be authorized pursuant to dissolution of the corporation, and in dissolution it seems clear that the distribution is governed by the contractual claim of each class, which would of course include any liquidation preference.

NEWMAN v. ARABOL MFG. CO.

New York Supreme Court, Special Term, 1963.
41 Misc.2d 184, 245 N.Y.S.2d 442.

MILTON M. WECHT, JUDGE. The defendant Arabol Mfg. Co., a duly organized corporation, existing under the laws of the State of New York, had issued an outstanding 3630 shares of common stock, and 3720 shares of preferred stock, of which 150 shares of its preferred stock is in the hands of plaintiff, a testamentary Trustee. It then sold all of [its] assets and goodwill to the Borden Co., another defendant, and received therefor 49,600 shares of common stock of Borden.

The plaintiff at no time objected to this sale, nor to the transfer of Arabol's assets for 49,600 shares of Borden common. After this transfer, Arabol proceeded to buy back 3570 of its preferred shares for 10,710 shares of Borden stock, or 3 shares of Borden for each share of Arabol preferred. With respect to the remaining shares of Borden, or 38,890, Arabol intends to distribute these shares to the owners of its 3630 shares of common stock, or a bit over 10 shares of Borden for each share of Arabol common.

To this planned transfer, plaintiff, the holder of the outstanding 150 shares of Arabol preferred, objects, and argues that all the shareholders of Arabol, both the common and preferred, are entitled to equal distribution. As a matter of fact, to further emphasize his objection, he refused to accept the 450 shares of Borden transferred to his name or the dividend check from Borden, representing such shares which he received on the basis of the exchange of 3 for 1, hereinbefore mentioned, and started an action for an injunction and a declaratory judgment. . . .

* * *

The statutes . . . empowering a corporation to sell its property and to pay a dissenting stockholder the appraised value of his stock have no application to Arabol's plan. The attempt to distribute its assets in such a way as to give a holder of common stock a greater share of the corporate assets than a preferred stockholder is improper since there is nothing in the stock certificates or the charter authorizing such a differentiation. Plaintiff is not restricted to alternate courses of agreeing to the plan, or seeking appraisal, but can contest the planned distribution of assets in equity. . . .

* * *

It is clear that the difference in distribution between the 3 shares to the preferred stockholders and the 10 shares to the common stockholders does not constitute a dividend, it being the expressed intention of the corporation not to declare it a dividend now or in the future. Therefore, the preferred and common stock should share equally in the assets upon liquidation. . . .

Accordingly, . . . summary judgment in favor of plaintiff is granted.

4. ALTERATION OF PREFERRED STOCKHOLDERS' LIQUIDATION PREFERENCE

GOLDMAN v. POSTAL TELEGRAPH, INC.[9]

United States District Court, D. Delaware, 1943.
52 F.Supp. 763.

LEAHY, DISTRICT JUDGE. Diversity and the requisite amount establish jurisdiction.

The occasion has never arisen for the Delaware courts to determine where a certificate of incorporation provides a preference stock is to be paid $60 per share upon liquidation before any distribution is to be made to the common stockholders whether an amendment [of the certificate] . . . which attempts to provide that such preferred stockholder shall receive on dissolution less than the stated figure of $60 a share is valid. Absent a precise holding by the state court, a federal court must examine all the available data as to what the state tribunal would probably decide under such facts.

I. *The Plan.* Postal Telegraph, Inc., incorporated under the laws of Delaware in 1939 (herein called "Postal"), agreed to transfer to Western Union Telegraph Company (herein called "Western Union"), another Delaware corporation, all its assets. At the time

---

9. Portions of the text and all the court's footnotes omitted.

of the agreement plaintiff owned 500 shares of non-cumulative preferred stock of Postal which, by the terms of Postal's certificate of incorporation, entitled all preferred stockholders to a payment of $60 a share on liquidation before any distribution could be made to its common stockholders. On July 5, 1943, defendant Postal proposed three resolutions authorizing (1) the sale of all its assets to Western Union, conditioned upon the approval by Postal's stockholders of an amendment to its certificate of incorporation referred to in (2); (2) the amendment of Postal's certificate of incorporation so as to provide that the holders of defendant's non-cumulative preferred stock would receive in lieu of $60 per share on liquidation one share of Western Union B stock; and (3) formal dissolution of Postal. At the stockholders' meeting held on August 10, 1943, these resolutions were passed by a requisite vote over plaintiff's express objection. This suit followed.

The Postal-Western Union agreement provides that for the transfer of all the assets of Postal to Western Union, Postal will receive as part consideration 308,124 shares of Class B stock of Western Union. The entire amount of Class B stock to be received from Western Union will have a value substantially less than the aggregate liquidation preference of the preferred stock of Postal. Consequently, under its certificate of incorporation Postal's common stockholders—whose equity is deeply under water—would be entitled to receive nothing if ordinary liquidation occurred. Subject to various adjustments which do not have my immediate attention, Western Union will assume approximately $10,800,000 of Postal's liabilities. Postal's economic position is shown by its steady losses, aggregating over $13,500,000 from February 1, 1940, to May 31, 1943. . . .

In order to complete the proposed transfer of assets to Western Union, the vote of a majority of the outstanding stock of Postal was required under the Delaware law. . . . Postal's outstanding preferred was 256,769.9 and the number of shares of common was 1,027,076.6. Hence, if all the preferred voted in favor of the plan, it would still be necessary to obtain the affirmative vote of approximately 400,000 shares of common. In order to obtain such vote, Postal's directors determined it advisable that the preferred's rights on liquidation be modified, so as to provide that out of the 308,124 shares of Class B stock of Western Union to be received by Postal, 256,770 shares would be distributed share for share for each of Postal's preferred and the balance of the Class B—51,354 shares—would be distributed to Postal's common stockholders, which was to be in the ratio of 1/20 of a share of Class B Western Union stock for each share of common stock of Postal.

As part of the plan, Western Union would also change its present 1,045,592 shares of capital stock into an equal number of shares of Class A stock without par value, which stock would be entitled to a non-cumulative dividend of $2 per share in each year before any dividends could be paid upon the Class B stock. After such dividend payment, the Class A and Class B stock are to participate on an equal basis in any dividends. . . .

Plaintiff here seeks, on behalf of himself and all other non-assenting shareholders, to enforce the liquidating rights which he contends are secured to him by the certificate of incorporation of Postal prior to the adoption of the resolution to amend it. . . .

Two issues are raised by the pleadings: (1) Whether the amendment to Postal's certificate of incorporation is authorized under Sec. 26 of the Delaware Corporation Law [the Delaware counterpart of MBA § 53, now Del. § 242], and (2) if Sec. 26 authorizes the present amendment whether the statute to this extent is constitutional.

II. *The Delaware Law.* The national and Delaware bars generally together with the legal literature especially have been unwilling to look directly at the radiations from the Delaware opinions which disclose what reclassification acts may be accomplished under Sec. 26 of the Delaware Corporation Law.

After much contemplation I concluded this is not the occasion to trace in limine the growth of the Delaware law in the field of corporate reclassification or rearrangement of stockholders' rights in order to show the development of a logical pattern of judicial thought on this and allied questions. Because the Delaware decisions are so crystalline in outline, I am mildly surprised there could be disagreement of interpretation as to just what may not be accomplished under the corporation statutes of that state.

Defendant's certificate of incorporation provides that, in the event of liquidation or dissolution, the holders of preferred stock are entitled to be paid $60 per share, plus all unpaid dividends (of which there are none), before any distribution is made to the holders of the common or junior stock. Sec. 26 provides that an amendment to a certificate of incorporation may alter or change "preferences" theretofore provided for a preferred stock, if the vote of a requisite majority is had. . . .

The right of preferred to priority in distribution of assets upon liquidation is clearly a preferential right within the meaning of the Delaware statutes. . . . I hold such right is subject to the amendment here involved under the particular language of Sec. 26. . . .

III. *The Constitutional Question.* Plaintiff's main contention is that if Sec. 26 authorizes the action taken by Postal it is unconstitutional, because such action will result in the destruction of what plaintiff calls his "vested" or "property" rights. Obviously, the determination of this question depends upon whether one accepts or rejects plaintiff's primary postulate of what is a "vested" or "property" right.

A person buying into a Delaware business corporation does so subject to the provisions of the particular charter and the Delaware Corporation Law. Delaware law assumes such person realizes Sec. 26 provides that *preferences* may be changed by a requisite majority vote. And preferred stockholders of a Delaware corporation when they buy into the particular enterprise accordingly consent in advance that whatever their preferences may be at the time they are subject to change by vote of the proper majority. . . . This is not a harsh rule. . . . It is one of the fundamental concepts of the Delaware law that protection is afforded against arbitrary action in the requirement that a majority of those affected by the amendment must vote in favor of it. This democratic principle, based, in reality, on a worldly or practical necessity, is that the voice of a majority must be accepted as an expression of what is best for the whole. Moreover, another concept established by the Delaware decisions is that, assuming a grant of power by statute, . . . exercise of such grant is always subject to the historical processes of the court of equity to gauge whether there has been an oppressive exercise of the power granted. . . . This is "fair and equitable" language. Where, as here, it is admitted there are no questions of unfairness involved, the only question remaining is one of classic constitutionality, involving only the contract clause and due process.

Plaintiff therefore contends that the rights of the preferred to priority of return of capital in distribution of assets upon liquidation are fixed, vested, or contractual rights and thus are constitutionally beyond reach of alteration by amendment under Sec. 26. Plaintiff presses the point that these preferential rights are analogous to the right of stockholders to accrued and unpaid dividends on preferred stock, and if it be said that Sec. 26 authorizes the alteration of such rights, then the statute is unconstitutional under the doctrine of Keller v. Wilson & Co.[10] . . .

* * *

It is clear on principle there can be no constitutional objections to the present amendment. Since the corporation is the creature of the state, and since the corporation law is a part of the corporate charter . . . it is self-evident the state has the right to reserve to itself, or a majority or more of the stockholders, the power to change the contract between the corporation and its stockholders or between its different classes of stockholders by an amendment to the charter after such contracts are made, even if a particular class of stockholders must suffer slightly. If a rationale is sought for this reservation of power, then a more cogent reason than that which exists in the case at bar would be difficult to find. Here, the public interest has a stake. We are concerned with two of the great communicating systems of this country. Duplicity of effort gone, an attendant increase in effi-

---

10. [Ed. note] See text at note 11, page 742 infra.

Sec. 1   LIQUIDATION OF ACQUIRED CORPORATION   741

ciency and decrease in waste will naturally make the public beneficiaries, in part, by the absorption of Postal by Western Union. Viewed against the undoubted reservation of right by the state and the public interest involved, changes in liquidating preferences seem mild.

* * *

Plaintiff argues, however, that execution of the contract of sale of assets by Postal and Western Union on May 13, 1943, gave to preferred a present right to payment of $60 per share, and that its right to such payment on dissolution or liquidation then became a "fixed and vested right". But the agreement of May 13, 1943, was not binding upon Postal, since by its terms it called for authorization by the vote of its stockholders. . . . A sale of assets does not constitute a dissolution or necessarily call for a liquidation. . . . Here, Postal might have continued to hold the Class B shares of stock of Western Union without distribution to its stockholders. In fact, such a course was suggested in its proxy statement which it sent to all its stockholders.

I conclude the execution of the May 13, 1943, contract for sale of assets to Western Union did not accelerate the preferential right of Postal's preferred stockholders to $60 a share on dissolution into a "vested right" which could not thereafter be altered by amendment under Sec. 26.

IV. *The Procedural Question.* At argument, plaintiff made his last contention that defendant could not agree to sell its assets conditioned upon the power of the corporation to amend its certificate of incorporation as a part of the transaction. There is no merit to this view. . . . This court and the Delaware courts have recognized the strategic position of common stock to hamper the desires of the real owners of the equity of a corporation, and the tribute which common stock exacts for its vote under reclassification and reorganization. . . . [S]eparate meetings of Postal's stockholders could have been called to (a) amend under Sec. 26 and (b) approve a sale of assets under Sec. 65; for purposes of convenience and the saving of expense, both steps were taken at one meeting. Nothing in the Delaware law forbids such a procedure. . . .

NOTE ON AMENDMENTS ALTERING THE RIGHTS
OF SHAREHOLDERS

NOTE: LIMITATIONS ON ALTERATION OF SHAREHOLDERS' RIGHTS BY CHARTER AMENDMENT *

69 Harv.L.Rev. 538 (1956).

The general corporation laws in the principal states of incorporation authorize majority interests to effect by charter amendment certain chang-

---

* Copyright (c), Harvard Law Review Association, 1956. Reprinted by permission. Portions of the text and most of the footnotes omitted.

es in the rights of shareholders. The validity of such amendments depends on the scope of the authorizing statute, on whether the corporate charter was obtained before or after enactment of that statute, and on the judicial construction of the state's power to authorize changes in the contract of the shareholders *inter se*.[2]

Interpretation of the Authorizing Statute.—Statutory interpretation does not pose serious problems where, as in New York, the statute enumerates specifically those rights of investors which may be altered by charter amendment. However, corporation laws containing general authorizing language are common. An early Delaware statute allowed a majority of shareholders to make "any . . . change or alteration in . . . [the] Charter of incorporation that may be desired," with the proviso that if "preferences" were altered it must be done by a class vote. In a case where all the proposed amendments had been approved by a class vote, a Delaware court construed this statute to permit amendments changing voting rights and authorizing the issue of prior preferred stock, but to prohibit one canceling accrued dividends. The statute was subsequently amended to authorize changes in "preferences, or relative, participating, optional or other special rights of the shares." Although a federal court construed the statute as amended to permit cancellation of accrued dividends, in a subsequent case the Delaware court still refused to allow such an amendment.[11] The divergent results reached by these and other courts construing similar language indicate that the meaning given to general statutory authorizations is dictated not so much by the statutory language as by criteria similar to those which courts employ to determine whether the statute as applied is constitutional.

Limitations on Amendments Authorized by Statutes Enacted Subsequent to Incorporation.—The Supreme Court in Trustees of Dartmouth College v. Woodward [13] held that a corporate charter constitutes a contract between the state and the corporation and that the Constitution protects such contracts against alteration by the state. The state's power over the charter as a contract of the shareholders *inter se* was not involved in the Dartmouth College case, but it is likely that if, subsequent to incorporation, the state had sought to impose a change in the substantive rights of the shareholders, or had authorized a majority interest to impose such a change, this too would have been declared unconstitutional. Although the Court in the Dartmouth College case rested its decision on the impairment of contracts clause, the fourteenth amendment had not yet been adopted; having largely absorbed the contract clause, due process would be the more likely basis for constitutional attack today.

Mr. Justice Story stated by way of dictum in the Dartmouth College case that the state could, as a term of its contract with the corporation, reserve a power to amend the charter; and most states, either by statute or constitutional provision, have reserved such a power. However, it is doubtful, under modern conceptions, whether there is any such contract

---

2. The courts have come to regard the corporate charter as embodying three contracts: between the state and the corporation, the corporation and the shareholders, and the shareholders *inter se*. . . .

11. Keller v. Wilson & Co., 21 Del.Ch. 391, 190 A. 115 (Sup.Ct.1936). . . .

13. 17 U.S. (4 Wheat.) 518 (1819).

in which the right to amend is reserved since the relationship of the state to the corporation would seem regulatory rather than contractual. Corporations are no longer created by franchise and special legislative grant, as in the time of the Dartmouth College case. Instead they are authorized and controlled by general statutes applicable to all who adopt the corporate form of business organization. But even if the charter is a contract between the state and the corporation, a term permitting the state to amend its own contract would not seem to provide it with power over the shareholders' contract. Nevertheless, it might be argued that the reserved power, like all other terms of the corporation laws, becomes part of the charter by force of law,[23] and therefore part of the shareholders' contract *inter se.* Thus the shareholders would be deemed to have consented in advance to the exercise by the state of a power to amend the charter or to authorize the majority to do so. . . .

New Jersey [25] and several other states hold that the reserved power does not extend to the contract among the shareholders and that this contract can only be altered by the state in the "public interest." Some commentators have construed this position to preclude any change in the shareholders' contract. However, recent New Jersey cases, applying equitable principles to enjoin as unfair amendments authorized subsequent to incorporation, indicate that New Jersey may not fully subscribe to this position today. And within the limits of fairness, whether it be defined in terms of due process or the equitable power of courts, state power to authorize reasonable charter amendments would seem desirable in order to enable businesses incorporated under an earlier statute to adjust to a changing economy.

The Delaware courts have set constitutional limits to the state's power to authorize amendments by holding that it cannot authorize impairment of "vested" rights, such as the right to accrued dividends. However, since the shareholder cannot sue for such dividends unless they have been declared, and since on dissolution creditors have a prior claim on corporate assets, "vested" in this context does not seem to connote an assured right of enjoyment to the shareholder, and so is largely a fictional concept raised by the courts to protect the fruits of the shareholder's past investment. Although this seems to be a due process consideration of fairness, it has not been applied in other contexts, the Delaware courts having allowed the practical elimination of accrued dividends as a result of merger or the issue of prior preferred. Nevertheless, what is important to the shareholder is not the form of the alteration but its result.

It would seem preferable to examine whether such benefits as the corporation is likely to derive from a charter amendment are outweighed by the probable injury to the minority shareholders, rather than to base de-

25. Pronik v. Spirits Distributing Co., 58 N.J.Eq. 97, 42 A. 586 (Ch. 1899); Zabriskie v. Hackensack & N. Y. R. R., 18 N.J.Eq. 178 (Ch. 1867). [Ed. note: In the Zabriskie case, the chancellor expressed the view that while the reserved power changed the rule of the Dartmouth College case and thus made it possible for the legislature to make changes in a corporate charter for the benefit of the public, the reserved power could not justify giving "a power to one part of the incorporators as against the other, which they did not have before".]

23. Most state corporation laws provide that they shall be automatically included in the terms of the charter. . . .

cisions on such tests as a fictional "vested" rights theory. If an injury to the minority would result, the amendment can only be justified on the ground that it is necessary to enable the corporation to make adjustments essential to its continued existence. And it should appear, considering the alternatives that are available, that the amendment sought will be likely to produce financial stability. Furthermore, it is important that the minority receive a reasonable *quid pro quo* for the rights which it will lose under the amendment. Where the interests cannot be readily valued in monetary terms, as is the case with voting rights, it will be difficult to determine what is a fair exchange.

The problems inherent in applying a fairness test can be mitigated to some extent by placing the burden of going forward with the evidence upon the corporation once the minority shareholder has shown that the amendment works to his detriment. Since the corporation has presumably already examined the factors relevant to the proposed amendment, it will be in a better position than the shareholder to furnish proof on the issues of financial necessity, possible alternative plans, and the value of the rights of the different classes before and after the proposed amendments. This change from present practice, by relieving the shareholders of the expense and difficulty of obtaining information on these issues, will facilitate suit by those not able or willing to seek relief because of the smallness of their interests. Furthermore, if the majority knows that in case of suit it will have the burden of showing that the proposed plan is fair, greater attention may be given to fairness at the time the plan is formulated.

Limitations on Amendments Authorized by Statutes Enacted Prior to Incorporation.—Courts seem more reluctant to impose due process or equitable limitations on amendments authorized by statutes in existence at the time the corporate charter was obtained than on those where the statute was enacted after the date of incorporation. The reason for this greater judicial self-restraint might be that where the authorizing statute is in existence at the time of incorporation, shareholders are thought to be able to determine in advance how their interests could be modified by charter amendment. However, it is hardly feasible for a purchaser of corporate securities to examine the corporation laws in existence at the date of the charter for each state where a business in which he plans to invest is incorporated. Moreover, if the authorizing statute is not specific and has not been widely litigated, it will not apprise him of the extent of the power which may be available to the majority. Nevertheless, justification may be found for treating amendments differently where the statute was in existence at the date of the charter since the public interest may require that within a narrow limit, such as that imposed by the date of incorporation, there be a clear formulation of corporate power so as to enable corporations to amend their charters unhampered by repeated litigation. However, it would still seem desirable to apply fairness principles which will afford some protection to the interests of the investor.

Other Possible Safeguards.—In addition to any fairness limitations which may be imposed on charter amendments, other safeguards are available in some states. In a few jurisdictions, shareholders objecting to an amendment can obtain appraisal and purchase of their shares. To allow a shareholder whose rights are to be modified by the amendment the alternative of an appraisal or of an attack on the ground of unfairness provides an additional deterrent to adoption of unfair amendments by the majority, who presumably will want to avoid the expenditure of large sums in purchasing the stock of dissenters. However, if appraisal is made the exclusive remedy of the dissenting shareholder, so that he cannot seek an injunction on the ground of unfairness and so retain his investment and interest in future earnings, he may be forced to choose between accepting an unfair modification of his rights and selling his shares at the appraised price. Another safeguard available in many states is the requirement that a majority of each class adversely affected vote in favor of the amendment. However, this may not assure fairness to the dissenter, because a majority of his class may be induced to vote for a plan by the offer of a present cash payment, or because a majority may also own securities of another class which will benefit from the amendment. Furthermore despite SEC proxy rules, proxy returns continue to be relatively automatic, so that majority acceptance is no guarantee of a reasoned choice. On the other hand, a requirement of a high majority vote of each class may make class voting an effective device by forcing proponents of a charter amendment to offer generous terms in order to secure the vote necessary to the adoption of the plan.

Consideration of Fairness in the Context of Specific Charter Amendments.—Plans requiring charter amendments usually call for the alteration of numerous rights, so that in determining fairness it is necessary to consider the cumulative effect of all proposed changes.

(a) *Amendments to Eliminate Accrued Dividends and the Right to Future Accruals.*—Amendments to cancel accrued dividends are usually sought on the ground that the corporation must free earnings from the claims of the preferred before needed capital can be raised by a sale of additional common or of securities convertible into common. However, such a change not only reduces the present value of the preferred shareholder's stock, unless he is entitled to an appraisal which will take into account the accrued dividends, but also denies him the chance to recover the accruals through future dividends or asset priorities on dissolution. In addition, where the outlook for future earnings is favorable, other practical means of obtaining capital are likely to be available which will not prejudice the interests of any class; thus, long-term borrowing may be possible since the preferred's claim to accrued dividends will neither prevent the payment of interest nor impair creditors' rights on dissolution. And where the prospect of earnings is unfavorable the cancellation of accrued dividends will not hide a poor financial position from a careful investor.

An amendment to remove only the right to future accruals will not be nearly as effective in attracting new capital as one which cancels past accruals. But a loss of cumulative dividend rights may have as much impact on the value of a preferred shareholder's investment as a cancellation of past accruals, since the decreased certainty of return on the investment lowers the value of the preferred shares to prospective purchasers.

(b) *Amendments to Authorize an Issue of Prior Preferred.*—A change in the charter which authorizes an issue of new preferred with priority in dividends and assets for the purpose of raising new capital will generally not be unfair to existing classes. Although the dividend and dissolution rights of the prior preferred will be paramount, new capital and hence an opportunity for increased earnings will be available. The holders of common and of the present preferred, if the latter have the right to vote, presumably will not approve the change unless the additional resources appear likely to provide earnings at least sufficient to satisfy the claims of the new shares to dividends.

On the other hand, where the proposed issue is part of a plan to exchange prior preferred for the original preferred, there may be danger of unfairness, for the object is likely to be the elimination of accrued dividends rather than the acquisition of new capital. To induce acceptance of the plan, holders of the original preferred are frequently offered cash or other securities in addition to shares of the new issue. And they are given little practical alternative but to accept the proposed exchange. If a holder of the original preferred retains his shares, . . . his claims to assets and dividends be subordinated to the claims of those who accept the exchange . . . ..

* * *

(d) *Amendment of Provisions for Redemption* . . . .—A reclassification of noncallable preferred shares as shares callable by the corporation at a certain price may be attempted when replacement capital can be obtained at a lower dividend rate, or when the corporation has cash or low yield securities which it could use in retiring preferred with a high dividend rate, thereby releasing more earnings for distribution to the common. Such a reclassification may also benefit the common by making it possible to retire preferred which has a right to participate in earnings in excess of its fixed dividend rate. However, the amendment providing for reclassification will be unfair unless the redemption price gives the preferred at least an amount which, when reinvested at the prevailing dividend rate of similar securities, will yield income equal to that received prior to redemption. Since the majority sets the call price, there is danger of unfairness unless the shareholder has the right to an appraisal which would take into account the possible loss of income to the preferred, or unless a high majority vote of each class is required. . . .

* * *

(e) *Amendments of Liquidation Preferences.*—Especially when used in conjunction with a contemplated sale of assets, alteration of liquidation preferences may substantially injure the holders of the preferred. An amendment may be passed changing the terms of the preference to specify that the shareholder of the vendor corporation shall receive instead of cash certain securities of the proposed vendee corporation, the value of which is lower than that of the original liquidation preference. Although such plans seem unfair, courts have nevertheless upheld them.

(f) *Amendments of Voting and Pre-emptive Rights.*— . . . Where the common has voting control, complete withdrawal of the right to vote will in most instances only be sought against the preferred, since the common is unlikely to surrender its power. The contention that there is no injury to the preferred in removing its right to vote where the preferred cannot gain control ignores the possibility that holders of preferred, if joined by dissatisfied holders of common, may be able to prevent corporate action which will adversely affect their interests. An amendment providing for a transfer of the right to vote from the common to the preferred in the event of dividend arrearages on the preferred would not seem unfair to dissenting common, since the transfer of control would be the class with the most immediate financial interest. In such situations, by advancing its own interests the preferred will also bring the common nearer to participation in earnings. . . .

(g) *Merger and Consolidation as a Means of Avoiding Limitations on Charter Amendments.*—Those of the above rights which the courts have not allowed to be altered directly by amendment can nevertheless frequently be changed through merger or consolidation.[71] Even where the corporation creates a subsidiary solely for the purpose of effecting a merger and altering the rights of a class through an exchange of shares, the courts have generally refused to enjoin the plan unless there is a showing of fraud. Yet to preserve the effect of fairness limitations on charter amendments of certain rights, it would seem necessary also to apply a fairness test to other methods designed to alter these rights.

SECTION 2. FAIRNESS IN COMBINATION TRANSACTIONS

A. FAIRNESS BETWEEN THE CONSTITUENT CORPORATIONS

STERLING v. MAYFLOWER HOTEL CORP.

Supreme Court of Delaware, 1952.
33 Del.Ch. 293, 93 A.2d 107, 38 A.L.R.2d 425.

SOUTHERLAND, CHIEF JUSTICE. The principal question presented is whether the terms of a proposed merger of Mayflower Hotel Corporation (herein "Mayflower") into its parent corporation, Hilton Hotels Corporation (herein "Hilton"), are fair to the minority stockholders of Mayflower.

The essential facts are these:

Mayflower and Hilton are both Delaware corporations. Mayflower's sole business is the ownership and operation of the Mayflower

---

[71]. Accrued dividends, the most frequently protected right in amendment cases, have been widely held subject to elimination by merger. . . . In Langfelder v. Universal Laboratories, Inc., 163 F.2d 804, 807 (3d Cir. 1947) (dictum), the court indicated that all shareholders rights may be subject to alteration by merger.

Hotel in Washington, D. C. It has outstanding 389,738 shares of common stock of $1 par value. Hilton and its subsidiary corporations are engaged in the business of owning, leasing, operating and managing hotel properties in many of the large centers of population in the country. Hilton has outstanding, in addition to an issue of Convertible Preference stock, 1,592,878 shares of common stock of $5 par value.

On December 18, 1946, Hilton acquired a majority of the outstanding shares of Mayflower. Thereafter it continued to make purchases of Mayflower stock. On or about February 4, 1952, it purchased 21,409 shares at a price of $19.10 a share, and on that date made an offer to all other minority stockholders to buy their shares at the same price. As of March 25, 1952, Hilton owned 321,883 shares, or nearly five-sixths of the outstanding stock.

From the time of the acquisition by Hilton of a majority interest in Mayflower, Hilton's management had contemplated a merger of Mayflower with Hilton. . . . In the early part of 1950 the Mayflower directors discussed the question of ascertaining a fair basis of exchange of Mayflower stock for Hilton stock. All of the Mayflower directors (nine in number) were nominees of Hilton, and it was the view of the board (as well as of the Hilton board) that an independent study should be made by competent and disinterested financial analysts for the purpose of evolving a fair plan of exchange. . . .

In the early part of 1950 Standard Research Consultants, Inc., a subsidiary of Standard & Poor, was retained to make the study, and Mr. John G. Haslam, its Vice President, undertook the work. Later he submitted a study which determined a fair basis of exchange of Hilton stock for Mayflower stock to be three-fourths of a share of Hilton for one share of Mayflower. No action was taken on the basis of this study.

. . . Mr. Haslam on January 7, 1952, was again retained to continue and bring up to date his prior study and to develop a fair plan of exchange. Thereafter he submitted his final study (hereinafter referred to as "the Haslam report"), which embodies his conclusion that a fair rate of exchange would be share for share. A plan for a merger upon this basis was approved by the boards of directors of both corporations. The directors—at least the Mayflower directors—appear to have relied largely on the Haslam report to justify their action. A formal agreement of merger was entered into on March 14, 1952, providing for the merger of Mayflower (the constituent corporation) into Hilton (the surviving corporation), . . . Each outstanding share of Mayflower is converted into one share of Hilton. A separate agreement between Hilton and Mayflower provides that for a limited period Hilton will pay $19.10 a share for any Mayflower stock tendered to it by any minority stockholder. At stockholders' meetings held in April the requisite approval of the merger was obtained. At the Mayflower meeting 329,106 shares were voted in favor; 4,645 against. Holders of 35,191 shares of Mayflower who objected to the merger did not vote. The Hilton stockholders voted overwhelmingly to approve the merger.

On April 7, 1952, plaintiffs below (herein "plaintiffs"), holders of 32,295 shares of Mayflower stock, filed their complaint in the court below, seeking injunctive relief against the consummation of the merger, on the ground that the terms of the merger are grossly unfair to the minority stockholders of Mayflower, and that the Mayflower directors entered into the merger agreement in bad faith.

* * *

Plaintiffs' principal contention here, as in the court below, is that the terms of the merger are unfair to Mayflower's minority stockholders. Plaintiffs invoke the settled rule of law that Hilton as majority stockholder of Mayflower and the Hilton directors as its nominees occupy, in relation to the minority, a fiduciary position in dealing with Mayflower's property. Since they stand on both sides of the transaction, they bear the burden of establishing its entire fairness, and it must pass the test of careful scrutiny by the courts. . . . Defendants agree that their acts must meet this test. We therefore inquire whether the facts sustain the conversion ratio of share for share which forms the basis of the merger agreement.

As the Chancellor observed, the Haslam report forms the principal justification for the terms of the merger. We accordingly examine it.

The report is an elaborate study of some forty pages (including charts) with a long appendix containing analyses of pertinent financial data. The principles upon which it is based are set forth in the Chancellor's opinion. See 89 A.2d page 867. Implicit in the report is the assumption that the legal principles governing the transaction require a comparison of the value of the stock of Hilton with the stock of Mayflower. Since the report is the basis of the conversion terms of the merger agreement, it is in effect directed to a determination of the question whether, upon the conversion of Mayflower stock into Hilton stock, the Mayflower minority stockholder will receive the substantial equivalent in value of the shares he held before the merger. Thus a comparison is required of factors entering into the ascertainment of the values of both stocks. In Haslam's opinion the problem reduces to "a comparison of the operating trends of each of the corporations and of the investment characteristics of the two stock issues." A summary of some of the more important comparisons developed in the report is set forth in the margin.[1] On the basis of these comparisons, as well as upon consideration of the past history and future prospects of the two corporations, Haslam concludes that the financial record of Hilton has been substantially superior to that of Mayflower, and that purely upon a statistical basis it could be argued that Hilton should not offer better than three-fourths of a share of Hilton for one share of Mayflower. Nevertheless it is his opinion that, because of the problems incident to Hilton's control of Mayflower and the advantages incident to complete ownership, a share-for-share exchange will be fair and reasonable to all concerned.

An affidavit of J. Sellers Bancroft, Vice President in charge of Trust Department investments of Wilmington Trust Company, sets forth his conclusion, reached after a review of Mr. Haslam's study and an examination of pertinent financial data, that a share-for-share exchange is unquestionably fair.

The Haslam report contains no finding of net asset value—a factor nevertheless proper to be considered. Plaintiffs submitted affidavits containing an appraisal of the Mayflower Hotel (including land) and an estimate of reproduction cost (less depreciation) of the hotel proper. These affidavits indicate a value of upwards of $10,000,000. If plaintiffs' figure of a minimum value of $10,500,000 [2] be accepted (it was accepted by the Chancellor), a share of Mayflower stock would have a liquidating or net asset value of about $27 a share. Defendants submitted an affidavit of J. B. Herndon, Jr., Vice President and Treasurer of Hilton, to the effect that two of the hotel properties of Hilton (the Conrad Hilton and the Palmer House in Chicago), which are carried on the books at $26,800,000, have a value of at least $60,000,000. Mr. Hilton gave some testimony to the same

---

1. Comparisons drawn from Haslam report:

Average Earnings Per Share

	Hilton	Mayflower
1947–1951 Average:		
Before income taxes and extraordinary items	4.31	2.17
After " " " "	2.79	1.17
1951 to Nov. 30:		
Before income taxes and extraordinary items	4.22	3.14
After " " " "	2.37	1.15

Dividends Per Share

	Hilton	Mayflower
1947–1951 Average	1.07	.34
1951	1.20	.40

Book Value Per Share

	Hilton	Mayflower
Nov. 30, 1951 Per books	18.26	14.38
Adjusted	18.42	13.98

Market Value Per Share

	Hilton	Mayflower
1950 average	12.88	11.25
1951 Average	15.46	15.56
Approximate current price [at date of study]	14.75	16.25

2. Arrived at by adding to the appraised value $500,000 in liquid assets.

effect. If the indicated increase of $33,200,000 be accepted, there is added to Hilton's per share book value about $20, making an asset value of about $38 a share. Haslam submitted a comparison of "indicated values" of the hotel properties, arrived at by assuming rates of capitalization of earnings derived from plaintiffs' appraisal of the Mayflower Hotel and applying such rates to the Hilton earnings, and, by two different methods, arrived at figures of $30.56 and $40.82 as "indicated" net asset values of a share of Hilton stock. Plaintiffs submitted no evidence of value of the Hilton hotel properties.

Now, it will be noted that all of the comparisons above set forth except that of market value are in favor of Hilton. As for the market value of Mayflower stock, it appears to be conceded by all parties to be fictitious, that is, higher than would be justified in a free and normal market uninfluenced by Hilton's desire to acquire it and its policy of continued buying. At all events, that is the natural inference from the evidence. If we lay aside market value, and also disregard the comparison of book values—a factor, as the Chancellor said, of little relevancy in this case—we find three comparisons of various degrees of importance—earnings, dividends and net asset value—all in favor of Hilton.

If, therefore, we should accept the findings in the Haslam report and the principles on which it is based, and also accept the evidence bearing on comparative net asset value of Mayflower and Hilton stock, we should have to conclude that a share of Hilton stock has a value at least equal to a share of Mayflower stock, and that no unfair treatment of the Mayflower minority stockholders has been shown.

But we are confronted at the outset with the contention of the plaintiffs, basic to their case, that the Haslam report and the comparisons of value therein developed are wholly irrelevant to the issues before us. This contention, urged with much vigor—and repetition—is that the transaction here assailed is in substance a sale of assets by a fiduciary to himself. That the transaction is cast in the form of a merger, they say, is of no consequence; it is in effect a sale, and the only relevant comparison to be made is the comparison of the value of the transferred assets—worth $10,500,000—with the value of the consideration—389,738 shares of Hilton stock of a market value of $5,846,700; a disparity so shocking as to stamp the transaction as a fraud upon the Mayflower minority stockholders.

If plaintiffs' contention should be accepted it would follow that upon every merger of a subsidiary into its parent corporation that involves a conversion of the subsidiary's shares into shares of the parent, the *market* value of the parent stock issued to the stockholders of the subsidiary must equal the *liquidating* value of the subsidiary's stock. On its face this proposition is unsound, since it attempts to equate two different standards of value. In the case of many industrial corporations, and also in the instant case, there is a substantial gap between the market value and the liquidating value of the stock; and to apply to the merger of such corporations the proposition advanced by plaintiffs would be to bestow upon the stockholder of the subsidiary something which he did not have before the merger and could not obtain—the liquidating value of his stock. . . .

What is the reasoning by which plaintiffs would lead us to sanction such a result?

Plaintiffs start with a quotation from the opinion of Chancellor Wolcott in the case of Cole v. National Cash Credit Ass'n, 18 Del.Ch. 47, 156 A. 183, 188, which involved a merger of several Delaware corporations. Preferred stockholders of National (one of the constituent corporations) charged that if the merger were effected the asset security underlying the preferred stock of the surviving corporation that was to be given in exchange for their preferred stock in National would be less in value than that which underlay their National stock; and that this reduction in value flowed from an undervaluation of National's assets in comparison with the assets of the other merging corporations. Plaintiffs' charge of unfairness was thus based upon alleged disparity in comparative net asset values. The Chancellor said:

> "The case therefore is one that rests on the sole fact of alleged undervaluation and overvaluation of the assets of two of the merging companies."

Announcing a rule embodying a test of fraud applicable to such a case, the Chancellor continued:

> "Where that is the case the rule adopted by this court as applicable to the sale of corporate assets would seem by analogy to supply a sound basis for guidance. While a consolidation is quite distinct from a sale, yet, *from the viewpoint of the constituent companies, a sale of assets is in substance involved.* Here it is the sale feature of the merger and that alone with which we are concerned. *Looking then at the transaction as one where the stockholders of the defendant are in substance selling its assets to another in exchange for securities issued by the latter,* what is the rule by which the value derived in exchange for the assets is to be tested for the purpose of discovering whether or not fraud can be said to have been shown? . . ." 18 Del.Ch. 57–58, 156 A. 188; emphasis plaintiffs'.

Seizing upon the emphasized language and disregarding the facts to which it was directed, plaintiffs say in effect: A merger is essentially a sale of assets; this transaction is a sale of assets by a fiduciary (Hilton) to itself for shares of stock worth shockingly less than the assets sold; therefore the transaction is a fraud. So runs the syllogism.

A manifest fallacy, we think, lurks in the basic premise of this reasoning. A merger may be said to "involve" a sale of assets, in the sense that the title to the assets is by operation of law transferred from the constituent corporation to the surviving corporation; but it is not the same thing. It is, as the introductory clause of Chancellor Wolcott's language affirms, something quite distinct, and the distinction is not merely one of form, as the plaintiffs say, but one of substance. A merger ordinarily contemplates the continuance of the enterprise and of the stockholder's investment therein, though in altered form; a sale of all assets (the type of sale referred to in the Cole case) ordinarily contemplates the liquidation of the enterprise. In the first case the stockholder of the merged corporation is entitled to receive directly securities substantially equal in value to those he held before the merger; in the latter case he receives nothing directly, but his corporation is entitled to receive the value of the assets sold. The scope of the applicable sections of our General Corporation Law (Section 59, relating to mergers and consolidations, and Section 65, relating to sales of all the corporate assets) may to some extent overlap; but this is not to say that the two procedures differ only in form. They are, in general, distinct and designed for different ends.

The instant case supplies an apt illustration. The Mayflower assets are not to be liquidated; the property is not for sale. Its directors and stockholders have determined, not that the venture should be terminated, but that it should be integrated completely with the Hilton enterprise. Having made this decision they had the right to avail themselves of the means which the law provides for just such a purpose, subject always to their imperative duty to accord to the minority fair and equitable terms of conversion.

Nor do we think that the Cole case supports plaintiffs' contention. The quoted language embodies, as Chancellor Wolcott indicated, an analogy and not a definition. The question actually before him was one of comparative net asset values. Thus, at the beginning of that portion of the opinion which deals with the objections of the preferred stockholders, he said:

> "The crucial point on which their complaint turns is one of value—whether or not they as stockholders in one of the constituents are to receive in exchange for their present holdings, *stock which has a value commensurate* with the *asset contribution which their company* is making to the common pool." 18 Del.Ch. 55, 156 A. 187; emphasis plaintiffs'.

Plaintiffs interpret the words "commensurate with" as meaning "equal to". Thus they say that the quoted language makes it plain that a comparison of the value of the assets transferred with the value (i. e., market value) of the stock issued in exchange is the only relevant factor to be considered.

But this is not what the language says nor what it means. The reference is to the value of the assets underlying the stock extinguished by the merger compared with the value of the assets which will underlie the stock to be received upon the consummation of the merger. Thus, in a later part of the opinion the Chancellor speaks of the question before him as one involving "the relative participations of the merging companies in the total assets thrown into the merger pool", 18 Del.Ch. 59, 156 A. 188, and ultimately resolves the question by comparing the net asset value of a share of the stock extinguished with a similar valuation of the stock to be received. There is no suggestion in the case that in determining the fairness of a merger net asset value of one stock should be compared with market value of the other.

The unsoundness of such a method of comparison is illustrated by the subsequent decision in Mitchell v. Highland-Western Glass Co., 19 Del.Ch. 326, 167 A. 831. In that case all of the assets of Highland were to be sold to Mississippi Glass Company for shares of stock of the seller. The consideration was alleged to be grossly inadequate. Plaintiffs' counsel argued that the number of shares issued in payment for the sale was based on a ratio of assets of two to one; whereas the assets were nearly equal in value, and the ratio was grossly unfair. To develop this argument he took the full book value of the seller's assets as their fair value, but refused to value the stock received by the same method. The Chancellor dismissed the argument with the terse comment: "Manifestly that is unjustifiable." 19 Del.Ch. 333, 167 A. 834.

Plaintiffs' attempt to push to extremes the analogy drawn from a sale of assets leads them to a wholly untenable position, viz., that upon a merger a stockholder of a subsidiary is entitled to receive securities equal in value to the liquidating value of his stock. As we have already indicated, this proposition is unsound. Speaking generally, a merger effects an exchange of shares of stock in a going concern for shares in another going concern. In determining the fairness of the exchange liquidating value is not the sole test of the value of either. In [Porges v. Vadsco Sales Corp., 27 Del.Ch. 127, 32 A.2d 148 (Ch. 1943)] preferred stockholders objected to a merger which accorded recognition to the common stock on the ground that the common shares were without value—that is, without liquidating value. Implicit in this objection was the assumption that liquidating value was the sole test by which the measure of recognition accorded to the common stock in the merger was to be evaluated. Vice Chancellor Pearson rejected the argument, pointing out that the preferred stockholders had no right to require liquidation of the corporation and that the rights of the two classes of stock must be viewed in the light of the fact that the corporation was a going concern. . . .

A similar rule obtains in ascertaining the value of stock in appraisal proceedings under the merger statute. In such cases the liquidating value of the stock is not the sole test of value; all relevant factors must be considered. . . .

* * *

Sec. 2   FAIRNESS BETWEEN CORPORATIONS   755

No case is cited to us holding that upon a merger of a subsidiary into a parent corporation the minority stockholders of a subsidiary are entitled to the liquidating value of their stock.

In the instant case the Chancellor held that in a case of merger "all relevant value factors must be considered in arriving at a fair value for comparison purposes." 89 A.2d 866.

For the reasons above given, we find no error in this ruling.

The main question of law having been resolved against the plaintiffs, we turn to their remaining contentions. *Criticisms of the Haslam report.*

Plaintiffs make some criticisms of the Haslam report designed to rebut or weaken its findings.

First, they say that the Haslam report is unacceptable because it was designed as a plan for a voluntary exchange and not in contemplation of a merger; the word "merger", say the plaintiffs, does not occur in it. Hence (plaintiffs apparently argue) it has no bearing on the fairness of a merger plan.

We think the argument wholly unsubstantial. It reduces to a criticism of the use of the word "exchange" instead of the word "conversion"—the term technically correct in describing the effect of a merger. Obviously comparisons used to determine, abstractly, the fairness of a voluntary exchange of one share of stock for another are equally pertinent in determining the fairness of a compulsory exchange, that is, a conversion of one share of stock into another. Moreover, it is scarcely to be supposed that the Haslam report was obtained for the purpose of inducing minority stockholders to make a voluntary exchange. From the beginning of Hilton's control a merger had been looked forward to.

Next, plaintiffs assert that the Haslam report contains certain errors in the figures developed. They say that the Haslam report uses the figure of $14.38 as the book value of Mayflower stock, whereas the testimony shows the correct figure to be $17.50; that the Haslam report uses the figure of $16.25 a share as the market price of Mayflower, whereas Hilton had paid $19.10 a share for the stock; and that the comparison of earnings of the two corporations appearing in the report is inaccurate in that a nonrecurring item of $70,000 of litigation expense was not eliminated from the computation and capital improvements amounting to about $41,000 had been charged to maintenance and repairs on Mayflower's books. All these criticisms were advanced in the court below and were carefully considered by the Chancellor, who found them all without merit. The comparison of book values, as we have above indicated, is of little relevancy here; the market value, as we have shown, is fictitiously high, and Hilton's purchases at $19.10 a share are, under the circumstances, no evidence of true market value. As for the other matters—if they represent anything more than a difference of accounting opinion—they are immaterial, since, if the soundness of the criticisms be conceded and the suggested corrections be made, the comparison of earnings would still be in favor of Hilton. We approve the Chancellor's findings on these matters.

An argument of more substance is directed to the question of the net asset value of a share of Hilton.

Noting the omission in the Haslam report of any comparison of such values, plaintiffs develop the contention that the defendants, having the burden to justify the terms of the merger, have failed to sustain it, since no proper appraisal of Hilton's physical assets has been made. As for the evidence submitted after the suit was filed, plaintiffs say that it is of little value and inadequate to supply the deficiency in the Haslam report. At the very least, they contend, defendants' failure to present formal appraisals of Hilton's assets calls for fuller investigation of the matter than was possible at a hearing on a motion for a preliminary injunction, and the status quo should be preserved until final hearing.

As we have already held, net asset value is one of the factors to be considered in determining the fairness of a plan of merger. But the requirement that consideration be given to all relevant factors entering into the determination of value does not mean that any one factor is in every case important or that it must be given a definite weight in the evaluation. . . . The relative importance of several tests of value depends on the circumstances. Thus, in some cases net asset value may be quite important. . . . But in the case at bar it is of much less importance than the factors analysed in the Haslam report. We are dealing here with corporations engaged in the hotel business, whose capital is invested largely in fixed assets. The shares of such corporations are worth, from the viewpoint of an investor, what they can earn and pay. A comparison of net asset values may have some weight, but it is of much less importance than demonstrated capacity of the corporation to earn money and pay dividends. In Allied Chemical & Dye Corp. v. Steel and Tube Co. of America, 14 Del.Ch. 64, 122 A. 142, Chancellor Wolcott, dealing with the relative importance of replacement costs and earning power as standards of value in connection with industrial property, expressed the view that earning power is by far the more important. 14 Del.Ch. 73, 122 A. 142. And compare 1 Bonbright, Valuation of Property, Ch. XII, pp. 240–244, "Bearing of Asset Valuations on an Enterprise Appraisal". In respect of earning power the superiority of Hilton stock is clearly shown. In these circumstances we deem the evidence adduced by defendants upon the issue of comparative net asset value to be sufficient to discharge whatever duty they were under in respect of the matter; and this notwithstanding the inconclusive nature of the "indicated values" arrived at by Haslam.

Plaintiffs say that the directors of Mayflower did not give proper consideration to the question of the value of Mayflower's assets in their approval of the terms of the merger. As we have shown, the only pertinency of this figure is to develop a comparison of net asset value per share between Mayflower stock and Hilton stock. Since the deficiency of the Haslam report in this respect is supplied by other evidence the effect of which is to corroborate the findings of the Haslam report, we think this omission (if it was an omission) of little significance.

Nor are we impressed with plaintiffs' claim that they were afforded in the court below insufficient time to controvert defendants' evidence in respect of the value of Hilton's assets. If the issue was then deemed important and the time available was believed to be inadequate for procuring and filing controverting affidavits, plaintiffs could have applied to the court for indulgence in this regard. But, apart from this consideration, it is difficult for us, in the light of plaintiffs' main contention, so earnestly pressed, to believe that a comparison of net asset value was deemed by them to be an issue of any consequence. They chose to pitch their case upon a theory of law—already examined and found to be erroneous—that dispensed with any consideration of comparative net asset values, as well as of values derived from comparisons of earnings and dividends. The record indicates that further investigation of comparative net asset values would yield no evidence favorable to Mayflower—much less evidence sufficiently weighty to overthrow the findings of the Haslam report.

We think that the foregoing contentions are without merit.

Hilton's offer to buy Mayflower stock at $19.10 a share.

The facts with respect to this offer are set forth above. The price derives from a purchase by Hilton in February, 1952, of 21,409 shares of Mayflower stock at $19.10 a share from a group headed by John E. Meyers, one of the interveners in the Washington litigation. A similar offer is now made to the remaining minority stockholders in connection with but not technically as a part of the plan of merger.

Upon these facts plaintiffs build an argument that the price thus voluntarily paid by Hilton, and still offered for Mayflower shares, shows the unfairness of converting one share of Mayflower into one share of Hilton. This argument assumes that the price in Hilton's offer is better evidence of value than the prices of the over-the-counter market and the values indicated by the Haslam report. This does not follow; on the contrary, the true inference would seem to be that, for whatever reason, Hilton paid for a large block of shares somewhat higher than real value. Messrs. Baxter and Fleming, two of the directors who had served under the prior management, are of the opinion that Mayflower stock is not worth $19.10 a share. After the Meyers purchase, Hilton may have determined to continue the offer to others in order to avoid any charge of having accorded the Meyers group special treatment. But Hilton's reasons for doing so are not here important; it is enough to say, as the Chancellor said, that the minority stockholders of Mayflower suffer no harm from the offer and have no ground of complaint.

Conclusion.

We have considered all of plaintiffs' objections to the fairness of the proposed merger, and find ourselves in accord with the Chancellor's conclusion that no fraud or unfairness has been shown. . . .

NOTE ON FAIRNESS BETWEEN THE CONSTITUENT CORPORATIONS

The court's approach to the issue of comparative valuation of the constituent corporations in the Sterling case has some rather puzzling features. First, there is the statement at the outset that the defendants must establish the "entire fairness" of the transaction. This seems a rather onerous burden to cast upon the defendants, bearing in mind that the appraisal remedy was available to dissenting shareholders. It may be, as suggested in the note on page 619 supra, that dissenting stockholders are not ordinarily limited to their appraisal remedy, although it should be noted that Hilton came very close to qualifying for use of the Delaware short-merger statute, § 253, under which appraisal probably is exclusive. See page 733, supra. But the availability of the appraisal remedy might at least serve to confine judicial relief to cases of gross disproportion. See generally, Vorenberg, Exclusiveness of the Dissenting Stockholder's Appraisal Right, 77 Harv.L.Rev. 1189 (1964).

In any event the plaintiffs in Sterling did charge that there was a gross disproportion in value, in that the appraised net asset value of the Mayflower property, alleged to be approximately $10,000,000, was almost twice as much as the market value of the Hilton stock received for it. But instead of meeting this charge of "gross disparity" head-on, the court veered off on the rather technical tack that the test of fairness in a merger was different than in the case of a sale of assets, and that in a merger the $10,000,000 figure, referred to by the court as the "liquidating value," did not have to be taken into account, at least so far as minority stockholders having no power to compel a liquidation were concerned. Such an approach scarcely gives the impression that the "entire fairness" of the transaction had been established.

However, it is submitted that any seeming departure from the court's fairness standard is more apparent than real, and that there was in fact no real disparity in value at all. For this $10,000,000 figure, which the plaintiff contended should be matched in market value of Hilton stock, was nothing more than the appraised value of the property based primarily upon reproduction cost, and hence was not really a significant measure of value. Certainly the term "liquidating value" was a complete misnomer, since the figure bore no relation whatever to the amount which might have been realized upon a liquidation of Mayflower. Therefore, the short answer to the plaintiffs' contention was that since the $10,000,000 figure was not a significant index to value, there was no reason why the defendants should have to match it in market value of Hilton stock. At a minimum,

Sec. 2   FAIRNESS BETWEEN CORPORATIONS   759

the court should have held that if the appraised value of the Mayflower property was to be taken into account, it should be weighed against the appraised values of Hilton property which underlay the stock transferred to Mayflower stockholders; and on this basis, as the court noted rather obliquely, there was certainly no disproportion.

Unfortunately, however, the court instead seemed to accept the premise that the $10,000,000 figure had some validity as a measure of "liquidating value", as indicated by both the court's use of that term and its stress upon the purported distinction between valuation for merger and valuation for a sale of assets. The clear implication of that distinction was that if Hilton had chosen to eliminate Mayflower by purchasing its assets for stock instead of by merger, the plaintiffs might well have a valid objection unless the market value of Hilton's consideration was substantially equal to this $10,000,000 figure. Of course the court's error becomes manifest at this point, since whatever the method used to determine the fair value of Mayflower property, that value could not vary by almost 100% merely because of the particular combination technique used. The answer is that this $10,000,000 was simply not a significant measure of value for any purpose.

A somewhat similar but much more troublesome question of valuation is presented by the recent case of Abelow v. Midstates Oil Corp., 189 A. 2d 675 (Del.Sup.Ct.1963). There Midstates was an operating company; Middle Corporation was a holding company whose only significant asset was 96% of the stock of Midstates. The two companies, under their common management, decided that the operating assets should be sold. They obtained expressions of interest from a number of prospective buyers, embracing a variety of different approaches, including the acquisition of the assets directly from the operating company, the acquisition of the stock of the operating company from the holding company and the acquisition of the stock of the holding company from its stockholders. One of the two offers endorsed by the companies' investment bankers took the latter form, and a deal was ultimately worked out involving an exchange of 45 shares of the buyer's stock for each 100 shares of the holding company's stock. This ratio was based upon the comparative market values of the two stocks. On this basis, the total market value of the holding company's stock was about $30,500,000, which seemed to indicate that the operating company's stock, which was its only asset, was worth approximately $1450 per share. After acquiring about 95% of the stock of the holding company in this exchange, the buyer caused the holding company to buy the operating company's assets, preparatory to merging the holding company into the buyer, as had been contemplated from the outset. The price paid for the operating assets was approximately $25,000,000 plus assumption of liabilities, which produced a liquidating dividend of approximately $1125 per share of the operating company's stock.

Minority stockholders of the operating company attacked the transaction, contending that if the acquisition had taken a different form, such as a direct sale of the operating company's assets to the buyer, they would have received a figure closer to $1450 per share, corresponding to the valuation inherent in the exchange ratio used in the exchange of stock between the buyer and the stockholders of the holding company. But the court held that the management had no obligation either to adopt any particular form of transaction for the sale or to make sure that minority stockholders of the operating company were ultimately paid on a basis comparable to that afforded the stockholders of the holding company in the exchange transaction. In effect, the court agreed with the contention of the defendants that the only issue was the fairness of the price paid by the holding company for the operating company's assets, and accepted the evidence of the defendants' appraisal experts that the assets were worth no more than the price at which they were purchased. As to the plaintiffs' contention that the ratio upon which the buyer's stock was exchanged for stock of the holding company fixed the value of the operating company's stock, and indirectly its underlying assets, the court commented as follows:

> Moreover, it is at least doubtful whether a comparison of a value based on market value of shares with asset value is of any assistance in this case. Cf. Sterling v. Mayflower Hotel Corporation, . . . (comparison of market value of stock and asset value in merger disapproved).

Citation of the Sterling case is somewhat ironic since in Sterling it was the appraised value which the court insisted upon ignoring (though for the wrong reasons), whereas in Abelow the court accepted appraised valuation and rejected the much more compelling evidence of the market value of stock actually paid to acquire (indirectly) the assets in question. Of course it may be that in some cases the total market value of the stock of a corporation can exceed the value of the underlying assets—in other words, the operation of the stock market may add some elements of value, as, for example, it seems to do in the case of stock dividends. Accordingly, it was presumably open to the defendants to show that there were elements of value in the stock of the holding company which were separate from and in addition to the value of the assets of the operating company. But mere appraisal evidence hardly seems a sufficient showing, particularly under the burden imposed by the Sterling case upon a parent corporation to establish the "entire fairness" of a purchase of assets from a controlled subsidiary.

Where there is no conflict of interest like that in Sterling and Abelow, the courts have generally been very reluctant to override the judgment of the managers of the respective constituent companies as to the comparative values of their respective contributions. Thus in the Cole case, referred to in the Sterling opinion, the court stated the rule as follows:

> The [disparity] must be so gross as to lead the court to conclude that it was due not to an honest error of judgment but rather to bad faith, or to a reckless indifference to the rights of others interested. There is a presumption that the judgment of the governing body of a corporation, whether at the time it consists of directors or majority stockholders, is formed in good faith and inspired by a bona fides of purpose.

The same test has been applied in cases involving an attack on the price at which substantially all of a corporation's assets were sold to a third party. E. g., Cottrell v. The Pawcatuck Co., 36 Del.Ch. 169, 128 A.2d 225 (Sup.Ct.1956) ("The plaintiff has failed to show any such gross inadequacy of price as would justify an inference of reckless disregard of the rights of the minority stockholders.")

This standard seems entirely sound where there is no self-dealing and the final bargain is the result of arms' length negotiations between the constituent concerns. It should also be clear that no indirect self-interest is present, such as a special side-deal for the managers of a selling corporation in the form of lucrative long-term employment contracts or the like. Cf. Smith v. Good Music Station, Inc., 36 Del.Ch. 262, 129 A.2d 242 (Ch. 1957), where a sale of assets was upheld despite a generous employment contract extended to a 50% shareholder-director by the purchaser; the court found that the employment agreement was bona fide and the amount to be received was not out of line. Query, should the existence of an improper side-deal serve as a basis for upsetting a completed transaction, or is it enough if the recipient of the special deal is required to share it with all his fellow stockholders? Cf. Perlman v. Feldmann, 219 F.2d 173, 50 A.L.R.2d 1134 (2d Cir. 1955).

B. FAIRNESS AMONG CLASSES OF STOCK OF THE SAME CORPORATION

1. IN GENERAL

Whenever a disappearing corporation in a merger has more than one class of stock, there may also be questions of fairness as between those classes. That is because the merger plan, in specifying the basis for conversion of the various classes of the disappearing corporation's stock into stock of the surviving corporation, fixes not only the total participation of the disappearing corporation but also the allocation thereof among its various classes of stock. (And the merger may also be used as an occasion to rearrange the interests of the various stock classes of the surviving corporation.)

Presumably the appropriate vehicle for objecting to the basis of allocation among the classes of one of the corporations would be an attack on the merger for unfairness, just as it is for complaining of the comparative treatment as between the constituent corporations. Here, however, the similarity between these two types of attack ends. For unlike the comparative treatment of the constituent corporations, the allocation among classes of stock of the same corporation is rarely the product of arm's-length negotiations of any kind. Obviously, the representatives of the other parties to the merger are concerned only with the total participation of each constituent; the allocation within each separate corporation plays no part in the bargaining process. So this allocation falls entirely to the management of the corporation, which is typically more closely identified with junior than with senior classes. And in some states, notably Delaware, there is not even the protection of the class vote which MBA § 67 seems to afford in all such cases.

Despite this important difference between the two situations, the courts have generally drawn no distinction between the inter-corporate and the intra-corporate aspects of a merger so far as the applicable fairness standard is concerned. Thus in the Cole case, page 752 supra, no point was made of the fact that the complainant was a preferred stockholder in one of the constituents, although perhaps there the plaintiff was only concerned with the adequacy of the total participation accorded to his corporation and not with its allocation among the various classes. But in MacFarlane v. North American Cement Corp., 16 Del.Ch. 172, 157 A. 396 (Ch.1928), the plaintiff preferred stockholders expressly disclaimed any complaint about the total participation of their corporation, and instead levelled their attack directly on the comparative treatment of the preferred and common stockholders. Nevertheless, the court applied the same "grossly unfair" standard adopted in the Cole case, and refused to upset the proposed allocation between the two classes.

At first blush it looks as though the court in MacFarlane applied a totally unsuitable standard to the inter-class allocation. But it must be borne in mind that the plaintiffs in that case, like all stockholders in a merger, had the alternative of an appraisal remedy; and as noted earlier, that might justify limiting judicial review to cases of gross unfairness, despite the absence of arm's-length bargaining.

If it were decided that greater judicial scrutiny of the inter-class allocation in merger was called for, where would one look for the appropriate standard of fairness? Perhaps the closest analogy is to the recapitalization of a single corporation, where too the comparative treatment of two or more classes of stock may be drawn into question, particularly when the corporation is to end up with only common stock outstanding, which means that the former senior classes are to be "collapsed" into, i.e., exchanged for, common stock. In effect, in a merger the disappearing corporation is "recapitalized" in shares of the surviving corporation. But there is the rather important difference that in a merger there is almost invariably a right of appraisal (though not always a class vote), whereas in a "straight" recapitalization pursuant to an amendment of the certificate of incorporation there would only rarely be an appraisal right (although there would almost always be a class vote).

However, the fact is that in the recapitalization cases too the courts have exhibited considerable reluctance to review for fairness. Instead, particularly in Delaware, there has been a tendency to apply the same "gross unfairness" standard used in the merger cases. This is perhaps understandable when the recapitalization actually takes the form of a merger, as for example in Porges v. Vadsco Sales Corp., 27 Del.Ch. 127, 32 A.2d 148 (Ch.1943), where the merger of a parent corporation with its wholly-owned subsidiary was used as the vehicle for recapitalizing the parent. Such mergers have often been utilized as a substitute for a straightforward certificate amendment, in part because of a supposed greater latitude to change the rights of the stockholders, particularly with regard to arrearages on preferred stock. And at least when the merger form is adopted appraisal rights for dissenting stockholders would normally be available, so it may do little harm to follow the merger precedents even though the transaction really amounts to a recapitalization of a single corporation. But unfortunately, the courts have tended to apply the same "gross unfairness" standard in cases of "straight" recapitalization pursuant to certificate amendment, despite the absence of any appraisal remedy. Indeed, in Barrett v. Denver Tramway Corp., 53 F.Supp. 198 (D.Del.1943), the court went so far as to sustain a plan of recapitalization even though it regarded the plan as unfair to the preferred stockholders. The plan was one designed to eliminate cumulative dividend arrearages on preferred stock by inducing the preferred stockholders to exchange their existing stock for new prior preferred. (See pages 745–746, supra.) However, the new stock gave the preferred stockholders virtually nothing additional by way of annual dividends or liquidation preference to compensate them for the loss of their arrearages. The court conceded that because of its voting control the common stock could exact some "tribute" from the preferred, but expressed doubt about a plan under which the "preferred receives nothing for what it is required to relinquish" while the common is not required to give up anything.

Nevertheless, the court concluded that since there was no "constructive fraud, bad faith, or gross unfairness," under the Delaware authorities the plan had to be upheld. And even in New Jersey, where the courts have often been more sympathetic to complaints by preferred stockholders, e.g., Wessel v. Guantanamo Sugar Co., 134 N.J.Eq. 271, 35 A.2d 215 (Ch.1944), affirmed Murphy v. Guantanamo Sugar Co., 135 N.J.Eq. 506, 39 A.2d 431 (Ct.Err. & App.1944), one case has indicated that the fairness of a recapitalization need not be considered at all, so long as the certificate amendment is authorized by the statute and adopted by the required vote. See Franzblau v. Capital Securities Co., Inc., 2 N.J.Super. 517, 64 A.2d 644 (1949).

This judicial reluctance to review the fairness of recapitalization plans has been the subject of considerable critical comment. See, e. g., Dodd, Fair and Equitable Recapitalizations, 55 Harv.L.Rev. 780 (1941); Walter, Fairness in State Court Recapitalization Plans— A Disappearing Doctrine, 29 B.U.L.Rev. 453 (1949). Admittedly, judicial invalidation of a recapitalization plan for unfairness could lead to an impasse if the common stockholders thereafter refuse to approve a plan which gives the preferred stockholders enough to escape judicial condemnation. But as a practical matter it is probably just as likely that judicial rejection of a plan would lead the parties to find some different accommodation of their respective interests which would be fair. This was undoubtedly the premise of the Nebraska

Legislature in adopting a statute requiring the court to enjoin certificate amendments if the proponents do not "show that, to a reasonable probability, they are fair, just, and equitable to all shareholders affected thereby." Neb.Rev.Stat. § 21–1,162 (1954). See generally, Latty, Exploration of Legislative Remedy for Prejudicial Changes in Senior Shares, 19 U.Chi.L.Rev. 759 (1952).

With the current decline in the use of preferred stock, the recapitalization battleground seems to have shifted to disputes between voting and non-voting classes of stock. Here again the Delaware courts have exhibited reluctance to upset transactions on account of unfairness. For example, Manacher v. Reynolds, 39 Del.Ch. 401, 165 A.2d 741 (Ch.1960), involved a holding company which had a closely-held class of voting stock, and 16 times as many shares of publicly-traded, non-voting, otherwise identical common. The holding company in turn owned a controlling block of the publicly-traded stock of a successful operating company. Since the non-voting stock of the holding company was selling at a price equivalent to only about two-thirds of the value of the equity they represented in the stock of the operating corporation, a minority holder bought an action to force the holding corporation to liquidate and distribute pro rata its shares of the operating corporation. The parties to the suit worked out a settlement under which, in contemplation of such a liquidation, the holding company was to be recapitalized by exchanging three shares of non-voting stock for each share of voting stock, which would give the holders of the voting stock about $40,000,000 more in stock of the operating company than they would have received in a pro rata distribution without any recapitalization. The plan was approved by a substantial majority of the disinterested holders of the non-voting stock. In sustaining the settlement against the objection that the plan of recapitalization was too generous to the holders of the voting stock, the court implied that a $40,000,000 premium was somewhat excessive, but upheld the transaction on the basis of the disinterested shareholder approval. See Case Comment, 109 U. of Pa. L.Rev. 887 (1961).

A somewhat similar situation was presented in Honigman v. Green Giant Co., 309 F.2d 667 (8th Cir.1962), where the corporation involved had 44 Class A voting shares and 429,000 Class B non-voting shares. The challenged recapitalization plan called for giving the Class B shares the right to vote, in consideration for allowing the Class A stock to be converted into Class B on the basis of 1000 to 1, the conversion to take place gradually over a period of ten years. The plan was approved by the overwhelming majority of Class B stockholders, as well as all the Class A stockholders. Minority Class B stockholders attacked the plan, but the District Court sustained it, and the Court of Appeals affirmed. The District Court expressly purported to review the fairness of the plan, but dwelt primarily upon the benefits which an increase in the number of voting shares might be expected to produce for the corporation, in connection with acquisitions or other equity financing. The court did not attempt to compare the value of the voting rights surrendered by the Class A stockholders with the amount of the premium which they received under the plan. And here, as in the Manacher case, the court obviously relied heavily upon the overwhelming approval by the holders of the Class B stock: "The court cannot ignore the persuasive fact that the holders of 92.3% of all outstanding Class B stock concluded that the plan was fair to them and likewise to the corporation. That fact speaks more persuasively than the arguments of those who attempt to theorize on unrealistic principles of so-called corporate democracy." 208 F.Supp. at 762. See Case Comment, 28 Mo.L.Rev. 512 (1963).

2. STANDARDS FOR TESTING INTER-CLASS FAIRNESS IN RECAPITALIZATIONS

a. THE ABSOLUTE PRIORITY APPROACH

If courts did undertake to review fairness as between senior and junior classes of stock in recapitalizations, what standards of fairness would be utilized? One possibility is the so-called "absolute priority" doctrine developed in reorganization proceedings under the Bankruptcy Act. Under that doctrine, the allocation of stock and securities of the reorganized company among the former creditors (and stockholders when the debtor is solvent) follows closely the pattern which would be used if the debtor corporation were forced to sell its assets and distribute the proceeds in liquidation. The first step is to value the enterprise, usually on the basis of capitalization of earnings, for the purpose of determining what classes are entitled to participate in the reorganization. Any class which would not receive anything if cash in the amount of the estimated enterprise value was distributed is excluded from the reorganization. Thus if a corporation being reorganized was valued at $5,000,000 and there were claims of creditors in excess of $5,000,000, no class of stock would be eligible to participate in the reorganization. On the other hand, if the claims of creditors amounted to only $3,000,000, at least the senior stock would be entitled to participate; the junior stock's right to participate would depend upon whether the total liquidation preference of the senior stock amounted to less than $2,000,000. In other words, under the absolute priority approach the corporation is treated "as if in liquidation", thus making the liquidation preference of senior stock (which of course normally includes any accrued but unpaid dividends) the measure of the claim of the senior stock; and junior stock is not entitled to participate in the plan at all unless the net enterprise value (in excess of claims of creditors) exceeds the total liquidation preference of the senior stock.

As between classes entitled to participate in the reorganization, the absolute priority doctrine requires that each senior class of claimants in turn receive full compensation for its claim before any junior class receives anything. This does not necessarily mean that each class must receive stock or securities having a present market value equal to the amount of its claim—as a practical matter, that would often not be possible, since the figure at which the market "values" the total of the new stock and securities of a reorganized company at the outset is generally less than the amount estimated as the enterprise value. But the plan must certainly aim at producing full compensation in the relatively near future if the reorganized company performs as is hoped. In addition, any class which is reduced in seniority must receive some compensation on that account. For example, if in a reorganization in which both preferred and common are entitled to participate, both classes are to receive new common stock so that the preferred are deprived of their former priority over the common, the preferred must receive compensation for such demotion in status as well as reasonable satisfaction of the amount of its liquidation preference. See generally Brudney, The Investment-Value Doctrine and Corporate Readjustments, 72 Harv. L.Rev. 645, 667–675 (1959).

While this absolute priority standard has the considerable advantage of providing a specific measure of the claim of senior stock, it seems clear that it would not constitute a feasible standard for fairness in voluntary recapitalization proceedings under state law. For one thing, a voluntary recapitalization, unlike a reorganization under the Bankruptcy Act, is not a substitute for liquidation, and hence the "as if in liquidation" measure of the competing claims seems out of place. Moreover, unlike a reorganization proceeding which under federal law does not require the approval of any junior class excluded from participation under the plan, a recapitalization under state law does need the approval of the necessary percentage of all stockholders entitled to vote; and there is no basis for excluding a class just because its "real" financial stake in the enterprise has dwindled or even disappeared. Accordingly, the consent of the junior stockholders, who typically have voting control, would be required for the adoption of any plan, and they could hardly be expected to approve a plan of recapitalization which provides for "as if in liquidation" treatment for the senior stockholders, particularly when that standard would call for total exclusion of the junior stock from participation in the plan. In this connection it is interesting to note the suggestion of the court in Barrett v. Denver Tramway Corp., page 763 supra, to the effect that new state legislation is needed to provide "for ascertainment of worthlessness of junior shares, after which, as a condition subsequent, the junior stocks' vote would not be necessary to effect an urgent reclassification plan."

b. THE INVESTMENT VALUE APPROACH

Perhaps a more apt test for fairness in recapitalization proceedings is represented by the so-called "investment value" approach which has been developed in connection with recapitalizations under the Public Utility Holding Company Act. In the simplification of corporate structures required by that Act, it was often necessary to determine whether and to what extent certain junior classes of stock might be entitled to participate in the revamped corporate structure. Here it was thought that the claims of the competing classes ought not to be measured on the "as if in liquidation" basis, regardless of the corporate technique actually used to achieve the simplification. Instead, it was held that the rights of the respective classes of stock should be determined on the basis of their "going-concern investment value"; and any class that was found to have some chance of ultimately receiving dividends was regarded as entitled to participate in the reorganized enterprise. Otis & Co. v. SEC, 323 U.S. 624, 65 S.Ct. 483, 89 L.Ed. 511 (1945).

BRUDNEY, THE INVESTMENT-VALUE DOCTRINE AND CORPORATE READJUSTMENTS [11]

72 Harv.L.Rev. 648–651, 657–660 (1959).

A. The Measure of the Surrendered Claim and Its Rationale

The claims of securities surrendered in corporate readjustments compelled by the simplification requirements of the Holding Company Act are determined, under the investment-value doctrine, by "the value of the securities on the basis of a going business and not as though a liquidation were taking place, except as it appears that liquidation could and would have taken place apart from the compulsion of [the Act]." This measure of claims is designed to make the readjustment a mechanism for transmuting the long-range going-concern value of the surrendered contract into equivalent value in another form, rather than a procedure for redistributing underlying values in satisfaction of the stated contractual commands of the security being surrendered. The "bundle of rights"—whether matured or unmatured—embodied in the surrendered security determines the scope or magnitude of its claim, not as it states obligations to be ful-

---

[11]. Copyright (c), Harvard Law Review Association, 1959. Reprinted by permission. Portions of the text, and most of the footnotes omitted.

filled, but only to the extent that those obligations are in fact underpinned by economic values in the enterprise. As a result, . . . the claim is measured neither by its *rights* on maturity nor by its *rights* in the going concern, but by its *value* on a going-concern basis. . . . In short, under the investment-value doctrine, "it is not the promise that a charter made to a stockholder but the current worth of that promise" that is the measure of the claim he is surrendering.

The doctrine was designed to meet the problem created by the disparity—often substantial—between the "value" of a security when it is assessed as a continuing claim on a going concern and the value of the corporation's available assets which the same security would, by its terms, be entitled to receive in a liquidation, recapitalization, merger, or other form of corporate readjustment compelled by . . . the Holding Company Act. To honor the contractual provision might be to entitle the security holder in any given case to more (or less) than the going-concern value of the security he is being forced to surrender. But except for the compulsion of [the Act], senior-security holders might not have the right to force, and junior-security holders might not have the desire to make, the proposed readjustment. The investment-value doctrine rests on the assumption that Congress did not intend enforcement of the overriding public policy of holding-company simplification to have "its effect visited on one class with a corresponding windfall to another class of security holders" or to result in shifting "investment values from one class of security holders to another." On that premise, both the Commission and the Supreme Court, after some preliminary fumbling, concluded that the act (1) overrides the security contract—i. e., precludes a corporate readjustment which it compels, from being a "maturing" event under the security contract merely by reason of such compulsion, even though the particular form of readjustment occurring was a contingency explicitly provided for in the contract; and (2) requires surrendering security holders to receive the long-term going-concern values which their securities have when the act compels their surrender—i.e., their claims are to be measured by their going-concern values rather than by the requirements of their contracts or by some other norm.

* * *

B. The Operation of the Investment-Value Doctrine . . .

Although the rationale on which the investment-value measure of claims is based has been made plain by the SEC and the courts, its operation in particular cases is not so plainly decipherable. Thus, initially, the Commission's inquiry was directed toward ascertaining whether at some future time—very often ten to twenty years later, and sometimes even longer—earnings could be expected, on concededly optimistic assumptions, to have paid off preferred-stock arrearages and to exceed preferred-dividend claims, so that at that time juniors might be expected to share in the earnings. If it so found, the Commission concluded that there was "some" value for the junior securities for which "some" participation in the reorganized enterprise was required to be allowed.[39] Later, the Commission developed a somewhat different technique in applying the investment-value concept. The assorted contractual rights of the surrendered senior security, both monetary and protective, were ascertained and the continuing economic values estimated to be available to satisfy those rights were examined; the results were either translated into dollar terms by capitalizing estimated future earnings or, as was most frequently the case, expressed descriptively in a comparison of the bundle of rights and long-term values surrendered with the bundle of rights and long-term values embodied in the new securities.

* * *

. . . [T]here is wide scope for the play of immeasurable judgment factors and, therefore, for a large range of equally correct results, in the determination of the "investment value" and the "equitable equivalent" of a surrendered security. The complexities and uncertainties intrinsic in valuing on an earnings basis and in determining equitable equivalence are not the only reasons for this. The dominant objective of transmuting continuing values in one form into the same values in another form results in the rejection of current market prices as the test of either the investment value of the old security or the equitable equivalence of the new security. . . .

As is indicated in note 39, supra, the standard for determining whether and to what extent a junior class is entitled to participate under the investment value doctrine is somewhat vague—and the early SEC authorities did not provide much guidance as to how the allocation was arrived at. For example, in Federal Water Service Corpora-

---

39. The permissible extent of such participation was determined by the Commission's "over-all judgment" which was "not susceptible of mathematical demonstration." . . . A finding of no value for a security (and therefore exclusion from participation) was made when estimated earnings would either not exceed the earnings claims of the securities prior in rank to that being valued or would not be sufficient to discharge such prior claims and arrearages on the prior securities within the "foreseeable" future. . . .

tion, 8 SEC 893, 10 SEC 194 (1941), a corporation with senior preferred, junior preferred, and common stock was being recapitalized into an all common stock structure. On the basis of estimated future earnings, the dividend arrearages on the senior preferred might have been cleared in about eleven years. The SEC concluded that the junior preferred had a "reasonable expectation of receiving earnings at some future time" and awarded them 5% of the new common, the other 95% of the new common having gone to the senior preferred. As to the old common, the SEC found that it had "no reasonable possibility of ever receiving anything", and it was excluded from participation.

In United Light and Power Co., 13 SEC 1 (1943), the corporation had preferred stock, with a total annual dividend requirement of $3,600,000 and arrearages of $38,700,000, ahead of the common stock. The SEC estimated the future earnings of the company at $6,185,000, on which basis "it would take approximately fifteen years for the preferred dividend arrearages to be paid in full, if all consolidated net earnings were to be applied toward the payment of current and accumulated preferred dividends". In rejecting a proposal to give the old common stockholders 8.8% of the new common, the SEC said: "Under all the circumstances it is our view that a participation for the common of approximately 5%, while representing the maximum, would not exceed the permissible limits of fairness, and to secure our approval the plan must be modified to reduce the common stockholders' participation accordingly". Just how 5% was arrived at is not explained. However, a concurring opinion by Commissioner Burke did offer a clue in the suggestion that the present value of the earnings to which the old common would be entitled after fifteen years might be arrived at by capitalizing those earnings, using a fairly low multiplier because of the high risk, and then discounting the resulting figure to present worth to take account of the fifteen year delay.

This suggestion does afford a basis for computing the relative investment values of senior and junior classes by comparing their relative interests in the estimated future earnings of the enterprise. The interest of the preferred stock consists of a perpetual right to its fixed annual dividend plus the right to receive the excess of annual earnings over the fixed dividend requirement until its arrearages have been paid. The interest of the junior stock consists of the right to receive that excess in perpetuity, once the preferred arrearages have been paid.

Following the line suggested by Commissioner Burke, the value of these various rights in future earnings can be computed by capitalizing the relevant earnings. The total estimated earnings for the company may be divided into two layers, the first consisting of the preferred's fixed annual dividend, and the second consisting of the excess of the total estimated earnings over that amount. The first layer of the earnings stream, to which the preferred have a perpetual right, would be capitalized in the normal way, at an appropriate capitalization rate. As to the second layer of the earnings, which of course is the riskier portion and must be capitalized at a higher rate, the preferred's interest would constitute a terminable annuity for whatever period is required to pay off the preferred arrearages. Thereafter, that second layer of the earnings stream would belong to the common stock in perpetuity; and this right can be valued, as Commissioner Burke suggested, in the normal fashion for a perpetual annuity, provided that the resulting figure is then "discounted" to present value to reflect the fact that the interest of junior stock does not vest until the preferred arrearages have been paid off.

One of the few concrete illustrations of this approach appeared in Appendix A to the Answering Brief of Securities and Exchange Commission, dated April 1950, in Matter of Eastern Gas and Fuel Associates, in the United States District Court for the District of Massachusetts, Civil Action, No. 50–168, in which an order was made approving and enforcing a Plan filed by Eastern with the SEC under § 11(e) of the Holding Company Act of 1935, as described in 30 SEC 834 (1950). In that recapitalization junior preferred, with dividend arrearages, and common were changed into a single class of new common. The plan, as approved by the SEC and the court, allocated 87% of the new common to the old junior preferred and 13% of the new common to the old common.

The figures used in the illustration, which follows, are hypothetical, although the indicated allocation works out to approximately the same as the allocation under the approved plan.

APPENDIX A

The following example illustrates the application of the two-discount technique as a check on the exercise of overall judgment. It assumes that the reasonably foreseeable income of a corporation is $2,000,000, that the corporation has outstanding 200,000 shares of $5 preferred stock with an annual dividend preference of $1,000,000, and that there are dividend arrearages on such stock aggregating $5,000,000. It further assumes that rates of 10% and 20% appropriately measure the risk factors attaching to the preferred and common stocks, respectively. The calculation of the relative present worths of the preferred and common stocks would then be made as follows:

Annual earnings	$2,000,000
Preferred dividend requirements	1,000,000
Balance applicable to arrears and common stock	$1,000,000

Number of years required to satisfy the preferred dividend arrearages of $5,000,000 on the assumption that all earnings would be applied in satisfaction of dividend arrearages— 5 years.

		Indicated allocation percentage
Preferred Stock:		
Present worth of $1,000,000 a year in perpetuity, discounted* at 10%	$10,000,000	
Present worth of $1,000,000 a year for 5 years, discounted at 20% ($1 per year for 5 years at 20% has a present worth of $2.99)	2,990,000	
Total Present Worth of Preferred Stock	$12,990,000	86.6%
Common Stock:		
Present worth of $1,000,000 a year in perpetuity, beginning after 5 years, discounted at 20% ($1 per year in perpetuity beginning after 5 years, has a present worth of $2.01)		
Total Present Worth of Common Stock	2,010,000	13.4%
Total Preferred and Common Stock	$15,000,000	100.0%

This approach to the relative valuation of senior and junior classes is sometimes referred to as the "double discount method", presumably a reference to the fact that the interest of the junior stock in the second layer of earnings is "discounted" twice, once in perpetuity, in a traditional capitalization of earnings, and again in discounting the figure arrived at back to present value. There are several items worth noting in this connection. First, the capitalization rate selected for the second layer of the earnings stream, here 20%, has a double impact on the participation of the junior stock. Of course, it determines the total value of the second layer of the earnings stream, in which alone the junior stock has any interest. But in addition the capitalization rate determines how large a portion of the total value of a particular earnings stream is attributable to the first few years

---

* [Ed. note] The word "discounted" as used here means the same as "capitalized", and the rate specified is, as the capitalization rate always is, the reciprocal of the multiplier.

of the stream. As you might expect, the greater the risk attaching to a particular layer of earnings, the greater the uncertainty about what the years beyond the immediate future will bring, and hence the greater the proportion of the total value of the earnings layer which is attributable to the first few years. For example, as the Appendix A illustration indicates, at a capitalization rate of 20%, approximately ⅗ of the total value of the earnings stream is attributable to the first five years. At a capitalization rate of only 15%, on the other hand, not only would the total value of the second layer of the earnings stream be greater (i. e., $6,667,000 instead of $5,000,000), but also the portion attributable to the first five years would only be approximately ½. Thus if a capitalization rate of 15% had been used for the second layer of earnings in Appendix A, the interest of the common stock would have amounted to approximately $3,333,500 (½ × $6,667,000) out of a total of $16,667,000 ($10,000,000 plus $6,667,000), or approximately 20%.

A second observation about the Appendix A illustration relates to the question of whether a terminable annuity for five years fully reflects the interest of the preferred stock in the second layer of earnings. Actually, the preferred's rights in that second layer continue until it has received its $5,000,000 in dividend arrearages, whether that takes five years or fifty. And the important corollary of this is that the interest of the junior stock does not necessarily start after five years, but rather only after the second earnings layer has totaled $5,000,000 (and it has been paid to the preferred). In effect then, the preferred's interest in the second earnings layer is substantially less risky than the common's interest in the same layer, and this suggests the need for using different capitalization rates for the two interests.

See Generally, Masson, New Shares for Old (1958) 288–301.

c. The Appraised Valuation Approach

Whatever the merits of the investment value approach, it is primarily useful only where a single type of consideration is being allocated between the senior and junior stock, and all that is needed is to determine the relative values of the respective classes. Where a recapitalization calls for the distribution of different types of consideration to the two classes, as where the old preferred are to receive a new class of preferred, while the old common retain common, in order to test fairness it may be necessary to value in absolute terms both the interest of each participating class and the consideration offered in satisfaction of that interest under the plan. Here the closest analogy is to appraisal of the stock of dissenting stockholders, where too the objective is to translate either preferred or common stock into absolute dollar terms. In the case of a simple one-class corporation, this may be simply a variant of enterprise valuation. But the treatment of senior stock under this approach may give rise to some additional problems, as the following case suggests:

JACQUES COE & CO. v. MINNEAPOLIS-MOLINE CO.
Court of Chancery of Delaware, 1950.
31 Del.Ch. 368, 75 A.2d 244.

SEITZ, VICE CHANCELLOR. An appraiser . . . appraised the preferred and common stock of stockholders who chose not to accept the terms of a merger. This is the decision on exceptions to the appraiser's report.

The defendant corporation's preferred stock contract provided for a liquidation price of $110 per share plus accrued dividends. They amounted to $29.60 as of February 21, 1949. The call price was of an equal aggregate amount. The contract had certain provisions for retiring the preferred stock, but the corporation was in substantial default thereon. So long as the dividend arrearages exceeded $6.50 per share, the preferred stockholders had exclusive voting power.

In determining net asset value for the preferred, the appraiser decided that in no event should it exceed $139.60—the liquidation value plus accrued dividends. The appraiser determined the net asset value of the common stock to be $32.54. This amount was based on the acceptance of an expert witness' net asset evaluation of $26.80 per share less $1.12 per share which represented an amortization item which the appraiser concluded the expert witness had improperly excluded. The appraiser then added $6.86 per share representing good will.

The appraiser decided that net asset value should be weighted at 40% for the preferred stock and 20% for the common. In stating his reasoning in connection with the weighting factor, the appraiser stated that the preferred had been weighted much more heavily than the common because of the substantial advantages which the preferred possessed over the common under the charter provision.

The appraiser decided that a fair market value, uninfluenced by the merger, existed on February 21, 1949—the date of merger. I find no error in this conclusion. The market price for the preferred on that date was $113 per share, while the common was $12.13 per share.

The appraiser weighted the market value of the preferred stock at 30% and the common at 45%. In explaining the weight given to the market price the appraiser stated that the common was entitled to more weight than the preferred because of the greater market activity of the common stock. He also pointed out that substantial weight was given the market value of the common because that price represented the considered judgment of numerous investors and speculators—backed up by their own savings. This is, of course, certainly true to a degree.

Finally, the appraiser capitalized the earnings and dividends by taking the average earnings for the preferred and common for a 5-year period.* Multiplying these yearly earnings by the factor of 5, the appraiser arrived at a figure of $149 per share as the earnings-dividends value for the preferred. The appraiser pointed out that arrearages were not included under this element because he had already taken them into account under net asset value. Capitalized for the same period, the per share value of the common stock based on earnings and dividends amounted to $16.90.

The appraiser weighted earnings and dividends at 30% on the preferred and 35% on the common. The appraiser stated that this element was not weighted more heavily as to the common stock because of the failure to pay dividends thereon. The earning prospects of the company did appear to be good.

In order to resolve some of the questions posed by the various exceptions, it is necessary to consider, in a general way, the appraiser's approach to his duties under the statute.

Conceivably, an appraiser in weighting various elements of value and arriving at an appraised value might not articulate his mental processes. However, I believe an appraiser should state the monetary value which he has ascribed to the more substantial elements of value considered and the weight he has given each such element in arriving at his appraised value. I shall not pause to discuss the many infirmities involved in any evaluation process. The important thing is that the appraiser must, under the statute, arrive at a dollar and cents' appraisal. Consequently, the appraiser should state the value of the elements given independent weight and the weight given to each in arriving at the appraised value. This procedure will render the valuation process a little less arbitrary and will permit a review at least on a degree basis.

The present appraiser first determined asset value, market value and value derived from earnings and dividends. He then weighted

---

* [Ed. note] The "average earnings for the preferred" used in this computation were computed by simply dividing the net income of the corporation each year by the number of preferred shares outstanding. For the five years 1944–1948 these figures were approximately $13 per share, $10, $17, $46, and $63, producing an average of $29.80. Of course, the preferred could not in fact receive these amounts; they were limited to their fixed annual dividend of $6.50 per share, plus any payments made on the accumulated arrearages (which payments averaged $1.50 per year during 1944–1948).

The average earnings for the common were derived by deducting the fixed annual preferred dividend from net income and dividing the remainder by the number of common shares outstanding. The average for the period 1944–1948 of approximately $3.40 included earnings per share for 1948 of $8 per share.

these elements and arrived at his appraised value. Counsel for the defendant corporation contends that the appraiser committed error in so doing because he contends that the Supreme Court in Tri-Continental v. Battye, Del.Ch., 74 A.2d 71, 72, held that where an active market exists, and is uninfluenced by "artificial" factors, such market price is controlling in fixing value under the appraisal statute. I do not so construe the Supreme Court's decision, despite certain features of that opinion, because the Supreme Court there said: "In determining what figure represents this true or intrinsic value, the appraiser and the courts must take into consideration all factors and elements which reasonably might enter into the fixing of value. Thus, market value, asset value, dividends, earning prospects, the nature of the enterprise and any other facts which were known or which could be ascertained as of the date of merger and which throw any light on future prospects of the merged corporation are not only pertinent to an inquiry as to the value of the dissenting stockholders' interest, but must be considered by the agency fixing the value."

I conclude that the appraiser properly considered elements other than market value in arriving at his evaluation. This consideration took the form of giving independent weight to some of them, and correctly so, in my opinion.

The preferred stockholders contend that the protective features of their stock were so great that they should have been considered by the appraiser as an independent element of value and weighted accordingly. Did the appraiser commit error in failing to treat the protective features of the preferred stock as an element of value to be weighted separately? I think not. It is apparent that, to a degree, many of the so-called "substantial" elements of value may and often do encompass each other. For example, market value may well reflect earnings and dividend prospects. However, in order to effectuate the object of the appraisal statute as construed by our Supreme Court, it is necessary that various factors be considered and, where appropriate, some of them given independent weight. It seems to me that in order to make the appraisal procedure work realistically the court should not disturb the appraiser's determination that a particular factor should not be given independent weight unless that determination is arbitrary or unreasonable in the premises. I say so because, as previously stated, a value factor may well be fairly reflected in an element of value given independent weight—as the appraiser here recognized. It seems to me that the value factor based on the protective features of the preferred stock is fairly reflected in varying degrees in the elements of value actually given independent weight by the appraiser.

The preferred stockholders contend that it was error to limit net asset value to the call or liquidation price when the asset value was more than twice that amount. They concede that the final appraised value should not have exceeded the call or liquidation price, but they urge that such a limitation should not have been placed on net asset value which constituted but one element of the appraised value. Obviously the more assets there are, the more the preferred is protected but this should not increase the amount of net assets attributable to the preferred. The appraiser properly limited net asset value to the call or liquidation price where the net assets were substantially in excess of such prices because he was seeking value at a particular time. The stockholders' contention, if here adopted, would result in a distortion of the ultimate value of the preferred stock.

* * *

Both the stockholders and the corporation have excepted to the weight which the appraiser gave net asset value in computing the appraised value of both the preferred and common stock. I have examined the arguments of counsel and the appraiser's report and I find nothing which would justify the conclusion that the weights assigned by the appraiser to this element were arbitrary or unreasonable. The appraiser committed no error.

The preferred stockholders took two exceptions to the appraiser's calculation of the earnings-dividends element of value. They say the appraiser should have included the $29.60 per share accrued dividends and should have multiplied the average earnings by a factor larger than 5.

The appraiser included accrued dividends in determining net asset value. The preferred stockholders urge that it should also have been included under earnings and dividends because the earnings were adequate to pay such arrearages. I find no error in refusing to consider this item under two elements of value. It is argued that by incorporating it under one item which was weighted 40%, the appraiser has necessarily weighted it only 40%. If other elements of value are weighted, then the same must be true of dividends arrearages. We are not dealing with a dissolution or liquidation.

In calculating the earnings-dividends value the appraiser multiplied average earnings by the factor of 5. The preferred think this factor was too small. The factor employed by the appraiser is within the range of reason and will not be disturbed. Substantially the same exceptions as to this element are taken by the common stock and my conclusion as to the preferred also applies to the common.

* * *

I find the per share value of the preferred to be $131.74 and the common $17.88.

NOTE ON VALUATION IN DELAWARE APPRAISAL PROCEEDINGS

Delaware has led the way in refusing to treat market value as controlling even where there is a full, free and active market, uninfluenced by the proposed transaction which gives rise to the right of appraisal. The leading case is Chicago Corp. v. Munds, 20 Del.Ch. 142, 172 A. 452 (1934), where the Chancellor said:

> When it is said that the appraisal which the market puts upon the value of the stock of an active corporation, as evidenced by its daily quotations, is an accurate, fair reflection of its intrinsic value, no more than a moment's reflection is needed to refute it. There are too many accidental circumstances entering into the making of market prices to admit them as sure and exclusive reflectors of fair value. The experience of recent years is enough to convince the most casual observer that the market in its appraisal of values must have been woefully wrong in its estimates at one time or another within the interval of a space of time so brief that fundamental conditions could not possibly have become so altered as to affect true worth. Markets are known to gyrate in a single day. The numerous causes that contribute to their nervous leaps from dejected melancholy to exhilarated enthusiasm and then back again from joy to grief, need not be reviewed. It would be most unfortunate indeed either for the consolidated corporation or for the objecting stockholder if, on the particular date named by the statute for the valuation of the dissenter's stock, viz., the date of the consolidation, the market should be in one of its extreme moods and the stock had to be paid for at the price fixed by the quotations of that day. Even when conditions are normal and no economic forces are at work unduly to exalt or depress the financial hopes of man, market quotations are not safe to accept as unerring expressions of value. The relation of supply to demand on a given day as truly affects the market value of a stock as it does of a commodity; and temporary supply and demand are in turn affected by numerous circumstances which are wholly disconnected from considerations having to do with the stock's inherent worth.

The "other factors" which the Delaware courts insist upon taking into account raise some questions of their own. For example, the earnings factor, which in practice amounts pretty much to a traditional capitalization of earnings, depends upon selecting an appropriate capitalization rate; and for this purpose resort is usually made to comparable price-earnings ratios in the market. But why should the market's price-earnings ratio for other stocks be relied upon, when its valuation of the stock being appraised is rejected as untrustworthy?

As to the other important factor, asset value, among the questions which arise are whether book value or "current" value should be used as the measure, and whether intangible assets are included. For the most recent struggle with the first issue, see Levin v. Midland-Ross Corp., 194 A.2d 50 (Del.Ch.1963). When the asset value factor was originally injected into the picture in the Chicago Corporation case, supra, it was with relation to an investment corporation, whose assets consisted in large measure of marketable stocks and debt securities with a readily ascertainable value; and the same was true in the

Tri-Continental case (cited in Jacques Coe), which stressed the fact that the stock of an investment company often sells at a discount from its underlying asset values. This is a far cry from the industrial area, into which this factor has been imported, where computation of asset value is no less complicated than making the overall determination of enterprise value itself.

As a postscript to the relationship between valuation for the purpose of appraising a dissenting stockholder's stock and valuation for the purpose of testing fairness in a recapitalization, note should be taken of the recapitalization of York Ice Machine Corporation which ultimately produced a proceeding of each type. At the time of the recapitalization in early 1941, York had outstanding 56,731 shares of 7%, $100 par, cumulative preferred stock with dividend arrearages of $88.25 per share, and 161,481 shares of common stock. The income of the company for its most recent five fiscal years, 1936–1940, had varied rather sharply, being respectively a profit of $165,000, a profit of $975,000, a loss of $119,000, a loss of $185,000 and a profit of $483,000. The plan called for a merger of the company into a wholly-owned subsidiary created expressly for that purpose, with an exchange ratio of 15 shares of new common for each share of old preferred, and one share of new common for each old common share. Thus the preferred received 83.2% of the new common, and the old common got 16.8%.

Objecting preferred stockholders brought an action in the federal district court attacking the plan, primarily on the ground that a Delaware corporation had no power to eliminate preferred stock arrearages in this fashion. However, the District Court sustained the recapitalization, so far as corporate power was concerned, and the Court of Appeals for the Third Circuit affirmed. Hottenstein v. York Ice Machinery Corp., 136 F.2d 944 (3d Cir. 1943).

The objecting stockholders also attacked the plan of recapitalization as unfair to the preferred stockholders. In dealing with this issue, the District Court first distinguished review of a plan of reorganization under the Bankruptcy Act, where court approval is affirmatively required; as to review of a merger under state law, the court held that an injunction could be granted only if "the plan is so unfair as to shock the conscience of the court and to amount to fraud", citing the MacFarlane case, page 762 supra. Nevertheless, the court then seemed to talk in "absolute priority" terms when it continued as follows:

> The value of the preferred stock, if the common stock has any value, is approximately $10,000,000, including accumulated dividends. Therefore, if the value of the interest which the preferred stockholders receive under the plan of merger is as much or more than $10,000,000, it certainly is not so grossly unfair as to shock the conscience of the court.

And insofar as the interest given to the preferred stockholders has less than that value, the plan approaches the point at which it must be deemed so unfair that the merger should be enjoined. [45 F.Supp. at 438.]

The reference to "$10,000,000," though never explained by the court, must surely have come from the liquidation preference of the preferred, which did amount to almost $10,000,000. Certainly, the figure had no relation to the market value of the stock, which at the time of the recapitalization was about $45 per share, for a total of less than $2,500,000.

In any event, the District Court concluded that, on the evidence submitted as to the total value of the enterprise, the value of the new common stock allocated to the preferred stockholders was not substantially less than $10,000,000. Looking first at the asset value factor, the court noted that while book value was substantially below $10,000,000, this figure was the product of an arbitrary writedown of asset values at a time long before the plan of recapitalization was contemplated. On the other hand, replacement cost (less depreciation) was apparently almost $15,000,000, although it was conceded that this was much higher than the fair value of the assets. The court observed that splitting the difference between book value and replacement cost produced a figure in excess of $10,000,000; and this seemed to satisfy the court that the asset value factor supported an overall enterprise value in excess of $10,000,000.

Turning to the earnings value factor, the lower court noted the difficulty of predicting future earnings for a corporation which had had such wide fluctuations in earnings in the past. However, the court observed that net income for the year 1941, in which the recapitalization occurred, had been at least $800,000, of which the 83% interest awarded to the preferred stockholders would have been entitled to approximately $665,000; in the court's view this confirmed that the stock received by the preferred was not worth substantially less than $10,000,000. (Notice that in effect the court applied a multiplier of about 15 times earnings.)

The District Court's decision on fairness was also affirmed. In a much briefer analysis of the issue, the Court of Appeals, while conceding that the book value of the corporation's assets was less than the liquidation preference of the preferred, stressed the facts that the earnings had increased substantially, that the recapitalization gave the preferred stockholders voting control, and that when the plan became public the preferred stock nearly doubled in price. The court concluded that "it is not unjust under all the circumstances of the case at bar to treat the equity of the common stockholders as being worth approximately 17% of the stock of the surviving corporation".

The objecting preferred stockholders then commenced a proceeding for the appraisal of their stock under the provisions of the Delaware statute. A majority of the appraisers fixed the value of the stock at $90 per share (approximately twice the market price of $45); the third appraiser fixed the value at $197.50, (apparently on the basis of the redemption price of the preferred, which included par of $100, a premium of $7.50, and accrued dividends of about $90). While the report of the appraisers was awaiting review by the Delaware Chancellor, the objecting stockholders filed a special bill with the Court of Appeals for the Third Circuit protesting the fact that in the earlier federal court proceeding the corporation had contended that its assets were worth more than $10,000,000, whereas in the state court appraisal proceeding the corporation had presented evidence that the assets were worth very much less. Hottenstein v. York Ice Machinery Corp., 146 F.2d 835 (3d Cir. 1944). The Court of Appeals commented as follows:

> Obviously, if the assets of York Ice Machinery Corporation were worth only $5,000,000 at the time of the merger, common stockholders should have received far less, if any, recognition. If the value found for the preferred stock by the appraisers is correct it seems probable that the value suggested for the assets . . . [during the earlier proceedings] was far too high. Conceding that the value of the assets is not invariably, or even necessarily, reflected in stock values, the . . . comparatively low value attributed to the stock by the appraisers does not coincide with the asset picture seemingly presented by the defendant to the District Court of Delaware.

However, the court reluctantly denied leave to file the bill of review on the ground that under state law commencement of appraisal proceedings terminated the petitioners' status as stockholders.

Subsequently, the report of the appraisers came on for review before the Chancellor. Root v. York Corp., 29 Del.Ch. 351, 50 A.2d 52 (1946). The Chancellor noted that "based on evidence of asset value, it is . . . evident that the corporation did claim in the injunction suit that the common stock of York Ice Machinery Corporation had some equity, while before the appraisers it claimed that the value of the preferred stock was worth less than par and the accumulated dividends thereon." However, the Chancellor was not unduly concerned about this apparent inconsistency. He observed that in the appraisal proceeding only the value of the preferred stock was pertinent, and that in valuing the stock, asset value was not the sole controlling factor. Instead, all relevant factors were to be taken into account; and since the appraisers had done that, their valuation was sustained.

SECTION 3. FINANCIAL ASPECTS OF CORPORATE COMBINATIONS

A. INTRODUCTION

One of the important questions in every corporate combination is how to account for the acquired assets on the books of the acquiring corporation. A related question is the effect of the combination transaction on the proprietary accounts of the acquiring corporation. To illuminate these issues, let us start with the simple case of a corporation which purchases a new asset, say a building, from an individual for cash. Obviously the building should be recorded on the books of the acquiring corporation at its cost, and thereafter treated in accordance with the corporation's normal practice for depreciable assets. The same would be true if the corporation acquired the building in exchange for its stock, except that, as we have seen before, there is no longer quite as ready a measure of the cost of the building. Ordinarily, the "cost" of property acquired for stock is the fair market value of the stock exchanged for it, which in turn, at least in an arm's-length transaction, is normally equal to the fair market value of the property at the date of acquisition. In other words, the end result is the same as if the stock had been issued for cash which was then used to acquire the assets. And just as in the case of an issuance of stock for cash, so when stock is issued for property any excess of the consideration received over the stated capital attributable to the stock is credited to capital surplus.

Should the transaction be treated differently if the building is acquired from a corporation rather than an individual? The answer seems clearly "no", if the acquiring corporation is simply obtaining an additional facility for the conduct of its operations. And it should make no difference whether the acquisition is for cash or for stock, or whether the building represents all or only a portion of the assets of the selling corporation. Accordingly, the figure at which the building was carried on the books of the selling corporation, and *a fortiori* that corporation's earned surplus or deficit, would be of no concern to the acquiring corporation.

However, suppose that the acquiring corporation, X, is a real estate corporation owning only one piece of property—and that X is acquiring from Y corporation the latter's only piece of property. Now the transaction begins to look more like a combination of two separate businesses into a single unified enterprise than a mere "purchase" of property. Assuming that the two pieces of property are of equal value, the old Y stockholders should end up owning one half of the stock of the combined enterprise (hereinafter referred to as "X–Y"). Such a combination transaction seems analogous to the formation of a partnership, although of course the enterprise is to be carried on in corporate form; in essence, the two groups of shareholders are "pooling their interests" for the future.

In such circumstances, there is must to be said for accounting for the transaction by simply combining the accounts of the two corporations (of course after eliminating any inter-corporate items which might exist.) This would treat the combination as nearly as possible as though the two enterprises had been carried on together from the outset. Thus the opening balance sheet for the combined enterprise would be derived by pooling the assets and liabilities of the two corporations, at the figures at which they appear on the books of the respective companies. Similarly, the net worth accounts, i. e., stated capital and the various types of surplus, for the combined enterprise might be derived by pooling the respective balances in such accounts on the books of the separate corporations. Here, however, some departure from a strict "pooling" approach would become necessary since the stated capital for the acquiring corporation after a combination transaction, like that of any other corporation, must be determined in accordance with the governing statute, and the figure called for might well be different from the arithmetic sum of the stated capital accounts of the constituent corporations. For example, if the acquiring corporation issued par stock in making the acquisition, the increase in its stated capital would be measured, under a typical statute like MBA § 19, by par times the additional number of shares issued; and it would be the sheerest coincidence if that figure was precisely equal to the stated capital of the acquired corporation.

To make our illustration more concrete, assume that the balance sheets for the two corporations being combined are as follows:

X

Cash	$200,000	Stat. Cap. (10,000 shares of $40 par)	$400,000
		Cap. Surp.	300,000
Building (net)	900,000	Earn. Surp.	400,000

Y

Building (net)	$1,100,000	Stat. Cap. (10,000 shares of $100 par)	$1,000,000
		Earn. Surp.	100,000

Assume further that Y is to be merged into X, with the Y shareholders exchanging their stock for X stock on a share for share basis. Under MBA § 19 X's stated capital after the merger would be $800,000 (20,000 shares of $40 par stock), absent some additional step affecting stated capital such as a transfer to that account from surplus under § 19. If all the other accounts of X and Y were pooled while the stated capital for the combination was fixed at $800,000, the balance sheet for the new X–Y corporation would not balance. This should not be surprising, since so far no account has been taken of the fact that in the course of the merger there was a reduction of the stated capital attributable to Y from its original $1,000,000 to the $400,000 figure corresponding to the X stock issued in exchange for the Y stock.

It is easy enough to see what adjustment should be made. If Y had reduced its capital from $1,000,000 to $400,000 prior to the merger, it would have produced $600,000 in capital surplus, which presumably would have been pooled with X's capital surplus on the books of X–Y. There is no reason to treat a reduction of capital in the course of the merger any differently, and accordingly, the decline in total stated capital should be offset by an equivalent increase in capital surplus:

X–Y

Cash	$200,000	Stat. Cap. (20,000 shares of $40 par)	$800,000
		Cap. Surp.	900,000
Buildings (net)	2,000,000	Earn. Surp.	500,000

Similarly, a combination transaction may result in an increase in total stated capital, if the par or stated value of the stock of the acquiring corporation issued to the acquired corporation's shareholders exceeds the stated capital of the acquired corporation. In that event there will be a corresponding decrease in the overall surplus of the combination—in effect there has been a capitalization (i. e., a transfer to capital) of some of the acquired corporation's surplus. In the absence of some statutory guidance, it would appear that the management is free to decide which type of surplus should be reduced, capital or earned.

The foregoing illustration of the pooling approach was simplified by assuming that the two corporations were equal both in actual value and in book value, and that a share for share exchange ratio was appropriate. However, the pooling approach may also be applied to more complicated transactions. For example, assume that in the previous illustration, on the basis of earnings, reproduction cost and any other relevant elements of value, X is regarded as worth $1,200,000, or $120 a share, while Y is valued at $2,400,000 or $240 per share. Presumably, under these circumstances Y's stockholders would insist upon receiving two-thirds of the total stock in the event of a combination with X, so that if X were to be the surviving entity, the Y stockholders would get 20,000 shares of X stock. The only difference that this would make in the application of the pooling approach is that now Y would be treated as having reduced its capital from $1,000,000 only down to $800,000 (20,000 shares of X's $40 par stock) instead of to $400,000, so that X-Y's stated capital would be $400,000 more than before, and its capital surplus would be $400,000 less. All other accounts for the combination would remain just as they were before. This is quite a small change in appearance for what is really quite a large difference in substance between the two transactions. The reason for this is that the pooling approach, consistent with its theory of reflecting the combination as though the separate corporations had been operated together from the outset, takes no direct account of the current value of either of the two enterprises.

Let us now consider how this transaction would look if it were treated as a "straight" purchase of Y's assets by X in exchange for its stock. As in any purchase, X would record the assets acquired from Y at their cost, measured by the sum of the value of the stock issued to acquire the property plus the amount of any liabilities assumed. Where the stock of the acquiring corporation is traded in a full, fair and free market, and there is no reason to believe the proposed acquisition will have a substantial impact on the market value of the stock, the quoted market price will commonly be used as the measure of the "cost" of the assets acquired. Where there is no such dependable quoted market figure for the stock of the acquiring corporation, or where the proposed issue is so large with relation to the amount of stock already outstanding that the quoted market price of the latter may no longer be significant, then as noted earlier the fair market value of the assets acquired may provide the best measure of the "cost" of those assets to the acquiring corporation.

Assuming a "cost" of $2,400,000 for Y's property here, it would be recorded at that figure on X-Y's balance sheet. In the typical case where the acquired corporation has a number of different assets, rather than a single item of property as in our illustration, it would be necessary to determine the value of the various assets in order to properly allocate this "cost" among them. And in many cases the total amount paid by the acquiring corporation will exceed the highest defensible value for the listed assets of the acquired corporation, which means that part of the price is being paid for the goodwill of the acquired corporation. The emergence of such a goodwill asset in a combination transaction is one of the most ticklish aspects in the whole combination area, in part because of the great uncertainty which presently exists as to the extent, if any, to which such goodwill should thereafter be amortized on the books of the acquiring corporation. See page 792 infra.

As to the effect viewing the transaction as a "purchase" has on the right-hand side of the acquiring corporation's balance sheet, of course stated capital is still increased by the total par value of the stock issued to acquire the assets, here $800,000. However, there is no longer any carryover of the earned surplus of the acquired corporation, and instead the entire excess of the value of the assets acquired over the increase in stated capital (plus any liabilities assumed), here $1,600,000, would be credited to capital surplus.

The differences between the pooling and the purchase approaches may thus be summarized as follows. Under the purchase approach, full recognition is given to the current value of the assets acquired, as measured by the bargain between the parties; but there is no carryover of any of the surplus accounts of the disappearing enterprise. Under the pooling approach, the surplus accounts of the constituent corporations, after adjustment for any change in the stated capital attributable to the acquired corporation, are carried over onto the books of the acquiring corporation; but no account is taken of the present value of the assets of any of the constituent corporations.

It should not be thought, however, that under the pooling approach the value of the assets of the acquired corporation can be ignored entirely. For example, in determining the total amount of par value stock which the acquiring corporation may issue in exchange for the acquired corporation's property under typical corporation statutes like MBA §§ 17 and 18, it is the actual value of the assets acquired which controls, not the book value, regardless of whether the transaction is accounted for under the pooling of interests approach. This means that if the acquiring corporation issues stock with a total par value in excess of the value of the net assets of the acquired corporation, such stock would be watered, even though that total par value did not exceed the book value of the net assets of the acquired corporation. Conversely, if the acquired corporation's assets have substantially appreciated in value, the acquiring corporation may issue stock having a total par value equivalent to the current value of the acquired corporation's assets without running afoul of the watered stock provisions; however, under the pooling of interests approach a deficit would emerge because the book value of the acquired corporation's assets carried over to the books of the acquiring corporation would not balance the par value of the stock issued.

It should be noted that the revaluation of the acquired corporation's assets under the purchase approach is regarded in some quarters as an important advantage of that approach. Remember that many people would like to see assets revalued generally because it results in a clearer picture of the "amount" of invested capital actually at work in the enterprise, and puts annual depreciation on a current price-level basis. And a primary obstacle to such general revaluation—the lack of objective criteria of value—is often thought to be overcome in cases where unrelated corporations are combined, since the terms of the combination transaction will provide a measure of the value of the assets of the acquired corporation. Accordingly, it has sometimes been urged that any combination transaction should be seized as an opportunity to put the assets of the acquired corporation on a current value basis. E. g., May, Business Combinations: An Alternative View, 103 J. Accountancy (April, 1957) 33.

There are, however, some difficulties with this view. For one thing, the terms of the combination transaction do not necessarily determine *absolute* values for either of the constituent corporations, since it is sufficient for combination purposes merely to determine the *relative* values of the contributions being made by the respective concerns. And so far as relative values are concerned, the terms of the combination transaction provide as much guide to the value of the assets of the acquiring corporation as for the acquired corporation. Therefore, there seems little reason to distinguish between the two corporations so far as using a combination transaction to put assets on a current value basis is concerned. This is all the more true when it is recalled that any distinction between acquired and acquiring corporations in this regard will raise the same type of issue—as to which is "really" which—as is presented in the *de facto* merger cases.

To be sure, where there are dependable market quotations for the stock of either or both of the constituent corporations, they would seem to afford a guide to *absolute* values. But here the point may prove too much. If, for example, the market price of the acquiring corporation's stock is used to measure the value of the assets of the acquired corporation, would it not *a fortiori* establish the value of the acquiring corporation's assets, since that is after all what the market value of the stock represents? On the other hand, if that is so, what turns on there being a combination transaction? Why shouldn't the market price of a corporation's own stock be used as a basis for revaluation of its assets from time to time whether or not any combination transaction is involved?

B. STANDARDS FOR DECIDING WHETHER A TRANSACTION IS A PURCHASE OR A POOLING

1. THE APPROACH OF THE AICPA

The AICPA has been struggling for some time with the question of the proper accounting for combination transactions, and more particularly the standards for deciding which should be accounted for as a "purchase", and which as a "pooling of interests". Here is the most recent official pronouncement on the subject:

BUSINESS COMBINATIONS
Accounting Research Bulletin No. 48 (1957).

1. Whenever two or more corporations are brought together, or combined, for the purpose of carrying on the previously conducted

businesses, the accounting to give effect to the combination will vary depending largely upon whether an important part of the former ownership is eliminated or whether substantially all of it is continued. This bulletin differentiates these two types of combination, the first of which is designated herein as a *purchase* and the second as a *pooling of interests*, and indicates the nature of the accounting treatment appropriate to each type.

2. For accounting purposes, the distinction between a *purchase* and a *pooling of interests* is to be found in the attendant circumstances rather than in the designation of the transaction according to its legal form (such as a merger, an exchange of shares, a consolidation, or an issuance of stock for assets and businesses), or in the number of corporations which survive or emerge, or in other legal or tax considerations (such as the availability of surplus for dividends).

3. For accounting purposes, a *purchase* may be described as a business combination of two or more corporations in which an important part of the ownership interests in the acquired corporation or corporations is eliminated or in which other factors requisite to a pooling of interests are not present.

4. In contrast, a *pooling of interests* may be described for accounting purposes as a business combination of two or more corporations in which the holders of substantially all of the ownership interests * in the constituent corporations become the owners of a single corporation which owns the assets and businesses of the constituent corporations, either directly or through one or more subsidiaries, and in which certain other factors discussed below are present. Such corporation may be one of the constituent corporations or it may be a new corporation. After a pooling of interests, the net assets of all of the constituent corporations will in a large number of cases be held by a single corporation. However, the continuance in existence of one or more of the constituent corporations in a subsidiary relationship to another of the constituents or to a new corporation does not prevent the combination from being a pooling of interests if no significant minority interest remains outstanding, and if there are important tax, legal, or economic reasons for maintaining the subsidiary relationship, such as the preservation of tax advantages, the preservation of franchises or other rights, the preservation of the position of outstanding debt securities, or the difficulty or costliness of transferring contracts, leases, or licenses.

5. In determining the extent to which a new ownership or a continuity of old ownership exists in a particular business combination, consideration should be given to attendant circumstances. When

---

* As used in this bulletin, the term "ownership interests" refers basically to common stock, although in some cases the term may also include other classes of stock having senior or preferential rights as well as classes whose rights may be restricted in certain respects.

the shares of stock that are received by the several owners of one of the predecessor corporations are not substantially in proportion to their respective interests in such predecessor, a new ownership or purchase of the predecessor is presumed to result. Similarly, if relative voting rights, as between the constituents, are materially altered through the issuance of senior equity or debt securities having limited or no voting rights, a purchase may be indicated. Likewise, a plan or firm intention and understanding to retire a substantial part of the capital stock issued to the owners of one or more of the constituent corporations, or substantial changes in ownership occurring shortly before or planned to occur shortly after the combination, tends to indicate that the combination is a purchase. However, where a constituent corporation has had two or more classes of stock outstanding prior to the origin of the plan of combination, the redemption, retirement, or conversion of a class or classes of stock having senior or preferential rights as to assets and dividends need not prevent the combination from being considered to be a pooling of interests.

6. Other attendant circumstances should also be taken into consideration in determining whether a purchase or a pooling of interests is involved. Since the assumption underlying the pooling-of-interests concept is one of continuity of all of the constituents in one business enterprise, abandonment or sale of a large part of the business of one or more of the constituents militates against considering the combination as a pooling of interests. Similarly, the continuity of management or the power to control management is involved. Thus, if the management of one of the constituents is eliminated or its influence upon the over-all management of the enterprise is very small, a purchase may be indicated. Relative size of the constituents may not necessarily be determinative, especially where the smaller corporation contributes desired management personnel; however, where one of the constituent corporations is clearly dominant (for example, where the stockholders of one of the constituent corporations obtain 90% to 95% or more of the voting interest in the combined enterprise), there is a presumption that the transaction is a purchase rather than a pooling of interests.

7. No one of the factors discussed in paragraphs 5 and 6 would necessarily be determinative and any one factor might have varying degrees of significance in different cases. However, their presence or absence would be cumulative in effect. Since the conclusions to be drawn from consideration of these different relevant circumstances may be in conflict or partially so, determination as to whether a particular combination is a purchase or a pooling of interests should be made in the light of all such attendant circumstances.

8. When a combination is deemed to be a purchase, the assets acquired should be recorded on the books of the acquiring corporation at cost, measured in money or in the event other consideration is given,

at the fair value of such other consideration, or at the fair value of the property acquired, whichever is more clearly evident. This is in accordance with the procedure applicable to accounting for purchases of assets.

9. When a combination is deemed to be a pooling of interests, a new basis of accountability does not arise. The carrying amounts of the assets of the constituent corporations, if stated in conformity with generally accepted accounting principles and appropriately adjusted when deemed necessary to place them on a uniform accounting basis, should be carried forward; and the combined earned surpluses and deficits, if any, of the constituent corporations should be carried forward, except to the extent otherwise required by law or appropriate corporate action. Adjustments of assets or of surplus which would be in conformity with generally accepted accounting principles in the absence of a combination are ordinarily equally appropriate if effected in connection with a pooling of interests; however, the pooling-of-interests concept implies a combining of surpluses and deficits of the constituent corporations, and it would be inappropriate and misleading in connection with a pooling of interests to eliminate the deficit of one constituent against its capital surplus and to carry forward the earned surplus of another constituent.

10. Where one or more of the constituent corporations continues in existence in a subsidiary relationship, and the requirements of a pooling of interests have been met, the combination of earned surpluses in the consolidated balance sheet is proper since a pooling of interests is not an acquisition as that term is used in paragraph 3 of chapter 1(a) of Accounting Research Bulletin No. 43 which states that earned surplus of a subsidiary corporation created prior to acquisition does not form a part of the consolidated earned surplus. Under the pooling-of-interests concept, the new enterprise is regarded as a continuation of all the constituent corporations and this holds true whether it is represented by a single corporation or by a parent corporation and one or more subsidiaries. If, however, prior to the origin of a plan of combination one party to the combination had been acquired by another such party as a subsidiary in circumstances which precluded the transactions from being considered a pooling of interests, the parent's share of the earned surplus of the subsidiary prior to such acquisition should not be included in the earned surplus of the pooled corporations.

11. Because of the variety of conditions under which a pooling of interests may be carried out, it is not practicable to deal with the accounting presentation except in general terms. A number of problems will arise. For example, if a single corporation survives in a pooling of interests, the stated capital of such corporation may be either more or less than the total of the stated capitals of the constituent corporations. In the former event, the excess may be deducted first from the total of any other contributed capital (capital

surplus), and next from the total of any earned surplus, of the constituent corporations. In the former event, the excess may be deporation is less than the combined stated capitals of the constituent corporations, the difference should appear in the balance sheet of the surviving corporation as other contributed capital (capital surplus), analogous to that created by a reduction in stated capital where no combination is involved.

12. When a combination is considered to be a pooling of interests, statements of operations issued by the continuing business for the period in which the combination occurs should ordinarily include the combined results of operations of the constituent interests for the part of the period preceding the date on which the combination was effected; if combined statements are not furnished, statements for the constituent corporations prior to the date of combination should be furnished separately or in appropriate groups. Results of operations of the several constituents during periods prior to that in which the combination was effected, when presented for comparative purposes, may be stated on a combined basis, or shown separately where, under the circumstances of the case, that presentation is more useful and informative. Disclosure that a business combination has been, or in the case of a proposed combination will be, treated as a pooling of interests should be made and any combined statements clearly described as such.

ARB No. 48 did not by any means lay the matter of accounting for combinations to rest. After considerable comment in the accounting periodicals over the years, the subject was assigned for special study by the Accounting Principles Board of the AICPA, and this resulted in Accounting Research Study No. 5: Wyatt, A Critical Study of Accounting for Business Combinations (1963). In summary, that study finds an increasing trend toward characterizing combination transactions as poolings of interests, primarily because of a desire to adopt the pooling accounting approach rather than because of the inherent characteristics of the transaction itself. One important reason for this is the fact that most of the combination transactions in recent years have been designed to qualify for tax-free treatment, which means that for tax purposes, as we shall see later, the assets of the acquired company are carried over at the same tax basis onto the books of the acquiring corporation, in a manner akin to the accounting treatment for a pooling of interests. Hence if for accounting purposes the transaction is treated as a purchase, with the assets of the acquired corporation recorded on the books of the acquiring company at the cost of acquisition to that corporation, which is typically higher than their book value on the books of the acquired company, the acquiring corporation would thereby incur higher depreciation and other charges against income without any corresponding tax benefit.

Moreover, during this period of prosperity the price paid (in stock of the acquiring company) has often far exceeded the highest defensible value of the tangible assets of the acquired company, so that if the transaction is accounted for as a purchase, a substantial goodwill or other intangible asset would emerge as a result of the combination. This problem is accentuated by the fact that in some quarters there has been increasing pressure for the systematic amortization of such intangible assets, which again would result in additional charges against net income without any corresponding tax benefit. Thus Professor Wyatt concludes that whereas earlier "the general approach seemed to be that for a combination to qualify as a pooling of interests, and to be accounted for in that manner, all of the various criteria [in ARB No. 48] should be present, . . . by the late 1950's, the approach to the analysis of a combination transaction appeared to be that the *absence* of a given criterion should not *prevent* the transaction from being a pooling of interests."

On the basis of his study, Professor Wyatt recommended that all combination transactions between independent enterprises should be treated as purchases, with the pooling of interests approach confined to cases involving the combination of previously related entities, such as a parent and subsidiary. Professor Wyatt also recommended that in the case of a combination of two constituents of approximately equal size, where it might be difficult to determine which one in fact acquired the other, it might be appropriate to apply the purchase accounting approach to both constituents, so that the assets of each would be reflected at current value and no earned surplus of either constituent would be carried forward after the combination.

At the request of the director of accounting research of the AICPA, Mr. Robert C. Holsen was asked to comment upon Professor Wyatt's views, which he did in Another Look at Business Combinations, Acc.Res.Study No. 5 at 109–114. Mr. Holsen differed sharply with Professor Wyatt, contending that the pooling of interests approach was entirely appropriate whenever both groups of shareholders continued their former ownership interests in the combined enterprise. Indeed, he would apparently go to the opposite pole from Professor Wyatt and permit the adoption of the pooling approach without regard to such factors as relative size and continuity of management. For him, the only critical element is whether the former owners of the basic equity in the acquired corporation continue to own a similar interest in the combined enterprise. Thus he would deny the pooling approach if the common stockholders of the acquired company receive only preferred stock in the combination.

2. THE VIEW OF THE SEC

The distinction between a purchase and a pooling of interests has proved just as elusive for the SEC as for the AICPA. But in general the Commission seems to have followed the approach taken in ARB No. 48. See generally, Rappaport, SEC Accounting Practice and Procedure (2d ed. 1963) 19.10–19.26. Here are some examples:

a. From Barr [Chief Accountant of the SEC], Accounting Aspects of Business Combinations, 34 Acc.Rev. 175, 180–181 (1959):

> An interesting example is found in a recent registration statement in which an exchange offer was described. As originally filed, purchase accounting was applied to the combination of two companies of which the proposed parent company was one-fifth the size of the company being acquired. The smaller company, which had some 400,000 shares of stock outstanding, was to issue 1,600,000 shares of its $.25 par value common stock for the entire outstanding stock of the larger company, assigning to its shares a value of $2 per share. The prospectus also carried a public offering of 250,000 shares at a price to net the company $2.10 per share. As originally proposed in the registration statement, $2,600,-000 of the excess of the ascribed value of the new shares was to be assigned to certain undeveloped real estate owned by the larger company.
>
> After reviewing the terms of the proposed combination our staff objected to the use of purchase accounting and the resulting substantial write-up in the value of the land. Prior to the exchange offer the registrant's then outstanding common shares were redesignated as Class A convertible stock. This class was convertible into debentures until a specified date after which, if not converted, Class A automatically became common shares. Class A stock and the debentures together had voting rights for the election of five directors, and the new common issued under the plan of exchange was limited to representation by five directors, making a total of ten directors. However, two members of this new group in the organization were to become president and secretary of the parent company.
>
> After discussions, an amended registration statement was filed in which the pooling of interests concept was applied to the combination and the investment in the subsidiary was recorded on the books of the parent at the underlying book value based on cost.

b. From 18 SEC Ann.Rep. 60 (1952).:

Preliminary proxy solicitation material, which was submitted by a food manufacturing company with total assets of approximately $95,000,000, contained a pro forma statement of financial position giving effect to the acquisition of the net assets of a company with total assets of approximately $15,000,000.

The registrant issued 115,000 shares of its common stock, $25 par value, for substantially all of the net assets of the company to be acquired. This represented the issuance of approximately 20 per cent additional stock. The sum of $2,296,300, representing the excess of the common stock equity of the company to be acquired over the aggregate par value of registrant's common stock issued therefor, was reflected in the registrant's account, 'Accumulated earnings retained and used in the business.' The accounting staff in the Division of Corporation Finance took the position that the accumulated earnings of the company to be acquired in excess of the credit to registrant's common stock account, $2,875,000, should be credited to capital surplus instead of to registrant's accumulated earnings account since the transaction appeared to be, and was represented as, a purchase of net assets. Consequently, the pro forma statement of financial position was amended to reduce the accumulated earnings account by $2,296,300 and to credit the capital surplus account with the same amount.

c. From 19 SEC Ann.Rep. 20 (1953):

In an application for the registration of additional shares a registrant described a merger resulting in the acquisition of the assets of another company by the issuance of preferred stock of the registrant in exchange for all of the common stock of such company, which was to be dissolved and its plant operated as a division of the registrant. The net assets to be obtained after assumption of liabilities amounted to $1,667,000 less than the aggregate par value of the registrant's preferred stock to be issued. The registrant indicated it would charge off this difference of $1,667,000 to earned surplus. The registrant was advised that the proposed accounting treatment appeared to be inappropriate in the circumstances since it appeared that the plan was developed primarily for the purpose of acquiring additional plant. Accordingly the registrant filed an amendment in which it was stated that the difference would be added to the cost of buildings. The registrant stated that the other company was acquired in order to obtain urgently needed building space and that the past earnings of the acquired company did not justify capitalization of any part of the consideration as having been paid for goodwill or for any other intangible. Acceptance of the originally proposed accounting would have resulted in an understatement of the assets to be acquired and thereafter in an understatement of depreciation charges, with a corresponding overstatement of income.

C. PARENT-SUBSIDIARY ACCOUNTING PROBLEMS

The parent-subsidiary relationship gives rise to a number of special accounting problems, many of which are imported into the combination area when the combination takes the form of a stock acquisition and the acquired corporation is kept in existence as a subsidiary. Most of the problems concern the treatment of the investment in the subsidiary on the books of the parent corporation. In the first instance, the parent's investment in the subsidiary would be recorded as an asset on the parent's balance sheet, at cost. Assuming for simplicity that 100% of the subsidiary's stock has been acquired, the amount paid by the parent should be equal to the current value of the subsidiary's net assets, since that is what has been acquired, at least indirectly. As a corollary, it would seem to follow that any dividends received by the parent out of surplus of the subsidiary which existed at the time of acquisition do not constitute income to the parent, but rather represent a partial return of the parent's investment and should be recorded as a reduction therein. See ARB No. 43, Ch. 1(A), Rule 3 ("Earned surplus of a subsidiary company created prior to acquisition does not form a part of the consolidated earned surplus . . . ; nor can any dividend declared out of such surplus properly be credited to the income account of the parent company.")

Of course, dividends received from the post-acquisition earnings of the subsidiary do constitute income to the parent. In addition, there is some accounting authority for the proposition that the undistributed earnings of a controlled subsidiary should be reflected in the statements of the parent, by a debit to the investment and a credit either to income or surplus, because of the parent's power to draw those earnings up as dividends virtually at will. This approach is often referred to as the "combined" method of accounting, since it constitutes a kind of informal combination of the operating results of the parent and its subsidiary.

A more formal method of combining the accounts of a parent corporation and its subsidiary is the use of *consolidated* statements for the two corporations. The object of consolidated accounting is to portray the operating results and financial condition of the total enterprise as nearly as possible as though it had been carried on by a single corporation. Normally, this would seem to call for literally combining the various accounts of the two corporations (after making an appropriate elimination of any inter-corporate items), just as is done in a combination transaction accounted for under the pooling of interests approach. But it is here that ARB No. 48 enters the parent-subsidiary arena, and applies the purchase-pooling dichotomy to the preparation of consolidated statements. Under ARB No. 48 the preparation of consolidated statements depends upon whether the acquisition transaction is viewed as a purchase or a pooling of interests. If the former, then for consolidated balance sheet purposes the net assets of the subsidiary should be recorded at the parent corporation's cost. But if the acquisition is viewed as a pooling of interests, then the assets of the subsidiary should be carried over to the consolidated statement at their book value; and the earned surplus (or deficit) of the subsidiary at the date of acquisition should be combined with the parent's earned surplus, which represents a departure from ARB No. 43, Ch. 1(A), Rule 3, supra.

For more on parent-subsidiary accounting problems, see Baker & Cary, Cases and Materials on Corporations (3d ed., unabridged 1959) 1333–1345; Hackney, Financial Accounting for Parents and Subsidiaries—A New Approach to Consolidated Statements, 25 Pitt.L.Rev. 8 (1963).

D. PURCHASE AND POOLING UNDER THE CORPORATION STATUTES

Until quite recently, there had been little attention paid to the purchase-pooling dichotomy in the corporation statutes. Indeed, as we have already seen, only in the case of statutory merger or consolidation did the statutes even take special note of combination transactions. Thus where a combination took the form of an acquisition of assets (or stock), it was treated just like any other purchase of property for stock, with the acquired property presumably recorded at its fair market value at the date of acquisition. And while there was perhaps no absolute mandate against carrying forward the acquired corporation's property at book value, there was certainly no warrant for any carry-over of the earned surplus of the acquired corporation.

However, in the case of merger or consolidation a few of the statutes did expressly contemplate carry-forward of the earned surplus of the acquired corporation (without, however, any corresponding dictate as to property valuation). A typical provision of this kind was former

§ 69(g) of the Model Act (which was dropped in the 1962 amendments, in conjunction with the addition of the last sentence of § 2(*l*) and the third paragraph of § 19, neither of which had any counterpart in the Act prior to 1962.) Prior to its elimination in 1962, § 69(g) read as follows:

> The net surplus of the merging or consolidating corporations which was available for the payment of dividends immediately prior to such merger or consolidation, to the extent that such surplus is not transferred to stated capital or capital surplus by the issuance of shares or otherwise, shall continue to be available for the payment of dividends by such surviving or new corporation.

As in the case of so many of the Model Act provisions, § 69(g) had come from the Illinois statute, where the counterpart provision is also § 69(g). The following commentary on this provision appears in 1 Ill.Bus.Corp.Act Ann. (1947) 281:

> *Dividends after merger or consolidation.* Paragraph (g) of section 69 was inserted in order to negative any intention that a merger or consolidation should of itself effect a capitalization or "freezing" of the earned surplus of the corporations losing their separate existence. Without this provision such a result might have been supposed to follow from the application of the definition of stated capital in § 2(k) [the counterpart of MBA § 2(j)]. Thus in the absence of special provision in the plan of merger or consolidation the stated capital and paid-in surplus, if any, applicable to the respective shares of the constituent corporations would determine the stated capital and paid-in surplus applicable to the shares of the surviving or new corporation into which they were transformed. Any alteration in such amounts should be provided for as part of the plan. . . .
>
> If one of the constituent corporations had a deficit prior to the merger or consolidation and another had a surplus available for dividends, only the net surplus, if any, remains available for dividends under paragraph (g).

As an aid to understanding the reasons for the aforementioned 1962 amendments to the Model Act, deleting § 69(g) and adding the last sentence of § 2(*l*) and the third paragraph of § 19, the following background items may be instructive. First, it appears that in 1961 the Committee on Corporate Laws of the American Bar Association, which prepared the Model Act and has responsibility for any amendments, received a letter calling attention to problems raised by § 69(g) in the following terms:

> 1. The use of the term "net surplus . . . available for the payment of dividends" is puzzling, since it raises the

question of why the terms defined in section 2, such as "earned surplus" or "capital surplus" were not employed. Prior to the amendment of section 69(g) [in 1957] to include the words "or capital surplus" after the words "stated capital", it seemed likely that the phrase was not limited to "earned surplus", not only because it would have been simple to say "earned surplus", but also because capital surplus is "available", at least for stock dividends. With the amendment to 69(g) to insert the words "or capital surplus" after the words "stated capital", it becomes much harder to construe the phrase "surplus . . . available for the payment of dividends" to include capital surplus, though it is far from clear that any change in coverage was intended by the aforementioned amendment. Perhaps this peculiar phrase is primarily attributable to the somewhat similar language used in the Illinois statute; but it may be noted that the phrase is just as troublesome there as in the Model Act.

2. Section 69(g) seems to eliminate the emerging distinction between a "pooling of interests" and a "purchase" by treating all mergers or consolidations pursuant to the Model Act as poolings, at least for the purpose of handling the surplus accounts. In view of the very sensible reliance upon accounting developments in other sections of the Act, it seems unfortunate to preclude correlation between Accounting Research Bulletin No. 48 and the Model Act in this area.

3. The difficulty referred to in paragraph 2 is heightened by the treatment accorded by the Model Act to acquisition transactions which take the form of a purchase of assets. There it appears that netting of earned surplus is not permitted, whether or not the transaction meets the accounting tests for a pooling of interests, since there is no counterpart of section 69(g) which is applicable in connection with purchase transactions. The result is that under the Model Act the form of the transaction becomes conclusive on the issue of whether the surplus accounts of the combining enterprises should be netted. Is it not sounder to attempt to minimize the differences between merger and purchase of assets, as the tax and accounting approaches do?

4. Finally, the addition of the words "or capital surplus" after the words "stated capital" in section 69(g) introduces another element of confusion. In the normal "pooling of interests" situation, which section 69(g) seems to contemplate, there is no occasion for a transfer of earned surplus (and *a fortiori* existing capital surplus), to capital surplus, whether on account of issuance of shares or for any other reason. It is true that if the par value of the new shares being issued by the surviving entity in a merger exceeds the par value of the

shares which are being replaced, a transfer to stated capital may be required. Otherwise, however, the process seems to be simply one of netting the respective surplus accounts, and there is no basis for the creation of any additional capital surplus.

Quite the reverse is true in the "purchase of assets" situation. There of course no netting of surplus accounts at all occurs; and the excess of the value of the net assets acquired over the par value of the new stock issued to acquire those assets does augment capital surplus. But since as already noted the whole pattern of section 69(g) seems to preclude the "purchase of assets" approach in a merger or consolidation, it is hard to see just what the significance of the addition of those words "or capital surplus" was intended to be.

In addition to this and perhaps other correspondence, the Committee had before it the example in Pennsylvania which in 1959 had taken the lead in amending its corporation statute to allow greater flexibility in accounting for combination transactions. Pa.B.C.L. § 704F; see Hackney, Financial Accounting For Parents and Subsidiaries—A New Approach to Consolidated Statements, 25 Pitt.L.Rev. 8, 15–18 (1963).

The 1962 amendments are analyzed in the following terms by the chairman of the committee which prepared them, in Gibson, Surplus, So What? — The Model Act Modernized, 17 Bus.Law. 476, 481–483 (1962):

> While the pooling of interests concept is defined in Accounting Research Bulletin No. 48 in terms realistic enough for accounting purposes, they lack the specificity of legal rules. Thus the new doctrine is said to apply whenever two or more corporations are "brought together" or "combined" for the purpose of carrying on the previously conducted businesses. The concept of being "brought together" sounds more like the law of domestic relations than corporation law, even suggesting problems of compatibility. "Combined" falls equally short of any known word of art in corporate practice. Were we to make the result depend on subjective inquiry into "purpose", we should depart altogether from the traditional technique of corporate law that, in the absence of fraud, everyone may rely on the form of the transaction.
>
> In addition to these dissimilarities of idiom, the accounting standards that operate in the pooling of interests doctrine are also remote from accepted corporate law requirements. For example, it is required that there be a continuity of ownership by "substantially all the ownership interests", that there be no material alteration of "relative voting rights"

and above all that there be a "continuity" of managerial personnel. It is quite apparent that no statute of familiar corporate form could be written in such terms and an effort to employ them would leave the availability of the statute, and the limits of its operation, open to serious doubt. It would be still less satisfactory to enact that earned surplus might be carried forward in any transaction where permitted by sound accounting practice, since this would in effect abdicate control by law and leave the whole matter to accounting rules as they might from time to time be administered. It is known, moreover, that judgments sometimes differ as to their effect. In short, unless definite standards were to be adopted in the Act, businessmen would never know in advance the legal consequences that might follow from an attempt to effect a "pooling of interests".

The real remedy, in the judgment of the Committee on Corporate Laws, was to look directly to the end sought—the carry forward of earned surplus. There appears to be no compelling reason of public policy or business necessity for not providing that in all transactions of merger or consolidation or acquisition of assets, or even in a mere acquisition of control, the earned surplus of both participating corporations may properly be considered as earned surplus, rather than capital surplus, of the resulting enterprise. The significance of earned surplus to the investment world is more important than any artistic incidents of legal technique, such, for example, as the theory of survival of corporate personality that might possibly have prompted the exception in the merger law. As in the case of the law merchant, the law should follow business rather than obstruct it unless some public policy requires otherwise.

On this premise, there is no reason from the point of view of corporate law why the continuation of earned surplus should not be permitted in every transaction of this general nature, so far as the policies of corporate law alone are concerned, even if the permission accorded by accounting practice is more limited in its effect. All that means is that, so far as the law is concerned, the privilege is unmistakably accorded in each such instance, though in some instances the accountants will not permit its utilization in full. So far from this being an objection, it is indeed a recommendation. The mere circumstance that accounting practice has recently changed and now necessitates an amendment of the Model Act shows that further changes, with consequential amendments, may be needed in the future. Room for further learning by accountants should be left. Moreover, corporate law has tended more and more in the direction of a simple set of workable ground rules for the corporate enterprise, leaving regulation either to the equitable jurisdiction of the courts or to regulation through statutes of a policing nature or through the informed judgment of administrative agencies. In short, corporate law should not attempt to particularize all foreseeable situations of the future, since they will look very different when the future comes. . . .

In analyzing these 1962 amendments to the Model Act, be sure to differentiate between the question of whether the earned surplus or deficit of the acquired corporation may (or must) be carried over, a subject with which the new provisions expressly deal, and the question of the basis on which the assets of the acquired corporation should be recorded on the books of the acquiring corporation, a subject that is not even alluded to in the statute (as it was not in the pre-1962 provisions either). To the accountants, as ARB No. 48 indicates, these two issues are always linked: carryover of the assets at book value goes with carryover of earned surplus (under the pooling approach); recording the assets at cost goes with no carryover of earned surplus (under the purchase approach). Consider whether the Model Act preserves this symmetry, and indeed whether the Act contemplates the carryover of asset book values under any circumstances. Cf. MBA §§ 18, 19.

SECTION 4. TAX INCIDENTS OF COMBINATION TRANSACTIONS

A. GENERAL BACKGROUND

Absent some special statutory provisions, the various exchange transactions which are inherent in corporate combinations, both those between corporations and those between corporations and stockholders, would presumably constitute taxable transactions under the basic exchange provisions of §§ 1001 and 1002. However, as we have already seen in connection with recapitalizations, a very important exception to ordinary exchange treatment is provided by the reorganization provisions of the Code, and the various modes of corporate combinations represent the most important, and complex, types of reorganization. Accordingly, a detailed analysis of the reorganization pattern applicable to combination transactions is in order at this point.

There are two important consequences which flow from qualification as a reorganization. One is of course complete or partial nonrecognition of gain, which is provided by §§ 354 and 361. The other is that usual corollary of non-recognition, the carryover of basis, which means that the basis of property in the hands of the new owner is either the same as it was in the prior owner's hands or the same as the new owner's basis in the property exchanged by him. It may be helpful to divide our analysis into two parts, looking first at the tax incidents to the corporations being combined, and then at the tax incidents to the stockholders (and security holders). See generally, Darrell, The Use of Reorganization Techniques in Corporate Acquisitions, 70 Harv.L.Rev. 1183 (1957); Sapienza, Tax Considerations in Corporate Reorganizations and Mergers, 60 Nw.U.L.Rev. 765 (1966).

1. NON-RECOGNITION AND BASIS FOR CORPORATE TRANSFERORS AND TRANSFEREES

Here the basic non-recognition section is § 361. Section 361(a) provides that no gain shall be recognized to a corporation which transfers its assets in a transaction constituting a reorganization under § 368. This would include the transfer of all or substantially all of its assets by the acquired corporation in an assets acquisition (hereinafter "C reorganization"); and it would also apply to a statutory merger or consolidation (hereinafter "A reorganization") if such transactions are regarded as including a transfer of property from the disappearing corporation to the surviving corporation, instead of being more in the nature of a "coalescence" of the two corporations. Section 361(a) is applicable only if the exchange is solely for stock or securities (plus assumption of liabilities, by virtue of §§ 368(a)(1)(C) and 357). If some other consideration passes to the acquired corporation in a C reorganization, as it may to a limited extent by virtue of §§ 368(a)(2)(B), § 361(a) becomes inapplicable. However, § 361(b)(1) will then apply, either to prevent recognition of gain to the corporation if the "boot" (i.e., the consideration other than stock, securities and assumption of liabilities) is distributed to shareholders of the acquired corporation *pursuant to the plan of reorganization*, or to limit recognition to the amount of the boot if it is not so distributed. Whether or not boot is present, § 361(b)(2) prohibits the recognition of loss by the acquired corporation.

Section 358 prescribes the basis of the acquired corporation in the non-recognition property received; as in the case of § 351 transactions, the basis is the same as the basis of the assets transferred, increased by the amount of any gain recognized, and decreased by the amount of any cash and the fair market value of any other boot received, plus the amount of any liabilities assumed or to which the transferred property was subject.

The basis of the acquiring corporation in the assets it receives is determined under § 362(b), which operates in the same manner as

§ 362(a)(1) in the case of the transferee corporation under § 351. That is, the acquiring corporation takes the assets at their basis in the hands of the acquired corporation, increased by the amount of any gain recognized by the acquired corporation. Thus both the acquiring corporation and the acquired corporation end up with a basis determined with reference to the original basis of the acquired corporation's property (aside from adjustments for boot or liabilities), so that the possibility of two gains or two losses exist.

2. NON-RECOGNITION AND BASIS FOR SHAREHOLDERS AND SECURITY HOLDERS

Here, as we have already seen in connection with recapitalizations, the basic non-recognition section is § 354, which provides that "no gain or loss shall be recognized if stock or securities in a corporation a party to a reorganization are, in pursuance of the plan of reorganization, exchanged solely for stock or securities in such corporation or in another corporation a party to the reorganization". Under this section the exchange by the acquired corporation's shareholders of their stock for stock of the acquiring corporation in an A reorganization or in a stock acquisition (hereinafter "B reorganization") would be tax-free.

In a C reorganization, unless the acquired corporation is liquidated there will be no tax incidents to its shareholders, since they will merely continue as shareholders of the acquired corporation. However, where the acquired corporation liquidates and distributes the stock of the acquiring corporation, in effect the shareholders of the acquired corporation exchange their stock for stock of the acquiring corporation; if the liquidation is "pursuant to the plan of reorganization", the transaction will be covered by § 354(a).

As noted in the analysis of recapitalization transactions, § 354 (a) applies only to an exchange which is solely for stock (and/or securities in a principal amount not exceeding the principal amount of any securities surrendered); the presence of any boot, (i.e., money, property, or principal amount of securities in excess of the principal amount of securities surrendered) prevents the application of § 354. In that event, § 356(a) would come into play and tax the gain on the transaction to the extent of the boot. And if the transaction has the "effect of the distribution of a dividend" within the meaning of § 356(a)(2), the boot, to the extent it does not exceed the amount of the gain on the transaction, would be taxed as a dividend. Whether or not boot is involved, §§ 354(a) and 356(c) prevent the recognition of any loss.

The basis of property received in exchanges governed by §§ 354 or 356 is prescribed by § 358(a). Under that section, the basis of any non-recognition property received is equal to the basis of any property given up, increased in the amount of any gain recognized and decreased by the amount of any cash or the fair market value of any other boot received in the transaction.

B. JUDICIAL LIMITATIONS ON QUALIFICATION AS A REORGANIZATION

1. IN GENERAL

It is important to note that unless a transaction fits one of the specific definitions in § 368(a), it cannot qualify as a reorganization —the operative words of § 368(a)(1) are that the term "reorganization" *means* rather than *includes*. On the other hand, the converse is not true—that is, not every transaction which literally complies with one of the specified definitions of reorganization in § 368 (a)(1) will qualify for the favorable reorganization treatment. Because taxpayers have often sought to cast in the reorganization mold transactions which really do not belong there, the courts have found it necessary to go beyond the bare words of the statute and try to determine whether the particular transaction comes within the spirit of the tax-free reorganization provisions. We have already seen one illustration in the recapitalization area, in the Bazley case, at page 412 supra, where the Supreme Court held that a transaction which concededly constituted a recapitalization under state law nevertheless did not qualify as a reorganization for tax purposes.

A number of the extra-statutory standards developed by the courts for testing purported reorganization transactions have crystallized into general principles. Foremost among these is the "business purpose" doctrine, which stems from the landmark case of Gregory v. Helvering, 293 U.S. 465, 55 S.Ct. 266, 79 L.Ed. 596, 97 A.L.R. 1355 (1935). There the Supreme Court held that a transaction which complied literally with the then-existing divisive reorganization provisions nevertheless did not qualify for tax-free treatment because the entire arrangement had no business purpose and was designed solely to accomplish what in effect was a dividend to the stockholder. The business purpose doctrine is now expressly incorporated in the reorganization regulations, Reg. § 1.368–1(b); and it has of course spread far beyond the reorganization area to become one of the basic principles in the tax field.

Another doctrine of general importance which has had a special impact in the reorganization area is the "step transaction" doctrine. Under this principle, purportedly separate transactions will be amalgamated into a single transaction when it appears that they were really component steps intended from the outset to be taken for the purpose of reaching the ultimate result. For example, in Heller v.

Commissioner, 2 T.C. 371 (1943), affirmed, 147 F.2d 376 (9th Cir. 1945), the stockholders of a Delaware corporation wanted to reincorporate under California law, which is a classic type of tax-free transaction. However, the stockholders wanted to recognize the unrealized loss they had on their stock in the Delaware corporation. Accordingly, they organized a California corporation and purchased its stock with cash borrowed from a bank which was also a creditor of the Delaware corporation. The California corporation then purchased the assets of the Delaware corporation for cash, augmented by a loan from the same bank. The Delaware corporation used the cash it received to pay off its bank loan, and then dissolved, distributing the balance of the cash in liquidation to its stockholders. Presumably, the stockholders then repaid their own bank loans. *Held*, the transaction constituted a reorganization so that no loss could be recognized by the stockholders upon the liquidation: "The effect of all the steps taken was that petitioner made an exchange of stock of one corporation for stock of another pursuant to a plan of reorganization."

2. CONTINUITY OF INTEREST

Perhaps the most important judicial doctrine in the reorganization area has been "continuity of interest", which is not only firmly embedded in the regulations, Reg. § 1.368–1(b), but has also played an important part in the development of the statutory definition of B and C reorganizations. The continuity of interest doctrine seems to stem from Cortland Specialty Co. v. Commissioner, 60 F.2d 937 (2d Cir. 1932), involving an earlier rudimentary definition of reorganization which included any acquisition by one corporation of substantially all the properties of another corporation. In the Cortland case, substantially all of the property of one corporation had indeed been acquired by another corporation, in exchange for cash and short-term promissory notes, but the court held that the transaction did not qualify as a reorganization for tax purposes since that term presupposes a "continuance of interest on the part of the transferor in the properties transferred." In effect, then, the continuity of interest doctrine constituted the instrument for preventing what was essentially a sale transaction from obtaining reorganization treatment.

Only one year later, in Pinellas Ice & Cold Storage Co. v. Commissioner, 287 U.S. 462, 53 S.Ct. 257, 77 L.Ed. 428 (1933), this question came before the Supreme Court, which held that to qualify as a reorganization "the seller must acquire an interest in the affairs of the purchasing company more definite than that incident to ownership of its short-term purchase-money notes." Two years later came Helvering v. Minnesota Tea Co., 296 U.S. 378, 56 S.Ct. 269, 80 L.Ed. 284 (1935), where a transfer of assets for common stock worth approximately $700,000 (and amounting to about 7% of the acquiring corporation's outstanding stock) plus cash of approximately $425,000 was sustained as reorganization. After referring to the statement in the Pinellas case that an "interest" must be acquired in the transferee, the Court said:

> And we now add that this interest must be definite and material; it must represent a substantial part of the value of the thing transferred. This much is necessary in order that the result accomplished may genuinely partake of the nature of merger or consolidation. . . .
>
> The transaction here was no sale, but partook of the nature of a reorganization, in that the seller acquired a definite and substantial interest in the purchaser.
>
> True it is that the relationship of the taxpayer to the assets conveyed was substantially changed, but this is not inhibited by the statute. Also, a large part of the consideration was cash. This, we think, is permissible so long as the taxpayer received an interest in the affairs of the transferee which represented a material part of the value of the transferred assets.

In the same year, in John A. Nelson Co. v. Helvering, 296 U.S. 374, 56 S.Ct. 273, 80 L.Ed. 281 (1935), the Court found the requisite continuity of interest where assets were transferred for preferred stock and cash. The preferred stock was non-voting except upon default in dividends. The Court commented as follows:

> The owner of preferred stock is not without substantial interest in the affairs of the issuing corporation, although denied voting rights. The statute does not require participation in the management of the purchaser.

The line between debt and equity never glowed more brightly than after the last of the important Supreme Court decisions in the continuity of interest field, Le Tulle v. Scofield, 308 U.S. 415, 60 S.Ct. 313, 84 L.Ed. 355 (1940), where the court held that bonds did not satisfy the requisite continuity, so that a transfer of assets for cash and ten-year bonds secured by a mortgage did not qualify as a reorganization. The Court said:

> In applying our decision in the Pinellas [case, supra], the courts have generally held that receipt of long-term bonds as distinguished from short-term notes constitutes the retention of an interest in the purchasing corporation. There has naturally been some difficulty in classifying the securities involved in various cases.
>
> We are of opinion that the term of the obligations is not material. Where the consideration is wholly in the transferee's bonds, or part cash and part such bonds, we think it cannot be said that the transferor retains a proprietary

interest in the enterprise. On the contrary, he becomes a creditor of the transferee; and we do not think that the fact referred to by the Circuit Court of Appeals, that the bonds were secured solely by the assets transferred and that, upon default, the bondholder would retake only the property sold, changes his status from that of a creditor to one having a proprietary stake, within the purview of the statute.

However, Congress had already decided not to leave the development of the continuity of interest doctrine entirely to the courts. Because of the multiplying efforts to fit what were essentially sale transactions within the protective reorganization cloak, Congress had acted in 1934 to substantially restrict the scope of the reorganization provisions. In effect, a rather extreme continuity of interest limitation was built directly into the statutory definition of the B and C reorganizations by the requirement that the acquisition must be *solely for voting stock.* (The exception for assumption of liabilities in C reorganizations came into the statute in 1939; the 20% leeway from the solely voting stock requirement for C reorganizations under § 368(a)(2)(B) came in 1954.) However, the definition of an A reorganization simply in terms of "a statutory merger or consolidation" was left unchanged.

Since Congress was clearly concerned with the continuity of interest concept at the time of the 1934 amendments, the absence of any reference to the matter in connection with A reorganizations might have led to the view that continuity of interest was not required for an A reorganization. Nevertheless, in Roebling v. Commissioner, 143 F.2d 810 (3d Cir. 1944), the court held that the continuity of interest requirement was applicable to an A reorganization, and hence rejected reorganization treatment for a merger when the stockholders of the acquired corporation received only bonds of the acquiring corporation. In Southwest Natural Gas Co. v. Commissioner, 189 F.2d 332 (5th Cir. 1951), continuity of interest was found lacking in a statutory merger despite the fact that the consideration received by the stockholders of the acquired corporation included 16% of the outstanding common stock of the acquiring corporation. However, the value of this 16% stock interest was only about $5500, out of a total consideration in cash, bonds, and stock of almost $600,000; moreover, some 41% of the acquired corporation's stockholders had elected to forego any continued participation in the combined enterprise in favor of receiving only cash. On the other hand, as the dissenting opinion pointed out, there was in fact a greater continuity of interest than there appeared to be, since a group owning 35% of the acquired corporation's stock before the merger also owned 85% of the acquiring corporation's stock, and they ended up with an 88% equity interest in the combination.

The Southwest Natural Gas opinion phrased the continuity of interest test as follows:

> While no precise formula has been expressed for determining whether there has been retention of the requisite interest, it seems clear that the requirement of continuity of interest consistent with the statutory intent is not fulfilled in the absence of a showing: (1) that the transferor corporation or its shareholders retained a substantial proprietary stake in the enterprise represented by a material interest in the affairs of the transferee corporation, and, (2) that such retained interest represents a substantial part of the value of the property transferred.

Taken literally, the first of these requirements would normally depend in the first instance on the relative size of the two corporations. Where the acquired corporation is very much smaller than the acquiring corporation, the stockholders of the acquired corporation might not have a "substantial" or "material" interest in the acquired corporation even if the consideration they received consisted solely of voting common stock. However, this *quantitative* aspect has not been stressed in the cases, and it does not presently appear to be a significant factor in Service policy.

The second requirement seems to look to the ratio of that part of the consideration received by the acquired corporation's shareholders which constitutes a continuing proprietary interest to the total consideration received. It is this *qualitative* aspect of the continuity of interest doctrine that was stressed in the Minnesota Tea case, supra, and of course the Southwest Natural Gas case itself turned primarily on this factor. Certain subsidiary questions arise here which are easier to state than answer: (1) Will a higher ratio of consideration providing a proprietary interest be required when the acquired corporation is substantially smaller than the acquiring corporation, so that the continuing interest of the stockholders of the former would be relatively small in any event? (2) Does the required ratio turn at all upon the type of proprietary interest consideration involved, so that a lower ratio might be permitted if voting common of the acquiring corporation is used than, say, if nonvoting preferred is used?

To some extent the importance of the qualitative aspect of the continuity of interest doctrine has been somewhat lessened by the addition of §§ 354(a)(2) and 356(d) in the 1954 Code, treating as boot any excess in principal amount of securities received over the principal amount of securities surrendered. And of course if only securities are received and none are surrendered, the transaction does not come under §§ 354 or 356 at all, but reverts to §§ 331, 346 or 302. These provisions, however, only relate to the tax consequences to the acquired corporation's stockholders. The basis to the acquiring corporation of the assets acquired in the merger still depends upon whether there has been a "reorganization". In addition, the question of whether boot might be taxable as a dividend under §§ 356(a)(2), rather than simply as part of the consideration in an exchange transaction, may turn on the presence of a reorganization.

There is one other aspect of the continuity of interest doctrine which was actually presented in the Southwest Natural Gas case but was not expressly referred to in the court's formulation of the test. Might the necessary continuity of interest be found lacking if a substantial number of shareholders, of either the acquired corporation or the acquiring corporation, refuse to participate in the merger and pursue the statutory appraisal remedy to obtain cash? In the Southwest Natural Gas case, the plan of merger itself afforded the stockholders of the acquired corporation the option of taking cash, and some 41% of the stockholder elected that alternative. Thus, even if all the other stockholders had received nothing but voting stock, the failure of almost half of the stockholders of the acquired corporation to continue any participation in the enterprise might have raised serious doubts as to the necessary continuity of interest. Of course in the absence of a cash alternative under the merger plan, the percentage of non-participating stockholders would normally be substantially lower, since typically the merger statutes require the approval of at least two-thirds of the stockholders; and in many situations even an approved merger could not be consummated in the face of any substantial body of dissenting shareholders, because of the lack of necessary cash.

While there do not appear to be any cases directly in point on this issue, some light may be gleaned from the authorities on an analogous issue under the 1939 Code version of a D reorganization. That section then, as now, dealt with a transfer of assets by one corporation to another, but prior to 1954 the control requirement was that the "transferor or its shareholders or both" have control of the transferee. In Reilly Oil Co. v. Commissioner, 189 F.2d 382 (5th Cir. 1951), 69% of the stockholders of the acquired corporation participated in a reorganization and secured control, while the remaining stockholders were paid off in cash. The court held that there was sufficient continuity of interest, affirming the Tax Court, 13 T.C. 919 (1949), where five dissenters would have required something more than 69%, though less than 100%. The court did not indicate how low it would go. See also Western Mass. Theatres, Inc. v. Commissioner, 236 F.2d 186 (1st Cir. 1956), accepting a 67% participation. In Civic Center Finance Co. v. Kuhl, 83 F.Supp. 251 (E.D.Wis. 1948), aff'd per curiam, 177 F.2d 706 (7th Cir. 1949), participation by 40% of the former stockholders was held insufficient to provide the necessary continuity of interest.

Even if a substantial number of dissenting shareholders would not in and of itself preclude the necessary continuity of interest, questions may still arise as to the impact of this factor upon the other aspects of continuity of interest discussed above. Thus, would the presence of a large number of dissenting shareholders result in requiring a higher ratio of proprietary-interest consideration for those stockholders who do participate? Could a substantial number of dissenting shareholders bring the relative size, or quantitative, aspect of continuity of interest back into focus?

Questions of what qualifies as "stock" may arise in connection with A reorganizations both as a matter of determining whether the necessary continuity of interest is present, and, assuming that hurdle is cleared, in determining whether there is "boot" which would require the recognition of gain under § 356. Thus, the question may be asked whether redeemable preferred stock provides the requisite continuity of interest, since if the stockholders of an acquired corporation received only redeemable preferred they would be subject to being ousted from the surviving corporation at any time. While there does not appear to be any authority dealing expressly with this question, it should be noted that according to the opinion of the Board of Tax Appeals, the preferred stock approved as providing the necessary continuity of interest in the John A. Nelson Co. case, page 806 supra, was in fact subject to redemption in accordance with an unspecified schedule. See 28 B.T.A. 529, 542 (1933). Moreover, in Atlantic City Electric Co. v. Commissioner, 288 U.S. 152, 53 S.Ct. 383, 77 L.Ed. 667 (1932), involving the question whether redeemable, voting preferred stock should be taken into account in measuring the extent of a parent corporation's control over a subsidiary for the purpose of applying an early version of the consolidated return regulations, the court stated that the owners of the redeemable preferred stock "were not in the position of creditors, but were stockholders with a proprietary interest in the corporate undertaking". On the other hand, if only redeemable preferred was issued and the stock was actually redeemed shortly thereafter, it seems likely that a serious question as to continuity of interest would arise; and this would certainly be true if it were shown that an early redemption had been contemplated from the outset.

As to stock options and warrants, according to Reg. § 1.354–1(e) they "are not included in the term 'stock or securities' ", which means that they not only do not contribute to the continuity of interest but in fact represent taxable boot. Bateman v. Commissioner, 40 T.C. 408 (1963). The Bateman case goes on to hold that although warrants received along with stock in a statutory merger do constitute boot, they cannot be taxed as a dividend under § 356(a) (2) because § 316 only taxes distributions of "property" as a dividend, and § 317 specifically excludes warrants from the definition of "property".

Questions may also arise in connection with such mechanical adjuncts to combination transactions as fractional shares and contingent interests in shares. As to the latter, Mr. Darrell noted, at page 688 supra, that such contingent interests may stem from an arrangement under which some of the stock to be issued to stockholders of the acquired corporation is temporarily withheld as security against the possibility of unknown or contingent liabilities. Not infrequently, such stock is placed in escrow and certificates representing the contingent interests in the stock are issued to the stockholders of the acquired corporation. Carlberg v. United States, 281 F.2d 507 (8th Cir. 1960), holds that such certificates constitute "stock" rather than boot, so that they do not occasion the recognition of gain.

Fractional shares pose an even more important practical problem, since they will be present in virtually every combination transaction, except where the exchange ratio calls for an even multiple of the acquiring corporation's stock for each share of the acquired corporation. As will be noted later, it has generally been assumed that fractional shares may even satisfy the "voting stock" test now imposed upon B and C reorganizations, so *a fortiori* they constitute "stock" rather than boot so far as non-recognition of gain is concerned; and the same is true of so-called "scrip", that is, certificates, representing fractional shares, which may be exchanged for full shares. E.g., Rev.Rul. 55–59, 1955–1 Cum.Bull. 35; Mills v. Commissioner, 331 F.2d 321 (5th Cir. 1964). Often the parties make arrangements to handle fractional shares by giving each stockholder entitled to a fractional interest the option of either purchasing a further fractional interest sufficient to make a full share, or selling his fractional interest; in the latter event, of course, the stockholder would realize gain or loss measured by the difference between the amount of cash received and the allocated cost basis of the fractional interest sold. However, if instead the plan of reorganization calls for the issuance of cash in lieu of fractional shares to all stockholders, the cash might then be regarded as boot in the reorganization transaction and thereby subject to taxation as a dividend under § 356(a)(2). Cf. Rev.Rul. 56–220, 1956–1 Cum.Bull. 191.

3. CONTINUITY OF BUSINESS ENTERPRISE

Reg. § 1.368–1(b) states that one requisite for a valid reorganization is "a continuity of the business enterprise under the modified corporate form". In some quarters this has been regarded as imposing a variant of the continuity of interest test, which in effect would require that any business enterprise carried on by the constituent corporations be continued by the combination, so that the stockholders would continue to have an interest in their former enterprise. Under this view the continuity of business enterprise requirement for a valid reorganization would be quite analogous to the test for a pooling of interests under ARB No. 48, which states that the "abandonment or sale of a large part of the business of one or more of the constituents militates against considering the combination as a pooling of interests".

This view received considerable support from Rev.Rul. 56–330, 1956–2 Cum.Bull. 204, which held that a transfer by three real estate corporations of all of their assets to a newly formed insurance company, solely in exchange for voting stock of the latter, did not qualify as a reorganization because the acquiring corporation was to engage in a new business entirely different from the activities carried on by the acquired corporations, and hence the continuity of business enterprise test was not satisfied. The ruling claimed to distinguish (but without explaining how) the case of Becher v. Commissioner, 221 F.2d 252 (2d Cir. 1955), which had sustained reorganization treatment, at the urging of the Commissioner, where the assets of a sponge rubber and canvas product manufacturing business were transferred to a new corporation formed to engage in the upholstered furniture business; in the Becher case, the court stated that there was no requirement of "identity of business before and after the reorganization".

However, in Bentsen v. Phinney, 199 F.Supp. 363 (S.D.Tex.1961), which apparently involved the very transaction to which Rev.Rul. 56–330 had been addressed, the court held that if the continuity of business enterprise test in the regulations required that the acquiring corporation engage in the same type of business as the acquired corporation, or a similar business, it went beyond the statute and was invalid. In the court's view, all that was required was a continuation of some business activity.

The Service has since renounced its earlier position and adopted the view expressed in the Bentsen case. In Rev.Rul. 63–29, 63–1 Cum. Bull. 77, a corporation formerly engaged in the manufacture of children's toys had sold practically all of its operating assets to third parties for cash and notes. Thereafter it acquired, solely for voting stock, all of the property of a corporation engaged in the distribution of steel products, and it used the proceeds of the sale of its toy business to expand its newly acquired steel products business. The ruling states that the continuity of business enterprise test is satisfied so long as "the surviving corporation was organized to engage in a business enterprise", and holds that "the surviving corporation need not continue the activities conducted by its predecessors". Notwithstanding the possible distinction between the instant situation, where at least a business enterprise previously carried on by one of the constituents was continued by the surviving entity, and Rev.Rul. 56–330, where the acquiring corporation was formed to carry on an entirely new and distinct activity, Rev.Rul. 63–29 went on to revoke Rev.Rul. 56–330, stating that the conclusions reached in the present ruling were equally applicable to the question involved in the earlier one.

4. USE OF A SUBSIDIARY IN REORGANIZATION ACQUISITIONS

One of the early judge-made limitations on qualification as a reorganization, with roots in the continuity of interest doctrine as well as the "party to a reorganization" requirement of § 354, precluded reorganization treatment where a subsidiary corporation effected an acquisition in exchange for stock of its parent. The same was true where a parent corporation acquired the assets or stock of a corporation for its own stock but promptly transferred what it acquired to a subsidiary in pursuance of the plan of reorganization. E. g., Groman v. Commissioner, 302 U.S. 82, 58 S.Ct. 108, 82 L.Ed. 63 (1937). However, in the 1954 Code these limitations were virtually eliminated so far as C reorganizations were concerned. Under § 368 (a)(1)(C), an asset acquisition by a subsidiary corporation qualifies as a C reorganization if the consideration given for the assets consists solely of voting stock of a corporation in control of the acquiring corporation. And the parent corporation would be a "party to the reorganization" under the language of § 368(b), second sentence. However, it should be noted that the subsidiary may not use both its own stock and its parent's stock in the same transaction. Reg. § 1.368–2(d)(1).

If the parent first acquires the assets of the acquired corporation itself but then transfers them to a subsidiary, the transaction still qualifies as a C reorganization by virtue of § 368(a)(2)(C); and again the parent corporation is a party to the reorganization under § 368(b), last sentence. Section 368(a)(2)(C) also permits the acquiring corporation in a A reorganization to place the acquired assets in a controlled subsidiary without disqualifying the transaction as a reorganization.

The Service has recognized that the 1954 amendments indicate a general intention on the part of Congress "to remove the continuity-of-interest problem from the section 368(a)(1)(C) reorganization area"; accordingly, a reorganization was found where assets received in exchange for the parent's stock were transferred to a wholly-owned subsidiary of the parent's wholly-owned subsidiary, even though that situation is not expressly covered by § 368(a)(1)(C). Rev.Rul. 64–73, 1964–1 Cum.Bull. (Part 1) 142.

Although for some unexplained reason the 1954 Code did not make these rules applicable to B reorganizations, happily that anomaly has been corrected by § 218 of the Revenue Act of 1964 which amended § 368, subsections (a)(1)(B), (a)(2)(C), and (b), to conform the treatment of B reorganizations to that afforded C reorganizations so far as use of a subsidiary is concerned.

C. SPECIAL PROBLEMS IN B REORGANIZATIONS

1. IN GENERAL

As previously noted, in response to the continuity of interest problem Congress provided express statutory standards governing the consideration which an acquiring corporation could use in a B (or C) reorganization. Needless to say, the resulting statutory formulation created some difficulties of its own.

COMMISSIONER v. TURNBOW [12]

Court of Appeals, Ninth Circuit, 1960. 286 F.2d 669.
Affirmed, 368 U.S. 337, 82 S.Ct. 353, 7 L.Ed.2d 326 (1961).

MERRILL, CIRCUIT JUDGE. This case presents the following question: whether gain realized by a taxpayer upon the transfer of his stock in a wholly owned corporation in consideration for voting stock in another corporation plus cash is recognizable in its entirety or only to the extent of the cash received. The Tax Court, following Howard v. Commissioner of Internal Revenue, 7 Cir., 1956, 238 F.2d 943, has ruled that the gain is recognizable only to the extent of the cash received. . . . We have concluded that this was error and that the gain is recognizable in its entirety.

The taxpayer, Turnbow, was the sole stockholder of International Dairy Supply Company, a Nevada corporation which had its principal place of business in San Francisco, California. In 1952, the taxpayer transferred his stock in that company to Foremost Dairies, Inc., a New York corporation which had its principal place of business in Jacksonville, Florida. This transfer was in exchange for 82,375 shares of the common stock of Foremost and $3,000,000.00 cash, socalled "boot". The Foremost shares were of a value of $1,235,625.00. Thus the shares constituted 29% of the total consideration received, while the boot constituted 71%.

The taxpayer reported a capital gain on the transaction limited to the $3,000,000.00 cash boot, less expenses which by agreement he had undertaken to assume. The Commissioner determined that the entire gain on the transaction was taxable, establishing that gain at $4,163,691.94. Tax deficiencies for the years 1952 and 1953 in the amounts, respectively, of $264,037.43 and $14,786.26 were determined. . . .

The problem presented involves construction of [the Code provisions dealing] with recognition of gain or loss.

---

12. Portions of the opinion and all footnotes omitted.

[§ 1002] * sets forth the general rule that "upon the sale or exchange of property the entire amount of gain or loss . . . shall be recognized, except as hereinafter provided . . . ."

Among the exceptions specified, . . . [§ 354] deals with exchange of stock for stock on reorganization. It provides:

> "No gain or loss shall be recognized if stock or securities in a corporation a party to reorganization are, in pursuance of the plan of reorganization, exchanged solely for stock or securities in such corporation or in another corporation a party to the reorganization."

The term "reorganization" . . . is defined in [the predecessor of § 368(a)], which, as amended in 1943, provides:

> "The term 'reorganization' means (A) a statutory merger or consolidation, or (B) the acquisition by one corporation, in exchange solely for all or a part of its voting stock, of at least 80 per centum of the voting stock and at least 80 per centum of the total number of shares of all other classes of stock of another corporation, or (C) the acquisition by one corporation, in exchange solely for all or part of its voting stock, of substantially all the properties of another corporation, but in determining whether the exchange is solely for voting stock the assumption by the acquiring corporation of a liability of the other, or the fact that property acquired is subject to a liability, shall be disregarded, ..."

In this case we are concerned with the definition set forth in Clause (B) . . . . Our discussion also deals with the definition set forth in Clause (C). Today these types of reorganization are known to the tax bar as (B) and (C) reorganizations and we shall take advantage of this terminology.

[The predecessor of § 356(a)] is the section upon which the taxpayer relies for his right to limit recognition of gain to the cash boot. As amended in 1943, [that section] provides:

> "If an exchange would be within the provisions [for nonrecognition] . . . if it were not for the fact that the property received in exchange consists not only of property permitted . . . to be received without the recognition of gain, but also of other property or money, then the gain, if any, to the recipient shall be recognized, but in an amount not in excess of the sum of such money and the fair market value of such other property."

---

* [Ed. note] Section references in brackets represent 1954 Code section numbers substituted for the section numbers of predecessor provisions which appear in the original.

The dispute before us is as to the method to be followed in applying [§ 356(a)] to the facts of a case. The Tax Court purported to follow its earlier decision upon this problem in Luther Bonham, 1936, 33 B.T.A. 1100, 1103–1104. It quoted that opinion (supplying its own emphasis) as follows:

"It is necessary therefore to determine whether or not the exchange of . . . stock for . . . stock *would be* within the provisions of [§ 354] *if the item of cash had been omitted* and only . . . stock had been received in exchange for . . . stock."

Howard v. Commissioner . . . was also quoted to the following effect:

"In the present case, *but for* the cash received in exchange for . . . common stock of Binkley, the transaction would have met the 'solely' requirement of [§ 368(a)(1)(B)] and fallen within the scope of [§ 354]. To the extent that 'boot' was received, gain would be recognized under our interpretation of the application of [§ 356(a)]."

Applying this method to the case at bar, the taxpayer reasons: but for the cash received, the transaction — solely stock for stock — would have met the "solely" requirements . . . and fallen within the nonrecognition provision of [§ 354]. Therefore, he says, under [§ 356(a)] the gain to be recognized is limited to the amount of the cash received.

The Commissioner contends that [§ 354] requires an actual and not a hypothetical reorganization before nonrecognition can result; that petitioner's method assumes the absence of boot not only to determine whether [§ 354] would apply but also to determine whether the [§ 368(a)(1)(B)] definition would apply; that this does violence to [§ 354], which expressly contemplates the existence of a reorganization.

The method . . . advocated by the Commissioner, is to ascertain first whether a reorganization exists. . . . If it does, then and only then can the nonrecognition provisions . . . become applicable. If it does not, [§ 354] cannot apply. Only when [§ 354] applies, can [§ 356(a)] operate to modify its consequences.

Applying this method to the case at bar, the Commissioner reasons that, since the presence of boot precludes a (B) reorganization, [§ 354] cannot apply and the gain is subject to taxation. . . . Under the Commissioner's construction, (B) and (C) reorganizations are forever excluded from the operation of [§ 356(a)]. The other types of reorganizations specified in [§ 368(a)], however, do remain subject to the operation of [§ 356(a)].

Upon this dispute, legislative history supports the Commissioner's position.

Prior to 1934, there were no (B) or (C) reorganizations as such. Section 112(i) of the Revenue Act of 1932 [an earlier version of § 368 (a)] read in pertinent part:

> "The term 'reorganization' means (A) a merger or consolidation (including the acquisition by one corporation of at least a majority of the voting stock and at least a majority of the total number of shares of all other classes of stock of another corporation, or substantially all the properties of another corporation)."

The provisions of [§§ 354 and 356(a)], however, existed in substantially their present form.

The reasons for the 1934 amendment of [368(a)] are clearly disclosed by congressional reports and discussion. The House Ways and Means Committee Report . . . states:

> "The reorganization provisions have been in effect for many years, having been adopted in substantially their present form in 1924. They state in detail how each step of a reorganization should be treated for tax purposes. The policy was adopted of permitting reorganizations to take a wide variety of forms, without income-tax liability. As a result, astute lawyers frequently attempted, especially during the prosperous years, to take advantage of these provisions by arranging in the technical form of a reorganization, within the statutory definition, what were really sales."

* * *

> "The committee decided that under present conditions, the wiser policy is to amend the provisions drastically to stop the known cases of tax avoidance, rather than to eliminate the sections completely." . . .

The House committee's solution was to eliminate from the definition of reorganization, as it then appeared in Clause (A), the parenthetical phrase following the words "merger or consolidation."

Had this solution been adopted, there would have been no (B) or (C) reorganizations and [§ 356(a)] obviously could have no reference to such transactions.

The Senate Finance Committee reported . . . :

> "Your committee is in complete agreement with the purposes of the House bill which aim at tax avoidance schemes in this connection. However, some modifications are recommended in order to bring about a more uniform application of the provisions in all 48 of the States. Not all of the States have adopted statutes providing for mergers or consolidations; and, moreover, a corporation of one State cannot ordinarily merge with a corporation of another State. The committee believes that it is desirable to permit reorganiza-

tions in such cases, with restrictions designed to prevent tax avoidance. Consequently, the committee recommends the insertion in the House bill of an addition to the definition of the term 'reorganization'. . . .

* * *

"It will be noted that the proposed amendment requires that . . . the acquisition, whether of stock or of substantially all the properties, must be in exchange solely for the voting stock of the acquiring corporation."

It is clear from this history that, with specific abuses in mind, Congress sought to eliminate them by requiring that, for an acquisition to qualify for the tax advantages of a reorganization, it must be in exchange solely for voting stock.

* * *

Certainly it could not have been intended by Congress that this result would be frustrated at birth by the already existing provisions of [§ 356(a)]; yet such would seem to be the effect of the taxpayer's construction.

The Commissioner's construction seems supported by subsequent congressional action. If (B) reorganizations can hypothetically exist notwithstanding boot, the same would apply to today's (C)-type reorganizations, which also were created by the 1934 amendments.

". . . the acquisition by one corporation, in exchange solely for all or a part of its voting stock, of substantially all the properties of another corporation . . . ."

Yet, in 1939, Congress saw fit to amend the definition of (C) reorganizations by providing:

". . . but in determining whether the exchange is solely for voting stock the assumption by the acquiring corporation of a liability of the other, or the fact that property acquired is subject to a liability, shall be disregarded . . . ." . . .

In § 368(a)(2)(b) of the Internal Revenue Code of 1954 . . . the definition was further amended to provide that only 80% of the assets of the acquired corporation need be obtained in exchange for voting stock; that boot could, without defeating reorganization, be the consideration for assets above 80%. Under the taxpayer's construction, neither of these amendments was necessary. That Congress felt it necessary so to amend the section indicates that the Commissioner's construction reflects the true congressional intent and understanding.

The taxpayer refers us to a point emphasized in Howard v. Commissioner of Internal Revenue, supra. Section [356(c)] is the counterpart of [§ 356(a)], the latter dealing with recognition of gains and the former with recognition of losses. Section [356(c)] has remained virtually unchanged since its original enactment as § 203(f) of the Revenue Act of 1924. It provides:

> "If an exchange would be within [§ 354] . . . if it were not for the fact that the property received in exchange consists not only of property permitted . . . to be received without the recognition of gain or loss, but also of other property or money, then no loss from the exchange shall be recognized."

Howard points out that if the presence of boot results in recognition of gains it likewise results in recognition of losses; that a taxpayer desiring that a loss be recognized might convert what otherwise would be a legitimate reorganization into a sale by the payment of a trifling amount of cash; that such a construction would thus defeat the 1924 legislative intent in enacting [§ 356(c)].

It would appear, however, that Congress in 1934 was aware that attempts might be made under the proposed amendment to secure recognition of losses notwithstanding actual continuity of interest. The House Ways and Means Committee, as we have noted, recommended that the "acquisition" type of transaction (the forerunner of today's (B) and (C) reorganizations) be completely eliminated from the definition of reorganization. At the same time the report stated:

> "Furthermore, the retention of the other reorganization provisions will prevent large losses from being established by bondholders and stockholders who receive securities in a newly reorganized enterprise which are substantially the same as their original investments." . . .

Thus it would appear that in the judgment of Congress the danger of tax avoidance (through securing recognition of losses notwithstanding continuity of interest) was avoided by the probability that the acquisitions resulting in loss could be treated as reorganizations under the remaining provisions of [§ 368(a)].

Whether this judgment was sound apparently still remains to be tested. However, Congress would seem to have weighed the desirable features of the proposed amendment (as to gains) against its undesirable potentialities (as to losses). For us to permit the possibility of tax avoidance under [§ 356(c)], to control our construction of [§ 356(a)], would be to overrule the apparent judgment of Congress upon this very question.

* * *

We conclude that, if the "solely for voting stock" requirement of (B) and (C) reorganizations is to be given the effect intended by Congress, [§ 356(a)] cannot operate to render a stock-plus-boot acquisition a (B) or (C) reorganization through a disregard of the existence of boot. In the case before us, then, the existence of boot prevents [§ 368(a)(1)(B)] from applying; since no reorganization exists, [§ 354] cannot apply; [§ 356(a)] is then also inapplicable.

NOTE ON B REORGANIZATIONS

a. Definitional Aspects

The present definition of a B reorganization in § 368(a) (1) (B) differs from the pre-1954 version which was applicable in the Turnbow case (as well as in the Howard case, referred to at several points in Turnbow). However, the problems of construction under the present wording of that definition can best be illustrated in terms of the pre-1954 language, which is repeated here for convenience:

> (B) the acquisition by one corporation, in exchange solely for all or a part of its voting stock, of at least 80 per centum of the voting stock and at least 80 per centum of the total number of shares of all other classes of stock of another corporation.

One of the questions presented in the Howard case was whether that statute was satisfied when a corporation acquired 80% of the stock of another corporation solely for voting stock, while purchasing the other 20% from other stockholders for cash. The court held that it was not, rejecting the taxpayer's contention that the 80% acquisition solely for voting stock constituted a B reorganization regardless of the presence of some additional purchases for cash. In reaching its conclusion, the court relied heavily upon the analogy to a C reorganization, where concededly the presence of any consideration other than voting stock (prior to the 1954 amendment permitting a 20% leeway) destroyed the reorganization. But query whether the court paid sufficient attention to the fact that by its very nature a type C acquisition (i. e., of all or substantially all of the assets of another corporation) constitutes a single transaction, whereas the B reorganization definition at least admitted of the possibility of separating the acquisition of the necessary 80% of the stock from the acquisition of any additional stock. It seems clear that if the stock purchased for cash had been acquired in a separate, unrelated transaction substantially before or after the acquisition for stock, the latter would have qualified as a reorganization. The real question, therefore, was whether the cash acquisitions should be *integrated* with the 80% acquisition for stock, so that all would be treated as parts of single transaction. In fact, in Howard there was substantial warrant for integrating the cash acquisitions with the acquisitions for stock, since both were encompassed within a single overall plan to acquire 100% ownership of the acquired corporation. Perhaps the court did not delve deeply into these issues because of its ultimate conclusion that the taxpayers, being among those who received only voting stock, were not required to recognize gain anyway, by virtue of the predecessor of § 356(a) (1). That view, of course, has subsequently been laid permanently to rest by Supreme Court's affirmance in the Turnbow case, supra.

At the opposite end of the single transaction spectrum from Howard is the later case of Lutkins v. Commissioner, 160 Ct.Cl. 648, 312 F.2d 803 (1963), where the taxpayers were trying to integrate apparently separate transactions in order to find a B reorganization. There the acquiring corporation obtained approximately 65% of the acquired corporation's stock in 1912 solely for voting stock. Between 1929 and 1951, in a series of unrelated transactions, the acquiring corporation purchased for cash approximately 2.5% more of the acquired corporation's stock. In 1952, the acquiring corporation decided to increase its holdings in the acquired corporation to at least 80%, and accordingly offered to exchange its voting stock for stock of the acquired corporation. Holders of some 29.5% of the acquired corporation's stock, including the taxpayers, accepted this offer, after which the acquiring corporation owned over 97% of the acquired corporation's stock. The taxpayers contended that the 1952 acquisition qualified as a B reorganization under the pre-1954 definition quoted above, on the ground that taking into account the 1912 acquisition the acquiring corporation had acquired more than 80% of the acquired corporation's stock solely for voting stock; but the court disagreed. The court found it unnecessary to decide whether the 1912 transaction could be combined with the 1952 transaction for the purpose of finding the required 80% acquisition, since even if so it would also be necessary to take the intervening cash purchases into account, and that would destroy the reorganization under the Howard case.

As to the question left open in the Lutkins case, it has generally been assumed that the required 80% of the stock of the acquired corporation had to be obtained pursuant to a single integrated plan of acquisition in order to achieve a B reorganization under the pre-1954 version of the statute. This meant that if a corporation already owned more than 20% of the stock of an enterprise it wanted to acquire, the parties would be precluded from a B reorganization. Certainly this was true if the earlier acquisition of stock had been for cash, since then not even a favorable integration view could save the transaction as a reorganization.

In 1954 Congress heeded complaints that the 80% requirement was unduly restrictive and amended the statute into its present form, under which no particular minimum amount of stock of the acquired corporation need be obtained to qualify as a reorganization, so long as the acquisition is solely for voting stock and thereafter the acquiring corporation is in "control" of the acquired corporation within the meaning of § 368(c).

Although this statutory authorization of so-called "creeping control" solves the problem of the acquiring corporation which already owns a substantial stock interest in the object of its combination affections, the present statute seems calculated to place even greater stress on the integration issue while affording no more guide to the resolution of the issue than its predecessor did. Thus, if a corporation owning 79% of the stock of another corporation acquires an additional 1% of the stock in exchange solely for voting stock, the latter transaction literally qualifies as a B reorganization. Yet if the "earlier" acquisition was made for cash only one day earlier, reorganization treatment seems doubtful — the integration concept could be imported into the word "acquisition" and the two transactions treated as parts of a single acquisition transaction, with the result that qualification under the "solely for voting stock" requirement would be lost. But suppose the cash deal was six months earlier? A year?

On the other side of the coin, if a corporation acquires solely for its voting stock the stock of another corporation from time to time over a period of years, finally reaching a position of 80% ownership after, say, eight years, reorganization treatment would not seem to be available for the earliest acquisitions; they would not be integrated with the later ones for the purpose of establishing the necessary control "immediately after the acquisition". Reg. § 1.368–2(c) refers to an acquisition "in a single transaction or in a series of transactions taking place over a relatively short period of time such as 12 months." But does it follow that only the last acquisition, the one which brings the acquiring corporation up to 80%, would qualify as a reorganization? Or could it be argued, perhaps by giving a reverse twist to the above-quoted regulation, that the last few transactions, say all acquisitions within the last twelve months, may come in under the tax-free umbrella?

And what about acquisitions by a corporation which is already in control of another? Again, literally, any acquisition of additional stock solely for voting stock would seem to qualify. But if the acquiring corporation embarked on a series of acquisitions from individual shareholders, indiscriminately using cash for some deals and solely voting stock for others, would the concurrent cash transactions taint the exchanges for voting stock?

See generally, on the foregoing issues, Vernava, The Howard and Turnbow Cases and the "Solely" Requirement of B Reorganizations, 20 Tax.L.Rev. 387 (1965).

b. The "Voting Stock" Requirement

Needless to say, there have been a number of questions of interpretation in connection with the "voting stock" part of the definition. First of all, the term "voting" looks to the power to vote for at least some of the directors. And of course the instruments must qualify as stock before they can be counted as voting stock, which means that warrants and options are excluded. Helvering v. Southwest Consolidated Corp., 315 U.S. 194, 62 S.Ct. 546, 86 L.Ed. 789 (1942). As to contingent rights to additional voting stock (which as noted earlier may result from an arrangement to secure the acquiring corporation against unknown or contingent liabilities of the acquired corporation), the Service has recently ruled that where the rights of the stockholders to receive additional stock are merely contractual, and are not assignable, they will not violate the "solely for voting stock" requirement. Rev.Rul. 66–112, 1966–19 Int.Rev.Bull. 8. The decision in Hamrick v. Commissioner, noted at page 78 supra, that such rights qualified under § 351 was approved in result. But the Ruling indicates that if transferable instruments, such as so-called "certificates of contingent interest", are issued to the stockholders to represent their contingent interests in the reserved shares, the "solely" requirement will not be satisfied.

Fractional shares and scrip also seem not to constitute voting stock themselves, but it appears that these items do not run afoul of the "solely for voting stock" requirement. See Rev.Rul. 55–59, 1955–1 Cum.Bull. 35 (involving issuance of scrip in a C reorganization). And apparently the acquiring corporation can help to facilitate the sale of fractional shares by the receiving shareholders, or their purchase of fractions to make whole shares, without disqualifying the transaction as a reorganization. This seems to have been conceded by the Government in Mills v. Commissioner, 331 F.2d 321 (5th Cir. 1964) (which actually involved the tax effect of distributing cash to all stockholders in lieu of fractional shares), where the court observed:

> Counsel for the Commissioner suggested in argument that the parties might have followed another course. He stated that the Internal Revenue Service has recognized procedures under which fractional shares may be handled in a qualifying reorganization. Thus he says that it would be proper for the corporation, at the direction of the person entitled to a fractional share, to buy an addi-

tional fraction to make a whole share for him or to sell the fractional share for his account to another shareholder or on the open market; or for the corporation to appoint an independent agent to carry out this task. And, since the Service recognizes that in a reorganization the acquiring corporation is responsible for distributing its stock in an appropriate number of shares, including fractions, to each exchanging shareholder, it has taken the position that such an agent's expenses may be paid by the acquiring corporation.

As to the question actually presented in the Mills case, literally a cash payment to every shareholder of the acquired corporation in lieu of fractional shares would seem to disqualify the reorganization, but the Court of Appeals, reversing the Tax Court, refused to adopt such a strict construction of the statute. The case involved three taxpayers who were equal stockholders of three small gas companies in the southeast. General Gas Corporation, a Delaware corporation with listed stock, was interested in acquiring those companies and obtained options from the stockholders to purchase their stock. The option agreements entitled General to acquire the stock at book value, as determined in accordance with an agreed-upon audit, in exchange for voting common stock of General, to be valued at $14 per share. The option agreements also provided that if the purchase price for any stockholder's stock of any corporation was not evenly divisible by $14.00 the difference would be paid in cash. In July, 1954, General exercised its options, and each taxpayer received for his stock in the three corporations respectively 1,321 shares of General stock and $10.88 in cash, 251 shares of General and $8.36 in cash, and 23 shares of General and $8.12 in cash. Immediately thereafter, General owned all of the stock of the three corporations, which were then liquidated and operated as divisions of General. The Tax Court took the view that the requirement of "solely for voting stock" under § 368(a)(1)(B) left no room for leeway, even under the *de minimis* doctrine; but the Court of Appeals held that the cash paid on account of fractional shares did not constitute "additional independent consideration" but was merely a mechanical adjunct to what was intended to be consideration composed exclusively of voting stock.

The "solely for voting stock" requirement must be carefully watched in other contexts, too. Thus if the acquiring corporation agrees to pay expenses of the transferor shareholders, such as lawyer's fees, that could constitute consideration other than voting stock and preclude reorganization treatment. However, it appears that the Service has issued an unpublished ruling that a promise by the acquiring corporation to pay the costs of the stockholders of the acquired corporation to register the stock they received from the acquiring corporation with the SEC will not disqualify the transaction as a reorganization. See Vol. XIX, No. 2, ABA Tax.Sec.Bull. 130 (1966). In any event, it would seem that the acquiring corporation could in effect pay some of the expenses of the acquired corporation's stockholders, while staying within the "solely for voting stock" bounds, by simply paying a larger acquisition price in voting stock, leaving the recipients to sell some of the stock received to obtain the money with which to pay the expenses.

c. Basis Aspects

Recently a question has been raised as to the acquiring corporation's basis in the acquired corporation's stock obtained pursuant to a B reorganization. Where the acquiring corporation deals exclusively with the stockholders of the acquired corporation, and does not obtain any stock from the acquired corporation itself, is the acquired corporation nevertheless a party to the reorganization within the meaning of § 354(a)(1)? Hays Corp. v. Commissioner, 331 F.2d 422 (7th Cir. 1964), confirmed the validity of the view, long taken in the regulations, that a corporation whose stock is acquired in a reorganization is a party to the reorganization, irrespective of the fact that the stock is acquired from the shareholders. Accordingly, the acquiring corporation's basis in the stock is governed by § 362(b), which provides for a carryover of the basis of the acquired corporation's stockholders from whom the stock was obtained. However, if the acquiring corporation uses stock of its parent to acquire the stock of the acquired corporation, as is now permitted pursuant to the 1964 amendments, and the subsidiary had a cost basis in its parent's stock, query whether the subsidiary's basis in the stock acquired would be the former basis of the transferors under § 362(b), or the subsidiary's basis in its parent's stock under § 358.

Obviously, it may prove rather inconvenient for the acquiring corporation to have to ascertain its basis from the stockholders of the acquired corporation. Fortunately, however, this carryover basis becomes relevant only if the acquiring corporation transfers the stock in a taxable transaction; as will be noted in the following subsection, the acquiring corporation's basis in the acquired corporation's stock drops out of the picture in the event the subsidiary is liquidated.

2. LIQUIDATION OF A SUBSIDIARY ACQUIRED IN A B REORGANIZATION

a. RECOGNITION OF GAIN OR LOSS

Although of course ordinarily the liquidation of a corporation is a taxable transaction to the stockholders, under § 332 a parent corporation may liquidate a subsidiary without recognition of gain or loss if the parent owns "at least 80 percent of the total combined voting power of all classes of stock entitled to vote and . . . at least 80% of the total number of shares of all other classes of stock (except nonvoting stock which is limited and preferred as to dividends)". It is to be noted that the stock ownership requirement of § 332 is almost identical to the control test of § 368(c) except that under § 332 non-voting preferred stock of the subsidiary may be ignored. Accordingly, if a subsidiary was acquired in a transaction which qualified as a B reorganization, it would presumably be eligible for liquidation under § 332.

However, § 332 reaches well beyond reorganization acquisitions, since under that section it makes no difference how or for what consideration the necessary stock ownership was acquired — a subsidiary acquired for cash is just as eligible for liquidation under § 332 as one acquired solely for voting stock. All that is required is that the necessary stock ownership exist on the date of the adoption of the plan of liquidation (and continue until the property has been received in liquidation). And the difference in the stock ownership requirement between § 332 and § 368(c), i. e., that non-voting preferred does not count under § 332 but does under § 368(c), affords another illustration of a transaction which may qualify for a tax-free liquidation under § 332 although the acquisition did not qualify as a tax-free reorganization under § 368(a)(1)(B).

While § 332 is not expressly elective, it appears that a parent corporation may avoid the section whenever it wants, as for example in order to recognize a loss, simply by selling enough of the subsidiary's stock to reduce the parent's stock ownership below the 80 percent line. See Commissioner v. Day & Zimmerman, Inc., 151 F.2d 517 (3d Cir. 1945) (sale at public auction to corporation's treasurer who purchased the stock with his own funds).

As to the relationship between §§ 337 and 332, see pages 648–652, supra.

b. BASIS ASPECTS IN THE TAX-FREE LIQUIDATION OF A SUBSIDIARY

The general basis provision in connection with the tax-free liquidation of a subsidiary is contained in § 334(b)(1), which provides for a carryover to the parent of the basis of the assets in the hands of the subsidiary. Under this provision, as previously noted, the parent's basis in the subsidiary's stock (as well as its economic investment in that stock, which of course may be very different from the basis) drops out of the picture. However, § 334(b)(2), added in the 1954 Code, provides a special basis rule in connection with the tax-free liquidation of a subsidiary under certain circumstances. The purpose and impact of this provision can best be understood in the light of the judicial development in this area prior to the 1954 Code, which is illustrated by the following decision:

KIMBELL-DIAMOND MILLING CO. v. COMMISSIONER

Tax Court of the United States, 1950. 14 T.C. 74.
Affirmed, per curiam, 187 F.2d 718 (5th Cir. 1951).

[In August, 1942, the taxpayer's milling plant was destroyed by fire and in November, 1942, it collected insurance as reimbursement for its loss. On December 26, 1942, it used the insurance proceeds and other cash to acquire all of the stock of Whaley Mill and Elevator Co., its sole intention in purchasing that stock being to acquire the milling plant of Whaley by liquidating Whaley as soon as possible.

On December 31, 1942, Whaley was liquidated. The basis of the milling plant in Whaley's hands was $139,521.62. The taxpayer's basis for the stock of Whaley was the cost of its destroyed milling plant, $18,921.90, plus $91,799.84, the cash outlay for the stock in excess of the insurance proceeds, or $110,721.74.]

OPINION

BLACK, JUDGE: . . . Petitioner argues that the acquisition of Whaley's assets and the subsequent liquidation of Whaley brings petitioner within the provisions of [the predecessor of § 332 (a)] and, therefore, by reason of [the predecessor of § 334(b) (1)], petitioner's basis in these assets is the same as the basis in Whaley's hands. In so contending, petitioner asks that we treat the acquisition of Whaley's stock and the subsequent liquidation of Whaley as separate transactions. It is well settled that the incidence of taxation depends upon the substance of a transaction. . . . It is inescapable from petitioner's minutes set out above and from the "Agreement and Program of Complete Liquidation" entered into between petitioner and Whaley, that the only intention petitioner ever had was to acquire Whaley's assets.

We think that this proceeding is governed by the principles of Commissioner v. Ashland Oil and Refining Co., 99 F.2d 588, certiorari denied 306 U.S. 661, 59 S.Ct. 790. In that case the stock was retained for almost a year before liquidation. Ruling on the question of whether the stock or the assets of the corporation were purchased, the court stated:

"The question remains, however, whether if the entire transaction, whatever its form, was essentially in intent, purpose and result, a purchase by Swiss of property, its several steps may be treated separately and each be given an effect for tax purposes as though each constituted a distinct transaction. . . . And without regard to whether the result is imposition or relief from taxation, the courts have recognized that where the essential nature of a transaction is the acquisition of property, it will be viewed as a whole, and closely related steps will not be separated either at the instance of the taxpayer or the taxing authority. . . ."

We hold that the purchase of Whaley's stock and its subsequent liquidation must be considered as one transaction, namely, the purchase of Whaley's assets which was petitioner's sole intention. This was not a reorganization within [the predecessor of § 332(a)], and petitioner's basis in these assets, both depreciable and nondepreciable, is, therefore, its cost, or $110,721.74 ($18,921.90, the basis of petitioner's assets destroyed by fire, plus $91,799.84, the amount expended over the insurance proceeds). Since petitioner does not controvert respondent's allocation of cost to the individual assets acquired from

Whaley, both depreciable and nondepreciable, respondent's allocation is sustained.

* * *

Decision will be entered for the respondent.

Reviewed by the Court.

NOTE ON THE KIMBELL-DIAMOND RULE AND § 334(b)(2)

The approach of the Kimbell-Diamond Milling Co. case, under which the transaction is regarded as basically a purchase of assets by the purchasing corporation, with the temporary stock acquisition and liquidation of the acquired corporation ignored tax-wise, has been followed in a number of cases. This includes not only cases where, as in Kimbell-Diamond, the cost of the stock to the purchasing corporation was less than the basis of the acquired corporation's assets, e. g., Tennessee, Alabama & Georgia Railway Co. v. Commissioner, 187 F.2d 826 (6th Cir. 1951), but also cases where the rule works in the taxpayer's favor because the stock cost is higher than the asset basis. E. g., Texas Bank & Trust Co. of Dallas v. Commissioner, 12 T.C.M. 588 (1953). Application of the rule may produce some important collateral effects—for example, in United States v. Mattison, 273 F.2d 13 (9th Cir. 1959), where an individual negotiated a sale of the assets of a corporation and then bought its stock, liquidated it and transferred the assets to the purchaser, the application of Kimbell-Diamond resulted in turning what would have been a long-term gain into short-term gain.

It was this Kimbell-Diamond rule which provided the example for § 334 (b)(2) of the 1954 Code. In essence, that section was designed to provide that a corporate purchaser of a corporate business will end up with the same basis in the property acquired when it buys the stock of a corporation and liquidates it as when the assets are bought directly. Like § 337 on the seller's side, § 334(b)(2) was designed to produce tax neutrality so far as choosing the form of acquisition is concerned.

Also like § 337, § 334(b)(2) has its special conditions and timetable. The necessary 80% stock ownership must be acquired by *purchase* (a technical tax term which *inter alia* excludes reorganization acquisitions) during a period of one year, and the distribution in liquidation must be pursuant to a plan of liquidation adopted not more than two years after the acquisition of the necessary 80%. Unlike § 337, however, § 334(b)(2) does not specify any particular time within which the distribution itself must be completed.

The important difference between § 334(b)(2) and the judicially-developed Kimbell-Diamond rule is that the statute applies whenever its conditions are satisfied, whether or not there was an intention to liquidate when the stock was acquired; the judicial rule did not apply if there was no intention to liquidate the corporation at the time of the stock acquisition. Distributors Finance Corp. v. Commissioner, 20 T.C. 768 (1953). In other words, the statute substituted compliance with a timetable for a showing of intent. Particularly because of this difference, the question arises as to whether the judicial Kimbell-Diamond rule has survived the enactment of § 334(b)(2) in cases not covered by that statute. For example, what about a purchase of stock by an individual, which was subject to the judicial rule but is outside the scope of the statute? And if the judicial rule has survived at all, could it also be applied to corporate acquisitions which would clearly be covered by § 334(b)(2) except for failure to satisfy the section's timetable?

See generally, Lewis, Cost-of-Stock Basis for Assets Received from Acquired Corporations, 19 U.Miami L.Rev. 159 (1964).

D. SPECIAL PROBLEMS IN C REORGANIZATIONS

1. EXCEPTIONS TO THE "SOLELY FOR VOTING STOCK" REQUIREMENT

As previously noted, two important exceptions have been engrafted onto the "solely for voting stock" requirement for C reorganizations. The first, which is embodied in the definition itself in § 368(a)(1)(C), provides that in applying the "solely for voting stock" test the fact that the acquiring corporation assumes the liabilities of the acquired corporation, or takes its property subject to liabilities, may be disregarded. This exception responds to the needs of business practice, as the acquiring corporation in a combination transaction normally must take over the liabilities of the acquired corporation one way or another. Since this does not disqualify an A reorganization (or the tax-free liquidation of a subsidiary after a B reorganization), there seems little reason why it should preclude the C form.

Under this exception, it appears that the acquiring corporation may issue its own securities in place of the securities of the acquired corporation. See Southland Ice Co. v. Commissioner, 5 T.C. 842, 850 (1945). However, the terms of the new securities should not vary too much from the old, lest the transaction be regarded as the issuance of new securities constituting boot rather than a mere assumption of the old securities.

The second exception to the "solely for voting stock" requirement is the provision in § 368(a)(2)(B), added in 1954, which permits some leeway for consideration other than voting stock so long as at least 80% of the *fair market value* of *all* of the property of the acquired corporation is obtained solely for voting stock. This 20% leeway is directly related to the assumption of liabilities provision, since any liabilities assumed by the acquiring corporation (or to which property of the acquired corporation is subject) must be counted as consideration other than voting stock for the purpose of measuring the 20%. Thus when the total of the liabilities assumed by the acquiring corporation (or to which property of the acquired corporation is subject) exceeds 20% of the fair market value of all the property of the acquired corporation, the 20% provision provides no additional leeway at all. Because of this, as well as the difficulty of ascertaining the value of the corporation's assets with certainty, this 20% provision seems destined to be of rather limited practical importance.

The 20% provision has no counterpart in B reorganizations. On the other hand, it still leaves C reorganizations well behind A reorganizations, which are not subject to the "solely for voting stock" requirement at all. Technical differences of this kind among the various types of reorganization transactions seems to be simply statutory aberrations, and there have been many calls, both inside and outside of Congress, for their elimination. But so long as these differences continue, they must be kept constantly in mind when selecting the form of reorganization in any particular case.

There are of course the same questions of what constitutes "voting stock" as were encountered in connection with B reorganizations, but with one possible difference so far as the problem of fractional shares is concerned. Theoretically, the acquiring corporation in a C reorganization is not directly involved with fractional shares since it simply issues the specified total number of shares to the acquired corporation in exchange for the latter's assets. The need for fractional shares arises when the acquired corporation is liquidated and the shares of the acquiring corporation are distributed to the stockholders of the acquired corporation in exchange for their stock, and the acquiring corporation could remain aloof from this aspect of the transaction. But as a practical matter the acquiring corporation must assist the acquired corporation in dealing with this problem, presumably by making fractional shares or scrip available to the acquired corporation. However, as in the analogous B reorganization case, it is not a violation of the "solely for voting stock" requirement for the acquiring corporation to include scrip or fractional shares in the consideration transferred to the acquired corporation, or to help in arranging for the sale or purchase of fractional interests, so long as the acquiring corporation does not itself, directly or indirectly, supply any cash in the transaction.

For a comprehensive analysis of the various problems involved in C reorganizations, including both the foregoing and those discussed below, see Goldman, The C Reorganization, 19 Tax L.Rev. 31 (1963).

2. ACQUISITION OF "SUBSTANTIALLY ALL" OF THE ACQUIRED CORPORATION'S PROPERTY

REVENUE RULING 57–518
1957–2 Cum.Bull. 253.

Advice has been requested as to the Federal income tax consequences of a reorganization between two corporations under the circumstances described below.

The M and N corporations were engaged in the fabrication and sale of various items of steel products. For sound and legitimate business reasons, N corporation acquired most of M corporation's business and operating assets. Under a plan of reorganization, M corporation transferred to N corporation (1) all of its fixed assets (plant and equipment) at net book values, (2) 97 percent of all its inventories at book values, and (3) insurance policies, and other properties pertaining to the business. In exchange therefor, N corporation issued shares of its voting common stock to M corporation.

The properties retained by M corporation include cash, accounts receivable, notes, and three percent of its total inventory. The fair market value of the assets retained by M was roughly equivalent to the amount of its liabilities. M corporation proceeded to liquidate its retained properties as expeditiously as possible and applied the proceeds to its outstanding debts. The property remaining after the discharge of all its liabilities was turned over to N corporation, and M corporation was liquidated.

* * *

The specific question presented is what constitutes "substantially all of the properties" as defined in [§ 368(a) (1) (C)] of the Code. The answer will depend upon the facts and circumstances in each case rather than upon any particular percentage. Among the elements of importance that are to be considered in arriving at the conclusion are the nature of the properties retained by the transferor, the purpose of the retention, and the amount thereof. In Milton Smith, et al. v. Commissioner, 34 B.T.A. 702 . . . (1936), a corporation transferred 71 percent of its gross assets. It retained assets having a value of $52,000, the major portion of which was in cash and accounts receivable. It was stated that the assets were retained in order to liquidate liabilities of approximately $46,000. Thus, after discharging its liabilities, the outside figure of assets remaining with the petitioner would have been $6,000, which the court stated was not an excessive margin to allow for the collection of receivables with which to meet its liabilities. No assets were retained for the purpose of engaging in any business or for distribution to stockholders. In those circumstances, the court held that there had been a transfer of "substantially all of the assets" of the corporation. The court very definitely indicated that a different conclusion would probably have been reached if the amount retained was clearly in excess of a reasonable amount necessary to liquidate liabilities. Furthermore, the court intimated that transfer of all of the net assets of a corporation would not qualify if the percentage of gross assets transferred was too low. Thus, it stated that, if a corporation having gross assets of $1,000,000 and liabilities of $900,000 transferred only the net assets of $100,000, the result would probably not come within the intent of Congress in its use of the words "substantially all."

The instant case, of the assets not transferred to the corporation, no portion was retained by M corporation for its own continued use inasmuch as the plan of reorganization contemplated M's liquidation. Furthermore, the assets retained were for the purpose of meeting liabilities, and these assets at fair market values, approximately equaled the amount of such liabilities. Thus, the facts in this case meet the requirements established in the case of Milton Smith, supra.

The instant case is not in conflict with I. T. 2373, C. B. VI–2 19 (1927), which holds that, where one corporation transferred approximately three-fourths of its properties to another corporation for a consideration of bonds and cash, it did not dispose of "substantially all the properties" owned by it at the time and, therefore, no corporate reorganization took place, so that the transaction constituted an exchange of property resulting in a gain or loss to the transferor for income tax purposes. I. T. 2373, supra, is obsolete to the extent that it implies that a corporate reorganization could have occurred where there was no continuity of interest. However, that ruling is still valid with regard to its discussion of the question of what constitutes "substantially all of the properties." From the facts as stated in that case, it appears that a major part of the 25 percent of the assets retained were operating assets, and it does not appear that they were retained for the purpose of liquidating the liabilities of the corporation. On the contrary, it seems likely that the corporation may have contemplated continuation of its business or the sale of the remainder of its operating assets to another purchaser. As a result, I. T. 2373, supra, is clearly distinguishable from the instant case.

Accordingly, since the assets transferred by M to N constitute "substantially all" of the assets of the transferor corporation within the meaning of that statutory phrase, the acquisition by N corporation, in exchange solely for part of its voting common stock, of the properties of M corporation pursuant to the plan will constitute a reorganization within the purview of section 368(a) (1) (C) of the Code. No gain or loss is recognized to the transferor as a result of the exchange of its property for common stock of the transferee under section 361 of the Code; and no gain or loss is recognized to the shareholders of M corporation, under section 354(a) (1) of such Code, as the result of their receipt of N common stock.

3. LIQUIDATION OF THE ACQUIRED CORPORATION

It is to be noted that the definition of a C reorganization does not include the liquidation of the acquired corporation (just as is true in connection with a B reorganization), and it is clear that qualification as a reorganization does not depend upon there being such a liquidation. E. g., Helvering v. Minnesota Tea Co., 296 U.S. 378, 56 S.Ct. 269, 80 L.Ed. 284 (1935). However, the liquidation of the acquired corporation can be included within the "plan of reorganization" (notwithstanding Reg. § 1.368–2(g) which purports to limit the plan "to such exchanges or distributions as are directly a part of the transaction specifically described as a reorganization" in § 368), thereby making § 354 applicable to the receipt of the acquiring corporation's stock by the stockholders of the acquired corporation upon the liquidation of the acquired corporation. E. g., Rev.Rul. 57–518, set out just above. Were this not so, it would not be possible to use the C reorganization route to get the stock of the acquiring corporation to the stockholders of the acquired corporation tax-free, since there is no counterpart of § 332 to provide non-recognition treatment for the liquidation of the acquired corporation in such circumstances.

The harder question is whether the parties are free *not* to include the liquidation of the acquired corporation in the plan of reorganization if they prefer. If so, it would mean that in a C reorganization the recognition of gain or loss by the stockholders of the acquired corporation would become elective, depending upon whether the liquidation was included within the plan. But it seems more likely that whenever liquidation of the acquired corporation is contemplated from the outset, it will be regarded as a part of the plan of reorganization whether or not the liquidation is expressly included in the plan and even if it does not occur until a substantial time after the acquisition transaction. See Wilson v. Commissioner, 20 T.C.M. 676 (1961) (liquidation of the acquired corporation three years after the transfer of assets held, at the urging of the taxpayer, to be pursuant to the plan of reorganization). See generally, Manning, "In Pursuance of the Plan of Reorganization": The Scope of the Reorganization Provisions of the Internal Revenue Code, 72 Harv.L.Rev. 881, 885–890, 910–917 (1959).

4. EFFECT OF OWNERSHIP BY THE ACQUIRING CORPORATION OF STOCK IN THE ACQUIRED CORPORATION

There has been a problem where the acquiring corporation in a C reorganization owns stock in the acquired corporation, a situation sometimes referred to as a "creeping acquisition" because the acquiring corporation has already moved partway down the path (though admittedly a different one) toward acquisition of the acquired corporation. In such cases, when the acquired corporation is liquidated the acquiring corporation (in its capacity as a stockholder of the acquired corporation) will receive back some of the stock it transferred in exchange for the acquired corporation's assets; accordingly, it might be argued that the acquiring corporation has in effect received some of the assets of the acquired corporation on account of the stock it owned in the acquired corporation rather than in exchange for its own stock. Bausch & Lomb Optical Co. v. Commissioner, 267 F.2d 75 (2d Cir. 1959), adopts this view, denying C reorganization treatment under the 1939 Code where corporation P, which earlier had acquired 79% of the stock of corporation S for cash, issued its stock for the assets of corporation S and then liquidated S, with P thus receiving back 79% of the stock it had issued. Accord, Rev.Rul. 54–396, 54–2 Cum.Bull. 147 (ruling on the Bausch & Lomb transaction). See generally, Seplow, Acquisition of Assets of a Subsidiary: Liquidation or Reorganization, 73 Harv.L.Rev. 484 (1960).

This is another of those very troublesome variations among the types of reorganization which often amount to a trap for the unwary. As we have seen, creeping control is now permitted for B reorganizations; and in A reorganizations, which are even more closely analogous to asset acquisitions, ownership of stock by the acquiring corporation in the corporation to be acquired does not seem to present any problem. Cf. Helvering v. Winston Bros. Co., 76 F.2d 381 (8th Cir. 1935). It is also possible to avoid the Bausch & Lomb result while still pursuing the C reorganization route. First, it appears that reorganization qualification can be achieved by not liquidating the acquired corporation, even if all of the stockholders other than the acquiring corporation turn in their acquired corporation stock and receive stock of the acquiring corporation in exchange. See Rev.Rul. 57–278, 1957–1 Cum.Bull. 124. Second, apparently the two corporations can safely combine in a C reorganization by both transferring their assets to a new corporation, and then liquidating. George v. Commissioner, 26 T.C. 396 (1956).

5. CLAIMS OF DISSENTING STOCKHOLDERS

While in a merger the appraisal claims of the dissenting stockholders of both corporations are usually lodged against the surviving, acquiring corporation, e. g., MBA § 74, in an asset acquisition if the stockholders of the acquired corporation who object to the sale of assets have any right to appraisal at all their claims must usually be filed against the acquired corporation. Ibid. This can lead to some significant tax complications. It is clear that if the acquired corporation attempted to supply the acquired corporation with the cash to pay the dissenting stockholders' claims it would represent boot which could disqualify the transaction as a C reorganization if the amount of the cash (together with any liabilities assumed) exceeded 20% of the fair market value of the acquired corporation's property. However, as a practical matter this is not a matter of any real concern since the amount to which the dissenting shareholders are entitled would rarely have been determined in time to have the acquiring corporation supply the cash anyway. Normally, it would be more feasible to simply have the acquiring corporation assume the acquired corporation's liability to dissenting stockholders, which would make the situation closely comparable to what occurs in a merger. But this approach runs head on into the decision in Helvering v. Southwest Consolidated Corp., 315 U.S. 194, 62 S.Ct. 546, 86 L.Ed. 789 (1942), which held that since the liability to dissenters arose out of the reorganization plan itself it did not constitute "a liability of the other" corporation within the meaning of § 368(a)(1)(C) and therefore its assumption constituted boot. In Southwest Consolidated the liability assumed was actually one to a bank for funds borrowed to pay the dissenting stockholders, but it could hardly be doubted that the result would have been the same if the acquiring corporation had assumed the liability to the dissenters directly.

The other obvious alternative for dealing with dissenters is to have the acquired corporation use its own assets to pay their claims. This approach seemed to be approved in Southland Ice Co. v. Commissioner, 5 T.C. 842 (1945), since the court sustained reorganization treatment where dissenters were paid with cash obtained by the acquired corporation from its operations during the reorganization period. To be sure, this means that the acquiring corporation would not be acquiring *all* of the acquired corporation's assets. But as the court in the Southland Ice case noted the statute only requires the acquisition of "substantially all" the assets; and the court was satisfied that this requirement was sufficient to police the acquired corporation's use of its own assets to pay dissenters.

Often the amount due to dissenters can not be determined by the time when the transfer of the acquired corporation's assets to the acquiring corporation is called for. In that event the acquired corporation can simply exclude from the property sold to the acquiring corporation enough of its liquid assets to meet the dissenters' claims. See Roosevelt Hotel Co. v. Commissioner, 13 T.C. 399 (1949). Presumably, this could be coupled with an arrangement to transfer any excess of the liquid assets retained over the amount ultimately required to meet the dissenters' claims to the acquiring corporation for additional stock, in accordance with some predetermined formula. Alternatively, the acquired corporation could transfer all of its assets to the acquiring corporation and then sell enough of the stock received from the acquiring corporation to obtain the amount needed to pay dissenters (subject to some possible SEC problems, to say nothing of the depressed market which might result from such an immediate, quasi-forced sale of stock). However, these approaches present some practical difficulties when, as is typically the case, it is contemplated that the acquired corporation will be liquidated promptly and the stock of the acquiring corporation will be distributed to the stockholders of the acquired corporation in exchange for their stock. Normally in such cases the plan submitted to the stockholders of the acquired corporation would be expected to specify the ratio upon which the stock of the acquired corporation would be exchanged for stock of the acquiring corporation in the liquidation, just as a plan of merger specifies the exchange ratio when the merger route is followed. But if the value determined for the dissenters' stock in the appraisal proceeding should turn out to be significantly greater than the amount allocated to them under the plan (and of course the dissenters are "betting" that they can show a substantially higher value for their stock), the amount available for distribution to non-dissenting stockholders upon the liquidation of the acquired corporation would be proportionately reduced, and the exchange ratio would be thrown askew. Indeed, what this means is that it may not be possible to fix an exchange ratio in advance. And if the acquired corporation can not tell its stockholders at the outset what they can expect to receive under the plan, it may be difficult to secure the necessary stockholder approval.

These uncertainties are inherent in any procedure which throws on the acquired corporation, rather than the acquiring corporation, the risk that dissenters will be awarded substantially more in the appraisal proceeding than they were to receive under the plan. Conversely, these difficulties evaporate under any plan which shifts that risk on to the acquiring corporation, where it is in a merger. For example, the plan might provide that as soon as the number of dissenting shares is known the acquiring corporation will transfer sufficient stock to take care of all the non-dissenting stockholders of the acquired corporation in accordance with the agreed-upon exchange ratio; but the acquired corporation would be permitted to retain enough cash to provide a safety margin in the event of a generous appraisal award, with any excess over the actual appraisal award to be remitted to the acquiring corporation. But the trouble with this approach, or any other one which shifts the risk of the appraisal award to the acquiring corporation, is that it is not really distinguishable from a direct assumption of the appraisal liability by the acquiring corporation and therefore runs a serious risk of disqualifying the reorganization under the Southwest Consolidated case.

An analogous problem arises in connection with the reorganization expenses of the acquiring corporation, which would also seem to produce a liability arising out of the reorganization plan itself within the meaning of the Southwest Consolidated case. But the Tax Court, in the Roosevelt Hotel case, supra, confined Southwest Consolidated to the assumption of the liability to dissenters and held that the acquiring corporation's assumption of the liability for other expenses of the acquired corporation did not constitute boot. (But see Stockton Harbor Industrial Co. v. Commissioner, 216 F.2d 638 (9th Cir. 1954), which interprets the Southwest Consolidated test as applicable to any liabilities "determined only in the reorganization" and seems to assume this would include "debts incurred as expenses of reorganization".) The decision in the Roosevelt Hotel case also suggests that at least the Tax Court may be expected to be sympathetic to efforts to escape the strictures of the Southwest Consolidated case even where the claims of dissenters are involved.

SECTION 5. CARRYOVER OF TAX ATTRIBUTES IN COMBINATION TRANSACTIONS

A. IN GENERAL

One of the most important tax questions in connection with combination transactions is to what extent the acquiring corporation succeeds to the characteristics, benefits, and obligations of the acquired corporation pursuant to a tax-free combination. Prior to 1954 what few rules there were in this area came mainly from the courts. There was no consistent judicial pattern, and the result seemed to depend primarily on the nature of the particular tax item involved. Most of the cases related to either earnings and profits or net operating losses, both of which will be considered in more detail below. However, it may be useful to illustrate the general problem with an example from outside those two areas. In Mendham Corporation v. Commissioner, 9 T.C. 320 (1947), the acquiring corporation in a combination transaction had received from the acquired corporation property subject to a mortgage which had been placed by the acquired corporation. Subsequently, the mortgagee foreclosed the mortgage and took over the property, but did not assert any deficiency. If this foreclosure had occurred while the acquired corporation still held the property, the transaction would have been viewed as a transfer of the property in satisfaction of the mortgage debt, giving rise to recognized gain in the amount of the difference between the mortgage debt and the depreciated basis of the property. Here, however, while the acquired corporation had obtained the money on the mortgage, it was the acquiring corporation which was yielding the property to satisfy the debt. Nevertheless, the Tax Court upheld the Commissioner's contention that the acquiring corporation should recognize the gain, on the ground that in a tax-free combination the acquiring corporation stepped completely into the shoes of the acquired corporation.

The 1954 Code in § 381 introduced the first statutory effort to deal comprehensively with the carryover of items from the acquired corporation to the acquiring corporation in a corporate combination. The transactions subject to § 381 are: A, C, and F reorganizations; D reorganizations which do not involve any corporate division; and tax-free liquidations of a subsidiary in which the parent takes the basis of the subsidiary's assets. In other words, the section applies generally where the acquiring corporation in effect absorbs the acquired corporation.

It is not clear whether in a C reorganization it is necessary that the acquired corporation be liquidated for § 381 to apply. If not, the section may lead to the rather anomalous result that the various attributes of the acquired corporation go over to the acquiring corporation even though the acquired corporation remains in existence.

The tax items covered by § 381 are specifically enumerated in subsection (c) and include such important attributes as net operating loss carryovers, earnings and profits, methods of accounting, and various elections. Although the statutory list is not exhaustive, there is no catch-all clause. However, the section is not intended to be exclusive, and the Senate Finance Committee Report, S.Rep.No. 1622, 83rd Cong., 2d Sess. 277 (1954), states that the section is "not intended to affect the carryover treatment of an item or tax attribute not specified in the section or the carryover treatment of items or tax attributes in corporate transactions not described in subsection (a)." Thus it would seem that such rules as that of the Mendham case, supra, which are not dealt with in the section, would continue to be applicable.

See generally, Reese, Reorganization Transfers and Survival of Tax Attributes, 16 Tax.L.Rev. 207 (1961).

B. CARRYOVER OF EARNINGS AND PROFITS

The pre-1954 judicial authorities relating to the carryover of earnings and profits, and the pattern adopted by § 381(c)(2), are well summarized in the following:

NESSON, EARNINGS AND PROFITS DISCONTINUITIES UNDER THE 1954 CODE*
77 Harv.L.Rev. 452–456 (1964).

A. Sansome, Phipps, and Frelbro

Commissioner v. Sansome,[8] uniformly recognized as the "leading case," posed the problem of the disappearing earnings account in its starkest form. In a tax-free reorganization, corporation N, with substantial earnings and profits, transferred all its assets to corporation

---

* Copyright (c), Harvard Law Review Association, 1964. Reprinted by permission. Most of the footnotes omitted.

8. 60 F.2d 931 (2d Cir. 1932).

M in return for all M's stock and then liquidated. The same shareholders thus owned the same business under a new name. Noting that a corporate distribution to be taxable as a dividend must be "out of its earnings or profits," and noting further that the new corporation had no earnings and profits of its own, the shareholders of M argued that since distributions made subsequent to the reorganization were not out of "its" — M's — earnings and profits, they were capital distributions. Judge Hand, however, refused to place so much weight on the statutory "its"; he reasoned that Congress could not have intended that by a nontaxable change in corporate form, earnings and profits — and thus dividend taxation — could so easily be eliminated. From this simple beginning great confusion developed. When corporate structure was more substantially changed by reorganization, as when new capital was introduced, or a corporation merged with another operating corporation, there was some judicial resistance to the survival of earnings after the transaction. On the other hand, some courts seem to have developed the notion that earnings and profits represent an obligation to the Government and that no tax-free transaction should impair that obligation. In Robinette,[13] Sansome was extended to apply to tax-free liquidations of subsidiaries; it was held that earnings and profits of the liquidated subsidiary should carry over to the parent. Then in Phipps[14] it was argued that earnings should be reduced when a parent corporation with substantial earnings and profits liquidated wholly owned subsidiaries having substantial deficits. Mr. Justice Murphy, fearful of tax avoidance, spoke for a unanimous Supreme Court in holding that the subsidiaries' deficits could not be allowed to offset the parent's earnings, and thus should be totally disregarded. It was evidently of no moment in the Court's view whether the parent had actually sought out and purchased deficit corporations intending to reduce the parent's earnings and profits, or whether the parent had purchased or formed the subsidiaries long before to carry on business enterprises which had subsequently soured. Rather, the controlling consideration was that, absent the tax-free unification, the parent could not have used its subsidiaries' deficits to reduce its earnings. The Court distinguished the converse situation in Harter,[15] in which a liquidated subsidiary's earnings were apparently allowed to offset the parent's deficit. Justice Murphy reasoned that since the Harter parent, without liquidation, could have made use of its deficit by having its subsidiary pay dividends to the extent of the parent's deficit, the deficit should be permitted to offset earnings on liquidation. The Phipps-Harter result seems to make the use or loss of a deficit depend on which corpora-

13. Robinette v. Commissioner, 148 F.2d 513 (9th Cir. 1945).

14. Commissioner v. Phipps, 336 U.S. 410 (1949).

15. Harter v. Helvering, 79 F.2d 12 (2d Cir. 1935). That a deficit was permitted to offset earnings is deducible only from the figures used in the opinion, not from the text of the opinion itself.

tion was the parent. Where the parent-subsidiary relationship has already been established, as will be the case when the parent acquired the subsidiary to carry on a business enterprise and thought of the benefits of liquidation only at a later time, the flexibility necessary to avoid Phipps has already been lost. But when a corporation with earnings begins with the more questionable motive of earnings reduction, it can structure the acquisition transaction so that the deficit corporation becomes the parent and survives. The simplest method would have a deficit corporation acquire the stock of a profitable corporation in a (B) reorganization and then liquidate the profitable corporation.

It would seem, then, that the reasoning of Phipps is weak and that its result — total elimination of a liquidated subsidiary's deficit when the parent has earnings — is extremely harsh. Nonetheless, as recently as 1961, the Tax Court extended the reach of Phipps to the point of absurdity. The Frelbro [17] case, arising under the 1939 Code, involved a merger of two deficit corporations. Clearly in such a case earnings reduction could not have motivated the consolidation since neither corporation had any earnings to reduce. Nevertheless the court refused to allow the deficits of the two corporations to cumulate. Its reasoning is, to say the least, questionable:

> Following petitioner's position to its logical conclusion would result in an inconsistency demonstrated by the following hypotheticals:
>
> 1. E corporation has a $1 credit balance and D has a $1 million debit balance in their respective earnings and profits accounts. In a tax-free reorganization the two are consolidated to form F and (under the Phipps doctrine) F acquires a $1 credit balance in its earnings and profits.
>
> 2. Same facts except that E has a $1 deficit in earnings and profits. F acquires $1,000,001 debit in its earnings and profits.
>
> What petitioner overlooks is that the evil which the Court was meeting in the Phipps case is still present if corporations are permitted to "pool" deficits and use them interchangeably.

The immediate "evil" in Phipps was that a parent corporation might wipe out its existing earnings and profits by liquidating its subsidiaries, and this without reference to any comparison between the parent's investment in a subsidiary's stock and the basis of the assets received on liquidation. This immediate "evil" certainly did not exist in Frelbro. If the court was worried about the "pooled" deficit offsetting future earnings, the opinion could not have been

---

17. Frelbro Corp., 36 T.C. 864 (1961), rev'd on other grounds, 315 F.2d 784 (2d Cir. 1963).

regarded as within Phipps. The court clearly recognized the harshness of Phipps as indicated by hypothetical (1); nonetheless, its decision goes a step beyond.

B. The 1954 Code

A further surprising aspect of the Frelbro opinion is its failure to make mention of the 1954 Code. Section 381 would have applied to the facts of Frelbro had they arisen after 1954, and it is clear that in section 381(c)(2) Congress substantially qualified Phipps, retaining the immediate results of Phipps but clearly rejecting the Frelbro implications. In all liquidations or reorganizations in which the acquiring corporation takes substantially all the assets of the acquired corporation with continuity of basis the new Code provides that earnings cumulate where both corporations have earnings and that deficits cumulate where both corporations have deficits. Where one corporation has earnings and the other a deficit, both the earnings account and the deficit account carry over but do not offset each other; rather the two accounts must be separately maintained, and any earnings of the resulting corporation subsequent to the unification must first exhaust the deficit account before accumulated earnings are increased. In this compromise both the harshness of Phipps and the upstream-downstream Harter-Phipps distinction are eliminated.

The section 381 compromise is by and large a good resolution of a difficult problem. However, its treatment of deficits is not totally beyond criticism. To the shareholders of a corporation with a sure earnings future it may make very little difference in the long run whether an acquired deficit offsets future rather than accumulated earnings; however, it should be kept in mind that the accumulated earnings account must be completely exhausted before shareholders benefit from a deficit. The section 381 compromise does prevent deficits from being directly subtracted from earnings, but if the earnings and profits of the acquiring corporation were low enough to begin with so that ordinary dividend distributions sufficient to exhaust them would not be prohibitively expensive to the shareholders, then future earnings of the corporation would be distributable as capital to the extent of the deficit. Arguments may be made to undercut this criticism. First, since regardless of deficits distributions are dividends to the extent of current earnings, the picture of the prosperous corporation distributing its earnings as capital is clearly exaggerated. Nonetheless, distributions in excess of current earnings will not be treated as dividends. Second, it may be argued that a corporation with low or nonexistent accumulated earnings is not likely to have enough assurance of future earnings to make a deficit acquisition worthwhile. However, this observation would not apply to a corporation formed to carry on a new enterprise, or to an existing corporation that develops new prospects. Third, it may be argued that the abuse possible under section 381 will be curbed by section 269. It is unclear, however, that the present section 269 would have such application.

C. NET OPERATING LOSSES

1. MECHANICS OF THE OPERATING LOSS CARRYOVER PROVISIONS

Before attempting to analyze the impact of combination transactions on operating loss carryovers, it would be well to examine the provisions governing the carryover of losses generally.

HAWKINS, MECHANICS OF CARRYING LOSSES TO OTHER YEARS*

14 West.Res.L.Rev. 241, 242-251 (1963).

GENERAL EXPLANATION

The basic rule is that a net operating loss can be carried back three years and forward five years,[2] being "used up" against the income of these years taken in chronological order. Thus, a loss incurred in 1959 is carried first to the third preceding year, 1956. If the 1956 income was not sufficient to completely use up the loss, the balance is then carried to the second preceding year, 1957. The remainder, not used up in that year, is then carried to 1958, and the then balance, if any, is carried to 1960, the first year following the loss, and so forth.

The chronological rule applies in carrying losses *to* a year as well as *from* a year. If 1960 is assumed to be a profitable year, the total amount which can be deducted from its profits on account of net operating losses carried over from all eight years (the five preceding years plus the three following years) is known as the net operating loss *deduction* for 1960. However, in determining which losses were actually used up in eliminating the 1960 profits, one begins with the losses from the earliest of the eight years, in this case 1955. If no operating loss was incurred in 1955, or if it was incurred but was used up against the income of the years before 1960 to which it could be carried, or if the balance not used up was insufficient to wipe out all

---

* Reprinted by permission of the Western Reserve Law Review. Portions of the text and footnotes omitted.

2. The Code refers to "taxable years." Thus, a short fiscal year counts as a full year for carrying purposes. Treas. Reg. § 1.172–4(a) (2). . . .

the 1960 profits, one proceeds to the losses, if any, from the next year, 1956, and then to the losses of 1957, and so forth.

A complication in the carryover procedure lies in determining how much of the loss from 1959 was "used up" in 1956, in order to know how much of the loss remains to be carried to 1957. The "used up" portion is not simply the 1956 taxable income, but the 1956 taxable income subject to a series of modifications.[4] These modifications include some, but not all, of the modifications made in computing a net operating loss in the first place.* In particular, the net operating loss deduction is allowed but only to the extent of losses carried to the year in question, 1956, from years preceding the loss year in question, 1959. . . .

A final basic point is the procedure involved. In preparing almost any timely income tax return, it will be possible to compute the net operating loss deduction only to the extent that this consists of loss carryovers from the five preceding years. If the succeeding three years give rise to losses the carryback of which reduces the tax due for the year in question, it is necessary to obtain a refund. This can be done either by an ordinary claim for refund or by means of a "tentative carryback adjustment." This adjustment is governed by section 6411, which provides that if the taxpayer applies for the adjustment on the proper form within twelve months of the end of the loss year, the Commissioner shall normally grant the refund within ninety days. The Commissioner need not allow the application, however, if he finds errors which he is unable or unwilling to correct within the ninety days. (The errors in question are those made in relation to the carryback: disagreement as to the merits of the return originally filed for the profitable year is not a proper gound for disallowing the application). In any event, proper or improper, the disallowance of the application for a tentative carryback adjustment is not an adequate foundation for a suit for refund. If the application procedure under section 6411 is not successful, the taxpayer must revert to a regular claim for refund.

* * *

SPECIAL PROBLEMS IN CARRYING LOSSES

Statute of Limitations

The general rule is that the statute of limitations is open for carrying back losses to earlier years as long as it is open for filing claims for

---

4. Code § 172(b) (2). . . .

* [Ed. note] In using this modified taxable income test both for computing the operating loss for a particular year and for measuring the amount of the operating loss carryover which is "used up" by the various years to which it may be carried, the 1954 Code is substantially more favorable to taxpayers than the pre-1954 "economic income" standard, which included such adjustments as adding back the 85% dividends received deduction. See United States v. Whitney Land Co., 324 F.2d 33 (8th Cir. 1963).

refund for the year in which the loss was incurred. The same rule applies in determining the limitations period for assessing deficiencies "attributable to the application to the taxpayer of a net operating loss carryback" (including a tentative carryback adjustment).

The extent to which the statute is opened up is uncertain. Under the statute governing deficiencies, assessments are limited to items "attributable to the carryback." The same test governs the Commissioner's review of an application for a tentative carryover adjustment. Both the Tax Court and the Commissioner agree that under this test, the merits of the return for the year to which the loss is carried are not opened up for re-examination: the only issue is whether the amount of the net operating loss deduction attributable to the carryback in question is correct. The Court of Appeals for the Second Circuit holds, however, that if a claim for refund is filed based on a loss carryback, the Commissioner can offset against the claim deficiencies arising from any other item for the year to which the loss is carried, even though the ordinary period of limitations on assessments for that year has expired.[20] It argues that otherwise, a taxpayer carrying back a loss is in a better position than a taxpayer actually incurring the loss in the earlier year.[21] The effect of its rule is to put taxpayers [who get a so-called "quickie" refund under the tentative carryback adjustment procedure] in a better position than taxpayers who have chosen [the regular refund approach].

* * *

Choice of Law

The loss year, the three preceding years, and the five following years, add up to a nine-year period which may be involved in a carryover problem. Since the fateful year 1913, our tax law has never survived any period of anything like this length without undergoing extensive changes. Accordingly, it is necessary to choose which of the tax laws shall prevail of those which obtained at different times during the carryover period.

While the authorities are not complete enough to permit absolute certainty, the "better view" would seem to be summed up by the following rules.

(1) The years to which a loss may be carried is determined by the law in effect in the year the loss was incurred.

---

20. Commissioner v. Van Bergh, 209 F. 2d 23 (2d Cir. 1954).

21. Id. at 24. This is probably not true. Under the Van Bergh rule, the Commissioner has a second chance to audit the earlier return, which he would not have had if the loss had been incurred in the earlier year. If the loss had been then incurred, there is no reason to suppose it would have *increased* the chance the first audit would have uncovered a different unrelated issue; it is more likely in practice that the reduction of reported taxable income would have *decreased* the revenue agent's interest. . . .

(2) All computations shall be made according to the law governing the year to which the computation primarily relates. By "computation" is meant the calculations relating to any one year, to wit, the calculation of the amount of the loss in the loss year, the calculation of the amount of the loss "used up" in an intervening year, and the calculation of the net operating loss deduction for the profitable year in question, but excluding any part of such calculation which relates primarily to another year.

(3) The statute of limitations applicable to the year of the loss determines the period for filing a refund claim based on carryback of the loss.

* * *

Carryover Destroyed by Capital Gain

If a corporation has a net operating loss deduction greater than its income apart from long term capital gain, the deduction may be "used up" in that year without producing any tax saving whatever.

Assume a long term capital gain of $100,000 and a net operating loss deduction which exceeds the corporation's ordinary taxable income (computed before such deduction) by $40,000. The corporation will use the "alternative tax" under which it must pay twenty-five per cent of its long term capital gain *unreduced by the net operating loss deduction.*[45] This tax would be $25,000. If the alternative tax were not used, the capital gain would be taxed as ordinary income,[46] *after* deduction of the net operating loss deduction, which would produce a tax of $25,700.

The alternative tax would be no greater and no less than if the corporation had not had a net operating loss deduction at all. Nevertheless, in computing the amount of the loss carried to the following year, the full capital gain is deducted from the loss even though the alternative tax was used.[47] On the assumed figures, accordingly, the loss would be completely wiped out in a year in which it did no good.

The same rules apply in determining whether in the year of the capital gain an excess of ordinary deductions over ordinary income gives rise to a net operating loss.[48]

NOTE ON OPERATING LOSS CARRYOVERS

A concrete example may help to illuminate the operation of the net operating loss carryover provisions. Suppose that X corporation incurred an

---

45. Code § 1201(a); Rev.Rul. 56–247, 1956–1 Cum.Bull. 383; Weil v. Commissioner, 229 F.2d 593 (6th Cir. 1956).

46. If an individual does not use the alternative tax he nevertheless includes only fifty per cent of the long term capital gain in ordinary income, Code § 1202, but this section does not apply to corporations. . . .

47. Code § 172(b) (2).

48. Code § 172(c).

operating loss of $20,000 in 1958. As noted above, the loss would first be carried to the earliest year to which it could apply, here 1955. Regardless of whether the year 1955 would be closed under the normal statute of limitations, it would be open for a claim for refund on account of the loss carryback from 1958 for as long as the year 1958 itself remained open for claims for refund. On the other hand, under the Van Bergh case, supra, even if 1955 were closed so far as assessment of a deficiency is concerned, the Commissioner would nevertheless be free to show that X's taxable income for that year was actually higher than the amount reported, and to use any such deficiency to offset the operating loss carryback and thereby reduce or eliminate any claim for refund.

Now suppose that X's reported taxable income for the year 1955 was exactly $0. In that event, *prima facie* none of the 1958 operating loss would be "used up" in 1955 and the entire $20,000 of loss would then be carried to 1956. Of course again in 1956 it would be open to the Commissioner to recompute X's taxable income and use any deficiency so determined to offset the loss carryback. Would it also be open to the Commissioner to recompute taxable income for 1955 for the purpose of offsetting the net operating loss carryback from 1958 by "using it up" in 1955 (although without any tax benefit to X), thereby reducing or eliminating the amount of the loss to be carried to 1956? Just this approach was sustained in Phoenix Coal Co. v. Commissioner, 231 F.2d 420 (2d Cir. 1956), where the court regarded it as a logical extension of the Van Bergh doctrine. The Phoenix Coal case was recently followed in Springfield Street Railway Co. v. United States, 160 Ct.Cl. 111, 312 F.2d 754 (1963), with a rather interesting reverse twist: the taxpayer was allowed to show that its actual taxable income for an earlier, barred year was in fact less than the amount reported, in order to reduce the amount of operating loss carryback "used up" in that year and thus increase the amount which could be carried to later, open years. Accord, Rev.Rul. 65–96, 1965–1 Cum.Bull. 126.

These same rules are operative in connection with loss carryforwards. Thus if X was seeking to carry forward the 1958 loss to subsequent years, the fact that 1958 itself had become closed under the statute of limitations would not prevent the Commissioner from recomputing the alleged loss in 1958 for the purpose of reducing or eliminating the loss carryover to later years. The State Farming Co., Inc. v. Commissioner, 40 T.C. 774 (1963); Phoenix Electronics, Inc. v. United States, 164 F.Supp. 614 (D.Mass.1958); Rev.Rul. 56–285, 1956–1 Cum.Bull. 134. Presumably the Phoenix Coal rule would be applicable to any year intervening between the loss year and the year to which the loss is being carried forward, so that even if such intervening year is itself closed the Commissioner is free to recompute taxable income for the purpose of "using up" the operating loss and reducing or eliminating the amount remaining to be carried forward to later years.

Returning now to our previous example, suppose that while there was no error in X's reported taxable income for either 1955 or 1956, X had had an operating loss in 1954 which could have been utilized as a carryforward to 1956 but was in fact never used by X at all. Assuming that it is now too late to use the 1954 loss as the basis for a refund for 1956, could the Commissioner nevertheless maintain that the 1956 taxable income had been "constructively" used up by the 1954 operating loss, so that there was no longer any 1956 income against which to apply the 1958 loss? While the Service has expressly ruled in the affirmative on this question, Rev.Rul. 218, 1953–2 Cum.Bull. 176, its position has recently been rejected in what appears to be the only litigated case on this issue. Brandon v. United States, 204 F.Supp. 912 (N.D.Ga.1962).

The Brandon opinion is rather disappointing in that it does not even mention Rev.Rul. 218, and indeed does little more than state the facts and hold for the taxpayer. But this much is clear — the Brandon case does not represent any basic departure from the general rule requiring an operating loss to be carried to other years in chronological order. For in the Brandon case the later operating loss which was the basis for the claim for refund was in fact being carried to earlier years in perfect chronological order. And the chronological requirement has been reaffirmed at least twice since Brandon (without any reference to that decision). Romer v. United States, 216 F. Supp. 832 (S.D.N.Y.1963); Eisenberg v. Commissioner, 22 T.C.M. 333 (1963).

What the Brandon decision seems to stand for is the proposition that a taxpayer may elect to waive a particular operating loss and not use it at all. At first blush, this certainly seems perfectly sensible. As Mr. Hawkins points out in a portion of his article not included in the foregoing excerpts, 14 West.Res.L.Rev. at 247, it would seem that the Commissioner could not defeat a refund claim for 1956 by showing that in that year the taxpayer overlooked some ordinary deduction, such as interest, which would have wiped out the taxable income for the year. If so, why should the result be any different where the overlooked deduction is an operating loss carryforward from 1954?

In addition, a rule contrary to Brandon could lead to an enormous proliferation of efforts to redetermine the income of barred years under the Phoenix Coal doctrine. Any time the taxpayer sought to carry a loss back to a prior year, the Commissioner could try to show that there had actually been a loss in some earlier year which could (and under a contra-Brandon view, *should*) have been carried to the year for which a refund was sought, thus "wiping out" the income of that year. Presumably, taxpayers would respond by attempting to establish that the income of some intervening year was actually higher than the amount reported, in order to absorb the loss established by the Commissioner before it could be carried to the refund year. Notice that among other things the parties' normal roles in tax litigation would be reversed, with the Commissioner trying to show that the taxpayer had a loss in some year and the taxpayer trying to show that for some other year his income was actually higher than reported.

On the other hand, the Brandon result presents the spectre of allowing a taxpayer to use the same operating loss twice. To illustrate in terms of the above example, assume that under the Brandon decision X was able to secure a refund for 1956 on the basis of the 1958 loss despite the unused 1954 loss. However, in determining whether any of the 1958 loss remained to be carried forward to 1957 and later years, X might be able to argue that none of that loss was used up in 1956, because the 1956 income was "wiped out" by the earlier 1954 loss. Such an argument is quite analogous to the one which the taxpayer successfully advanced in the Springfield Street Railway Co. case, supra. Moreover, the express language of § 172(b)(2) seems to support the argument. After providing that the "portion of [a] loss which shall be carried to each of the other 7 taxable years shall be the excess, if any, of the amount of such loss over the sum of the taxable income for each of the prior taxable years to which such loss may be carried", the statute goes on to provide that the "taxable income for any such prior taxable year" shall be adjusted to take account of the net operating loss deduction for any year prior to the loss year in question. In terms this would seem to mean that in our example the amount of the 1958 loss used up in 1956 would be no more that the 1956 income *less* the 1954 operating loss.

Hawkins, op. cit. supra, at 247–248, reached the conclusion that the same operating loss could be used twice under the Brandon rule. He did not regard this as objectionable because it would merely put the taxpayer where he would have been if he had in fact taken advantage of the earlier loss. Nevertheless, it is hard to believe that such a double use of an operating loss would be permitted. See Sanden, Techniques and Computations of the Net Operating Loss Deduction, 21 N.Y.U. Inst.Fed.Tax. 1227, 1231 (1963). It seems more likely that if the Brandon approach is to be followed, the earlier operating loss would be regarded as waived for all purposes, and therefore not be taken into account in the computation under § 172(b)(2). The same result would be reached by adopting the view that the actual use of a net operating loss carryover to secure a refund for a particular year necessarily "uses up" the loss to that extent, thereby reducing or eliminating the amount left to be carried to later years.

2. CARRYOVER OF OPERATING LOSSES IN CORPORATE COMBINATIONS

The question of the impact of a combination transaction on the operating loss carryovers of the constituent corporations is really but one aspect of the broader question as to how changes in the stockholders and/or business of a corporation affect its operating loss carryovers. Thus, for example, the merger of a profitable corporation into a loss corporation is in the first instance no more than a particular illustration of the acquisition of a new business by a loss corporation plus a significant change in its stockholders. Nevertheless, it is worth singling out tax-free combinations for special attention at the outset because so much of the early development concerning operating loss carryovers involved cases of this kind.

a. SURVIVAL OF OPERATING LOSSES UNDER PRIOR LAW

Originally, the only statutory standard for judging whether a particular corporate transformation affected an existing loss carryover came from the words of the predecessor of § 172 allowing "the taxpayer" to utilize its operating losses. In the case of a corporation it was generally assumed that the corporate entity, rather than its owners, constituted "the taxpayer". Thus when a new corporation was organized to take over another corporation's business, the successor could not carry forward the operating loss of its predecessor even though the creditors and stockholders remained identical, because the successor was not "the taxpayer" which had sustained the loss. New Colonial Ice Co. v. Helvering, 292 U.S. 435, 54 S.Ct. 788, 78 L.Ed. 1348 (1934). The corollary of this strict entity approach seemed to be that so long as the corporation which suffered the loss did remain intact, its operating losses could be carried forward even though there had been a complete change in its stockholders and its business. Alprosa Watch Corp. v. Commissioner, 11 T.C. 240 (1948).

An important departure from this strict entity concept came in Stanton Brewery, Inc. v. Commissioner, 176 F.2d 573 (2d Cir. 1949), which held that upon the merger of a wholly-owned subsidiary into its parent, the parent was the same "taxpayer" as the subsidiary and was therefore entitled to carry forward the subsidiary's operating losses. Since the New Colonial Ice case was distinguished on the ground that no statutory merger had been involved, Stanton seemed to mean that a statutory merger (or consolidation) could be relied on to preserve the loss carryovers of each of the constituents. But in 1957 the Supreme Court laid this notion to rest in Libson Shops Inc. v. Koehler, 353 U.S. 382, 77 S.Ct. 990, 1 L.Ed.2d 924 (1957), which involved a statutory merger of sixteen separate corporations, each operating a single retail store, into the taxpayer, which performed management services for the others. All seventeen corporations were owned by the same stockholders in the same proportions. Three of the 16 retail corporations had operating loss carryovers which the taxpayer sought to carry forward against the post-merger profits of the combination. The three loss stores continued to lose money. In disallowing the carryovers, the Court rejected the view that the surviving corporation in a merger was automatically the same "taxpayer" as each of the constituents and thereby entitled to carry forward their operating losses. Instead, the Court adopted the contention of the Government that pre-merger loss carryovers could be offset against post-merger income "only to the extent that this income is derived from the operation of substantially the same business which produced the loss." Thus was born the "same business" test, which has plagued the operating loss carryover area ever since.

However, so far as tax-free combinations were concerned, the Libson Shops approach was in effect still-born, since some three years earlier the 1954 Code had already adopted a specific solution to the New Colonial Ice-Stanton hassle about the "same taxpayer" in such cases.

b. The 1954 Code Treatment

As previously noted, § 381 of the 1954 Code provides for a carryover of certain tax attributes of a corporation whose assets are acquired in a tax-free liquidation or reorganization, and net operating losses are expressly included, under § 381(c)(1). As we have just seen, in 1954 when the new Code provisions were adopted there had as yet been little judicial development of the rules under the 1939 Code, and in particular the Libson Shops decision was still three years away. Thus the new provisions were probably directed primarily at the conflict over corporate entity, and the major thrust was to make it clear that in the transactions covered by § 381 the operating loss carryovers of the constituent corporations could be preserved regardless of which was the surviving entity. (However, as we shall see there may still be some differences in result depending upon which corporation survives.)

Turning to the operation of § 381(c)(1), it should first be noted that the statute is not needed when the loss corporation is the surviving entity. The loss corporation can simply continue to carry forward its own operating losses against "its own" income, although of course that income is now augmented by the earnings produced by the assets obtained from the acquired profit corporation. The only special provision of note here is § 381(b)(3) which prohibits carrying back pre- or post-combination losses of the acquiring corporation against the pre-combination profits of the acquired corporation.

It is when the loss corporation is the one acquired that § 381(c)(1) is called into play. The mechanics of § 381(c)(1) are somewhat complex (although happily not as much so as they look, except where more than one of the constituents has losses to carry forward) primarily because the acquired corporation's losses may be carried forward only against the post-combination income of the acquiring corporation, and cannot be applied to any income of the acquiring corporation accrued prior to the combination date. Accordingly, unless the combination occurs on the last day of the acquiring corporation's fiscal year, it is necessary to allocate the acquiring corporation's income for that year between the pre-combination period and the post-combination period. Instead of leaving this to an actual accounting determination, the statute calls for dividing the acquiring corporation's fiscal year into two parts, referred to as the "pre-acquisition part year" and the "post-acquisition part year", and allocating the total income of the acquired corporation for the year (which would include the post-combination income or loss from the assets obtained from the acquired corporation) in proportion to the number of days in each part. The post-acquisition part year (running from the day after the acquisition to the end of the fiscal year of the acquiring corporation) then becomes the first year of the acquiring corporation to which operating losses of the acquired corporation can be carried.

As already suggested, § 381(c)(1) does not make it entirely immaterial which corporation is the surviving entity. For one thing, it will make a difference if the acquiring corporation suffers post-combination losses. Since such losses can only be carried back against the acquiring corporation's pre-combination profits, and not those of the acquired corporation, there is a distinct advantage in making the profitable corporation the surviving entity.

On the other hand, making the profitable company the acquiring corporation may result in a significant disadvantage in connection with the period for which that corporation's losses can be carried forward. That is because by virtue of § 381(b)(1) the taxable year of the acquired corporation ends on the date of the acquisition, which means that unless the acquisition takes place on the last day of the acquired corporation's year, a short taxable year for the acquired corporation will result. But that short taxable year still counts as one of the five years for which an operating loss may be carried forward under § 172(b)(1), see Reg. § 1.381(c)(1)–1(e)(3); and the post-acquisition part year of the acquiring corporation to which the loss carryover of the acquired corporation is first carried also counts as one of the years in the § 172(b)(1) computation. Accordingly, whenever the loss company is the acquired corporation and the acquisition does not occur at the end of that company's fiscal year, the result will be some reduction in the permissible carryover period; and in the common case where the two corporations are both on a calendar year (or otherwise have the same fiscal year), the carryover period will be reduced by a full year, from five years to four. To illustrate, if two calendar year taxpayers were combined on June 30, 1964, the acquired loss corporation's short taxable year 1/1/64–6/30/64 would count as one of the five years under § 172(b)(1), and the post-acquisition part year of the acquiring corporation, 7/1/64–12/31/64, would also count as a year. If instead the loss corporation were the surviving entity, all of 1964 would only count as one year in the computation of the five year carryover period.

It may help to illustrate the operation of § 381(c)(1) with a concrete example. Suppose that X corporation's operating history for the five years prior to 1964 was as follows:

Year	(Net Loss)
1963	0
1962	($30,000)
1961	(60,000)
1960	(50,000)
1959	(35,000)

Suppose further than on November 1, 1964, at which time X's net income before taxes for the year to date amounts to $30,000, X is merged into Y corporation in a transaction to which § 381 applies. Y's total income before taxes for the calendar year 1964 (including the contribution made by X's assets during the last one-sixth of the year, November 1 to December 31) turns out to be $408,000.

In computing the loss carryover from X to Y, it should first be noted that none of the 1959 loss of $35,000 can be included. That loss expired in X's short taxable year ending October 31, 1964, which constituted the fifth year after the year of the loss. Of course $30,000 of that $35,000 loss served to offset the income earned by X during its short taxable year ending October 31, 1964; but the remaining $5,000 of loss would expire without producing any tax advantage. If the amount of carryover wasted in this way was more substantial, consideration would have to be given to making the loss corporation the acquiring corporation, which as noted above would eliminate the short taxable year for the loss corporation and allow the remainder of the 1959 loss to be applied against the earnings of the combined enterprise for the period November 1 to December 31, 1964. Alternatively, where, as here, the loss corporation is currently producing earnings, the waste of loss carryover could be avoided (or at least reduced) by postponing the combination transaction until December 31, 1964, thereby again eliminating the short taxable year for X and making it possible to at least apply the remaining balance of the 1959 loss against X's own earnings for the rest of the year 1964.

Assuming, however, that the merger of X into Y on November 1, 1964 took place as assumed, the loss carryover from X to Y would total $140,000; and the first year to which that amount could be carried would be Y's post-acquisition part year, running from November 1, 1964 to December 31, 1964. Y's income before taxes for that post-acquisition part year would be computed by determining the amount which bears the same ratio to Y's total income before taxes for 1964 ($408,000) as the number of days in the post-acquisition part year (61) bears to the total number of days in the year (366), or one-sixth of $408,000. The resulting figure, $68,000, would represent the amount of Y's 1964 income which could be offset by X's loss carryover. (Notice that if this figure had been less than $50,000, so that less than $50,000 of X's loss carryover could be used in 1964, the difference between the amount actually so used and $50,000 would be wasted, since X's 1960 loss of $50,000 would have expired in any event in Y's post-acquisition part year, that being the 5th year after the year in which the $50,000 loss was incurred.) The remaining $72,000 of X's loss carryover would be available to be carried forward against Y's income for 1965 and subsequent years.

3. LIMITATIONS ON LOSS CARRYOVERS IN COMBINATION TRANSACTIONS

a. SECTION 382(b)

After granting broad authority to carry over operating losses in combination transactions in § 381, the 1954 Code expressly limits this privilege by providing in § 382(b) for a reduction in the loss carryovers unless the stockholders of the loss corporation end up with at least 20% of the fair market value of the outstanding stock of the combined enterprise. An excellent analysis of § 382(b) appears in the following:

COMMENT, NET OPERATING LOSS CARRYOVERS AND CORPORATE ADJUSTMENTS: RETAINING AN ADVANTAGEOUS TAX HISTORY UNDER LIBSON SHOPS AND SECTIONS 269, 381, AND 382 [13]

69 Yale L.J. 1249–1257 (1960).

For example, where X, a loss corporation, was merged into Y Corporation in an (A) reorganization, Y Corporation — the survivor — will inherit X's carryover without limitation by section 382(b) only if X's former shareholders receive at least a 20 per cent interest in Y. Section 382(b) also affects transactions not governed by section 381(a) since carryforwards of the acquiring corporation are expressly made subject to its provisions; section 381(a) deals only with the tax attributes of the transferor corporation.

Thus, if Y Corporation merged into X Corporation, a loss corporation, in an (A) reorganization, . . . unless X's former shareholders retain a 20 per cent interest in X, section 382(b) would limit X's own carryover. Stated differently, if Y's former shareholders receive more than 80 per cent interest in X pursuant to the plan of reorganization, X's carryover will be reduced. Section 382(b) does not apply to tax-free liquidations of subsidiaries (although they are included within 381(a) (1)), taxfree transactions other than those described in section 381(a) (2),* or any taxable transaction. Additionally, section 382(b) has no applicability to carrybacks.

Underlying section 382(b) is an apparent belief that certain shifts in ownership indicate abuse of the corporate carryover privilege. Congress did not want a totally new group of shareholders to reap the benefit of a loss incurred by a corporation under different ownership even though the loss corporation's shareholders have benefited by receiving a premium as a result of the carryover. Thus, the statute attempts to ensure that the corporation which ultimately utilizes the carryover be at least one-fifth owned by persons on whom the loss "really" fell. Congress might have left prevention of manipulation of losses to section 269. But the difficulties of proving a principal tax avoidance purpose highlighted the need for an "objective" test

---

13. Copyright, Yale Law Journal, 1960. Reprinted by permission. Portions of the text and most of the footnotes omitted.

* [Ed. note] Thus a transaction consisting of a stock acquisition qualifying under § 368(a) (1) (B) followed by a liquidation qualifying under § 332 would literally be free of § 382(b). However, the regulations warn that such a two-step acquisition may well be viewed as a § 368(a) (1) (C) reorganization "for purposes of § 382 (b)." Reg. § 1.382(b)–1(c).

which could be used to disallow carryovers. Perhaps the search for objectivity also prompted the failure to adopt any type of "same business" test. Whatever the rationale, many problems of construction arise under section 382(b) which may diminish its value as an objective supplement to section 269.

The first hurdle in determining whether the stockholders of the loss corporation own less than a 20 per cent interest of the acquiring corporation is ascertainment of the "stockholders" of the loss corporation. Section 382(b) might be interpreted to require that every shareholder of the loss corporation receive stock in the acquiring corporation. But under the usual "continuity of interest" test applied in reorganizations only the group as a whole is considered. Thus if any shareholder of the loss corporation, or any group of shareholders, own the requisite 20 per cent, section 382(b) will probably be satisfied. . . .

The continuity of interest might be rendered nugatory unless section 382(b)'s reference to "immediately after the reorganization" is given an expansive meaning. . . . To prevent avoidance of section 382(b), "immediately after the reorganization" should be interpreted in the same manner as those words are read under section 351. Under this reading, a sale of stock shortly after the reorganization which is deemed an integral part of the transaction will disqualify the shares sold from being counted toward the 20 per cent since "momentary control" would not be sufficient. . . .

In one situation, the requirement that the loss corporation's *shareholders* own stock in the acquiring corporation "immediately after" the reorganization may make the allowance of a carryforward under section 381(a) illusory. . . . If the transferor-loss corporation retains the stock, its stockholders would not "own" the stock of the acquiring corporation "immediately after" the transaction and the 20 per cent continuity of interest requirement would not be satisfied. . . . This problem may be avoided if the transaction is cast so that the loss corporation is the acquiring corporation in the (C) reorganization. The loss corporation's shareholders would continue to "own" the same stock which they had previously owned; whether the transferor remained in existence would be unimportant since ownership of stock by the nonloss corporation's shareholders is irrelevant under section 382(b).

* * *

If no problems of ownership arise, owners of the loss corporation will still have to demonstrate that their interest in the acquiring corporation qualifies as "stock." For purposes of section 382 "stock" is defined, in section 382(c), as "all shares except nonvoting stock which is limited and preferred as to dividends." Thus either voting or financial equity in the acquiring corporation will suffice. The theory underlying section 382(b) was apparently that the loss corporation's shareholders must retain a significant economic stake in the acquiring corporation so that "too much" of the carryover's benefit does not accrue to outsiders. The right to vote, however, does not seem sufficiently related to enjoyment of the carryover. Additionally, the statute does not give specific content to the phrase "nonvoting stock" and it could be interpreted narrowly so that any stock with a contingent right to vote would qualify as "stock." On the other hand, if the construction of a similar phrase in section 1504 which defines the type of stock ownership required for consolidated returns "affiliation" will be applicable to section 382(c), stock possessing the right to vote only when dividend arrearages or other contingencies occur will probably not qualify. In any event, use of voting preferred stock to acquire a carryover is limited by section 382(b)'s requirement that the stock represent 20 per cent of the fair market value of the acquiring corporation's "stock." When a profitable corporation acquires a loss corporation's assets many shares of such nonparticipating stock will probably have to be issued for the value to equal 20 per cent of all outstanding "stock."

Owning stock in the acquiring corporation will not satisfy section 382(b), however, unless persons holding such stock acquired it "as a result of owning stock of the loss corporation." Apparently section 382(c)'s definition of "stock" applies to the stock previously owned as well as to that acquired, so that the new shareholders of the acquiring corporation must have held either voting stock in the loss corporation or stock which was not limited and preferred as to dividends. This requirement creates a strict continuity-of-interest test, since only the interest of persons with voting or financial equity in both the loss corporation and the acquiring corporation will be counted toward the requisite 20 per cent. Curiously, however, a person with a financial equity in the loss corporation and only voting equity in the acquiring corporation will, under the statutory language, be counted, even though his interest has been drastically altered. The Senate Committee Report on section 382(b) indicated that the section was designed only to force the acquiring corporation to give up a 20 per cent share. This result could have been achieved by focusing solely on the stock given up, without regard to the prior interest of the new owners. But even if the statutory definition of "stock" is applied to the interest given up by the loss corporation's shareholders, the restriction may be circumvented. Knowing that a merger is imminent, the shareholders of the loss corporation can agree to a recapitalization which will give the preferred stock voting rights. Stock subsequently obtained by the preferred holders will thus be counted toward the 20 per cent requirement. The extent to which the Service must recognize this transaction is speculative.

Section 382(b) (6) may provide another method of avoiding the requirement that the 20 per cent be held by former holders of the loss corporation's "stock." This subsection was designed to mesh the general 20 per cent requirement with three party transactions qualifying as (C) reorganizations. . . . In contrast to section 382(b) (1) (B) which applies to two party transactions, section 382(b) (6) only refers to a 20 per cent interest obtained "as a result of the reorganization" and not "as a result of owning stock in the loss corporation." Thus section 382(b) (6) seems to ignore the quality of stock given up by the loss corporation's stockholders. Under this construction, the limitations of section 382(b) (1) (B) on the type of stock which must be surrendered by the loss corporation's shareholders could be evaded by recasting an ordinary two-party (C) reorganization as a three-party transaction. . . . This evasion can be frustrated, however, if "stockholders" in section 382(b) (6) is construed to incorporate section 382(c)'s definition of "stock." The difference in language between section 382(b) (6) and section 382(b) (1) (B) was probably inadvertent and no difference in outcome was intended.

The entire 20 per cent problem is moot if the reorganization involves two corporations owned by the same economic group. Under section 382(b) (3) the limitation of the carryforward "shall not apply if the transferor corporation and the acquiring corporation are owned substantially by the same persons in the same proportion." [248] Congress must have assumed that such transactions do not involve tax avoidance, because the people whose corporation sustained the loss are the persons who will ultimately benefit from the carryforward. In any event, section 382(b) (3) may have little significance in the light of section 382(b) (1) (B). Assume that individuals A and B each own 50 per cent of loss corporation X and profitable corporation Y. If X is merged into Y in a (C) reorganization so that A and B surrender their stock in X for stock in Y, section 382(b) (1) (B) is satisfied if the new stock they receive in Y is equivalent to 20 per cent of the value of Y's outstanding stock. This requirement presents no difficulty since A and B's equity interests will be unaffected if Y Corporation prints new stock certificates to satisfy the 20 per cent requirement. Therefore, while section 382(b) (3) eliminates the need to issue new stock in this situation, it is not needed to transfer the carryover.[250] Even for this limited purpose section 382(b) (3) may

248. This language seems to have meant "owned by *substantially* the same persons in *substantially* the same proportions." In the statute as written it is arguable that "substantially" (an adverb) modifies "owned"; therefore "same persons in the same proportion" means exactly the same. [Ed. note: The regulations contain examples indicating that where two persons each own 50% of the stock of one corporation, ownership of 48% and 52% respectively of the second corporation's would qualify under § 382(b) (3), but ownership of 60%, and 40% would not. Reg. § 1.382(b)-1(d) (2), Ex. 1 and 2.]

250. If X Corporation is worth substantially less than Y Corporation, however, the Commissioner could argue, in the absence of § 382(b) (3), that the 20% interest was not acquired as a result of the surrender of X stock but only to meet the statutory requirement. Such an argument would be based on the origin of the 20% requirement. The original House bill denied nonrecognition treatment to reorganizations of closely held companies where, in general, one of the two combining corporations was worth more than four times as much as the other. Hence, the 20% test of § 382

be difficult to apply because no content is given to the word "own." Suppose that an individual owns stock in the acquiring corporation and bonds in the transferor. In some circumstances a bondholder may be viewed as an owner, but section 382(b) (3) does not indicate whether "ownership" includes ownership of stock or securities other than those defined in 382(c). Additionally, there is no indication whether ownership in "substantially . . . the same proportion" is to be measured by financial equity or by voting equity. Since voting equity is sufficient for other parts of section 382(b), a substantially similar share of voting power in both corporations may satisfy section 382(b) (3) although financial interests are disparate. Or, perhaps only financial interests are to be considered, irrespective of voting rights.* Once the measuring factors are ascertained, what is "substantially . . . in the same proportion" will still have to be determined.

If section 382(b) (3) is inapplicable and the 20 per cent requirement of section 382(b) (1) (B) is not satisfied, section 382(b) (2) provides for a proportional reduction of the amount of the available carryforward. The carryforward will be reduced 5 per cent for every one per cent less than 20 which the loss corporation's shareholders obtain or retain in the acquiring corporation. For example, if these shareholders obtain twelve per cent, the acquiring corporation will inherit $^{12}/_{20}$ (60 per cent) of the carryover. . . .

NOTE ON MECHANICS OF § 382(b)

The mechanics of reducing an operating loss carryover pursuant to § 382 (b) are somewhat complicated by the need for integrating the reduction into the general carryforward process, under which the operating loss of each prior year is applied in chronological order and expires after a period of five years. One way of handling this would be simply to reduce the operating loss of each prior year by the percentage called for under § 382(b) and then just follow the normal procedure for "using up" the balance of each such loss. To illustrate, suppose that at the time of its acquisition on November 1, 1964, X had a total operating loss carryover of $140,000, consisting of $120,000 which was incurred in 1960 and was due to expire in the post-acquisition part year of 1964 of the acquiring corporation, Y, and $20,000 incurred in 1961 and therefore not due to expire until Y's year 1965. Suppose further that the stockholders of X received 13.4% of the stock of Y, which would make the § 382(b) reduction 33%. If this reduction percentage was simply applied to each year's losses, the carryovers from X would become $80,400 due to expire in Y's 1964 post-acquisition part year, and $13,400 due to expire in 1965, making a total carryover of $93,800. These losses would first be carried to Y's post-acquisition part year, in which, let us assume, the income before

---

(b). The Government could, on this theory, argue that "as a result of owning stock in the loss corporation" requires a comparison of the values of the transferor and acquiring corporations. . . .

*[Ed. note] The regulation examples indicate that "fair market value", which is expressly the factor to which the basic 20% test is applied, will also be used in applying the § 382(b) (3) test. Reg. § 1.382(b)–1(d) (2).

taxes (computed in accordance with § 381(c)(1)) amounted to $68,000. In that event, only $68,000 of the loss carryover would be effectively "used" in Y's post-acquisition part year; but the entire $80,400 from the 1960 loss would be gone, having expired by the passage of time, and only the $13,400 from the 1961 loss would be available as a carryforward to 1965.

While the foregoing would seem to be an entirely appropriate method for handling the § 382(b) reduction, the statute in fact calls for a different procedure. Under § 382(b)(1) the reduction is applied in gross to "the total net operating loss carryover from prior taxable years of the loss corporation to the first taxable year of the acquiring corporation ending after the date of transfer". However, as a corollary to this approach § 382(b)(4) provides that in computing the loss carryovers to subsequent taxable years, the income for that first taxable year of the combined enterprise must be constructively increased by the total amount of the § 382(b) reduction.

Applying this procedure to the foregoing example, the total loss carryover from X to Y's post-acquisition part year would be reduced to $93,800, just as before; and again $68,000 of that amount would be offset against Y's net income for that period. The difference comes in computing the amount of loss carryover which can be carried forward to 1965. Here the § 382(b) reduction is ignored, and the computation is made upon the basis of the original, unreduced amount of the loss carryovers; but in determining how much of the loss carryovers was "used up" in Y's post-acquisition part year the income of that period is treated as though it was actually larger by the amount of the § 382(b) reduction. Thus the amount of X's loss carryover used up in Y's post-acquisition part year would amount to $114,200 (actual net income of $68,000 plus constructive increase of $46,200), thereby apparently leaving $25,800 of loss to be carried forward to 1965. Actually, of course the full $25,800 could not be carried to 1965, since the entire $120,000 loss from 1960 would have expired by the passage of time, regardless of how much of it had been "used up" in Y's post-acquisition part year, and only the $20,000 loss from 1961 would remain eligible for carryforward. But the important point is that since under the statutory procedure the § 382(b) reduction is only applicable as such in the first year of Y to which X's losses are carried, and not to any subsequent years, the entire $20,000 loss from 1961 could be carried to 1965, whereas under the previous approach the carryforward to 1965 was limited to $13,400.

What this means is that the mechanics adopted by the statute throw the major brunt of a § 382(b) reduction upon the losses of the earliest years, instead of spreading it pro rata among all of the losses of prior years. This approach is quite favorable to taxpayers, since it does not seem that it could ever produce any disadvantage, and it may often materially benefit the taxpayer, as it does in the foregoing case where all of the § 382(b) reduction is offset against losses which would have expired by the passage of time anyway.

b. SECTION 382(a)

Section 382(a) represents an effort to establish objective criteria for limiting a corporation's carryover of its own operating losses where there has been a substantial change in the stock ownership of the corporation *and* it has not continued to carry on substantially the same business conducted before the change in stock ownership. This of course is the classic case of "trafficking in loss corporations" with which Congress was particularly concerned in 1954. See S.Rep.No. 1622, 83d Cong., 2d Sess. 53 (1954). However, § 382(a) has no application to tax-free combination transactions even if the loss corporation remains in existence (as where it is the acquiring corporation, or where it is the acquired corporation in a B reorganization and is not liquidated), since § 382(a)(4) expressly confines this provision to cases when the change in stock ownership does not involve any carryover basis; in a tax-free combination, of course, the change in the loss corporation's stock ownership would involve a carryover basis. Accordingly, further consideration of § 382(a) will be postponed until the discussion of operating loss carryovers in non-reorganization transactions, in paragraph 4 below.

c. The Libson Shops Doctrine

Although the Libson Shops case, page 848 supra, was decided under the 1939 Code, the Service has insisted that the "same business" test announced there may also be applicable under the 1954 Code. However, as the following excerpt indicates, the Service has not sought to import this doctrine into the tax-free combination area, so here again further discussion of the issue will be postponed until paragraph 4 below.

REVENUE RULING 58–603

1958–2 Cum.Bull. 147.

In Libson Shops, Inc., v. Koehler, . . . the Supreme Court of the United States announced the principle that, under the Internal Revenue Code of 1939, a surviving corporation in a merger may not carry over and deduct pre-merger net operating losses of one business against post-merger income of another business which was operated and taxed separately before the merger. The principle announced in that case will not be relied upon by the Internal Revenue Service under the Internal Revenue Code of 1954 as to a merger or any other transaction described in section 381(a) of the 1954 Code. However, see sections 382(b) and 269 of the 1954 Code for the possible disallowance of net operating loss carryovers in such transactions . . . ..

d. Section 269

An analysis of the development of § 269 as an anti-avoidance tool appears at pages 168–169, supra, and should be reviewed at this point. In recent years the Service has had a good deal of success in relying upon § 269 in the area of loss carryovers. See generally, Feder, The

Application of Section 269 to Corporations Having Net Operating Loss Carryovers and Potential Losses, 21 N.Y.U.Inst.Fed.Tax 1277 (1963). Moreover, in 1962 the final regulations under § 269 finally appeared, and they clearly confirm the Service's intention to apply this section quite broadly to limit "trafficking" in loss carryovers. Needless to say, however, there remain a number of unanswered problems in connection with § 269, quite apart from the always troublesome questions associated with determining purpose.

The potential impact of § 269 on combination transactions can best be illustrated by a series of examples. Consider first the typical case in which a loss corporation is acquired in a merger (or assets acquisition) to which § 381 applies. Such a transaction would obviously be subject to § 269(a)(2), since the acquiring profit corporation would take the acquired loss corporation's property at the latter's basis. Would it make any difference if the loss carryovers had already been reduced to some extent (but not eliminated) under § 382(b)? The Senate Finance Committee Report, S.Rep.No.1622, 83d Cong., 2d Session 284 (1954), contains an implication that once § 382(b) applies to limit a carryover, § 269 "shall not also be applied". But this would mean that by planning for a small reduction under § 382(b), complete immunity from § 269 could be obtained. Reg. § 1.269–6 flatly rejects this position and requires that to whatever extent a carryover survives § 382(b) it must also pass the screen of § 269.

Suppose that the combination takes the form of the loss corporation acquiring the profitable one. Assuming that the former stockholders of the profit corporation end up with at least 50% of the stock of the loss corporation, the transaction would be subject to § 269(a)(1) — unlike § 382(a), § 269(a).(1) is equally applicable to tax-free acquisitions of control. Presumably, § 269(a)(2) could also be applicable, since the loss corporation has acquired the profit corporation's property and holds it at a carryover basis. To be sure, that acquisition of property from the profit corporation did not itself produce or increase any loss carryover, but it does enable the loss corporation to enjoy the benefit of its already-existing loss carryover, and under the Coastal Oil approach to § 269(a)(2), see page 169 supra, that may be enough to bring this section into play.

However, this example serves as another illustration of the flaw in the Coastal Oil interpretation of § 269(a)(2). If the loss corporation acquires profit-making assets in a taxable transaction, § 269(a)(2) would clearly be inapplicable even though the tax benefit would be exactly the same. In other words, in this situation the carryover of asset basis, despite being the operative condition for the application of § 269(a)(2), is actually irrelevant to the tax benefit achieved. It may make more sense to confine § 269(a)(2) to cases where the tax benefit in question is related to the carryover of asset basis, either directly, as in the case of high basis, low value assets, or collaterally, as in the case of a corresponding carryover of losses. See Feder, op. cit. supra, at 1297–98.

Curiously, the regulations contain no example of a combination transaction involving the acquisition of a profit corporation by a loss corporation. But this much seems clear: one way or another, § 269 should be no less applicable when the combination transaction proceeds in this direction as when the profit corporation acquires the loss corporation.

Suppose that the combination takes the form of an acquisition of the stock of the loss corporation by the profit corporation. What alternatives are available for offsetting the loss carryovers against the profits of the acquiring corporation (apart from using consolidated returns, which will be discussed in the next section)? One possibility is to liquidate the subsidiary loss corporation and try to transfer the loss carryovers to the parent profit corporation under § 381(c)(1). But that is possible, per § 381(a)(1), only if the parent takes the assets from the subsidiary at the latter's basis under § 334(b)(1) (rather than at the parent's cost of the stock under § 334(b)(2)) — and in that event, § 269(a)(2) would be operative, just as it would in the case of a direct asset acquisition in an A or C reorganization. To be sure, the exception for common control in § 269(a)(2) would be literally applicable, but the fleeting control involved in these circumstances would probably be ignored under the step transaction doctrine.

Another possibility would be for the parent corporation to transfer some of its own profit-making assets to its newly-acquired subsidiary. Under the Coastal Oil interpretation, § 269(a)(2) would seem to be applicable: the transfer of assets would enable the loss corporation to "enjoy" its existing carryovers. And the exception for common control would not apply since neither the transferee (subsidiary) corporation nor its stockholders would have been in control of the transferor (parent) corporation immediately before the transfer. The regulations, § 1.269–6, Ex. 3, expressly provide that this type of case is subject to § 269(a)(2), thus confirming the Coastal Oil approach. However, it should be noted that the regulation example specifies that it is dealing with a case in which if the loss subsidiary was liquidated its assets would be taken by the parent at the latter's stock cost under § 334(b)(2), and the operating losses would not carryover under § 381(c)(1). This seems to be an effort to make it clear that acquisition of the stock of the loss corporation did not qualify as a B reorganization (since a reorganization acquisition would not constitute a "purchase" under § 334(b)(3) and hence a § 334(b)(2) basis would not be possible); but the example gives no clue as to what difference it would make, if any, if the circumstances were otherwise so that the losses would carryover in a liquidation.

Presumably § 269(a)(1) could also apply to this type of case, under a kind of step transaction approach, if the purpose of the profit corporation's acquisition of control of the loss corporation was to obtain the benefit of the latter's loss carryovers by transferring profit-making assets to it.

What is the role of § 269(c) in combination transactions? As is true of the rest of § 269, subsection (c) applies equally to tax-free acquisitions. But it is difficult to fathom just what this provision was designed to accomplish. Reg. § 1.269–5 indicates that "substantially disproportionate to" is intended to mean "substantially less than". Applying this interpretation to a purchase of high basis, low value assets, it would appear that the presumption arises if the purchase price is based primarily on value, and does not include any additional element for the attractive tax attributes. In other words, the section seems to treat the beneficial tax attributes as property which the purchaser *should pay for*, although the general theme of § 269 would seem to cut the other way, i. e., that the purchaser should not be buying the tax attributes as such. This curious inconsistency has been noted by the Tax Court on several occasions. See H. F. Ramsey Co. Inc. v. Commissioner, 43 T.C. 500, 517 (1965); The Wallace Corporation v. Commissioner, 23 T.C.M. 39, 53, note 6 (1964). In any event, it seems likely that a purchaser who is not swayed by tax factors and sticks to asset value will not run afoul of § 269, no matter how "disproportionate" the price within the meaning of § 269(c). This means that the onus of § 269(c) may fall most heavily upon the purchaser who does pay something extra on account of the tax attributes, so that he can not deny that the potential tax advantages were in the picture, but does not pay enough extra to escape the "substantially disproportionate" price test. And what standards are available for determining how much is "enough" in this context, bearing in mind the uncertainty of the value of the prospective tax benefits in view of their dependence on the purchaser's future income?

e. CONSOLIDATED RETURNS

The following case serves as both a postscript to the preceding material on § 269 and an introduction to the subject of consolidated returns.

ZANESVILLE INVESTMENT CO. v. COMMISSIONER [14]

United States Courts of Appeals, Sixth Circuit, 1964. 335 F.2d 507.

LEVIN, DISTRICT JUDGE. The question presented for decision is whether Section 269 of the Internal Revenue Code of 1954 or some judicially enunciated principle of law prevents the offsetting in a consolidated return of cash operating losses and losses realized on

---

14. Portions of the opinion and all of the footnotes omitted.

the sale of physical assets sustained after affiliation by one corporate member of an affiliated group with the post-affiliation profits of another corporate member thereof, where it could be anticipated that such operating losses would be incurred.

The cases principally relied on by the Government are not apposite, as they all concern situations where a taxpayer was attempting to utilize built-in tax losses (i. e., losses which had economically accrued prior to the affiliation but which had not as yet been realized in a tax sense), whereas the taxpayer in this case is attempting to offset actual cash losses incurred both economically and taxwise after the affiliation.

Since the Government cites no authority in point and independent research discloses none, it will be necessary to review the history of Section 269 and the consolidated returns provisions to determine whether the interpretation sought by the Commissioner is correct. The facts of this case are as follows:

During the period 1951 through August 31, 1955, a coal mine corporation (Muskingum Coal Company), which in prior years had been highly profitable (almost four million dollars of net income in the period 1945 to 1950), sustained operating losses of about $730,000 in an attempt to develop a new mine opening to replace the prior mine opening which had been exhausted. These losses had been financed in part by loans from the taxpayer and its wholly-owned subsidiary, Earl J. Jones Enterprises, Inc., totaling $320,268.68, during the period from September 1953 to August 1955, of which $42,930.79 was repaid. Enterprises was profitably engaged in operating a newspaper.

In September 1955, Muskingum was in the process of attempting to solve its problems through a new type of mechanization, but encountered continuing difficulty. Muskingum did not have adequate funds either to finance the purchase of such equipment or absorb the operating losses that almost certainly would continue to be sustained before profitable operations might be expected.

At this juncture, on September 1, 1955, Earl J. Jones, the sole stockholder of Muskingum since 1945, transferred all the stock thereof to the taxpayer (of which, since 1948, he was also the sole stockholder).

The Tax Court found (38 T.C. at p. 414) that the principal purpose of the transfer to the taxpayer of the stock of Muskingum (the losing coal mine business) was to utilize Muskingum's "anticipated" losses on a consolidated return to be filed with the other members of the affiliated group, including the profitable newspaper publisher (Enterprises) and that this was interdicted under the provisions of Section 269 . . . .

The taxpayer, Enterprises, and Muskingum filed consolidated returns for 1955 and 1956. Muskingum sustained an operating loss of $176,806 during the period September 1 to December 31, 1955, and an operating loss of $369,950 during the period January 1 to July 10, 1956. In July 1956 Muskingum sold its mine properties at a net loss of about $480,000 and later filed a petition in bankruptcy. Enterprises' taxable income in 1955 was $175,283.61 and during the first seven months of 1956 was $102,496.46. Enterprises operated profitably also in subsequent periods.

Both prior and subsequent to affiliation, Muskingum's operations were extensive, its sales were at an annual rate in excess of two million dollars, and it employed several hundred persons throughout the period in question. Muskingum attempted to sell its properties between October 1955 and June 1956, and various transactions were discussed, negotiated, and, in two cases, documented; but none was consummated. Had any been consummated, Muskingum's properties would have been disposed of at a tax gain rather than a loss.

It is not disputed that Muskingum and the other members of the affiliated group that were financing it were engaged in a good faith but unsuccessful attempt to overcome the engineering problems and thereby render operations at the second mine opening economically profitable. In this connection, the taxpayer and Enterprises made further advances of $161,359.28 to Muskingum in the post-affiliation period, of which $44,966.59 was repaid. The total investment in physical assets, in an attempt to bring in the second mine opening, was $1,026,610.30, of which $247,309.01 was spent in the post-affiliation period. It would thus appear that approximately $247,000 of the $480,000 net loss realized on the sale of Muskingum's properties was paid for in cash after affiliation. The Government has not contended that such loss was incurred in an economic sense prior to affiliation.

Section 129 of the Internal Revenue Code of 1939, now Section 269 of the I.R.C. of 1954, was added in early 1944 to prevent the distortion through tax avoidance of the deduction, credit, and allowance provisions of the Code and, particularly, the then recently developed practice of corporations with large incomes acquiring corporations with built-in losses, credits, or allowances . . . . Most of the cases that have arisen under Section 269 and its predecessor, Section 129, have dealt with the sale by one control group to another of a corporation with, typically, a net-operating loss carryover, and the efforts of the new control group to utilize this carryover by funneling otherwise taxable income to a point of alleged confluence with the carryover.

Until this case, the Commissioner made no attempt in the approximately twenty years since enactment of Section 129 (now Section 269), so far as the reported cases indicate, to deny a taxpayer the right to offset an out-of-pocket dollar loss incurred after affiliation with post-affiliation income. We do not believe that Section 269 requires such a result.

An examination of the Senate Finance Committee report accompanying the Revenue Act of 1943, which enacted Section 129 of the I.R.C. of 1939, reveals that the statutory language cannot be mechanically interpreted and that all acquisitions that result in tax saving are not prohibited. The test, according to the Senate Finance Committee, is:

". . . whether the transaction or a particular factor thereof 'distorts the liability of the particular taxpayer' when the 'essential nature' of the transaction or factor is examined in the light of the *legislative plan* which the deduction or credit is intended to effectuate." 1944 Cum.Bull., p. 1017. (Emphasis added.)

* * *

In deciding whether the essential nature of the transaction before this court violates the "legislative plan," the fact that the Tax Court's decision is the first in the heavily litigated tax field where a court was asked to deny a taxpayer the right to use real post-affiliation losses, incurred and paid in cash after affiliation, against post-affiliation income suggests that the legislative plan may not be violated by allowing the deduction.

Individuals, partnerships, and corporations have long been permitted to offset the losses incurred in one business of the taxpayer against profits realized by another business of the same taxpayer. Thus, there is no "legislative plan" that prohibits such offsetting. In fact, the Internal Revenue Code permits an individual, partnership, or corporate taxpayer to do just that.

But here, the loss was incurred by one entity, and the profit was realized by another. What is the legislative plan in this regard?

Congress first required and now permits certain affiliated corporations to file consolidated returns and to offset the losses of one against the profits of another. The consolidated return regulations forbid the use of pre-affiliation losses of one entity against pre- or post-affiliation consolidated income (Reg. 1.1502–31(b) (3)) but have never suggested that post-affiliation losses may not be utilized against post-affiliation consolidated income. In fact, these regulations specifically permit the use of post-affiliation losses against post-affiliation consolidated income. (Reg. 1.1502–31(b)).

All the cases cited by the Government where consolidation was denied involved situations where the taxpayer sought to take advantage of the realization after affiliation of losses which in an economic sense had occurred prior to the affiliation. In J. D. & A. B. Spreckels Company, 41 B.T.A. 370 (1940), after the loss corporation had contracted to sell its remaining asset at a tax loss of $192,000, its sole stockholder transferred all its capital stock to the taxpayer there before the court. The sale was consummated, and the economic loss of $192,000 incurred prior to the affiliation was realized in a tax sense.

The Tax Court (then the Board of Tax Appeals) refused to permit such loss (which, to repeat, had accrued prior to the affiliation) to be utilized against the income of other members of the new affiliated group.

In Elko Realty Company, 29 T.C. 1012 (1958), affirmed in Elko Realty Company v. Commissioner, 260 F.2d 949 (3rd Cir. 1958), the taxpayer corporation acquired for a nominal consideration the stock of two separate corporations each owning apartment houses which were subject to FHA insured mortgages in excess of their cost, and an attempt was made to utilize the large depreciation losses against consolidated income. It was found that there was no intent that the apartment house corporations could ever be made to operate profitably. There was no showing that the value of the apartment houses at the time of the acquisition equalled the bases for depreciation. Compare Regulation 1.1502–31(b) excluding in the determination of the consolidated income deductions with respect to the sale or exchange of capital assets to the extent that such deductions are attributable to events preceding the affiliation.

R. P. Collins & Co., Inc. v. United States, 303 F.2d 142 (1st Cir. 1962), was concerned with an acquisition by one control group from another of stock of a corporation owning property with a built-in tax loss. A deduction for the tax loss was claimed on the subsequent sale of the property and realization of the economic loss incurred prior to affiliation. Post-affiliation operating losses were also suffered and a majority of the court thought that their utilization should also be denied because once it was determined that the acquisition was within the coverage of Section 269 all losses, including post-affiliation economic losses, must be denied. The dissenting judge would have allowed the post-affiliation operating loss. Collins, however, is not authority for the proposition here advanced by the Government because even the majority would not have disallowed the post-affiliation operating loss if it stood by itself, as it does in this case, and only denied the post-affiliation operating loss because it was thought to be tainted as in respect to the built-in loss the use of which, as we have seen, Section 269 was designed to prevent. The fact that the dissenting judge in Collins would have allowed the post-affiliation operating loss and the two majority judges denied it only because it was tainted ("They are tarred by the same brush," 303 F.2d at p. 146), as incidental to the built-in loss, tends to support the taxpayer's view that post-affiliation operating losses standing by themselves are not within the coverage of Section 269.

An individual or corporate member of a partnership is entitled to offset the losses of the partnership (except to the extent they exceed the basis of the member's interest in the partnership) against income derived by such member from other sources, including from other partnerships. . . . An individual stockholder of a tax option

(Sub-Chapter S) corporation is permitted, to the extent of his investment, to utilize the losses of such a corporation against other income.
. . .

Similarly, had Earl Jones dissolved all three corporations he could have utilized the Muskingum losses against the publishing company's profits; or if he had dissolved Muskingum and contributed its property to the taxpayer or to Enterprises he could have accomplished a similar result.

In Revenue Ruling 63–40, 1963–1 Cum.Bull. 46, the Internal Revenue Service stated its view that where there is no change in the control group, Section 269 was not applicable to the addition of a new profitable business to a loss corporation, which had discontinued the money losing business, even if the means by which this was accomplished was the purchase by the loss corporation of the stock of the money-making business and the transfer of its assets in liquidation to its new stockholder. Compare Kolker Brothers, Inc., 35 T.C. 299 (1960).

Section 382 of the Internal Revenue Code of 1954 expressly permits the use of historical losses against the income of other businesses where either there has not been a change in the control group (as defined therein) or there has not been a substantial change in the trade or business conducted before the change in control. One would think that if the same control group could, after the loss, add new income (Revenue Ruling 63–40, supra), there would be no objection to the offsetting of a future loss against future income. The latter case, which is the case before this court, would appear to be a stronger one for the taxpayer.

Although the Government is correct in stating that the transaction must be viewed in the light of what was done, rather than on the basis of what might have been done, one is left with the definite impression that there is no legislative plan to deny the utilization of post-affiliation losses against post-affiliation income and one suspects that one of the basic reasons why taxpayers consolidated corporations and paid the two per cent penalty that prior to the enactment of the Revenue Act of 1964 was payable on consolidated taxable income, was to be able to offset the losses of one corporation against the profits of another. Inherent in the concept of consolidation is the offsetting of loss against income.

The legislative plan is perhaps best revealed by the following excerpts from the Senate Finance Committee report accompanying the Revenue Act of 1928:

> "The permission to file consolidated returns by affiliated corporations merely recognizes the business entity as distinguished from the legal corporate entity of the business enterprise. Unless the affiliated group as a whole in the conduct of its business enterprise shows net profits, the individuals

conducting the business have realized no gain. The failure to recognize the entire business enterprise means drawing technical legal distinctions, as contrasted with the recognition of actual facts. The mere fact that by legal fiction several corporations owned by the same stockholders are separate entities should not obscure the fact that they are in reality one and the same business owned by the same individuals and operated as a unit. To refuse to recognize this situation and to require for tax purposes the breaking up of a single business into its constituent parts is just as unreasonable as to require a single corporation to report separately for tax purposes the gains from its sales department, from its manufacturing activities, from its investments, and from each and every one of its agencies. It would be just as unreasonable to demand that an individual engaged in two or more businesses treat each business separately for tax purposes. . . ."

The Regulations promulgated pursuant to such authority have, as appears above, only prohibited the association of pre-affiliation losses with pre- or post-affiliation consolidated income, and have never prevented the offsetting of post-affiliation consolidated income with post-affiliation losses. The legislative plan has clearly been to encourage the filing of consolidated returns . . . .

This legislative attitude also finds expression in the House and Senate reports accompanying the Revenue Act of 1964, both of which contain the following statement:

"General reasons for provision.—The bill removes the special 2-percent penalty tax on the privilege of filing a consolidated return, in part because the return of commonly controlled corporations as a single economic unit for tax purposes is in accord with the reality of the situation. Moreover, there appears to be no reason why, where a group of commonly controlled corporations are willing to have their operations consolidated for tax purposes, the mere presence of more than one corporate organization in the group should result in any penalty tax. No such penalty, for example, is exacted in the case of other corporate organizations operating through divisions rather than separate corporations."

We have seen that the principal purpose of Section 269 was to deny those losses, credits, deductions, etc., which could only be obtained by acquiring (generally, by buying) a corporation which, because of its own history, had obtained such benefits and which benefits the acquiring person could not otherwise obtain.

* * *

It is noteworthy that the cases construing Section 269 to date have all involved situations where the loss sought to be utilized flowed from the corporation's individual past history or from the fact that the corporate rather than some other form of business organization was involved and was otherwise unobtainable under any other provision of the Code. But, as we have seen, that is not the case here, as Muskingum's losses could have been realized and offset against other income if the several businesses had been conducted in non-corporate forms or if Muskingum's assets had been dissolved into the taxpayer.

In this case, it may well be, as the Tax Court found, that the taxpayer desired to offset anticipated losses against income; but there is no evidence that such objective is violative of the legislative plan which permits just that in an effort to counter-balance profits with losses. The over-all purpose of Section 269 was to prevent distortion of a taxpayer's income resulting from the utilization of *someone else's loss* or a *built-in but unrealized loss* . . . ; but there is no indication that Section 269 was designed to prohibit the utilization of future losses against future income merely because a corporate rather than a partnership or individual proprietorship form of business enterprise was involved. We believe that it would be a distortion to deny the utilization of these losses which were incurred in good faith to save a business and that Section 269 does not require any such result.

In a recent decision, Naeter Brothers Publishing Co., 42 T.C. 1, decided April 2, 1964, the Tax Court, in an almost identical fact situation held that consolidation would be permitted. The following appears in the court's opinion:

"We think the anticipated consequences were Missourian's continued operating losses for a short time to be followed by profitable operation. It can hardly be said this was not realistic for it is exactly what did happen."

Actually, the portion of the business that caused the losses in the cited case never did become profitable. ". . . Missourian, apparently despairing of any profitable operations in the printing division, sold the . . ." same. The portion of the loss corporation's business that was profitable after said disposition was profitable before it. In any event, there is no basis for reaching different results based on whether the hoped-for ultimate profitable operation is in fact realized. Hindsight is always better than foresight, but should not be elevated to a standard for determining those consolidations that will be permitted and those that will be denied.

In view of this court's decision, it is unnecessary to consider taxpayer's alternative arguments that there was no acquisition because Earl J. Jones (the underlying controlling person) owned the stock of Muskingum many years before the prohibited purpose could come to mind, or that a loss deduction should be allowed alternatively at least to the extent of the loss realized on the sale of the physical assets in July 1956; the Government does not contend that this is a built-in loss (Regulation 1.1502–31(b) (9)). . . .

This case is remanded to the Tax Court for the entry of a judgment not inconsistent with this opinion.

Reversed.

NOTE ON CONSOLIDATED RETURNS

As the Zanesville case illustrates, consolidated returns may make it possible to offset the losses of one corporation against the profits of another even though the two corporations remain in existence and maintain their separate identities. Thus in the combination area consolidated returns could come into play when the combination takes the form of a B reorganization, and the acquired corporation is not liquidated. However, quite apart from § 269, there are some limitations on the use of consolidated returns to achieve tax advantages, particularly in connection with net operating loss carryovers; accordingly, a brief review of the rules governing consolidated returns is appropriate at this point.

While the primary source of authority for the use of consolidated returns is the statute, §§ 1501–1504, most of the rules governing the operation of consolidated returns are to be found in the regulations, which have a kind of semi-legislative status since the statute specifically delegates such rule-making power to the Secretary in this area. During 1964–1965 these regulations were the subject of a lengthy study by the Treasury and late in 1965 the Treasury promulgated proposed new regulations which represented a substantial revision. See generally, Cohen, The New Consolidated Return Regs: A Bird's-Eye View of the Extensive Changes, 24 Journ. of Tax. 82 (1966). Since there is little reason to expect that the final regulations will differ much from these proposed regulations, this analysis will focus principally on the proposed regulations.

As a starting point, it should be noted that consolidated returns may be filed by any "affiliated" group of corporations, which means any group of corporations connected through stock ownership with a common parent corporation if at least 80% of the voting stock and 80% of the non-voting common stock of each subsidiary is owned by one or more members of the group, and the common parent corporation owns that percentage of the stock of at least one other member of the group. When an affiliated group has remained the same throughout the taxable years involved, it is treated taxwise much the same as a single corporation, and any operating loss incurred by the group can be carried backwards and forwards in the same manner as for a single corporation. But when a group is newly formed (as in an acquisition transaction), or a corporation is added to (or dropped from) an existing consolidated group, the regulations impose certain limitations on carrying losses to or from a separate return year. Under Prop.Reg. § 1.1502–21 (as well as under the prior regulations), losses sustained by a corporation prior to the time of joining in a consolidated return (unless the corporation was a member of the affiliated group on every day of the year in which the loss occurred, even though it did not join in a consolidated return for that year) can only be carried forward against income produced by the loss corporation after consolidation, and cannot be applied against the income of other corporations in the group. Thus, for example, in the straightforward case of a profitable corporation acquiring the stock of a corporation with operating loss carryovers in a B reorganization (or in a taxable transaction, for that matter), the loss corporation's carryovers can only be applied against the future income of the loss corporation; and the same would be true if the transaction took the form of the loss corporation acquiring the stock of the profitable corporation.

However, there is still some room for maneuver. For example, after acquiring the stock of the loss corporation the profitable corporation might transfer some of its own profit-making assets to the loss corporation, thus assuring the loss corporation of income against which to apply its existing loss carryovers. In a sense, permitting this would seem to be inconsistent with the bar in the regulations against using pre-consolidation losses of one corporation against the post-consolidation income of the other. On the other hand, that bar is itself inconsistent with the fact that under § 381(c)(1) such losses and profits can be offset against each other if the two enterprises are combined into a single corporation, either pursuant to an A or C reorganization, or upon the liquidation of the acquired corporation after a B reorganization. Even more important, acquiring a loss corporation and injecting profit-making assets into it is not really a consolidated return problem anyway, since that can occur just as well if the corporations are filing separate returns. In other words, this is actually a variation of the single corporation case, where the question is to what extent the corporation's own loss carryovers survive a significant change in stock ownership and/or business operations. Assuming the acquisition took the form of a B reorganization, so that the change in stock ownership occurred in a non-taxable transaction, § 382(a) would not apply; but as we saw above, § 269 could be applicable, and, if it is still alive under the 1954 Code, so could the Libson Shops doctrine, discussed below, which was applied under the 1939 Code in just this type of situation. Commissioner v. Virginia Metal Products, Inc., 290 F.2d 675 (3d Cir. 1961).

Suppose the parent corporation of an affiliated group with existing loss carryovers acquires the stock of a profitable corporation. Literally, the limitation in the regulations on carrying forward pre-consolidation losses would not bar the utilization of this *consolidated loss*. But Prop.Reg. § 1.1502–21(d) provides in effect that where there has been a 50% change in the stock ownership of a consolidated group with loss carryovers (whether by purchase or tax-free reorganization), those losses may be carried forward only against the income of the old members of the group. This provision will normally operate to prevent offsetting existing loss carryovers against the profits of a new member of the group since the acquisition of a profitable corporation will generally result in its stockholders owning more than 50% of the acquiring loss parent's stock.

Under the prior regulations there were some special problems with regard to the operation of the loss carryover provisions in cases where the subsidiary had been created by the parent rather than acquired by it. Thus in Ruppert Plumbing & Heating Co. v. Commissioner, 39 T.C. 284 (1962), the question was whether the bar in the regulations against applying the pre-consolidation losses of one corporation against post-consolidation profits of a different corporation meant that a loss corporation which had transferred some of its assets to a newly-formed subsidiary could not carry forward its losses against the profits subsequently earned by the subsidiary. The Tax Court held that the regulation applied; but this decision has been overruled by Prop.Reg. § 1.1502–1(f), which provides, in effect, that losses of the common parent of an affiliated group may be carried forward without limitation against consolidated income, even though the parent's losses were incurred before the consolidated return period, subject of course to the 50% change of ownership limitation described above.

As to loss carrybacks, the general rule is that losses suffered during the consolidation period by a corporation which filed separate returns in prior years can only be carried back against the separate income of the loss corporation. However, if the loss corporation was not in existence in the prior years, then the loss incurred in the consolidation period can be included in the amount carried back against the consolidated income of the group in those prior years. Prop.Reg. § 1.1502–79(a)(2).

As the Zanesville opinion indicates, the consolidated return regulations have also sought to limit the use of consolidated returns to take advantage of so-called "built-in" losses, that is, losses which have already been economically incurred but have not yet been recognized for tax purposes. The classic "built-in" case is the corporation with high basis, low value assets whose stock is acquired by a profitable corporation which then files consolidated returns in an effort to utilize this built-in loss as it is recognized by the subsidiary either by sale of the assets or through the deduction for depreciation. Under Prop.Reg. § 1.1502–15 such built-in losses are not automatically disallowed, but are treated as if they were in fact recognized before the acquisition or affiliation date, and are then subjected to the limitations applicable to the carryover of net operating losses from pre-consolidation years. However, this limitation is not applicable (1) if the corporation with the built-in loss has been a member of the affiliated group for more than ten years at the start of the year in which the loss in question is actually recognized for tax purposes, or (2) if immediately before the date the corporation became a member of the group "the aggregate of the adjusted basis of all the assets (other than cash and good will) of such corporation did not exceed the fair market value of such assets by more than 15%".

When a loss subsidiary is liquidated, problems may arise with regard to the relationship between (1) the parent's utilization of the subsidiary's operating loss carryovers, and (2) any loss suffered by the parent in its investment in the subsidiary. Particularly in the case where the parent corporation itself organized the subsidiary and was the sole stockholder, there would often be a close economic relationship between the amount of the subsidiary's operating losses and the amount of the parent's investment loss. Normally, a corporation is entitled to an ordinary loss deduction for any advances made to its subsidiary; and by virtue of § 165(g)(3) a parent corporation which owns 95% of the stock of a subsidiary may also obtain an ordinary loss deduction for losses sustained on its investment in the stock or securities of the subsidiary. But in Charles Ilfeld Co. v. Hernandez, 292 U.S. 62, 54 S.Ct. 596, 78 L.Ed. 1127 (1934), a parent corporation which had offset the operating losses of its subsidiaries against its own income through the use of consolidated returns was not permitted to later deduct its investment losses in the subsidiaries, the Court stating that the parent should not be allowed to deduct twice what was in effect the same loss.

In a similar vein, suppose there are no consolidated returns in the picture, so that upon the liquidation of a loss subsidiary the parent is entitled to deduct its losses upon its advances to or investments in the subsidiary;

but the parent also seeks to carry over the subsidiary's operating losses, in accordance with § 381. Although nothing in § 381 limits the carryover in such circumstances, Marwais Steel Co. v. Commissioner, 354 F.2d 997 (9th Cir. 1965), refused to permit the carryover because it would result in a double deduction, the court relying principally on the Ilfeld case.

4. LIMITATIONS ON LOSS CARRYOVERS IN NON-REORGANIZATION TRANSACTIONS

It is in connection with non-reorganization acquisitions that most of the current furor relating to operating loss carryovers has arisen, particularly with regard to the question of the continued vitality of the Libson Shops doctrine under the 1954 Code:

REVENUE RULING 63–40
1963–1 Cum.Bull. 46.

Advice has been requested whether either the rationale of the decision in Libson Shops, Inc. v. Koehler, . . . or the provisions of section 269 of the Internal Revenue Code of 1954 prevent the use of a net operating loss carryover under the circumstances described below.

1. The M corporation was organized in 1947 by three individuals who owned an equal number of shares of its authorized and outstanding stock. From the date of its incorporation until the early part of 1958 it was engaged in the fabrication and sale, through distributors, of household light steel products. The business was successful during its early years of operation. However, commencing in 1953 it sustained losses in each of its taxable years and over the period ending December 31, 1957, had accumulated substantial net operating losses.

In 1958 M corporation purchased for cash, at fair market value, all of the assets of N corporation, which had a history of successful operation of drive-in restaurants. M and N were unrelated corporations and none of the shareholders of M corporation owned, directly or indirectly, any stock of N corporation. The funds for the cash purchase were derived in part from M corporation's own business assets and in part from an equal contribution to its capital of cash by its three stockholders. Shortly thereafter, M corporation discontinued its former business activity, sold the assets connected therewith, and engaged exclusively in the business of operating the chain of drive-in restaurants formerly operated by the N corporation.

Under the facts presented, neither section 269 nor section 382 of the Code is applicable and the sole question raised is whether the rationale of the Libson Shops decision bars the allowance of the net operating loss deduction attributable to losses incurred prior to the acquisition of the new business activity for M corporation's taxable year ended December 31, 1958.

In cases, like the one discussed above, arising under section 122 of the Internal Revenue Code of 1939 or section 172 of the 1954 Code in which losses have been incurred by a single corporation and there has been little or no change in the stock ownership of the corporation during or after the period in which the losses were incurred, the Internal Revenue Service will not rely on the rationale of the Libson Shops decision to bar the corporation from using losses previously incurred by it solely because such losses are attributable to a discontinued corporate activity. Accordingly, since there was no change in stock ownership in M corporation either before the discontinuance of its former business activity or after the commencement of its new business activity, a net operating loss deduction is allowable for its taxable year ended December 31, 1958.

However, if there is more than a minor change in stock ownership of a loss corporation which acquires a new business enterprise, the Service may continue to contest the deductibility of the carryover of the corporation's prior losses against income of the new business enterprise. . . .

2. Advice has also been requested whether the Service would apply different treatment to a case involving the same facts as are set out in the foregoing except for a difference in the method of acquisition by M corporation of the assets of N corporation. In this second case M corporation first attempted in extended negotiations to purchase the assets of N corporation, but the shareholders of N corporation were unwilling to consummate the transaction except by way of the sale of their stock to M corporation. M corporation purchased the stock of N corporation for cash, at fair market value, solely for the purpose of acquiring its assets to earn a profit with those assets and *immediately* liquidated that corporation under such circumstances that the basis of the assets to M corporation will be determined by the amount it paid for the stock of N corporation.

Under the facts of this second case, the Service will not contend that the acquisition of control of N corporation has as its principal purpose the evasion or avoidance of Federal income tax for purposes of section 269(a) of the Code. Accordingly, section 269 of the Code will not, under these facts, bar the M corporation from carrying over its prior losses and the conclusion reached with respect to the first case is equally applicable here.

No opinion is expressed as to other cases where the facts show that the purchase price is payable over a substantial period of time (whether or not specifically payable only out of earnings of the business) or exceeds fair market value or where other circumstances may justify the application of section 269 of the Code. . . .

MAXWELL HARDWARE CO. v. COMMISSIONER [15]

United States Court of Appeals, Ninth Circuit, 1965. 343 F.2d 713.

Before HAMLEY and MERRILL, CIRCUIT JUDGES, and THOMPSON, DISTRICT JUDGE.

THOMPSON, DISTRICT JUDGE. This is a petition for review of a decision of the Tax Court . . . . The Tax Court disallowed to Petitioner, Maxwell Hardware Company, a corporation, net operating loss carryover deductions taken for its tax years ending January 31, 1957 to 1960, inclusive.

In summary, the facts are that Maxwell Hardware had sustained approximately $1,000,000 of losses in a hardware business. It entered into an agreement with two partners, Beckett and Federighi, who were engaged in numerous real estate development activities as partners and controlling stockholders of corporations, whereby a real estate department was established in Maxwell Hardware to develop a subdivision, the funds therefor being furnished by the two partners through purchases of non-voting preferred stock in the corporation for an amount which was approximately two-fifths of the then value of the common stock of the corporation. The real estate department was accounted for independently of the other corporate business. The agreement provided that the real estate department should not be discontinued for a period of six years, that the preferred stockholders should not sell their stock for this period, and thereafter, if the department were discontinued at the option of either the corporation or preferred stockholders, the preferred stock should be redeemed by distribution in kind of ninety per cent of the department's assets to the preferred stockholders. A voting trust agreement was established to restrict the control of the common stockholders over the corporation for a period of five years. The voting trust agreement did not, however, transfer such control to the new investors. The hardware business was discontinued and the real estate business (Bay-O-Vista Subdivisions) operated at a profit. The net operating losses which had been previously sustained by the hardware business were deducted as loss carryovers from the real estate profits. The agreement between the corporation and the new preferred stockholders was entered into on October 18, 1954, and was therefore governed by the provisions of Internal Revenue Code of 1954.

The transactions and events giving rise to this dispute are complicated and extensive. The Findings of Fact and Opinion of the Tax Court are published (Arthur T. Beckett v. Commissioner, 41 T.C. 386). Inasmuch as this decision will be of interest primarily to the tax bar, to whom the referenced publication is readily available, we

---

15. Portions of the opinion and all footnotes omitted.

Sec. 5   CARROVERS OF OPERATING LOSS   875

see no justification in reprinting here the twelve odd pages of Findings of Fact there published. They are adopted by reference. Neither have we undertaken here to repeat in detail all the contentions and arguments discussed in the Tax Court Opinion. With one exception, the findings of the Tax Court have not been contested on this appeal. Petitioner complains that the finding that the "primary purpose of Beckett and Federighi in entering into the agreement of October 18, 1954 with Maxwell Hardware was to enable the profits which they anticipated would be made in the development of the Bay-O-Vista Subdivision to be offset by net operating losses which had been sustained by Maxwell Hardware in prior years" is contrary to the evidence. We think the finding to be amply sustained by substantial evidence and not subject to review by this Court. . . . Our review of the decision, therefore, is restricted to an interpretation and application of the law to the facts as found.

Preliminarily, we should note that in the Tax Court, three petitions for redetermination of deficiencies assessed by the Commissioner, involving the tax liabilities of Arthur T. Beckett and Gertrude E. Beckett, #93309, of Frederick J. Federighi and Mary Helen Federighi, #95310, and of Maxwell Hardware Company, #95311, arising out of the related transactions, were consolidated for trial on a single common fact issue. The Tax Court trial was a complete trial with respect to the tax liability of Maxwell Hardware Company, but only a partial trial with respect to the tax liability of the individuals, Becketts and Federighis. The common issue of fact consolidated for trial was whether the income of the real estate department of Maxwell Hardware Company should have been returned by Maxwell Hardware Company or by the partnership of Beckett and Federighi, and derivatively, by the partners individually. The Government contended that the transactions were a sham, and that the operation of the real estate business under the corporate cloak was pure subterfuge, without factual substance.

The Tax Court, relying upon substantial evidence, resolved this issue in favor of the bona fides of the transactions in the sense that they were not sham, that there was a genuine business purpose for using a corporation for the real estate development enterprise, and that the resulting transactions were corporate actions of Maxwell Hardware, not actions of Beckett and Federighi carried on under a corporate name. The Tax Court held that the subdivision income was properly returned as the income of Maxwell Hardware Company. This conclusion is not excepted to by either party on this appeal and constitutes the foundation for our consideration of the case.

The reported opinion and decision of the Tax Court (Judge Scott) demonstrates careful and thorough analysis of the facts, understanding of the law, and clarity of expression. We do not, however, agree with the conclusions of the Tax Court in applying the law to the established facts.

APPLICABILITY OF THE LIBSON SHOPS DOCTRINE

The Tax Court relied upon the decision of the Supreme Court in Libson Shops, Inc. v. Koehler . . . . The Commissioner, the Tax Court and Petitioner all agree that if Libson Shops had arisen under the 1954 Code, the same decision could not have been made inasmuch as Section 381 of the 1954 Code would expressly allow the net operating loss carryover and the limitations of Section 382 would be inapplicable.

Whenever a Court adopts a rule of decision to sustain a conclusion, interpreting statutory law then applicable, and the legislative authority amends or changes the statutory law to the effect that the same decision could not be reached if the new statute were applied to the same facts, the case is not controlling precedent for judicial interpretation of the new law. By enacting the 1954 Code, Congress destroyed the precedential value of the rule of decision of Libson Shops; that is, that for a loss carryover deduction to be allowed, the income against which the offset was claimed must have been produced by substantially the same businesses which incurred the losses. This is not now the law. It seems to us irrelevant that Libson Shops was decided in 1957, long after the enactment of the 1954 Code. The Supreme Court, in Libson Shops, decided the case by deliberately interpreting and applying the Internal Revenue Code of 1939, as amended, and, while noting a minor change in the 1954 Code . . ., did not comment upon or consider how the case should be decided if the 1954 Code were applicable.

SECTIONS 172 and 382 LIMITATIONS

Recognizing the frailty of Libson Shops as a precedent for decision in this case, the Government suggests alternative bases to sustain the Tax Court. One is the contention that Section 172, which establishes the net operating loss carryover deduction does not apply to Maxwell Hardware. The argument is that, viewed realistically, the transactions amounted to placing "two separately owned business entities under a single corporate roof", and that the net operating loss carryover deduction inures only to the business entity which generated it. As a matter of statutory interpretation, we find nothing in § 172 which justifies such a conclusion. We cannot disregard the finding of the Tax Court that Maxwell Hardware Company, a corporation, is the taxable entity in this case and that it is the entity which suffered the losses as well as generated the subsequent income sought to be taxed. The corporation is the "taxpayer" as defined in the Code [26 U.S.C., § 1313(b), § 7701(a) (14)], and we see no justification for a judicial departure from the carefully devised and integrated concepts of the Code which would require a judicial recognition of a taxable entity or "taxpayer" different from those identified by Congress.

Sec. 5   CARRYOVERS OF OPERATING LOSS   877

With respect to the limitations applicable to the deductibility of net operating loss carryovers, the Government says that the deduction is disqualified in this case by the special limitation provisions of Section 382(a).

The Tax Court found Section 382(a) to be inapplicable, and we agree. The conditions of subsection (C) have been fulfilled, i. e., Maxwell Hardware did not continue to "carry on a trade or business substantially the same as that conducted before any change in the percentage ownership of the fair market value" of the stock. It is also clear, however, that these complicated transactions did not result in persons, as defined, owning fifty percentage points more of the total fair market value of the outstanding stock of such corporation than theretofore. The Tax Court found that the stock acquired by Beckett and Federighi was "nonvoting stock which is limited and preferred as to dividends" [. . . § 382(c)], and said: "It is clear that the issuance of the preferred stock to Beckett and Federighi does not come within any of these provisions." (T.C. 417.) Its concise statement of the problem remaining is (T.C. 417): "The problem is whether by specifying the various circumstances in section 382 in which net operating loss deductions would be disallowed in whole or in part where a change in stock ownership has occurred followed by a change in corporate business, Congress intended to provide that in all other instances the loss corporation would be entitled to deduct its net operating loss carryover from earnings from a different business enterprise unless such deduction fell within the prohibition of section 269." We disagree with the Tax Court's negative answer to this inquiry. We conclude from the legislative history that it was the clearly expressed intention of Congress to attempt to bring some order out of chaos, and, in effect, to countenance "trafficking" in operating loss carryovers except as affected by the special limitations of Section 382 and the general limitations of Section 381. (Other Code sections, such as Section 269, are disregarded in this discussion and will be hereinafter considered separately).

By adopting Section 172(a), Congress created a net operating loss deduction, applicable to taxpayers generally. In Section 381, Congress dealt specifically with the transfer of a variety of deductions, including net operating loss carryovers [Sec. 381(c) (1)] in cases of corporate reorganizations and acquisitions; and in Section 382, Congress provided special limitations by careful and specific definition upon the right to take a net operating loss carryover deduction where there had been a change in ownership of the corporate stock and a change in the corporation's trade or business. Section 172 is a substantial revision of Section 122 of the 1939 Code. . . . Sections 381 and 382 are entirely new, and had no counterpart in the 1939 Code. Idem. pp. 4273, 4281 (House Report); pp. 4914, 4922 (Senate Report). We cannot ascribe to a Congress which, after years of thorough and careful committee consideration aided by the solicited advice of the finest students of taxation, has adopted a fully integrated revenue code, the intention that its provisions should be lightly disregarded by the courts. Neither can we conclude that new and unanticipable judge-made rules are contemplated by a Congress which declares: "As a result, present practice rests on *court-made law* which is *uncertain* and frequently *contradictory*. Moreover, whether or not the carryover is allowed should be based upon economic realities rather than upon such artificialities as the legal form of the reorganization" (emphasis added), Idem. p. 4066 (House Report), p. 4683 (Senate Report). The Reports respecting Section 382 even more clearly demonstrate Congressional intent to substitute statutory rules for judge-made law. It is quite unlikely that the stated purposes of certainty, consistency and objectivity are to be achieved if each court considering a loss carryover problem adds a gloss of judicial exceptions reflecting what a particular judge or group of judges thinks Congress should have done, rather than what it did. An expression like "trafficking in loss carryovers" is a question-begging epithet which clouds reason. A dispassionate consideration of the 1954 Code must lead to the conclusion, we believe, that Congress has deliberately sanctioned such so-called "trafficking" in those situations where it is not expressly abjured.

This is not to say that the language of the 1954 Code is to be given a sterile, mechanical, literal application. The courts must give sense and vitality to that language, but this must be done within the framework of the Code to achieve the Congressional design.

APPLICABILITY OF SECTION 269

As a second alternate basis for affirmance, the Government invokes the applicability of . . . § 269. . . . [T]he Tax Court found that the Maxwell Hardware acquisition by Beckett and Federighi was made for the avoidance of Federal income tax by securing the benefit of the net operating loss deduction. Just as Section 382(a) requires more than proof of a substantial change in the trade or business conducted to disqualify the deduction, so does Section 269 require more than proof of a purpose to evade or avoid taxes. The additional requirement is the acquisition directly or indirectly of control of a corporation, specifically, the ownership of stock possessing at least fifty per cent of the voting power or at least fifty per cent of the total value of shares of all classes. The purchase by Beckett and Federighi of preferred shares for $200,000 of a corporation whose common shares were found to have a fair market value of $500,000 on its face did not satisfy the requirement of acquisition of fifty per cent of the total value of the shares outstanding, and there is nothing in this record which would justify a conclusion that the true fair value of the preferred shares at the date of acquisition exceeded the amount paid therefor.

Invoking Section 269, the Government argues that the complex transaction between Maxwell Hardware and Beckett and Federighi, viewed realistically, resulted in the indirect acquisition by Beckett and Federighi of fifty per cent of the total combined voting power of the corporation. An integral component of the entire transaction was the voting trust agreement which, although not mentioned in the basic agreement of October 18, 1954, bore even date therewith. The agreement created an irrevocable voting trust of all the common shares of Maxwell Hardware until January 31, 1961 and invested the trustee, The San Francisco Bank, with all voting rights, limiting its authority only in respect of the selection of the Board of Directors. The agreement required the trustee to vote for T. P. Coates, an officer of the Bank, and John M. Bryan, as two members of the three man board. The trustee's selection of the third member was unfettered. The agreement accomplished a relinquishment by the common stockholders of their voting control; but the condition for the invoking of Section 269 is the acquisition by persons (here, Beckett and Federighi) of fifty per cent voting control. This is an integrated voting trust agreement which controlled the trustee's powers and responsibilities. It cannot fairly be construed as an acquisition by Beckett and Federighi of any voting control.

True, the evidence proved and the Tax Court found that it was understood that Federighi would be the third director of Maxwell Hardware (T.C. 399), and that there was an oral agreement that Bryan would not be vetoed on any reasonable business investment he wished to make on behalf of Maxwell Hardware. Such evidence was probative and relevant on the issue of sham, an issue which has been permanently resolved against the Government, and on the issue under Section 269 of purpose to evade or avoid, an issue which has been conclusively determined against Petitioner, Maxwell Hardware. Such evidence, however, does not, in our view, justify an inference, as the Government asserts, that fifty per cent voting control was thereby acquired by Beckett and Federighi. A voting trust agreement is too valuable a vehicle for the effectuation of innumerable commercial transactions to be thus lightly impugned; and the eagerness of the Commissioner to collect taxes, a duty imposed on him by law, should not lead the courts arbitrarily to disregard established and useful forms of business relationships. The voting trust agreement invested the voting control in the trustee, not in Beckett or Federighi. If the evidence were such as to justify a finding that, under all the circumstances, either the trustee bank or T. P. Coates, a designated director, was under the domination and control of Beckett and Federighi, the case would be different. There is no such evidence. The Tax Court correctly said: "We think it clear that the provisions of Section 269 are not applicable here because of the absence of the type of acquisition provided for therein." (T.C. 414.)

APPLICABILITY OF SECTION 482

* * *

The Government, in its arguments based on Sections 382(a) and 269, infra, has repeatedly reemphasized that under the carefully designed legal relationships established by these facts, two separate businesses owned and managed by separate interests were being conducted under one corporate roof.

The Tax Court found that the transactions were not a sham, that Maxwell Hardware was the corporate taxpayer, and that the subdivision profits were the taxable income of Maxwell Hardware.

With respect to the tax liability of Maxwell Hardware, no reliance may be placed on Section 482 to justify a decision because the Commissioner did not rely upon it and gave no notice of such issues in his Notice of Deficiency to Maxwell Hardware. . . .

. . . [But] we have not alluded to it in this case just to raise a strawman and then blow him down. Sometimes plain statutory language is distorted by courts to achieve what appears to be a just result in a particular case. The Government seeks to have this Court do that with respect to Sections 172, 382 and 269 to attain what it deems to be the just result in this case. We decline to do so, and to justify ourselves to the fainthearted, we have wondered whether Congress actually did leave the Commissioner helpless in this situation.

The opening statements of counsel before the Tax Court show that the Commissioner did rely upon Section 482 in his notices of deficiency to the Becketts and Federighis as individual taxpayers. Congress has not defined the meaning of "owned or controlled" under Section 482 as it has in Section 382(a) and 269, and a broad definition has been adopted in the Regulations [Regs. 1.482–1(a) (3)]:

> "The term 'controlled' includes any kind of control, direct or indirect, whether legally enforceable, and however exercisable or exercised. It is the reality of the control which is decisive, not its form or the mode of its exercise. A presumption of control arises if income or deductions have been arbitrarily shifted."

It is arguable that the combination of factors in this case, such as the basic agreement, the preferred stock, the management contract with Federighi, the voting trust, the election of Federighi to the board of directors, the carefully drafted dissolution provisions allocating ninety per cent of the subdivision profits to the preferred stock, are sufficient to justify a conclusion that the subdivision business of Maxwell Hardware was controlled by Beckett and Federighi if the Commissioner, in his discretion, had properly so determined . . . and if the Commissioner had also properly determined that it was necessary to allocate ninety per cent of the subdivision income to the individuals to "prevent evasion of taxes" (Sec. 482).

This, however, is not an issue before this Court on this petition for review and our comment is only a comment and not a judgment.

Nor do we suggest that the Section 482 issue is still alive in the Tax Court's consideration of the petitions for redetermination of the individual taxes of the Becketts and Federighis. The opening statements before the Tax Court make it clear that the consolidated trial before the Tax Court would definitely determine the common issue of whether the subdivision income was properly taxable to the corporation or to the individuals, and both parties on this appeal have accepted the Tax Court determination that the subdivision income was properly taxable to Maxwell Hardware.

SUMMARY

This decision is reached in a straight-jacket. We are bound by the Tax Court finding that the Maxwell Hardware transaction was a bona fide business transaction creating substantial, and not illusory, business relationships. We are concerned only with the tax liability of Maxwell Hardware, which, the Tax Court found, properly reported as its income the profit from the subdivision business. We are faced only with the problem of whether the net operating loss deduction generated by the hardware business may be taken against the income from its subdivision business.

The Tax Court considered this a special case, and said: "In so holding, we do not intend to establish a broad legal principle but merely to apply already established principles to an unusual factual situation." We think special cases are to be processed under Section 482 if applicable.

Libson Shops, decided under the 1939 Act, is no longer law. It has been superseded by the 1954 Internal Revenue Code which, in Section 382, dealt specifically and differently with the concept of continuity of business enterprise upon which the Libson Shops decision was based.

Taxation is peculiarly a matter of statutory law, and in applying that law to the determination and computation of income and deductions, the Courts do not make moral judgments. There is nothing perfidious or invidious in enjoying a statutory deduction from reportable income. It is not a matter of conscience but of statute and the determination of Congressional intent. In our opinion, Congress has quite plainly said that net operating loss deductions should be allowed unless the special circumstances interpreted within the letter and spirit of Sections 382(a) and 269 obtain. The conditions disallowing the deduction have not been established here. It is of much more importance that businessmen, accountants, lawyers and revenue agents should retain confidence that plain statutory language means what it says and what it reasonably implies than that a particular deficiency assessment should be sustained. We cannot, within the statutory framework applying a fair and reasonable interpretation to the language used, disallow to Maxwell Hardware the net operating loss deduction.

The decision of the Tax Court is reversed.

T. I. R. 773

1965 CCH ¶ 6751.

The United States Internal Revenue Service today announced that it will not follow the decision of the United States Court of Appeals for the Ninth Circuit in the case of Maxwell Hardware Co. v. Commissioner, 343 F.2d 713 (1965).

In that case, the circuit court held that the Supreme Court's decision in Libson Shops, Inc. v. Koehler, 353 U.S. 382, 77 S.Ct. 990, 1 L.Ed.2d 924 (1957) has no precedential value under the 1954 Code, and that the net operating loss carryovers involved therein were not subject to disallowance under sections 172, 269 or 382. The court, by way of dictum, stated that the Commissioner might have successfully applied section 482 in this case.

It is the position of the Revenue Service that in cases similar to Maxwell Hardware, sections 269 and 382, as well as section 482, are applicable in dealing with the carryover of losses. The Revenue Service believes that the foregoing statutory provisions must be construed to effectuate congressional intent in combating "trafficking in loss carryovers". Moreover, the Service also believes that the loss carryover in cases similar to Maxwell Hardware should be denied under the rationale of the Libson Shops decision since to permit a loss carryover in such cases would run counter to the legislative objectives of the carryover privilege.

The cornerstone of the Libson Shops decision was a searching examination of the purposes of the carryover privilege. Thus, in approaching the question of whether the taxpayer was entitled to a loss carryover, the Supreme Court held that the loss carryover provision was not automatic and that the "availability of . . . [the loss carryover] privilege depends on the proper interpretation to be given to the carryover provisions". The Service believes that this fundamental type of statutory analysis was not made obsolete by the enactment in 1954 of provisions limiting or denying loss carryovers in certain situations involving abuses that were specifically brought to the attention of Congress. It is the view of the Service that the basic approach of the Supreme Court in Libson Shops retains vitality under the 1954 Code in interpreting the application of section 172.

Accordingly, the Service will apply Libson Shops in any loss carryover case under the 1954 Code, not contemplated by the announcement in Revenue Ruling 58–603, C.B. 1958–2, 147, where there has been both a 50 percent or more shift in the benefits of a loss carryover (whether direct or indirect and including transactions having the effect of shifting the benefit of the loss by shifting assets, stock, profit interests or other valuable rights) and a change in business as defined in section 382(a) and the regulations thereunder. The Service will not rely on Libson Shops under the 1954 Code in any loss carryover case where there has been less than a 50% change in the beneficial ownership of the loss or where there has been no change in business as defined in section 382(a) and the regulations thereunder. However, the Service will continue to rely on sections 269 and 482, where appropriate, in dealing with the carryover of losses. Revenue Ruling 63–40, C.B. 1963–1, 46 will be modified to the extent inconsistent herewith.

The Revenue Service stated that certiorari was not requested in Maxwell Hardware due to the absence of a direct conflict between the circuits. The decision will not be followed as a precedent in the disposition of similar cases.

NOTE ON § 382(a) AND THE LIBSON SHOPS DOCTRINE

As a matter of statutory interpretation, the one thing that is clear about the relationship between § 382(a) and the Libson Shops doctrine is that no particular intention on the matter can be ascribed to Congress, since § 382(a) was enacted prior to the Libson Shops decision. On the merits, it is true that the specificity of § 382(a), when taken together with the express purpose proscription of § 269, certainly cuts against the existence of any general judicial doctrine like that of Libson Shops. On the other hand, there is no evidence that § 382(a) was intended to be a kind of reverse "safe harbor", making every transaction not covered by it (or § 269) immune from attack. See generally, Comment, The Loss Carryover Deduction and Changes in Corporate Structure, 66 Col.L.Rev. 338 (1966); Comment, Loss Carryovers and the Libson Shops Doctrine, 32 U. of Chi.L.Rev. 508 (1965).

Looking more closely at the mechanics of § 382(a), it should be noted that the change in stock ownership test is actually a good deal more complex than just a 50% shift. It is formulated in terms of whether at the end of a corporation's taxable year any one or more of the ten largest stockholders own a percentage of the total fair market value of the outstanding stock which is at least 50 percentage points more than such persons owned at the beginning of that taxable year or at the beginning of the prior taxable year. The reference to "percentage points" looks to the amount of the stockholders' increase in percentage ownership: for example, an increase in a stockholder's ownership from 10% to 15% would constitute an increase of 5 percentage points. Only increases in percentage points resulting from a purchase, directly or indirectly, of stock in a taxable transaction, or a redemption of stock by the corporation (except a redemption to which § 303 applies), are included in the computation. Stock ownership is to be determined in the light of the attribution rules of § 318 (subject to a minor modification); but a taxpayer may not acquire stock in order to create an attribution which would aid the taxpayer under the § 382(a) formula.

Obviously, this formula has some troublesome aspects. For example, the statute applies as well where the change in ownership results from a series of transactions as where it occurs in one fell swoop; and apparently it does not matter whether the series of transactions are at all related. Thus if A purchased 40% of the stock of a loss corporation and set about rejuvenating it, a sale by another stockholder of 10% of the stock could result in the elimination of the corporation's carryovers (if the requisite change in business was present) whether or not A had anything to do with the subsequent transfer or indeed even knew of it.

In addition, as the Maxwell Hardware case illustrates, the change of stock ownership test is bound to involve special problems whenever there is more than one class of stock. In addition to the inherent difficulty of valuing the different classes of stock, there is the fact that the relative values of the different classes may change without any change in the ownership of the stock. For example, suppose that A purchases a majority of the common stock of an unsuccessful corporation which also has outstanding voting preferred stock — under § 382(a), as under § 382(b), non-voting preferred stock does not count — and at the time of A's purchase the preferred stock accounts for most of the total value of the corporation's stock. If A is able to improve the operations it is quite possible that within the two year period in which change in stock ownership is tested the common stock's value vis-a-vis the preferred could rise enough to make A's block of common stock worth more than 50% of the total value of all the stock.

While the rules as to change in stock ownership are relatively precise, the change in business test is quite general, and hence questions are bound to arise. Under the statute, the critical question is whether the corporation's previous business was continued — it makes no difference whether a new business is added. And it appears that the old business need only be continued for two taxable years after the change in stock ownership, counting the year in which the change occurred as one of those years. In other words, a change of ownership near the end of a year in effect reduces the period for which the old business must be continued to just over one year.

The difficulty of course comes in determining what kinds of adjustments, such as a discontinuation of a portion of the business, or a change in location, employees, products or customers, will constitute a failure to continue the old business for the purposes of § 382(a). Some guidance is afforded by Reg. § 1.382(a)–1(h), which contains a number of examples, together with the ultimate warning that "all the facts and circumstances of the particular case shall be taken into account . . . [and] evaluated in the light of the general objective of section 382(a) to disallow net operating loss carryovers where there is a purchase of the stock of a corporation and its loss carryovers are used to offset gains of a business unrelated to that which produced the losses". Notice that this "general objective" which the regulations purport to find in § 382(a) is not readily discernible from the words of the statute, and smacks more of an attempt to import the Libson Shops rationale than a construction of § 382(a).

To date, judicial attention has been focused primarily upon the extent to which some hiatus in the continuation of the predecessor business will be permitted without disqualification under § 382(a). In Glover Packing Co. of Texas v. United States, 164 Ct.Cl. 572, 328 F.2d 342 (1964), it was conceded that some interruption was permissible, as, for example, if a corporation's plant was destroyed by fire shortly before a change in the ownership of its stock, see Reg. § 1.382(a)–1(h) (6); but the court held that since the corporation had terminated its business and remained inactive for over four years prior to the change in stock ownership, the attempt to revive the old business was not a continuation of that business but the inauguration of a new one. On the other hand, in H. F. Ramsey Co., Inc. v. Commissioner, 43 T.C. 500 (1965), the Tax Court found a "continuation" of a contracting business although the corporation had been substantially inactive for about a year. Where the loss corporation has terminated its active business prior to the change in stock ownership and is merely leasing its facilities, continuation of the leasing activity does not satisfy the test of § 382(a). Euclid-Tennessee, Inc. v. Commissioner, 352 F.2d 991 (6th Cir. 1965).

*

Chapter 6
CORPORATE DIVISIONS

Introduction

The division of a corporation into two or more separate entities may occur for a variety of reasons and may take a number of different forms. For example, X corporation might transfer one of its operating divisions to a newly-formed subsidiary, Y, in exchange for all of Y's stock, which X would then distribute to its stockholders. The distribution of Y stock might take the form of an ordinary dividend (a "spin-off", in tax jargon); or it might be in redemption of X stock from its stockholders (a "split-off"). A third route to the same end-point would be for X to transfer all of its assets to two new corporations, Y and Z, and then distribute their stock to its stockholders in complete liquidation (a "split-up"). See generally, Siegel, When Corporations Divide: A Statutory and Financial Analysis, 79 Harv. L.Rev. 534 (1966).

It should be noted that a corporate division does not always entail pro rata ownership of the new entity by the stockholders of the original enterprise. To be sure, any "spin-off" would normally result in pro rata ownership of the two entities. But either a split-off or a split-up could be the vehicle for a non-pro-rata division. To illustrate, assume that X corporation in the foregoing example had two equal stockholders, A and B, and two operating divisions of roughly equal size. If X transferred one of the operating divisions to Y in exchange for all Y's stock, and then transferred all of the Y stock to B in exchange for all of B's X stock, the result would be a completely non-pro-rata division of the original enterprise.

A corporate enterprise may also be divided without organizing any new corporation. For example, the foregoing non-pro-rata division could be accomplished by distributing one of X's two divisions in kind to B in exchange for all of his X stock. Thereafter, B could either operate that division as a proprietorship or, if he preferred the corporate form, he could transfer it to a new corporation and end up exactly where he would have been under the split-off procedure (apart from possible tax differences).

The split-up approach could be used to effect a non-pro-rata division without creating any new corporations. Thus X could adopt a plan of liquidation under which (subject of course to the rights of creditors) one of its divisions would be allocated to A as his liquidating distribution and the other to B as his. However, this approach would be available only where the stockholders have been able to agree in advance as to the manner of allocating the assets of the corporation upon liquidation. Otherwise, each of the stockholders would presumably become a tenant in common of all the corporation's assets; or more likely, the plan of liquidation would call for the sale of all of the corporation's assets, leaving only cash to be distributed in the liquidation.

SECTION 1. DISSOLUTION UPON DEADLOCK

The relationship between liquidation and corporate division is particularly highlighted in cases involving deadlock between the owners of a closely-held corporation, where normally at least some of the parties are anxious to part company and go their separate ways. If the enterprise lends itself to a reasonable allocation between the parties, and they can lay aside their differences long enough to reach an agreement to that effect, a corporate division may constitute the best resolution of the situation. But often the dissension is too sharp for this to be feasible; in addition, the question of whether and how to continue the enterprise may be one of the substantial bones of contention between the parties. In that event, one of the parties may seek to compel a dissolution of the enterprise.

JACKSON v. NICOLAI-NEPPACH CO.
Supreme Court of Oregon, 1959.
219 Or. 560, 348 P.2d 9.

ROSSMAN, JUSTICE. This is an appeal by the plaintiff, owner of 50 per cent of the corporate stock of the defendant, Nicolai-Neppach Co., an Oregon corporation, from a decree of the circuit court which denied the plaintiff's prayer for the appointment of a receiver to liquidate the business of the corporation and distribute its assets to its shareholders. The principal ground of the complaint is that the shareholders are deadlocked in voting power and for three successive years have been unable to elect successors to the members of the board of directors. The suit was brought under a section of the Oregon Business Corporation law, ORS 57.595(1) (a) (C) which authorizes liquidation in the event of shareholder deadlock.

The section of our laws just cited provides:

"(1) The circuit courts shall have full power to liquidate the assets and business of a corporation:

"(a) In an action by a shareholder when it is established:

"(A) That the directors are deadlocked in the management of the corporate affairs and the shareholders are unable to break the deadlock, and that irreparable injury to the corporation is being suffered or is threatened by reason thereof; or

"(B) That the acts of the directors or those in control of the corporation are illegal, oppressive or fraudulent; or

"(C) That the shareholders are deadlocked in voting power, and have failed, for a period which includes at least two consecutive annual meeting dates, to elect successors to directors whose terms have expired or would have expired upon the election of their successors; or

"(D) That the corporate assets are being misapplied or wasted."

The circuit court, after hearing the evidence, dismissed the suit and from that order this appeal was taken.

The Nicolai-Neppach Co. is located in Portland. It is a close or family corporation. The business is the manufacture of lumber products such as sash, doors, cabinets and store fixtures. The business was begun in 1866 and the company was incorporated in 1887. Herbert Jackson, brother-in-law of the plaintiff, joined the company as an employee in 1928. At that time the principal shareholder was the president and general manager of the company, C. E. Cowdin. In 1931 Herbert Jackson married Eva Jackson, who was employed by the company as a stenographer and secretary to Mr. Cowdin. After her marriage she ceased her employment.

In 1945 Herbert Jackson was offered opportunity to purchase the stock of Nicolai-Neppach Co. Upon that development he consulted his brother, Arthur Jackson, who was familiar with the lumber industry, and the two of them together with Mr. Cowdin incorporated in August 1945 the Jackson Company. Five hundred shares of stock of no-par value were authorized and 51 of the shares were issued, 25 to each of the Jacksons and one to Cowdin. No further shares have been issued. The directors then elected Herbert Jackson president, Cowdin vice president and Arthur Jackson secretary and treasurer.

September 1, 1945, the Jackson Company entered into an agreement to purchase the stock of Nicolai-Neppach Co. for $180,000 payable over a term of twelve years. In October 1945 the Jackson Company changed its corporate name to Nicolai-Neppach Co.

The three years following 1945 were boom years in the construction industry and the Nicolai-Neppach Co. earned large profits, enabling it by 1949 to complete payments under the stock purchase agreement. At that time C. E. Cowdin surrendered his share of stock and withdrew from the company. Mr. Robert R. Rankin, attorney for the company, thereupon accepted this share of stock in trust for the Jacksons in order to comply with a provision of the by-laws that all members of the board of directors must be shareholders and was then elected to membership upon the board. The other two directors were Herbert and Arthur Jackson. Herbert Jackson retained the presidency. Mr. Rankin became vice president and Arthur Jackson continued as secretary and treasurer.

Herbert and Arthur Jackson jointly managed the business of the company. From 1945 onward each received a salary of $11,000 which was increased by a resolution of the board of directors in December 1949 to $13,750. Harmony apparently prevailed.

April 7, 1950, Arthur Jackson died and the plaintiff, his wife, inherited his shares of stock. In the light of that fact Rankin delivered his one share of stock, one-half to Herbert Jackson and one-half to Hazel Jackson who is now the plaintiff in this suit. Thereupon Mr. Rankin resigned from the company. At that juncture there were two vacancies in the membership of the board of directors which were filled May 18, 1950, by the election of Hazel Jackson and Eva Jackson. Herbert Jackson had assigned one share of his stock to his wife, Eva, in order to qualify her as a director. The shareholdings, which since have remained static are as follows:

> Herbert Jackson 24½ shares
> Eva Jackson 1 share
> Hazel Jackson 25½ shares

Since the death of Arthur Jackson, Herbert Jackson has been the sole active manager of the corporation and the only shareholder-officer to draw a salary. Hazel Jackson, the plaintiff, served as vice president and treasurer from 1950 to 1952 and Eva Jackson during those years as secretary. At the directors meeting of December 6, 1952, Hazel Jackson yielded the office of treasurer to Eva Jackson in order to facilitate record keeping, and since that time has held only the office of vice president. In 1951 the company loaned to Hazel $8,000 to help her finance Myrtle Creek Building Supply, Inc., a company which is operated by her brother.

Dissension between Hazel and Herbert Jackson receives its first mention in the minutes of the stockholders meeting that was held December 6, 1952. The by-laws that were adopted by the Jackson Company in 1945 called for the corporation to be governed by a board of three directors, all of whom were required to be shareholders. In the 1952 meeting Mrs. Hazel Jackson (the plaintiff) assisted by her attorney, Carl Davidson, demanded that the by-laws be amended to add a fourth director, and explained that thereby her 50 per cent interest would have equal representation with that of Herbert Jackson. Robert

Rankin, for the company, objected on the grounds that it was customary to have an odd number of directors, that Hazel Jackson had had no experience in company management and that it was for her benefit as well as that of the others to leave the affairs of the company in Herbert Jackson's control. The plaintiff then moved that the three Jacksons be re-elected "with the understanding that her action was not to prejudice her request for equal representation on the Board of Directors." The plaintiff stated "that there was no complaint against the management or service of the president, Herbert W. Jackson, but that the request of representation was based solely on her desire for equal representation on the Board." At the directors meeting which immediately followed the plaintiff suggested, through her attorney, that a dividend of $12,000 for the year was justified, but Mr. Jackson stated that large sums would shortly have to be spent upon repairs to the plant. Action upon the plaintiff's question was thereupon postponed until Jackson collected data upon which a sound decision could be made.

In the course of the meeting of the shareholders November 16, 1953, the plaintiff was represented by Ralph H. King and Robert S. Miller as her counsel. An amendment of the by-laws to require four directors was again proposed by her. When a vote was taken the proposal was defeated by an equal division. According to the minute book the three Jacksons then elected themselves directors for the ensuing year. However, the complaint filed by the plaintiff alleges that no election of directors occurred in 1953; its words are:

> "At the postponed annual meeting of defendant held November 16, 1953, no successors to the then directors were elected by affirmative vote of the shareholders."

The defendant's answer admits that averment. Notwithstanding that state of the pleadings, the minutes of the meeting of the stockholders that was held November 16, 1953, show the election of all three Jacksons; their words are:

> "The election of directors was then called and stockholder Eva B. Jackson nominated Herbert W. Jackson and Hazel M. Jackson for directors and Herbert W. Jackson nominated Eva B. Jackson for director.
>
> "There being no other nominations or other stockholders from whom nominations could be had and the law requiring three directors of this corporation, the three were unanimously declared elected as directors of Nicolai-Neppach Co., an Oregon corporation."

At the meeting of the directors which followed Mr. King, on behalf of the plaintiff, proposed a dividend of $11,985. Mr. Jackson, however, stated that he "felt some dividend should be declared, but not that much, and that he would like consideration given to an advance in salary for the reasons that had been previously cited and discussed." Mr. King replied that "they had a motion before the Board for dividends and that they were not going to bargain on that motion in connection with the request for increase in salary of Herbert W. Jackson." A vote for the dividend was lost by an equally divided number. Two additional votes for reduced dividends were lost by equally divided votes, until finally agreement was reached on a dividend of $150 per share or $7,650. Mr. Jackson then moved that his salary be increased from $13,750 a year to $20,000. Although a by-law provides that "The salaries of all officers shall be fixed by the stockholders," this motion was lost by a one to one vote of the directors. Mr. Jackson had abstained from voting on account of his personal interest. A motion to increase his salary to $15,000 was also defeated. Mr. Jackson declined to ask for a smaller increase.

At the shareholders meeting in 1954 Mr. Jackson again refused to allow a change in the by-laws for a board of directors of four members. The plaintiff then proposed Mr. King, Mr. Miller and Orval O. Hager, all three of the law firm of King, Miller, Anderson, Nash and Yerke, as directors. Mr. Jackson proposed as directors the three Jacksons. The vote failed to yield a majority for either of the proposed slates and thereupon under the by-laws the old board of the three Jacksons continued in office. At the directors meeting which followed, the plaintiff proposed a dividend of $235 a share or $11,985, but this was defeated along with five other motions for reduced sums until all agreed on a dividend of $75 a share or a total of $3,825. In the meantime Mr. Jackson had emphasized that as much as $10,000 would be needed for modernizing the plant by replacing steam power with electricity. He invited the directors to go through the plant with him for inspection, but "This they refused on the grounds of lack of qualification to pass upon the project."

Apparently, 1954 was not a particularly successful year for the company. The net earnings were $8,235.69. Some of the company's competitors were liquidating. The directors authorized Mr. Jackson to borrow up to $20,000 for use in the business, but he found it unnecessary to borrow anything. Mr. King and Mr. Miller suggested liquidation. Mr. Jackson objected, "maintaining that there could and would be better years but as it was, the company was not liquidating as many of its competitors were and that the old uses of wood, lost through competition with steel, were now coming back, as some of the new orders being received, would show." Mr. King, on behalf of the plaintiff, then proposed a resolution directing the president of the company to "investigate and assemble facts regarding dissolution of the corporation and report what he learned at a special meeting of the directors to be held December 6." This was defeated, as was a similar proposal that the corporation employ outsiders to survey the possibilities of liquidation.

April 27, 1955, the plaintiff instituted the suit now under review for involuntary liquidation. At the shareholders meeting November 12, 1955, a motion to increase the number of directors was defeated for the third time. The stockholders were once again deadlocked on the election of a board of directors. At the directors meeting a dividend of $12,750 was declared. A dividend of $17,850 had been requested earlier by the plaintiff, but Mr. Jackson again protested that funds were required for modernization. At this meeting the plaintiff, upon her own volition, moved that Mr. Jackson's salary be increased $3,000 for the term of one year.

The year 1956 was prosperous for Nicolai-Neppach Co. An unprecedented dividend of $25,500 was declared and Mr. Jackson's increased salary was continued for another year. However, the deadlock continued. The plaintiff again cast her votes for Messrs. King, Miller and Hager as directors and Mr. Jackson cast his for the three Jacksons. The minute book of the corporation introduced in evidence ends with this year.

Mr. Jackson testified that the firm employed about 65 men among whom were "many that have been there longer than I have." He expressed the belief that "the future is very good" and that "things really look pretty good." He expressed a hope of obtaining orders from the State Board of Higher Education and from various construction projects about Portland.

The recent history of the Nicolai-Neppach Co. is thus one of continuing prosperity marred, however, by the dissensions of the two 50 per cent shareholders. Owing to that deadlock and the fortuity which saw two directors of Mr. Jackson's faction in power at the time the deadlock began, he is in control and the plaintiff, as a director, is without power equal to his. There is no evidence that Mr. Jackson has abused his dominating position to the injury of the plaintiff or that he has managed the company other than for the good of all the shareholders as he understands their good. In her complaint the plaintiff alleged that the acts of Herbert and Eva Jackson have been arbitrary and oppressive. She averred abuse of discretion in several aspects such as failure to pay larger dividends, to increase the board of directors, to vote for liquidation. At the trial, however, plaintiff moved to strike all allegations of oppression and mismanagement. Her counsel stated, "We are not undertaking to charge the management with oppression or mismanagement or any illegal acts."

The plaintiff's position at the trial was that ORS 57.595(1) (a) (C) is mandatory and that a corporation must be liquidated when it is shown that there is a deadlock in voting power and a failure to elect directors for two consecutive years. Consistently with that position plaintiff's counsel stated that no evidence of dissension would be offered and that the plaintiff's only evidence would be directed at a showing of deadlock over dividends, liquidation and election of directors. To that end the plaintiff introduced in evidence minutes of the corporation and rested. Objection was then made to all efforts of the defendant to interpose equitable considerations. Plaintiff's counsel made clear her position that:

> "In our view of the case there is only one issue here: It is deadlock; that there were no successors elected to the directors in the years '53, '54, '55 and '56. So we would like to interpose an objection at this time to all evidence going to any aspect of the case other than whether or not a deadlock in fact exists, because we feel that any such evidence as was outlined in the opening statement of counsel is immaterial and irrelevant."

Although the position taken by the plaintiff upon this appeal is not entirely clear, she argues that liquidation must be without regard to benefit or detriment to the shareholders.

ORS 57.595 was taken haec verba from Section 90 of the American Law Institute's Model Business Corporation Act. The present section 90 first appears in the 1953 revision of the model act. In turn, section 90 of the model act was taken haec verba from a section of the Illinois Business Corporations Act, 32 Smith-Hurd Illinois Ann.Stat., ch. 32, § 157.86, amended by Laws, 1951, p. 1299, § 1 so that the Illinois shareholder deadlock provisions and those of Oregon are identical. The Model Business Corporation Act is largely based on Illinois experience, the Illinois Business Corporations Act of 1933 serving as the "parent act." See Whitney Campbell, "The Model Business Corporation Act," 11 Business Lawyer No. 4, pp. 98, 100 (1956); Ray Garrett, "Model Business Corporation Act," 4 Baylor Law Review 412 (1952); American Law Institute, Model Business Corporation Act (1953 revision) p. 84.

At common law petitions for dissolution presented by 50 per cent shareholders were often dismissed with the statement that a court of equity lacked "power" or "jurisdiction" to dissolve a solvent corporation in the absence of statutory authority. . . . The only exception was when the dissension between groups of stockholders was so serious as to lead to waste, corporate paralysis or oppression of one group by another. Under those circumstances some states held that a court of equity could appoint a receiver and wind up the affairs of the company. . . . Illinois does not appear to have had a case calling for the application or rejection of that exception.

When Illinois enacted its shareholder deadlock statute in 1951, it had before it . . . such cases as . . . . The decisions of its own appellate courts in Lush'us Brand Distributors, Inc. v. Fort Dearborn Lithograph Co., 1946, 330 Ill.App. 216, 70 N.E.2d 737 and Gidwitz v. Cohn, 1925, 238 Ill.App. 227. In the Gidwitz case one of two equal shareholders in a solvent corporation demanded the appointment of a receiver to liquidate the company on the ground that the stockholders could not agree to fill a vacancy in the board of directors. It was provided by statute that failure to fill a vacancy did not effect a dissolution. The court cited the following language of People v. Weigley, 155 Ill. 491, 40 N.E. 300, 303, as controlling:

" . . . It is well settled by the decisions of this court, as well as the authorities generally, that courts of chancery are without jurisdiction to decree the dissolution of corporations, except in so far as that jurisdiction is conferred by statute . . .."

Since the statutes at the time did not provide for liquidation in the event of deadlock, the suit was dismissed. Lush'us Brand Distributors v. Fort Dearborn Lithograph Co. was an action by a corporation, of which Novak had practical control and in which he owned 50 per cent of the stock, against Adler, a 50 per cent stockholder in the same corporation, to prevent Adler from using a company trademark, and for an accounting. Adler counterclaimed for dissolution of the company. The court found against Adler on the original claim and dismissed the counterclaim on the authority of Gidwitz v. Cohn.

It was in the light of this background that Illinois enacted the shareholder deadlock provisions of its corporation act, granting the courts of equity "full power" to liquidate a corporation whose shareholders are deadlocked in voting power and fail for two successive years to elect successors to directors. This "full power" is described in the title of the section—a title adopted by the Model Business Act and Oregon Business Corporation Law—as a matter of "jurisdiction." The actual title is "Jurisdiction of court of equity to liquidate assets and business of corporation."

Although the Oregon courts have not been called upon to decide whether there is a common law right to wind up a corporation at the suit of a 50 per cent stockholder, it is likely that they would have followed the general rule in denying relief. . . .

The shareholder deadlock provisions of the Illinois Business Corporation Act, of the Model Business Corporation Act, and of the Oregon Business Corporation Law are clearly couched in language of permission. It is incredible that the many able lawyers who worked from time to time on these three identical acts would have used such phraseology to express a mandate. The statute contemplates that the court of equity shall take jurisdiction once a requisite showing of fact is made and contemplates further that having taken jurisdiction it will bring its discretion to bear in granting or refusing to grant equitable relief. The very fact that the legislature has made the remedy of liquidation a matter of discretion for the courts is a mandate to us to use discretion, and we would not be carrying out the legislative will by simply decreeing liquidation as a matter of course once the jurisdictional facts and nothing more are proven. The common law rule was thought to be an insufficient safeguard of the rights of the half-owner of a corporation who happened to be out of power. The drafters of the shareholder deadlock provision apparently thought that any statutory rule which provided for liquidation as a matter of law would insufficiently safeguard the rights of the half-owner who happened to be in power. As we read the statute its intent is to obligate the courts to thread their way from case to case without the assistance of sweeping generalizations.

In arguing for liquidation of the Nicolai-Neppach Company, appellant places her principal reliance on Strong v. Fromm Laboratories, 1956, 273 Wis. 159, 77 N.W.2d 389, which construed the shareholder deadlock provision of the Wisconsin business corporation law, Wis. Ann.Stat. 180.771(1) (a) (4). Wisconsin had adopted the Model Business Corporation Act and the shareholder deadlock provision is in every material respect identical to our own, ORS 57.595(1) (a) (C). In the Strong case the Supreme Court of Wisconsin decreed liquidation of a prospering corporation, and it is appellant's argument that the decision ought to be followed here. We think, however, that the facts of the Strong case and the reasoning of the Wisconsin court set the case apart from the one that is before us.

Strong v. Fromm Laboratories was an action by Harland Strong, trustee of 50 per cent of the share of Fromm Laboratories, Inc., for liquidation of the company. Fromm Laboratories was a Wisconsin corporation created in 1933 by Edward and Walter Fromm and Dr. Robert Gladding Green. Strong represented the Green interests. The Fromm interests owned the other 50 per cent stock interest. The company manufactured vaccines used in the fur farming business and at the time of the petition for dissolution was prosperous. However, the corporation had never paid a dividend. Dr. Green drew a salary as active director of the laboratories and the Fromms were salaried officers. The by-laws of the corporation provided that only stockholders were to be directors. Moreover, as stated in the opinion [273 Wis. 159, 77 N.W.2d 391]:

> "The by-laws . . . contain no provision permitting the members of the board of directors to fill a vacancy on the board. Instead, such by-laws expressly provide that, in the case a vacancy should occur on the board of directors, the board shall call a special meeting of the stockholders for the purpose of filling such vacancy, and that *until such vacancy is filled the board 'shall transact no other business than to authorize the calling of the special meeting' for the purpose of filling the vacancy.*"

Dr. Green died in 1947. By will he left his stock in trust to Strong for the benefit of his niece Gale Green. The trust was to last until Strong should sell the stock. The Fromms were granted first purchase rights. Green had also entered into an inter vivos written agreement with the Fromms, granting them a first option to purchase his stock, which was to be binding on his estate. The Fromms apparently made no move to purchase the Green interest. Strong had a disagreement with the Fromms which became acute in 1951.

The by-laws of the corporation called for a board of four directors. Although Wisconsin law requires an annual election of directors (Wis. Ann.Stat. 180.32(2)), no meeting of stockholders was held, after a single meeting to elect Dr. Green's successor in 1947, until the year 1953. The 1953 stockholders meeting was "abortive." A vote on only one director was taken which resulted in a tie. In 1954 another shareholders meeting was called. Strong cast his share for himself as director and "against any other candidate for director"—doing this because all of the other eligible shareholders were members of the Fromm party and Strong, as trustee, could not assign any of his shares to an ally. The Fromms cast their votes for three other shareholders and declared Strong's negative ballot a nullity, but the Supreme Court held that it was valid, and deadlocked the election.

On the above facts the trial court denied dissolution but the Supreme Court reversed with orders to liquidate the company. To an argument that there was no showing of benefit to the stockholders the court replied as follows:

"Because of the extensive research made by the committee of eminent Wisconsin corporation lawyers who sponsored the 1953 addition of par. 4 of section 180.771(1) (a) to our new corporation code, we must assume that its members were familiar with the New York and Minnesota deadlock statutes and court decisions interpreting the same, and that they preferred to word the Wisconsin statute so as not to make dissolution or liquidation, because of a stockholders' deadlock, contingent upon a finding that the same will be beneficial to stockholders. We, therefore, hold that whether or not a liquidation of Fromm Laboratories, Inc., will be beneficial or detrimental to the stockholders is not a material factor to be considered in exercising the power of liquidation conferred by par. 4 of section 180.771(1) (a) Stats."

The further argument was made that the power of dissolution was discretionary by statute, "and that there was no abuse of discretion on the part of the trial court in refusing to exercise such power." The opinion of the Supreme Court makes it clear that reversal was based on abuse of discretion rather than absence of discretion, and furthermore, that the primary reason for which dissolution was granted was lack of a legally functioning board of directors—a situation not present in Nicolai-Neppach Company. We quote from the relevant paragraphs of the opinion:

"Section 180.30, Stats., provides that, 'The business and affairs of a corporation shall be managed by a board of directors.' The by-laws of Fromm Laboratories, Inc. expressly prohibit the board of directors of such corporation from transacting any business after a vacancy occurs on the board, except to call a meeting of the stockholders to elect a successor director, until such vacancy has been filled. This by-law was undoubtedly adopted for the purpose of insuring that neither the Green nor Fromm interest should be able to manage the corporate business, in the event of the death of a director, as a result of having two members to the other's one among the other three members of the board. We thus have a situation where, ever since Dr. Green's death on September 6, 1947, the board of directors has been without legal power to manage the business of the corporation. The fact that the two directors representing the Fromm faction have usurped such power and may have capably exercised the same is wholly beside the point.

* * *

"In the instant case there is no *alternative corrective remedy*, other than that provided by section 180.771(1) (a) 4, Stats., which will permit Fromm Laboratories, Inc., to function and be legally managed as required by section 180.-30, Stats., and the corporate by-laws. It, therefore, was an abuse of discretion for the trial court not to have decreed a liquidation."

The by-laws of Nicolai-Neppach Co. provide that the board of directors shall consist of three members "who shall hold office until the next annual meeting and until their successors are elected and have qualified." At a time long before any dispute arose, the incorporators, Herbert and Arthur Jackson and C. E. Cowdin, construed this provision to mean that the directors were "to hold office until the next annual meeting of stockholders, *or* until their successors were duly elected and qualified." This appears from the "Incorporators' Certificate of Election" of August 31, 1945, which appears in the company minute book. Moreover, ORS 57.185 provides that:

". . . Each director shall hold office for the term for which he is elected and until his successor shall have been elected and qualified, unless removed in accordance with the provisions of the by-laws."

ORS 57.141 provides that:

". . . The bylaws may contain any provisions for the regulation and management of the affairs of the corporation not inconsistent with law or the articles of incorporation."

Therefore, whether by act of the legislature or by virtue of the by-laws of the company — which, it is unnecessary to decide — the board of directors of Nicolai-Neppach Co. in office at the time of the deadlock continued to function legally thereafter. Strong v. Fromm Laboratories held, on the other hand, that under Wisconsin law the by-laws of a company may be drawn so as to paralyze effectively the corporate function. In addition, the by-laws of Nicolai-Neppach Co., by requiring three directors, indicate that the stockholders of that concern placed a higher value on effective corporate action than on equal representation of their equal interests while the by-laws of Fromm Laboratories, by requiring four directors, indicate that the stockholders insisted on equal representation even at the risk of deadlock.

Appellant argues that we can not consider benefit to the stockholders as a factor in decreeing or withholding liquidation since the shareholder deadlock provision of our statute fails to require it, citing the language of Strong v. Fromm Laboratories which we have quoted above. She notes that Virginia, which has adopted section 90 of the model act, changed the shareholder deadlock provision to require "That as shown by the proceedings at any meeting of the stockholders the stockholders are deadlocked in voting power and that irreparable injury to the corporation is being suffered or is threatened by reason thereof . . .."

Benefit to the shareholders is a condition precedent to the granting of dissolution on the grounds of shareholder deadlock in some jurisdictions, notably New York. The New York Gen.Corp.Law, ch. 23, § 103, provides:

> "Unless otherwise provided in the certificate of incorporation, if a corporation has an even number of directors who are equally divided respecting the management of its affairs, or if the votes of its stockholders are so divided that they cannot elect a board of directors, the holders of one-half of the stock entitled to vote at an election of directors may present a verified petition for dissolution of the corporation as prescribed in this article."

Section 117 provides that the court must make a final order dissolving the corporation if upon application it appears that a dissolution "will be beneficial to the stockholders or members and not injurious to the public . . .." In re Radom & Neidorff, 1954, 307 N.Y. 1, 119 N.E.2d 563, 566, denied dissolution of a corporation on facts outlined by Justice Fuld in a dissenting opinion:

> ". . . Neidorff died in 1950, at which time respondent, through inheritance, acquired her present 50% stock interest in the business. Since then, all has been discord and conflict. The parties, brother and sister, are at complete loggerheads; they have been unable to elect a board of directors; dividends have neither been declared nor distributed, although the corporation has earned profits; debts of the corporation have gone unpaid, although the corporation is solvent; petitioner, who since Neidorff's death has been the sole manager of the business, has not received a penny of his salary—amounting to $25,000 a year—because respondent has refused to sign any corporate check to his order. More, petitioner's business judgment and integrity,

never before questioned, have been directly attacked in the stockholder's derivative suit, instituted by respondent, charging that he has falsified the corporation's records, converted its assets and otherwise enriched himself at its expense. . . ."

The appellate division, 282 App.Div. 854, 873, 124 N.Y.S. 424, 922, dismissed the petition and this was affirmed in the court of appeals by a four to three vote. The majority said that "The prime inquiry is, always, as to necessity for dissolution, that is, whether judicially-imposed death 'will be beneficial to the stockholders or members and not injurious to the public.' " *

If the Wisconsin court, in ruling that benefit to the stockholders is not a material factor to be considered in proceedings for dissolution, had in mind the "benefit" that exists by virtue of mere solvency, which apparently was that contemplated by the New York Court of Appeals in In re Radom & Neidorff, we tend to agree with its position. If, on the other hand, it means to suggest that we can not consider actual benefits to the stockholders in the form of such matters as payment of regular and substantial dividends, then we can not accept its viewpoint. We must remember that Strong v. Fromm Laboratories was a case in which the complainant was receiving no dividends from the company while the faction in power were drawing substantial salaries. We think that actual benefit to the stockholders is a factor which may properly be considered in determining whether dissolution is to be granted. We say this not because we think the petitioner in such cases has a duty to be satisfied in spite of himself, but because we must consider the rights of the 50 per cent interest which is in control of the company as well as that which is out of control.

Appellant argues that because the director deadlock provision of our act, ORS 57.595(1) (a) (A), requires a showing of "irreparable injury to the corporation" before the court can liquidate a company by reason of a deadlocked directorate which the shareholders can not break, and because such a requirement is absent from the shareholder deadlock provision, a further reason is thus provided why we can

---

* [Ed. note] Accord, Kruger v. Gerth, 22 A.D.2d 916, 255 N.Y.S.2d 498 (1964), affirmed per curiam (with two dissents), 16 N.Y.2d 802, 263 N.Y.S.2d 1 (1965) (holding that it was not a sufficient reason to justify dissolution at the suit of the minority stockholders that the business earned little more than enough to pay the compensation of the chief officer-majority stockholder, so long as that compensation was fair). The New York provision dealing with dissolution upon deadlock was completely rewritten in the 1963 revision. N.Y.B.C.L. § 1104. The new law bears some resemblance to MBA § 90, but there are several important differences. First, § 1111 provides expressly that in an action for dissolution by a shareholder or director, "the benefit to the shareholders of a dissolution is of paramount importance"; moreover, "dissolution is not to be denied merely because it is found that the corporate business has been or could be conducted at a profit." Second, § 1104 includes as an independent basis for seeking dissolution "that there is internal dissension and two or more factions of stockholders are so divided that dissolution would be beneficial to the shareholders."

not consider benefit or detriment to the stockholders. We do not understand the statute in this way. We can not equate "irreparable injury" and "benefit to the shareholders." The former is a much more restrictive idea. The absence of a requirement of "irreparable injury" from the jurisdictional facts which must be proven in a petition for dissolution by reason of shareholder deadlock certainly does not indicate that we must dismiss from our consideration of the equities of the case any showing of actual benefit to the stockholders from the operation of the company. We think that it is only persuasive of the fact that "irreparable injury" is not properly a decisive factor. We take note of the fact that the shareholder deadlock provision did not appear in the 1950 revision of the model act. It was added to the 1953 revision after Illinois had included such a provision in its Business Corporation Act. To this extent, therefore, Section 90 is not made up of integrated subsections, and reasoning from one subsection to another must therefore be done with caution.

Appellant also cites two recent New Jersey cases as supporting her view that the corporation ought to be dissolved. The corporation act of New Jersey, R.S. 14:13–15, N.J.S.A., provides that corporations "may be dissolved" in the event of shareholder deadlock. Petition of Collins-Doan Co., 1949, 3 N.J. 382, 70 A.2d 159, 163, 13 A.L.R.2d 1250, presented a situation in which the stock of the company was divided into preferred and common, each of which was to be represented by two directors. Doan took the preferred and Collins the common. The company was a prosperous printing house. The factions became deadlocked over non-payment of dividends on the preferred stock. Collins, without authorization from the directors, ruled the corporation as a personal desmesne for the benefit of himself and his son. They received salaries and moved the business into a building owned by the son at an annual rental of $4,200. It is clear from the opinion that dissolution was granted because of corporate paralysis.

". . . Collins concedes that the differences are irreconcilable. Thus, dissension has rendered the directorate impotent; and the like equal division of interest and voting power among the stockholders put it beyond their power to cure this paralysis of function by the election of a directorate of an uneven number.

* * *

"There is no alternative course. For ten years or more the Company has not functioned as ordained by the law; and irreconcilable differences between the equally divided shareholders and directors render a resumption of function impossible. . . . RS 14:7–1 N.J.S.A. provides that the 'business of every corporation shall be managed by its board of directors, not less than three in number.' And the statute has in view also the protection of the interests of the shareholders. There is no corporate function here. The business is under the management of one who happened to be serving in that capacity when the deadlock occurred; and the direction has become personalized to the exclusion of all other interests. . . ."

In re Evening Journal Ass'n, 1951, 15 N.J.Super. 58, 83 A.2d 38, 41, granted a petition for dissolution of a solvent daily newspaper. Dissension among the shareholders, however, lost it business that it might have enjoyed. The Dear and Newhouse factions were at odds. The directors, four in number and evenly divided between the two factions, were holding over since no nominees at subsequent elections received a majority. There was interference with payment of salaries. By virtue of his position as president and editor Dear had arrogated to himself the entire control of the company. There was evidence that both parties could protect themselves at a public or private sale of the newspaper. Again the court relied on paralysis of corporate function as a basis for dissolution. It said:

"Defendants have not proved bad faith on the part of the plaintiffs. They charge that they are attempting to ruin the company but not the newspaper. But where is the proof? There is resistance by plaintiffs to Dear's attempt to be the sole manager of the association, but is not that something which they may properly do? If the stockholders are impotent to elect a board of directors by reason of the equal division of the stock into two independent ownerships or interests, if the directors are equally divided respecting the management of the corporation and the president of the association and editor of the newspaper assumes to act as the sole manager, what is more natural for the ownership of one-half of the stock of the association to do than seek the remedy of dissolution? Plaintiffs have a very substantial investment in the association and they have the right to protect it.

* * *

". . . Due to the equal division on the board of directors that body has been unable to control and manage the operation of the business. In the absence of action by the directors, Dear has assumed the general management of the corporation. To an extent Newhouse has tolerated this. He has resisted in some respects. But is he required to suffer control and management by the Dear half-interests indefinitely? . . ."

Reviewing Petition of Collins-Doan Co., supra, the court concluded:

"Hence the test is not whether routine business is carried on or not, or whether business is being conducted at a profit or a loss, but whether there is a paralysis of corporate function."

Appellant also cites and relies upon the reasoning of a scholarly article by Carlos L. Israels, "The Sacred Cow of Corporate Existence—Problems of Deadlock and Dissolution," 19 U. of Chic.L.Rev.

778 (1952). It is Mr. Israels' position that courts should be reluctant to "put themselves in business" for reviewing the equities of cases involving deadlock among shareholders, and that the model act is susceptible of a mechanical and "pragmatic" interpretation. Mr. Israels apparently would permit dissolution whenever the jurisdictional facts are proven. If we assume, arguendo, that a mechanical rule is desirable, if only from the standpoint of facility of administration, we have nevertheless already expressed our view that the statute contemplates that courts shall consider the equities of the individual case. If this were not true, the shareholder deadlock provision would have been expressed in terms of mandate rather than permission.

Viewed in this light we do not think that appellant has made out a case for liquidation of the Nicolai-Neppach Co. While her sole purpose in introducing the minute book of the corporation into evidence was to show deadlock and failure of the stockholders to elect a board of directors, the minute book as well as other evidence furnishes us with a broader view of the activities of the company. Even so, there is nothing in evidence which persuades us to enter an order winding up the company. We think that the plaintiff has not only the burden of proof to establish jurisdictional facts under the shareholder deadlock provision, but the further burden of proving equitable grounds for dissolution. She has failed to meet that burden.

The evidence before us is that Herbert Jackson has refused to allow the board of directors to be increased to four members—which would certainly result in further deadlock—and that he has refused to consider liquidation of the company. We do not think that it is lack of equity for a stockholder who is in control of a deadlocked company to refuse to vote against his own interests, even though the effect is to perpetuate him in office. The evidence shows affirmatively that Herbert Jackson has ably administered the company for the benefit of all of the stockholders, and that he has agreed to the distribution of profits in dividends in so far as they were not required for the repair or development of the plant. These profits have been substantial. The plant employs about 65 men and there is a public interest in preserving it as a going concern.

The evidence shows, moreover, that Hazel Jackson has an effective weapon of corporate management through her control over Herbert Jackson's salary. The power to fix officers' salaries is vested in the stockholders by virtue of the by-laws. There is thus no danger, so long as the company remains prosperous, that the incumbent management will be able to siphon off profits of the corporation through salaries rather than dividends.

We need not decide at what point we would hold that dissolution must be granted as a matter of right. Traditionally a court of equity will not interfere with the exercise of business discretion by the directors and officers of a company. Perhaps this is a branch of the law where we will find it necessary to do so under proper circumstances. But such circumstances are not present in this case. The proper solution of the impasse reached in Nicolai-Neppach Co. appears to be for one of the two shareholders to purchase the other's shares. We think an equitable adjustment will be reached by denying rather than granting dissolution in this case. To decree liquidation would give Hazel Jackson a club to hold over the head of Herbert Jackson. To deny liquidation imposes upon each party a certain amount of burden and uncertainty so long as their differences continue. There is a possibility that Hazel and Herbert Jackson may compose their differences amicably—it does not appear so far that either has attempted to oppress or unfairly deal with the other. If they can not settle their disagreement, then we think that denial of relief at the present time may well lead to a fairer buy-sell agreement than the remedy of enforced liquidation, a remedy which might destroy the going concern value of the plant and give both parties an unduly small return for the value of their investment.

The judgment of dismissal is affirmed.

In 1960, this dissolution pattern originally fashioned under the Illinois statute was finally presented for construction by the courts of that state, in Gidwitz v. Lanzit Corrugated Box Co., 20 Ill.2d 208, 170 N.E.2d 131 (1960). The decision in that case is thoughtfully analyzed in the following case comment in 74 Harv.L.Rev. 1461 (1961)[1]:

The plaintiff controlled fifty per cent of the shares and two of the four directorships in the defendant corporation. Control of the other half interest was held by the plaintiff's cousin, who was also president. Since 1950, when the cousins had had a falling out, substantially all business decisions had been made by the president alone, despite vigorous informal protests by the plaintiff. During this time almost no directors' or shareholders' meetings were held, and no election of directors was conducted. The corporation had continued to earn profits, though a slight business decline had recently been experienced. The plaintiff sued to obtain liquidation pursuant to [§ 157.86(a) of the Illinois Business Corporation Act, which is virtually identical to MBA § 90(a) except that subparagraphs (2) and (3) are reversed]. After lengthy proceedings before a master, during which each party refused to sell his interest to the other, the chancellor ordered sale of the business and liquidation of the proceeds. On appeal, *held*, affirmed. The deprivation of the plaintiff's right to participate

---

1. Copyright (c), Harvard Law Review Association, 1961. Reprinted by permission. Footnotes omitted.

in the management of the corporation constitutes oppression under subparagraph [2] * and entitled him to a decree of dissolution. . .

Despite the equal division of shares and directors between antagonistic parties, it is questionable whether the statute authorized liquidation in the present circumstances. Subparagraph (1) was probably inapplicable because of its requirement of irreparable injury, which has ordinarily been interpreted to necessitate a showing of imminent insolvency. Subparagraph [3] might have applied since the present directors had carried over in office without election for more than a decade; however, it is doubtful that the shareholders can be considered to have "failed" to elect new directors since no election had been attempted and since, because of the Illinois cumulative-voting requirement, the evenly divided shareholders could never have failed to elect a complete four-man board.

The "oppression" required by subparagraph [2] has normally been read to mean abuse of corporate position for private financial gain at the expense of other shareholders. Although there was evidence in the present case that the president had engaged in some such conduct, the court seems to have rested its determination of oppression upon its conclusion that the plaintiff had been excluded from his rightful participation in management. The plaintiff's right as a director to vote on matters requiring board approval does seem to have been invaded by the president's action undertaken without securing such approval, and the plaintiff's informal protests seem sufficient to negate any inference of acquiescence in this conduct. However, the plaintiff also had authority to call board meetings to consider presidential action and, if necessary, could have sought a court order enjoining actions which a deadlocked board had failed to approve. The continued availability of these less severe remedies seems to make a grant of liquidation unnecessary to halt infringement of the authority provided the plaintiff in the corporate charter and by-laws. Although affirmative action in accord with the plaintiff's preferences might still be prevented by deadlock of the directors, the statutory relief available for this circumstance seems dependent on subparagraph (1). By its extension of the meaning of "oppression" the court seems to have produced the anomaly that although dissolution is unavailable in the absence of threatened insolvency when the directors have been unable to agree, when there has been no demand that they attempt agreement it becomes available without regard to this limitation.

On the other hand, the present result seems responsive to the special characteristics of a close corporation, the dissolution of which has increasingly been recognized as desirable whenever its shareholders have ceased to cooperate. Regardless of their constitutive provi-

---

* [Ed. note] Subparagraph numbers in brackets have been changed from the original to conform to the appropriate subparagraphs of MBA § 90(a).

sions, such corporations are commonly formed upon the understanding that business decisions will be reached cooperatively. In the present case, the parties were successors to their parents who had managed the corporation by means of informal conferences, and they themselves had evidenced a desire to perpetuate this equality by dividing representation on the board of directors instead of simply filling a single vacancy on the prior three-man board. Thus, the subsequent inability to share in the executive functions of the corporation or to exercise an affirmative influence on its policies would result in a frustration of the plaintiff's expectations. Moreover, since the marketability of a one-half interest in an unharmonious family corporation is considerably restricted, the plaintiff may be effectively locked into an investment over which he lacks control. An insistence that the antagonistic parties resolve their differences within the corporate framework would, in addition, seem inconsistent with the traditional hesitance of courts of equity to enforce unwelcome personal relationships. Continuation of the business in this state of animosity would be likely to reduce its efficiency and profitability, and might well lead to recurrent litigation.

Previous efforts of the Illinois legislature to liberalize the dissolution requirements have been interpreted very restrictively by the courts. The addition in 1951 of the present subparagraph [3] seems to have been for the purpose of establishing a precise rule to prevent shareholders owning half the stock from perpetuating their control to the exclusion of other shareholders having an equal investment. However, since the manner in which the section was drafted seems to limit its application to corporations with odd-numbered directorates — a consequence probably not intended by the legislature — the extension of subparagraph [2] may be justified as in accord with the apparent aims underlying the amendment. . . .

Although the language of the present opinion seems to indicate that a shareholder who can establish the existence of any of the enumerated circumstances has an absolute right to dissolution, the statute should probably be construed to confer only discretionary power to grant the remedy. Dissolution has been denied under an identical statute when it was feared that such an order would allow the petitioning shareholder to acquire the assets of the corporation at less than a fair price, [citing the Jackson case, supra]. There was no indication in the present case, however, that either party was without sufficient funds to insure competitive bidding for the assets. Moreover, the degree of managerial skill required in the manufacture of corrugated boxes seems insufficient to preclude either party from seeking to reacquire the business. Since no adverse interest of employees, creditors, or the general public was brought to the attention of the court, the affirmative exercise of discretion in the present case seems to have been appropriate.

See generally, Israels, the Sacred Cow of Corporate Existence — Problems of Deadlock and Dissolution, 19 U. Chi. L. Rev. 778 (1952); Barkin, Deadlock and Dissolution in Florida Closed Corporations: Litigating and Planning, 13 U.Miami L.Rev. 395 (1959); Comment, Deadlock and Dissolution: Problems in the Closely Held Corporation in Illinois, 56 Nw.U.L.Rev. 525 (1961).

SECTION 2. ROLE OF GOODWILL AND COVENANTS NOT TO COMPETE

A. IN GENERAL

As was noted earlier in connection with valuation of a business, goodwill and other intangibles may be among an enterprise's most valuable assets. However, in the case of a relatively small business of the sort usually carried on by a closely-held corporation, such intangible values are often intimately related to the skill or reputation of one or more of the individual participants in the enterprise. Indeed, in many cases the goodwill is so personal to the individuals that there is no enterprise goodwill as such. And even where the enterprise does have goodwill (or at least momentum) which could survive the departure of the individuals, such goodwill would be either greatly impaired or eliminated if the individuals went into competition with their former enterprise. In such cases any buyer of the enterprise would normally insist upon a covenant against competition by the individuals formerly associated with it. Such covenants would also be useful in cases like the one hypothesized above, where an enterprise with two divisions is divided between the former stockholders — each of the stockholders would agree not to compete with the business transferred to the other.

What happens to enterprise goodwill in cases of involuntary dissolution where the parties are not in a position (or the mood) to bargain about anything? Here the absence of any vehicle for restricting competition by the former participants in the enterprise may substantially affect the situation, particularly when the participants vary widely in their ability to compete. This problem is nicely illustrated in the following excerpt:

CHAYES, MADAM WAGNER AND THE CLOSE CORPORATION*

73 Harv.L.Rev. 1545–1548 (1960).

Another Look at the "Sacred Cow"

Dissolution of the close corporation has been given increasing attention since Mr. Israels' much-cited article.[55] It has not been remarked, however, that refusal to dissolve may amount to enforcing specifically against the petitioner the respondent's version of the relationship. Nonetheless, cases in New York and elsewhere seem to say that as long as the company pays the rent — in the form of immediate profits for the shareholders — it cannot be disturbed in its lease on life.

This kind of judicial solicitude for the lives of fictional persons, creatures of the law, has already been criticized as somewhat misplaced in the close-corporation field. A large measure of agreement with such criticism is implicit in the position taken in this Comment. A judicial treatment of the close corporation which is responsive to the underlying reality of a personal, intimate, ongoing association among the enterprisers will be somewhat readier to dissolve the corporate shell, rather than leave the parties in an Ugoline embrace. And this despite the continuation of satisfactory noises from the direction of the cash register.

It does not necessarily follow that the close corporation should become as soluble as the partnership.[59] Muslim divorce is not the only alternative to "till death do us part." The very instability of the partnership form is often one of the reasons dictating a corporate incarnation for the business. Again the question is essentially one for resolution through the familiar balancing processes and flexible remedial resources of courts of equity.

To take an example, the refusal to dissolve the deadlocked company in In the Matter of Radom & Neidorff, Inc.[61] is the kind of thing that reduces the brave new close-corporation lawyer to a helpless rage. Radom and Mrs. Neidorff were brother and sister, and were sole and equal shareholders in a profitable music-printing and lithographing company. She had come into her half upon the death of her husband. When the two brothers-in-law had run the show, all had

---

* Copyright (c), Harvard Law Review Association, 1960. Reprinted by permission. Most of the footnotes omitted.
55. Israels, The Sacred Cow of Corporate Existence—Problems of Deadlock and Dissolution, 19 U.Chi.L.Rev. 778 (1952).
59. Indeed, the partnership itself is not as fragile as is sometimes assumed. True, a partner can always withdraw. But monetary penalties can be embodied in the partnership agreement which exert a powerful suasion for the partners to patch up their difficulties. Similar techniques might well be employed by close-corporation planners.
61. 307 N.Y. 1, 119 N.E.2d 563 (1954).

gone swimmingly. Consanguinity, as is not infrequently the case, thickened the air. Mrs. Neidorff sued her brother for breach of fiduciary duty, refused to sign his salary checks, failed to show up at meetings, and generally left to him the burden of running the business. One can hardly fail to sympathize with Radom when he brings suit to dissolve. Yet the New York Court of Appeals not only refused his petition but held that there was no discretion to appoint a referee to hold a hearing on it.

Was this result wholly unjustified? In early 1950, Radom offered Mrs. Neidorff $75,000 for her interest in the company. Three years later, accumulated profits (before his salary) were $242,000. This suggests that the shares may have been worth more than $75,000 in 1950. Further, in a court ordered dissolution, Mrs. Neidorff would have had to content herself with one-half the liquidating value of the corporate assets, $150,000 at the outside. But Radom would have had the going-concern value, since he had the skill and associations to continue to operate the business while his "partner's" widow did not. Surely, when they organized the business the two men did not contemplate this kind of bet on survivorship. Moreover, apart from their wishes, the law is clear-cut that a majority shareholder will not be permitted to siphon off going-concern value by exercising his power to bring about voluntary dissolution of the company. Why should one lacking such power be permitted to enlist the court in his aid?

In this view, there is something to be said for denying Radom's petition for dissolution: it is one way to force him to offer his sister a fair price for her interest.[63] More generally, where the company whose demise is sought continues to earn tidily, it is not unlikely that one of the parties (usually the petitioner) will capture the lion's share of the value on liquidation.

The answer to this argument is that there are much better ways of achieving a result consonant with fairness. Dissolution could be granted conditioned upon petitioner's offering to buy out the respondent at a fair price. This result is expressly sanctioned by statute in some states. In others, courts of equity have occasionally managed to approach it under their own steam. Once such a condition is recognized as potentially appropriate, others, more or less fancy, are seen also to be imaginable.

The dissolution problem ties in still more directly with the theme of this Comment. Co-owners of a business enterprise are unlikely to resort to litigation of any kind with each other unless the existence of amicable business relations between them has been gravely threatened. Thus when a case of the types discussed earlier — disputes over shareholders' contracts, pooling agreements, charter provisions

---

[63]. Cf. Jackson v. Nicolai-Neppach Co., 219 Or. 560, 348 P.2d 9, 22 (1959).

or by-laws — comes before a court, the decree, whether or not it grants specific performance, is likely to remit the loser to his statutory or contractual rights to dissolve the company. The availability of such a recourse may be a proper factor for the court to consider in fashioning its relief.

Does the parties' agreement include a liberalized method of voluntary dissolution by compulsory buy-out or otherwise? If so, it may make specific enforcement of the operating arrangement, say, a pooling agreement, that much easier, since they have provided their own safety valve for the pressures of enforced intimacy. Similarly, where statutory authority to dissolve is relatively leniently administered, the judge need not be so concerned about the threshold of tolerance in enforcing a shareholders' contract. There is a ceiling on the advantage the winner can extract from a favorable decree.

More often, however, it will be apparent that the integument of friendship, cooperation, profit, or even common civility has so far decayed that the organism of the enterprise is no longer viable. At that state, it seems pointless to try to prolong its life by enforcing the portions of the agreement of the parties designed to govern operations. . . .

B. IMPLIED COVENANTS NOT TO COMPETE

When may a covenant not to compete be implied in connection with a transaction in corporate stock? An important recent Massachusetts decision in this area is analyzed in the following case comment in 77 Harv.L.Rev. 368 (1963)[2]:

Cody and Tobin, Inc., was engaged in the scrap metal business in New Bedford, Massachusetts. In 1956, as sole shareholders, Paul Tobin and his brother owned fifty shares, William Cody owned forty-nine, and one share was owned by William Cody, Jr., who in 1942 had left the business for a long period before returning to its employ. During negotiations among the shareholders and the Codys' attorney, the corporation's assets were evaluated without mentioning goodwill, and the Codys sold their stock to the corporation. In 1959 Cody, Jr., who had left the state shortly after the sale, returned to Massachusetts and activated Cape Cod Iron Works, Inc., operating it as a scrap metal business in New Bedford, a short distance from the business premises of Cody and Tobin, Inc.; he solicited some of the latter corporation's customers. Paul Tobin and the former corporation were

---

2. Copyright (c), Harvard Law Review Association, 1963. Reprinted by permission. Portions of the text and all of the footnotes omitted.

granted a decree permanently enjoining both Codys and Cape Cod Iron Works from engaging in the scrap metal business in Bristol County and from soliciting customers of the plaintiff corporation. On appeal, *held*, affirmed, subject to a further hearing on whether the decree should be limited to New Bedford. The defendants' complete divestment of interest in the corporation is presumed to include their interest in its goodwill. Such a transfer, by active participants in the business, implies an agreement by the sellers not to compete so as to derogate from the value of the goodwill sold. The master's finding that defendants' activities derogate from the 1956 sale was justified, and in view of the small area involved and the similarity of names, the lower court properly concluded that the need for such protection will continue throughout the individual defendants' lives. Tobin v. Cody, 343 Mass. 716, 180 N.E.2d 652 (1962).

Except for a few instances involving personal-service occupations, apparently no state other than Massachusetts has held that the sale of a proprietor's or partner's interest in a business may preclude the seller from engaging subsequently in a similar business, in the absence of an express covenant to that effect. The present decision is the first to extend to a sale of capital stock the rule in Massachusetts prohibiting such competition as an impairment of a prior transfer of goodwill. Judicial definitions of goodwill have in general focused on favorable customer relationships and their continuance, emphasizing the factors responsible for such advantages — trade names, business location, secret methods, excellence of goods and services, the personality and ability of those connected with the business, reputation, and customer habits and prejudices. Courts which permit the transferor of goodwill to compete have even in the absence of an explicit agreement nevertheless prohibited him from interfering with the buyer's succession to these advantages by using a name deceptively similar to that of the old business or otherwise holding himself out as its successor, by discouraging former customers from continuing to deal with the old business, or by direct solicitation of such customers; the transferor may, however, advertise generally and deal with old customers who come to him voluntarily. This majority rule thus treats as a derogation from the goodwill which the seller has transferred only his competitive use of those relationships built up by and for the old business, and not merely his subsequent competition "as a stranger."

The doctrine seems grounded on the policy that the right to carry on a business should not be held to be lost by implication, in view of the traditional judicial distrust of and limitations upon agreements in restraint of trade and the public policy favoring competition and individual economic opportunity. To be sure, express covenants not to compete have been enforced, notwithstanding these objections, partly because they have been regarded as reasonable safeguards to protect a buyer of a business interest in his investment, an objective which would also tend to support the creation of implied covenants. But an equally important reason for their enforcement has been the contention that such express agreements often are necessary to enable a seller to dispose advantageously of his business interest — sales which the law should not discourage. And this policy is presumably inapplicable when the buyer has not seen fit to demand an express covenant.

If the issue is posed in terms of satisfying the normal expectations of parties bargaining for the sale of a business interest, it would seem proper to place upon the buyer the burden of laying express ground rules, if there are to be any, in regard to the seller's future competition. This may not follow so readily, however, in a jurisdiction such as Massachusetts with well-established precedent for inferring the covenant, or in a case like the present one, where the buyer was not represented by counsel in the negotiations. Despite the objections to implied covenants, the Massachusetts rule may gain some support from the recognition that in practice a former owner who immediately enters into a nearby competing business, even if restrained from direct solicitation of old customers and holding himself out as a successor, is still likely to interfere with the patronage of the old business not merely "as a stranger" but rather because of his reputation and associations developed in the former business. Yet this result, rather than being presumed, might be made to depend on the nature of the business — whether its patronage depended significantly on the ability or personality of persons connected with it.

Whatever the merits of the Massachusetts rule, its present application to stock transfers seems logical. Such an extension would be objectionable if applied indiscriminately, for example to transfers of shares in a widely held corporation. But often a shareholder, by reason of prominence in management and especially in customer relationships, is personally responsible for corporate goodwill and can therefore substantially affect it by subsequent activities. If, as in the present case, his sale is part of a transaction in which a substantial percentage of corporate ownership is transferred, the Massachusetts policy of protecting the purchaser of goodwill seems equally apposite. It is arguable that to find a basis for inferring a covenant in a transfer by the holder of a relatively insubstantial percentage of corporate ownership would be inconsistent with the settled refusal, both in Massachusetts and elsewhere, to infer such a covenant by an employee upon his leaving the business. Hence no basis might be found for inferring a covenant by Cody, Jr., seller of only one share. But the court might reasonably have regarded the Codys as joint transferors for this purpose. In light of the family relationships involved, the fact that Cody, Jr. initiated the negotiations, the designation of the Codys as joint owners in the contract, and the fact that payment was made to Cody, Sr. in one check, it appears that the parties treated the families as units. As to any technical objections arising out of the corporate form, it is noteworthy that in upholding express covenants not to compete made in connection with sales of stock, the courts have swept aside contentions that a prominent shareholder has no vendible interest in goodwill. Moreover, failure to mention goodwill in the sale contract or in valuing business assets to determine a sale price should no more preclude the creation of implied restrictions, designed to protect goodwill transferred, in the sale of corporate shares, than in the transfer of a partnership or proprietorship interest. Complete divestment of the seller's stockholdings should carry with it his interest in all attributes of the business. . . .

See generally, Levin, Implied Covenants Against Competition Created by Transaction in Corporate Stock: Some Thoughts on Tobin v. Cody, 43 B.U.L.Rev. 20 (1963).

C. TAX ASPECTS OF COVENANTS NOT TO COMPETE

NOTE, TAX TREATMENT OF COVENANTS NOT TO COMPETE: A PROBLEM OF PURCHASE PRICE ALLOCATION*

67 Yale L.J. 1261 (1958).

Conflicting tax interests of the vendor and vendee of a going business influence the amount of purchase price allocated to goodwill rather than to an accompanying covenant not to compete.[1] Embracing reputation and customer loyalty, goodwill may rest largely on the owner's individual personality or skill and, after sale of the business, its retention may therefore depend upon the purchaser obtaining a promise from the seller not to open a competing business. Since an excess of purchase price over the value of all tangible and identifiable intangible assets must be attributed either to goodwill or the covenant, pricing the covenant is primarily a task of apportionment between it and goodwill rather than of valuing the covenant alone.

---

* Copyright, Yale Law Journal, 1958. Reprinted by permission. Most of the footnotes omitted.

1. In addition to the physical assets, the purchaser of a going business generally acquires goodwill, which may be an important source of earning power. When goodwill is based primarily on general reputation of the business rather than personal qualities of the proprietor, the purchaser ordinarily has little difficulty obtaining the benefits of the firm's good name. Many customers may, however, be attracted by an individual proprietor and will not necessarily patronize his successor. Frequently, the purchaser's ability to retain the seller's goodwill depends upon the seller's withdrawal from competition; accordingly, the seller's covenant not to compete often accompanies the sale of a personalized business. . . .

The vendor, seeking capital gains, will demand a high price for goodwill — a capital asset — and a correspondingly low price for the covenant — taxable as ordinary income.** The vendee, on the other hand, prefers a high basis for the covenant which, unlike goodwill, has a limited life furnishing depreciation deductions.[9]

Similarly, when an incorporated business is transferred through sale of corporate stock, goodwill represents that part of the stock's value not allocable to any specific asset. A low price on a selling shareholder's covenant will therefore permit a high allocation to the stock with attendant capital gains for the vendor-shareholder. Because stock is nondepreciable and resale ordinarily is not contemplated, the vendee, obtaining no immediate tax benefit from a high basis for stock, will prefer a large allocation to the depreciable covenant. In any event, whatever the price agreed upon when a business is transferred through sale of stock, inclusion of a separate covenant from the selling shareholder [will normally deprive] him of capital gains to the extent of the price of the covenant.

In Richard Ullman,[15] this dilemma confronted the joint owners of three corporations who, on selling their stock, executed seven-year covenants not to compete. After agreeing to $1,000,000 as the total purchase price, the vendee suggested allocating $400,000 to the covenants. The vendors, fearful of losing the sale, agreed to an apportionment of $350,000 to the covenants and $650,000 to the cost of the stock. When capital gains treatment was sought for the full $1,000,000, the Tax Court held the $350,000 ordinary income on two grounds. That the covenant was separately bargained for was considered evidence of its severability from goodwill. In addition, the court postulated that stockholders cannot own corporate goodwill and concluded that proceeds from the sale of a shareholder's — as distinguished from a sole proprietor's — covenant cannot be income from the sale of goodwill but only compensation for personal services, taxable as ordinary income.

Under present law, each of the two grounds on which Ullman rests is insufficient in itself to support the result. The fact that stockholders have no direct proprietary interest in corporate goodwill does not, standing alone, make the covenant price ordinary income; in the absence of a stated allocation to stock and covenant, courts have attributed the entire purchase price to the stock, taxable at capital gains rates.[21] Nor does mere agreement by the parties on a separate price for the covenant, without more, produce ordinary income

---

** [Ed. note] See note 32 infra.

9. . . . No deduction for depreciation is allowable with respect to good will. . . . Depreciation deductions for goodwill are disallowed because of difficulty in determining when and to what extent they become exhausted in use. . . .

15. 29 T.C. 129 (1957). [Ed. note: Affirmed, 264 F.2d 305 (2d Cir. 1959).]

21. Sidney Alper, P-H 1956 T.C.Mem. Dec. ¶ 56271 (despite allocation, covenant ignored as not separately bargained for because necessary to assure transfer of goodwill: no mention of stockholder status). George H. Payne,

taxation. And since failure to fix a price may result in a judicially determined covenant value taxed as ordinary income,[23] neither inclusion nor omission of a covenant price by the parties has alone been the determining factor in prior case law. Apparently unwilling to break new ground, the Ullman court conformed with previous decisions by relying both on its finding that the covenant was specially bargained for and on the status of taxpayers as shareholder-vendors rather than proprietors.

The Tax Court's distinction between proprietors and shareholders ignores the actual function and effect of a covenant not to compete. The covenant enables the vendee to acquire those customers who presumably will do business with him so long as the covenantor does not become a competitor. Reputation and customer loyalty being elements of goodwill, the covenant is a means of protecting goodwill transferred with the business and is enforceable only if adopted for that purpose. Since goodwill can be equally protected whether the covenant is that of a proprietor, stockholder or key employee, differences arising from status are differences not in the operation of the covenant but in the ease with which its value is ascertained. In an arm's length transaction, the price allocated to an employee's covenant — which protects goodwill sold by another — is automatically taxed as ordinary income, for the price can only reflect the value of the covenant, the taxpayer having conveyed nothing else. In contrast, the proprietor-vendor's covenant maintains transferred goodwill which he owned directly, while the promise of the shareholder-vendor conserves purchased stock-value flowing from goodwill. Thus, the close relation of the proprietor or shareholder covenant to goodwill makes a price apportionment between them difficult. Irrespective of the covenantor's identity or of complexity in allocation, however, the covenant always fulfills precisely the same function of safeguarding goodwill — without altering the essential nature of either goodwill or the covenant.

Accordingly, a covenant with a separately stated price should always produce ordinary income to the extent of that price regardless of the status of the covenantor. Although a sale of property — good-

---

22 T.C. 526 (1954) (allocation in unsigned memorandum but not in formal contract; covenant not separately bargained for held nonseverable from goodwill; no mention of stockholders lacking direct proprietary interest).

23. See Rodney B. Horton, 13 T.C. 143 (1949) (goodwill and covenant held severable). Courts have often held the covenant severable and permitted a vendee depreciation deductions when no allocation was made by the parties. Wilson Athletic Goods Mfg. Co. v. Commissioner, 222 F.2d 355 (7th Cir. 1955) (lack of express segregation by parties not binding); Frances Silberman, 22 T.C. 1240 (1954) (business had no goodwill) . . . More often, however, courts have accepted the absence of allocation as evidence of nonseverability and disallowed depreciation deductions. Radio Medford, Inc. v. United States, 150 F.Supp. 641 (D. Ore.1957) (parties did not treat covenant having little value as distinct item); Dauksch v. Busey, 125 F.Supp. 130, 133 (S.D.Ohio 1954) (parties did not treat covenant separately from goodwill). . . .

will — accompanies the covenant, the covenant itself is not property and therefore not a capital asset, but a promise of certain conduct supported by consideration.[32] Moreover, ordinary income treatment for the covenant would create no special hardship. Favorable tax rates accorded capital gains are intended to mitigate the burden of telescoping into one year gain resulting from appreciation in value over many years and to preserve liquidity for those capital items whose transfer might be unduly discouraged by heavy taxation. But a taxpayer wishing to sell a business, besides being likely to have a reason for the transfer which outweighs the inhibiting high taxation of incidental covenants, can mitigate the harsh effects of telescoping by arranging to receive compensation for noncompetition in installments over the life of the covenant. Such an arrangement should be satisfactory to the vendee, who would make a smaller initial outlay while retaining the ability to stop payments on breach of the covenant. The vendor, on the other hand, might be apprehensive of vendee insolvency or simply prefer immediate payment. Unwillingness to assume ordinary commercial risks, however, is an unpersuasive reason for conferring capital gains advantages on payments for nonperformance of activity which, if performed, would produce ordinary income. Furthermore, capital gains rates would remain applicable to the stock of selling shareholders [38] and to transferred business assets other than inventory and accounts receivable.

Taxing the covenant as ordinary income and honoring the contracting parties' price allocation would achieve predictability of tax treatment in an area currently marked by needless uncertainty.[40]

32. . . . No doubt exists that proceeds from a contract, other than for a sale of capital assets or § 1231 assets, constitute ordinary income under this broad statement. Covenants not to compete, when unaccompanied by, or separable from, a sale of other assets, have consistently been held to be compensation for services, taxable as ordinary income under present § 61(a)(1). See e. g., Beals' Estate v. Commissioner, 82 F.2d 268, 270 (2d Cir. 1936). However, the covenant becomes depreciable property in the hands of the vendee and, on sale of the business by the vendee, proceeds from the sale of the covenant would probably be taxed as capital gains. . . .

38. . . . Prior to sale, a stockholder-vendor might covenant not to compete with his corporation for a nominal consideration. This would raise the value of the stock transferred to include the value of the covenant. On selling his stock, the vendor would then receive the same amount for the stock as he would have received for the stock plus a personal covenant. Thus, the price of the covenant becomes part of the price of stock yielding capital gain to the vendor. The vendee, however, may dislike this arrangement because he receives no depreciation deductions. . . . And the court may well look through form to the substance of the transaction, especially if the shareholder covenant to the corporation was executed solely for tax-avoidance purposes. . . .

40. At present, no clearly defined standard exists by which vendors and vendees can predict tax treatment accorded a covenant not to compete. *Compare* Richard Ullman, 29 T.C. 129 (1958) (stockholder-vendor ineligible for capital gains treatment of covenant), *with* George H. Payne, 22 T.C. 526 (1954) (stockholder-vendor's covenant accorded capital gains). *Compare* Hamlin's Trust v. Commissioner, 209 F.2d 761 (10th Cir. 1954) (allocation a ground for taxation of covenant as ordinary income), *with* Toledo Newspaper Co., 2 T.C. 794 (1943) (de-

Since vendor and vendee ordinarily bargain with their net position after taxes in mind, the proposed rule would avoid unnecessary disappointment of their legitimate expectations while saving the Commissioner the difficult task of attempting to apportion between covenant and goodwill or stock. Thus, Ullman is to be commended for confirming the principle that allocation by stockholder-vendors results in ordinary income for the stipulated price of the covenant. In simultaneously basing the decision on the vendor's shareholder status, however, the court supplied inconsistent criteria for cases involving either shareholder-vendors with an unallocated price or nonshareholder-vendors with an allocated figure. Specifically, the court's reliance on allocation contradicts prior nonshareholder cases ignoring an allocation; and the court's statement that a stockholder-vendor cannot receive capital gains for a covenant conflicts with previous nonallocation cases according capital gains treatment to shareholders. Ullman therefore lays the ground for later decisions to hold that stipulated allocations do not reflect true values or, in the opposite situation, that failure to allocate must be remedied by judicial apportionment.

Had the Ullman court viewed allocation by the parties as the sole determining factor, future vendors and vendees irrespective of status would know the tax consequences of covenants and could plan accordingly. Moreover, tax revenue would not be significantly impaired by failure to allocate or by allocations not reflecting true values. No price for the covenant, or an understated one, though increasing the proportion of capital gains for the vendor, reduces depreciation deductions available to the vendee. Conversely, excessive depreciation deductions produced by undue allocation to the covenant are balanced by the increased amount of ordinary income received by the vendor. While parties in different tax brackets may achieve an overall tax saving by careful allocation, potential revenue loss does not appear great enough to justify expenditures for investigation and litigation on the question of true value.

The suggestion made in the foregoing Note that the parties' allocation (or lack thereof) of consideration to a covenant not to compete should be virtually conclusive for tax purposes has not been adopted by the courts. For example, in Annabelle Candy Co., Inc. v. Commissioner, 314 F.2d 1 (9th Cir. 1962), the two equal stockholders of a successful corporation decided to resolve their differences by having the corporation purchase all of the stock of one of them for $115,000.

spite allocation, covenant found non-severable from goodwill and taxed as capital gains). *Compare* Estate of Masquelette v. Commissioner, 239 F.2d 322 (5th Cir. 1956) (absence of allocation a ground for giving capital gains), *with* Rodney B. Horton, 13 T.C. 143 (1949) (despite failure to allocate, covenant found severable from goodwill and taxed as ordinary income). . . .

The selling stockholder gave an express covenant not to compete for a period of five years, but in the agreement of sale no portion of the total consideration paid to him was allocated to that covenant. Nevertheless, the corporation-taxpayer allocated approximately $80,000 of the $115,000 purchase price to the covenant and sought to amortize that amount over the covenant's five-year term. The Commissioner disallowed the deduction, and was sustained by the Tax Court on the basis of its finding that no separate or severable consideration was bargained for or paid for the covenant not to compete. Noting that the parties had not even discussed the covenant until after the purchase price had been preliminarily agreed upon, the Tax Court held that there was no convincing proof that the parties treated the covenant "in a separate and distinct manner"; accordingly, the court was "unable to find as petitioner contends that it was the intent of the agreement . . . that a portion of the $115,000 which petitioner agreed therein to pay . . . was in consideration for [the] promise not to compete . . . .."

The Court of Appeals reversed, on the ground that the Tax Court's emphasis upon whether or not the contract was "severable", or whether the covenant was "treated in a separate and distinct manner", constituted an erroneous theory of law. The proper test, according to the Court of Appeals, was whether the parties *intended* to allocate a portion of the purchase price to the covenant not to compete. The court noted that the failure to allocate any consideration to the covenant was "pretty good evidence that no such allocation was intended", but held that "it is not conclusive on the parties as would be the case if there had been an express affirmance or disavowal in the agreement". Accordingly, the Court of Appeals remanded the case for "a clear-cut decision as to what [the parties'] intent was, as evidenced by the agreement and all the surrounding circumstances".

Upon rehearing, the court modified its decision in a *per curiam* addendum to its previous opinion which seems likely to have particular application wherever a covenant not to compete is implied rather than express:

> The petition for rehearing and reply thereto establish more clearly than was heretofore apparent, that at the time the contract for the purchase of . . . stock was executed there was no expressed intention one way or the other as to allocation and tax consequences. It follows that the petitioner failed to sustain its burden of proving that, notwithstanding the lack of any recital to that effect in the agreement, the parties intended to allocate consideration to the covenant.
>
> Accordingly we are now of the view that there is no need of remanding the matter to the tax court for a rehearing on the question of intention. . . .

SECTION 3. TAX ASPECTS OF CORPORATE DIVISIONS

A. IN GENERAL

The tax treatment of corporate divisions has long been a ticklish problem because of the potential for bail-out of earnings and profits which divisions afford. To take a polar example, suppose that a prosperous corporation with substantial "investment" assets, such as marketable securities, could transfer those assets to a new corporation and "spin off" (or "split off") the new stock to its stockholders pro rata without subjecting them to tax at ordinary income rates. The stockholders would then be in position to sell the stock of the new corporation without surrendering any part of their ownership or control of the operating assets.

Understandably, therefore, corporate divisions have been the subject of considerable attention, both legislative and judicial. For present purposes, it is unnecessary to recount the developments in this area prior to 1954. For an excellent review, see Bittker, Federal Income Taxation of Corporations and Shareholders (1959) 321–328. But it should be noted that in general corporate divisions were prima facie eligible for tax-free treatment. This was based primarily on the predecessor of present § 368(a)(1)(D), under which a transfer of assets by one corporation to another corporation controlled either by the transferor or its shareholders constituted a reorganization. To the extent that the transfer of the stock of the new corporation to the shareholders of the original corporation, whether by spin-off, split-off or split-up, could be brought within the "plan of reorganization" under the predecessor of § 368(a)(1)(D), the transaction qualified for tax-free treatment under the predecessor of § 354.

The 1954 Code adopted an entirely new approach to the problem of corporate divisions. Basically, the present pattern is to make § 355 the exclusive vehicle for tax-free treatment of a corporate division — and to control such treatment by including in § 355 certain strict conditions for qualification. Section 355 does not depend upon the presence of a reorganization, either under § 368(a)(1)(D) or otherwise, but applies to any distribution of the stock of a subsidiary, whether in the form of a spin-off, a split-off or a split-up, which otherwise meets the tests of that section. Except that it does not depend upon there being a reorganization, § 355 is a kind of counterpart of § 354; and like the latter section, § 355 refers to § 356 for the treatment of any transaction which would have qualified under § 355 but for the presence of boot.

The effort to channel all divisive transactions through § 355 is evidenced by a number of subsidiary provisions in the Code. First, under the present version of § 368(a)(1)(D) a transfer of assets to a controlled corporation constitutes a reorganization only if the stock or securities received from the transferee are distributed to the transferor's stockholders in a transaction which qualifies under § 354, § 355 or § 356. And § 354(e) provides that § 354 is not applicable to transactions pursuant to a § 368(a)(1)(D) reorganization unless the transferor corporation transfers substantially all of its assets to the transferee, and the transferor thereafter distributes all of its property to its stockholders, including the stock and securities received from the transferee corporation. In effect, this means that whenever there is any vestige of a corporate division, a distribution to the stockholders pursuant to a § 368(a)(1)(D) transaction can not qualify under § 354 and must therefore pass the screen of § 355 to obtain tax-free treatment. And to make sure that the C reorganization route could not be used to achieve a division, § 368(a)(2)(A) expressly provides that any transaction which could constitute either a C or a D reorganization must be treated as a D reorganization, with the result that, as just noted, the test of § 355 becomes applicable.

It should be observed that the 1954 pattern leaves little scope for the operation of § 368(a)(1)(D). Even where a corporation seeking to divide does not already have an existing subsidiary, it would not have to depend upon § 368(a)(1)(D) to avoid the recognition of gain upon the transfer of assets to a new corporation — § 351 would be available for that purpose. And of course the subsequent transfer of the stock of the new corporation to the stockholders of the original corporation would be governed by § 355. Actually about the only independent function which § 368(a)(1)(D) can perform for taxpayers occurs when the transferor corporation receives some boot upon its transfer of assets to a controlled corporation. Then if a § 368(a)(1)(D) reorganization is present and the boot is distributed, § 361(b)(1)(A) would provide non-recognition to the transferor corporation; but if only § 351 was available, the transferor corporation would have to recognize gain to the extent of the boot, even if the boot was distributed to the transferor's stockholders. However, § 368(a)(1)(D) may perform an additional independent function from the Government's point of view by serving as a barrier against certain tax avoidance schemes based on a liquidation followed by a reincorporation. See pages 652–654, supra.

B. QUALIFICATION UNDER § 355

BONSALL v. COMMISSIONER

United States Court of Appeals, Second Circuit, 1963. 317 F.2d 61.

J. JOSEPH SMITH, CIRCUIT JUDGE. Albany Linoleum & Carpet Company was organized in 1924 and since that time has engaged in the wholesale distribution of various floor covering materials. Its largest supplier has been Armstrong Cork Company. Henry and Martha Bonsall, husband and wife, have at all pertinent dates been the controlling shareholders and principal officers of Albany Linoleum. C. Jordan Vail and his wife Nancy were minority shareholders, and he was an employee of the company. Albany Linoleum acquired its principal place of business at 64 Northern Boulevard in Albany, New York, in 1945, at a cost of roughly $75,000. The gross usable floor area of this building was 40,200 square feet. At the same time, it acquired a small adjoining building located at 231 Elk Street. The gross usable floor area of these premises was 3,312 square feet. From 1946 to 1956 Albany Linoleum leased 2,770 square feet of its Northern Boulevard building to Armstrong Cork Company. From 1949 to 1954 the Elk Street building was leased to Albany Poultry Company. Rental income in comparison to corporate income as a whole can be summarized as follows:

Year	Gross profit from sales	Gross rental income	Net income
1952	$318,650.55	$1,710.00	$40,955.17
1953	333,118.52	1,350.00	43,309.75
1954	322,412.45	1,158.00	32,865.77
1955	351,479.74	1,054.00	36,853.84
1956	388,890.81	628.00*	38,951.81

In 1956 it was decided to tear down the Elk Street building and put up an addition to the Northern Boulevard property. To raise construction funds and pay off the current mortgage, a new mortgage was financed through the Albany Savings Bank for $90,000. The bank required that a new corporation be formed to take title to the property with Albany Linoleum as tenant, as a condition to making the loan, and that the lease rentals be assigned by that new corporation to the bank as collateral for the loan. In compliance with this requirement, the shareholders of Albany Linoleum voted to form Abon, Inc. to acquire its buildings on Northern Boulevard and Elk Street. The certificate of incorporation was filed with the Secretary of State of New York on July 27, 1956, providing for 1,500

---
* [Footnote by the court] Through August 31, 1956 only.

shares of stock at $100 par value. On August 2, 1956 a meeting was held at which Bonsall and his wife and three others were elected directors, and Vail, Bonsall's son, and one Jones were elected as officers. It was then resolved to accept an offer from Albany Linoleum to convey the properties to Abon in return for assumption of an existing mortgage of $54,000, obligations pursuant to the building of the addition, and issuance of its stock to the Albany Linoleum shareholders, one share for every twenty shares of Albany Linoleum stock owned. Bonsall and his wife each owned 9,300 shares of Albany Linoleum stock, entitling them to 466 shares each of Abon stock; Vail and his wife owned a total of 700 shares of Albany Linoleum stock entitling them to 35 shares of Abon stock.**

A meeting of Abon stockholders was held on September 12, 1956 at which the prior acts of the incorporators and directors were ratified. Vail, Bonsall, and Bonsall's wife signed the minute book of this meeting. Mr. and Mrs. Bonsall also executed a written waiver of notice. The next day, title to the properties at 64 Northern Boulevard and 231 Elk Street was conveyed to Abon and accepted by its directors, and a lease of the premises was executed between Abon and Albany Linoleum. Abon then drew a mortgage loan of $90,000 from Albany Savings Bank, and assigned its future rentals due as collateral, pursuant to the prior agreement. The fair market value of net assets transferred to Abon was $9,707.87 or $7.96 per share, computed on the basis of 1219 shares required to be issued under the agreement with Albany Linoleum. A special meeting of shareholders, held February 20, 1957, attempted to rectify the patent illegality of issuing $100 par shares for this consideration by amending the certificate of incorporation to increase capital stock to 150,000 shares and decrease par value to $1 per share. Waivers of notice to shareholders for this meeting were executed by Mr. and Mrs. Bonsall and by Vail. A certificate of amendment executed February 26 was filed April 2, 1957, in which the original subscribers stated that they were the only subscribers, that no stock had been issued, and that no officers had been elected. However, a stock ledger for Abon had apparently existed from the previous September containing entries showing Henry Bonsall, Jr. and his wife to be owners of 466 shares each of Abon stock, C. Jordan Vail to own 380 shares and his wife Nancy 405—and the date that each of them became owner of these shares to be September 12, 1956. The first stock certificates were executed, representing the $1 par shares on April 5, in the amounts listed in the stock ledger.

Abon filed a corporate income tax return for 1956 reporting an entry for common stock of $1,219 on March 15, 1957. Albany Linoleum's balance sheet as of December 31, 1956 showed no stock or other ownership in Abon but did reflect decreases in land and buildings and other

---

** [Ed. note] Apparently, other minority stockholders of Albany Linoleum owned 5040 shares, entitling them to 252 shares of Abon stock, so that a total of 1219 shares of Abon were to be issued.

Sec. 3   TAX ASPECTS OF CORPORATE DIVISIONS   923

fixed depreciable assets. Bonsall and his wife and Vail and his wife did not report any Abon stock received from Albany Linoleum as a dividend for 1956 on their returns for that year. The Commissioner of Internal Revenue asserted that Bonsall and his wife received an added $7,418.72 in dividend income—the value of the Abon stock—and determined an income tax deficiency of $4,027.91. Vail and his wife were likewise found to have failed to report $278.60 in dividend income with a resulting deficiency of $50.25. Petitioners argued in the Tax Court that no distribution of Abon stock was made to them until 1957, and even if made in 1956, that it was tax-free within the Internal Revenue Code of 1954, § 355. The Tax Court rejected these contentions and sustained the deficiencies. Taxpayers petition to review that decision. We affirm.

* * *

The petitioners assert that even if the stock was transferred to them in 1956 it is not taxable as a dividend because of the effect of Internal Revenue Code of 1954 § 355. (It should be noted that they concede that the distribution was made to them by Albany Linoleum even though it never actually owned the stock.) That section provides, as relevant here, that if a corporation distributes to a shareholder with respect to his stock, stock of a corporation which it controls immediately prior to the distribution and (1) the transaction was not used primarily as a device for distributing the earnings and profits of either corporation, (2) the requirements of subsection (b) relating to the active conduct of businesses are satisfied, and (3) at least a controlling percentage (as defined) of the stock of the subsidiary is distributed, then no gain or loss shall be recognized to the shareholder on receipt of the stock. The requirements of subsection (b) are, in part, that the distributing corporation and the subsidiary corporation both be engaged in the "active conduct of a trade or business" immediately after the distribution. A corporation can be so regarded only if "such trade or business has been actively conducted throughout the 5-year period ending on the date of the distribution." Other limitations are set down that are not applicable here. The Tax Court found that Albany Linoleum had not been engaged in the active conduct of a real-estate rental business for five years prior to the distribution and therefore that Abon was not engaged in the active conduct of a trade or business within the meaning of the statute.

There is ample support for the factual determination that Albany Linoleum was not actively conducting a real-estate rental business. As the table above indicates, the portion of its income realized from real estate rentals was minute. There was testimony by Bonsall himself tending to negate active efforts at promoting rentals: the buildings had never been listed with an agent, nor were there even signs on them indicating that space was available. No activity appeared beyond a few casual conversations with prospective tenants. Moreover, most of the floor-space of the two buildings combined was occupied by the floor-covering business. Only a very small part was available for rental, and an even smaller part actually leased. The continuing rental to Armstrong Cork Co. which provided most of the rental income appeared to be an accommodation to a large supplier of the floor-covering business and thus an adjunct to it, rather than indicative of an independent business, for the Tax Court found that the premises were let at less than fair rental value over the five-year period. Finally, no separate records of rental income and expenses were kept. Absence of such records is at least probative of the fact that the managers of Albany Linoleum did not regard it as engaged in an independent rental business. The Tax Court was plainly justified in concluding that the small amount of rental activity was merely an incidental part of the sole business of the corporation — wholesale floor-coverings. See Theodore F. Appleby, 35 T.C. 755 (1961), aff'd per curiam, Appleby v. C. I. R., 296 F.2d 925 (3 Cir.), cert. denied 370 U.S. 910, 82 S.Ct. 1256, 8 L.Ed.2d 404 (1962); Isabel A. Elliott, 32 T.C. 283 (1959).

Petitioners argue in reply that even if Albany Linoleum is found to have been conducting but one business, the recent decision of the Tax Court in Edmund P. Coady, 33 T.C. 771 (1960), aff'd per curiam, C. I. R. v. Coady, 289 F.2d 490 (6 Cir., 1961), permits the tax-free division of that business as has been done in this case. This is to misconceive the scope of that decision. Coady only decided that the division of a single business into two operating halves, each continuing the previous activity (which had been carried on for more than five years) could fall within § 355, invalidating the Regulation that stated that the section did not apply to division of a single business as unauthorized by the statute. See Regs. § 1.355–1(a). Each corporation was engaged in the "active conduct of a trade or business" within the statute because it could be traced back through five years or more to the same activity, whether it was an old or new corporate entity. That is not true here. As the Tax Court properly found no prior real estate rental business, Abon must be taken to have embarked on a wholly new venture when it was formed. It is lacking the five-year history that the statute requires for "active conduct of a trade or business".

It is clear that careful scrutiny of purported "real-estate rental" businesses is necessary to prevent evasion of the purposes of the statute. The possibility of the shareholders abstracting accumulated earnings at capital gains rates is present whenever a corporation owns its own factory or office building. Under taxpayers' interpretation, all that need be done is to transfer the building to a new corporation and distribute the stock received in return. The shareholders would then be free to sell their stock and pay a capital gains rate on the proceeds while the corporation can rent or purchase another building and reduce its accumulated earnings. The present case is little more than that, and it is noteworthy that the two prior cases decided under this section other than Coady, Theodore F. Appleby, supra, and Isabel A.

Elliott, supra, were likewise factually similar. Only long application may completely clarify the difficult terminology of section 355. But obvious cases such as presented here plainly must be excluded from tax-free treatment.

The Commissioner also urged before the Tax Court that the transaction was disqualified from tax-free treatment by the express provision of section 355(a) (1) (B) as it was "used principally as a device for the distribution of the earnings and profits of the distributing corporation." As the Tax Court found it unnecessary to pass on this point, the Commissioner argued in this Court that a remand for further findings should be made if his contention that there was no active rental business were not sustained. In view of our disposition of the case, we need not pass on this question. It should be noted, however, that there was no valid shareholder business purpose for the distribution of the Abon shares. The reasons for the creation of Abon were adequate, but no necessity for the distribution of its stock was shown. See Parshelsky's Estate v. Commissioner, 303 F.2d 14 (2 Cir., 1962).

The distribution of Abon stock to Albany Linoleum shareholders was taxable as a dividend in 1956. It being undisputed that Albany Linoleum had earnings and profits on December 31, 1956 far in excess of the fair market value of the stock, the dividend is properly taxable at ordinary income rates. See Internal Revenue Code of 1954, §§ 301, 316.

The decision of the Tax Court is affirmed.

COMMISSIONER v. WILSON

United States Court of Appeals, Ninth Circuit, 1965. 353 F.2d 184 (1965).

MADDEN, JUDGE. The Commissioner of Internal Revenue seeks review and reversal by this court of a decision of the Tax Court of the United States setting aside income tax deficiencies which the Commissioner had assessed against these taxpayers. No problem relating to the jurisdiction of the Tax Court or of this court is involved.

Our question is whether the Tax Court was right in concluding that when a corporation in which the taxpayers were the sole stockholders formed another corporation, transferred certain assets of the existing corporation to it, and then transferred the stock in the second corporation to the taxpayers, that was not a distribution taxable to the taxpayers as a dividend paid by the first corporation, but was a tax-free transaction pursuant to Section 355 of the Internal Revenue Code of 1954, 26 U.S.Code, 1958, ed., § 355.

One William C. Wilson operated a furniture store business. He died in 1950. His widow and his two sons, who are the taxpayers in this litigation, continued the business as a partnership. In 1955 Wilson's Furniture, Inc., hereinafter called Wilson's Inc., was formed. The assets of the partnership were transferred to the corporation, and all of the stock of the corporation was issued to the two sons, the father's widow being paid for her partnership interest by a note of the corporation to her for $49,310.31.

In 1958 Wilson's Inc. formed another corporation, Wil-Plan, and transferred to it the conditional sales contracts which Wilson's Inc. had on hand as a result of selling furniture on deferred payments. An automobile owned by Wilson's Inc. was also transferred to Wil-Plan in this transaction. All of the stock in Wil-Plan was distributed to the two taxpayers herein, who, as we have seen, were the sole stockholders in Wilson's Inc. The fair market value of the stock in Wil-Plan delivered to each of the two taxpayers was $69,020.07. The accumulated earnings and profits of Wilson's Inc., at the time of the incorporation of Wil-Plan, were $48,889.98.

The taxpayers did not, in their tax returns for 1958, include any income attributable to the stock in Wil-Plan which had been distributed to them in that year. The Commissioner of Internal Revenue mailed timely deficiency notices to each of them, asserting a deficiency against each of some $11,000. The taxpayers filed in the Tax Court timely petitions for redetermination of the deficiencies. As we have seen, the Tax Court decided in favor of the taxpayers, and the Commissioner seeks, in this court, review and reversal of that decision.

Section 355 of the Internal Revenue Code of 1954 is difficult reading and will not be reproduced in this opinion. Its purpose and the purpose of its predecessors is to give to stockholders in a corporation controlled by them the privilege of separating or "spinning off" from their corporation a part of its assets and activities and lodging the separated part in another corporation which is controlled by the same stockholders. Since, after the spin-off, the real owners of the assets are the same persons who owned them before, Congress has been willing that these real owners should be allowed, without penalty, to have their real ownership divided into smaller artificial entities than the single original corporation, if the real owners decide that such a division would be desirable. Congress early learned, however, that shareholders would select the part of the assets of an original corporation which could most readily be converted into cash or its equivalent, spin off those parts into the second corporation, distribute the stock in that corporation to themselves and thus have available for sale and capital gains tax treatment the stock in that corporation, though in fact what they sold represented accumulated earnings of the original corporation, which earnings, if they had been paid directly to the shareholders of the original corporation, would have been fully taxable to them as dividend income.

Section 355 contains, as did its predecessors, a prohibition against the use of the spin-off as a "device for the distribution of the earnings and profits of the distributing corporation or the controlled corpora-

Sec. 3   *TAX ASPECTS OF CORPORATE DIVISIONS*   927

tion." § 355(a) (1) (B). The section also contained other requirements which had to be complied with in order to qualify a spin-off as a tax-free transaction. The Commissioner urges that some of these requirements were not complied with but, in view of the position which we take in this opinion, we find it unnecessary to resolve those problems.

As we have indicated above, the general purpose of Congress in sanctioning in proper cases, tax-free spin-offs was to permit the real owners of enterprises to rearrange their units and evidences of ownership to suit their own ideas of how best to carry on their businesses. This purpose of Congress was not expressly written into section 355, but the legislative history of the section shows that it underlay the drafting of the section. In his opinion in Parshelsky's Estate v. C. I. R., 303 F.2d 14 (C.A.2), Chief Judge Lumbard recounts the pertinent legislative history of section 355 and its predecessors. We will not indulge in useless repetition of the same material.

Both parties to this litigation recognize that, in addition to the requirements for tax-free spin-offs expressly written into section 355, the requirement stated for the Supreme Court of the United States by Mr. Justice Sutherland in the case of Gregory v. Helvering, 293 U.S. 465, 55 S.Ct. 266, 79 L.Ed. 596, is and has been an essential part of the law. That requirement is, briefly stated, that a literal compliance with the provisions of the statute relating to tax-free corporation reorganizations is not enough; that there must be a valid business purpose for the reorganization. We refer again to Parshelsky's Estate, supra, for citations to the extensive literature on this subject.

As we have said, both parties recognize the business purpose requirement stated in Gregory v. Helvering, supra. The taxpayers assert that they had three business purposes in separating the ownership and management of the conditional sales contracts acquired by Wilson's Inc. in the furniture store business and placing them in Wil-Plan. Here the taxpayer's difficulty is that the Tax Court expressly stated that none of the three business purposes asserted in the Tax Court litigation as the motive for the formation of Wil-Plan was, in fact, a bona fide motive, 42 T.C. 914, 922. We can read no other meaning into the Tax Court's language than that these asserted reasons were nonexistent when Wil-Plan was created, but were afterthoughts presented in the litigation.

In view of the Tax Court's conclusion that the several business purposes asserted by the taxpayer were nonexistent, and the fact that the Tax Court did not find any other business purpose, the taxpayers, in view of their recognition of the necessity of satisfying the Gregory v. Helvering requirement, would have expected to lose their case in the Tax Court. But they won their case. The Tax Court found that they did not have a tax-avoidance purpose in creating Wil-Plan. The Commissioner argued that the tax advantage sought by the taxpayers in creating Wil-Plan was that it gave them the opportunity to sell the stock of Wil-Plan or to liquidate it at some future time and thereby receive a distribution of the earnings and profits of Wilson's Inc. as a capital gain. Answering this argument, the Tax Court wrote:

> The answer to that position is that in the present case we have found that there was no plan or intention to achieve any such result and no attempt to do so has in fact been made.

We seem to be confronted with what may be a unique situation, that of a corporation reorganization which had no business reason and which had no tax avoidance purpose, but which had the effect of removing from the risks and vicissitudes of a retail furniture business accumulated earnings in a form readily convertible by the shareholders into cash, by selling their stock in the spin-off corporation or by liquidating it and receiving and selling those easily liquidated assets. The shareholders have and will continue to have a tax advantage whenever they choose to make use of it, even though, as the Tax Court found, they never thought of the reorganization in terms of a tax advantage.

We think that, in this practical area of taxation, so much in the way of liability for taxes can hardly be allowed to depend solely upon what goes on in someone's mind. If the assets transferred to Wil-Plan had been United States or municipal or high grade corporate bonds, the purpose of the spin-off might well have been the removal of these assets from the risks of the retail furniture business, with the motive of creating security for old age or for their families and without any thought of tax consequences. Yet it would be unfair to shareholders who are fully taxed upon dividends received by them to give such an advantage to the beneficiaries of a spin-off without a business purpose. We suppose that is the reason for the Gregory v. Helvering doctrine. Congress, in enacting section 355 and its predecessors, was trying to give to business enterprisers leeway in readjusting their corporate arrangements to better suit their business purposes. If the rearrangement had that purpose, Congress was willing to concede them some possible tax advantages. If the rearrangement had no business purpose, let the taxes fall where they might.

As we have said, the taxpayers urge in this court, as they did in the Tax Court, that there were business reasons for the creation of Wil-Plan. But the Tax Court held that there were none, and that holding is well supported by the Tax Court's discussion of the evidence. The Commissioner urges in this court, as he did in the Tax Court, that there was a tax avoidance motive in creating Wil-Plan. But the Tax Court held that there was no such motive. Its holding was based upon the oral testimony of one of the taxpayers, which testimony the court said "rang true." We cannot find that that holding is clearly erroneous.

We conclude, however, that even if there is no tax avoidance motive, a reorganization having no business reason does not result in the tax advantages which section 355 confers upon those who satisfy the legal requirements for its benefits.

The decision of the Tax Court is reversed, and the case is remanded to the Tax Court with a direction to dismiss the taxpayers' petitions for redetermination of deficiencies.

NOTE ON § 355

1. The "Active Conduct of a Business" Requirement

As indicated in the Bonsall opinion, the position taken in the Regulations, § 1.355–1(a), is that not only must each of the corporations resulting from a corporate division be actively engaged in business, but also the respective businesses must have been *separately* carried on for the five year period prior to the division. It is this position which, as the Bonsall opinion notes, was rejected in the Coady case, where it was held that § 355 was satisfied so long as after the division each of the corporations was carrying on a business which had been carried on for five years prior to the division, regardless of whether those businesses had been conducted separately in the past. In effect, Coady permits the tax-free division of a single business, a doctrine which has been followed in United States v. Marett, 325 F.2d 28 (5th Cir. 1963), and was finally acquiesced in by the Service, in Rev.Rul. 64–147, 1964–1 Cum.Bull. (Part 1) 136. See generally, Jacobs, Spin-Offs: The Pre-Distribution Two Business Rule — Edmund P. Coady and Beyond, 19 Tax.L.Rev. 155 (1964). Notice that under the Coady view it may be the Service in some cases which is arguing that a particular activity constituted a separate business, in order to lay a basis for the contention that *that business* was not carried on for five years before it was spun-off. See Burke v. Commissioner, 42 T.C. 1021 (1964).

In the Bonsall case, the court held that the Coady doctrine was inapplicable on the ground that the real estate business in which one of the two corporations was engaged after the division had not been carried on *at all*, separately or otherwise, during the prior five year period. However, this would seem to be a more arguable proposition than the Bonsall opinion suggests. Since it is both feasible and common for an operating business to rent premises instead of owning them, and of course renting property to others can constitute a business, an operating business which owns its premises might be regarded as in effect carrying on two businesses: (1) operating its facilities; and (2) renting its property (albeit to itself). To be sure, these two businesses would not be separately conducted — but the one thing that the Coady doctrine does make clear is that the absence of separate operation in the past is no bar to tax-free division under § 355. See also Estate of Lockwood v. Commissioner, 350 F.2d 712 (8th Cir. 1965), in which a corporation engaged in the manufacture and sale of agricultural equipment was permitted to spin-off the portion of its business carried on in the state of Maine, although the corporation had engaged in substantial activity in Maine for only about two years. If the single construction business in the Coady case could be regarded as including the two constitutent construction businesses into which it was divided, and the single manufacturing and selling business in the Lockwood case could be treated as including the two manufacturing and selling businesses into which it was divided, it is far from clear why the Bonsall business could not be regarded as including both the operating component and the "rental" real estate component into which it was divided.

2. The Special Problem of Real Estate in Corporate Divisions

One answer to the question posed at the end of the last paragraph may lie in the special nature of real estate in the divisive transaction area. As noted earlier, since the "active conduct of a business" requirement is intended to forestall the use of a divisive transaction to achieve a bail-out, the distinction between business and non-business assets, or as it is sometimes termed, "active" and "inactive" assets, becomes very important. Nowhere is the line between these two more difficult to draw than in the area of real estate held for rental purposes. While of course the renting of property can constitute an active business, in many cases rental property constitutes an inactive, "investment" asset, little different from marketable securities. This is particularly true of property rented under a "net lease", that is, a fairly long-term lease which relieves the lessor of virtually all responsibility by requiring the lessee to pay taxes, make repairs, and otherwise generally manage the property. Cf. Rev.Rul. 56–512, 1956–2 Cum.Bull. 173. When the rental property is of the investment type, a tax-free pro rata division of an enterprise into an operating business and a holding company for the real estate could constitute a classic bail-out.

The borderline nature of rental real property becomes particularly critical when a corporation carrying on an operating business begins to invest in unrelated real property held for the production of income. The question presented is whether the corporation has embarked upon a second business activity, or whether it is simply "investing" its surplus funds. Incidentally, this same distinction would be critical under the accumulated earnings tax, on the issue of whether such acquisitions of rental property constituted a justification for the accumulation of earnings. In any event, in view of the difficulty of dealing with actual rental property, a court would be understandably reluctant to import that issue into a case like Bonsall by finding a constructive real estate business in the corporation's ownership of its own operating premises.

Somewhat related to the foregoing is the question of whether and when the operation of several pieces of rental property can constitute the conduct of more than one business. This issue has become less significant now that the Coady doctrine permits tax-free treatment for the division of a single business. Thus the division of a real estate corporation owning and operating two pieces of rental property could presumably qualify under § 355 whether or not the two pieces of property are regarded as separate businesses. But there may still be some question as to whether the Coady doctrine would support tax-free treatment for the spin-off of less than all of one business by a corporation which does have two or more businesses. In other words, if a corporation carrying on an industrial business also owns a number of pieces of rental property, query whether it would be possible to spin off just one piece of property under § 355 unless that piece of property itself constituted a separate business.

It seems likely that where the pieces of rental property owned by one corporation are widely dispersed geographically, as, for example, where each is located in a separate state, or at least in a separate city, each parcel of property could constitute a separate busines. A number of examples in the regulations, § 1.355–1(d), indicate that where a corporation carries on similar activity at several locations, each location may constitute a separate business unless operations at the various sites are substantially integrated. While none of the regulation examples deals with rental property, Rev.Rul. 57–334, 1957–2 Cum.Bull. 240, holds that each of two rental properties located in different cities constitutes a separate business within the meaning of § 346(b), which has an active business test much like that of § 355 (except that § 346(b) seems clearly to require the presence of *separate* businesses, thus leaving no room for the Coady doctrine).

Even where a particular piece of rental property otherwise constitutes a separate business, at least one other obstacle to a tax-free spin-off is posed by Rev.Rul. 59–400, 1959–2 Cum.Bull. 114. That ruling involved the spin-off of a hotel by a corporation which had been operating it since 1920. The corporation had concededly also been in the rental real estate business since 1934, having acquired a number of rental properties since that time. During the five year period prior to the division, the earnings of the hotel business had amounted to more than three times the earnings of the real estate business. Shortly before the division, the corporation had acquired a large new piece of rental property. In holding that the division did not qualify under § 355, the ruling stated:

> It is the position of the Internal Revenue Service that where a corporation which is devoted to one type of business also engages in the rental business, and substantial acquisitions of new rental property are made within the 5-year period preceding the separation of these businesses, a "spin-off" transaction will not qualify under section 355 unless it can be shown that the property acquisitions were substantially financed out of the earnings of the rental business and not out of the earnings of the other business.

See generally, Cohen, Partial Liquidations and Spin-offs of Real Estate Corporations, 21 N.Y.U. Inst.Fed.Tax. 685 (1963).

3. Non-pro-rata Divisions

Under the pre-1954 law, the status of non-pro-rata corporate divisions was not entirely clear. In order to eliminate any doubt about the eligibility of such divisions for tax-free treatment, the 1954 Code, in § 355(a)(2)(A), expressly makes it immaterial whether "the distribution is pro rata with respect to all of the shareholders." (The provision in § 368(a)(1)(D) to the effect that the control requirement is satisfied if it exists in "one or more" of the transferor's stockholders serves the same purpose.)

However, it should be noted that at least so far as completely non-pro-rata divisions are concerned, the statute might well have gone beyond mere "neutrality". That is, the fact that the enterprise was divided between two groups of stockholders might have been made an independent basis for tax-free treatment under § 355. After all, there is no real bail-out threat in such cases, even in the polar situation where one of the two corporations resulting from a corporate division ends up with nothing but inactive assets — for by hypothesis, in a non-pro-rata division, the stockholder group which receives the corporation with the inactive assets would receive no interest in the corporation with the operating assets. *A fortiori,* there is no bail-out threat when a single business is divided between two dissident groups of stockholders, as occurred in the Coady case.

To be sure, it is not quite as serious if a non-pro-rata division fails to qualify under § 355 as it would be in the case of a pro-rata division where the result would normally be the imposition of a dividend tax on all the stockholders if § 355 does not apply. A non-pro-rata division, on the other hand, would presumably constitute a redemption in complete termination of the interest of one group of stockholders, so that the only tax incidents (absent § 355) would be at capital gains rates on those stockholders who gave up their old stock in exchange for the stock of the new corporation. Nevertheless, the failure to obtain complete tax immunity in such circumstances could seriously impede the resolution of deadlock situations, since it would add to the other issues in controversy the question of which group of stockholders should bear this capital gains tax.

To some extent, of course, this issue can be resolved by allocating a larger amount of assets to the corporation to be split off. See Rev.Rul. 64–102, 1964–1 Cum.Bull. (Part 1) 136. However, this approach can become rather complicated in situations where it is uncertain whether § 355 will be applicable. Here some type of contingent obligation from one of the corporations to the other (or from one group of individual stockholders to the other) seems called for; but the tax status of such arrangements is at best very uncertain.

Under the actual language of § 355, there seems little room to distinguish between pro rata and non-pro-rata divisions. Nevertheless, there might still be some temptation to give § 355 a broader reading where a non-pro-rata division is involved. For example, it is perhaps no coincidence that the Coady decision, which first sustained tax-free treatment for the division of a single business, involved a non-pro-rata division arrived at by the parties in a last-ditch effort to resolve their deadlock. But there would be real danger in "stretching a point" for non-pro-rata divisions. Since § 355 does not draw any distinction between pro rata and non-pro-rata divisions, any construction of § 355 adopted in the latter type of case becomes equally applicable to pro rata divisions, as is illustrated in the Marett case, supra, which applied the Coady doctrine in a pro rata division without so much as noting this issue.

4. Device for the Distribution of Earnings and Profits

As a further guard against using divisive transactions to avoid taxes, § 355(a)(1)(B) includes as an express condition for tax-free treatment a showing that "the transaction was not used principally as a device for the distribution of the earnings and profits of the distributing corporation or the controlled corporation or both . . . ." Although it seems likely that one prime target for this "device" language is the pro rata division followed by a sale of the stock of one of the corporations, the statute rather narrowly confines its operation in this area with the provision that such a sale of stock after a divisive transaction "shall not be construed to mean that the transaction was used principally as such a device" unless the sale was pursuant to an arrangement "negotiated or agreed upon prior to" the division. In Rev.Rul. 59–197, 1959–1 Cum.Bull. 77, a corporation owned by a husband, wife and son, carried on both a manufacturing business and a brokerage business in the same products. When customers of the brokerage business objected, it was decided to separate the two businesses. The brokerage business depended largely upon a key employee who insisted on obtaining some proprietary interest. As a first step in accomplishing these objectives, the wife sold part of her stock in the original corporation to the employee. Then the brokerage business was transferred to a new corporation, and its stock was distributed to the husband and the key employee in exchange for their stock in the original corporation. The ruling indicates that the wife's sale of stock in the original corporation to the key employee before the division was in effect the same as making a binding contract to sell the new stock to be received in the divisive transaction. Nevertheless, qualification under § 355 was sustained because only a portion of the new stock was "sold" in this way, and then only to the extent necessary to retain the services of the key employee. Compare Curtis v. United States, 336 F.2d 714 (6th Cir. 1964), where a spin-off, which was followed immediately by a tax-free acquisition of the parent corporation by another corporation, was held not to qualify under § 355 because the parent was no longer in existence carrying on a business.

In any event, the court in the Wilson case, supra, was not satisfied to rely upon this "device" mechanism to police corporate divisions, and instead insisted upon importing the general business purpose doctrine (as do the regulations, in § 1.355–2(c)). The Wilson opinion is somewhat unclear as to whether shareholder purposes will satisfy the "business purpose" requirement, or whether some corporate purpose must be established. In this connection, the court's two references to Parshelsky's Estate v. Commissioner, 303 F.2d 14 (2d Cir. 1962), become particular puzzling. That case, decided under the 1939 Code counterpart of § 355, rejected the Tax Court's effort to distinguish between corporate and shareholder purposes and held that it was erroneous not to consider the personal interests of the sole stockholder in determining the validity of a spin-off. On remand, the Tax Court found that the spin-off served a legitimate personal business purpose of the stockholder in connection with the administration, conservation, and ultimate disposition of his estate. 22 T.C.M. 911 (1963). But there is reason to wonder whether the Wilson court would have reached the same result, in view of the hypothetical case which it put of a spin-off of bonds for the purpose of removing them from the risks of the retail furniture business, or creating security for the old age of the stockholders. The court made clear its view that such a case should not qualify for a tax-free division; yet it comes perilously close to the personal estate considerations which motivated the stockholder in the Parshelsky case.

5. Allocation of Earnings and Profits

The allocation of earnings and profits between or among the corporations involved in a corporate division under § 355 is governed by Reg. § 1.-312–10, promulgated pursuant to § 312(i) of the Code. See generally, Nesson, Earnings and Profits Discontinuities under the 1954 Code, 77 Harv. L.Rev. 450, 474–490 (1964). For corporate separations which do not qualify under § 355 the allocation of earnings and profits is governed by Reg. § 1.-312–11. See Lyons, Some Problems in Corporate Separations Under the 1954 Code, 12 Tax.L.Rev. 15, 23 (1956).

C. THE LIQUIDATION-REINCORPORATION PROBLEM

Reference has already been made to the problem of using § 368 (a)(1)(D) to prevent the bail-out of earnings and profits through the device of liquidating a corporation at capital gains rates and then reincorporating the operating assets. See page 920 supra. For a thoughtful recent analysis of this subject, see Lane, The Reincorporation Game: Have the Ground Rules Really Changed?, 77 Harv.L.Rev. 1218 (1964). A variant of this problem which is equally troublesome involves the transfer by a corporation of some of its assets to a corporation controlled either by it or its shareholders, followed by the liquidation of the transferor corporation. See Surrey & Warren, Federal Income Taxation (1960 ed.) 1649–1653.

INDEX

References are to Pages

ACCOUNTING
Combination transactions,
    See Corporate Combinations.
Stock dividends, this index.
Tax accounting,
    See also Consolidated Returns.
  Deferred payment transactions, this index.
    Installment method, 519–526.
  Tax-free incorporation,
    See Incorporation.
Treasury stock,
    See Repurchase of Stock.
Unrealized appreciation, 326–328.

ACCUMULATED EARNINGS TAX
In general, 558–565.
Burden of proof, 565–578, 580.
Credit for reasonable business needs, 578–580.
Impact of a redemption, 420–422, 582–594.
Proof of reasonable business needs, 580–582.
Purpose, 565–580.
Reasonable business needs issue, 565–580.

ACQUISITION TO AVOID TAX
See Multiple Corporations; Net Operating Loss Carryover.

AFFILIATED CORPORATIONS
See Consolidated Returns; Multiple Corporations; Parent and Subsidiary.

AMENDMENT OF CERTIFICATE
Mechanics in general, 389–393.
To change rights of preferred, 737–747.
    Vested rights doctrine, 742–744.
To reduce capital,
    See Reduction of Capital.

APPRAISAL REMEDY
Effect on tax-free reorganization, 809–810, 833–835.
Exclusivity of the remedy, 691.
Mechanics, 683, 691–692.
Under de facto merger doctrine, 698–723.

APPRAISAL REMEDY—Cont'd
Valuation of dissenting stockholder's stock,
    See Valuation.

ASSET ACQUISITION
See Corporate Combinations; Reorganization.

ASSUMPTION OF LIABILITIES
As "adequate provision" for creditors upon dissolution, 628–629.
By operation of law in merger, 687–688.
Effect on C reorganization, 828–829, 833–835.
Effect on tax-free incorporation, 78–80.
    Liabilities in excess of basis, 79–80.

ATTRIBUTION OF INCOME TO RELATED CORPORATION
See Multiple Corporations.

ATTRIBUTION OF STOCK OWNERSHIP
See Redemption.

BAD DEBT DEDUCTION
Business vs. non-business bad debts, 124–132.
Payment by guarantor, 132.

BAIL-OUT
See Recapitalization; Section 306 Stock.

BASIS
See Incorporation; Liquidation; Redemption; Reorganization.

BLUE SKY LAW
See Securities Regulation.

BUSINESS PURPOSE
See Corporate Divisions; Redemption; Reorganization.

CLASSIFICATION OF STOCK, 31–34

COLLAPSIBLE CORPORATIONS, 657–678
Liquidation of, applicability of I.R.C. section 337, 646–648.

Herwitz Cs.Bus.Planning UCB   935

COMMON STOCK
Compared with other types of stock and securities, 44–49.

COMPENSATION
Stock issued as,
    Corporate aspects,
        See Issuance of Stock.
    Deductibility by the grantor, 76, 276–277.
    Tax treatment to the recipient, 56–58, 76–77, 262–278.
        Effect of transfer restrictions, 277–278, 284–286.
Stock options, issued as,
    See Stock Options.

COMPLETE LIQUIDATION
See Liquidation.

CONSOLIDATED RETURNS
Tax law,
    Effect on multiple surtax exemptions, 166–167.
    Eligibility to file, 166, 869.
    Limitations on net operating loss carryover, this index.

CONSOLIDATION
See Corporate Combinations; Reorganization.

CONTINUITY OF INTEREST DOCTRINE
See Reorganization.

CONTROL
Allocation of managerial control, 38–44.
Allocation of voting power, 29–38.
Test for loss of surtax exemption under section 1551.
    See Multiple Corporations.
Test for tax-free incorporation,
    See Incorporation.

CORPORATE COMBINATIONS
Accounting, 782–801.
    Effect of corporation statutes, 796–801.
    Parent-subsidiary consolidated return, 795–796.
    Pooling vs. purchase, 787–795.
Asset acquisition,
    See Mechanics, comparison of methods, infra; see also Sale of Assets.
Consolidation,
    See Mechanics, comparison of methods, infra.
De facto merger doctrine, 697–723.

CORPORATE COMBINATIONS—Cont'd
Dissenting shareholders' appraisal rights,
    See Appraisal Remedy
Fairness,
    Between classes of the same corporation, 761–765.
        See also Recapitalization.
    Between the corporations, 747–761.
For tax treatment,
    See Reorganization.
Mechanics, comparison of methods, 679–691, 720–723.
Merger,
    See Mechanics, comparison of methods, supra.
Securities regulation, this index.
Stock acquisition,
    See Mechanics, comparison of methods, supra.

CORPORATE DISTRIBUTIONS
See Dividends; Reorganizations; Repurchase of Stock.

CORPORATE DIVISIONS
Allocation of earnings and profits, 933.
Corporate aspects,
    See Liquidation.
Qualification for tax-free treatment, 919–920.
    Active business requirement, 921–925, 929–931.
    Business purpose requirement, 925–929, 932–933.
    Device for distribution of earnings and profits, 932–933.
    Division of a single business, 929–931.
    Non-pro-rata division, 931–932.
    Real estate, 930–931.
Role of covenant not to compete,
    See Covenant Not to Compete.

COVENANT NOT TO COMPETE
Implication from sale of stock, 910–913.
Role in deadlock and dissolution situations, 907–910.
Tax treatment of payments on account of, 913–918.

CUMULATIVE VOTING, 29–31

DEBT
See also Securities.
Corporate law,
    Issuance of debt in exchange for stock, 393–398.
    Limitations on stockholder-owned debt, 67–76.
        Subordination, 69–75.

INDEX

DEBT—Cont'd
Debt obligations received in exchange for property,
    See Deferred Payment Transactions.
Tax law,
    Comparison of debt and stock, 120–124.
    Deductibility of loss on debt,
        See Bad Debt Deduction.
    Limitations on stockholder-owned debt, 133–147.
        Effect of pro rata holding of stock and debt, 136–138.
        Incorporation of a going business, 145–147.
        Riskiness of the investment, 138–145.
        Substitutes for debt, 147–149.

DEFERRED PAYMENT TRANSACTIONS
Effect of accounting method on tax treatment, 493–496.
Existence of a discount, 499–511.
Gain on repayment of an obligation, 496–503.
"Open" vs. "Closed" transaction approach, 490–493.
Tax treatment of interest and discount on installment obligations, 503–519, 526–532.
Unstated interest under section 483, 526–532.

DISCOUNT
On installment obligations,
    See Deferred Payment Transactions.

DISSOLUTION
See Liquidation.

DIVIDENDS
Corporate law,
    Capital surplus, 318–319.
    Effect of quasi-reorganization, 358–362.
    Fund available, 313–319.
    Liability of directors for improper distributions, 324.
    Preferred stock,
        See Preferred Stock.
    Reduction surplus,
        See Reduction of Capital.

DIVIDENDS—Cont'd
Corporate law—Cont'd
    Unrealized appreciation,
        Aftermath of Randall v. Bailey in New York, 328–332.
        Outside New York, 332–335.
        Randall v. Bailey, 320–325.
        Role of accounting, 326–328.
        Under the Model Act, 335–340.
Stock dividends, this index.
Tax law,
    Definition, 371–373.
    Disguised dividends, 374.
    Distributions having effect of,
        See Reorganization.
    Earnings and profits, 373–374.
    Essential equivalence to,
        See Redemption.
    In kind, 374–379.

EARNINGS AND PROFITS
Allocation of in corporate divisions,
    See Corporate Divisions.
Carryover in corporate combinations, 837–841.
Computation of, 373–374.
Effect of a redemption, 554–557.

ENTERPRISE VALUATION
See Valuation.

INCORPORATION
See also Issuance of Stock.
Applicability of section 1239, 81.
Tax-free under section 351,
    Accounting aspects, 97–98.
    Basis, 77–81.
    Control test, 77–78, 81–97.
        Effect of disproportionate issuance of stock, 96–97.
        Effect of proposed transfer of stock, 92–95.
        Effect of public offering, 90–92.
        Effect of stock issued for services, 62–63, 86–87.
        Several classes of stock, 95–96.
    Receipt of debt not qualifying as security, 106–116.
    Receipt of securities, 106–107, 116–120.
    Reserve for bad debts, 97–98.
    Transfer of property requirement, 86–90.

INSTALLMENT METHOD OF ACCOUNTING, 519–526

INDEX
References are to Pages

INTEREST
Accounting for interest on installmment obligations,
  See Deferred Payment Transactions.

INTERNAL REVENUE SERVICE
Administrative policy, 101–102.
Professional responsibility in practice before, 102–105.
Rulings, 98–101.

ISSUANCE OF STOCK
Corporate law,
  Authorization, 49.
    In stock or asset acquisition, 683, 721–723.
    Type and amount of consideration required, 49–56.
      Effect of liquidation preference, See Preferred Stock.
      Prohibition against issuance for future services, 49–56.
Securities regulation, this index.
Tax law,
  For services,
    See Compensation.
  Tax incidents to corporation, 76.
  Tax incidents to recipient, 76–81.
    See Incorporation.

LIQUIDATION
  See also Partial Liquidation.
Corporate law,
  Dissolution compared, 613–615.
  Liability of directors, 627–629.
  Liquidation of controlled subsidiary, 723–730.
    Short-form merger as a substitute, 730–735.
  Relation to sale of all assets, 613–615.
  Rights of creditors, 624–629.
  Rights of preferred stockholders, 290–291, 723–724.
  Upon shareholder deadlock, 888–907.
Liquidation preference,
  See Corporate law, Rights of preferred stockholders, supra.
Tax law,
  Controlled subsidiary, 648–652, 824–828.
    Basis of assets received, 825–828.
  Deductibility of related expenses, 540.
  Followed by reincorporation, 652–654, 934.

LIQUIDATION—Cont'd
Tax law—Cont'd
  Tax-free sale of assets under section 337, 630–657.
    Exceptions to tax-free treatment, 638–646, 656–657.
    Problems of timing, 632–637, 654–656.
    Requirement of a complete liquidation, 654–656.

MERGER
  See also Corporate Combinations; Reorganization.
Short-form merger of controlled subsidiary, 730–735.

MULTIPLE CORPORATIONS
Allocation of income and deductions under section 482, 183–187.
Attribution of income of one to another under section 61, 181–183.
Limitation on surtax exemptions,
  Controlled corporations under sections 1561–1563, 164–167.
    Allocation of one surtax exemption, 166–167.
    Election of multiple surtax exemptions, 166–167.
  Section 269, 168–176.
    Purpose, 170–176.
  Section 1551, 177–181.
    Purpose, 180–181.
Use in allocating managerial control, 43–44.

NET OPERATING LOSS CARRYOVER
In combination transactions, 847–851.
  Limitations,
    Consolidated returns, 861–872.
    Libson Shops doctrine, 858, 872–885.
    Section 269, 858–861.
    Section 382(a), 857–858, 883–885.
    Section 382(b), 851–857.
Mechanics in general, 841–847.

ORGANIZATION OF CORPORATION
See Incorporation.

PARENT AND SUBSIDIARY
See also Consolidated Returns; Corporate Combinations; Liquidation; Merger.

PARTIAL LIQUIDATION
  See also Redemption.
Corporate aspects,
  See Repurchase of Stock.

INDEX

PARTIAL LIQUIDATION—Cont'd
Deductibility of expenses, 540–545, 546–554.
Distribution in kind, 538–540.
Historical development of tax treatment, 464–471.
Qualification as, 482–486.

PERSONAL HOLDING COMPANIES, 594–612

PREFERRED STOCK
As a stock dividend,
   Corporate law, 307–308, 312–313, 348–349.
   Tax law, 379–385.
     See also Section 306 Stock.
Characteristics, 46–47, 287–302.
Compared with debt securities, 287–302.
Issuance,
   Effect of liquidation preference on amount of stated capital, 303–313.
   Effect of liquidation preference on required consideration, 303–313.
Recapitalization, 389–392.
   Tax aspects,
     See Reorganization.
Terms of, 287–302.
   Contractual restrictions on corporate action, 300–302.
   Convertibility, 293–296.
   Dividends, 287–289.
   Liquidation rights, 290–291.
     Change in,
       See Amendment of Certificate.
   Redemption, 297–299.
   Voting rights, 291–293.

PROFESSIONAL RESPONSIBILITY
In practice before service,
   See Internal Revenue Service.

RECAPITALIZATION
Exchange of debt for stock, 393–398.
Fairness between different classes of stock, 761–765.
   Absolute priority approach, 765–766.
   Appraised valuation approach, 773–781.
   Investment value approach, 767–773.
For tax treatment,
   See Reorganization.
Non-pro-rata, 392.
To eliminate dividend arrearages on preferred stock, 389–391, 745–746, 761–764.

REDEMPTION
   See also Partial Liquidation.
By related corporation, 482.
Corporate aspects,
   See Repurchase of Stock.
Deductibility of expenses,
   By the corporation, 540–545.
   By the stockholders, 545–554.
     Fees paid to tax counsel, 546–554.
Distribution in kind, 538–540.
Effect on accumulated earnings tax,
   See Accumulated Earnings Tax.
Effect on basis, 480–481.
Effect on earnings and profits, 554–557.
Historical development of tax treatment, 464–471.
Impact on the remaining stockholders, 532–538.
Rulings, 481.
Tax treatment of selling shareholders, 471–482.
   Attribution of stock ownership in applying tests, 476–479.
     Waiver of family attribution rules under complete termination test, 477–479.
   Complete termination of interest test, 477–479.
   Disproportionate redemption test, 476–477.
   Not essentially equivalent to a dividend test, 471–476, 479–840.
   Redemption to pay estate taxes, etc., 481.

REDUCTION OF CAPITAL
Mechanics, 350–358.
Reduction surplus,
   Respective rights of preferred and common, 365–370.
Rights of creditors, 358–362.
Rights of preferred stockholders, 362–371.

REORGANIZATION
Asset acquisition, 828–835.
   Claims of dissenting stockholders, 833–835.
   Expenses of the acquired corporation, 828–829, 833–835.
   Liquidation of the acquired corporation, 831–832.
   Requirement that substantially all the assets be acquired, 829–831.
   "Solely for voting stock" requirement, 828–829.

REORGANIZATION—Cont'd
Basis,
    Corporations, 802–803, 824.
    Stockholders, 803–804.
B reorganization,
    See Stock acquisition, infra.
Business purpose requirement, 804.
Carryover of earnings and profits,
    See Earnings and Profits.
Carryover of net operating losses,
    See Net Operating Loss Carryover.
Continuity of business enterprise, 811–812.
Corporate aspects,
    See Corporate Combinations.
C reorganization,
    See Asset acquisition, supra.
Divisive,
    See Corporate Divisions.
Merger and consolidation, 805–811.
    Continuity of interest doctrine, 805–810.
Non-recognition,
    Corporations, 802–803.
    Shareholders, 803–804.
Recapitalization,
    Definition, 398–400.
    Having the effect of a dividend, 400–403.
    Preferred stock, 403–405.
    Non-pro-rata, 406–410.
    Relation to stock dividend, 405.
    Securities, 410–413.
Step transaction doctrine, 804–805.
Stock acquisition, 814–824.
    Expenses of the acquired corporation's stockholders, 823.
    Liquidation of subsidiary acquired corporation,
        See Liquidation.
    "Solely for voting stock" requirement, 820–822.
        Meaning of "voting stock", 822–823.
Use of a subsidiary, 813.

REPURCHASE OF STOCK
Accounting for treasury stock, 422–426.
    Cancellation of treasury stock, 425–426.
Because of overcapitalization, 461.
Fund available, 414–420, 426–441.
    Test for installment repurchase, 426–441.
Ousting troublesome stockholders, 441–458, 461–463.

REPURCHASE OF STOCK—Cont'd
Preserving control, 441–458.
    Liability of directors, 461–463.
Preventing take over, 441–458, 461–463.
Requirement of pro rata offer to all stockholders, 458–460.
Tax treatment,
    See Redemption.

REVALUATION
See Accounting; Dividends.

RULINGS
See Internal Revenue Service.

SALE OF ASSETS
Distinguished from liquidation and dissolution, 613–615.
Pursuant to dissolution,
    Corporate requirements, 622–623.
    Tax-free sale under section 337,
        See Liquidation.
Requirement of stockholder approval, 615–623.

SECTION 306 STOCK, 385–389

SECTION 1244 STOCK, 121–123

SECURITIES
Characteristics of debt securities, 45–46, 48.
Tax law,
    Effect on tax-free incorporation,
        See Incorporation.
    Qualification as, 116–120.
    Recapitalization,
        See Reorganization.
Terms of,
    Compared with preferred stock, 287–302.
    Contractual restrictions on corporate action, 300–302.
    Convertibility, 293–296.
    Interest, 289.
    Liquidation rights, 291.
    Redemption, 297–299.
    Sinking fund, 299–300.
    Voting rights, 292.

SECURITIES REGULATION
Corporate combinations, 693–697.
    "No sale" doctrine, 695–697.
Securities Act of 1933, 192–197.
    Analysis, 197–202.
    Exemptions,
        Combining exemptions, 245–246.
        Intra-state offering, 219–223.
        Private offering, 202–218.
        Regulation A, 223–226.
    Stock issued for services, 246–249.

SECURITIES REGULATION—Cont'd
State Blue Sky laws,
    Techniques of regulation, 249–259.
    Uniform Securities Act, 259–261.

SERVICES
Effect of stock issued for services,
    See Compensation; Incorporation.

SPIN-OFF
See Corporate Divisions.

STOCK
See Common Stock; Issuance of Stock; Preferred Stock.

STOCK ACQUISITION
See Corporate Combinations; Reorganization.

STOCK DIVIDENDS
Accounting for, 341–343.
Analysis of, 343–349.
Out of revaluation surplus, 337, 349–350.
Tax treatment,
    Current law, 381–385.
    Disposition of the dividend stock, 385–389.
    Historical development, 379–381.

STOCK OPTIONS
Qualified stock options, 281–282.
Restricted stock options, 281.
Unrestricted stock options,
    Current tax treatment, 282–284.
    Effect of transfer restrictions on the stock received, 284–286.
    Historical development of tax treatment, 279–281.

STOCK OPTIONS—Cont'd
Unrestricted stock options—Cont'd
    Received by independent contractor, 286–287.

SUBCHAPTER S, 149–157

SURTAX EXEMPTIONS
See Multiple Corporations.

THIN INCORPORATION
Corporate law,
    See also Debt.
    In general, 67–68.
    Loss of limited liability, 75–76.
    Subordination of stockholder-owned debt, 69.
Tax law, 133–149.
    See Debt.

TREASURY STOCK
See Repurchase of Stock.

UNREALIZED APPRECIATION
See Accounting; Dividends.

VALUATION
In general, 1–7.
Dissenting stockholder's stock, 691, 773–781.
For dividend purposes, 340.
Large enterprise, 7–26.
Preferred stock, 773–781.
Small enterprise, 26–29.
Techniques,
    Asset valuation, 2, 19–26.
    Asset value factor, 24–26.
    Capitalization of earnings, 3–5, 7–19.

END OF VOLUME